With the Compliments

of the

International Institute of Islamic Thought

P.O. BOX 669, HERNDON, VA 22070, USA
Telephone: (703) 471-1133 Telex: 901153 IIIT Wash

THE CULTURAL ATLAS OF ISLAM

THE CULTURAL ATLAS OF ISLAM

Isma'īl R. al Fārūqī

and

Lois Lamyā' al Fārūqī

MACMILLAN PUBLISHING COMPANY
New York

Collier Macmillan Publishers
London

MACMILLAN PUBLISHING COMPANY
866 Third Avenue, New York, NY 10022

Collier Macmillan Canada, Inc.

Library of Congress Catalog Card Number: 85-27501

Printed in the United States of America

printing number
2 3 4 5 6 7 8 9 10

Library of Congress Cataloging in Publication Data

Al-Faruqi, Isma'il R., 1921–
Cultural atlas of Islam.

1. Civilization, Islamic. 2. Civilization, Islamic—
Maps. I. Faruqi, Lois Ibsen. II. Title.
DS36.85.A39 1986 909'.097671 85-27501
ISBN 0-02-910190-5

Illustration opposite Part One (p. 1):
Interior of the Umawī Mosque of Dimashq (Damascus), built under Caliph 'Abdul Malik ibn Marwan (66-86/685-705).
Illustration opposite Part Two (p. 71):
Interior of Mosque of Qurṭubah, Spain, eighth century C.E.
Illustration opposite Part Three (p. 93):
Mausoleum of Ruku al 'Alam, Multan, Pakistan, c. 1320.
Ilustration opposite Part Four (p. 181):
Masjid Kuala Kangsar, Malaysia, twentieth century.

Editorial and Production Staff:

Charles E. Smith, Publisher
Elly Dickason, Project Editor
Morton I. Rosenberg, Production Manager
Joan Greenfield, Designer

Contents

List of Maps

Acknowledgments

We wish to express our deep gratitude to Temple University, the International Institute of Islamic Thought, and the American Trust Publications for making the writing and publication of this work possible. Numerous persons contributed their expertise during the development of the manuscript. It is impossible to name them all, but we would like to acknowledge the much-valued assistance of Taymā' al Fārūqī, Laila Latib, Maysam al Fārūqī, Cecelia Larsen, and David Layman for their help with many details connected with the project. Finally, we wish to thank the members of the staff at Macmillan Publishing Co., particularly Charles E. Smith, who gave us his unwavering support, and Elly Dickason, who edited the manuscript and who offered invaluable help through the many stages of its production.

Introduction

Most Western and Muslim scholars who have written on the culture and civilization of Islam have treated their topic either territorially or chronologically. Territorial arrangement is the favorite method of Western authors, who divide the relevant materials according to the various regions, emphasizing the particular features of the history of a given area. Chronological arrangement is the preference of Muslim authors, who organize their data according to the main events or accomplishments of a single period or of successive periods. Both betray the grave shortcoming of taking no account of the essence of Islamic culture and civilization. The geographic arrangement misses that element which unites the regions and makes them provinces of one World of Islam and hence integral parts of Islamic culture and civilization. The chronological treatment ignores the substance that has persisted through the events of centuries and generations and that has forged the dazzling diversity of expressions into an organic cultural and civilizational unity. There are other books on Islam that combine the geographic arrangement with the historical; but they succeed only in combining the shortcomings of both methods.

The answer to these shortcomings lies, of course, in the phenomenological method, which requires that the observer let the phenomena speak for themselves rather than force them into any predetermined ideational framework; let the eidetic vision of essence order the data for the understanding and be corroborated by them. These essentials of the phenomenological method were known to and meticulously observed by the Muslim scholar Abū al Rayḥān al Bīrūnī (440/1048) in his classical study of the religion and culture of India. The methodological principles he established were continued in a long tradition of comparative learning and writing by Muslims. The phenomenological method was first introduced into Western philosophy by Edmund Husserl, and into the study of ethics and religion by Max Scheler. Still more recently, the method has come into vogue with the publication of *The Journal of the History of Religions* and the appointment of Mircea Eliade to the chair of Comparative Religion at the University of Chicago.

For the past generation or more, the discipline of the history of religions has benefited from the breakthrough of phenomenology. Although many authors have applied the phenomenological method to the study of extinct or living traditional religions, few have applied it to the study of world religions; and none has applied it to the study of Islam. The latter has been the exclusive domain of Western Islamicists who seem never to have heard of phenomenology. For them, the principle of *epochē* required by phenomenology—that is, the suspension of all preconceptions, prejudgments, and biases in interpreting the data of another religion or culture and distilling their meanings—seems an impossible demand. Though using this method in the editing of an ancient manuscript, or in identifying and describing an archeological remain or a work of art, the Orientalists have never proven themselves capable of *epochē* in interpreting the religion and culture of Islam. Their commitment to epistemological ethnocentrism, or the perception of reality as determined by ethnicity, commits them to territoriality in understanding history. Furthermore, the so-called scientific method, which regards as true only the sensory, material, quantitative, and measurable given, binds them to the phenomenal manifestation and blinds them to the essence manifested in the phenomena. As students of other religions and cultures, they are ever suspicious of everything, valuational or universal, and they regard such data as relative, subjective, and even personal. Finally, the millennial legacy of enmity and confrontation between Islam and the West of which these authors are heirs constitutes another barrier to objectivity in dealing with the data of Islam.

Muslim authors, on the other hand, have a natural sensitivity to the values of Islam; but they have hardly begun the articulation of the relationship between the essence of Islam and the phenomena of its concretization in history. The assumed perception and understanding of that essence by the Muslim reader leads them to gloss over the need to analyze it and impels them to proceed to their description and/or evaluation of phenomena without identifying its relevance to the materials under study.

Moreover, in the writings of many authors Islam is confused with the Muslims. Such authors understand the legacy of thought, action, and expression by Muslims as constitutive of Islam itself, just as they regard Christianity and Judaism to be little else besides their historical traditions. The fact that Islam is not its history does not catch their attention because of its contrast with what they know of Christian or Jewish history. To distinguish between Islam and its history therefore seems to run against their empiricist assumptions and bent of mind. They seem unaware that, unlike Christianity and Judaism, Islam was born complete—complete in the vision of its Prophet, complete in the Qur'ānic revelation he received, and complete in the *Sunnah* he exemplified. This claim is not that of any human or humans; it is Qur'ānic (3:19; 5:4; 2:132) and thus God-given. Claiming to be the perfect and primordial religion of God, Islam cannot be identified with any Muslims' history. It is the ideal to which all Muslims strive and by which they would and should be defined. Hence, true objectivity demands that Islam be distinguished from Muslim history and instead be regarded as its essence, its criterion, and its measure.

Islam did not teach an imminent eschaton and hence the irrelevance of history. Neither did it advocate withdrawal from the world and from history into the subjective flights of consciousness. It commanded total involvement in the process of history as the only theater in which felicity or damnation might be achieved. As entertained by the Prophet, the vision of Islam meant to take history, as it were, by the horns; to direct it so as to produce culture and civilization. Its association with Muslim history is hence crucial; for Islamic culture and civilization were indeed its offspring, nourished and perpetually sustained by it in every realm of human endeavor. But this fact has no meaning without the analysis indicating whether the phenomenon in question is an actualization, approximation, or violation of the essential vision. The exact content of that relationship—the influence of Islam on its manifestation in history—has yet to be properly discerned and adequately analyzed.

The present work is a beginning in that direction. The treatment of Islam and its civilization is at once fitting and novel. It does not ignore the relationship of civilizational materials to Islam, but at the same time it does not equate Islam with any historical materials. Understanding the essence of Islam in terms that pertain exclusively to the Qur'ān and the *sunnah,* the study aims at presenting the civilizational materials as concretizations of that essence in space and time. It may be rightly claimed that this book is the first application of the phenomenological method to Islam and its civilization as a whole. It opens with an examination of the crucible, the historical reality in which Islam — the religion, the culture, and the civilization — was born. It then proceeds to a definition of the essence of Islamic civilization or *tawḥīd,* its first principle and core. This is based on an eidetic vision of the faith of Islam. Analysis of the essence is followed by that of its form-giving into a system of ideas, a system of exemplary actualizations, and a system of social institutions. All three have jointly molded Islamic culture and civilization, given them their character and form, marked their depths and other dimensions, and served to anchor and undergird their development in history. Finally, the manifestations of Islam in the phenomena of culture and civilization are surveyed under the categories of action, thought, and expression, thus giving a systematic account of the relevant fields of human activity. Chapters 9 and 10 deal with manifestation in action. Chapters 11 through 18 describe manifestation in thought. And Chapters 20 through 23 examine manifestation in expression.

The materials presented were selected from an infinite variety of data. The principle guiding this selection was proximity to the ideal, or the degree to which the data of history may be said to have instantiated the essence. Hence every chapter seeks to relate its materials to *tawḥīd,* the essence of Islamic civilization, and to show how the essence acted as ground and conditioning prius of the manifestation in question. From a phenomenological standpoint, the essence is indeed a principle of sufficient reason, of understanding of both the figurization and manifestation.

Finally, an explanation of the title of this book is necessary. The word "Atlas" can refer to a book of maps that represent geographical features of a physical, agricultural, urban, political, economic, or military nature. Cultural geography, however, is still young; and the methods for translating cultural phenomena into visible form are far from being fully established and perfected. Mapping cultural information is a difficult affair because of the complexity and diversity of the constitutive materials and the factors influencing their development. Realizing the hazards of such a pioneering task, we have made this first attempt to produce a comprehensive "Atlas" of Islamic culture and civilization. "Atlas" can also be used to designate a book of visually represented information on a specific subject. The title is therefore further justified, since included here is a wealth of information on Islamic culture and civilization presented in tables, charts, chronologies, figures, and photographs.

Naturally, this study is not immune from the shortcomings usually affecting "first" productions. But we hope that it may open the road to a better understanding of Islam and the culture and civilization it produced, and will stimulate others to complete and perfect the task.

A Note about Dates and Qur'ānic References

Wherever possible and appropriate, two dates have been given to indicate the year of a person's death, the time of an event or action, or the boundaries of a period of time. Separated by a slash, the first is the year according to the *Hijrah* lunar calendar which began in 622 with the setting up of the first Muslim community in Madīnah; the second is that of the corresponding year of the Common (Christian) Era. Whenever a single date without further specification is cited, it should be understood as pertaining to the Common Era. If a single date is followed by B.C.E., it will apply, as is customary, to a year prior to the birth of Christ.

Qur'ānic references are usually given between parentheses. The first figure is the number of the *sūrah* or chapter. The number following the separating colon indicates the *āyah* or verse.

PART ONE
THE CONTEXT

CHAPTER 1

Arabia: The Crucible

The first look at the map of Southwest Asia (Map 1) reveals a number of significant facts. A huge land mass—the Arabian Peninsula—dangles from Asia into the surrounding seas. At its widest, it measures about 1,200 miles; at its longest, 1,500 miles. It hangs onto Asia by a neck consisting of a desert center and a crescent of green and fertile land. On the west end of the crescent bordering on the Mediterranean, the rainfall is sufficient to permit regular vegetation of cereals and vegetables; in the higher altitudes, olive and fruit trees grow. At the crescent's southern extremity, the point where the continents of Asia and Africa meet, namely, the strait of Suez and the Isthmus of 'Aqabah, the rainfall diminishes to nothing, making the desert continuous to the Mediterranean shore. On the east end, the cause of verdure is a twin-forked river—the Tigris and Euphrates. Springing from the highlands beyond the north edge, the river twins meander through the plain and empty their waters into the Arabian (Persian) Gulf, the water sleeve that bounds the Peninsula on its east side. To the north and east, beyond this green crescent crown, are forbidding mountains which the inhabitants of the Peninsula never crossed before Islam. On the other sides are bodies of water: the Mediterranean to the northwest, the Red Sea to the west, the Arabian Sea and Indian Ocean to the south and east. On the western shores of the Peninsula stands a range of mountains known as the Ḥijāz (literally, "enclosing elevation") which shields the desert plateau of the mainland from the coast and catches an amount of rainfall which increases further south, making the southwest corner as green and fertile as the northern reaches. In this corner stood al Yaman, literally "the blessed land," or "Arabia Felix," as it was known to the ancients precisely on account of its fertility and capacity to support life.

Geographically speaking, "Arabia" is the Peninsula as well as its crown and neck, the "Fertile Crescent." Each is the continuation of the other and is inconceivable without it. The Peninsula desert extends to the extremities of the overarching Crescent thinning its extremities to nothing. Likewise, it extends northward into the Crescent, widening its cavity and making it coalesce with the Peninsula which it closely and continuously hugs. Contrary to common usage, we shall henceforth apply the name "Arabia" to both the Arabian Peninsula and the Fertile Crescent. Beside the foregoing, there is a plethora of evidence to corroborate this novel application.

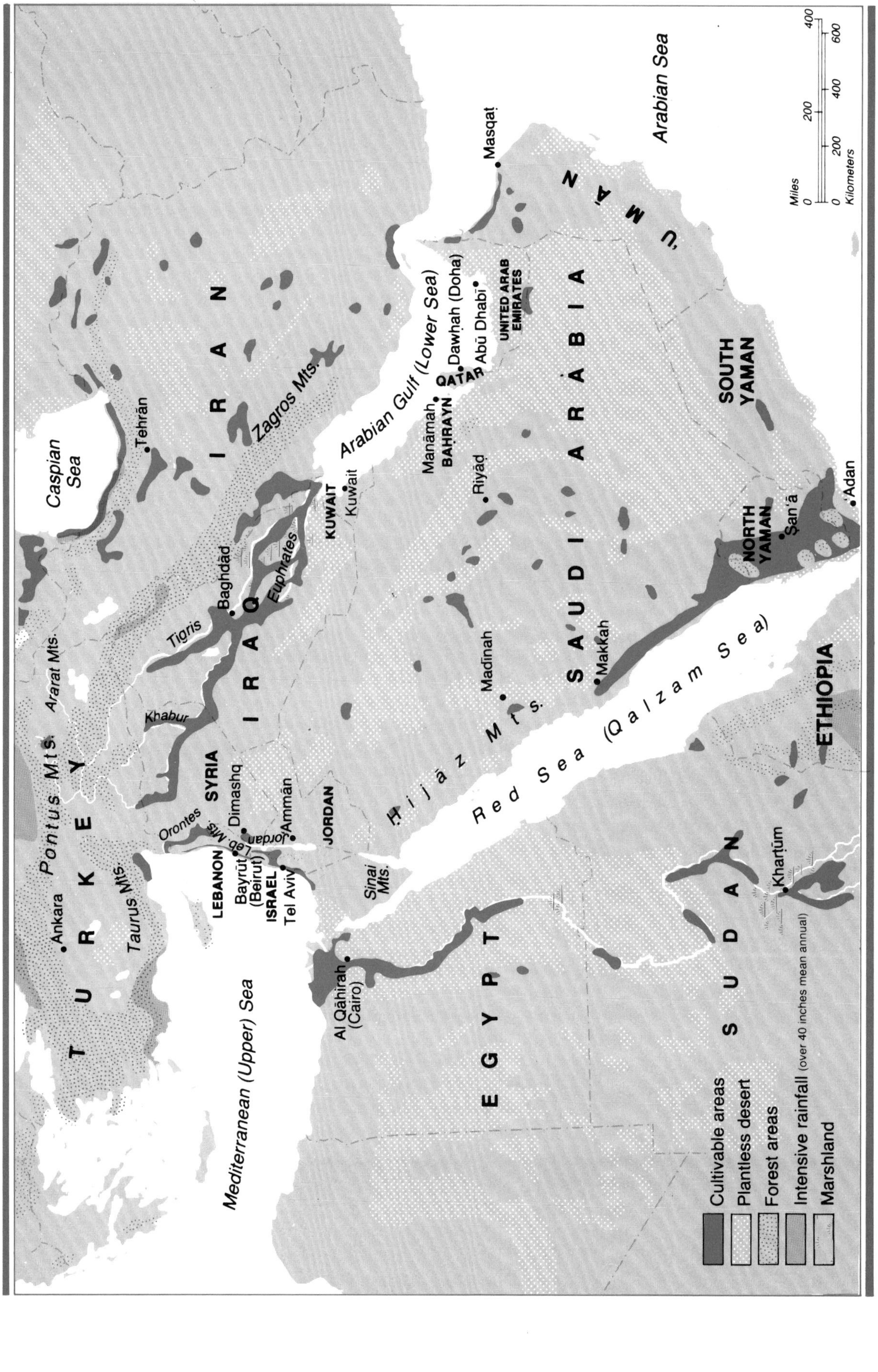

Map 1. The Arabian Theater: Physical Features and Modern States

TOPOGRAPHY

The theater in question is both a desert and a fertile land. The former is the larger unit and constitutes the main body; the latter — the crescent to the north, the Ḥijāz to the west, and al Yaman in the southwest — is the smaller and constitutes the extremities. The life and history of the two regions have been their interaction with each other. Certainly they are different in topography, indeed opposites. The desert is sparsely populated; the fertile land is dense, teeming with people. The desert, however, has numerous oases, with lavish vegetation and abundant water, punctuating its stretches and marking the routes of interregional communication. Water and the green it produces were never too far away to make life impossible, or to form a radically differing consciousness. On the other hand, the desert was always close at hand, never so far as to be "alien." In this Arabian theater, the dominant theme is interpenetration, not contrast of opposites.

The green was of many a variety. The mountainous regions of the northwest and southwest consisted of small valleys planted with cereals and vegetables and flanked by mountains covered with deciduous fruit trees, with forests of evergreen pines; or, in the higher reaches, with barren rocks and winter snow. The flat northeastern region was covered with a tropical evergreen wherever it was not intensively cultivated to produce food for humans and fodder for cattle. In its southern extremity it resembled a jungle, a thick marshland in which the waters of the river and the sea mixed and the animals of the land, water, and sky shared in a tropical and wild paradise. The date palm was omnipresent; so were the cereals of wheat and white maize, all of which constituted staple foods for the region as a whole. Certainly, the green regions produced many other foods; but these were all known to the desert dwellers, who either grew them in the oases or imported them in dried form. The difference was one of volume, the agricultural products of both regions being common and the same. If this was not literally true of the hearts of the two regions, it was certainly so on the edges where no one could clearly perceive where one region ended and the other began. Unlike the common perception of the desert as the sand dune where nothing grows and nothing lives, the Arabian desert presents a wide variety of flora supporting an equally wide variety of fauna, both of which co-existed in the two regions, in the one scantily and in the other abundantly.

Around 1500 B.C.E. the horse made its appearance in Arabia, both as an aesthetic creature and as a terrible tool of war. It was as a weapon that the horse made its entry in the hands of the "people of the mountains" who invaded the region in waves between 1500 and 900 B.C.E. These were a new amalgam of natives who populated the lands north of the Fertile Crescent — Asia Minor and the Caucasus — spurred by deposits of the larger migration of Aryan tribes from west to east. The Aryan tribes fertilized ancient Greece and Anatolia to the northwest, as well as Armenia and Persia to the northeast. They played havoc with the security and stability of the region for centuries. The warrior on horseback or in the horse-driven chariot could not be stopped by the foot soldier. However, it was not long before the horse became the standard accoutrement of the vanquished. Indeed, in Arabia, it became the object of the greatest admiration. Long genealogies of horses were kept and memorized to establish their thoroughbred character, and stately races were organized to prove their peaceful use for sport and beauty. No wonder the Arabic language has given the horse over 200 names.

Being not native to the region, the horse is not adapted to its topography. It is quick in running, but for a short while. It needs regular meals of green and cereal, and frequent drinks of water. Its hoofs need a relatively hard ground to run upon. They sink in sand and slow down the animal considerably.The camel, on the other hand, is perfectly adapted to the region. Its hoofs are flattened and especially designed not to sink in sand. Its stomach is large enough to store food for as long as a week, its humps of fat acting as a reserve store of food. It can go without water for as long as two weeks or more. A camel tolerates a much greater depletion of body water (up to 30 percent of its total weight!) than most other mammals. While a camel can drink as much as 25 gallons of water at a time, which it distributes evenly throughout its body quickly, it keeps the water content in its blood constant in case of desiccation, allowing the body cells to lose their water as the blood continues to function normally. It is thus capable of traveling long stretches of waterless desert. The longer the span it sustains itself without water, the more watery and saltier its milk becomes, which is just what is needed by its accompanying human master. Moreover, the camel is a beast of burden, capable of carrying a load of 270 kilograms across a distance of 50 kilometers in one day.

The camel was first domesticated in Arabia about 2000 B.C.E. Camel remains have been found in ancient urban sites of the region dating back to the Middle Bronze Age. Remains of Bactrian camels were found at Shah Tepe in Iran and Turkestan which go back a whole millennium earlier, to about 3000 B.C.E. Sporadic and nonurban domestication of the camel may have taken place much earlier in both regions. The earliest cuneiform inscriptions or monumental

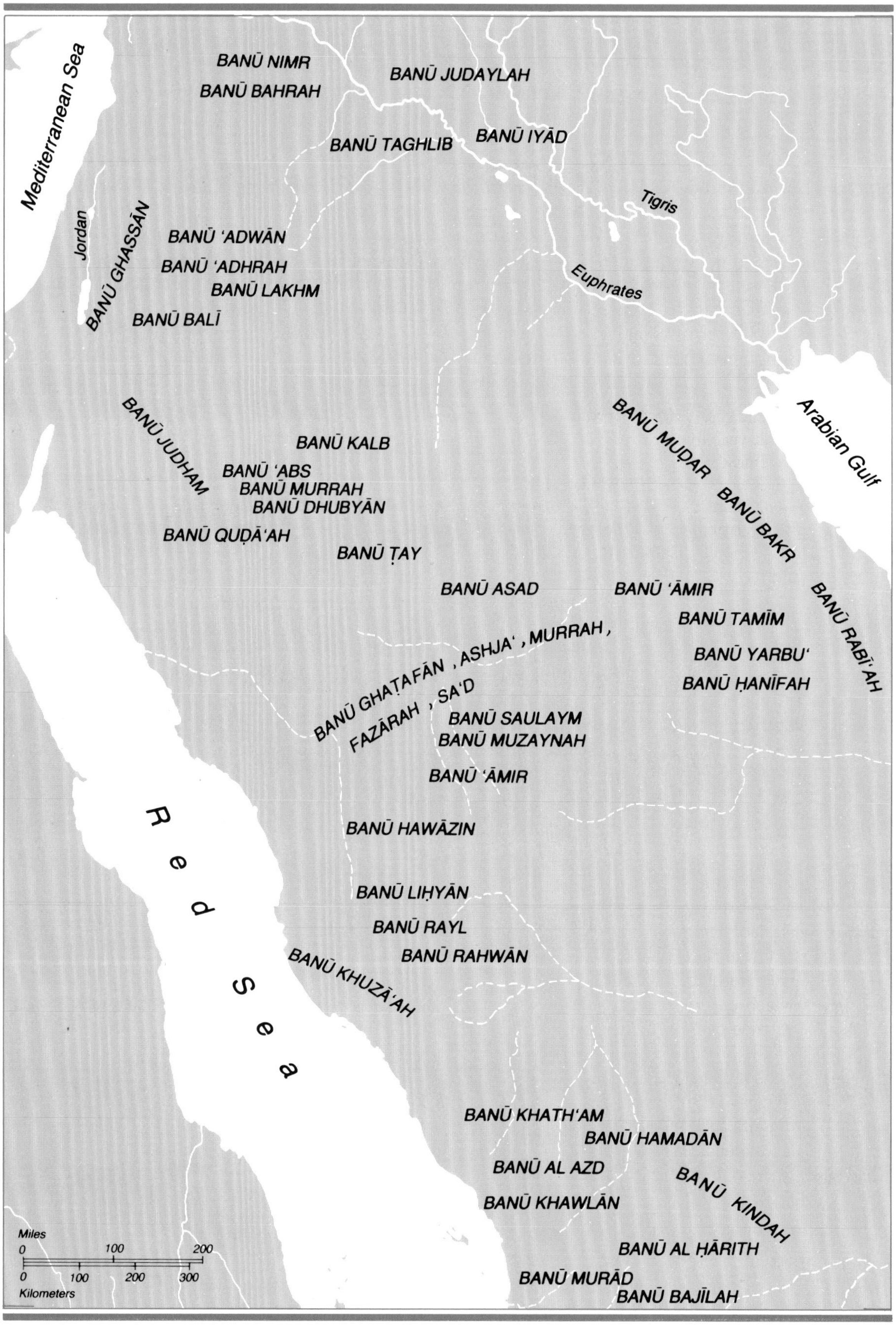
Mediterranean Sea
BANŪ NIMR
BANŪ BAHRAH
BANŪ JUDAYLAH
BANŪ TAGHLIB
BANŪ IYĀD
Tigris
Jordan
BANŪ GHASSĀN
BANŪ 'ADWĀN
BANŪ 'ADHRAH
BANŪ LAKHM
BANŪ BALĪ
Euphrates
Arabian Gulf
BANŪ JUDHAM
BANŪ KALB
BANŪ 'ABS
BANŪ MURRAH
BANŪ DHUBYĀN
BANŪ QUḌĀ'AH
BANŪ ṬAY
BANŪ MUḌAR
BANŪ BAKR
BANŪ ASAD
BANŪ 'ĀMIR
BANŪ TAMĪM
BANŪ RABĪ'AH
BANŪ YARBU'
BANŪ ḤANĪFAH
BANŪ GHAṬAFĀN, ASHJA', MURRAH,
FAZĀRAH, SA'D
BANŪ SAULAYM
BANŪ MUZAYNAH
BANŪ 'ĀMIR
Red Sea
BANŪ HAWĀZIN
BANŪ LIḤYĀN
BANŪ RAYL
BANŪ RAHWĀN
BANŪ KHUZĀ'AH
BANŪ KHATH'AM
BANŪ HAMADĀN
BANŪ AL AZD
BANŪ KINDAH
BANŪ KHAWLĀN
BANŪ AL ḤĀRITH
BANŪ MURĀD
BANŪ BAJĪLAH
Miles
0
100
200
0
100
200
300
Kilometers

THE ARAB TRIBES: GENEALOGY

AL 'ARAB AL 'ĀRIBAH
(The Arabizing Arabs)

- Qaḥṭān
  - Ya'rub
    - Yashjub
      - Saba'
        - Ḥimyar
          - Quḍā'ah
            - 'Adhrah (S. Ḥijāz)
            - Juhaynah (N. Ḥijāz)
            - Tanūkh (N.E. Baḥrayn)
            - Kalb (N.E. Arabia, Kūfah)
            - Bahrā' (N. Ḥijāz)
            - Jarm (Central Arabia)
            - Nahr (Yaman)
        - Al Azd
          - 'Ātik
          - Thumālah
          - Banū Naṣr (Al Ḥīrah, Tihāmah)
          - Azd 'Umān ('Umān)
          - Khuzā'ah (Makkah), Banū Ḥārithah
          - Al Aws and Al Khazraj (Yathrib), Banū Tha'labah
          - Ghassān (Syria)
        - Kahlān
          - Lakhm (Al Ḥīrah)
          - Judham (Yaman)
          - 'Āmilah (N. Syria, 'Āmilah Mts.)
          - Madhḥaj (Yaman)
          - Hamadān (Central Yaman, Arabia)
          - Khath'am (Yaman)
          - Bajīlah (Yaman)
          - Ṭay (Central Hijaz)
          - Jabal Shammar

representations of camels go back to 1100 B.C.E., as evidenced on the Broken Obelisk and earliest orthostates of Tall Ḥalaf.[1] From that time on, camels played very important war roles. The confederacy of Hebrew, Midianite, Horebite, and other northwest Arabian tribes which entered Palestine in the twelfth century B.C.E. rode camels; and so did the Amurru irruptions into the Fertile Crescent six to eight centuries earlier. As it did to the horse and the lion, the Arabic language gave the camel a great abundance of names, denoting its age, color, special physical characteristics, descendence, and the number of offspring it had sired, carried, or nursed.

Map 2. The Arab Tribes on the Eve of Islam

DEMOGRAPHY

The people who have inhabited the geographic theater of Arabia belong to one race of humans, the Caucasian, or West Asian, otherwise known as "Semite" or "Semitic." The term "Semite" was invented by Old Testament scholars of the eighteenth century who first became aware of the presence of "Semitic" peoples, languages, and civilizations other than the Hebrew, Arabian, and Ethiopic, as a result of archeological discoveries made in the territories of the Fertile Crescent. Guided by the genealogies of the Old Testament (Genesis 10), Johann Gottfried Eichhorn attributed the name "Semite" to the descendants of Sem or Shem, son of Noah, whom he presumed to be the Hebrews, descendants of Isaac, son of Abraham; the Arabs, descendants of Isaac's elder brother Ishmael; and all other peoples of the ancient Near East who spoke languages that are sisters of Hebrew and Arabic and for which no other name could be found.[2]

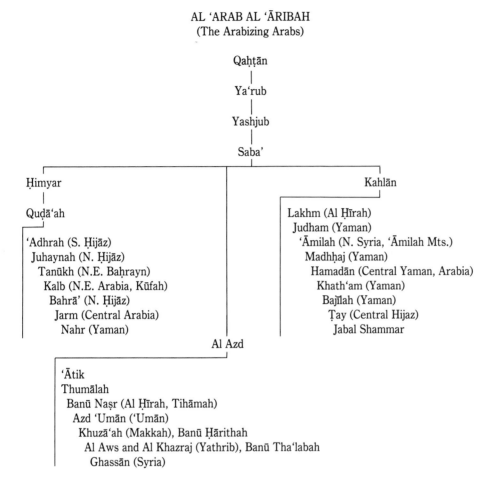

AL 'ARAB AL MUSTA'RIBAH I
(The Arabized Arabs I)

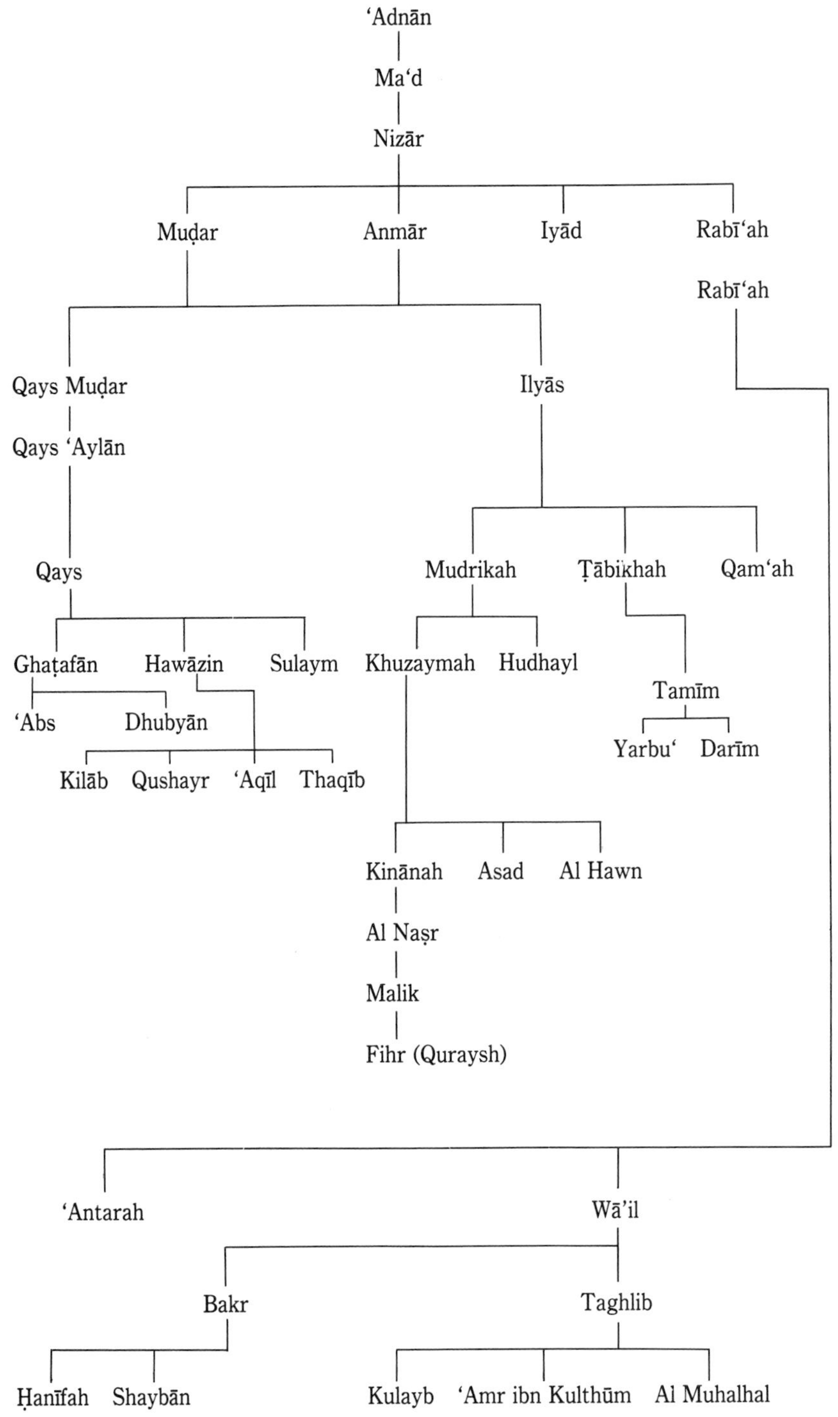

AL 'ARAB AL MUSTA'RIBAH II
(The Arabized Arabs II)

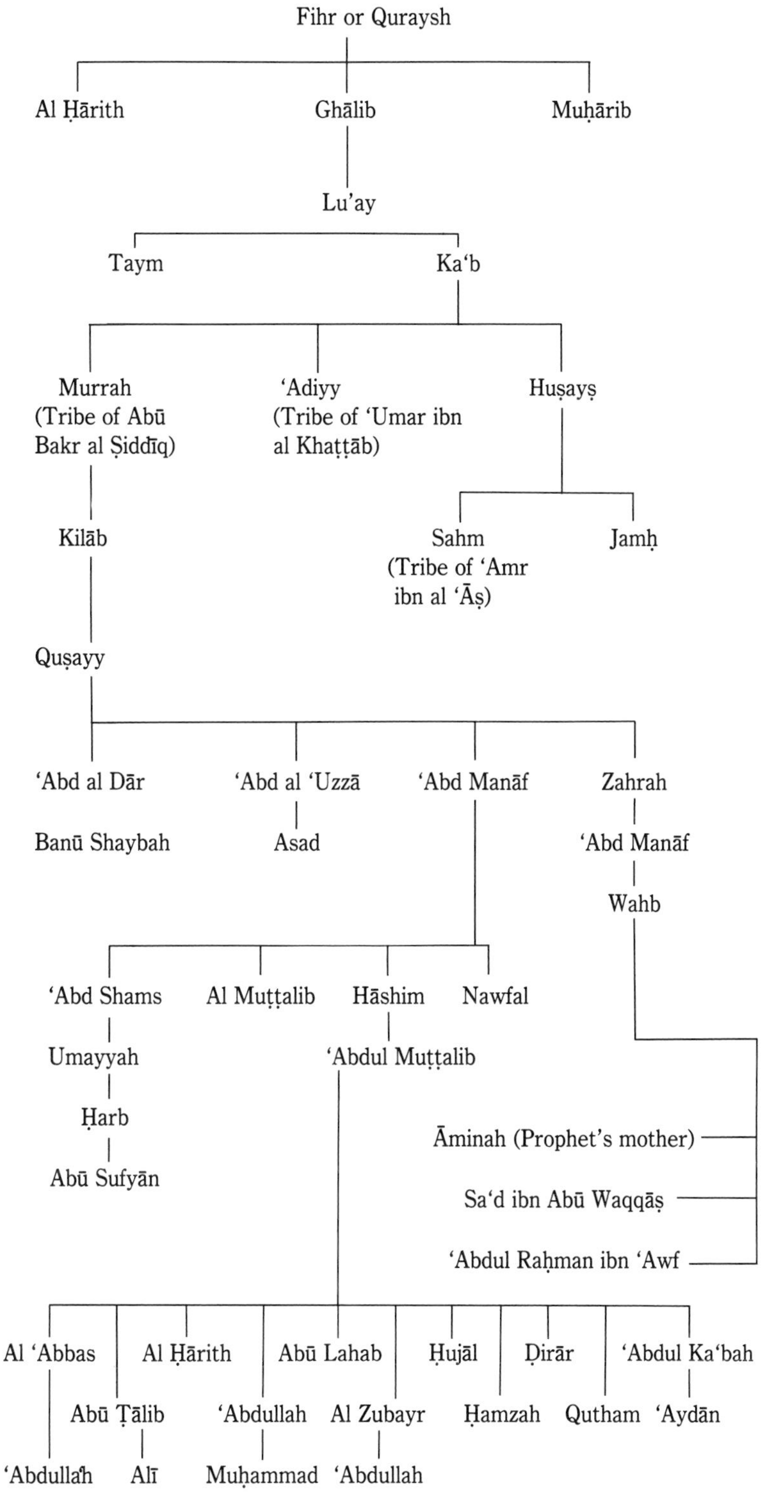

Illustration 1.1

Inlaid column from Tall al'Ubayd (limestone, shell, and mother-of-pearl), c. 4000 B.C.E. [Courtesy The University Museum, University of Pennsylvania.]

Although the appellation is almost universally accepted, it is unworthy for two reasons. First, it is founded on the Old Testament claim that the Deluge was a universal, cosmic event in which all humans except Noah and his children perished, a claim which only faith in the literal word of the Old Testament can support.[3] Although it is certain that the city Orim (Biblical Ur) in lower Mesopotamia prospered in two periods of history separated by a flood that occurred about 3000 B.C.E., there is no evidence that a universal flood took place at that time. Hence, the Old Testament claim must be cut down to size, as describing Noah's locality and community alone. Second, none of the peoples called "Semite" have ever perceived themselves in terms of this biological descendance from Shem, son of Noah, except the Christians and Jews of the modern West. The perception is ethnocentric, a creation of romantic Europe. The peoples of the ancient Near East certainly perceived themselves as people in terms of the languages they spoke, the religions or cultures they adhered to, or the political regime under which they lived, not their biological descendance or race. Only the Hebrews have done so; and except for them, the perception of race is absent from Arabia.

The actors of the Arabian theater were, in the main, all native to the area. They moved from one part to other parts, but not from outside the theater into it, nor from within the theater to the outside world, except, under the Phoenicians (1730–1570 B.C.E.), to Egypt, and under Islam.

Internal Population Movements

From desert nomadism to settled farming. Within the theater, the population has never been still. Movement from farmland to pasture land and from pasture land to farmland took place constantly and characterized every phase of the theater's history. In fact, the history of the whole area is little more than the causes and consequences of such domestic demographic movements.

The Arabian desert has never been a desolate area free of population. Its oases and other lands adjoining the fertile areas have always supported populations. True, desert scarcity imposed a very strict lifestyle which helped mold human character and develop mental and social traits that gave its people many of their peculiar distinctions. The self-discipline required to keep one's instincts under ascetic control, the raising of generosity and hospitality to the rank of cardinal virtue, observance of the most cohesive group loyalty, preoccupation with precision in description and depth in self-analysis, the predilection for contemplation, for self-transport by appeal to the imagination through language—these and many more distinctive characteristics owe their intensive development in Arabia partly to the conditions of life the desert imposes. Desert scarcity therefore did not make life impossible, though it may have contributed toward building population pressures that made immigration indispensable. Such pressures may have even caused explosive immigration to the adjoining fertile lands. However, the flow out of the desert into the fertile areas has taken place throughout the ages.

This flow of humans from the desert into the farmland was responsible for a wide tradition of literature depicting relations between farmer and shepherd. The most famous account is the story of Dumuzi and

Enkimdu, which dates back to the earliest Sumerian times and which comes to us as a love story of two gods seeking the hand of the same goddess. What we have of the poem begins with the assumption that Inanna, who had already committed herself to Enkimdu, the farmer, is entreated by her brother Utu to marry Dumuzi, the shepherd. She refuses haughtily, declaring marriage to Dumuzi below her dignity. Dumuzi then introduces himself and lists his good points against those of the farmer Enkimdu. This delights Inanna who is now charmed by Dumuzi's eloquence and convinced of his worthiness to be her husband. Dumuzi becomes full of joy. He challenges the farmer to a fight; the farmer declines; and reconciliation and happiness for all ensue. The farmer permits the shepherd to graze his flocks on the farmland, the shepherd invites the farmer to his wedding, and they exchange gifts in friendship and reciprocal esteem.[4]

Of course, on other occasions the advent of shepherds upon the sedentary populations of the fertile zones was not as peaceful. A Sumerian hymn to the god of the West gives a warlike description of the Amorites (Amurru) who migrated from the Arabian desert into Mesopotamia and Syria around 2000 B.C.E.

> The weapon is his companion
> Who knows no submission
> Who eats uncooked flesh
> Who has no house in his life-time
> Who does not bury his dead companion.[5]

This, however, was the exception. The incontrovertible fact about these migrations is that they took place slowly, over very long periods of time during which penetration by intermarriage and assimilation were the rule. A tribe never moved *in toto* like a modern mechanized army. The movement was always slow, extending over generations during which countless members of the moving tribe experienced the sedentary life; learned trades, handicrafts, and farming; intermarried with the natives and settled down and grew roots. Evidently, some stayed behind when the tribe moved and became the tribe's human deposit, embodying its language or dialect and perpetuating its customs, culture, and values.

The people of the Arabian desert migrated to the Fertile Crescent in the north from the earliest times. They traveled on foot or on donkey back on a path circumscribing the northern reaches of the desert in a clockwise direction. The western parts of the peninsula were always the more densely populated. From that region, the path of migration would naturally run straight north to east Jordan and Syria, turn east at the northernmost hump of the desert and descend on the west side of Mesopotamia all the way to the Arabian Gulf. Since their means of transportation was the donkey, they could not wander too far into the desert, but had to remain close to the land with water, hugging it throughout their journey along the periphery of the desert. Their course, starting from the Ḥijāz, would ultimately bring them to Mesopotamia, descending on it, as it were, from the north. This fact accords with Sumerian descriptions of the Akkadians as migrants coming from the north. A west–east crossing of the desert was impossible before the domestication of the camel, and eastern Arabia was always too scarcely populated to launch any large-scale migration.

From settled farming to desert nomadism. Population movement was not limited to migration from the desert to the Fertile Crescent in the north. A similar migration took place in the opposite direction. Sociologists have always regarded the former movement as usual and justified because it was seen to lift people to a more developed level of life, from the harsh conditions of the desert to the temperate mode of lands fertilized by rain or river. It changed their scarcity into abundance, their wandering into settlement; and it obviated their need for perpetual raiding and hostility. It opened for them avenues other than war, namely, law-abiding trade and production and exchange of goods. But why would anyone want to move in the opposite direction?

Three major causes may pressure population to do so. The first may have been a natural catastrophe such as a strong earthquake or flood. Arab tradition is alive with the memory of the destruction of the great dam in Ma'rib in the Sabaean Kingdom in southwest Arabia in the fifth century C.E., which brought about vast destruction and caused havoc among the population. Arab tradition tells of many tribes from the fertile south who migrated to the desert in the north because of that disaster. The Azd tribe, for instance, with all its clans in the Fertile Crescent traces its genealogy to a settled ancestry in Yaman.

The second major cause of migration into the desert by the settled population of the fertile land is ideological disagreement with the ruling regime. Religious difference led to persecution in Ur (the case of Abraham and Nimrod) toward the beginning of the second millennium B.C.E. as well as in Yaman in 523 C.E. (the Christians and Dhū Nuwās). In both cases, which we shall have occasion to discuss separately and in detail later, the persecuted had to flee. The Arabian desert with its trackless expanse and rugged terrain provides excellent hiding places. The ubiquitous cult of hospitality among its dwellers provides shelter for the newcomer who may prove a great help in future relations with the settled people whence he migrated.

The third major cause of migration into the desert is that life in the desert is superior to that of the fertile land. Its harshness and privation are compensated by the freedom and simplicity it provides, the leisure to contemplate, the meticulous care for pronunciation and diction, the love and ecstasy of poetry and eloquence, the single-minded pursuit of *murū'ah*— the virtues of manliness, courage, fidelity, and hospitality — indeed, the very capacity to rise above the stream of existence, to reach a fresh perspective of truth and reality. The Arabian desert is certainly not an expanse of sand dunes. It is, rather, a steppe with some rain, a wide variety of flora and fauna, capable of supporting herds of camels, sheep and goats, and humans. The desert dweller has always regarded himself purer in genealogy and speech than the settled farmer, stronger in war, more resolute in peace, firmer in the face of adversity, truer in friendship, and, generally, of a nobler frame of mind. Moreover, the desert was never so far away that the settled people hardly knew it. The latter ventured into the desert frequently and on a regular basis, especially in the spring; and the desert people were to them no strangers but cousins and relatives, whether close or distant. Life in the farmland showed higher technology and material prosperity, but lower dignity and greater commercialism. The more sensitive nature could find in desert life the greater appeal and the richer self-realization.

The last two causes may very well coalesce into a new vision of life; or the persecuted dissenters may make common cause with such vision born out of the desert man's constant preoccupation with the questions of identity and destiny. Population pressure or historical pretexts become tools and instruments in the hands of a movement bound to forge new paths for history.

External Population Movements

Invasions from the outside. Certainly the theater has witnessed some invasions by outsiders. Hittites, the "peoples of the mountains" mentioned earlier, entered Arabia from Asia Minor as early as 1535 B.C.E. under Mursulis I, who raided Babylon and thus opened the way to its domination by the Kassites from the east (Persia). The Hittites continued to harass the region from their bases in Syria, and Hurrians entered north Mesopotamia from the Caucasus. For three whole centuries after their political emergence about 1500 B.C.E., the Hurrians, Hittites, and Kassites dominated the scene and set up governments to rule the territories they conquered. The state of Mitanni in north Mesopotamia was established by the Hurrians about 1500 B.C.E., with its capital at Wassukkanni, but it collapsed 150 years later. It extended almost to the Mediterranean and included the cities of Nuzi and Arrapkha in Assyria and Alalakh in Syria. The state prospered and had such good relations with Egypt that the pharaohs Thut-mose IV (1406–1398 B.C.E.) and Amen-Hotep III (1398–1361 B.C.E.) took Mitanni princesses in marriage. But those good relations collapsed in 1365 B.C.E. in consequence of a succession war which forced Mattiwaza to sign a treaty of vassaldom to Suppiluliumas, king of the Hittites.

The "peoples of the mountains" were mixtures of natives and Indo-Europeans deposited there by the Aryan migrations. In every case, the rulers and nobles were Indo-European (by evidence of their names) who set themselves up as a ruling class apart from the others and who monopolized the new strategic weaponry of the age: the horse and the chariot. They used an elaborate system of political, juridical, and diplomatic relationships to perpetuate the class difference. The rulers themselves, however, succumbed to the influence of the natives on all fronts, using their language to write their official documents and adopting their religions, cultures, and mores. The Kassites

Illustration 1.2

Jar with stylized animals, Jamdat-Naṣr type, found at Kaffājah, c. 2500 B.C.E. [Courtesy The University Museum, University of Pennsylvania.]

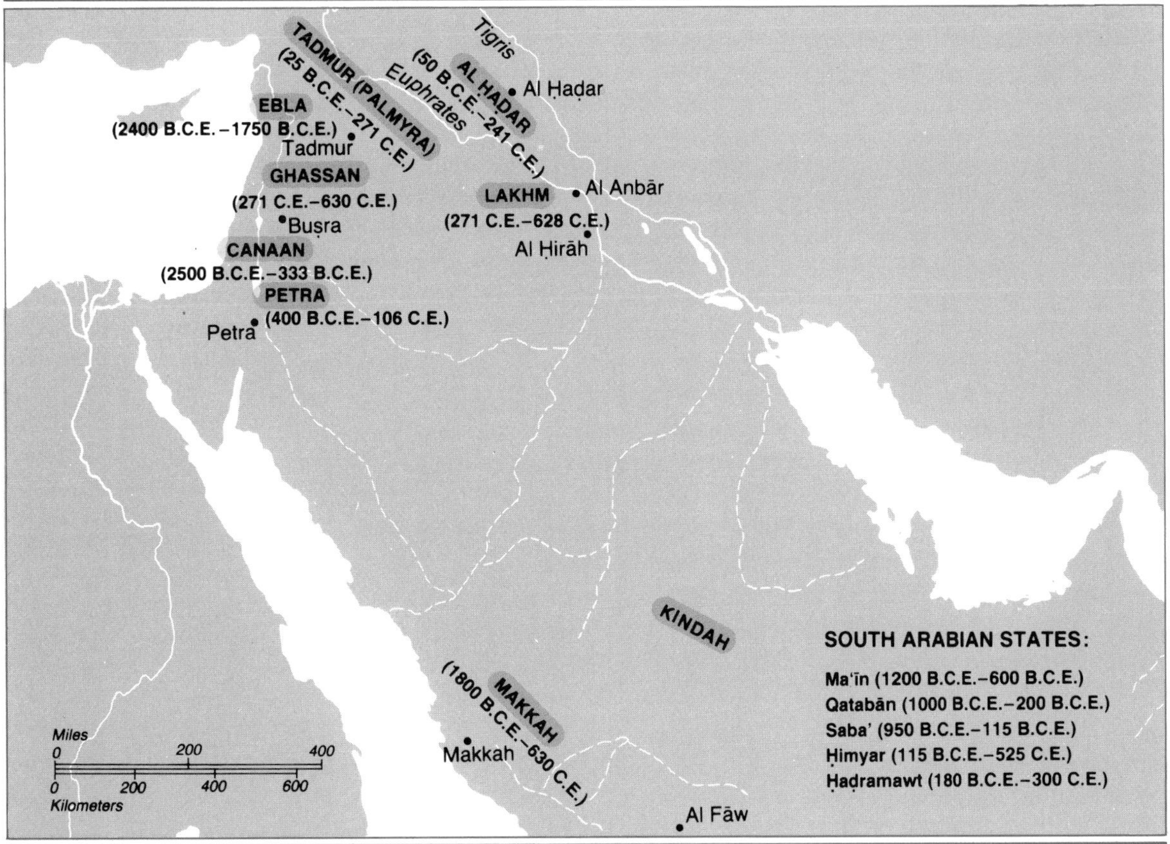

Map 3. Arab Pre-Islamic States

were the first to assimilate themselves entirely to Mesopotamian religion and culture. Gradually, all the others did likewise, and adopted the language, culture, and religion of the people they conquered. Indeed, their assimilation helped spread the language of the natives (Akkadian) and their culture among people who never spoke it, including the Egyptians, as the evidence of the Amarna (Akhetaton) letters indicates. Cuneiform script spread all over the Near East, and the great literary works of Mesopotamia, embodying its culture, religion, artistic motifs, and themes, not only were adopted by the invading conquerors but were spread by those conquerors to distant lands and peoples. "Thus," wrote Sabatino Moscati, "the new civilization has neither victors nor vanquished. Like Rome in the Middle Ages, despite its political decadence, Mesopotamia in the age of the "peoples of the mountains" celebrates the triumph of its culture."[6]

After a period of self-consolidation in Anatolia, the Hittites under Hattusilis I sent an expedition against Aleppo around 1750 B.C.E., and two centuries later

TADMUR (PALMYRA)

Tribes:	Banū Ghassān and Tanūkh groups, Banū Baḥrah, etc.
Capital:	Tadmur
Religion:	Mostly Christian Monophysite and Mesopotamian
History:	Tadmur of Amurru 1100 B.C.E.
	Hadriana Palmyra (Hadrian's visit in 130 C.E.)
	Flowering: 130–270. Included Egypt and Asia Minor up to Ankara.
	Trade to China, heir to Petra
	Vassal to Rome from 117 C.E.
	Destroyed by Aurelian in 272 C.E.

PETRA: NABATAEAN STATE

Tribes:	Midyan, Judhām, Banū Baliy, Banū 'Adhrah
Religion:	Mesopotamian
Capital:	Petra, founded in 5th century B.C.E.
History:	Flowering in 1st century B.C.E.
	Trade center in North and South traffic
	Invaded by Romans in 105 C.E.
Features:	Petra: City carved in rock

AL ḤAḌAR (HATARA) 85–241 C.E.

Tribes:	Banū Nimr, Banū Taghlib, Banū Judaylah
Religion:	Mesopotamian; a few Christians and Zoroastrians

Capital:	Al Ḥaḍar, 50 km west of Ashur
History:	Began in the 1st century B.C.E.
	Flourished on trade, controlling traffic between Mesopotamia and Asia Minor, Persia, and Byzantium
	A vassal of Persia
	Persian anger over her prosperity brought destruction to the state in 241 C.E.
Features:	Shamash (The Sun) is principal god. Outstanding architecture and statuary at capital.
	Poets: Ṭarafah ibn al 'Abd, Ḥārith ibn Ḥillizah, 'Amr ibn Kulthūm, all Mu'allaqāt winners
LAKHM	
Tribes:	Tanūkh, Banū Bakr, Banū Taghlib, Banū Muḍar
Religion:	Mesopotamian; some Zoroastrians and Christian Nestorians
Capital:	Al Ḥīrah, 3 miles south of Kūfah
History:	Vassal to Persia from 400 C.E.
	Direct Persian Rule 602–635
	End of state: Islamic Futūḥāt, 635 C.E.
Features:	Al Khawarnaq, the Great Palace of Bahram Gur, son of Yazdigird
GHASSĀN	
Tribes:	Banū Ghassān
Religion:	Mostly Monophysite Christian; some Mesopotamians and Jews
Capital:	Buṣra, al Jābiyah, Jillīq
History:	Flowering in 6th century C.E.
	Battle with Lakhm in 545, 554, 580
	Invaded by Persia, 613–614
	Liberated by Byzantium in 629
Features:	War hero-poets: Labīd, Mu'allaqah winner; Ḥassān ibn Thābit, the Prophet's poet
Last king:	Jabalah ibn al Ayham
KINDAH	
Tribes:	Banū Bakr, Banū Asad, Banū Ghaṭafān, Banū Kinānah
Religion:	Makkan/Mesopotamian
Capital:	Alfaw in south
	Al Anbār in north (on Euphrates)
History:	0–529 C.E.
	Flowering 480–529 C.E.
	Vassal to Ṭubba' Kings of Yaman
	Hero-Poet: Al Samaw'al
Features:	Poets: Umru' al Qays (d. 328 C.E.) (Mu'allaqah winner); Samaw'al, the Jew at Taymā'
MAKKAH	
Tribes:	Quraysh
Religion:	Makkan/Mesopotamian
Capital:	Makkah
History:	Major religious center
	Ka'bah—Repository of 365 idols of all Arabs
	Pilgrimage center
	Trade capital of Arabia
Features:	Sūq 'Ukāẓ, the annual national competition of poets
	Preeminent prestige in all aspects among Arabs
	Moral hegemony over Peninsula

felt sufficiently strong to send a raid against Babylon. This was the Old Empire which lasted until 1380 B.C.E., when succession problems provided an occasion for Suppiluliumas to take over the reins of power (1380–1346). The weakness of Egypt as a result of Akhenaton's reforms provided another chance for Suppiluliumas to extend his empire into upper Mesopotamia, upper Syria, and Lebanon. In 1250 B.C.E. the Hittite empire came to its end at the hand of "the peoples of the sea" armed with the new weapons of the Iron Age, who descended upon the whole region from Greece, the Aegean Sea islands, Crete, and Cyprus. These came to the region at a period of great weakness and division. Egypt and Mesopotamia were in eclipse, suffering from invasion by the "peoples of the mountains." Moreover, several centuries of competition in the western arm of the Fertile Crescent or geographic Syria had weakened both parties and left Syria open to whosoever could wield the power to grab it. The Hittites contended for it; and so did "the peoples of the sea," who arrived with equal if not superior arms and mastered the sea lanes between the eastern shores of the Mediterranean and their island homes.

Like their cousins to the north—the Hittites, the Hurrians, and the Kassites—the "peoples of the sea" were quickly assimilated by Mesopotamian civilization. Their greatest contribution was in neither religion, language, nor culture but in their political formation, which enabled them to establish their hegemony by making effective use of their new iron weaponry. Their chief was a ***primus inter pares,*** a chief with limited powers put at the helm of the state by a class of nobles who supported as well as controlled him. Like the "peoples of the mountains," the "peoples of the seas" had chiefs who were neither gods, as in the case of Egypt, nor god's vicars on earth, as in Mesopotamia. Upon conquering another people, they did not kill or spoil wantonly, nor did they enslave their victims. They entered with them into a treaty that defined their status as overlords and turned the defeated into vassals. The subservient status of the vanquished was defined in the treaty, which also served as juridical document or source of law and authority. This was a form of federalism hitherto unknown. The conquerors'authority was established alongside the local authority of the natives, thus precluding any imperialist expansion and opening the gates to acculturation. The cultures and religions, the customs and mores, began to intermingle, allowing the stronger to emerge victorious over both conqueror and vanquished. Whereas some elements of the conquerors' culture were assimilated into Mesopotamian culture, their separate identity as a group was doomed. As soon as their political hegemony subsided, their separate identity collapsed and they became one with the indigenous people of the land.

It was otherwise with the Egyptians who, following the Hyksos invasion during the 18th Dynasty (1570–1305 B.C.E.) occupied the western arm of the Fertile Crescent and resisted assimilation. Their purpose was then to safeguard the frontiers of Egypt and punish those who defied the pharaoh or flouted his command. During the Empire (1465–1090 B.C.E.), their purpose was still the same, but the political turbulence of the period and the advent of the "peoples of the mountains" and "peoples of the seas" demanded a more stable Egyptian presence. Whereas Egyptian expansion southward into Nubia and westward into Libya meant annexation, expansion toward Asia meant only extension of military and political power. The Asian lands occupied by Egypt were never incorporated into the Egyptian kingdom. To the Egyptian, the Asiatic was forever alien, forever in need to be subjugated militarily and politically, but never to be an associate. Hence, Egypt was content to appoint a commissioner to exercise control over the Asiatic sovereigns and their peoples and to extract tribute from them as ordered by the pharaoh. This Egyptian imperialism had its periods of glory and weakness. In both, it never meant assimilation except to those Egyptians whom official duty brought to Syria for long periods of time. The majority, however, could and did return home to their people, their land, and their culture, having regarded their presence among the Asiatics as a necessary but transient military expedition. The few whom circumstances forced to remain in Asia were, like all other non-Asiatics, assimilated and dissolved in the crucible of "Arabia." Assimilation of these Egyptians went so far as to cause the pharaoh's officers in Asia to correspond with their superiors back home in Akkadian, the Mesopotamian language of the Fertile Crescent.

Not exactly the same fate awaited the Persians. Under the Achaemenid Empire (550–330 B.C.E.), Cyrus invaded Babylon and Cambyses led his forces to occupy the whole length and breadth of Syria as well as Egypt. Direct Persian rule in Egypt lasted over a century, and was overthrown only in 401 B.C.E. with the establishment of the 27th Dynasty. In Syria, however, it continued unchallenged until Alexander the Great put an end to it in 332 B.C.E. The fate of the Persians in Egypt does not concern us here since Egypt was then no part of the civilization of Arabia. But in the Fertile Crescent, the Persians had assimilated themselves to Mesopotamian civilization; and they contributed to it in numerous significant ways. For the first time in history, they united Western Asia except the Arabian Peninsula proper under one empire. From India to the Danube, from the Caspian Sea to Nubia—all these territories were united for the first time under one administration. An administrative system of satraps with identical instructions and policies, the opening of communication between the provinces, the introduction of coinage to facilitate commerce, indeed, the building of the interprovince 1,500-mile highway from Susa to Sardis all helped to establish a fair measure of unity, security, and prosperity for all inhabitants.

Whereas Cyrus, the founder, followed a policy of tolerance, allowing native dynasties and institutions to operate under Persian hegemony, his son Darius and grandson Xerxes imposed an exclusivist version of the religion of Zarathustra, earning for both the title of cruel tyrant. In an inscription of Xerxes unearthed at Persepolis, the king proclaimed: "Some of the countries . . . revolted; but I crushed them with the aid of Ahuramazda. . . . Under the shadow of Ahuramazda I uprooted the temples of the wicked god and made proclamation: No more must ye worship the wicked gods."[7] Nonetheless, the Persian presence in the theater of Arabia dissolved through assimilation. This was due to two reasons: First, there was the tremendous capacity of Mesopotamian civilization to influence, acculturate, and assimilate the newcomer. Second, the process of Mesopotamianization or Arabization of the Persian peoples had begun centuries before their arrival on the scene as conquerors, so that the ideological difference between conqueror and conquered was too small to be significant. That is especially evident in the artistic and literary forms they brought to Arabia. In addition, the arrival of the Greeks and the defeat of the Persians severed the Persian presence in Arabia from the Persian heartland. Whatever remained of that presence within the Arabian world quickly completed its Mesopotamianization and became indistinguishable.

The conquerors of later times present us with much more straightforward cases. The Greeks were responsible for much Hellenization in the Fertile Crescent. This notwithstanding, those that remained within the area were acculturated and assimilated by a process that began with Alexander the Great and that had claimed him toward the end of his life. The fate of the Romans was identical. So was that of the Tatars, Mongols, and Turkmen who arrived in Arabia as immigrants in successive waves beginning in the eighth century C.E. or who did so as conquerors in the thirteenth century. The latter practiced some variety of shamanism which they dropped as they learned the culture and religion of Islam. The grandson of Genghis Khan became a Muslim, and his sons rallied the forces

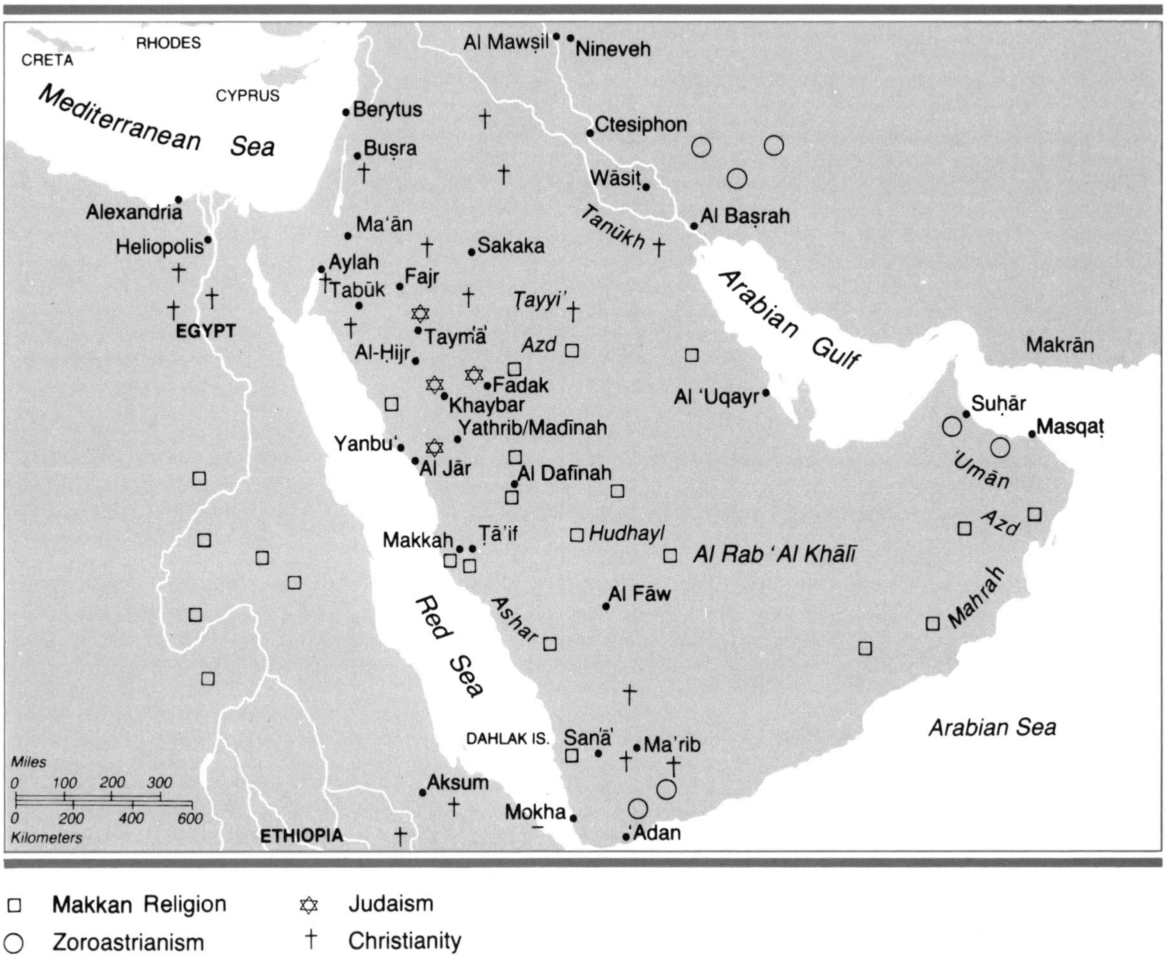

Map 4. Religion in Pre-Islamic Arabia

of the Muslim community *(ummah)* to march behind them on a new wave of conquests in Russia, the Balkans, and central Europe. The Muslims of the world acclaimed the house of 'Uthmān and elected its members caliphs, not as alien Turks but as Muslims who had become thoroughly assimilated into the culture of the region, Islam.

The same facts are equally true of the Crusaders who arrived from Europe in several waves in the twelfth–fourteenth centuries C.E. They marched through, occupied large areas of geographic Syria, and succeeded in establishing a number of petty states. The Crusader state of Jerusalem was in its day one of the strongest in the region, and the Crusaders themselves were the most close-knit religious and political community in an alien land. As an autonomous state, theirs lasted over 100 years. Eventually, however, Europe lost interest in the Crusaders and their adventure; some returned home, but most decided to stay and make it on their own. In a generation or two, their acculturation and assimilation were complete. They intermarried with the natives and became indistinguishable from them.

More recently, the British, French, and Italian peoples invaded, occupied, and colonized vast regions of Arabia which had since, and by virtue of Islam, spread to include the whole of North Africa. Their arrival was the effect of the industrial expansion of Europe, and their colonization of that area was carried out in a romantic consciousness of the superiority of their race over that of the area's inhabitants. Their military, political, and economic power was unchallengeable, and the Arab world groaned under their yoke for almost a century. The ties of the colonizers with their mother countries remained extremely strong throughout their expatriation. Hence, when their occupation was no longer tenable, practically all of them returned home. Two exceptions, however, must be recorded: the French expeditionary force of Napoleon, which occupied Egypt, and the French *colons* of Tunisia, Algeria, and Morocco. The former stayed in Egypt largely because of the destruction of their fleet (Abū Qīr Bay, 1798 C.E.) and frustration of their whole campaign by the British. The latter did so largely because of the socioeconomic hardship involved in self-uprooting and resettling. The former were completely acculturated and assimilated in a generation, and the latter are currently undergoing the same process.

Thus Arabia has suffered the influx into it of a large variety of ethnic elements. But it has digested them all, converting them to its religion and worldview, acculturating and assimilating them. The invasions and colonizations certainly brought about some physical changes in the racial complexion of the native inhabitants. But to the spirit, the language, the categories of consciousness, the religion and ideology of Arabia, they contributed nothing. Arabia was enriched more or less significantly by the original elements that each wave of invasions brought with it, from the horses and chariots of the "peoples of the mountains" to the gnostic philosophy and natural sciences of the Hellenes, and the technologies of ancient Egypt as well as of the modern West. Throughout five or six millennia, Arabia has maintained a continuing demographic unity. No addition was large enough or significant enough to alter the nature or composition of that unity. Hence, it is indeed proper to speak of an Arabian ethnicity, although almost every ideology that "Arabia" has subscribed to during its long history (the ideologies of some Hebrews and some pre-Islamic peninsular Arabs excepted) has preached the anti-ethnocentric lesson of universalism.

Semitic invasions of the outside (Egypt, Africa, Phoenicia, and Islam). Since the theater of the early history of humankind was assumed by the Bible and its scholars to be the Fertile Crescent, it followed that Ham and his descendants originated there and moved to Africa under their father Noah's curse.[8] The decipherment of Egyptian hieroglyphs revealed a number of similarities with Semitic languages, and this spurred a long controversy as to the relations of the languages and of the peoples that spoke them.[9] Some scholars regarded Egyptian as a member of the Semitic family of languages and explained the differences as due to time and living conditions. Others regarded it as Hamitic and explained the similarities as due to invasion of one group by the other, leading to the opposite theory that the Semites were once the inhabitants of the Nile Valley.[10] History has recorded Mesopotamian influences on Egypt in consequence of trade in the last 500 years of the

MAKKAN/MESOPOTAMIAN RELIGION

Throughout Peninsula

Idols: Wadd at Maʻīn; Sacred Palm at Najrān; Dhāt Anwāṭ (tree) at Makkah; al ʻUzzā at Nakhlah; Al Lāt at Ṭā'if; Dhū al Sharā at Petra; Manāt (Black Stone) at Qudayd, between Makkah and Yathrib; Hubal, chief deity at the Kaʻbah
Great Days Remembered and Celebrated:
Day of Buʻāth: Aws vs. Khazraj, 610 C.E.
Days of Fujār: Quraysh and Kinānah vs. Hawāzin, 585 C.E.
Day of al Basūs: Banū Bakr vs. Banū Taghlib, 498 C.E.
War hero-poets: Al Jassās ibn Murrah vs. Al Muhalhil
Day of Dāḥis and Ghabrā': ʻAbs vs. Dhubyān, 530 C.E.
War hero-poet: ʻAntar ibn Shaddād, 615 C.E.
Day of ʻUkāẓ: Annual day of national poetry competition at Nakhlah and Ṭā'if

CHRISTIANITY

Byzantine Empire: Dominant throughout

Fertile Crescent:	Common in Ghassān state from 500 C.E. (Monophysite Rite); Yaʻqūb al Bardaʻī (Jacob Baradeus), "Prelate of all Arabs," at Edessa; Jabalah ibn al Ayham, last king of Ghassān, converts into and out of Islam, 634 C.E.
	Scattered through Lakhm State (Nestorian Rite); Saint: Simeon, living on pillar, 400–418 C.E.
	A few adherents in North Arabia
Arabian Peninsula:	A few in Yaman (Coptic Church); Aryāṭ (Abyssinian Invasion of Yaman), 523; Abrahah (2nd Abyssinian Invasion), 565, 570; Massacre of Christians by Jews under Dhū Nuwās in Yaman (Qur'ān 85:4), 560 C.E.; Persia invades Jerusalem, 613–614; Persian expeditionary force under Wahrāz evicts Christian Abyssinians from Yaman, 575 C.E.

JUDAISM

Qaraites and Samaritans
Loci: Yibna (Jamnia), Safad, Babylon, Taymā', Khaybar, Madīnah, Yaman
In Yaman, state religion under Dhū Nuwās, 560–570 C.E.

ZOROASTRIANISM

Throughout Iran
Scattered through Lakhm, ʻUmān, Baḥrayn, and Qaṭar
Some adherents in Yaman, 560–632 C.E.

pre-dynastic period (3200–2700 B.C.E.), peaceful infiltration by Asiatic immigrants in the First Intermediate Period (2200–2050 B.C.E.), and a Semitic invasion (the Hyksos) which ruled Egypt from 1730 to 1570 B.C.E., it knows of no incursion from Egypt or Africa into Asia until after that time. It stands to reason that in the earliest times, the fourth millennium and earlier, movement from Asia to Africa was more likely than the opposite. Civilization had blossomed in Mesopotamia earlier than in Egypt, since its effects show their genesis and gradual development in Mesopotamia and their full development in Egypt. A whole series of Semitic elements constituted "a visible stimulus" contributing effectively to the crystallization of pre-dynastic Egyptian culture.[11] The cylinder seal, monumental architecture, bricks in decorative paneling, artistic motifs such as symmetry and antithesis, composite or stylized animals, Mesopotamia-type boats, the potter's wheel, advanced metallurgy, and, most important of all, writing, came from Asia to Egypt and helped lift her from prehistory to history.[12] There is no evidence of a reciprocal influence, which means that cultural leadership was all on the side of Mesopotamia. It is safe, therefore, to conclude that the Semites who were used to crossing the desert, crossed into Egypt as tradesmen, invaders, or immigrants and were responsible for the similarities between the two languages and civilizations.

The Canaanites were a subgroup of the great Amorite movement from the Arabian Peninsula into the Fertile Crescent in the third millennium B.C.E. They settled themselves in the western arm of the Fertile Crescent, the lands of Syria, Lebanon, Palestine, and Jordan. Theirs was another layer of migrations from Arabia over earlier layers of the same, deposited as far back as the fourth millennium B.C.E., as witness the names of Jericho, Beth-Shean, Megiddo, Akko, Tyre, Sidon. Their name, Canaanite, designated their main industry and export, namely, purple dye. The same connotation is responsible for their other name, Phoenicians, given to them by the Greeks (*phoinix* = purple red). Their culture was Mesopotamian and is reflected in the names of their cities, which are repetitions of Amorite cities in Mesopotamia, as well as in their pottery and sculpture. Besides purple dye, the Phoenicians exported timber (especially cedar wood), wheat, oil and wine, cloth, and metalwork. Cedar wood and the resins collected from the pine trees of Lebanon enabled the Phoenicians to build seaworthy ships, which increased their trade and industry. Learning how to navigate by means of the stars, their ships began to ply the Mediterranean, and they planted trading colonies on its shores.

The Persian Gulf, the Red Sea, and the East African coast, penetrated by the Nile and a canal dug by Pharaoh Necho (609–593 B.C.E.), were equally navigated and their trade mastered by the Phoenicians. According to Herodotus, they sailed around Africa, having the sun on their left side going south on its east coast and on their right on its west coast.[13] Wherever they traded, they planted factories and built colonies and connected them all with sea communications. Phoenician colonies dotted the shores of the Mediterranean. Gades (Cadiz), Malaga, Cordoba, and Barcelona in the Iberian Peninsula, Utica (Tunis) in North Africa, Baal-Lebanon in Cyprus, Hippo and Carthage, Tarsus in Cilicia, Mahon (capital of Minorca), and Corinth (whose god was Melikertes or Melkarth) were all Phoenician colonies. Europa, whom Zeus, the god of the Greeks, carried away and married, was a Phoenician princess, daughter of King Agenor. Her brother, Cadmus, king of Tyre, worked the gold mines of Thrace. To all these distant places, Semitic names, letters, and writing; arts and crafts; gods and rituals were exported along with the goods of trade. The Phoenician sailors certainly brought back silver, gold, and goods, mostly objects they themselves manufactured from materials mined, grown, or found in the colonies. But they never brought back culture. They always gave it; for theirs was the higher, the more advanced.

The expansion of Arabia under Islam was the greatest. The Mediterranean Sea and the Indian Ocean and the shores of Asia, Africa, and Europe became the object of a movement seeking their transformation into the pattern of Arabia developed under Islam. The Islamic expansion was the prototype of all Arabian expansions, the most successful as well as the farthest-reaching. The Muslims of Arabia brought

Illustration 1.3

Golden vessels of Queen Shubad, from Royal Cemetery at Ur, c. 2650–2550 B.C.E. [Courtesy The University Museum, University of Pennsylvania.]

with them the first principles of ideology and the language in which they were cast in inseparable unity. They also brought their own people to mix and intermarry with the natives and provide the actualization of the principles they preached. They were ready to learn — and they certainly did learn — all that the natives had to offer which they could adapt and digest, transform and recast so as to fit into the pattern of Islam. As we shall see, the main principles of Islam were almost identical with those of earlier Semites or emigrants from the Arabian Peninsula, a fact that so facilitated the process of Islamization that it turned it into one of Arabization as well.

NOTES

1. A. F. Albright, *From the Stone Age to Christianity* (Garden City, N.Y.: Doubleday, 2nd ed. 1957), p. 165.

2. Johann Gottfried Eichhorn, *Algemeine Bibliothek* (Leipzig, 1794), Vol. VI, p. 772. Here Eichhorn assumes the credit of invention and first use of the term. Evidently, Eichhorn believed the Old Testament claim that the peoples of the world as well as their languages are ultimately classifiable as Semitic, Hamitic, or Japhetic, following the three sons of Noah as given in Genesis 10.

3. Interestingly, the Qur'ān places the Deluge within the experience of Noah and his people exclusively. Noah and a few other believers in God and morality were saved from a flood which God inflicted upon Noah's people for their disbelief and disobedience, as a lesson to the other people (Qur'ān 25:37; 26:121; 29:15). As if to dispel any claim for nepotistic merit in religion or morality, the Qur'ān took care to mention that one of Noah's children continued to disbelieve and act unjustly despite his father's warning, and that he got what he deserved — he perished in the flood (Qur'ān 11:42–48).

4.

"Her brother, the hero, the warrior, Utu
Says to the pure Inanna:
Only sister, let the shepherd marry thee
O maid Inanna, why art thou unwilling?
His fat is good, his milk is good,
The Shepherd, everything his hand touches is bright."

"Me the shepherd shall not marry.
In his new garment he shall not drape me.
Me, the maid, let the farmer marry,
The farmer who makes plants grow abundantly,
The farmer who makes grain grow abundantly. . . ."

"The Farmer (more) than I,
I, the farmer, what has he more (than I)?
Should he give me his black garment,
I would give him, the farmer, my black ewe for it.
Should he pour me his prime date wine,
I would pour him, the farmer, my yellow milk for it. . . .
He rejoiced . . . on the riverbank he rejoiced,
The shepherd moreover led the sheep on the riverbank."
The shepherd, Dumuzi, in his plain starts a quarrel with him.

"I against thee, O Shepherd, against thee
Why shall I strive?
Let thy sheep eat the grass of the riverbank
in my meadowland let thy sheep walk about,
In the bright field of Erech let them eat grain
Let thy kids and lambs drink the water of my Unum canal."

"As for me who am a shepherd, at my marriage,
O farmer, mayest thou be counted as my friend. . . ."

"I would bring thee wheat, I would bring thee. . . ."

James B. Pritchard, ed., *Ancient Near Eastern Texts* (Princeton, N.J.: Princeton University Press, 1955), pp. 41–42.

5. E. Chiera, *Sumerian Religious Texts,* p. 20, quoted in Albright, *From the Stone Age,* pp. 165–66.

6. Sabatino Moscati, *The Face of the Ancient Orient: A Panorama of Near Eastern Civilization in Pre-Classical Times* (Garden City, N.Y.: Doubleday, 1962), p. 164.

7. Pritchard, *Ancient Near Eastern Texts,* pp. 316–317.

8. Living in an age in which the Hebrews lived in hostile relation with practically all their neighbors, and reflecting this obsessive hatred for them, the biblical redactor identified the enemies of the Hebrews (the Canaanites, Egyptians, Sebaites, Cushites, Babylonians, Akkadians, Assyrians, Jebusites, Amorites, Philistines, Caphtorites, Phoenicians, etc.) as descendants of Ham, the evil one, who saw and mocked his father's nakedness (Genesis 9:18–28; 10:1–20).

9. Adolph Erman launched the controversy by his article, "Das Verhältnis des ägyptischen zu den semitischen Sprachen," *Zeitschrift der Deutschen Morgenlandischen Gesellschaft* 46 (1892), pp. 93ff; and George A. Barton argued for the Hamitic origin in his *Semitic and Hamitic Origins* (Philadelphia: Univ. of Pennsylvania Press, 1934), pp. 85–87. Aaron Ember, *Egypto-Semitic Studies* (Leipzig, 1930); William F. Albright, "Notes on Egypto-Semitic Etymology," *American Journal of Semitic Languages and Literatures* 34 (1917), pp.81–98, 215–255, and 47 (1927), pp. 198–237; Franz Calice, *Grundlagen der ägyptisch-semitischen Wortvergleichung* (Vienna, 1936); and Otto Rossler, "Der semitische Character der Libyschen Sprache," *Zeitschrift für Assyriologie* 16 (1952), pp. 121–150, have argued the question to the point that Hamitic has become a geographical term synonymous with north and northeast Africa. The remoteness of the period of connection — pre-3000 B.C.E. — and the lack of adequate materials make any conclusion a speculative hypothesis.

10. John A. Wilson, *The Culture of Ancient Egypt* (Chicago: University of Chicago Press, 1951), p. 37.

11. Ibid., p. 39.

12. Wilson, *The Culture of Ancient Egypt,* p. 39.

13. Herodotus, Book IV, ch. 42. This was the report of the sailors which Herodotus mentioned and belied, but which confirms their circumnavigation of the continent.

CHAPTER 2

Language and History

LANGUAGE AND LITERATURE

The previous chapter has shown that geographically as well as demographically, the lands of the Arabian Peninsula and the Fertile Crescent constituted a single theater, and were continuous with one another. Their integrity or unity is further demonstrated by another kind of evidence, the linguistic, which this chapter will explore.

The Semites as a Linguistic Family

As we have seen in Chapter 1, it was the archeological discoveries of the eighteenth and nineteenth centuries C.E. that established the existence of peoples and languages to which Old Testament scholars applied the name Semitic as determined by the genealogical table of nations of Genesis 10. The languages furnished grounds for this appellation in that they were found to be similar, which led scholars to the conclusion that the languages belonged to one demographic family. Further study revealed more intimate relations between languages hitherto not thought to be related. Today, the so-called Semitic languages may be classified as follows:

1. Belonging to the northern half of the theater:
   - Eastern: Akkadian or Babylonian; Assyrian
   - Northern: Aramaic with its eastern varieties of Syriac, Mandean, and Nabatean, and its western varieties of Samaritan, Jewish Aramaic, and Palmyrene
   - Western: Phoenician, Biblical Hebrew, and other Canaanite dialects
2. Belonging to the southern half of the theater:
   - Northern: Arabic
   - Southern: Sabean or Ḥimyarī, with its varieties of Minaean, Mahrī, and Hakilī dialects; and Geez or Ethiopic, with its varieties of Tigré, Amharic, and Hararī dialects.

Almost all of these languages are today defunct, Arabic being the only one with real life.[1] The waves of emigration from the Arabian Peninsula to the Fertile Crescent—the Akkadian and Amoritic waves, 3000–1800 B.C.E.—spread the Akkadian language over the area. This was still the case down to 1400 B.C.E., to which the Amarna (Akhetaton) tablets of Egypt give evidence, when Akkadian was the language of common discourse as well as of government, spoken and written by natives as well as by their Egyptian overlords.[2] Aramaic began to replace Akkadian after 1200 B.C.E., established itself throughout the Fertile Crescent, and began to develop dialectic, peculiarities in each subarea. Aramaic displaced Hebrew, the language of Canaan, and became the vernacular of the Jews in West Asia, as the papyri of Elephantine (Egypt) of the sixth century show, as well as of the whole area until the advent of Islam in the seventh century C.E.[3] Arabic then displaced Aramaic throughout West Asia.

Today Arabic is the vernacular language of some 150 million people in West Asia and North Africa making up the twenty-two countries that are members of the League of Arab States. Under the influence of Islam, it has determined the Persian, Turkish, Urdu, Malay, Hausa, and Sawāḥilī languages, giving them 40–60 percent of their vocabularies and affecting indelibly their grammar, syntax, and literatures. Furthermore, it is the religious language of a billion Muslims around the world, recited by them in daily rituals. It is equally the language of Islamic law, which, at least in the area of personal status, dominates the lives of all Muslims. Finally, it is the language of Islamic culture taught in thousands of schools outside the Arab world from Senegal to the Philippines as the medium of instruction and as literature and thought in the fields of history, ethics, law and jurisprudence, theology, and scriptural studies.

Arabic is the language of the Qur'ān. In that form, it was spoken by all the inhabitants of the Arabian Peninsula and the Fertile Crescent lands immediately adjoining it a millennium before Islam. Unfortunately, there are very few written records of it anteceding Islam, and the oral tradition presents it perfect and complete in its development when the Qur'ān was revealed. There is no doubt that it had developed and acquired a large number of Persian, Egyptian, and Sanskrit words. But it had assimilated those elements and Arabicized them before Islam. Qur'ānic Arabic, we are told by tradition, was the language of the North Arabians, *al 'Arab al musta'ribah* or self-Arabized Arabs. As their name indicates, the North Arabians must have learned the Arabic language from others. Tradition also tells us that the North Arabians were the descendants of Isma'īl (Ishmael), first-born son of Ibrahīm (Abraham of Genesis), who settled in

Map 5. The Arabic Alphabet

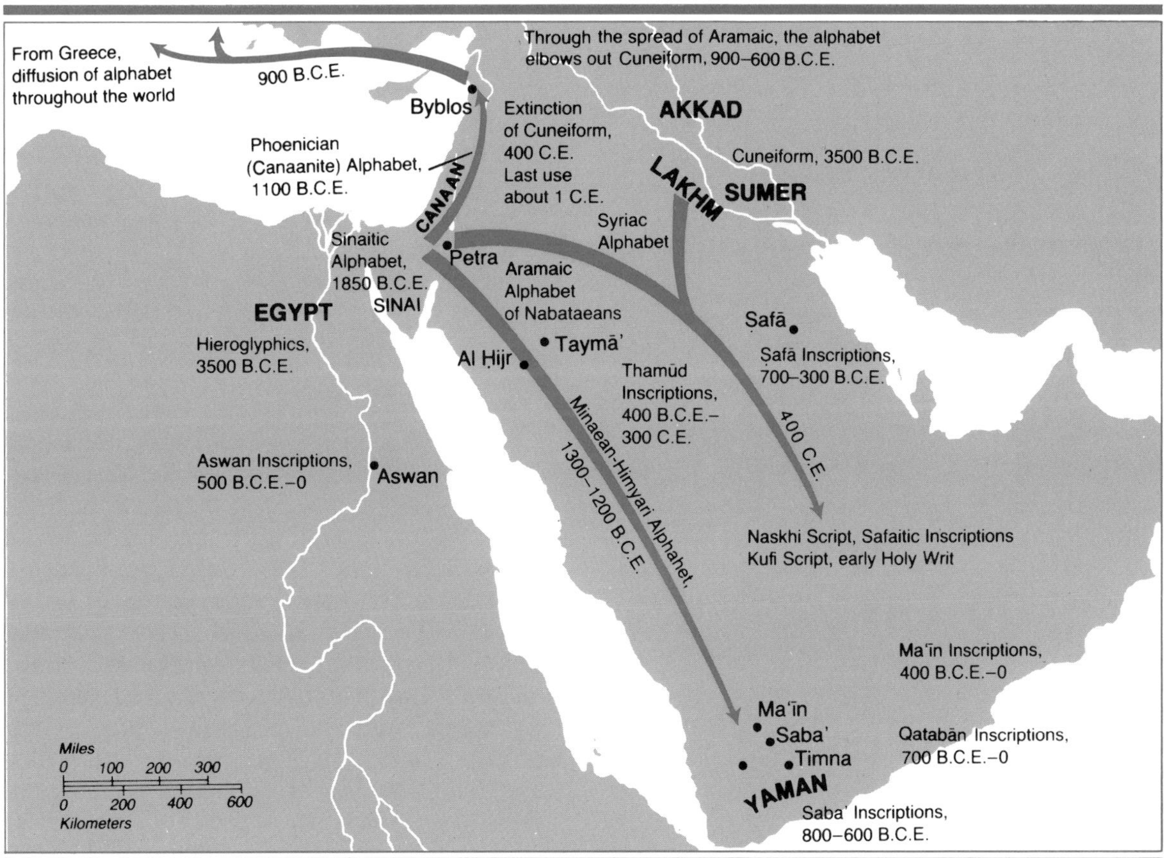

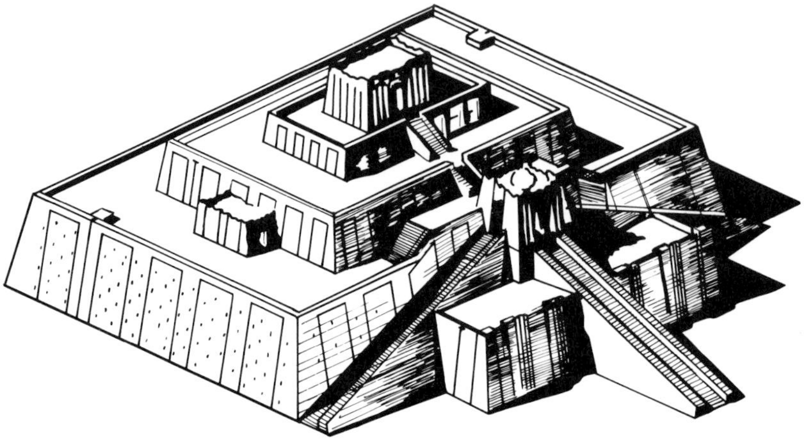

Figure 2.1
The Ziggurat of Ur: A Reconstruction

Makkah and built the Ka'bah as a house of worship of the one God. Isma'īl married into the tribe of Jurhum, natives of the area, and sired twelve sons who became the founders of the tribes living across the whole peninsula except its south and southwest areas. The Jurhumīs readily adopted the language, religion, and culture of Isma'īl, thus deserving the title *musta'ribah,* and pointing to a source of Arabic other than themselves. Such must have been the source to which Isma'īl and Ibrahīm belonged.

Another genealogy offered by the tradition is that the first king of the first Arabian kingdom in the peninsula was Ya'rub, son of Qaḥṭān, king of the South Arabians. The very name Ya'rub (literally, he eloquizes) points to such Arabicization as he might have suffered or led his countrymen to undergo. Tradition corroborates this by calling the South Arabians *al 'Arab al muta'arribah* (the Arabized-by-others Arabs), and tells how a tribe descended upon the south from the north, mixed with its native population and built the first kingdom whose first king was Ya'rub ibn Qaḥṭān. The process of Arabicization initiated by him must therefore be the cause of the disappearance of the languages or dialects of the south (Ma'īnī or Minaean, Sabaean or Ḥimyarī, Mahrī, and Hakilī). This process may have coincided with the decline of the South Arabian Kingdoms in the second half of the first millennium B.C.E.

The second genealogical tradition explains the origin of the Arabic language no more than the first. Both point to an "other" point in space and time, other than Makkah at the time of Isma'īl, and other than South Arabia under Ya'rub. This point is to be found in a third genealogical claim which the Arabic tradition has saved with equal tenacity, namely, that the origin of all Arabs, those who descended from Isma'īl as well as from Ya'rub, lies in a more distant source, namely, *al 'Arab al 'Āribah* (the Arabizing Arabs) whose habitat was the northern part of the Arabian Peninsula but who are also called *al 'Arab al Bā'idah* (the extinct Arabs). Being extinct, even in legendary times, means that very little is known about them except for their role as originators of the Arabs.

Which of the three traditions is true? All three, despite their apparent contradictions. One part of the "extinct Arabs" of the desert may have migrated south into Yaman, intermixed with the southerners, and constituted a kingdom first reigned over by the man responsible for that vision, Ya'rub ibn Qaḥṭān. The Akkadians' emigration to the north and the establishment of their kingdom at Agade under Sargon, is another such tradition. Another tribe, a branch of the Amoritic migration from the Arabian desert into the Fertile Crescent in the nineteenth century B.C.E., might well have descended upon Makkah after a stop in lower Mesopotamia, Padan Aram, eastern Syria and Jordan, and founded the city of Makkah. In fact, scholars agree that the exodus of Abraham from Ur was indeed part of a much larger wave of migration from the desert to the Fertile Crescent, which broke up into sections continually moving from one arm of the Crescent to another, or to the outside, that is, to Egypt. Ishmael might well have been the symbol of a whole tribe or clan that sought another place in which to settle, namely, Makkah.

It is certainly proper that these migrants be remembered by those who stayed behind and did not emigrate as the "extinct Arabs," for they had left the desert, mixed with other peoples, and, as far as the desert-dwellers are concerned, disappeared. Their advent into the territories was the start of new life, a new regime, and a new religious culture based upon language. The new orientation, we can safely presume, was not radically new; for it was of the same kind as earlier deposits left by earlier migrations from the same source. The new injection must have been seen as a reaffirmation of older truths and values, a purge or reformation, a change to something classical, to a purer form unsullied by the admixtures and pollutions of the particular locality or time, and therefore welcome and appreciated by the majority. This is why the "injection" lives in the people's consciousness as their own, as the formative event of their collective identity.

We may therefore conclude that the Arabic language in which the Qur'ān was revealed was the language of all Arabs in the Peninsula; that it was acquired by the Makkans and south Arabians in distant times, as a consequence of population movement into those areas; and ultimately, that the desert is the birthplace and cradle of the migrating tribes as well as of their language, Arabic.

The Nature of the Semitic Languages

Semitic languages are indeed members of one and the same family. As such, they enjoy a number of essential characteristics by which they can be identified and which constitute their core. This core is not affected by novel peculiarities which the language develops as it assimilates new experiences and accommodates the changes of history. As long as it is itself, it reveals the following elements:

Triliterality. Semitic languages share in the linguistic characteristic of triliterality, that is, their words consist of roots of three consonants each and of the derivatives from these roots. This is peculiar to the members of this family; no other language or linguistic family has such a feature. The list of stems or root-words may vary from one language to another, some roots having been dropped from use and others added in loan from other languages as life and history had made necessary. However, the Semitic languages have managed to continue to have the majority of their root-words in common with one another. From these tri-consonantal roots, words are formed through a process called "conjugation" or "foliation," consisting of changing the vocalization of the three consonants according to rule, or of adding one or more consonants as prefix, suffix, or infix and changing its vocalization as well. This process of conjugation of consonantal roots is the heart and core of the language and the mirror of consciousness of its speakers. It gives the language a formal structure: each conjugated form connotes a modality of the meaning of the consonantal root, which is one and the same with all other roots.[4] Were these modalities placed as headings on a horizontal dimension, and the consonantal roots on a vertical dimension, we would have a grid on which all the nouns and verbs, and therefore, almost the whole language can be spread out for inspection and clearer understanding. Only prepositions and pronouns escape conjugation, although Muslim philosophers have conjugated them (***anniyyah, huwwiyyah,*** et cetera). The degree of conformance of each of the Semitic languages to the grid may differ; but the structural grid remains true of all of them. The grid constitutes their "blood-relation" to one another. If the commonality of the majority of their root-words points to their common fund of human experience, their structural conformance points to the identical methodology of their thinking. In no language are all the conjugational forms of every root available and in use. The extent to which they are is determined by the experience and needs of the people of that language. In this respect, the Arabic language comes closest to filling up the whole grid, which supports the claim that it is, in its classic form, the *Ursemitisch* or original tongue out of which the various Semitic languages have sprung and from which they vary according to new ranges of experience.

Phonetics. The Semitic languages share an alphabet consisting of six gutturals (a, h, j, kh, ', gh), two palatals (k, j), two labials (p, b), five uvulars (q, ṭ, ẓ, ṣ, ḍ), two linguo-dentals (t, c), three sibilants (th, s, z), six liquids (r, y, l, w, m, n), and six spirants (m, g, t, d, p, b) whose pronunciation is slightly different from that known in English. No existing Semitic language or dialect has them all. Arabic has the most, twenty-nine out of a total of thirty-two. The history of Hebrew, or Canaanite, reveals how in time letters combined together to produce one, such as z with s, g with '.[5] The loss of one or more letters by a language is a natural phenomenon. It may be due to a need for simplicity and ease in pronunciation, brought about by the immigrant speaker's desire to make himself understood, or the inability of the native learner to pronounce the letter or to distinguish it phonetically from a similar letter in his own tongue. But the theory that new letters may have been developed by the South Arabians or the Fertile Crescent peoples runs against the evidence that Arabic, the language of the desert,

Value	Phoenician[a]	Aramaean[b]	Hebrew	Syriac (old)	Syriac (common)	Chaldean	Arabic
ʼ	𐤀	𐡀	א	ܐ	ܐ	ܐ	ا
b	𐤁	𐡁	ב	ܒ	ܒ	ܒ	ب
g	𐤂	𐡂	ג	ܓ	ܓ	ܓ	ج
d	𐤃	𐡃	ד	ܕ	ܕ	ܕ	د
h	𐤄	𐡄	ה	ܗ	ܗ	ܗ	ه
v	𐤅	𐡅	ו	ܘ	ܘ	ܘ	و
z	𐤆	𐡆	ז	ܙ	ܙ	ܙ	ز
ḥ	𐤇	𐡇	ח	ܚ	ܚ	ܚ	ح
ṭ	𐤈	𐡈	ט	ܛ	ܛ	ܛ	ط
y	𐤉	𐡉	י	ܝ	ܝ	ܝ	ي
k	𐤊	𐡊	ך כ	ܟ ܟ	ܟ ܟ	ܟ ܟ	ك
l	𐤋	𐡋	ל	ܠ	ܠ	ܠ	ل
m	𐤌	𐡌	ם מ	ܡ	ܡ ܡ	ܡ ܡ	م
h	𐤍	𐡍	ן נ	ܢ ܢ	ܢ ܢ	ܢ ܢ	ن
ṣ	𐤎	𐡎	ס	ܣ	ܣ	ܣ	س
ʻ	𐤏	𐡏	ע	ܥ	ܥ	ܥ	ع
p	𐤐	𐡐	פ	ܦ	ܦ	ܦ	ف
ẓ	𐤑	𐡑	ץ צ	ܨ	ܨ	ܨ	ص
ḳ	𐤒	𐡒	ק	ܩ	ܩ	ܩ	ق
ṛ	𐤓	𐡓	ר	ܪ	ܪ	ܪ	ر
sh	𐤔	𐡔	ש	ܫ	ܫ	ܫ	ش
t	𐤕	𐡕	ת	ܬ	ܬ	ܬ	ت

Figure 2.2

The Alphabet: A Near Eastern contribution to human civilization

[a] Baal Lebanon and Moabite inscriptions, 11th–9th centuries B.C.E.
[b] In use from 5th to 1st century B.C.E.
NOTE: The first writing was in cuneiform, the script invented by the Mesopotamians at the very rise of civilization. Cumbersome as it may have been, it was a great advance over hieroglyph and ideograph, and it paved the way for the Canaanites to give the world its first complete phonetic alphabet. The Canaanite alphabet served as the basis for most languages of the world; and these improved on it for simplicity, clarity, and efficiency. Only the Arabs, under Islam, developed the alphabet for aesthetic as well as pragmatic reasons, and thus rendered writing into the worthiest of all arts.
SOURCES: James Hastings, *Dictionary of the Bible* (1905); *Al Munjid* (Beirut: Catholic Press, 1956); Safwan al Tall, *Taṭawwur al Ḥurūf al 'Arabiyyah* ('Ammān: University of Jordan Press, 1401/1981), p. 107; Wendel Philips, *Qataban and Sheba* (London: V. Gollancz, 1935), p. 55.

had more letters than any other Semitic language. It is on this account that scholars agree that "it is probable that the original Semitic alphabet was nearly identical with that of the classical Arabic."[6]

Grammar. The Semitic languages are inflecting, that is, they change the ending of a noun depending on its case, whether it is subject or direct or indirect object, and of a verb depending on the tense. Only three languages today are inflecting: Arabic, Amharic, and German. Many languages of the past were inflecting, for example, Akkadian, Greek, Latin, and Sanskrit. Modern languages have for the most part dropped their inflections. Within the Semitic family, Syriac and Chaldean lost their inflections; and within the Latin family, French, Italian, and Spanish did likewise. English too lost its inflection whereas German preserved it. The fact that Akkadian and Arabic preserved their inflection and that their daughters—Syriac, Chaldean, and colloquial Arabic—have lost it points to the close relationship maintained by the parents among themselves in their heyday. On the other hand, inflection is a sign of a more exacting, precision-seeking tendency in the fastidious; its absence, a sign of a less exacting, pragmatic tendency.

Vocabulary and precision. Semitic languages have a profuse vocabulary, with many words for the same object. In this regard, all of them do better than the European languages; and Arabic surpasses them all. The latter gives light 21 names, the year 24, the sun 29, the clouds 50, darkness 52, rain 64, the water-well 88, water 170, the snake 100, the camel 255, and the lion, 350. The same profusion exists in regard to the other animals, the desert, the sword, as well as to the human characteristics of tall (91 words), short (160), courageous, generous, avaricious, and so on. The writer of prose or poetry is hence free to choose, from the rich spectrum, the word that suits his composition best as to form, sound, length, rhyme, and affinity.

Besides sheer profusion of words, Semitic languages show extraordinary precision in their uses of proper diction. The connotative shades of meaning the Semites perceive are often too subtle for others.[7] Again Arabic has developed this characteristic to the ultimate degree, giving a different name for each hour of the day and night, for every night of the lunar month, for every lock of hair according to its location on the human body, for every variety of seeing, of sitting, of walking, of sleeping, of loving.

Syntax, style, and literature. In the Semitic languages, syntax consists of articulative simplicity and perceptual clarity. In Arabic, eloquence is often defined in terms of fitness, precision, or clarity. Brevity of expression is always a literary virtue; and compressing great meanings into a few words that can be easily understood and memorized is a particular strength of all Semitic literary products. In the condensation of piety, morality, and wisdom into the fewest and yet most powerful words, the Hebrew Bible and the Qur'ān are second to none. With such literary capacities latent in them, it is no wonder that the Semitic languages have been the media of prophecy from the earliest times.

Another syntactical characteristic common to all Semitic languages is the near total absence of compound words. Apparently, the profusion of synonyms and availability of a separate word for any denotative or connotative meaning on any level have obviated the need for compounding. Compounding did exist in the old Semitic languages and continues to exist in those languages that survive, but only in proper names, such as God-has-given, God-has-blessed, servant-of-Provider-God.

Since the invention of writing, the Semites were the first to produce literary prose and poetry, to commit them to writing, and to preserve them impressed on clay for posterity. They gave the world its first *Edubba* or library in which they kept large collections of their scientific, commercial and historical, as well as literary, religious, and legal texts. Their literatures encompassed an immense range, from knowledge of nature to the deepest perceptions of human emotions.

Literary aesthetics consists in the combination of precision and clarity with beauty and emotional effect. Aesthetic quality pertains therefore to a phrase, a verse, or a sentence and is not necessarily the function of the broad movement of action or plot. This is why the Semitic literary legacy is free of drama and is not on that account the poorer. That is also why all Semitic poetry is of the lyric type, characterized by the parallelism of its parts, the autonomy of its verses and the nondevelopmental nature of its sequence. It may not be described in terms of dramatic unity but rather in its loose-endedness or unfinishedness. Instead of close-knit overall unity of plot, the Semitic literary product is annalistic and repetitious (Hebrew Book of Kings, Psalms, and Song of Songs; Akkadian royal inscriptions, *The Epic of Gilgamesh;* the Arabic *qaṣīdah,* the Qur'ān, the *maqāmāt,* or *The Thousand and One Nights*). All compositions equally give the impression of their own infinity, of the absence of a beginning or of an ending. The buildup of emotional pressure is never sustained through the whole length of the composition, reaching climax and relief at the end. Emotions are expressed in every constitutive member of the composition, in every verse or sentence, tableau or *maqām,* or group of verses and sentences.[8]

Figure 2-3

Two roadsigns engraved in stone from the caliphate of 'Abdul Malik ibn Marwān, builder of the Dome of the Rock in Al Quds (Jerusalem), 66-86/690-710. Matḥaf Al Quds (Jerusalem Museum).

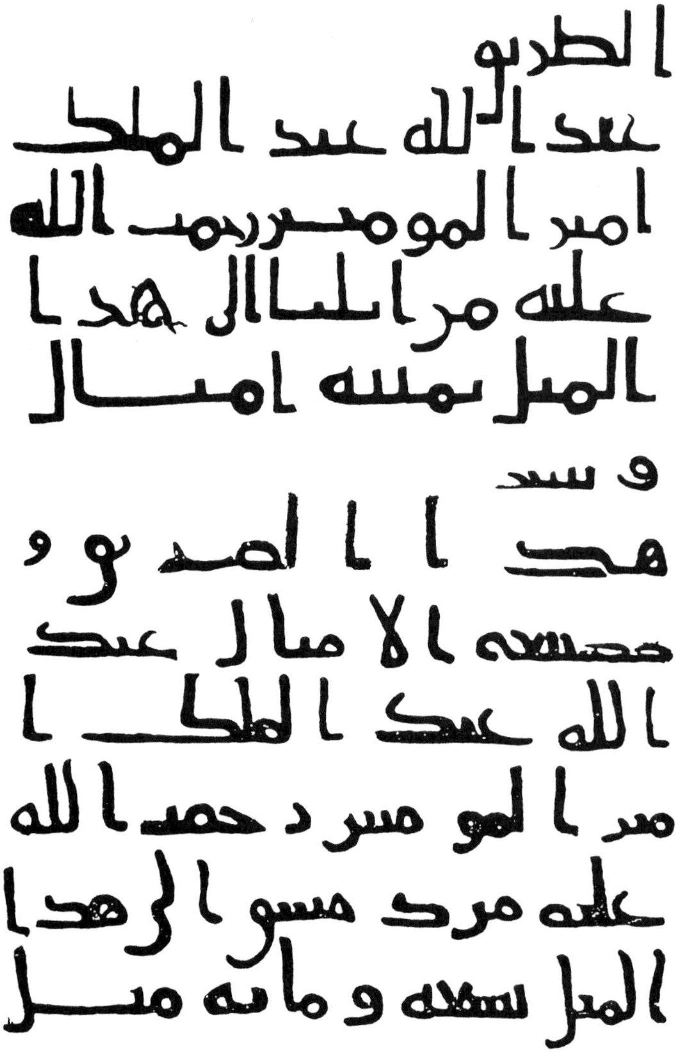

Another most essential characteristic of all Semitic literature is its moral tone. Whether the Semite is describing outward nature, human life and action, or past history, his objective is never description for its own sake. As we saw earlier, his will to precision, accuracy, and adequacy of description is unsurpassed. In addition, he always seeks to bring out a moral, to guide his audience or readers to virtue. To the Semite the aesthetic and the moral are inseparable twins, indeed a unity, where description and prescription are one whenever value is concerned. The Semite has always subscribed to the view that to understand value is to be moved and affected by its appeal.

HISTORY: SCENES AND DRAMATIS PERSONAE

Proto-Akkadian (to 2800 B.C.E.) and Early Dynastic Period (2800–2360 B.C.E.)

Long before the migrants from the Arabian desert established their first Akkadian world-state in Mesopotamia in 2360 B.C.E., perhaps a whole millennium before that date, countless waves of them had arrived in Mesopotamia, mixed with its natives, and become indigenized. Migrants from the Arabian desert had been flowing into the Tigris-Euphrates basin. The direction of this flow must have been from north to south along the Euphrates, and from west to east across northern Mesopotamia and then southward along the Tigris River. The migrants settled in the northern areas first. Later migrants who found these areas saturated with their predecessors extended their migration further south. Thus the north and central areas witnessed larger concentrations of migrants than the south. Upon arrival, the migrants mixed with fellow tribesmen who had arrived earlier, with the descendants of earlier waves of migrants, and with the Sumerian natives.

The processes of immigration, settlement, and integration were certainly slow and peaceful. There is no record of a violent advent. Adaptation to the new sedentary style of life— learning agriculture, the professions, and crafts— and disciplining oneself into the observance of a new ethos appropriate to the new life cannot have been easy. Nor could this process be hastened. Every migrant, young or old, male or female, had to undergo this double change of lifestyle: de-nomadization and sedentarization. The natives themselves were already a mixture. The Sumerians were only one element in that mixture in which "proto-Akkadians speaking some early Semitic dialect also belonged."[9] The process was old enough to make it possible for many Arab migrants to rise to royal positions in several city-states. Their names, obviously Semitic, are easy to spot in the king-lists of the early dynastic period. The state of Mari was ruled by an Arab dynasty in 2500 B.C.E.; that of Kish in northern Mesopotamia presents us with three or four Akkadian dynasties in pre-Sargonic times; and so do the tablets of Shuruppak. Sumerian is older than Akkadian; and yet, it presents us with a wealth of Akkadian terms which Sumerians must have borrowed and used long enough to make them popular. As the documents of Lagash (2500 – 2400 B.C.E.) indicate, Arab penetration must have been in progress for several generations to allow Akkadian terms to be so incorporated into the Sumerian language. Indeed, there is as yet no evidence that Sumerian was at any time the sole language of the whole of Mesopotamia.[10] It is even uncertain that Sumerian was the dominant language during the al 'Ubayd period (to 3900 B.C.E.), as non-Sumerians were present in sufficient numbers to give their language a palpable presence.[11] These non-Sumerians were Akkadians, or Arabs from the Arabian desert, and this fact explains the continuity of style, religion, and culture in Mesopotamia.[12] It is equally certain that there were neither gaps nor disruptions in Mesopotamian civilization. The typical constituents of the later Akkadian period, namely, the oblong shape of the sanctuary, the altar and offering table, the platform under the temple, the walls with symmetrical piers, recesses and niches making a rhythmic decoration internally and externally,[13] the style of pottery decoration, would not be found in the proto-literate period unless the Akkadians themselves had been there already.[14]

This Akkadian presence has no explanation other than the continual flow of migrants from the Arabian desert south and west of Mesopotamia. The concentration of several waves of migration enabled the Akkadian language to gain popularity and later supremacy and the power to determine all other aspects of Mesopotamian life beside language. As the foremost Assyriologist of this century has affirmed, the earliest speakers of the Semitic dialects found in Mesopotamia all moved "as all later Semites did — from Northern Arabia across the middle course of the Euphrates and eastward across the Tigris into the region between that river and the mountain ranges."[15] Evidence of the coalition of migrant tribes following their settlement in Mesopotamia was the fusion of their loyalties together as the necessary step to initiate the larger political formation — the world-state — that superseded the city-states in the twenty-fourth century B.C.E.[16]

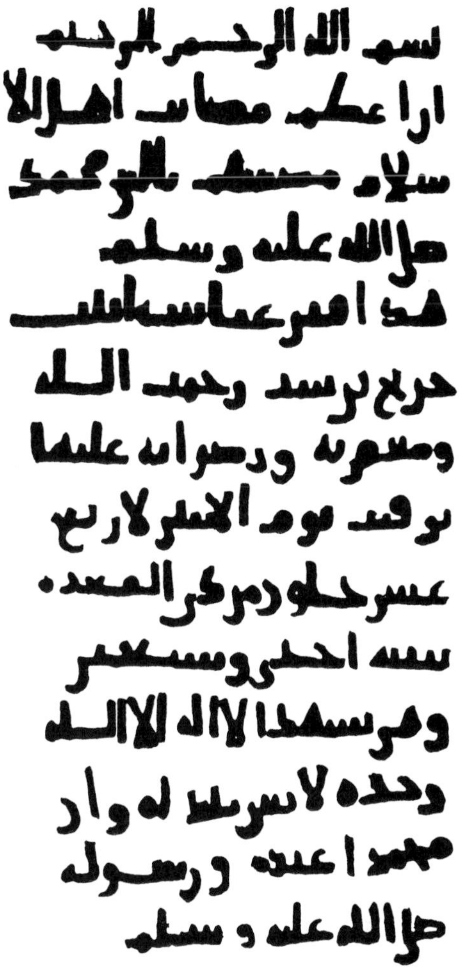

Figure 2-4

Tombstone inscription of 'Abbāsah bint Ḥudayj at Aswān (Egypt), dated 71/695. Islamic Museum, Cairo.

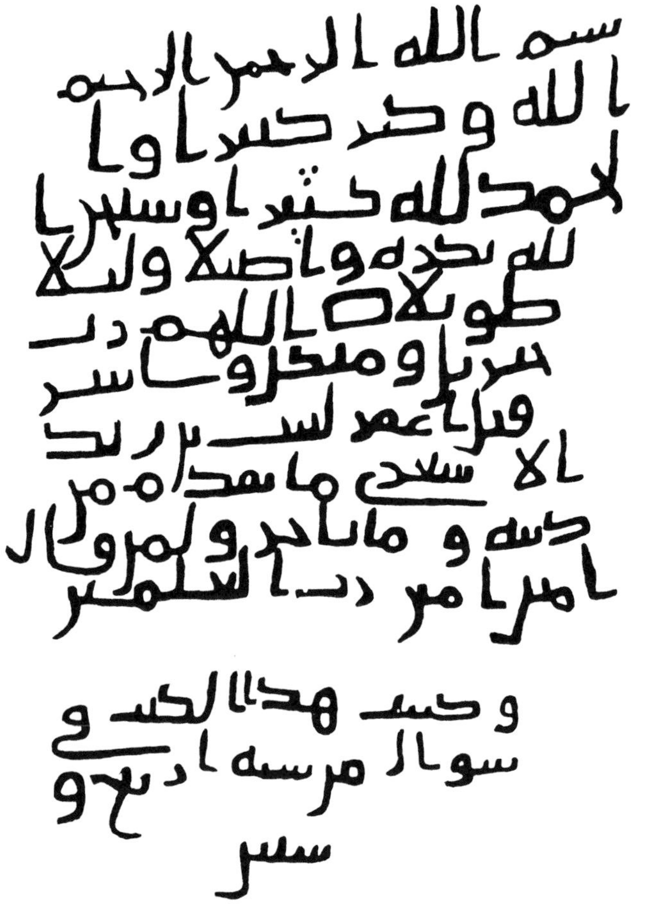

Figure 2-5

Tombstone inscription of Thābit ibn Yazīd al Ash'arī near Karbalā' (Iraq), dated 64/688. Iraq Museum, Baghdād.

The Akkadian World-State (2360–2112 B.C.E.)

After the middle of the third millennium, the pace of migration quickened and immigrants from the desert poured into Mesopotamia. Their numbers reinforced the Akkadian presence. Their common loyalty to the Akkadian identity prompted them to join cause with the Akkadians who preceded them and who were already settled on Mesopotamian farmland or on their way to sedentarization. Most important, however, was the pure Akkadian view of the world and reality, the fresh affirmation of the Akkadian ethos of life which the latest migrants brought. Their input rejuvenated the spirit of the settlers, confirmed and enriched their aspirations, and intensified their will to seize power and launch a new political existence commensurate with their worldview. The city-state was too small, too limited, too narrow, too provincial, too particularistic in every aspect. Each of the city-states had its own god and its own king. It was built on a "congregationalist" loyalty which bound the citizens to their own city and their own cult. The energies of the government were all focused upon and in the city. Obviously, the Arab desert dweller could not identify with such a politico-religious entity. His loyalty extended to his fellow tribesmen throughout the land and beyond it, in the desert and other lands to which the migrants had gone. When the migrants' numbers grew, this supra-city loyalty grew bolder and came to constitute a base for a universal linkage reinforced by common religion, common language, and common culture. If the migrants were already everywhere in the land, if they were strong — nay, dominant — in so many city-states, if they felt no or little attachment to these petty loyalties of the city-states, then surely the time had come to go beyond the city-state as the unit of political life. Indeed, the migrants furnished the vision for a wider association than the city-state provided: a vision of a universal association to actualize the good, to build culture and civilization, to lead the world toward a fuller self-realization of humanity. That this greater vision predated the migrants' arrival in Mesopotamia and constituted, as it was to do in the Islamic expansion, the very motivation for migration, cannot be demonstrated because of the absence of adequate archeological records in the Arabian desert. However, it is certain that upon arrival in Mesopotamia the migrants agitated and pressed for the formation of a state that would hold them, the previous migrants, the desert people, the desert migrants to other lands, and the natives all together. Indeed, their vision was large enough to include the whole world they then knew, and it gave birth to the first world-state that history has known.

The person who rose to the historical occasion was Sargon of Agade. He was a man of low birth. "My mother was a changeling, my father I knew not [except that his brothers 'loved the hills'] . . . in secret she bore me."[17] The gods picked him up to guide history. "Ishtar granted me [her] love. . . . Sargon, King of Agade, overseer of Ishtar . . . great ensi of Enlil . . . [who] did not let anybody oppose Sargon [and] . . . gave him (the region from) the Upper Sea to the Lower Sea."[18] Legend wove around him a beautiful story which became typical of the great man in the Semitic tradition. "She [Sargon's mother] set me in a basket of rushes, with bitumen she sealed my lid. She cast me into the river which rose not (over) me. The river bore me up and carried me to Akki, the drawer of water . . . [who] lifted me out as he dipped his ewer . . . took me as his son and reared me . . . [until] Ishtar granted me her love."[19]

According to the chronicle carrying his name, Sargon, founder of the first universal state, "spread his terror-inspiring glamor over all the countries. He crossed the sea in the East, and he himself conquered the country of the West in its full extent. . . ."[20] The chronicle goes on to list the cities and countries and peoples which Sargon conquered and integrated into his kingdom. These include far-off places in Syria, Asia Minor, Susiana (Elam), southeast Arabia, and Dilmun in the Gulf, besides all the main city states of Mesopotamia. "For the first time is achieved the kingdom of the known world, of the four quarters of the earth."[21] Having established this world-state and its government machinery, Sargon and his supporters infused it with a new mission: to unite mankind in common effort toward peace and prosperity, to spread culture and civilization, to institute law and justice. Sargon, and the new and old migrants who were his prime constituency, felt free of the traditional framework in which the city-state operated, and soared with their imagination to a worldwide civilizing mission. Surely "Sargon made sedentary this nomadic Society"[22]; but this was not done at the cost of limiting their worldview or their notion of identity as did the city-states. In the new order, the king's name was invoked in oath-making and became an expression of popularity. The practical consequence of such invocation was to make the king for the first time the protagonist of the weak, it being his duty to enforce the agreement for which he was invoked as witness and guardian. Equally, the new world-state abolished the individual calendars of the city-states and introduced a new and unified calendar for the whole region. The names of the months as well as the celebration of festivals became unified.

The new vision was equally evident in new forms of art, surpassing as well as transforming what was hitherto known in Mesopotamia. The Akkadian language, as vehicle of the new spirit, spread throughout the new state, not only as language of government, which was true even before Sargon, but as language of the people. The process of Akkadianization of Sumer, which had begun in earlier centuries, could now proceed at greater pace. By the time of the Hammurabi dynasty (nineteenth century B.C.E.), the Sumerian language had become extinct and Akkadian had taken its place. This was a process of acculturation marked by neither racial conflict nor power competition between native and foreigner.[23] Moreover, when the Sargonic state collapsed under the invasion of the Gutians (Persian highlanders), it was supplanted by a new state called Kingdom of Sumer and Akkad which lasted through the third dynasty of Ur (Shulgi) until 1950 B.C.E., after which the realm broke up into a number of semi-autonomous dynasties in the south, center, and north. However, despite invasion by foreigners and the subsequent fragmentation, Mesopotamia continued every cultural, religious, and linguistic trend established by the Akkadian state. The Akkadian character of the Mesopotamian state persisted without significant change throughout its history, down to the Persian conquest by Cyrus in 539 B.C.E.

The Amurru (20th–14th century B.C.E.)

The Guti invasions weakened the Mesopotamian state and fragmented it politically. Culturally, the Gutians could not affect it because they were inferior to the Mesopotamians. The political vacuum thus created invited a new wave of immigration from the Arabian desert. Strangely, the Mesopotamianized Semites referred to the new migrants as "Amurru" (Amorites) or Westerners. Not only was Mari, their capital, the westernmost point on the Euphrates in central and southern Mesopotamia, but they had filled up the whole western area of the Fertile Crescent before descending upon its eastern arm. So much were the whole western extremities of Asia other than Asia Minor saturated with the Amurru people that even the Mediterranean came to be known to the Mesopotamians as "the great sea of Amurru." Evidently, Syria, Lebanon, Palestine, and Jordan had

Figure 2-6

Inscription on dam at Ṭā'if (Hijāz, Saudi Arabia) built by Mu'āwiyah ibn Abū Sufyān, first Umawī Caliph, dated 58/681.

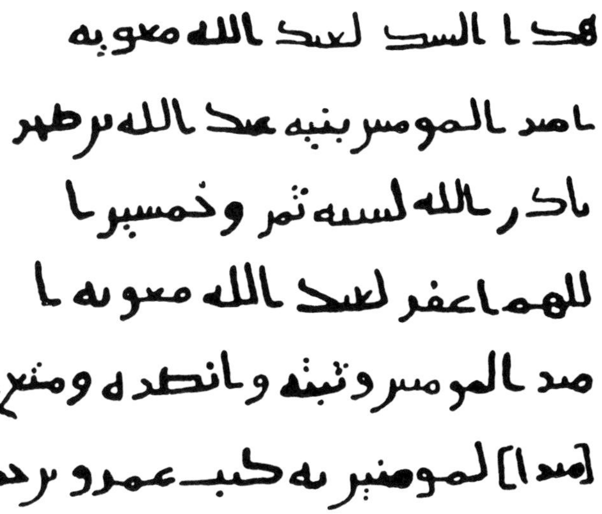

been undergoing Arabization for a very long time. Indeed, migration from the Arabian desert to the western arm of the Crescent preceded that to the eastern arm because the former is easier and closer to reach from the Ḥijāz and from central and south Arabia. Under the Amorite migration, this process of Arabization of the whole Fertile Crescent was completed.

The Amorites, however, were no strangers to the Akkadians. They spoke the same language, namely, Akkadian, and belonged to the same Arabian stock from which the Akkadians had emerged. While it is possible to speak of an Amorite wave of migration, it must be borne in mind that, like all other migrations from the Arabian desert, this one consisted of numerous and successive waves. Mari was a kind of stopover or base for the Amorites' infiltration of Mesopotamia. The Amorites' fighting spirit and reputation tempted both the Akkadians and their enemies, the Gutians, to employ Amorites as mercenary soldiers. Some Amorites lent their services as fighters. But when the waves multiplied and their density thickened, they took over the local governments and reestablished the unified state of Sargon. Isin, Larsa, Mari, Eshnunna, Babylon, Assur, and Carchemish fell one after another into Amorite hands; and Babylon became the capital of the new Amorite world-state. The state

Figure 2-7

Letter from the Prophet to the Ruling Archbishop of Egypt, dated 5/627. Topkapi Museum, Isṭanbūl.

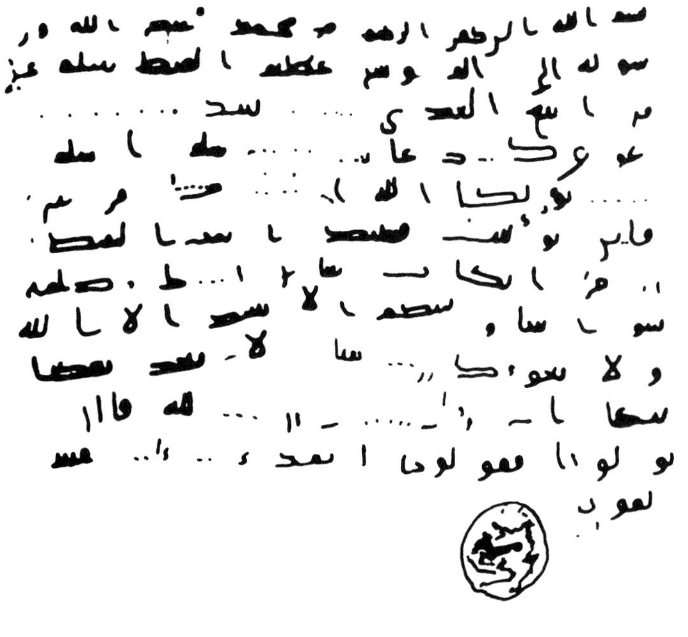

itself was in every respect identical to the Akkadian state it supplanted, except that it was larger and included more territories to the west as well as more people. The language of the new state was Akkadian; and the Amorite state took upon itself the task of spreading the language throughout the new territories of Syria, Lebanon, Palestine, Jordan, and Anatolia. The new architecture followed the same principles but became more imperial and the decoration more stylized. The literature, of which the tablets of Mari have given us numerous samples, followed the same genres and realized all the requisites of Semitic literary aesthetics.

The most salient characteristic of the new world-state and its most important achievement was its political philosophy. Sargon had dreamed of a state that would include the whole known world, and he came very close to achieving it. There were numerous territories to the west which, though known to the Sargonic state, lay beyond its effective boundaries. Not so the Amorite state. It included everything, even those parts of distant Anatolia reached by the farthest traveling Amurru. The will to expand the world-state to all-inclusive proportions was part of a universalist vision of human society.

Among the Amurru chiefs of state, this vision had its first try with Lipit-Ishtar. A "humble shepherd," an obvious reference to his desert upbringing, "was called by the god Enlil to the princeship of the land, to banish complaints, to turn back enmity and rebellion by the force of arms, to bring well-being to the Sumerians and Akkadians."[24] In obedience to the word of Enlil, Lipit-Ishtar "procured the freedom of the sons and daughters of Nippur, . . . of Ur, . . . of Islin, . . . of Sumer and Akkad upon whom slaveship had been imposed."[25] All the peoples of the region, whether Sumerians, Akkadians, or others, citizens of this, that, or another state—all were equal candidates for citizenship of the new state. The godhead—whatever deity happened to be uppermost at the time—wanted all humans to be free and prosperous and to deal with one another with justice. The purpose of the state was moral, and its extent or jurisdiction universal. This took place in the middle of the nineteenth century B.C.E.

A century and a half later, new migrants from the Arabian desert arrived, bringing with them the same vision but with new clarity and intensity. Having spread far and wide in all known territories, this wave of migrants was better prepared than their predecessors to fulfill the vision and give it embodiment in their new state. As soon as he came to power (in the second year of his forty-three-year reign, 1728–1686 B.C.E.), Hammurabi promulgated a new law. This law

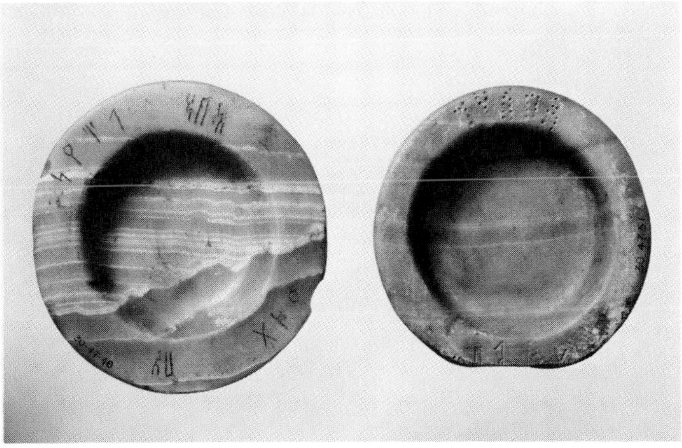

Illustration 2.1

Inscribed alabaster plates, South Arabia, Sabaean, first millennium B.C.E. [Courtesy The University Museum, University of Pennsylvania.]

was not of his making, but of God's. It was handed to him complete by the God of justice, the sun-god Shamash who was prominent in the pantheon when the stela was made. Hammurabi perceived himself as directed by God to bring the "four quarters of the world" under his arm and to make their cities and governments subservient. According to the prologue of the Code of Hammurabi, the god Marduk commissioned him "to guide the people aright, to direct the land, to establish law and justice in the land, thereby promoting the welfare of the people."[26] The state then was a world-state, ordained in heaven from the beginning, indeed from creation.

> When lofty Anu, King of the Annunaki
> And Enlil, Lord of heaven and earth
> The Determiner of the destinies of the land
> Determined for Marduk, the first born of Enki
> Dominion over all mankind
> Then did Anu and Enlil name me, Hammurabi . . .
> To make justice rule in the land . . .
> To destroy the wicked and unjust,
> That the strong might not oppress the weak
> To promote the well-being of the people.[27]

The king was himself no god but a servant of God, appointed to rule in God's name, to enforce the law which is God's will for men. The world-state was to be a replica of the cosmic state where Marduk, the chief god, reigns among the Annunaki, or the divine collectivity. The might and power of the king were to be at the service of "orphan and widow," of the oppressed throughout the world-state, to deliver them from their oppression and restore to them their rights. The king's great temptation to think of himself as god, or as a sort of demi-god, here was knocked out once and for all. In other areas of the world where civilization had developed, notably in neighboring Egypt or among the Hittites, Kassites, Gutians, and Elamites, hero worship had already turned political leaders into gods. In Mesopotamia, the temptation was equally strong; but the religio-cultural complex of the migrating Arabs resisted that idea. The new vision militated against it, and finally put it completely out of circulation. This was done by defining power to be executive only, not legislative. The king was not the legislator; God was. The king merely executed what God had commanded, and adjudicated disputes according to laws God had revealed. The law which had come from God was all justice, equity, righteousness, and goodness. Because it was divine, the law was above and binding on all—ruler and ruled, citizen and noncitizen, male and female, great and small. As executor of the law, the king was *ipso facto* prosecutor of anyone accused of injustice, *ipso facto* defender of anyone falsely accused. Besides the material verdict of the law, the whole weight of God's vengeance and power was hurled against the unjust, the oppressor, the criminal. The king was to be "like a real father to the people, a good shepherd and protector of his flock"; in

Figure 2-8

Tombstone inscription of 'Abdul Raḥman al Ḥijrī at Aswān (Egypt), dated 31/654. Islamic Museum, Cairo.

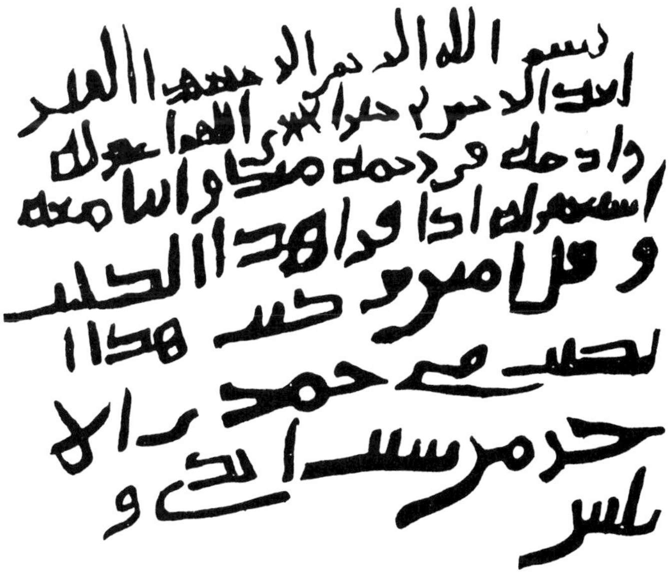

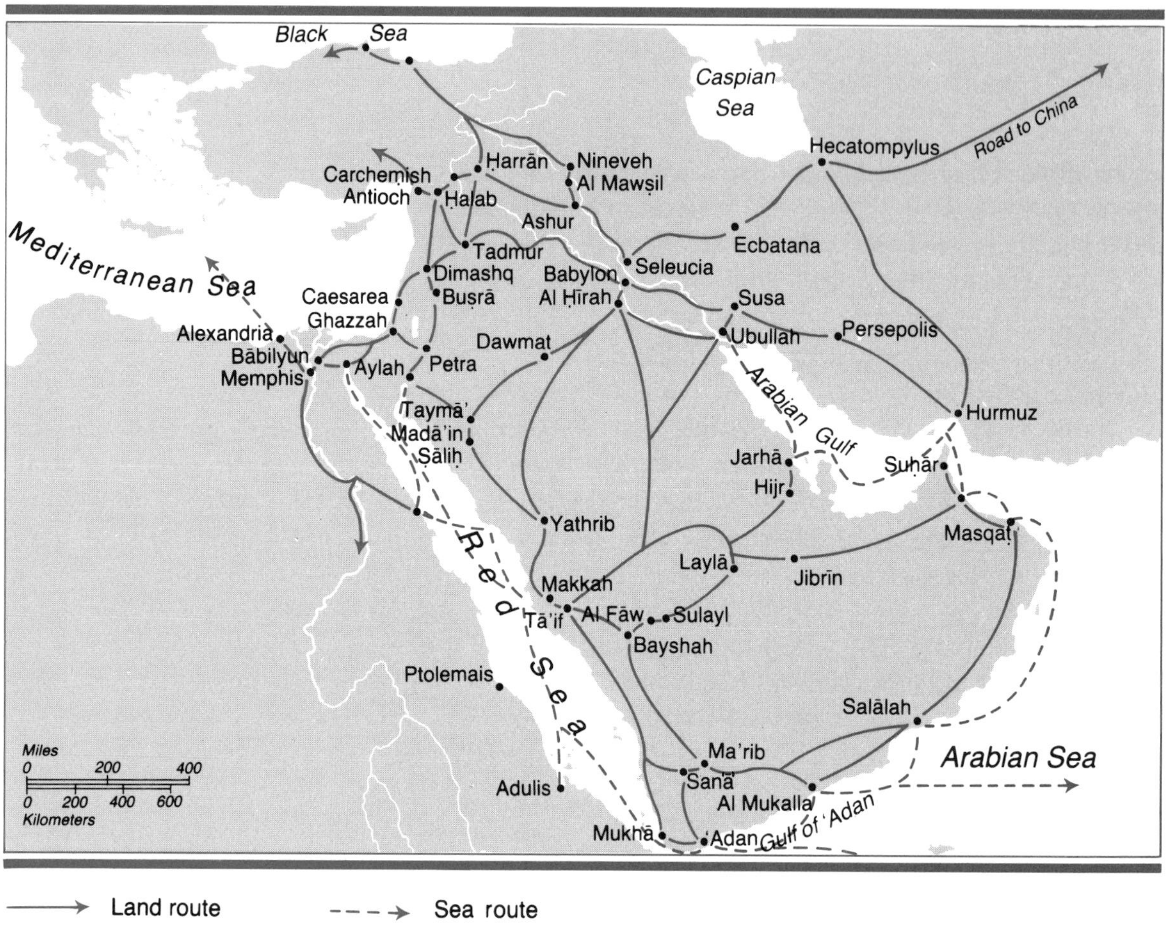

Map 6. Trade Routes, 1/622

ordering their affairs, nothing shall move him but the commonweal; for he shall be "bestirred by the word of Marduk" alone.[28] Whenever in human history royal government got mixed up with divine governance, or was identified with it as in the case of divine kingship, it became a source of great oppression. Certainly, it was a great step forward when Hammurabi, by separating God and the Law from himself, repudiated divine kingship and put a tremendous obstacle in the way of oppression.

The Canaanites (from the 20th century B.C.E.)

The Amorites who settled in the western arm of the Fertile Crescent and who gave the whole group of migrants their collective name Amurru or Westerners, because of their location in relation to the desert, came to be known also as Canaanites. The distinction was caused by the land in which they came to settle and the natives with whom they had assimilated. The "natives," or original inhabitants of the eastern Mediterranean shoreland, may well have been truly indigenous, like the Sumerians in southern Mesopotamia. Or, they may have been human deposits, layer upon layer, of earlier waves of migration from the Arabian desert, and hence representing varying degrees of assimilation and change, of distance from the new migrants. Such distance on the ideological, social, or linguistic level, however, was never large enough to hide the common origin and heritage of all groups that came to the region from the Arabian desert.

The western Amurru (redundant as the expression may be!) spread over the whole area of Syria, Lebanon, Jordan, and Palestine. The sea littoral was the ground in which the shell *murex trunculus* prospered and was found in great numbers. The *murex* mollusk contained a liquid from which a purple dye was extracted. The dye was called *kina'ni* (Akkadian), *knaggi* (Hurrian), *kinakhkhi* (Tall al 'Amarnah), *kena'* (Phoenician), thus giving us the Hebrew word *ken'an*, or land of purple. The Greek name Phoenicia derives from *phoinix,* meaning purple. It was the most prestigious dye of the ancient world and became associated with royalty. Purple was the imperial color everywhere. The term Canaan was applied to the whole land and to its peoples whose geographical location caused them to look toward the sea and seek a livelihood from trade. The Canaanite language was the same as that which all Amorites spoke, namely, Akkadian. Local conditions produced differences in dialect but no substantial change. The same was true of religion, the arts, and culture.

The Canaanites founded great cities but no nation. Gaza and Ascalon, Gezer, Lachish, Hazor, Schechem, Jericho, Beth Shan, Megiddo, Akko, Tyre, Sidon, Gubla, Byblos, Arka and Simyra, Tripoli, Ugarith, Botys, Berytus, Aradus — all were founded or rebuilt by the Canaanites as autonomous city-states with strong fortifications and a prosperous economic life based on industry, trade, and/or agriculture. Their rapid assimilation and absorption into industry, trade, and agricultural pursuits, along with the dominating presence of mighty neighbors (Egypt, the Hittites, Mesopotamia) must have pulled them away from the task of building a unified state. Certainly, they were active agriculturists, industrious craftsmen (textiles and metallurgy), and ambitious entrepreneurs in trade beyond their borders.[29] Strabo's account of them makes them the first humans ever to tap fresh water from submarine springs.[30] Likewise, their engineering feats made them the builders of Solomon's temple, and their navigational knowledge and skill in shipbuilding made them the first expeditionary colonizers of the Mediterranean shores.

The Aramaeans (from the 13th century B.C.E.)

The city-states of Canaan found little peace or security, despite their fortifications which in Jericho were 21 feet tall and in Gezer as thick as 16 feet. Besides the occasional invasions of each of the three great powers surrounding them and their own intercity feuds, they were periodically attacked by new waves of migrants from the Arabian desert. The Amorites' settlements in the cities and villages of the Fertile Crescent's western arm were the target of later migrants desiring to follow in their footsteps, that is, to settle down in the farmlands and reestablish their lives on a new basis. The imperial world-state of Babylon had been attacked and infiltrated by the peoples of the mountains, the Hurrians from the northeast, the Kassites from the east, and the Hittites from the northwest. These were invasions by people whose objectives were to stay and colonize. Their lands of origin were in turn the object of invasion and colonization by the Indo-European tribes which had been moving from west to east for centuries and had assimilated with some natives and pushed others out.

About 1500 B.C.E., the Hurrians became powerful enough to carve out a state of their own called Mitanni, out of northern Mesopotamia and northwest Syria, with a capital at Washshukanni. Their leadership was mostly Indo-European, invoking in their treaties with their neighbors Indian deities such as Mithra, Varuna, and Indra. Their official language,

Figure 2-9

Inscription from the Muwaqqar Palace, in the Jordanian desert, dated 115/733. Jordan Museum, 'Ammān.

Illustration 2.2

Cuneiform tablets carrying portions of the Code of Lipit Ishtar, Sumerian king of Isin, who lived about 1900 B.C.E. [Courtesy The University Museum, University of Pennsylvania.]

however, was Akkadian, as witness the letters to Amenhotep III and IV sent by their King Tushratta.

The raids and resultant fragmentation of the world-state the Amorites had built rendered it vulnerable to further attack and penetration by the new *dramatis personae,* the Aramaeans. These were Arab tribesmen like their predecessors, the Amurru and the Akkadians. They were known by several names. A group of them were known as "Khabiru" or "Epiru," names applied as early as Naram-Sin (c. 2300 B.C.E.) to mercenaries on the frontiers who would fight on behalf of anyone for pay or booty. Mursilis of the Hittites (c. 1600 B.C.E.) hired them to do his bidding against Mitanni. In 1367 B.C.E., they were known to have captured Schechem in Palestine; and Abd-Khiba, the vassal king of Jerusalem, wrote to Akhenaton, his overlord in Egypt, for help against them. The same description of roving mercenaries is also found in a Mari letter (18th century B.C.E.) and on a Nuzi tablet (15th century B.C.E.). Evidently, they were the unattached, opportunist ends of the tribal formations migrating form Arabia. Unlike their fellows, they had no loyalty to the settled populations and their states.

Figure 2-10

Carved inscription from 'Anjar, Lebanon, dated 123/740.

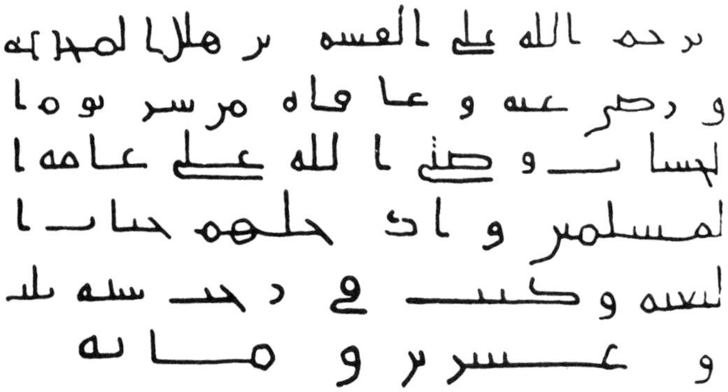

Another group, obviously the main one, was known as the *Akh-lamu* (the brethren). These were a confederation of migrant tribes banding and working together for a common cause. Assyria declared war upon them and sought to check their advance under Adad-Nirari (1297 – 1266 B.C.E.); and the Hittite King Hattushilish (1275 – 1250 B.C.E.) did likewise and advised Babylon to resist them. The Akh-lamu made common cause with the natives wherever they went, reestablishing older ties of genealogy and culture, and cooperating with them to bring about a new regime and new embodiment of a traditional ideal to which they subscribed. By 1200 B.C.E., the Aramaeans were practically everywhere, leading majorities made up of themselves and the natives whom they had reawakened to the Arabian ideal. Aram Naharaim, comprising northern Syria and Mesopotamia west of the Khābūr River, was the first Aramaean state. It lived from the thirteenth to the ninth century B.C.E. Its center of gravity was the land between the Khābūr and the Euphrates. Paddan-Aram, another Aramaean state, followed as the center shifted to Ḥarrān in north Syria. It was to this state that, according to biblical tradition, the patriarchs belonged, where Abraham sought a wife for his son, where Jacob found and married his two cousins, Leah and Rachel. Certainly, these patriarchs spoke Aramaic, until they assimilated with the Canaanites and adopted their dialect. A third Aramaean state was centered on the middle region of Syria between Damascus (Dār Meshek) and Ḥamāh on the Orontes River, and extended north into the Euphrates basin, south into the Jordan basin, and west to the Mediterranean.

The Aramaean state in Syria contended with the Hebrew monarchy from Saul to Jehu, and dodged between Egypt's pressure from the south, and Assyria's

Illustration 2.3

Alabaster slab from the palace of Ashurnasir-pal II, king of Assyria from 883–859 B.C.E. The inscription over the sculptured figure glorifies the king. [Courtesy The University Museum, University of Pennsylvania.]

from the northeast. The king of Judah paid tribute to Ben-Hadad (879–843 B.C.E.), its king, and allied Judah to the kingdom of Damascus that the latter may keep its presssure on the northern kingdom, Israel. Ben-Hadad was able to rally all the city-states and kingdoms of the area to withstand the invasion of Assyria under Shalmanezer III in 853 B.C.E. Hazael, Ben-Hadad's successor, extended the kingdom to the Dead Sea region and the coastal plain of Palestine, and came close to conquering Judah. Under Tiglath-Pilezer III (744–727 B.C.E.), a generation later, Assyria recouped its forces and marched again, leveling everything in its way as far south as the outskirts of Jerusalem in 734 B.C.E.

The Aramaeans spread their language, really a dialect of Akkadian, throughout the area, indeed, among their friendly as well as hostile neighbors. They popularized tha alphabet invented by the Canaanites. Hebrew, Syriac, Pahlawi, and Sanskrit scripts owe their origins to the Canaanite script popularized by the Aramaeans. In its written and oral forms, Aramaic reigned supreme throughout the whole area. Later, when the Persians under Cyrus and Darius included the Aramaean regions in their empire, Aramaic became the language of trade and government from India to the Nile, while its alphabet was destined to circumscribe the globe.

The Assyrians (14th century to Fall of Nineveh (612 B.C.E.)

Northern Mesopotamia had seen the assimilation of migrants from the Arabian desert with the Sumerian natives, and the generation of many Akkadian-speaking, Akkadian-acculturated city-states. It also witnessed the growth and decline of Sargon's world-state. The same process was repeated after the decline of Hammurabi's universal state, in which the Amurru invasions were integrated and settled. Now came the people of the mountains, who invaded, mixed with the natives, and integrated themselves into Akkadian culture. This new blood was vigorous enough to generate a new political entity. But, having been Mesopotamianized in outlook and Akkadianized in language, the new state was new only in that it had different persons leading or embodying it. The ethnic mixture became irrelevant; and the emergent state was fully "Semitic," affirming the same Arabian ideology as the earlier states and the Akkadian language.

Following the weakness of the Amoritic state of Hammurabi, caused in part by the Kassite invasions from the Iranian plateau, Mesopotamia experienced a shift of political power from the center and south to the north. In the eighteenth century B.C.E. Shamsi-Adad laid the foundation of the Kingdom of Assyria which was to witness a significant rise in the fourteenth under Asshur-uballit I (1354–1318 B.C.E.). The growth continued in the twelfth century when Tiglath-Pilezer I (1115–1077 B.C.E.) conquered Anatolia as far as the Black Sea, and Syria as far as the Mediterranean. His dream was no less than those of

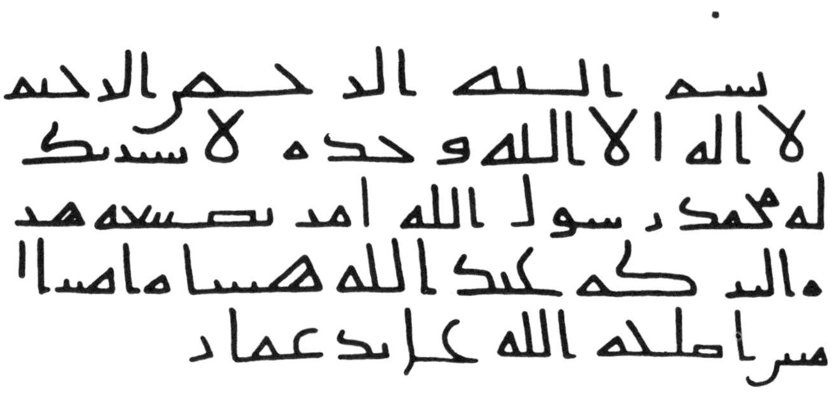

Figure 2-11

Commemorative stone inscription on water reservoir built by the Umawī caliph Hishām at ʻAyn Ḥāzim (Syria), 105-125/723-742.

Illustration 2.4

A procession of sculptured animals on the towering brick walls built by Nebuchadnezzar (605–562 B.C.E.) at Babylon. [Courtesy Arab Information Center, New York City.]

his predecessors, Sargon, Lipit-Ishtar, and Hammurabi. "I am Tiglath-Pilezer, the legitimate king, king of Assyria, king of the four parts of the earth . . . [who] guided by the oracles of Asshur . . . and the command of my lord Asshur . . . conquered . . . the thirty kings of the Nairi countries . . . the Amurru country . . ." and launched this new kingdom.[31] The king was no god, but the agent whom God chose and commanded to establish a new kingdom. The new state was not to be another petty state, but a world-state embodying the universal community. It was an ideological state insofar as it meant to carry out the will of God. In state as well as king, religious and political powers were united. Thus, the kingdoms the Assyrian state replaced, especially Babylon, were not annihilated but exalted, since their tradition, language, religion, culture, and mission were taken intact as Assyria's own. Indeed, the new state presented itself as a reaffirmation of Babylonia and of her gods. Assyria continued to expand within the Fertile Crescent. In 671 B.C.E. it invaded Egypt and subjected it to Assyrian rule, the first time that one of the two ancient civilizations subjugated the other; and the "four corners of the earth" assumed a new meaning.

Assyria remained in control of Egypt for twenty years. Thereafter, its clutch loosened because its own capital, Nineveh, fell under the blow of another Mesopotamian emergent state, Babylon II. Allied with the Medes from the Persian highlands, a resurgent Babylon took to war against Assyria and wrestled the reins of power from her, again to reaffirm the mission of bringing mankind in the four quarters of the earth to heed and implement the word of God.

The Chaldaeans (626–539 B.C.E.)

In 671 B.C.E., Assyria stood at the zenith of its power. It had conquered Egypt and brought the whole of the Fertile Crescent under its dominion. "The lordship of the four corners of the earth," the aspiration of most Mesopotamian leaders since Sargon, had never been truer. However, this glorious achievement was short-lived. The Medes, inhabitants of the Persian highlands to the east, had been infiltrating Mesopotamia for two millennia, but never in such quantities as to produce more than a weakening of the Mesopotamian state or states. In 612 B.C.E. they sought and obtained alliance with a renascent Babylonia anxious to avenge its subjection to Assyria under Tiglath-Pileser III (740 B.C.E.). Now, they descended upon Mesopotamia in swarming hordes directing their fury against Assyria which had extended itself to the "four corners of the earth" from the Black Sea to Aswan. The heart of the Assyrian empire, Nineveh, lay too close to them. The capital was inadequately protected, and it could not take much hammering. The battle was swift and decisive.

Despite their great numbers and crucial role in bringing about this change, the Medes were already sufficiently Mesopotamianized in culture and religion to permit themselves to be assimilated. Leadership in all fields belonged to the resurgent Babylonians (referred to as Neo-Babylon or Babylon II) or Chaldaeans (a geographic designation). Babylon again was dominant; and it assumed the imperial charge of "the four corners of the world" where Assyria had left off. However, Mesopotamia's hold upon the distant provinces, which had been weakening in the last decades of Assyria's rule, was further weakened by the change of power at home. Taking advantage of this temporary weakness, Psammeticus I (663–609 B.C.E.) established the 26th dynasty on the throne of Egypt and shook off the Assyrian influence altogether. His successor, Neco II (609–593 B.C.E.), thought Egypt strong enough to rebuild its Asian empire, and entered the scene as ally of a defeated Assyrian government in Carchemish. Anxious first to secure its northern frontier, Babylon's Nebuchadnezzar (605–562 B.C.E.) spent the first years of his kingship campaigning in Armenia. Once the northern flank was secured, he turned all his power south and west, inflicting one defeat after another against the Assyrian remnants, Egypt, and her ally Judah (Carchemish, Hamath 605; Megiddo, Ashkelon 604; Egypt 601; Jerusalem 589–587 B.C.E.).

The meteoric rise of Babylon II did not last long. The migration of Medes, which had helped it attain power, was apparently the result of pressures generated farther in the Persian hinterland. Beyond Media, Mesopotamian influence was too weak to be effective; and the Persian tribes (Moraphii, Maspii, Pantialaci, Derusiaei, Germanii, Dai, Mardi, Sogartians, etcetera) perched on the higher elevations of the Persian plateau were regrouping themselves under the leadership of the Achaemenidean kings of Pasargadae. Media was their first objective. Having conquered it, the king of Parsa, Cyrus, continued his exploits into North Mesopotamia. Asshur, Nineveh, Arbela, and Harran fell in 547. Conquest of the Lydians, the Greeks, the Lycians to the northwest, and Hyrcania, Parthia, Zaranka, Bactria, and all the lands to the east, up to Gandara (India), followed, thus giving inexhaustible resources and strategic depth to Cyrus's power. Upon conclusion of these campaigns, Cyrus returned to Babylon. In 539, he commanded Gobryas (Gubaru), satrap of Gutia, to march on Babylon, who entered it without battle, paving the way for a new empire to stretch from the Balkans to India, and, a little later, to include Egypt and all the lands in between.[32]

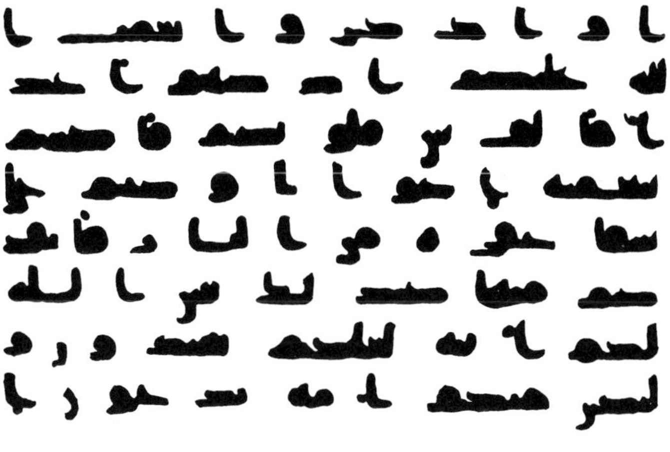

Figure 2-12

Passage from the Qur'ān on deerskin ascribed to 'Umar ibn al Khaṭṭāb, second Rāshidūn Caliph. Topkapi Museum, Iṣtanbūl.

The Hebrews (19th to 1st century B.C.E.)

The Hebrews had their origins in the migrations of the Amurru.[33] They must have been one of the tribes that drifted from Arabia to Mesopotamia, and settled a short while in the southern half. Their inability to assimilate their neighbors or be assimilated by them caused the Hebrews to reenter the nomadic life in the northern part of the Arabian desert. Genesis is absolutely silent on the causes of nonassimilation, and God's order to Abraham to uproot himself and go appears rather arbitrary. This arbitrariness received only theological explanation. It is held that it was a "chosen-ness," or "election" to a plan to make of Abraham's descendants a "chosen" or "special" people. Christians, who adopted the Torah as their Scripture, explained the arbitrary action as divine mercy meant to initiate a long cursus of history culminating "in the fullness of time" in the "incarnation of God in Jesus," and in his "death on the cross and resurrection." The Qur'ān was the first to give a historical explanation. Abraham, or Ibrahīm as he is called in Arabic, it taught, outgrew the *shirk* or associationism of other beings with God which was held by his ancestors in Chaldaea. Having discovered monotheism by his own effort, he disputed the matter with his peers, who then plotted to kill him by fire, from which he was saved. This account of Abraham became popular among Jews in the Muslim World in the Middle Ages and was adopted by Rashi (13th century C.E.). The *Midrash Hagadol,* written after Rashi and discovered in Yaman in the eighteenth century, rendered an account of Abraham's exit from Ur that is almost a literal translation from the Islamic source.[34]

Abraham and his tribesmen left Ur and joined the nomadic tribes roving the Arabian desert. The course of their travels was the reverse of the movement that had brought them into Mesopotamia, namely, north alongside the Euphrates valley, crossing into Paddan-

Map 7. Arab Overseas Trade in 1/622

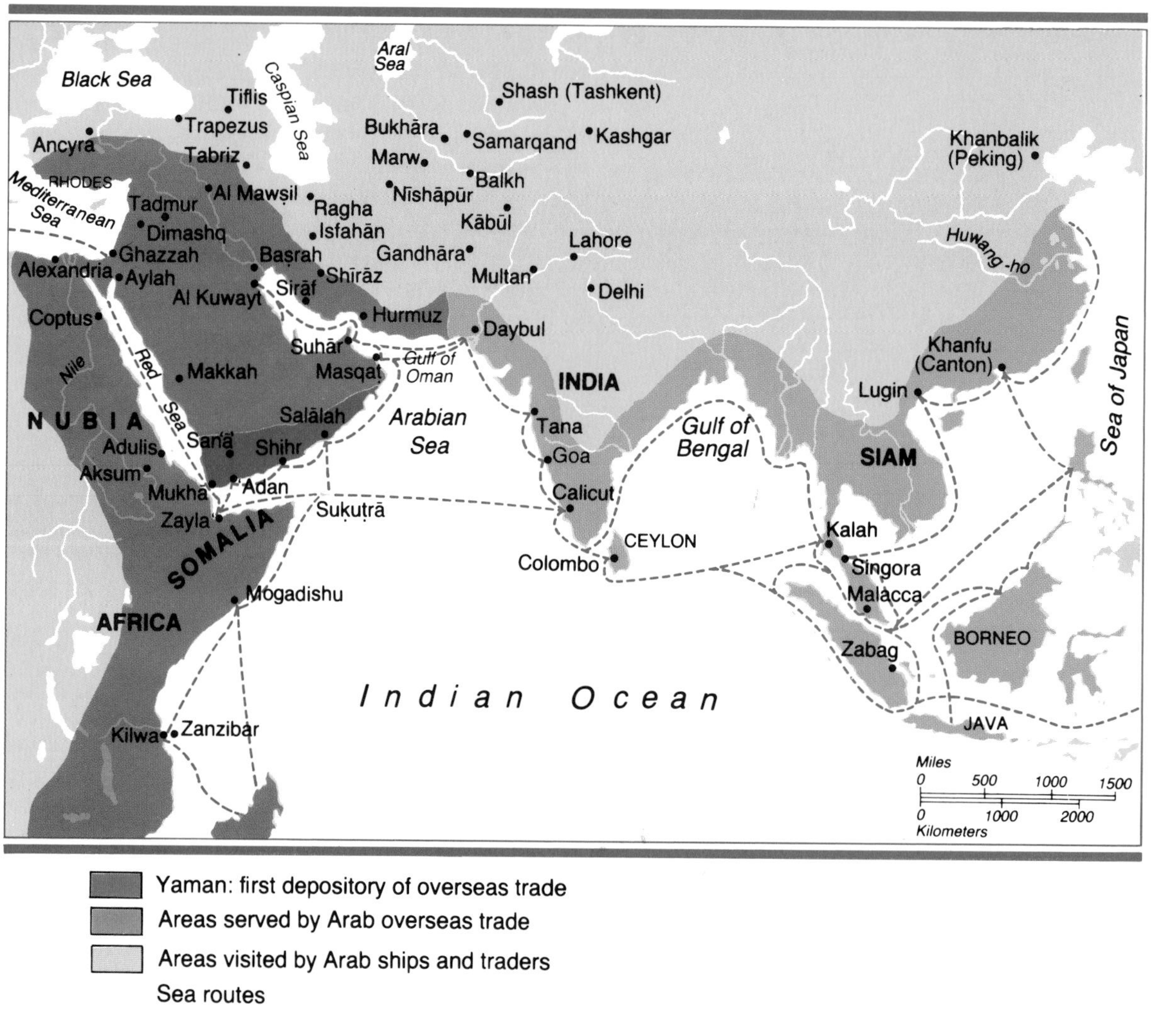

Aram, and south along the edge of the desert all the way to Egypt. Their nonassimilation was the hallmark of their character, as the episodes of Jacob at Paddan-Aram,[35] of his children at Shechem,[36] and of their descendants in Egypt indicate.[37] Coming out of Egypt through a chastizing experience, the Hebrews assimilated with the tribes of Midyan, Horeb, and other elements in northwest Arabia to form an amphictyony of tribes which proceeded north on the desert road east of Palestine for further assimilation. The entry of the amphictyonic tribesmen into Palestine was not always violent, as later redactors of the Bible wished their readers to believe. In particular, archeologists have found no evidence or large-scale destruction during the thirteenth and twelfth centuries.[38]

Spreading first in the arid lands around the Dead Sea and south of Jerusalem, they multiplied and became thoroughly acculturated before the tenth century. The language of Canaan, its calendar, temple, rituals and sacrificial system, its arts and crafts, they adopted and made their own. Some of them maintained a stubborn attachment to a separate identity, while others became more and more indistinguishable from the motley of Arabian and other tribes that made up the population of the Jordan River basin. There was enmity and friction between them and the "people of the sea" or Philistines who, arriving from Caphtor and beyond, began to settle the length of the coastland from Ugarith to Egypt.

About 1000 B.C.E. David was able to consolidate the disparate provinces into a united kingdom which lasted less than a century, 1000–922 B.C.E. He moved the capital from Hebron to Jerusalem, a non-Hebrew city, in order to placate those parts of the population that were not Hebrew and constituted the majority. By military campaign or diplomatic maneuvering, he succeeded in putting together under his suzerainty most of the Jordan River basin south of and including Damascus. The area was never totally Hebrew and many city-states, like Sidon and Damascus, merely paid a tribute to the distant monarch. The nomads' opposition to the temple worship prevented David from erecting one to give focus to his kingdom, and their lack of *savoir faire* sent his son Solomon after Canaanite engineers to build it. Judahite particularism angered the northern tribes, who were far more ready to assimilate with the surrounding peoples. Upon the death of Solomon, the kingdom split in two. Israel, the northern half, which was excluded from participating in building the Temple because of the charge of impurity arising from racial mixture, built a temple of its own and continued its steady march toward assimilation. When in 722 Assyria marched toward it in conquest and dethroned its king, no more was needed for Israel to dissolve once and for all into surrounding Canaan. Liberated from the shackle of a universalizing north, Judah, the southern half, affirmed its separate identity with ever stronger emphasis. It sought, but never succeeded, to bring back the old Davidian glory. In fact, it turned itself into a football puppet, tossed between the great powers of Egypt and Assyria. Finally, in 587 B.C.E., as heir and ideological continuation of the same Assyrian empire, Babylon II put an end to Judah and sent its king, aristocracy, and intelligentsia into exile.

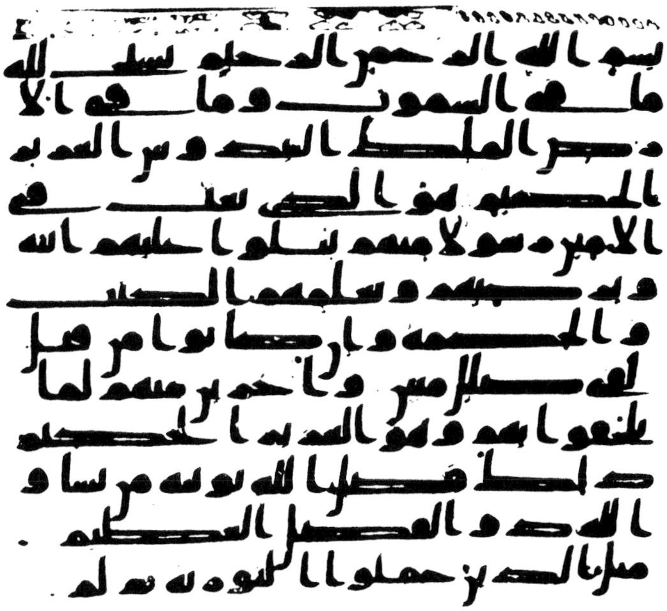

Figure 2-13

Passage from the Qur'ān on deerskin ascribed to 'Uthmān ibn 'Affān, third Rāshidūn Caliph. Topkapi Museum, Istanbūl.

Cyrus's edict of restoration, permitting the Hebrews to return and rebuild Jerusalem, fell on little more than deaf ears. What they fought to preserve, namely, their separate religion and culture, fell under the strongest influences of Babylon and its new faith, Zoroastrianism. Judaism then acquired its eschatology, its absolute monotheism, the ethical tone of its godhead, its angelology and demonology, as well as its messianism and theory of redemption. The exiles liked Babylon; and very few of them ever returned to Judah. About 450 B.C.E. another attempt was made by Ezra and Nehemiah (cupbearer to Darius) to rebuild the kingdom, with little avail. A very conservative remnant continued to agitate for racial purity among the Hebrews—now called Judah-ites or Jews—

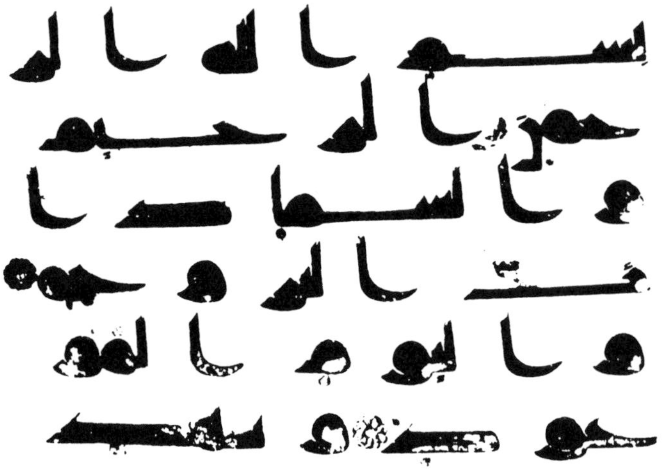

Figure 2-14

Passage from the Qur'ān on deerskin ascribed to 'Ali ibn Abū Tālib, fourth Rāshidūn Caliph (Najaf, Iraq).

within, and for autonomy for their fledgling state in relation to the mighty empires surrounding them. That autonomy was granted by the Greek Seleucid Empire in 142 B.C.E., following a series of uprisings which the Greek Seleucus could not put down because of preoccupation with bigger enemies on other frontiers. Dissension between the heir-presumptives to the throne broke down the unity and prosperity the new kingdom had enjoyed under the Hasmoneans. By 64 B.C.E. the disputing parties had inflicted enough massacres on one another to invite Pompey, the Roman general, to judge between them. As might be expected, he favored the Hellenizing, universalizing party to the dismay of the conservative ethnocentric party. The latter rebelled the following year. They were crushed, and Judah became a province of the Roman Empire. Domestic turbulence continued because the Romans permitted the Jews to be governed by themselves, and Roman patience was exhausted. The ethnocentric zealots made their last stand in the Masada fortress, which they seized from the Romans. The Roman generals Vespasian and Titus, and after them Severus, met the rebellions one after another and brought crushing defeat in 70 C.E. Jerusalem was plowed over; a new city was built and given a new name, Aelia Capitolina, which the Jews were forbidden to enter. This order remained effective throughout the Roman and Byzantine periods, until after the city passed under Islamic rule in 635 C.E. By immigration of Arab tribes from the desert and conversion of natives to Islam, Jerusalem acquired a Muslim population large enough to change its anti-Jewish character and repeal the law as inconsistent with their own faith, Islam.

Mesopotamian Satellites

Three satellite non-Semitic civilizations developed around Mesopotamia. They were the Elamite, Urartian, and Hittite civilizations, with capitals at Susa, Lake Van, and Hattusha, respectively. Their durations were impressive. Elam lasted the longest, about 2,000 years, and was a constant parallel to Mesopotamia. Urartu lasted two centuries, and the Hittite civilization about seven. All three entered into relations of peace and war with Mesopotamia, and all three were at the receiving end as far as language, culture, art, and religion were concerned. They all accepted cuneiform and, in differing measure, Akkadian and its literary tradition.[39] In later times, they accepted Aramaean and its alphabet. Throughout, the literary styles and aesthetic standards embodied in Akkadian became dominant in their literatures.

Relations with Other Civilizations

Mesopotamia, all scholars agree, has been a giving civilization. All those that came into it brought some-

Figure 2-15

Inscription at Qasr al Burqu' in the Jordanian desert, dated 81/706.

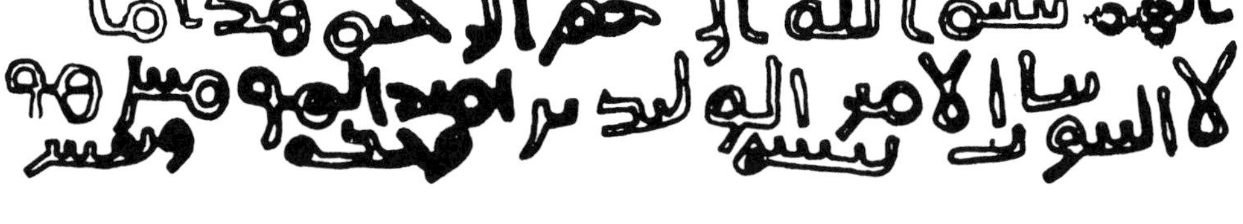

thing with them, but they received from it far more than what they gave. The universal index of Mesopotamian giving was its language, Akkadian, and its writing, cuneiform. Along with language and writing must have gone literary style and form, historical tradition, popular wisdom, law, and finally religion. The Hurrians, for instance, continued to show their peculiar characteristics for a long time after their entry into Mesopotamia; but they nonetheless were eventually completely acculturated. The Kassites, Gutians, Hittites, Medes, and others suffered the same transformation; and so, it is often mistakenly added, were the Akkadians, Amorites, and Aramaeans.

Mesopotamia did give to and did acculturate the aliens that entered its territory as warriors and invaders or as migrants and settlers. But it did so to the non-Semites. The assimilating Mesopotamian identity or culture was itself received from the Arabian desert migrants. True, there was an interaction between the culture of the migrants and that of the Sumerians; but in the resultant culture, the Arabian elements were undoubtedly predominant. The migrants' language, Akkadian, being the vehicle of the new culture, supplied it with its categories and values. Coming about half a millennium after the Akkadians, the Amurru's original language was not markedly different from Akkadian and had no script of its own. And since the ideology was one, it was natural for them to adopt Akkadian as the written language of trade and government, and to continue to speak the Amoritic dialect as colloquial language of kitchen or street. It was otherwise with the Aramaeans. Although the linguistic differences from Akkadian and Amoritic were slight, the Aramaeans came with a superior script which they had learned from the Canaanites, and with ink and parchment, which were far superior to stylus and clay which had to be wet and malleable and had to be fired to be preserved. Thus equipped, Aramaean was destined to elbow out Akkadian and its cuneiform script and take their place. As to the other aspects of culture and religion, the differences between the fresh desert migrants and their predecessors who had arrived at an earlier time were always slight. History knows of no significant difference between them through the three millennia of recorded history.

NOTES

1. Exceptions: Aramaic is spoken as an esoteric, sacred language by a handful of people in Syria and Iraq. Geez has been displaced by its subdialects — Amharic and Harari — which divide the 20 million Abyssinians among themselves. Hebrew is the sacred language of Jewish Scripture, in which most Jews recite their Torah readings. While the vernacular of Arab Jews is Arabic — and these compose two-thirds of the Jewish population of Israel — European and American Jews use English and other European languages as their vernacular. In addition to the vernacular, Western Jews speak Yiddish, a mixture of Hebrew, German, and Slavic, and modern Hebrew — the official language of Israel. The latter, however, is the language of daily discourse for about two million people or less, most of whom live in Israel.

2. James B. Pritchard, ed., *Ancient Near Eastern Texts* (Princeton, N.J.: Princeton University Press, 1955), pp. 483-490.

3. Ibid., p. 491-492.

4. For example, the root *k-t-b,* when conjugated, yields the words: ***kataba,*** to write; ***kutiba,*** to be written; ***kātaba,*** to correspond with someone; ***kattaba,*** to make one write; ***kātib,*** writer; ***kitāb,*** book; ***maktab,*** a place to write; ***maktabah,*** a library; ***kuttāb,*** the place where one is made to write, that is, a school; ***istaktaba,*** to invite one to write to the author; ***katībah,*** a list or those included in the list; ***iktataba,*** to subscribe; ***inkataba,*** to have been written; etcetera. The conjugated words may in turn become roots and be conjugated again to yield new words. The roots *ḍ-r-b* (strike), *f-'-l* (act), *q-w-l* (say), etcetera, would yield the same modalities of meaning when conjugated in the same forms.

5. William J. Moran, "The Hebrew Language in Its Northwest Semitic Background," *The Bible and the Ancient Near East,* ed. G. E. Wright (London: Routledge & Kegan Paul, 1961), p. 65.

6. Crawford Howell Toy, "Semitic Languages," *Schaff-Herzog Encyclopedia of Religious Knowledge* (Grand Rapids, Mich.: Baker Book House, 1977), Vol. 10, p. 352.

7. "The Semites multiply words for objects and acts which we do not care to particularize. . . ." (ibid.).

8. "Repetition and parallelism," writes Samuel Noah Kramer, "metaphor and simile . . . static epithets, lengthy repetitions, recurrent formulae . . . little feeling for close-knit plot structure . . . mark Sumerian literature. Their narratives tend to ramble on rather disconnectedly and monotonously — their poets lack a sense of climax; they did not appreciate the effectiveness of bringing their stories to a climactic head . . . [of] intensification of emotion and suspense as the story progresses . . . the last episode is no more moving or stirring than the first" (Wright, *The Bible,* p. 254). The greatest authority in the field and father of Sumerology is so enwrapped in his Greek and Western aesthetic values that he must judge Sumerian literature by them. Apparently, having never heard of *épôché,* of the need to suspend one's categories and empathize with the alien civilization in order to understand it, he rendered himself incapable of appreciating a literature based upon a different set of values.

9. A. Leo Oppenheim, *Ancient Mesopotamia: Portrait of a Dead Civilization* (Chicago: University of Chicago Press, 1946-1967), p. 49.

10. A. F. Albright, *From the Stone Age to Christianity* (Garden City, N.Y.: Doubleday, 1957), p. 141.

11. Were "the Sumerians" a people or was "Sumerian" only a language? Scholarship is still divided on this question because the evidence is not conclusive either way. The unquestionable fact is that the population of Mesopotamia has been a mixture from the earliest times. Henri Frankfort, *The Birth of Civilization in the Near East* (Garden City, N.Y.: Doubleday, 1956), p. 51; Albright, *Stone Age*, pp. 145ff., 165ff., 174ff., 189ff.; Thorkild Jacobsen, "The Assumed Conflict of Sumerians and Semites in Early Mesopotamian History," *Journal of American Oriental Society* 59 (1939), pp. 485–495.

12. Oppenheim, *Ancient Mesopotamia*, p. 34.

13. E. A. Speiser, *Bulletin of the American School of Oriental Research*, 66 (1937), pp. 2ff.

14. Frankfort, *Birth of Civilization*, pp. 46–48.

15. Oppenheim, *Ancient Mesopotamia*, p. 54.

16. Sidney Smith, *Early History of Assyria* (New York: E. P. Dutton, 1924), p. 93; Frankfort, *Birth of Civilization*, p. 85; Albright, *Stone Age*, pp. 148–149. Lugalzaggizi, king of the Sumerian city of Kish, had some of his inscriptions written in Akkadian (Albright, *Stone Age*, p. 149).

17. Pritchard, *Ancient Near Eastern Texts*, p. 119.

18. Ibid., pp. 119, 267.

19. Ibid., p. 119.

20. Ibid., p. 266.

21. Sabatino Moscati, *The Face of the Ancient Orient: A Panorama of Near Eastern Civilization in Pre-Classical Times* (Garden City, N.Y.: Doubleday, 1962), p. 60. Scholars agree that this was the first bid for a world-state based on a universal community in human history. See Albright, *Stone Age*, p. 149.

22. Pritchard, *Ancient Near Eastern Texts*, p. 266.

23. The claim that Akkadian came to dominate in Mesopotamia by virtue of conquest by aliens was finally laid to rest through the researches of Jacobsen, "The Assumed Conflict."

24. Pritchard, *Ancient Near Eastern Texts*, p. 159.

25. Ibid.

26. Ibid., p. 165.

27. Ibid., p. 164.

28. Ibid., p. 178.

29. The blade of an ax from the fourteenth-century Ugarith gives evidence of smelting iron as well as of mixing it with other metals to form steel (C. F. A. Schaeffer, *Ugaritica*, Vol. 2 [1949], p. 110).

30. Walafrid Strabo (c. 808–849 C.E.), *De Exordiis et Incrementis Quarandum in Oservationibus Ecclesiasticis Rerum*, Bk. xvi, ch. 2, p. 13.

31. Moscati, *The Face*, pp. 65–66.

32. A. T. Olmstead, *History of the Persian Empire* (Chicago: University of Chicago Press, 1959).

33. See above, pp. 29ff.

34. See details in I. al Fārūqī, *On Arabism: 'Urūbah and Religion* (Amsterdam: Djambatan, 1962), pp. 23–28; 51–57.

35. Genesis 29.

36. Genesis 34. For an analysis of Hebrew opposition to the universalist claim of the king of Schechem, see al Fārūqī, *On Arabism*, pp. 31–37.

37. Exodus 1. The account of Exodus 1 contrasts starkly with that of Genesis 46:18–22, where Pharaoh welcomed the Hebrews and offered them "the fat of the land." The radical change in Egypt's attitude toward them is inexplicable except in terms of Hebrew resistance to assimilation. Martin Buber rejected Sigmund Freud's analysis of Moses (*Moses and Monotheism* [New York: A. A. Knopf, 1939]) precisely because he (Buber) perceived Hebrew ethnocentrism as patriarchal rather than Mosaic (*Israel and the World: Essays in a Time of Crisis* [New York: Schocken Books, 1948], pp. 217–218).

38. W. F. Albright, *The Archaeology of Palestine* (Baltimore: Penguin Books, 1960), p. 113; Kathleen Kenyon, *Archaeology in the Holy Land* (London: Ernest Benn Ltd., 1960), pp. 207–210.

39. "According to the evidence we have," writes A. Leo Oppenheim, "in Urartu and in Elam the native texts parallel their Akkadian prototypes quite slavishly" (*Ancient Mesopotamia*, p. 68).

CHAPTER 3

Religion and Culture

MESOPOTAMIAN RELIGION

A Question of Method

In an essay entitled "Why a 'Mesopotamian Religion' Should Not Be Written," A. Leo Oppenheim has argued that the materials on which to base such a work do not lend themselves to clear understanding.[1] The archeological materials may yield a-religious descriptions of Mesopotamian temples and rituals, but the meaning of these buildings and rituals will necessarily escape us (pp. 172–173). One cannot accept this premise without casting doubt on the whole discipline of archeology and its reconstruction of ancient history. True, since we are dealing with humans who no longer exist, we have to deduce and extrapolate from the little material evidence in our hands to reach their religious ideas and vision. From this there is no escape.

However, our position as students of history is not desperate on this account. Besides the archeological, there are the textual materials which tell us about the gods, their activities and dispensations, and their imperatives for men. Oppenheim suggests these to be largely literary in character, and asks—the answer being indubitably negative in his mind—"What conceivable light can a body of texts shed . . . on the perplexing diversity of what we are wont to call 'Mesopotamian religion'? . . . To what extent and with what degree of reliability can written sources impart to us . . . individual and group reactions to things considered sacred, to such existential facts as death, disease, and misfortune . . . what is commonly meant by religion?" (pp. 174–175). One can appreciate the sensitivity behind these candid questions. This notwithstanding, the historical truth about Mesopotamian religion may still be distilled out of the thousands of texts, literary, historical, mythical, as well as legal. Literariness of a composition does not render it inexpressive of human hope, fear, or aspiration. Nor does it necessarily make it untrustworthy as a report of such emotions. Indeed, religious feeling always inclines to the literary form of expression and is nearly always distorted by descriptive, behavioral, or scientific ways of expression. The sublime in literature expresses the human soul's deepest religious emotions. What is myth if not a climactic combination of religion and literary form?

There are valid reasons why the modern student of Mesopotamian religion finds his work frustrating. Besides the ever-present threat to correct comprehension of materials which ignorance of the nuances of the alien language poses, there is always the danger of

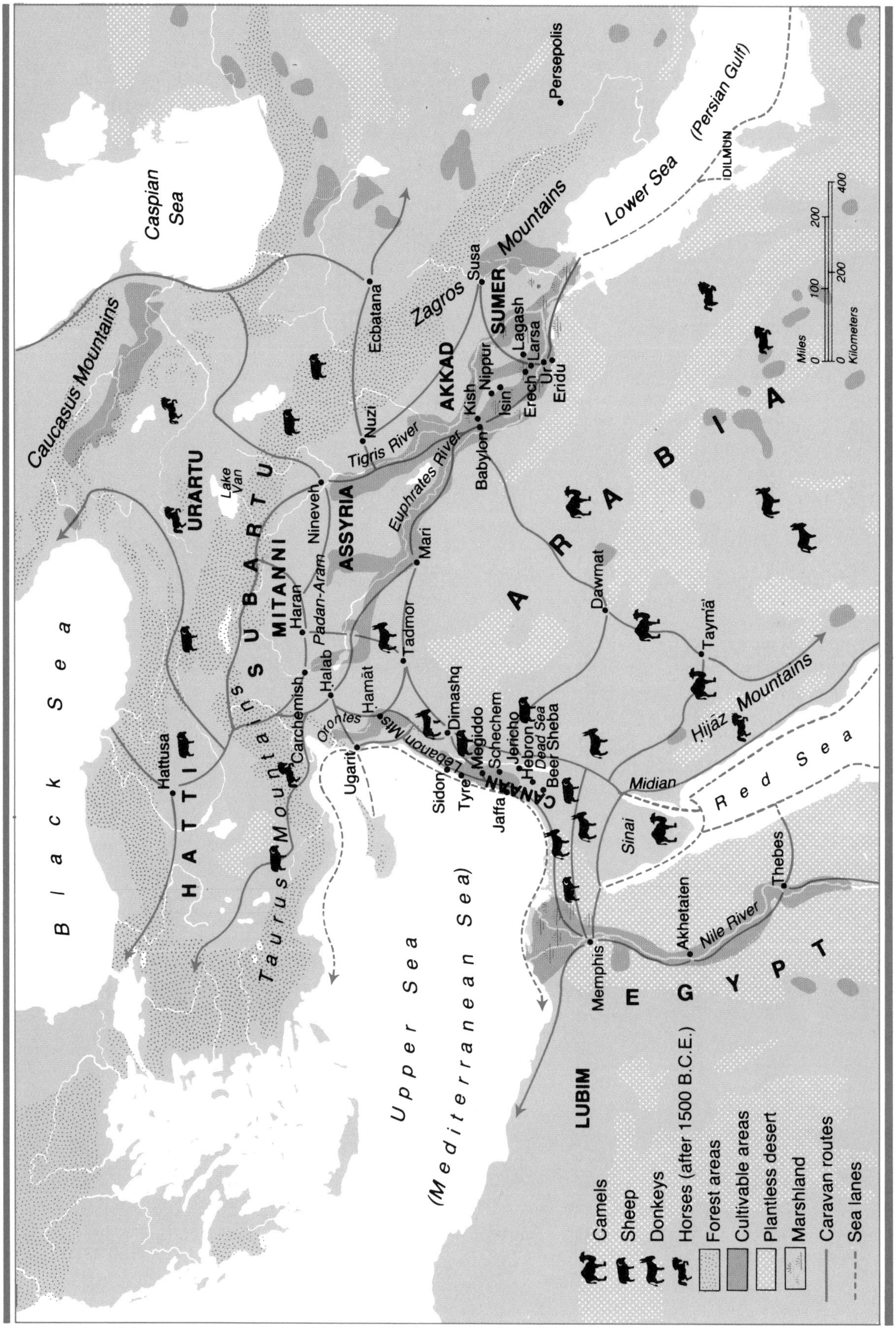

Map 8. Ancient Near East—General

apprehending the strange materials under one's own built-in categories, and thus subjecting them to distortion. Three conditions must be met if genuine understanding of another faith is to be achieved. The first is *epoché,* the suspension or neutralization of all the examiner's religious, ethical, and cultural categories. One should never impose upon religious materials any category not derived from them, and avoid judgment of them. The effort should be primarily devoted to understanding, not to judging, whether positively or negatively. The second is empathy, or the openness to determination by the materials under examination. Religious data are "live materials" whose perception means determination by them of the emotive faculties of the perceiving subject. Knowledge of them comes only through reflection upon the experience of determination. Like sensitive beings, religious data do not speak out; they reveal themselves only to the sympathetic listener. The third is experience or previous familiarity with religious materials, with the sort of affection that religious values bring upon the man of religion. Such experience facilitates empathy and is almost always its prerequisite. This is especially so if the experience falls in a religious tradition whose worldview and ethic are akin to that of the data under study. The secular-minded student, for instance, has learned to shield himself from all religious calls whatever their source. In an atmosphere where religion is banished from public life and relegated to the realm of secret personal relation with whatever one assumes to be ultimate reality, the secularist's consciousness becomes compartmentalized into two separate chambers. In the one are to be found critical knowledge and truth, understanding of cultures, public loyalty to nation and state, exercise of power, acquisition of property, and consumption of the materials of pleasure and life. In the other reside uncritical knowledge and dogmatic truth, loyalty that hardly ever transcends the individual, an escapist eschatological hope, and a phantasmagoric world of ethereal spirits! How could such a consciousness begin to understand Mesopotamian or Semitic religion, where God is the real cause and end of everything, where human activity—cultural, social, economic, or physical—is deeply religious, where the state, the law, war and peace, and politics are the highest expressions of religious relevance? How could the secularist begin to perceive relevance in legal texts, political annals, or "literary" pieces that sing the praises of spring or of the moon?

It is otherwise with the person who fulfills the prerequisites of comparative study. His position is not desperate. While *epoché* would suspend his inherited or acquired notions, his empathy and experience would enable him to appreciate the realms of religious meanings in Mesopotamian legal, political, and mythological materials. That is precisely what many illustrious scholars have done for us. Needless to say, openness to new evidence, modesty in laying down claims, and intellectual integrity in probing the evidence must characterize the scholarly effort if it is to be worthy. Of equal importance, in religious study, as in every other academic pursuit, a creative imagination is an absolute necessity.[2]

The Essence

The essence of religious experience characteristic of Mesopotamia through its three millennia of history may be described as consisting of five core principles. First is the perception of reality as ultimately composed of two kinds of ontologically disparate beings, one divine, absolute, and everlasting, numinous, creaturely, and, above all, commanding; and another, material, human, creaturely, changing and ephemeral, subject to the divine imperatives. Second, the realm of the divine is relevant to that of creation in that the will of the former is the ought-to-do of the latter; this will is knowable through divination or revelation. Third, humans are created neither in vain nor for their own sakes, but to serve their Creator; and the content of their service is obedience to or fulfillment of the divine imperatives. Fourth, since they are indeed capable of such obedience or fulfillment, and since the content of the imperative is what ought to be, humans are responsible. Hence, they will be rewarded with prosperity and happiness if they obey, and punished with suffering and privation if they do not. Fifth, the divine plan concerns a world in which humanity acts as an organic unity. Hence, society, not the individual, is the constitutive unit of reality. It is the object of cosmic action on the part of the deity. The steps of society are those of the cosmos. Membership in society, and cooperation with it, are definitive of humanism and of morality.

The first principle may be called ontological dualism. It guarded Mesopotamia against union of the two ultimate realms and never permitted their fusion into one being. However, the Mesopotamians found ways to associate the two realms together, by pairing the function of the god with a force or phenomenon of nature while keeping the god's being utterly "other," or transcendent. Dualism of creator and creature distinguished Mesopotamia from ancient Egypt, where the basic view of reality was the opposite, namely, monophysitism.[3] There, Pharaoh, *en chair et en os,* was god; the sun disk, with its light and heat, was the god Atum. The blade of grass growing up from the earth following the flood, with its green and freshness, was the god Osiris. Primacy belonged to nature in whose image the god and the divine order were conceived and with which they were ontologically equated. This principle raised naturalism above its ordinary meaning and transformed it into theology.

Per contra, the Mesopotamians believed Enlil to be the god of the storm; Inanna the goddess of the reed, or of the moon; but they did not identify the god with its hierophany. The storm, the reed, the moon, were not themselves the gods associated with them. The gods did not disappear with the disappearance of their natural expressions. The forces of nature were hence mere indices of the presence of the gods, instruments of their power. Ontological dualism contrasts equally with the Indian religion, where the principle *Tat twam Asi* is as general and absolute as its Egyptian counterpart. Both perceive reality as single-natured. However, in India, the primacy is laid on the side of the divine, not the natural, resulting in an ethic diametrically opposed to that of Egypt. The highest desideratum of the moral life in Egypt was to become nature-like, to do "what comes naturally," to attune oneself with nature. The ideal of the moral life in India was to disengage oneself from nature, to escape from life and to merge oneself into Brahma. In contrast to both, Mesopotamia maintained a dualistic doctrine in which only God was divine, and the creature, creaturely. Despite many temptations and pressures to identify the divine with the creaturely, Mesopotamia consistently maintained their separateness.

In the Mesopotamian view, the ontological disparity between Creator and creature posited by the first principle did not amount to isolation of the two realms from each other. The divine was deeply relevant to the world which is its creation. The will of the Creator is what creation ought to be; His commandment, what creation ought to do. This will was perceived as built into nature, where it may be discerned through divination and the reading of omens, or as immediately revealed by the divine in the form of the law. This act of disclosure was undertaken by God in order to make His will known and obeyed. Fulfillment of the will of God by nature is necessary; and this necessity is precisely what makes of creation a cosmos rather than a chaos. In the case of man, the divine will has to be actualized voluntarily if its moral content is to be fulfilled. It was to this end that humans were created, namely, "to serve the gods."[4] God "created mankind to set them [the gods] free" from reconstructing the world and making it productive, a task which the Mesopotamians saw devolving upon mankind.[5] Humans were hence obliged always to praise God,[6] to "provide for their [the gods'] maintenance . . . and take care of their sanctuaries . . . to make on earth a likeness of what he [the God] made in heaven."[7] To serve God meant therefore to fulfill His directives as they are received through revelation, and to do so voluntarily.

Such fulfillment constitutes a very important role for humans in this divine drama of the creation. Fulfillment is necessary for maintenance of cosmic order without which the latter would collapse. Humans are a cosmic bridge through which the divine will must pass if it is to be fulfilled. Humans are the only creatures whose fulfillment of the divine will is self-conscious and voluntary and hence satisfying to the divine imperative. Theirs is the greater destiny.

The fourth principle constitutive of the essence of Mesopotamian religion affirms the human capacity to perceive and understand the revelation of divine will, to implement it and bring about the goals and objectives it contemplates. Since these goals and objectives are normative, obligatory, and desirable, and since humans are capable of realizing them, it follows that humans are responsible. Responsibility demands that humans be rewarded with prosperity and happiness for their obedience and service, and punished for their dereliction and violation with privation and suffering. The gods look with favor upon the obedient, and with disfavor upon the others.

In a Sumerian version of creation honored in Mesopotamia down to 800 B.C.E., when it was committed to a clay tablet found in the ruins of Asshur, the poet exclaimed on behalf of God:

> Let us create mankind. The service of the gods be their portion for all times. To maintain the boundary ditch, to place the hoe and basket into their hands . . . to water the four regions of the earth, to raise plants in abundance . . . to fill the granary . . . to increase the abundance in the land . . . to celebrate the festivals of the gods . . . to increase ox, sheep, cattle, fish and fowl. . . . [Thus God] ordained for them great destinies.[8]

The fifth and last principle concerns the social order, and sums up the whole Mesopotamian worldview. The social order is the absolute category by which the worldview is governed. Unlike Egypt where nature presents constant regularity and is positively constructive even when it is on a rampage (the annual Nile flood, the daily burning sunshine), nature in Mesopotamia presents an arbitrary, whimsical will — the rain storm or sand storm — which is always destructive. Humans must always team up together, organize and assign to each citizen up- and down-river the specific duties of maintaining the irrigation and drainage canals and their banks and watergates for agriculture to become at all possible. They must mobilize themselves to undo the effects of a storm. Otherwise, agriculture would fail and any concentration of life would become impossible. It is this self-discipline which man imposes upon himself that makes him a citizen, a member of a social order. Society is a mode of life where somebody rules and others voluntarily obey to fulfill the common objective. Social order is so necessary for prosperity, for life itself, that the Mesopotamian saw it as old as creation, and saw both himself and the godhead as equally subjected to it. He credited the organized society — the state — with responsibility for all the advances of human civilization then achieved: the invention of writing, the ziggurat sanctuaries where food was stored and distributed, the construction of large cities, the institution of the calendar and festivities, and the success of large-scale agriculture capable of supporting large urban populations. Humans without the orderly state, the Mesopotamians thought, are "like sheep without shepherd."[9] The vision of an ideal social order moved the desert peoples and prompted them to emigrate to "the four corners of the world," to establish therein a *modus vivendi* where justice and prosperity would prevail and where humans could lead a felicitous existence.

The Manifestation

The gods. The Mesopotamians had many gods. Highest among them was Anu, god of the sky, whose authority was moral and yet supreme, for no being, divine or other, could question it. It was believed that Anu was begotten by Anshar and Kishar, the children of Apsu and Tihamat, the gods of sweet and salty waters. His divine pedigree was high, and so was his place in the hierarchy. Like the sky which represented him, Anu was the object of great awe and wonder, commanding obedience by his sheer presence. Ultimately, all authority derived from him, be it the authority of the head of a household or that of a ruler of state. Yielding to him was seen as submission to what "ought-to-be" in its most general sense, inclusive of all laws, customs, and wisdom. To recognize and acknowledge Anu was perceived as the first prerequisite of humanity, meant to attune the individual to a commanding ultimate reality. Not only humans bowed to Anu; everything that is did so. The birds in the sky, reptiles on earth and fishes in the water, the elements, mountains, rivers, and trees — aye, the gods themselves constantly acknowledge Anu. Obedience to him is voluntary, as in the case of humans, or necessary, as in nature.

"What thou has ordered [comes] true! The utterance of prince and Lord is [but] what thou hast ordered, [that with which] thou art in agreement. O Anu! thy great command takes precedence, who could say no [to it]? O father of the gods, thy command, the very foundation of heaven and earth, what god could spurn [it]?"[10]

Great and exalted as the authority of Anu was, the universe still needed a forceful ruler to administer it. Unfortunately, not all humans listen to the voice of moral authority and some openly defy it. Great as man may be when he voluntarily yields to Anu, he can sink in his disobedience lower than animals and trees, who obey him instinctively. Moreover, the world is not a leisurely pastime, but a theater where Anu's will must be realized. Hence, the need is never obviated for a powerful agency that will crack down on delinquents and recalcitrants and force them to abide by the law of heaven. The Mesopotamians believed this agent to be Enlil, god of the storm, who can whip up the necessary force to coerce anyone into obedience. Enlil was originally a Sumerian god. His identity and name were assumed by the Akkadians and Amorites. The Assyrians assumed the Sumerian-Babylonian god and ascribed his qualities and functions to their god, Asshur.

The association of Anu with the sky expressed man's deepest wonder at the firmament above, the most available theater of infinity and locus of transcendental intuition. Association of Enlil with the storm grew out of the Mesopotamian's terror at the devastating might of the sudden storm. The natural catastrophe as well as the raid of a cruel enemy were perceived as Enlil's whip unleashed against those guilty of injustice, oppression, and social disorder. While Anu's authority was responsible for social order, Enlil's accounted for the coercive power of the state. Without the former, the social order was devoid of norms or moral authority; without the latter, it remained a utopian dream, hardly capable of entering the course of history. Together, they complemented each other and provided the framework of organization and power necessary for a society bent upon making history.

The third and fourth most important gods were Ki and Ea (also called Enki). Ki was associated with the earth, and was represented by its passive fertility. Ki was the mother of all the newborn, the generator of all living things. As "Nimmah," she was the exalted "queen of the gods," the "lady who determines . . . heaven and earth." Ea, or Enki, was associated with fresh water and hence with the power of creativity which acts upon the earth to make it blossom forth and produce. As water is devious and will always reach its destination whatever the impediment in its way, Ea was regarded as the hypostasis of intelligence, wisdom, and knowledge. Ea therefore became the god of the craftsman, the engineer, the farmer, the wise counselor. The earth, indeed the whole of creation, the Mesopotamian held, is the material substrate of all life, all action, and all history. It is fertile, malleable, capable of being fertilized and of producing whatever it is called upon to produce by agents of creativity. Patterns or laws are built into its very constitution; and they are ready to be discerned by the intelligent and the creative, and put under productive harness. This is also the objective of all humans: to understand the laws of nature and to engineer nature's processes creatively so as to satisfy human need. The earth is alive with potentiality which requires the creative agent to bring it to actuality.

The other members of the Mesopotamian pantheon responded more directly to man's need for explaining origins (the gods Enlil and Ninlil, originators of the moon and stars; Kingu, of man; Ninsar, of plants; Uttu, of cloth and weaving; Ninmah, of the disabled), or for explaining natural and social phenomena (Apsu and Tihamat, gods of fresh and salt waters, respectively, and their son Mummu, god of clouds and mist; Dumuzi and Enkimdu, gods of shepherd and farmer). Most important, however, was the "primordial" assembly of the gods and the investiture of Marduk with the kingship of the gods designed to explain the social order and the state.

The cosmic order. The criterion, or basic reality, through which all truth is perceived is the social order. It is an order of wills, where the wills or desires of beings have been bent in order to make life and happiness possible for all. Before the emergence of social order, life was impossible, and so were truth and knowledge and civilization. All came to be at once, when humans and/or gods agreed to deny their individual wills and to submit to one authority to organize their activities so as to produce life and civilization. This greatest moment in human history became, in the mythopoeic mind, the birth moment of cosmic order. Before this time, in heaven as on earth, chaos predominated and life was impossible. Even God Himself, insofar as He was an object of human knowledge, was numinous but vague. But once cosmic order was established, together with its replica on earth, the divine character of the deity emerged clear and distinct.

A petty dispute arose between the gods and their offspring at which Apsu, the father of the gods, was slain. His wife Tihamat sought vengeance and the whole pantheon was thrown into turmoil. Tihamat was so mighty that none could subdue her. The whole realm was threatened and chaos reigned supreme. The grandfather of the gods called all the members of the divine realm to a meeting at which they decided to send Marduk, the youngest son of Ea, to face Tihamat. But Marduk demurred, asking for absolute authority over all things. The gods voted to grant him his request. Marduk accepted the investiture, confronted Tihamat and slew her, and established order. Chaos was terminated. The gods were placed in their stations, and Marduk became absolute ruler and judge of the universe. He created man to serve in His manor, that order may continue and divine peace be established everywhere. While Marduk reigned supreme, humans were established for service, agriculture and industry, culture and civilization; the gods were to receive that service from humans under the ever-watchful, ever-caring, ever-merciful, ever-just eye of Marduk.

The dramatic elements of the story were created by a mythopoeic mind that could not understand metaphysical matters except as causally connected and crassly anthropomorphized. For our part, we may and should drop these dramatic and mythological elements. The Mesopotamian conception of God, man, and history and of their mutual relations constitutes the lesson to be gleaned from Ancient Mesopotamia.

The transformation from chaos to cosmos brought many significant changes in the world. The first and most important of these was the emergence of Marduk as sole king, which meant his transformation from a god among gods to the one and only God. The Sumerians had set up city-states, each with its own patron god. If a group had its own god, it was inevitable that other groups should have their own gods too. Polytheism thus became inevitable. The arrival of desert migrants to the scene for the first time made possible a state of "the four corners of the world" under one king. The world-state was perceived as a replica of the cosmic state, the prior normative archetype. Hence the polytheism of the cosmic constituency must give way to monotheism, the unity of the godhead. One and only one god can be God; the other gods must be discharged and discredited, "assigned to their minor posts." The ascendancy of Sargon as king of Sumer and Akkad complemented the ascendancy of Marduk as God of all the gods.

Marduk's unique and distinctive status was there even before his investiture. He was "the wisest of the wise," "*the* god," surpassing all other gods in everything.[11] But he would not save the gods from destruction until all power had been yielded to him alone. The gods had to vote that henceforth Marduk's command was the most authoritative, the highest; that it was solely his judgment "to exalt and to abase," that "kingship over the totality of the universe was exclusively his own."[12] Order and safety ensued. Marduk assigned the various "stations for the gods," determined the year, defined its divisions. He caused the moon "to shine forth," assigned the months and their days, created man and assigned him to service.[13] He established Babylon, as Enlil had established Agade before, as a sanctuary for himself and as capital of the world-state. Marduk now enjoyed dominion over all, including the gods. He "dispose[d] of all destinies," "exercise[d] shepherdship over mankind" whom he taught "to fear him" and to make on earth "a likeness of what he made in heaven." As to the gods, they shall henceforth declare him "their God," "proclaim his fifty names," "quake . . . at the mention of his name," shine only by His light, acknowledge Him as the one who "restored them to life," "the creator of grain and legume," "who causes the green herb to spring up," "who waters the fields," who "commands . . . creation, destruction, mercy" and ultimately, the god "besides [whom] no god whatever knows the appointed time," the God Who "created the four [known] groups of mankind [Akkad, Elam, Subartu and Amurru]."[14]

Under the influence of the desert migrant, the Mesopotamian mind—really the same migrant's mind, but finding itself in the new context of farming, industry, and interaction with other humans—rose to a monotheistic conception of the godhead and a unified view of humankind. No Mesopotamian could recite or hear the creation poem, *Enuma Elish,* without perceiving Marduk as absolutely unique, unlike all other gods. The gods owed their life, their

Map 9. The Fourth Millennium B.C.E.: *Akkadian Penetration of the Fertile Crescent*

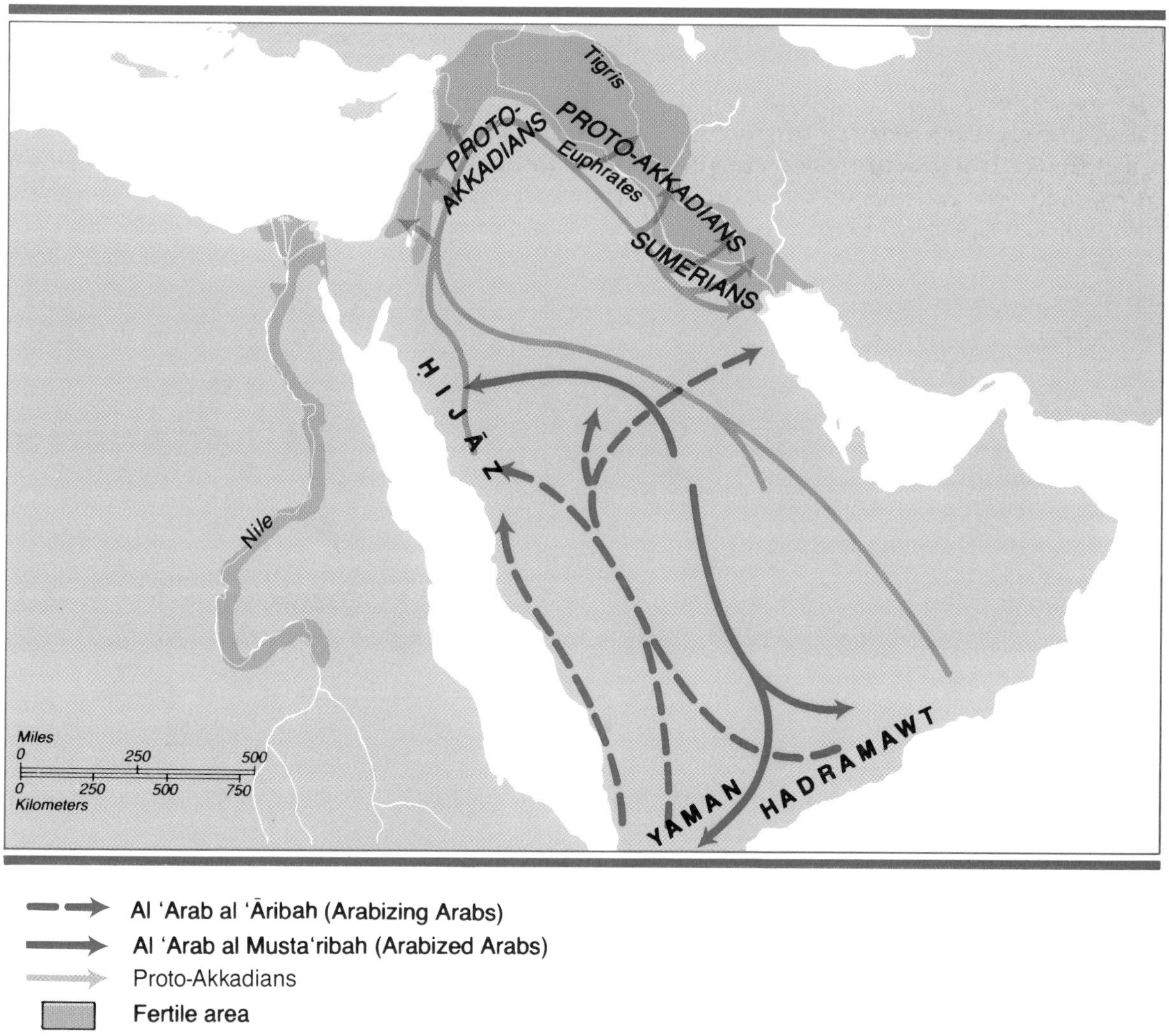

position, their sustenance, and their destinies to Him alone. He ruled and they did not. Obviously, they must have been the cosmic counterparts of the earthly feudal lords. As the former were associates of God but certainly not God, the latter were nobility but not king. Only Marduk, as the one and only God, was worthy of praise and worship by humans as well as by the gods themselves. Certainly this is monotheism; but it is confused, beclouded, and vitiated with *shirk* or association of other beings with God. This Mesopotamian *shirk* is lessened in significance by the uniqueness of God as disposer of destiny, which was not the case with the demi-gods of pre-Islamic Arabia, which we will have occasion to examine below. The Mesopotamian mind equally rose to the conception of God as transcendent, however locked it remained in the old anthropomorphisms. *Enuma Elish* described Marduk in the opposite of empirical terms: "double-equal of the gods," "beyond comprehension were his members," "not-fit for human understanding," "four were his eyes and four were his ears . . . to see and hear everything," "fire blazed forth when his lips moved." Evidently, in the absence of the highly abstract concept of transcendence, the Mesopotamian mind was content to describe God in terms borrowed from human experience but qualified in such way as to deny their empirical character. Their "not like" the things of nature or creation is tantamount to our modern expression, "the totally other."

Mesopotamian Religion in Peninsular Arabia

Following the rise of Cyrus and his Persian Empire, Mesopotamia became part of that empire that was influenced by its religion. Zoroastrianism contributed its eschatology and angelology, and introduced messianism, ideas that penetrated Judaism and, through it, Christianity. The culture of Mesopotamia suffered little change, because Persia had already been influenced by Mesopotamia for two millennia. At a very early stage, Persia had adopted the cuneiform script. The association of the two lands with each other over the centuries in wars, occupations, and joint states had equally acculturated Persia and reduced its cultural differences with Mesopotamia. Later, Persia adopted the Pahlawi or Avestan script. Aramaic and ancient Pahlawi borrowed heavily from each other. When Mesopotamia became part of Cyrus's empire, Persian influence fell mainly in the religious domain, the other realms of human life having already sustained all the mutual influence possible.

The new Persian element in Mesopotamian religion did not convince Peninsular Arabia, which continued in its older Mesopotamian associationist forms of religion. Eschatology and messianism did not appeal to the Arabs and were rejected, the former as superstition and the latter as impotence in the here and now. Within Arabia, associationism remained the rule. However, a voice within maintained the vision of Abraham. Abraham, the Mesopotamian Amorite from Ur, settled his second wife Hagar and his eldest son Ishmael in West Arabia. He entrusted them with the new faith for the sake of which he was persecuted in Ur and which prompted his emigration. This was the monotheistic vision of God and the ethical, universalist vision of humanity. Though faint, as it certainly was, the Abrahamic vision preserved itself in the midst of associationist Arabia and awaited the advent of prophets to vindicate and proclaim it again.

JUDAISM

The Essence

The essence of religious experience in Judaism was the same as that of the Amoritic tribes of which they were one, and of which Hammurabi's code was the best expression. However, that experience was affected by the discovery of transcendent monotheism. The Amorites arrived in Mesopotamia with a developed monotheistic concept which served as base for their demand for a single government of "the four corners of the world," and the equal citizenship of all humans under the divine law promulgated by the king of the world-state, Hammurabi. But, as we saw earlier, that monotheistic concept was adulterated with *shirk* (association of other gods with God). Abraham discovered that if Marduk was truly God, he would not need any of the other gods. Neither in creating nor in governing the universe would God need helpers. Therefore, Shamash as sun god, Enlil as storm god, and Inanna as moon goddess were not gods but figments of the imagination. Since God is indeed God, humans do not owe the lesser gods anything, certainly not worship. This was more than Abraham's people, the Amorites, could understand or accept at the time, and they condemned Abraham to death. Abraham then took leadership of his clan and separated them from Ur. They reentered the Arabian desert as migrants, and moved toward another region and another destiny.

This alienation from the Amurru consensus, which established Amorite hegemony over the whole Fertile Crescent in the nineteenth century B.C.E., forced the Hebrews to separate themselves from all the inhabitants of the region. They redefined themselves in terms of Abraham's great discovery, as the people who worship God alone and none beside Him. Absolute, transcendent monotheism possessed their consciousness and prepared them to accept suffering and disadvantage for the sake of a great idea, a noble cause. The God of monotheism required that all other gods be repudiated; that worship and service be exclusively His. This imposed upon the adherents the duty of calling other humans to God, and of working *with* them with all possible sympathy and persuasion to bring about conversion. Monotheism is impossible without universal mission, without engagement of self with the adherents of other faiths.

However, instead of reinforcing the Amorite consensus with the Abrahamic vision by purging Mesopotamian monotheism of its *shirk,* the Hebrews' vision of their superiority dictated physical separatism. The covenant with God became a covenant "in the flesh," causing the Hebrew to regard himself as physically different from the rest of humanity. Two generations later, this exaggerated separatism began to undo the original vision that was its cause. The Hebrews' religious experience shifted from the unique transcendent God of Abraham to the monolatrous god of the biblical patriarchs. The patriarchs' god was "theirs" alone while other peoples could have, and indeed had, their own gods—the very polytheism of the pre-Sargonic Mesopotamian city-states. Thus, the Hebrews refused to assimilate themselves with any tribe or clan among whom they came to live, and they were rejected by those tribes. Indeed, the Hebrews rejected the offer of their non-Hebrew hosts "to dwell in the land . . . to become [with them] one people . . . to take their daughters to us for wives and let us give them our daughters . . . and be circumcised as they are circumcised" and convert to the Hebrew faith.[15]

In Paddan-Aram, in Ḥarran, in Schechem, in Edom, in Beth El, in Hebron, the Hebrews time and again had to flee because, as the biblical redactor put it on the lips of Jacob addressing his sons: "Ye have troubled me to make me to stink among the inhabitants of the land, among the Canaanites and the Perizzites; and I being few in number, they shall gather themselves together against me, and slay me; and I shall be destroyed, I and my house."[16]

Begun as self-distinction on account of the higher vision of divine transcendence, Hebrew separatism, by force of its own extremism, caused transcendent monotheism to degenerate into monolatry and launched the Hebrew people on a career of ethnocentrism.

The essence of religious experience of the Hebrews and of their descendants, the Jews, has remained the same since the patriarchal age. It contained both the Abrahamic vision with its transcendence and universalist ethics and the ethnocentric particularism and separatism. The two views were always in constant tension, the one asserting its dominion over the other through the ages, but never succeeding enough to destroy it. History tells us that for the most part it was ethnocentric particularism that predominated; and while it did, it adversely affected the vision of divine transcendence.

The Manifestation

The patriarchal period. Little is known about the religious life of the Hebrews during the patriarchal age besides the adverse influence their self-separation from the whole society of the ancient Near East exercised over their conception of the godhead. First their attachment to the one God caused them to regard God as their "Father," as belonging to them as they belonged exclusively to Him. This is amply indicated by the ubiquitous appellation, "God of our fathers," "God of our ancestors," "God of Abraham," "God of Jacob," and so on, and their referring to themselves as the "sons of God." The unique, very special relationship to God was thus anthropomorphized. The simile—if it ever began as a simile—came to be taken literally. Such literal understanding is certainly capable of pressuring the mind to think of others as belonging to other gods, and hence to assume that "our" god is one among many. Certainly, "our" god remains strong enough to vindicate us against our enemies; but this does not counter the existence of other gods. Gradually, the mind comes to tolerate other gods, regard their existence and patronage of the others as de jure. Such development must lie behind the biblical usage of the plural term Elohim throughout the Torah. Biblical scholars acknowledge that the use of Elohim for God was representative of a strand within the Hebrew religious tradition, and that it coalesced in the Hebrew mind with the "Yahwist" strand and formed the Torah. Neither the Deuteronomic reform of the seventh century B.C.E. nor the priestly reedition of the Scripture could remove the term, or the idea associated with it, from the religious tradition. The ratio of the biblical use of Elohim as compared with the tetragrammaton יהוה (Yahweh) is 2,222 to 398. Indeed, when the Jew, in reading the Bible in Hebrew, comes across the tetragrammaton, he reads "Elohim." As if this were not enough, the Torah affirmed that the "Beni Elohim," or sons of God, "saw the daughters of men that they were fair; and they took them wives of all which they chose;" that "the Beni Elohim came in unto the daughters of men, and they bore children to them."[17]

The Mosaic period. The Hebrews' counterclockwise movement around the inside edge of the Fertile Crescent left behind at every station some tribesmen who were better disposed than the majority to assimilate with the natives. Granted that desert migrants penetrated and settled in the whole region, those who inhabited the inside edge of the Fertile Crescent maintained closer relations with the Arabian desert than those who lived deeper in the innerland. Such people preserved the purity of the desert's original ideology better than those who ventured further afield and were exposed to conditions much different from those in the desert. That is why, when separatism rendered their residence in Egypt impossible, the Hebrews could find welcome and shelter among those who lived on the desert edge.

Hebrew ethnocentrism forced Moses — who grew up as an Egyptian, was given an Egyptian name, and was adopted by an Egyptian princess — to side with a Hebrew who ran into trouble with an Egyptian overseer, kill the overseer, and flee for his life.[18] He took shelter in Midyan, married the daughter of the chieftain, and learned his religion, which must have been very close to the Hebrew religion to enable Moses to assimilate with the Midyanites. Indeed, the purity and intensity of Midyanite religion must have aroused basic intuitions in Moses, and rekindled in him a passion for desert religiosity. He began to agitate for the return of the Hebrews to their origins, away from the "corruptions" of Egypt to desert religion. The voice he heard at the mountain of God (Horeb) mirrored very deep stirrings within his soul aroused by the religious renewal which Jethro, his father-in-law, and the Midyanites induced in him.[19] This was sufficient to send him back to Egypt to plead with Pharaoh to permit the Hebrews to emigrate.

Upon the return of the Hebrews, under Moses' leadership, to their primordial habitat, the desert, another religious experience took place. This experience was collective, involving all Hebrews as well as their desert hosts, primarily the Midyanites, whose chief priest (Moses' father-in-law) led in a sacral meal of burnt offering[20] to the "God of the Mountain" who "came from Sinai, and rose up from Seir unto them [and] shined forth from Mount Paran."[21] The group was "a mixed multitude" of the afore-mentioned, other Hebrews who did not go to Egypt, bedouin Habirus roaming the region, and several tribes of south Palestine and northwest Arabia. Many of these tribes preserved their pre-amphictyonic identities even after settlement in Palestine, as witness a number of biblical passages.[22] Kenites, Kenizzites, Jerahmeelites (probably the Jurhumī tribesmen who dominated the Ḥijāz at the time of Ishmael's settlement) had gathered at the volcanic mountain of Horeb, whose eruptions were perceived as theophanic occasions.[23] It was there that an amphictyony or "sacred alliance" of tribes was forged between them, committing them to worship Yahweh and order their lives in harmony with His commandments. Since the desert had no shrines, an ark was constructed to contain the law as well as the instruments that created the amphictyony. The "Covenant of Sinai" was the agreement of this multitude of tribes to stick together under Moses' leadership, sanctioned by the God of the Mountain and given concrete direction by the newly promulgated law. This "new" law was not new. It was couched in a form identical to that of covenants of vassaldom concluded between the various powers of the area and was similar in content to the law of Hammurabi.

The Davidic period. The entry and settlement of the "mixed multitude" into Palestine in the eleventh and twelfth centuries B.C.E. was not one of bloody conquest, as the later editors of the biblical narratives chose to present it, determined as they were by later Hebrew hatred for their neighbors. Although some conflict and some battles certainly took place, the majority came and settled in the manner of Dumuzi, the shepherd, intermarrying and assimilating with the inhabitants. That is why penetration into Palestine could not proceed through the Amalekite south, but had to take the longer route of the desert, through Edom and Moab with whom assimilation was possible and who in all likelihood reinforced the amphictyony forces with their own. The more significant aspect of this period was acculturation of the migrants in Palestine and the emergence of extreme Hebrew ethnocentrism in reaction to acculturation.

Palestine was full of Hittites, Perizzites, Jebusites, Moabites, Edomites, Philistines, Phoenicians, Syrians, and Canaanites. Its dominant religion and culture were Canaanite. Those who did not partake of this religion and culture were being assimilated when the amphictyony tribesmen entered the area. On the religious level, "the nation of priests," where every human ministers unto himself on the open and free highway to God, became a nation whose religious life was dominated by priests.[25] Paralleling this was a gradual change from the worship-anywhere attitude of the desert to the localization of worship in a shrine or immobile building in village or city, as well as adoption of the elaborate sacrificial system of the Canaanites. The desert worship-as-you-need attitude equally gave way to the Canaanite religious calendar based upon the rhythm of the seasons in response to the needs of settled farmers.

On the cultural level, the Hebrews were gradually learning the language of Canaan, namely, Hebrew. They must have come with some other dialect of Aramaic which they had retained from patriarchal days and which called them to cooperate with the tribes of northwest Arabia and south Trans-Jordan. Their clothing, eating, marrying, and other living habits were being attuned with those of Canaan as they retransformed themselves from desert nomadism to settled farming. The tribal confederacy and its rule by chieftains or "judges" gave way to kingship (Samuel, Saul) and dynastic rule (David). King Solomon, David's son, sought and obtained Canaanite help in designing and building the Temple.[26] Hiram of Tyre and his people furnished most of the specialized labor as well as the timber and other building materials. Moreover, Solomon married "many strange women, together with the daughter of Pharaoh, women of the Moabites, Ammonites, Edomites, Zidonians and Hittites."[27] Those women and the religious and cultural influences they represented succeeded in turning Solomon's heart "after other gods." Solomon's court was so Canaanized that he "went after Ashtoreth the goddess of the Sidonians, and after Milcom the abomination of the Ammonites."[28] Solomon's wives exercised no little authority over his court and government, and filled the land with "high places for Chemosh . . . for Molach," with statues and altars devoted to his wives' gods.[29] Indeed, the difference between the Hebrew and Canaanite ways of life has been blurred and almost obliterated.[30] This pushed the conservative elements into stronger conservatism and brought about the split of the kingdom into Israel and Judah. Israel's greater momentum toward assimilation made it possible for its people to dissolve without a trace within the Fertile Crescent society once its royal government, rent by dynastic and domestic disputes, was knocked out by Assyria in 722 B.C.E. Judah's stronger ethnocentrism stretched out its life to 587 B.C.E. when it too was destroyed by Babylon and its leadership driven into exile.

The Exilic period. In Babylon, acculturation continued, despite the fact that the exiles were for the most part the most ethnocentric-minded and conservative of the lot. New religious influences had by then come to Babylon from the East, the most appealing of them being eschatology—with its attendant angelology and demonology, Paradise and Hell, and final judgment—and messianism. The Mesopotamians had become weary of their long struggle and began to doubt the values that had created their civilization three millennia earlier. Hence, they succumbed to the promise of a Saoshyant or savior who at the end of time would resurrect all humans and restore the world to its pristine innocence and goodness, and enter humankind into Paradise after purging them of their sins through immersion into molten metal. Obviously, their new religious view was that of the desperate and the downtrodden. It appealed to those incapable of making their kingdom on earth a replica of God's, of trusting that the social order was fully capable of controlling itself and maintaining its own equilibrium. Most of the exiles, therefore, grew roots in Mesopotamia and resisted all appeals to return to Judah.

A few of them turned to the new religious vision—messianism—to bolster their ethnocentric hope for return to Judah and vindication against their enemies. Their leader in this trend was Isaiah who reinterpreted the rise of Persia, Babylon's enemy, as the rise of a messiah (anointed or king) to lead the Exiles victoriously to Jerusalem and rebuild the glory of the Davidic kingdom.[31] In Babylon, the exiled Judahites relearned the old Mesopotamian desire of a universal community and a world-state. They witnessed Babylon's attempt to achieve this ideal; and they heard Persia's claim that it too was engaged in the same pursuit. Gradually, the actualization of the world-state unfolded before their eyes as Cyrus joined one province after another to his empire. This prompted the Judahites to emulate their Babylonian captors and Persian liberators; and the vision dawned on Isaiah that the reconstituted kingdom of Judah would be the capital of a world-state, the center of power out of which "shall go forth the law . . . [in] judgment [of] the earth . . . the isles . . . the gentiles."[32] Likewise, the power and jurisdiction of the monolatrous god grew to challenge the other gods, to expose their impotence, even to declare them inexistent.[33] But the conception of the ideal remained as ethnocentric as before; indeed, it became more so. For the raising of the Hebrews and restoration of their power demanded that the omnipotent God use His power to crush and subjugate the nations of the world.[34] He will order "the Gentiles . . . to bring thy sons in their arms and thy daughters shall be carried upon their shoulders. And kings shall be thy nursing fathers and their queens thy nursing mothers; they shall bow down to thee with their face toward the earth and lick up the dust of thy feet."[35] Obviously, resentment against the enemy had combined with ethnocentric bombast to reach this fantastic proposition.

The post-Exilic period. The plan to restore the Judahic kingdom did not work. Few people responded to Isaiah's appeal and the others preferred to stay in Babylon. Other attempts also failed; and this con-

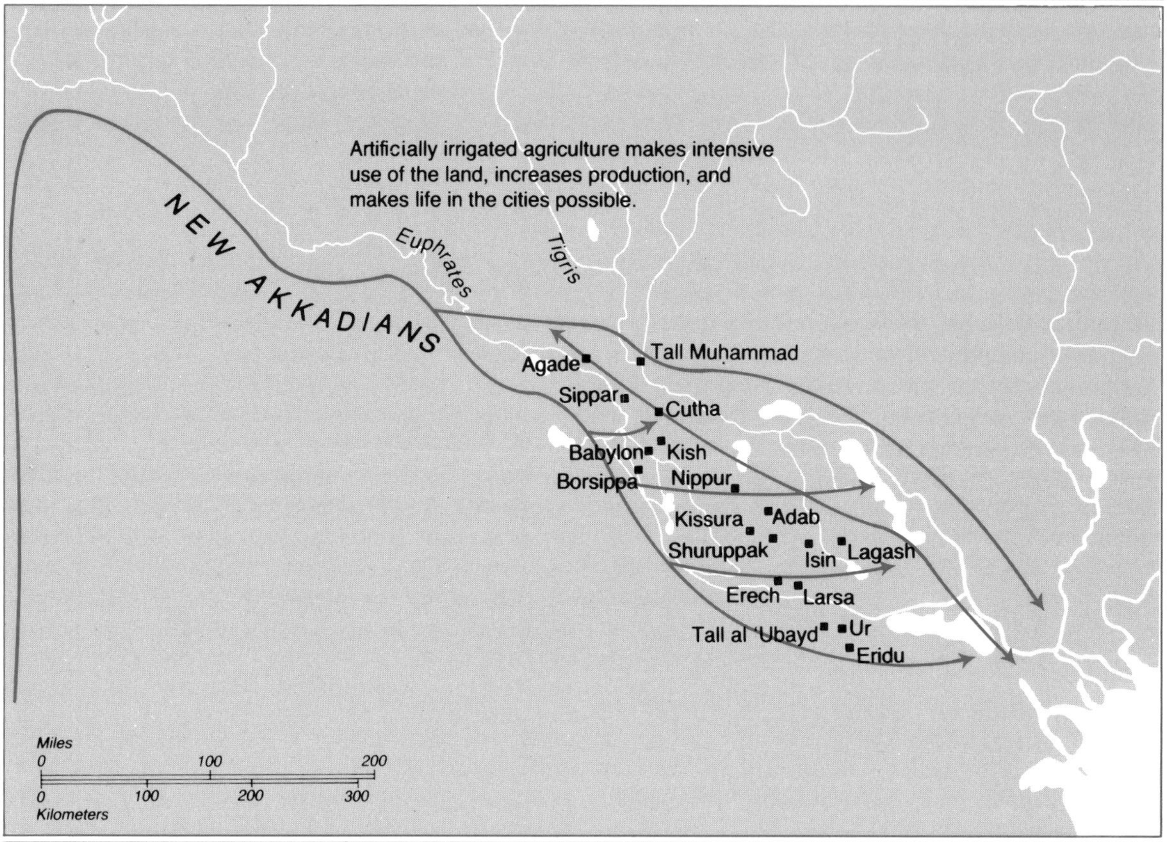

Map 10. The Third Millennium B.C.E.*: The Birth of Civilization*
A. The First City-States (3000–2360)

vinced those who believed in the vision that it was impossible of realization in time. Gradually, the Davidic kingdom was idealized, spiritualized, and pushed beyond time. The eschatology learned at Babylon was wedded to the kingdom of David to constitute a universal messianic hope. This hope, with its object completely purged of material, political, ethnocentric content, became the seed out of which Christianity was to grow. Spiritualization of the kingdom and internalization of the struggle for it was a powerful antidote to the tragic reality.

The other alternative taken by the ethnocentrists was to resume the political-military struggle against the masters that supplanted Persia. Successive rebellions by Judahite zealots under the Greeks and Romans exacerbated the failure. Destructive countermeasures were taken to blot out Zion and disperse those who still believed in her as focus for a political, ethnocentric kingdom. With Temple and Jerusalem finally destroyed, the Judahite priesthood declared an end to the sacrificial system of Temple worship. Henceforth, Jewish worship was to consist only of reciting the Torah, observing the Sabbath and the dietary laws, and where possible the personal status laws.

Judaism in peninsular Arabia. The desert roamings of the patriarchs, as well as the repeated persecutions they suffered at the hands of other Hebrews within Palestine or non-Hebrews without, and the destruction of Judah and Israel, provided many Hebrews with the impetus to settle in northwest Arabia. Their engagement in metal works and trade earned them a place and a livelihood. They were never autonomous tribes but had to exist as protégés or clients of one or another of the dominant Arab tribes in the region. That was the situation in which the Prophet Muḥammad found them.

A group of them had found their way to Yaman where they proselytized the king and seized control of the state. There they began a cruel persecution of Christians who were previously converted to Christianity by Abyssinian missionaries accompanying the Byzantine expeditionary force under Abrahah about 570 C.E., incurring the condemnation of Christians, pagan Arabs, as well as the future Muslims.[36] The Jews of Arabia never succeeded in winning the Arabs' respect. Partly this was due to their ethic, which focused on survival rather than on the values of chivalry; and partly, to their attachment to the Torah, which they often hid, would not teach to others, and often violated in their own conduct.[37]

It is quite evident that the Hebrews produced no civilization in ancient times. Rather, they were part of the greater Semitic whole composed of Arabia and the Fertile Crescent. As migrant tribes in the patriarchal age, they belonged to and carried the civilization of the Amorites. Following their exodus from Egypt, they were reacculturated into the Semitic stream by the amphictyony of northwest Arabian Sinaitic and Jordanian tribes. Later, they were nearly completely Canaanized in Palestine. In Babylon, they underwent another acculturation, this time by a Zoroastrianized Mesopotamian people who had lost faith in themselves and in their ancient tradition. Later still, they were Hellenized. Nowhere in this long history does one meet with creativity except in the all-important spheres of religion and religious literature. However, they were incapable of spreading the good they had, namely, the transcendental monotheism of Abraham. Instead of doing so, they thought, wrote, and lived the strongest ethnocentrism.

Once they bound themselves to the letter of the law, they produced one of the greatest legalistic traditions of all time. In legal thought, however, they never produced a systematic jurisprudence, or elaborated a universal legal ethic or theory for the benefit of humanity. We shall have occasion to consider the question of the contribution of the Judeo-Christian tradition to Islam below.

CHRISTIANITY

It is obvious that the religious situation of the Jews at the time immediately preceding the advent of Jesus called for a prophet to reform it. The time was ripe for a movement to break the dominion of ethnocentric particularism on Jewish minds and to reaffirm their equality with all other humans, to purge their theology of its anthropomorphisms and restore divine transcendence to its rightful place at the core of the faith; to liberate the Jews from the tyranny of the law which kept its letter but had lost its spirit. A divine dispensation was certainly due to bring the internalizing and spiritualizing tendency in Judaism to full development, if the moral decay of the ancient world was to be arrested and humanity reoriented to religious felicity.

To fulfill this great task, God sent Jesus, the son of Mary. Born and raised in the midst of these problems, he dedicated the last three years of his life to teach and exemplify the new faith. His call was shaped by the situation of his contemporaries, Jews and Gentiles. The former had convinced him of their hypocrisy and narrow legalism; the latter, of their materialism and cynicism. Hence, his two-pronged attack against both.

The Essence

Insofar as it can be elicited from the Gospels of Matthew, Mark, and Luke, and insofar as this can be checked against the religious needs of the age and the region, the essence of religious experience as Jesus understood and taught it was that salvation is a state of consciousness dominated by faith in God almighty and merciful, and attunement with His will through purity, self-denial, and charity. This internalization of religion, Jesus taught, was the antidote to Jewish legal literalism, hypocrisy, and ethnocentric particularism, as well as to Roman materialism and cynicism. The internal personalist values restored the focus of the law to its role of reforming the individual. It recaptured the spirit which literalism had lost, and challenged the hypocrite by referring him to the agency that knows him best, namely, his conscience. Moreover, internalization put the prime religious values of piety and obedience on a level where all men are equal before God. Where they are the criteria, no man may be discriminated for or against since only God is the Judge. No ethnic or other peculiarities can have any bearing on the net worth of the person. Jesus' religious call was directed equally to those Jews who observed the ethic of materialism and cynicism in imitation of their Greek and Roman teachers, and to the whole of classical antiquity. Jesus' reform was divinely guided. It answered the terrible but real need of humanity at its time.[38]

The Manifestation

The Jews' response to the reformative ministry of Jesus was meager. His call was perceived by the ethnocentric leadership as diametrically opposed to them, and they took it as designed to undermine their hold over the Jewish people. It appealed to the uprooted, the slaves, and the destitute; for they saw in it a genuine compensation for their misery. It restored to them their confidence in themselves as the call shifted attention from the external, of which they had none, to the internal, which they could develop in plenty. To the more sensitive, the call of Jesus reestablished religion as it ought to be—as personal faith in God and commitment to do His will on earth. These factors combined to constitute a reform of Judaism under the leadership of a master—Jesus—whom all Jews expected as a savior from the apparently hopeless predicament in which they had been languishing since the Exile, from the *Untergang* in which they had been drifting since Solomon's death. However, the zealots and conservatives were in the majority; and they rose in defense of their power which was threatened by the reform. They trumped up charges of blasphemy and rebellion against Jesus and persuaded the Romans to get rid of him.

Paul, a Romanized Jew at the service of the Romans in their persecution of members of the new faith, converted to Christianity. The countless plebeian converts to Christianity practicing their faith in hiding from authority and prosecuted by Paul now became a great potential for turning the Roman Empire, its religion, and its ideology upside down. But first, the message of Jesus had to be transformed into something Hellenistic that would appeal to the vast millions of the empire around and beyond the Mediterranean shores. This had already been done to the Old Testament by Philo of Alexandria, and in the Gospel of John. The dominant ideology was gnosticism; the dominant culture, Hellenism. Both were spreading throughout the provinces of the Roman Empire on a foundation previously laid down by the Greeks. The methodology was that of *eisegesis,* or allegorical interpretation of what is revered as scripture or holy text, which had precedents in the attempts of late Greek thinkers to make sense out of Greek pagan religions. Thus began the transformation of the religion of Jesus.[39]

The focus of the mission shifted from Palestine and the Jewish people, who were the very object of the reform, to the main urban centers of the Roman Empire where the masses of slaves and uprooted lived. The language changed also—from Aramaic to Greek—and with it, the categories of thought embedded in the language. The internalist emphasis of the reform remained. But instead of being the prerequisite condition for fulfilling the works of obedience to God, it became the *ipso facto* constituent of salvation. The content of faith was likewise expanded. God remained the center of it. But in addition, it acquired faith in His incarnation in Jesus, in Jesus' death as an oblation and atonement for human sins, in his resurrection and victory over his enemies, and in the Holy Spirit as the third person of a divine trinity. The obligation to do the works commanded by God remained, but only as a consequence of faith which was declared sufficient even if it had no such consequences. This axiological denigration of "works" was coupled with the institution of sacraments and a sacramentally ordained priesthood to administer them. The state, because it happened to be the enemy, was condemned as the work of Satan. The Christian was to owe it no positive loyalty, but to suffer its taxation or authority with patience, awaiting the second advent of Christ when the fallen would be saved and all the enemies would be vanquished.

This transformation of Christianity was brought about by John and Paul. It was not the only one. In the absence of a central authority, churches were formed in town after town on the basis of a sermon which a Christian missionary had delivered or an epistle he had sent. Every church was autonomous, depending upon its own constituents in all matters, including doctrine and nature of the faith. Thus many "Christianities" arose, each developing according to its own spiritual and other determinants. Since all of them were missionary—Jesus himself had repudiated Jewish particularism—it was inevitable that the churches would multiply themselves and come into conflict with one another as to what was and was not Christianity.

Thus, three main lines of thought emerged, each of which in various forms was defended by churches scattered over the whole Eastern Mediterranean. Unfortunately, heretication, excommunication, persecution, and sometimes open genocide have left us no traces of these churches and their leaders except in the memories of their enemies. The Roman Church contended for supremacy over all the churches of Christ. When it finally achieved this status, it eradicated the other churches by forcing them all to adopt its doctrine and its tradition alone as canonical. There were numerous bones of contention between the churches, such as those revolving around the nature of man, sin, and grace; or that of the Church, ministry, and sacraments; or the authority of the Church of Rome, but the most important controversies revolved around the nature of Jesus. These were the most determinative, for their conclusions affected every other aspect of Christian doctrine and practice.

The first and oldest controversy grew from the Semitic background of Jesus. Its adherents believed that Jesus was indeed the expected Christ or Messiah, sent to deliver the Jews from their predicaments, but that he was human, all too human. He was to achieve his deliverance by teaching true religion and by good example. His mission was like that of previous prophets: to convey the divine message whose con-

Illustration 3.1

An alabaster cylinder seal depicting the Sun-God emerging from the Gates of the East, Babylonian, c. 2000 B.C.E.

[Courtesy The Metropolitan Museum of Art, Purchase, 1886.]

tent is salvific if observed. In the first century, this must have been the view of all or most Jews who heard of and believed in Jesus and who constituted the first Christian Palestinian churches. It was also the view of Cerinthus (c. 100) who taught that Jesus was indeed human; that at his baptism "the Christ"—a high divine power—had descended upon him and was the cause of his delivery of the message. Once the message was delivered, the Christ left him to die like any other human.[40]

This first view of Christianity must have traveled with the Jews throughout the Roman Empire where it won converts among Jews as well as others. Some of them called themselves Ebionites and chose poverty as their lifestyle, devoting their energies to self-purification and worship. Regarding Jesus as a human prophet with a message from God, they learned his lesson on internalism best, and may be regarded as the first exemplification of monastic and ascetic life in Christianity.[41] In Rome, in the middle of the second century, Hermas, brother of Pius, bishop of Rome, wrote an essay—*The Shepherd*—giving classical expression to this view.[42] Another major exponent of this view was Paul of Samosata (third century) whose followers, the Paulicians, survived until the ninth century when Empress Theodora sent her army to exterminate them in Armenia.

The second view of Christianity was born in Alexandria, and was the outcome of a peculiar synthesis between the internalizing messianism of the Jews and gnosticism. Assuming creation to be a descending degradation from the eternal Absolute One Who is wholly spirit to the changing relative plurality which is imprisoned in matter, gnosticism saw salvation as a release of the spiritual from its prison and return to its primordial source. Matter being absolutely evil for its contradiction of and distance from spirit, the world- and life-denying gnosticism accorded with Jewish despair and eschatology. Such release from matter certainly occurred at death. In life, it had to be attained in *gnosis,* the moment at which the soul of man detached itself from every material connection, pulled itself upward and away from creation by disciplined meditation or contemplation, and became illuminated by the presence of the Absolute. This was thinking, the very process of salvation.

The Absolute, for its part, could only think, since it is all spirit. Moreover, it could think only of itself, since it was originally all that existed. Through its thinking, another *logos* or mind emanated from it, and from this, a third emanated until all nine *logoi,* minds or heavenly lights (the Ennead), emanated from one another and made possible the emanation of the active mind that created the universe. Thinking, then, is a cosmic activity. It is identical with the process constitutive of creation as well as of its maintenance by which things come to be—the downward process—as well as that by which they can return to their origin. The latter, when achieved by humans, is salvation. The activity of the Absolute, of God, may hence be described in the following terms: the *logos* or word of God, which is as divine as God because it is consubstantial with the Absolute, is the creative principle in its downward motion. It is also the saving principle because its activity in the upward motion, namely, human thought, is redeeming. This sophisticated language of Neoplatonism was Christianized by casting it into popular Greek terms borrowed from the adherents of the mystery religions. Jesus became the Word of God, for whom the world was created. His advent and teaching were constitutive of salvation. There neither was nor could be another way to restore man who, because of matter, lost knowledge of God except through knowledge of the word of God.[43] An enthused apologist for this Christianity could even say that Christ equals *logos* or mind or reason; that whoever activates his mind is a Christian and is saved; that Socrates was the archetype of intelligence, as well as of Christian salvation.[44]

The Christian churches to which Neoplatonism gave rise were numerous. However, the growing power of the Church of Rome eventually hereticated, excommunicated, and supplanted all of them. Throughout their existence, these churches never permitted their lofty intellectualism to be marred by the plebeian ideas of the mystery religions. As adherents of Docetism, they believed that Christ, being divine, of the Father Who is God or the Absolute, cannot suffer or die. Hence, any historical Jesus was a phantasm, an appearance designed to cover the divine and saving message. Cerinthus, Saturninus (c. 120), and Basilides (c. 130) taught that another person was crucified in place of Jesus, who "flew back" to heaven. Marcion (c. 160) followed the same view with the demand that the Old Testament be abolished because its god is "a worker of evil, delighting in wars, inconstant in judgment and self-contradictory."[45] In rather emphatic terms, all of them affirmed the absolute unity of God, which merited them the appellation of Monarchianism. The farthest they would go to meet their opponents was the admission that the trinity was no more than three manifestations of the Absolute, "Father, Son and Holy Spirit [being] one and the same being, in the sense that three names are attached to the one substance . . . as the sun: it is one substance, but it has three manifestations, light, heat and the orb itself."[46] This explanation of the trinity was advocated by Sabellius, an early third-century theologian, and was named after him.[47] None of them doubted that the Christ was God, but none of them meant by the Christ the earthly, human, historical Jesus. The Christ was the Word (*logos* or mind) of God. Hence, they reasoned, "God always, Son always; the Son exists from God Himself . . . [He is] unbegotten . . . not born-by-begetting . . . [not even] by thought . . . does God precede the Son."[48] Arius went farther, repudiating with a syllogism that carried his name the idea of a begotten Christ as logically self-contradictory, since the begetter must always be prior in being and time to the begotten.[49]

Arianism, as a variety of gnosticism, almost dominated Christendom for several centuries. However, the coincidence of imperial interests as well as those of some members of the Byzantine royalty with those of the Church of Rome led eventually to the destruction of all churches that said no to Rome's assertion that Jesus was both God as well as man, that he suffered death in atonement for vicarious guilt, and that he rose three days later in triumph, as the gods of the mystery religion and fertility cults did in their spring rituals.

This position of the Church of Rome was the third view of Christianity, which came to supplant the other two views. It sought and found authority for its doctrine in the Gospel of John and the epistles of Paul, but more clearly in the essays of some apostolic fathers such as Ignatius (c. 107) and Athanasius (c. 373).[50] It was Augustine that gave the view its final crystallization,[51] in his controversy with Pelagius (c. 400), an Irish monk, and his pupil Celestius. These two asserted man's innocence as well as his capacity to achieve the good without divine grace. The implication is evident that without necessary sin—and hence the need for divine intervention—Christians need not assert either Jesus' divinity or his atoning death. That is why, after some hesitation, Augustine rose to the defense of Pauline Christianity and launched against Pelagius the most virulent attack in the formative history of the Christian faith.

Victory of the Roman view, however, was not easy. For centuries the Byzantine Imperial Government backed the Church of Rome and imposed its view upon the people. The Council of Nicaea (325) put together a creed combining the gnostic elements with the Pauline, and hardly anybody accepted it. Later, at the Council of Constantinople (381), the authority of the Church of Rome was challenged by the Church of Constantinople, which called itself "the New Rome," and again at Chalcedon in 451. The conversion of the churches to the Roman position continued, at least publicly. However, Christians with a Semitic bent of mind could not reconcile themselves either to trinitarianism or to the notions of vicarious guilt, vicarious suffering, salvation through death, or the unquestionable authority the Church of Rome had arrogated to itself. While confessing their adherence to the Church of Rome, they continued secretly to entertain their age-old ideas.

Christianity in Arabia

Most people in the western arm of the Fertile Crescent and in Africa had in time converted to Christianity. The northern tribes which lived in the adjoining desert had also been converted. Few conversions took place in Mesopotamia, but Christians were numerous as a result of immigration. Fleeing Byzantine persecution, Christians ran away by the thousands to the edge of the desert, or to the Persian Empire across the desert, where the hand of the persecutors could not reach them. For their part, the Persians welcomed them because of their knowledge and experience. Heretical monks were the carriers of the legacy of ancient learning. Christian condemnation of that learning (the Academy of Athens and all of the philosophy schools in the Empire were closed in 529 by order of Justinian) sent its protagonists to the desert or Persian Empire for shelter. In Edessa, Jundishapur, Bosra, and other localities, colonies of exiled Christians prospered and kept alive the tradition of Greek learning under the aegis of a liberal, non-Roman Christianity.

In the Arabian Peninsula there was hardly any Christian presence. Byzantium was interested in Peninsular Arabs as tradesmen or carriers of goods from distant Asia and Africa. The missionary spirit of Byzantium was weak or nonexistent, and, at any rate, its center was the Mediterranean and Europe, not the east. Some Arab tribes (Ghassān, Banū Taghlib, Lakhm) counted a number of Christians and some had Christian chieftains. They were all on the edge between Peninsular Arabia and Byzantium, or between Arabia and Persia. The two great powers were interested in them either as buffer satellites to protect their frontiers, or as refugees capable in the arts and sciences who hated their persecutors, the enemies of Persia. An Arab Christian from the Nabataean tribe of southeast Jordan was brought to Yaman as a slave, and he succeeded in converting those who came into contact with him to his faith. His name survived in Islamic annals as Yaʻqūb al Sarrūj; and his faith was probably a monophysite version of Christianity.[52] The Christians of Arabia could not keep themselves away from the political winds blowing upon the region as a whole. As they regarded Byzantium, their patron, and

Map 11. The Third Millennium B.C.E.*: The Birth of Civilization*
B. The First World State (2360–2180)

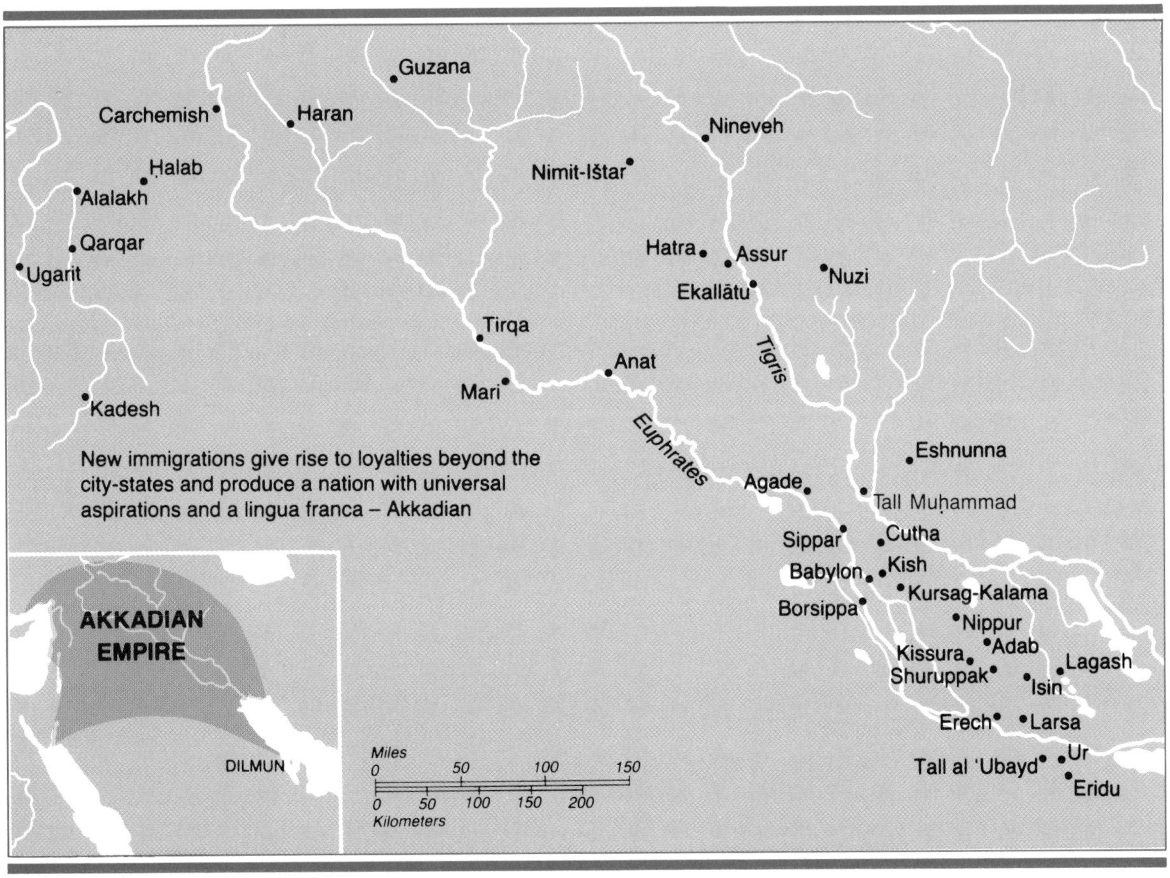

looked to it for protection, they invited interference by the Persian Empire. The latter favored the Jews of Yaman, as enemies of the Christians. A Jewish persecution of Christians under Dhū Nuwās, Jewish king of Ḥimyar, took place in 523. Its cruelty left a bad memory throughout the Peninsula and was immortalized by a mention in the Qur'ān (85:4) in support of the persecution of Christians. When Justin I heard of it, he ordered Abyssinia to send an expeditionary force to Yaman, partly to avenge the Christians and partly to seize the trade route for Byzantium. The Abyssinians achieved a brief victory in Yaman and built a cathedral in San'ā', the capital. Realizing that the second objective could not be met without the subjugation of Makkah, they set out to conquer it, but met with disaster. The year (570) was the year of the Prophet's birth, also called "the year of the elephant" because the Makkans saw the animal for the first time in the service of the invading Abyssinians.[53]

The Christian inhabitants of the western Fertile Crescent as well as the Christians of the Peninsula adhered to their own traditions, most of which were inimical to Roman doctrine. The area continued to burst into "heresies" questioning, if not the divinity and humanity of Jesus, the relationship between the two natures (Apollinarianism, Nestorianism, Eutychianism, Monophysitism, Monothelitism), the nature of man, sin, salvation (Pelagianism), the authority of the Church and the "Holy See of Rome" (Montanism, Donatism), and the legitimacy of images (iconoclasm). When Islam knocked at their door, they were only too glad to accept its call, and they converted *en masse.* Not only were they embittered by the exploitative and tyrannical policies of Byzantium, whose yoke they wished to shake off, but they also resented the religious imperialism evident in the forced supremacy of Roman doctrine. The fact that Islam confirmed Jesus' prophethood and humanity and spoke of him in the most respectful way did the rest.

Eastern Christians who converted to Islam brought with them their ideas, crafts, and customs which were later to enrich Islamic civilization. Western writers often accuse the eastern churches of fossilism, pedantry, and backwardness. To reduce the glory of Islam's victories, they describe those churches and Byzantium itself as corrupt, inept, and ready to fall when Islam came on the scene. The truth is that up to the advent of Islam, the pedantry, irrationalism, and backwardness of Byzantine Christianity were equally true of all Christendom. Islam reformed Christianity in the regions it incorporated into its empire, purging it clean of petty theological disputation and superstitious doctrines. After Islam arrived, the Christians' genius and energies poured themselves into the culture and civilization of Islam. The soul of the Fertile Crescent under Islam rediscovered itself and reaffirmed its Ancient Mesopotamian legacy. It was temporarily (nearly a millennium!) alienated from its own identity by the Greeks and Romans, on one side, and by the Persians, on the other. The former imposed first their naturalism and idolatry, and then their trinitarian, sacramentalist version of the religion of Christ. The latter imposed their dualism and caste system. Under the impetus of Islam, both were shaken off and the Fertile Crescent Arabs now joined with the Peninsular Arabs to rebuild Semitic civilization.

CONTRIBUTION OF THE JUDEO-CHRISTIAN TRADITION TO ISLAM

Were the contribution of the Judeo-Christian tradition to that of Islam to be measured by the co-existence in both of identical religious personalities, events, ideas, and principles, it would be enormous. But co-existence is not contribution; and the fact that Islam came later in history than either Judaism or Christianity constitutes no proof of same. Western scholars, however, not only affirm such contribution but even call it "borrowing," thus exacerbating Muslim dissatisfaction with Western interpretations of Islam. It is repugnant to speak of "borrowing" between any two movements, an earlier and a later one, when the later sees itself as a continuation and reform of the earlier. The same scholars do not speak of "borrowing" by Christianity from Judaism, or by Buddhism from Hinduism, or by Protestantism from Catholicism. Yet that is precisely how Islam sees itself regarding Judaism and Christianity, namely, as their very same identity but reformed and purged of the accumulated tamperings and changes of their human leaders and scribes.

Islam does not regard itself as a new religion but as the oldest religion — indeed, as the eternal religion of God, of Adam in Paradise and on the earth, of Noah and his progeny. It sees itself as the religion of Abraham and his descendants, of all the prophets God had sent to the Hebrews as well as to other peoples, and of Jesus, the son of Mary. Moreover, Islam assumes the religious legacy of Mesopotamia as its own and does so rightly, since Mesopotamian civilization was the product of Arab migrants from the Peninsula as they settled in Mesopotamia and were reinforced by the continuous flow of humans from the desert into the Fertile Crescent. What is commonly called Semitic language, Semitic religion, and Semitic civilization is a product of which the Arabs of the Peninsula were prime movers, authors, practitioners, and objects. The Mesopotamian tradition, as well as its monotheistic reform by Abraham, became the tradition of all Arabs, those of the Peninsula as well as those of the Fertile Crescent. The Hebrews were one of the tribes composing this great conglomerate of peoples. It is certainly repugnant to claim that the Mesopotamian or Abrahamic tradition belongs to a minority of Abraham's descendants rather than to all the peoples of the Arabian theater who are the physical and spiritual heirs to both. It cannot be denied that both Hebrews and Arabs are acutely aware of their legacy, that both regard Abraham and his progeny as their ancestors, and his faith and tradition as their own, but it must be equally affirmed that both traditions are entitled to draw from that legacy as they please. What is usually charged as borrowed by Islam from Judaism is exactly what may be charged as borrowed by Judaism from the Semitic Arabian Mesopotamian tradition. James Pritchard's *Ancient Near Eastern Texts* and Abraham Heidel's *Babylonian Genesis* popularized what the Hebrew Bible had "borrowed" from Ancient Mesopotamian literature, and James A. Montgomery's *Arabia and the Bible* shows what the biblical redactors borrowed from the religious literature of their contemporary Arab neighbors.

As we saw earlier, the Mesopotamian tradition was formed in Mesopotamia by migrants from Peninsular Arabia whose flow was constant across the centuries, from the thirtieth to the thirteenth century B.C.E. However, the ideas carried by the migrants to the Fertile Crescent were known and adhered to by the folks who stayed behind and did not emigrate.

Like the Mesopotamian tradition, the religious tradition of the Peninsula was subject to Abraham's reformative ideas which came to it through Ishmael, Abraham's eldest son, whom he chose to bring back to the Peninsula and settle in Makkah (Paran or Faran) and who became the ancestor of many great peoples (Genesis 17:20; 21:20–21). From Arab tradition, we know that Isma'īl—the Arabic version of Ishmael—married into the Jurhum tribe, that he scioned founders of the twelve tribes of Arabized Arabs, and that these were the prime carriers of the "Arab" tradition of language and ideas.

Unlike the Jewish tradition in whose genesis Hebrews and Arabs participated, Christianity developed as a strictly Jewish and Christian affair. No Arabs were responsible for its genesis which may be totally credited to the Jews and their traditions. It acquired the Mesopotamian legacy by virtue of its growth out of the Jewish tradition. However, large numbers of its early adherents were non-Jewish Fertile Crescent Arabs who joined the faith partly for its own spiritual merit and partly in reaction to the tyranny and crass materialism of the Romans, as well as in Semitic resistance to Hellenistic culture. In the first two centuries C.E., Arabs constituted the majority of Christians. These were universalist missionaries by double virtue: that of their Arab heritage and that of their new Christian faith which opposed Jewish ethnocentrism. They took their Christianity farther east to Persia and India, to Egypt and Abyssinia, north into the Caucasus and wherever around the Mediterranean their ancestors had planted colonies for trade or settlement. As we have seen, the ascendancy of the Church of Rome backed by the Byzantine Empire had alienated these Semitically oriented Christians. When they were hereticated by the Church of Rome, and persecuted by the Byzantine Empire or its puppets on the scene, they took refuge in the desert. There, they swelled the ranks of Jewish refugees and reinforced the Abrahamic tradition with their monotheistic and spiritualizing version of Christianity.

Both Jews and Christian immigrants to the desert found a ready welcome among those Arabs who upheld the Mesopotamian-Abrahamic tradition. Together, they consolidated that tradition in Peninsular Arabia which came to be known as *Ḥanīfiyyah.* Its adherents, the *ḥanīf(s),* resisted every association of other gods with God, refused to participate in pagan rituals, and maintained a life of ethical purity above reproach. It was common knowledge that the *ḥanīf* was a strict monotheist who paid no tribute to tribal religion, that he was of impeccable ethical character, and that he kept aloof from the cynicism and moral lasciviousness of other Arabs. The *ḥanīfs* always stood above tribal disputes and hostilities. Everybody knew of their presence since they belonged to nearly all tribes. Moreover, they had the reputation of being the most learned in religion. The Prophet knew the *ḥunafā'* well enough to say: "Islam is identical with Ḥanīfiyyah," and above him stood the Qur'ān's authoritative identification of Abraham as a *ḥanīf.*

In Aramaic, the *ḥanīfs* were called *hanepai,* meaning "separated." The term must have been coined by their enemies, the adherents of contrary religious views, who held power or were in the majority and who observed the phenomenon of some dissenting members of their own group separating themselves. Such phenomena must have happened throughout Hebrew and Christian history before the Hijrah. As the religious establishment, whether Jewish or Christian, deviated from the Abrahamic transcendentalist faith and persecuted the dissenters, the latter had little choice but to run away to the desert where their relatives, clan-members, or fellow tribes-

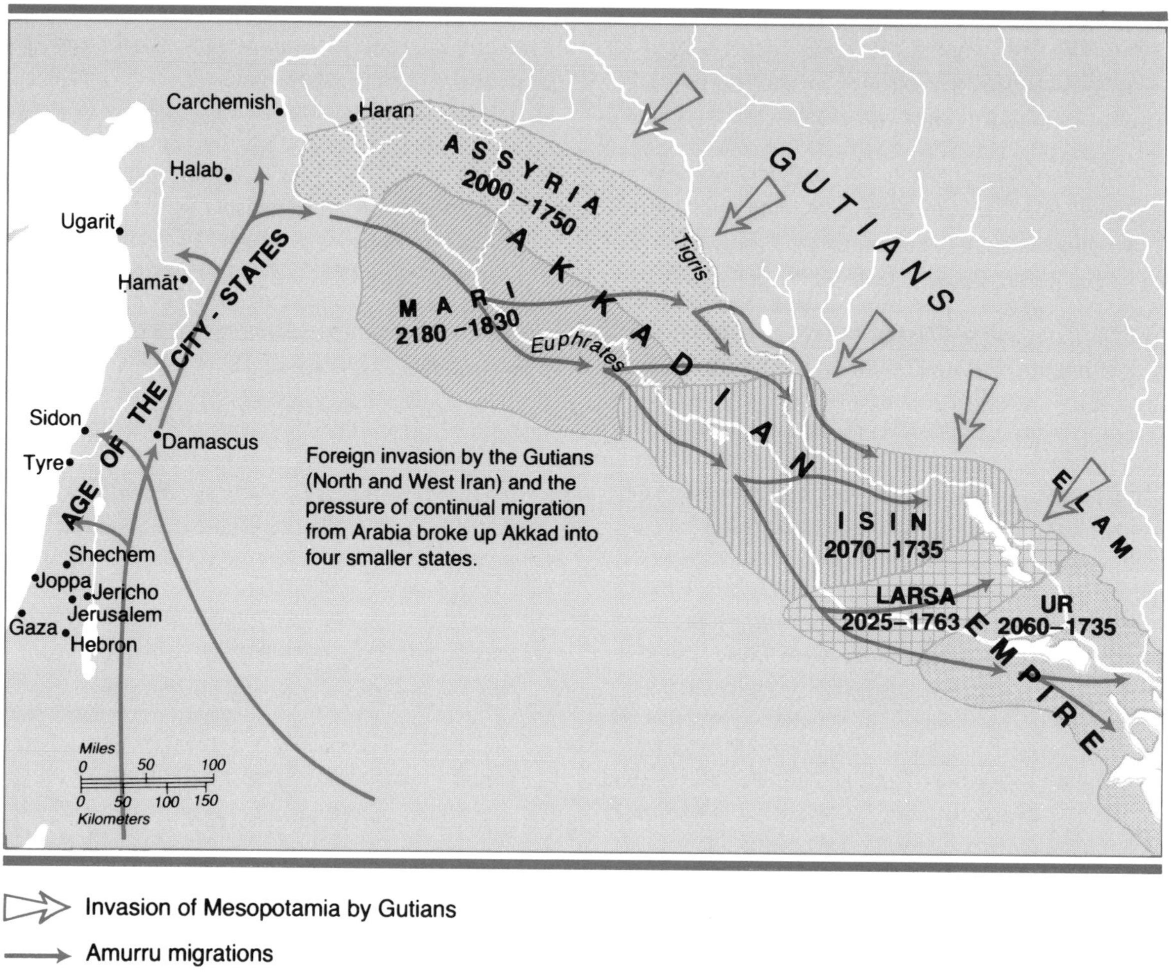

Map 12. The Second Millennium B.C.E.
A. Fragmentation of the World State

men would grant them shelter. The desert peoples' faith would more likely have remained the purer—and hence closer to the Abrahamic faith—than those Hebrews whose settlement resulted in Canaanization; or those Christians who allowed the religion of Jesus to be transformed into the trinitarian, sacramentalist religion of John and Paul. As followers of Abrahamic Judaism and Jesus' Christianity, the dissenters would thus have found affinity of view and sympathy among those who remained loyal to the transcendent unity of God. Naturally, what was regarded by the establishment as "separated" was viewed by the desert people as "pure," thus constituting the two apparently contradictory meanings of the word *ḥanīf* in Aramaic and Arabic.

Long before the Prophet's age, a call for an Abrahamic monotheistic reform arose in the Peninsular tribes of 'Ād (N. Ḥaḍramawt), Thamūd and Shu'ayb (Ḥijāz) at the hands of the prophets Hūd, Ṣāliḥ, and Shu'ayb. The memory of their calls remained; but their movements toward reinstituting Abrahamic monotheism did not succeed and were drowned in Arab *shirk* or associationism.

MAKKAN RELIGION

When Abraham came with Hagar and Ishmael to Makkah (whom the Qur'ān calls Ibrahīm, Hājar and Isma'īl, respectively), there was no plantation in the area. The Qur'ānic account described the place as desolate.[54] Together, they built the Ka'bah, a square room with one aperture, and dedicated it to the worship of the one God. The fountain of Zamzam, which sprang miraculously at the feet of the baby Isma'īl as his mother scrambled between Ṣafā and Marwah in search of water, continued to flow, and the place became a caravan stop. Centuries later, the Ka'bah became a pantheon of numerous idols or gods; and Makkah became the main center binding together the whole of Arabia religiously, culturally, politically, and economically. The tradition of its foundation by Ibrahīm and Isma'īl as a sanctuary for the one God remained a living memory throughout Arabia.

The transcendental unity of God which Ibrahīm and his family taught was not easy to keep in mind. It required a level of sophistication that was not always available. How many generations it did survive in Makkah after Isma'īl, nobody knows. It was transformed into the ***shirk*** or polytheism of Makkah by a combination of forces. ***First*** was the human desire for a deity in close proximity in case of need. The needs of daily living are many: to foretell the future; to consult and obtain advice whether the time is auspicious to undertake war, a business undertaking, a hunt, a long journey; to appease when tragedy strikes in the hope of having it lifted; to thank when bliss and good fortune arrive. When any of these needs is felt, it requires a rather strong mind and will to resist the temptation to seek satisfaction through the close and concrete if available. The tendency is operative even with the knowledge that ultimate power lies with another being, in which case the nearby deity is regarded as an intercessionary agency. "We worship them [the deities] but for their power to bring us closer to God."[55] ***Second*** was the tendency to aggrandize the deceased good man whether ancestor, chieftain, patriarch, or benefactor to the point where his humanity passed into divinity. It is a peculiarly human temptation not only not to see the bad sides of the deceased but to idealize their good qualities. Idealization is a very potent idol-making inclination in all humans. Unless it is kept in check, the deceased could easily suffer apotheosis. ***Third*** was the perpetual fear humans felt upon realization of their helplessness in front of the inexplicable mighty forces or tragic events of nature. Unless their nerve-resistance capacity is adequate, it is not surprising that suffering and tragedy may bend or break the person's will and corrupt the mind. In such cases, numinous perception shifts from God, the real cause of the event, to the force of nature that acted as vehicle or locus for it. The transcendent God is likely to be perceived as distant simply because His transcendence may be construed as distance. It was in militancy against this tendency that transcendentalist faith took special care to emphasize the nearness, accessibility, and availability of God to anyone who calls upon Him. ***Fourth,*** and last, was the near total absence from the scene of any transcendentalist faith. True, the transcendentalist tradition was kept by the ***ḥanīfs;*** but these were too few to be effective. The Abrahamic faith was poorly maintained. While the Jews were perceived as having reduced transcendent monotheism to monolatry by their anthropomorphism and ethnocentrism, the Christians, by their incarnation and trinitarianism, their sacramentalism and ***theotokos***-theology, were perceived as having reduced it to polytheism. Wherever they turned, the pre-Islamic Arabs saw the transcendence of God violated. Those Arabs who inclined in that direction became bolder by the example of their neighbors. It was their Byzantine Christian neighbors who sold them the human statues of the Ka'bah.

The Essence

The essence of religious experience in pre-Islamic Arabia revolved around two axes. The first was hedonism, or the pursuit of a material, personal, worldly happiness during one's lifetime. This life was the only opportunity one had to do so. When life passed or was lost, everything dissolved into oblivion; there was nothing outside this life. Existence was hard enough in the desert. Its travails as well as those of life in general were to be drowned in wine, women, and poetry. Many children, many wives, many friends, large herds of sheep and goats, camels and horses, a prosperous trading business, a victorious booty-laden raid, wine and poetry for a pastime—these were the components of happiness.

The second axis was romanticism. On the individual level it was expressed in ***murū'ah,*** or the values of chivalry. These included bravery in battle, hospitality even in poverty, fidelity even at the risk of one's life, and, above all of these, eloquence. Eloquence glorified these values and idealized them, making them the ultimate ends of human life. Nothing was greater than the poet's craft; for poetry intensified the beauty and appeal of the valuable deeds. It made them worthy of remembrance, immortal. On the societal level, romanticism made up the internal solidarity of the tribe. It rested on the consciousness of identity of the tribesman which was given to the member by the tribe. His being and existence, his legitimacy and reputation, and finally his very security could be assured only within the tribe. Outside of it, the Arab of the Peninsula was an outlaw; his life and property were a free and easy prey for anyone who could take them. As a tribesman, the whole might of the tribe was his very own. Any offense against his person was at once an offense against every other member; and everyone stood obliged to avenge it against any member of the offending tribe. In the member's life, the tribe was supreme. Its prosperity, reputation, honor, greatness were all the member's; and so were its misery, ill reputation, dishonor, or defeat. No wonder then that the tribe monopolized the member's loyalty. The land was not a constituent, since the tribe moved constantly and shifted from one area to another. But the poetry the tribe had produced, and the deeds of its members which poetry immortalized — these defined the tribe, classified it among other tribes and determined the honor and self-esteem of the individual. Indeed, the tribe has never been so mystified and made so beautiful through poetical idealization of its heroes as in Peninsular Arabia. This was romanticism founded upon tribal discipline, tribal loyalty, tribal responsibility, and all of these were made immemorial in the most exquisite poetry ever produced in any language. To live in the atmosphere this poetry created,

Illustration 3.2

Clay tablets containing part of the 135-line text of a Sumerian version of the Job essay on a man's suffering and submission to his god. The poem has been pieced together from six clay tablets and fragments excavated at Nippur, about 100 miles south of Baghdād. [Courtesy The University Museum, University of Pennsylvania.]

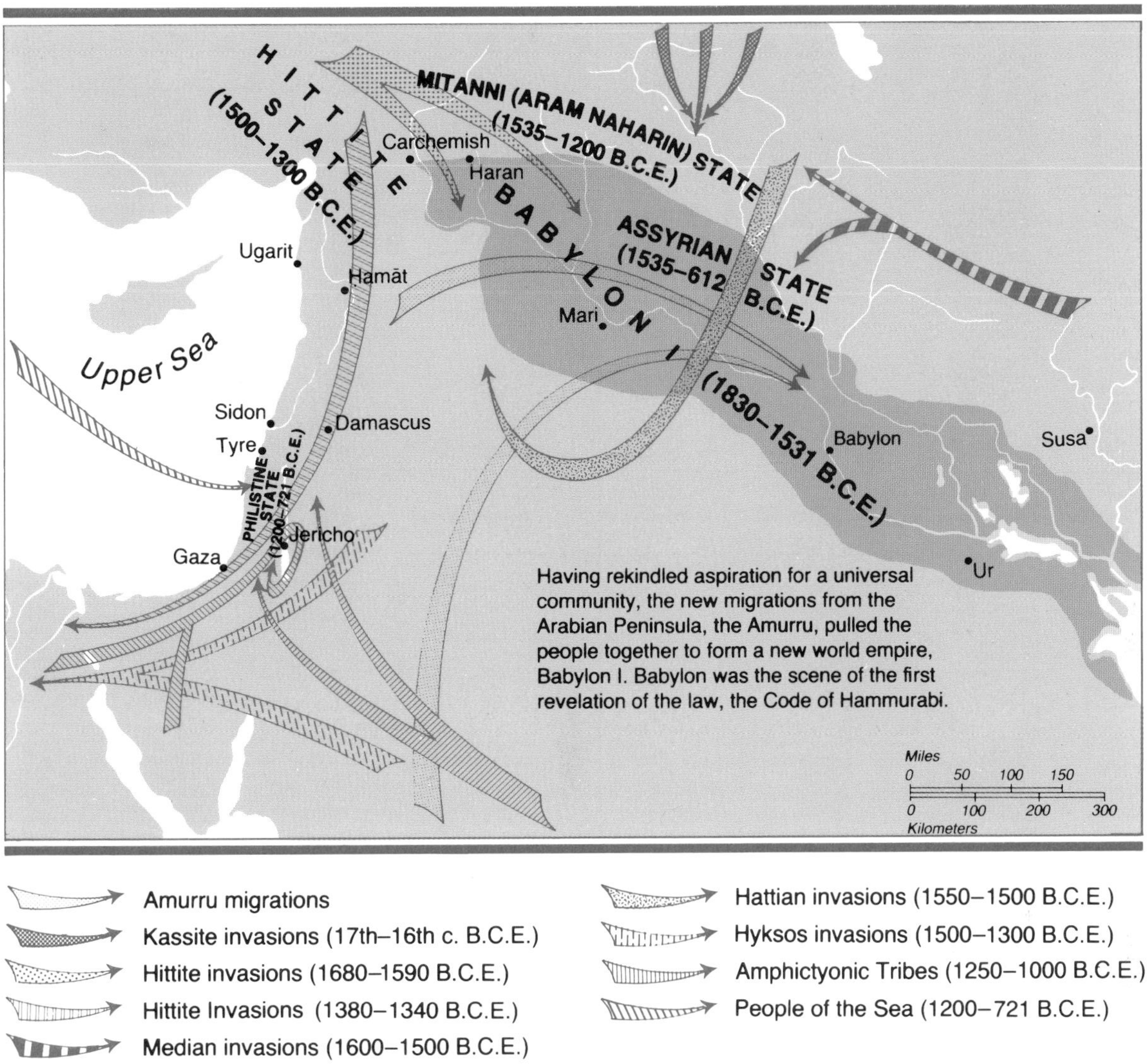

Map 13. The Second Millennium B.C.E.
B. The Second World State; the Second Fragmentation

and to move in pursuit of material well-being and contentment under the *murū'ah* values it glorified, was for the pre-Islamic Arab of the Peninsula the meaning and purpose of life.

The Manifestation

South Arabian (Ma'īn, Saba', and Qaṭabān) as well North Arabian (Liḥyān, Thamūd, and Ṣafā) inscriptions give evidence that a supreme deity called *al Ilah* or *Allah* was worshipped from time immemorial. This deity watered the earth, made the crops grow, the cattle multiply, and the springs and wells yield their life-giving waters.[56] In Makkah as well as throughout Peninsular Arabia, "Allah" was acknowledged as "the creator of all," "the Lord of the world," "the Master of heaven and earth," "the ultimate Controller of all."[57] "Allah" was the most frequently mentioned divine name.[58] However, His functions were delegated or assumed by other minor deities; and His wondrous effects were expressed in the sun and the moon, for example. His qualities were hypostasized and turned into gods and goddesses beside Him. Thus a whole pantheon came to exist, each member cater-

Illustration 3.3

Tablet of light brown clay with three columns of script. Included are the Sumerian Epic of Paradise, the Flood, and the Fall of Man. Nippur, Isin Period, c. 1830 – 1530 B.C.E. [Courtesy The University Museum, University of Pennsylvania.]

ing either to a special need or a special tribe and representing a special feature, site, object, or force that suggested His numinous presence, provision, or might. Allāt, a goddess, was described as the daughter of Allah and identified with the sun by some, with the moon by others.[59] Al 'Uzzā was a second divine daughter, associated with the planet Venus; Manāt, the third daughter, represented fate. Dhū al Sharā and Dhū al Khalāṣah were gods that took the names of places of divination; Dhū al Kaffayn and Dhū al Rijl were associated with bodily organs of some special — though unknown — significance. Wudd, Yaghūth,

Ya'ūq, and Suwā' were gods who took the names of the divine functions of loving, helping, preserving, and inflicting of hard punishment, respectively. The god Hubal, who had the most prominent statue in the Ka'bah, had a hand made of solid gold. Al Malik (the King), al Raḥman (the Merciful), and al Raḥīm (the Always-Merciful) identified gods or perhaps represented supreme divine functions of a god of another name. Proper names abound in ancient inscriptions where the divine name is joined to words such as "servant of," "friend of," "protected by," "favored by," and so on.[60]

When these gods and goddesses had a shrine, or a marked spot of earth associated with them, they were attended to by a part-time priesthood. The priests functioned only when worshippers called for their services. Otherwise, they were private persons, like their fellow tribesmen. Their function was to draw arrows or throw stones or interpret dreams and omens of nature when the purpose was divination of the god's opinion or judgment; to perform the sacrifice or help in the offering when the object was propitiation or thanksgiving. And they were not needed at all when the object was daily or occasional respect effected by the worshipper's circumambulation of the sacred precincts. Service of all the gods of the Ka'bah belonged exclusively to Quraysh, the dominant tribe of Makkah. This honor and prestige among all Arabs belonged exclusively to the Makkans, though even there, the priestly function was a part-time affair. The Makkans combined the priesthood with the leadership of the state and distinguished six functions, each of which they assigned to each one of the Quraysh clans. The *Ḥijābah* was for the maintenance of the Ka'bah and guardianship of its keys; the *Siqāyah,* for the provision of fresh water to daily worshippers and seasonal pilgrims; the *Rifādah,* for providing food for the pilgrims; the *Nadwah,* for organizing and chairing all convocations; the *Qiyādah,* for leading the military forces in war; the *Liwā',* for holding the flag and other deities or symbols wherever prescribed.[61]

Tribal internecine wars were the general rule whose interruption brought relatively short periods of peace. Poetry fanned the fires continuously, proclaiming death for the tribe as the highest peak of heroic achievement. *Ayyām al 'Arab* (Moments of Arab Glory) developed almost like a cult, wherein the worshippers were any Arab audience listening with rapture as the priest—in this case, the narrator—told in eloquent poetry and prose the legacy of anecdotes of the warring heroes of one tribe after another. This cult took complete possession of the imagination of those who participated.

Tribal wars broke out between North and South in the Arabian Peninsula, as the Southerners encroached upon the Northerners and sought to establish hegemony over them. The Northerners, Banū 'Adnān, were divided against themselves and thus made the task easier for the Southerners. However, tyrannical exploitation by the South prompted the 'Adnānī group of tribes in the North to rally and achieve their independence. The South's leadership was in the hands of the kingdom of Ḥimyar, whose wars with Abyssinia eventually rendered it weak enough for the northern dependencies to challenge its authority. In its war of independence, fought toward the end of the fifth century C.E., the North was led by Kulayb, chieftain of the twin tribes of Bakr and Taghlib. The oldest hostility on record took place about 350 C.E., between 'Adwān (a northern tribe) which was led by 'Āmir ibn al Zarb, and Madhḥaj (a southern tribe). The Battle of Khazzāz (c. 400 C.E.) was the subject of "poetical fights" between Farazdaq (Madhḥaj poet of Baṣrah, d. 732 C.E.) and Jarīr (Muḍar poet of Yamāmah, d. 733 C.E.). Such poetical fights rocked the Umawī caliphate and stirred up the people from Yaman to Persia. Between the northern tribes themselves, many battles were fought, the most important taking place between the Rabī'ah group of tribes and the Muḍar group. Each group accounted for six victories over the other, thus providing the poets with twelve battles to depict in poetry, singing the exploits of their heroes. Within the Rabī'ah group, hostilities broke out and battles were fought continually. Between Bakr and Taghlib, a whole series of battles took place in which al Muhalhil (d. 570), one of the greatest poets of pre-Islamic Arabia, participated, lost his brother Kulayb, and composed some of the most beautiful poetry in the language in the latter's eulogy. Within the Muḍar group, to which the Makkan Quraysh tribe belonged, hostilities were likewise continuous. The tribes of 'Abs and Hawāzin accounted for the famous battles of Raḥraḥān (c. 420 C.E.) and of Dāḥis and Ghabrā' (c. 423). Imru' al Qays (d. 431), the king-poet of 'Abs who authored one of the *mu'allaqāt* memorized and recited by all Arabic-speaking peoples, was involved in the first battle. As a young man of fourteen, the Prophet Muḥammad was involved in the Battle of al Fijjār (584 C.E.), fought between his tribe, Quraysh, and the tribes known as Kinānah and Qays-'Aylān. The battle received its name, which means "desecration," because the enemies of Quraysh broke the taboos commonly agreed upon by all Arabs not to fight within the *ḥaram* area or during the holy months. Unlike all other battles, this one did not produce heroic poetry, but shook all Arabs into awareness of the futility of these struggles. Voices were raised in all quarters demanding an end to the bloodshed, which prepared the ground for the call of the Prophet to repudiate tribalism and unite all Arabs under the banner of Islam.

The Arabs' love of poetry caused them to hold an annual competition at the 'Ukāẓ Fair on the occasion of the annual pilgrimage to the Ka'bah. The most competent literary critics and authoritative poets would sit in judgment, and new poetic compositions were recited in competition for prizes. When the new compositions did not measure up, the prizes were awarded to the former prize winners. The prize entailed permission for the best composition to be written in gold and hung on the walls of the Ka'bah. Hence, the name *mu'allaqāt* or "suspended." The generations delighted in learning and reciting these poems, which set the standard for literary eloquence. When Islam arrived, the practice was two centuries old, during which time only ten poems had been awarded the distinction of *mu'allaqāt*.[62] The prize-winning poems sang the praises of the tribes of their authors, the glories of a chivalrous engagement, the greatness of personal honor and tribal fidelity, the tenderness of love, the warmth of friendly discourse with wine and song, the sweetness of revenge, the ephemeral nature of all life. Each excelled in one form or another; and everyone agreed that Zuhayr had no match when he composed, inspired by desire; al Nābighah, when he was inspired by fear; al A'shā, by musical pleasure; and 'Antarah, by anger.

NOTES

1. A. Leo Oppenheim, *Ancient Mesopotamia: Portrait of a Dead Civilization* (Chicago: University of Chicago Press, 1964–1967), pp. 171ff.

2. Thorkild Jacobsen, "Ancient Mesopotamian Religion: The Central Concerns," *American Philosophical Society Proceedings,* 107 (1963), pp. 473–484; idem, "Formative Tendencies in Sumerican Religion," *The Bible and the Ancient Near East: Essays in Honor of William Foxwell Albright,* ed. G. E. Wright (London: Routledge & Kegan Paul, 1961), pp. 267–278; idem, "Mesopotamia," in Henri Frankfort (ed.), *Before Philosophy: The Intellectual Adventure of Ancient Man* (Baltimore: Penguin Books, 1964), pp. 137–236; E. Dhorme, *Les Religions de Babylonie et d'Assyrie* (Paris, 1945); S. Moscati, *The Face of the Ancient Orient* (Garden City, N.Y.: Doubleday, 1962); idem, *Ancient Semitic Civilizations* (London: Elek Books, 1957), especially pp. 43–98.

3. I am using the term of John A. Wilson, "Egypt: The Function of the State," in Henri Frankfort et al., *Before Philosophy: The Intellectual Adventure of Ancient Man* (Baltimore: Penguin Books, 1967, p. 75) which he borrowed from Christian theology where it refers to the single nature of Christ, to mean the Egyptian principle that the divine is itself the worldly and vice versa, the two being continuous and identical.

4. Thorkild Jacobsen, "Mesopotamia: The Function of the State," in *Before Philosophy,* p. 200.

5. Alexander Heidel, *Babylonian Genesis: The Story of Creation* (Chicago: University of Chicago Press, 1963), p. 55.

6. "Throughout the days to come, let them without forgetting make mention of his [God's] deeds" (Heidel, *Babylonian Genesis,* p. 50).

7. Ibid.

8. Ibid., pp. 70–71.

9. Jacobsen, "Mesopotamia," p. 218.

10. Ibid., p. 153.

11. The Mesopotamian poet described Marduk as enjoying "double equality with the gods," and affirmed his divine status to be "beyond comprehension," "not fit for human understanding," the very idea of transcendence proper to divinity (Heidel, *Babylonian Genesis,* pp. 21–22; James B. Pritchard, ed., *Ancient Near Eastern Texts* (Princeton, N.J.: Princeton University Press, 1955), pp. 60ff.

12. Heidel, *Babylonian Genesis,* p. 36; Pritchard, *Ancient Near Eastern Texts,* pp. 66ff.

13. Heidel, *Babylonian Genesis,* pp. 44–46.

14. Ibid., pp. 50–59.

15. Genesis 34:16, 21–22.

16. Genesis 34:30.

17. Genesis 6:2–4.

18. Exodus 2.

19. Exodus 3:1–10.

20. Exodus 18:12.

21. Deuteronomy 33:2.

22. I Samuel 27:10; 30:29; Judges 1:16ff.

23. Martin Noth, *The History of Israel* (London: Adam and Charles Black, 1958), p. 132.

24. George Mendenhall, "Covenant Forms in Israelite Tradition," *The Biblical Archeologist,* 17 (1954), pp. 50–76.

25. Exodus 19:6.

26. I Kings 7:13ff.

27. I Kings 11:1.

28. I Kings 11:4–5.

29. I Kings 11:7–8.

30. Noth, *History of Israel,* p. 218.

31. Isaiah 40.

32. Isaiah 2:3; 42:1–4.

33. Isaiah 40, 41, 45. The other gods "are all vanity; their works are nothing; their molten images are wind and confusion" (Isaiah 41:29).

34. Isaiah 40:15; 49:25–26.

35. Isaiah 49:22–23.

36. Qur'ān 85:1–10.

37. Qur'ān 2:101, 187; 5:71; 62:5.

38. For further elaboration of this understanding of the essence of the religion of Jesus, see Isma'īl Al Fārūqī, *Christian Ethics: A Historial and Systematic Analysis of Its Dominant Ideas* (Montreal: McGill University Press, 1962).

39. Cyril of Alexandria quoted Julian reproaching a colleague in the following words: "But you, unfortunately, do not abide by the tradition of the apostles, which in the hands of their successors deteriorated into great blasphemy. Neither . . . Matthew, nor Luke, nor Mark had the audacity to say that Jesus is God. But the worthy John, realizing that by that time a vast number of people in many of the Greek and Italian cities were infected with the disease . . . was the first to have the audacity to make this assertion" (*Contra Julianum,* X, quoted in Henry Bettenson, *Documents of the Christian Church* [Oxford: Oxford University Press, 1956], p. 29).

40. Irenaeus, *Contra Heresies,* I, xxvi, 1-2.

41. Adolph Harnack, *History of Dogma* (New York: Dover Publications, n.d.), Vol. I, pp. 289ff.

42. *The Shepherd of Hermas, Ante-Nicene Fathers,* Vol. II.

43. To the question, how could man be saved, Athanasius (296-373) answered: "By God's Word," and added: "What else was needed to restore man from corruption but the Word of God, Who in the beginning made everything from nothing" (*De Incarnatione,* vii; quoted in Bettenson, *Documents,* p. 47).

44. Justin Martyr, *Apology,* I, xlvi, 1-4, quoted in Bettenson, *Documents,* p. 6.

45. Irenaeus, *Contra Heresies,* I, xxvii, 2-3, quoted in Bettenson, *Documents,* p. 53.

46. Epiphanius, *Against Heresies,* lxii, 1, quoted in Bettenson, *Documents,* p. 54.

47. Ibid.

48. Theodoret (458), *Historia Ecclesiastica,* I, v, quoted in Bettenson, *Documents,* p. 55.

49. Socrates (440), *Historia Ecclesiastica,* I, v, quoted in Bettenson, *Documents,* p. 56.

50. *Ante-Nicene Fathers,* Vol. I, pp. 45ff; *The Nicene and Post-Nicene Fathers,* Vol. IV.

51. *The Nicene and Post-Nicene Fathers,* Vol. III, pp. 17ff.

52. Philip Hitti, *History of the Arabs* (London: Macmillan, 1963), p. 61.

53. Qur'ān 105.

54. Qur'ān 14:37.

55. Qur'ān 39:3.

56. F. V. Winnett, "Allah before Islam," *The Muslim World,* XXVIII, No. 1, pp. 239-248.

57. Qur'ān 17:69; 23:86, 89; 29:61, 63-65; 31:31; 35:40; 6:139-41; 16:40.

58. Theodor Noldeke, "Arabs (Ancient)," *Encyclopaedia of Religion and Ethics,* Vol. I, pp. 659-673.

59. Ibid., p. 664.

60. Ibn al Kalbī, *Kitāb al Aṣnām,* ed. Aḥmad Zakī (Cairo, 1914, 1924); Y. Moubarac, *Les Etudes d'épigraphie sud-sémitique et la naissance de l'Islam* (Paris: Paul Geuthner, 1957); A. Jamme, "Le Panthéon sud-arabe préislamique d'après les sources épigraphiques," *Le Muséon,* 60 (1947), pp. 57-147.

61. Jawād 'Alī, *Tārīkh al 'Arab Qabla al Islām* (Baghdad, 1951), Vol. I, pp. 416ff; Jurjī Zaydān, *Al 'Arab Qabla al Islām* (Cairo: Dār al Hilāl, n.d.), pp. 275ff; Muḥammad Ḥusayn Haykal, *The Life of Muḥammad,* trans. I. R. al Fārūqī (Indianapolis: American Trust Publications, 1976), pp. 31-32.

62. These were the compositions of Imru' al Qays (d. 540 C.E.), Zuhayr ibn Abī Salmā (d. 615 C.E.), al Nābighah al Dhubyānī (d. 604 C.E.), al A'shā (d. 629 C.E.), Labīd ibn Rabī'ah (d. 662 A.C.), 'Amr ibn Kulthūm (d. 600 C.E.), al Ḥārith ibn Ḥillizah (d. 580 A.C.), Ṭarafah ibn al 'Abd (d. 500 C.E.), 'Antarah ibn Shaddād (d. 615 C.E.), and 'Ubayd ibn al Abraṣ (d. 555 C.E.).

PART TWO
THE ESSENCE

CHAPTER 4

The Essence of Islamic Civilization

There can be no doubt that the essence of Islamic civilization is Islam; or that the essence of Islam is *tawḥīd,* the act of affirming Allah to be the One, absolute, transcendent Creator, Lord and Master of all that is.

These two fundamental premises are self-evident. They have never been doubted by those who belonged to this civilization or participated in it. And only very recently have missionaries, Orientalists, and other interpreters of Islam subjected them to doubt. Whatever their level of education, Muslims are apodictically certain that Islamic civilization does have an essence, that this essence is knowable and capable of analysis or description, that it is *tawḥīd.*[1] Analysis of *tawḥīd* as essence, as first determining principle of Islamic civilization, is the object of this chapter.

Tawḥīd is that which gives Islamic civilization its identity, which binds all its constituents together and thus makes of them an integral, organic body which we call civilization. In binding disparate elements together, the essence of civilization—in this case, *tawḥīd*—impresses them with its own mold. It recasts them so as to harmonize with and mutually support other elements. Without necessarily changing their natures, the essence transforms the elements making up a civilization, giving them their new character as constitutive of that civilization. The range of transformation may vary from slight to radical, depending on how relevant the essence is to the different elements and their functions. This relevance stood out prominently in the minds of Muslim observers of the phenomena of civilization. That is why they took *tawḥīd* as title to their most important works, and they pressed all subjects under its aegis. They regarded *tawḥīd* as the most fundamental principle which includes or determines all other principles; and they found in it the fountainhead, the primeval source determining all phenomena of Islamic civilization.

Traditionally and simply expressed, *tawḥīd* is the conviction and witnessing that "there is no God but God." This negative statement, brief to the utmost limits of brevity, carries the greatest and richest meanings in the whole of Islam. Sometimes, a whole culture, a whole civilization, or a whole history lies compressed in one sentence. This certainly is the case of the *kalimah* (pronouncement) or *shahādah* (witnessing) of Islam. All the diversity, wealth and history, culture and learning, wisdom and civilization of Islam is compressed in this shortest of sentences *"Lā ilaha illā Allah."*

TAWḤĪD AS WORLDVIEW

Tawḥīd is a general view of reality, of truth, of the world, of space and time, of human history. As such it comprehends the following principles:

Duality

Reality is of two generic kinds, God and non-God; Creator and creature. The first order has but one member, Allah, the Absolute and Almighty. He alone is God, eternal, Creator, transcendent. Nothing is like unto Him; He remains forever absolutely unique and devoid of partners or associates. The second is the order of space-time, of experience, of creation. It includes all creatures, the world of things, plants and animals, humans, jinn and angels, heaven and earth, paradise and hell, and all their becoming since they came into being. The two orders of Creator and creation are utterly and absolutely disparate as far as their being, or ontology, as well as their existence and careers are concerned. It is forever impossible that the one be united with, fused, con-fused or diffused into the other. Neither can the Creator be ontologically transformed so as to become the creature, nor can the creature transcend and transfigure itself so as to become in any way or sense the Creator.[2]

Ideationality

The relation between the two orders of reality is ideational in nature. Its point of reference in man is the faculty of understanding. As organ and repository of knowledge, the understanding includes all the gnoseological functions of memory, imagination, reasoning, observation, intuition, apprehension, and so on. All humans are endowed with understanding. Their endowment is strong enough to understand the will of God in either or both of the following ways: when that will is expressed in words, directly by God to man, and when the divine will is deducible through observation of creation.[3]

Teleology

The nature of the cosmos is teleological, that is, purposive, serving a purpose of its Creator, and doing so out of design. The world has not been created in vain, or in sport.[4] It is not the work of chance, a happenstance. It was created in perfect condition. Everything that exists does so in a measure proper to it and fulfills a certain universal purpose.[5] The world is indeed a "cosmos," an orderly creation, not a "chaos." In it, the will of the Creator is always realized. His patterns are fulfilled with the necessity of natural law. For they are innate in the very nature of things. No creature other than man, acts or exists in a way other than what the Creator has ordained for it.[5] Man is the only creature in which the will of God is actualized not necessarily, but with man's own personal consent. The physical and psychic functions of man are integral to nature, and as such they obey the laws pertinent to them with the same necessity as all other creatures. But the spiritual functions, namely, understanding and moral action, fall outside the realm of determined nature. They depend upon their subject and follow his determination. Actualization of the divine will by them is of a qualitatively different value than necessary actualization by other creatures. Necessary fulfillment applies only to elemental or utilitarian values; free fulfillment applies to the moral. However, the moral purposes of God, His commandments to man, do have a base in the physical world, and hence there is a utilitarian aspect to them. But this is not what gives them their distinctive quality, that of being moral. It is precisely the commandments' aspect of being fulfillable in freedom, that is, with the possibility of being violated, that provides the special dignity we ascribe to things "moral."[7]

Capacity of Man and Malleability of Nature

Since everything was created for a purpose — the totality of being no less so — the realization of that purpose must be possible in space and time.[8] Otherwise, there is no escape from cynicism. Creation itself and the processes of space and time would lose their meaning and significance. Without this possibility, *taklīf,* or moral obligation, falls to the ground; and with its fall, either God's purposiveness or His might is destroyed. Realization of the absolute, namely, the divine raison d'être of creation, must be possible in history, that is, within the process of time between creation and the Day of Judgment. As subject of moral action, man must therefore be capable of changing himself, his fellows or society, nature or his environment, so as to actualize the divine pattern, or commandment, in himself as well as in them.[9] As object of moral action, man as well as his fellows and environment must all be capable of receiving the efficacious

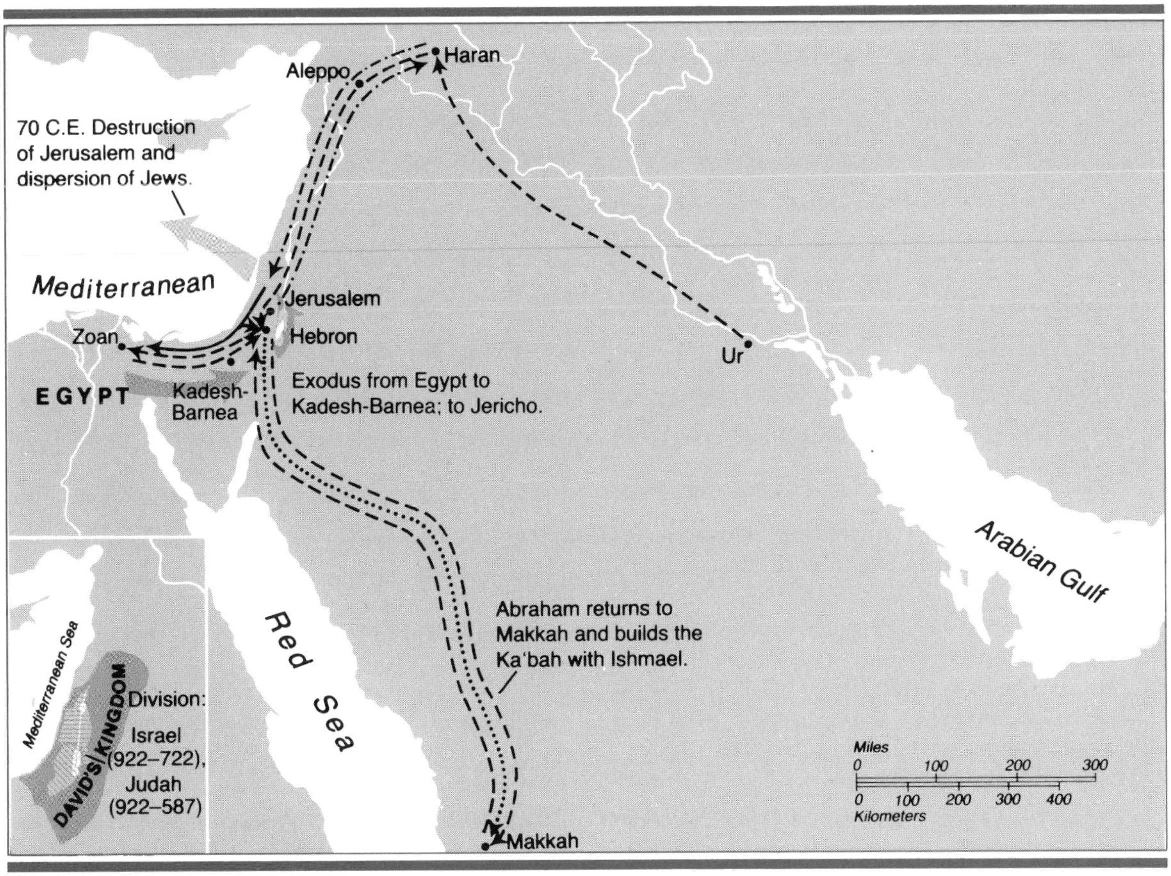

- - → Abraham's migrations

······→ Abraham, Hagar and Ishmael migrate to Makkah

—·→ Jacob to Haran; on return his son Joseph is carried off by Arab caravan to Egypt

——→ Jacob's children to Egypt and return to Hebron

Map 14. Makkan and Hebrew Origins (1800 B.C.E. - 622 C.E.)

action of man, the subject. This capacity is the converse of man's moral capacity for action as subject. Without it, man's capacity for moral action would be impossible and the purposive nature of the universe would collapse. Again, there would be no recourse from cynicism. For creation to have a purpose — and this is a necessary assumption if God is God and His work is not a meaningless *travail de singe*— creation must be malleable, transformable, capable of changing its substance, structure, conditions, and relations so as to embody or concretize the human pattern or purpose. This is true of all creation, including man's physical, psychic, and spiritual nature. All creation is capable of realization of the ought-to-be, the will or

The Makkans and the Hebrews are cousins. Both descend from one ancestor, Abraham or Ibrahīm, of Ur in Lower Mesopotamia. Rebelling against the idolatry of his people and escaping miraculously from their judgment against him, Abraham joined the roaming Amurru tribesmen and came to Canaan. He settled his eldest son, Ishmael or Isma'il, in Makkah, where they built the Ka'bah and Isma'il scioned the Makkan tribe of Quraysh. Abraham's other son, Isaac, and his progeny sought to settle in Canaan but could not do so for almost a millennium, during which time they either roamed the area or went to Egypt. They settled in Canaan in the following millennium, but they were torn between assimilation with Canaan and separation from it. Their stay in Canaan ended with destruction, and the survivors dispersed throughout the world during the next two millennia.

pattern of God, the absolute in this space and in this time.[10]

Responsibility and Judgment

If man stands under the obligation to change himself, his society, and his environment so as to conform with the divine pattern, and is capable of doing so, and if all that is object of his action is malleable and capable of receiving his action and embodying its purpose, then it follows with necessity that he is responsible. Moral obligation is impossible without responsibility or reckoning. Unless man is responsible, and unless he is accountable for his deeds, cynicism becomes once more inevitable. Judgment, or the consummation of responsibility, is the necessary condition of moral obligation, of moral imperativeness. It flows from the very nature of "normativeness."[11] It is immaterial whether reckoning takes place in space-time or at the end of it or both, but it must take place. To obey God, that is, to realize His commandments and actualize His pattern, is to achieve *falāḥ* or success, happiness, and ease. Not to do so, to disobey Him, is to incur punishment, suffering, unhappiness, and the agonies of failure.

Illustration 4.1

An Afghan pilgrim in Makkah. [Courtesy Saudi Arabian Ministry of Information.]

TAWḤĪD AS ESSENCE OF CIVILIZATION

As the essence of Islamic civilization, tawḥīd has two aspects or dimensions: the methodological and the contentual. The former determines the forms of application and implementation of the first principles of the civilization; the latter determines the first principles themselves.

The Methodological Dimension

The methodological dimension includes three principles, namely, unity, rationalism, and tolerance. These determine the form of Islamic civilization, a form that pervades every one of its departments.

Unity. There is no civilization without unity. Unless the elements constituting a civilization are united, woven, and harmonized with one another, they constitute not a civilization but a hodgepodge conglomeration. A principle unifying the various elements and comprehending them within its framework is essential. Such a principle would transform the mixture of relations of the elements with one another into an orderly structure in which levels of priority or degrees of importance are perceivable. The civilization of Islam places elements in an orderly structure and governs their existence and relations according to a uniform pattern. In themselves, the elements can be of either native or foreign provenance. Indeed, there is no civilization that has not adopted some elements foreign to it. What is important is that the civilization digest those elements, that is, recast their forms and relations and thus integrate them into its own system. To "in-form" them with its own form is in fact to transform them into a new reality where they exist no more in themselves or in their former dependency, but as integral components of the new civilization in which they have been integrated. It is not an argument against any civilization that it contains such elements; but it is a devastating argument against any civilization when it has merely added foreign elements; when it has done so in disjointed manner, without re-formation, in-formation, or integration. As such, the elements merely co-exist with the civilization. They do not belong organically to it. But if the civilization has succeeded in transforming them and integrating them into its system, the integrating process becomes its index of vitality, of its dynamism and creativity. In any integral civilization, and certainly in Islam, the constitutive elements, whether material, structural, or relational, are all bound by one supreme principle. In Islamic civilization, this supreme principle is *tawḥīd.* It is the ultimate measuring rod of the Muslim, his guide and criterion in his encounter with other religions and civilizations, with new facts or situations. What accords with it is accepted and integrated. What does not is rejected and condemned.

Tawḥīd, or the doctrine of absolute unity, transcendence, and ultimacy of God, implies that only He is worthy of worship, of service. The obedient person lives his life under this principle. He seeks to have all his acts to conform to the pattern, to actualize the divine purpose. His life must therefore show the unity of his mind and will, the unique object of his service. His life will not be a series of events put together helter-skelter, but will be related to a single overarching principle, bound by a single frame which integrates them together into a single unity. His life thus has a single style, an integral form — in short, Islam.

Illustration 4.3

Mosque of the Prophet in Madīnah. [Photo by L. al Fārūqī.]

Illustration 4.2

A pilgrim in Makkah studying the Qur'ān. [Courtesy Saudi Arabian Ministry of Information.]

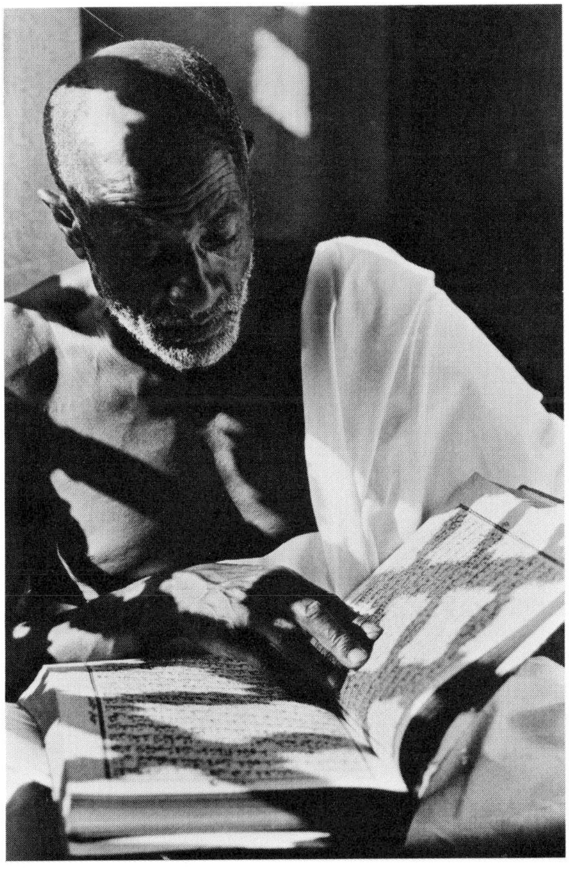

Rationalism. As methodological principle, rationalism is constitutive of the essence of Islamic civilization. It consists of three rules or laws: first, rejection of all that does not correspond with reality; second, denial of ultimate contradictories; third, openness to new and/or contrary evidence. The first rule protects the Muslim against opinion, that is, against making any untested, unconfirmed claims to knowledge. The unconfirmed claim, the Qur'ān declares, is an instance of *ẓann,* or deceptive knowledge, and is prohibited by God, however slight is its object.[12] The Muslim is definable as the person who claims nothing but the truth. The second rule protects him against simple contradiction on one side, and paradox on the other.[13] Rationalism does not mean the priority of reason over

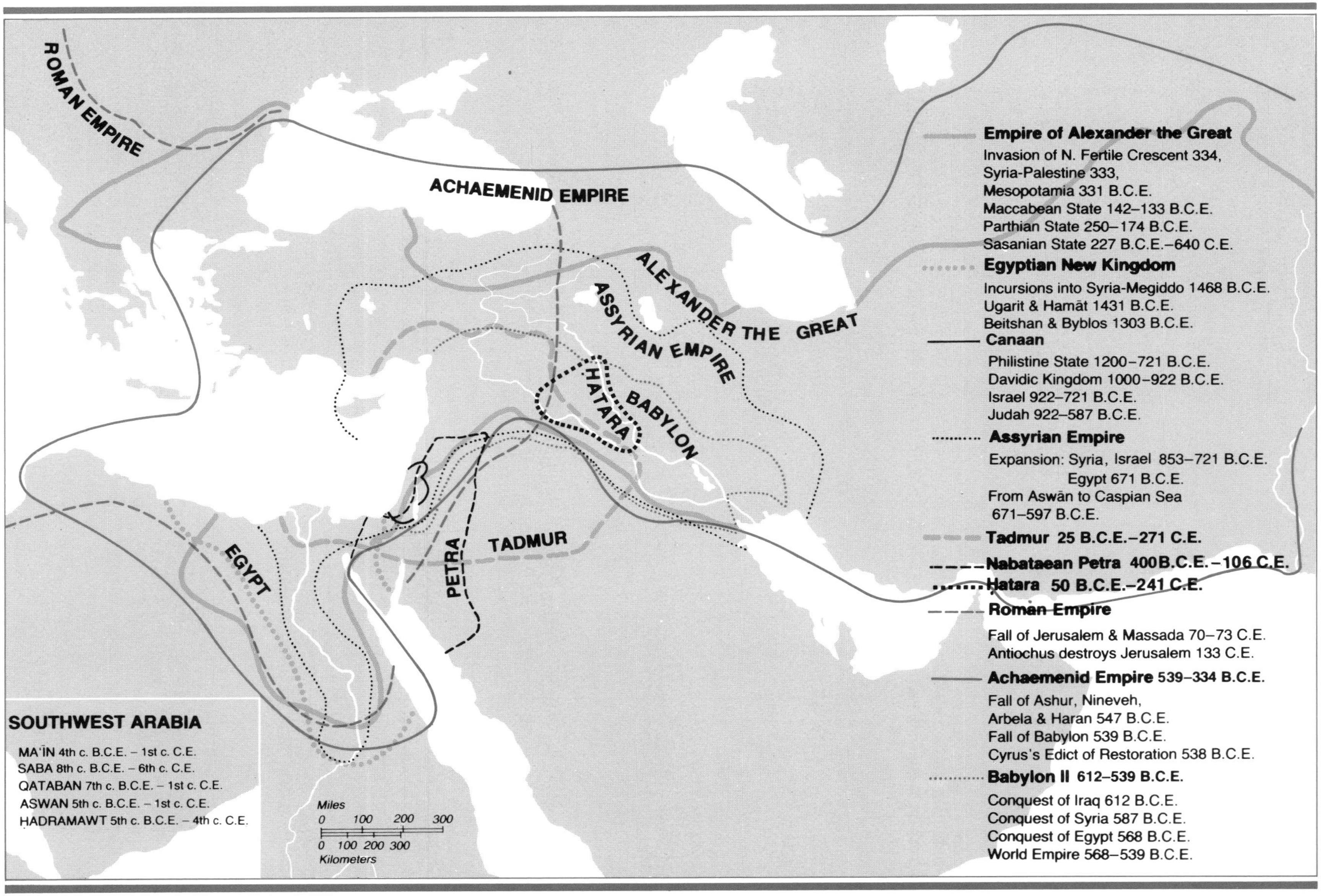
ROMAN EMPIRE
ACHAEMENID EMPIRE
ALEXANDER THE GREAT
ASSYRIAN EMPIRE
HATARA
BABYLON
EGYPT
PETRA
TADMUR
Empire of Alexander the Great
Invasion of N. Fertile Crescent 334,
Syria-Palestine 333,
Mesopotamia 331 B.C.E.
Maccabean State 142–133 B.C.E.
Parthian State 250–174 B.C.E.
Sasanian State 227 B.C.E.–640 C.E.
Egyptian New Kingdom
Incursions into Syria-Megiddo 1468 B.C.E.
Ugarit & Hamāt 1431 B.C.E.
Beitshan & Byblos 1303 B.C.E.
Canaan
Philistine State 1200–721 B.C.E.
Davidic Kingdom 1000–922 B.C.E.
Israel 922–721 B.C.E.
Judah 922–587 B.C.E.
Assyrian Empire
Expansion: Syria, Israel 853–721 B.C.E.
Egypt 671 B.C.E.
From Aswān to Caspian Sea
671–597 B.C.E.
Tadmur 25 B.C.E.–271 C.E.
Nabataean Petra 400 B.C.E.–106 C.E.
Hatara 50 B.C.E.–241 C.E.
Roman Empire
Fall of Jerusalem & Massada 70–73 C.E.
Antiochus destroys Jerusalem 133 C.E.
Achaemenid Empire 539–334 B.C.E.
Fall of Ashur, Nineveh,
Arbela & Haran 547 B.C.E.
Fall of Babylon 539 B.C.E.
Cyrus's Edict of Restoration 538 B.C.E.
Babylon II 612–539 B.C.E.
Conquest of Iraq 612 B.C.E.
Conquest of Syria 587 B.C.E.
Conquest of Egypt 568 B.C.E.
World Empire 568–539 B.C.E.
SOUTHWEST ARABIA
MA'ĪN 4th c. B.C.E. – 1st c. C.E.
SABA 8th c. B.C.E. – 6th c. C.E.
QATABAN 7th c. B.C.E. – 1st c. C.E.
ASWAN 5th c. B.C.E. – 1st c. C.E.
HADRAMAWT 5th c. B.C.E. – 4th c. C.E.
Miles
0 100 200 300
0 100 200 300
Kilometers

Map 15. The First Millennium B.C.E.: Power and Turbulence without Idealism

In the first millennium B.C.E. the Arabian theater saw the rise and fall of five world empires: the Assyrian, Second Babylonian, Persian, Hellenistic, and Roman. None of the twelve states in the area had a sense of mission.

revelation but the rejection of any ultimate contradiction between them.[14] Rationalism studies contradictory theses over and over again, assuming that there must be an aspect that had escaped consideration and that, if taken into account, would expose the contradictory relation. Equally, rationalism leads the reader of revelation—not revelation itself—to another reading, lest an unobvious or unclear meaning may have escaped him which, if reconsidered, would remove the apparent contradiction. Such referral to reason or understanding would have the effect of harmonizing not revelation per se—revelation stands above any manipulation by man!—but the Muslim's human interpretation or understanding of it. It makes his understanding of revelation agree with the cumulative evidence uncovered by reason. Acceptance of the contradictory or paradoxical as ultimately valid appeals only to the weak-of-mind. The intelligent Muslim is a rationalist as he insists on the unity of the two sources of truth, namely, revelation and reason.

The third rule, openness to new or contrary evidence, protects the Muslim against literalism, fanaticism, and stagnation-causing conservatism. It inclines him to intellectual humility. It forces him to append to his affirmations and denials the phrase *"Allahu a'lam"*(Allah knows better!). For he is convinced that the truth is bigger than can be totally mastered by him.

As the affirmation of the absolute unity of God, *tawḥīd* is the affirmation of the unity of truth. For God, in Islam, is the truth. His unity is the unity of the sources of truth. God is the Creator of nature whence man derives his knowledge. The object of knowledge are the patterns of nature which are the work of God. Certainly God knows them since He is their author; and equally certainly, He is the source of revelation. He gives man of His knowledge; and His knowledge is absolute and universal. God is no trickster, no malevolent agent whose purpose is to misguide and mislead. Nor does He change His judgment as men do when they correct their knowledge, their will, or their decision. God is perfect and omniscient. He makes no mistakes. Otherwise, He would not be the transcendent God of Islam.

Tolerance. As methodological principle, tolerance is the acceptance of the present until its falsehood has been established. Thus, it is revelant to epistemology. It is equally relevant to ethics as the principle of accepting the desired until its undesirableness has been established.[15] The former is called *sa'ah;* the latter, *yusr.* Both protect the Muslim from self-closure to the world, from deadening conservatism. Both urge him to affirm and say yea to life, to new experience. Both encourage him to address the new data with his scrutinizing reason, his constructive endeavor, and thereby to enrich his experience and life, to move his culture and civilization ever forward.

As methodological principle within the essence of Islamic civilization, tolerance is the conviction that God did not leave people without sending them a messenger from among themselves to teach them that there is no God but God and that they owe Him worship and service,[16] to warn them against evil and its causes.[17] In this regard, tolerance is the certainty that all men are endowed with a *sensus communis,* which enables them to know the true religion, to recognize God's will and commandments. Tolerance is the conviction that the diversity of religions is due to history with all its affecting factors, its diverse conditions of space and time, its prejudices, passions, and vested interests. Behind religious diversity stands *al dīn al ḥanīf,* the primordial religion of God with which all men are born before acculturation makes them adherents of this or that religion. Tolerance requires the Muslim to undertake a study of the history of religions with a view to discover within each the primeval endowment of God, which He sent all His apostles at all places and times to teach.[18]

In religion—and there can hardly be anything more important in human relations—tolerance transforms confrontation and reciprocal condemnations between the religions into a cooperative scholarly investigation of the genesis and development of the religions with a view to separating the historical accretions from the original given of revelation. In ethics, the next all important field, *yusr* immunizes the Muslim against any life-denying tendencies and assures him the minimum measure of optimism required to maintain health, balance, and a sense of proportion, despite all the tragedies and afflictions that befall human life. God has assured His creatures that "with hardship, We have ordained ease *[yusr].*"[19] And as He commanded them to examine every claim and make certain before judging,[20] the *uṣūliyyūn* (doctors of jurisprudence) resorted to experimentation before judging as good and evil anything desired that is not contrary to a clear divine injunction.

Both *sa'ah* and *yusr* devolve directly from *tawḥīd* as a principle of the metaphysic of ethics. God, Who

Illustration 4.4

Interior of the Ḥaram in Makkah. [Courtesy Saudi Arabian Ministry of Information.]

created man that he may prove himself worthy in the deed, has made him free and capable of positive action and affirmative movement in the world. To do so, Islam holds, is indeed man's raison d'être.[21]

The Contentual Dimension

***Tawḥīd* as first principle of metaphysics.** To witness that there is no God but God is to hold that He alone is the Creator Who gave to everything its being, Who is the ultimate Cause of every event, and the final End of all that is, that He is the First and the Last. To enter into such witnessing in freedom and conviction, in conscious understanding of its content, is to realize that all that surrounds us, whether things or events, all that takes place in the natural, social, or psychic fields, is the action of God, the fulfillment of one or another of His purposes. Once made, such realization becomes second nature to man, inseparable from him during all his waking hours. One then lives all the moments of one's life under its shadow. And where man recognizes God's commandment and action in every object and event, he follows the divine initiative because it is God's. To observe it in nature is to do natural science.[22] For the divine initiative in nature is none other than the immutable laws with which God had endowed nature.[23] To observe the divine initiative in one's self or in one's society is to pursue the humanities and the social sciences.[24] And if the whole universe itself is really the unfolding or fulfillment of these laws of nature, which are the commandments of God and His will, then the universe is, in the eye of the Muslim, a living theater set in motion by God's command. The theater itself, as well as all it includes, is explicable in these terms. The unization of God means therefore that He is the Cause of everything, and that none else is so.

Of necessity, then, *tawḥīd* means the elimination of any power operative in nature beside God, whose eternal initiative are the immutable laws of nature. But this is tantamount to denying any initiative in nature by any power other than that which is innate in nature, such as magic, sorcery, spirits, and any theurgical notion of arbitrary interference into the processes of nature by any agency. Therefore, *tawḥīd* means the profanization of the realms of nature, their secularization. And that is the absolutely first condition of a science of nature. Through *tawḥīd,* therefore, nature was separated from the gods and spirits of primitive religion. *Tawḥīd* for the first time made it possible for the religio-mythopoeic mind to outgrow itself, for the sciences of nature and civilization to develop with the blessing of a religious worldview that renounced once and for all any association of the sacred with nature. *Tawḥīd* is the opposite of superstition or myth, the enemies of natural science and civilization. For *tawḥīd* gathers all the threads of causality and returns them to God rather than to occult forces. In so doing, the causal force operative in any event or object is organized so as to make a continuous thread whose parts are causally — and hence empirically — related to one another. That the thread ultimately refers to God demands that no force outside of it interferes with the discharge of its causal power or efficacy. This in turn presupposes the linkages between the parts to be causal, and subjects them to empirical investigation and establishment. That the laws of nature are the inimitable patterns of God means that God operates the threads of nature through causes. Only causation by another cause that

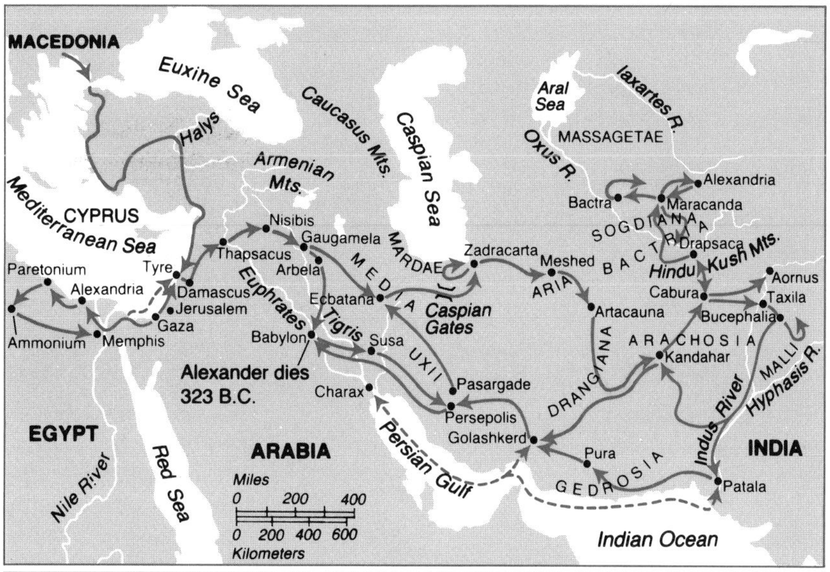

Map 16A. The Campaigns of Alexander the Great

is always the same constitutes a pattern. This constancy of causation is precisely what makes its examination and discovery—and hence, science—possible. Science is none other than the search for such repeated causation in nature, for the causal linkages constitutive of the causal thread are repeated in other threads. Their establishment is the establishment of the laws of nature. It is the prerequisite for subjecting the causal forces of nature to control and engineering, the necessary condition for man's usufruct of nature.

***Tawḥīd* as first principle of ethics.** *Tawḥīd* affirms that the unique God created man in the best of forms to the end of worshipping and serving Him.[25] This means that man's whole existence on earth has as its purpose the obedience of God, the fulfillment of His command. *Tawḥīd* also affirms that this purpose consists in man's vice-gerency for God on earth.[26] For, according to the Qur'ān, God has invested man with His trust, a trust which heaven and earth were incapable of carrying and from which they shied away with terror.[27] The divine trust is the fulfillment of the ethical part of the divine will, whose very nature requires that it be realized in freedom, and man is the only creature capable of doing so. Wherever the divine will is realized with the necessity of natural law, the realization is not moral, but elemental or utilitarian. Only man is capable of realizing it under the possibility of doing or not doing so at all, or doing the very opposite or anything in between. It is this exercise of human freedom regarding obedience to God's commandment that makes fulfillment of the command moral.

Tawḥīd affirms that God, being beneficent and purposive, did not create man in sport, or in vain. He endowed him with the senses, with reason and understanding, made him perfect—indeed, breathed into him of His spirit[28]—to prepare him to perform this great duty.

Such great duty is the cause for the creation of man. It is the final end of human existence, man's definition, and the meaning of his life and existence on earth. By virtue of it, man assumes a cosmic function of tremendous importance. The cosmos would not be itself without that higher part of the divine will which is the object of human moral endeavor. And no other creature in the cosmos can substitute for man in this function. Man is the only cosmic bridge by which the moral—and hence higher—part of the divine will may enter the realm of space-time and become history.

The responsibility or obligation *(taklīf)* laid down upon man exclusively knows no bounds. It comprehends the whole universe. All mankind is object of man's moral action; all earth and sky are his theater, his *matériel*. He is responsible for all that takes place in the universe, in every one of its remotest corners.

For man's *taklīf* or obligation is universal, cosmic. It comes to end only on the Day of Judgment.

Taklīf, Islam affirms, is the basis of man's humanity, its meaning, and its content. Man's acceptance of this burden puts him on a higher level than the rest of creation, indeed, than the angels. For only he is capable of accepting responsibility. It constitutes his cosmic significance. A world of difference separates this humanism of Islam from other humanisms. Greek civilization, for instance, developed a strong humanism which the West has taken as a model since the Renaissance. Founded upon an exaggerated naturalism, Greek humanism deified man, as well as his vices. That is why the Greek was not offended by representing his gods as cheating and plotting against one another, as committing adultery, theft, incest, aggression, jealousy and revenge, and other acts of brutality. Being part of the very stuff of which human life is made, such acts and passions were claimed to be as natural as the perfections and virtues. As nature, both were thought to be equally divine, worthy of contemplation in their aesthetic form, of adoration — and of emulation by man of whom the gods were the apotheosis. Christianity, on the other hand, was in its formative years reacting to this very Greco-Roman humanism. It went to the opposite extreme of debasing man through "original sin" and declaring him a "fallen creature," a *"massa peccata."*[29]

Illustration 4.5

Basmalah in mirrored symmetrical design. [Photo by L. al Fārūqī.]

The degrading of man to the level of an absolute, universal, innate, and necessary state of sin from which it is impossible for any human ever to pull himself up by his own effort was the logical prerequisite if God on High was to incarnate Himself, to suffer, and die in atonement for man's sinfulness. In other words, if a redemption has to take place by God, there must be a predicament so absolute that only God could pull man out of it. Thus human sinfulness was absolutized in order to make it "worthy" of the Crucifixion of God. Hinduism classified mankind into castes, and assigned the majority of mankind to the nethermost classes — of "untouchables" if they are native to India, or *malitcha,* the religiously unclean or contaminated of the rest of the world. For the lowest as well as for the others, there is no rise to the superior, privileged caste of Brahmins in this life; such mobility is possible only after death through the transmigration of souls. In this life, man necessarily belongs to the caste in which he is born. Ethical striving is of no consequence whatever to its subject as long as he is alive in this world. Finally, Buddhism judged all human and other life in creation as endless suffering and misery. Existence itself, it held, is evil and man's only meaningful duty is to seek release from it through discipline and mental effort.

The humanism of *tawḥīd* alone is genuine. It alone respects man as man and creature, without either deification or vilification. It alone defines the worth of man in terms of his virtues, and begins its assessment of him with a positive mark for the innate endowment God has given all men in preparation for their noble task. It alone defines the virtues and ideals of human life in terms of the very contents of natural life, rather than denying them, thus making its humanism life-affirmative as well as moral.

***Tawḥīd* as first principle of axiology.** *Tawḥīd* affirms that God has created mankind that men may prove themselves morally worthy by their deeds.[30] As supreme and ultimate Judge, He warned that all men's actions will be reckoned[31]; that their authors will be rewarded for the good deeds and punished for the evil.[32] *Tawḥīd* further affirms that God has placed man on earth that he may colonize it,[33] that is, that he may strike out on its trails, eat of its fruits, enjoy its goodness and beauty, and cause it and himself to prosper.[34] This is world-affirmation: to accept the world because it is innocent and good, created by God and ordered by Him for human use. Indeed, everything in the world, including the sun and the moon, is subservient to man. All creation is a theater in which man is to perform his ethical action and thereby implement the higher part of the divine will. Man is responsible for satisfying his instincts and needs, and every individual is responsible for the same satisfaction for all men. Man is obliged to develop the human resources of all men to the highest possible degree, that full use may be made of all their natural endowments. He is obliged to transform the whole earth into productive orchards and beautiful gardens. He may in the process explore the sun and the moon if necessary.[35] Certainly he must discover and learn the patterns of nature, of the human psyche, of society. Certainly he ought to industrialize and develop the world if it is eventually to become the garden where the word of God is supreme.

Such world affirmation is truly creative of civilization. It generates the elements out of which civilizations are made, as well as the social forces necessary for its growth and progress. *Tawḥīd* is anti-monkery, anti-isolation, anti-world-denial, and anti-asceticism.[36] On the other hand, world affirmation does not mean unconditional acceptance of the world and nature as they are. Without a principle to check man's implementation or realization, affirmation of the world and nature may run counter to itself by the exaggerated pursuit of any one value, element, or force, or group of them, to the exclusion of all others. Balancing and disciplining man's pursuit so that it results in harmonious realization of all values, under the priority system properly belonging to them, rather than under any haste, passion, zeal, or blindness of man, is a necessary prerequisite. Without it, the pursuit may wreck itself in either tragedy or superficiality, or may unleash some truly demonic force. Greek civilization, for instance, exaggerated its pursuit of the world. It asserted that all that is in nature is unconditionally good and hence worthy of pursuit and realization. Hence, it declared all that is actually desired, the object of a real interest, to be *ipso facto* good, on the grounds that desire itself, being natural, is good. That nature often contradicts itself, that and the pursuits of such desires or elements of nature may counter one another, did not have enough appeal to warrant a revision of the first assumption. The need for a supernatural principle overarching all the tendencies and desires of nature, and in terms of which

Map 16B. The Empire of Alexander the Great

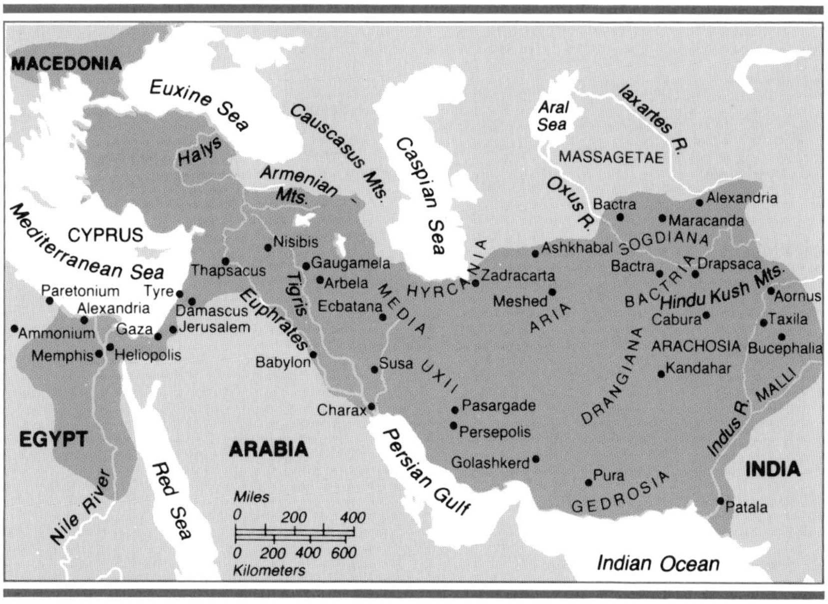

Illustration 4.6

Calligraphy design (eight Allah repetitions). [Photo by L. al Fārūqī.]

their contradictions and differences may be understood, must be recognized. But instead of realizing this truth, Greek civilization was too intoxicated with the beauty of nature per se and regarded the tragic outcome of naturalism itself natural. Since the Renaissance, modern Western civilization has paid the highest regard for tragedy. Its zeal for naturalism took it to the extreme of accepting nature without morality as a supernatural condition. Since the struggle of Western man has been against the Church and all that it represents, the progress of man in science was conceived as a liberation from its clutches. Hence, it was extremely hard even to conceive of world-affirmation or naturalism as attached to normative threads stretching from an a priori, noumenal, absolute source. Without such threads, naturalism is bound to end up in self-contradiction, in conflicts within itself that are *ex hypothesi* insoluble. The Olympus community could not live with itself in harmony and had to destroy itself. Its world-affirmation was in vain.

The guarantee of world-affirmation, which secures it to produce a balanced, permanent, self-redressing civilization, is morality. Indeed, true civilization is nothing but world-affirmation disciplined by an a priori, or supernatural, morality whose inner content or values are not inimical to life and the world, to time and history, to reason. Such morality is furnished by *tawḥīd* alone among the ideologies known to man.

***Tawḥīd* as first principle of societism.** *Tawḥīd* asserts that "this ummah of yours is a single ummah whose Lord is God. Therefore, worship and serve Him."[37] *Tawḥīd* means that the believers are indeed a single brotherhood, whose members mutually love one another in God, who counsel one another to do justice and be patient[38]; who cling together without exception to the rope of God and do not separate from one another[39]; who reckon with one another, enjoining what is good and prohibiting what is evil[40]; who, finally, obey God and His Prophet.[41]

The vision of the *ummah* is one; so is the feeling or will, as well as the action. The *ummah* is an order of humans consisting of a tripartite consensus of mind, heart, and arm. There is consensus in their thought, in their decision, in their attitude and character, and in their arms. It is a universal brotherhood which knows neither color nor ethnic identity. In its purview, all men are one, measurable only in terms of piety.[42] If any one of its members acquires a new knowledge, his duty is to teach it to the others. If any one acquires food or comfort, his duty is to share them with the others. If any one achieves establishment, success, and prosperity, his duty is to help the others do likewise.[43]

There is hence no *tawḥīd* without the *ummah.* The *ummah* is the medium of knowledge, of ethics, of the caliphate (vice-gerency) of man, of world-affirmation. The *ummah* is a universal order comprehending even those who are not believers. It is an order of peace, a *Pax Islamica,* forever open to all those individuals and groups who accept the principle of the freedom to convince and to be convinced of the truth, who seek a world order in which ideas, goods, wealth, or human bodies are free to move. The *Pax Islamica* is an international order far surpassing the United Nations, that child of yesteryear, aborted and warped by the principles of the nation-state and the dominion of the "big powers," both of which are constitutive of it. These principles are, in turn, based upon "national sovereignty" as it has evolved in the ideological history of Europe since the Reformation and the demise of the ideal of the universal community the Church had so far half-heartedly carried. But national sovereignty is ultimately based on axiological and ethical relativism.

The United Nations is successful if it fulfills the negative role of preventing or stopping war between the members. Even then, it is an impotent order since it has no army except when the Security Council's "big power" members agree to provide it ad hoc. *Per contra,* the *Pax Islamica* was laid down in a permanent constitution by the Prophet in Madīnah in the first days of the *Hijrah.* He made it inclusive of the

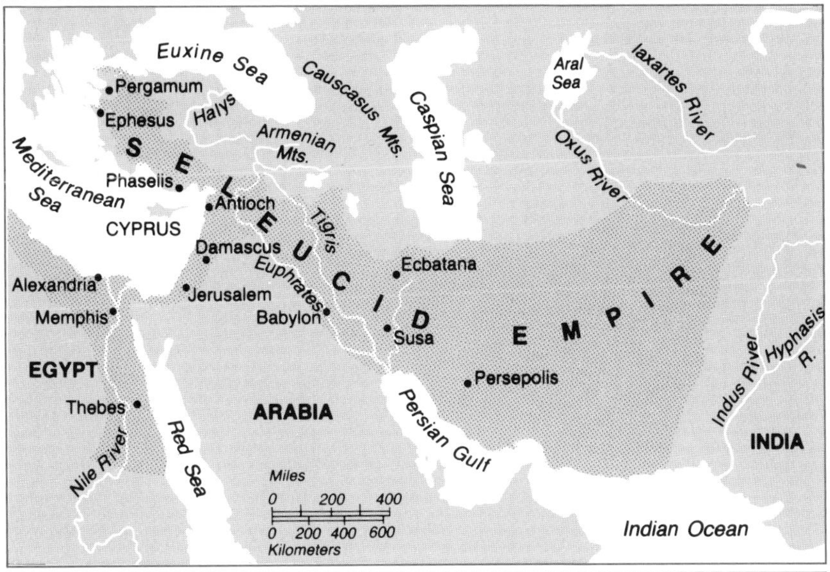

Map 16C. The Seleuci Empire

Jews of Madīnah and the Christians of Najrān, guaranteeing to them their identity and their religious, social, and cultural institutions. History knows of no other written constitution that has honored the minorities as the constitution of the Islamic state has done. The constitution of Madīnah has been in force in the various Islamic states for fourteen centuries and has resisted dictators and revolutions of all kinds—including Genghis Khān and Hulagu!

The *ummah* then is a world order in addition to being a social order. It is the basis of Islamic civilization, its *sine qua non.* In their representation of human reason in the person and career of Ḥayy ibn Yaqẓān, philosophers had discovered that Ḥayy had by his own effort grown to the point of discovering the truth of Islam, and of *tawḥīd,* its essence. But having done so, Ḥayy had to invent or discover the *ummah.* He therefore made for himself a canoe out of a hollowed trunk and set forth on the unknown ocean, to discover the *ummah* without which all of his knowledge would not cohere with the truth.

Tawḥīd is, in short, *ummatism.*

Tawḥīd as first principle of aesthetics. *Tawḥīd* means to exclude the Godhead from the whole realm of nature. Everything that is in or of creation is a creature, nontranscendent, subject to the laws of space and time. Nothing of it can be God or godly in any sense, especially the ontological which *tawḥīd,* as the essence of monotheism, denies. God is the totally other than creation, totally other than nature, and hence, transcendent. He is the only transcendent being. *Tawḥīd* further asserts that nothing is like unto Him,[44] and hence, that nothing in creation can be a likeness or symbol for God, nothing can represent Him. Indeed, He is by definition beyond

Illustration 4.7

Mosque of Ẓāhir in Alor Star, Malaysia. [Photo by L. al Fārūqī.]

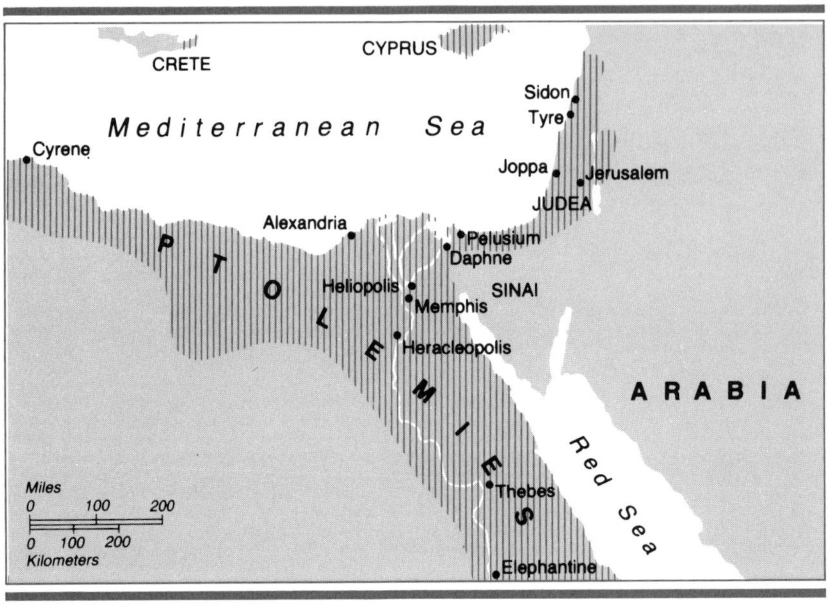

Map 16D. The Ptolemaic State

representation. God is He Whom no aesthetic intuition whatever is possible.

By aesthetic experience is meant the experience through the senses, of an a priori, metanatural essence that acts as the normative principle of the object beheld. It is what the object ought to be. The nearer the visible object is to that essence, the more beautiful it is. In the case of living nature, of plant, animal, and especially man, the beautiful is that which comes as close to the a priori essence as possible, so that whoever is capable of judging would be right in holding that in the aesthetic object nature has articulated itself eloquently, clearly; that the beautiful object is what nature meant to say, as it does so rarely among its thousand-and-one shortcomings. Art is the process of discovering within nature that metanatural essence and representing it in visible form. Evidently, art is not the imitation of created nature; nor is it the sensory representation of *natura naturata,* the objects whose "naturing" or natural reality is complete. A photographic representation may be valuable for illustration or documentation, for the establishment of identity. As a work of art, it is worthless. Art is the reading in nature of an essence that is nonnature, and the giving to that essence of the visible form that is proper to it.

As it has been defined and analyzed so far, art is necessarily the presumption to find in nature that which is not of it. But that which is not of nature is transcendent; and only that which is divine qualifies for this status. Moreover, since the a priori essence which is the object of aesthetic appreciation is normative and beautiful, man's emotions are especially affected by it. That is why humans love the beautiful and are determined by it. Where they see the beautiful in human nature, the a priori metanatural essence is humanness idealized to a transcendent degree. This is exactly what the Greeks called *apotheosis,* or the transfiguration of a human into divinity. Humans are particularly prone to adore such transfigured humans and regard them as gods. Modern Western man has little tolerance for any deity as far as metaphysics is concerned. But as far as ethics and conduct are concerned, the "gods" that he creates out of his idealization of human passions and tendencies are the real determinants of his action.

This explains why among the ancient Greeks the arts of representing the gods as apotheoses of human elements, qualities, or passions, visually as in sculpture and imaginatively as in poetry and drama, were the foremost aesthetic pursuits. The objects they represented—the gods—were beautiful because they were idealizations of what human nature ought to be. Their beauty did not hide the innate conflict of each with the other gods, precisely because each was the real object of nature absolutized to its divine, supernatural level.

It was only in Rome, the theater of Greek decadence, that the supreme Greek art of sculpture degenerated into realistic, empirical portraiture of the various emperors. Even there, however, this would not have been possible without the deification of the emperor. In Greece, where the theory remained pure for centuries, the art of drama developed alongside that of sculpture precisely in order to represent the eternal conflicts of the gods with one another by means of an unfolding of a series of events in which the characters were involved. The overall purpose was the representation of their individual characters which the spectators knew were human, all too human, but which were the source of immense delight. If the dramatic events unfolding before their eyes led to a tragic end, this was regarded as necessary and innate. Its necessity removed its sting and through catharsis it helped remove from them the guilt they felt at their immoral affirmations and pursuits. That is why the art of tragedy, born and perfected in Greece, was the apex of the literary arts as well as of all the humanities. In a rare statement of truth, the Orientalist G. E. von Grunebaum said that Islam had no figurative arts (sculpture, painting, and drama) because it is free of any gods incarnated or immanent in nature, gods whose activities conflict with one another or with evil.[45] Von Grunebaum meant it as a reproach to Islam, though it is in reality Islam's prime distinction. For it is the unique glory of Islam that it is absolutely free of idolatry, of the mistaking of the creature for the Creator. However, the statement remains true; for it shows the intimate relation between the figurative arts, the pagan reli-

Illustration 4.8

Mosque of Sulṭān Aḥmad, Isṭanbūl. [Courtesy Embassy of Turkey, Washington, D.C.]

Illustration 4.9

Nigerians standing for *ṣalāt.* [Courtesy A. R. Doi.]

gions of antiquity, and the incarnational theology of the West.

The Jews had previously asserted that the transcendence of God precluded any making of "graven images," and committed themselves, in obedience to that divine commandment, to a whole history of near total withdrawal from any visual art.[46] They produced some minor works only under the influence of Egypt, Greece and Rome, and Christendom. In modern times, especially since their emancipation under Napoleon and assimilation into Western culture, they have abjured their original Semitic position for the naturalism of the West.

Tawḥīd is not against artistic creativity; nor is it against the enjoyment of beauty. On the contrary, *tawḥīd* blesses the beautiful and promotes it. It sees absolute beauty only in God and in His revealed will or words. Accordingly, it was prone to create a new art befitting its view. Starting from the premise that there is no God but God, the Muslim artist was convinced that nothing in nature may represent or express God. Through stylization, he removed every object as far as possible from nature. Indeed, the object of nature was thereby so far removed from nature that it became almost unrecognizable. In his hand, stylization was a negational instrument by which he said No! to every natural thing, to creation itself. By denying its naturalness altogether, the Muslim artist expressed in visible form the negative judgment that there is no God but God. This *shahādah* (witness) of the Muslim artist is indeed the equivalent of the denial of transcendence in nature.

The Muslim artist did not stop there. His creative breakthrough came when it dawned on him that to express God in a figure of nature is one thing, and to express His inexpressibility in such a figure is another. To realize that God—May He be glorified in His transcendence—is visually inexpressible, is the highest aesthetic objective possible for man. God is the absolute, the sublime. To judge Him unrepresentable by anything in creation is to hold His absoluteness and sublimeness seriously. To behold Him in one's imagination as unlike all that is in creation is to behold Him as "beautiful—unlike any other object that is beautiful." Divine inexpressibility is a divine attribute, whose meaning is infinity, absoluteness, ultimacy or nonconditionedness, limitlessness. The infinite is in every sense the inexpressible.

In pursuit of this line of Islamic thought, the Muslim artist invented the art of decoration and transformed it into the "arabesque," a nondevelopmental design that extends in all directions *ad infinitum.*

The arabesque transfigures the object of nature it decorates — whether textile, metal, vase, wall, ceiling, pillar, window, or page of a book — into a weightless, transparent, floating pattern extending infinitely in all directions. The object of nature is not itself but is "trans-substantiated." It has become only a field of vision. Aesthetically, the object of nature has become under the arabesque treatment a window onto the infinite. To behold it as suggestive of infinity is to recognize one of the meanings of transcendence, the only one given — though only negatively — to sensory representation and intuition.

This explains why most of the works of art produced by Muslims were abstract. Even where figures of plants, animals and humans were used, the artist stylized them in such a way as to deny their creatureliness, to deny that any supernatural essence is resident within them. In this endeavor, the Muslim artist was assisted by his linguistic and literary legacy. To the same end, he developed the Arabic script so as to make of it an infinite arabesque, extending nondevelopmentally in any direction the calligrapher chooses. The same is true of the Muslim architect whose building is an arabesque in its façade, elevations, skyline, as well as floor plan. *Tawḥīd* is the one denominator common to all artists whose worldview is that of Islam, however geographically or ethnically separate they may be.[47]

Map 16E. The Eastern Roman Empire

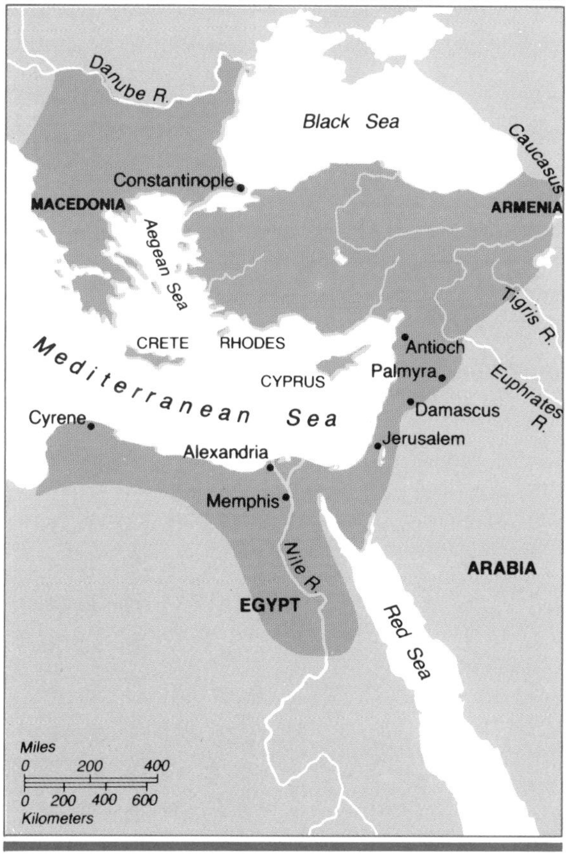

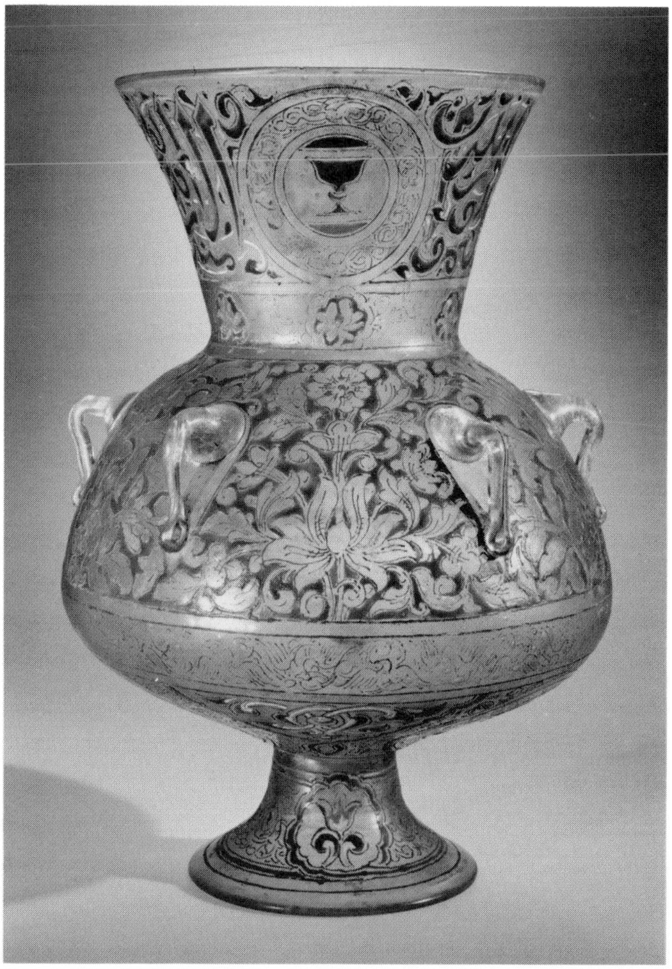

Illustration 4.10

Mosque lamp, Syria, c. 1355 C.E. [Courtesy The Corning Museum of Glass.]

NOTES

1. See my refutation of the Orientalists who raise doubt that Islam has an essence or that it is known or knowable, in "The Essence of Religious Experience in Islām," *Numen,* 20 (1973), pp. 186–201.

2. In this regard, *tawḥīd* distinguishes itself from Sufism and some sects of Hinduism, where the reality of the world

is dissolved into God, and God becomes the only reality, the only existent. In this view, nothing really exists except God. Everything is an illusion; and its existence is unreal. *Tawḥīd* equally contradicts the ancient Egyptian, Greek, and Taoist views that run in a direction diametrically opposed to that of India. In that view, the Creator's existence is dissolved into that of creation or the world. Whereas Egypt maintained that God is indeed Pharaoh, and the green grass blade rising from earth in the spring, and the Nile River with its water and bed, and the disc of the sun with its warmth and light, Greco-Roman antiquity maintained that God is any aspect of human nature or personality magnified to a degree that places it above nature in one sense but keeps it immanent in nature in another. In either case, the Creator is con-fused with His creation. Under the influence of its priesthood, Christianity separated itself from *tawḥīd* when it claimed that God incarnated Himself in the body of Jesus and asserted that Jesus is God. It is Islam's unique distinction that it emphasized the ultimate duality and absolute disparity of God and the world, of Creator and creature. By its clear and uncompromising stand in this matter of divine transcendence, Islam became the quintessence of the tradition of Semitic prophecy, occupying the golden mean between Eastern (Indian) exaggerationism, which denies nature, and Western (Greek and Egyptian) exaggerationism, which denies God as other.

3. This principle points to the absolute ontological separation of God and man, to the impossibility of their union through incarnation, deification or fusion. The principle, however, does not deny the possibility of communication between them. In fact, it is inseparable from prophecy, or the communication by God to man of a commandment which man is expected to obey. Nor does it rule out the possibility of communication through intellect or intuition, as when man observes the creatures, ponders their whither and why, and concludes that they must have a creator, designer, and sustainer Who deserves to be heeded. This is the avenue of ideation or reasoning. In the final analysis, it is this principle of ontic separation of God and the world that distinguishes *tawḥīd* from all theories that apotheosize man or humanize God, whether Greek, Roman, Hindu, Buddhist, or Christian.

4. As the verses 3:191 and 23:116 indicate.

5. As contained in the verses 7:15; 10:5; 13:9; 15:29; 25:2; 32:9; 38:72; 41:10; 54:49; 65:3; 75:4, 38; 80:19; 82:7; 87:2–3.

6. Qur'ān 17:77; 33:62; 35:43; 48:23; 65:3.

7. Any deed that is done "by nature" is *ipso facto* amoral, deserving neither reward nor punishment. Examples are breathing, digestion, or an act of charity or injustice entered into under coercion. It is completely otherwise with the act entered into in freedom, with the possibility of its author doing or not doing it, or doing some other act beside it.

8. This is attested by the verses that speak of the perfection of God's creation (see notes 4, 5 above), and those that stress man's moral obligation and responsibility. The latter are too numerous to count.

9. This is the meaning implied in the verses that speak of the subservience of creation to man, namely, 13:2; 14:32–33; 16:12, 14; 22:36–37, 65; 29:61; 31:20, 29; 35:13; 38:18; 39:5; 43:13; 45:11–12.

10. As the ubiquitous emphases of moral obligation in the Qur'ān indicate.

11. The verses dealing with the Final Judgment are very numerous, and there is no need to cite them all; some examples: man will not be left alone without reckoning (75:36), but will be brought to account by God (88:26, 4:85).

12. God prohibited man from doubting his fellows in 4:156; 6:116, 148; 10:26, 66; 49:12; 53:23, 28.

13. This Greek term has no equivalent in Arabic, which illustrates the difference between the minds behind the two languages. The Greek term refers to an irrational dogma adhered to by the Christian.

14. The philosophers have raised reason above revelation and have given it priority status when judging religious claims. Certainly they are wrong in doing so. The Islamic thinker is certainly capable of defining reason differently and to use his definition as premise of all other claims. The question of validity of either definition may certainly be raised, and we have no doubt regarding the philosophic viability, or reasonableness—nay, superiority!—of the Islamic definition. The definition given here, that rationalism is the rejection of ultimate self-contradiction, has, in addition, the value of continuing the tradition of the righteous fathers.

15. Evidence for this can be found in the verses questioning arbitrary prohibition, e.g., 5:90; 7:13; 66:1, as well as the *uṣūlī* (juristic) principle agreed upon by all that "Nothing is *ḥarām* (prohibited) except by a text." Consider also the verse, "God has indeed detailed for you what He has prohibited" (6:119, 153).

16. Qur'ān 6:42; 12:109; 13:40; 14:4; 15:9; 16:43; 17:77; 21:7, 25; 23:44; 25:20; 30:47; 37:72; 40:70.

17. Ibid., 4:162; 35:23. "We have sent before you [Muḥammad] no prophet but We revealed to him that there is no God other than Me. Adore and serve Me."

18. Ibid., 30:30.

19. Ibid., 94:6.

20. Ibid., 49:6.

21. See below, Chapter 14.

22. The natural sciences did not develop until the principle was accepted that natural events constantly follow the same immutable laws. That is precisely what Islam has contributed for the development of natural science among its adherents. Its insistence on the orderliness of the cosmos under God provided the atmosphere necessary for the growth of the scientific spirit. The opposite faith, namely, that nature has no constancy but is the field of action of arbitrary deities incarnated therein, or of magical forces manipulating it, can lead to no science.

23. Unlike history, which studies a particular event and analyzes it into its individual constituents and establishes their mutual relations, the natural sciences are concerned with the general pattern, the universal law applicable to all

particulars of a given class, or to all members of a class, or to all classes.

24. The same is true of the social sciences and the humanities where the object is the establishment of the laws governing or determining human behavior, individual or collective.

25. In accordance with the verse, "And I have not created jinn or humans but to worship and serve Me" (Qur'ān 51:56).

26. As in ibid., 2:30; 6:165; 10:14.

27. Ibid., 33:72.

28. As in ibid., 15:29; 21:91; 38:72; 66:12.

29. To use the term of St. Augustine.

30. Qur'ān 11:7; 18:7; 47:31; 67:2.

31. Ibid., 9:95, 106.

32. Ibid., 99:7–8; 101:6, 11.

33. Ibid., 11:61.

34. Ibid., 2:57, 172; 5:90; 7:31, 159; 20:81; 67:15; 92:10.

35. As God had said in the Qur'ān, "You may penetrate the regions of heaven and earth if you can. You will not do so except with power and authority" (55:33).

36. Qur'ān 57:27. Indeed, we stand under the divine commandment, "And do not forsake your share of this world" (28:77). God taught humans to pray to Him that they "may be granted advantage in this world as well as in the next" (2:201; 7:156). Moreover, He assured them that He will answer their prayers if they do the good deeds (16:30; 39:10).

37. Qur'ān 21:92; 23:53.

38. As Sūrah Al 'Aṣr (103) indicates. See also 49:10.

39. Ibid., 3:103.

40. Ibid., 3:110; 5:82; 9:113; 20:54, 128.

41. As God has commanded in the verses 3:32, 132; 4:58; 5:95; 24:54; 47:33; 64:12.

42. As the *ḥadīth* said, quoting the Prophet's farewell sermon on his last pilgrimage. By tripartite consensus we mean the sameness of vision or mind or thinking, the agreement of will or decision and intention, and the agreement of action or human arms.

43. The Prophet likened the Muslims to a well-constructed building whose parts consolidate one another; and to an organic body that reacts in its totality whenever any organ or part of it is attacked.

44. Qur'ān 42:11.

45. For further details of this question, see Isma'īl al Fārūqī, "Islam and Art," *Studia Islamica,* 37 (1973), pp. 81–109.

46. I. R. al Fārūqī, "On the Nature of the Religious Work of Art," *Islam and the Modern Age,* 1 (1970), pp. 68–81.

47. For further reading on the relation of *tawḥīd* to the other arts, see below Chapters 19–23; and Lois Lamya' al Fārūqī, *Aesthetic Experience and the Islamic Arts,* Islamabad: Hijrah Centenary Committee, 1405/1985.

PART THREE
THE FORM

CHAPTER 5

The Qur'ān

DATA REVELATA AND THE HISTORY OF PROPHECY

Revelation, or the communication of God's will to man, has a long history, and has taken various forms. In the earliest times, God, or the being assumed to be divine, revealed his will indirectly through the omens of nature, or directly through visions and dreams, which the priesthood was initiated to decipher and charged to communicate and implement. The *data revelata* were preserved by being committed to memory. They were recalled, recited, or invoked on ceremonial occasions. Some were thus translated into and had become a living tradition; others were forgotten or transformed into something else after the passing of the original recipients of revelation. Naturally, all were subject to forgetfulness, personal interpretation, and the shifting vicissitudes of the needs and conditions of the carriers. Their recording or textualization was late and, at any rate, had to await the invention of writing. The idea that the *verba* of a divine message is holy and hence object of a religious taboo against tampering with it, may be as old as revelation itself. However, the earliest text of a divine message containing a claim of such holiness or taboo — and thus establishing by internal evidence that the promulgators of that message regarded it as such — is the Code of Hammurabi. Its evidence is partly graphic and partly verbal. The former presents Hammurabi in reverential posture before the god of Justice, Shamash, Who hands to him the law. The latter consists in Hammurabi's own affirmation that the law was committed to him by the god who remains its ultimate executor and keeper, and the code's threat to those who would tamper with its text.[1] In a passage reflecting the Ḥanīfī tradition of Peninsular Arabia, the Qur'ān refers to *ṣuḥuf* (revealed texts) of Ibrahīm (Abraham).[2] Although archeology has not yet uncovered a physical proof of their existence, it is not unreasonable to assume their existence. Since historians have agreed to place Ibrahīm in the patriarchal age — 2000 – 1400 B.C. — it is likely that he knew how to read and write, and regarded the text of a divine message as reverently as did Hammurabi's contemporaries who were themselves Ibrahīm's compatriots and fellows.[3]

The next claim of this kind is one made on behalf of King Hezekiah who reigned in Judah from 715 to 687 B.C.E. Hezekiah's claim to fame is the reform he achieved, which sought to centralize the cultic observances of the Hebrews, a reform alleged to fulfill a requirement of a Deuteronomic text and hence implying both the existence of the text and its being held

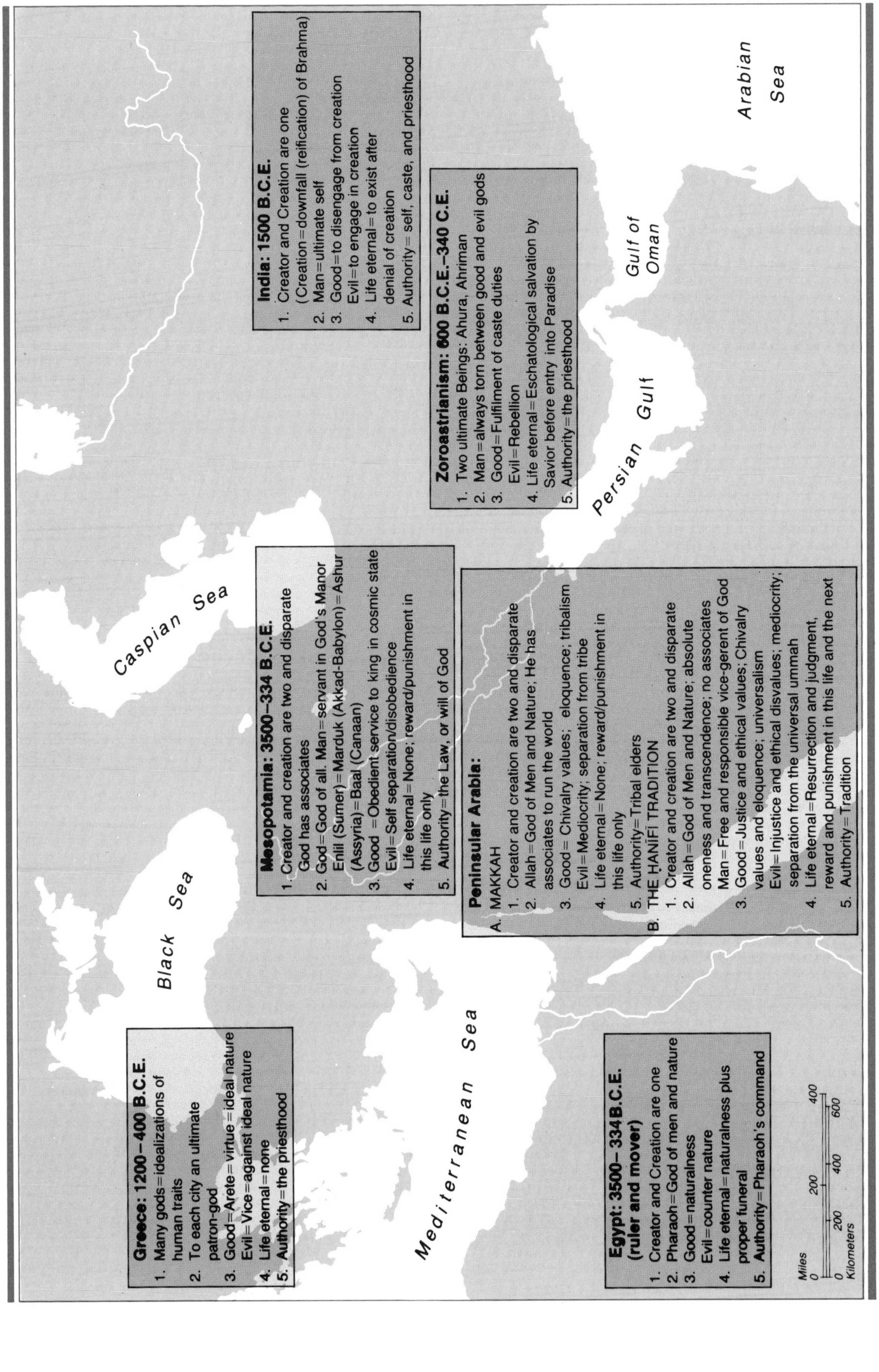
Greece: 1200–400 B.C.E.
1. Many gods=idealizations of human traits
2. To each city an ultimate patron-god
3. Good=Arete=virtue=ideal nature
Evil=Vice=against ideal nature
4. Life eternal=none
5. Authority=the priesthood
Egypt: 3500–334 B.C.E. (ruler and mover)
1. Creator and Creation are one
2. Pharaoh=God of men and nature
3. Good=naturalness
Evil=counter nature
4. Life eternal=naturalness plus proper funeral
5. Authority=Pharaoh's command
Miles 0 200 400
0 200 400 600 Kilometers
Black Sea
Mediterranean Sea
Caspian Sea
Persian Gulf
Gulf of Oman
Arabian Sea
Mesopotamia: 3500–334 B.C.E.
1. Creator and creation are two and disparate God has associates
2. God=God of all. Man=servant in God's Manor
Enlil (Sumer)=Marduk (Akkad-Babylon)=Ashur (Assyria)=Baal (Canaan)
3. Good =Obedient service to king in cosmic state
Evil=Self separation/disobedience
4. Life eternal=None; reward/punishment in this life only
5. Authority=the Law, or will of God
Peninsular Arabia:
A. MAKKAH
1. Creator and creation are two and disparate
2. Allah=God of Men and Nature; He has associates to run the world
3. Good=Chivalry values; eloquence; tribalism
Evil=Mediocrity; separation from tribe
4. Life eternal=None; reward/punishment in this life only
5. Authority=Tribal elders
B. THE ḤANĪFĪ TRADITION
1. Creator and creation are two and disparate
2. Allah=God of Men and Nature; absolute oneness and transcendence; no associates
Man=Free and responsible vice-gerent of God
3. Good=Justice and ethical values; Chivalry values and eloquence; universalism
Evil=Injustice and ethical disvalues; mediocrity; separation from the universal ummah
4. Life eternal=Resurrection and judgment, reward and punishment in this life and the next
5. Authority=Tradition
India: 1500 B.C.E.
1. Creator and Creation are one (Creation=downfall (reification) of Brahma)
2. Man=ultimate self
3. Good=to disengage from creation
Evil=to engage in creation
4. Life eternal=to exist after denial of creation
5. Authority=self, caste, and priesthood
Zoroastrianism: 600 B.C.E.–340 C.E.
1. Two ultimate Beings: Ahura, Ahriman
2. Man=always torn between good and evil gods
3. Good=Fulfilment of caste duties
Evil=Rebellion
4. Life eternal=Eschatological salvation by Savior before entry into Paradise
5. Authority=the priesthood

Map 17. Religion in the Ancient Near East

sacred by the people. However, no law book is even hinted at in connection with that reform.[4] A "book" is indeed mentioned in connection with the reform of a later successor to Hezekiah's throne, Josiah (640–609 B.C.E.), and this constitutes the third claim of its kind (II Kings 22:8). Instructed by the king to bring out the hoard of silver from the Temple's vault to spend it on repairing its walls, Hilkiah, the high priest, found a "book of the law" for which he could not vouch.[5] The king ordered his ministers as well as Hilkiah to go out to the people and ask "all Judah concerning the words of anybody regarding this book" unto which "our fathers have not hearkened." None rose to the bait but a certain Huldah, a "prophetess" of doubtful reputation, seized the occasion to defend the anti-Canaanization, anti-assimilation view of the book which neither king nor high priest ever knew (II Kings 22:11–20). Later, a fourth claim presented itself. "The word of God" which came to Jeremiah was thrown into the fire by King Jehoiakim around 598–597 B.C.E. because it threatened dire punishment for Judah at Babylon's hands (Jeremiah 36:20ff). This did not destroy it because Jeremiah could recite it from memory. However, the redactor of the Book of Jeremiah saw fit to warn the reader that to that very word of God that came to Jeremiah, "there were added besides unto them many like words" (Jeremiah 36:32). Two centuries later, a fifth claim was made when Ezra introduced yet another version of the law of God which scholars classify as P in contrast to the earlier versions of J and E, as well as D, the above-mentioned law book of Josiah, Hilkiah, and Huldah.[6] Throughout the two millennia of pre-Christian history, the Hebrews certainly received numerous revelations. But there is no evidence that they ever agreed upon or kept a text in a way worthy of its divine provenance. It was at the Council of Jamnia (Yibna) in 100 C.E. that a body of old inherited texts, redacted and edited numerous times by unknown persons, was declared holy and hence "defiling the hands" that touched them.[7] Even then, the texts known as "Latter Prophets" and "Writings" were not finally fixed but were to suffer addition. Canonization was a long process in which the Pentateuch was first to be recognized as canonical, followed by the other parts of the corpus.

This development in the texts of revelation was in large part determined by changing attitudes toward the phenomenon of prophecy. In Mesopotamia, the king and the provincial governors he appointed acted as receivers of the messages from Heaven, and as conveyors of its contents to the people. Reverence for the divine was thus joined to reverence for the state and its officers. This reverence never waned but continued regardless of the growth or decline of the state and its power. Although the Hebrews issued from the same Mesopotamian background, they seem to have lapsed into more primitive forms during the centuries following their exodus from Ur. Jacob's stealing the gods of his employer-uncle (Genesis 31:19–22), his wrestling with God-as-ghost near the Jordan River (Genesis 32:24–32), and the intermarriage of the Beni Elohim (literally the sons of gods) with the daughters of men (Genesis 6:2–4)—granted the antiquity of the J and E sources—point to the level of Hebrew popular religiosity in Canaan rather than to the lofty one of their ancestors in Mesopotamia.

Through his association with Jethro, High Priest of Midyan, Moses, who grew up as an Egyptian in religion and culture, quickly undid his upbringing and recaptured his Mesopotamian inheritance. He saw God as speaking to him directly in a message containing the essentials of the law, not unlike Hammurabi. However, as the Hebrews and their colleagues, the Amphictyonites who rallied with and accompanied them in their drive toward Canaan, settled there, they returned to the Canaanite practices they had learned before they went to Egypt. In the period of the Judges and down to David (1200–1000 B.C.E.), whole villages practiced prophecy with trumpet and drum and singing and dancing (II Kings 4:1). The whole populace would plunge into an orgy of "prophesying" (I Samuel 10:5, 10; 19:18). Under Samuel, David, and Solomon, the Old Testament evidence shows, prophecy became tame, and the prophets, now turned almost into priests—Samuel, Jeremiah, Ezekiel, and Pashhur were both (Isaiah 8:2; Jeremiah 20:1–6)—invariably advocated the monarchy and its policies like state functionaries. State functionaries they certainly became under David, who used them to voice the plea that his kingdom was God's and his dynasty was eternal. During Solomon's reign dissatisfaction with his policies expressed itself through some dissenting voices critical of the monarchy. After his death, prophecy disengaged itself from the state and established itself as the authoritative autonomous voice of God. For several centuries the prophets relayed to the people divine pronouncements that were critical and often condemnatory of royalty, state policy and administration, and popular religious and social practices. It was in this period that prophecy attained greater heights than were achieved in Mesopotamia. Jeremiah compared the word of God to a ball of fire that cannot be conjured and that, when it comes, can only be passed on with all its integrity. This apogee did not last. Soon prophecy degenerated with the decay of Israel until nobody could differentiate between the true prophet and the false ones who

Illustration 5.1

Calligraphy panel from a contemporary mosque in Kuwait. Central medallion: *Basmalah;* middle circle: Qur'ān 33: 35; outer circle: Qur'ān 91: 1–15. [Courtesy 'Iṣām Tājī.]

were circulating among the Hebrews everywhere by the hundreds.

Jesus came in the midst of this degeneration of the phenomenon of prophecy. Hebrew scripture had already been canonized, and Jesus invoked it on every occasion. Both speaker and audience must have assumed its divine origin and sacredness, its authority and unchangeableness. This notwithstanding, no one of Jesus' disciples, who were all Jews well acquainted with the taboo of a revealed message, revered the new revelation of Jesus enough to commit it to memory or record it. Obviously, this could not be expected of his detractors and enemies, or generally of the unbelievers. But the strange fact is equally true of his believing followers. A few anecdotes from his life, coupled with a few of the parables he taught, some proverbs and common sayings he quoted along with his recollection of some passages of Hebrew scripture, are all that survived of his message. Nothing of this was kept in the original tongue Jesus spoke, namely Aramaic. All came down filtered through Greek, a tongue alien to Jesus and his audience in its vocabulary as well as its categories of thought. Scholars speak of a "Jewish" or "Palestinian" Christianity battling Hellenic Christianity and the form which the message of Jesus had taken soon after its appearance. The latter triumphed and dominated; and the "Aramaic message" of Jesus disappeared forever.

These circumstances, unfortunate for the historian of the texts of revelation, moved Ibn Ḥazm, the greatest comparativist before modern times and the first textual critic of the Old and New Testaments, to open his analysis of the New Testament with a feeling of relief. "The Torah," he wrote,

> is claimed by its adherents to be the verbatim word of God conveyed by Him to Moses and written down by his own hand. That is why I had to write the foregoing long and assiduous analysis of its text to establish the contrary. Fortunately, no Christian makes this kind of claim regarding the New Testament. All Christians agree that the New Testament text is a composite of works by the four evangelists—Matthew, Mark, Luke, and John—and a number of other writings by humans.[8]

CLIMAX OF THE PHENOMENON OF PROPHECY

In a sense, Hammurabi, Moses, and Jeremiah represent apogees of the phenomenon of prophecy. Each one of them regarded God as revealing to him His will through words which are absolutely His—verbatim—absolutely commanding, imperative, and carrying

Illustration 5.2

Mosque, Ottawa, Canada, completed 1981. [Courtesy 'Abdullah Khandwānī.]

a measure of numinousness to make them at once sacred and unalterable. However, were the three messengers to return to earth today, they would not recognize what is attributed to them as their own. Perhaps Hammurabi alone might recognize the code bearing his name as his own. The text of the code we have comes from a stela that was carried away from Mesopotamia to Susa by raiding Elamites between 1207 amd 1171 B.C.E., more than five centuries after Hammurabi. Whether the stela was a true copy of the original we will never know. Even so, it was disfigured by the Elamites; and the missing parts had to be filled in from still later copies of the code.[9]

Moses and Jeremiah, on the other hand, would be hard put to find in the texts of the Old Testament anything that is in language, form, or content truly their own, communicated by them as the message from Heaven. Not only were the texts of their messages heavily altered by countless collectors and editors, but their very language has long been dead and forgotten. Whatever is attributed to them passed through numerous languages, peoples, and ages, each of which conceived it in its own idiom or language, and molded and repatterned it in different modes of feeling and thinking different from those of the messengers themselves or of their first audiences. Even if the Old Testament is to be trusted in its ascriptions, the real messages of these prophets, like those of all divine messengers before them, lie buried under impenetrable and forever insoluble hermeneutical problems — linguistic, idiomatic, syntactical, formal (lexicographic, grammatical, redactional, stylistic, ideational), structural, and historical.

Illustration 5.4

Spiral minaret of Grand Mosque of Al Mutawakkil, Sāmarrā, Iraq. [Courtesy Joseph P. Metelski.]

Illustration 5.3

Al Rashīd Mosque, Canadian Islamic Centre, Edmonton, Alberta, completed 1982. [Courtesy 'Abdullah Khandwānī.]

We have a completely different case in the message of Muḥammad conveyed in the last two decades before his death in 10/632. Both the Prophethood of Muḥammad and the Qur'ān he conveyed as the message dictated to him by the angel on behalf of God represent the highest and ultimate development of the phenomenon of prophecy. Unlike any prophet before him, were Muḥammad to return today, he would doubtless acknowledge the Qur'ān to be the selfsame text he received from God and conveyed to his companions.

The text has been preserved absolutely intact. Not one jot or tittle has changed. Diacritical marks have been added and the calligraphy has been improved to facilitate its correct reading and recitation. Its parts stand today in exactly the same order in which the Prophet was instructed by the Angel to arrange them. Moreover, the language the Prophet and his contemporaries spoke is still alive. It is read, written, and spoken by the millions. Its grammar, syntax, idioms, literary forms — the media of expression and the constituents of literary beauty — all are still the same as they were in the Prophet's time. All this makes of the Qur'ān a phenomenon of human culture without parallel.

The Qur'ān as Divine *Ipsissima Verba*

The Qur'ān is a text of 114 *suwar* (sing. *sūrah*) or chapters, 6,616 *āyāt* or verses, 77,934 words, and 323,671 letters. It was revealed in Makkah and Madīnah and their environs — hence the characterization of its *suwar* as Makkī or Madanī — several verses at a time. Except for the first few revelations, which took the Prophet Muḥammad completely by surprise, each of the revelations had a situational context to which it spoke. Most of these, if not all, are known to scholars as *asbāb al nuzūl* (the situational causes of revelation). From the first to last, each revelation was first impressed upon the Prophet's memory, who then conveyed the revelations verbatim to his relatives or companions, who memorized and recited them in turn, and finally recorded them in a text. At the end of his life, Muḥammad had about 30,000 contemporaries who had heard and memorized the Qur'ān in whole or in part. Several of them could read and write and had committed the Qur'ān to writing in part or in toto. Certainly, writing materials were crude: leather, bones, stone or wood, cloth, and papyrus.

Map 18. Makkah al Mukarramah at the Time of the Prophet

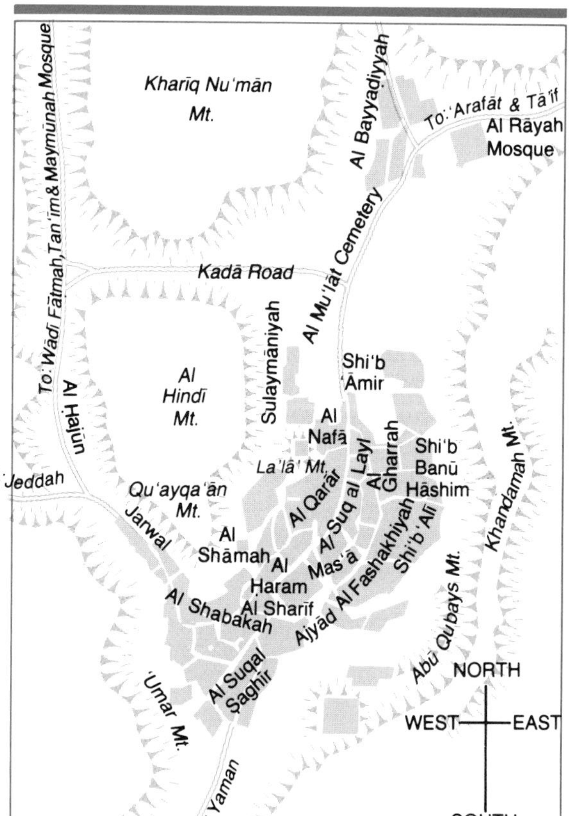

Since revelation of the Qur'ān was a cumulative process over some twenty-three years, the Prophet arranged and rearranged the revelations year by year. This took place during the month of fasting — Ramaḍān — when the Angel Gabriel would instruct the Prophet where to intercalate and include the new passages, and the Prophet would then recite liturgically and publicly all that had been revealed up till then in the new order given to him by the Angel. For fourteen centuries, following this practice of the Prophet, Muslims by the hundreds of thousands have liturgically and publicly recited the Qur'ān from memory. Under Islamic law, recitation of the Qur'ān in *ṣalāt* — the ritual of worship — may not be interrupted except by loss of ritual purity or death; but it can and should be interrupted in case of error in the recitation. In that case any other worshipper may raise his voice with the correct recitation of the misread, omitted, or mispronounced passage.

The Qur'ān was also committed to writing. Being illiterate, the Prophet engaged a scribe to write down the revelation. Many others wrote it down as well. In the year Muḥammad died, all the revelations written by the Prophet's scribe were collected and stored in the house of 'Ā'ishah, the Prophet's wife and daughter of Abū Bakr, the first khalīfah (caliph). Twelve years later, as many non-Peninsular Arabs and non-Arabic-speaking peoples converted to Islam and recited the Qur'ān with some mistakes, the Prophet's scribe was ordered to head a commission of the Prophet's literate companions, of those who were most able in memory, to prepare a written text of the Qur'ān. This was completed within the year, and several copies were made and distributed. One of these old copies is extant and is kept in Bukhārā. Except for the diacritical marks and some improvements of orthography and calligraphy, the Qur'ān extant in every Muslim home around the world today, or kept and recited from memory by the millions, is identical to the material that was recited and conveyed by the Prophet to his companions fourteen centuries ago.

There is no history of the text of the Qur'ān. Nor can there be one other than that which traces the

Illustration 5.5
Mosque of Sulaymān the Magnificent, Iṣtanbūl, Turkey. [Photo by L. al Fārūqī.]

shape and use of diacritical marks and calligraphic forms. Some Orientalists have misunderstood the fact that a few words of the Qur'ān could be read with slightly differing accentuation, or replaced by others of the same length, construction, and, in most cases, meaning. These variants of recitation were authorized by the Prophet himself, and were kept as exegetical footnotes in commentaries, or passed from generation to generation as a *qirā'ah* or "recitation tradition." These variants affect neither the form nor the substance nor meaning of the Qur'ān. They exist at all because they were tolerated by the Prophet, who may have authorized a variant pronunciation because it agreed with the reciter's tribal or local linguistic tradition. Muslims agree that the Qur'ān was revealed in the linguistic tradition of Quraysh, the dominant tribe of Makkah. That is why the Quraysh recitation is basic, and the others are tolerated and included in footnotes and commentaries for use by the interested. None of this warrants the appellation "history."[10] Other Orientalists have investigated the problem and have concluded with William Muir that "we might beyond the strongest presumption affirm that every verse in the Kor'an is the genuine and unaltered composition of Muhammad himself, and conclude with at least a close approximation to the verdict of von Hammer that we hold the Kor'an to be as surely Muhammad's word, as the Muhammadans hold it to be the word of God."[11] Thus, accordance between the judgment of history and scholarship, on one side, and the pronouncement of faith, on the other, is complete and total. The historicity and integrity of the text of the Qur'ān stands absolutely beyond question.

Muḥammad proclaimed, and the Qur'ān (7:156–57) confirmed, what his contemporaries already knew, namely, that he was illiterate, and could not have composed the Qur'ān. The words and verses of the Qur'ān must have come to him from an outside source, which revelation identified as the Angel Jibrīl (Gabriel), the messenger from heaven. Thus Muslims believe the Qur'ān to be verbatim revelation. The

Prophet's consciousness was the recipient, a passive patient that suffered the divine words to be indelibly impressed upon it. "The prophet as tape-recorder" is a theory of prophecy which Jeremiah proclaimed for the first time in the history of the Hebrew prophets and which Islam seconded and fulfilled par excellence.[12] The very word of God is "put in the mouth" of the prophet.[13] It is like a "ball of fire" which, having come, cannot but be conveyed by the prophet to the people in all its power and holiness.[14] In vain did Jeremiah warn against those who "stole" the word of God, tampered with it, or those who would "use their tongues and say, He saith."[15] In an identical, yet more emphatic vein, the Qur'ān proclaimed: "The Qur'ān is but a revelation, sent down as such by Us. . . . We have revealed it in Arabic . . . in the Arabic tongue, clear and precise. . . . As We recite it, you [Muḥammad] shall follow Our recitation of it. . . . Do not seek to bring revelation to yourself. . . . Had the Prophet ascribed to Us anything which We did not reveal, We would have seized him with power and cut off the arteries of his heart."[16]

The Muslims took the revelation in dead earnest. They regarded the Qur'ān holy and divine both in its meaning-content and in its language and form. They held it in the highest honor possible. To express their esteem of it, they invented the arts of Arabic calligraphy, manuscript illumination, and book-making, arts that gave to humanity its noblest and richest creations in the visible aesthetics of the word.[17]

Illustration 5.6

Grand Mosque of Dimashq, interior mosaic decoration, early eighth century C.E. [Courtesy 'Iṣām Khalīfah.]

Illustration 5.7

Plaited Kūfī script *(Basmalah)*. [Photo by L. al Fārūqī.]

Earlier revelations in the Semitic stream of history were codes of law composed in mundane and practical prose. The later revelations were narrations and exhortations to piety and virtue, but were similarly composed in plain common-sensical style. The Hebrew Old Testament contains many passages of exquisite literary beauty. But no one who believes in the divine source of the Hebrew Bible has rested his claim for its divinity on its literary beauty. On the contrary, appreciation of any literary beauty was a consequence of faith in the text's divine origin. The same dependence of beauty upon faith characterizes the Christian view that the Bible — whether Hebrew, Greek, or English — is the word of God. When faith in the divine origin is absent, or when "divine origin" is understood as meaning inspiration not unlike the inspiration of human genius in poetry and letters, the common view is that the King James version, with its Elizabethan penchant for flowery language and rhymed prose, has added considerably to the literary beauty of the Hebrew Bible.

The case of the Qur'ān is the reverse of that of the Bible. Without a doubt, the Qur'ān is beautiful, indeed, the most beautiful literary composition the Arabic language has ever known. Its beauty, however, is not the consequence of faith but its very cause. The aesthetic judgment — that the Qur'ān is beautiful, nay, sublime — is not a pronouncement of faith. It is a critical judgment, reached through literary analysis. Hence, its beauty is not only held by Muslims but also by non-Muslims conversant with the literary aesthetics of the Arabic language. Instead of beauty depending upon the divine origin and flowing out of faith in that origin, the divine origin of the Qur'ān is the reasoned consequence of its literary beauty. Beauty is the cause and evidence for its divine origin. Islam is unique among the religions of humankind in that it rests the veracity of its scripture (the claim that it is revelation) on the fact of its sublime beauty. It trusts the judgment of the critical mind, familiar with Arabic literary beauty, to acquiesce unconditionally to the Qur'ānic claim upon presentation.

Indeed, this was the argument raging between the Prophet and his opponents in Makkah. The Prophet called upon them to abandon the false gods of Makkah and the debauched style of life of its people, and claimed for his call the very authority of God. It is God Himself, the Prophet claimed, Who sent the revelation commanding this radical change. Reluctant to forsake their gods, to abandon their traditions and alter their customs, the Makkans resisted. They denied the authority of the new teaching, alleging that rather than God, the source and author of the Qur'ān

Illustration 5.8

Calligraphy design, Kūfī script, sixteenth century C.E., written in gold and black ink. The text is Qur'ān 112: 1–4. [Photo by L. al Fārūqī.]

بسم الله الرحمن الرحيم
المغضوب عليهم ولا الضالين

Illustration 5.9

Page of a Qur'ān, Muḥaqqaq script, copied for Sulaymān the Magnificent in the sixteenth century C.E. Opening ***sūrah,*** "Al Fātiḥah" (The Opener). This page comes from a copy of the Qur'ān preserved in the Topkapi Saray Museum, Isṭanbūl. [Courtesy Research Center for Islamic History, Art, and Culture, Isṭanbūl.]

was Muḥammad or some teacher from whom the Prophet borrowed these words. The so-called word of God or revelation was not divine but human, all too human, and hence devoid of commanding authority. What proof did Muḥammad have that it was divine? Could he produce a miracle such as Moses and Jesus had performed?[18] The Qur'ān answered them that he was unable, that he commanded no superhuman power, and that in the process of revelation, he was a passive patient receiving what was given by the divine source.[19] The proof that the Qur'ān was the word of God devolved upon the Qur'ān itself. It constituted its own proof by its inimitability, its superior beauty, and its moving appeal which no human composition can match. Thus, the Prophet seems to have argued, with

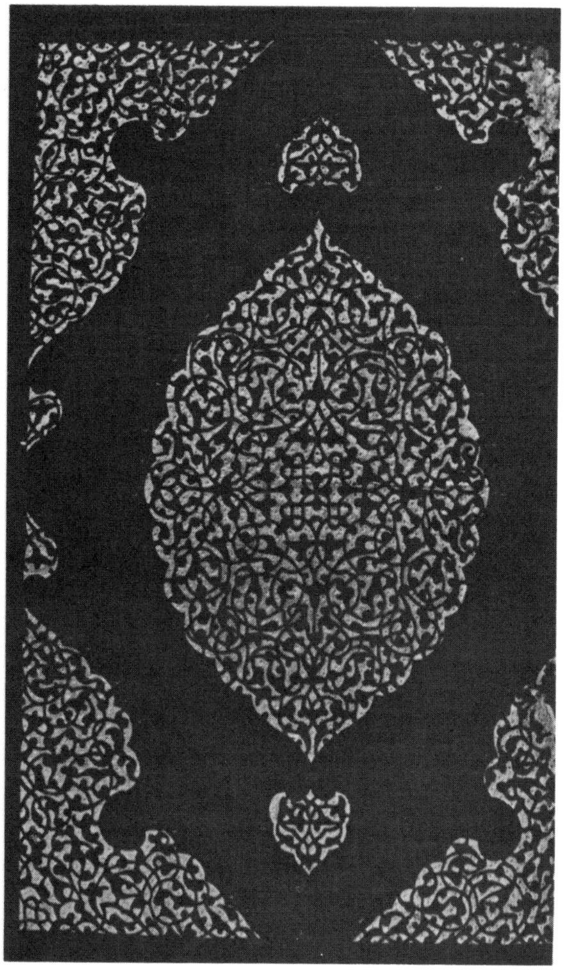

Illustration 5.10

Leather-tooled Qur'ān cover, held in the Library of Sulaymāniyyah Complex, Iṣtanbūl. Dated 1025/1616. [Courtesy Ministry of Culture and Tourism, Government of Turkey.]

the revelation's own backing, that the Qur'ān is divine because it is beautiful. The veracity of Muḥammad, of his call or religion, as well as that of its supporting base, the Qur'ān—that the Qur'ān is indeed revelation from God—hung by a single thread, namely, the beauty of the Qur'ānic text. The Qur'ān, Muḥammad claimed with Qur'ānic approval, indeed dictation, is so beautiful that it is inimitable; it is so inimitable that it is miraculous. It is therefore not the work of humans but of God. This character of the Qur'ān is called its *i'jāz.*

The opponents of the Prophet in Makkah sought to repudiate the claim of this inimitability, and to affirm that the Qur'ān was a human product that could be imitated and even surpassed. The Qur'ān provoked this defiance further by inviting the opponents to produce a similar book,[20] ten *suwar* like any in the Qur'ān.[21] But none would rise to the bait, despite the fact that the Arabs regarded themselves the pinnacles of poetry and literary eloquence, and the Makkans, the very head of that pinnacle. The Qur'ān reduced the challenge, asking them to produce even one *sūrah* like any of the Qur'ān whose short *suwar* had fewer than thirty words, and inviting them to bring their own gods to help.[22] The terrible struggle which the Makkans waged against Muḥammad, with all its cost in blood and injury, in tribal division and hatred, in economic hardship, in its threat to Makkah's leadership of Arabia, could have been stopped and finished by a Makkan victory if they could only compose a few verses that would equal or surpass the Qur'ān in literary beauty and eloquence.

If the Makkan poets and literati were frightened by the prospect of such competition, Makkan leadership was not. Poets and men of letters from all over Arabia were called to the rescue and were promised the greatest prizes for their compositions. One of them, al Walīd ibn al Mughīrah, listened to the Qur'ān recited by the Prophet and felt admiration for it. Abū Jahl, the Makkan leader, approached him to bolster his resistance and promised him the wealth of Makkah. Al Walīd listened again to the Qur'ān and spoke out without hesitation: "I am the first connoisseur of poetry and letters in Arabia, and I speak with unquestionable authority. This Qur'ān is not the work of humans, nor of *jinn.* It has a very special beauty, a very special ring. It is replete with light and beauty, surpassing everything known." Abū Jahl insisted still more. Under pressure, al Walīd finally declared that the Qur'ān was extraordinary but human, the work of magic, not God; but that it was inimitable just as the Prophet had claimed.[23] Other poets and contenders presented their compositions as well, only to be declared failing by one another and their own sponsors. By its words, the Qur'ān wielded an awesome power, fascinating, shattering, composing, and moving. Whatever their predicament or social position, those who heard it and apprehended its meanings fell prostrate before the divine presence it signified.

The Freezing of the Arabic Language and of Its Categories

Being the verbatim word of God, the Qur'ān was the object of the greatest veneration by Muslims. It signified the divine presence itself and commanded the greatest honor. The first and perennial duty of every Muslim was to appropriate it. To memorize it, to recite its verses, to analyze its sentences and grasp their meanings—these were for the Muslim the deeds with the greatest merit. The non-Arabic-speaking converts to Islam applied themselves to learning Arabic with all the earnestness of which they were capable. Many of them mastered it better than the Arabs. Too numerous to count were the non-Arab poets, prose writers, critics, and men of letters who stood at the pinnacle of Arabic literary achievement. And many more were those who contributed in major and significant ways to the elaboration and establishment of Arabic grammar, syntax, lexicography, and literary criticism. Without them, the Arabic legacy would not be itself. The Muslim Arabs, for their part, found the propagation of their mother tongue a great blessing and honor conferred upon them by the advent of Islam. To belong to the people of Muḥammad, to speak his tongue, to think in the language of the Qur'ān was an honor they guarded most avidly. To be closer to Arabic and hence to the Qur'ān meant for all Muslims to be closer to God. This caused the Muslims to preserve Arabic, to make it the language of daily discourse in order to maintain and increase their familiarity with its idioms, its figures of speech, its eloquence, the more to appreciate the beauty of the Qur'ān.

The fact that the Qur'ān was assumed to be the very word of God produced another very grave and significant result. Since the Qur'ānic word is divine, it is eternal and cannot change. Muslims may not allow their usage of it to change. Otherwise, the cumulative effect of change would alienate them from the Qur'ān to the point of rendering it liable to misunderstanding. The Qur'ānic words should be attached to their meanings forever if they are to be eternal. Otherwise, they would be dated human conventions that become obsolete as soon as their meanings shift in the flux of time and space. Rather than conveying something eternal, they would then point to something that once was and is no more. They would lose their normativeness, as human interest in them becomes academic and historical.

This issue was at the root of the controversy that raged under al Ma'mūn (197–217/813–833) when he appointed Ibn Abū Du'ād as chief justice. That jurist belonged to the Mu'tazilah school, which held the Qur'ān to be the created word of God because it feared that the contrary (namely that the Qur'ān is the eternal word of God) would compromise the divine unity. Ibn Abū Du'ād used his position to promote this view, and he was opposed by Aḥmad Ibn Ḥanbal (240/855), who led a popular resistance against the Mu'tazilah position. The opposing populace correctly perceived that to declare the Qur'ān created is to subject it to space and time and all the conditioning of history, to divest it of its holiness and thus to liberate Muslim consciousness from its determining power and normativeness. The upshot was the downfall of the Mu'tazilah school and repudiation of its doctrine. The Qur'ān emerged victorious, and the masses accepted it as uncreated not only in its meaning or content but also in its form, in the Arabic words in which it is composed. Every idea of translating the Qur'ān was laid to rest as every Muslim regarded learning Qur'ānic Arabic as the paramount religious duty. In handling its words and phrases, the Muslim believed he was in contact with the divine.

A third implication of the conviction that the Qur'ān is the word of God was that the Qur'ān objectified all the norms of the Arabic language. The rules of grammar and syntax, of conjugation of words, of literary construction and beauty, in short, all that is con-

Map 19. Al Madīnah al Munawwarah and Vicinity

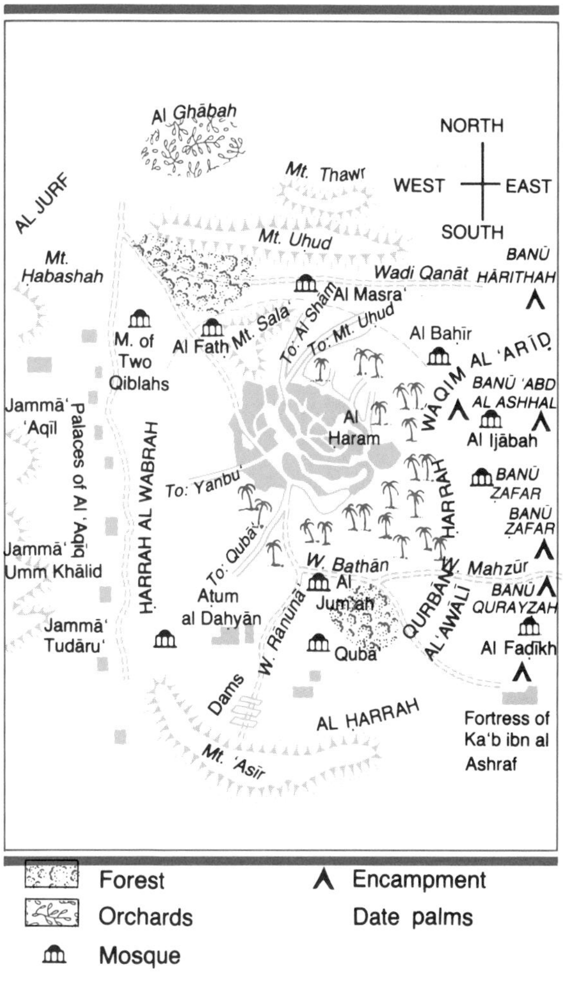

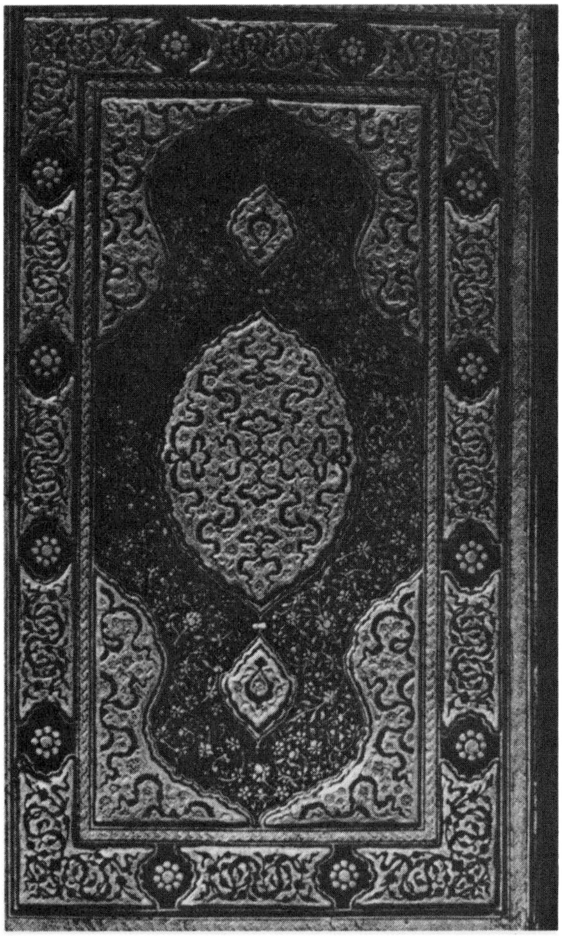

Illustration 5.11

Leather-tooled Qur'ān cover, held in the Library of Sulaymāniyyah Complex, Isṭanbūl. [Courtesy Ministry of Culture and Tourism, Government of Turkey.]

stitutive of the language, was there, concretized in the Qur'ān as it had never been before. It was from the Qur'ān that the Arabist derived his grammar, the linguist his morphology, the poet his figures of speech. It was the standard and norm of all that pertains to Arabic. Some pre-Islamic poetry, common sayings and proverbs, a few narratives of history, or passages of famous oratory survived. Where these deviated from the Qur'ān, the Qur'ānic form overruled. A total coalescence took place between the Qur'ān and the Arabic language. Thus attached to the Qur'ān as its sublime instance, the Arabic language passed beyond the flux of time and became as eternal and unchangeable as the Qur'ān itself, its ideal exemplification. Indeed, the Muslim mind never permitted any separation of the Qur'ān from its Arabic language. Arabic was nothing else besides the language of the Qur'ān. The two were equivalent and convertible since neither was possible without the other. Both remained alive, always co-present and mutually reinforcing each other. To learn the one meant to live and think in the other. To possess and understand the one was to possess and understand the other. Both remained alive as well as interdependent. Arabic could not change. It stood beyond history, beyond change. Its words and lexicography, its structure and order, its forms and norms, all froze and became immune to change. Fourteen centuries after the revelation of the Qur'ān, anyone with an average knowledge of Arabic can understand the Qur'ān as clearly and certainly as its audience did when it was first revealed. Between the Arabic-speaking Muslim and the Qur'ān there can be no ideological gap brought about by change in language or shifting of the categories of thought embedded in it. All those who know the Arabic language stand the same chance of understanding the Qur'ān as the Prophet's contemporaries had done. The only difference between them lies in the extent of one's vocabulary. Given a dictionary, their understandings

Illustration 5.12

Contemporary Kuwait mosque. [Courtesy 'Iṣām Tājī.]

Illustration 5.13

Calligraphy arabesque (Qur'ān 13: 28). [Photo by L. al Fārūqī.]

must be equal if their mastery of Arabic grammar and syntax is assured. That is why understanding of the Qur'ān knows of no hermeneutical problems such as affect the Bible. The only hermeneutic the Qur'ān knows is lexicographic; the only possible question concerns the meaning a given word had at the time of revelation, which the word is then assumed to have had throughout the fourteen centuries.

THE IDEOLOGICAL CONTENT OF THE QUR'ĀN

The "How" and "What" of Revelation

The Islamic revelation described itself as a message defining *"al Dīn"* or "the definitive religion." It presented its principal idea or essence, namely *tawḥīd,* as the witness of God about Himself.[24] As regards humans, Islam regarded itself as *dīn al fiṭrah,* or "innate" or "natural religion,"[25] the religion God had implanted in humankind as He endowed them with cognitive faculties with which to discern His norms or patterns in all fields of life and activity. The foregoing descriptions imply that Islam was not a new religion but an old one, indeed, the oldest, since God, in His eternity, could not but have the same description of Himself. They also imply that the same religion must have been revealed before Islam. Indeed, it was the religion of all the prophets, the religion God conveyed to Adam when "He taught him the names of things."[26] In relating itself to the previous revelations, the Islamic revelation distinguished itself as one concerned with the norms of religion and ethics, a figurization *in abstracto,* a statement of principles and patterns. Unlike the previous revelations of the Semitic legacy which, as we saw earlier, were revelations of the law, the divine will in prescriptive form, the Islamic revelation focused on principles; and it relegated to man the task of translating them into guides and precepts for daily action and living. These

Illustration 5.14

"Mirrored" calligraphy design (Qur'ān 17: 84). [Photo by L. al Fārūqī.]

guides were designated as *sharī'ah* (law) or *minhāj* (program). The revelation acknowledged, further, that the law is susceptible to change in time and place, conditioned as it must be by the status quo of the addressees. The needs of various societies must determine the nature of the laws they may be expected to observe. The principles of the law and its ends, on the other hand, stand above change and must remain the same throughout creation, since they represent the ultimate purposes of the Creator.

This self-view of the Islamic revelation enabled it to explain the repetition of messages from God in history. The revealed prescriptions of the past were corrupted or outgrown. They had to be superseded by new revelations responsive to the changed needs of their respective societies. That is why every society must have received more than one revelation, each progressively different from the other as far as it addressed specific prescriptions to specific circumstances of a given society, but all of them identical as far as the ultimate purposes of first principles are concerned. Revelation was a process of revocation *(naskh)* of the old law, and promulgation *(tashrī')* of the new. Hence, the succession of the prophets.

The same need for restatement has affected the divine purpose or first principles whenever the message, figurized in a language for the benefit of a specific society, fell into misunderstanding and misinterpretation. This might have been caused by change in language, or the massive migration of people, or both, rendering the meanings of the message unreachable. By suffering change, both the "what" and the "how" of the past divine messages necessitated the repetition of prophecy as God's means of communication with humanity.

The Islamic revelation separated the "what" from the "how." The latter became the prerogative of humans. They were the trustees expected to undertake the elaboration of the law and to maintain its relevance for all times and places by developing it as the varying circumstances of societies dictated. However, if this effort of humans is not to issue eventually in completely different religions, there must be an immutable statement of the core, of religious and ethical principles, which everybody can refer to as the ultimate basis of all legislation. Such a statement is precisely what the Qur'ān purported itself to be. It is the sole and ultimate authority, containing all the first principles of creation, of human life. Unlike the *sharī'ah,* which is subject to change (and necessarily so), the Qur'ān was meant to provide continuity and identity. That is why the text of the Qur'ān, as well as the cognitive tools necessary for its understanding (the Arabic language with all its principles and structures, the categories of thought imbedded in it, its words, their forms and meanings) had to be frozen, had to remain the same throughout the centuries. The Qur'ān's view of itself as the verbatim word of God, and the attachment of the Arabic language to the divine word as something inextricable from it, fit well into this overall divine scheme.

Illustration 5.15

The doors of the Ka'bah, Makkah, and its embroidered, calligraphy-design cover. [Photo by L. al Fārūqī.]

Many thinkers have wondered how it came about that all the parts of the divine scheme fitted so well together. Some have speculated that the growth of the Arabic language to its level of perfection and precision, the addiction of the Arabs to the appeal of the word, the fulfillment of their genius in the aesthetics of poetry and literary eloquence, were stages in an unfolding *Heilsgeschichte.* The question of the divine choice of placing the definitive revelation in Arabia where the situational context fitted the purpose had been raised and answered in the Qur'ān. "God knows best where to place His message" was the answer of faith. But it is also an item of the faith that God operates through material and situational causes, a fact that legitimizes the above-mentioned speculation as a fallible attempt by humans to grasp more penetratingly the nature of the divine mission.

Ideational Structure

Although the Qur'ān is indeed an ideational figurization of the essence of Islam couched in sublime Arabic form, not every word of its text pertains to that essence in the same degree and belongs, as it were, on the same level of priority. Disparity of importance between its constitutive ideational elements is due in part to its comprehensiveness. "We have not left out anything in this Book" (Qur'ān 6:38). If the book is to include everything, it must order them differently because by nature they do not all belong to the same rank. Second, the Qur'ān contains principles of religion and ethics as well as prescriptive legislation for everyday living. Some of these prescriptions have a place in the Qur'ān because of the capital importance of their content for the overall divine plan. These are the "Qur'ānic laws of marriage and divorce, of dependence and inheritance. They govern the family, an institution which Islām treats with a seriousness as if it were of the essence of human life. Since human life is not possible without the institution of the family, the regulations governing its formation and dissolution, its proper development and functioning, its growth and felicity, are equally of the essence. Other Qur'ānic laws were given as illustrative of the legislation to be made by man on the basis of Qur'ān-given principles. Such are the laws pertaining to the organization of society. That society and social order and human relations must be ordered in justice and equity to all is of the essence. But the forms social order may take can and do vary. The Qur'ān's pronouncements in this regard are conditionally normative, in contrast to those first principles such as *tawḥīd,* justice, human freedom and responsibility, and so on, which are absolute and universal.

One must keep in mind that the Qur'ān does not treat its subject matter systematically. Fulfilling a requisite of the aesthetic sublime in letters, a subject to be examined below, the Qur'ān is a book in which principles and precepts are strewn like a string of pearls that has become unfurled. The ordering of its chapters, and of its verses in the chapters, is not meant to give the Qur'ān a topical structure. The order given by the Prophet on instruction from the Angel, which Muslims have always regarded as essential to the Qur'ān, fulfills the condition of the literary sublime in Arabic and most legacies of Semitic literatures. It is not developmental, not organic; it does not work itself toward a culmination or conclusion at specific points. Rather, it is composed of a series of clusters of verses, each cluster treating a different topic, but constituting a complete unit even if it is only one or two lines. As a whole, the Qur'ān is a book without beginning or end. It can be read or recited by beginning at any verse and stopping at any verse. It is infinite, or rather, a window to the infinite, a window through which the reader can peek at the supernal plenum, the infinite space of values and principles constituting the divine will.[27] Any systematization such as we have attempted in our analysis of the essence of Islam (see Chapter 4) is the outcome of fallible endeavor.

At the very center of the Qur'ān's edifice of ideas stands God, the Absolute, the One, the Transcendent, the Creator, the Cause and Judge of all. His existence, His nature, His will and His creation, His purpose for humanity and His conveyance of that purpose and will through all the prophets including Muḥammad, the last of the prophets, constitute the content of the faith, the *'aqīdah* of Islam.

Surrounding this center of Qur'ānic ideas about the divine being and its relevance to creation is a body of methodological principles governing man's response to divinity. In their sum, these principles establish a worldview constituted by the following:

1. Rationalism or the subjection of all knowledge, including religious knowledge, to the dictates of reason and common sense, the repudiation of myth, of paradox, of ultimately contradictory positions, acqui-

Illustration 5.16

Calligraphy design by Ṣādiqayn (Qur'ān 55: 26 – 28). [Photo by L. al Fārūqī.]

Illustration 5.17

Young Muslims studying the Qur'ān in Ningxia Autonomous Region, People's Republic of China. [Courtesy Dru Gladney.]

escence to proof and evidence, and openness to further evidence and readiness to alter one's knowledge and attitude according to the demands of new evidence.

2. Humanism, or the doctrine, first, that all humans are born innocent, there being neither original sin nor guilt; second, that they are free to determine their individual destinies since neither matter nor social order can or should restrict their movement or efforts to order their lives in accordance with the best dictates of their own consciences; third, that they are equal before God and the law since no discrimination is legitimate that bases itself upon race, color, language, inherited culture, religion, or inherited social position; fourth, that they are all by nature capable of making judgments of truth and falsehood, of good and evil, of desirableness and its opposite, since without such capacity for judgment and action, neither humanity nor moral merit nor demerit are possible; fifth, that they are all responsible, certain to be accountable and will receive from their Creator, whether in this world or the next, exactly what their deeds have earned for them.

3. World- and life-affirmation, or the doctrine that God created life to be lived and not denied or destroyed, and the world to be enjoyed; that Creation is subservient to man, malleable and transformable by him according to his wishes and design; that both life and the world are to be promoted and developed, culture and civilization to be nurtured and to issue in human self-realization in knowledge, in *taqwā* and *iḥsān* (piety and righteousness), and in beauty.

4. Societism, or the doctrine that man's cosmic value lies in his membership in and contribution to human society; that his individual self is certainly an end-in-itself, yet more ennobled, and hence conditioned, by its subjection to humanity as an end-in-itself.

Beyond these methodological principles, but lying within the essence of the Qur'ānic figurization, is a body of ethical principles sometimes given explicitly and sometimes to be inferred from their concrete instantiations narrated or described by the Qur'ān. They constitute Islam's personal and social ethics, the moral precepts to guide the conduct of individuals and groups. The Qur'ānic text is, in the main, a phenomenology of moral values or precepts.

Finally, the Qur'ānic essence includes the institutions of Islam. These cover all fields of human activity: the religious and the ethical, the political and the economic, the cultural and the educational, the judicial and the military, as we shall have occasion to see below.

NOTES

1. As indicated by "The Prologue" and "The Epilogue" of the Code of Hammurabi, J. Pritchard, *Ancient Near Eastern Texts* (Princeton, N.J.: Princeton University Press, 1955), pp. 164–165 and 177–180, respectively.

2. Qur'ān 87:18–19.

3. John Bright, *A History of Israel* (London: SCM Press, 1960), pp. 62–63; George E. Mendenhall, "Covenant Forms in Israelite Tradition," *The Biblical Archeologist* 17 (1954), pp. 58–60; Stanley B. Frost, *Patriarchs and Prophets* (Montreal: McGill University Press, 1963), pp. 15–16.

4. H. H. Rowley, *The Growth of the Old Testament* (London: Hutchinson University Library, 1960), pp. 30–31.

5. Ibid; H. Wheeler Robinson, *The Old Testament: Its Making and Meaning* (London: University of London Press, 1961), p. 189.

6. Bright, *History of Israel,* pp. 374–375; Rowley, *Growth of the Old Testament,* pp. 34–36; Nehemiah 8. The redactor's insistence that intermediaries were used to "cause the people to understand the law," "to understand the reading" as Ezra was reciting it to them, suggests that the law (scripture) Ezra carried with him from Babylon (Ezra 7:14) was not in Hebrew but in some language the people could not understand (Nehemiah 8:7–8).

7. "Until the Council of Jamnia [c. 90 C.E.] . . . it is improper to speak of them [certain books which were venerated but which cannot be identified with any certainty] as a Canon." So writes H. H. Rowley, and he quotes Oesterley, Robinson, and Holscher approvingly.

8. 'Alī ibn Ḥazm, *Kitāb al Faṣl fī al Milal wal Niḥal* (Cairo: Mu'assasat al Khānjī, 1321/1903), Vol. II, p. 22.

9. Pritchard, *Ancient Near Eastern Texts,* pp. 163-164.

10. Labīb al Sa'īd, *Al Muṣḥaf al Murattal* (Cairo: Dār al Kātib al 'Arabī, 1387/1967), pp. 68-69; 'Abdullah ibn Abū Dawūd al Sijistānī (d. 316/930), *Kitāb al Maṣāḥif* (Cairo: Al Maṭba'ah al Raḥmaniyyah, 1355/1936).

11. William Muir, *The Life of Muhammad* (Edinburgh: John Grant, 1923), p. xxviii.

12. Qur'ān 53:4; 38:70; 18:110; Jeremiah 23:29-30.

13. Qur'ān 18:110, 14; Jeremiah 5:14.

14. Jeremiah 23:29.

15. Jeremiah 23:31.

16. Qur'ān 4:104; 26:195; 12:2; 20:113; 3:7; 75:16, 17; 69:45-46.

17. See Chapter 20, "Calligraphy."

18. Qur'ān 17:90-93.

19. Qur'ān 41:6.

20. Qur'ān 18:110; 52:34.

21. Qur'ān 11:13.

22. Qur'ān 17:88.

23. Muḥammad ibn Isḥaq (151/769) and Muḥammad ibn Hishām (218/834), *Sīrat al Nabiyy Ṣallā Allahu 'Alayhi wa Sallam,* edited by M. M. 'Abd al Ḥamīd (Cairo: Muḥammad 'Alī Ṣubayḥ, 1383/1963), Vol. I, pp. 174-175. The event was confirmed by revelation in Qur'ān 74:11-31.

24. Qur'ān 3:18.

25. Qur'ān 3:19; 30:30.

26. Qur'ān 2:31.

27. The implications of the Qur'ānic commands to various aspects of thinking and living were elaborated in I. R. al Fārūqī, *Tawḥīd: Essays on Life and Thought* (Kuala Lumpur: A.B.I.M., 1982).

CHAPTER 6

The Sunnah

THE TEXTUAL BASE

The burden placed upon man by the Islamic revelation, namely, henceforth to translate the *data revelata* into laws or precepts for action, was a heavy one indeed. At least in the stream of Semitic religious consciousness, it was the first time that law was desacralized — and by religion itself; it was divested of its holiness as direct revelation. Henceforth, law was declared to be a human responsibility in the exercise of which humans were fallible. When done right, law is man's greatest accomplishment; when done wrong, his greatest downfall. At any rate, law-making was to be a human activity, capable, like every other human activity, of being right or wrong. When wrong, it is equally man's responsibility to discover the locus of error, to amend that law, and bring it into accord with the divinely given principles of which the law is the translation. Certainly it is an act of mercy that God chose to aid man in fulfillment of this obligation when He provided him with an example and clarification, an exegesis of the general principles of the revelation. For that is precisely what the *sunnah* is.

Technically, the *sunnah* is a collection of the Prophet's sayings and deeds. It includes his opinions about matters good or evil, desirable or otherwise, as well as the practices of which he approved as becoming for Muslims to follow. The *sunnah* quotes the words and phrases attributed directly to the Prophet or to his companions who witnessed his attitudes and deeds and reported them. Every unit of the *sunnah* conveying a report about the Prophet is called a *ḥadīth.* The *sunnah* occupies a place second to the Qur'ān. Its function is to clarify the Qur'ān's pronouncements, to exemplify and illustrate its purposes. Where the Qur'ānic statement is general, the *sunnah* particularizes it to make it applicable; and where particular, the *sunnah* generalizes it in order to make possible its extrapolation to other particulars. The *sunnah* was first memorized by the companions of the Prophet as many of them found the time to record the Prophet's sayings in writing. Afraid that the new Muslims might confuse the word of God with the word of Muḥammad, the Prophet had first prohibited the writing down of his own sayings. Later, when the possibility of confusing the two was removed by the majority's memorization of the Qur'ān, the Prophet permitted his companions to write the *sunnah.* Among those companions who recorded some parts of the *sunnah* were Sa'd ibn 'Ubādah al Anṣārī (15/637), 'Abdullah ibn Abū Awfā, Samrah ibn Jundub (60/680), Jābir ibn 'Abdullah (78/698), Wahb ibn Munabbih (114/732) who inherited the collection of

Abū Hurayrah (58/678); 'Abdullah ibn 'Amr whose writing recorded 1,000 or more *ḥadīth* preserved in the *Musnad* of Ibn Ḥanbal; and 'Abdullah ibn 'Abbās (69/589) who left us a "camel load" of writing materials covered with *ḥadīth* of the Prophet. Besides these, there was the covenant of Madīnah, the constitution of the first Islamic state and the first constitution ever to be written. Dictated by the Prophet, its principles have remained operative throughout Islamic history. The main bulk of the *sunnah,* however, was not written until later. The first generation of Muslims memorized the sayings of the Prophet, taught them to one another, observed what they prescribed, and emulated what they described as the practice of Muḥammad.

The value of the *sunnah* and its relevance to Islam was universally recognized by all Muslims. The need for it to help the Muslim fulfill the requirements of his faith in liturgical, legal, ethical, social, economic, political, and international affairs was felt by all. Hence, the *sunnah* came to be regarded, from the beginning, as a second authoritative source of Islam, whose dicta were binding on all Muslims. The Qur'ān commanded obedience to the Prophet and equated that obedience with obedience to God.[1] It ordered the Muslims to refer their disputes to him and to abide by his judgment.[2] The Prophet's companions, for their part, obeyed that command and voluntarily fulfilled everything the Prophet had asked of them. It was their unanimous consensus that the *sunnah* of the Prophet is normative, that its precepts are binding on all Muslims. Indeed, the Muslims had no other source to provide them with the specific rituals of worship and institutions of their faith, and to legislate for them in matters on which the Qur'ān is silent, save the *sunnah.* Naturally, there can be no contradiction between the Qur'ān and the *sunnah.* Everyone of the latter's provisions must be either confirmed or implied by the Qur'ān, whether explicitly, by a direct passage of the text, or implicitly, by a Qur'ānic principle or desideratum whose realization necessitates the provision commanded by the *sunnah.*

However, not all that the Prophet said or did, approved or disapproved of, is normative and hence obligatory for Muslims to follow. The Prophet was not superhuman or divine but a human, all too human, being. The Qur'ān repeated this fact many times, and the Prophet himself never tired of reaffirming this basic truth. As a human being he did, said, approved and disapproved of many things outside of his function as executor of Qur'ānic commands, as exemplar of the ethic of Islam, or as embodiment of the Islamic lifestyle. In this regard, Muslims distinguish between those items that issue from his prophethood and mission, and those that issue from his humanity. The former are accepted as normative without hesitation. The latter, in absence of evidence to the contrary, are treated as peculiar to him as a shepherd, tradesman, farmer, husband, general, statesman, paramedic, engineer, and so on. Muslims regard the former as normative and the latter, otherwise; and in doing so, they are backed by the Prophet himself, who acknowledged and accepted on numerous occasions the contrary counsel or action of his companions. The *sunnah,* as a technical term or source of Islamic law and ethics, includes only those items that are proven to have been meant by the Prophet to be followed and obeyed in loyalty to his divine message.

The foregoing differentiation in normativeness divided the *sunnah* into two great divisions; one containing all those items that give rise to law and obligation *(sunnah ḥukmiyyah),* and one containing all those that do not *(sunnah ghayr ḥukmiyyah).* Within

Map 20. The Prophet's Migration to Yathrib: Al Hijrah, 1/622

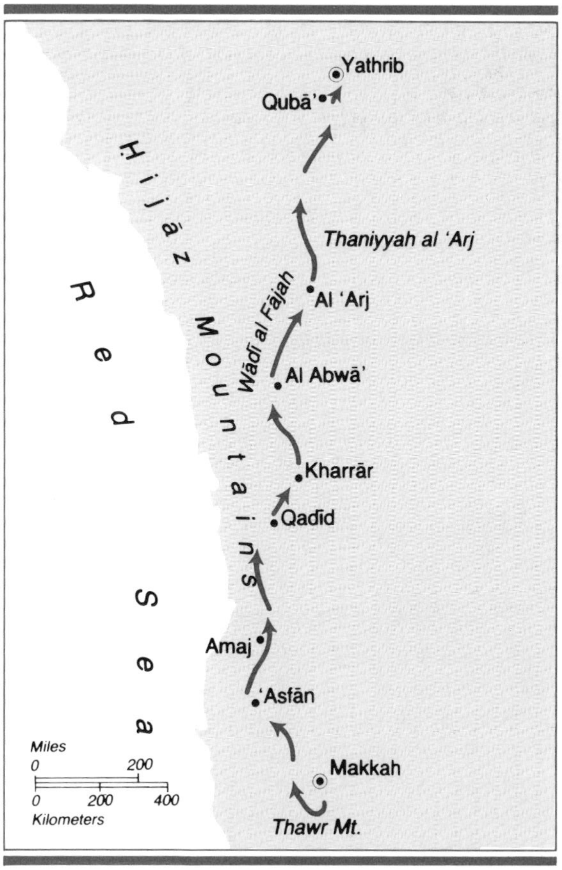

Illustration 6.1

A calligraphic design ("Muḥammad" repeated 5 times) by the contemporary Turkish calligrapher Emin Berin. [Photo by L. al Fārūqī.]

the former, various degrees of normativeness were discerned following two criteria: first, the degree of certainty of provenance *(wurūd)* or the quality of our knowledge that those items issued from the Prophet and did so for the purpose of clarification or exemplification of the divine message; and second, the degree of certainty with which the specific connotation *(dalālah),* the exact identity, meaning, or form of that which is commanded, is known. This differentiation divided the *sunnah ḥukmiyyah* into *qat'iyyah* (absolutely certain) and *ẓanniyyah* (probable), and these divisions applied to both provenance and connotation. Obviously, legal obligation attached only to those items fulfilling the criteria of certainty in both respects.

During the lifetime of the Prophet, the *sunnah* was for the most part something witnessed in public. As it issued from the Prophet, people heard, saw, and understood. When they were not present and sought reassurance, they could and did refer to the Prophet and asked him directly, face to face, to satisfy their quest. After his death, the companions asked one another. When all those who attended or witnessed the event agreed, their unanimity was tantamount to certainty. For it is not possible that the Prophet's companions, with all their loyalty and sincerity, their personal differences and distinctions, could come up with the same report unless the event was real and its meaning was absolutely clear. Items of the *sunnah* that fit this description were called *sunnah mutawātirah.* The *sunnah mashbūhah* refers to those items that were reported by some companions — not all — whose consensus could not have involved mistake, error, or misrepresentation; while *sunnah āḥād* includes items reported by one companion known for his good memory, fidelity, and moral integrity.

Across these divisions lies the distinction between *fi'liyyah* (actional) and *qawliyyah* (verbal). The former refers to deeds of the Prophet, done once, occasionally, or repeatedly under the witness of the public. To this group belong the rituals and institutions of Islam which continue to be practiced throughout the Muslim world with astounding identity despite the centuries that separate their practice from the Prophet and the total discontinuity of geography, ethnicity, language, and culture among the world's followers of the Prophet. The latter comprises the Prophet's sayings heard by others and necessarily involving a lesser degree of certainty than something witnessed, unless — again like the rituals and institutions — they were repeated on a daily, weekly or yearly basis.

The *sunnah* thus was heard, witnessed, memorized, recorded, and transmitted to posterity. Since the third century A.H., it has been known through six canonical collections called the *ṣiḥāḥ* (sing. *ṣaḥīḥ*). By order of the rigor with which they carried out their sifting and classification, the collectors of the *ṣiḥāḥ* were al Bukhārī (256/870), Muslim (251/865), Abū Dā'ūd (275/888), Ibn Mājah (273/886), al Nasā'ī (303/915), and al Tirmidhī (279/892). Among these, the first two stand apart, acknowledged by all Muslims as more critical and authoritative than the rest. Those items commonly found in both their texts are most authoritative of all.

THE CONTENT

Following the death of the Prophet, the Muslims found themselves a people with a cause, a people endowed with a mission as radical as it was universal (Qur'ān 3:19, 85). The whole world had to be remade in the likeness of the divine pattern. The world within — the self — and the world without — nature — had to be transfigured into that pattern. The Muslims themselves had already undergone a radical transformation at the hands of the Prophet in the course of their conversion to Islam and their companionship with the Prophet in his lifetime. This was the justification of the name "Muslim" which revelation conferred upon them (Qur'ān, 22:78). The Prophet made certain to impart to them his vision, his cause; and they were the excellent pupils who appropriated that vision and dedicated their lives to it. The vision of the

Prophet lay complete in the Qur'ān, ready for the understanding to appropriate. The last verse to be revealed affirmed: "Today I have completed for you your religion, assigned to you My total blessing, and established Islam henceforth as your religion."[3] It signified that, as idea, principle, and representation the whole life- and worldview of Islam was complete, ready to be taken in its entirety by any intellect willing to appropriate it and possessing the minimum requisite powers of theoretical and axiological cognition. Understanding of the Qur'ān and the power to produce in oneself the self-shattering, self-reconstructing, and self-mobilizing required for joining the company of the Prophet are not readily available to all. Those who are capable of being moved by a vision presented *in abstracto* are always few; and those who, being so affected, are so moved that they cannot rest unless and until their "vision is realized in history or they perish in the process"—to use Muḥammad's own phrase—are fewer still. For, as educators have always realized, cognitive appeal presumes a strong imagination capable of representing to the consciousness a vision in the concrete where the values may exercise their appeal upon the heart with all their power. Without such imagination, the apperception remains theoretical; and theory, in the sense of ideation, does not affect the heart, the source of all movement. But, the stronger an imagination is, the more vivid its representation will be and, consequently, the more real the value represented, the stronger will be the affective emission or moving appeal. The case of the Prophet's companions could not be different from that of humanity at large. Nor could their special sensitivity to the religious and ethical plight of humankind, or their specially developed imagination as the most poetry-possessed people in the world, absolve them from the need for another aid, a nontheoretical, nonideational aid. This aid was the *sunnah.* It supplied the needed concretization of the ideal of Islam.

The *sunnah* as concretization of the vision, or materialization of the ideal, translated theory into reality. In it, the values of Islam were given form and became alive. They throbbed with moving power. In their presence, the inert became alive, lost its ontological poise, and began to move in the direction to which the values pointed. From their concrete instantiations, the values of Islam commanded the actualization of materials that fulfill their patterns; and in their presence, humans could only obey. The *sunnah* was the ministry of Muḥammad. It extended over the last twenty-two years of his life. In his life as well as after his death, the *sunnah* of Muḥammad supplied the missing link between thinking and doing, between ideational apperception and action, between thought and life and history. That is why the *sunnah* of Muḥammad became the teacher of the millions. It constituted the richest mine from which every person in a position of leadership drew to exhort or to convince, to inspire or to move. It furnished the emulatory material that dominated all Islamic celebrations, and indeed, decorated and ornamented all Muslim convocations.

Illustration 6.2

Anatolian prayer rug (eighteenth century), Turkish and Islamic Art Museum, Isṭanbūl, Turkey. [Photo by L. al Fārūqī.]

The *sunnah* materials may be grouped into four categories, each of which built an image of Muḥammad in the imagination of Muslims. First were the ritualistic materials which formed the image of the Prophet as worshipper of God, as His pious servant. Second were those texts pertaining to Muḥammad's role as missionary and caller to the new faith, as a man of the world with all kinds of relations with other people of the world but living by and for his mission alone. Third were the materials pertaining to Muḥammad as a human being and hence as husband,

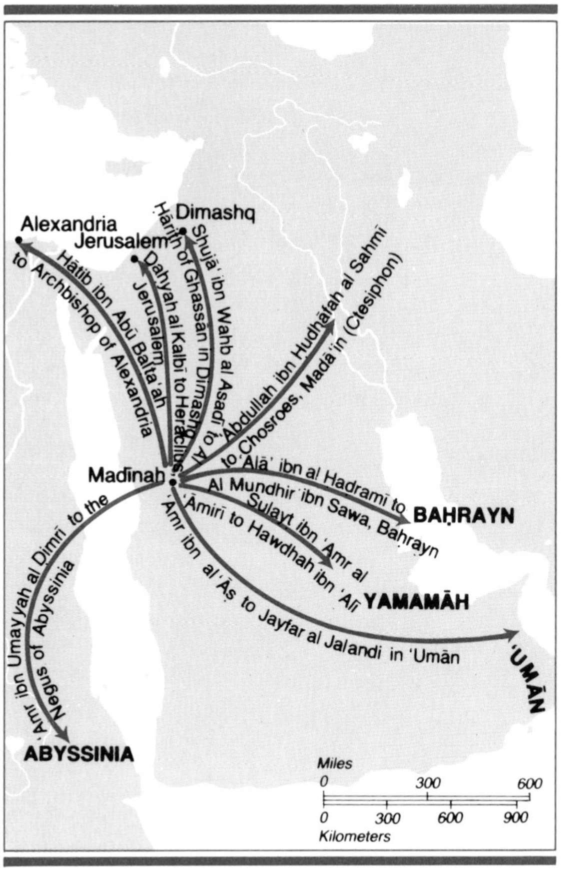

Map 21. The Prophet's Delegates to Neighboring Sovereigns, 6/628

father, relative, neighbor, and friend. Fourth were the materials pertaining to the Prophet as leader of men whether in the state, the battlefield, the marketplace, the classroom, or the mosque.

Muhammad as Worshipper Servant of God

The principal act of worship—*ṣalāt*—was imposed by God directly on Muḥammad on the occasion of the *Isrā'* and *Mi'rāj* (the night journey to Jerusalem and ascent to heaven in the year 6 B.H./616). *Ṣalāt* is also commanded in the revelation a countless number of times, as are the other rituals of fasting, *shahādah, zakāt,* and *ḥajj.* Muḥammad taught his followers the details of *ṣalāt,* as well as of all other rituals, following the instruction given him by God. The Prophet's observance of these rituals was meticulously observed, reported, tried, and repeated in the practice of the companions. The latter performed under the eye of the Prophet who corrected every deviance from what he knew to be the norm. From the smallest detail of bodily purification to the highest spiritual meanings, these rituals constitute a fair part of the *sunnah.* Every Muslim learns them as a child, and has Muḥammad constantly in mind in his performance of them throughout his life.

Important as they certainly are for the religious life, punctuating as they do human life five times a day *(ṣalāt),* a whole month every year *(ṣiyām),* touching every unit of wealth beyond what is absolutely necessary for subsistence *(zakāt),* and providing a culmination of the Muslim's personal and corporate piety *(ḥajj),* the rituals of Islam have a restricted place. They may be neither increased, reduced, or changed because the *sunnah* has taught them in their exact and precise dimensions (or *maqādīr*). Those who flout or neglect to observe them are guilty; those who overdo and exceed the proper dimensions are perhaps not as guilty as the former, but guilty nonetheless. When asked whether it would not earn a person greater merit to fast all year and pray all night, the Prophet answered: "God did not prescribe it. . . . As for me, I pray and I sleep; I fast and I eat; I work and I keep women company." Unlike the "holy men" of other religions, Muḥammad was not therefore an ascetic denying the world and mortifying his flesh, nor a monk spending most of his hours in prayer or meditation. The rituals of Islam were acts of obedience and self-discipline, closed to indulgence of any kind. It is therefore elsewhere that we have to look for Muḥammad's pietism.

Long before any revelation came to him, the Prophet was in the habit of isolating himself and meditating over the predicament of humanity. The plight of humans everywhere distressed him; the status quo of other religions left much to be desired, for these religions had been disfigured by their guardians, the monks, priests, and rabbis. They had long since stopped to inspire and move humanity toward the great goals. And yet, the signs of God in creation were everywhere, arousing wonder and pressing the human mind to break through to its Creator. The patterns of God within the self, in the world of nature and history, were obvious if humans would only shake off the inherited stereotypes and open themselves to the ever-fresh evidence of the facts of creation.

Following revelation and Muḥammad's absolute conviction that God is, that He is indeed God, One, Absolute, Almighty, and Beneficent, he became a man possessed. Everything in the world of humans—the past, the present, the future—and everything in that of nature—the sun, moon, stars, trees, and animals big or small—moved and lived and died by God's action. Belief in God is not religious until one sees

Illustration 6.3

A class of students performs during Commencement program at Clara Muḥammad School, Philadelphia, 1983. [Photo by L. al Fārūqī.]

everything as the creation, work, and providence of God. Muḥammad did see the world this way and did so par excellence. Prophethood placed Muḥammad in contact with this divine Being in a special way. God was the Creator of Muḥammad and all else, as well as the Master constantly watching over and guiding everything. Above all, God as God of the universe is to be acknowledged through His works, contemplated through the events of nature and history, which fill the mind of anyone who thinks. Furthermore, He is to be loved, honored, and obeyed, not just acknowledged and held in contemplation. For what is perceived as divine is *ipso facto* understood as normative and commanding. To love, honor, and obey God is to conscript oneself voluntarily into His service, which is nothing less than transforming oneself, other selves, and the whole of creation into a harmonious whole fulfilling His will. And His will is the plenum of values, material, utilitarian, moral, religious, aesthetic. Many of these are already actualized in creation, and many others remain to be actualized by man.

This then was the meaning of worship for Muḥammad: to perceive God through His works, to acknowledge Him precisely for what He is — namely, God, the One, Absolute in all respects, ever-living, ever-present — and to fulfill His will. Worship, hence, was not something to be done at one time or place rather than another. It was a full-time occupation, a job never *accompli,* never stopped. No reason may justify a relaxation of worship except death. As long as life is, the obligation to worship continues. Such was the preoccupation of the Prophet. If he performed a ritual, he would shorten it to accommodate those observing it with him, or would lengthen it if he were alone and inclined toward contemplation. But he would never permit contemplation to disturb his penchant for the other forms of worship. He saw and heard God wherever his senses turned, and he was ever-restless in seeking to do His will.

Muḥammad's spirituality was of a new kind. The world had known a spirituality that knew the eternal only as the antipode of the material, and sought it only at the cost of self, of world and history. Hinduism and Buddhism taught such spirituality. Such too was the spirituality of Christianity, which integrated into itself that of Alexandrian Hellenism, with all its antagonism to matter and the world. The affirmation of life, the world, and history was irreconcilable with these religions. It could be affirmed only in the pagan religions; but these were really little more than that will projected onto the supernatural and mythologized. Hu-

Illustration 6.4

Two examples of Indian calligraphy from the *Ḥadīth* literature. Both read: "Whoever builds a mosque for the sake of God, God will build for him a house in Paradise." The example on top appears on a mosque commissioned by Rukn al Dīn Barbak Shāh (fifteenth century), Hatkhola, Sylhet, Bangladesh. The one at the bottom is from a mosque in Gaur commissioned by Shams al Dīn Yūsuf Shāh (fifteenth century). [Courtesy Department of Antiquities, Government of Bangladesh.]

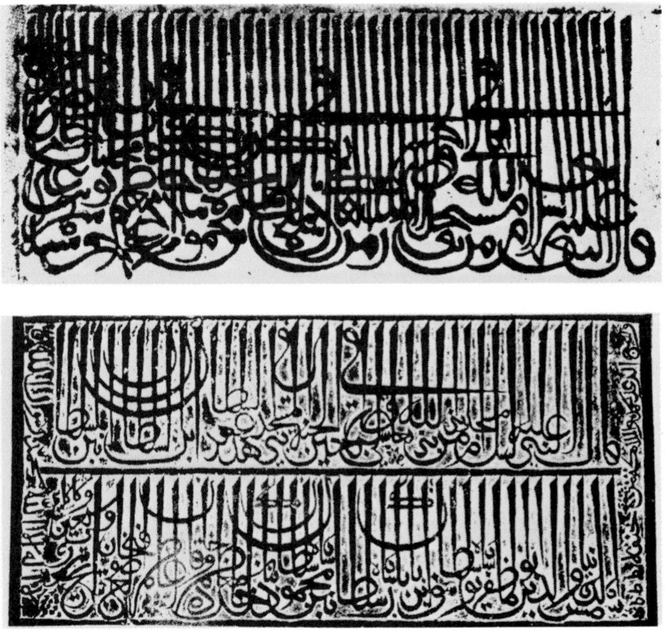

manity yearned for a spirituality that would reconcile the two: a religion that affirmed life and the world but disciplined their pursuit with morality; that affirmed the personalist values of purity, faithfulness, and devotion but disciplined their pursuit with measured rituals and engagement in the making of history.

Pondering, wondering, and meditating took most of Muḥammad's energies before the Qur'ānic revelation. Thereafter, every moment of his life was an acknowledgment of God, an act of acquiescence to the Creator-Master of the universe. Every moment was an active affirmation of life, a reconstruction of culture and civilization, a remolding of the world into the divine pattern. The last two decades of his life were a continuous struggle, a constant self-exertion in the path of God. But by living in God's presence and working under His command, the struggle and exertion became rest and reassurance — the *sakīnah* which is more precious than any and all gifts. Muḥammad was in the habit of withdrawing to His Master and pleading for this *sakīnah* whenever events took a turn for the worse. But never did that recourse to God deter him from fulfilling whatever task was due, whether to himself, his family, his environment, or to the least of his people.

Muḥammad as Caller

The divine command dictated that Muḥammad should be a caller of men to God. It was to be his most solemn duty to convey the revelation to the world.[4] The command cautioned that his duty did not go beyond conveyance, that is, informing, warning, and guiding others. How the call fared, whether it succeeded or not, was not his responsibility but God's.[5] He alone disposes, guiding or not permitting to be guided whomsoever He wills.[6] In perfect obedience, Muḥammad conveyed all that was revealed to him and lost no time in calling to the new faith all those he could contact. The unique incident in his career, in which he failed to call a blind pauper to the faith because he was preoccupied by a man of influence,[7] was not a case of failure to call. For his business with the notable was equally a call to Islam. This was an error in judgment as to who was more important at that moment of time. The obligation to call, the concern for the faith quality of everyone, never left Muḥammad's consciousness. He turned every occasion into an opportunity for mission. And the image of the Prophet as *dā'iyah* or "caller to God" has commanded the imagination of Muslims ever since. In this image, and in the anecdotes and direct sayings of which it is composed, the *sunnah* concretized the vision of Islam as the valued personal quality and lifestyle of Muslims.

The Prophet was armed with the most formidable — indeed miraculous and irresistible — weapon, namely, Qur'ānic eloquence. The power of the Qur'ān to persuade and to convince was a great *tremendum,* a moving *fascinosum,* without match. As sublime presentation of Islam, the Prophet allowed it to speak for Islam on every occasion, thus giving the call the numinous power of the divine voice. Thus, when 'Utbah ibn Rabī'ah and the Quraysh tribe offered Muḥammad

Illustration 6.6

Interior of mud mosque, Zaria, Nigeria. [Courtesy A. R. Doi.]

Illustration 6.5

At prayer *(ṣalāt)* in the Masjid Negara (National Mosque) in Kuala Lumpur, Malaysia. [Photo by L. al Fārūqī.]

kingship, money, wealth, and medication, assuming that those things would cause him to desist from his opposition to Makkan religion, Muḥammad answered them with verses from the Qur'ān. Those verses did not only ward off the suspicion that Muḥammad was in search of kingship and wealth, or was sick and needed medication, but also converted the Makkan delegate, Rabī'ah, to Islam. For those who understand Arabic, the Qur'ān is truly mighty. A phrase or two of it well woven into the text of a speech or an essay could set the composition on fire, make it vibrant and penetrating. Muḥammad's speech relied heavily on the Qur'ān and often was composed exclusively of Qur'ānic verses.

Qur'ānic quotations aside, Muḥammad's own human speech was eloquent. He used to say that, having been brought up in the camp of Banū Sa'd bin Bakr, he spoke Arabic precisely and eloquently. He

Illustration 6.7

Pilgrim in prayer. [Courtesy Saudi Arabian Ministry of Information.]

appreciated literary eloquence highly and admitted that "literary beauty is a fascinating art." Certainly, he was a master of the Arabic language, capable of manipulating it to touch the hearts of his audience and stimulate their imagination. Added to his personal conviction of God and of His attributes and actions, and to the zeal he felt in his attachment to the cause, the Prophet was preeminently successful in convincing the people of the truth. His words, as 'Ā'ishah has reported, were always so well measured that they were easy to memorize from the first hearing; and none had touched the strings of the heart and elicited such emotions as did Muḥammad.

Muḥammad lent his ear readily to everyone who sought it. He listened with a smile expressing sympathy, and with eyes focused on the speaker in candid interest. When his time to respond came, he did so to the point, never ambiguously. If he did not know the answer, "God knows better" was the reply. If the matter was controversial, he would reassure the speaker and win his acquiescence to the principles underlying the problem, principles that were always religious. Anyone who talked to Muḥammad emerged not only convinced of his judgment in the matter at hand but also of the greater issue, and became a new recruit for the cause of Islam. Still more, such a person emerged fully in love with and admiration for the Prophet's person. This was the case with his fiercest opponents, such as the aforesaid 'Utbah ibn Rabī'ah and 'Umar ibn al Khaṭṭāb.

The latter drew his sword in rage over the Prophet's "blasphemies" against the gods of the Quraysh, and went looking for Muḥammad to put an end to this scourge once and for all. That very trip ended in his conversion to Islam, and he became one of its staunchest defenders. The Qur'ān and Muḥammad's call vanquished the voice of paganism in 'Umar and replaced it with the voice of Islam. Muḥammad's ministry was a perfect exemplification of the divine commandments: "Argue with them with fairer and more comely saying. . . . Respond to evil with good, and the enmity between you and the evil-doer will be transformed into warm friendship.[8]

The Prophet took great risks in conveying his message. The early years in Makkah brought terrible reaction. The Makkans jeered at him and his friends. They threw their refuse in his face and boycotted his whole tribe regardless of whether they were Muslims or not. Muḥammad took his call to Ṭā'if, was pelted with stones and chased away, and almost perished on that mission. His failure weighed heavily on his conscience, causing him to pray to God like one defeated but still loyal and faithful. In the service of mission, Muḥammad spared neither himself nor his compan-

Illustration 6.8

Woodcarving on traditional houses of Saudi Arabia. [Courtesy Saudi Arabian Ministry of Information.]

ions. So great was his enthusiasm to respond favorably to any invitation to present Islam that his enemies took it as a way to fight Islam by killing its adherents. Once, he sent six of his companions to the Hudhayl tribe (Ḥijāz) at the tribe's request. At al Rajī', the said tribesmen fell upon the Muslims, killed four, and sold two to Makkah. The latter were also executed. He sent a number of his dearest companions, under the protection of Abū Barā' 'Āmir ibn Mālik, to teach Islam to the tribes of Najd. At the well of Ma'ūnah, the tribesmen of Banū 'Āmir fell upon the Muslims and decimated them. One Muslim, taken for dead among the corpses, survived to tell the story.

For the sake of this mission, Muḥammad was always prepared to forgive. He forgave all the Makkans — including those who opposed him most — and invited them to join the new faith, at the time of his greatest victory. Custom prescribed their enslavement and confiscation of all their wealth; but for Muḥammad, the higher interest of mission came first and last. Similarly, the Prophet would not execute 'Abdullah ibn Ubayy, who had vilified and cheated him, committed treason against the Islamic state, and fought the movement on every occasion. When the

Map 22. The Riddah *(Apostasy) Wars, 10 – 12/632 – 634*

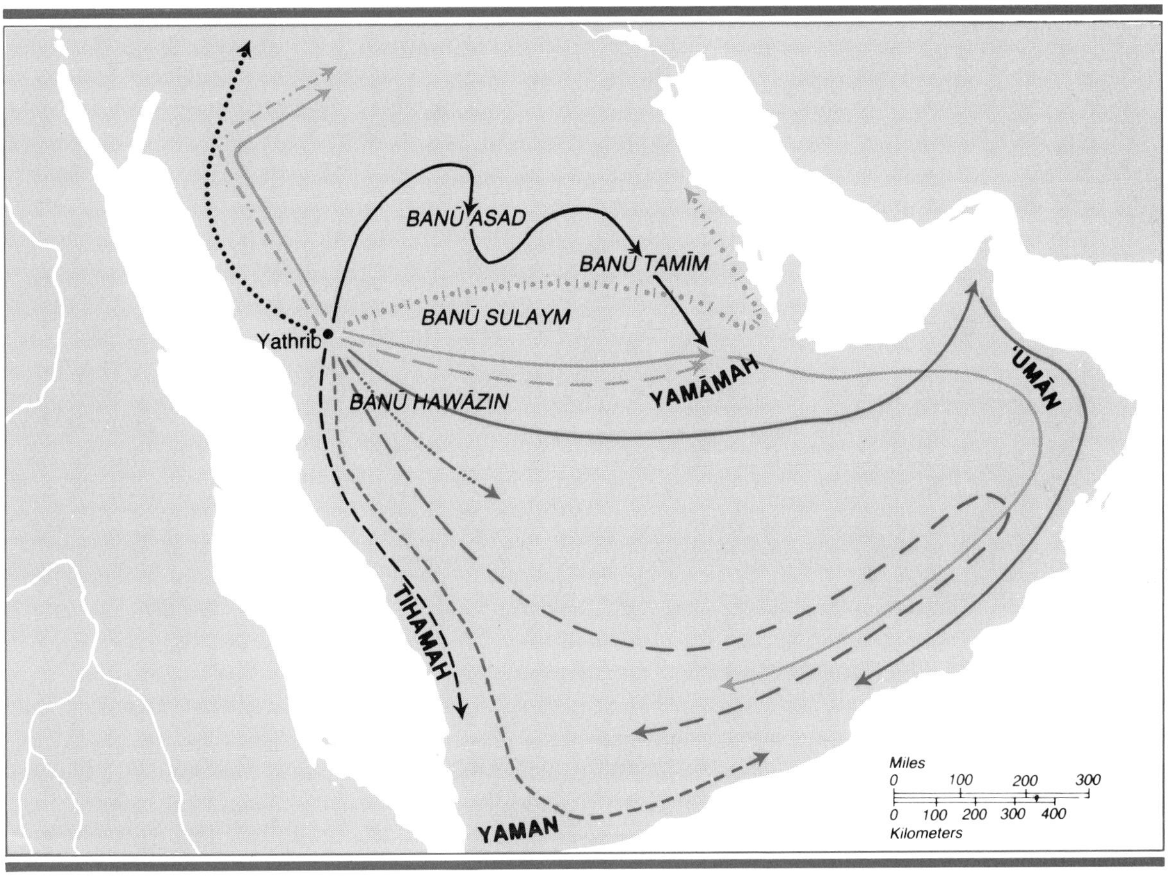

COMMANDER		AGAINST
⟵	Khālid ibn al Walīd,	Ṭulayḥah ibn Khuwaylid al Asadī, Banū Asad, Bazākhah.
		Mālik ibn Nuwayrah, Banū Tamīm, Biṭāḥ
⟵ — —	'Ikrimah ibn Abū Jahl,	Musaylimah at Yamamah
⟵———	Shuraḥbil ibn Ḥasanah,	– to help 'Ikrimah and 'Amr ibn al 'Āṣ
⟵-----	Muhājir ibn Abū Umayyah,	al Aswad al 'Ansī 'Amr ibn Ma'dī Karib and Qays ibn Makshūḥ in Yaman
⟵ - - -	Suwayd ibn Muqrin,	to Tihāmah of Yaman(western plain) vs. Al Ḥakam ibn Ḍabī ah at Baḥrayn
⟵|•|•|•|	Al 'Alā' ibn al Ḥaḍrami,	
⟵———	Hudhayfah ibn Muḥsin,	Dhū al Tāj Laqīṭ ibn Mālik in 'Umān
⟵ — —	'Arfajah ibn Harthamah,	to Mahrah
⟵ - - -	'Amr ibn al 'Āṣ,	Quḍā'ah
⟵•••—	Ma'an ibn Ḥājiz al Sulamī,	Banū Sulaym and Hawāzin
⟵••••••••	Khālid ibn Sa'īd ibn al 'Āṣ,	to outskirts of Byzantium

son of ibn Ubayy, a fervently committed Muslim, heard that his father had been condemned by the Prophet, he asked that he be the executioner, lest somebody else's execution create in him a will to vengeance. Indeed, when ibn Ubayy died, the Prophet offered a shroud for his remains, led the funerary prayer for him, and walked in his funeral, thus convincing his son and all those who witnessed these events that propagation of the faith could and should vanquish all thoughts of retribution. Following the Muslims' victory at Ḥunayn (8/630), the Makkans helped themselves to the greater part of the war booty; when the Madīnans complained, the Prophet offered himself as compensation, saying, "Are you not the happier that the Makkans are running away with the material things and you with the Prophet of God?"[9]

Muḥammad taught every Muslim to be a missionary for Islam; and he taught them well. Whether in high or low position, missionaries emulate their prophet well. The Muslim has consistently made a commendable presentation of the message of Islam. This is partly due to the normative nature of the message and partly to the teaching of the Prophet. Ja'far ibn Abū Ṭālib was brought into the presence of the Negus of Abyssinia to answer the Makkan charge and request for extradition to Makkah of himself and the few Muslims who escaped thither. Ja'far presented the case of Islam truthfully and yet in a way that could not but win the pleasure of the king. "O King," he said, "we were in a state of ignorance and immorality, worshiping idols, eating carrion, committing all sorts of iniquities. . . . The strong among us exploited the weak. Then God sent us a prophet. . . . He called us to worship naught but God . . . to tell the truth, to hold to trust and promise, to assist the relative or neighbor . . . to avoid fornication and false witness. . . . We believed and followed him. . . . The Makkans tried to dissuade us and inflicted upon us great suffering. That is why we came hither. . . . As for Jesus, our Prophet brought us this revelation concerning him." Here Ja'far recited verses from *sūrah* "Maryam," which fell upon the ears of the audience like sweet music. The Negus and his Patriarchs were moved to tears and vowed never to extradite the Muslims or molest them.[9]

Muḥammad as Family Man

Muḥammad was twenty-five when someone first suggested that he should get married. He was a poor man, a dependent of his uncle Abū Ṭālib. Young men in Makkah were in the habit of frequenting its bars and flirting with the barmaids. Not Muḥammad! He led a life of chastity and purity. Nothing of the petulance of youth or the debauchery of adult life in Makkah was known of him. In the last two years of his bachelorhood, Muḥammad was in the employ of Khadījah, a widow and a merchant, whose interest he had served well enough to deserve her praise as well as that of Maysarah, her long-trusted and faithful servant. The latter went on the trading trips with Muḥammad looking after the interests of his employer. The successful ventures were as much his as Muḥammad's; but Maysarah modestly put Muḥammad ahead of himself, reporting to Khadījah that the successes were exclusively Muḥammad's.

The fact that nobody had spoken to Muḥammad about marriage indicates that marriage was not on his mind. That explains his stupefaction when Nafīsah bint Munyah, a friend of Khadījah, suggested that if he would entrust the matter to her, she would secure for him the hand of Khadījah with all the wedding expenses prepaid. Muḥammad was elated, and he and Khadījah were married. Khadījah gave Muḥammad all his children but one: Fāṭimah, who married Muḥammad's cousin 'Alī and bore him his only grandsons, Ḥasan and Ḥusayn. Fāṭimah alone survived her father's two sons, Qāsim and Ṭāhir, who died in infancy. Three daughters, Zaynab, Ruqayyah, and Umm Kulthūm, all married and died without children before 8/630.[10] In 9/631, another son, called Ibrahīm, was born to Muḥammad from his Egyptian wife Maryam. That child also died in infancy. Khadījah remained the only wife of Muḥammad as long as she lived. Their marriage lasted until her death in 1 B.H./621. It was during this period that many of the most important events of the life of Muḥammad occurred. It was indeed a happy marriage for both.

Khadījah's wealth relieved Muḥammad of the burden of working for a living. It liberated him from material concern for himself and his family, and provided him with the leisure requisite for long meditations, one of which was the occasion for the first revelation. When those first revelations came, Muḥammad thought himself sick or possessed. He could not bring himself to believe what the Angel had conveyed to him, that he was to be a prophet. It fell to Khadījah to prop up her husband's spirits, to reassure and inspire him, to help him gain confidence in himself and in those extraordinary experiences. With the repeated return of the vision, Khadījah herself needed reassurance. She sought this from Waraqah ibn Nawfal, a distant uncle of hers, reputed for his religious knowledge and wisdom. After hearing a full report, Waraqah exclaimed, "By Him Who dominates my soul, Muḥammad is the Prophet of this nation. The great Spirit that has come to Moses has now come to

TABLE 6.1. GENEALOGY OF THE PROPHET

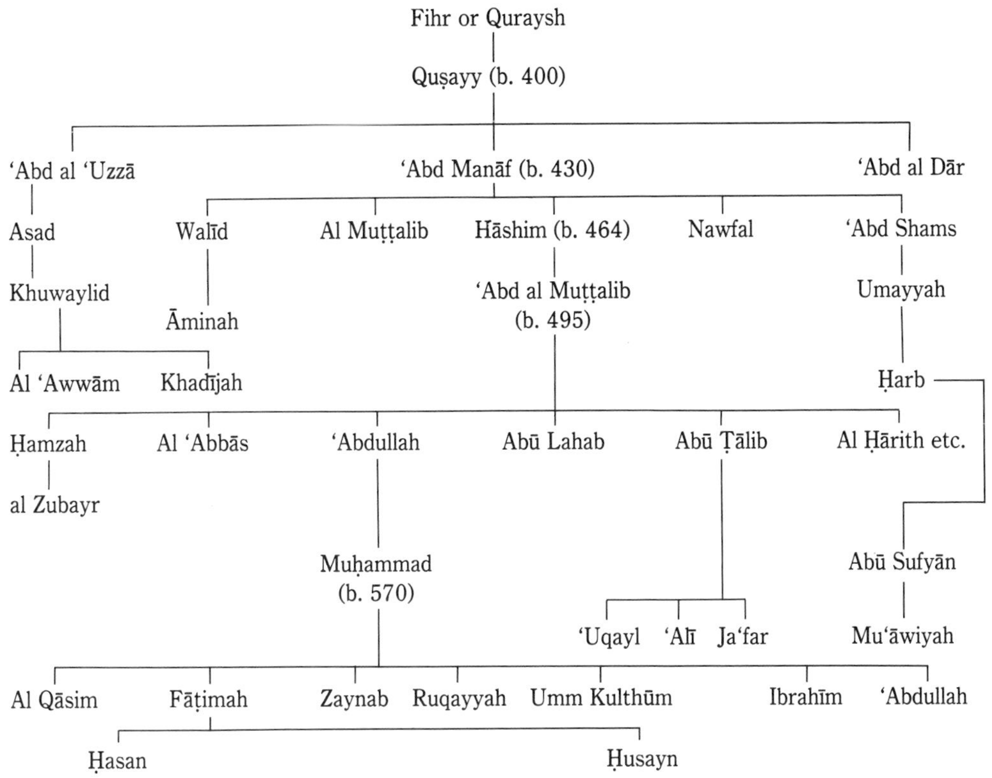

him. . . . May he be firm!" Khadījah was certainly encouraged; but it was a tremendous burden that she had henceforth to carry as wife of someone who was to be a prophet. Muḥammad loved his wife dearly. He poured on her all the affection of which he was capable. He cried when she died; and he kept her memory on every occasion. Later, his youngest wife, 'Ā'ishah said, "I have never been more envious than I am of Khadījah, long dead as she may be."

Though Muḥammad married eight times after the death of Khadījah, only one of them was a real marriage. That was his marriage to 'Ā'ishah, daughter of his closest companion, Abū Bakr. The others were marriages for political and social reasons. The Prophet entered into them as an exemplification of a new value Islam taught. A few examples will illustrate. Zaynab bint Jaḥsh, a cousin of his whom Muḥammad knew well, was given by him in marriage to Zayd ibn Ḥārithah, Khadījah's slave whom Muḥammad had manumitted. Incompatibility of the spouses made them miserable, and the marriage broke down. This was a double tragedy, since Arab custom made the divorced wife of a slave a social pariah, forever unmarriable. Although this custom was abolished by Islam, no Muslim would condescend to marry the woman despite her young age. To raise her status and teach the Arabs a lesson against social stratification, Muḥammad took her in marriage. Ḥafṣah was a widowed daughter of 'Umar ibn al Khaṭṭāb, a close companion of the Prophet. She was in her forties and was poor. Her father was even poorer. He offered her to a number of friends and acquaintances, but all declined. It grieved him deeply that his daughter was homeless, unprotected, and liable to fall into trouble. To uplift them both and teach the Muslims that it is necessary for them to give the needed protection to their single women, especially the widows, the Prophet joined her to his household as his wife.

Sawdah was the Muslim wife of Sakrān ibn 'Amr, one of the first converts to Islam. The Prophet married the couple when Sawdah converted to Islam. She had to run away from her family to avoid their vengeance. The same had happened to her husband. The Prophet ordered them both to emigrate to Abyssinia. On their return, Sakran died. Sawdah had to choose between staying in the streets or returning to her family and their retribution. Muḥammad had to give her the protection due and reassure his other fol-

TABLE 6.2. CHRONOLOGY OF THE PROPHET'S LIFE AND ACTIVITIES

570 C.E.	Abraha's abortive attack on Makkah, "The Year of the Elephant."
	Death of 'Abdullah, the Prophet's father.
	Muḥammad's birth (August 20).
570–575	Muḥammad's nurture by Ḥalīmah and residence at Banū Sa'd.
	Persian conquest of Yaman.
	Expulsion of the Christian Abyssinians.
575–	Persecution of Christians in Yaman by the Jewish King Dhū Nuwās.
575–597	Persian dominion in Yaman.
576	Death of Āminah, the Prophet's mother.
578	Death of the Prophet's grandfather, 'Abdul Muṭṭalib.
	Guardianship of the Prophet passes to his uncle Abū Ṭālib.
580–590	The Fijjār War.
582	Muḥammad's first journey to Syria. Meeting with Baḥīrah.
586	Muḥammad's employment by Khadījah.
595	Muḥammad's second journey to Syria.
	Muḥammad marries Khadījah.
605	Muḥammad helps rebuild the Ka'bah.
610	Call to Prophethood (June). Beginning of the revelation of the Qur'ān.
	Khadījah, 'Alī, and Abū Bakr accept Islam in that order.
613	Public preaching of Islam begins.
	Confrontation with the Makkans.
615	Ḥamzah accepts Islam.
	First Muslim migration to Abyssinia.
	'Umar accepts Islam.
616	General boycott of Banū Hashim.
	Return of the first emigrants.
617	Second migration of Muslims to Abyssinia.
619	Death of Abū Ṭālib.
	Death of Khadījah.
	Muḥammad seeks tribal protection and preaches Islam in Ṭā'if.
620	Muḥammad's engagement to 'Ā'ishah bint Abū Bakr.
	First converts of Aws and Khazraj from Yathrib.
621	First meeting of al 'Aqabah.
	Al Isrā' and al Mi'rāj (night journey and ascent to heaven).
622	Second meeting of al 'Aqabah.
	Attempted assassination of the Prophet by the Makkans.
	July 16, the *Hijrah,* the Prophet's migration to Yathrib, henceforth called Madīnah al Nabiyy, or The City of the Prophet, 1/1/1 A.H.
1 A.H./ 622 C.E.	The Prophet builds a mosque and residence.
	Establishment of Islamic brotherhood as new social order
	The Prophet founds the first Islamic state.
	The Covenant of Madīnah.
	Muḥammad marries 'Ā'ishah.

lowers that their families would not be left to the mercy of their enemies, should they fall as martyrs in the raging conflict.

Juwayriyyah was the daughter of al Ḥārith, chief of the Banū al Musṭaliq tribe. She was a widow, and she fell captive in the war her people waged against the Muslims. The Prophet took her as his portion of the booty, manumitted her in respect to her father, and offered to take her in marriage. Her father left the choice to her, and she decided in favor of Islam and marriage to Muḥammad. Her honor was thus kept. She proselytized for Islam with her people and brought them all into the faith a few months following her marriage.

These and other women were elevated through their marriage to Muḥammed to the rank of "mothers of the Believers." Each one played an important role in the formative period of Islam and contributed to the social cohesiveness of the new society. Having declared the old tribal ties illegitimate in the new universalist *ummah,* Muḥammad used every other cohesive to consolidate the fledgling society. The honor of belonging to the house of the Prophet or of being related thereto by marriage was part of the great reform Islam had introduced in man–woman relations. Prior to Islam, a woman was regarded by her parents as a threat to family honor and hence worthy of burial alive at infancy. As an adult, she was a sex object that could be bought, sold, and inherited. From this position of inferiority and legal incapacity, Islam raised women to a position of influence and prestige in family and society. Regardless of her marital status, a woman became capable of owning, buying, selling, and inheriting. She became a legal entity whose marriage was impossible without her consent, and she was entitled to divorce her husband whenever there was due cause. All religious obligations and privileges fell equally upon women as well as upon men. Adultery

	The call to worship *(ṣalāt)* is instituted.
	ʿAbdullah ibn Salām accepts Islam.
	The Jews attempt to split the Aws-Khazraj coalition.
1/623	Ḥamzah's campaign against the Makkans near Yanbuʿ.
	Campaign of al Kharrār.
2/623	Campaign against Waddān.
	The incident of Finḥāṣ.
	Campaign of Buwāṭ.
	Campaign of al ʿUshayrah.
2/624	Institution of Kaʿbah in Makkah as *Qiblah* (orientation) in worship.
	Campaign of Badr (first Muslim victory).
	Campaign of Banū Qaynuqāʿ.
3/624	Campaign of Banū Sulaym.
	Campaign of Dhū Amarr.
	Campaign of al Qaradah.
3/625	Muḥammad's marriage to Ḥafṣah, widow, daughter of ʿUmar.
4/625	Campaign of Ḥamrā' al Asad.
	Marriage of ʿAlī to Fāṭimah, the Prophet's daughter.
	Campaign of al Rajīʿ.
	Treachery against Islam at Bi'r Maʿūnah.
	Campaign of Banū al Naḍīr.
4/626	Campaign of Uḥud; martyrdom of Ḥamzah.
5/626	First campaign of Dawmat al Jandal.
5/627	Campaign of al Muraysiʿ.
	Ḥadīth al Ifk (libel) against ʿĀ'ishah.
	Campaign of al Khandaq (The Ditch).
	Campaign of Banū Qurayẓah.
6/628	Second campaign of Dawmat al Jandal.
	Campaign of Fadak.
	Campaign of Khaybar.
	Al Ḥudaybiyah Peace Treaty with Makkah.
	The Prophet sends delegates to present Islam to the neighboring monarchs.
7/629	First Islāmic *Ḥajj.*
	Khālid ibn al Walīd and ʿAmr ibn al ʿĀṣ accept Islam.
8/629	Killing of Muslim missionaries at Dhāt al Ṭalḥ.
8/630	Campaign of Makkah.
	The Makkans accept Islam.
	Destruction of the idols and cleansing of the Kaʿbah.
	Conversion of the Arab tribes in the Ḥijāz.
	Campaign of Hawāzin at Ḥunayn.
9/631	Second Muslim pilgrimage (led by Abū Bakr).
10/631	The Christian delegation of Najrān (Yaman) visits Madīnah and is incorporated into the Islamic state as a constituent ***ummah*** in that state.
	The Year of Deputations: The Arab tribes enter Islam and pledge their loyalty.
10/632	Death of Muḥammad's son Ibrahīm.
	Last pilgrimage of the Prophet.
	Completion of the revelation of the Qur'ān.
11/632	Death of the Prophet.
	The campaign of Mu'tah.

being looked upon by Islam as a capital and most degrading crime, Islam protected women and guided them against all that may lead to their downfall. It exempted a woman from having to earn her livelihood by obliging her male relatives to support her at all times. It further decreed that in any matter a woman should be entitled to at least as much as she was obliged to give, and so always with kindness.

All these legal reforms were radical in their day; and they remain radical in much of the world today. Muḥammad and his household provided the exemplification of these reforms, and added to it the embodiment of the new ethic. His wives testified that Muḥammad's sympathy for them never waned; that they never saw him except with a smile on his face. And they in turn made his home an abode of peace and contentment. As Prophet and head of state, he did not regard it beneath his dignity to help them in their daily house chores. On the contrary, he made them think of

Illustration 6.9

Interior, Mosque of Sulaymān, Isṭanbūl, Turkey, 1569–1575. [Photo by L. al Fārūqī.]

Al Awzā'i (d. 158/774) was the founder of the school of law known by his name. The majority of Syria, Lebanon, Jordan, and Palestine belonged to his school from 134 to 300 A.H. Beginning in 150 A.H. Abū Zar'ah introduced the school of Shāfi'i; and that of Ibn Ḥanbal began to spread after 250 A.H. Today, the whole area is overwhelmingly Ḥanafī, a school that, having conquered Iraq from 100 A.H. on, began to spread in Syria in 150 A.H., with a sprinkling of Ḥanbalīs and Shāfi'īs among the Sunnīs. Substantial minorities (Druze, Shi'ah Twelvers or Ithnā 'Asharis, and Seveners or Isma'īlīs) emerged under Fāṭimī rule and continue to the present day.

Spain was all Ḥanafī until 200 A.H. The Mālikī school became predominant by 250 A.H. and continued unchallenged until the end of Muslim rule in that country (898/1492).

India is predominantly Ḥanafī. Small Shi'ah minorities (mostly Isma'īlīs) continue to survive in the region around Bombay.

Map 23A. Law and Jurisprudence, 41–200/661–815

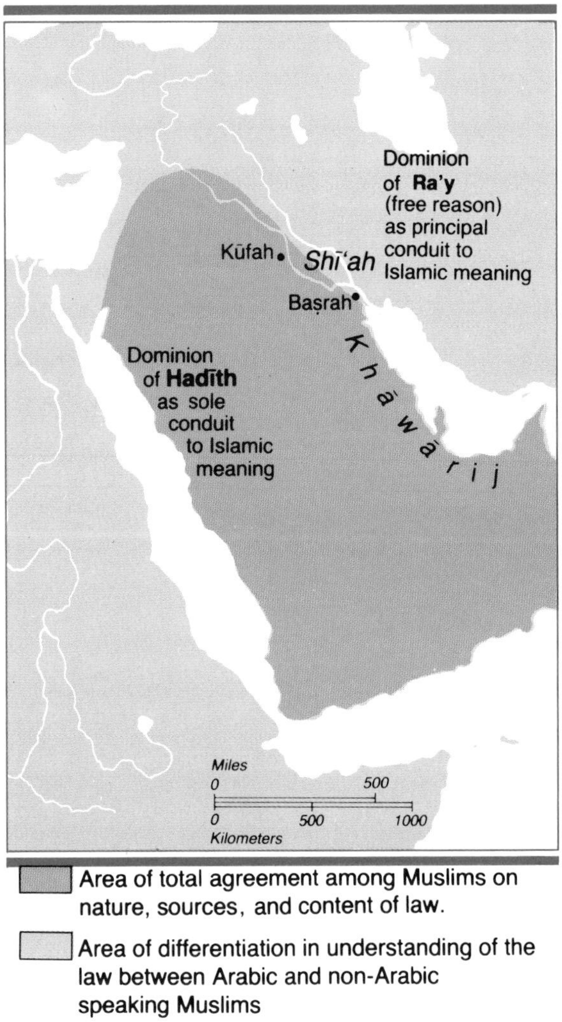

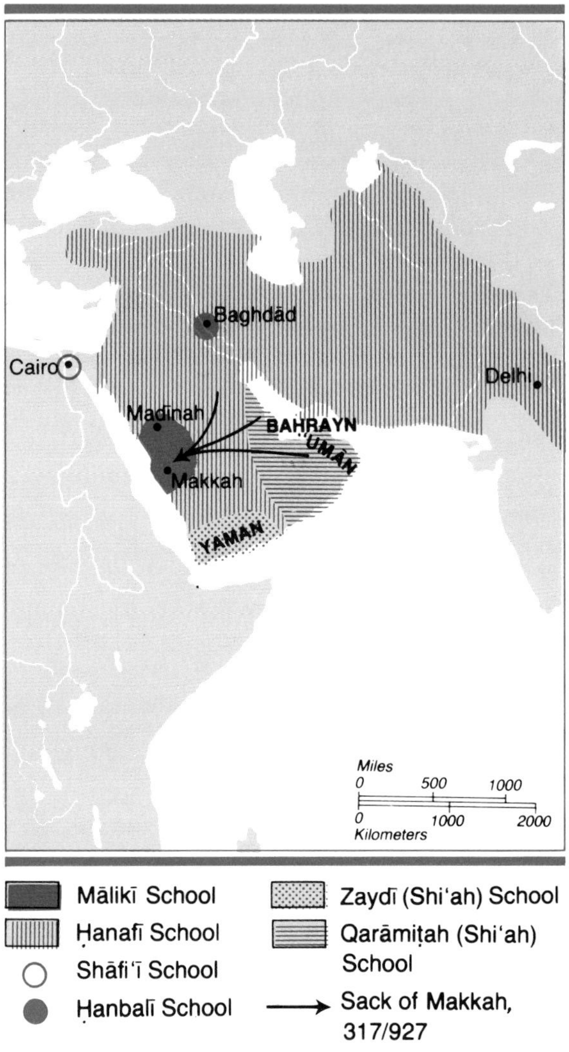

Map 23B. Law and Jurisprudence, 201–350/816–963

him as their equal. One of them was bold enough once to say to him, "Alright now, it is your turn to speak. But please say only the truth." The remark infuriated her father, 'Umar, who was present and who castigated her severely for her offensive tone. Muḥammad interfered, saying: "We did not invite you here for this purpose." Muḥammad spent long hours with his children and grandchildren. He lengthened his prostration once in order not to push away a grandchild who saw his position as an invitation to ride on his back. He counseled his followers to be good to their families, declaring that "surely the best among you in the eye of God are the best toward their families." Muḥammad called earning a livelihood for one's dependents an act of worship and raised its value to the level of martyrdom. The Qur'ān condemned monkery (57:27), and the Prophet used to add: "Marriage is of my *sunnah.*" He encouraged the young Muslims to marry, often contributing to their dowries or reducing those obligations to affordable amounts. The Qur'ān condemned killing one's children, whether out of fear for family honor, or out of fear of poverty and famine. The Prophet urged the Muslims to procreate, saying: "Allah will provide for them"; their numbers are "pleasing to God and His Prophet."

This great emphasis on the necessity and value of the family coincided with the destruction by Islam of the tribe and the loyalties and commitments to which it had given rise. First, the family was a matter of nature. Based upon the bond of blood, it harbored feelings of love, of trust, and of concern that may not be violated without injury to the human personality. Hence, Islam acknowledged and girded it with law. Second, by regulating inheritance and dependence, Islam enabled the family to exist and prosper in its extended form, so that three generations could live together and eat from the same kitchen. Third, the large membership prevented any gap from forming between the generations and facilitated the processes of socialization and acculturation of the members.

Map 23C. Law and Jurisprudence: Spread of the Schools

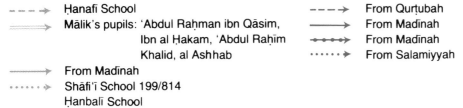

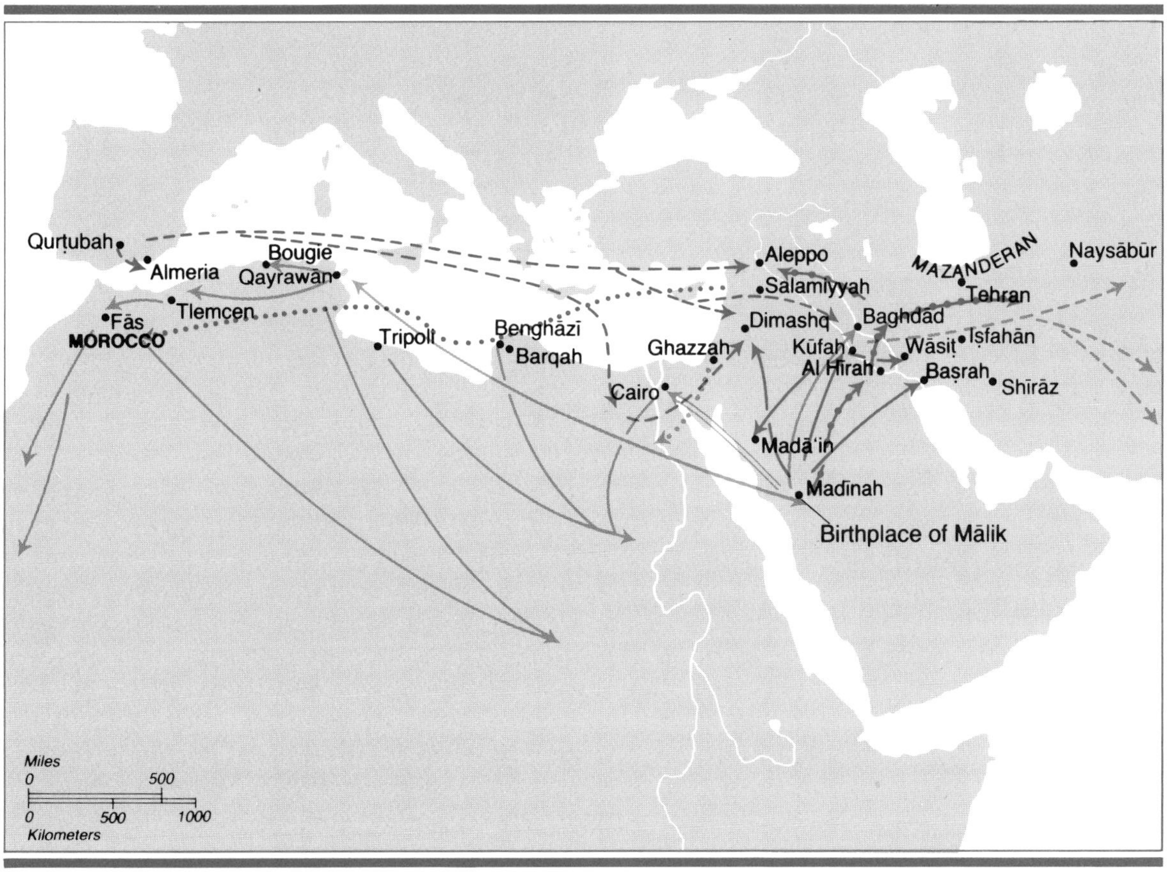

Ḥanafī School
Mālik's pupils: 'Abdul Raḥman ibn Qāsim, Ibn al Ḥakam, 'Abdul Raḥīm Khalid, al Ashhab
From Madīnah
Shāfi'ī School 199/814
Ḥanbalī School
From Qurṭubah
From Madīnah
From Madīnah
From Salamiyyah

Fourth, Islam made available in any household a wide variety of talents and temperaments so that the members might complement one another; and it disciplined them to adjust to one another's needs.

Beyond the family, there was only the universal *ummah,* Islam having done away with the tribe and its institutions. The *ummah* was both the universal community and the universal state. It was an open and egalitarian society which any individual or group could join by an act of decision. Unlike the world-empires which are built upon power and designed to exploit the slave and subject populations for the benefit of the elite few, the *ummah* was classless. The bond holding it together was a rational one, built upon the consensus which members shared in the vision of Islam. It depended upon education in that vision and training in its implementation on the local and universal levels. The family bond, on the other hand, is a blood call affecting humans willy-nilly, regardless of their ethical or rational maturity. Certainly, it can also rise to the level of rationality and carry some of the noblest and most ethical meanings of which man is capable. But there is no denying that without this rationality the family bond is both necessary and universal, unlike the "ummatic" bond which is exclusively acquired and rational.

Muḥammad as Leader

Perhaps the most essential quality of leadership is the capacity to perceive and to assess correctly all the factors given in a situation, to decide upon the desired objective, to design the best strategy for execution, to convince those involved of the appropriateness of the whole scheme, and to move them to desire it with the strongest will of which they are capable. Muḥammad had this capacity to a very high degree. Had there been no Islam, he would have been the ablest statesman Makkah ever knew. Islam added its own worldview as a new objective, and expanded the scope of leadership to humanity and the world.

A single event in the early *sunnah* of the Prophet gave evidence of his leadership qualities. While the Makkans were rebuilding the Ka'bah following a flood that cracked its walls, the chieftains disputed among themselves who should have the honor of laying the cornerstone. This was the Black Stone which the Makkans had honored for generations. Since all the chiefs were involved, the suggestion of Abū Umayyah that they bind themselves to accept the arbitration of the first comer to the site, was accepted but with apprehension. When the first comer turned out to be Muḥammad, they felt reassured that his judgment would bear no prejudice to anyone. Entrusted with the task, Muḥammad decided to roll the Black Stone onto a canvas and to have each of the tribal chiefs hold on to a corner of the canvas as they carried the stone to its place. Each chief emerged satisfied that the honor was his, and that none had surpassed him in that honor. All were deeply grateful to Muḥammad who turned a threatening occasion into one full of joy.

The same astute perception of Muḥammad was present when he first arrived in Madīnah. The Muslims welcomed him warmly. Each wanted to have the honor of receiving Muḥammad in his home; and toward this end, the tribal chiefs competed with one another. The Prophet said he was not going to make a decision; rather, he would stop wherever his camel would stop. After wandering in the streets of Madīnah for a while, the camel came to rest on the empty lot of Sahl and Suhayl, the sons of 'Amr. The Prophet paid for the land and upon it built his first mosque.

Just as he would not favor one chief or section of the community over another, Muḥammad was always careful not to claim any privilege for himself. He regarded himself as an equal among equals. When mealtime approached as he marched on a campaign, his companions declared they would prepare the meal. They apportioned the tasks among themselves and left nothing for the Prophet to do. Noticing that they had omitted the collection of wood for the fire—the hardest and least pleasant chore—Muḥammad declared: "And I will gather the wood." Among subordinates, his position was that the chief should always be worthy of their love and esteem. This he expressed in the *ḥadīth* that says: "The prayer of the *imām* (leader) who is hated by the people is unacceptable to God"; "whoever assumes the leadership of a people against their will, his prayer never reaches beyond his ears." Neither His prophethood nor his status as chief of state prevented Muḥammad from treating others as his equals. Indeed, it was he who taught the Muslims to have their servants and slaves eat at the same table, to give them the same clothes to wear, to call them "son" rather than "servant" or "slave," and be called by them "uncle" rather than "master." One day in the marketplace, a merchant whom Muḥammad patronized took his hand and kissed it. Muḥammad pulled his hand back saying, "That is what the Persians do to their king. I am not a king, and you are not a Persian." Likewise, when the Muslims were mobilized to dig a ditch in front of the vulnerable part of Madīnah as defense against cavalry attack, Muḥammad insisted on joining them with his own hands. Long before his prophethood, this quality caused Muḥammad to be loved by his companions and acquaintances. Zayd was an adult slave brought to Makkah for sale. Khadījah bought him and presented him to Muḥammad, who manumitted him forthwith and made him his assistant. Soon Zayd's father arrived to ransom his son; but, finding him free, he offered to take him home. Muḥammad gave Zayd the choice of staying or returning to his home and family, but Zayd chose to remain with Muḥammad.

For his personal security in Makkah, Muḥammad relied on tribal loyalties. His tribe, Banū Hāshim, could and did protect him for many years against the rest of Makkah. This protection was not without its price in vituperation and ridicule, in injury and social and economic boycott. Makkan opposition was gaining momentum while Muslims were still too few and weak in Makkah. Soon, the situation became critical; and Muḥammad's tribal chief had to ask his nephew — Muḥammad — to drop the cause. But Muḥammad refused, pledging his own life to pursue the struggle to the end. Although the uncle supported Muḥammad and rejected Makkah's ultimatum, Muḥammad knew that the time of decision was near and that the men of Banū Hāshim were no match for all the Makkans now united against them because of him. It was his prescience of this situation that prompted him to negotiate and enter into two successive covenants with the Muslims of Madīnah. Thus he would replace the tribal relationship, should Banū Hāshim give up their support, and bolster his forces against the Makkans with those of Madīnah. Certainly, his premonition was right and his strategy timely. Both were precious components of his leadership.

Upon arrival in Madīnah in the summer of 622, Muḥammad reconciled the two main tribes of the city and merged them together to form the first Islamic polity. Their alienation and mutual antagonism were traditional. Muḥammad replaced hatred with respect, love, and esteem; estrangement with concern; and division with unity. He then merged the Madīnese *(al Anṣār)* with the Makkans *(al Muhājirūn)* who had come to Madīnah bare-handed and destitute. Every home in Madīnah responded to the appeal by opening its hearth to a Makkan individual or family. It was the first time that chiefs and aristocrats, plebeians and slaves, rich and poor, citizens and aliens merged together to form a new society in which the bond of faith transcended the differences of birth and history; where religious loyalty created for itself an organic socioeconomic, political, and military unity. The union was not restricted to Muslims. Muḥammad persuaded the Jews to join, and they became integral members of the new social order. They too had their differences among themselves, as well as with the Arab and Muslim Madīnese. They were clients of the two dominant tribes, al Aws and al Khazraj, and were involved with the latter in all their disputes and wars. Muḥammad's leadership was strong enough to bring them all under one roof and to weld them together into the first ecumenical, pluralistic society. To formalize their union and record their agreement, Muḥammad dictated the Covenant of Madīnah — the first written constitution in human history. Promulgation of this constitution launched the first Islamic state, the first multireligious world order.[11]

Muḥammad brought all this about with his own wisdom and power of persuasion. Of the power to coerce anyone, he had none. He knew well that a union not fully desired by its members cannot stand, just as the ruler undesired by his people will never succeed. The new society was based on *shūrā* (con-

Illustration 6.10

Interior view of the Sathgumbad Mosque, Bagerhat, District Khulna, Bangladesh, c. 1459. [Courtesy Department of Antiquities, Government of Bangladesh.]

TABLE 6.3. THE EARLY CALIPHS

A. The Rāshidūn Caliphs, Al Madīnah (11-41/632-661)

	Date
Abū Bakr al Ṣiddīq	11-13/632-634
'Umar Ibn al Khaṭṭāb	13-24/634-644
'Uthmān ibn 'Affān	24-36/644-656
'Alī ibn Abū Ṭālib	36-41/656-661

B. The Umawī Dynasty, Dimashq (41-133/661-750)

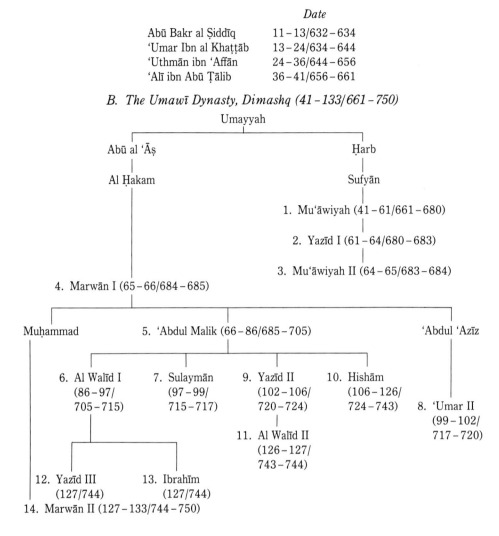

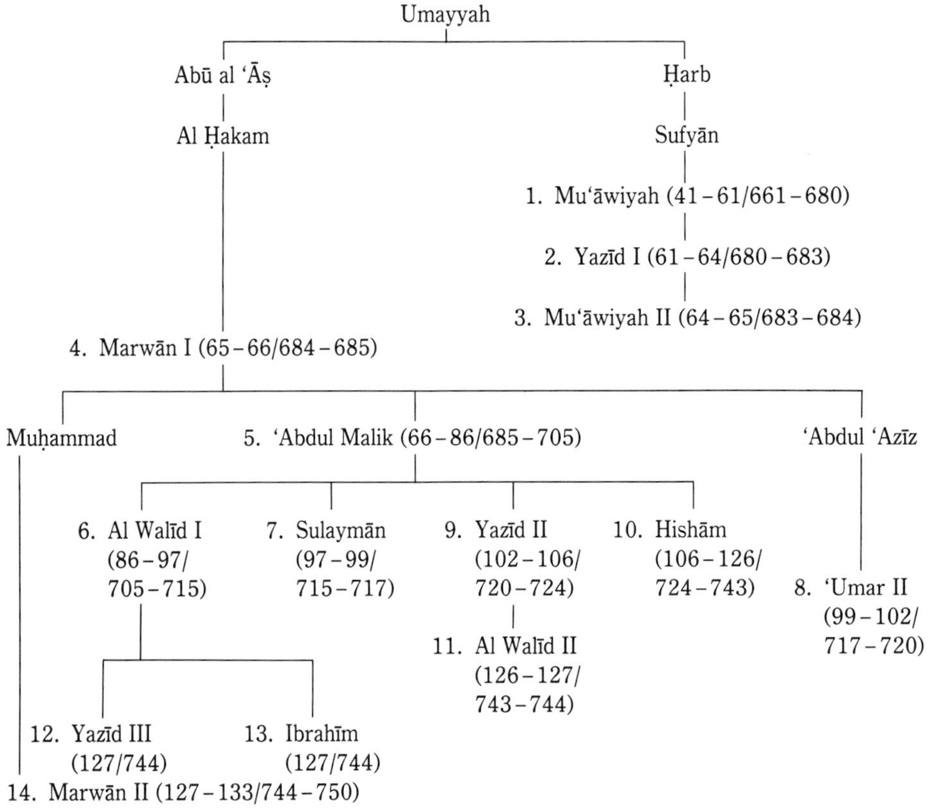

sultation among peers with a view to achieve consensus, as described in the Qur'an 42:38) as well as upon a number of principles that have continued to serve as norms of political activity throughout Muslim history. Among others, these principles include the following. Social order is absolutely necessary. "If as few as three of you go out on a mission, you should designate a *khalīfah* (leader), a first successor, and a second successor."[12] This is the old Mesopotamian principle which regards social order as the *conditio sine qua non* of life; the group without a leader is like sheep without a shepherd.[13] The *ummah* is a people with a cause, a mission to be accomplished in space and time, and hence it must be ordered. "Even an unjust *imām,*" Muḥammad said, "is better than chaos or no-order . . . where anybody may take the law into his own hand. . . . Naturally, neither case, as such, is felicitous; and yet, an unjust government that maintains order does fulfill an essential good for society." Best of all is the government that fulfills both order and justice. In such a state, obedience to the ruler is a religious and civil duty as long as what is commanded does not contravene the law of God. Where the state departs from the law of God, no obedience is necessary. Because of potential abuse of this condition, Muḥammad carefully warned against

C. The Umawī Dynasty, Qurṭubah (139-423/756-1031)

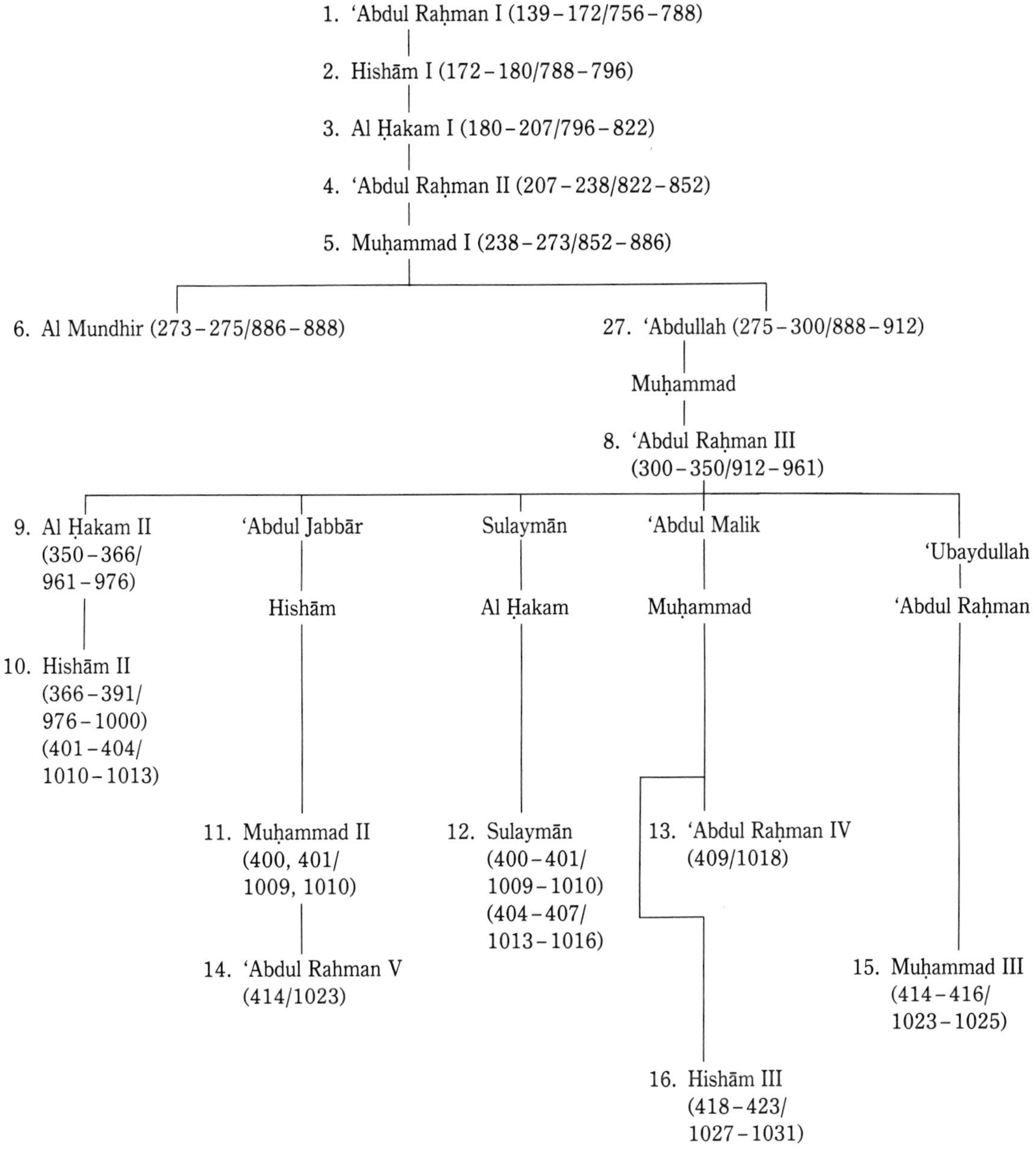

(Continued on next page)

it. We should never question the legitimacy of a government's action, he commanded, unless it is obviously *kufran bawāḥan fīhi burhān* (a departure from the law of God confirmed by unquestionable evidence of its occurrence).[14] Within these limitations, every Muslim or citizen is a pastor responsible for his pastorate, the ruler for his state as well as the father for his home, the mother for her children and household, the employee for the interests of his employer.[15] Besides orienting the ship of state toward the goals

Table 6.3 *(Continued)*

D. The 'Abbāsī Dynasty, Al Kūfah (133-149/750-766)
Baghdād (149-657/766-1258)

1. The Makkan Lineage

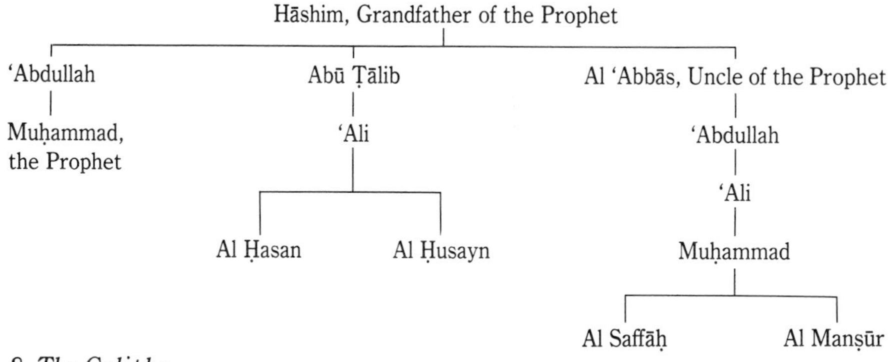
Hāshim, Grandfather of the Prophet
'Abdullah
Abū Ṭālib
Al 'Abbās, Uncle of the Prophet
Muḥammad, the Prophet
'Ali
'Abdullah
'Ali
Al Ḥasan
Al Ḥusayn
Muḥammad
Al Saffāḥ
Al Manṣūr

2. The Caliphs

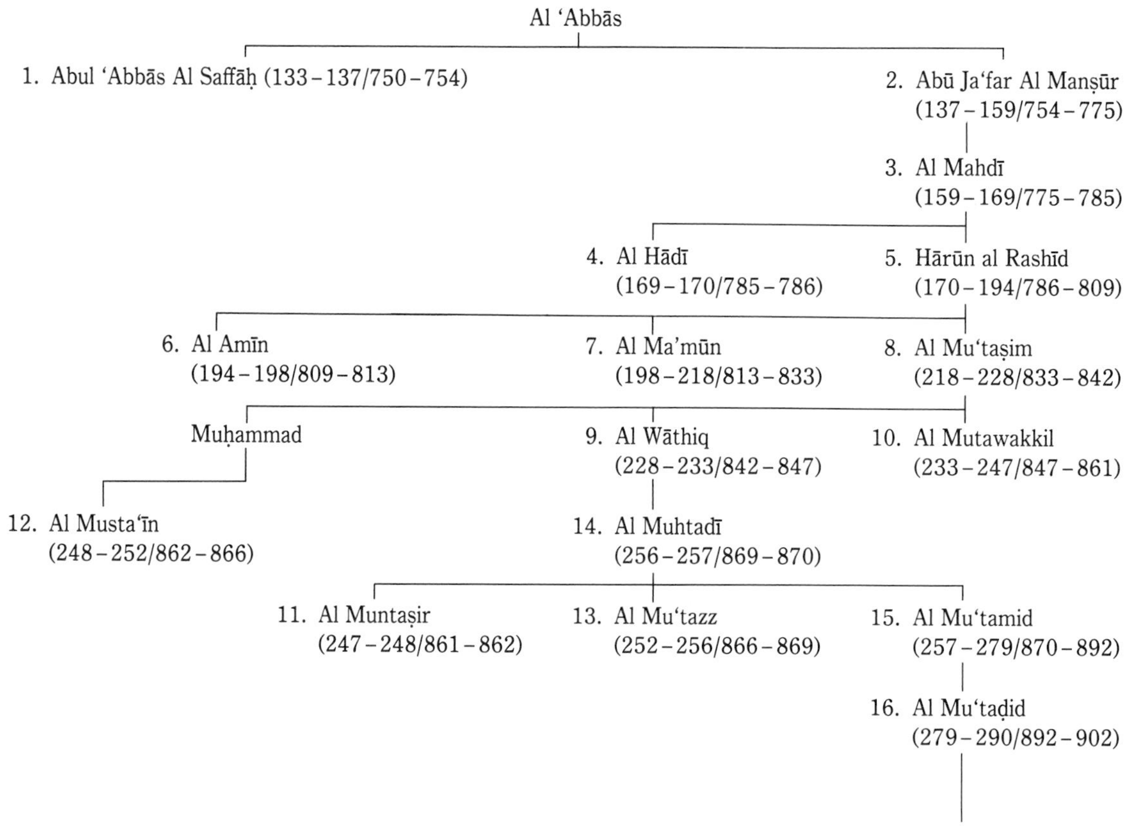
Al 'Abbās
1. Abul 'Abbās Al Saffāḥ (133-137/750-754)
2. Abū Ja'far Al Manṣūr (137-159/754-775)
3. Al Mahdī (159-169/775-785)
4. Al Hādī (169-170/785-786)
5. Hārūn al Rashīd (170-194/786-809)
6. Al Amīn (194-198/809-813)
7. Al Ma'mūn (198-218/813-833)
8. Al Mu'taṣim (218-228/833-842)
Muḥammad
9. Al Wāthiq (228-233/842-847)
10. Al Mutawakkil (233-247/847-861)
12. Al Musta'īn (248-252/862-866)
14. Al Muhtadī (256-257/869-870)
11. Al Muntaṣir (247-248/861-862)
13. Al Mu'tazz (252-256/866-869)
15. Al Mu'tamid (257-279/870-892)
16. Al Mu'taḍid (279-290/892-902)

Islam had prescribed for it, the prime duty of the leadership is to care for the weak, the poor, and all those who need help to fulfill the ultimate and personal goals. "Those leaders who fulfill this function," Muḥammad proclaimed, "earn for themselves a guarantee against the Fire." And history has no regard for those societies that did not care for the weak among them. "Indeed," the Prophet said, "God will provide and give assistance and victory in the measure to which societies show concern for their weak. . . . Whoever shows no mercy to the small among us, and no respect to the great, does not belong to us." Above

17. Al Muktafī (290-296/902-908)
18. Al Muqtadir (296-320/908-932)
19. Al Qāhir (320-323/932-934)
20. Al Raḍī (323-329/934-940)
21. Al Muttaqī (329-333/940-944)
23. Al Muṭī' (335-364/946-974)
22. Al Mustakfī (333-335/944-946)
24. Al Ṭā'i' (364-381/974-991)
25. Al Qadīr (381-423/991-1031)
26. Al Qā'im (423-468/1031-1075)
Muḥammad
27. Al Muqtadī (468-487/1075-1094)
28. Al Mustaẓhir (487-512/1094-1118)
29. Al Mustarshid (512-530/1118-1135)
31. Al Muqtafī (531-555/1136-1160)
30. Al Rashīd (530-531/1135-1136)
32. Al Mustanjid (555-566/1160-1170)
33. Al Mustaḍī' (566-576/1170-1180)
34. Al Nāṣir (576-622/1180-1225)
35. Al Ẓāhir (622-623/1225-1226)
36. Al Mustanṣir (623-640/1226-1242)
37. Al Musta'ṣim (640-656/1242-1258)

all, social order should issue in justice for all. To respond to the cry of the victims of injustice—whether Muslim or non-Muslim—is of paramount importance. "Nothing separates that cry from the hearing of God," the Prophet affirmed.

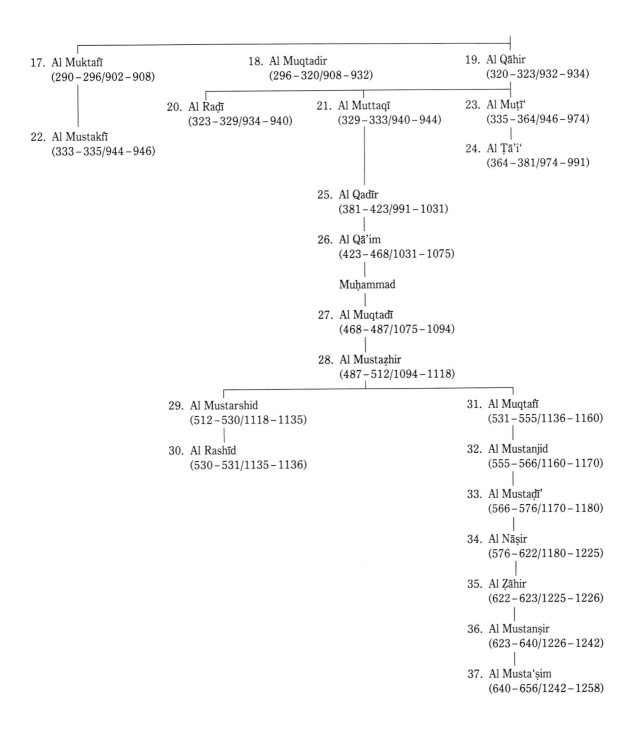

The leadership of the social order must organize its administration so as to maximize its service to the people and minimize the cost. To achieve this objective, competence should be the criterion of employment. "To appoint any leader of any public service, however small, on any other basis," the Prophet declared, "is an act of treason to God, His Prophet and the *ummah*." The ruler should hold everyone responsible for his deeds and leave the reckoning of intentions to God. But if he starts suspecting people, or pushing them to suspect one another, corruption will spread within that state and bring it to ruin. The ruler should always aim at reconciliation and unity. When a dispute arises between two factions, he should bring them to a just settlement; should any rebel against the settlement, the whole *ummah* should oppose the rebel faction and bring it to its senses.[16] Justice is certainly the first social ideal of Islam. The indignation its violation generates in the Muslim and the enthusiasm for its defense and maintenance know little or no limit in the heart committed to *tawḥīd.* However, like every value, the pursuit of justice can also become oppressive. That is why one should not omit to temper such pursuit with compassion and mercy. This realization, together with his usual sensitivity to the need of the hungry, the weak, and the oppressed, prompted Muḥammad to declare: "When He created humanity, God pledged to himself that He would always exercise mercy. 'My mercy is stronger than My wrath'—God said." As to his own rule, Muḥammad said: "God did not send me to be a zealot as ruler, nor a fanatic, but an educator and guide to make life easier for humans."

All the foregoing facts of the *sunnah* concretize the values relating to the personal and internal social ethic of Islam. This was an achievement of the Makkan period. The external social ethic of Islam, however, could not come into play until after the Hijrah to Madīnah and the setting up of the *ummah* as a sovereign state. Prior to this event, the *ummah* existed *in potentia.* Even so, it was subject to such persecution that it could not exercise its prerogatives as an *ummah.* Hence, the first concern of the Prophet after the Hijrah, once internal order was established and everybody was assigned to his station, was to turn to the outside world. Obviously the most immediate external problem was the warlike hostility of Makkah, whose leadership had decided to assassinate Muḥammad on the eve of the *Hijrah.* On that night, learning of their plan, the Prophet decided to divert their attention by putting 'Alī, his cousin, in his bed and covering him with Muḥammad's own green mantle. Muḥammad and Abū Bakr slipped away in the darkness of night. The Makkans forced the door open, pulled the mantle with their swords drawn and found 'Alī instead of the man they wanted.

Most of the Muslims had by then left Makkah for Madīnah. They left behind them their relatives and properties. The Makkans resorted to harassing the former and confiscating the latter. The Muslim emigrants from Makkah were destitute and had to depend on the hospitality of their hosts. It was natural for them to think of ways of getting back at the Makkans. The caravans of Makkah passed through Madīnah, carrying goods north and south. The Muslims sought to seize what they could, and Makkah mobilized for war. In consequence, the Muslims were dragged into their first military confrontation with their enemies. Three hundred Muslims led by the Prophet met a Makkan army of over one thousand at Badr. Both sides thought that the encounter would be decisive for all time. While the Makkans readied the cream of their men for battle, the Prophet lifted his followers' morale to the highest possible level. He prayed to God aloud, saying, "O God, here is Makkah come to belie Your Prophet and stamp out Your servants. If they win today, You will not be adored in this land. Grant us Your assistance and victory. You alone are our Master, our Help and Succour." Then he turned to the Muslims and said to them that God would answer his prayer and grant them victory; that whoever fell in the coming battle would achieve Paradise and life eternal.[17]

The Prophet's military strategy was questioned by his followers after he declared to them that whereas the cause was divine, the strategy would be human. In consultation with one another, the Muslims decided upon a different deployment of their forces. The battle raged in the afternoon, and losses were heavy on both sides. The Muslims emerged victorious. In fact, it was a miraculous infusion of unusual energy that made the Muslims fight so valiantly as to defeat their enemies despite their preponderous numbers and equipment. However, the Muslims were exhausted and could not press their victory by pursuing the Makkans. They returned to Madīnah satisfied with their victory in a battle, if not in the war. A year later, the Makkans returned for another engagement, which took place outside of Madīnah, at the foot of Mount Uḥud. There, the Muslims lost the battle but inflicted heavy losses upon the Makkans, who could not pursue their victory and occupy Madīnah. Desperate as well as wise from their mistakes, the Makkans launched another last attempt against Muḥammad and his movement. This time they mobilized practically the whole of Arabia and arrived at the gates of Madīnah to destroy the Islamic state, eradicate the Muslims, and finish off their scourge once and for all. With such vastly superior numbers the Muslims could not contend, and they had to stay within their city. In haste, one vulnerable side of the city had to be defended by digging a ditch in front of it, which gave the battle its name.[18] Fortunately for the Muslims, they did not have to fight. A terrible sandstorm swept over the region. It did not affect the Muslims who were inside their own houses and fortresses; but it played havoc with their enemies who were camped in tents over a wide arch on the southern flank of Madīnah right in the path of the storm. The storm uprooted their tents, dispersed and killed most of their mounts, and destroyed their supplies. Those who could managed to run away and the campaign collapsed.

The constitution of the Islamic state (the Covenant of Madīnah) regarded the Jews as an autonomous *ummah* within the state. It endowed the rabbinic court with ultimate authority to adjudicate and settle all Jewish affairs. Since their defeat and dispersion by the Romans, this was the first time that Jewish communal existence and the Torahic law were recognized as legitimate by any state. Nonetheless, the Jews' allegiance to the Islamic state wavered. The Prophet warned them first, then banished some of them, then banished others and confiscated their properties. In the Battle of the Ditch they again played a treacherous role; but it was thwarted only by collapse of the enemy in the sandstorm. This time the Prophet was compelled to execute a number of them and send the rest out of Madīnah. From their exile in Khaybar, their plotting against the Islamic state continued. In time it necessitated a campaign to dislodge and banish them from the Arabian Peninsula altogether. Their fate under Christian Byzantium was no better. However, when the Fertile Crescent was conquered by the forces of Islam, the status under the Covenant of Madīnah was again offered to them without regard to their past relations with the Muslims in the Arabian Peninsula.

Several months after the Battle of the Ditch, on the occasion of the *ḥajj* (pilgrimage), the Prophet decided to perform the pilgrimage ritual with his companions. He invited all the Arab tribes to join him, partly to pay tribute to the Ka'bah and the Abrahamic tradition which it expressed, and partly to disprove Makkah's claim that the Muslims have no regard for Makkah and its tradition. Upon reaching the outskirts of Makkah, the Makkans came out in force to defend their city against what they thought to be a Muslim invasion. The Prophet had previously declared the religious intention of the trip; but the Makkans did not trust his statement. They feared that once inside the city, the Muslims would take over. Hence, they decreed that there would be no entry for Muslims and no pilgrimage. The occasion called for some negotiation between the two parties, which led to an agreement known as the Treaty of Ḥudaybiyah.

The terms of the covenant spelled humiliation for the Muslims. First, the Muslims were to perform no pilgrimage that year but could return for pilgrimage the following year provided they came devoid of arms and stayed no more than three days. Second, any Makkan who joined them was to be returned to Makkah and any Muslim who defected to Makkah was not to be returned to Madīnah. Third, the Arabs from outside Makkah who wished to join with the city could do so, and those wishing to join with Muḥammad could do so. Fourth, neither side was to attack the other in the next ten years. The Prophet acquiesced in these terms. He calculated that, since Islam was a matter of personal conviction and faith, the Makkan convert to Islam would not apostasize if he were compelled to reside in Makkah; that the presence of the Muslim apostate in Madīnah would be useless and even harmful. He also realized that the tribes were autonomous entities. If they wished to join Makkah, no one could stop them by force; but the possibility of persuading them to join the ranks of Islam might prove to be a distinct advantage. As to the ten years of peace, the Prophet took them to be a tremendous gain because peace was exactly what he needed to bring the message of Islam to the whole of Arabia. He equally agreed to postpone the pilgrimage one year in order

Illustration 6.11

Jāmi' Mosque, Brunei. [Courtesy Government of Brunei.]

to have a peaceful pilgrimage at which all Arabs would gather and be informed of the message of Islam first-hand. He was therefore agreeable to signing the treaty. Not so were the senior companions, who regarded the whole treaty as an insult worthy of a violent response. Division and rebellion within Muslim ranks were close at hand. Moreover, the treacherous past of Makkah left no room for Muslim confidence. The Makkans overkept the Muslims' delegate, 'Uthmān ibn 'Affān, and the rumor spread that they had killed him. What if they took the Muslims by surprise right now and started a battle whose time, place, and conditions were all of their own choosing? How could they be trusted to enter into a covenant of peace?

While the delegates of both camps waited, the Prophet gathered his closest companions under a tree and sat down to reason with them. He asked them to trust in God, in Him and in peace. Equally, he asked them to be ready to fight to the last man should the Makkans cheat. Finally, Muḥammad reasserted his authority as Prophet and reminded them of their covenant to accord him obedience in everything, including laying down their lives. As in all other times of crisis, Abū Bakr was the first to renew his pledge and warned 'Umar ibn al Khaṭṭāb not to violate his own, which he made when he first entered the ranks of Islam. So 'Umar renewed his pledge to obey, and the other companions followed suit. Having restored unity to his camp by this new covenant—later called *Bay'at al Riḍwān* or the Covenant of Contentment—the Prophet proceeded to sign the pact with Makkah. The delegates returned safely to their camps, and the Muslims began their journey back to Madīnah.

On the way home, *sūrah "Al Fatḥ"* was revealed, opening with the verse: "We have granted you a clear and certain victory; and We have forgiven you all your shortcomings, past and present. We have proffered unto you Our total blessing; and We have guided you onto the straight path."[19] This revelation dissipated whatever doubt remained in the minds of the Muslims concerning the value of the Treaty of Ḥudaybiyah. The following years proved them right.

For the first time, Islam, its Prophet, and its *ummah* as sovereign state were no longer looked upon by the Makkans and their allies as nonentities or runaways from the Quraysh tribe, but as equals with acknowledged title, legitimacy and rights, and a political entity as prominent as Makkah. Second, the pact acknowledged the right of access of Muslims to the Ka'bah, and their right to perform the pilgrimage and to worship within the holy sanctuary of Makkah. Third, the peace permitted Muḥammad to send his messengers to the tribes of Arabia without fear for their lives. In two years of Islamic mission in Arabia after the Treaty of Ḥudaybiyah a near majority were converted. When Muḥammad called the Muslims to march on Makkah following Makkah's violation of the Ḥudaybiyah treaty, the numbers that rallied to the call were so preponderant that Makkah was overwhelmed without battle. The peace which Ḥudaybiyah ushered in gave Muḥammad the confidence to send his delegates even outside of Arabia, to Abyssinia, Egypt, Byzantium, Persia, and the tribes on the edges of the Peninsula. Without Ḥudaybiyah, the conquest of Makkah would not have happened so soon, nor would it have been so bloodless.

By instituting peace, the Ḥudaybiyah Treaty allowed the Muslims to present Islam without being regarded as a threat. Since war and hostility were ruled out, the conflict resolved itself into an ideational one presented to reason and conscience, to each individual person as such. Is God God or not? If He is the only Creator, ought He not to be the only Master or Judge? Must not worship and adoration, obedience and service, loyalty and faith be exclusively His? If justice and mercy and temperance are virtues, must they not be God's commandments and hence be obeyed under all circumstances? And if literary eloquence is the noblest and greatest value, is not the Qur'ān so sublime that it must be a revelation from God, a supernatural work by the divine Author? This cool logic of Islam quickly convinced the Arabs of the Peninsula, as it was to convince the millions to whom it was presented later. The ranks of the *ummah* swelled with new recruits every day, and soon Islam became the preponderant voice of most of Arabia.

Abū Baṣīr, a Makkan, converted to Islam and ran away to Madīnah. The people of Makkah asked for his extradition in accordance with the terms of the treaty. Muḥammad called Abū Baṣīr and told him: "We Muslims do not cheat. We pledged to return the runaways, and we must therefore return you to Makkah. Be firm and go back. God will provide for you." Abū Baṣīr surrendered to the Makkan delegates and left. On the way to Makkah, Abū Baṣīr wrestled with his captor, seized his sword, killed him, and ran away. The number of Makkan converts to Islam continued to increase. Since by remaining in Makkah they would expose their lives to danger, they ran away to the desert and lay in wait for Makkan caravan traffic. They disrupted that traffic so badly that Makkah, being unable to contain them, pleaded with the Prophet to alter the terms of the treaty so that the Makkan converts to Islam would fall under Muḥammad's responsibility and he would have to contain them under the terms of the treaty. It was ironic that the term of the treaty that the Muslims found humiliating and objectionable turned out to be advantageous to the Muslims and harmful to Makkah. The Makkans sent Suhayl ibn ʻAmr, the delegate who had dictated that ruling, to plead for its repeal.

The next pilgrimage season soon arrived, and Muḥammad called on all Muslims to perform the *ḥajj* with him. Thousands responded and readied themselves to go. Muḥammad taught them how to dress for the pilgrimage, how to perform the ritual, what to say and do. Their procession and entry into Makkah with their *iḥrām* garb, consisting of two white unsown pieces of cloth, their chanting *Labbayka Allahumma Labbayka* (At your call O God, here I come) must have been awe-inspiring to all the Arabs who saw them. It engendered profound respect for them and reverence for their new religion, Islam. The Makkans evacuated their city and positioned themselves on the mountain overlooking the sanctuary. As the Muslims circumambulated the Ka'bah, Muḥammad taught them to chant:

Allahu Akbar, Allahu Akbar, Allahu Akbar
(God is Greater, God is Greater, God is Greater)
Allahu Akbar, Allahu Akbar, Wa Lillahi-l-ḥamd
(God is Greater, God is Greater, to God belongs the praise)

Allahu Akbaru Kabīran, wal ḥamdu lillahi kathīran
(God is Greater, truly Greater; to God belongs all the praise)
Wa subḥāna Allahu bukratan wa aṣīlan
(To God belongs the glory every morning and evening)
Lā ilaha illā Allahu waḥdah
(There is no God but Allah alone)
Ṣadaqa wa'dah, wa a'azza jundah
(His promise was true; He reinforced with His army)
Wa hazama al aḥzāba waḥdah
(And He alone brought defeat to Makkah and her allies)
Lā ilaha illā Allahu wa la na'budu illā iyyāh
(There is no God but Allah. We shall adore none but Him)
Mukhlisīna lahuddīna walaw kariha al mushrikūn
(We shall be candid in our religion to Him, however opposed the associationists may be).

This confession of faith was as candid as it was terrifying and fascinating. Its defiant tone inspired terror in the heart of the enemy without show of arms; and yet it moved those hearts to agree with it by its certain candidness, its firm resolution to adore but one God, its reassurance and optimism that God will give Islam ultimate victory. Equally, the ritual of the *ḥajj* itself confirmed the Muslims' high regard for the Ka'bah, for Makkah and her Abrahamic tradition. All this made Islam irresistible, at least to two of Makkah's greatest generals, Khālid ibn al Walīd and ʻAmr ibn al ʻĀṣ, who abandoned their fellow Makkans and rushed in front of them to declare their conversion to Islam. Muḥammad received them with open arms and invited them to join in the ceremony.

It was only a few months after this pilgrimage that a tribe allied to Makkah aggressed upon an ally of Madīnah. The Muslims asked the Makkans to fulfill their responsibility under the Ḥudaybiyah Treaty. But the Makkans declined. The Muslims mobilized and called for war. Ten thousand or more horsemen and thousands more on camel back and foot behind them stood at the gates of Makkah within days, ready to lay down their lives at the Prophet's command. Overwhelmed, the Makkans surrendered. The Prophet entered the city and went straight to the Ka'bah. With his own hands, he struck the idols down, removed the debris from the holy precinct, cleansed and reconsecrated the Ka'bah to the unique God, Master and Creator of all. As he labored he recited: "The truth has become manifest; falsehood is confuted, as it should be."[20] The Makkan leaders stood by, watching and trembling in fear for their lives. Then the Prophet called them to come forth to hear his verdict. They advanced and knelt before him. The Prophet said: "Rise and go forth; you are free," signifying his general pardon to them and to all Makkans. This magnanimity of Muḥammad at his finest hour of triumph dissipated the last resistance in their hearts. First their leaders and then the rank and file came to declare their conversion to Islam. Makkah became a Muslim city; its sanctuary became the holiest shrine of Islam, and its people its foremost defenders.

Finally, the *sunnah* was the concretization of Islam's relevance to international order and relations. The covenant of Madīnah had acknowledged the Jews as an *ummah* and had granted them constitutional autonomy to order their lives as the Torah dictated and as it was interpreted by their own judicial courts and institutions. This constitutional provision did not change when some Jews committed acts of treason against the Islamic state because Islam rejects any theory of vicarious guilt. The acts of treason were the acts of those who committed them, not of their descendants. The same constitutional provision was extrapolated by the Prophet for application to the Christians of Najrān. These had sent a delegation to Madīnah seeking a reassurance regarding their own status and inquiring about Islam. The Christian delegation was met and entertained by the Prophet, who also presented Islam to them. Some of them converted and joined the ranks of the Muslim *ummah*. Those who did not convert were established by the Prophet as another *ummah* within the Islamic state and under its constitution. He sent the delegates back to their people in Yaman guarded from the hazards of the road by Muslims and accompanied by Abū 'Ubaydah, whom he appointed as state representative in their midst.

The Islamic state, therefore, was by the Prophet's own design and implementation a multireligious order which brought together under the order of peace and legitimacy Muslims, Jews, and Christians. This pluralism was not a matter of courtesy but was constitutional; not a matter of tolerating the alien customs of food, dress, or music, but the whole corpus of laws that governed the life of the non-Muslim religious community. The pluralism of the Islamic state was a pluralism of laws, an innovation unheard of elsewhere in the history of mankind. The Islamic state of Madīnah was a microcosm of the world order to be. The act of bringing the Christians of Najrān under the Constitution was to be repeated by his companions in favor of the Zoroastrian Persians, and by their successors in favor of the Hindus and Buddhists, and of all other religions.

Following the peace with Makkah, Muḥammad had sent delegations to the kings around Arabia inviting them to join Islam. If they did not accept to convert, after hearing the presentation of the delegates, they were invited to join the *Pax Islamica,* the international order of peace under which ideas are free to move and humans are free to convince and be convinced of the truth while preserving their political, economic, social, cultural, even military establishments intact. The Islamic state sought an opportunity to present Islam to all humans everywhere and would honor their personal decisions to accept or reject it. It was not interested in subjugating them, nor in exploiting them in any way. It sought not its own interest but their own as equal human beings, as creatures of God like themselves, entitled to have the revelation conveyed to them. The Islamic state's mission was restricted to conveying that message from God. The decision to accept or reject it was to be entirely man's, just as God had said (Qur'ān 18:29). But no power, institution, or tradition may prevent humans from hearing and considering the divine call. That would be to assume their incapacity to judge for themselves, which, besides being both false and insulting, is a kind of spiritual tyranny over them.

This is why the Prophet's delegates were instructed to tell the kings and chieftains that every ruler must bear responsibility for the spiritual welfare of his subjects. The emperor of Byzantium, the ruler of Egypt, and the Negus of Abyssinia responded with kind words. The emperor of Persia and the chieftains of the buffer states in Northern Arabia rejected the call with contempt and defiance. The ruler of Dhāt al Ṭalḥ, a vassal of Byzantium, killed all fifteen of the Prophet's companions who were sent to present Islam to him and his people. The governor of Buṣrā, another agent of Byzantium, killed the Muslim delegate upon hearing him deliver his message. Some Muslim historians have reported that Emperor Heraclius himself gave the order to the provincial governors to mobilize and engage in hostilities.[21] This response from Byzantium and its satellites prompted the Muslims to seek to break the authority obstructing the promulgation of the divine message. The options of these defiant rulers were further restricted by their foolhardy actions. The Muslim armies gathering at their door offered them three possibilities: to accept Islam; to accept the world order of Islam in which they would exist as a constituent *ummah,* free to exercise their religion and guaranteed their human and corporate rights; or war. As for the Muslims themselves, their spirit was typified by 'Abdullah ibn Rawāḥah, a companion of the Prophet in command of the army at Ma'ān, southeast of the Dead Sea. Before engaging the enemy, he told his men: "Brothers! That which some people fear might happen to us is precisely the reason why we came here; namely, martyrdom. We Muslims fight neither with numbers nor equipment. Our only power is in our faith, which God has graciously granted to us. Rise to battle and march forward! One of the two greatest blessings shall be ours: either victory or martyrdom. In either case we are the winners." A similar spirit moved the Muslims confronting the Persian Empire. The Persian supreme commander, in an attire so resplendent and covered with gold that he could hardly move, sent after the Muslim commander who was clad in the usual desert attire. "What brings you here to fight us?," the Persian asked. The Muslim commander answered: "That humans may stop worshipping humans and offer worship to the Creator of humans. To fulfill this end, our men are as eager to die as your men are eager to live."[22]

In the tenth year of the *Hijrah* (632 C.E.) the Prophet led a procession of over 100,000 Muslims from Madīnah to Makkah to perform the *Ḥajj.* These thousands had come from all corners of the Peninsula to accompany the Prophet on his pilgrimage. Thousands more joined the procession en route, and others went directly to Makkah. On this occasion, the Prophet delivered the sermon that was to be his last. In it he summed up the message of which he was the divinely appointed trustee.

Mounted on his camel and with Rabī'ah ibn

Umayyah by his side on another camel to repeat his words so that everyone would hear, the Prophet said:

O Men, listen well to my words, for I do not know whether I shall meet you again on a like occasion. Until you meet your Lord, the safety of lives and of your property shall be as inviolate as this holy day and holy month. . . . You will indeed meet your Lord and He will reckon your deeds. Whoever is keeping anything that does not belong to him must return it to its rightful owner. . . . All interest is abolished; and all interest due shall be waived; only your capital is yours. . . . You will neither inflict, nor suffer any injustice or iniquity. . . . God has commanded that all interest due to ʻAbbās ibn ʻAbd al Muṭṭalib and his clan [to which Muḥammad was heir] in pre-Islamic days shall be waived. . . . O Men, Satan has lost hope of ever being worshipped in your land. Nevertheless, he is still capable of determining the lesser of your deeds. . . . O men, to you a right belongs with respect to your women, and to your women a right with respect to you, plus kindness. . . . Do treat them well and be kind to them, for they are your partners and committed helpers. . . . I am leaving with you the Book of God and the *sunnah* of His Prophet. If you follow them, you will never go astray.[23]

Eighty-one days after he delivered this sermon, the Prophet died. He had been ill for ten days, and he suffered from a strong fever. Before he was buried, his companions gathered to ponder their fate after his departure. His death was a terrible shock which caused some of them to lose their common sense. In their grief, they were responsive to the plea of ʻUmar, which he voiced at that meeting, that Muḥammad had not died, that God had lifted him up to Heaven as He did Jesus before, and that he continued to live. Abū Bakr arrived late to that meeting. Overhearing ʻUmar, Abū Bakr nudged him to sit down and keep quiet. But ʻUmar persisted, and spoke even louder. Abū Bakr rose and addressed the assembled Muslims: "O People, if you have been worshipping Muḥammad, then know that Muḥammad is dead, dead, dead. But if you have been worshipping God, then know that God is eternal and never dies. God said in His Holy Book: ʻMuḥammad is but a human messenger like other messengers before him. If he died or were killed, would you then forsake your faith [that only God is God?]" (Qur'ān 3:144). That was the last time the Muslim world heard of any attempt to deify Muḥammad, or to ascribe to him any of the supernatural qualities that belong exclusively to God.

Before that occasion, on the death of his son Ibrahīm, born to him of his Egyptian wife Maryam, Muḥammad was struck with overwhelming grief. Since he had no male progeny, the birth of Ibrahīm had meant a great hope for him, which he expressed by choosing the ancestral name for the child. His premature death as an infant of only a few months depressed Muḥammad severely. At that moment, some companion suggested that the baby did not die, but was taken by God and lived with Him. Looking at the dead infant he held in his arms, Muḥammad said: "O Ibrahīm, the fact that you are the son of Muḥammad, the Prophet of God, is of no avail to you whatever, as you meet your Creator. The sun and the moon are signs of God. They neither shine nor set for anyone; nor are they eclipsed for the death of anyone. Nothing avails a human except his deeds."

Illustration 6.12

Ince Minare Madrasah, Konya, Turkey, 1260–1265. [Courtesy Embassy of Turkey, Washington, D.C.]

NOTES

1. Qur'ān 3:32, 132; 4:58, 79.
2. Qur'ān 4:58; 33:36, 8:1, 13.
3. Qur'ān 5:4.
4. Qur'ān 5:70, 102.
5. Qur'ān 42:48, 10:99.
6. Qur'ān 2:142; 10:25; 6:88; 22:16; 24:35.
7. Qur'ān 80:1–10.
8. Qur'ān 16:125; 41:34.
9. Ibn Isḥaq, *Sīrat,* Vol. I, pp. 223–224.
10. Muḥammad Ḥusayn Haykal, *The Life of Muḥammad,* trans. I. R. al Fārūqī (Indianapolis: American Trust Publications, 1396/1976, Chap. 26, pp. 429–442.
11. Ibn Isḥaq, *Sīrat,* Vol. II, pp. 348–357; Haykal, *Life of Muḥammad,* pp. 180–183.

12. Narrated on behalf of 'Abdullah ibn 'Amr ibn al 'Āṣ by Aḥmad ibn Ḥanbal in *Al Musnad* (Cairo: Dār al Ma'ārif, n.d.), Vol. 2, p. 176. The same *ḥadīth* was reported by Abū Dawūd in *Al Sunan.*

13. Thorkild Jacobsen, "Mesopotamia: The Good Life," in H. Frankfort (ed.), *Before Philosophy* (Baltimore: Penguin Books, 1964), p. 217.

14. As reported by al Bukhārī, Muslim, and Aḥmad ibn Ḥanbal.

15. This *ḥadīth* was reported by Muslim.

16. Qur'ān 49:9.

17. Ibn Isḥaq, *Sīrat,* Vol. 2, p. 457; Haykal, *Life of Muḥammad,* pp. 226–227.

18. Ibn Isḥaq, *Sīrat,* Vol. 3, pp. 699ff; Haykal, *Life of Muḥammad,* pp. 299ff.

19. Qur'ān 48:1ff.

20. Qur'ān 17:81.

21. Haykal, *Life of Muḥammad,* pp. 338–389.

22. See Chapter 10.

23. Ibn Isḥaq, *Sīrat,* Vol. 4, pp. 1022ff.; Haykal, *Life of Muḥammad,* pp. 486–488.

CHAPTER 7

Institutions

The essence of Islam was not only laid down in the words of the Qur'ān — for the ready use of the understanding, and as sublime literature to move the deepest emotions. It was also expressed in the concrete deeds and judgments of the Prophet as recorded in the *sunnah* and taught to and practiced by a stream of generations. In addition, the essence of Islam was laid down in social institutions founded by the Prophet and continued after him to the present day. Islam meant to be observed, to be preserved perpetually as befits its claim to be the last revelation. Hence, the *sharī'ah,* or Islamic law, incorporated these institutions and devoted its attention to their protection and to the regulation of their operation. The institutions of Islam cover most of life's activities — the personal, the familial, the communal, and the international. And they do so with regard to Muslims as well as non-Muslims. Insofar as non-Muslims relate to the Islamic community and/or state, the *sharī'ah* has devoted undivided attention to them.

THE *SHAHĀDAH*

The *shahādah* (witnessing) is the solemn recitation of the words, "There is no God but God and Muḥammad is the Prophet of God." These words may be recited alone or with the words, *"Ashhadu anna"* (I witness that), prefixed to them. They are the first words the Muslim newborn baby hears as the parents or attendants recite them upon birth; and they are the last words the Muslim hears in his hour of death. If they are capable, the dying recite the words to themselves; if incapable, they are recited by others for them. At burial, the dead are reminded by the attendants that God is their God, that there is no God but He, that Muḥammad is the Prophet of God. Thus the life of the Muslim begins and ends with the *shahādah.*

Between life and death, the *shahādah* is recited by Muslims countless times. Some occasions for the recitation are official and public. In a court of law, before any testimony is given, the *shahādah* is recited to establish the Muslim faith of the person involved. No more may be required, as the *shahādah* is regarded by the *sharī'ah* as sufficient evidence of the person's adherence to Islam. Not being a sacramental religion, Islam has no ritual of initiation. The only requirement is the solemn declaration of acquiescence to the essence of the faith, made by a conscious subject understanding the meaning of the terms recited. Other occasions for reciting the *shahādah* are personal and private. The liturgy of Islam prescribes that the words of the *shahādah* be the first words pronounced

Illustration 7.1

Religious instruction for young Muslims of Toronto, Canada. [Courtesy ʿAbdullah Khandwānī.]

by the Muslim upon waking in the morning and the last before going to sleep; upon conclusion of every *wuḍū'* (ablution) or *ghusl* (bath); in every *rak'ah* (prayer unit) during *qu'ūd* (sitting on one's legs) as part of the prayer recited at that stage of *ṣalāt* (worship). The Muslim who performs his five daily rites would thus have occasion to recite the *shahādah* fourteen times a day. The *shahādah* is also recited by Muslims nonliturgically, whenever the occasion calls for it. It is used as an opener in speeches and letters, prefaces and introductions, as well as intermittently in any conversation as a means of punctuation, exclamation, or an expression of surprise, bewilderment, or reassurance. In the Muslim's mind, the notable states of consciousness are all associated with the presence of God and the subject's awareness of that presence, and therefore the *shahādah* is a suitable accompaniment. In most Muslim homes, the *shahādah* is present in beautiful Arabic calligraphy in every room, and sometimes on every wall.

The meaning of the *shahādah* is affirmation of divine existence and unity, transcendence and absoluteness, presence and proximity of God. Its value is identical with that of *tawḥīd,* of which it is the expression. Its meaning also comprehends the affirmation of the prophethood of Muḥammad and, consequently, acceptance of all that he conveyed as revelation from God. The *shahādah* therefore is the confession of faith. As we saw earlier, the Islamic confession of faith is not itself an "act of faith." Rather, it is a declaration of an intellectual-cognitive and intuitive-emotional *fait accompli,* namely, the conviction of the truth that God is indeed God and that Muḥammad is indeed His Prophet. This conviction may be arrived at in different ways — sensory, empirical, rational, a priori, emotional, and intuitive — until one reaches a state of perfect certainty called *yaqīn;* and the *shahādah* is an affirmation or proclamation that *yaqīn* has been reached.

ṢALĀT

Ṣalāt is the supreme act of worship in Islam. It is mistakenly referred to as "prayer." The latter is an act of adoration or worship possible in any shape, form, language, or condition. The child's petitional request for a toy is as much a "prayer" as the meditative act of the mystic saint. *Per contra, ṣalāt* may be performed only at certain times, in a prescribed way, under certain conditions. It is entered into five times a day, at dawn, noon, mid-afternoon, sunset, and an hour after sunset. At times other than these, the *ṣalāt* is a compensatory make-up exercise whose value is less than when it is recited at its proper time. *Ṣalāt* must be preceded by ablution, consisting of a solemn declaration of one's intention to perform it and of washing with clean water one's hands, mouth, nostrils, ears, face, neck, and head; one's arms to the elbows and feet to the ankles; and a recitation of the *shahādah.* Without ablution, there is no *ṣalāt* at all. *Ṣalāt* is always recited in Arabic. Recited in any other language, *ṣalāt* loses its liturgical status and becomes an invocational prayer. *Ṣalāt* consists of units *(rak'āt)* of which the dawn *ṣalāt* has two; the noon, mid-afternoon, and night *salāt,* four, and the sunset *salāt,* three. The *rak'ah* or unit consists of recitation of *Allahu Akbar* (God is greater), of the opening *sūrah* of the Qur'ān, and of praising and glorifying God and invoking His blessing upon the Prophet Muḥammad in specific terms. The *rak'ah* also consists of genuflection and prostration performed in one and the same way by all Muslims. One *ṣalāt* a week, the noon *ṣalāt* of Friday — has to be performed in congregation. For transients and travelers, congregation is recommended but not obligatory. Any two or more worshippers constitute a group for *ṣalāt* purposes. Every group *ṣalāt* must be led by an *imām* (leader) whose movements the congregation follows without exception. The group must stand behind the *imām* in straight rows, foot to foot and shoulder to shoulder without discrimination between the worshippers. Once the *ṣalāt* is begun, it must be completed in all its parts, unless the worshipper loses consciousness or unless the state of sacral purity in which his ablution had placed him is undone. *Ṣalāt* or worship in Islam has but this one definite and specific form as assigned to it by revelation to the Prophet Muḥammad. Any change in its form nullifies it.

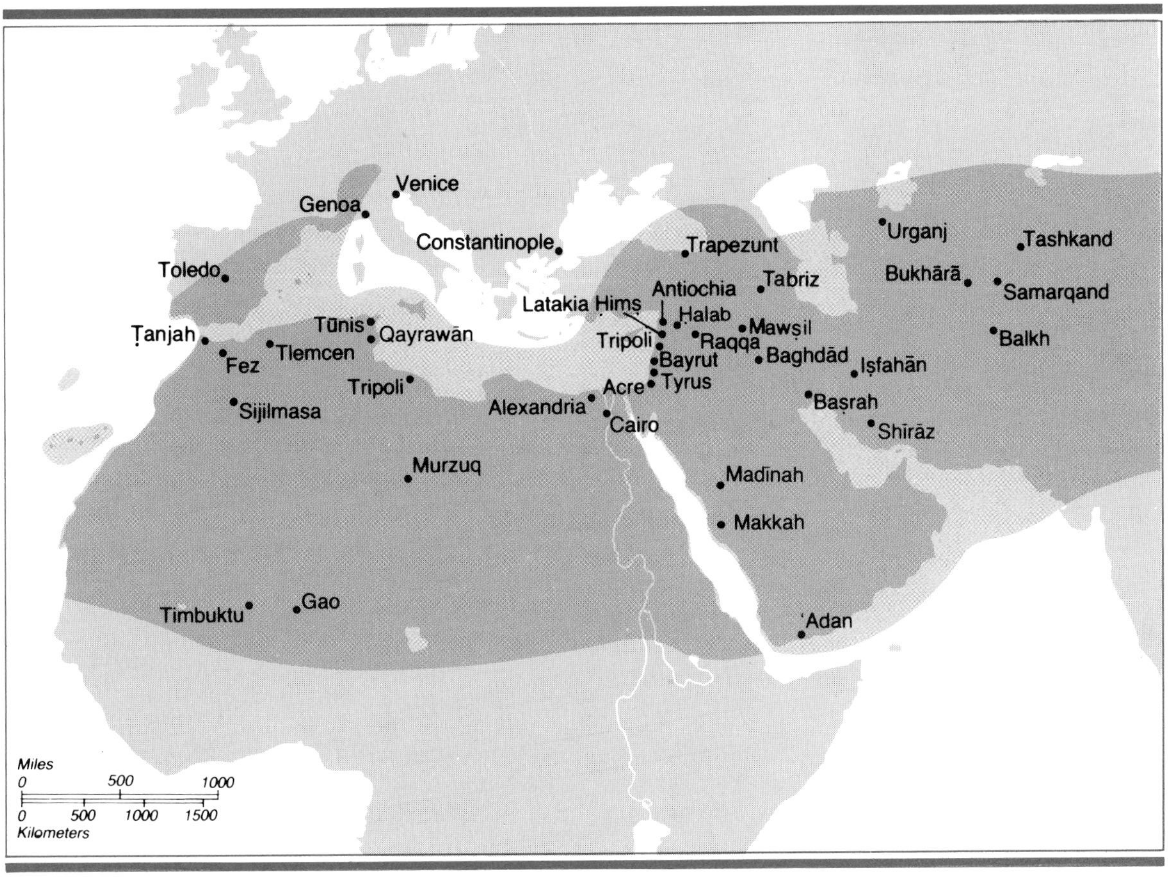

Muslim

Map 24A. Islam and Christianity, 442/1050

Formal as it is, *ṣalāt* in Islam is a discipline imposed upon all Muslims. By subjecting the worshipper to it, Islam sought to discipline its adherents and keep them ever conscious of the presence of God. *Ṣalāt* punctuates the time and habituates the Muslim to a healthy rhythm of life. Through ablution in fresh water, *ṣalāt* acts as a refreshener and cleanser; and through the alternation of standing up, genuflection, prostration, and sitting down, it serves as an exercise for the body. *Ṣalāt* brings psychic satisfaction and emotional fulfillment. To empty the consciousness of its daily cares, to concentrate upon God and His presence and will, is an uplift of the self to the realm of the absolute and universal. From such an exercise, the worshipper emerges more ready to face life and its problems than before. The content of the *ṣalāt,* the ideas presented to the mind through the liturgical recitation, strengthen the self in its determination to will and do the good, to avoid evil, to fill the world with value. Finally, when performed in congregation, the packed straight lines readily suggest and exhort the Muslim to uphold egalitarianism, universalism, brotherhood, and concern for the others.

Ṣalāt made necessary the establishment of mosques (from *masjid*—place of worship) in Islamic towns and cities. Every city quarter has its mosque where the residents of the vicinity hold their congregational *ṣalāt.* Usually, mosques stand no farther away from one another than the distance that can be covered by the human voice. For it is the muezzin (*mu'adhdhin*—caller to the *ṣalāt*) that calls the worshippers in the vicinity to prepare and congregate for worship five times a day. In order to reach a larger distance, the call to *ṣalāt* is proclaimed from the highest place in the locality. This made necessary the attachment to the mosque of a *mi'dhanah* (a high tower from which the call to *ṣalāt* is made). In English this tower has been misnamed "minaret" (from the

Arabic *manārah,* lighthouse). The skyline of any Muslim city is punctuated with "minarets" of varying shapes and heights. Every town has its *masjid jāmi'* (congregational mosque), where the *Jumu'ah* (Friday noon worship by the totality of Muslims present in any locality) is performed. More than any other institution, the *ṣalāt* has determined Islamic architecture and the character of Islamic cities.

Illustration 7.3

Part of the *shahādah,* or declaration of faith. Contemporary design by Emin Berin, Iṣtanbūl, Turkey. [Photo by L. al Fārūqī.]

ṢIYĀM

Islam prescribes fasting during the month of Ramaḍān, the ninth month of the lunar year. On each of the twenty-nine or thirty days of the month, Muslims abstain from food, drink, smoking, and sex from dawn to sunset. Before retiring, the Muslim solemnly commits himself to fast the following day and to observe total abstinence from all alimentation of the body, and from satisfaction of its sexual desires. At sunset, the fast is broken and the Muslim celebrates the victory achieved over self during the day by making the meal a ceremonial occasion for the whole family and sometimes for the neighborhood as well. Obviously, *ṣiyām* changes the rhythm of daily life, spurring activity in the morning and night, and slowing it down in the afternoon. In Muslim towns, the proximity of dawn and the setting of the sun are announced by the beating of drums, chanting of songs, and the *adhān* (call to *ṣalāt*), or, in bigger towns and cities, by all these and the firing of cannon at central squares. In every congregation, Ramaḍān witnesses the public recitation of the whole Qur'ān, in thirty equal parts, as supererogatory exercises of worship, *ṣalāt al tarāwīḥ,* held after the night *ṣalāt.* During one night in the second half of Ramadān, which the Qur'ān had called *Laylat al Qadr* ("the night of power") as commemoration of the advent of the first segment of the Qur'ānic revelation, Muslims address their invocations and prayers to God, and rededicate their lives to His service and obedience with special determination and warmth. On every day of Ramaḍān, Muslims make a point of giving in charity, of doing good deeds, of bringing consolation and reconciliation to all around them, besides offering daily hospitality to the needy and the wayfarer. Before the end of the month, they distribute to the poor an amount of charity equivalent to a day's feeding of an adult person on behalf of each member or dependent in their households.

Illustration 7.2

Calligraphy design in the shape of a boat. "I believe in God, and His angels, and His books, and His prophets, and the Day of Judgment, and in His providence with what it includes of fortune and misfortune, and in the resurrection after death." [Photo by L. al Fārūqī.]

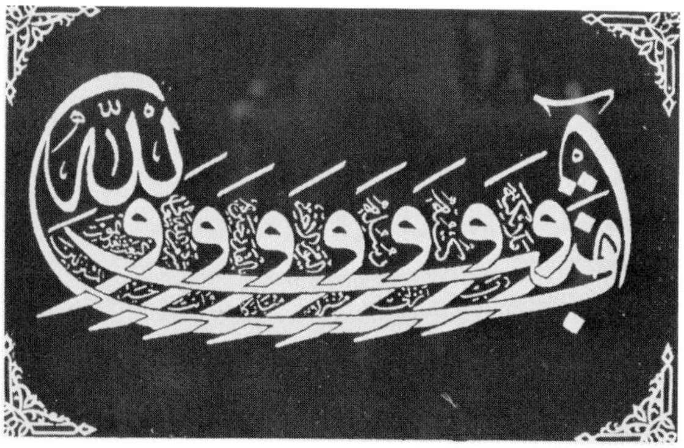

Muslims call Ramaḍān the blessed month, a month of mercy and compassion. Certainly, it is a month of self-purification and rededication to the cause; a month of commiseration with the poor and hungry, the majority of mankind. Above all, it is a month of self-mastery and discipline during which the most basic instincts and needs of the body are consistently denied. If they are sated at the end of the day or in the night, they are denied again the next dawn — a repetition that ideally fulfills the requirements of disciplining the human self, of mastering one's instincts and desires to the point of determining when and how they may be satisfied. Ramaḍān is for Muslims a month of reckoning with oneself, a unique month to take stock

Illustration 7.4

'Īd Prayers, Toronto, Canada. [Courtesy 'Abdullah Khandwānī.]

of one's moral and spiritual assets and liabilities. The end of the month is celebrated with an *'Īd* or feast, which is to the month what the sunset meal is to the day of fasting. It is celebrated with a special *ṣalāt* consisting of two *rak'āt* (sing. *rak'ah*), in which the whole community participates. Where weather permits, it is held in an open field to accommodate the thousands of worshippers who gather, clad in their new or best apparel, chanting the *takbīrāt.*

After *ṣalāt al 'Īd,* Muslims exchange congratulations and good wishes, distribute presents to children and the poor, and treat one another to an elaborate feast. The *zakāt* (tithe) of Ramaḍān comes appropriately at the end of the month to help the poor celebrate the *'Īd* and bring about a change from their daily privation.

ZAKĀT

Ramaḍān and the *'Īd* are not the only occasions at which Muslims contribute to their poor. Practically on every page of the Qur'ān, and hence in almost any portion of the Qur'ān they recite within or outside of their daily *ṣalāt,* they read that God commands them to give *ṣadaqah* (alms) to the poor and the needy. *Ṣadaqah* is formless; any amount given at any time in any circumstance of poverty or need is a commendable and meritorious act, the more so the purer the motive behind it. Islam teaches its adherents that the poor and deprived have a "title" to the wealth of the rich (Qur'ān 70:24–25), and exhorts the rich incessantly to meet that obligation.

In addition to *ṣadaqah,* Islam has founded the institution of *zakāt* for the purpose of giving charity and concern for the poor a permanent and definite establishment. Being formless and depending solely upon the good will of the donor, *ṣadaqah* could not be trusted to satisfy the needs of society fully, regularly, and permanently. The need is certainly permanent, for as long as humans are humans, endowed with differing capacities and motivations for economic action, there will be some who, whether deservedly or otherwise, are poor. Indeed, the majority of humankind belongs to this class. Abject as poverty may be (the Qur'ān calls it "the promise of Satan"— 2:268), the human predicament is that it is, and most likely will continue to be, universal. To transform the elements of nature into sources of nutrition and comfort, of wisdom and beauty, efficiency and enjoyment, is the content of the divine *amānah* every human carries. So many humans will fail in achieving a satisfactory level of *amānah* and will consequently suffer poverty in their lives that to help them in their deprivation and misery is indeed built into the *amānah* itself and con-

Illustration 7.5

A pilgrim in Saudi Arabia for the *Ḥajj.* [Courtesy Saudi Arabian Ministry of Information.]

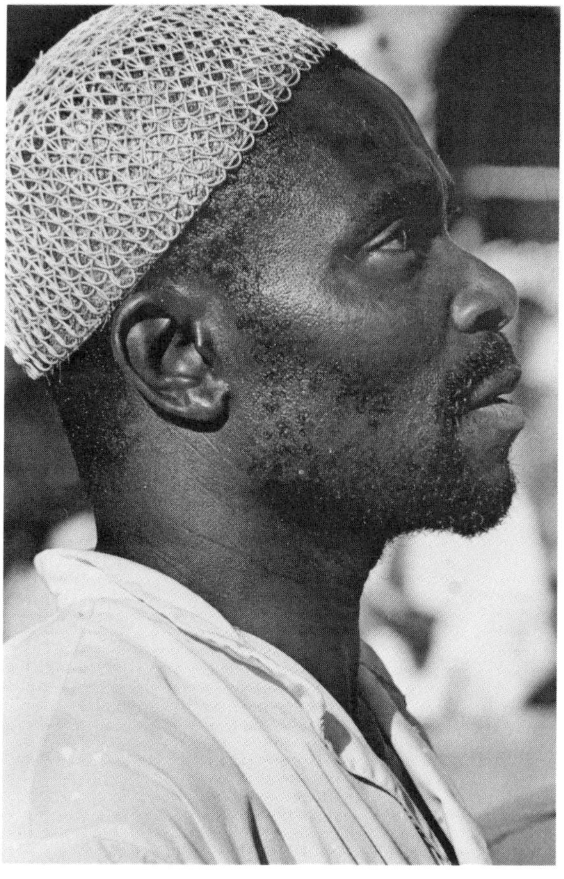

stitutes a fair part of the moral vocation. And nothing is more conducive to happiness in the recipient, and to self-discipline and transcendence in the donor, than the act of charity. Hence no morality could do without it. Religion may back up morality in this regard and all religions have done so. Islam went beyond other religions by institutionalizing charity in addition to giving its voluntary form *(ṣadaqah)* the greatest possible promotion.

Zakāt consists of an annual contribution of 2½ percent of one's appropriated wealth to public welfare. It is incumbent upon minors and adults, males and females, living or dead. After debts, *zakāt* is deducted from the inheritance of any deceased Muslim. Although it can be more than 2½ percent if the donor so wishes, it cannot be less. To cheat in its calculation is, under Islamic law, a punishable crime. "Appropriated wealth" excludes debts and liabilities; house and household effects (except jewelry) required for living; and land, buildings, and capital materials used in or for production. *Zakāt* is due on the current year's income as well as on the accumulated incomes of the past if held by the same person who acquired them, and on all stocks in trade, including lands and buildings and capital goods if they are owned (not kept on credit) and stocked for trade, not production. *Zakāt* is obligatory for all Muslims, whether permanent or transient residents of the Islamic state. Islamic law empowers and obliges the Islamic state to collect the *zakāt,* and keep a distinct account of it, separate from the public funds of the state treasury. *Zakāt* funds must be spent on the categories the

Map 24B. Islam and Christianity, 1009/1600

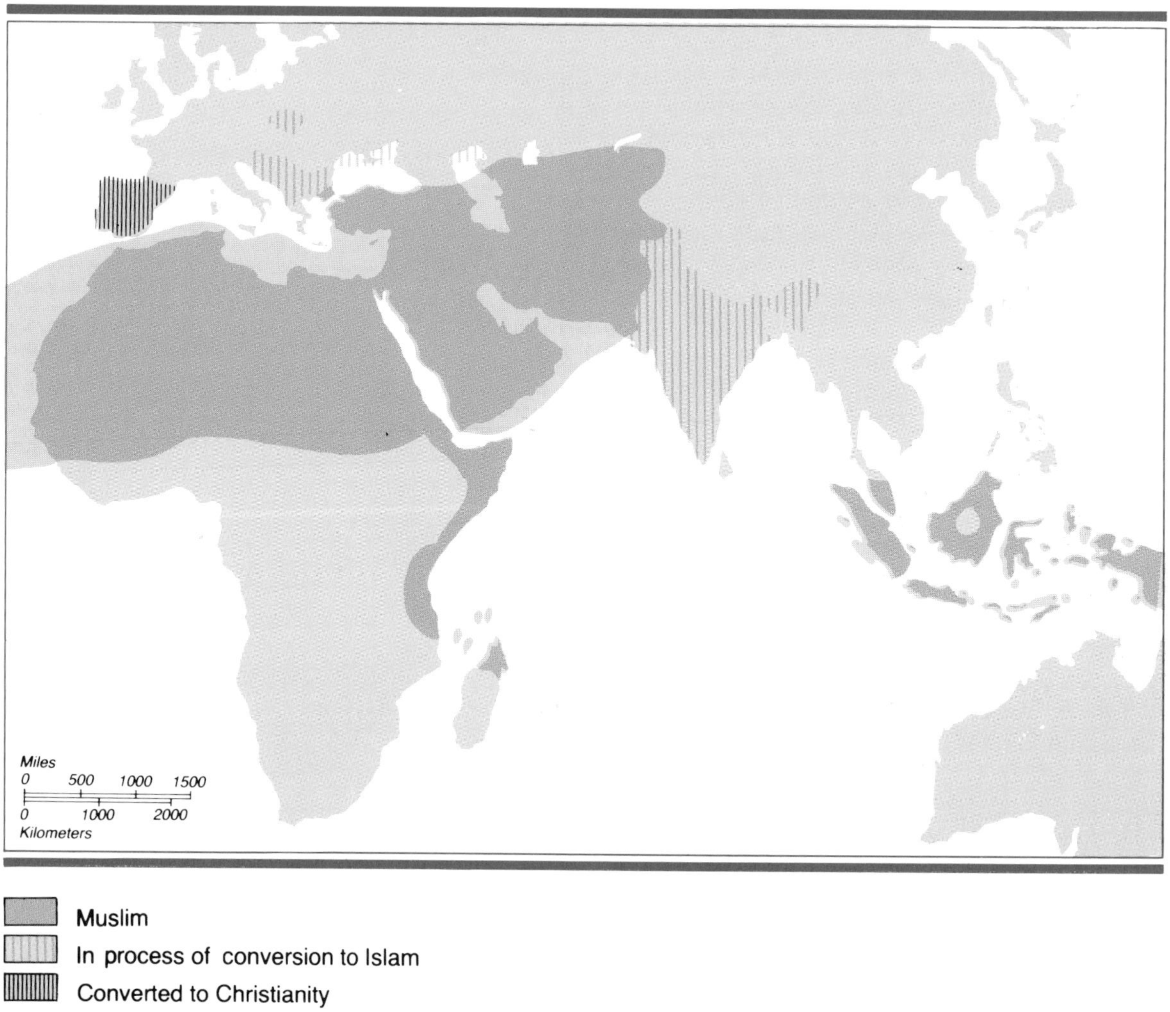

Qur'ān has specified, namely, the poor and the destitute, the wayfarer, the bankrupt, the needy converts, the captives, the collectors of *zakāt,* and in the path of God. With the exception of the last, all these categories are specific, capable of strict definition. The last category is deliberately ambiguous to allow *zakāt* funds to be used for the general welfare of the community. The *sunnah* has allowed use of *zakāt* funds for education of the people, for public works, and for defense of Islam and the *ummah.*

The institution of *zakāt* has offered numerous advantages to Muslims. Being a religious duty, it offers the donor the inner satisfaction of a duty accomplished. It induces a feeling of pleasure in giving up wealth by teaching that only those funds on which the due *zakāt* has been paid are *ḥalāl* (legitimate) for appropriation or consumption. The very word *zakāt* means "sweetening," and it implies that those funds on which no *zakāt* has been paid are "bitter." The funds on which *zakāt* has been paid are promised to give satisfaction and reward in this world and the next; those on which no *zakāt* has been paid will bring suffering and punishment in this world and the certain fire of Hell. Economically, *zakāt* has proven to be a tremendous stimulus to investment of income in productive enterprise, for the appropriated and not-invested capital would disappear in 2½ percent annual *zakāt*-levies in thirty years. Invested in production, it adds to society's wealth, creates jobs, and produces more than 2½ percent *zakāt* tax for appropriation by the owner. Moreover, *zakāt* is a great promoter of wealth circulation, a prime objective of any healthy economy.

Under Islamic law, *zakāt* is obligatory to Muslims alone. Non-Muslim citizens are exempt but have to pay a different kind of tax (the *jizyah,* an annual poll tax levied on the lay, adult, free, and capable males exclusively). The Islamic state collected the *zakāt* under the Prophet. After his death, some Muslims resisted the collection. They were declared apostates, and were fought by the majority until they acknowledged the legitimacy of the institution and paid the dues. The practice of enforceable collection of the *zakāt* continued throughout the Umawī and early 'Abbāsī periods, but was abandoned later, as it was replaced by the usual direct and indirect taxes levied by the government. From then on, it became a voluntary institution upheld by local Muslim communities by its sheer moral power.

ḤAJJ

Islam prescribes that all capable Muslims perform pilgrimage to the Ka'bah in Makkah once in a lifetime. Besides commanding his companions to perform it, the Prophet exhorted them to prepare for it, and taught them the specific way in which each of the rituals involved was to be done. The Prophet established it as an institution with which all Muslims should involve themselves even if they do not perform the *ḥajj.* The *sunnah* raised the religious and ethical value of pilgrimage so high that it became the ultimate worldly hope and crowning finale of the Muslim's life.

Illustration 7.6

A pilgrim from Africa in Makkah. [Photo by L. al Fārūqī.]

Pilgrimage to the Ka'bah in Makkah is meant to be undertaken as an affirmative response to God's calling. The refrain which the pilgrim chants throughout the pilgrimage is an expression of this acquiescence to God's call. The *ḥajj* is therefore a self-presentation before God. Muslims prepare for it as if they were leaving this world altogether. They have to pay their debts and the *zakāt* due on their wealth; to return whatever was given them in trust; and to provide for their families and dependents during their absence. They must have earned enough to cover the expenses of the journey and the sacrifice it includes. No *ḥajj* is valid if performed "on credit." In a sense, the *ḥajj* is a rehearsal of the Day of Judgment when all humans will return to God in their creatureliness, shorn of all their

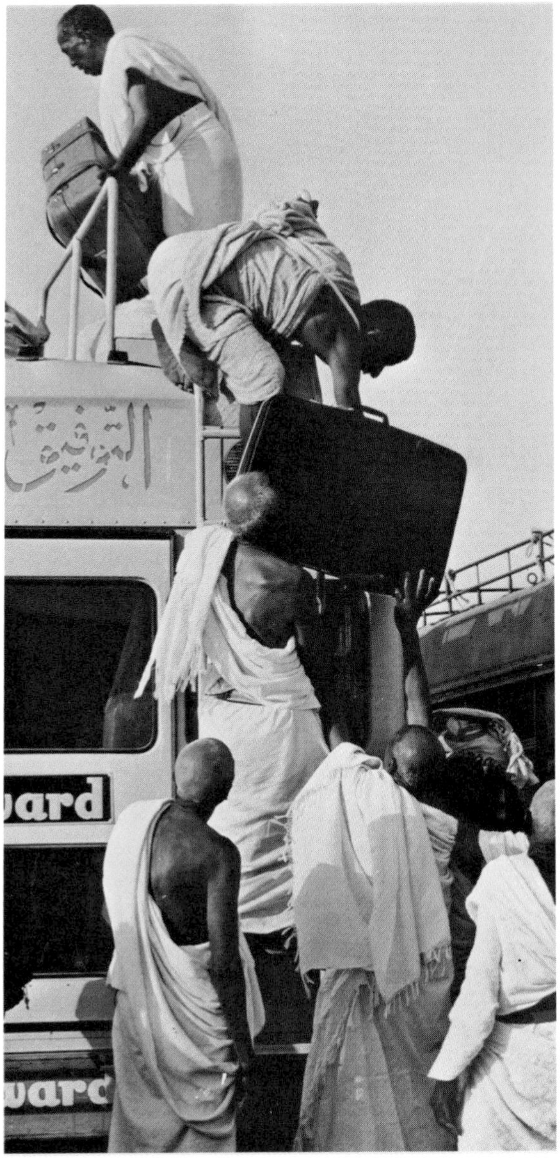

Illustration 7.7

Pilgrims preparing to travel from Jiddah to Makkah. [Courtesy Saudi Arabian Ministry of Information.]

worldly differentiations. Before God, there are neither rich nor poor, neither kings nor beggars, neither refined nor crude. All are equal. All will have nothing but the record of their deeds on earth to show; and nothing else will avail them.

To express this awareness, the pilgrim sheds his clothes and ornaments before reaching Makkah, dons the two pieces of white unsewn cotton, takes ablutions, performs a *ṣalāt* of two *rak'āt,* and declares solemnly his intention to perform the *ḥajj.* Women pilgrims do likewise without shedding their clothes, but they wear one piece of unsewn cotton over the upper part of their bodies on top of their ordinary clothes. Pilgrims then proceed to Makkah where they circumambulate the Ka'bah seven times, jog between the two hills of Ṣafā and Marwah seven times, and perform another *ṣalāt* of two *rak'āt.* They proceed to the plain of 'Arafāt outside of Makkah the following day and spend it totally in worship. This is the core of the ritual without which no *ḥajj* may be said to have been performed, in contrast to other rituals of the *ḥajj* which may be missed without nullifying the pilgrimage. On that evening, the pilgrims proceed from 'Arafāt to Muzdalifah and thence to Minā, where they sacrifice an animal, give its meat to the poor, and cast stones at a pillar symbolizing the devil in expression of their resolution henceforth never to entertain his counsel or succumb to temptation. They then return to Makkah, repeat the circumambulation of the Ka'bah, and desacralize themselves by clipping some of their hair and putting on their usual clothes.

On the occasion of the *ḥajj,* the chief of state, accompanied by other chiefs of state and dignitaries from the Muslim world, enters the Ka'bah for the purpose of washing its walls and floor and performing one brief *ṣalāt* inside the building. Following the *ḥajj,* these dignitaries and leaders convene to review the state of Islam and the Muslim world, as do the pilgrims of lesser rank. The *ḥajj* then becomes the largest and most spectacular social and political convention the world has ever seen. Hundreds of thousands (and in modern times, millions) of people coming from countless villages and towns, representing the widest possible variety of ethnicities, languages, cultures, customs, and points of view interact with one another. Having divested themselves of the differences which history has placed in them, they seek to renew their commitments to serve God. No wonder that the *ḥajj* has played such a capital role in the history of Islam and the *ummah.* It has served as educator, crystallizer, informant and communicator, reconciler of millions on the grandest scale. Before leaving for Makkah, the relatives and fellow townsmen of the pilgrims visit with them in order to wish them well. The pilgrims are usually sent off on their journey after a long celebration and joyful procession. When they return from Makkah, the celebrations are renewed, this time to hear the news of the pilgrim as well as of the world of Islam. The pilgrim is henceforth accorded a special prestige and honor among his peers, expressed in the title *Ḥājj* or *Ḥājjī* (masc.) or *Ḥājjah* (fem.), which he/she affixes to his/her name.

For those who do not perform the *ḥajj*— and they are always the majority — the occasion is celebrated as a feast. It is given the name *'Īd al Aḍḥā* (Feast of the Sacrifice). It lasts three days and begins with a *Ṣalāt al 'Īd* similar to that of *'Īd al Fiṭr* at the end of Ramaḍān, the month of fasting. Following the *ṣalāt,* an animal is sacrificed and most of its meat is given to the poor. The families celebrate with banquets and exchange visits, gifts, and good wishes. In their minds, as in those of the pilgrims, the occasion recalls the experience of Ibrahīm, the great prophet and patriarch, who brought his eldest son Isma'īl and his Egyptian mother, Hājar, to settle in Makkah, as yet a desolate place in the desert. Hājar deposited the child and wandered in the wilderness looking for water. She ran back to the baby's cries, to venture out again in search of water. This is reenacted by the pilgrim's *sa'y* (jogging) between the two hills of Ṣafā and Marwah. At her return, she found a spring of water, Zamzam, jutting under the foot of the child. Zamzam is now within the *Ḥaram* precinct. The story of Ibrahīm's sacrifice is told in the Qur'ān (37:100–113). When Isma'īl grew up, Ibrahīm received the command from God to sacrifice his son. He acquiesced, and at the moment he was about to execute the command, God stopped him and provided a lamb to be sacrificed instead.[1] All this, the Islamic tradition holds, took place on the site where the Ka'bah stands. In gratitude to God, Ibrahīm, the father, and Isma'īl, the son, built the Ka'bah and consecrated it as the "House of God," the house where God alone would be adored and worshipped. Isma'īl grew up, married a Jurhum tribeswoman from the vicinity, and scioned the Arabs of the northern regions of the Peninsula. Later on, the Makkans lapsed into idolatry; but the tradition of their origin and descendance from Isma'īl and Ibrahīm never died. To the Muslim, the *ḥajj* is a reaffirmation of the faith of Ibrahīm, whom the Qur'ān called the first Muslim, the *ḥanīf par excellence.*

Illustration 7.8

View of the Prophet's Mosque in Madīnah. [Courtesy Ministry of Information, Saudi Arabia.]

THE FAMILY

As regards male–female relations, Islam proclaimed the divine pattern as consisting of their cohabitation under the law. The Creator, the Qur'ān asserted, has constituted humanity into male and female, established mutual affection between them, and prepared them to find quiescence and love in each other (Qur'ān 31:21). Celibacy is condemned and marriage is encouraged. Islam blesses the couple that opts for marriage. Muslims regard it as noble and universally necessary because it brings quiescence, progeny, and continuation of life with purity and responsibility. Marriage also facilitates constructive participation in society's corporate life and mission through socialization of the children which the family institution achieves. Furthermore, Islam is free of the preconception of woman as temptress, as source of evil and death, or as cause of the fall of humanity. Sex and procreation carry no stigma, being in themselves natural like food, growth, and death, and having been instituted by God as integral elements of the process of existence and life, the very medium and *matériel* of ethics and religion.

In the Muslim world, prearranged marriages have been the rule, though marriages of two individuals committed to each other have always been known and accepted. In all cases, agreement of the parties to the marriage is an indispensable prerequisite. A child marriage contracted by the parents may be annulled by either spouse on demand upon reaching puberty. With the spouse's consent, the parents, guardians, or relatives negotiate the terms of the contract of marriage. Marriage not being a sacrament, its contract is a civil agreement, whose terms may be anything agreeable to the two parties. Once executed, the contract regulates the life of the married couple, their interrelations on the economic or any other level, as well as the termination of marriage. In order to be valid, a contract must include, besides the spouses' express consent, specification of an immediate and a deferred dowry due to the female from the male. The first is a consideration in jewelry and/or cash to be spent on the bride's trousseau or house furnishings; the second is a consideration in cash or kind which becomes due and payable by the male upon divorce. This dowry serves as a deterrent as well as an insurance policy against the male's arbitrary decision to

Illustration 7.9
The Ka'bah in Makkah, Saudi Arabia. [Courtesy Nasīm Ḥusayn.]

terminate the marriage. As the divorced wife's compensation is decided on before the marriage takes place, at a time of mutual love and esteem between the would-be spouses, the wife stands the best chance of a favorable settlement.

Under Islamic law marriage does not alter the Muslim woman's legal status as a full personality, capable of owning and disposing of income and property as she pleases. Neither does marriage alter the woman's name. Her residence and conduct in life are regulated by the contract of marriage. She can initiate divorce proceedings against her husband if there is cause, which the *sharī'ah* defines as incompatibility, cruelty, injustice, prolonged absence, adultery, insanity, and incurable or contagious diseases. She can make her marriage monogamous if she chooses to include a clause in her contract annulling her marriage in case the husband contracts another. Islam regards men and women as absolutely equal in their religious and civil duties, although it does not understand this equality as implying equivalence of natural capacities and talents, or as identity of roles. Islam's view, therefore, is one of equality, not equivalence. Men and women were created differently and were destined for different roles in creation. Both roles call for the greatest possible intelligence and exertion if they are to realize the ultimate purposes of creation. This notwithstanding, Islam imposes upon men always to deal with women *bil ma'rūf*(with sympathy, kindness, and in the noble way). As mistresses and managers of the household, as mothers and educators of the children, and as sources of *sakīnah* (quiescence, bliss, benediction, beauty), women have played a capital role in the making of Islamic society.

The Islamic family is not a nuclear one, consisting of only parents and children. It is extended to include the grandparents, grandchildren, uncles and aunts, and their progeny. Islam has guided the family in its extended form by the laws of dependence and inheritance. The former regard as the male's dependents all

TABLE 7.1. THE *Kiswah* (COVERING) OF THE KA'BAH

The *kiswah* is put together of 54 strips of cloth of 14 meters each, covering an area of 875 m². The cloth is 2 mm thick. The lining is made of white linen. The belt around the *kiswah* is 61 meters long and 94 cm wide.

220 B.H.	Ṭubba' Abū Karib As'ad, king of Ḥimyar, first to cover the Ka'bah with silk and make a door for it.
10 A.H.	The Prophet covers the Ka'bah with a Yamani cloth; after that, the caliphs put on a new cover every year.
160	Al Mahdī orders one *kiswah* per year. Al Ma'mūm orders a *kiswah* in white silk. In consecutive years, he orders yellow, green, and black coverings.
570	Isma'īl ibn al Nāṣir organizes a *waqf* of three villages in Egypt for the making of the *kiswah*. 'Uthmanlī rulers added seven villages to the *waqf*.
1226	Muḥammad 'Alī dissolves the *waqf*. The government assumes responsibility.
1341	Dispute between Sharīf Ḥusayn and Egypt. Istanbul makes *kiswah* and sends it by sea via Rābigh.
1346	Dār al Kiswah in Makkah organized with twelve looms.
1347	First *kiswah* made in Makkah.

the women in the extended family, regardless of their financial status, thus relieving them of having to earn their livelihood; the latter regard all the members of the extended family as heirs in varying degrees, assigning to the males double the share of females. If anything, Islam's law of inheritance has done women a favor — their property is theirs to keep or to sell; they are entitled to half the share of males; and they are forever dependents whose sustenance is obligatory upon the males. Islamic law has laid down the responsibility for the maintenance and prosperity of the household at the door of men, and Islamic ethics extol the value attached to this responsibility to the highest level of honor and felicity. By living together, the members of the extended family overcome any gap between the generations; they acculturate and socialize the new generation with efficiency and ease, and provide for each member a companion, confidant, playmate, or fellow to enable that member to overcome the hardships of life. Individualism, egotism, and loneliness are thus banished from Islamic family life. Furthermore, because the extended family readily provides a replacement for almost any function, it makes it possible for any of its members — including the women who have such inclination and aptitude — to pursue vocational goals outside the home without damage to children or to household harmony and beauty. Thus the Islamic family system is the best equipped to face and overcome the problems of modernity.

Islam assigns responsibility for bringing up children totally to the parents. Their duties include, besides physical care and nourishment, acculturation into Islam and socialization into the *ummah*. The *sharī'ah* prescribes that parents must arrange to give their children instruction in the Islamic rituals and Islamic law and ethics, and to initiate them into membership in the *ummah*. In case of inability or failure, the responsibility must be shouldered by society. The parents recite the *shahādah* into their children's ears when born; give them their Islamic names; arrange for their circumcision if males, for their learning "the pillars of Islam," and for their correct reading and recitation of the Qur'ān; prepare them for a life of service to the extended family and society; correct them when they err; and advise and provide them with a good example at all times. For their part, the *sharī'ah* prescribes for the children to honor and obey their parents and elders, and to support them in their old age.

The Muslim family is individually and corporately responsible for the *ummah*. It is the family's task to populate the state, to prepare the generations to uphold the social, cultural, political, and economic systems of the *ummah*, to contribute to the welfare of all citizens, and to defend the *ummah* in time of need.

Illustration 7.10

The famous Black Stone, encased in the east corner of the Ka'bah. [Courtesy Ministry of Information, Saudi Arabia.]

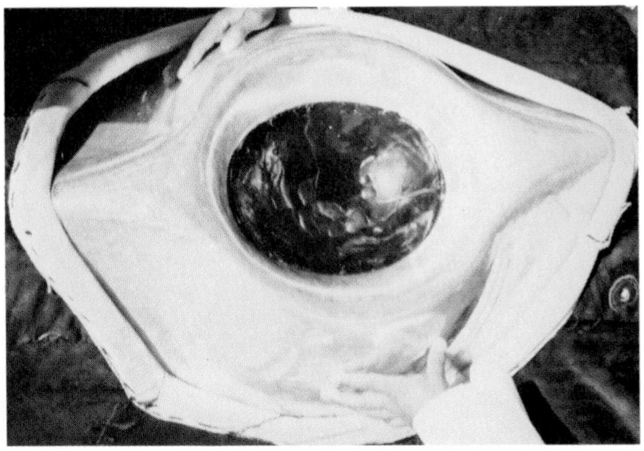

THE MOSQUE, THE *MADRASAH*, AND THE *WAQF*

In Islam, the mosque occupies a place of central importance. Regardless of its size, location, or splendor, the mosque has fulfilled the same function everywhere. Once built, the mosque belongs to no human owner. Its owner is literally God, making the expression "House of God" not only figuratively but legally true. There is no such a thing as membership in or of a mosque; every Muslim in the world is equally entitled to attend all functions, to use all facilities. There is no "admission" or initiation, no fees or subscription, no quota, limit, or restriction for anyone. This is the practical result of the mosque being *waqf,* a perpetual trust which the donor gave to God and then relinquished all control over. The mosque is run by a *mutawallī* (manager) who is appointed to the post by the *qāḍī* (judge) of the district. His duty is to receive the donations of the people and to maintain the mosque building, keeping it open, clean, well lit, and in good repair. In order to provide for the mosque, its *mutawallī,* and its *imām,* the original or other donors contribute other properties or, better still, build shops around the mosque, the income from which covers the mosque expenses. The *mutawallī* "manages" the *waqf* under the supervision of the *qāḍī.*

Every mosque has a *mu'adhdhin* (caller to *ṣalāt*) and an *imām* (*ṣalāt*-leader). Both are members of the community who recite the Qur'ān well and enjoy an impeccable reputation among their peers. They are neither priests nor ministers; and there is neither ordination nor sacrament to administer. The *imām*'s liturgical leadership is meant to synchronize the movements of the worshippers (beginning and ending of *ṣalāt,* genuflection and prostration), to recite aloud the Qur'ānic passages of the *ṣalāt,* and to deliver the sermon on Friday—functions which any member of the community could perform. Sometimes the *imāms* fulfill other functions as well, such as being the school teacher, or the social and political leader of the community; but these are not necessary concomitants of their liturgical leadership. The *waqf* was the earliest instance of a moral, nonhuman personality recognized by law. On behalf of the *waqf,* the *mutawallī* could sue; receive and administer funds; enter into contracts of service, repair, supply, or construction. The *waqf* is always perpetual; once made, it cannot be revoked or canceled. *Waqf* property cannot ever be sold, but it can be exchanged under special conditions. In most cases, neither *mutawallī* nor *imām* are full-time employments. Often they are honorific.

During the times that it was not used for the five daily *ṣalāt* exercises, the mosque often served as a place of "continuing education" for the worshippers, a community center in which the local members held their meetings. The Prophet's headquarters were in his mosque in Madīnah, and it remained the headquarters of the Rāshidūn caliphs (10–39/632–660). The mosques were also centers of mission. Non-Muslims were admitted to be taught the fundamentals of Islam. Naturally, they soon developed into colleges with permanent teachers and pupils. The colleges were first housed within the mosque, and the classes were held between the *ṣalāt* exercises. Later, the colleges came to occupy independent buildings adjoining or attached to the mosques. Unless someone else was appointed to head the college, the *imām* of the mosque carried that responsibility. He, the other teachers, and the students all received their respective stipends from the income of the *waqf* of the mosque or from a special *waqf* for the *madrasah* (school).

Mosque and *madrasah* contributed immensely to the growth of *awqāf* (plural of *waqf*); and these contributed in equal measure to the growth of colleges and learning among Muslims. Here were young and adult Muslims dedicating their lives to the study of the Islamic sciences: Qur'ān and ḥadīth; criticism and exegesis; every branch of the *sharī'ah;* history, astronomy and geography; Arabic grammar and letters. Certainly they deserve, the Muslim donor thought, to be relieved of the task of earning a living so that they may devote all their energies to their noble pursuits. The *madrasah* became autonomous. Each college was endowed with a constitution all its own, and it was

Illustration 7.11

Overview of the Plain of 'Arafāt, site of the principal rituals of the Ḥajj. [Courtesy Ministry of Information, Saudi Arabia.]

internally governed and regulated. The college was supported by its own *waqf.* Nobody exercised authority over the internal affairs of the college but its own *shaykh* or dean in consultation with his faculty. Muslims regarded it as an inviolable institution, worthy of their greatest respect and unlimited donations. Pursuit of knowledge and wisdom was for the first time recognized by society as a whole as an institution worthy of their material and moral support without touching its internal autonomy and integrity.

UKHUWWAH (BROTHERHOOD)

Islam declares all Muslims to be the brothers of one another; all of them together constitute but one *ukhuwwah* or brotherhood (Qur'ān 10:4). It elaborates the meaning of brotherhood and translates this into precepts for action. These precepts have been the substance of Islamic preaching throughout history, and have been regarded as laws, integral to the *sharī'ah.* However, most of them are laws without specific sanctions for their violation, except in the cases where material damage to others issues from the Muslim's failure to fulfill them. Islamic law treats such cases as "crimes of neglect," punishable at the discretion of the court according to the gravity of the consequent damage.

As in the Mesopotamian social order, the new Islamic religion regarded every person as a shepherd responsible for his/her pastorate; as standing at the center of several circles subject to his/her influence and therefore dependent upon that person's will and action to bring about felicity. Islam constantly combated individualism and isolationism, and commended

Map 24C. Islam and Christianity, 1358/1939

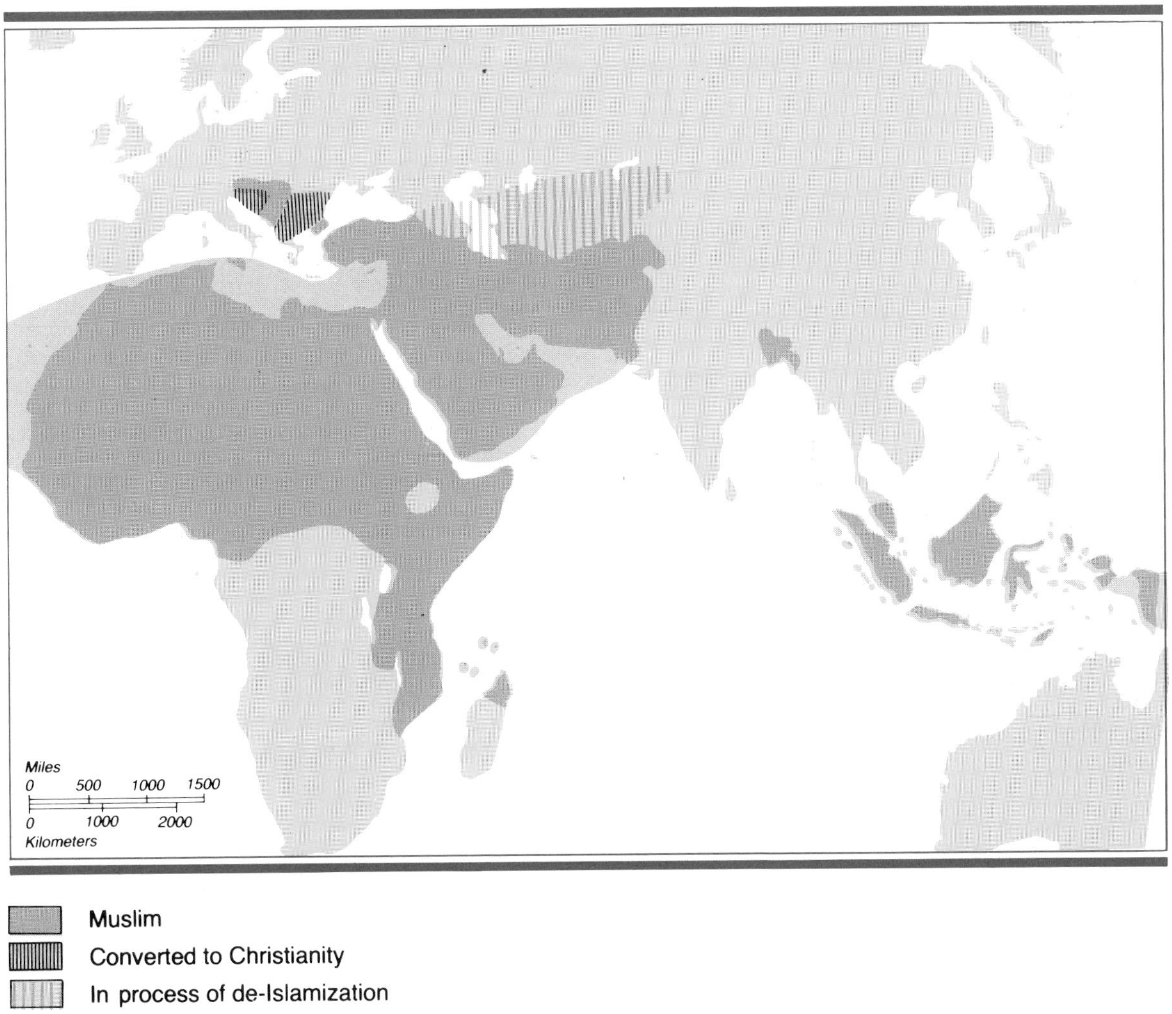

Illustration 7.12

Sa'y, the running back and forth between Ṣafā and Marwah seven times as part of the Ḥajj ritual. [Courtesy Ministry of Information, Saudi Arabia.]

interference in the lives of others to bring about their good. "Whoever witnesseth an evil," the Prophet said, "let him undo it with his own hands. If unable, with his tongue; and if unable still with his heart — the least of the actions of faith." The first of these circles is the family; the second is the neighborhood; the third is the collegium of profession or vocation; the fourth is the village, the town, or the city; and thereafter the people, the world *ummah,* humankind.

The duties to members of society include the following: greeting; visiting in sickness; consolation in tragedy; cooperation to resist aggression and evil; sharing in joy; forgiveness of misdemeanor; arrest of gossip about the neighbor in his absence (whether good or bad); cover-up of shortcomings; protection of the neighbor's family and property in his absence; advice and counsel on all occasions; instruction in all fields of knowledge whether religious, moral, or technical; charity in need; reconciliation in dispute, whether with self or others; and finally, participation in the funeral in case of death. Islamic law calls for the punishment of any Muslim whose neglect of these duties issues in actual damage to the neighbor.

These precepts have helped to establish the bonds of *ukhuwwah* or brotherhood among Muslims, however diverse their backgrounds. The servant or slave is to be given food and clothing as a member of the family, the neighbor feels reassured that behind him stands a whole mass of people ready to help avert any evil, or to undo its effects; the poor are reassured of relief; the ignorant, of good counsel and guidance; the wayfarer and the refugee, of hospitality; the orphan and widow, of the full protection of the law, the court, and the executive; the bankrupt and the captive, of assistance and ransom. The environment of Islam is indeed a brotherhood in which the Indonesian, the Central Asian, the European, the North African, the sub-Saharan African, the Indian can recognize as brothers the Syrian, the Egyptian, the Makkan, and find in their homes a haven and a refuge. The effects of this mixture of the races is obvious in most Muslim cities, as one watches the passers-by in the marketplace, whose physical characteristics betray their diverse origins. Moreover, the *zakāt* fund, and its offices and men, are always on the ready to offer their help.

THE *ḤĀRAH* (HABITAT)

The foregoing institutions of Islam make it necessary for Muslims to live close to one another. Of course, they have been doing so since before Islam but for other reasons, namely, security, descendance from a common ancestor, or in satisfaction of common economic needs. Islam accepted the status quo; but it infused it with its own values and thereby enlarged and strengthened the social milieu. New elements were incorporated into the community as the new political order of Islam enabled or caused large shifts and movements of population to take place. Most important was Islam's removal of political frontiers and customs barriers between the various sections of its territories. Islamic egalitarianism wiped out the social differentiations of previous cultures. The king or

Illustration 7.13

View of Minā. [Courtesy Ministry of Information, Saudi Arabia.]

chieftain, the nobleman, and the plebeian found themselves all equal in Islam. Moreover, their equality was given form in their rituals as well as in the treatment accorded to them by the *sharī'ah* and its guardians, whether in the mosque, in the community, or in any state organ or social institution. New trades developed and new associations sprang up which prompted the people to move and venture out, to initiate new undertakings. These migrants descended upon a community and necessitated the reorganization of its habitat, or chose a new site to build a new city, town, or village incorporating the new values of Islam.

The center of a *ḥārah* (locality) was a complex that included the mosque, the *madrasah,* the public bath, and the water supply. Close to these and making up a sort of outer sphere was the *sūq* (market), consisting of one or more rows of shops along several winding streets. The streets were covered to protect the shops and the shoppers from the weather, and were divided into sections, each of which housed one of the professions or trades—grocerers, jewelers, blacksmiths, carpenters, tanners, textile merchants, and so forth. Each section had at least one, and often more than one, baker, restaurant, coffee house, inn, or rest house. Beyond this center of the city lay the residential quarters. These consisted of dead-end streets on the sides of which stood the homes of the citizens. The streets were always crooked, providing alternate places of sun and shade, differing lot shapes for houses, inner courts and gardens, and perhaps greater security against attack. Usually, there was one access to each *ḥārah,* and no through passage on its streets to the outside. If the town was big enough to include several *ḥārāt* (sing. *ḥārah*), each one had a bakery, a grocery, and a small mosque on one or another of its winding streets.

The *ḥārah* was administered by a *mukhtār* (chosen), an elected or appointed notable who knew everyone. He ruled by moral authority derived from his status as elder of the community, and by his moral reputation. The *ḥārah* had no police. Usually, the *ḥārah* housed no stranger who was not the guest of one of its residents. The residents, for their part, knew one another and followed the development of one another's lives with brotherly curiosity and concern. They met one another in the market and in the mosque on a daily basis, and they did so on their way to or from their shops and factories within or close to the city, or on their farm or pasture lands which were normally at a distance from the town. The children went to the *kuttāb* (elementary school) attached to the *ḥarah* mosque; or, if older, to the *madrasah* attached to the city mosque, and interacted with one another there. The women gathered in discharging a number of household chores, such as fetching water, washing clothes, taking their dairy products and handicrafts to market, manufacturing the same, or processing foods for storage. In farming communities, numerous families moved to the land and lived in tents or under roofs of dry branches and leaves during the harvest season. Whatever the lifestyle, the young, the old, the men, and the women of the *ḥārah* had many occasions every day to interact with one another, and to put into practice the values of Islamic brotherhood for the benefit of all.

The Muslim habitat provided countless opportunities to promote and consolidate the bond of common-

Illustration 7.14

The Green Dome of the Prophet's Mosque, Madīnah. [Courtesy Ministry of Information, Saudi Arabia.]

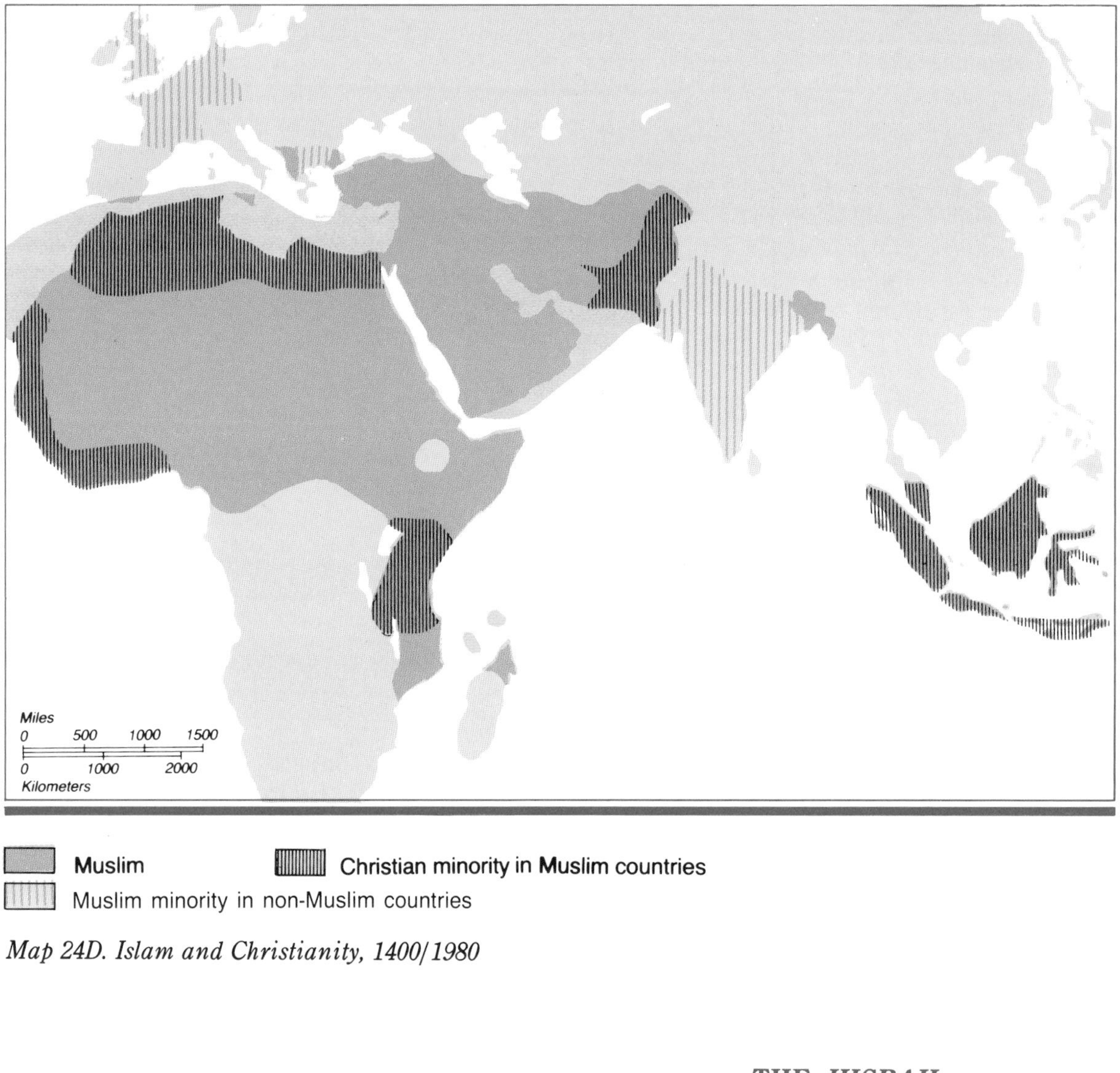

Map 24D. Islam and Christianity, 1400/1980

wealth and brotherhood among the people. Ramaḍān drilled them all into a new rhythm of life which increased social and cultural homogenization. So did the daily and Friday *ṣalāt* at the mosque, and the processional celebrations and festivities punctuating the year. The inhabitants of the *ḥārah* enjoyed the privacy of their house enclosure, to which they could retire whenever they wished. And they were compelled by co-presence in the *ḥārah* to interact with and interfere in one another's affairs. Birth and death, circumcision and marriage, graduation from school, building a masonry roof, sowing, harvesting and storing, starting and returning from a long trip, the *ḥajj* —all these and countless more events contributed to this solidification of disparate individuals into the *ummah* of Islam. This was not only true on the *ḥārah* level. Many of these factors worked on the inter-*ḥārah*, inter-town, and regional levels as well.

THE *ḤISBAH*

The *ḥisbah* is another institution unique to Islam. Every district in rural areas and every town and city is supposed to have an office that carries this name. In most cases, the *ḥisbah* office consists of one person; in some, where the work load is heavy or the area under jurisdiction too large; the *muḥtasib* (holder of the office of *ḥisbah*) has one or more assistants, one of whom wears a policeman's uniform. Normally, the *muḥtasib* has ready access to the records and services of all government departments. Above all, he holds in his hand the executive power of the district governor, the judicial power of the district court, as well as the coercive power of the district police. Concentration of such powers in the hands of a single man would be baffling were it not for Islam's commandments to all adherents to enjoin the good and prohibit the evil. For their part, the Muslims take this commandment quite seriously. To the end of fulfilling the obligation it lays upon them, they have invented the institution of the *ḥisbah,* and delegated to the *muḥtasib* the powers which they hold individually and as a community. What they personally cannot do is by that means guaranteed to be carried out by another acting as their agent in the prevention of evil and actualization of the good. The *muḥtasib,* therefore, is generally responsible for the Islamic welfare of the people at the grassroots level. Since, in the purview of Islam, both the worldly material and the otherworldly spiritual concerns constitute welfare, the *muḥtasib*'s jurisdiction is in effect limitless. Everything God has ordained and everything man has legitimately recognized as desirable have fallen within the *muḥtasib*'s concern; and that also includes prevention of any and all evil.

Illustration 7.15

Ibrahīm's Shrine in the Holy Mosque in Makkah. [Courtesy Ministry of Information, Saudi Arabia.]

The *sharī'ah* specifies that to hold the office of *ḥisbah,* one has to be of impeccable character, and known and acknowledged as such by one's peers. The *muḥtasib* should be a man of great experience and wisdom, physically fit and morally trustworthy, an elder who knows personally all the people under his care. The *muḥtasib* should command a fair knowledge of the *sharī'ah* and its provisions, a fair command of the vision of Islam, a sound understanding of the problems of the people, and a deep sympathy for their circumstances. To fulfill his function, the *muḥtasib* cannot sit in an office in expectation of complaints. He is always out of office and "in the field," inspecting and looking into everything, to guarantee observance of the *sharī'ah.* A good part of his day is usually spent in the marketplace, the scene of a large part of human relations — the economic — where most disputes and acts of injustice take place. He inspects the weights and measures to prevent cheating. He checks the notaries who write down the contracts on behalf of the contracting parties, and the deeds of sale. He listens to the complaints of the public and attends to them on the spot, paying special attention to children and women. Next in the *muḥtasib*'s order of priority are the public services, the freedom of passage on the streets, maintenance, lighting, and cleanliness of the thoroughfares, as well as the orderliness and cleanliness of the mosques, restaurants, and public baths. He inspects the *kuttāb,* the law court, and all places where people congregate to enforce observance of Islamic law and ethics. He examines the goods and services of the whole village or town in order to prevent cheating in their quality and/or measurement, keeping the standard units of measurement in his office. And it is his duty to see that the beasts of burden and the ships were not overloaded, thereby exposing the lives of humans and animals to danger. The *muḥtasib* is also accountable to the *qāḍī* and governor for the non-Muslims. It is his duty to see to it that they are not molested by anyone, that they enjoy the freedoms granted to them by, and fulfill their obligations under, the *sharī'ah.* Finally, the *muḥtasib* is responsible for the noncitizens present in his territory, their entry and exit, as well as their enjoyment of their rights under the *sharī'ah.*

Generally speaking, everybody can appeal to the *muḥtasib* to undo a wrong. And the *muḥtasib* has all the judicial and executive powers necessary to deal with the complaint. However, the *muḥtasib* cannot resort to spying on the citizens under his care; nor can he set himself as a judge and listen to witnesses and evidence in a dispute involving controversy. The wrongs with which he is empowered to deal are the manifest ones only.

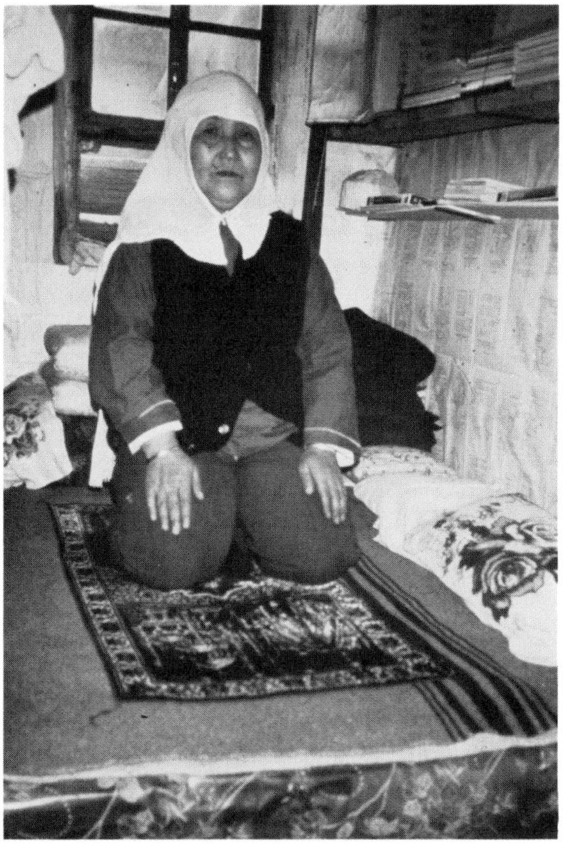

Illustration 7.16

A woman during *ṣalāt* in her home in Ningxia Autonomous Region, People's Republic of China. [Courtesy Dru Gladney.]

AL KHILĀFAH: THE STATE AND WORLD ORDER

Last but not least of the public institutions of Islam is *al khilāfah* or *al imāmah,* synonymous terms referring to the state or government. *Al khilāfah* is the mother of all other institutions, their *conditio sine qua non,* without which all the other institutions lose their grounds and support. Internally, the *khilāfah*'s justification is the enforcement of the *sharī'ah* whose comprehensive individual and institutional application constitutes the first means for bringing about justice. Externally, the *khilāfah* is responsible for the well-being and security of the *ummah,* for calling humanity to God and to submission to His will, and for establishing the new world order of peace and justice on earth. All these purposes flow from the essence of religious experience in Islam. They are readily recognized by all Muslims as necessary implications of *tawḥīd.* Having created the world as theater and malleable material for humans to prove their moral worth by doing the good works, and having equipped them with all the necessary perfections, faculties, capacities, and an authentic, permanently comprehensible revelation of His will, humans are obliged to reconstruct themselves and the world in the likeness of the divine pattern, to build culture and civilization in the process, and to add to the total value of the cosmos. And since both the pattern of God and its actualization in history are individual and societal, intentional and actional, spiritual and material, internal and external, the Muslims must organize themselves corporately, set up a system to regulate interhuman relations, to adjudicate disputes with fairness and equity, and to carry out the purpose of God in the world, in history.

Except for the few in modern times who have lost their Islamic roots through a Western education and/or association, the Muslims of all ages and places have acknowledged the Islamic state as necessitated by Islam and have understood its justification as *sharī'ah*-based. Jurists point to the numerous departments and/or provisions of the law required to be upheld and enforced by the state. Without the state, they conclude, these segments of the *sharī'ah* would not be observed, a failure clearly condemned by the Qur'ān as tantamount to forsaking the whole of religion and hence, resulting in apostasy (Qur'ān 5:44; 2:85). The *mutakallimūn* (Islamic thinkers) have regarded the state as a purely rational necessity. Both have argued that state organization of defense and protection of mission are absolutely required if life itself, with its culture and civilization, are to survive and develop. They all conclude that the state is an Islamic as well as human necessity.

Still others regard the state as dictated by consideration of trade and security, of general utility and public welfare. This makes it not a rational necessity but an indispensable means of human vicegerency on earth. Whatever the line of justification, all Muslims regard formation of the state and participation in its affairs as a moral and religious duty, a requisite of the Islamic faith itself. They see their position confirmed in the *ḥadīth* of the Prophet that it is of the essence of Islam to participate in one's lifetime in at least one *bay'ah* (caliphal election), that is, in the political process. Islam's original vision of the necessity of the state shows its Mesopotamian inheritance where, a people without ruler, and hence devoid of social order, were regarded as sheep without a shepherd, destined for destruction.

This vision of the state in Islam implies a number of principles of nature and structure; and these are relevant for its domestic organization and external interrelations.

Illustration 7.17

Prayer during Ramaḍān in Beijing, People's Republic of China. [Courtesy of Dru Gladney.]

Universalism and Egalitarianism

Al khilāfah is a social order whose actualization is commanded by God. God's will or commandment is one and universal. It applies to all humans as humans — hence to all lands and continents — and does not discriminate between them. Therefore, Islam saw the state as cosmic and universal. Muslims knew, no less than their Mesopotamian ancestors, that humans differed from one another in many ways, physical and mental, giving rise to tribalism, nationalism, racism, and every kind of corporate particularism. But they regarded none of these as constituting grounds for interhuman discrimination. The East and the West, the North and the South, the blacks and the whites, the Asians and the Africans — all were equally the creatures of God, obliged to do His will. Hence, all must be included in the social order set up to fulfill that will. The ultimate ground of the Islamic state being transcendent, the state cannot but be universally applicable to and inclusive of all humankind, the whole of creation. *Al khilāfah* is therefore a world order in which all humans are citizens, or citizens-to-be; all states are federal provinces, or federal-units-to-be. Whether actually or *in potentia,* the Islamic state is to cover the globe.

Totalism

The Islamic state is totalist insofar as the imperatives of God are not only morally binding on all humans but are also relevant to every human activity. Human life and existence is not divisible into a religious sphere where God's commands obtain, and a secular sphere where they do not. All life and existence are pervaded by values or moral "oughts" as laid down in the divine commandments. The *sharī'ah,* whose application is the raison d'être of the state, is comprehensive, covering every field and every action. There is no department of human activity that can properly be excluded from the relevance of the divine pattern. The will of God for man is, according to Islam, the transformation of creation by humans into the prescribed divine pattern, and in the course of such transformation, the proving of themselves as morally worthy. In the purview of the divine commandment, everything is relevant. All activities of life are subject to the law, because they are all expressions of self, of other selves, and/or of nature. In all cases, therefore, every change counts because it can and should be a change for the better. That is why Islam regards every act as an act of worship, an act of obedience or disobedience, in harmony or disharmony with the divine will. The state is man's corporate attempt to make all activities accord with and actualize the divine will. The range of state activities must therefore be limitless, just as its action must always be calculated to bring humanity and the world to a closer and more perfect actualization of the divine pattern. Thus, the more the state rules and governs and interferes in the lives of the citizens in order to make them adhere to the divine pattern, the more successful it will be. This is the opposite of the Anglo-Saxon view that the less the state governs, the better it is.

Freedom

The Islamic state must be free inasmuch as the desired actualization of the *sharī'ah,* the instantiation of the divine pattern on earth, is moral, that is, is to be achieved deliberately in obedience to God and in pursuit of His will. A coerced actualization may bring about a utilitarian, not a moral achievement. It cannot therefore satisfy the requisite of morality, however great the advantage it brings about. Totalitarianism and regimentation may be responsible for highly desirable change in humans and nature. But the change they bring about is vitiated by the lack of freedom, the absence of a will committed to bring about these changes out of love for them as constitutive of the divine will. In order to be moral, change and the act that brings it about must be free; it must be conscious and deliberate, knowing and desiring its objective and the means to that objective. This is the essence of the *amānah* (trust) God had offered to heaven, earth, and mountains, and which they "rejected" because by nature they did not possess the requisite freedom of action. Man accepted the trust because he is a free and capable being. In and throughout nature, the divine will is actualized by necessity, through the working of natural law. Nothing in nature can be otherwise than it is. Only man has a choice. Only he has the freedom to do or not to do the will of God.

Education

Since the Islamic state cannot be totalitarian, and since the obedience of its citizens must be free, it follows that the only legitimate influence it can exercise is that which seeks to convince and persuade, to obtain acquiescence and reassurance at once. The state is therefore a school on a grand scale where the ruler is teacher and the ruled are students; indeed, the entire community is a school where everybody is at once teacher and pupil, teacher of what he knows to those who know less, and pupil of what he does not know under those who know more. In the Islamic state, as in any good school, teaching is by both word and example. In the Islamic society, enjoining the good, encouraging emulation of the good deed, and prohibiting and preventing evil are everybody's business. The Prophet said: Everyone is a shepherd; and everyone is responsible for his/her pastorate. All are anxious to seek the highest virtue, the greatest piety, namely, knowledge and application of the truth, the content of the divine will. Hence, the Islamic state is truly *al imāmah* (literally, leadership), a leadership of humans to their ultimate felicity and well-being, a leadership that propels and guides the people, rather than coercing them.

Illustration 7.18

Ṣalāt in the Xining Mosque, Qinghai Province, People's Republic of China. [Courtesy Dru Gladney.]

Pluralism

Since doing the will of God on earth must be free, deliberate, and voluntary, it follows that dissent in the Islamic state must be legitimate and receive the protection of the state. The dissenter may not be coerced. Criminal or other activity prejudicial to the security of other citizens or of the state may and should be barred; but this is not regarded as limitation of freedom, for freedom does not imply the possibility of the agent's self-destruction, or of the destruction of others. Where dissent is a matter of principle and conviction, it can be answered only by argument and persuasion, the avenues of which must never be blocked. Hence, the *sharī'ah* created the *dhimmah.* This is a constitutional institution which permits the non-Muslim to be a citizen of the Islamic state, and to order his life under any system of law he desires. Islamic law is the only law that allows other laws to stand and be observed. In the Islamic state, where Islamic law is sovereign, Christian, Jewish, Hindu, and whatever other laws the non-Muslims wish to observe, are *de jure.*

The Islamic state is therefore a free state just as its society is an open and free society in which anyone is welcome provided aggression and war are renounced and a commitment to peace and reason is declared. It is equally open to Muslims and non-Muslims, the latter being free to observe their own laws in ordering their personal and communal lives. The lives of the Muslim citizens are ordered by Islamic law. And so is the Islamic state itself in the conduct of its affairs. War and peace, citizens and noncitizens, public morals and communal order fall likewise under Islamic law which is the source of the social order in its entirety.

Rule of Law

In *al khilāfah,* sovereignty belongs not to the people as a nation or collective but to the law. Nobody in the Islamic state "legislates"; only God does; and He did so for the last time in the revelation of the Qur'ān and the exemplification of the Prophet Muḥammad. There is hence no legislature and no need for one. Every citizen is an executive of the law in his own sphere, the *khalīfah* or chief of state being responsible for directing the common effort as a whole. Interpretation of the law is the prerogative of the *ummah* as a whole, and its *'ulamā'* (literally, the learned) devote their lives and energies to that pursuit. However, they do not constitute a priesthood or a legislature. They are neither elected nor appointed nor ordained. Each one of them establishes his credibility separately through his personal knowledge and wisdom. They are the product of the Islamic educational system. If it is at all proper to call them a "class," it must be borne in mind that they are an absolutely "open" class ready to grant its membership to anyone who cares to learn and master the law, whether by going through the educational system or by doing the work in the privacy of his home with or without the help of the learned. Being the guardians of the law, the *'ulamā'* constitute a large reservoir of brain- and manpower for the recruitment of the judiciary. The court in Islam is absolutely autonomous. It judges by the law. In the Islamic state, the non-Muslim court enjoys exactly the same power over non-Muslims as the Islamic court enjoys over Muslims.

Shūrā

The executive branch of government in the Islamic state runs on the basis of *shūrā* (consultation) between ruler and ruled. The process is institutionalized in *Majlis al Shūrā* (the *Shūrā* Council), whose members are the best qualified for exercising *shūrā*. However, the method of election to membership has never been specified, allowing the Islamic state to seek the form that best suits its situation, mission, and temper. To curb the power of the executive, Islamic law permits any court in the realm to look into any case involving the Islamicity of any law. In the past, the *shari'ah* set up a special court — *Al Maẓālim* — to hear complaints against the ruler or his delegated representative.

The government of the Islamic state has three main functions. First, it must uphold Islamic law in the daily life of its Muslim subjects. This means it has to organize corporate observance of the Islamic calendar, where the hours of the day and the days of the year are punctuated by Islamic rituals, memorials, and other special events. It has to help the Muslims implement the *sharī'ah* in their dealings with one another, and to adjudicate their disputes with justice and equity. Second, the Islamic government must uphold the freedom and integrity God has granted the non-Muslims in the Islamic state, and to protect them in their setting up of their religious leadership and courts of law to adjudicate their own disputes. Third, the Islamic government must carry out the sacred task of calling all humans to God and His law. To this end, it must seek to maintain the peace of humankind to the full extent of its power and by all means at its command. It must enable all people to hear the Word of God, but never to coerce them to accept it. Their decisions must always be honored. It must also lend its assistance wherever possible to the victims of injustice, whether Muslim or otherwise; and bring peace and reconciliation to any conflicting factions whether within or outside its territory. Finally, the Islamic state must be instrumental in setting up a new world order in which every human on earth can live in security and peace, improve himself with knowledge, share in God's bounty, and be free to convince and be convinced of the truth.

NOTES

1. The Islamic story runs parallel to that of Genesis 22:1 – 15, except that in the Qur'ān, Isma'īl is the sacrificial son, and Isḥaq is promised Ibrahīm in reward for his demonstrated faith. Muslims find corroboration of this in Genesis' assertion, "Your only son," which is not true in the case of Isḥaq.

CHAPTER 8

The Arts

In dealing with any aspect of Islamic civilization, its final raison d'être and creative base must be seen as resting on the Qur'ān, the Holy Scripture of Islam. Islamic culture is, in fact, a "Qur'ānic culture"; for its definitions, its structures, its goals, and its methods for execution of those goals are all derived from that series of revelations from God to the Prophet Muḥammad in the seventh century of the common era. It is not only the knowledge of Ultimate Reality that the Muslim derives from the Holy Book of Islam. Equally compelling and determining are its ideas on the world of nature, on man and all other living creatures, on knowledge, on the social, political, and economic institutions necessary for the healthy running of society — in short, on every branch of learning and activity known. This does not mean that specific explanations and descriptions of every field of endeavor are literally spelled out in that small book of 114 *suwar* (sing. *sūrah*) or chapters. It does mean that in it the basic principles are provided for a whole culture and civilization. Without that revelation, the culture could not have been generated; without that revelation, there could have been neither an Islamic religion, an Islamic state, an Islamic philosophy, an Islamic law, an Islamic society, nor an Islamic political or economic organization.

Just as surely as these aspects of Islamic culture may be rightly seen as Qur'ānic in basis and motivation, in implementation and goal, the arts of Islamic civilization should also be viewed as aesthetic expressions of similar derivation and realization. Yes, the Islamic arts are indeed Qur'ānic arts.

This statement may be startling to non-Muslims who have long viewed Islam as an iconoclastic and conservative religion that denied or prohibited the arts.[1] It may be equally strange to some Muslims who have misunderstood the efforts of the *'ulamā'* (learned men) and the *ummah* to guide aesthetic participation toward certain forms and types of art, and away from others. Some Muslims have thought that that guidance implied a rejection of, rather than a guidance for, Islamic art. Both of these views are misunderstandings of Islamic art and its genesis.

How then are the Islamic arts to be seen as "Qur'ānic" expressions in color, in line, in movement, in shape, and in sound? There are three levels on which such an interpretation rests.

LEVEL I: THE QUR'ĀN AS DEFINER OF *TAWḤĪD* OR TRANSCENDENCE

The Message To Be Aesthetically Expressed: *Tawḥīd*

The Qur'ān was a revelation sent to mankind and intended to reteach the doctrine of monotheism, a message conveyed to numerous Semitic prophets of earlier times—Abraham, Noah, Moses, and Jesus, for example. The Qur'ān comprised a new statement of the doctrine of monotheism, of the one God Who is the unique, unchanging, and eternal Creator as well as Guide of the universe and all that exists within it. Allah is described in the Qur'ān as a transcendent Being of Whom no visual or sensory experience is possible. "No vision can grasp Him, . . . He is above all comprehension (Qur'ān 6:103). . . . Nothing is like unto Him" (Qur'ān 42:11). He is beyond exhaustive description, and incapable of being represented by any anthropomorphic or zoomorphic image. In fact, Allah is that which defies answers to the questions of who, how, where, and when? It is this idea of the utter oneness and transcendence of Allah that is known as *tawḥīd* (literally, "making one").

The Qur'ānic statements regarding the nature of God certainly preclude God's representation through sensory means, whether in human or animal forms or in figural symbols from nature; but this is not all that the Qur'ānic message contributes to the Islamic arts. We find that the whole iconography of Islamic art has been significantly influenced by the Qur'ānic doctrine of *tawḥīd* or Islamic monotheism. If God was so completely nonnature, so ultimately different from His creation, it was not just a negative prohibition of naturalistic images of Him that was necessary as Islam began its new career. That was an aesthetic achievement of the Semitic soul which had been made in an earlier period by the followers of Judaism. Images of Yahweh were strongly condemned by all the Hebrew prophets, as well as in the well-known Second Commandment of the Mosaic Code. Even setting down the name of God was discouraged. Instead, the four consonants of the name "Yahweh," or other abbreviations, often served as written symbol for the God of the Hebrews.

Arising after the aesthetic influence from an alien tradition (that of the Greco-Romans and their Hellenistic offspring) had exerted itself for centuries over many regions of the Semitic East, Islam brought a demand for a new manner of aesthetic expression. The new Muslims needed an aesthetic mode that could supply objects of aesthetic contemplation and delight that would reinforce the basic ideology and structures of the society and be a constant reminder of its principles. Such art works would reinforce the awareness of that transcendent Being, the fulfillment of Whose will was the end-all and be-all, the raison d'être, of human existence. This orientation and goal of Islamic aesthetics could not be achieved through depiction of man and nature. It could be realized only through the contemplation of artistic creations that would lead the percipient to an intuition of the truth itself that Allah is so other than His creation as to be unrepresentable and inexpressible.

This challenge for aesthetic creativity was taken up by the early Muslims. They worked with motifs and techniques known to their Semitic, Byzantine, and Sassanian predecessors; and they developed new motifs, materials, and techniques as the need and inspiration arose. Even more important was their creation of new modes of artistic expression which were to be adopted and adapted in various parts of the world as Muslim individuals and political power spread with the religion in the regions from Spain in the West to the Philippines in the East. These new modes have provided a basic aesthetic unity within the Muslim world without suppressing or prohibiting regional variety.

Islamic art was to fulfill the negative implications behind the declaration of *Lā illaha illā Allah*—that there is no God but God and He is completely other than human and other than nature. But it also was to express the positive dimension of *tawḥīd*—that which emphasizes not what God is *not,* but what God *is.* Probably the most salient aspect of the Transcendent which the Islamic doctrine taught was that God is infinite in every aspect—in justice, in mercy, in knowledge, in love. However fully one might try to enumerate His many attributes, or describe any one of those attributes as applied to Him, the attempt would end in failure.[2] His qualities are always beyond human comprehension and description. The pattern which has no beginning and no end, which gives an impression of infinity, is therefore the best way to express in art the doctrine of *tawḥīd.* And it is the structures created for this purpose that characterize all the arts of the Muslim peoples. It is these infinite patterns, in all their ingenious variety, that provide the positive aesthetic breakthrough of the Muslims in the history of artistic expression. It is through these infinite patterns that the subtle content of the Islamic message can be experienced.

The art of the Muslims has often been designated as the art of the infinite pattern or as "infinity-art."[3] These aesthetic expressions have also been called "arabesques."[4] The arabesque should not be limited

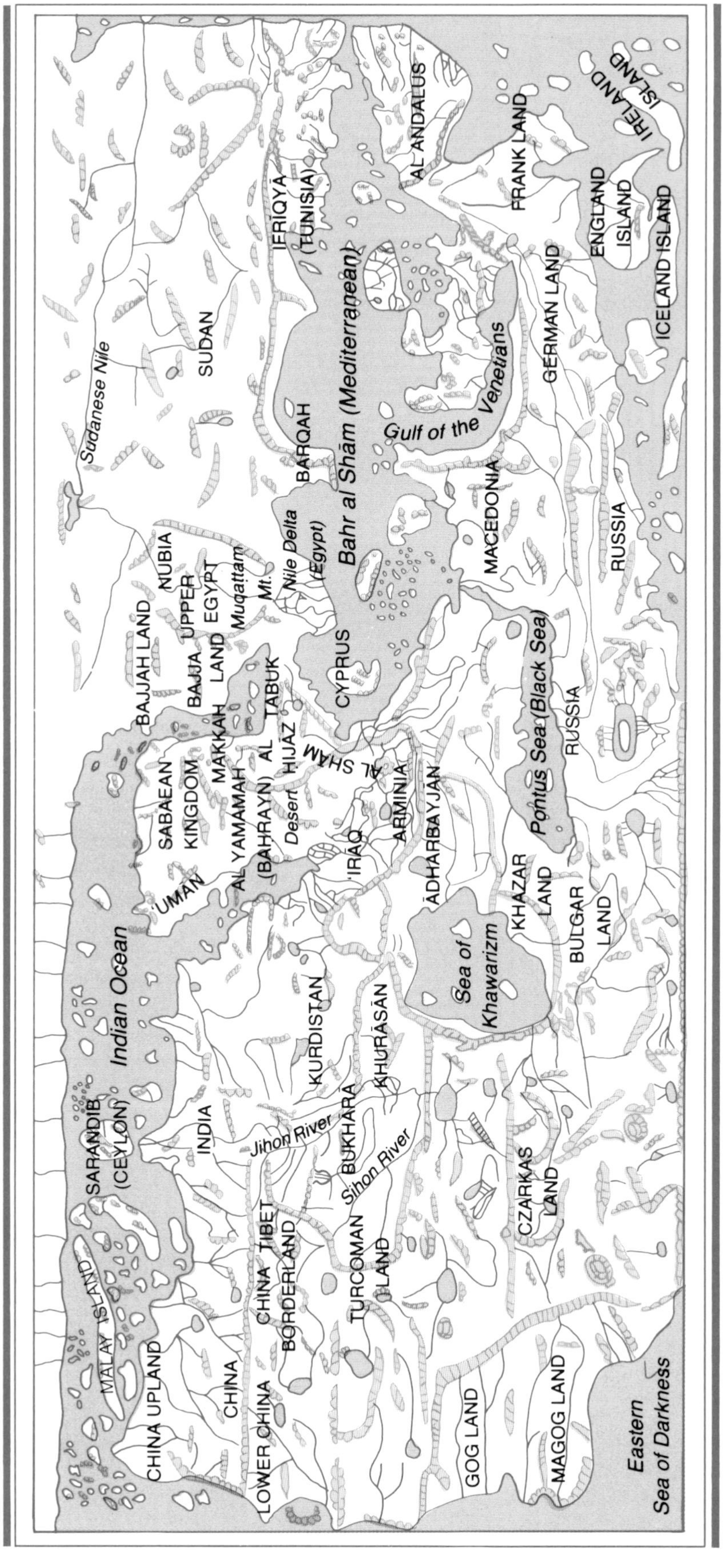

Map 25. The Earth According to Al Sharīf al Idrīsī, 562/1177

to a particular kind of leaf design perfected by the Muslim peoples, as has sometimes been maintained.[5] It is not simply any abstract two-dimensional pattern that uses calligraphy, geometric figures, and stylized plant forms.[6] Instead, it is a structural entity that accords with the aesthetic principles of the Islamic ideology. The arabesque generates in the viewer an intuition of the quality of infinity, of that which is beyond space-time; but it does so without making the — to the Muslim — absurd claim that the pattern itself stands for that which is beyond. Through contemplation of these infinite patterns, the recipient's mind is turned toward the Divine, and art becomes a reinforcement and reminder of religious belief.

This interpretation of the raison d'être of Islamic art rules out many common misconceptions regarding this art's rejection of figural art and the concentration instead on abstract motifs. For example, it denies the notion that nature is regarded by the Muslim as an illusion. For the Muslim, nature is part of God's tangible creation, equally as real and valid and marvelous as humanity and the animal world. In fact, nature is regarded as a proof of the Creator's power and beneficence (Qur'ān 2:164, 6:95 - 99, 10:4 - 6, and so on). Neither can one maintain that it is an Islamic idea to regard nature as an evil to be derogated. How could the Muslim think of God's creation as evil? Instead, nature is described by the Qur'ān as a field of perfect and beautiful marvels presented for mankind's use and benefit (Qur'ān 2:29, 78:6 - 16, 25:47 - 50, etcetera). For the Muslim, nature, although glorious in its variety and perfection, is only the theater in which humans operate to fulfill the will of a higher realm or cause. God, for the Muslim, is this highest Cause, "the greater One." *Allahu Akbar* is the ubiquitous Muslim exclamation of appreciation, admiration, thanks, and inspiration that expresses this belief. While other cultures and peoples may have regarded man as "the measure of all things" or nature as the ultimate determiner, the Muslim's concentration has been on God in His uncompromising transcendence.[7] Islamic art then has a goal similar to that of the Qur'ān — to teach and reinforce in mankind the perception of divine transcendence.

Characteristics of the Aesthetic Expression of *Tawḥīd*

That is not the only way in which a bond exists between the Qur'ān and Islamic art. It is also embodied in the aesthetic characteristics which the Muslims devised in order to create the impression of infinity and transcendence demanded by the Qur'ānic doctrine of *tawḥīd*. How is this doctrine emphasized

Illustration 8.1

Geometric arabesque, inlaid tabletop, twentieth century, Syria. [Photo by L. al Fārūqī.]

through aesthetic content and form to stimulate the impression of infinity and transcendence?

Abstraction. The infinite patterns of Islamic art are, first of all, abstract. While figural representation is not totally absent, there is generally little argument that naturalistic figures are rare in the Islamic arts. Even when figures from nature are used, they are subjected to denaturalization and stylization techniques that render them more suitable for their role as deniers of naturalism than as faithful depictions of natural phenomena.

Modular structure. The Islamic art work is composed of numerous parts or modules which are combined to produce the larger design. Each of these modules is an entity carrying a measure of climax and perfection which allows it to be perceived as an expressive and satisfying unit on its own as well as an important part of the larger complex.

Successive combinations. The infinite patterns of sound, sight, and movement evidence successive combinations of the basic modules and/or their repeti-

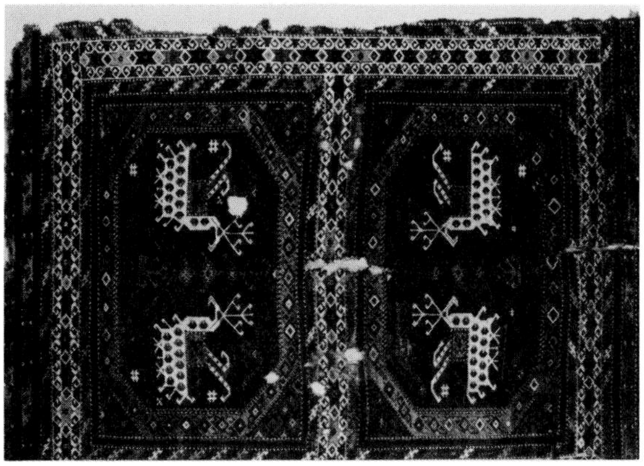

Illustration 8.2

Stylized animal design on thirteenth-century rug from Konya, Turkey. [Courtesy Ministry of Culture and Tourism, Government of Turkey.]

Illustration 8.4

Copper plate (niello) with Qur'ānic inscription, Cairo, twentieth century. [Photo by L. al Fārūqī.]

tions. In this way, larger additive combinations are formed which carry their own independent status and identity. The successively larger combinations in a work of Islamic art in no way destroy the identity and character of the smaller units of which they are made. Even such larger combinations may, in turn, be repeated, varied, and joined to other smaller or larger entities in order to form still more complex combinations. Thus the infinite pattern has numerous centers of aesthetic interest, numerous "views" to be experienced as the successive combinations of smaller modules, entities, or motifs are experienced. No design has a single point of aesthetic departure or a progres-

Illustration 8.3

Detail of ceramic decorations on the Shāh Zindah Tomb, Samarqand, fourteenth century. [Photo by L. al Fārūqī.]

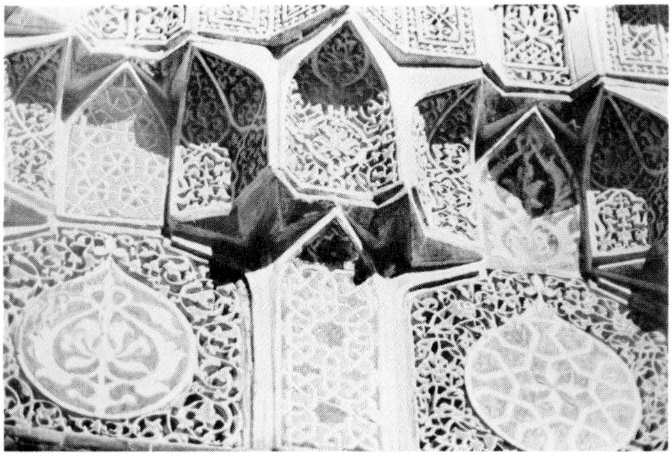

Illustration 8.5

Prayer rug from Turkey, eighteenth century, which includes many "successive combinations" of design motifs and modules. [Courtesy Ministry of Culture and Tourism, Government of Turkey.]

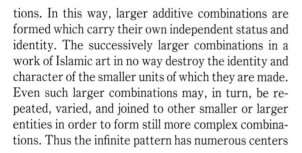

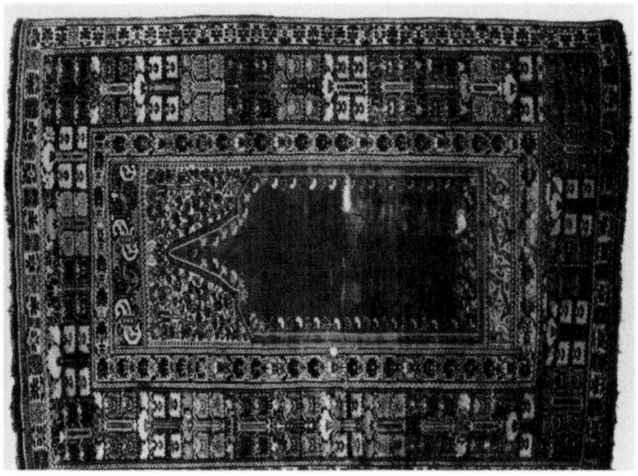

Illustration 8.6

Ṭalā Kārī Madrasah, Samarqand, 1646–1660. [Photo by L. al Fārūqī.]

sive development to a culminating or conclusive focal point. Instead, the Islamic design has an inexhaustible number of interest centers or foci, and a mode of internal perception that defies assignment of a beginning or conclusive end.

Repetition. A fourth characteristic which is demanded in order to create the impression of infinity in an art object is a high level of repetition. The additive combinations of Islamic art use repetitions of motifs, of structural modules, and of their successive combinations which seem to continue *ad infinitum.* Abstraction is enhanced and reinforced by this curbing of the individuation of the constituent parts. It prevents any one module in the design from taking precedence over another.

Dynamism. The Islamic design is "dynamic," that is, it is a design that must be experienced through time. Boas has described art works as being based either on time or on space.[8] For him the time-based arts include literature and music, while the arts of space are those of the visual arts and architecture. Dance and drama are categorized by Boas as arts utilizing both time and spatial elements. Although this description may prove meaningful for classifying the arts of Western culture, it proves misleading for an understanding of the Islamic arts. The superficial or obvious aspects of time and space do apply here, of course. A literary or musical composition, for example, is normally experienced through a series of temporal aesthetic events. In the case of literature, the art product is experienced either through reading or listening to its recitation; and in the case of music, through participating in or listening to a performance. Less commonly, the musical performance might be "read" from a score. On the other hand, the visual arts and architectural monuments all make use of space. They occupy physical space and use spatial elements (points, lines, shapes, and volumes) for their creation.

While granting these characteristics as pointed out by Boas, one needs to go further in qualifying the Islamic arts if they are to be properly understood. In addition to having the external temporal or spatial characteristics mentioned above, characteristics that may be regarded as universally relevant, every work of Islamic art partakes, on a more subtle level, of a strong and perhaps unique temporal orientation. In fact, the visual arts in Islamic culture, though dealing with spatial elements, cannot be properly experienced except through time. The infinite pattern can never be comprehended in a single glance, in a single moment, with a single view of its multifarious parts. Instead, it draws the eye and the mind through a series of views or perceptions that must be comprehended serially. The eye moves from pattern to pattern, from center to center of a two-dimensional design. The architectural monument is experienced in the successive movement through its rooms, aisles, dome chambers, or subdivisions. Even the building or complex of buildings is not comprehended from afar as a totality, but necessitates its being experienced through time as the visitor moves through its many segments and quarters.[9] The pictorial miniature art likewise presents a series of characters or scenes that must be experienced successively and sequentially, as in the time arts of literature, musical expression, or dance. Whether belonging to the so-called space arts or the time arts, the Islamic art work is comprehended serially and cumulatively. The imagination is pushed to supply the continuation of an evolving, repeating pattern which seems even to extend, by im-

Illustration 8.7

Central Asian prayer rug (Milhim Mubārak Collection), displayed at an Exposition of Islamic Art organized by the Nicholas Sursuq Museum, Beirut, Lebanon, 1974. [Photo by L. al Fārūqī.]

plication, beyond the edge of a plate, the page of a book, the panel of a wall, or the façade of a building. No overall understanding of even the architectural infinite pattern is possible except after the actual or imagined movement over its surfaces and through its spaces in a temporal sequence. Ardalan and Bakhtiar speak of "a moving architecture . . . that reads like a musical composition."[10] The totality cannot be comprehended simultaneously; instead, one only knows the whole after experiencing and savoring its many parts.[11]

The arabesque therefore can never be a static composition as has sometimes been charged by mistaken interpreters.[12] On the contrary, appreciation of it must involve a dynamic process that investigates each of its motifs, modules, and successive combinations serially. For those who understand its message and structures, it is the most dynamic, most aesthetically active, of all art forms.[13] It is an expression in which both the arts of time and those of space require a temporally determined experience and apprehension.

Intricacy. Intricate detail is a sixth characteristic that defines Islamic art. Intricacy enhances the ability of any pattern or arabesque to capture the attention of the viewer and force concentration on the structural entities represented. A straight line or a single figure, however gracefully executed, could never be the sole iconographic material of the Islamic pattern. It is only with the multiplication of internal elements and the increased intricacy of execution and combination that the dynamism and momentum of the infinite pattern can be generated.

Illustration 8.8

Calligraphy and arabesque wall and furniture decorations, Dimashq, Syria. [Courtesy Embassy of Syria, Washington, D.C.]

Illustration 8.9

Persian Miniature, "Bahram Killing a Dragon," illustration from a copy of the ***Khamsah*** of Niẓāmī dated 1574. [Courtesy The University Museum, University of Pennsylvania.]

LEVEL II: THE QUR'ĀN AS ARTISTIC MODEL

In addition to being determined by the ideological message of the Qur'ān, Islamic art is also "Qur'ānic" in the sense that the scripture of the Muslim peoples has provided the first and prime model for aesthetic creativity and production. The Qur'ān has been described as "the first work of art in Islām."[14] This is not to be understood as meaning that the Qur'ān is regarded as the creation of the literary genius of the Prophet Muḥammad, as has been repeated so many times by non-Muslims and so vigorously denied by Muslims. On the contrary, Muslims hold that the Holy Scripture is divine in its form as well as its content, in its letters as well as its ideas; that it was revealed to Muḥammad in the exact words of God; and that its present arrangement in *āyāt* (verses) and *suwar* (chapters) was dictated by God.

This content and this form of the Qur'ān have provided all the distinguishing characteristics which, as we have noted above, are representative of the infinite patterns of the Islamic arts. The Qur'ān itself is the most perfect example of infinite patterning—the example that was to influence all future creations in the literary arts, the visual arts (both decoration and architectural monuments), and even the arts of sound (see Chapter 21) and movement.[15] As a literary work, the Qur'ān has had a tremendous aesthetic and emotional impact on Muslims who read or heard its poetic prose. Many conversions to the new religion were in fact made through the aesthetic power of its recitations, and many are the accounts of people weeping or even dying from listening to its recitation.[16] Even non-Muslims have been deeply impressed by its literary excellence. This inimitable perfection of the Qur'ān has been designated as its ***i'jāz,*** or "power to incapacitate." But the inability to match its eloquence has not kept it from being a model for all the arts. This contribution to Islamic culture has shaped the adoption and use of countless artistic motifs and techniques borrowed from many cultures and many peoples over the centuries. It is this core or model that molded the adoption of those materials and ideas and determined the creation of new motifs and techniques. The sublime embodiment of the Islamic message of *tawḥīd* was to be the norm and the ideal for all future examples of Islamic art (see Chapter 19).

The Qur'ān provides the first model for the six characteristics of Islamic art mentioned above. First, instead of emphasizing realistic or naturalistic depiction, the Qur'ān evidences a rejection of narrative development as a literary organizational principle. References to certain events are treated segmentally

Illustration 8.10

Mausoleum of Muḥammad V, Rabāṭ, Morocco, carved stucco ornamentation, lambrequin arch. [Photo by L. al Fārūqī.]

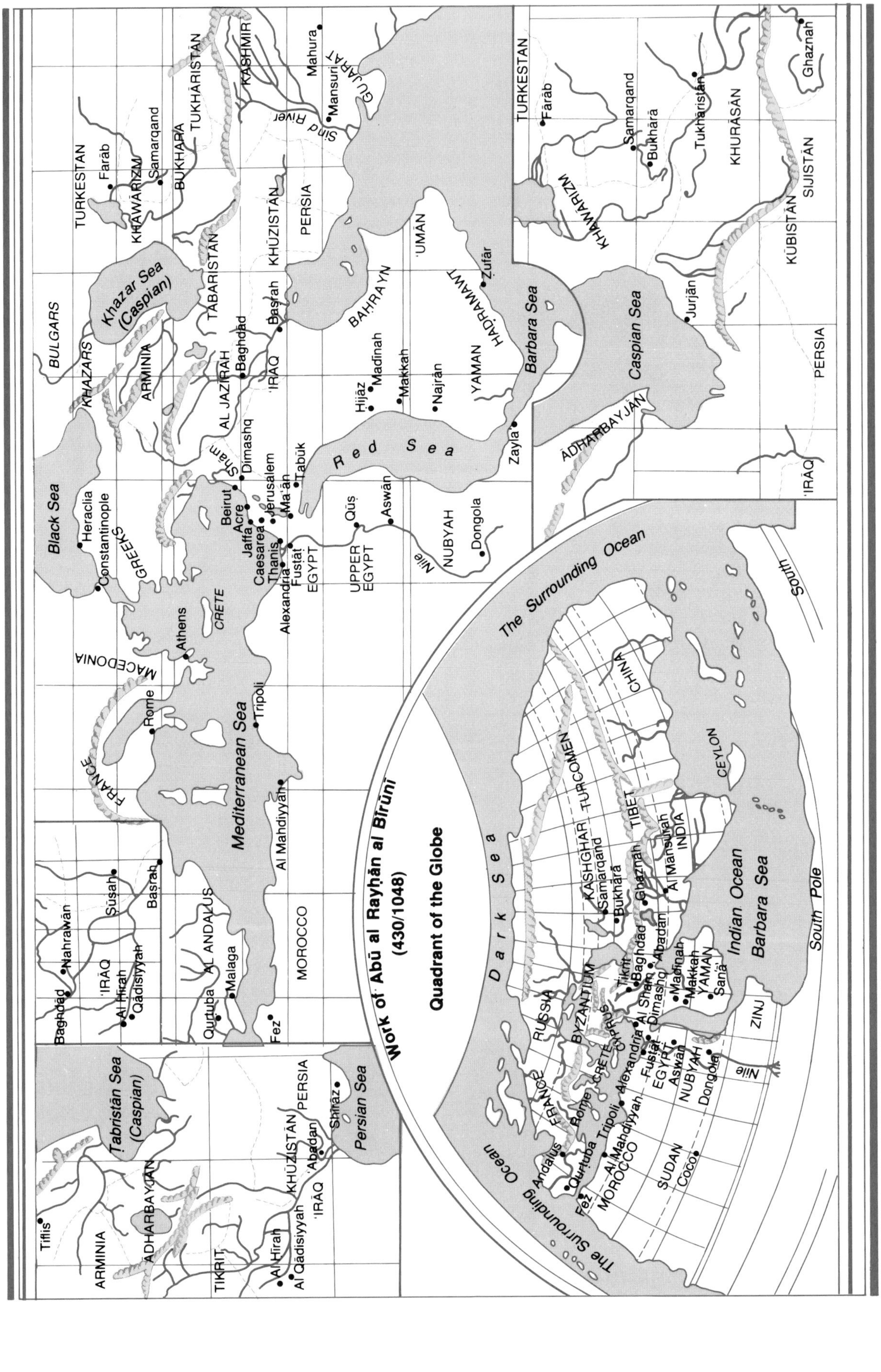

Map 26. The Earth According to Abū al Rayḥān al Bīrūnī, 430/1048

and with repeated mention, as if readers were already familiar with the stories and characters. The main purpose is not narrative, but didactic and moral. The very ordering of the work (the longer, more proselike Madīnan *suwar* near the beginning, and the shorter, strongly poetic Makkan *suwar* near the end) contributes, as well, to the Qur'ān's abstract quality. Verses do not lead the reader through a series of contrasting and dramatically stimulated moods. Instead, the reader is moved by emotions that seem abstracted or divorced from specific characterization. The *āyāt* and *suwar* certainly arouse the emotions of the listener, but they do so without evoking specific moods.

Second, the Qur'ān, like the Islamic work of art, is divided into literary modules *(āyāt* and *suwar)* which exist as satisfying segments standing on their own. Each one is complete, and not dependent on what went before or comes after it. The modules have little or no organic relationship that would necessitate a particular sequence. In its cantillated recitation, periods of silence *(waqfāt)* provide a clear division of the musical rendering into aural modules (see Chapter 23).

Third, Qur'ānic lines and verses are combined to form longer entities or successive combinations. These may be short chapters or sections within a longer chapter. For example, ten *āyāt* constitute a *'ushr.* A series of *'ushr* divisions make a *rub'* or "quarter." Four "quarters" combine to form a *ḥizb.* Two *aḥzāb* (pl. of *ḥizb*) constitute a *juz'* ("part"), and thirty *ajzā'* (pl. of *juz'*) are contained in the complete Qur'ān. Even the *āyāt* modules are further subdivided into separate lines by end rhymes and assonance.

So long as the meaning is not distorted, stopping places for these combinations of verses may be varied. A reading *(qirā'ah)* of the Qur'ān may end with the completion of a *sūrah* or may stop after any verse or cluster of verses, even if they overarch two or more *suwar.* The Muslim reads or hears *mā tayassara* ("what transpires"), that is, whatever he/she is moved to read or hear at that particular time. The recitation is therefore without predetermined length or beginning and end. It leaves no impression of conclusive development or finality.

The fourth characteristic that can be found in all the arts of Islamic culture — the profusion of repetitive means — is equally represented in the Qur'ānic prototype. Poetic devices resulting in sound or metrical repetitions abound in the Qur'ān. In addition to frequent instances of single- or multisyllable end-rhymes, the Qur'ān contains numerous rhymes internal to the lines. Repetitions of metrical units and of vowel and consonant sounds abound and poetically enliven this literary work. Refrain phrases and lines return again and again to reinforce both the didactic and the aesthetic message. The repetition of ideas and of patterns of speech are counted among the elements of eloquence or *balāghah.* It is this eloquence that has provided substantiation for the argument of the Muslims that the Qur'ān is indeed miraculous, and therefore the eternal word of God.

The fifth outstanding characteristic of the visual arts of Islamic culture — the necessity of experiencing them through time — is to be expected in the Holy Qur'ān, since all literary works are considered to be time arts. In this case, however, as in all the Islamic arts, there is a serial process of perception and appreciation that defies development to a single major climax and subsequent conclusion. The impression of overall unity is weak, and only through experiencing its individual parts in succession does the reader or listener grasp a sense of the whole.

Illustration 8.11

Muslim woman carrying Qur'ān on her head, Jolo, Sulu Province, Philippines. [Courtesy I. E. Winship.]

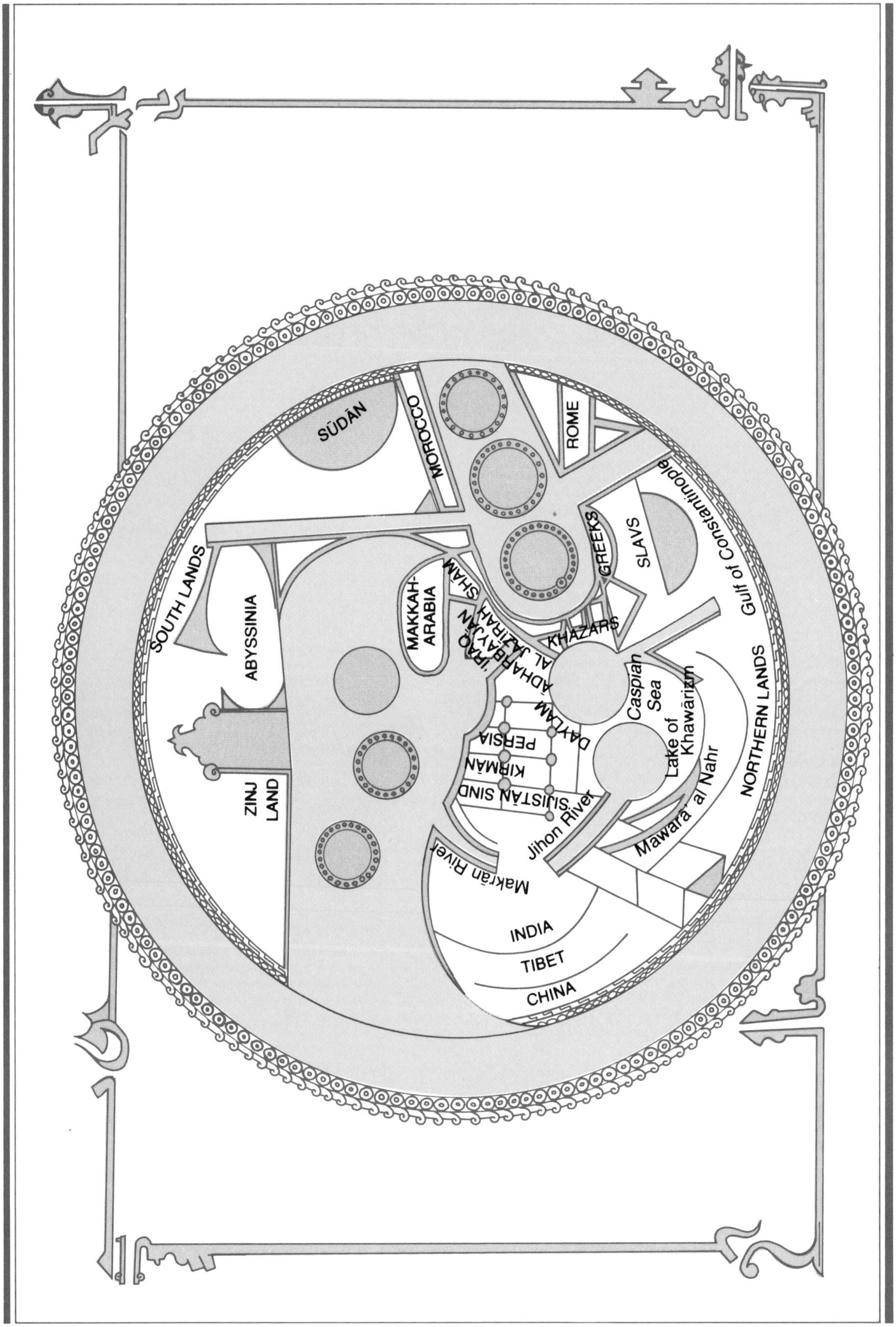

Map 27. The Earth According to Ibrāhīm ibn Muḥammad al Iṣṭakhrī (4th/10th century)

Intricacy, the sixth characteristic of the arts of the Muslim peoples, is equally modeled after the Qur'ān. Parallelism, antithesis, congery, metaphor, simile, and allegory are only some of the many poetic devices that provide verbal richness and elaboration in the Qur'ān. The proliferation of these elements causes those who hear or read its passages to marvel at its beauty and eloquence.

LEVEL III: THE QUR'ĀN AS ARTISTIC ICONOGRAPHY

The Qur'ān not only provided Islamic civilization with an ideology to be expressed in its arts; it not only furnished the first and most important model of artistic content and form; but it also provided the most important material for the iconography of the Islamic arts.

The long tradition of literary emphasis and excellence among the Semitic forerunners of the seventh-century Muslims is well known. Following their interest and excellence in literary creation, the art of writing had been developed by the Semitic peoples at an early stage. Writing was used for millennia in the pre-Islamic Mesopotamian cultures as a component of the visual arts. Accompanying bands of script have been found on numerous artistic reliefs and statues of the Sumerians, the Babylonians, and the Assyrians, to name but a few of these peoples.[17] The function of those pre-Islamic calligraphic inclusions was, however, primarily discursive. Writing was used as a logical accompaniment to explain the meaning of a visual representation. Such use of writing in artistic products continued in Byzantine art. With Islam, however, writing and calligraphy were to undergo a profound metamorphosis which changed them from merely discursive symbols into aesthetic and fully iconographic materials.

It was not by chance that this development took place. Rather, it can be seen as another dimension of the basic "Qur'ānic" influence on the aesthetic sense and behavior of the Muslims. The aim of art for the Muslim is to direct human beings, as vicegerents of the one transcendent God, toward contemplation and remembrance of Him. Toward this goal, no more suitable agent could be found than the poetically inspiring passages from the Holy Qur'ān. Though God is indeed beyond nature and beyond representation, His Word as revealed to the Prophet Muḥammad carries remembrance of Him to the viewer or listener without fear of violating divine transcendence. It is therefore the iconographic material *par excellence* for the work of Islamic art. Already in the seventh century C.E., this tendency had become manifest, as is so clearly demonstrated in the decoration of the Dome of the Rock *(Qubbah al Ṣakhrah)* in Jerusalem. This monument, which has an extensive decorative program incorporating Qur'ānic quotations, was completed by the Umawī caliph 'Abd al Malik in 71/691. Through continued and prolific use of Qur'ānic expressions and passages, the art objects of the Muslim peoples were to be constant reminders of *tawḥīd.*

Illustration 8.12

Qubbah al Ṣakhrah ("The Dome of the Rock"), Al Quds, completed 691 C.E. [Courtesy Ministry of Tourism and Antiquities, Government of the Hashemite Kingdom of Jordan.]

Realization of the effectiveness, ennoblement, and suitability of Qur'ānic visual and discursive motifs brought in its wake a wealth of correlative influences on Islamic culture and the arts. These include the astonishingly rapid development of the Arabic script, its elaboration into a highly malleable catalog of forms, the incredible proliferation of distinctive styles, and the widespread use of calligraphic materials in artistic works.

Inclusion of Qur'ānic passages was never to be executed without care, reverence, and perfection. Consequently, the art of beautiful writing, or calligraphy, developed among the early Muslims with astonishing inventiveness and rapidity. No pre-Islamic or post-Islamic calligraphy has demanded of itself the cursiveness, malleability and plasticity, as well as legibility, that was demanded of the Arabic script. Elongations and contractions in height as well as width were essayed as the letters were molded into various shapes and sizes. Numerous styles of script were used alone or were combined with noncalligraphic motifs. Scripts of every imaginable angular and rounded mien

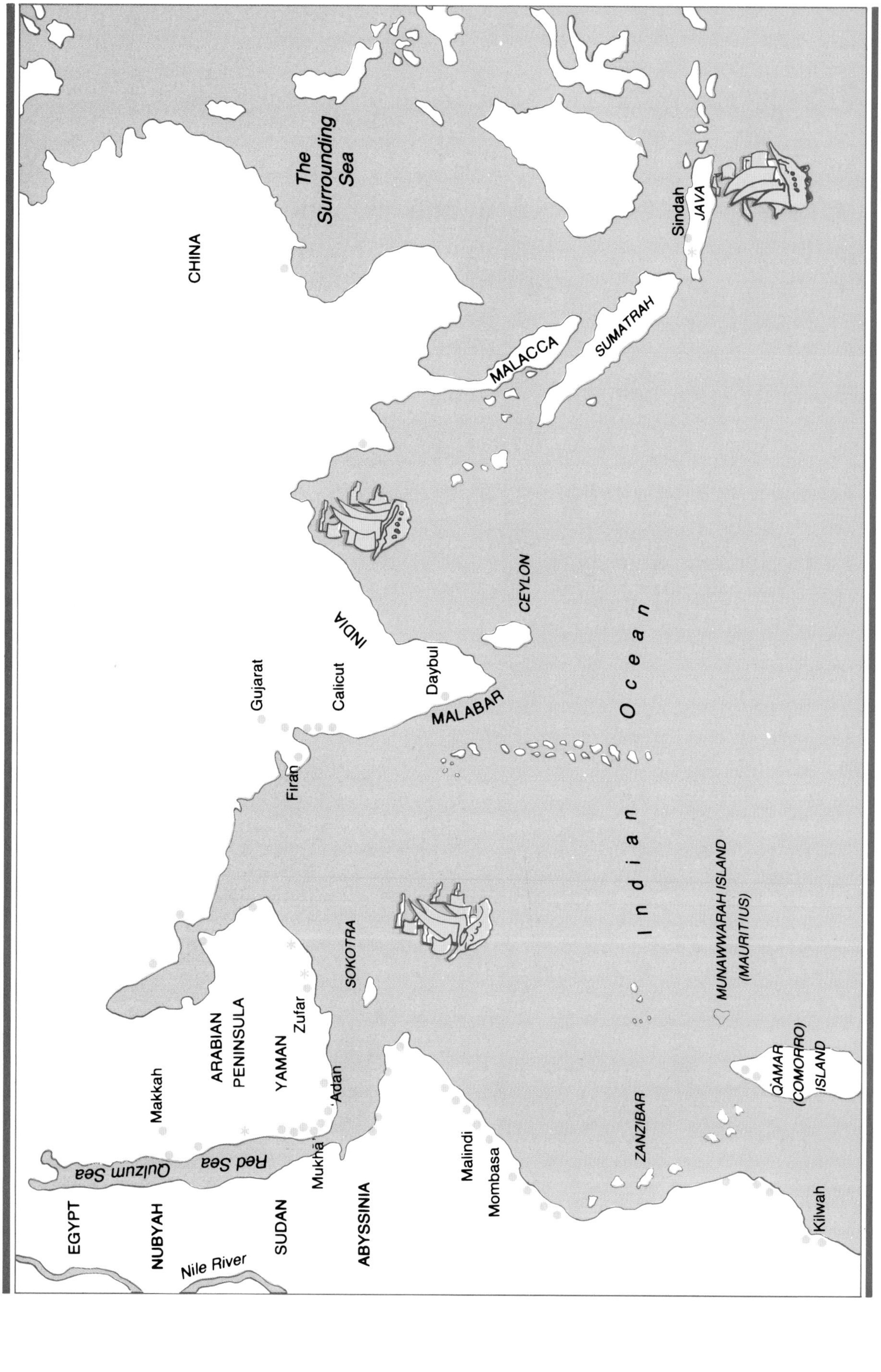

Map 28. The Indian Ocean, by Ahmad ibn Majid (10th/17th century)

Illustration 8.13

Malaysian brocade with Qur'ānic passage (2:255) executed in *Kūfī* script, contemporary. [Photo by L. al Fārūqī.]

have been created by the Muslim peoples. Some of the most interesting contemporary aesthetic efforts in the Muslim world are indeed those developing around this most popular artistic subject matter of the Muslim peoples.

Since every act and thought of the Muslim carries a religious connection or determination, the incorporation of the words of God in every possible decorative scheme, in every aural and visual experience, is a desired objective.[18] Qur'ānic passages have been used as decorative motifs not only on religiously significant items but also on fabrics, garments, vessels and service trays, boxes and furniture, walls and buildings, even the lowly cooking pot, in every century of Islamic history and in every corner of the Muslim world. It is no less prevalent and prominent in the literary and vocal arts. With the inclusion of beautiful calligraphy reproducing passages from the Qur'ān, the Islamic work of art derives not only a discursive influence from the Qur'ān but also a Qur'ānic aesthetic determination. Even when the writing conveys material other than passages from the Holy Scripture—pious sayings; proverbs; names of God, the Prophet, or religious persons; or details of construction, patronage, or artist—there has been an emphasis on imaginative and beautiful exemplifications of Arabic script. From Rabat to Mindanao, from Kano to Samarqand, the Qur'ānic passages executed in Arabic script have provided the most revered ingredient of the arts. In no aesthetic tradition of the world has such a decisive role been played by the art of calligraphy or by a single book.

A number of scholars have written in recent years about the symbolic nature of Islamic art.[19] Some of them are non-Muslims; others are Muslims. In both cases, however, these writers, almost exclusively, have been born or educated in a Western environment. Their attribution of symbolic significance to the Islamic arts does not merely imply the universally accepted notion that the arts are a way of expressing an abstract idea in poetry, color, lines, shapes, sounds, movements, and so on. In this sense, of course, all art is symbolic. These writers claim much more for what they see as the symbolic implications of Islamic art. For them, the forms, shapes, objects, scenes, and even letters and numbers used in Islamic art have a hidden *(bāṭinī)* significance. As the *mandala,* the

Illustration 8.14

Calligraphy *(Thuluth)* sculpted in wood, southern Thailand, nineteenth century. Unidentified eulogy passage. [Courtesy Asian Art Museum, University of Malaysia, Kuala Lumpur.]

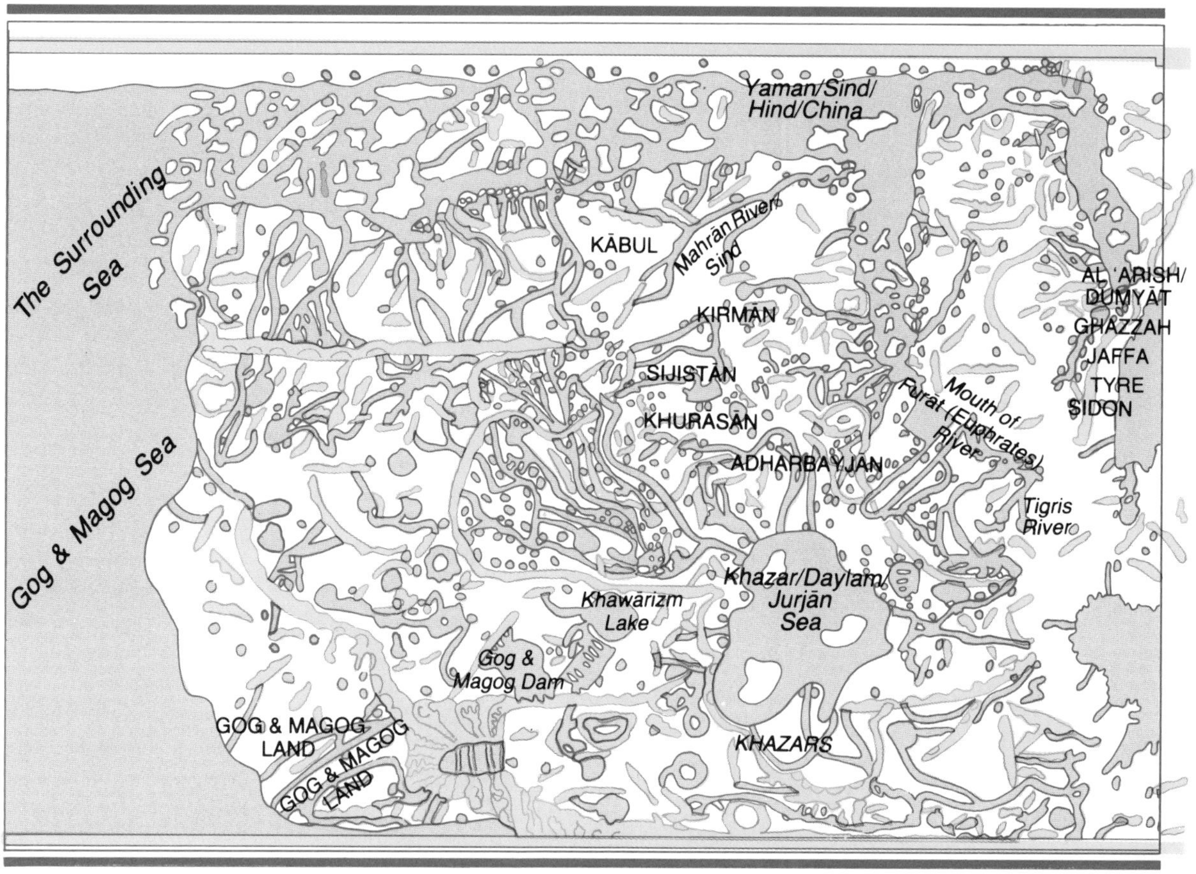

Map 29. The Earth According to Al Ṣafaqṣī (4th/10th century)

phallic pillar, or the anthropomorphic representations of gods and goddesses hold special religious significance for the Hindu, or the cross, the Crucifixion scene, and the statue of Christ are powerful symbols for the Christian, so their argument goes, there are specific "Islamic symbols" which visually represent a wealth of meanings to be grasped and understood by the viewer. Although the motifs or symbols of which these scholars speak are judged to be peculiar to Islamic culture, the aesthetic *logique* is identical to that which pertains to certain other artistic traditions. The dome is to be regarded as the dome of heaven, it is claimed[20]; the medallion at the center of a carpet is a representation of the passageway into heaven[21]; the blue of the manuscript illumination is a symbol of the Infinite, of God[22]; the epigraphic decoration including the ruler's name is a symbolic stand-in for the political state,[23] or even a manifestation of Allah.[24] Even emptiness or the "void" is regarded as "the symbol of both the transcendence of God and His presence in all things."[25]

All of these ascriptions of literal symbolic content are antagonistic to the essence of Islamic art and to its abstract quality. Islamic art was born and developed in a Semitic environment which forswore and condemned all representations of the transcendent realm. It is an art based on an ideology — *tawḥīd* — that cannot be aesthetically expressed by real or imagined linkages between nature and God. Such linkage would be a kind of *shirk* or "associationism" of other beings and objects with Allah; and this has been judged as the most hated practice, the major sin, in Islam.

These beliefs and premises have generated a uniquely asymbolic quality in the religion and culture of Islam. It has frequently been noted that even the rituals of Islam are functional rather than symbolic in essence. The call to prayer, even the minaret itself, are not symbolic aural or visual elements. They are, respectively, an act to help the Muslims congregate for prayer at specific times of the day and an architectural member to facilitate that act.[26] The *miḥrāb*

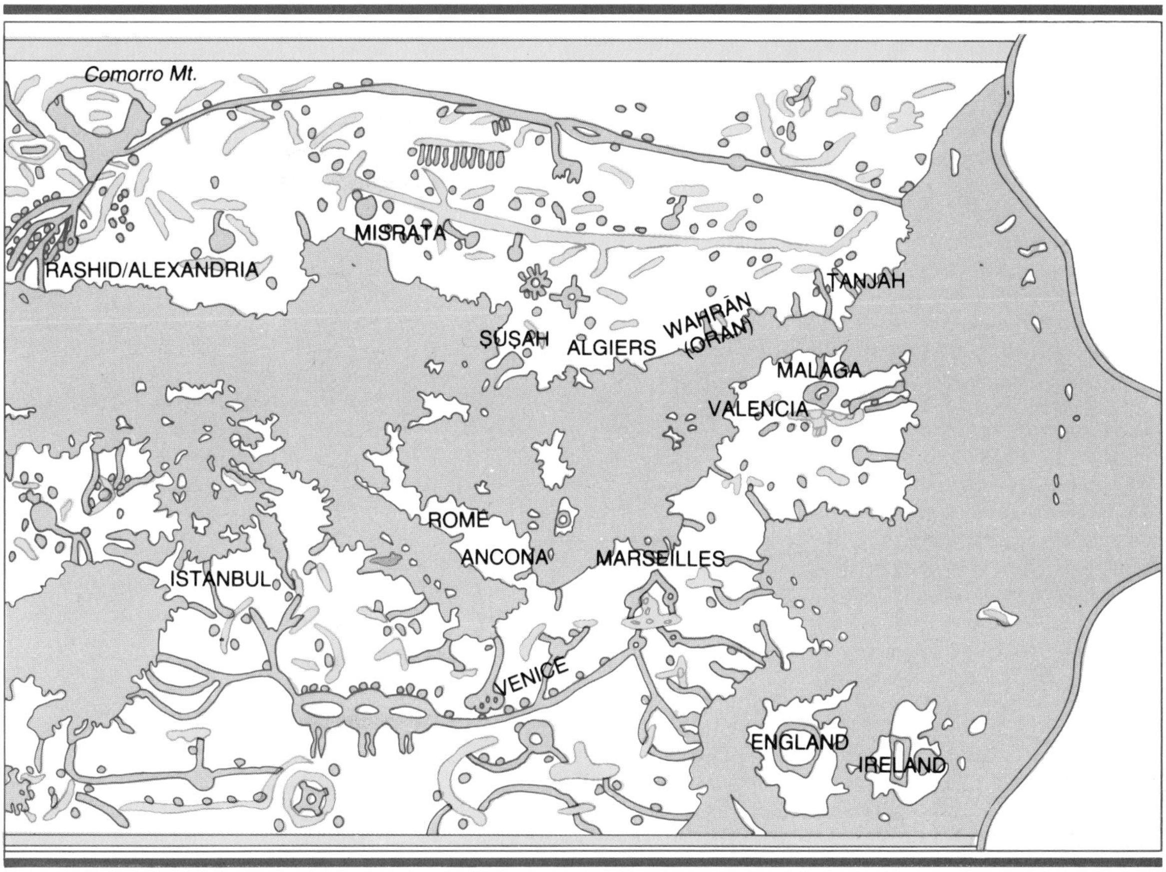

niche of the mosque commands no special deference on the part of the worshipper; the area is not holier than any other in the mosque.[27] The crescent, which has often been associated with Islam by non-Muslims, has no significance as a visual symbol of the faith within Islamic culture.[28] It is rather an insignia of the Ottoman army which the Europeans mistakenly regarded as a symbol of the religion of Islam. Since the cross had much earlier come to symbolize Christianity, they jumped to the conclusion that Islam had adopted the crescent as its comparable symbol.

Surely these facts are known to the non-Muslim as well as Muslim scholars of Islamic art. It is strange, then, that these scholars persist in interpreting that art in a way that is inconsistent with the rest of the culture. The following hypotheses may help explain their adherence to such explanations of aesthetic meaning in Islamic art.

One hypothesis is that the authors are so indoctrinated by Western interpretations of art that it is difficult, if not impossible, for them to escape those civilizational biases when dealing with the art of Islam. Unfortunately, premises that may fit perfectly for interpreting the Christian art of Europe seem to have been transplanted to the field of Islamic art, where they are patently out of place. This certainly underlines the need for extreme caution, deep knowledge, and empathy to be exercised when dealing with comparative and intercultural studies in general and with Islamic art in particular.

A second reason for the prevalence in recent publications of symbolic interpretations of Islamic art is that the field of aesthetics and art history is dominated either by Western scholars or those with Western training. The field has been held in such low esteem in the Muslim world that it has attracted few significant talents from within, necessitating its control by religio-cultural outsiders. In addition, since colleges and universities in the Muslim world have been negligent in fostering studies in aesthetics and art history, Muslims interested in those disciplines, practically without exception, have been trained in Western institu-

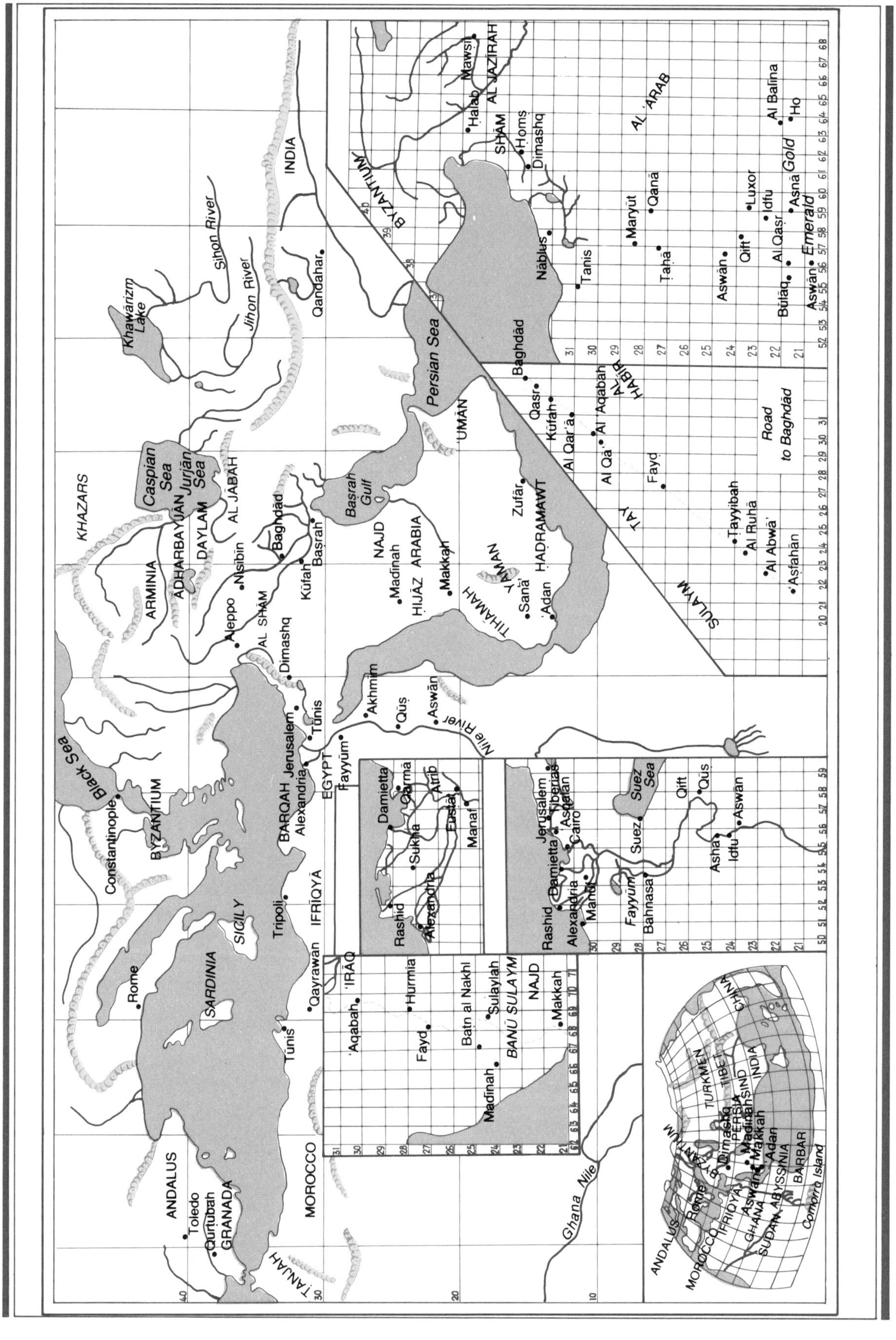

Map 30. The Earth According to Iban Yunis al Miṣrī (339/951)

tions, under the influence of Western tutors and Western art principles. The Muslim scholars, therefore, whether converts or Muslims by birth, are often as affected by the exogenous misinterpretations of Islamic art as are their non-Muslim counterparts.

There is a third reason for the recent attributions of a blatantly literal symbolic content to Islamic art, in contradiction to its inherent abstract quality. This is the influence of Ṣūfism, the mystical current within Islam. Mysticism, in addition to its stress on the personal, inward experience of religion, is a doctrine or persuasion that emphasizes the mysterious, the esoteric, and the magical qualities of religion. Such ideas are true of mystical thought in Islam, as well as in Christianity, Hinduism, Jainism, Judaism, and other religious traditions. Mystics have commonly ascribed hidden meanings to letters, words, and phrases as well as to all types of visual motifs and figures. As they have sought, by various means, to achieve union with the divine, they have been much less careful to maintain the clear distinction between the transcendent and the natural realms which is a hallmark of orthodox Islam and *tawḥīd* (see Chapter 16).

No one can deny the existence of such ideas within Islamic history or the proliferation of certain occult practices and interpretations which they brought in their wake. But these facts should not be blown out of proportion to explain the whole phenomenon known as Islamic art. Though mystics have tried to argue that the originator of Ṣūfism was Muḥammad himself, it was only centuries after the Prophet's death that the movement gained any statistical significance. Its wider acceptance in certain periods of Islamic history cannot be adduced to explain the genesis and whole history of Islamic art. The presence of a uniquely Islamic art was already evident in the first century A.H., a period certainly antedating widespread Ṣūfī influence. 'Abd al Malik's Qubbah al Ṣakhrah (Dome of the Rock) in Jerusalem (71/691) has all the ingredients and characteristics of Islamic art — of Qur'ānic art — long before Ṣūfism proliferated and began to attach its interpretations of literal symbolism to the Islamic arts. The Dome of the Rock was certainly not a product of mystical Islamic ideology. Therefore, it must be accorded an aesthetic interpretation that accords with Islam as a whole.

Exaggerations (both religious and social) of some mystical groups have given Ṣūfism a bad name in many parts of the Muslim world. Its inward-looking, personalist tendencies have been regarded by the Islamic modernists as one of the prime causes for the subjugation and degradation of the Muslim peoples at the hands of internal and external powers. It is argued that an overemphasis on personal piety was achieved at the expense of the traditional Islamic stress on individual and collective achievement, development, and progress. This transvaluation diminished the striving for cooperation between *dīn* and *dunyā* (between "religion" and "this world"), and brought an exaggerated concern instead for the afterlife. Recent

Illustration 8.15

Carved calligraphy decoration (from Qur'ān 2:285) on dome of Mausoleum of Sulṭān Qayt Bay, Cairo, 1472–1474 C.E. [Photo by M. Ashraf.]

Illustration 8.16

Excerpt from a glazed tile calligraphic frieze used to decorate the Sa'dian Tombs, Marrākish, Morocco, 1578–1603 C.E. [Photo by L. al Fārūqī.]

Islamic reform and revival movements are therefore generally opposed to mysticism, and the leadership of the contemporary Muslim *ummah* is largely nonmystical or even antimystical.

Although the majority of Muslims living in the Muslim world are not adherents of mystical brotherhoods, and although those organizations and their activities are regarded with some suspicion by many in the Muslim world, it would certainly be erroneous to say that the mystical movement of Islam is dead. However, the power Ṣūfism held over the people after the disruptions of the Mongol invasion and the Crusades, and the influence it exerted during the subsequent decline in power and increase of political fragmentation, is no longer widely evident. In fact, it is primarily in Europe and America that Ṣūfism flourishes, whether in actual communities or in scholarly interest, research, and publication. It is there that Muslim Ṣūfīs find a sympathetic ear and attain power and prestige. It is there that Westerners—divorced from their former religious traditions and cast adrift without religious moorings—have taken an interest in the ecstatic and exotic practices of Islamic mysticism and espoused its emphasis on the inner spirit. A latent background in Christian or Jewish mysticism often provides a bridge for the Westerner to the mystical elements in Islam. In fact, a considerable number of the Anglo-Saxon converts to Islam in recent decades have entered through the influence of Ṣūfī movements. Contributors of writings expounding the symbolic interpretations of Islamic art have come mainly from this group of white, upper-class, educated Western converts or their non-Muslim Western counterparts.

The mystical, literally symbolic interpretations of recent writings are in opposition to the abstraction so deeply imbedded in the aesthetic consciousness and production of the Muslim peoples. They are also antagonistic to the Islamic aversion to any practice that hints of divine immanence or compromises divine transcendence. Although they may attract the Western-trained scholar and the mystic, they do not satisfy the need for a comprehensive and internally consistent interpretation of the Islamic arts.

An acceptable theory of Islamic art is one that assigns its premises to factors internal to the religion and culture rather than to those imposed by an alien tradition. It is also one that bases itself on the most significant rather than on the minor or accidental elements affecting that culture. Given such demands, the Holy Qur'ān provides a ready and logical source of inspiration for aesthetic creation. The Qur'ān has been as influential of the arts as it has been of the other aspects of Islamic culture. The Qur'ān has provided the message to be expressed aesthetically, as well as the manner of expressing it as evidenced in the six characteristics of its literary form and content. It has even supplied its own expressions and passages as most important subject matter for the iconography of the arts. The Islamic arts therefore can rightfully be designated "Qur'ānic arts."

NOTES

1. This negative view is exemplified by such statements as the following: "The Islamic doctrine of the unity of God, and its correlative, the menace of *Shirk,* or deification, have demanded the prohibition of all representational art. In the realm of worship Islam enforces, often with a puritan severity, a total veto on artistic joy in shape and image, music and iconography" (Kenneth Cragg, *The House of Islam* [Belmont, California: Wadsworth Publishing Co., 1975], p. 15).

2. The *ṣifāt* or attributes of God are traditionally considered to be ninety-nine, though the implication is that they are infinite.

3. Isma'īl R. al Fārūqī, *Islām and Culture* (Kuala Lumpur: Angkatan Belia Islam Malaysia, 1980), p. 44.

4. The "arabesque" is most narrowly defined as a particular form of stylized leaf and vine design created by the Arabs/Muslims. According to Ernst Kühnel (*The Arabesque: Meaning and Transformation of an Ornament,* tr. Richard Ettinghausen [Graz, Austria: Verlag für Sammler, 1949], p. 4), it was in the late nineteenth century that Alois Riegl wrote a book in which he limited the term to this specific category of design. It has generally had a much wider meaning which included a whole range of ornamental designs, including calligraphic, geometric, and vegetal motifs. A still wider significance for this term has been claimed by Lois Ibsen al Fārūqī in "Ornamentation in Arabian Improvisational Music: A Study of Interrelatedness in the Arts," *The World of Music,* 20 (1978), pp. 17–32; idem, "The Islamization of the Hagia Sophia Plan," paper delivered at the Symposium on *The Common Principles, Forms, & Themes of Islamic Art,* Istanbul, April, 1984; and Isma'īl R. al Fārūqī, "Islam and Art," *Studia Islamica,* 37 (1973), pp. 102–103.

5. Kühnel, *The Arabesque.*

6. Ernst Kühnel, "Arabesque," *The Encyclopaedia of Islam,* new ed. (Leiden: E. J. Brill), Vol. I, pp. 558–561.

7. See for a more detailed discussion, Lois Ibsen al Fārūqī, "An Islamic Perspective on Symbolism in the Arts: New Thoughts on Figural Representation," *Art, Creativity, and Religion,* ed. Diane Apostolos Cappadona (New York: Crossroad Pub. Co., 1983), pp. 164–178.

8. Franz Boas, *Primitive Art* (Oslo: Instituttet for Sammenlignende Kulturforskning, 1927).

9. See the description of the city of Isfahan in Nader Ardalan and Laleh Bakhtiar, *The Sense of Unity: The Sufi Tradition in Persian Architecture* (Chicago, 1973), pp. 97ff.

10. Ibid., p. 95.

11. See Marshall G. S. Hodgson's description of Jalāluddīn Rūmī's *Mathnawī* in *The Venture of Islam* (Chicago: University of Chicago Press, 1974), Vol. II, pp. 248–249.

12. Ernst Diez, "A Stylistic Analysis of Islamic Art," *Ars Islamica,* 5 (1938), p. 36; Arthur Upham Pope, *Persian Architecture: The Triumph of Form and Color* (New York: George Braziller, 1965), p. 81.

13. See David Talbot Rice, "Studies in Islamic Metal Work—VI," *Bulletin of the School of Oriental and African Studies* (University of London), 21 (1958), pp. 225–253.

14. I. R. Al Fārūqī, "Islam and Art," pp. 95–98.

15. Lois Ibsen al Fārūqī, "Dance as an Expression of Islamic Culture," *Dance Research Journal,* 10 (Spring–Summer, 1978), pp. 6–13.

16. 'Alī B. 'Uthmān Al-Jullābī Al Ḥujwīrī, *Kashf Al-Maḥjūb of Al Ḥujwīrī,* tr. Reynold A. Nicholson, in *E. J. W. Gibb Memorial Series,* 17 (London: Luzac & Co., 1976), pp. 396–397.

17. See Giovanni Garbini, *The Ancient World* (New York: McGraw-Hill, 1966); André Parrot, *The Arts of Assyria,* tr. Stuart Gilbert and James Emmons (New York: Golden Press, 1961); *The Great King: King of Assyria,* photographs by Charles Wheeler (New York: Metropolitan Museum of Art, 1945).

18. See René A. Bravmann, *African Islam* (Washington, D.C.: Smithsonian Institution Press, 1983), chap. 1; and Clifford Geertz, "Art as a Cultural System," *Modern Language Notes,* 91 (1976), pp. 1489–1490.

19. For example, Martin Lings, *The Quranic Art of Calligraphy and Illumination* (London: World of Islam Festival Trust, 1976); Titus Burckhardt, *The Art of Islam* (London: World of Islam Festival Trust, 1976); Nader Ardalan and L. Bakhtiar, *The Sense of Unity* (Chicago: University of Chicago Press, 1973); Anthony Welch, *Calligraphy in the Arts of the Muslim World* (Austin: University of Texas Press, 1979); Erica Cruikshank Dodd, "The Image of the Word," *Berytus* 18 (1969), pp. 35–58; Seyyed Hossein Nasr, "The Significance of the Void in the Art and Architecture of Islam," *The Islamic Quarterly,* 16 (1972), pp. 115–120; Annemarie Schimmel, "Schriftsymbolik im Islam," in *Aus der Welt der islamischen Kunst: Festschrift für Ernst Kühnel,* ed. Richard Ettinghausen (Berlin, 1959), pp. 244–254; Schuyler van R. Cammann, "Symbolic Meanings in Oriental Rug Patterns," *The Textile Museum Journal,* 3 (1972), pp. 5–54; idem, "Cosmic Symbolism on Carpets from the Sanguszko Group," *Studies in Art and Literature of the Near East in Honor of Richard Ettinghausen,* ed. Peter J. Chelkovski (Salt Lake City and New York, 1975), pp. 181–208.

20. Burckhardt, *Art of Islam,* chap. 4.

21. Cammann, "Symbolic Meanings" and "Cosmic Symbolism on Carpets."

22. Lings, *Quranic Art,* pp. 76–77.

23. Welch, *Calligraphy* p. 23.

24. Ibid.

25. Nasr, "Significance of the Void," p. 116.

26. In contrast with the sacraments of Christianity and the libation ceremonies of the Hindus.

27. In contrast with the significance of the altar of the Catholic cathedral and the statue of the god in a Hindu temple.

28. Thomas Arnold, "Symbolism and Islam," *The Burlington Magazine,* 53 (July–Dec., 1928), pp. 155–156.

PART FOUR
THE MANIFESTATION

CHAPTER 9

The Call of Islam

Having come into history, the religion of Islam sought to convince humans of its truth and to recruit them for its fellowship. The essence of religious experience being what it is, Islam entertained the greatest plan ever, namely, to convert the whole of humanity and to mobilize them for the achievement of justice, truth, well-being, saintliness, and beauty. We have already seen that Islam does not discriminate between people except for their virtue, their righteousness, and their piety. And we have seen that Islam sees the divine imperative as touching every range of human activity and concern; that everything is relevant to religion, not just the rituals of worship or sacraments. And we have seen that Islam is neither a religion of contemplation, nor one of monkery and ascetic withdrawal from the world. It is rather a religion of involvement in the world, in its kitchens and marketplaces as well as in its mosques and on the battlefields.

Islam came to one man, Muḥammad. It asked him "to rise and warn his next of kin and people" (26:214). When he cowered in fear of the burden—and wrapped himself against the shivering of that fear, the voice called out to him, "O [You! who are] wrapped in your mantle . . . Arise" (74:1–2). Muḥammad obeyed the call. He converted his wife and his cousin, and called his personal friends to the new faith. The process had begun; but it was a long way from its objective of converting the world. As a new movement seeking to reform the established religion, Islam was hated and combated, and its few adherents were persecuted. Insults and curses were heaped upon them. Every means of pressure was exerted to dissuade them from their faith. And when all these tactics failed, the enemy hatched a plot to do away with the leader, Muḥammad. With God's help, the Prophet outwitted them and escaped. They began open warfare against him and his followers. Many battles were fought and many lives were lost; but the cause of Islam continued to advance and finally overcame the opposition.

This story of Islam is commonplace in the history of religions. Practically every religion has had a similar beginning. The majority religion seeks to safeguard itself by preventing other religious movements to grow in its midst. If a new religion does succeed and gains a foothold, the older, established religion persecutes the new one. The same tragic history is true of cultures and ethnicities. Wherever there happen to be minorities, the majority culture or ethnicity tries hard to absorb them; and when it fails, it resorts to tyranny and coercion. It is a sign of health and vitality for a majority to seek to expand itself and absorb the minor-

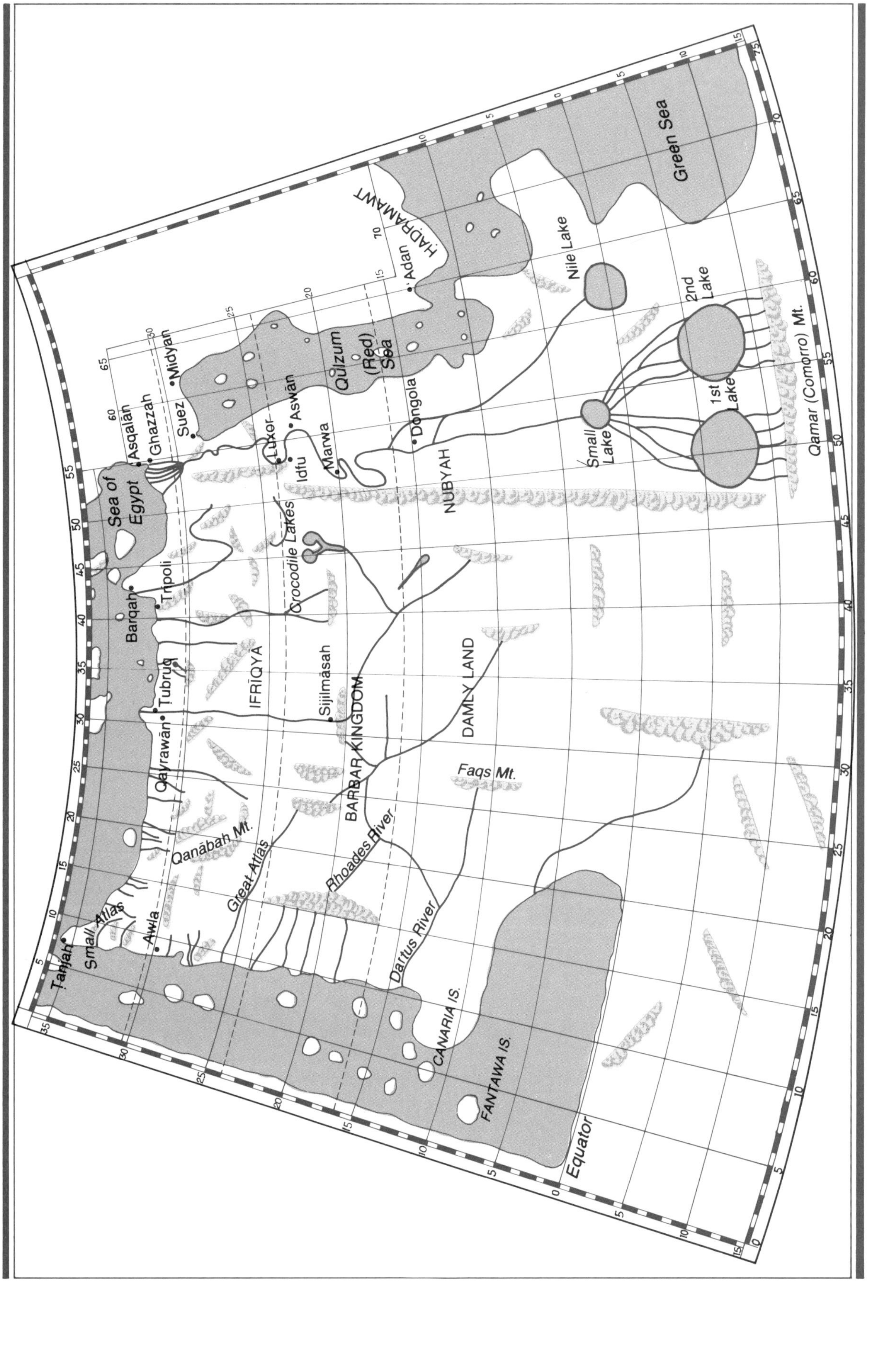

Map 31. A Map of Africa by Al Khawarizmi (236/851)

ity. There is nothing wrong with that universal appetite. Rather, the fault is in the method of absorption, in its recourse to persecution, to coercion and tyranny, to the "carrot" or the "big stick" to achieve its end.

Practically all the religions of the world are guilty in this respect—all except Islam. For Islam has a unique theory of mission, a unique theory of other faiths, and a unique theory of the other religions and their adherents within Islamic society.

ISLAM'S THEORY OF MISSION

God's Commandment

The Muslim regards himself as commanded by God to call all humans to a life of submission to Him, to *islām* as a present participial act (42:15). His life goal is that of bringing the whole of humankind to a life in which Islam, the religion of God, with its theology and *sharī'ah,* its ethics and institutions, is the religion of all humans. In the Qur'ān, God has commanded the Muslim: "Call men unto the path of your Lord with wisdom and goodly counsel. Present the cause to them through arguments yet more sound" (16:125). *Da'wah* is the fulfillment of this commandment. It includes the tasks of teaching the truth to those who are ignorant of it; proclaiming the good news of worldly blessing and otherworldly paradise; and warning against the impending punishment of hell in the hereafter and of misery in this world (22:67). Fulfillment of the command is declared by the Qur'ān to be the apex of virtue and felicity. "Who is better in speech than he who uses it to call men to God?" (41:33). The Prophet too regarded mission as the noblest virtue, its consequence—conversion to Islam—the greatest of all prizes. Since obedience to God is of the essence in Islam, to fulfill the commandment of calling men to obedience to God must be the nearest fulfillment of that essence, a burden all Muslims carry with pride and resolution.

Da'wah Is the Greatest Charity

There is no doubt concerning the centrality of *da'wah* to Islam nor of the value of its end-product as far as the fate of man is concerned. Knowledge of the truth is the greatest possession; *da'wah* is the imparting and teaching of truth. The caller seeks to dispense the truth, and the called is invited to appropriate it. Obviously, *da'wah* is the giving away of the most precious gift possible to give. Moreover, *da'wah* is warning against imminent danger. To alert one's fellows or neighbors to a fire that is spreading is regarded by all as an obligatory charity. How much greater a charity it is to alert one's neighbor against the infinitely more ominous fire! Finally, human life presents hardly any pleasure greater than that of aiding another human to perceive the truth. Comprehension of the truth and the grasping of reality expand both the mind and the heart at once, in both pupil and teacher. No wonder then that Muslims have undertaken the tasks of *da'wah* with enthusiasm.

Mission Is Necessary for Religion

No religion can avoid mission if it has any kind of intellectual backbone. To deny mission is to deny the need to demand the agreement of others to what is being claimed to be the truth by the religion. Not to demand agreement, when a claim is made as to what is true or good and what is not, is either to be not serious about the claim or to declare the claim to be absolutely subjective, particularist, or relative and therefore inapplicable to anyone other than those who make the claim. Obviously, this is the extreme case of tribalism, of religious relativism, of ethnocentrism and parochialism. In religion, as in other matters, relativism provides a poor defense against contention by other views and claims; and even the most tribalist or ethnic religions have had to go beyond it to make themselves worthwhile even among their own adherents. Relativism implies the presentation of a claim as "true only for the adherent, and contrary claims may be equally true for others." But religions make the most significant assertions about life and death; existence and nature; past, present, and future; the world and creation; virtue and vice; happiness and damnation; knowledge and truth. When such assertions are declared not necessary by their claimants, the seriousness of the assertion is put in doubt. Still graver, however, is the assumption that the claim is made in all candidness. In that case, it becomes an invitation to juxtapose contradictory propositions, to claim them to be true, and to accept their contradiction as ultimate and forever irreconcilable. Such a position, to which the religious relativist reduces the assertions of his faith, can by nature appeal only to a mediocre mind. The mind with any amount of intelligence rebels at such a claim, because the truth by nature is exclusivist. Certainly any person, including the man of religion, may propose a hypothetical statement, a proposition of doubtful value, of limited application or validity, of uncertain truth. But in religion, especially as regards the fundamental premises of the faith, one cannot equivocate about truth, with all its power, universalism, and exclusiveness. But when convinced of the truth of one's claims one needs to defend them against contention, and thus becomes involved in convincing the nonadherent of their truth — which is the intellectual side of mission.

Islam is indeed a missionary religion, perhaps more so than any other, precisely because the claims it makes are rational and critical. Moreover, Islam claims to be the final revelation, the definitive reform of all religions, especially of Judaism and Christianity which preceded it in the same religious tradition. Its claims are naturally directed against the contrary assertions of other religions. Intellectually speaking, therefore, the mission of Islam is a necessary corollary of its affirmations and denials. Anybody is invited to contend; and the Muslim is epistemologically bound to prove the truth of Islam's propositions, and obtain the consent of the contender.

NATURE OF ISLAMIC MISSION

Freedom

Being an invitation to consider the most important claims regarding life and death, eternal bliss or punishment, happiness in this world or misery, the light of truth or the darkness of falsehood, virtue and immorality, *da'wah* or mission must be conducted with absolute integrity on the part of both caller and called. For either party to tamper with that integrity, by asking for or receiving bribes or advantages, applying or suffering any kind of coercion or pressure, using it for any purpose other than the discovery of truth and for the sake of God, is a capital crime, vitiating and invalidating the call. The call of Islam must be made in dead seriousness; and it is always expected to be received with equal commitment to the truth. The called must feel absolutely free of fear, absolutely convinced that the judgment he reaches is his very own.

Muslims do not therefore see themselves commanded to call men to Islam *simpliciter.* The conditions of their call have been set by God, and they carry the same authority as the command to call. "No coercion in religion. Truth is manifest; and so is falsehood. . . . Whoever wills, let him believe; and whoever does not will, let him disbelieve . . . whoever accepts the call does so to his own credit; whoever rejects it does so to his own discredit (Qur'ān 2:256, 18:29, 39:41). Certainly, "calling" is not coercing. Rather, it is an invitation whose objective can be fulfilled only with the free consent of the called. Since the objective is to convince the called that God is his Creator, Master, Lord, and Judge, a forced judgment is a contradiction in terms. Humanistic ethics regard coerced *da'wah* as a grave violation of the human person, second only to homicide, if not equal to it. And the judgment of Islam is no less severe. That is why the Qur'ān specified the means of persuasion to be used. If the case is argued with the non-Muslims and they are not convinced, they must be left alone (5:108, 3:176–177, 47:32). When the Prophet's enthusiasm in calling men to Islam overstepped the boundary, God stopped him reprovingly (10:99), teaching us the lesson that even a prophet may not go beyond what preserves the integrity of the call. Moreover, the gravity of what is being asked demands that the person making the decision do so in full consciousness of all consequences, spiritual, social, and material. And in order to reassure the Muslims that their duty is not to guarantee the result, the Qur'ān told them that it is not they who convert men to Islam but God, and once their presentation is made, to leave the matter to Him (28:56, 7:154). Certainly, the Muslim is to try again and never give up, that God may guide his fellowmen to the truth. The example of his own life, his commitment to the values he professes, and his engagement constitute his final argument. If the non-Muslim is still not convinced, the Muslim is to rest his case with God. The Prophet himself allowed those Christians who were not convinced by his own presentation of Islam to keep their faith and return home in dignity.

Rationality

Islamic *da'wah* is an invitation to think, to debate and argue, and to judge the case on the merits presented to the mind. It cannot be met with indifference except by the cynic, nor with rejection except by the fool or the malevolent. The right to think is innate and belongs to all men. No man may preemptively deny it to any human including himself. It can be denied only at one's loss of integrity or respect.

Since what is being sought here is judgment, it follows from the nature of judgment that *da'wah* cannot have for objective anything but a reasoned, deliberate, and conscientious acquiescence to its contents on the part of the called. This means that if the consciousness of the called is in any way vitiated by any of its common defaults or defects, the *da'wah* is itself equally vitiated. That *da'wah* which involves in any way forgetfulness, transport of emotion, or an artificially induced lapse or "Psychopathic expansion" of consciousness, is not legitimate. Da'wah is not the work of magic or illusion, not a mere appeal to the emotions so that the response is rather affectation than judgment. It must be a cool presentation to the consciousness, one wherein neither reason nor heart overrule each other. The decision must be an act of discursive reason supported by an emotional intuition

Illustration 9.1

A Chinese Muslim of Xining, Qinghai Province, People's Republic of China. [Photo by Dru Gladney.]

of the values involved, the former disciplining and the latter enriching the other. Judgment should be arrived at only after consideration of the alternatives, their comparison and contrast with one another, after the precise, unhurried, and objective weighing of evidence and counterevidence. Without tests of internal coherence, of consistency with other knowledge, of correspondence with reality, the response to the call of Islam would not be rational. The call of Islam cannot therefore be made in secret; for it is not an appeal to the heart.

The call of Islam, therefore, is a critical process of intellection. It is in its nature never to be dogmatic, never to stand by its contents as if by its own authority, or that of its mouthpiece, or that of its tradition. It keeps itself always open to new evidence, to new alternatives; and it continually casts and recasts itself in new forms, in cognizance of the new discoveries of human science, of the new needs of human situations. The Islamic caller is not the ambassador of an authoritarian system, but the co-thinker who is cooperating with the called in the understanding and appreciation of God's double revelation, in creation and through His prophets. It is inhuman for the process of intellection to stop at all; for the mind to close itself up against the light of new evidence. Whatever its present affiliation, it should continue to be dynamic, always growing in intensity, clarity of vision, and comprehension. Hence no healthy mind can afford to reject the call a priori. The mind that is so satisfied with its own truth that it wishes to hear no other evidence is doomed to stagnate, to become impoverished, and to lose viability.

Universalism

No human may be excluded from the call of Islam. God's existence, transcendence, and unity, His relevance to this world and life, His commandments, are everybody's concern. Nobody may be precluded from the debate about matters of religion. God has called all humans to Him, because all humans are equally his creatures and He is equally their Creator and Master. Any limitation of His call is equally a limitation of Himself and His power, or an arbitrariness that cannot be reconciled with His justice and impartiality. Partiality may be a characteristic of a tribal, ethnocentric God. It is certainly not one of Islam. The tribalist God can escape the charge of arbitrariness no more than He can escape the charges of irrationality and mediocrity. Racism, election, parochialism, or favoritism do not become stronger when they attribute their judgment to God. They only denigrate themselves and their god in the eye of humanity. There are those who divide humanity, including their own adherents, into castes and assign "spirituality" and "talent" to some and deny them to others on the basis of their birth in these castes. Such theories are even more offensive than tribalism because they are built on the flimsiest and most pretentious notions.

Islam knows no such limitations. It absolves nobody from the tasks of hearing the evidence and rendering judgment. It has called humanity to listen to and consider its claim. It regards with contempt those who do not accept Islam but cannot put up a valid counterargument. If to accept Islam is wise, Islam regards counterarguments as honest and worthy of all respect (as it does counter-counterarguments). Whether among its adherents or in the world at large, Islam regards all humans as equal creatures, equally descendant from Adam and Eve. "O People," the Qur'ān proclaimed, "We have created you all from a single pair of male and female; and We have differentiated you into tribes and nations that you may know

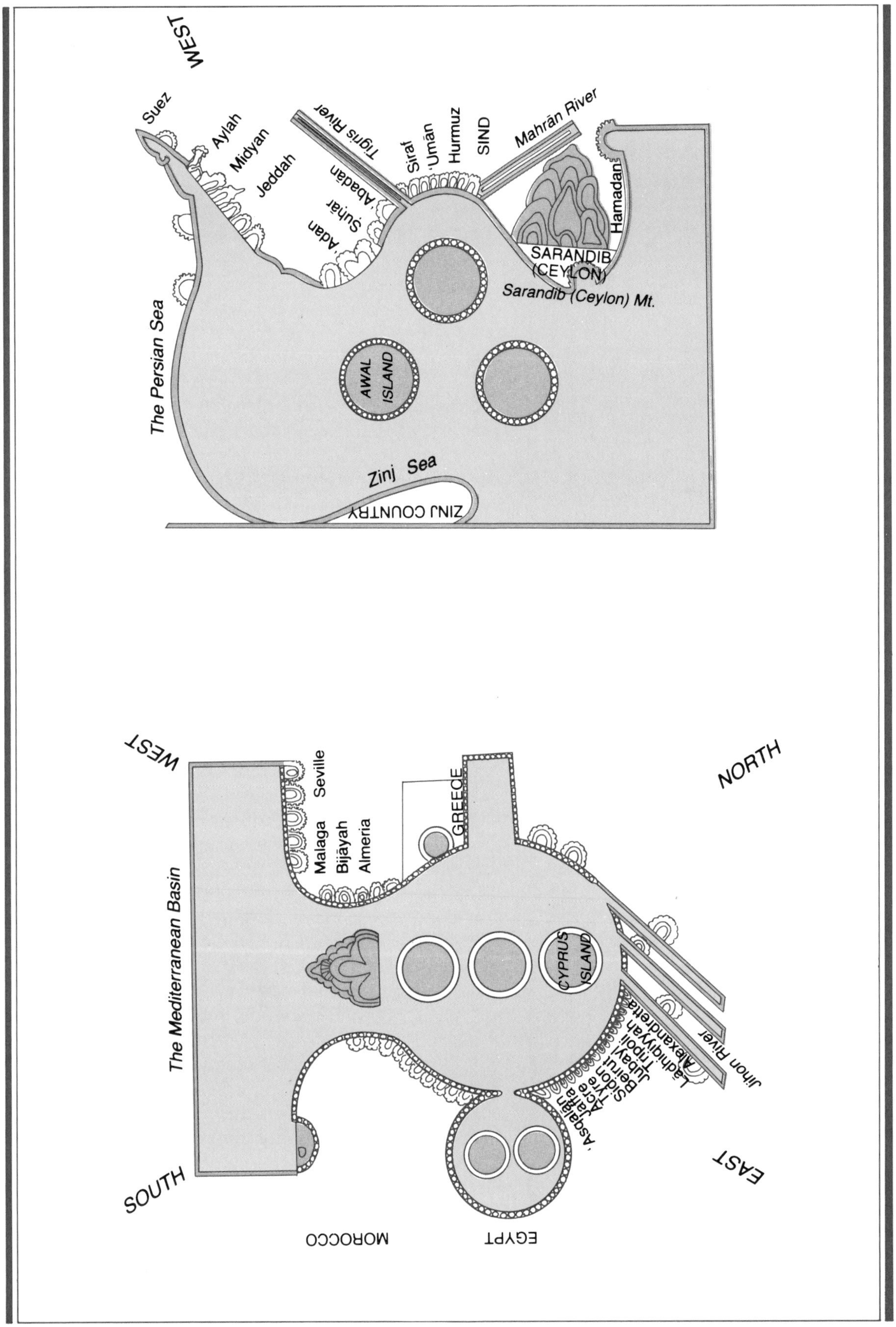

Map 32. The Persian and Mediterranean Seas by Ibrāhīm ibn Muḥammad al Iṣṭakhrī (4th/10th century)

one another. Priority in the eye of your Lord is a function of virtue [not of tribe or nation] (49:13). The Prophet Muḥammad's last sermon included the admonition: "All of you descend from Adam and Adam proceeded from dust. No Arab has any priority over a non-Arab, and no white over a black except in righteousness." All men are equally *mukallafūn,* that is, obliged to respond to God's call with obedience. God's divinity lays a universal claim on the whole of creation.

ISLAM'S THEORY OF OTHER FAITHS

On the Level of Ideas

For the Muslim, the relation of Islam to the other religions has been established by God in His revelation; and for him, the Qur'ān is the ultimate religious authority, the final and definitive revelation of His will. What Islam teaches in this regard has been confirmed by Muslim practice throughout the centuries. Its continuity constitutes an irrefutable testament to Muslim understanding of the meanings attributed to the Qur'ānic verses. Despite the widest possible variety of ethnic cultures, languages, races, and customs characterizing the Muslim world, from Morocco to Indonesia and from Russia to the heart of Africa, the understanding and the practice have been the same. Islam's ideational relation to the non-Muslim will be discussed as it pertains to Judaism and Christianity, to the others religions, and to mankind in general.

Judaism and Christianity. Islam accords to these two religions special status. First, each of them is the religion of God. Their founders on earth—Abraham, Moses, David, Jesus—are the prophets of God. What they have conveyed—the Torah, the Psalms, the Evangels—are revelations from God. To believe in these prophets, in the revelations they have brought, is integral to the very faith of Islam. To disbelieve them—nay, to discriminate between them—is apostasy. "Our Lord and your Lord is indeed God, the One and Only God" (Qur'ān 20:88). God described His Prophet Muḥammad and his followers as "believing all that has been revealed from God"; as "believing in God, in His angels, in His revelations and Prophets"; as "not distinguishing between the Prophets of God" (2:285).

Arguing with Jews and Christians who object to this self-identification and claim an exclusivist monopoly on the former prophets, the Qur'ān says: "You claim that Ibrahīm, Isma'īl, Isḥaq, Ya'qūb and their tribes were Jews or Christians [and God claims otherwise]. Would you claim knowledge in these matters superior to God's?" "Say, [Muḥammad], We believe in God, in what has been revealed by Him to us, what has been revealed to Ibrahīm, Isma'īl, Isḥaq, Ya'qūb, the tribes; in what has been conveyed to Moses, to Jesus and all the prophets from their Lord" (3:84). "We have revealed [Our revelation] to you [Muḥammad] as We did to Noah and the Prophets after him, to Ibrahīm, Isma'īl, Isḥaq, Ya'qūb, the tribes, to Jesus, Job, Jonah, Aaron, Solomon, and David" (4:163). "It is God indeed, the living and eternal One, that revealed to [Muḥammad] the Book [Qur'ān] confirming the previous revelations. For it is He Who revealed the Torah and the Evangels as His guidance to mankind . . . Who revealed the Psalms to David" (3:2–4). "Those who believe [in you, Muḥammad], the Jews, the Christians and the Sabaeans—all those who believe in God and in the Day of Judgment, and have done the good works, will receive their due reward from God. They have no cause to fear, nor will they grieve" (5:69).

The honor with which Islam regards Judaism and Christianity, their founders and scriptures, is not mere courtesy but acknowledgment of religious truth. Islam sees them not as "other views" which it has to tolerate but as standing *de jure,* as truly revealed religions from God. Moreover, their legitimate status is neither sociopolitical nor cultural nor civilizational but religious. In this, Islam is unique. For no religion in the world has yet made belief in the truth of other religions a necessary condition of its own faith and witness. Christianity accepts the scripture of Judaism as its own, and some Christians regard the Torah, or Jewish law, as binding. However, the majority of Christians consider themselves free from the laws of Judaism, following St. Paul's understanding that the mission of Jesus was essentially a liberation *(apolytrosis)* from the law. All Christians subject the Hebrew scripture to "Christian" interpretation and regard Judaism as a mere prelude to God's salvation plan, a *preparatio* for Christianity, not as an autonomous religion, valid in and of itself.

Consistently, Islam has pursued this acknowledgment of religious truth in Judaism and Christianity to its logical conclusion, namely, identification with them. Identity of God, the source of revelation in the three religions, necessarily leads to identity of the revelation and of the religions. Islam does not see itself as coming to the religious scene *ex nihilo,* but as a reaffirmation of the same truth presented by all the preceding prophets of Judaism and Christianity. It regards them all as Muslims, and their revelations as one and the same as its own. Together with Ḥanīfism, the monotheistic and ethical religion of pre-Islamic Arabia, Judaism, Christianity, and Islam constitute crystallizations of one and the same religious con-

Illustration 9.2

Mosque of Xining, Qinghai Province, People's Republic of China. [Photo by Dru Gladney.]

sciousness whose essence and core is one and the same. The unity of this religious consciousness can be easily seen by the historian of civilization concerned with the ancient Near East. It is traceable in the literatures of these ancient peoples and is supported by the unity of their geography, their languages (for which they are called "Semitic"), their demography, their history and their artistic expression. It is relevant to recall here the conclusion we drew in our earlier discussion of ancient Near Eastern religiosity (see Chapters 2 and 3). There we discovered that the unity of the religious consciousness of the Near East consisted of five dominant principles which characterize its known literature: the disparate ontic reality of God from His creatures; the purpose of man's creation as service to God; the relevance of Creator to creature; the law as content of God's will; man's capability to transform the world into what ought to be; and finally, happiness and felicity resulting from man's fulfillment of the divine command, with suffering and damnation as the result of human failure in this pursuit.

Islam has taken all this for granted. It has called the central religious tradition of the Semitic peoples "Ḥanīfism" and identified itself with it. The Islamic concept of "Ḥanīf" should not be compared to Karl Rahner's "anonymous Christians." "Ḥanīf" is a Qur'ānic category, not the invention of a modern theologian embarrassed by his church's exclusivist claim on divine grace. It has been operating within the Islamic ideational system for fourteen centuries. Those to whom it is attributed are the paradigms of faith and greatness, the most honored representatives of religious life, not the despised though tolerated approximators of the religious ideal. Islam's honoring of the ancient prophets and their followers is not to be affected by any diminution of respect or loyalty to them by either Jews or Christians. In Islam, the Christians are exalted for their asceticism and humility, and they are declared the closest of all believers to the Muslims. If, despite this commendation of them, their prophets, and their scriptures, Jews and Christians persist in opposing and rejecting the Prophet and his followers, Muslims see themselves nonetheless bound to call the Jews and Christians in these words: "O People of the Book, come now with us to rally around a fair and noble principle common to both of us, that all of us shall worship and serve none but God, that we shall associate naught with Him, that we shall not take one another as lords beside God. But if they still persist in their opposition, then warn them that We shall persist in our affirmation" (3:63–64).

Islam has given the maximum that can reasonably

be given by any religion to another. It has acknowledged as true the other religion's prophets and founders, its scripture and teaching. It declared its God and the God of that religion as One and the same, and the adherents of the two religions as mutual friends under God.

The other religions. Islam teaches that the phenomenon of prophecy is universal, that it has taken place throughout all space and time, and that there will be no judgment unless a prophet has been sent to each people (Qur'ān 17:15). God's absolute justice requires that no one will be held responsible unless His law has been conveyed and promulgated. Such conveyance and/or promulgation is precisely the phenomenon of prophecy. Some of these prophets are widely known; others are not. Neither Jewish nor Christian nor Muslim ignorance of them implies their nonexistence. Islam teaches that God has not differentiated between His messengers; that the prophets of all times and places have taught one and the same lesson — namely, that worship and service are due to God alone, and that evil must be avoided and the good pursued (16:36). Islam thus lays the ground for a relation with all peoples as recipients of a revelation identical to that of Islam. But if all prophets have conveyed one and the same message, where did the religions of mankind obtain their historical variety? To this question, Islam furnishes a theoretical and a practical answer.

Islam holds that the messages of all prophets have but one essence composed of two elements: *tawḥīd,* or the acknowledgment that God alone is God and that all worship, service, and obedience are due to Him alone; and morality or the doing of good and avoidance of evil. Each revelation has come in a code of law applicable to its people, and hence relevant to their historical conditions. Such particularization does not affect the essence of the revelation, only the "how" of service. This Islamic theory of revelation rallies humanity around common principles of religion and morality which it removes beyond contention.

The second cause of religious diversity is that the revelations of God are not always welcomed by all men. *First,* some with vested interests do not agree with divine dispensations that persistently advocate charity and altruism, and giving of the rich to the poor. *Second,* being in support of ordered social living, revelation always counsels obedience of the ruled to the law, but under the assumption of a rule of justice, which may not always be agreeable to rulers and kings who seek to have their own way. *Third,* divine revelation reminds man to measure himself by reference to God and His law, not to himself. But man is vain, and self-adoration is for him a constant temptation. *Fourth,* revelation demands that humans discipline their instincts and keep their emotions under control. But humans are inclined to indulgence, and their inclination pushes them against revelation. *Fifth,* where the contents of revelation are not judiciously and meticulously remembered, taught, and observed publicly and by the greatest numbers, they tend to suffer from dilution, shift of emphasis, change; or they are completely forgotten. *Finally,* when the divine revelation is moved across linguistic, ethnic, and cultural frontiers, indeed, even to generations within the same people but far removed from its original recipients in time, it is exposed to change through interpretation. Any or all of these circumstances may bring about a corruption of the original revelation. That is why God has seen fit in His love and mercy to repeat the phenomenon of prophecy, to send forth prophets to reconvey the divine message and reestablish it in the minds and hearts of humans.

Islam's relation to all humans. Islam has similarly felt a bond between itself and all other religions, indeed, even with areligionists and atheists, whom it aims to rehabilitate as integral members of a universal human society. This relation constitutes Islam's universalism and humanism. At its root stands the purpose of creation, which Islam defines in terms of innate capacity to discover the will of God — the ethically imperative — by reason, as well as through the faculty of innate religion, *dīn al fiṭrah,* which was implanted by God in every human to enable him to recognize the Creator and to acknowledge His law. Everybody is endowed with an inherent talent to consider and to perceive the truth. Thus, behind the dazzling religious diversity of mankind stands an innate religion which is inseparable from human nature, a primordial religion, the one and only true religion (Qur'ān 30:30; 3:19). All men possess a faculty with which they can perceive God as God and the moral law as imperative, unless misguidance had taught them otherwise. Under this view, Islam rehabilitates all humans as genuine instances of *homo religiosus.* This view makes a clean sweep of prophecy and of all history and trusts that in their innate form, humans may still agree on a naturally available religion and morality not different from Islam. Indeed, in its beginning Islam identified itself with natural religion or *dīn al fiṭrah,* which it praised as the religion of God.

On the Level of Practice

Based on these precepts, the Prophet Muḥammad founded the first interreligious social order in human history. He had barely arrived in Madīnah in July 622 when he brought together all the inhabitants of the city and its environs and promulgated with them the Islamic state and its constitution. This event was of capital importance for the relation of Islam to the other religions, and of non-Muslims to Muslims in all times and places. Four years after the Prophet's demise in 10/632, 'Umar ibn al Khaṭṭāb, the second caliph, ordered that the date of promulgation of this constitution be the beginning of the Islamic calendar since it was indeed the beginning of Islamic history.[1]

The constitution was a covenant between the Prophet, the Muslims, and the Jews. It abolished the tribal system of Arabia under which the Arab defined himself and by which society was governed. Henceforth, the Arab was to be defined by Islam; and his personal and social life to be governed by Islamic law, the *sharī'ah*. The old tribal loyalties gave way to a new social bond which tied every Muslim to all other Muslims across tribal lines, to form the *ummah*. The *ummah* is an organic body whose constituents mutually sustain and protect one another. Their personal, reciprocal, and collective responsibilities are all defined by law. The Prophet was to be its chief political and juristic authority; and, as long as he lived, he exercised this power. After his death, his successors exercised political authority, while juristic authority devolved exclusively upon the jurists who had by then developed a methodology for interpretation, renewal, and expansion of the law.

The Jewish *ummah*. We have already seen how the Prophet founded the first Islamic state, and made it inclusive of the Jews and Christians of Arabia. Suffice it here to recall those features that are pertinent to the status of the non-Muslim in Islamic society. Alongside the *ummah* of Muslims in Madīnah stood the *ummah* of the Jews. Their old tribalist loyalties to the Arab Aws and Khazraj tribes were supplanted by the bond of Judaism. Instead of their citizenship being a function of their relationship to this or that Arab tribe, it was now a function of their Jewishness. Their life was structured around Jewish institutions and governed by the Torah, their revealed law. Political authority was vested in them collectively as Jewish people, and juristic authority rested with their own rabbinic institutions. Overarching both *ummah* of Jews and Muslims was a third organization, also called *"al ummah,"* or *"al dawlah al Islāmiyyah"* (the Islamic state), whose purpose was the protection of the state, the conduct of its external affairs, and the carrying out of Islam's universal mission. The state could conscript the Muslims in its services, whether for peace or for war, but not the Jews. However, Jews could volunteer their services if they wished. Neither the Muslim nor the Jewish *ummah* was free to conduct any relation with a foreign power, much less to declare war or peace with any other state or foreign organization; which was the exclusive jurisdiction of the Islamic state. The Jews of Madīnah entered freely into this covenant with the Prophet and his Muslim followers. The new constitution raised their status from tribal clients on sufferance to citizens *de jure* of the state. In all Islamic states through history, wherever the law of Islam was sovereign, the Jews never lost that status. Their position could not come under attack or be denied because it was ordained by the Prophet Muḥammad. Even when the Jews betrayed that status, the Muslims continued to acknowledge it because of its religious sanctity. When the Islamic state expanded to include northern Arabia, Palestine, Jordan and Syria, Persia and Egypt, where numerous

Illustration 9.3

Two Nigerian pilgrims just returned from the *Ḥajj*. [Courtesy A. R. Doi.]

Jews lived, they were automatically treated as legal citizens of the Islamic state. This explains the harmony and cooperation that characterized Muslim–Jewish relations throughout the centuries that followed.

For the first time in history since the Babylonian invasion of 586 B.C.E., and as citizens of the Islamic state, the Jew could model his life after the Torah and do so legitimately, supported by the public laws of the state where he resided. For the first time, a non-Jewish state put its executive power at the service of a rabbinic court. For the first time, the state assumed responsibility for the maintenance of Jewishness, and declared itself ready to use its power to defend the Jewishness of Jews against the enemies of Jewishness, be they Jews or non-Jews. After centuries of Greek, Roman, and Byzantine (Christian) oppression and persecution, the Jews of the Near East, of North Africa, of Spain and Persia, looked upon the Islamic state as liberator. Many of them readily helped its armies in their conquests and cooperated enthusiastically with the Islamic state administration. This cooperation was followed by acculturation into Arabic and Islamic culture, and produced a dazzling blossoming of Jewish arts, letters, sciences, and medicine. It brought affluence and prestige to the Jews, some of whom became ministers and advisers to the caliphs. Indeed, Judaism and its Hebrew language developed their "golden age" under the aegis of Islam. Hebrew acquired its first grammar, the Torah found its jurisprudence, Hebrew letters achieved their lyrical poetry, and Hebrew philosophy found its first Aristotelian, Mūsā ibn Maymūn (Maimonides), whose thirteen precepts, couched in Arabic first, defined the Jewish creed and identity. Judaism developed its first mystical thinker as well, Ibn Gabirol, whose "Ṣūfī" thought brought reconciliation and inner peace to Jews throughout Europe. Under 'Abd al Raḥman III in Cordoba, the Jewish prime minister, Ḥasdai ben Shapirūt, managed to effect reconciliation between Christian monarchs whom even the Catholic Church could not bring together. All this was possible because of one Islamic principle, namely, the recognition of the Torah as revelation and of Judaism as God's religion, as proclaimed in the Qur'ān.

The Christian *ummah*. Shortly after the conquest of Makkah by Muslim forces in 8/630, the Christians of Najrān in Yaman sent a delegation of chieftains to meet the Prophet in Madīnah. Their purpose was to clarify their position vis-à-vis the Islamic state, and that of the state vis-à-vis them. The conquest of Makkah had made the Islamic state a power to reckon with in the region. The delegates were the guests of the Prophet; he received them in his house and entertained them in his mosque. He explained Islam to them and called them to convert to his faith and cause. Some of them did and instantly became members of the Muslim *ummah.* Others did not. They chose to remain Christian, and to join the Islamic state as Christians. The Prophet constituted them a Christian *ummah,* alongside the Jewish and Muslim *umam* (pl. of *ummah*), within the Islamic state. He sent with them one of his companions, Abū 'Ubaydah, to represent the Islamic state in their midst. They converted to Islam in the period of the second caliph (2–14/624–636).

When the Muslims defeated the Byzantines on the battlefields, the latter abandoned the territories of the Fertile Crescent to their native peoples. Having heard of the Muslims and of their attitude toward Christianity, the archbishop of Jerusalem refused to surrender the keys of the city except to the caliph in person. 'Umar journeyed to Jerusalem and, after agreeing

Illustration 9.4

Façade and minaret of The Islamic Center, Washington, D.C. [Courtesy The Islamic Center, Washington, D.C.]

with the archbishop, signed the following treaty which remained the *typos* of Muslim tolerance and good will on the religious as well as on the social and cultural levels.

In the name of God, the Compassionate, the Merciful. This charter is granted by Umar, Servant of Allah and Prince of the Believers, to the people of Aelia. He grants them security for their persons and their properties, for their churches and their crosses, the little and the great, and for adherents of the Christian religion. Neither shall their churches be dispossessed nor will they be destroyed, nor their substances or areas, nor their crosses or any of their properties, be reduced in any manner. They shall not be coerced in any matter pertaining to their religion, and they shall not be harmed. Nor will any Jews be permitted to live with them in Aelia. Upon the people of Aelia falls the obligation to pay the jizya, just as the people of Mada'in (Persia) do, as well as to evict from their midst the Byzantine army and the thieves. Whoever of these leaves Aelia will be granted security of person and property until he reaches his destination. Whoever decides to stay in Aelia will also be granted same, and share with the people of Aelia in their rights and the jizya. The same applies to the people of Aelia as well as to any other person. Anyone can march with the Byzantines, stay in Aelia or return to his home country, and has until the harvesting of the crops to decide. Allah attests to the contents of this treaty, and so do His Prophet, his successors and the believers.

Signed: Umar ibn al-Khattab.

Witnessed by: Khalid ibn al-Walid, 'Amr ibn al-'As, 'Abd al Rahman bin 'Awf, and Mu'awiyah ibn Abu Sufyan.

Executed in the year 15 A.H.[2]

Map 33A. Al Futūḥāt of the Prophet I: Quraysh Caravan (Battle of Badr), 2/624

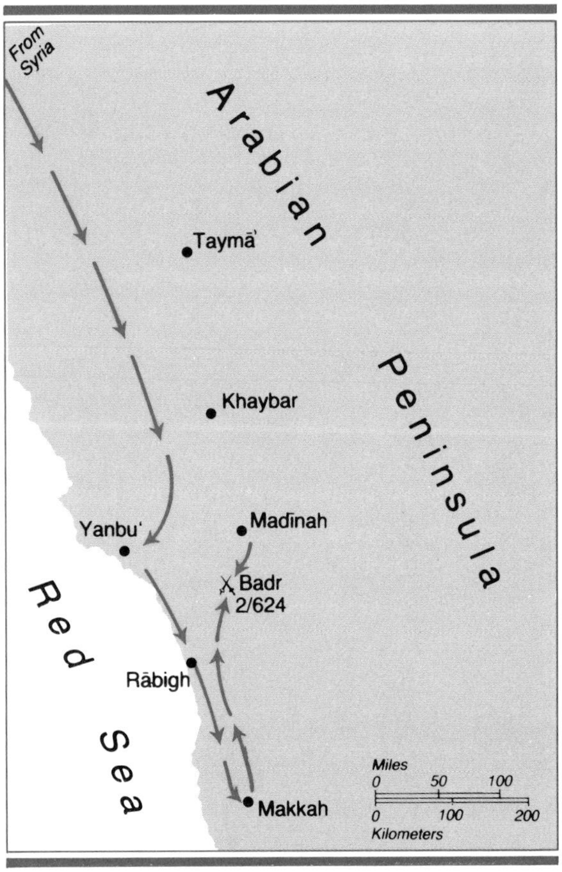

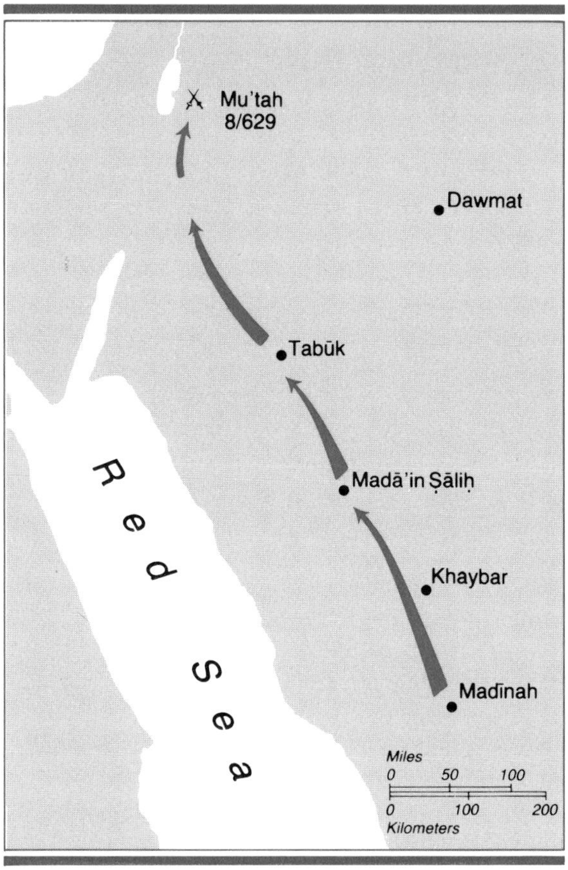

Map 33B. Al Futūḥāt of the Prophet I: Battle of Mu'tah, 8/629

The Christian *ummah* in the Islamic state continued to grow by the expansion of its frontiers to the north and west. Indeed, for the greater part of the first century A.H., the majority of the citizens of the Islamic state were Christians, enjoying respect, liberty, and a new dignity which they had not enjoyed under either Christian Rome or Greek Byzantium.

Both these powers had been imperalist and racist. They had colonized the territories of the Near East and tyrannized their non-Roman, non-Greek subjects. Under Islam on the contrary, Christians lived in peace and prospered for centuries, during which time the Islamic state saw righteous as well as tyrannical sultans and caliphs. Had it been a part of Islamic sentiment to do away with the Christian presence within the Islamic state, it could have been done without a ripple. But it was Islam's respect for and acknowledgment of Jesus as Prophet of God and of his Evangel as revelation that safeguarded that presence.

The same is true of Abyssinia, a Christian neighboring state which harbored the first Muslim emigrants from the wrath of Makkah. When, in the early years, Makkan persecution became unbearable for his followers, the Prophet ordered them to seek refuge in Ethiopia, the Christian kingdom, confident that the followers of Jesus Christ were moral, charitable, and friendly, and promoters of the worship of God. His high regard for them was well justified. The Christian emperor rejected Makkah's demand for extradition of the Muslim refugees and acclaimed the Qur'ānic recognition of the prophethood of Jesus, the innocence of his mother, and the oneness of God. Abyssinia maintained with the Islamic state at the time of the Prophet a covenant of peace and friendship. In consequence of this, the expansive designs of the Islamic state never included Abyssinia.

Map 33C. Al Futūḥāt of the Prophet I: Battle of Tabūk, 9/630

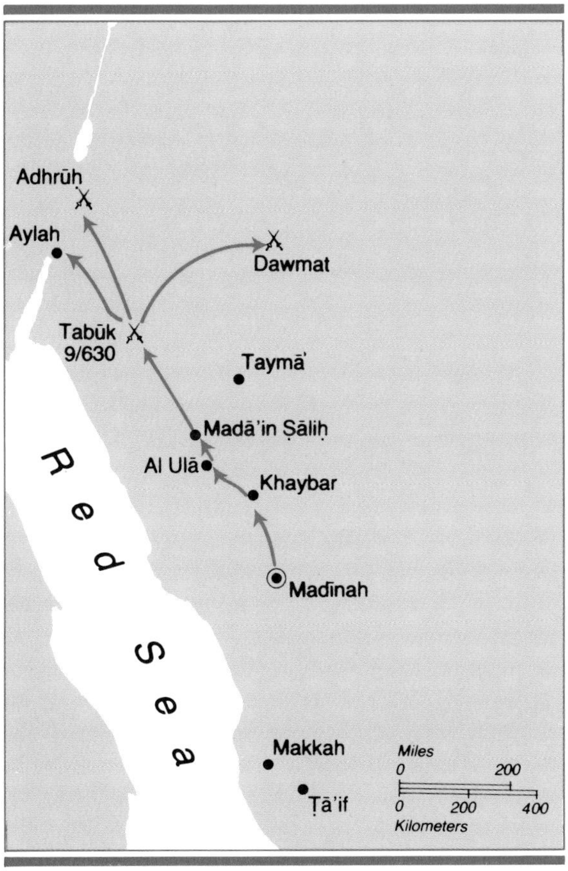

Nothing is further from the truth and more inimical to Muslim – non-Muslim relations than the claim that Islam spread by the sword. Nothing could have been and still is more condemnable to the Muslims than to coerce a non-Muslim into Islam. As noted earlier, the Muslims have been the first to condemn such action as mortal sin. On this point, Thomas Arnold, an English missionary in the Indian Civil Service of colonial days, wrote:

> . . . of any organised attempt to force the acceptance of Islam on the non-Muslim population, or of any systematic persecution intended to stamp out the Christian religion, we hear nothing. Had the caliphs chosen to adopt either course of action, they might have swept away Christianity as easily as Ferdinand and Isabella drove Islam out of Spain, or Louis XIV made Protestantism penal in France, or the Jews were kept out of England for 350 years. The Eastern Churches in Asia were entirely cut off from communion with the rest of Christendom throughout which no one would have been found to lift a finger on their behalf, as heretical communions. So that the very survival of these Churches to the present day is a strong proof of the generally tolerant attitude of the Mohammedan governments towards them.[33]

Compared with the histories of other religions, the history of Islam is categorically different as far as toleration of nonbelieving communities is concerned. Fortunately, we have on record many witnesses from those days of Muslim expansion to whom we should be grateful for clearing this matter once and for all. Michael the Elder, Jacobite patriarch of Antioch, wrote in the second half of the twelfth century: "This is why the God of vengeance . . . beholding the wickedness of the Romans who, throughout their dominions, cruelly plundered our churches and our monasteries and condemned us without pity—brought from the region of the south the sons of Ishmael, to deliver us through them from the hands of the Romans."[4] Barhebraeus is author of an equally powerful witness in favor if Islam.[5] Ricoldus de Monte Crucis, a Dominican monk from Florence who visited the Muslim East about 1300, gave an equally eloquent witness of tolerance, nay, friendship, to the Christians.[6] And yet, if the Muslims were so tolerant, the Christian persist-

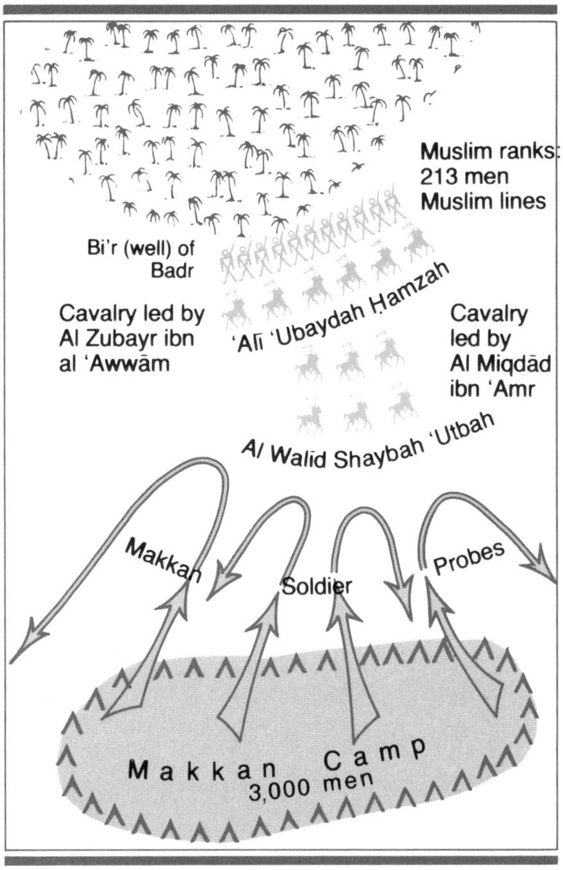

Map 34A. Al Futūḥāt of the Prophet II: Badr

ently asks, why did their co-religionists flock to Islam by the millions? Of these co-religionists the Arabs were the smallest minority. The rest were Hellenes, Persians, Egyptians, Cyrenaicans, Berbers, Cypriots, and Caucasians.

In making the same point Thomas Arnold reported approvingly from the speech of a Christian missionary leader—Canon Taylor of the Anglican Church—delivered at a church congress to consider mission to Muslims. He wrote in his *Preaching of Islam* that Taylor said:

> It is easy to understand why this reformed Judaism [sic!] spread so swiftly over Africa and Asia. The African and Syrian doctors had substituted abstruse metaphysical dogmas for the religion of Christ: they tried to combat the licentiousness of the age by setting forth the celestial merit of celibacy and the angelic excellence of virginity—seclusion from the world was the road of holiness, dirt was the characteristic of monkish sanctity—the people were practically polytheists, worshipping a crowd of martyrs, saints and angels; the upper classes were effeminate and corrupt, the middle classes oppressed by taxation, the slaves without hope for the present or the future. As with the besom of God, Islam swept away this mass of corruption and superstition. It was a revolt against empty theological polemics; it was a masculine protest against the exaltation of celibacy as a crown of piety. It brought out the fundamental dogmas of religion—the unity and greatness of God, that He is merciful and righteous, that He claims obedience to His will, resignation and faith. It proclaimed the responsibility of man, a future life, a day of judgment, and stern retribution to fall upon the wicked; and enforced the duties of prayer, almsgiving, fasting and benevolence. It thrust aside the artificial virtues, the religious frauds and follies, the perverted moral sentiments, and the verbal subtleties of theological disputants. It replaced monkishness by manliness. It gave hope to the slave, brotherhood to mankind, and recognition to the fundamental facts of human nature.[7]

***Umam* (sing. *ummah*) of other religions.** Persia's incursion into Arabia had left behind it some Persians and some, though very few, Arab converts to the Zoroastrian faith. A larger number of these lived in the buffer desert zone between Persia and Byzantium, and in Shaṭṭ al 'Arab, the lower region of the confluence of the Tigris and Euphrates, where Arabia and Persia overlapped. Notable among the Persian Zoroastrians in Arabia was Salmān al Fārīsī, who converted to Islam before the Hijrah and became one of the illustrious companions of the Prophet. According to some traditions, it was the Prophet himself who, in the "Year of Delegations" (8–9/630–631), the year that witnessed the tribes and regions of Arabia sending delegations to Madīnah to pledge their fealty to the Islamic state, recognized the Zoroastrians as another *ummah* within the Islamic state. Very soon afterward, the Islamic state conquered Persia and included all its millions within its citizenry. Those who converted to Islam joined the *ummah* of Muslims; the millions of others who chose to remain Zoroastrian were accorded the same privileges and duties accorded by the constitution to the Jews. The Prophet had already extended their application to the Christians eight years after the constitution was enacted. They were extended to apply to the Zoroastrians in 14/636, following the conquest of Persia by the Prophet's companions if not sooner by the Prophet himself.

Following the conquest of India by Muḥammad bin Qāsim in 91/711, the Muslims came in contact with new religions, Buddhism and Hinduism. Both religions co-existed in Sind and the Punjab, the regions conquered by Muslims and joined to the Islamic state. Muḥammad bin Qāsim sought instruction from the caliph in Damascus on how to treat Hindus and Buddhists. They appeared to worship idols, and their doctrines were at the farthest remove from Islam. Their founders were unheard of by Muslims. The caliph called a council of *'ulamā'* and asked them to render judgment on the basis of the governor's report. The judgment was that as long as Hindus and Buddhists did not fight the Islamic state, as long as they paid the *jizyah* or tax due, they must be free to "worship their gods" as they please, to maintain their temples and to determine their lives by the precepts of their faith. Thus, the same status as that of the Jews and Christians was accorded to them.[8]

The principle governing Islam and the Islamic state's relations with other religions and their adherents had thus been established. It was implemented as the Islamic state entered into relations with those adherents, a process that took place either during the Prophet's life or very soon after it. When the *sharī'ah* crystallized in prescriptive form, the status, rights, and obligations of Muslim and non-Muslim citizens were already included. For fourteen centuries in many places, or less because of the later arrival of Islam or the imposition of Western law by colonial administrations, the *sharī'ah* successfully governed Muslim-non-Muslim relations. It created a *modus vivendi* that enabled the non-Muslims to perpetuate themselves—hence their continuing presence in the Muslim world—and to achieve felicity as defined by their own faiths. The atmosphere of the Islamic state was one replete with respect and honor to religion, piety and virtue, unlike the tolerance of modern times—where such may exist—born of skepticism regarding the truth of religious claims, of cynicism and unconcern for religious values. The Islamic *sharī'ah* is otherwise known as the *millah* or *millet* system (meaning "religious communities"), or the *Dhimmah* or *Zimmi* system (meaning the covenant of peace whose *dhimmah* or guarantor is God). Evil

Map 34B. Al Futūḥāt of the Prophet II: Uḥud Mountain

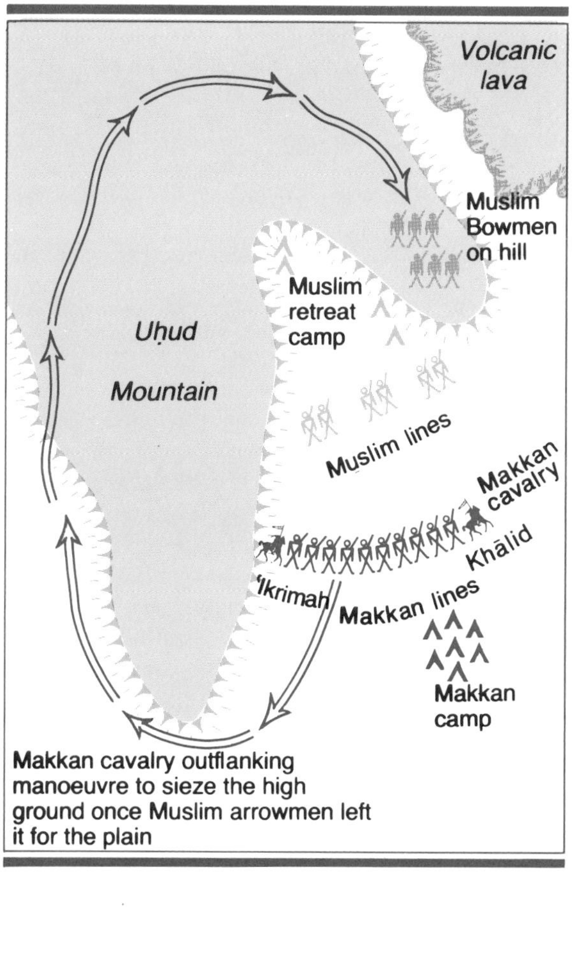

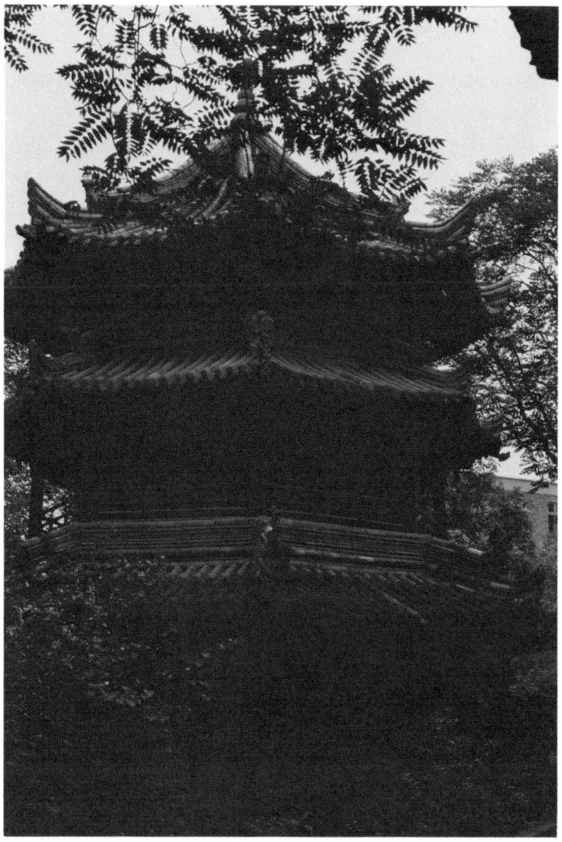

Illustration 9.5

Minaret, Qingzhen Mosque, People's Republic of China. The mosque was founded in the eighth century; the present buildings date from the fourteenth century. [Photo by S. M. Chiu.]

rulers cannot be denied to have existed in the Muslim world; and where they existed, Muslims as well as non-Muslims suffered. Nowhere in Islamic history, however, were non-Muslims singled out for prosecution or persecution for their adherence to their faiths. The constitution that protected them was taken by Muslims to be God-inspired, God-protected. The Prophet had already warned: "Whoever oppresses any *dhimmī* (non-Muslim peace-covenanter with the Islamic state), I shall be his prosecutor on the Day of Judgment." No other religion or societal system has ever regarded the religious minority in a better light, integrated it into the stream of the majority with as little damage to either party, or treated it without injustice or unfairness as Islam did. Indeed, none could. Islam succeeded in a field where all other religions failed because of its unique theology which recognized the true, one, and only religion of God to be innate in every person, the primordial base of all religions, identical with the Ḥanīfī tradition, with Sabaeanism, Judaism, and Christianity.

Far from being a national state, the Islamic state is a world order in which numerous religious communities, national or transnational, co-exist in peace. It is a universal *Pax Islamica* which recognizes the legitimacy of every religious community, and grants it the right to order its life in accordance with its own religious genius. It is superior to the League of Nations and the United Nations because, instead of national sovereignty as the principle of membership, it has taken the principle of religious identity. Its constitution is divine law, valid for all, and may be invoked in any Muslim court by anyone, Muslim or non-Muslim.

Map 34C. Al Futūḥāt of the Prophet II: Al Khandaq

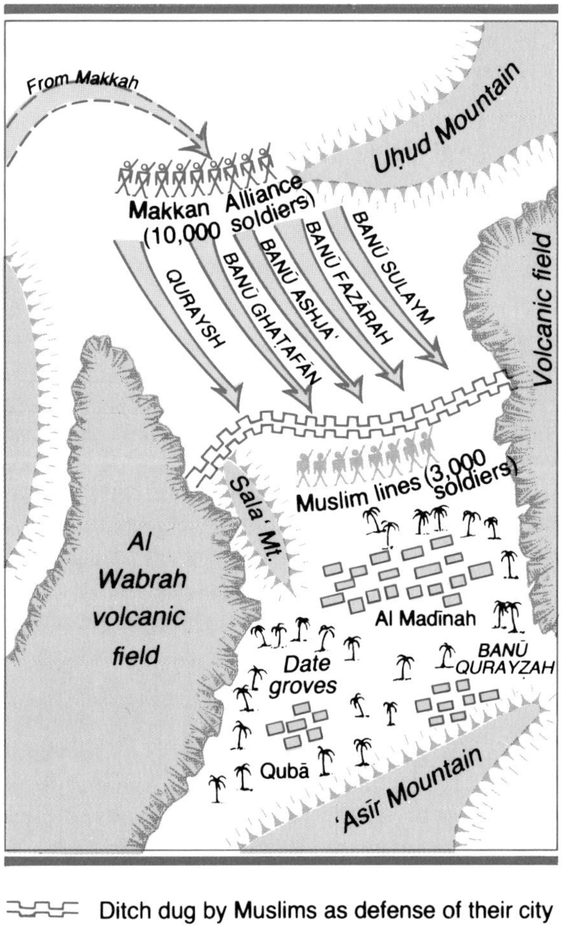

Ditch dug by Muslims as defense of their city

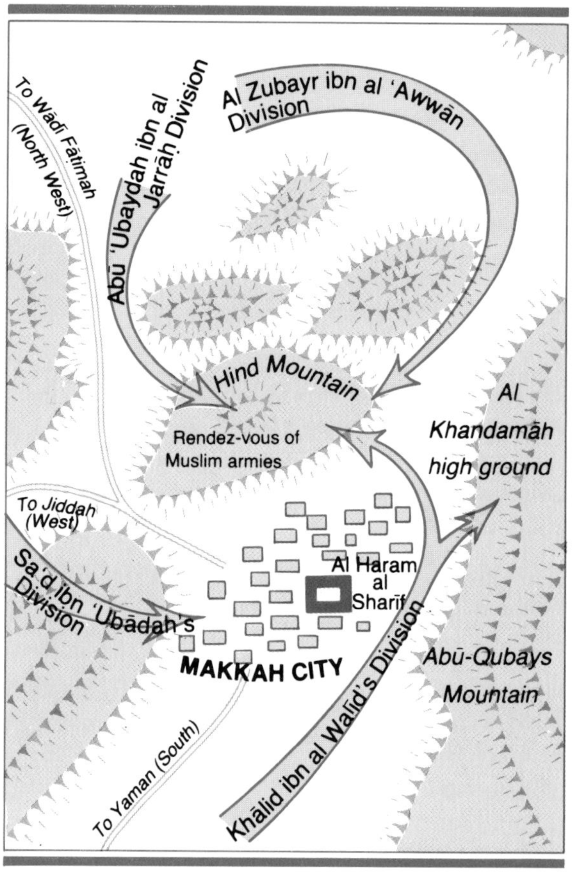

Map 34D. Al Futūḥāt of the Prophet II: Makkah

NOTES

1. The "Covenant of Madīnah" was the constitution of the first Islamic state. It was dictated and enacted by the Prophet in the first week following his emigration from Makkah to Madīnah. For the full text, see Ibn Hishām, *Sīrat Rasūl Allah,* tr. Alfred Guillaume under the title *The Life of Mohammed* (London: Oxford University Press, 1955), pp. 231–234.

2. Quoted in Alistair Duncan, *The Noble Sanctuary* (London: Longman Group, 1972), p. 22. Also in Thomas W. Arnold, *The Preaching of Islam: A History of the Propagation of the Muslim Faith* (Lahore: Sh. M. Ashraf, 1961, first pub. 1896), pp. 56–57.

3. Arnold, *Preaching of Islam,* p. 80.

4. Michael the Elder, *Chronique de Michel le Syrien, Patriarche Jacobite d'Antioche (1166–1199),* ed. J. B. Chabot (Paris, 1899–1901), Vol. II, pp. 412–413. Quoted in Arnold, *Preaching of Islam,* p. 55.

5. Gregorii Barhebraei, *Chronicon Ecclesiasticum,* ed. J. B. Abbeloos and T. J. Lamy (Louvain, 1872–1877), p. 474.

6. *Et ego inveni per antiquas historias et autenticas aput Saracenos, quod ipsi Nestorini amici fuerunt Mochometi et confederate cum eo, et quod ipsi Machometus mandavit suis posteris, quod Nestorinos maxime conservarent. Quod unique hodie diligenter observant ipse Saraceni"* (J. C. M. Laurent, *Peregrinatores Medii Aevi Quatuor* [Leipzig, 1864], p. 128).

7. Quoted by Arnold, *Preaching of Islam,* pp. 71–72.

8. Muḥammad 'Alī bin Ḥāmid ibn Abū Bakr al Kūfī, *Shah Namah: Tarikh-i-Hind wa Sind,* tr. A. M. Elliott, in *The History of India as Told by Its Own Historians* (Allahabad: Kitab Mahal Private, Ltd., n.d.), Vol. I, pp. 184–187.

CHAPTER 10

Al Futūḥāt: The Spreading of Islam

The word *al Futūḥāt* is the plural of *fatḥah* which means "opening." In the figurative sense, it is often used to refer to the victorious campaigns carried out by the Prophet and his followers under the flag of Islam. In this usage, however, the term does not mean conquest, in the literal or material sense. Rather, it refers first to the opening of the heart and mind to the truth of Islam; and second, to a change in the configurations of history that makes it possible for the message of Islam to overcome obstacles and reach the hearts and minds of men. The evidence for this meaning is in the Qur'ān where *Sūrah Al Fatḥ* begins with a verse that is the source of usage in this figurative sense. The passage reads: "We have opened for you [Muḥammad] a manifest opening; that Allah may forgive you your previous sins, complete His blessing, guide you to the straight path, and grant you a great victory" (48:1–3). These and subsequent verses were not revealed after a military victory but upon conclusion of the peace treaty of Ḥudaybiyah with the Makkans. It was a peace that all the companions found humiliating to themselves, to the Prophet, and to Islam; a peace whose acceptance by the Prophet incited them to disobedience and outright rebellion. The Prophet found it agreeable because it was a treaty of peace, and peace was most needed if people were to stop and listen to the call of God. The Qur'ānic revelation confirmed Muḥammad's understanding of the treaty and called it a "manifest opening." The accounts presented in this chapter are regarded by Muslims as *futūḥāt* in this moral sense. That they rested upon, or were associated with, operations of a military nature belongs to their aspect as events in mundane history. Their significance, however, stood beyond those operations precisely because the world —with all its power and sovereignty, its joys and material wealth—was no part of the objective at all. That is why these Muslims were ready to keep political, economic, social, and cultural power where it was. Their only concern was to reach the heart and mind of their enemy—plebeian or king—and convince him of the Islamic truth. If the person was not convinced, all they asked was the freedom to reach and convince others. The thrones of the world and material wealth were nothing in their eyes, which were full of the Islamic vision of the love of God and fulfillment of the divine imperative.

THE CAMPAIGNS OF MUḤAMMAD

Aware that the Banū Hāshim, which had given Muḥammad the protection needed to survive in a society divided by tribal loyalties, had lost their powerful position, Muḥammad concluded a new security pact with the Muslim converts from Madīnah. Despite their own tribal loyalties, these new Muslims covenanted with Muḥammad twice at al ʿAqabah to defend Muḥammad against his enemies as if they and he were a new tribal unit of their own. This pact paved the way for Muḥammad to send his followers to Yathrib (later Madīnah); and he followed in July 622, after foiling the Makkan plan to assassinate him. These developments coincided with the progress of the revelation. Having begun with the call to abandon the multiplicity of gods and idols and give worship to the one God to Whom alone service is due, the Qur'ānic revelation had elaborated the cosmology of a theocentric universe, the eschatology of certain judgment and eternity of reward and punishment, and the anthropology of human reasonableness, innocence, and responsibility, of life-affirmation and positive achievement as the works of salvation and felicity. The revelation was now ready to turn its attention to society and to crystallize its place and function in the divine plan of creation.

Therefore, upon his arrival at Madīnah, Muḥammad gave his attention to the establishment of the first society of Islam. The pacts of ʿAqabah were supplanted by a new agreement, the "Covenant of Madīnah." This covenant boldly affirmed the solidarity of the Muslims as an integral, autonomous community, and repudiated their old tribal loyalties. It invested them with a new identity, Islam. No more would they be known as Banū Hāshim, Quraysh (the Makkans), and as Aws or Khazraj (the Madīnese). The covenant buried that tribalist tradition with all its rights and obligations once and for all; and it established in Madīnah a new sociopolitical, military order based upon the members as Muslims. The non-Muslim members of the tribe were invited to join the new order — they had no choice after the dissolution of the tribalist order by the Muslim majority. The Jews of Madīnah constituted by themselves no tribal entity, but lived as clients of the Aws and Khazraj tribes. The Covenant of Madīnah formed them into an autonomous, integral community of their own; and, as such, made them a constituent member of the new Islamic polity. Henceforth, the revelation was to spell out the laws under which the new order was to operate, and the purposes and patterns of social behavior it was expected to achieve. The Muslims, with the Prophet as their leader and chief of state, were to actualize the revelation and provide the example for all other peoples at all times.

Muḥammad began by setting the house in order. Since the Makkan émigrés *(al Muhājirūn)* were destitute, he suggested that they be adopted by the Madīnese and given a new start in life. This done, the new polity, the Islamic state, was ready to turn its attention to the outside. Two challenges posed themselves. First, now that the Muslims were protected by the new Islamic state, they should call all the Arabs to Islam. Second, Makkah, the persistent enemy, must not be permitted to send its caravans across the territory of Madīnah without reckoning for its past deeds.

In January 623, barely six months after the Hijrah, the Muslims launched their first raid to intercept a Makkan caravan traveling north to Syria. The Muslim force consisted of forty riders under the command of Ḥamzah, the Prophet's uncle. The caravan was under the command of Abū Jahl. They met at al ʿĪs where Majdiy ibn ʿAmr al Juhanī separated them. At the same time, another Muslim force of sixty riders was sent to Rābigh, where a Makkan force of 200 led by Abū Sufyān had come to protect the caravan. The Makkans withdrew before the Muslims' arrival and no engagement took place. Saʿd ibn Abū Waqqās, who shot the first arrow under Islam at Rābigh, was commissioned by the Prophet to probe for the Makkans deeper into the Ḥijāz. He had a force of only twenty riders. Saʿd returned without engaging the enemy. In June 623, another Muslim force set out for al Abwā' with the Prophet himself in command. They reached Waddān, but no Makkans were there to engage them in battle. The Prophet talked to Banū Ḍamrah, the

Illustration 10.1

Pietra dura decorations of columns, the Fort, Lahore, Pakistan, seventeenth century. [Photo by L. al Fārūqī.]

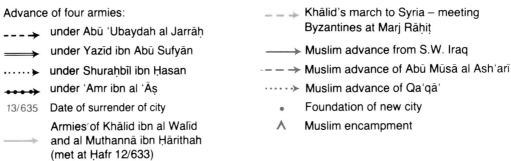

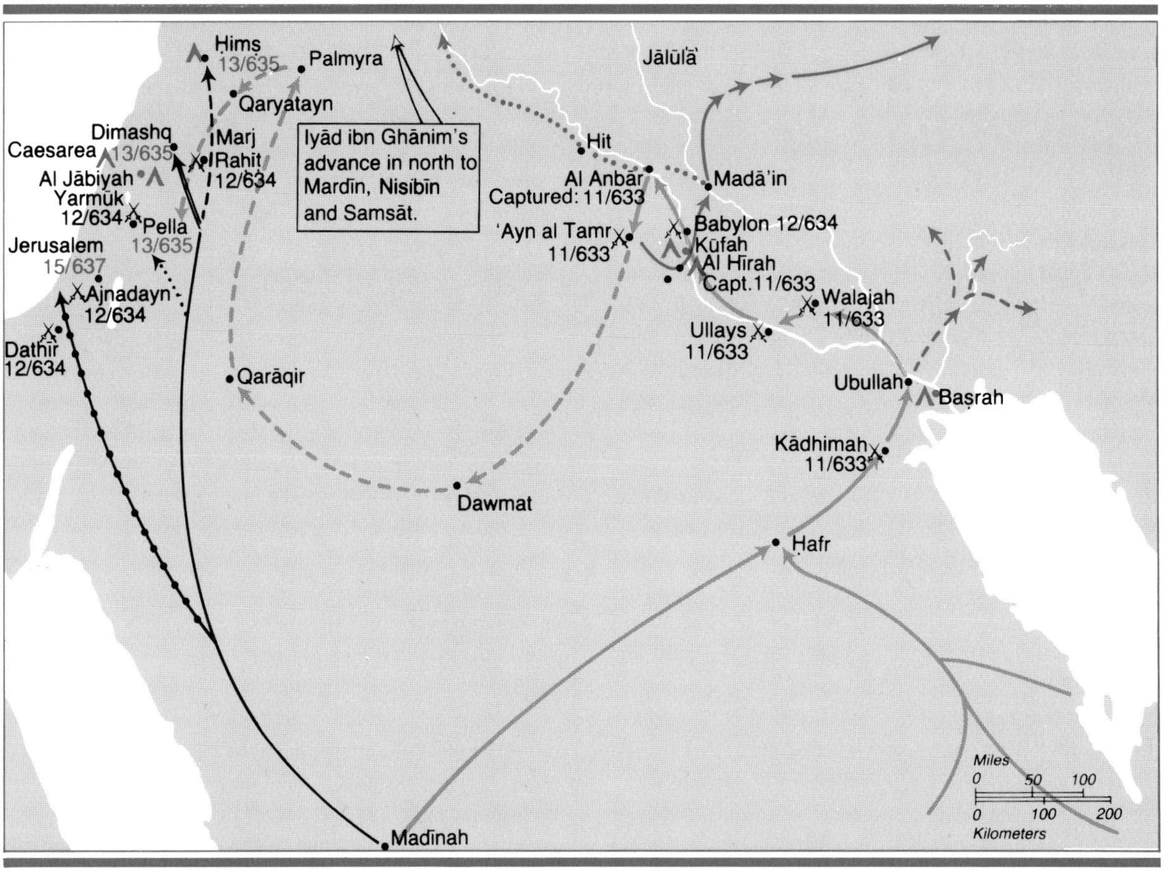

Advance of four armies:

- under Abū 'Ubaydah al Jarrāḥ
- under Yazīd ibn Abū Sufyān
- under Shuraḥbīl ibn Ḥasan
- under 'Amr ibn al 'Āṣ
- 13/635 Date of surrender of city
- Armies of Khālid ibn al Walīd and al Muthannā ibn Ḥārithah (met at Ḥafr 12/633)
- Khālid's march to Syria – meeting Byzantines at Marj Rāḥiṭ
- Muslim advance from S.W. Iraq
- Muslim advance of Abū Mūsā al Ash'arī
- Muslim advance of Qa'qā'
- Foundation of new city
- Muslim encampment

Map 35. Al Futūḥāt: The Fertile Crescent, 11–18/633–640

inhabitants of the locality, and caused them to join the Muslim alliance. In July 623, another expeditionary force marched against a Makkan caravan led by Umayyah ibn Khalaf, without success. In the autumn of the same year (October 623), the Prophet led another force to 'Ushayrah in the district of Yanbu'. The expedition produced no engagement, but it brought Banū Mudlaj to join their neighbors and allies, Banū Ḍamrah, and to participate in the general security pact of Islam. A month later, another expedition set out for Badr in search of Kurz ibn Jābir al Fihrī, who had raided Muslim cattle. Again they failed to catch up with the pursued party.

The same season witnessed a reconnoitering mission near Makkah which was led by 'Abdullah ibn Jaḥsh. It netted the Muslims a donkey caravan loaded with goods and two Makkan captives. Its timing provided the Makkans with the argument that the Muslims had no respect for the holy months of the Arabian tradition. The raiders were hence chastized by the Muslims until a revelation justified fighting injustice even in the holy months (Qur'ān 2:217).

The first serious encounter between Makkah and the Muslims took place in the spring of the following year, 624. Abū Sufyān led the Makkan caravan from Syria. Sensing that the Muslims were following him, he sent Ḍamḍam al Ghifārī to mobilize the Makkans. These were fearful of a stab in the back by their neighbor tribe, the Kinānah. When the chief of Kinānah reassured them, they marched to face Muḥammad and his party of 305 riders. The Muslims, who had set out in search of a caravan guarded by thirty or forty riders, now confronted a force of nearly 2,000. At any rate, the caravan had already escaped. The Prophet gave the Muslims the choice of withdrawing or pressing ahead for a confrontation with Makkah; the decision to press on was unanimous and enthusiastic. The Muslims encamped at Badr, where they awaited arrival of the enemy. The enemy soon arrived, and the battle began. The losses were heavy, but the Muslims triumphed as the Makkan force withdrew in defeat.

The Battle of Badr had significant consequences. It consolidated the position of Islam in the minds and hearts of the people, and of the fledgling Islamic state. The non-Muslims in and around Madīnah had now become convinced that Islam was a force to reckon with. They called meetings at which old divisive poetry was recited to split the unity which Islam had forged between the Aws and Khazraj tribes. People repudiating unity between Muslims and Jews, Makkans and Madīnese, were given a hearing. Ka'b ibn al Ashraf, a Jewish leader, bemoaned the Makkan defeat loudly and traveled to Makkah to incite the Makkans to renew the fight—a betrayal of the Covenant of Madīnah which he had signed. This treachery resulted in his execution. Muslim–Jewish relations deteriorated rapidly. An attack on the honor of a Muslim woman in a jeweler's shop was revenged by a Muslim killing a Jew of the Qaynuqā' tribe and that tribe's disposal of the life of the attacker. The incident then aroused the Muslims to attack the Banū Qaynuqā' and blockade their quarter in Madīnah. The Prophet's companions urged him to banish, rather than kill, the captives; and the Qaynuqā' tribesmen left Madīnah for Adhri'āt in northwest Arabia. The remaining Jews of madīnah and vicinity were invited to remain, and were reassured by the Prophet that the Covenant of Madīnah would be honored; that they would enjoy Islam's protection, peace, and security if they would observe their obligation and not betray their covenant. Ostensibly they gave the Prophet a new pledge to abide by their agreement; but their fear of the Muslims and their plotting to overthrow the Islamic state continued.

Unable to contain his grief after the Makkan defeat, Abū Sufyān and a few of his men attacked al 'Urayḍ, a suburb of Madīnah, burned its orchards, killed two of its inhabitants, and withdrew to Makkah. The Prophet gave them pursuit but never caught up with them. In order to hasten their escape, they unloaded the grain and flour their camels carried. The Muslims were therefore able to pick up their trail. Despite the fact that there was no engagement, the Muslims referred to their expedition as the campaign of al Sawīq (literally, flour). Following what seemed to be a dislodgment of Makkan hegemony over the area, several tribes prepared for war, out of fear for their future. The Ghaṭafān and Sulaym tribes mobilized and set out in the direction of Madīnah. The Muslims prepared to meet them at Qarqarat al Kudr, only to find that their enemies had retreated and dispersed before the Muslims' arrival. The Tha'labah and Muḥārib tribes gathered at Dhū Amarr. A Muslim army led by the Prophet sought them there without avail.

A year after Badr (623 C.E.), Makkah was ready to march again, having put in the field an army of 200 horsemen, 3,000 camel riders, and about 1,000 men in heavy armor. The Makkans advanced to the vicinity of Madīnah. The Prophet thought that for better defense, the Muslims had better remain in their city and reinforce it. His companions, however, prevailed upon him to let them go out to meet the Makkans in the open fields. They prepared to engage the enemy at the foot of Mount Uḥud, just outside of Madīnah. The Muslims took the higher ground and sent one formation to the low ground to meet the advancing Makkans. The armored infantry of Makkah was defeated in the melée while the cavalry was kept at bay by Muslim bowmen on the higher ground. When these abandoned their positions to retrieve booty from the fallen enemy, Makkan cavalry led by Khālid ibn al Walīd quickly outflanked the battlefield, seized the higher ground and fell upon the Muslims from behind. Muslim ranks fell into disarray, and the Prophet would have been killed were it not for a handful of fiercely loyal companions who shielded him with a ring of steel. Nonetheless he received at least one blow which knocked out one of his molars. The Makkans were too apprehensive to push their luck further, and they retreated without achieving a conclusive victory. The Muslims rallied and pursued the Makkans for three days and three nights. But the Makkan retreat was swift. No engagement ensued; and the Muslims returned with a more viable claim to victory than their adversaries (Qur'ān 8:42).

In the following months several other campaigns were carried out. The Banū Asad marched against the Prophet. A force mobilized to meet them included three notable companions (Abū 'Ubaydah ibn al Jarrāḥ, Sa'd ibn Abū Waqqās, and Usayd ibn Ḥuḍayr) under the leadership of Abū Salamah ibn 'Abd al Asad. The campaign netted the Muslims a large amount of cattle which they herded into Madīnah as spoils of war and evidence of victory. Sent by the Prophet to reconnoiter the Banū Liḥyān's preparations for war, 'Abdullah ibn Unays single-handedly killed the leader of the tribe and threw the enemy force into confusion. In 625, six of the Prophet's companions who were well-versed in the Qur'ān were lured to al Rajī' by the Hudhayl tribe, which had requested men to teach them Islam. These delegates were betrayed and attacked by their hosts. Four died and two were sold into slavery to Makkah, where they were crucified. At Bi'r Ma'ūnah, in the same year, another party of Muslims was led by al Mundhir ibn 'Amr and protected by Abū Barā', one of the chieftains of the Banū 'Āmir. The first Muslim to set foot in Banū 'Āmir's territory was put to death immediately by the other chieftains who ordered their men to mete out the same fate to the other Muslims. Abū Barā''s prestige was put to the test and the tribesmen refused to kill the Muslims. Banū 'Āmir's allies responded with enthusiasm and killed all the Muslims, who had come not to fight but to teach. Later, Abū Barā' avenged himself against his fellow-chieftain who was mainly responsible for the Muslim tragedy.

In the summer of 626, Banū Muḥārib and Banū Tha'labah, both of Ghaṭafān, took to the field against the Muslims taking with them their women and property, thus forcing the Prophet to march with his companions to meet them. The encounter took place at Dhāt al Riqā'. The non-Muslims gave up their ground and ran away at the sight of the adversary, leaving their families and properties to fall into the hands of Muslims.

In the fall of the same year, the Prophet led a Muslim force of 1,000 riders to Dawmat al Jandal (today's al Jawf) in the north-central desert, halfway between the northern tip of the Ḥijāz and Iraq. The Prophet's purpose was above all to establish Islam and its state as the dominant religion and power in the Peninsula, to deter the Arab tribes from adopting the cause of Makkah. Every occasion was for him one to spread the word of God and invite men to join the ranks of those who make His service supreme.

The Muslims had reason to believe that, after all these military activities, they could feel secure, settle down for some rest, and give attention to their internal affairs. The Prophet, on the other, had to keep his eyes and ears open for any move by the Arab tribes directed against the Muslims. The Quraysh, the masses of Hudhayl and Ghaṭafān tribes, and the Jews, who had never stopped their plotting, all sat in wait for an opportunity to pounce on Madīnah. Indeed, Ḥuyayy ibn Akhṭab and Sallām ibn Abū Ḥuqayq traveled to Makkah to plead with the pagans that their religion was better than Islam, that dominion should belong to Makkah because of its idolatrous tradition, and that the whole of Arabia was anxious and ready to march with them to stamp Islam out once and for all. Having convinced the Makkans to try once more in the coming spring, they proceeded to the tribes and convinced Banū Kinānah, Ghaṭafān, Banū Sulaym, and Banū Asad to join. A force of over 10,000 riders concentrated itself on Madīnah as their target. The Muslims decided this time to stay put in Madīnah and to fortify their houses, block the alleys and streets, and wait for the unbelievers to attack. Salmān, a companion of the Prophet, suggested that a ditch ought to be dug wide and deep enough to stop any cavalry assault.

Illustration 10.2

Window screen, the Fort, Lahore, Pakistan. [Photo by L. al Fārūqī.]

The Prophet approved and a corvée was mobilized and put on the job at once, with the Prophet himself digging shoulder to shoulder with his people.

The allied tribes now surrounded Madīnah but could not advance. The Banū Qurayẓah were afraid of the consequences in case the Muslims won, and did not move. But when the Muslims asked them in turn to provide men for sentry duty, which was being kept around the clock, and invoked the Covenant of Madīnah, the Banū Qurayẓah turned the request down and repudiated the agreement they had committed themselves to honor. Fortunately, a sandstorm blew over the area. It was so strong that it dispersed the enemy's animals and destroyed their tents. The Makkans were the first to pack up what was left of their belongings and returned to Makkah. The rest of the tribes dispersed as well.

The danger of war lifted, the Muslims found themselves victorious, not by their own might but by what they believed to be the help of God. Turning to the Qurayẓah traitors in their midst, the Muslims laid siege to their quarters and offered them the choice of an arbitrator. Banū Qurayẓah chose the Aws chief, Sa'd ibn Mu'ādh, as arbitrator. His judgment was that they should get the full punishment they deserved for their treason.

Under the Treaty of Ḥudaybiyah (March 628), peace reigned between the Muslims and Makkah for ten years. The treaty was broken less than two years after its conclusion when Makkah refused to compensate the Muslims for an attack launched against them

Illustration 10.3

Salīmiyyah Mosque, Edirne, Turkey, Sinān's great masterpiece, built during the reign of Sulṭān Salīm II, 1569–1576 C.E. The dome rests on eight heavily decorated columns. [Courtesy Embassy of Turkey, Washington, D.C.]

by one of Makkah's allies. The missionary efforts of the Prophet and his companions had won the Arabs to Islam by the thousands. Thus, it was possible for the Prophet to mobilize an overwhelming force, march with it to Makkah, and overtake the city without a fight.

Another consequence of Ḥudaybiyah was that it called upon the Muslims to give attention to their northern frontier. The Khaybar Jews, among whom the exiles from Madīnah lived, had been architects of the grand tribal rally that had been defeated at the campaign of the Ditch, a year before. They now convinced the numerous Ghaṭafān clans, indeed the whole northwest of Arabia, to join the Makkans. In pursuit of his call to Islam, the Prophet sent messengers to present the new religion to Heraclius, emperor of Byzantium; to the archbishop of Alexandria; to al Ḥārith, chief of Ghassān and king of al Ḥīrah; to the king of Yaman; and to the Negus of Abyssinia. He sent identical messages to Chosroes, to the kings of Yamāmah and Baḥrayn, and to the chieftains of the Arab Christian and Zoroastrian tribes in the regions separating Byzantium and Persia in northern Arabia. These initiatives set the whole Fertile Crescent buzzing with reports and predictions of what the Muslims might do next. The Jews of the North (Khaybar, Fadak, Taymā', and Wādī al Qurā) lost no time in initiating a plot to counter the Islamic moves and, in anticipation of war, to strengthen their fortresses at Waṭīḥ, al Sulālim, Na'īm, Qāmūs, al Shaqq, Zubayr, and Naṭāṭ. Sallām ibn Mishkam, first leader of the Jews, had made his headquarters at Naṭāṭ; but when the Muslims advanced, he came out to meet them and was killed by men of the Khazraj, of whom he was once a client. Al Ḥārith ibn Zaynab, another Jewish leader, perished the same way before the fortress of Na'īm; and so did Ṣa'b ibn Mu'ādh at the fortress of Qamūs, and the Jewish poet Marḥab, who recited Arabic battle poetry before engaging the Muslims.

News of their anti-Islamic activities prompted the Prophet to launch a military campaign against the Jews of the North of Arabia. The campaign ended with an agreement that the Jews would remain in their places but would have to share half of their crops with the Islamic state. The older leaders, Sallām ibn Abū al Ḥuqayq and Yāsir ibn Razzām, were seized and executed for their treason. The local leaders fell in battle, and the Jewish presence in Arabia was reduced to insignificance. No more would the Jews enjoy any political power in Arabia. This fact caused the Muslims, especially the Anṣār of Madīnah, to mellow their attitude toward the Jews and to reestablish friendly relations. The Prophet himself inclined in this direction. He saw fit to attend a memorial to 'Abdullah ibn Ubayy and present his personal condolences to his son, and to warn his deputy in charge of the Jews not to interfere in their religious life or molest them in any way. Likewise, the Prophet extended the protection of the Islamic state to the Jews of Banū Ghāziyah and Banū 'Arīḍ who had not been involved in the hostilities.

These events reached the ears of the authorities in Byzantium, who then ordered a partial mobilization for war. At the same time, the Prophet sent five of his companions to Banū Sulaym in the North, the present Islam to them. That tribe had been patronized and protected by Byzantium. Four of the delegates were summarily executed, only one escaping to tell the story. Of the party of fifteen missionaries the Prophet sent to Dhāt al Ṭalḥ for the same purpose, all were killed. He also sent a messenger to the Byzantine governor of Buṣrā, who met the same fate. The Prophet returned with his men to Madīnah and began to organize a larger army. Under the leadership of Zayd ibn Ḥārithah and including such notable companions as Khālid ibn al Walīd, 'Abdullah ibn Rawāḥah, and Ja'far ibn Abū Ṭālib, the army began its march in late 629.

Illustration 10.4

Grand Mosque of Dimashq, early eighth century. [Courtesy Embassy of Syria, Washington, D.C.]

The Byzantines had indeed assembled a tremendous army made up of Greek soldiers as well as Arab recruits from the buffer territories of Lakhm, Judham, al Qayn, Bahrā', Baliyy, and so on. Three leaders of the Muslim force fell in battle, and Khālid ibn al Walīd assumed leadership. He resorted to a ruse to make the Byzantines believe that large Muslim reinforcements had arrived, whereupon the Byzantines decided to withdraw. The Muslims returned to Madīnah. The Prophet organized another army under 'Amr ibn al 'Āṣ and sent it northward, partly to avenge the dead of the Mu'tah campaign, and partly to deter Byzantium from further anti-Islam adventures. The Muslim force camped at Dhāt al Salāsil in Judham territory (which gave the name to the campaign). The Muslims achieved another victory and returned with loads of war booty (March 630).

The Islamization of Makkah that followed the Prophet's magnanimous pardon of his previous enemies did not please the tribe of Hāwāzin. They mobilized and marched upon hearing of the news of Makkah's surrender. The Muslims, their ranks reinforced by new Makkan converts, marched to meet them. Despite their numbers, the Muslims nearly lost the battle when they were trapped in an ambush in a narrow strait (Wādī Ḥunayn) between two mountain ranges on which the Hāwāzin tribesmen perched themselves. The Prophet stood firm, recouped the Muslim forces around him, and concluded the engagement with a resounding victory (Qur'ān 9:25–26).

Six or seven months later (September 630), the Prophet heard news of an impending military move by Byzantium against Arab tribes that had shown friendship to Islam and the Muslims; a large army was on the ready at Tabūk. He ordered the preparation of an expedition to the north and led it out of Madīnah in person. The force was called *jaysh al 'usrah* ("the army of hardship") because it was hard to raise and equip, and because it undertook an even harder task at the most difficult time of the year for man and animal, namely, at mid-summer. The Muslim army encamped at Tabūk, and the Prophet invited Bishop Yūḥannā ibn Ru'bah, governor of Aylah at the northeast extremity of the Red Sea, to visit him. The governor came and was handed a covenant by the Prophet. It contained a promise that the governor's Christian subjects, their guests, their ships and their properties, their religion, their culture, and their customs were all to be honored and protected by Islam. The Prophet gave the governor a Yamanī mantle and showed every courtesy. The news of the Muslim army's arrival at Ḥijr caused the Byzantines to withdraw to the hinterland. The first purpose of the expedition being obviated by their withdrawal, and the entry of Aylah into the Islamic covenant of peace secured, the Prophet decided to return home.

The following year (631) was one of peace for the whole of Arabia. It was called the Year of Deputations. One tribe after another sent its representatives to Madīnah to convey to the Prophet of God news of the entry of their people into the faith of Islam and their joining the Islamic state. Tribes that fell under the protection of Byzantium or Persia, or under other stronger tribes, no longer felt the need to remain in their tutelage. The Islamic state and the peace of Islam were one; and every Muslim felt the new safety enveloping him. Everybody was keen to join the new order, if not for its ideological aegis, then surely for the social, economic, and political well-being it promised.

Especially worthy of mention is the delegation of the Thaqīf tribe, people of the city of Ṭā'if, perched on the highest peaks of the Ḥijāz, southeast of Makkah. The Prophet had laid siege to Ṭā'if following the campaign of Ḥunayn, without subduing it. Most of its people, the tribesmen of Thaqīf, continued to worship the idol of the goddess al Lāt. Now they had to reckon with the Islamic state, whose power extended over almost the whole of the Peninsula. They decided to send a delegation of three of their chiefs to negotiate their terms with Muḥammad. These pleaded for saving the idol of al Lāt, and for continuation of her worship along with Allah for three years or less. The Prophet rejected all their terms and ordered the immediate destruction of the idol. He did accept a last appeal from the delegation to save themselves from the opprobrium of their people if they were to break up the idol with their own hands. He assigned Abū Sufyān ibn Ḥarb and al Mughīrah ibn Shu'bah to that task.

Seventy-four tribes sent delegations to the Prophet to assure him of their faith and obedience. The whole of Arabia had entered Islam, united itself under the aegis of the first Islamic state, and stood poised to bring the blessings of faith and peace to a troubled world outside Arabia.

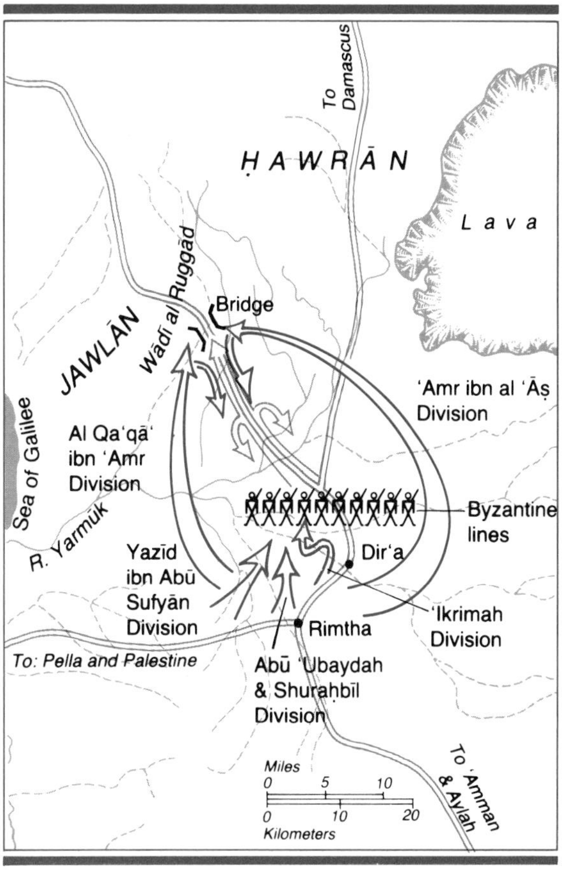

Map 36. The Battle of Yarmuk, 14/636

THE MUSLIMS' HISTORICAL CAMPAIGNS

In the Arabian Peninsula: The Apostasy Wars

The news of the Prophet's death in 632 spread quickly among his companions and followers. Abū Bakr had taken leave of him at the dawn prayer to spend the day in a nearby oasis, and had believed that the Prophet's sickness was passing. On hearing the news, he returned immediately to Madīnah. The Muslims had already gathered in the guest hall of Banū Sā'idah, shocked by the death of their Prophet and leader and wondering how to proceed. Being mostly Madīnese, the gathered people were inclined to elect their tribal chief, Sa'd ibn 'Ubādah (of the Khazraj tribe), as successor to the Prophet. Then Abū Bakr, 'Umar ibn al Khaṭṭāb, and Abu 'Ubaydah ibn al Jarrāḥ arrived. Their presence altered the course of history. Had tribal feeling crystallized around Sa'd, it would have resurrected the pre-Islamic particularism which Islam had condemned so severely. As the conversation progressed, the Madīnese suggested that two successors be elected at once, a Madīnese for the Anṣār (literally, helpers) and a Qurayshī for the Makkans. The three Makkans objected that this would split the *ummah,* which God had declared to be one (Qur'ān 21:92). 'Umar then boldly nominated Abū Bakr to succeed the Prophet on the grounds that He was the Prophet's oldest and most trusted companion whom the Prophet had delegated to lead the Muslims in prayer in almost every one of his absences from Madīnah. 'Umar asked Abū Bakr to stretch forth his hand, placed his hand on it as was the custom, and gave his oath of fealty to him. Abū 'Ubaydah followed and gave his oath of fealty to Abū Bakr. Overwhelmed by a feeling of Islamic solidarity and unity, the Anṣār present followed the example of the two Makkans, one after another. The trustworthiness of Abū Bakr, his closeness to the Prophet, and the tremendous esteem in which he and 'Umar were universally held, were obviously irresistible.

Abū Bakr accepted their oaths, thanked them, and returned to the Prophet's house to arrange for the funeral and burial. It was Abū Bakr's decision that the Prophet should be buried at the very spot where he died, in 'Ā'ishah's chamber, which adjoined the mosque and was later incorporated into it. On the following day, Abū Bakr took his place at the pulpit in the mosque and delivered his inaugural speech. He said: "Oh Men! I am assigned the duty of leading you when I am not the best of you. Therefore, if I do well, help me; if I do wrong, redress me. . . . The weak shall be mighty in my eye until I have restored to them their right; the mighty shall be weak until I have restored from them the rights of the weak. . . . Obey me as long as I obey God and His Prophet. But if I disobey them, then no obedience is incumbent upon you."[1] The whole assembly rose and, filing past Abū Bakr, rendered to him their oath of fealty. This was the public *bay'ah* (election) of the *khalīfah* (successor) which was to become the pattern of caliphal election in Islam. The decision of the previous day was the "first *bay'ah*" acting as a nomination of the caliph by *ahl al ḥall wal 'aqd* (the decision-makers of the community).

The first political decision Abū Bakr took was to send the Muslim army back to al Shām (Syria). The Prophet had sent the army to Syria in response to Byzantine mobilization. Its leader was Zayd ibn Ḥārithah who received reinforcement of a cavalry force under Khālid ibn al Walīd. The first force lost the battle at Mu'tah, in Jordan; and its three leaders fell one after the other. The Byzantines were equally exhausted and withdrew, not caring to press their victory on the battlefield. Khālid's arrival on the scene was late and resulted in no engagement. The Prophet then led the same army back north, covenanted peace with Aylah in south Jordan, and thus secured the northwest flank. Khālid was sent to Dawmat where he secured the central north flank after subduing Ukaydir, its chief, and bringing him captive to Madīnah. When news of further troop deployment by Byzantium reached the Prophet shortly before he died, he sent the same army under the leadership of Usāmah, the teenage son of the fallen general who had led the force on the earlier expedition. The army returned to Madīnah without engaging the enemy. In fact, it had marched for two days when the news of the Prophet's death reached it and its commander decided to return home. The new chief-of-state, Caliph Abū Bakr, decided to reinforce the army and send it back north to fulfill the mission entrusted to it by the Prophet. Abū Bakr rejected arguments that Usāmah was too young

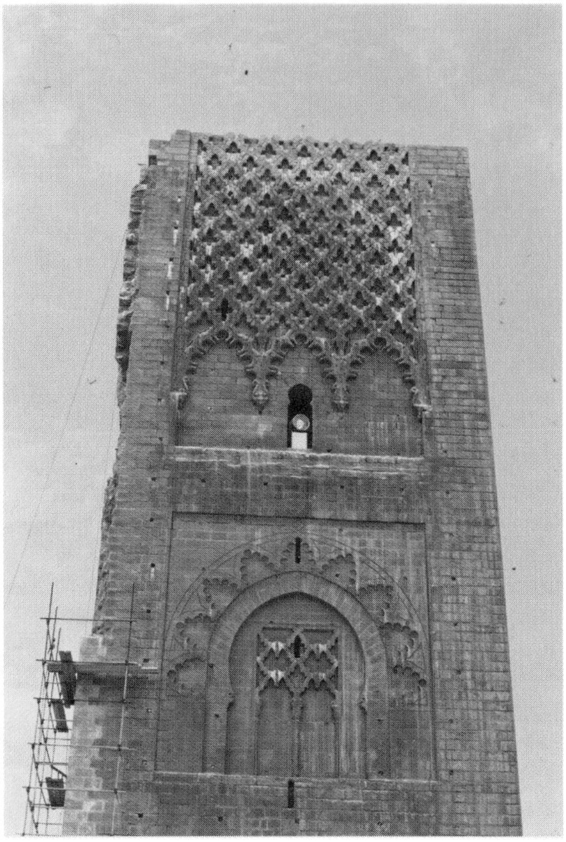

Illustration 10.5

The Tower of Ḥasan, Rabāṭ, Morocco, 1196 C.E. [Photo by L. al Fārūqī.]

to lead, and that the time called for Muslim unity, for presence of the army closer to home. He argued that no action started by the Prophet could be altered or interrupted; and he probably thought that the presence of the army in the northern regions constituted a better defense against the only real dangers confronting the Islamic state, namely, Byzantium and Persia.

The news of the Prophet's death produced another crisis of far greater proportion. A number of tribes defaulted on paying the *zakāt* to its collectors, arguing that it had been a tribute to Muḥammad; since he died, the tribute was no longer due. Obviously, this was either a misunderstanding of the institution of *zakāt* or a cloak behind which the old tribalism and separatism reasserted themselves. In either case, it drew Abū Bakr's fury and caused him to prepare for war. When his opponents objected that no war was legitimate against those who witnessed to the unity of God and the Prophethood of Muḥammad, Abū Bakr replied that *zakāt* was of the essence of Islam and could not be denied without denying the religion itself. The 'Abs and Dhubyān tribes, who held an unorthodox view of the *zakāt,* camped at Dhul Qaṣṣa, thirty miles east of Madīnah. Abū Bakr quickly ordered every available man to take up arms, surprising the two tribes and vanquishing their main force in battle while putting the rest to flight. The fleeing remnant joined Ṭulayḥah, chief of Banū Asad, who camped farther east and who had declared himself a prophet. Abū Bakr put Khālid ibn al Walīd at the head of his force, and he returned to Madīnah after commanding Khālid to win back to Islam every recalcitrant in Arabia. The Ṭay tribesmen from the area joined with Khālid. The Muslims scored a great victory at Buzākha and dispersed their enemies. Ṭulayḥah himself escaped to Syria but later repented and was forgiven. His defeat reverberated throughout Arabia. The Banū Asad came out *en masse* to give fealty, and their surrender prompted the Banū Sulaym and Hawāzin tribe to follow suit and pay the *zakāt.* Abū Bakr readily pardoned all upon their return to the fold of Islam.

Farther east, Banū Tamīm and Banū Ḥanīfah lent their support to Musaylimah who also claimed to be a prophet. Khālid marched against them. One branch of Banū Tamīm, the Banū Yarbu', resisted under their leader Mālik bin Nuwayrah. Khālid gave them battle until they returned to Islam. Their leader, Mālik, fell captive and was killed. The Banū Ḥanīfah gave battle to the Muslims and killed a number of the Prophet's older companions. Zayd ibn al Khaṭṭāb, Thābit ibn Qays, al Barā', and Abū Dujānah, among numerous others, laid down their lives. The Banū Ḥanīfah were cornered in a garden at Yamāmah, and its members were killed to the last man. The encounter came to be known as the Battle of Yamāmah. Musaylimah was killed by Waḥshī, now a fervent Muslim and the same Makkan who, before his conversion to Islam, had fought for Makkah against the Muslims and had, in fact, killed the Prophet's uncle Ḥamzah at Uḥud. His javelin had killed "the best and the worst of men," as he bemoaned during the rest of his days. The number of companions killed was so large—some historians claim it was half the force of 5,000—that the Muslims feared for the loss of the Qur'ān itself, which the fallen heroes had kept in their memories.

The Battle of Yamāmah was the major engagement of the *Riddah* (Apostasy) Wars which raged after the death of the Prophet. But it was not the last one. 'Ikrimah, son of Abū Jahl, and two tribal chieftains, Hudhayfah and Arfajah, joined forces to subdue 'Umān and succeeded in adding that large province to the Islamic state. Later, in their march, they added the province of Mahrah. A number of tribes living in the South and Southwest joined the successful cause. The Christian Najrān renewed the covenant they had made with the Prophet. Their neighbors, however,

Illustration 10.6

Ferhadija Mosque in Banja Luka, Yugoslavia. [Photo by S. Balić.]

the Zubayd and Kindah tribes, rebelled under the leadership of ʻAmr ibn Maʻdī Karib and al Ashʻath ibn Qays, respectively. The news reached Abū Bakr, who immediately dispatched al Muhājir ibn Abū Umayyah with a small force to Yaman and ordered ʻIkrimah and his men to proceed thither in all haste. The two joined forces at Maʼrib, the site of the great dam, and moved westward against the rebellious tribes in Yaman. They laid siege to al Ashʻath in Nujayr; al Ashʻath was seized and sent captive to Madīnah where Abū Bakr forgave him and gave him his sister in marriage. The other chief, ʻAmr ibn Maʻdī Karib, surrendered to al Muhājir and repented. This brought the *Riddah* Wars to an end, and Arabia stood once more united, this time into an indissoluble religious as well as administrative unit. Henceforth, the tribal wars of Arabia stopped, having been condemned religiously and politically by Islam, as religion and as state.

On the Persian Front

Al Muthannā ibn Ḥārithah, chief of Banū Shaybān, a clan of Banū Bakr, having distinguished himself as one of the heroes of the battle of Dhū Qār against the

Map 37. Al Futūḥāt in Asia, 28-40/650-661

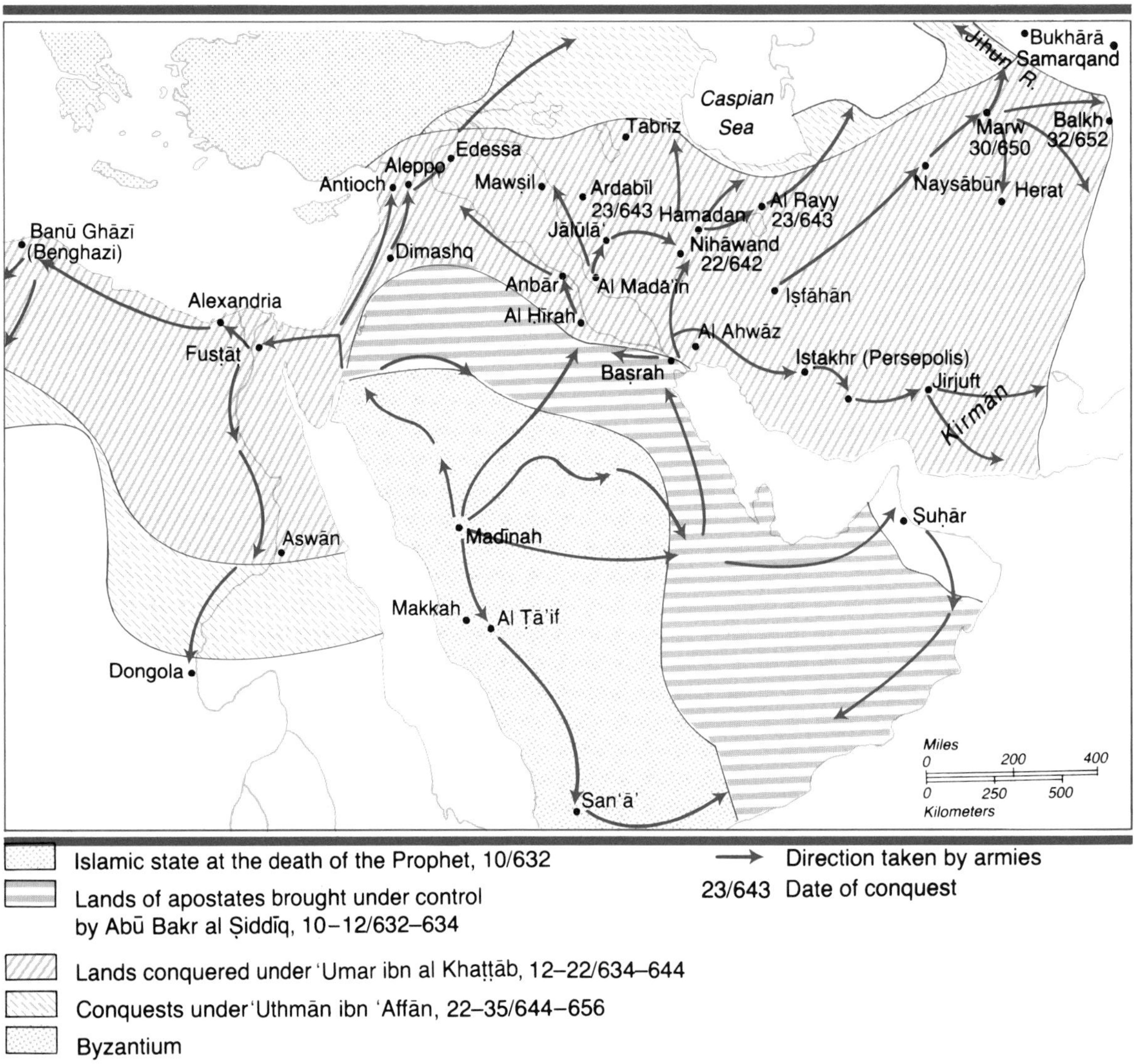

Persians, had risen in esteem among Banū Bakr. He was largely responsible for the reconciliation of the various clans of Banū Bakr when Khālid ibn al Walīd was sweeping through their territories. These clans, living in the shadow of the Persian Empire, had formed the satellite state of Lakhm, with its capital at al Ḥīrah. They were adversely affected when Persia revoked the semi-autonomous status they had enjoyed and subjected them to direct colonialist rule by Persia. Full of resentment against their imperial master, these tribesmen welcomed the opportunity al Muthannā's leadership provided to rally together under the Islamic state and face the Persian Empire as a new unity with a separate identity, a new purpose, and a new mission. The reconciliation among the clans of Banū Bakr was a direct result of their allegiance to Islam and the Islamic state. Naturally, the tribesmen saw in all this, in addition to the promise of Islam, an occasion to restore their dignity and assert their will against Persia. However, Caliph Abū Bakr did not trust them, precisely on account of their previous apostasy, and forbade Khālid ibn al Walīd to recruit any of them into the Islamic army. Only the few clans who never apostasized were permitted to join the Muslim army, and these included al Muthannā and his men. Al Muthannā's men joined with Khālid's forces at al Ḥafīr in the Northeast (about 100 miles southeast of modern Kuwait). Together with the forces of the Ṭay tribe who lived farther east in Jabal Shammar and rallied under Khālid's command, they made a formidable army.

With these reinforcements, the Muslim army moved to Kādhimah (present-day Kuwait) and defeated the Persians in 11/633. Pushing north toward the Euphrates estuary, the Muslims took Ubullah, the port city on Shaṭṭ al 'Arab, and brought its largely Christian Arab inhabitants under the protection of the Islamic state. Skirting the Euphrates, the Muslim army proceeded north. But before engaging the Persians at Ullays, it crossed the Euphrates to give battle to the Persians at Walajah (near modern Shaṭrah). Both cities were seized and entered under the same covenant of peace. The stage was set for an advance on al Ḥīrah. At the approach of the Muslims, the Persian commander fled to Madā'in (Ctesiphon) and left the city to its inhabitants, who were quick to welcome the Muslims, to agree to pay the *jizyah,* and to enjoy peace under the Islamic flag. Khālid then advanced toward al Anbār, on the northwestern edge of Sawād, the alluvial plain between the Tigris and Euphrates rivers. The capital of the region had been inhabited for centuries by the Arab tribes of Taghlib, Namīr, and Iyād. Following its conquest, Khālid moved in the direction of 'Ayn al Tamr, which he took after a brief battle with its desert garrison. It was at this site that he received the caliph's order to march with his men to Syria.

Illustration 10.7

Minaret of Ūlūgh Bak Madrasah, Samarqand, U.S.S.R., 1420 C.E. [Photo by L. al Fārūqī.]

On the Byzantine Front

The ruler of Dawmat al Jandal, a Christian, had embraced Islam in the course of the Prophet's last campaign to Tabūk and Aylah. At Muḥammad's death, he lapsed and renounced his allegiance. Together with the news of further military moves by Byzantium, this was the prime reason behind Abū Bakr's decision to send the Islamic army back to the north. Three columns were ordered to march under

Illustration 10.8

Garden, Xian Mosque, People's Republic of China. [Courtesy Robert H. Garvin.]

the command of 'Amr ibn al 'Āṣ, Shuraḥbīl ibn Ḥasanah, and Yazīd ibn Abū Sufyān in the direction of Palestine, Jordan, and Syria, respectively. Yazīd engaged and defeated the Byzantines at Wādī 'Arabah, southwest of the Dead Sea, killing the Greek commander Sergius. The rest of the Byzantine army retreated to Ghazzah; but on their way, 'Amr at Dathīn engaged them in another battle which nearly annihilated them. That battle took place south of Bi'r al Sab' or Beersheba. The two columns then turned back to the desert route in the east and marched parallel to the column of 'Amr toward Dir'ah and Buṣrā. These cities commanded the narrow passage to Damascus, between the mountain chain of al Shaykh (Hermon) and Ḥawrān. There, their march was stopped by the bulk of the Byzantine army, reinforced by fresh recruits under command of Heraclius's brother Theodorus.

It took Khālid only eighteen days to cross the desert from east to west and surprise the enemy by emerging behind his lines. The march took place in March 634, and was regarded as the greatest military feat in the history of the area. Going southwest from Ḥīrah, Khālid arrived at Dawmat and brought it back to the fold of Islam. He then proceeded through Wādī Sirḥān to Qurāqir. There he prepared to cross one of the driest deserts in the world, outflanking the Byzantines and the other Muslim columns. Five days later, his army arrived at Suwā or Sab' Ābār, where they found some water below the surface near an acacia tree. Replenishing themselves and their animals, the men drove to Tadmur (Palmyra), seized it, and moved southwest to meet the Byzantines from behind their lines. On the way, Qaryatayn and Marj Rāḥiṭ were the scenes of bloody encounters with the Byzantines, from which the Muslims emerged victorious. The march continued southward, and the cities of Buṣrā and al Fiḥl (Greek Pella) surrendered. The retreating Byzantine force was attacked again at Marj al Suffār; and in the fall of 23/635 the Islamic army entered Dimashq (Damascus). Ba'albak, Ḥimṣ, Ḥamāh, and the other towns of Syria met the same fate.

Undaunted by this defeat, Heraclius thought of another strategy to counter the Muslim army. Just as the Muslims were invincible when fighting under desert conditions, Heraclius, with his heavily armored army, could move safely within Palestine. The route south was shorter, and he could reach Wādī 'Arabah before any Muslims could. There he hoped to cut off the Muslim supply lines to Madīnah, and the road of their possible retreat.

Having raised another army, Heraclius marched south via Caesarea on the coast, aiming at the elimination of the guardian force the Muslims had left at Bi'r al Sab' (Beersheba) in south Palestine. Khālid learned of this march, and hastened to meet him. The Muslim commander took the longer and more arduous road, passing through Karak and 'Ayn Ḥaṣb at the head of Wādī 'Arabah. He joined with the other Muslim forces under 'Amr ibn al 'Āṣ and arrived at Bi'r al Sab' long before Heraclius. Without delay, he marched northward to meet Heraclius halfway between Caesarea and Bi'r al Sab'. The two armies fought at Ajnādayn, between the Mediterranean coast and Bayt Jibrīn, and another Muslim victory was scored.

After all these encounters, only the Byzantine force at Dir'ah remained. Khālid returned to that front forthwith, rallied all the Muslim forces, and confronted the enemy. With their defeat at Ajnādayn and their loss of the territories to the north, the Byzantine position at Dir'ah became untenable. Heraclius ordered a retreat to a small plain on the banks of the Yarmūk River which was surrounded with high cliffs, a position he regarded as defensible. A sandstorm — a common phenomenon at that time of the year — blinded the Byzantines and their horses and gave advantage to the Muslim troops who were used to desert conditions. Khālid rallied all the Muslim forces he could muster. The Muslim army attacked and routed the enemy in one day. Byzantium was driven from the Fertile Crescent once and for all.

A few days after news of the Muslim victory had reached him, Abū Bakr died. He had been caliph for a little more than two years. 'Umar ibn al Khaṭṭāb succeeded him as ***khalīfah.*** The new ruler appointed Abū 'Ubaydah ibn al Jarrāḥ governor of Syria, and proceeded in person to inspect the new territories, the garrisons, and their generals, and to define their status, rights, and obligations. He arrived at al Jābiyah, one of the camps of the Muslim army north of the Yarmūk battlefield. Abandoned by the Byzantines, Jerusalem, which was until then under siege, offered to open its gates. Ready to make peace with the Muslims, the bishop of Jerusalem requested 'Umar to take charge of the city in person. 'Umar acquiesced to his request, journeyed to Jerusalem, and took over its keys in the fall of 25/637. It was on this occasion that he executed the covenant mentioned earlier (see Chapter 9).

Return to the Persian Front

On the eastern front, Khālid's departure to Syria with half or better of the Muslim armed forces had left that area unprotected. Al Muthannā had come to Madīnah to ask for help, and Abū Bakr, on his deathbed, had ordered recruitment of a new army to be sent to the eastern front against Persia. His successor, 'Umar, fulfilled the order by calling for fresh recruits. Abū 'Ubaydah ibn Mas'ūd of Ṭā'if, being the first to volunteer, was appointed a general. Al Muthannā returned to the eastern front, ahead of his colleague, to recruit more men from the tribes en route, who had been forbidden by Abū Bakr to join because of their earlier apostasy. 'Umar had issued a new edict permitting their recruitment. The new Persian emperor Yazdigird appointed Rustum to the command of the front against the Muslims. Rustum began by sending delegates to the cities that had made covenants of peace with the Muslims, urging them to renege on their agreements.

Soon the two armies confronted each other near al Ḥīrah. There they fought the Battle of the Bridge, which resulted in the loss of several thousand Muslim lives. The rest of the army withdrew under the command of al Muthannā following the fall of Abū 'Ubaydah in battle. Reinforcements soon arrived from Madīnah. A month later, the two armies stood again face to face at al Buwayb (between Kūfah and Najaf) on the west side of the Euphrates. The Persians were now in the same position as the Arabs had been in the previous battle. The bridge was seized by al Muthannā. Denied access and a passage for retreat, the Persians were decimated. The Muslims reoccupied al Anbār and 'Ayn al Tamr, advanced to and took al Ḥīrah, and penetrated deeply into the plain between the two rivers. In a short time they stood before the gates of al Madā'in.

Al Muthannā did not recover from the wounds he suffered at Buwayb and died a month after his victory. Caliph 'Umar appointed a close companion of the Prophet to assume command of the eastern front. This was Sa'd ibn Abū Waqqās, a veteran of the Battle of Badr, a man about forty years old. He was sent forth with an army of 5,000 men, with the promise that more would come later. The lifting of the ban on the tribes who were guilty of apostasy increased the army's manpower resources. Even Ṭalḥah, the false prophet, converted to Islam and arrived at the scene heading 3,000 men from his tribe of Banū Asad. The Muslim forces, agile and quick of foot because they wore no armor, were perfectly at home in the deserts adjoining the Euphrates. In addition, they had been resting during the last two to three months of winter and spring, the wounded among them recovering and their horses and camels feeding on the spring pastures at the oases of Sharaf, Sulmān, Thalabiyyah, and Ghuday some eighty miles from the Euphrates, well beyond the reach of Persian cavalry. The Persians, on the other hand, were laden with armor. For a "tank regiment," they brought to battle a force of thirty-three elephants to lead the attack. Yazdigird, the Persian king, had impetuously ordered Rustum, his commanding general, to waste no time and to attack the Muslim force. Against his better judgment, Rustum gave the order, and the army crossed to Qādisiyyah, forty-five miles from the Euphrates, in the desert. The engagement took place there in the spring of 15/637. The Muslims won, and pursued their enemies to and beyond Madā'in (the twin cities of Seleukia and Ctesiphon, on either bank of the Tigris). Although the caliph had instructed Sa'd to stop there and not to advance deeper into Persia, the Persians' preparation of another army to recapture Iraq forced the caliph to rescind his order and to permit the Muslim armies to advance. An engagement at Jālūlā', in the north, followed by another at Mawṣil piled further defeat on the Persians. The last effective engagement took place at Nihāwand (ancient Ecbatana), and the remnant of Yazdigird's army was completely destroyed. Khūzistan, Elam, Pars, and Persepolis followed in 28/649–29/650. Khurāsan, Makrān, and Balūchistān were also subdued; Yazdigird was assassinated by one of his own generals at Marw in 29/651.

Nothing is more indicative of the spirit that moved the Muslims in these battles than the conversation, as reported by al Balādhurī, between Rustum, the commanding general of the Persians, and al Mughīrah ibn Shu'bah, the Muslim delegate. Without ceremony, al Mughīrah entered the carpeted hall riding on his horse and seeking to sit at the side of Rustum. When he was prevented from doing so, he remained standing by his horse. Rustum suggested that, since the Arab tribesmen were moved to this war by their poverty and lack of food, the Persians would gladly give them wealth and food in plenty, provided they promised to return home. Al Mughīrah answered: "We are here neither for food nor wealth, but to reorient your men from adoration of men to adoration of the one God. Our men are as eager to lay down their lives for this cause as your men are eager to preserve theirs. I call you to Islam. If you accept, you are one of us. If you do not, I offer you the peace of Islam and ask you to pay the *jizyah.* If you do not accept this, then war."[2]

Futūḥāt in Egypt and North Africa

Caliph 'Umar ibn al Khaṭṭāb prepared an army, gave its command to 'Amr ibn al 'Āṣ, and commissioned him to take Islam to Egypt. The march began in the winter of 18/639. After taking al Farāmah (Pelusium), the army moved to Babilyūn (Babylon), where the Byzantine army was routed. Cyrus, the archbishop of Alexandria and representative of the emperor who came to defend Babylon, returned to Alexandria after the fall of Babylon with the following description of the Muslims:

> We have witnessed a people to each and every one of whom death is preferable to life, and humility to prominence, and to none of whom this world has the least attraction. They sit not except on the ground, and eat naught but on their knees. Their leader *[amīr]* is like unto one of them: the low cannot be distinguished from the high, nor the master from the slave. And when the time of prayer comes none of them absents himself, all wash their extremities and humbly observe their prayer.[3]

To save Alexandria from a similar defeat, Cyrus agreed to pay tribute to 'Amr ibn al 'Āṣ, to keep the peace, and to maintain a Muslim garrison in the city. 'Amr reopened the ancient canal linking the Nile to the Red Sea. Popular dissatisfaction with the Byzantine government of Alexandria caused the Greek emperor to send a naval force under Manuel, an Armenian general, to subdue the city. The Greeks succeeded in taking the city and they slaughtered the Muslim garrison. However, the Muslim army returned, engaged and defeated the Byzantine army at Nikiu (25/646), and then proceeded to evict the Byzantines from Alexandria. This time, they established a permanent Muslim administration. This campaign was the occasion of 'Abdul Laṭīf al Baghdādī's false charge — repeated blindly by a number of Muslim and Orientalist historians after him — that Caliph 'Umar had ordered the destruction of Alexandria's famous Ptolemaic library. In fact, that library was first burned in 48 B.C.E. by Julius Caesar and then destroyed completely in 389 C.E. by an edict of Emperor Theodosius.

In 28/649 the Muslims built a fleet. From Alexandria and other ports of the eastern Mediterranean shore, they launched an attack upon Cyprus and wrenched it from Byzantium. In 34/655 the maritime battle of Dhū al Sawārī, in which 500 Greek ships were destroyed, put an end to Greek hegemony in the eastern Mediterranean. The fall of Alexandria opened the way for the Muslims to march westward toward Libya. Barqah (Pentapolis) was conquered by 'Amr ibn al 'Āṣ with little or no resistance. The people of Tripoli offered tribute the same year; and 'Amr's successor, 'Abdullah ibn Sa'd ibn Abū Sarḥ, moved westward into Ifrīqyah (Africa) and forced Carthage to pay tribute as well. In 31/652 'Abdullah pushed southward and entered into a covenant of peace with the Nubians.

Futūḥāt in the East and West

Subsequent developments were to take place in the east under the leadership of al Ḥajjāj ibn Yūsuf al Thaqafī (95/714) and in the west under Mūsā ibn Nuṣayr (97/716). Having distinguished himself in the service of the Umawī dynasty in the Ḥijāz, al Ḥajjāj was appointed governor of the eastern provinces in 74/694 in order to pacify them. He did so with an arm of steel, and mobilized the region to undertake further expansion of Islam in Asia. Al Ḥajjāj picked three outstanding generals and sent them in different directions with three well-equipped armies. 'Abdul Raḥman ibn al Ash'ath went to Kabul and subdued its king, Zunbil, in 80/700. Qutaybah ibn Muslim conquered Balkh in 85/705 and Bukhārā, Samarqand, and Khawārizm (modern Khiva) in the short period of two years (91/710 – 93/712). Farghānah was conquered a year later, and Kashgar (in Chinese Turkestan) in 96/715. In 133/751, al Shāsh (Tashkand) was added to the Islamic Empire. The third general, Muḥammad bin Qāsim, pacified Mukran and entered Sind in 92/711 to rescue a shipload of Muslim merchants whose boat was shipwrecked at Daybul at the mouth of the Sind River (near present Karachi). He advanced to Nīrūn (modern Hyderabad) and established an Islamic administration as far as Multan.

On the western front, Mūsā ibn Nuṣayr appointed the general 'Uqbah ibn Nāfi' to lead an army into Ifrīqyah. In 50/670, 'Uqbah founded the city of Qayrawān (modern-day Tunis), near Carthage, for use as a Muslim base. 'Uqbah overran the whole of North Africa and reached the shore of the Atlantic Ocean. Muslims remember his statement: "If I knew of a land beyond this sea, I would cross it on horseback and conquer the land for Islam!" But he did not live to conquer the Maghrib (Northwest Africa) for Islam, for he died in 63/683. Mūsā ibn Nuṣayr took charge of Ifrīqyah by a direct commission from the caliph in Damascus. He extended the frontier to the Atlantic and brought the hinterland under direct control. The Berber inhabitants were exposed to Islam and began to join its ranks *en masse.* In 92/711, Ṭāriq ibn Ziyād, a Berber convert to Islam, landed near the rock at the southern end of the Iberian Peninsula. The rock has since that time been known as "Jabal Ṭāriq" (the mountain of Ṭāriq)—or in its later corrupted form, Gibraltar. King Roderick with an army of 25,000 met the Muslim force at nearby al Buḥayrah, was dealt a crushing defeat, and lost his life. With this victory, any possibility of a centralized resistance was removed, and only local garrisons in the cities remained. These fell one after the other either after a brief siege or through direct assault. Ṭāriq marched toward Toledo, the capital, taking Ecija on the way. Another column took Archidona, a third seized Elvira, and a fourth led by Mughīth al Rūmī took Cordova. The following year, Mūsā ibn Nuṣayr himself arrived on the scene with 10,000 fresh troops. His objectives were the fortified towns which Ṭāriq had avoided on his march. Madīnah, Sidonia and Carmona, Seville, and Merida were all in Muslim hands before the end of the year. Muslim troops continued their advance into Aragon, Leon, the Asturias, and Galicia. The conquest of Saragosa sealed the fate of Spain, which the Muslims renamed al Andalus.

The Muslims did not stop in Spain but continued their march into France until they reached Poitiers/Tours, where the battle with Charles Martel stopped their northward thrust in 113/732. Their move into France, however, was not stopped. Avignon fell into their hands two years later (115/734); Lyons, Narbonne, and most of the area of the Provence down to the Mediterranean, two years thereafter. In 176/792 two armies were raised by order of Hishām I (172/788–180/796) to carry the flag of Islam deeper into the northwest and northeast corners of the Iberian Peninsula. The latter column met with greater success than the former. Having subdued Catalonia, it marched straight into southeast France and joined ranks with the remnants of the Muslim forces that had retreated from Poitiers/Tours. They reoccupied Narbonne and Carcassonne. Arles and Nīmes followed. Having occupied the islands of Majorca, the Muslims of Spain and those of Africa carried out a number of raids against Corsica and Sardinia in 191/806–193/808. They were aided by their co-religionists from Nice. But it was not until the end of the century that the Muslims made a serious advance into southeast France. The Muslims chose another area east of Marseilles, around the bay of Grimaud, and established a base for their operations at Fraxinet (today's Garde-Frainet) because of its strategic location: accessible by sea, guarded by a dense forest of ash *(fraxini),* and providing passage to the Alps. The Muslims seized the passages of the Alpine chains, one after another, and spread their dominion over the countryside. By 288/900, the regions of Provence, Dauphiné, Piedmont, Monferrat, and La Maurienne, and up the Rhine including St. Gall, Great St. Bernard, St. Rémy, and south to the Mediterranean slightly east of Nice, all were under Muslim control. The Muslims were forced out of these areas by the invading Huns from the north and Hungarians from the east. The Castle of Fraxinet was captured by the French in 365/975, and Muslim presence in France and Switzerland was over by the end of the fourth/tenth century. The Muslims seized the island of Sicily in 217/832, and they ruled it until the arrival of the Normans in 450/1058. However, the Normans allied themselves to the Muslims, who kept the actual government of their realm in their own hands for another two centuries, admittedly with a gradual waning of their influence in government, trade and industry, agriculture, local government, and the arts. The last remnant of Muslims was evacuated from Sicily by order of the German King Frederick.

Futūḥāt in the North

In the sixth–seventh/thirteenth–fourteenth centuries, the Muslim presence in Spain was losing ground; it came to a virtual end with the fall of Granada in 901/1492. Simultaneously, an 'Uthmānlī (Ottoman) state was founded in Anatolia in 699/1299 by 'Uthmān I, as a successor to the waning Byzantine power in that region. It consisted of Turkomen who had emigrated from Central Asia and arrived in the Muslim world in repeated waves as "Tatars" or Mongols under Genghis Khan and Tamerlane. The Turks who founded the 'Uthmānlī state were the converted grandchildren of the invaders. Since they arrived in waves, their numbers and density in central and eastern Turkey had been increasing for years, and the lands that had come into their possession had been expanding steadily. They formed a number of petty states under diverse dynasties. In Turkey proper (Asia Minor), the Artukis dominated Diyārbakr from 495/1102–811/1408, when the Karkoyunlu displaced them and united the lands of both tribes. The Danishmandis ruled in central and eastern Anatolia from 464/1071–563/1178, when the Saljūqs of Rūm, who first founded their power in Anatolia, expanded their domain and joined that of the Danishmandis to theirs. The Saljūks of Rūm dominated Anatolia until they were displaced by the Mongol invasion under the leadership of the children of Genghis Khan. The rest of Anatolia which did not fall in the foregoing conquests was under the dominion of the Qaramanis from 654/1256 to 888/1483, when the 'Uthmānlī state added it to its own territory.

The 'Uthmānlī state had a vigorous leadership which expanded its dominion constantly for three centuries. Bursa was conquered and made the capital in 715/1315; Iznik (Nicaea) was conquered in 730/1329. An alliance was made between the 'Uthmānlī state and Kantakuzinos, the Byzantine regent (whose daughter Theodora was married to the 'Uthmānlī Sulṭān Orhān Ghāzī). This alliance, made against the rebellious Greek constituents of the Byzantine regent, occasioned the arrival of Turkish troops in Europe. The 'Uthmānlī state moved its seat to Adrianople in 768/1366. Finally, Constantinople itself was conquered in 857/1453, and its name changed to Istanbul (a corruption of Islampul, or city of Islam). The conquered city became the capital of a vigorously growing Muslim Empire. Before the conquest, the Muslims had brought most of Bulgaria, Serbia, and Rumania under 'Uthmānlī rule. In the following century, the Muslims continued their advance into the Balkans, central Europe, and south Russia. By the middle of the sixteenth century, the Black Sea had become a Muslim lake, Muslim soldiers laid siege to Vienna, the island of Rhodes was conquered, and Islam was firmly rooted in the central Balkans.

Futūḥāt in South Asia

In South Asia, as the 'Abbāsī state power declined, autonomous Muslim states emerged in Baluchistan, Afghanistan, Multan, and Sind. Sebuktigin had established himself in Ghazna in 367/977 and consolidated the provinces surrounding it when the neighboring Indian state took to war against the Muslims. The Indians were defeated by Sebuktigin's son Maḥmūd. Nonetheless, the states of Ujjayn, Gwalior, Kalinjar, Kannawj, Delhi, and Ajmer confederated in order to make war against the Muslims; but they were defeated in the battle of Peshawar in 399/1008. Anxious to secure the kingdom for the future, Maḥmūd then took the initiative to expand his dominion into these Indian states. His army gave battle to the Hindus and marched victorious into Nagarkot, Thanesar, Kannawj, Kalinjar, and Somnath. Ghaznawī power passed into the hands of the Ghūrīs a century later; and under Ghiyāth al Dīn Muḥammad, Muslim power spread over most of North India. Ucch and Gujarat were conquered in 573/1178, Lahore in 582/1186, Bhatinda in 587/1191, Delhi and Ajmer in 588/1192, Kannawj and Banaras in 590/1194. Under Shihāb al Dīn, the successor, a small expeditionary force led by Bakhtiyār Khaljī conquered Bihar and Bengal. The Khaljī Sultanate based itself in Delhi (659/1196–720/1320) and secured Devagiri (Dawlatabad) which had been added to Muslim dominion two years earlier; it had conquered Warangel, Madura, and Dvarasamudra in 710/1310. Ghiyāth al Dīn Ṭughluq, a provincial ruler, had come to Delhi to punish the Hindu slave who usurped power from the last Khaljī Sultan. He established a new sultanate which carried his name. The Ṭughluq sultanate (723/1323–801/1398) did not add new territory to the domain of Islam, and it carried only one expedition into Hindu lands—Kangra, in the Himalaya Mountains. The Sayyid and Lodi dynasties ruled the Muslim provinces of India after the Ṭughluq Sultanate; but it did not add to Muslim territories.

The Moghul Dynasty was founded by Bābūr following his victory over the Lodis at Panipat in 932/1516. A period of consolidation followed. In 971/1564, Gondwana was annexed, and Akbar marched against Chitor and conquered it. The only territorially significant addition after that was Jinji in 1110/1698, and Koukan in 1112/1700. This followed the successful termination of the Maratha's resistance to Muslim Moghul power. From then on, Muslim political and military power went on the decline, but not the power to convince of the truth of Islam.

THE CONTINUING *FUTŪḤĀT*

Nothing is further from the truth than the claim that Islam was spread by the sword, or that Hollywood image of the Muslim rider or foot soldier charging the enemy with a view to kill, subdue, or convert. Unfortunately, in their resentment, the enemies of Islam did much to implant that image in the minds of generations of people. The Muslim faithful who is supposed to lay down his life in such process of forceful conversion of others knows only too well that God has commanded him never to coerce anyone into the faith (Qur'ān 2:256). He knows that God even warned his Prophet against any such practice (10:99, 88:22) and that the responsibility of the faithful cannot go beyond presentation of the claims of faith. Finally, he knows only too well that it is God Who guides, not he; and that God guides some and permits others to go astray (13:27). If he did not, how could he be the "faithful" in question? And if he did, how could he indulge in such condemnable crimes? Logic, however, is not the forte of the falsifiers of history.

Thomas Arnold, whom we mentioned earlier in this book and to whose excellent work, *The Preach-*

ing of Islam, we referred, cited fact after fact to bury the malicious claim once and for all.[4] In describing the events of the *futūḥāt,* Arnold wrote:

> These stupendous conquests which laid the foundations of the Arab Empire, were certainly not the outcome of a holy war, waged for the propagation of Islam, but they were followed by such vast defection from the Christian faith that this result has often been supposed to have been their aim. Thus the sword came to be looked upon by Christian historians as the instrument of Muslim propaganda, and in the light of the success attributed to it the evidences of the genuine missionary activity of Islam were obscured.[5]

Islam is a missionary religion. Its lack of an organized church made the task of teaching Islam to non-Muslims incumbent upon every member of the community. Every Muslim regarded himself as a caller of men to God, and took personal pride in the effort and its results. He was careful to match profession and speech with action. And he tried to the full extent of his capacities to be a model unto men, just as his Prophet was a model to him. The sincerity of his commitment, the candidness of his judgments, and the consistency and perseverance of his deeds exerted a disarming effect upon his neighbors.

The second reason for this massive entry into the faith of Islam was the order of justice which the Muslims brought with them. The swiftness, discipline, and efficacy of the Islamic judiciary system and its ready availability to rich and poor, aristocrat or plebeian, free of charge, made a deep impression on people accustomed to the colonialist exploitation by the Greeks and the Romans for many centuries. For generations, workers and farmers, landlords and merchants, were never certain of the state's whimsical power dominating purse and property. The provinces were never treated on a par with Byzantium, the Greek mainland. The Semite populations were subject peoples whose exploitation the state pursued with unabated diligence. The Muslims entered the land as genuine liberators from this colonialist yoke. In any case presented to them, they came down harshly and swiftly on the side of justice. For the first time since even their grandparents could remember, the people felt that their properties and incomes were secure, that justice was not a mere ideal or claim, that it was theirs for the asking.

The third reason explaining the early mass conversions to Islam must be sought in the new authority associated with religion. The papacy, the supreme church authority, and its representatives were perceived as temporal rulers in search of power and property which they obtained and kept with impunity. Their history of heretication, excommunication, persecution, and forceful conversion was long and well remembered. In the second half of the twelfth century, five centuries after the advent of Islam to these lands, Michael the Elder, Jacobite Patriarch of Antioch, wrote:

Illustration 10.9

The Fort, Lahore, Pakistan, seventeenth century. [Photo by L. al Fārūqī.]

> This is why the God of vengeance, who alone is all-powerful, and changes the empire of mortals as He will, giving it to whomsoever he will, and uplifting the humble—beholding the wickedness of the Romans who, throughout their dominions, cruelly plundered our churches and our monasteries and condemned us without pity—brought from the region of the south the sons of Ishmael, to deliver us through them from the hands of the Romans. And, if in truth, we have suffered some loss, because the Catholic churches, that had been taken away from us and given to the Chalcedonians, remained in their possession; for when the cities submitted to the Arabs, they assigned to each denomination the churches which they found it to be in possession of (and at that time the great churches of Emessa and that of Harran had been taken away from us); nevertheless it was no slight advantage for us to be delivered from the cruelty of the Romans, their wickedness, their wrath and cruel zeal against us, and to find ourselves at peace.[6]

The Muslims neither persecuted nor coerced the people to believe. Despite the utmost respect for religion and the crucial place it occupied in their lives, the *sharī'ah* stood guard against any infringement by them of the Qur'ānic prescriptions for protecting "the People of the Book" and for respecting the religious convictions of their neighbors.

The fourth reason for the mass conversion of Christians and Jews to Islam had to do with the nature of the mentality of the provincial subjects of the Byzantine Empire. In Western Asia, these people were mainly of Semitic (Near Eastern or Arab) stock; and their minds had been formed by the same visions that produced the Mesopotamian civilization. Indeed, they were the descendants of the Akkadians, Amurru, and Arameans. Many spoke Syriac, Aramaic, Hebrew, or Arabic in addition to the Greek language which had been forced upon them by the Greeks since Alexander. When the Seleucis, Alexander's successors, enforced their program of Hellenization in religion, language, and culture, many peoples rebelled. Some reacted silently by pushing stylization of their sacral objects to new heights in defense of their transcendentalist view of the godhead against Greek naturalism, as their archeological remains prove. Others reacted with armed struggle like the Maccabean Jews, or the Christians under Justinian who rebelled in 532 C.E. against Byzantine ecclesiasticism which looked upon the emperor and his court as Divine Majesty, privileged with the right to oppress, and paid for it with 35,000 lives massacred by the emperor's army. The war cry was: "we will become Jews . . . or return to Grecian paganism" rather than submit to such tyranny.[7]

There is a fifth reason that helps to explain the sudden conversion of the masses to Islam in the century of the *futūḥāt*. That is the unenviable situation to which the religion of Christ had sunk. It is common to most histories of the Church to describe what they call "Eastern Christianity" in condemning terms. Dean Milman wrote:

> Sect opposed sect, clergy wrangling with clergy upon the most abstruse and metaphysical points of doctrine. The Orthodox, the Nestorians, the Eutychians, the Jacobites [and, we may add, the so-called Catholics who were fighting all of these at once] persecuting each other with inexhausted animosity. . . . It had not been wonderful if thousands had not, in their weariness and perplexity, sought refuge from these interminable and implacable controversies in the simple, intelligible truth of the Divine Unity, though purchased by the acknowledgement of the prophetic mission of Mohammed.[8]

The contrast between Christianity and Islam was dazzling to the eyes of the Christian Near Easterner, who pined after an ideology that would accord with his innermost consciousness so long alienated from itself, first by Hellenistic paganism, then by Hellenistic Christianity. The same was true of the Jews. It should be recalled that the Christians had prohibited the Jews from entering or living in Jerusalem. This order had been a tradition since the destruction of Jerusalem by the Romans in 70 C.E. The Christian bishop of Jerusalem made its observance a condition of his surrender of the city to 'Umar ibn al Khaṭṭāb, and the Muslims had to honor it because Jerusalem was then a completely Christian city. It was under the Umawīs that this ban on the Jews was gradually lifted. Not until the vast majority of its residents had converted to Islam did adherence to the ban become pointless. Jews were first permitted to visit Jerusalem, and later to reside within its walls, after its inhabitants had converted to Islam. It is therefore thanks to Islam, to its tolerance, and to its universalism that the Jews succeeded in reestablishing their presence in the holy city.[9]

Illustration 10.10

Entrance to Shīsh Maḥal ("Mirror Palace") inside Lahore Fort, built by Mughal Emperor Shāh Jahān. [Photo by L. al Fārūqī.]

The Fertile Crescent

The lands situated in the belly of the Fertile Crescent and the desert surrounding it on three sides were inhabited by Arab tribes who spoke Arabic and whose culture was as Arab as that of Makkah. Politically they had fallen under the influence of the two giants, Byzantium and Persia, for whom they acted as proxies, and by whom they were proselytized. Most of the Banū Ghassān in the West converted to Christianity, and some of the tribesmen of Bakr, Taghlib, Lakhm, and Tanūkh, who inhabited the eastern regions, converted to Christianity and others to Zoroastrianism.

When Islam appeared, in 13/635, common cultural bonds with the Arabs of the Peninsula combined with the five reasons mentioned above to persuade most of the Arabs of the Fertile Crescent to convert to Islam. The Zoroastrians converted first, partly because they had recently lost their semi-autonomous status as buffer state and had become a direct colony of Persia, and partly because the injustice of the Persian order and the inner corruption of Zoroastrian society were even greater than those of Byzantium. The spread of Islam in Syria and Persia was just as fast, once the imperial power of Byzantium and Persia was broken. Some Christians in Syria have preserved their faith to the present day, enjoying not only the tolerance of Islam but also the friendship of the caliphs and their governments. The annals of Muslim history are replete with records of Christians in high offices in Muslim governments. From the days of Mu'āwiyah, the first Umawī caliph (41-61/661-680), whose treasurer was the father of John of Damascus, to the later 'Abbāsī caliphs and Buwayhī sultans, the secretaries of state, of war and defense, and of the treasury were often Christians.[10]

The Crusades whose numerous campaigns may be read on Map 48, left thousands of European and other crusaders in the territories they occupied. The treatment these unfortunates received at the hands of their own commanders, or at the hands of the Greek escorts, the Venetian shipowners, and the Byzantine hosts, contrasted shockingly with that of the Muslims when they passed under their dominion. Odo of Deuil,

Map 38. Al Futūḥāt in Asia, 41-133/661-750

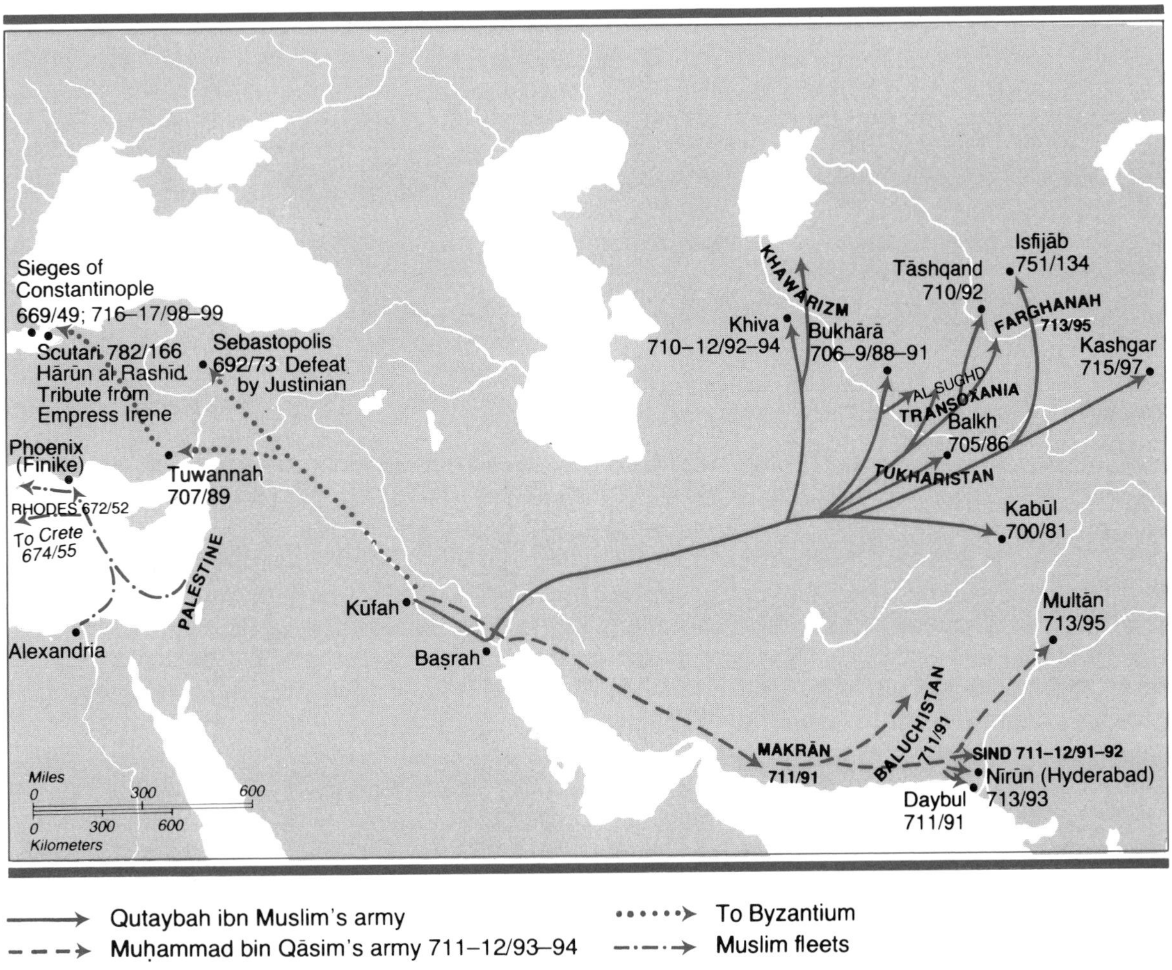

a monk of St. Denis and chaplain to Louis VII, accompanied his patron on the Second Crusade and gave a moving account of the conversion to Islam of a large number of crusaders. Following a fierce attack by the Muslims in Phrygia (543/1148), the wealthy and influential crusaders satisfied the exorbitant demands of Greeks and Venetians and took to the sea, leaving behind thousands of poor, wounded, or exhausted crusaders. Their misery moved the Muslims to pity and compassion. They tended to the sick and wounded and fed the hungry, and this kindness and liberality caused the crusaders to abandon the crusade as well as their faith and join their enemies both in rank and in faith. "Avoiding their co-religionists who had been so cruel to them," wrote Odo of Deuil, "they went in safety among the infidels who had compassion upon them, and, as we heard, more than three thousand joined themselves to the Turks when they retired. Oh, kindness more cruel than all treachery! They gave them bread but robbed them of their faith, though it is certain that contented with the services they performed, they compelled no one among them to renounce his religion."[11] The manifest superiority of the Muslims — in social, cultural, ethical, and religious matters — was equally effective in converting many of the crusading commanders as well. Robert of St. Albans, an English Templar, gave up Christianity and joined Islam out of love and admiration for its ethic and refinement. He married a granddaughter of Ṣalāḥuddīn.[12] Benedict of Peterborough reported that on the eve of the great battle of Ḥiṭṭīn, six of the knights of Guy, king of Jerusalem, "possessed with a devilish spirit, deserted the King and escaped into the camp of Saladin, where of their own accord they became Saracens."[13]

North Africa and Spain

The same influences that affected the Christian presence in the Near East were present in North Africa, perhaps to an even greater degree. Persecution of dissenting churches was carried out more systematically and with greater ferocity in Africa than in the West Asian territories. Justinian is said to have ordered the massacre of 200,000 Copts in Alexandria, and his predecessors had subjected the Jacobites (as Copts were identified) to indignities that have never been forgotten. Muslim victory over the Byzantines achieved by 'Amr ibn al 'Āṣ and his successors who carried the banner of Islam to Tunis brought the Christian population under an Islamic dominion characterized by the same terms 'Umar ibn al Khaṭṭāb had granted to the Christians of Jerusalem. Instead of persecution and interference in their internal church affairs, the Muslims granted them total autonomy in all matters pertaining to religion. Instead of bitterness and rancor, the Christians found respect for their religious views and justice in their relations with the Muslims. In the first years of the *futūḥāt* in North Africa, the revenue from the *jizyah* (the poll tax levied by the Islamic government on adult male and capable non-Muslims in return for the protection and security which the *Pax Islamica* provided) amounted to 12 million *dirhams* from Egypt alone. During the caliphate of Mu'āwiyah, ten years later or less, the amount fell to 5 million; and in the caliphate of 'Umar ibn 'Abdul 'Azīz (62/682) the amount dwindled to nothing, causing the governor to seek authority to raise new taxes to cover the expenses of his administration.

Add to these factors the influx of Arab tribes from the Peninsula and their settlement in North Africa. Blinded by their religion to any discrimination based on race, color, ethnicity, or language, permitted by Islamic law to marry non-Muslims, and encouraged by their vision to practice miscegenation and unite with humanity, these Arab immigrants mixed with the natives with great enthusiasm. The natives, for their part, were anxious to mix with them because of the additional prestige such alliances provided. Arab tribes poured into North Africa and spread nearly everywhere, especially southward along the Nile and westward along the Mediterranean coastline. By the fourth century A.H. their penetration had reached Soba, twelve miles north of modern Khartoum, where they built a large mosque. In the fourteenth century the Juhaynah tribe in particular had already converted most of the Dongola, according to the world traveler Ibn Baṭṭūṭah. Establishment of the Funj Empire in the ninth century A.H. signified the near extinction of Christianity in the northern area of the present Sudan.

In 1502 an edict by Ferdinand and Isabella pronounced Islam illegal in Spain and its practice criminal. Thus the Islamic presence of eight centuries was brought to an end in a country that shone like a jewel, bringing some of the greatest contributions of learning and civilization to Europe. This glorious chapter of human history began in 92/711 when converted native North Africans launched an expedition across the Strait of Gibraltar to back up a Muslim missionary group which had met death at the hands of the Spanish authorities the year before. The Catholic Church of Spain had just assumed full power over the monarchy, following its battles with Arianism, and exercised unrestricted power over all the affairs of the realm. This power was especially oriented toward wiping out all the vestiges of Arianism and toward the persecution of the Jews, the only non-Christians in view. Catholic victory, however, was achieved at tremendous cost in the attitudes of Arian Christians toward the Catholic Church. In his history of Visigothic Arianism, Adolph Helfferich correctly stated that its doctrinal remains in the consciousness of the Spanish people had predisposed them to accept Islam. Like Arianism, Islam rejected any duality of being in Christ as well as his crucifixion and resurrection, while the Arian doctrine of a divine nature in Christ might be interpreted as God's spirit or word breathed into Jesus.[14]

Because of this theological war waged by the Catholic Church against the Arian Church, large numbers of clergy converted to Islam, setting an unprecedented example to their pastorates. Thus Alvar, a monk and historian of the Church of Cordoba, moaned in 240/854:

> While we are investigating their [the Muslims'] sacred ordinances and meeting together to study the sects of their Philosophers not for the purpose of refuting their errors, but for the exquisite charm and for the eloquence and beauty of their language—neglecting the reading of the Scriptures, we are but setting up an idol the number of the beast (Apoc. xiii, 18). Where nowadays can we find any learned layman who, absorbed in the study of the Holy Scriptures, cares to look at the works of any of the Latin Fathers? Who is there with any zeal for the writings of the Evangelists, or the Prophets, or Apostles? Our Christian young men, with their elegant airs and fluent speech, are showy in their dress and carriage, and are famed for the learning of the gentiles; intoxicated with Arab eloquence they greedily handle, eagerly devour and zealously discuss the books of the Chaldeans [Muslims], and make them known by praising them with every flourish of rhetoric, knowing nothing of the beauty of the Church's literature, and looking down with contempt on the streams of the Church that flow forth from Paradise; alas! the Christians are so ignorant of their own law, the Latins pay so little attention to their own language, that in the whole Christian flock there is hardly one man in a thousand who can write a letter to inquire after a friend's health intelligibly, while you may find a countless rabble of all kinds of them who can learnedly roll out the grandiloquent periods of the Chaldean tongue. They can even make poems, every line ending with the same letter, which display high flights of beauty and more skill in handling metre than the gentiles themselves possess.[15]

Eastern Europe

While the tide of Islam was receding in Western Europe, Islam made history in Eastern Europe. There, Islam spread its dominion, beginning in 753/1353 when Adrianople was made capital of the emerging 'Uthmanlī state. In the first half of the following century, that dominion spread all the way to the Danube and included most of Greece; and in the second half, which also witnessed the capture of Constantinople and its renaming Islāmpul, that dominion spread to the Adriatic Sea. Under Sulaymān (926/1520–974/1566), Hungary, southern Poland and southern Russia, the Caucasus, and Crete were added, and the Aegean and the Black Sea became Muslim lakes.

As in other areas, centuries-old inter-Christian disputes and struggles had left their scars on the minds and hearts of the people. Here, the antagonism was between Catholic and Orthodox, Greeks and Russians, Greeks and their Frankish and Venetian overlords, and finally between the Greek masses and their feudal lords who were installed by distant foreign rulers and who had exploited and tyrannized the people. Above all, the administration of the Byzantine Empire was corrupt to the core and had left many malcontents, full of resentment and desire for revenge.

The new regime of the 'Uthmanlī Muslims brought order and dignity to these people; and the administration was far more just than it had ever been under Byzantium. Greek merchants preferred to sail under the 'Uthmanlī flag and they readily gave up their tongue and clothing style for those of the 'Uthmanlīs. On the doctrinal level, between Islam and Paulician Christianity there was far more than affinity. Their Christologies were identical, both regarding Jesus as a human and a prophet, sent by God to teach the supreme religious truth of divine unity and justice. This "Paulician" call of Islam evoked memories that were fresh among the people whose emperors had fought the Paulician Church with tooth and claw, and had massacred them by the hundreds of thousands. Although very few in number, some Christians called themselves Paulicians after they passed under the dominion of Islam. They were known as iconoclasts and strict unitarians. Add to this the fact that the 'Uthmanlī administration not only removed all obstacles to migration between the Asiatic and European provinces but encouraged it. Christian migrants were always well received, rehabilitated, and helped by the Muslims, and a great social and ethnic mixture took place as a result of intermarriage.

In Albania, for instance, the Muslims first arrived in 789/1387, but they were not recognized as sovereign until 827/1423. Christians and Muslims cooperated harmoniously while the Christians enjoyed autonomy in their internal affairs. Conversion was slow, but by the sixteenth century the Muslims outnumbered the Christians. Farther to the north, in modern Yugoslavia, the Muslims fanned out in large numbers, and Islam spread with them in Bosnia, Serbia, Montenegro, Herzegovina, and Croatia. The spread of Islam was greatly assisted by the mass conversion of the Bogomiles under Muḥammad II (855/1451–886/1481). Bogomile Christianity had a great affinity to Islam. It abhorred the worship of Mary, the institution of baptism, and every form of priesthood. It repudiated the cross as religious symbol, the bells, the gaudy decorations of the Catholic Church; and it condemned any bowing before the cross as idolatry. Like the Paulicians and the Arians generally, the Bogomiles rejected the doctrines of the incarnation, crucifixion, and resurrection. They drank neither wine nor spirits, kept their beards and said only the Lord's prayer. Passage to Islam was relatively easy for them, and their example prompted others to follow their course.

Crete first came under Muslim rule from 210/825 to 350/961. In this period all its inhabitants converted to Islam. When Byzantium reconquered Crete, an Armenian monk was sent to proselytize it, and in time the population converted again. In the early twelfth century, when the Cretans were all Greek Orthodox, the island was purchased by the Catholic Venetians from its French "owner," the Duke of Montserrat, to whom it had fallen following the partition of the Byzantine Empire. A rebellion was put down with such ferocity that half the island or better lay fallow and deserted for a century. The people who survived consisted of serfs, cruelly exploited by their Venetian overlords. Therefore, the Cretans longed for a liberator to end their misery. As soon as the Muslims arrived, Greek authority in religious and secular affairs was immediately restored. Reconversion to Islam progressed in peace and freedom until the Greek revolution and the passing of Muslim dominion from the island in the nineteenth century.

Persia

The same place the Qur'ān accorded to "the People of the Book" (Christians, Sabeans, and Jews) and the same treatment the *sharī'ah* accorded to them was extended by the Muslims to the Zoroastrians as soon as Persia passed under the dominion of Islam. Religious legitimacy and autonomy regarding internal affairs, especially those pertaining to personal status, were a constitutional matter, and were granted readily. Intermarriage turned the "vanquished" into the in-laws of Islamic leaders and commanders. Ḥusayn, the grandson of the Prophet, married Shahrbanu, a daughter of Yazdigird, the fallen monarch of the vanquished kingdom. The situation of the Christians in Persia was worse than that of their Arab co-religionists in Byzantium. When Byzantium defeated Persia, Khusro II brought his Christian subjects under a terrible wave of persecution. As for the Zoroastrian masses, their situation was one of servitude to the castes of royalty and priesthood.

Islam's entry onto the scene was therefore believed to be a genuine liberation from certain misery, enlightenment, and revival of piety after the darkest religious decay. Large numbers converted immediately. Islamic tolerance, however, enabled the conservative to practice and keep their faith. Toward the end of the second century A.H., Sāmān, a nobleman from Balkh, converted to Islam, and renamed his son Asad. The son later founded the Sāmānī dynasty (261/874–390/999). In 260/873, the whole city of Daylam converted to Islam through the effort of a Muslim missionary, Abū Muḥammad Nāṣir al Ḥaqq; and the province of Ṭabaristān did so in 300/912 through the effort of Ḥasan bin 'Alī. At Samarqand, destruction of a popular idol by Qutaybah ibn Muslim disproved the belief that whoever touched it would perish, and the Magian spectators embraced Islam by the thousands. By the time of Al Mu'taṣim, the vast majority of the people of Transoxania had joined the ranks of the faithful. The Sāmānī dynasty was responsible for bringing Islam to neighboring Turkestan by converting its prince Satuq Bughra Khān in 349/960. Emulating their prince, 200,000 families professed Islam on the same day. The prospects of matrimony between the House of Ghaznah and the pagan Ilik-Khānīs of Central Asia brought the latter into the fold of Islam in 1042, and most of their realm followed. The king of Kābul converted to Islam in the caliphate of Al Ma'mūn; but the bulk of Afghanistan did not join Islam until 258/871, when Ya'qūb ibn al Layth brought Kābul under the dominion of the Saffārī dynasty.

China

The Arabs had established trade relations with the Chinese before Islam. Their seafarers had plied the Indian Ocean, passed through the Straits of Malacca between Sumatra and peninsular Malaysia, crossed the South China Sea, and established trading posts on the southeast coast of China, as well as en route, for example, in Sumatra and on the Malabar Coast of India. Under the T'ang Dynasty, which came to power in 618 C.E., Chinese annals made the first mention of the Arabs, called their kingdom Madīnah, and described their faith as Islam. The same annals acknowledged the presence of Chinese Muslims in Canton, called them Hui Hui, and described their mosques. Muslim annals mention that Qutaybah had sent ambassadors to China after Islam was established in Samarqand and Shash (modern Tashkent). But Chinese annals mention an ambassador called Sulaymān who was sent by Hishām in 108/726 to Emperor Hsuan Tsung. This may be a legend explaining the Arab origins of the Chinese Muslims. Supposedly, Al Manṣūr sent a body of Muslim troops at the request of the Emperor's son, Su Tsung, in 139/756 to help him recover his throne from a usurper, and the Muslim force decided to stay in China rather than return home.

The widespread dislocation of people produced by the Mongol invasions of Central, South, and West Asia caused many Muslims to emigrate to distant, safer places. Some emigrated to China, or to the lands leading to it. On the other hand, the Mongol conquest of Central Asian Muslim lands produced a number of Muslims who befriended the Mongols and worked for them. In 642/1244 'Abdul Raḥman became head of the imperial finances and collected the taxes imposed on China. His successor, another Muslim named Sayyid Ajall, appointed in 658/1259 by Qublā Khān, became the governor of Yunnan where he built both mosques and Buddhist temples for his subjects. In 1335 Ajall sought and obtained an imperial proclamation that Islam was "the true and pure religion." In 1420 mosques were built in the capitals Singnanfu and Nankin, and Muslim presence was conspicuous enough to be observed by Marco Polo (1275–1292) in Yunnan and its capital, Talifu. A few decades later, that presence was evident throughout the south coastal region of China. Finally, under the Ming Dynasty (1369–1644), its founder Emperor Hungwu recognized his Muslim subjects and conferred upon them numerous privileges.

India

Pre-Islamic Arab seafaring in the Indian Ocean had established traders' colonies on the southwest coast of India known through its Arabic name of Ma'bar (Malabar). These must have converted to Islam when it was established in Arabia and began to spread in Western Asia. They were individuals or small communities at best, living under a Hindu government. The arrival of Muḥammad bin Qasim with an army at Daybul in 93/711 marked the beginning of the first Muslim government on the subcontinent. His pacification of the area and his inquiry of the Caliph in Damascus how to treat strangers who were not "people of the Book" but who agreed to pay tribute and live in peace with the Muslims, gave rise to an extension of this legal category *(dhimmī)* to Hindus and Buddhists, thus defining Islam's attitude to these two religions.

Sindī scholars were responsible for introducing Sanskrit knowledge and wisdom into the Near East. Muslims from Arabia and local converts began to spread Islam in the areas adjoining Sind. Thus Islam began its career in the subcontinent.

The first Muslim city in India was al Manṣūrah, founded c. 112/730 on an island in the Indus river near Shahdadpur. Multān, further to the north, became an Islamic center soon thereafter, and capital of a Muslim state by 236/850. Ibn Ḥawqal visited the city in 367/977 and described its population as all Muslim. From there Islam spread to Punjab in the north and Gujrat in the east and south. Islam made another influx from the northwest. Maḥmūd of Ghaznah (998–1030) invaded India from Afghanistan and established a base in Lahore. He placed his generals as governors of large areas including Punjab and Multān. From there Islam began to spread in all directions and, at the hand of Muḥammad 'Alafī, as far as Kashmir, where he had found refuge from unfriendly Muslims and Hindus. When Mas'ūd of Ghaznah arrived in Kashmir in 425/1033, there were already a prospering community of Muslims in that province.

In the southwest, Makrān was a Muslim state before the end of the tenth century. In the following century, Islam made significant inroads into Gujarat through two famous missionaries of Islam, 'Abdullah and Mulla 'Alī; in Pirana Imām Shah established friendly relations with the Hindus and succeeded in

Illustration 10.11

Qābūs Mosque, Brunei. [Photo by L. al Fārūqī.]

Illustration 10.12

Arcade of courtyard, The Islamic Center, Washington, D.C. [Courtesy The Islamic Center, Washington, D.C.]

converting thousands of them. Imām Shah had no match in missionary zeal until Malik 'Abdul Laṭīf who in the reign of Maḥmūd Begarah (863/1458-917/1511) converted thousands of Hindus to Islam. Mu'īnuddīn Chishtī arrived in Ajmer when it was completely Hindu. Before he died in 644/1246, he had transformed it single-handed into a base for Islam and made it the capital of a large Ṣūfī order which radiated Islam in all directions.

In Bengal, Chittagong had for centuries been a center of Arab maritime trade. Surrounding it was a strong Buddhist community whose religion had fallen into a primitive pattern and involved human sacrifices. Islam did not progress with any great speed until after the death of King Kans (796/1393) who ordered his son to be a Muslim and to take his place on the throne as King Jalāluddīn, and then changed his mind, dethroned his son, and had him reconvert to Hinduism. When he died, his son reascended to the throne as an enthusiastic and committed Muslim sovereign. Within the space of a century, the overwhelming majority of the people had converted to Islam.

East, Central, West, and South Africa

The Berbers made a last stand against the Muslim army in 84/703 and lost. In consequence, they were to supply 12,000 troops to the army of Islam. In military service, they would keep their dignity and honor, learn Islam and get disciplined in the law, and share in the spoils of war. Learned men were assigned to teach them and to accompany them on their war expeditions. Those who accompanied Ṭāriq ibn Ziyād in the campaign against Spain were such fresh converts. Their career found fulfillment in Spain. In the African hinterland, however, Islam made slow progress. In the eleventh century, a Ṣanhājah chieftain brought with him a learned Muslim to teach Islam to his recalcitrant tribesmen. The man was 'Abdullah bin Yasin. He tried with little avail to make the faith of the people more than lip-service. He retired to an island in the Senegal river with a few followers. Soon, others joined and the ranks of his pupils swelled. When they reached a thousand, he set them out to reform through teaching; but resolved with them that in case of failure, they would return to him to attempt the task by force. The teaching experiment failed again and 'Abdullah bin Yasin prepared to march with his followers as if to war. His campaign was successful, and he found himself at the head of a continentwide movement in control of the land. The movement was called al Murābiṭūn.

From the land of the Berbers, Islamization extended to the pagan tribes of the Sudan. The Lamtuna and the Jadala, two clans of the Ṣanhājah, distinguished themselves in bringing Islam to the pagans. Through their efforts, the whole Fulbe tribe became Muslim before the end of the eleventh century. Most of the citizens of Jenne and Timbuktu, founded in 494/1100, were Muslim. These cities became great centers of Islamic learning and they taught Islam to the Mandingos who conquered Ghana and became the greatest Muslim activists, bringing Islam to the Hausa people. Islam was also brought into the Western Sudan by Egyptians and Nubians coming to dwell or to trade. Their presence and missionary activity brought Islam to the Lake Chad area. In the fourteenth century, Muslim missionary efforts were strengthened by the Tunjar Arabs emigrating from Tunis to Darfur and other southern lands. One of them, Aḥmad, was liked by the heathen king of Darfur, and he was taken into his employment and patronage. He later married his patron's daughter and established a dynasty which continued the task of proselytizing the natives. By 1017/1608 most of the Wadai and Baghirmi peoples were converted to Islam, making possible the establishment by 'Abdul Karīm in 1021/1612 of Wadai as the center of Islamic influence throughout West Africa.

The Fulbe people mobilized and dedicated themselves to the propagation of Islam under the leadership of Shaykh 'Uthman dan Fodio in the late eighteenth century. They were eminently successful as they introduced Islam as far as Adamana in the southeast, founded the city of Ilorin in Yoruba land, and made the centers from which Islam radiated to the south and southwest. The Ṣūfī orders of Mīrghaniyyah (founded by Muḥammad 'Uthman al Amīr Ghānī in 1251/1835, the older Baghdād-originated Qādiriyyah from its centers at Walata and Timbuktu, the Tījāniyyah stemming from Algiers, and the Sanūsiyyah from its bases in Kufrah and Jaghbūb in southeast Lybia consolidated and continued the gains made earlier.

On the African east coast, contacts were made with the Arabs before Islam and continued to grow vigorously thereafter. Maqdisu (Maqdishu, Magadoxo) was founded c. 339/950 by Muslim immigrants who called themselves Ummah Zaydiyyah (Emozaydij) or the followers of Zayd ibn 'Alī. Other immigrants founded cities of their own farther south. 'Alī, son of Sulṭān Ḥasan of Shīrāz, emigrated with his black mother and followers, and founded the city of Kiloah. The news of their prosperity encouraged many more to emigrate, thus reinforcing the Islamic presence and mission to the tribes inhabiting the hinterland. Their efforts were assisted by those Muslims descending from the north through the Nile valley. Notable among their missionary achievements was the conversion of the Galla and Zayla' peoples reported by ibn Ḥawqal in the ninth century to be Christians, and by Abūl Fidā in the fourteenth to be Muslims.

The Dutch encouraged Muslims from the Malay Basin to emigrate to South Africa in order to work in the new plantations they were operating near the Cape of Good Hope. These intermarried with their Dutch masters as well as with the native Africans, and multiplied their numbers. Together with Muslim immigrants from India who settled on the east coast of South Africa, they constitute a significant presence in the land.

The Malay Basin

The circumstances of the spread of Islam in the Malay Basin are so similar to those in Africa that they can be merged into a single account. The most important element in this account is the encounter of Islam with the primitive mentality of the pre-Islamic Malay. That mentality fragmented human existence into countless separate tribes. It pictured the world as alien, frightful, and above all full of spirits which it had to appease and placate. These tribes relied on food gathering, or the least agriculture to survive, and related their miseries to fantastic myths in terms of which they understood themselves and the reality around them. They lived on cannibalism, instituted human sacrifice, tolerated infanticide, and never saw the nakedness of the body or the need to clean it. They never realized the need to read and write, to record human experience, and they existed without civilization, or even awareness of human culture. Where the West impinged upon it before Islam, as in Africa, Westerners bartered goods without ever developing native trade or industry and, besides bringing with them hitherto unknown diseases which debilitated the people, introduced gin and rum with all their attendant consequences. Where the first outside influence upon the primitive mentality came from Hinduism or Buddhism, as in the Malay archipelago, it provided no exposure or link to the outside world and formed neither society nor empire. Instead of developing native trade and industry or laying down foundations for the development of learning and civilization, Hinduism pushed primitive mythology to a higher degree of complexity and sophistication. As to the impact of Buddhism, it may have taught the Malay how to build temples and carve statues to the Buddha (although it is by no means certain that Borobudur is the work of natives; rather it seems the work of imported craftsmen who left behind them no tradition of sculpture or architecture!). But as in the other cases of contact, the primitive mentality remained primitive.

Islam transformed the primitive mentality completely. It eliminated superstition and spirits and ascribed all causation to one supreme Creator Whose will is orderly and Whose patents in creation are eternal. It divested the tribal chiefs and elders of their unscrupulous whimsical judgment and binding power, and it vested all normativeness in a permanent and unique law, backed by worldly and other-worldly sanctions. It dissolved the tribe, repudiated its loyalties, and grouped the people into nations and empires, imbuing them with loyalty for causes greater than themselves. It ended cannibalism, human sacrifice, and infanticide once and for all. It outlawed alcohol and nakedness, imposed cleanliness, and made necessary the wearing of shoes. It banned *ghazw* (raiding) and plunder, and safeguarded life and property. It ordered the family and its internal relations on a footing of justice, and raised women to a status not reached by many of the civilized nations of modern times. It established schools and imposed literacy on all its adherents, giving them a *lingua franca* with which to communicate internationally, and made possible the translation of books on religion and law to make their observance wider and deeper. It ordered them to build houses that lent privacy to their families and mosques in which to congregate for worship and the conduct of public affairs. It encouraged travel, trade, and industry and brought to the converts the best and most advanced learning known to other Muslims in the world. In short, conversion to Islam meant for the primitive a leap into civilization, from a miserable existence shorn of decency and dignity to one replete with both, and beautified with the products of Islamic poetry and art.

Islam came to the Malay Basin soon after its advent in Arabia, for Arab contacts and trading colonies in the area were pre-Islamic. Bases in Sumatra, at the Malacca straights, must have been founded to make the trade with Canton (China) possible. The period from the seventh to the thirteenth centuries witnessed a steady influx of traders and immigrants who settled in the region to conduct its prospering foreign trade. These arrived from Arabia as well as Persia, Afghanistan, and India where Islam had already established a strong and expanding presence. These traders married native women, learned the native tongues, and preached Islam to those with whom they came into contact. Gradually, they developed a viable measure of security and popularity. Although the annals mark 'Abdullah 'Arīf as founder of the first Muslim state in Atcheh in Sumatra in the mid-twelfth century, it is likely that pettier kingdoms of Muslims must have been formed earlier and that "Sri Paduka Sulṭān" 'Abdullah's monarchy was the high point of a long development. Marco Polo reported that Perlak (northeast corner of Sumatra) was already a Muslim kingdom in 692/1292.

The dislocations which the Mongol invasions had caused produced many emigrants to Southeast Asia. Hence, from the thirteenth century, the area witnessed a great expansion of Muslim power. 'Ulamā', Ṣūfīs, disbanded soldiers, craftsmen, and people of all walks of life and many races poured into the Malay Basin in search of peace and security, away from Tatar holocausts and other wars. Islam made its entry in large numbers into Palembang, South and Central Sumatra, and North Java in the first half of the fourteenth century. Minak Kamala Bumi is credited with spreading it into Java, after it had taken root among the Lampongs in the west of the island. It was mainly from Sumatra that Islam spread in Malaysia in the thirteenth and fourteenth centuries. Smaller colonies of Muslims were also set up by seafarers on the east coast of Malaysia, and these developed into the modern states of Trengganu (which has the oldest Muslim inscription of the area, the Trengganu Stone bearing the date of 702/1303), and Kelantan, and planting other Muslim colonies in Thailand, Cambodia, and Vietnam.

Western Europe and the New World

This discussion would not be complete without at least a brief allusion to the spread of Islam in Western Europe and America in the last hundred years. Colonialism had opened the gates for the colonized to migrate to the colonial country as cheap labor; and the developed industries of the West after World War II were hungry for working hands that could not be found in Europe. In consequence, between ten and fifteen million Muslims now live in Western Europe. The Muslims came to North America after World War II, to study or seek fortune, and in time took root in the New World. Their missionary activity led to the conversion of some two or three million native Americans. Together, they form an active, fast-growing community of about five or six million people. Smaller groups exist in Canada and the other countries of the New World.

NOTES

1. Haykal, M. H. *The Life of Muḥammad,* trans. I. R. al Fārūqī (Chicago: American Trust Pubs., 1976), pp. 510–511.

2. In forms slightly varying from one another, the speech of al Mughīrah is reported by al Ṭabarī (*Tārīkh al Umam wal Mulūk,* Cairo, 1358/1939, Vol. 3, p. 36); Ibn al Athīr (*Al Kāmil fī al Tārīkh,* Cairo, 1303–1318/1885–1900, Vol. 2, p. 179); Abū Yūsuf (*Kitāb al Kharāj,* Cairo, 1346/1924, p. 35); and Abū Ḥanīfah al Dīnawarī (*Al Akhbār al Ṭiwāl,* Cairo, Wizārah al Thaqāfah, 1380/1960, p. 120).

3. The report is from Ibn 'Abd al Ḥakam's *Futūḥ Miṣr wa Akhbāruhā* and is quoted by P. K. Hitti in his *History of the Arabs* (London: Macmillan, 1950), p. 163.

4. Thomas W. Arnold, *The Preaching of Islam: A History of the Propagation of the Muslim Faith* (Lahore: Sh. M. Ashraf, 1961), pp. 56–57.

5. Ibid., p. 46.

6. *Michael the Elder,* Vol. II, pp. 412–413. Barhebraeus, about a century later, wrote in a similar strain (*Chronicon Ecclesiasticum,* ed. J. B. Abeloos and Lamy, p. 474). Quoted in Arnold, *The Preaching of Islam,* pp. 54–55.

7. Arnold, *The Preaching of Islam,* pp. 72–73.

8. *History of Latin Christianity,* Vol. II, pp. 216–217, quoted in Arnold, *The Preaching of Islam,* p. 70.

9. D. Barāmkī, "From Ancient Times to the Beginning of the Muslim Era," in *Jerusalem: The Key to World Peace* (London: Islamic Council of Europe, 1980), pp. 103, 143.

10. Under al Mu'taḍid (892–902), 'Umar b. Yūsuf, a Christian, was governor of al Anbār; Naṣr ibn Hārūn, another Christian, was prime minister of 'Aḍud al Dawlah (949–982); even the Muslim army was more than once under the command of a Christian general, as in the cali-

phate of al Mu'tamid (870–982), when the command was entrusted to Israel, a Christian military officer, or the caliphate of al Muqtadir (908–932), when another Christian was charged with the defense of the Empire.

11. Odo de Diogilo, *De Ludovici* vii, Itinere. Migne, *Patrologia Latina.* Quoted in Arnold, *The Preaching of Islam,* pp. 89–90.

12. Roger Hoveden, *Chronica Magistri Regeri de Hovedene,* ed. W. Stubbs (London, 1868), Vol. II, pp. 307–308. Arnold, *The Preaching of Islam,* p. 91.

13. *Gesta Regis Henrici Secundi Benedicti Abbatis* (London, 1867), Vol. II, pp. 11–12.

14. Adolph Helfferich, *Der Westgothische Arianismus und die Spanische Ketzer-Geschichte.* Quoted in Arnold, *The Preaching of Islam,* p. 136.

15. Alvar, *Alvari Cordubensis Epistolae* (Migne, *Patrologia Latina*) xxi, 2. Quoted in Arnold, *The Preaching of Islam,* pp. 139–140.

CHAPTER 11

The Methodological Sciences

ISLAM AND THE DISCIPLINED PURSUIT OF KNOWLEDGE

Islam identified itself with knowledge. It made knowledge its condition as well as its goal. It equated the pursuit of knowledge with *'ibādah* (worship) and poured its most lavish praise on those who committed themselves to its cultivation, making them the saints and friends of God, and raising their ink above the blood of the martyrs in value. Islamic knowledge, however, was not some Upanishadic insight which one obtains from a guru-master. Nor was it an involuntary flash in the consciousness of an adherent undergoing a mystical experience, though some Muslim Ṣūfīs have defined it that way. Nor was it some esoteric information obtained on authority after initiation, or an illumination arrived at subjectively through contemplation. Rather, Islamic knowledge is the rational — empirical and intuitive — apprehension of every realm of reality. It is the critical knowledge of man and history, of earth and heaven. It is the tested, practical knowledge that produces results and leads to virtue, the object of the Muslim's prayer, "O God, grant us a knowledge that is useful and beneficial!" It is at the farthest possible remove from speculation, which Islam condemns as vain and idle. Islam's aversion to speculative knowledge is not anti-intellectualism. Rather, it is the apogee of criticality. The human quest will never be successful or worthwhile without strategy and economy. Pursuit of impossible knowledge is certainly futile; use of the wrong methodology annihilates the enterprise before it starts. *Ghayb,* the transcendent realm — the ultimate questions of metaphysics, the domain of God, of His heaven, His angels, His activity, of after-time and beyond-space — are forever beyond our ken. By nature, we can have no knowledge of them other than what God has revealed. Stealing knowledge from heaven like Prometheus is ridiculous and naïve; desiring it as did Adam and Eve regardless of consequences is futile. The mature, the responsible, and the wise among humans are those who are satisfied with their human condition. They accept it gratefully, knowing their limitations; and they move on to undertake the great task of establishing the truth men can establish — namely, knowledge of themselves and of their environment.

Knowledge is infinite because the truth is infinite. There is no shortcut to it; the road leading to it is hard and hazardous, requiring disciplined self-application and dedication. Above all, it is lengthy, extremely so, consuming the better years of a man's life. Fortunately, man does not start on the quest of knowledge *ex nihilo.* He stands equipped with a number of gifts which make the pursuit easy and bring the object within reach. He is endowed with the senses and the faculties of memory and imagination, of theoretical and axiological perception. And above them all stands the critical faculty of reason to guide, to collate and harmonize, to correct and corroborate, and finally to systematize the acquired knowledge and relate it to action. These are all gifts for which humans can never be too grateful.

To make the quest still easier, Islam regards prophecy as an aid to the human quest. Revelation, Islam holds, is not the disclosure of God but the making known of His will and commandments. Its object is knowledge, and only knowledge. It is offered as a warning against error and pitfall, as guidance to the truth, the same truth that is the object of the human quest and which the faculties of knowledge seek. It is recorded in a book — the Qur'ān — as a summation of the general principles and purport of all knowledge. The Qur'ān constitutes a ready reference for all who seek an open, public source of truth. It lays one condition upon the seeker, namely, mastery of the Arabic language, which anyone can achieve given the requisite aptitude and resolution. The Qur'ān stands as a book alongside another "book," nature or reality, which is equally open, public, and available to the seeker. The contents of the two "books" are identical: the laws of nature are the patterns the Creator has imbedded in His creation. They are hence His will, whether they apply to nature — to earth and sky, to things and organisms — or to history — to the intentions and deeds of men. Whereas the Qur'ān requires linguistic competence for access to its contents, that of nature needs more to "read" and understand it. It calls for use of all cognitive faculties at once. Despite the equivalence of the two books, priority belongs to the Qur'ān, because it posits the base of knowledge as such, the very thesis of the place of God, man, nature, and knowledge in the overall scheme of things. Moreover, linguistic competence and the ability to read the Qur'ān are a window to an infinite realm of meanings. To grasp these meanings and understand their interrelations, to discover the realities of creation to which they apply and those which they project for man to bring about, one needs all the faculties of cognition as well as all the cumulative legacy of human knowledge.

The Muslims called *al 'ulūm al shar'iyyah* those sciences that seek to master the meanings of revelation. They included in that category the sciences of language, the sciences of the Qur'ān, those of the *ḥadīth,* and those of the *sharī'ah.* The sciences of language were the first in importance because they constituted the key to the data of revelation, texts as well as meanings. The sciences of the Qur'ān revolved around the text of the word of God — its verba, grammar, syntax, and lexicology — and of the contemporary history as the situational context of revelation, as well as the meanings apparent and/or implicit in the text. The sciences of the *ḥadīth* dealt with the *sunnah* of the Prophet Muḥammad as clarifying, exemplifying, and concretizing the Qur'ānic meanings. The sciences of the *ḥadīth* also dealt with the problems of establishing the authenticity of the traditions and their texts. Finally, the sciences of the *sharī'ah,* taking all the foregoing sciences for granted, sought to specify the imperatives of Islam, to translate them into prescriptive legislation, and to devise institutions as well as methodologies for the *sharī'ah*'s perpetual observance.

Illustration 11.1

Muslim students going to the Central Mosque in Offa, Nigeria. [Courtesy A. R. Doi.]

THE SCIENCES OF LANGUAGE

Introduction

Being the language of revelation, the Arabic language was the first to come under scholarly study. It did so under the pressure of millions of new converts who wished to have access to the revelation which they believed was the divine message. Some of them spoke languages close to Arabic, for the Semitic languages were known by many people in Western Asia.

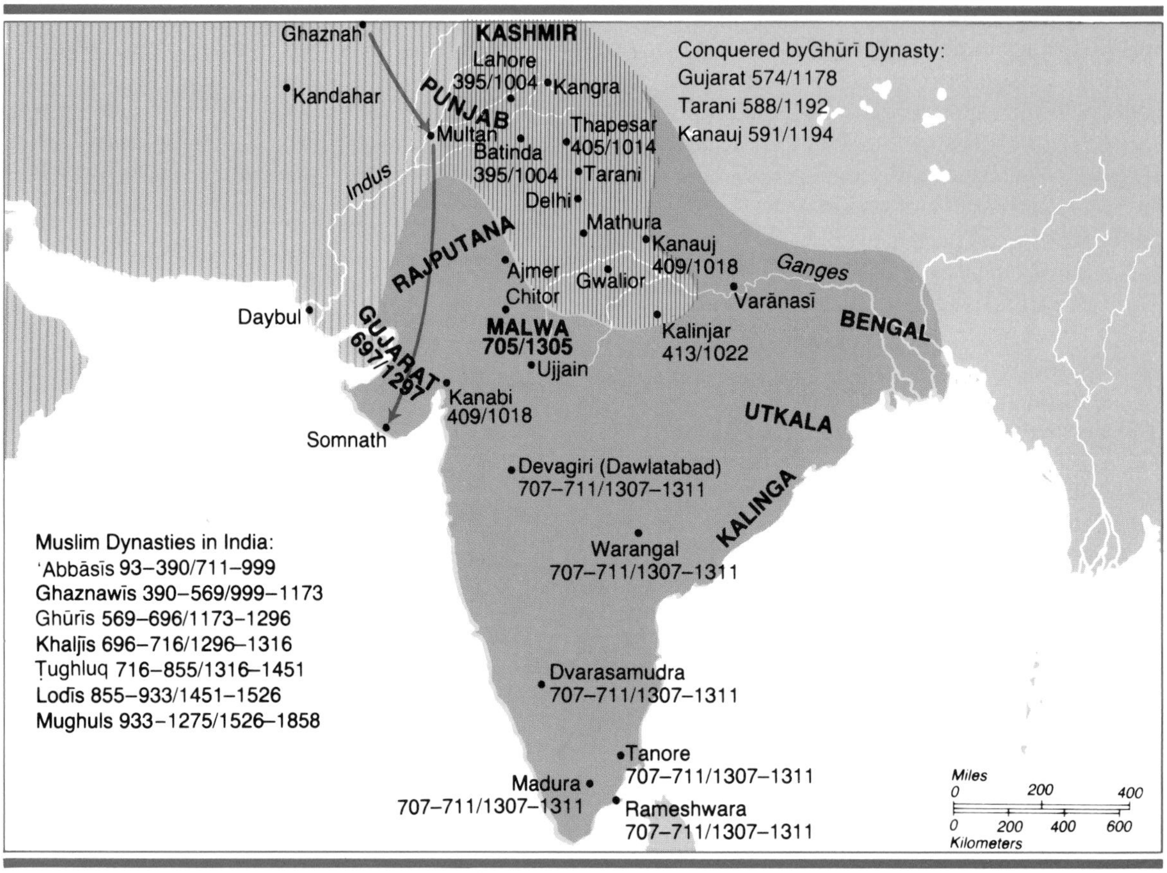

Area conquered by Muslims under Umawīs and 'Abbāsīs, 93–390/711–999
Sultan Maḥmūd's campaign, 415–416/1024–1025
Area conquered by Sultan Maḥmūd, 395–413/1004–1022
Area conquered by Khaljī Dynasty 696–716/1296–1316

Map 39. Al Futūḥāt in India, 93-1112/711-1700

They or others may even have known Arabic as a second language. However, understanding the Qur'ān and mastering its meanings, which was the desideratum of everyone, required greater competence than they could command. Hence their intense desire to learn.

History has never witnessed a similar phenomenon. Millions of converts, of all ages and ethnic backgrounds, rushed to put themselves through an Arabic training program. The Arabs were under divine command to bring the message of Islam to all peoples. For the majority, that was the justification for their being outside Arabia in the new lands to which Islam had come. Now that hostilities stopped and public security was reassured, the Arabs had little to occupy themselves. The mosque was instantly turned into a classroom, and so were the streets, marketplaces, and private homes. The Arabs had no text to teach except the Qur'ān which they had memorized and which they utilized as the standard of grammatical rules and their exemplification. Everywhere, the new Muslims gathered around an Arab to learn from him directly, and then perhaps to teach others who had no Arab teacher.

In time, the demand for teaching Arabic to non-Arabic-speaking Muslims produced the science of the language, namely, grammar, orthography, syntax, lexicology, linguistics, and poetics. Had the message been restricted to the Arabic-speaking people, development of the Arabic sciences may not have taken place as early as it did.

The first scholar to rise to the task of laying down a

grammar of the Arabic language in systematic form was Abū al Aswad al Du'alī (69/689). He belonged to the class of *Tābi'ūn* (second generation of Muslims), and had been a companion of 'Alī ibn Abū Ṭālib, the fourth caliph, at the Battle of Ṣiffīn. Al Du'alī was also responsible for devising the vocalization signs, which are determined by the grammatical status of the words and which constitute indices to that status and make understanding possible. The first vocalization signs used in Arabic were those used in Syriac and later adopted by Hebrew: one dot above for the short "a" of the direct object; one dot within the letter for the nominative "u"; and one dot under the letter to indicate the terminal "i" sound of the indirect object. This system did not last long. Before the first century of the Islamic period was over, the signs presently used were introduced. The same time witnessed the establishment of signs to denote the joining of two words or their separation, doubling of a consonant, and dots to differentiate letters having the same shape. By the time of al Ḥajjāj, the governor of Iraq and the eastern provinces, these processes were completed. It was he who introduced them into the Qur'ānic script during the caliphate of 'Abdul Malik ibn Marwān (66–86/685–705).

The Umawī caliphs encouraged the talented among their subjects to lay down the foundations of the Arabic language, and generously rewarded those who made worthy contributions. Caliph 'Abdul Malik asked his attendants: "Who could list organs of the body beginning with the letters of the alphabet in their own order?" Suwayd ibn Ghaflah rose and said, "Prince of the Believers, I am equal to it"; and he recited "A is for . . . , B is for . . . ," down to Z. When another attendant rose and said, "I can cite two organs for each letter," Suwayd retorted, "I can cite three"; and he did. The books of al Aṣma'ī on the animals and plants were not works of zoology or botany but linguistic treatises that identified, analyzed, and classified the names of animals and plants and their usage. Such works were specialized lexicons, in which words were arranged according to their meaning rather than their spelling. The Arabs produced them by the hundreds and thus laid the foundations for Arabic linguistics. Beside the works of al Aṣma'ī, the most famous were *Fiqh al Lughah* of al Tha'ālibī and *Al Mukhaṣṣaṣ* of Ibn Sayyidih.

The earliest and possibly the greatest master of the Arabic language was Khalīl ibn Aḥmad (180/796), the teacher of Sībawayh and a score of the greatest grammarians and men of letters of the second century A.H. He discovered, theorized, and established the rhythmic modes of Arabic poetry and gave them their names. He wrote *Kitāb al 'Ayn,* the first thesaurus of Arabic words and book of grammar and syntax. He surveyed and counted the words of the Arabic language and found them to be 1,235,412 words. Abū Bakr al Zabīdī (379/989), who published a summary of Ibn Aḥmad's masterpiece, gave the census of the language and arrived at the following table:

Number of Words	*Form of Roots*	*In Use*	*Not in Use*
750	Two letters	589	161
19,650	Three "	4,269	15,381
33,400	Four "	2,820	30,580
6,375,600	Five "	42	6,375,558
6,429,400		7,720	6,421,680

The Science of *Adab*

Besides being a general term referring to all studies pertaining to the Arabic language, the word *adab* has acquired two technical meanings, both of which were differentiated from *'ilm* (science). To contrast the *'ālim* (man of science) with the *adīb* (man of *adab*), the former is defined as "whoever specializes in any branch of the sciences and perfects his knowledge of it," while the latter is "whoever familiarizes himself with every branch of knowledge, takes the best part of it and digests it." To be a man of *adab* is to

SOME MUGHUL RULERS:

Bābur	932– 937/1525–1530
Humāyūn	937– 964/1530–1556
Akbar	964–1014/1556–1605
Jāhangīr	1014–1037/1605–1627
Shāh Jahān	1037–1069/1627–1658
Aurangzeb	1069–1119/1658–1707

FIRUZ ṬUGHLUQ (752–790/1351–1388) BUILT:

200 towns
40 mosques
30 colleges
30 reservoirs
50 dams
100 hospitals
100 public baths
150 bridges

'ALĀ'UDDĪN KHALJĪ (696–716/1296–1316):
attracted musicians from all over India;
under him Indo-Muslim music was created.

FAMOUS URDU POETS:

Maẓhar	1111–1195/1699–1781
Sauda	1130–1194/ 717–1780
Dard	1132–1200/1719–1785
Mīr	1137–1223/1724–1808

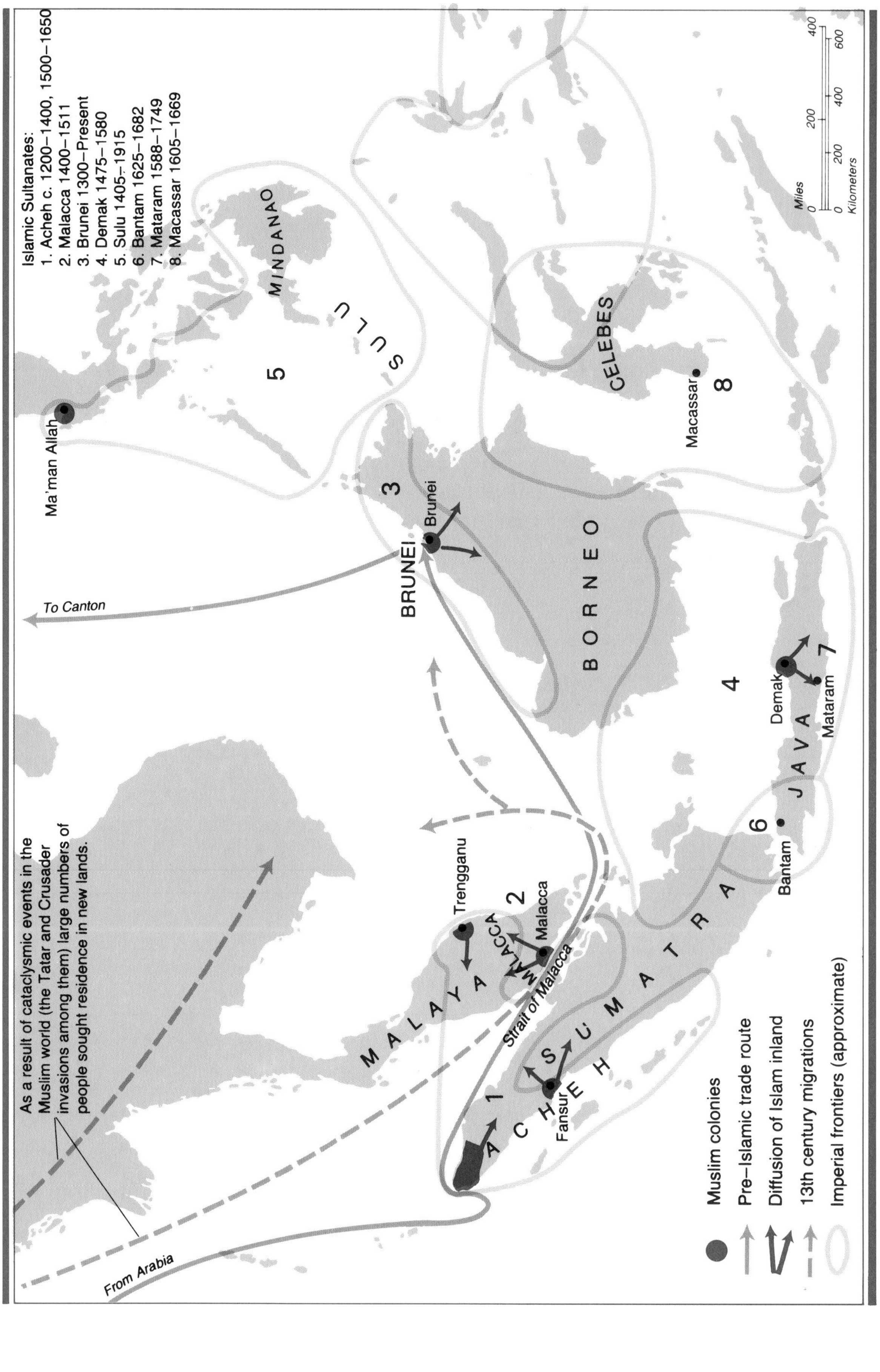
Islamic Sultanates:
1. Acheh c. 1200–1400, 1500–1650
2. Malacca 1400–1511
3. Brunei 1300–Present
4. Demak 1475–1580
5. Sulu 1405–1915
6. Bantam 1625–1682
7. Mataram 1588–1749
8. Macassar 1605–1669
As a result of cataclysmic events in the Muslim world (the Tatar and Crusader invasions among them) large numbers of people sought residence in new lands.
Muslim colonies
Pre-Islamic trade route
Diffusion of Islam inland
13th century migrations
Imperial frontiers (approximate)
Miles 0 200 400
Kilometers 0 200 400 600
From Arabia
To Canton
Ma'man Allah
MINDANAO
SULU
CELEBES
Macassar
BRUNEI
Brunei
BORNEO
JAVA
Demak
Mataram
Bantam
SUMATRA
ACHEH
Fansur
MALAYA
MALACCA
Malacca
Trengganu
Strait of Malacca

Map 40. Al Futūḥāt in Southeast Asia, 1–1112/622–1700

Illustration 11.2

A Qur'ānic school in Nigeria. [Courtesy A. R. Doi.]

know all fields of learning enough to realize their fundamental principles, methods, problems, objectives, achievements, and hopes, and to know these so well as to relate them meaningfully to the enterprise of human thought and life. The second technical meaning was a later invention. It applied to the man of science whose specialization consisted of prose and poetry.

In the early period of Islamic history, *adab* referred to the first technical meaning. It was particularly used to mean the collection, organization, and dissemination of the sayings, wisdom, poetry, history, and cultural materials of the Arabs as aids to understanding of the Qur'ān. It was Ibn 'Abbās, the first Qur'ānic exegete, who advised the Muslims to look for an explanation of anything they found problematic in the Qur'ān, in the poetry, and in the *adab* of the Arabs. When non-Arabs converted to Islam and sought to learn the Arabic language, the materials necessary for confirmation and exemplification of the rules of grammar, lexicology, syntax, and so on, were sought in the culture of the Arabs. Pursuant to the goals of Arabization so keenly desired by the Umawīs, the caliphs encouraged the theorizers of Arabic and offered great prizes to a new breed of collectors, the *ruwāt al adab,* those who searched the Arabic Peninsula for cultural materials, memorized them, and conveyed them to the students.

Kūfah and Baṣrah, standing between the Persian-speaking and Arabic-speaking worlds, became the vital centers of *adab* activity. The Persian clients of Banū Asad distinguished themselves as the foremost students and teachers of Arabic and *adab.* They and others with similar commitment to teach the Qur'ān used to travel to the heart of Arabia in search of the *adab* materials. And they did this voluntarily in order to excel in spreading Islam and its language. The more the caliphs rewarded the famous among them, the more *adab* and its *riwāyah* (collection and intellectual distribution) became professions whose men expected to be paid for their services. In his *Al Fihrist,* Ibn al Nadīm has given the names of scores of early Arabic teachers *(al fuṣaḥā')* and of collectors and distributors of *adab.* The first two generations of these collectors were immigrants from the central and western parts of the Peninsula; the third generation comprised, in the main, clients of one Arab tribe or another, a good number of them clients of Banū Asad. Among the first generation the most famous were Abūl Jāmūs Thawr ibn Yazīd, the teacher of Ibn al Muqaffa', Shubayl ibn 'Ara'arah (a Khārijī), Abū Thawābah al Asadī, Naṣr ibn Muḍar (of Banū Asad), Abū Maḥlam al Shaybānī, al Faq'asī (of Banū Asad); and Khalaf al Aḥmar (180/796), client of Abū Mūsā al Ash'arī. Among the second and third generations of masters of *adab* and *riwāyah* were: Qatādah ibn Da'āmah (117/735); Abū 'Amr ibn al 'Alā' (154/770); Abū 'Ubaydah Mu'ammar ibn al Muthannā (209/824); 'Abdul Malik al Aṣma'ī (214/829), author of more than forty books on poetry and on the names of animals, camels, horses, goats, plants, date palms, and so on; Abū Zayd al Anṣārī (215/830), author of *The Pearls of Language, Book of Rain,* and *Book of Milk;* and Abū 'Ubayd al Qāsim ibn Salām (223/837), author of *Gharīb al Muṣannaf,* which took forty years of labor to complete. Another group of *ruwāt* specialized and excelled in the collection and dissemination of poetry. Among them were Ḥammād al Rāwiyah (156/772), a client of Banū Bakr; Mufaḍḍal al Ḍabbī (168/784), author of the famous anthology *Al Ḥamāsah,* and of *Al Mufaḍḍaliyyāt,* another anthology of 126 poetical compositions and other materials; Abū 'Amr al Shaybānī (206/821); Muḥammad ibn Salām, creator of the science of classification of poets; and Ibn Abul Khaṭṭāb, the author of the classic *Jamharat Ash'ār al 'Arab.*

The Muslims were the first to systematize literary criticism, to identify its standards, principles, and rules, and to write textbooks for education of the students. The first of these was Ibn Qutaybah (267–880), author of *Adab al Kātib.* He was followed by 'Abdul Qāhir al Jurjānī, whose *Asrār al Balāghah fi 'Ilm al Bayān* covered more ground and carried the critical analysis to higher levels. Finally, Ḍiyā' al Dīn ibn al Athīr al Jazarī wrote his *Al Mathal al Sā'ir* and with it perfected the discipline.

The Science of Grammar and Syntax

The people of Baṣrah launched the discipline of Arabic grammar through Abūl Aswad al Du'alī, who identified and organized its principles and rules. The first to give explanation and justification for the rules of grammar was Ibn Abū Isḥaq al Ḥaḍramī (117/735). 'Īsā ibn 'Umar al Thaqafī (149/766) and Ḥārūn ibn Mūsā were the first to write textbooks, and Sībawayh (183/799) was the first to set it to verse. His book was the first to present grammatical knowledge in literary form, thus making its pursuit a high intellectual pleasure. His book quickly became a classic and was appreciated by everyone. It won the titles of *al Kitāb* (the book) and *"al Baḥr"* (the ocean). 'Alī ibn Ḥamzah al Kasā'ī (189/801), a student of Banū Asad, was the favorite of the 'Abbāsī caliph Hārūn al Rashīd and teacher of his son, al Amīn. After the latter became caliph, he sided unjustly with his teacher against Sībawayh in a public debate between the two masters. Yaḥyā ibn Ziyād al Farrā' (207/822), another Banū Asad student, excelled to the point that posterity acknowledged him as the greatest champion of the Arabic language. He was the favorite of Caliph al Ma'mūn, whose princely children vied with one another for the privilege of bringing the scholar his shoes whenever he left the court. He dictated two works on grammar, *Al Ḥudūd* and *Al Ma'ānī*. Finally, Ya'qūb ibn Isḥaq Ibn al Sākit (244/858), teacher of Caliph al Mutawakkil's children, wrote *Iṣlāḥ al Manṭiq* and *Tahdhīb al Alfāẓ*.

The work of Khalīl ibn Aḥmad in grammar was so fundamental and so perfect that it satisfied the need of several generations. Many works were written as commentaries and amplifications of his *Kitāb al 'Ayn*. Ibn Aḥmad and his contemporaries Abū 'Ubaydah and al Aṣma'ī graduated hundreds of great grammarians who led the field after them. Together, they developed *taṣrīf* (conjugation of verbs and foliation of words) into a science and wrote it down. Abūl 'Abbās Tha'lab (291/903) was another of the students of Ibn Aḥmad, Abū 'Ubaydah, and al Aṣma'ī. He wrote

Map 41. Al Futūḥāt Around the Mediterranean, 11–133/632–750

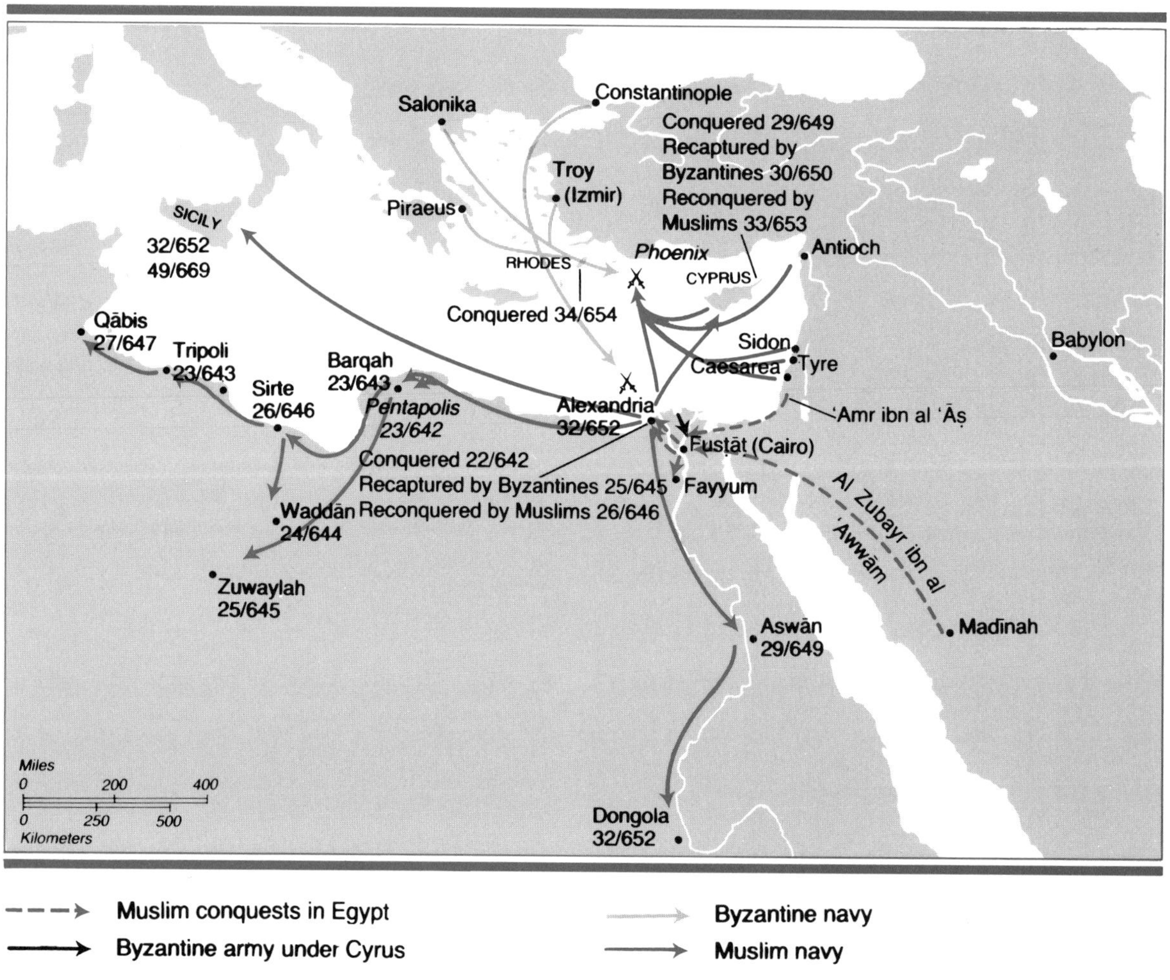

Illustration 11.3

Young Indonesian Muslims learning to pray. [Courtesy Indonesian Islamic Library Center, Masjid al Istiqlāl, Jakarta.]

Illustration 11.4

Courtyard, Madrasah al Sharrātīn, Salé, Morocco, 1341 C.E. [Photo by L. al Fārūqī.]

twenty-two books on grammar, among them *Kitāb al Faṣīḥ* and *Kitāb Qawā'id al Shi'r.* Abū Isḥaq al Zajjāj (311/923) wrote *Kitāb Sirr al Naḥw* in which he included an analysis of the "conjugable and non-conjugable"; he also produced a book on the human body, *Khalq al Insān,* and another on the meanings of the Qur'ān, *Ma'āni al Qur'ān.* Abūl 'Abbās Muḥammad al Mubarrad (285/898) contributed his classic work, *Al Kāmil.* Arabic grammar continued to occupy the greatest minds, and production of great works in the field continued. In the succeeding century, Ibn Khālawayh (370/980) led the discipline of parsing, which he applied systematically to thirty *suwar* of the Qur'ān, recording them in a book entitled *Parsing of the Qur'ān.* He also produced a book on the negative copulative *laysa.* 'Uthmān ibn Jinnī (392/1001), the son of a Greek slave, crowned the century with twelve illustrious works on grammar.

The next great age of grammarians was the seventh century A.H. It witnessed the work of Muḥammad ibn Mālik (672/1273), *Alfiyyat ibn Malik,* a summation of Arabic grammar in 1,000 verses of beautiful poetry, and that of Muḥammad ibn Ājarrūm (723/1323), *Al Ājarrūmiyyah,* which has remained the standard text of Arabic grammar throughout the Arab world till the present.

The Science of Lexicology

Lexicology, or the science of establishing the meanings of words, is as old as the language which it serves. The need to teach the correct diction, and to understand the correct purport of a statement, is universal. In the case of the Arabic language this need is crucial; for Arabic has a different word for each subdivision or nuance of the meaning, and for each member of a class which a word connotes. Every hour of the day, for instance, has a different name; and so does every night in the cycle of the moon. The hair on every identifiable area of the head, every shortcoming of the human eye, each has its proper term. Every action has a variety of degrees of intensity and other qualifications, each of which has a different word to designate it. To see, to sit, to stand, to walk, to eat, to drink—each has dozens of words referring to the same action generally meant by these words, but every one of the words qualifies the action in a way that ensures its special identity. Likewise, ordinary objects have numerous names which refer to the same object and yet distinguish slightly variant examples of it. Thirteen names belong to milk, thirteen to honey, twenty-one to light, twenty-four to the year, twenty-nine to the sun, fifty to various kinds of clouds, fifty-two to darkness, sixty-four to rain, eighty-eight to the well, one hundred to wine, one hundred to the serpent, one hundred and seventy to water, two hundred and fifty-five to the she-camel, three hundred and fifty to the lion. The horse, the donkey, the wild beasts, the desert, the sword, the tall man, the short man, the hero, the hospitable, the stingy, the noble — all have a great number of terms to designate them. Add to this the fact that Arabic is unique in having several hundreds of words that carry a meaning and its opposite at the same time, making usage and context determine which meaning the hearer should perceive as that intended. As if this were not enough, some words carry three or more meanings at the same time. Lexicologists have reported one hundred and fifty words with three meanings, one hundred and fifty with four, another one hundred and fifty words with five, and so on up the scale until they reach thirty-five meanings for the word *'ayn* (eye) and sixty for the word *'ajūz* (old person).

Understandably, a language such as Arabic, when it is learned by an adult, requires a lexicon. But in Arabic, because of the conjugation and foliation of words, the lexicon user must be a lexicologist, capable of breaking down a word and reducing it to its root form. Then he must find the meaning of the root, and apply the structural formal meaning to that root in order to find out the meaning of the word in question.

The advent of Islam altered the meanings of some

Map 42. Al Futūḥāt in North Africa and Europe, 11–133/632–750

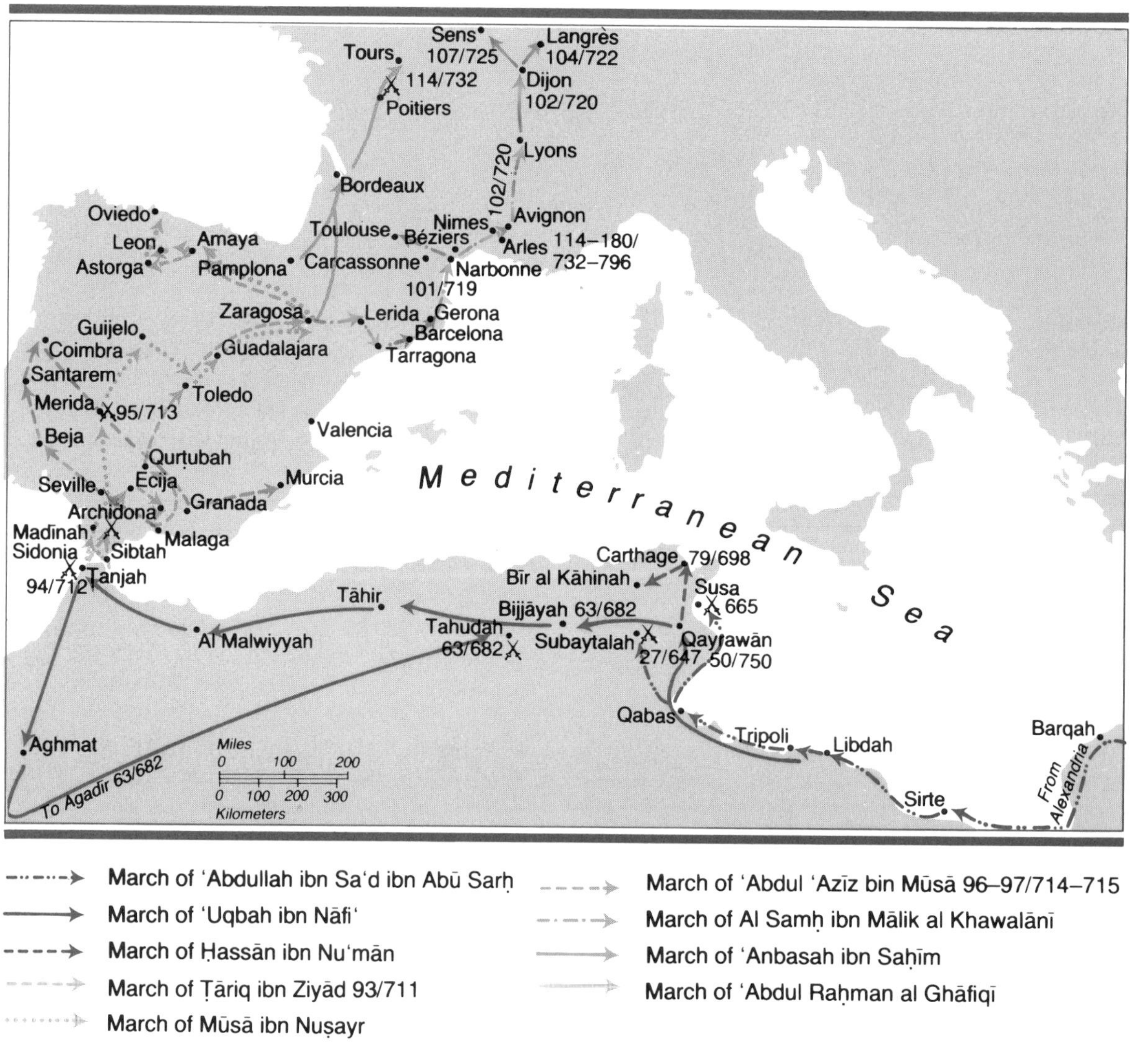

Illustration 11.5

Calligraphic carving, Quṭb Minạr, Delhi, India, 1206 C.E. [Photo by L. al Fārūqī.]

words and introduced new words with new meanings. The Qur'ānic usage determined these changes. Similarly, a number of words acquired a new juristic connotation, a liturgical connotation, a religious and ethical, political, economic, or social connotation, following the definitions of the *sharī'ah* or the requirements of Islamic personal and/or social ethics. These had to be learned by both Arabic-speaking and other Muslims. The shift from the old meanings to the new was easier to grasp by the Arabic-speaking people of the Peninsula; and it was doubly difficult for those who commanded only half-mastery of the language in the provinces adjoining the Arabian Peninsula.

In consequence of the advent of Islam and its rapid spread in the known world, a whole range of new meanings was attached to old words, or new words were "foliated" out of old roots, to refer to the requirements of the new situation. Administrative terms, economic and financial terms, military terms, diplomatic terms, and terms expressing new problems, new states, and new experiences made their way into the language and required lexicologists to establish them and regulate their use.

Al Jurjānī (816/1413) prepared the first compendium of lexicology, entitled *Al Ta'rīfāt* (Paris, 1845). He was followed by al Tahānawī (1158/1745) in his *Kashshāf Iṣṭilāḥāt al Funūn* (Calcutta, 1861). The mystics developed a lexicon of their own, and Ibn 'Arabī included one in his *Al Futūḥāt al Makkiyyah.* More important, a new methodology for writing and speaking in any science or branch of learning was developed and observed by everyone. Naturally, the methodology was first used in the exegesis of the Qur'ān. It involved the identification of, first, each word in the sentence as to its grammatical form, function, and interrelation with other parts of the sentence; second, the literal meaning of the words, that is, of their roots and of their structural forms; third, the lexicological meaning of the terms in the context of their usage; fourth, the technical meaning of the terms in relation to the science, discipline, or field of inquiry in which they fell.

By the end of the third century A.H., a huge collection of lexicological works had accumulated, making it necessary to organize them into a comprehensive dictionary of the Arabic language. The earlier attempts at producing a dictionary—Khalīl ibn Aḥmad's *Kitāb al 'Ayn,* Ibn Durayd's *Jamharah,* and al Qālī's *Al Badī'*—were incomplete. Soon a new generation of dictionaries, more complete and better organized, was produced. Muḥammad ibn Aḥmad al Azharī (370/980) wrote his *Al Tahdhīb* after a sojourn of twenty years among the tribes of central Arabia. Ṣāḥib ibn 'Abbād (385/995) produced *Al Muḥīṭ;* Aḥmad ibn Fāris (390/999) his *Al Mujmal;* Isma'īl al Jawharī (398/1007) his *Al Ṣiḥāḥ;* and 'Alī ibn Sayyidih, his *Al Muḥkam* and *Al Mukhaṣṣaṣṣ.* The last two, the former ordered alphabetically and the latter according to meaning, were the most complete and best ordered of all Arabic dictionaries for centuries to come. *Al Muḥkam* reigned over the field until Muḥammad ibn Manẓūr (711/1311) produced his *Lisān al 'Arab;* Majduddīn al Fīrūzabādī (817/1414), his *Al Qāmūs al Muḥīṭ;* and Murtaḍā al Zabīdī (1206/1791), his *Tāj al 'Arūs. Al Muḥkam* and the later three works are still widely used today, and they are regarded as the ultimate lexicological references for the Arabic language.

The academies of Arabic language of Cairo, Baghdād, Damascus, 'Ammān, Fās, and, more recently, the Arabic Language Committee of the League of Arab States, have been busy in expanding the Arabic language vocabulary to accommodate the inventions, discoveries, and products of modern science and technology. Observing the classical rules of the language, the impressive new lexicons they have produced contain new words that fill the modern needs. These were created either by conjugating existing roots, or by adopting new roots and conjugating them according to Arabic rules to obtain the desired modalities of meaning. *Al Lisān al 'Arabī* ("The Arabic Tongue"), published in Rabat, Morocco, on behalf of the League of Arab States, has so far produced over thirty volumes with several thousand new words in each.

CHAPTER 12

The Sciences of the Qur'ān

THE SCIENCE OF *QIRĀ'AH* (RECITATION)

Being the literal word of God, the Qur'ān was the object of the greatest reverence among Muslims. It continues to be so to the present day. Naturally, to recite it correctly is the first prerequisite of the man of learning as well as of the worshipper. The first discipline to develop in this regard was *'Ilm al Qirā'ah,* the science of reading or reciting the Qur'ān. The word *qāri'*(reader or reciter) is an honorific title. The Prophet had approved a number of variant recitations, according to accents and dialects of some of the tribes of Arabia, but he ruled that the standard was that of Quraysh. Consequently, a number of recitation traditions developed following the variants permitted by the Prophet. To distinguish between them, and to recite according to the Quraysh standard, was the first discipline. The traditions included the recitations of 'Abdullah ibn Kathīr (120/737), 'Āṣim ibn Abū al Nujūd (127/744), 'Abdullah ibn 'Āmir (118/736), 'Alī ibn Ḥamzah (189/804), Abū 'Amr ibn al 'Alā' (155/771), Ḥamzah ibn Ḥabīb (156/772), and Nāfi' ibn Abū Nu'aym (169/785). Their knowledge remained an oral tradition passed from teacher to pupil, generation after generation. The oldest written record came at the turn of the fourth century A.H., when Muḥammad ibn Qāsim al Anbārī (328/939) wrote his *Al Īḍāḥ fī al Waqf wal Ibtidā'.* Ibn al Ṣayrafī (444/1052) wrote *Al Taysīr fī al Qirā'āt al Sab', Jāmi' al Bayān,* and *Mufradāt al Qirā'āt,* thus establishing the oral tradition as a science. It has been alleged by the uninstructed that the seven variant recitations constitute several versions of the Qur'ān. Nothing could be farther from the truth. The "seven" are not even dialects, though some of the variations are due to dialects. They are little linguistic indulgences which the Prophet permitted in order to ease the recitation for those whose upbringing made the Qurayshī pronunciation of some words difficult.

THE SCIENCE OF *ASBĀB AL NUZŪL* (THE CONTEXTS OF REVELATION)

The second science to develop out of Qur'ānic study was *'Ilm Asbāb al Nuzūl* (the historical contexts of revelation). In learning the Qur'ān the Muslims realized that it is not possible to understand the word of God without knowledge of the time in which it was revealed, of the circumstances that brought it about, and of the real situations it had addressed. All revelation is contextual, situational. Even when revelation speaks of God and His angels and the heavenly king-

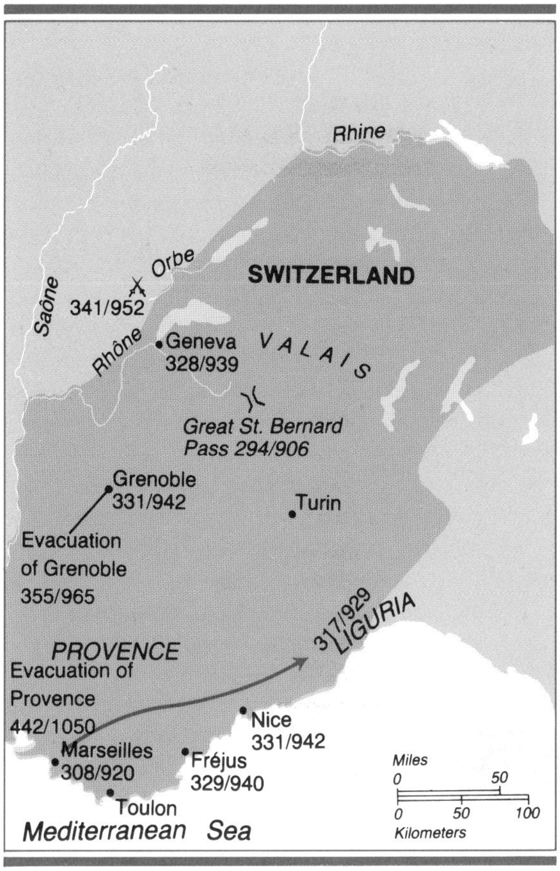

Map 43. Muslim Conquest of the Provence and Switzerland up to the Rhine, 225–294/839–906

dom, it is so that humans may recognize and acknowledge Him as their Creator and Lord. This does not make the revelation relative to history, but related to it, the relative and the relational being disparate. The absolute which is the opposite of the relative may well be relational. The Qur'ān is absolute since it is the will of God and His word; but it is relational to the world and history since it addresses the world.

The *asbāb al nuzūl,* causes or occasions of revelation, add considerably to our understanding of any verse, and for verses carrying a judgment, an imperative, or a sanction, a knowledge of them is crucial. This is an autonomous science, for which grammatical, linguistic, and lexicological analyses are necessary, but which goes beyond them. The discipline depended upon the oral tradition and applied all the known canons of critique to ascertain authenticity of the reports it received. It accepted those traditions that had been witnessed and reported by several channels. The variants were checked against one another, compared with the form aspects of the reports. Assuming their relation to the Qur'ānic verses in question, the resultant meanings obtained were compared and contrasted with similar verses and their certain contexts of revelation.

'Alī ibn Aḥmad al Wāḥidī (427/1035) was the first to collect and systematize bits of information and data scattered in numerous volumes dealing with the Qur'ān as well as other subjects, under the title *Asbāb al Nuzūl.* The same title was used by Jalāluddīn al Suyūṭī (911/1505) for his work to which he prefixed the words *"Lubāb al Nuqūl."* The expanded title alerted the reader that the work was only a selection from the available data. Ibrahīm al Ja'barī (732/1331) and Ibn Ḥajar al 'Asqalānī (852/1448) wrote books on *asbāb al nuzūl.* The greatest amount of pertinent materials, however, was included in the books of exegesis. Despite this fact, the contexts of revelation remained an autonomous science distinct from exegesis.

THE SCIENCE OF MAKKĪ AND MADĪNĪ (HISTORICAL CRITICISM)

The third science to develop from study of the Qur'ān was *'Ilm al Makkī wal Madīnī* (knowledge of the locus of revelation—Makkah or Madīnah). Like the contexts of revelation, the study of the locus of revelation may be subsumed under exegesis. Most of the pertinent materials were included in the exegetical works. However, the study is independent and autonomous, because it deals with historical materials different from those of the science of *asbāb al nuzūl.* The latter takes into consideration the particular historical materials in the individuals and their interrelationships, and the events, deeds, and circumstances that constitute the real matrix of the specific verse or verses in question. These, however, are not the only historical materials relevant for a correct understanding of revelation. The Makkī and Madīnī science was developed in order to answer three different inquiries.

First, granted that the verse or verses in question refer to this or that person and to this or that deed or event, the revelation of the verse or verses so related was meant as an address to the Makkans, that is, to the non-Muslims. This address provided a wider context, a background to which the revelation could be related. Why did God choose that particular person or deed? To what use was the particular event put by such revelation? What were the divine purposes behind such utilization? How were those purposes related to the general situation of the Makkans? Evidently, if the addressees of revelation were the

Muslims and not the non-Muslin Makkans, a different set of meanings might be perceived in them. Perhaps better than any other, this Qur'ānic science arouses the scholar's historical sense and prompts him to raise the most far-reaching questions of historical criticism. For the Makkah – Madīnah bifurcation is not merely geographical. It is equally — and we might even say, uppermost — chronological or historical. Second, raising the question of Makkah – Madīnah is necessarily to look at Islam as a movement in history and to question our perception of it as falling in stages, in different places and times, and in varying degrees of development within the last twenty-two or twenty-three years of the Prophet's life. The relevance of such historical knowledge of Islam as a movement goes far beyond the knowledge of who the addressees were. In the broad steps of a great movement, even the addressees as a group might be a context for an address directed at humankind in general. This may and may not include the Makkans or Madīnans, but it must surely pertain to the state of religion and culture during that portion of the lifetime of the Prophet. There are many verses of the Qur'ān which scholars have affirmed to be either Makkan or Madīnan, but which actually speak to neither. The only way to identify those verses is to ask the geographical and chronological question, whether the revelation was Makkan or Madīnan.

Illustration 12.1

Copper niello platter with calligraphy and arabesque patterning, contemporary Egyptian craftsmanship. Clockwise, beginning at 9 o'clock position, are eight exclamations to God: "Oh Just One; Oh Judge; Oh Great Glorious; Oh Merciful; Oh Beneficent; Oh Most High; Oh Rich One [Oh] Lord; Oh Guardian," surrounding a central "Action [good deeds] is obligatory." [Photo by L. al Fārūqī.]

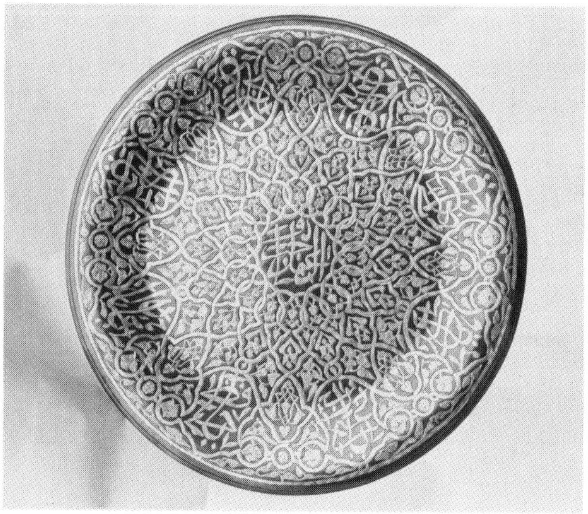

Some verses were revealed neither in geographic Makkah nor in Madīnah. This class includes verses revealed in Jerusalem, Ṭā'if, Ḥudaybiyah, and Juḥfah. When Makkah and Madīnah are taken chronologically, scholars try to establish whether the revelation took place during the day or the night, whether the Prophet was alone or in company of others. In fact, Muslim scholars gave full vent to their imagination, raising all sorts of detailed questions and seeking critical answers to them. Was the Prophet in a tent, in a house, or in the open? Was he stationary or in motion? What activity engaged him at that time? If the revelation took place when he was in company, who were the companions and what brought them together with the Prophet? Even the weather at the time of the revelation was an object of inquiry. Its relevance to some verses is a matter of fact.

Third, while geographically speaking some verses were certainly revealed in Madīnah, they addressed or were meant for the Makkans. Other verses were certainly revealed in Makkah, but they were meant for a projected society of Muslims, and hence to a would-be Madīnah. Respectively, these were designated by the scholars as Madīnan with Makkan status *(Madīniyyah ḥukmuhā Makkiyyah)* or Makkan with Madīnan status *(Makkiyyah ḥukmuhā Madīniyyah).* So too, there were verses that addressed neither the Makkans nor the Madīnans but the Christians and Jews, the "People of the Book." Their assignment to Makkah or Madīnah may have a geographical or chronological significance. But its real import may be elsewhere, in the fact that they were addressed to the People of the Book everywhere. Still others went beyond any Makkan, Madīnan, or People-of-the-Book reference. They were addressed to mankind and they touched upon universal human themes and problems.

A proper understanding of the Qur'ān requires the raising of the question Makkan or Madīnan for it is the spearpoint of historical questioning of a higher order. Raising and seeking to answer all these questions constituted an enterprise which Islam blessed, thus enabling it to gather its materials and blossom forth as a science. Historical criticism was never a science before the Muslims undertook this enterprise; and none has been as critically managed. Complemented with the sciences of language, it performed its task with thorough-going scholarship. The effort was prompted by a sophisticated and fastidious historical sense which Islam instilled in its adherents by teaching them that the truth is critically, rationally knowable; that Islam has no esoteric secrets and nothing to hide; that it does not fear a total and complete disclosure of all that pertains to it. For it is neither mythical nor dogmatic, neither particularist nor gnoseological. The Qur'ānic scholars were perfectly aware of the relatedness of their revelation to desert, village, and city; to Arabs and non-Arabs, Muslims and non-Muslims; to Christians and Jews and others. Their work on the Makkan and Madīnan question was their best exercise in historical criticism. The description of al Ḥasan ibn Ḥabīb al Naysābūrī is certainly true: "Knowledge of the advent and place of revelation, and ordering the revelations as belonging to an early, middle, late or conclusive period constitutes one of the noblest sciences."[1]

THE SCIENCES OF *TAFSĪR* (EXEGESIS)

Exegesis through Tradition *(Bil-ma'thūr)*

In a general sense, the Muslims regard the *sunnah* as a clarification or exegesis of the Qur'ān. This was the purport of Chapter 6, in which the *sunnah* was treated as a form of the essence of Islam. Since the Qur'ān is that essence stated in discursive propositions for better understanding, it follows that what clarifies and amplifies that essence, what exemplifies and concretizes it, fulfills the same function for the Qur'ān. Besides this general sense, the *sunnah* contains specific materials pertaining to specific Qur'ānic verses for the purpose of exegesis. Being the first and highest authority for understanding the Qur'ān, the Prophet made numerous statements explaining the contents of Qur'ānic verses in response to the inquiries of his companions. Nobody dared to explain the Qur'ān during the lifetime of the Prophet. His ready availability to perform this function obviated the need.

No one could better qualify for the task than the Prophet. Naturally, he knew best the situation to which the Qur'ān spoke, and the meaning of what it said. Unless the revelation was absolutely clear and immediately understood by the people it addressed, it was natural for somebody to ask for an interpretation, as well as for the Prophet to oblige. The Prophet's interpreting words were kept in mind to be passed to others who did not witness the revelation. Also, if the revelation was immediately comprehensible to the people present and witnessing the occasion, it may not have been so for the absent. When the revelation was brought by the companions to those removed from it, it was natural for the reporters to give a clarifying description or analysis in order to show its relevance. Likewise, after the Prophet had died, and the revelation was taught to the millions near to and far from the scene, the companions volunteered an explanation or gave it upon request in order to facilitate comprehension and observance. It is also natural that the need and demand for clarification of the revelation would increase in direct proportion to four factors: geographical distance from Makkah and Madīnah; time distance from the life of the Prophet;

Illustration 12.2

Bāb al Mardūn Mosque, Toledo, Spain, 999 C.E. The mosque was later converted into a church. [Photo by L. al Fārūqī.]

Illustration 12.3

Bāb al Mardūn Mosque, entrance. [Photo by L. al Fārūqī.]

direct involvement with the Prophet's activities and/or the progress of the Islamic movement; and linguistic distance from the Arabic language and the dialect of Quraysh. Clarifications must have numbered in the thousands. They were memorized and circulated at their time and passed to the second, third, and fourth generations of Muslims. Dependence upon them created the first school of exegesis named after the process that created it, *Tafsīr bil Ma'thūr,* or Exegesis through Tradition.

Some companions were more disposed than others to rendering the service of exegesis, and some excelled. As to the quantity and quality of their reports, Muslim scholars regard the following ten as outstanding: the four Rāshidūn caliphs (Abū Bakr, 'Umar, 'Uthmān, and 'Alī), Ibn Mas'ūd, Ibn 'Abbās, Ubayy ibn Ka'b, Zayd ibn Thābit, Abū Mūsā al Ash'arī, and 'Abdullah ibn al Zubayr. Among these, Ibn Mas'ūd stands out as the ablest companion, since his exegesis was repeatedly approved by the Prophet; the Prophet had called him "the exegete of the Qur'ān" and prayed that Allah might increase and guide him in this pursuit. The next class of companions involved with exegesis included Abū Hurayrah, Anas ibn Mālik, 'Abdullah ibn 'Umar, Jābir ibn 'Abdullah, and 'Ā'ishah, the Prophet's wife. The companions constituted the first *ṭabaqah* or class or generation of exegetes, the next generations constituting the second and third *ṭabaqāt.* Exegetes were also divided according to their place of activity. The scholars recognize four schools: those of Makkah, Madīnah, Baṣrah, and Kūfah. Ibn Taymiyah, among others, preferred the Makkan school on the ground that Ibn 'Abbās, Mujāhid, 'Aṭā' ibn Abū Riyāḥ, 'Ikrimah, Sa'īd ibn Jubayr, and Ṭāwūs belonged to it. Others preferred the school of Kūfah on account of its association with Ibn Mas'ūd; or that of Madīnah because of its association with Zayd ibn Aslam, whose son 'Abdul Raḥman ibn Zayd was the teacher of Mālik ibn Anas, the founder of the Mālikī school of law and author of one of the earliest records of *ḥadīth.*

Among the third generation of exegetes, the following stand out: Sufyān ibn 'Uyaynah, Wakī' ibn al Jarrāḥ, Shu'bah ibn al Ḥajjāj, Yazīd ibn Hārūn, and 'Abd ibn Ḥamīd. These were the authorities from whom the greatest work of "Exegesis through Tradition" drew, *Jāmi' al Bayān fī Tafsīr al Qur'ān* by Ibn Jarīr al Ṭabarī (310/922). Of equal importance—and greater clarity—is *Tafsīr al Qur'ān al 'Aẓīm* of 'Imād al Dīn ibn Kathīr (774/1372). Next in importance come the following works: *Al Durr al Manthūr fī al Tafsīr bil Ma'thūr* of Jalāluddīn al Suyūṭī (911/1505); *Baḥr al 'Ulūm* of Naṣr ibn Muḥammad al Samarqandī (375/985); *Ma'ālim al Tanzīl* of Ḥusayn ibn Mas'ūd al Baghwī (516/1122); and *Al Muḥarrar al Wajīz* of 'Abdul Ḥaqq ibn 'Aṭiyyah (546/1151).

Exegesis through Reason *(Bil-Ra'y)*

Claiming itself to be the religion of reason and common sense, whose disciplines honor the critical use of human faculties of intellection, Islam consistently opened the gates for those inclined to let the Qur'ān speak for itself as to the meanings it intended to convey. Exegesis of the Qur'ān by the Qur'ān, wherever it is possible, must take precedence over tradition. This is the first criterion. Second, the traditions were so numerous and varied, coming from different persons, places, times, and schools, that a higher criterion was necessary to reconcile their differences or to detect and discard the inapplicable. Such higher criterion must be the coherent understanding of reason. Surely, it must be disciplined by language and history and must take due account of all that linguistic, formal, and historical criticism have to offer. But ultimate judgment must belong to reason in light of the message of Islam as a whole. Third, exegesis must fill the need for doctrinal understanding, for juristic deduction of laws or for extrapolation of prescriptions for action. Such processes must assume and be founded upon a critical understanding of the underlying concepts and precepts of the revelation, which is impossible without reason.

For these reasons, another school of exegesis developed in addition to that which relied on tradition—the school of *al Ra'y* (reason). Its foremost promoters were those concerned with the elaboration of laws. Next to them stood the teachers of Islam entrusted with presentation of the faith to the non-Muslims and defending it against their attacks. These tasks fell upon the companions and their descendants generally. But with the diversification and multiplication of the issues, specialization emerged. The first task became the province of the jurists; the second, that of the Mu'tazilah, the first dialecticians of Islam. The productions of both were absolutely necessary. The brilliant successes of Islam in its early history, whether in the field of guiding action and solving practical problems or in converting the masses of the continents by the millions, are standing monuments to its viability and common sense, to the reasonableness and healthy-mindedness of its call.

Obviously, exegesis by reason could not be permitted to proceed without criteria to govern its application. In order to prevent the Qur'ān from being taken beyond its real intention, Islamic scholarship identified a number of prerequisites for the exegete. First, he must be an accomplished linguist, perfectly at home with the Arabic language, especially with its usage among the Arabs who were the contemporaries of revelation. Second, he must have unquestionable mastery of the message of Islam, of its essence and thrust in the history of religion and revelation, so that his exegesis may stand coherent with Islam as the final crystallization of prophecy. Third, the exegete must have an understanding capable of perceiving meanings, abstracting relations, and generalizing principles resident in the various passages of the revelation. This is the capacity to organize and order ideas, to discover their order of rank and relations, and to present to the consciousness the most coherent arrangement. Fourth, he must take into consideration the reports of tradition stemming from the Prophet and his companions. But he must be able to distinguish between the genuine and the spurious, as well as between the differing degrees of validity that the true traditions often represent.

The foremost works of exegesis through reason are: *Al Kashshāf 'an Ḥaqā'iq al Ta'wīl* of Maḥmūd al Zamakhsharī (538/1143); *Mafātīḥ al Ghayb* of Fakhr

Map 44. Al Futūḥāt in West Africa to 700/1300

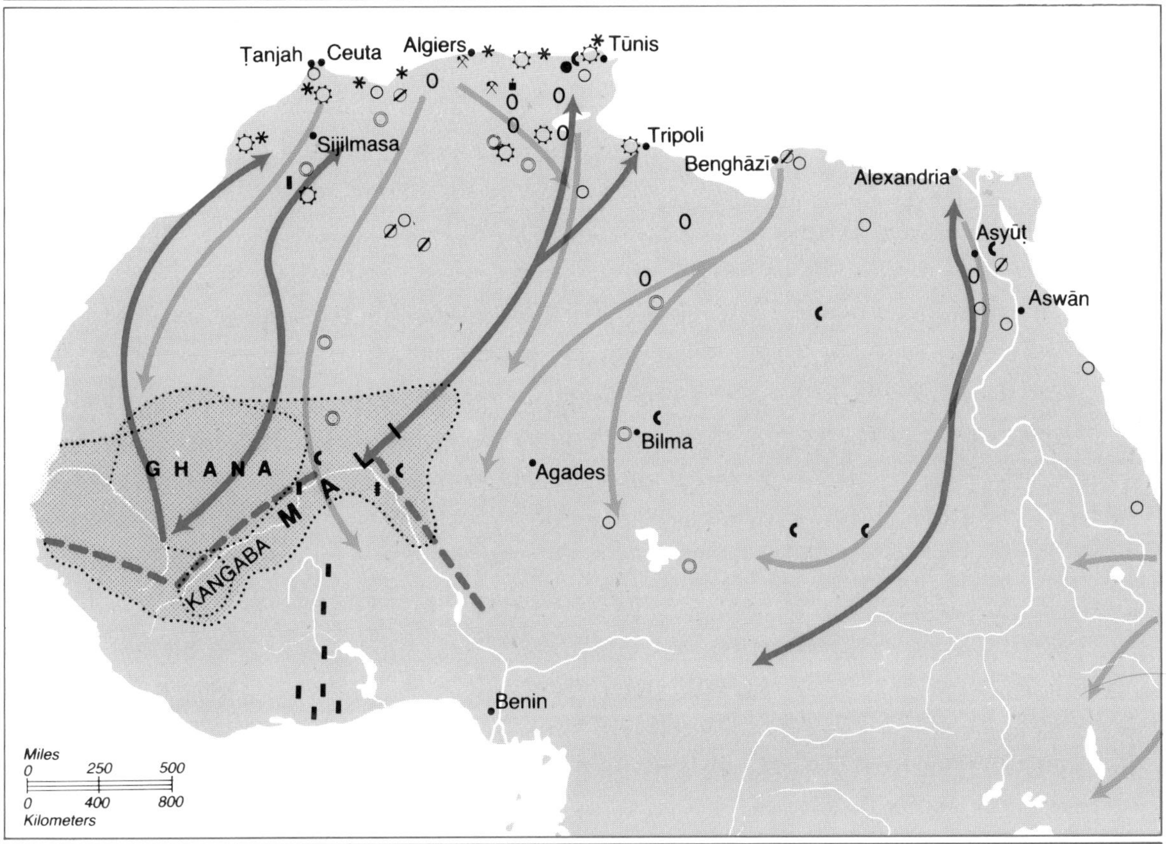

Routes of penetration of Islam

Trans-Saharan trade routes

River routes

Earliest centers of Islamic activity

Commodities produced and traded:

Gold	● Copper	▪ Lead	⚒ Iron ore	✳ Olives
○ Fruits / Foodstuffs	⟨ Ivory	✿ Cotton	⊘ Wool
○ Hides	▮ Naphtha & Bitumen	0 Dates

Illustration 12.4

Calligraphic design by Emin Berin, Turkey. "Allah" in the center with repetitive border chain of "Muḥammad." [Photo by L. al Fārūqī.]

al Dīn al Rāzī (606/1209); *Anwār al Tanzīl* of 'Abdullah al Bayḍāwī (691/1191); and *Madārik al Tanzīl* of 'Abdullah al Nasafī (701/1301).

A variety of exegetical works on the Qur'ān sought to interpret the revelation from a preconceived view of an author or a school. Such were the exegeses of the Mu'tazilah, the Ṣūfīs, the Shī'ah and their sects, and the modernists. Although all of them may claim to fall under the category of exegesis through reason since each has its own rationalization for following its school, the fact that each is sectarian, or that it interprets according to one view, brands it as an illegitimate application of exegesis through reason. No dogmatic observance of any view is true to reason. Rational exegesis is, above all, critical and open. It accepts evidence wherever it may come from and wherever it may lead. It never prejudges. It cannot therefore have any loyalty to a school, except to the anonymous school of reason and truth. The value of these works lies therefore not in their consistent presentation or defense of their sectarian views but in their demonstration of the wealth of facets of meanings which the verses of the Qur'ān often carry, those which escape ordinary observation.

THE SCIENCE OF *ISTINBĀṬ AL AḤKĀM* (EXTRACTION OF LAW)

Islam recognized the Qur'ān as the first source of Islamic law; and Muslims have always understood it as the commanding, imperative will of God. What the Qur'ān describes as desirable and good is so; and what it describes as undesirable and evil is so. However, Muslims have recognized the imperatives and desiderata of the Qur'ān as falling into different orders of rank or priority. Although they all belong to the divine will and are constitutive of it, Qur'ānic values do not all enjoy the same degree of normativeness. Some are more fundamental and important than others. Some are direct and specific in what they demand of man; some are indirect, pointing to general directions. Some are explicit and comprehensible on first reading; others are implicit and have to be deduced from one or more Qur'ānic premises. The Qur'ān was revealed so that it may be a guide. Anxious to order their lives in accordance with its model, the Muslims applied themselves to the task of eliciting from its text the imperatives and prescriptions which they can observe. It was hence necessary to elaborate a system of principles or rules by which imperatives may be reached, a methodology for translation of the Qur'ānic texts into laws for application, or practical precepts for the guidance of the people.

Juristic Categorization

The Qur'ān has been analyzed by the jurists for their own purposes, and the relevant parts of it have been divided into the following categories: (1) doctrine or first principles; (2) religious obligations; (3) ethical imperatives; and (4) laws in the strict sense of rights and obligations. All of these categories were regarded as relevant to the *sharī'ah* which was assumed to be reforming of all aspects of human life. The relevance of Qur'ānic laws is obvious enough. That of the others is built upon the fact that the Qur'ān contains general rules for behavior as well as for rendering justice. It is the juristic base that makes all other sources of Islamic law—the *sunnah, qiyās* (extrapolated laws), *ijtihād* (creative interpretation), *ijmā'* (consensus), *'urf* (custom), and *maṣlaḥah* (commonweal)—legitimate.

On the other hand, jurists divided the Qur'ānic laws (in the strict sense of rights and obligations) into three main divisions: (1) the laws that define the Muslim and his faith; (2) those that govern ethics or morality; and (3) the practical laws that govern human action and interhuman relations directly and immediately. The last category was divided into ritualistic and nonritualistic laws. The nonritualistic laws comprised the following subdivisions: (1) personal status (marriage, divorce, legitimacy, inheritance, dependence, etcetera); (2) civil laws, economic laws (financial, commercial, industrial); (3) criminal laws; (4) constitutional laws; (5) international laws; and (6) laws of juristic procedure. As to the legal evidence that the Qur'ānic provisions furnish in legal processes, Muslim scholars distinguished between categoric or terminal evidence *(qaṭ'ī)* and likely or supporting evidence *(ẓannī).*

Immediate and Mediate Meanings (*Al Manṭūq* and *al Mafhūm/Al Lafẓ* and *al Ma'nā*)

The immediate meaning is defined as that which the understanding apprehends upon presentation of the term. Some terms in the language are susceptible to one interpretation only. They carry a meaning associated with them and commonly known to all. No additional statement is necessary to identify or clarify the meaning. Such, for instance, are the verses commanding the performance of a certain thing in specific quantities. Scholars have also distinguished two subcategories of immediate meanings: first, those whose meaning is specifically given in the pronunciation of the term; second, those whose pronunciation confirms the meaning intended above all others, either by itself or by its place in the sentence.

The mediate meaning is defined as that which the understanding learns from a factor other than the presentation of the term. Its apprehension implies some intellection besides sensing with the ear or the eye. Mediate meaning may be confirmed by presentation of the term, or it may differ from it. Jalāluddīn al Suyūṭī confirmed this distinction and assigned the title *faḥwā al khiṭāb* (the content of communication) to the first kind, and *laḥn al khiṭāb* (the reference of communication) to the second, on the basis of presence and absence of equivalence between them. The former are simple, and their understanding is easy because of the equivalence of the meaning proclaimed in the pronunciation and the meaning understood by intellection. The latter, however, are the more complex, because many factors may contribute to their disparity with the presentational meanings of their terms. Qur'ānic scholarship recognized three kinds of disparity: that which is due to qualification by an adjective; that which is due to qualification by condition or hypothesis; that which is due to qualification by exclusion. In the first kind, scholars distinguish three kinds of adjectival qualifications due to the intrinsic state of a thing, its number or quantity, and its circumstance or condition.

While keeping all these distinctions separate and applying them to the understanding of any Qur'ānic passage, Islamic scholarship has devised rules for extraction of law in any category and has assigned to each extraction a place on the scale of validity. For example, from Qur'ān 2:223, which says "upon the father falls [the burden of] the mother's sustenance and clothing," jurists have extracted two laws: dependence *(nafaqah)* and descendance *(nasab).* The first meaning is immediately clear upon presentation; for one could not hear these words and understand something other than dependence, or the obligation upon the father to support the mother. The second is arrived at through a mediate understanding, passing from the relation of the newborn to the obligation of the father to support the infant and mother, to the public acknowledgment that the newborn is indeed his own progeny. Evidently, the former kind of evidence

Illustration 12.5

Glass jar, nineteenth century, Turkish and Islamic Art Museum, Isṭanbūl. [Photo by L. al Fārūqī.]

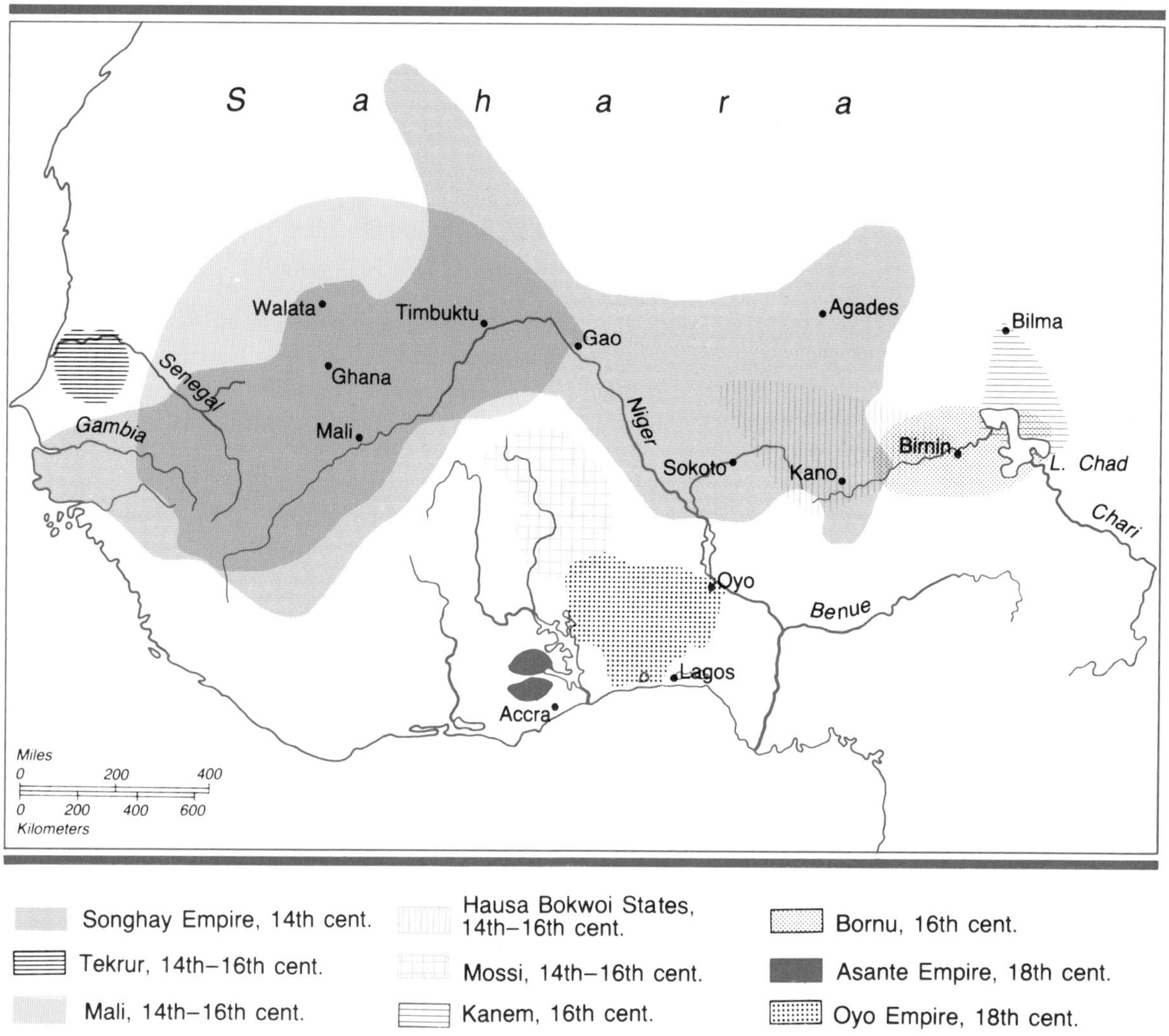

Map 45. Al Futūḥāt in West Africa, 7th-12th/14th-18th centuries

is stronger than the latter and carries a higher degree of validity.

Another species of mediate meanings is that which is understood from the sentence as a whole or from the compositional context which may include more than the sentence in question. Islamic scholarship has devised rules for understanding these meanings, for deriving laws from them, and for settling contention by differing jurists applying these rules.

The General and the Particular

Perhaps the most complex issue in the matter extraction of laws from statements composed as codal propositions is the matter of determining the extent of application of what is commanded or desired to be done. The issue is intimately connected with formal logic, which is in turn imbedded in the Arabic language and is expressible only in its terms. That is partly the reason why the ***uṣūliyyūn*** (philosophers of law) rejected Aristotelian logic and had to develop their own in order to govern lawmaking. Islamic scholarship called "general" *(ʿām)* the term that comprehends a plurality, and distinguished two varieties of it—generality in the term itself, and generality in the meanings to which the term may refer. It called particular *(khāṣṣ)* the term that comprehends only one object, and distinguished three varieties of it—the particularity of a genus, of a species, or of a single being. The jurists expanded and added to these distinctions a tremendous amount of detail, all to the end of specifying the applicability of a legal injunction. They divided themselves into generalists (advocating the priority of the general term), particularists (advocating that of the particular term), and the medianists (refusing to incline to one or the other without additional evidence).

The particularists held strongly to the view that the law derived from the general term must apply to the minimum required to maintain the truthfulness of the term. Extension of the law beyond that minimum requires ad hoc evidence. In the absence of such evidence, the applicability of the law is questionable, and in Islam no law is valid when its evidence or base is in doubt. The generalists held that the law derived from the general term must apply to all the members denoted by that term since comprehensiveness follows analytically from the general term. What requires special evidence is, rather, the restriction of the law to some members. However, the generalists disagreed among themselves as to the nature of the evidence for comprehensiveness, whether it was categorical or whether it admitted of qualification and exception, with serious consequences for the applicability of the laws. The medianists *(al wāqifiyyah),* for their part, refused to go either way, thus casting doubt upon what the others had taken as analytically, and hence necessarily, implied in the terms in questions. The discussions of the jurists led them to assign differing degrees of validity to the laws, and thus to make justice all the more certain. They classified the particular, wherever it served as base for law, as highest in validity, the more so the more specific the particularism of its foundation. They equated its validity to that of the general in the absence of any express exclusion, bearing in mind the time factor in revelation. The general followed by the particular was weaker than the particular followed by the universal.

Command and Prohibition

The same variety of distinctions and categories has affected the commands and prohibitions of the Qur'ān as to their obligatoriness. Obviously, there are gradations that affect any command or prohibition. Above all, it was necessary to define the good as object of enjoinment and evil as object of prohibition. The relation of ethical terms to law was fully analyzed and all the possible positions were defined and their consequences identified. It is in these discussions that one meets Islam's axiology or theory of value, as well as its deontology, or theory of morality. Islamic jurisprudence has known schools that regarded goodness and evil as intrinsic to objects (al Mu'tazilah, Abū Ḥanīfah) and others that regarded them as functions of the law (al Ash'arī, Ahl al Ḥadīth). Distinctions were made as to the nature of good and evil, whether the obligation was for one or repeated observance, for immediate or protracted execution, and whether any command implied the doing or not-doing of its opposite. In this connection, Muslim scholars have distinguished acts as voluntary *(ikhtiyārī),* involuntary *(muwallad),* and a whole spectrum of categories between these two poles. They have distinguished between the obligatory *(wājib)* and the prohibited *(ḥarām),* placing

Illustration 12.6

Goblet with geometric and Naskhī calligraphy decoration, enameled glass, Syria, 1200 C.E. [Courtesy Continental Oil Co.]

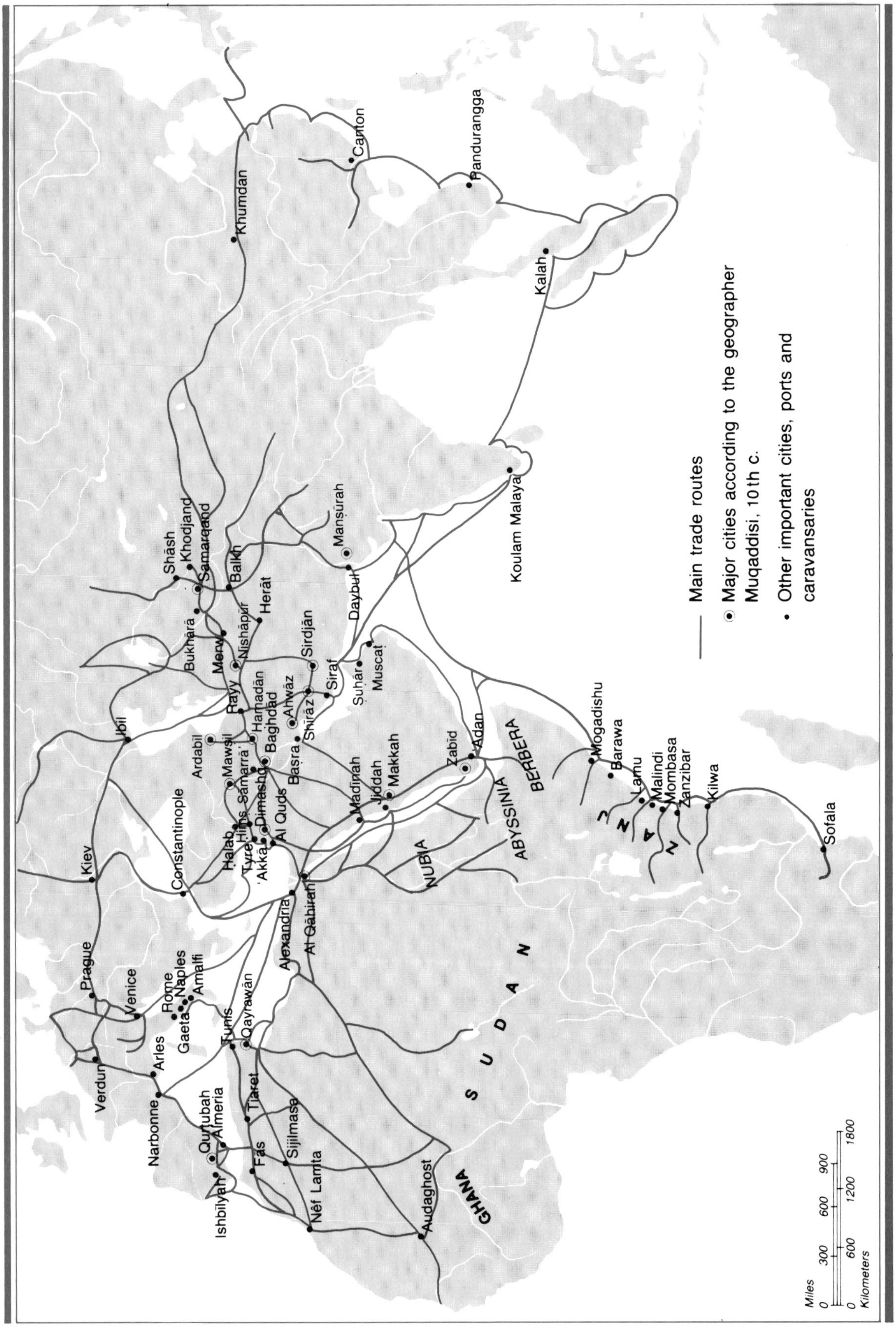

Map 46. Trade Routes of the Muslim World, 4th–10th centuries

between these poles the recommended *(mandūb),* the neutral or permissible *(mubāḥ),* and the recommended against *(makrūh).* They have also elaborated rules to govern the interrelations of all these categories. The problem of the relation of good and evil to law was moved toward solution by distinguishing between intrinsic and instrumental goodness, between the object-in-itself and the object-*in-percipi,* and between commands and prohibitions involving rewards or sanctions and those that do not. Good and evil were rationally perceptible in objects; and the *sharī'ah* was rationally discoverable as well, for it was capable of justifying itself on the basis of its beneficence for humanity. Between the given of reason and the given of revelation, there is hence an equivalence that rules out any ultimate discrepancy. This is complemented by the principle that there can be no sanction or punishment without a law grounded in text, though there can be blame or praise without such a law. The *sharī'ah* instituted the former in the *ḥudūd* (capital crimes with specific sanctions) and the *ta'āzīr* (lesser crimes punishable at the discretion of a judge). The same was true of the rights and obligations that issue from good and evil regardless of their agreement or disagreement with the *sharī'ah.*

The science that studies the methods and rules of extracting law from the text of the Qur'ān is the domain of *uṣūl al fiqh.* The *uṣūlīs* produced a legacy of tremendous proportion and importance. And it may be said that this is unique to Islam since in no other religion or culture was the discipline of methodology of law derivation as well developed. The science began as an oral tradition from the days of the Prophet's companions. Al Shāf'ī gave it its first text in the *Risālah.* Subsequently Muslim scholars produced a deluge of works. Of these, we can only mention the greatest classics in chronological order.

1. *Uṣūl al Fiqh,* by 'Ubaydullah al Karkhī (340/951)
2. *Al Fuṣūl fī al Uṣūl,* by Aḥmad al Rāzī al Jaṣṣāṣṣ (370/980)
3. *Al Taqrīb min Uṣūl al Fiqh,* by Muḥammad al Bāqillānī (403/1012)
4. *Al Ikhtilāf fī Uṣūl al Fiqh,* by al Qāḍī 'Abdul Jabbār (415/1024)
5. *Taqwīm al Adillah fī al Uṣūl,* by 'Ubaydullah al Dabbūsī (430/1038)
6. *Al Iḥkām fī Uṣūl al Aḥkām,* by 'Alī ibn Ḥazm (456/1063)
7. *Al Mu'tamad fī Uṣūl al Fiqh,* by Muḥammad ibn 'Alī al Baṣrī (463/1070)
8. *Al Burhān fī Uṣūl al Fiqh,* by 'Abdul Malik al Juwaynī (478/1085)
9. *Uṣūl al Fiqh,* by 'Alī Muḥammad al Bayḍāwī (482/1089)
10. *Uṣūl al Fiqh,* by Muḥammad Aḥmad al Sarakhsī (490/1096)
11. *Al Mustaṣfā min 'Ilm al Uṣūl,* by Abū Ḥāmid al Ghazālī (505/1111)
12. *Al Maḥṣūl fī Uṣūl al Fiqh,* by Fakhruddīn al Rāzī (606/1209)
13. *Al Iḥkām fī Uṣūl al Aḥkām,* by Sayfuddīn al Āmidī (631/1233)
14. *Al Muwāfaqāt fī Uṣūl al Fiqh,* by Ibrahīm al Shāṭibī (790/1388)

I'jāz al Qur'ān

We should not omit to mention here that the knowledge of the aspects of *i'jāz* (sublime nature) of the Qur'ān was regarded as one of the principal Qur'ānic sciences. The literary analysis of the Qur'ānic text was certainly an autonomous science which required the highest degree of linguistic competence and literary knowledge. (See Chapter 5 for details of Qur'ānic *i'jāz.*)

NOTE

1. 'Alī ibn Aḥmad al Wāḥidī al Naysābūrī (468/1075), *Asbāb al Nuzūl* (Beirut: Dār al Kutub al 'Ilmiyyah, 1400/1980), p. 4.

CHAPTER 13

The Sciences of the Ḥadīth

THE *SUNNAH* AS SECOND SOURCE OF ISLAM

We have seen that the *sunnah* of the Prophet Muḥammad—his actions, sayings, judgments, and attitudes—constitute the exemplification of the message of Islam. And we have seen that the *sunnah* consisted of oral reports which the companions of the Prophet passed to the second generation of Muslims, and these to the third and fourth. Some of this information was written down from the very beginning, by some of the companions; but the bulk of it was retained in practices which the whole *ummah* observed (as in the rituals) and in reports committed to memory. The *sunnah* received its normativeness from the Qur'ān. By direct Qur'ānic command, all Muslims stand obliged to obey the Prophet, to honor his word, and to follow his example. Indeed, the *sunnah* made specific the general imperatives of the Qur'ān. It provided explanation and clarification of the purposes of revelation.

Naturally, a source of Islam as authoritative as the *sunnah* deserved all the attention Muslims could give to it. Like the Qur'ān, the *sunnah* covers almost every subject, and its coverage ranges from the most abstract and general to the most concrete and particular. Naturally, the Muslims looked to it to answer their own inquiries concerning religion, morality, trade, contracts, crimes, the state, and so on. The more problems they faced, and the more varied these problems were, the more they looked to the *sunnah* for the answer or for directions leading to the answers. As the need for the *sunnah* increased, and as the number of people experiencing this need increased, the verbal reports of the *sunnah* proliferated. The more they proliferated, the more apt were its reporters to fall into error in their reporting, and its audience in their hearing and understanding of its materials. Even with the best of intentions, it was not possible to save the *sunnah* from incorporating materials extraneous to it. It did not have a character and style uniquely its own; it was not *mu'jiz* (miraculous and inimitable) like the Qur'ān; nor was it ordered by the Prophet to be memorized and transmitted literally like the Qur'ān.

As long as the Prophet was alive, it was possible to turn to him for explanation and information, or to check on any reports received about him. After his death, this was no longer possible. His departure was itself occasion for the followers to expand the *sunnah* in good conscience. As to those who willed such expansion in bad conscience (and no tradition is entirely free of them), they could do so after the Prophet's death with impunity until the tools were developed by which it became possible to test and evaluate the reports of the *sunnah*. To these instrumental sciences we shall now turn.

The Science of *Riwāyah* (Reportage)

The sciences of the *ḥadīth* are divided into two main groups. One group, with a membership of one, is the science of *riwāyah*, or reportage. It consists of learning the texts of the *ḥadīth* and the chains of reporters, of classifying them in some way in order to make them more easily retrievable. *Riwāyah* is the capacity to recall and report upon demand any *ḥadīth* for which the situation asks. It is a positive discipline, carrying by itself no critical apparatus. *Riwāyah* is a discipline peculiar to the Arabs, and they have cultivated it to the point of making it an autonomous science. Before Islam, their innate inclination and capacity for *riwāyah* concentrated on poetry, descendance and lineage of humans and animals, proverbs and common sayings, orations and proclamations of the *kuhhān* (sing. *kāhin*, oracular priest). After the birth of Islam, they added to these materials the Qur'ān and the *ḥadīth* of the Prophet and his companions. The second group of sciences is called *dirāyah;* it includes all disciplines concerned with the knowledge of a *ḥadīth*'s validity and all that pertains to authentication of oral traditions. It comprises the six disciplines which will now be introduced.

The Science of *Rijāl Al Ḥadīth* (Biography)

The discipline seeks to establish the full biographies of the *ḥadīth* reporters. Thanks to the concern of Muslim scholars for the *sunnah*, biography became

Map 47. The Tatar Holocaust

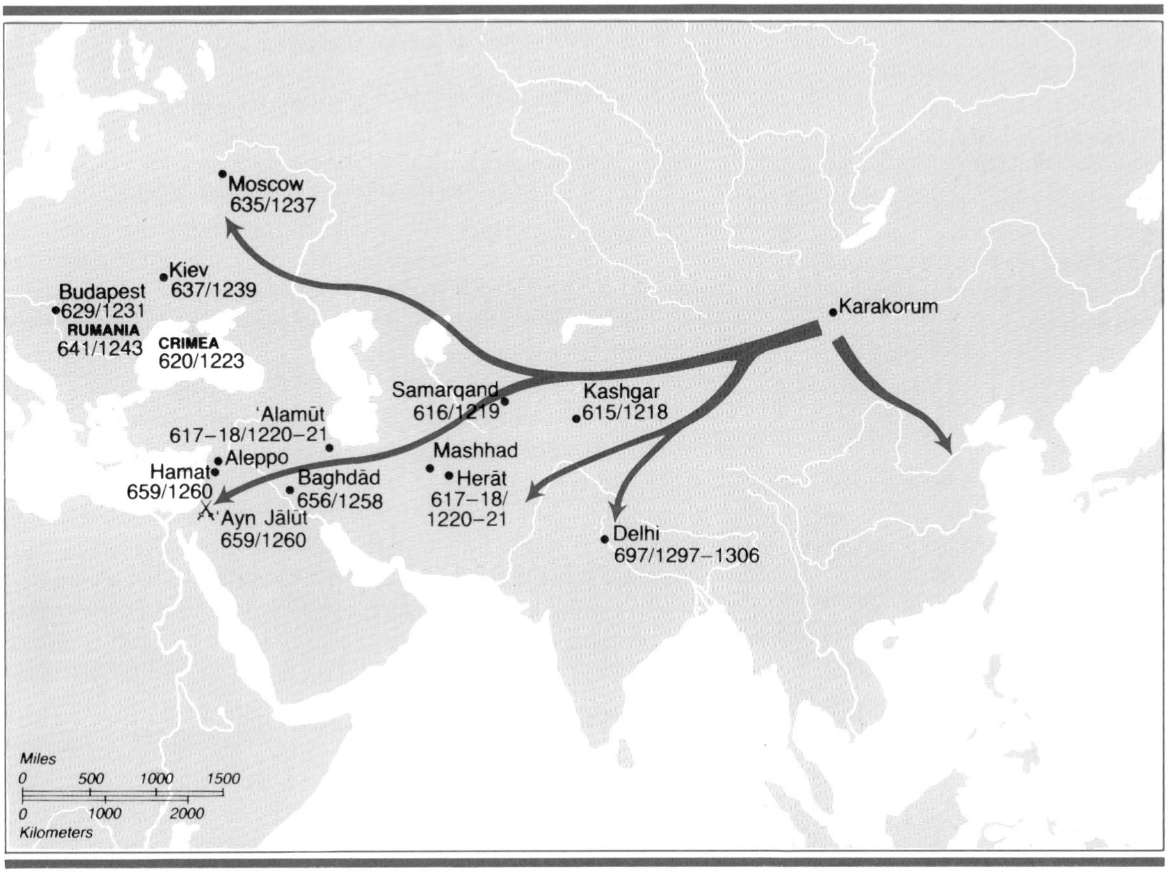

Advance of Tatars (under Genghis Khan and Hulagu)

659/1260 Date of fall into Tartar hands

Illustration 13.1

Badshahi Mosque, Lahore, Pakistan. Built by Mughal ruler Aurangzeb, 1674 C.E. [Photo by L. al Fārūqī.]

Illustration 13.2

Contemporary calligraphy design including ten representations of the word "Allah," designed by Emin Berin, Turkish calligrapher. [Photo by L. al Fārūqī.]

a science with its own research and critical methods. It consisted of collecting and classifying data about the reporters. Their births and deaths, their descendance and that of their spouses, their occupations and personal status, their economic and social conditions, their residences and travels, their friends and acquaintances, their likes and dislikes, their attitudes and judgments, their intelligence and memory, their political and cultural affiliations, what aroused and pacified them — all these were useful data, the collection, classification, preservation, and retrieval of which were of crucial importance to the critical evaluation of the *ḥadīth.* Considering that the companions of the Prophet numbered about 10,000 people, the gathering of adequate information about those who were in any way connected with a reported *ḥadīth* was a tremendous task. The greatest works produced in this field are the following:

1. *Al Istī'āb fī Ma'rifat al Aṣḥāb,* by Yūsuf ibn 'Abd al Barr (463/1070). In it, the author listed every person who met the Prophet even once in his life, even as an infant.
2. *Usd al Ghābah fī Ma'rifat al Ṣaḥābah,* by 'Izzud-

dīn ibn al Athīr, in which the author included 7,500 full biographies. The same scholar produced a sequel entitled *Tajrīd Asmā' al Ṣaḥābah,* in which he included 8,000 persons.

3. *Tajrīd Asmā' al Ṣaḥābah,* by Muḥammad ibn Aḥmad al Dhahabī (748/1337), containing 8,000 biographies.
4. *Al Iṣābah fi Tamyīz al Ṣaḥābah,* by Aḥmad ibn Ḥajar al 'Asqalānī (852/1448), in which the author included over 10,000 biographies.

The *Riwāyah* scholars classified the methods by which any person in the chain of reporters had received his *ḥadīth,* and they assigned to it a degree of authority. The first and most authoritative form of transmission was that of hearing the "higher link" in the chain tell the tradition to the "lower link" in person, thus enabling the latter to preface his report with the statement "I have heard X telling me that. . . ." Second in authority was the *ḥadīth* received through *qirā'ah* (reading), which means in this context: "I have recited before X and he has approved my recitation, that. . . ." Third in authority was the *ḥadīth* obtained through *ijāzah,* which means that the higher link, who was the teacher of the lower, permitted the latter to recite on the former's behalf and with his authority. Fourth in authority was *munāwalah,* or "the giving by the higher authority to the lower, expressly for the purpose of *riwāyah.*" Fifth was *mukātabah* (learning by correspondence); sixth was *i'lām* (public proclamation for the purpose of information); seventh was *waṣiyyah* (leaving something written by a will); eighth was *wajādah* (finding something through research in written documents).

Islamic scholarship has classified the reporters after application of these and other criteria into a dozen classes of progressive trustworthiness, and has assigned to their reports a qualifying title indicating the degree of trustworthiness of their narrator.

Illustration 13.3

Double-niche Ushak carpet, Turkish, seventeenth-eighteenth century, Dennis R. Dodds Collection, Philadelphia. [Photo by L. al Fārūqī.]

The Science of *Al Jarḥ Wal Ta'dīl* (Character Examination)

This science seeks to examine all available data for the purpose of determining the trustworthiness of the person as a reporter of *ḥadīth.* It is the critical apparatus of the previous science, for its objective is to elaborate a thorough set of criteria with the purpose of assigning to each reporter varying degrees of trustworthiness.

The first rule was that all criticism of personal character should be the work of the living on the dead. Any criticism by the living of the living was *ipso facto* unacceptable. Second came the criteria of rationality, precision, legal innocence or righteousness *('adl),* and adherence to Islam. Rationality or reasonableness was presumed if the reportage occurred in the reporter's adulthood, which was defined as sexual maturity for hearing a *ḥadīth,* and the age of fifteen or over for reporting it. Rationality was also supposed to mean that the reporter conducted his personal and family life, his economic and social activity in a coherent and sensible manner. He should not be known for irrational flights of temper in which he lost self-control.

By precision *(ḍabṭ)* the critics meant the capacity of the reporter to distinguish between correct and spurious data, whether in relation to reporter or to the text reported. According to one scholar, a re-

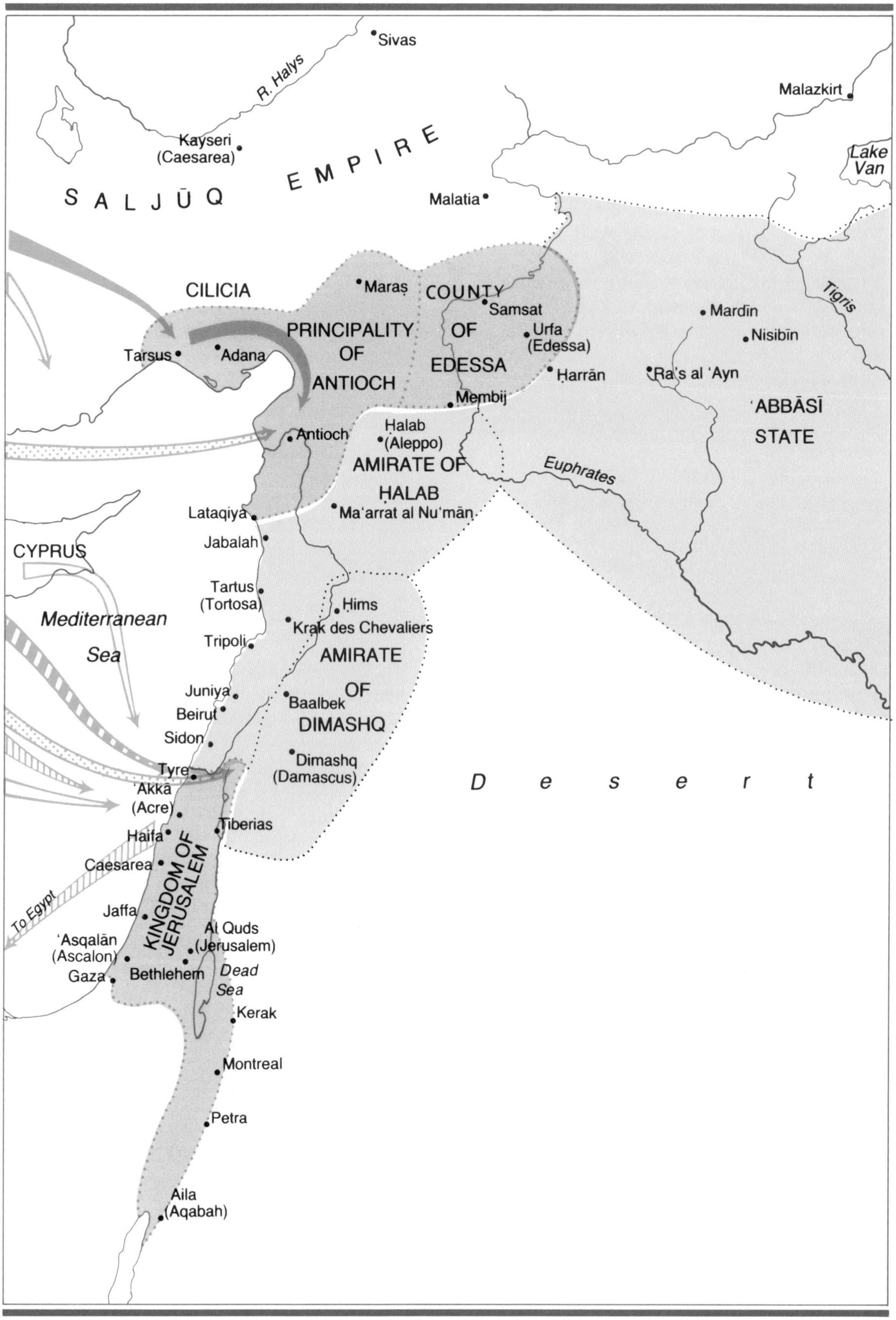
Sivas
R. Halys
Malazkirt
Kayseri
(Caesarea)
SALJŪQ EMPIRE
Lake Van
Malatia
CILICIA
Maraş
COUNTY OF EDESSA
Samsat
PRINCIPALITY OF ANTIOCH
Urfa
(Edessa)
Tarsus
Adana
Harrān
Mardīn
Nisibīn
Tigris
Ra's al 'Ayn
Membij
'ABBĀSĪ STATE
Antioch
Halab
(Aleppo)
AMIRATE OF HALAB
Euphrates
Lataqiya
Ma'arrat al Nu'mān
Jabalah
CYPRUS
Tartus
(Tortosa)
Hims
Mediterranean Sea
Krak des Chevaliers
Tripoli
AMIRATE OF DIMASHQ
Juniya
Baalbek
Beirut
Sidon
Dimashq
(Damascus)
Tyre
'Akka
(Acre)
Desert
Tiberias
Haifa
KINGDOM OF JERUSALEM
Caesarea
To Egypt
Jaffa
'Asqalān
(Ascalon)
Al Quds
(Jerusalem)
Gaza
Bethlehem
Dead Sea
Kerak
Montreal
Petra
Aila
(Aqabah)

porter lost his credibility if he reported about the famous (known) companions what was not commonly known about them; if he reported a single *ḥadīth* that was suspect on other grounds; if his report included mistakes of language, diction, composition, or of ordering of the reporters in the chain; or, finally, if he reported a *ḥadīth* otherwise known to be false. Legal innocence was defined as having a record of conduct without blemish. Especially vitiating to legal innocence was any previous conviction of crime *(ḥadd),* perjury, or any misconduct involving moral turpitude. Public failure to perform the duties of the *sharī'ah,* to be upright in both action and speech, were also vitiating. Legal innocence could be established by the solemn witness of any legally innocent person; but to this end it was prescribed that he who witnessed to another person's legal innocence must be either his lifetime neighbor, his partner in some major economic enterprise, or his fellow in some long and hazardous journey—thus establishing good character empirically, not merely on good faith. The critics ruled that good character established through unquestionable evidence of just dealings with one's fellows, freedom from any breach of promise, or any violation of the principal virtues of Islam was stronger than legal innocence established by someone's recommendation.

Under such rigors, however, Islamic scholarship was realistic enough to provide rules for trusting those reporters whose records left something to be desired. They devised a calculus of virtue by means of which the good points might be weighed against the bad points; and they ruled in favor of that reporter whose net balance was pro-virtue. Application of these criteria yielded the assignment to each link in the chain of reporters of a place on a graded scale of twelve levels. Imām al Bukhārī (256/869) and Ibn Sa'd (230/844), Yaḥyā ibn Ma'īn (233/817), Ibn Ḥanbal (241/855), and Mālik ibn Anas (179/795) were among the greatest in this field who wrote down the results of their researches for the benefit of later generations.

The Science of *'Ilal Al Ḥadīth* (Vitiating Causes of *Ḥadīth*) and of *Gharīb Al Ḥadīth* (The Insufficiently Known)

Both of these disciplines seek to examine each *ḥadīth* to ascertain its freedom from any vitiating cause. The former searches the data for any historical discrepancy, the latter examines the *ḥadīth* in question in light of all other *aḥādīth* to ascertain its strangeness or oddity. In order to complete its work, the science of *'Ilal al Ḥadīth* examines the situational contexts in which the *ḥadīth* occurred. In a sense, the historical circumstances in which the deed of the Prophet was done, his statement made, or his judgment passed constituted documentation for *'ilal* being attributed or not to each *ḥadīth.* The investigations of both these disciplines complemented knowledge of the meaning of the *ḥadīth,* its historical purport, its agreement with or difference from other *ḥadīth.* Such knowledge was indispensable for extraction of law from any given *ḥadīth.*

Muslim scholars, however, did not lay out criteria for determination of *'ilal,* as they did in the case of criticism of the reporters. Historical situations were so infinite in variability that causes for impairment

CONSEQUENCES OF THE CRUSADES

1. Destruction to Muslims and their cities; to Eastern Christians and their churches, including Constantinople; and to European Jews in the Crusaders' path.
2. Hatred and resentment between Europe's Christians on the one hand, and Christians, Muslims, and Jews of the East, on the other; falsification of Islam in Christian minds. Both evils continue today.
3. A flow of culture and civilization from East to West. The Crusaders brought back with them medical arts and hospitals; public baths; books on astronomy, geometry, and literature; musical instruments; the military arts and heraldry; chivalry values and sports tournaments; dyes and gunpowder; fruits and vegetables; perfumes and sugar; windmills and waterwheels; textiles; gold coinage; the compass; and the arts of navigation.

Map 48. The Crusades

First Crusade, 1096–1099
Second Crusade, 1147–1149
Third Crusade, 1189–1192
a) by Philippe Auguste of France
b) by Richard of England
c) by Frederick Barbarossa of Germany
Fourth Crusade (not shown on map), 1202–1204
Fifth Crusade, 1217–1221
Sixth Crusade, 1228–1229
Crusader states, ca. 1100
Muslim states

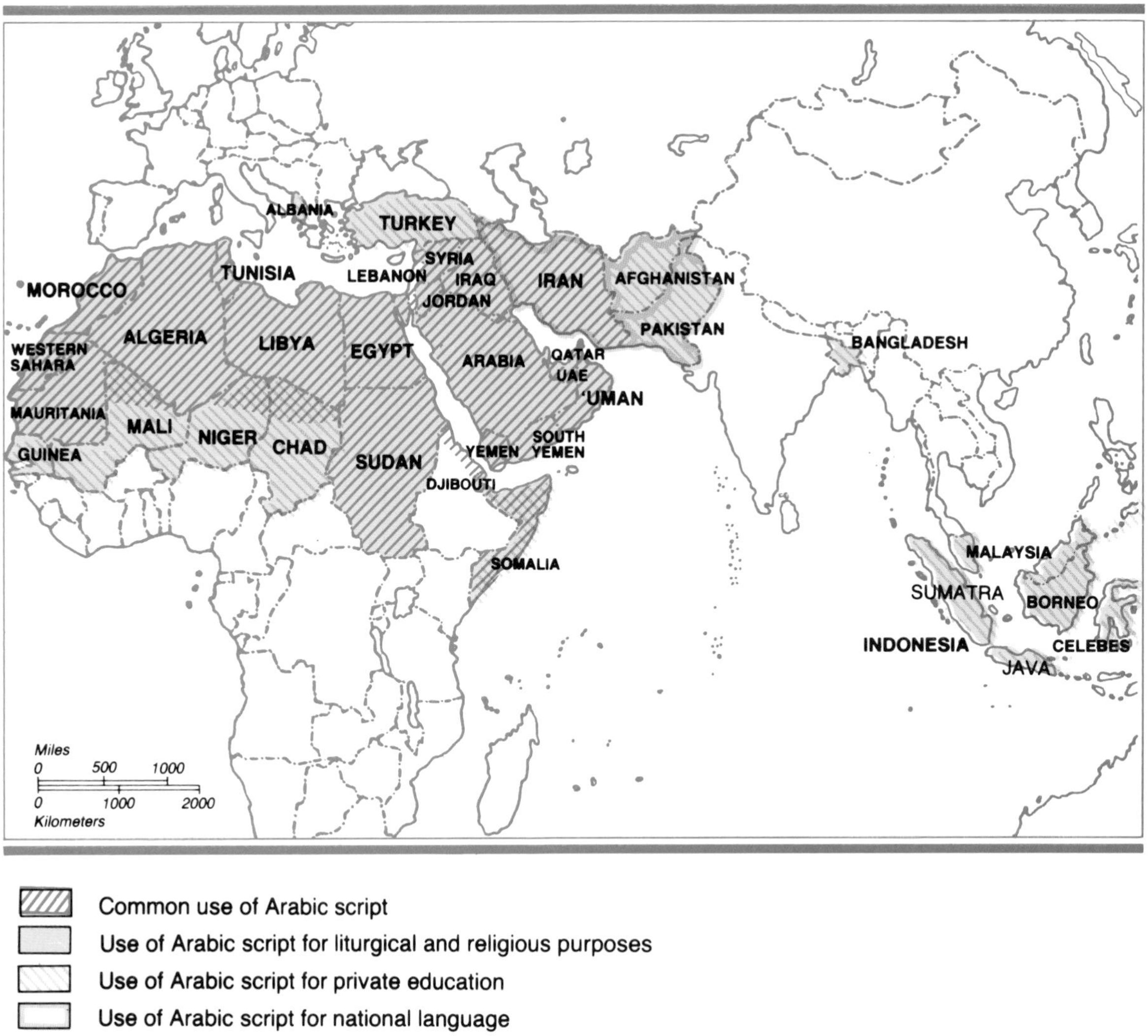

Map 49. Arabic Script in the Muslim World

could not be properly enumerated or classified. The reasons for categorization of *ḥadīth* as *gharīb* or not was equally unspecified because of the infinite number of possible reasons for judging a *ḥadīth* as "strange." When asked to name such criteria, the scholars of *ḥadīth* specializing in these two branches of knowledge have answered in the words of Ibn Ḥajar, one of the greatest authorities in the field: "This is one of the most difficult branches of knowledge, because it requires the most acute vision, and the widest possible knowledge of history, of the reporters, of the addressees of the *ḥadīth,* of the texts and chains of all other *aḥādīth.* Some of us do have the knowledge and others do not."[1] However, in his *Ma'rifat 'Ulūm al Ḥadīth,* al Ḥākim al Naysābūrī dared to attempt this impossible task and arranged the causes of invalidity under ten categories, ordering them according to their degree of gravity.

Islamic scholarship has produced a number of excellent works in the two fields mentioned here. They are *Kitāb al 'Ilal,* by 'Alī ibn al Madīnī (234/818), the teacher of Imām al Bukhārī; *Al Zahr al Maṭlūl fī al Khabar al Ma'lul,* by Ibn Ḥajar al 'Asqalānī (853/1449); and *Al 'Ilal al Mutanāhiyah,* by Ibn al Jawzī (655/1257).

The Science of *Mukhtalaf Al Ḥadīth* (*Ḥadīth* Harmonization)

Even after passing all the foregoing tests, *aḥādīth* may contradict one another, or present themselves in such a way as to reduce one another's validity. Such

Illustration 13.4

Minaret, Sulṭān Aḥmad Mosque, Isṭanbūl, Turkey, 1617 C.E. [Photo by L. al Fārūqī.]

ARABIC SCRIPT

1. Cultural legacy: From the advent of Islam to the present.
2. Liturgical use: whole Muslim world
3. Religious education: whole Muslim world
4. For all purposes: Arab world
5. Aesthetic decorational use: whole Muslim world
6. Private elementary and secondary education: all areas other than the Arab world.

CHANGE TO LATIN SCRIPT

1. Change by British Colonial Administration:		
Language:	*Country:*	*Date:*
Hausa	Ghana, Nigeria	After World War I
Swahili	Kenya, Tanzania	After World War I
Malay	Malaysia	After World War I
2. Change by French Colonial Administration		
Bambara, Malinke	Senegal to Ivory Coast	After World War I
Teda, Tamachek	Chad, Niger, Mali	After World War I
3. Change by Dutch Colonial Administration:		
Malay	Indonesia	After World War I
4. Change by National Administrations:		
Turkish	Turkey	After World War I
Albanian	Albania	After World War I
Serbo-Croatian	Yugoslavia (Serbia, Croatia, Montenegro)	c. 1890

CHANGE TO CYRILLIC SCRIPT

By U.S.S.R. Colonial Administration:

Language	*Country*	*Date*
Adharbayjani	Adherbayjan	1922–1937 (Latin script since 1937)
Kazakh	Kazakhstan	1927
Kirgiz	Kirgizistan	1927
Tadjik (Farsi)	Tadjikistan	1940
Tatar, Bashkir	Tatar Asian Soviet Socialist Republic	1927
Turkic	Turkmenistan	1940 (Latin 1928–1940)
Uzbek	Uzbekistan	1930 (Latin 1920–1930)

discrepancy, variation, or outright contradiction may be genuine; or it may be only apparent, and a harmless mistake. In the former case, one of the *ḥadīth* must be false or less valid than the other; or the one may have been revoked through the other in a real change of judgment by the Prophet *(naskh)*. In the latter case, the mistake should be corrected and the contradiction removed. The reports may concern two events in the Prophet's life rather than one; or the difference may be accounted for with linguistic analysis.

Numerous *ḥadīth* scholars wrote works in this field, and devised rules and methods for dealing with the various problems. They classified the possibilities of error as well as their solutions; and they assigned grades of validity to the *ḥadīth* according to the measure in which they fulfill the testing requirements. Imām al Shāf'ī (204/819) wrote *Ikhtilāf al Ḥadīth;* 'Abdullah ibn Qutaybah (276/889) wrote *Kitāb Ta'wīl Mukhtalaf al Ḥadīth;* Abū Ja'far al Ṭaḥāwī (321/933), *Mushkil al Āthār;* and Abūl Faraj ibn al Jawzī (597/1290), *Al Taḥqīq fī Aḥādīth al Khilāf.* These works are the best in the science of *ḥadīth* harmonization.

The Sciences of Language and Those of the Qur'ān

All the sciences discussed in chapters 11 and 12, whether those of the Arabic language or those of the

Illustration 13.5

Double Pavilion, Topkapi Palace, Isṭanbūl, Turkey. [Courtesy Embassy of Turkey, Washington, D.C.]

Qur'ān, apply equally to the *ḥadīth* except one — the science of *i'jāz al Qur'ān* — since the *sunnah* is not divine but human. The principles, methodologies, and criteria developed by all these sciences were applied to the *ḥadīth* with excellent results.

The Results of Islāmic Scholarship in the Sciences of the *Ḥadīth*

One million or more *aḥādīth* were in circulation by the end of the second century A.H. The tasks of collecting, classifying, and appraising them were formidable. However, Muslim scholars worked on them with diligence. Often they had to travel thousands of miles in order to ascertain the probability of one link in the chain of reporters, or the veracity of one word or expression in the text of a *ḥadīth*. But they were more than willing to pay the price, for the matter concerned their religion and their Prophet. The study took several generations to complete, and resulted in universal acceptance of six collections as authoritative. These are the works of al Bukhārī, Muslim, Abū Dāwūd, al Nasā'ī, al Tirmidhī, and Ibn Mājah. Two other collections were regarded by some Muslims as equally authoritative: those of Mālik ibn Anas and Aḥmad ibn Ḥanbal. Beyond these, there were many other collections which scholars classified as untrustworthy because their authors were lax in applying the criteria of the disciplines. These untrustworthy collections included some true *aḥādīth* as well as those that were weak, problematic, or doubtful. Other collections were notorious for their sectarianism and prejudice.

As for the six authoritative collections, some scholars have recognized that the collection of Ibn Mājah was not as critical as the other five; and they have therefore replaced it with those of Mālik and Ibn Ḥanbal, thus making the authoritative collections seven in number in their categorization. Among these, the collections of al Bukhārī and Muslim are especially trustworthy and stand apart, above the others. Between the collections of these two scholars, that of al Bukhārī takes precedence in reliability and authority. A still higher level of authority belongs to those *aḥādīth* reported by both al Bukhārī and Muslim.

The number of *aḥādīth* considered and passed as valid shed much light on the validity of the collections. Ibn Ḥanbal examined 750,000 *aḥādīth* from which he selected 40,000 as valid. Al Bukhārī examined 300,000 reported by 1,000 authorities and selected only 7,275 as valid. Among the valid accepted by al Bukhārī, there were numerous repetitions which, if eliminated, would bring the number of his accepted *aḥādīth* to 2,602. If the same criteria were applied to the collection of Muslim, we would find that that author accepted about 4,000 *aḥādīth* as valid. Those *aḥādīth* judged authentic by both al Bukhārī and Muslim numbered about 1,500.

As regards validity or authenticity, *ḥadīth* scholars have classified the *ḥadīth* into four main categories: *Ṣaḥīḥ* or authentic; *Ḥasan,* or good, likely to be authentic; *Ḍa'īf,* weak, or likely to be inauthentic; and *Mawḍū',* or forged and hence not a *ḥadīth.* Laws derived from the first two are binding to all Muslims; laws derived from *Ḍa'īf* are not binding but are recommended for observance.

The qualities that justify classifying a *ḥadīth* in the

Map 50. Languages of the Muslim World

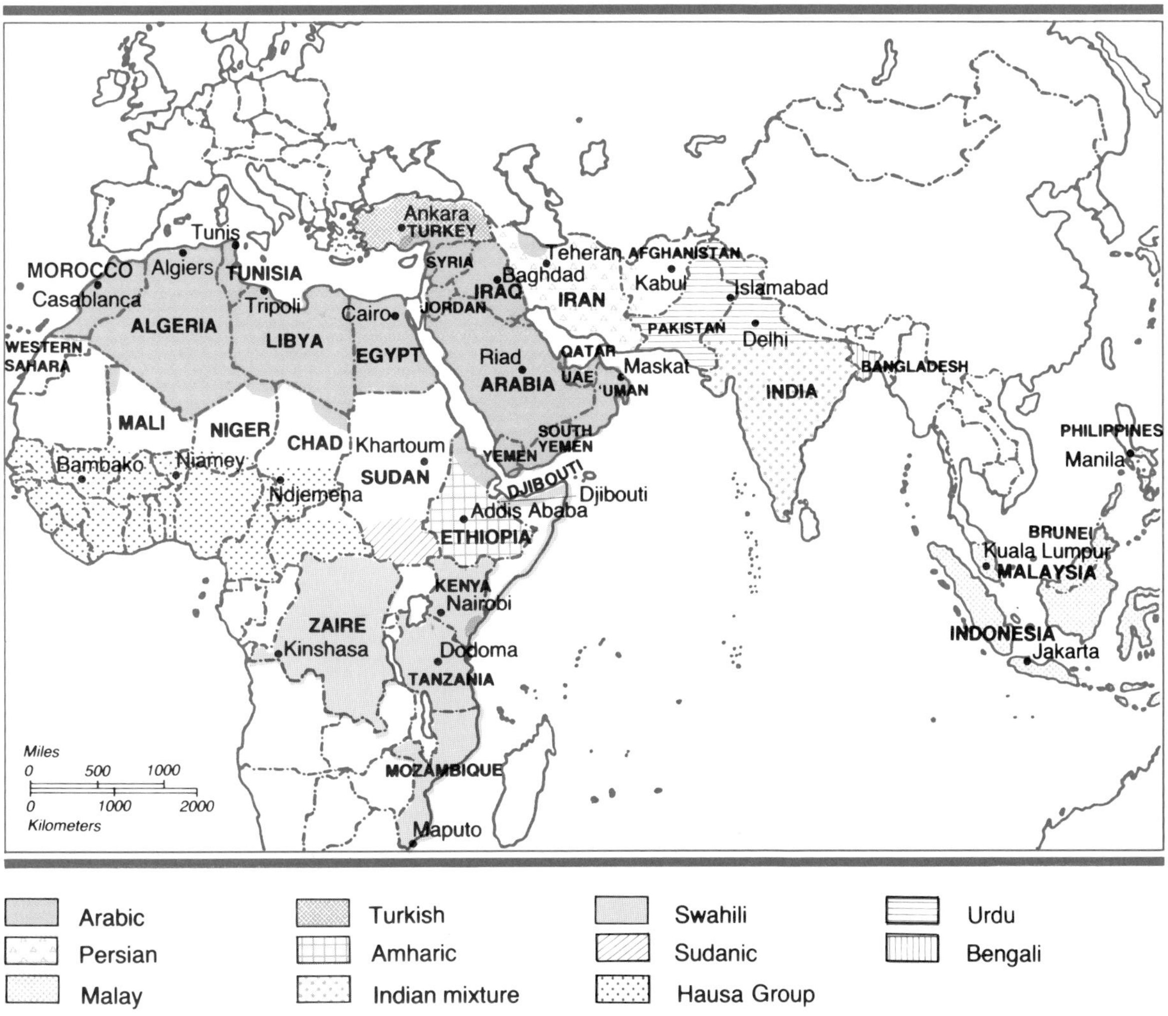

Ṣaḥīḥ category, the highest in authenticity, are the following: (1) ***musnad,*** meaning that it was reported by an unbroken chain of qualified reporters going back to the Prophet, every member of which had heard it personally from the next link in the chain (hearing being the most reliable form of transmission); (2) ***mutawātir,*** or universally related by at least four but sometimes as many as 310 different reporters in exactly the same form or meaning, without contradiction by any; (3) absolutely free of any vitium arising out of historical context, or in relation to other *ḥadīth,* and satisfying every demand of rationality, coherence, correspondence with historical fact, and conformance to acceptable language and style; and (4) all links in the chain of reporters fulfill all requisites, and thus constitute an unchallengeable chain, whose members cannot rationally be assumed to have agreed on falsehood, forgery, or an innocent mistake.

The *ḥadīth* qualifying for the second category, *Ḥasan,* fulfilled the same requirements as the *Ṣaḥīḥ* but one, namely, precision. Some reports of it showed imprecision in reportage. The *Ḍa'īf* examples are the most complex. They fall into as many kinds and classes as there are points contributing to their weakness. Most books of *ḥadīth* count about twenty such categories, and some go as high as seventy-five kinds or grades of weakness.

In their absolute honesty in matters of religion, the scholars of Islam dared not destroy the *aḥādīth* which their tests had proven to be weak or forged. They

Map 51. Ethnography of the Muslim World

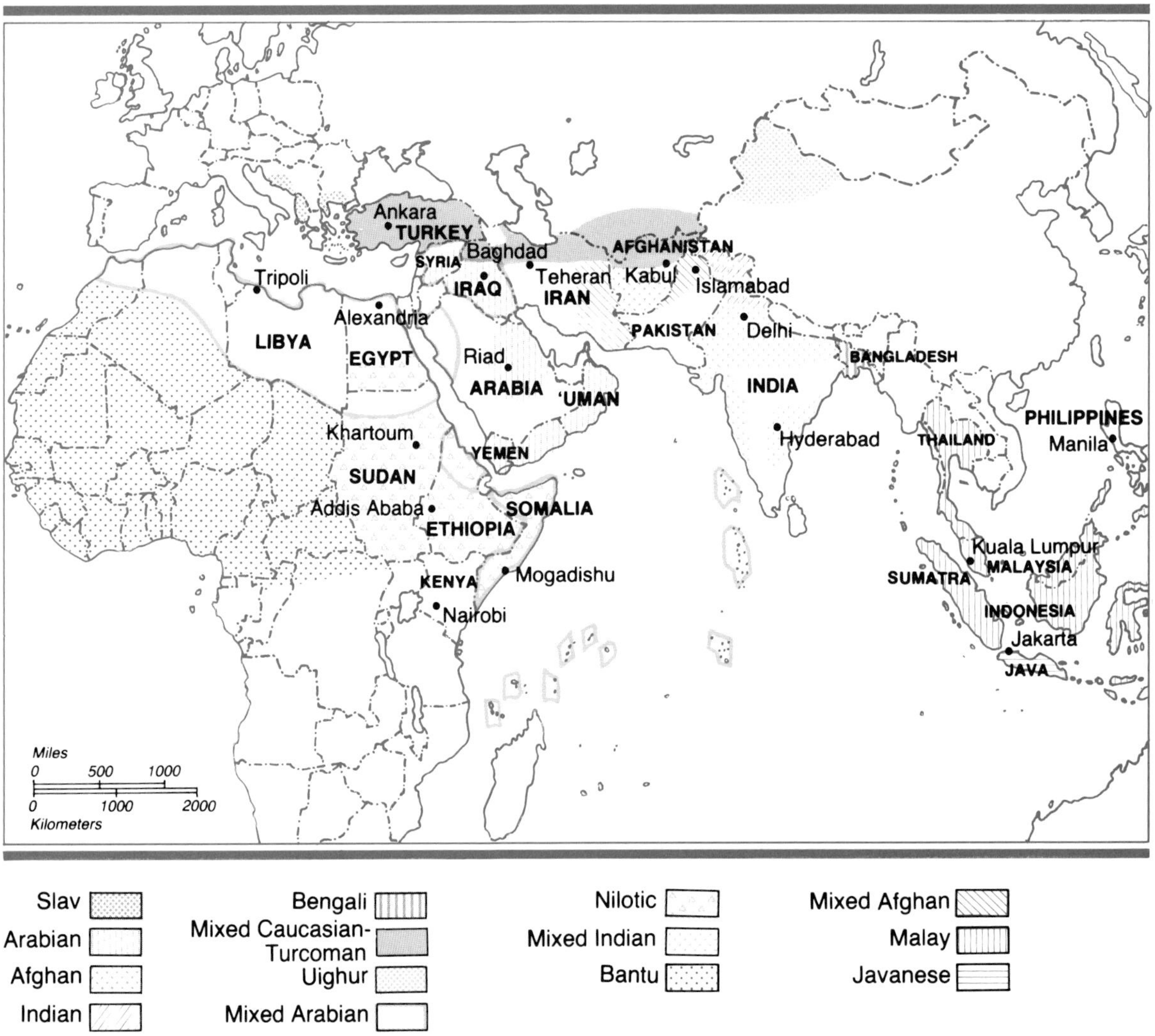

kept them and classified, recorded, and published them in special collections. They gave the causes or evidence of their judgments and even assigned degrees of inauthenticity to them, from the avowedly forged *aḥādīth* to those including words or ideas simply unbecoming of the Prophet.

CONCLUSION

There is no doubt that the methodological sciences of Islam were among their greatest achievements. Nor can there be any doubt that the religion of Islam, because of these sciences, achieved for itself the most authentic status among the religions of the world. Were the founders of the world's religions to return today, none but the Prophet Muḥammad would feel at home with what has come down through the centuries as coming from him. Who could tell what the other religions may have become had their followers developed and applied the critical methodological sciences of the Muslims in the first or second century of their history? The West has succeeded in developing biblical criticism in the last two centuries. One must acknowledge that that discipline has attained brilliant accomplishments, but the fact that it came eighteen centuries late removes the possibility of the religion's historical presence being affected in accordance with those accomplishments. Instead, it has resulted in the juxtaposition of two alternatives: skepticism and naïve fundamentalism.

NOTE

1. Quoted in Subḥī al Ṣāliḥ, *'Ulūm al Ḥadīth wa Musṭalaḥih* (Beirut: Dār al 'Ilm lil Malāyin, 2nd ed., 1378/1959), p. 180.

CHAPTER 14

The Law

THE NEED FOR LAW

God and creation are two ontologically disparate realms of being. Between them only one relation is possible, namely, that creation fulfill the will of the Creator; for the latter is its ultimate norm or ought-to-be. In nature, fulfillment of the divine will is built-in and necessary. Nature's compliance with the divine will is precisely what scientists call "natural laws." Another realm of divine laws is the social order, where humans interrelate with one another according to moral and social laws which revelation presented as imperatives, and compliance with which is free. Indeed, compliance with them is without value unless it is free. Man may violate them; or he may realize them voluntarily for the sake of God, their Author. Such fulfillment gives man an additional, higher merit than all other creatures. It is this merit that Muslims call the moral; its opposite is the immoral. For this reason, the Qur'ān tells: "God offered His trust to heaven and earth and mountain; but they shied away in fear and rejected it. Man alone carried it" (Qur'ān 33:72). For this reason, the Qur'ān adds, "God taught man the names of things [revealed to him their essences] and then commanded the angels to prostrate themselves before him" (Qur'ān 2:34). Thus man is higher than the angels on account of his capacity to act morally. His is a cosmic function, to actualize in space-time the higher part of the divine will—the moral—which only he can do.

Five conditions must be met if the purpose of creation is to be realized. First, the content of the divine imperative must be known or, at least, knowable. Second, man must be capable of action, of actualization of the divine imperatives in space-time. Third, space-time, nature or creation, must be malleable, that is, capable of being changed by human action into the desired ought-to-be. Fourth, there must be judgment, so that action is not in vain but entails significant consequences. Fifth, the reckoning of man's fulfillment of the ought-to-be must be done on a scale of absolute justice.

In support of the first condition, Islam taught that man is endowed with all the equipment necessary for the discernment of the divine imperatives. He has been given sight and hearing, smell, taste and touch, a heart, and understanding as faculties of cognition with which to discern the theoretical and axiological patterns of creation, within and outside of himself, in nature and in other humans. He has been endowed with language as a tool of discursive expression, and with colors and forms, light and shade, sound and imagination as media of aesthetic expression. Above all, he has been endowed with reason, with which to weigh and consider, to coordinate and judge all things. In addition to all this, God in His love and mercy revealed to man His will. "Unto every people," the Qur'ān affirms, "God had sent prophets to teach them the divine imperatives in their own tongue" (Qur'ān 14:4). Reason and revelation are "two open books" available to man to discern the divine imperative. Although human reasoning is fallible, yet it is trustworthy as an avenue of truth, since it can reconsider and correct its previous findings. And although revelation is not fallible, man's understanding of it is, and therefore stands to be corrected by reason. The two sources thus become equivalent in the sense that no contradiction between them can ever be final. Where there is fault, reconsideration by reason is the only recourse. Fortunately, it is an open, free, public, self-conscious, and critical avenue.

In support of the second condition, Islam taught that man is indeed the author of his deeds whether good or evil, and that this fact is a hard datum of consciousness. Man becomes conscious of it when facing several possibilities of action and/or inaction and he decides in favor of one; when, in the very exercise of action the subject becomes aware that he could or could not disturb and alter the status quo in question; when, having done the deed, the subject becomes aware of his responsibility, of either guilt or merit for the action undertaken, and for its results in space-time.

In support of the third condition, Islam taught that the whole of creation, with its suns and moons and stars, is subservient to man (Qur'ān 22:65; 31:20) to the end of proving his moral worth. Both science and metaphysics teach the necessity of adequate cause to produce any effect, as well as the necessity of the effect once the adequate cause is there. Neither affirms that the causal nexus is closed to any further determination by outside forces if there be such; or that when such forces enter the nexus, they do not generate but only deflect the movement of the nexus to an end other than that to which it would have moved without the additional interference. This openness of nature to determination by human initiative acting as additional causation is precisely what is meant by her subservience; and no more is needed to prove its malleability.

Finally, in support of the fourth condition, Islam taught that every human will get his or her due whether in or beyond space-time; that the reckoning starts at birth, not before it. Hence, Islam rejected as unjust — and hence untrue — any doctrine of original sin, any attempt to weigh down the scale before birth, whether against man (as in Christianity, Hinduism, Jainism, and Buddhism) or in his favor (as in Greek religion). Man's merit and demerit, it held, were functions of his own works, never transferable. Further, Islam taught that God is the ultimate Judge Whose scale is that of absolute justice, one which never loses an atom's weight of good works — or of evil works; one which admits of no intercession by anyone, no favoritism to anyone.

This vision of Islam was not a piece of utopian thinking. Nor was it left to the personal effort of the noble-minded, to be actualized when they were so inclined, and to suffer neglect or violation when they were not. It had to be, and was, translated into the *sharī'ah,* the system of laws that cover human life from the cradle to the grave. The values of Islam, therefore, did not remain ethical desiderata which could not be invoked in a legal process. As *sharī'ah* the ideal values enjoyed the full force of established law, and became facts of everyday life. They became known to the literate and illiterate alike a whole millennium before the age of printing. They were understood and pursued by the masses. Kings and cobblers appreciated and invoked their provisions on a daily basis to correct injustice, to justify possession, or to restore a right. The social ideal became so much a part of life that no spirituality was conceivable that did not begin with the fulfillment of the law. This realism protected Muslim piety against empty moralism, and Muslim morality against the speculative flight of the mystics.

Except in a few cases, the letter of the prescriptive elaborations of the values of Islam was not declared sacrosanct and hence absolutely unalterable. The qualities of eternity and immutability belonged to the values or principles behind the prescriptive elaboration, not to the legal form given them by translation of the purposes of the law into legislative prescriptions. Eternity and absoluteness belonged, in the main, to the axiological postulates. With the exception of these postulates and directions, all deontological elaborations were open to reinterpretation by humans. This openness was dictated by the ever-changing conditions and situations of human life which demanded, in turn, a readiness on the part of the law to meet them in pursuit of its eternal objectives. The *sharī'ah* was divine and eternal not in its letter but in its spirit. The letter of the law was honored because of its derivation from that which is divine and eternal.

To govern the process of translation of the values of Islam into legislative prescriptions, and to enable the *sharī'ah* to accommodate the changing human conditions, revelation provided both the law and the mechanism for its renewal. The fundamental principles, the values and groundwork for both the law and

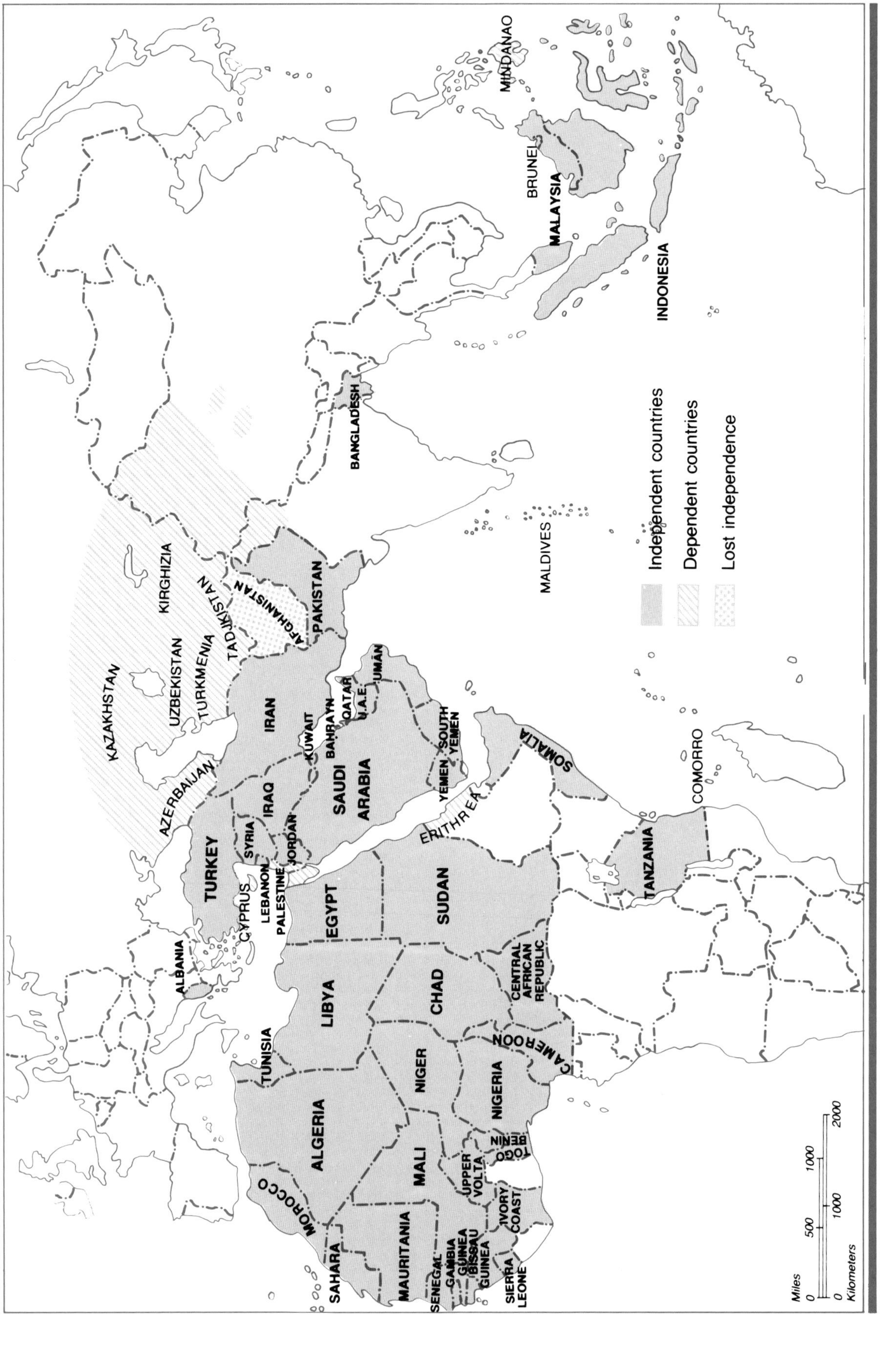

Map 52. Political Independence in the Muslim World

the methodology for its dynamic development were given by Islam under divine authority. Muslims invented the science of *uṣūl al fiqh* to systematize development of the law to meet new situations and problems, to institutionalize the continuous adaptation of the law to historical change. It was the task of *uṣūl al fiqh* to distinguish between the changeable and the changeless, and to develop a methodology out of the relevant principles laid down in the Qur'ān and the *sunnah* for governing change. The changeless included the prescriptive *(maqādīr)* laws of the Qur'ān and *sunnah,* bound as they were by their texts. As Muslims were absolutely certain of the divine provenance as well as of the unadulterated transmission of their texts, the prescriptive laws of the Qur'ān and *sunnah* were susceptible to linguistic hermeneutics only, the mere clarification of their grammatical, syntactical, and lexicographic meanings. These were universally accepted as obligatory and changeless by Muslims at all times. The rest of the juristic content of the Qur'ān and *sunnah* was regarded, again by all Muslims, as capable of change and development, though differences arose concerning application of the methodological principles governing change. *Uṣūl al fiqh* arose in order to establish criteria of validity for the development of new laws from their sources in the revelation.

Ijmā' and *qiyās* found no disagreement among Muslims and were accepted as valid principles of law-making by all schools. *Ijmā'* consists of the agreement of all jurists in any given period on a matter of law. *Qiyās* consists of subsuming a new matter under an established law because of the equivalence of the causes underlying them. To these principal criteria, *uṣūl al fiqh* added the following:

1. *Al tamassuk bil aṣl,* the rule that originally and essentially all beneficial actions are legitimate, all harmful ones illegitimate.
2. *Istiṣḥāb al ḥāl,* the rule that laws are permanently valid unless there is evidence challenging their beneficial nature.
3. *Al maṣāliḥ al mursalah,* the rule that a benefit is deemed legitimate if the *sharī'ah* is not known to have established or denied it.
4. *Al dharā'i',* the rule that the legitimacy of that which is instrumental is directly affected by the benefit or harm implicit in the final end to which it leads.
5. *Al istiqrā' al nāqiṣ,* the rule that a universal law may be derived from a particular law through ascending generalization, if no exception is known to challenge the generalization.
6. *Al istiḥsān,* the rule that a weaker *qiyās* may be

POPULATION OF INDEPENDENT MUSLIM COUNTRIES

Country	*Total Population*	*Muslim Population*	*Percentage Muslims*
Democratic Republic of Afghanistan	16,640,940	16,474,531	99
People's Socialist Republic of Albania	2,920,067	2,190,050	75
Democratic and Popular Republic of Algeria	20,131,891	19,729,253	98
State of Bahrain	424,000	424,000	100
People's Republic of Bangladesh	96,178,846	81,752,019	85
People's Republic of Benin	3,689,192	2,213,515	60
Brunei	173,000	131,000	76
United Republic of Cameroon	9,087,157	4,997,936	55
Republic of Chad	4,895,826	4,161,452	85
Federal and Islamic Republic of Comoros	424,424	411,691	97
Republic of Djibouti	424,763	420,515	99
Arab Republic of Egypt	44,756,157	41,623,226	93
Ethiopia	33,686,800	21,896,420	65
Republic of Gambia	850,703	723,098	85
People's Revolutionary Republic of Guinea	5,759,245	5,471,283	95
Republic of Guinea-Bissau	888,280	710,624	80
Republic of Indonesia	161,679,203	153,595,243	95
Islamic Republic of Iran	40,735,800	39,921,084	98
Republic of Iraq	14,090,771	13,386,232	95
Republic of Ivory Coast	8,868,193	4,877,506	55
Hashemite Kingdom of Jordan	3,451,222	3,278,661	95
State of Kuwait	1,486,692	1,486,692	100
Republic of Lebanon	3,308,472	1,885,829	57
Socialist People's Libyan Arab Jamahiriya	3,263,104	3,263,104	100
Republic of Malawi	6,531,720	3,592,446	55
Malaysia	14,929,273	7,912,515	53
Republic of Maldives	216,770	216,770	100
Republic of Mali	7,481,395	7,107,325	95
Islamic Republic of Mauritania	1,609,313	1,609,313	100
Kingdom of Morocco	22,237,740	22,015,363	99
People's Republic of Mozambique	12,751,800	7,651,080	60
Republic of Niger	5,836,678	5,311,377	91
Federal Republic of Nigeria	89,922,874	67,442,155	75
Sultanate of Oman	964,494	964,494	100
Islamic Republic of Pakistan	91,793,774	89,039,961	97
State of Qatar	227,900	227,900	100
Kingdom of Saudi Arabia	9,849,520	9,849,520	100
Republic of Senegal	6,145,774	5,838,485	95
Republic of Sierra Leone	3,751,340	3,001,072	80

POPULATION OF INDEPENDENT MUSLIM COUNTRIES (Continued)

Country	*Total Population*	*Muslim Population*	*Percentage Muslims*
Somali Democratic Republic	4,216,680	4,216,680	100
Democratic Republic of Sudan	19,728,720	16,769,412	85
Syrian Arab Republic	9,016,360	8,114,724	90
United Arab Republic of Tanzania	19,889,840	12,928,396	65
Republic of Togo	2,696,640	1,483,152	55
Republic of Tunisia	6,891,060	6,546,507	95
Republic of Turkey	47,658,660	47,182,073	99
United Arab Emirates	1,060,625	1,060,625	100
Republic of Upper Volta	7,271,600	4,072,096	56
People's Democratic Republic of S. Yemen	2,080,780	1,976,741	95
Yemen Arab Republic (North)	7,654,260	7,577,717	99

POPULATION OF DEPENDENT MUSLIM COUNTRIES

Country	*Total Population (in thousands)*	*Muslim Population (in thousands)*	*Percentage*
Azerbaijan	10,353	8,076	78
Erithrea	3,450	2,588	75
Kashmir	7,613	5,939	78
Kazakhstan	13,777	10,048	68
Kirghizia	3,373	3,103	92
Palestine	3,450	3,003	87
Sinkiang	10,706	8,665	82
Tadjikistan	3,375	3,268	90
Turkmenia	2,482	2,234	90
Uzbekistan	47,919	42,169	88

MUSLIM MINORITIES

Country	*Total Population (in thousands)*	*Muslim Population (in thousands)*	*Percentage*
Angola	6,870	1,717	25
Argentina	28,571	559	2
Armenia S.S.R.	2,618	343	13
Australia	15,128	152	1
Austria	7,656	41	.5
Belgium	10,243	200	2
Bhutan	1,337	63	5
Botswana	802	39	5
Brazil	124,950	242	.01
Bulgaria	8,898	1,388	16
Burma	35,269	3,529	10
Burundi	4,318	863	20
Byelorussia S.S.R.	9,183	621	7
Cambodia	7,500	805	1
Canada	24,399	824	3.5
Central America and the Carribean	37,595	120	.03

preferred to a stronger one if it fulfills the general purposes of the *sharī'ah* better.

7. *Al 'urf wal 'ādah,* the rule that custom and established practice may be legitimate sources of law.

By these means, the science of *uṣūl al fiqh* established a methodology of logical deduction and analogical extrapolation from the *data revelata,* as well as criteria for an empirical discovery of the common welfare of the people. For the overwhelming majority of Muslims, to actualize justice and fulfill equity, to establish critically the requisites of public welfare, and to subsume them — either through direct or indirect deduction, juristic preference, or juristic consideration of the commonweal under the general purposes of the law — was regarded as the pinnacle of juristic wisdom and Islamic piety.

We are therefore dealing neither with a fossilized law whose form or letter is immutable, nor with a flux of precepts that change with every situation. Rather, Islam's laws were anchored in eternal principles or values whose applications developed following human situations, but only with critical guarantees for the permanence of those principles and values.

THE VALUES OF THE *SHARĪ'AH*

Sharī'ah and Justice

Muslims believe that the *sharī'ah* is the property of all humanity, that everyone is entitled to adjudicate his disputes with his peers under its provisions. Nobody may be stopped from taking recourse to it if he so wishes, whether male or female, rich or poor, king or tramp, black or white, Muslim or non-Muslim, resident or transient, citizen or noncitizen. Equally, no Muslim is immune from being charged under its provisions. Anybody can bring such a charge to court and the court is obliged to consider the charge. On the other hand, unless he is guilty of a crime prejudicial to the state or against the *ummah* as a whole, or unless he has committed a bodily injury against others or aggressed upon another's property, no non-Muslim may be tried under the *sharī'ah* unless he expressly asks for it. The *sharī'ah* prescribes that the non-Muslim be tried under his own law, be it Jewish, Christian, Hindu, Buddhist, or whatever. That is the non-Muslim's prerogative which the *sharī'ah* acknowledges by recognizing non-Muslim laws as equally valid under its own dominion.

In this the *sharī'ah* is unique in all the legal systems history has known. It alone recognizes other laws as valid for those who wish to uphold them, and does so constitutionally or de jure. It alone makes Muslim society pluralistic in the only sense that really counts. No other system of laws or national constitution has ever considered the possibility of instituting another law beside it as equally valid, legal exclusivism being of the very essence of national or political sovereignty. The *sharī'ah,* on the contrary, never felt threatened by the co-existence of other laws in the territory it dominated, and gave its full blessing to their observance and application. At the same time, the Muslims continued to believe in the truth and worthiness of the *sharī'ah* and felt obliged to call humanity to convert to Islam and the *sharī'ah.* Their exclusivism was a matter of epistemology, metaphysics, and ethics, not of personal or state action. On the level of action, tolerance and pluralism were the rule.

Justice is so important in Islam that the *sharī'ah* prescribed that it be meted out freely and swiftly in order for it to be readily available to all. Of all the contributions of Islam, the universal right to justice which the *sharī'ah* has upheld throughout its fourteen centuries of history is perhaps the greatest. Islam taught that to establish justice on earth is the supreme duty of every human. Every man is religiously obliged to rise — nay, to lay down his life — in the establishment and defense of justice. Indeed, justice is so hallowed and cherished that everybody, however lowly, poor, or miserable, must feel absolutely certain that justice is his for the asking. That is why the *sharī'ah* prescribed that the meting out of justice be absolutely free. There are no fees and no costs; and any court is constitutionally qualified to look into any case, and seek the expert advice of anyone. Islamic practice has separated the cases where the defendant is the state or any of its officers and has assigned them to a special court called *maḥkamat al maẓālim* (the court for acts of injustice). Islamic law did not resort to imposition of fees to discourage litigation; but it imposed very stiff penalties for those who present false claims, including permanent legal disenfranchisement, the loss of the natural status of *'adl* (legal personality), or the right to be heard in court at all.

Giving witness is regarded by the *sharī'ah* as an obligation, with the greater merit belonging to the witness given voluntarily and before asking. Having prescribed the absolute equality of all those who stand before it, the *sharī'ah* postulates their innocence until legal evidence has established the contrary. It recognizes everybody's right to arbitrate and settle one's dispute out of court; and it holds man responsible only for his own personal deeds, firmly rejecting every suggestion of vicarious guilt or group culpability. In the meting out of justice, the Muslims are commanded to be its first exemplars and witnesses (Qur'ān 2:143), even if the whole world should act otherwise. Islamic justice was built on a principle it inherited from Meso-

MUSLIM MINORITIES (Continued)

Country	*Total Population (in thousands)*	*Muslim Population (in thousands)*	*Percentage*
Chile	11,173	57	.5
China	1,052,000	107,525	10.2
Congo	1,583	172	11
Cyprus	652	241	37
Equatorial Guinea	256	86	34
Fiji Islands	642	69	11
Finland	4,812	4	.08
France	54,120	1,360	2.5
Gabon	669	269	40
Georgia S.S.R.	4,781	1,130	24
Germany (West)	62,528	1,012	1.6
Ghana	12,329	5,047	45
Greece	9,595	310	3
Guyana	857	131	15
Hong Kong	4,243	48	1
Hungary	10,817	120	1
India	693,680	79,243	11
Italy	57,446	631	1
Japan	118,777	255	.02
Kenya	16,567	4,234	26
South Korea	39,928	86	.02
Liberia	1,877	572	30
Laos	3,560	37	1
Lesotho	1,370	138	10
Malagasy Republic	8,766	1,552	18
Malawi	6,155	1,928	31
Malta	354	52	15
Mauritius	969	162	17
Moldavia S.S.R.	3,643	123	3
Mozambique	10,531	2,535	24
Namibia	703	39	5.5
Nepal	15,338	553	3.6
New Zealand	3,169	33	1
Panama	1,969	58	2.9
Philippines	50,061	5,551	11
Poland	35,931	382	1
Portuguese Timor	672	147	22
Reunion	493	108	22
Rumania	22,498	216	1
Russian S.F.S.R.	132,600	8,976	6.7
Rhodesia-Zimbabwe	7,544	1,017	13.5
Singapore	2,250	382	17
South Africa	29,189	545	1.9
Sri Lanka	15,031	1,374	9
Surinam	424	123	29
Swaziland	562	53	9
Taiwan	17,980	155	.08
Thailand	48,087	6,406	13
Trinidad & Tobago	1,207	146	12
Uganda	13,621	4,460	33
Ukrania S.S.R.	48,078	6,505	14
United Kingdom	57,019	2,800	5
United States	224,113	4,344	1.9
Vietnam	54,212	245	.5

MUSLIM MINORITIES (Continued)

Country	*Total Population (in thousands)*	*Muslim Population (in thousands)*	*Percentage*
Yugoslavia	22,617	4,821	21
Zaire	29,494	2,742	9
Zambia	5,931	800	13

POLITICAL INDEPENDENCE IN THE MUSLIM WORLD

Independent Countries

Continent	*Country*	*Year of Independence*
Africa	Egypt	1922
	Libya	1951
	Moroco	1956
	Sudan	1956
	Tunisia	1956
	Guinea	1958
	Cameroon	1960
	Central African Republic	1960
	Chad	1960
	Mali	1960
	Mauritania	1960
	Niger	1960
	Nigeria	1960
	Senegal	1960
	Somalia	1960
	Togo	1960
	Upper Volta	1960
	Sierra Leone	1961
	Tanzania	1961
	Algeria	1962
	Gambia	1965
	Comorro	1975
	Rio de Oro	1976
Asia	Iran	1921
	Iraq	1932
	Saudi Arabia	1921
	Turkey	1290
	Yaman	1911
	Jordan	1945
	Lebanon	1945
	Syria	1945
	India	1947
	Pakistan	1947
	Indonesia	1949
	Malaysia	1957
	Kuwait	1961
	South Yaman	1968
	'Umān	1970
	Bahrayn	1971
	Bangladesh	1971
	Qatar	1971
	United Arab Emirates	1971
	Maldives	1977
	Brunei	1983
Europe	Albania	1913
South America	Surinam	1975

potamia: "A life for a life, an eye for an eye, a nose for a nose, an ear for an ear, and a tooth for a tooth, and for other injuries, equitable retaliation" (Qur'ān 5:47, 42:21).

Sharī'ah and Rationalism

Islam claims that the truth is one, just as God is One, and that it is knowable to humans by any of the twin avenues of reason and revelation. Translated into law, this Islamic value prescribes that all humans are entitled to know the truth; and no censorship or restriction may be imposed by anyone. The *sharī'ah* recognizes that all humans are entitled to inquire, to search, to learn, and to teach one another, and prescribes research and learning as universal duties from which no one is exempt. Under the *sharī'ah,* human society is regarded as a school on a grand scale where everyone is student and teacher at the same time. The *sharī'ah* declares ideological skepticism to be false, a defiance of God, and it prescribes that none may promote it to destroy the tradition of human knowledge and wisdom, or prevent anybody from appropriating it or contributing to its growth. *Al 'aql* (reason or rational knowledge) was honored by the *sharī'ah* as one of the six *maqāṣid al sharī'ah* (ultimate purposes of the law) along with life, property, family, religion, and honor.

Sharī'ah and World-Affirmation

Islam holds that God has created life and the world for a purpose; that they are prime values whose actualization is desirable. Life, the *sharī'ah* maintains, ought to be lived, the world developed, instincts satisfied; talents, faculties, and potentialities ought to be realized, and happiness sought and achieved. The result of all these activities should be the building and growth of culture and civilization. The human pursuit of these objectives is the very matrix in which law and ethics may be fulfilled. They are therefore necessary if the divine purpose of creation itself is to be realized.

Translated into the *sharī'ah,* the affirmation of life and the world prescribes that to be born is to have the right to be, to live as long as God permits; that none may be deprived of life except for legitimate cause. The *sharī'ah* also prescribes that to be born is to be entitled to the father's name, to his care and support or to that of the state in case of orphanhood or inability, to a free education and protection by society and/ or its institutions. Every human is entitled to the vocation of his choice, to partake of God's bounty on earth, to marry and raise a family, to acquire and enjoy wealth.

Sharī'ah and Universal Egalitarianism

Islam affirms the relation between God and all humans to be one and the same, that relation being a function of their creatureliness, or place in the cosmos. It rejects therefore all claims of favoritism or chosenness of any humans, and regards such claims as threats to divine transcendence and ultimacy.

Translated into law, this egalitarianism prescribes that none may be exempted from the imperatives of the *sharī'ah* on the ground of identity. All Muslims are *mukallafūn* (required to obey the law) and are so equally. Neither race nor ethnicity, neither sex nor position in society, neither wisdom nor wealth can alter their equality before the law. The fact that Muḥammad was their father, the Prophet admonished his children, avails them nothing; and 'Umar, the Caliph, could not exempt his son from enforcement of the law upon him. Governors of provinces and newly converted kings were subject to retaliation by the least person whose rights they had violated. Even the Muslim collectivity as a whole — the *ummah* — has no recourse against the law, and was sentenced by the least judge when it was found in violation of the law.

The *sharī'ah*'s egalitarianism did not apply solely to the Muslims among themselves, or to the citizens of the Islamic state regardless of their religious affiliation. It applied to all humans on earth entitling them — Muslim or non-Muslim, citizen or noncitizen, resident or nonresident, individual or group — to enter into a covenant of peace, of trade, of mutual security and friendly relation with the Islamic state. The "law of nations" has never witnessed anything comparable. For the *sharī'ah* recognizes the right not only of all nations, or peoples, or sovereign governments, to enter into a pact of peace and friendship with the Islamic state, but also of individuals, and this solely on the grounds of their humanity. In case the noncitizen covenanter is a Muslim, the *sharī'ah* would apply in all its provisions; in the case of a non-Muslim, the law of the covenanter's *millah* (community) applies during residence within the Islamic state. According to the *sharī'ah,* the Islamic state has no right to refuse entry, or a covenant of peace and friendly relations, to anyone who applies, without due cause. The *sharī'ah* entitles such a person to bring a lawsuit against the state in any Islamic court.

In order to bring about mutual understanding and cooperation between the nations — a condition necessary for the conveyance of the word of God — the *sharī'ah* forbids any ridicule or derision of any people, nation, or religion by another, and declares such acts punishable. Aggression of one nation against another is more ominous. It is regarded by the *sharī'ah* as an injustice and crime that must be stopped. The *sharī'ah* imposes upon the Islamic state and all Muslims to rise against the aggressor. It entitles the victim of injustice to apply to any Islamic court for redress, and the Islamic state is duty-bound to execute the judgment even if it leads to violent confrontation. Moreover, it entitles the victim of aggression and injustice to seek refuge within the Islamic state. The Islamic state cannot treat the noncitizens on the basis of ad hoc agreements with their respective states or on that of reciprocity. Being God's law, the *sharī'ah* is not subject to the whims or interests of governments or nations, even if these were Muslim.

POLITICAL INDEPENDENCE IN THE MUSLIM WORLD (Continued)

Dependent Countries

Continent	*Country*	*Dependent Since*
Africa	Erithrea	1918
Asia	Mindanao	c. 1500
	Pattani	19th century
	Cyprus	1878
	Central Asian Khanates	1884
	Palestine	1918
	Kashmir	1947
	Afghanistan	1980

MUSLIM AND CHRISTIAN MINORITIES

Muslims in Europe	
United Kingdom	2,800,000
France	1,400,000
Germany	1,100,000
Netherlands	400,000
Switzerland	300,000
Belgium	200,000

Christians in Muslim Countries	
Malaysia	120,000
West Africa	10-15 million
East Africa	10-15 million
Indonesia	1-2 million
North Africa	1,000,000
Pakistan	250,000

Sharī'ah and Society

Islam taught that all humans were created to serve God, and that their fate would ultimately rest on their accomplishment of that service. It defined this service in moral terms, and made freedom its *conditio sine qua non.* Translated into law, freedom prescribed

Illustration 14.1

Terra cotta floral decoration on a *miḥrāb* (orientation niche) of the Bagha Mosque, District Rajshahi, Bangladesh, 1523 C.E. [Courtesy Department of Antiquities, Government of Bangladesh.]

that the life of the individual or group may not be regimented or coerced in any way except in an extraordinary and temporary emergency. The *sharī'ah* imposed grave punishment upon the violators of men's freedom, and entitled the coerced person to return to his original position unharmed. The *sharī'ah* declared any witness or information flowing out of coercion, cheating, or spying as null and void, inadmissible in any legal process.

Islamic law entitled every citizen, Muslim or non-

Muslim, to choose and pursue the career of his choice, to move his person, family, and goods and wealth anywhere, to reside wherever he wishes, to practice the religion of his/her choice, to observe and develop his culture without hindrance from any source. The *sharī'ah* protected him against any interference in his affairs, and offered him its court of law to lodge his complaint free of charge and to receive vindication. Moreover, the *sharī'ah* held no man responsible for the deed of another. Unless the other was a dependent minor or legally insane, it recognized neither vicarious guilt nor merit and regarded group condemnation and punishment unjust and immoral.

The *sharī'ah* regarded the human person as a member or head of a household, and hence as dependent on or responsible for the household and its members. It defined the rights and mutual obligations of husband and wife, parents and offspring, brothers and sisters, uncles and aunts, grandparents and grandchildren, and cousins. It declared all of them dependents of the head of the household in case of need or inability to be heads of household of their own. The family in its extended form was the constitutive unit of society, disciplining its members into mutual loyalty and cooperation for the welfare of all members.

Moreover, the *sharī'ah* defined the person in terms of religious affiliation, and hence as a member of a religious community. Such membership determined the law applicable to that person and placed him within a circle of rights and obligations pertinent to that religious community. Citizenship in the Islamic state further imposed the responsibility of participating in the political process, of providing to the ruler advice as well as correction where needed. However, no social entity — whether the family, the *millah* or community, or the state — may absolutize itself and become the source or criterion of law. On the contrary, all these circles of influence remain subject to the overall dominion of the *sharī'ah*.

Sharī'ah and Charity

It is universally recognized that helping the weak, the underprivileged, and the deprived and seeking voluntarily to improve the quality of life for all is an objective of human morality. Few cultures, however, have sought to institutionalize it, and none to legislate it.

The *sharī'ah* dared this apparently impossible task. It legislated a specific minimum contribution by all owners of wealth, and recommended an indefinite additional amount. The latter is called *ṣadaqah* (charity). It is always personal and infinite in scope, nature, variety, and application. The prescribed contribution is called *zakāt*. It is collectible by state authority and amounts to 2½ percent of all appropriated wealth beyond the owner's personal need and that of his dependents. It is collected annually.

Comprehensiveness of the *Sharī'ah*

Islam developed a comprehensive law that covered the whole span of human life. This comprehensiveness flowed from Islam's conception of human life as created for the fulfillment of imperatives constituting the divine will. All acts, therefore, are seen as falling within the purview of the law and are either *wājib* (obligatory), *mubāḥ* (permissible), *mandūb* (recommended), *makrūh* (recommended against) and *ḥarām* (prohibited). At the same time, the law of Islam acknowledged the general welfare of humans to

Illustration 14.2

Key for the Ka'bah, twelfth century C.E., held in the Topkapi Saray Museum, Isṭanbūl. [Photo by L. al Fārūqī.]

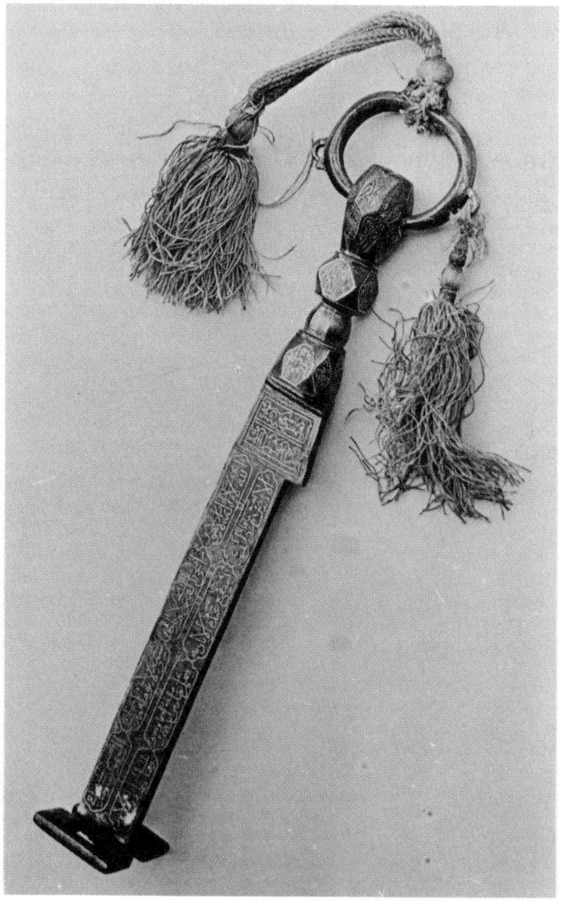

be its purpose. It divided that purpose as consisting of *ḍarūriyyāt* (universal necessities), *ḥājiyāt* (personal needs), and *taḥsīnāt* (desirables).

While ethics recommended the kind treatment of wife, children, and relatives, the law prescribed that feeding, sheltering, and caring for them be equal to one's treatment of oneself. In the same spirit, the law abolished all interest and instituted interest-free financing for all. It granted the captive the power to ransom himself by contract, the ignorant the right to be taught, and the deprived the right to partake of the wealth of the affluent.

The law further declared it a punishable sin to speak evil of one's neighbor even when the evil was true; to reject the neighbor's compensation and apology; to fail to visit him in sickness. One must help a neighbor in want, return his greeting with a better one, give him good counsel at all times, whether he asks for it or not; even to bless him when he sneezes. A Muslim is obliged to protect his neighbor's family and property in his absence, to attend his funeral and burial when he dies, or perform his obsequies in case of need.

Islamic law prohibits man from spying, lying, and being deceptive. It forbids speaking without knowledge, loud speech, entering another's house without knocking, and the assumption of airs of pride and superiority. It commands to keep oneself clean, to put on one's best when in congregation, to fulfill one's promise under all conditions, to maintain one's decorum at all times, and to bend one's head to parents and elders, to men of knowledge and those in authority.

Thus the corpus of laws constituting the *sharī'ah* is usually divided into twelve departments:

1. rituals and liturgy
2. personal status
3. contracts
4. torts
5. criminal law
6. constitutional law
7. taxation and public finance
8. administrative law
9. land law
10. law of trade and commerce
11. international law
12. ethics and personal conduct

Law is often said to be the mirror of civilization in the sense that when it has grown mature and complete, civilization reflects itself in its laws. This view assumes that law is a product of civilization, produced like other features of civilization by the forces operating within it. The opposite is the case with the *sharī'ah*. Rather than being a product or reflection of Islamic civilization, the *sharī'ah* is its first cause. Its observance by the Muslims of the world is the source that generated Islamic civilization, that nursed and protected it in history. The *sharī'ah* was and continues to be the civilizing force among Muslims.

THE LAW IN HISTORY

Formation

Being the medium of a continual stream of revelation, the Prophet provided the Muslims with answers to their inquiries regarding what they ought to do. The revelation was speaking to all occasions. The Qur'ān contains little prescriptive legislation but many principles and schemata for morality. However, the Prophet clarified, instantiated, and exemplified these principles and thus translated them into concrete guidelines and laws for action. Even in his lifetime, and before completion of the Qur'ānic revelation, the Prophet approved of his companions' recourse to their own reasoning, under the guidance of the divine imperatives, of a certain proposal or problem not mentioned in the revelation. After his death, and after the establishment of Islam in other lands through the *Futūḥāt,* a wide range of problems presented themselves for solution, which the Muslims of the Prophet's time had never confronted before. Pressing for a solution and in the absence of fresh revelation the Muslims began the task of translating ethical principles into legal prescriptions and extrapolating or deducing from the given instances of the Qur'ān and the *sunnah* the new legal directives they needed. This process was not centralized; and it soon led to the emergence of different schools in Madīnah and the provincial cities of Kūfah, Damascus, Fusṭāṭ, and Baghdād.

Under the Rāshidūn caliphs, twenty-seven companions of the Prophet distinguished themselves in the formation of legal opinion. Scholars have divided them into two groups according to the amount and quality of legislation for which they were responsible. Seven belonged to the first group: 'Umar Ibn al Khaṭṭāb, 'Alī Ibn Abū Ṭālib, 'Ā'ishah, 'Abdullah Ibn Mas'ūd, Zayd Ibn Thābit, 'Abdullah Ibn 'Abbās, and 'Abdullah Ibn 'Umar. The second group included: Abū Bakr al Ṣiddīq, Umm Salamah, Anas Ibn Mālik, Abu Sa'īd al Khudriyy, Abū Mūsā al Ash'arī, Sa'd Ibn Abū Waqqās, Abū Hurayrah, 'Uthmān Ibn 'Affān, 'Abdullah Ibn 'Amr, 'Abdullah Ibn al Zubayr, Salmān al Fārisī, Jābir Ibn 'Abdullah, Mu'ādh Ibn Jabal, Ṭalḥah, Al

Zubayr, 'Abdul Raḥman Ibn 'Auf, 'Imrān Ibn Ḥuṣayyin, Abū Bakrah, 'Ibādah Ibn al Ṣāmit, and Mu'āwiyah Ibn Abū Sufyān.

The method they used was dictated by their circumstances. Being fully familiar with the *data revelata* and trained by the Prophet, they first resorted to the Qur'ān, and then to the Prophet's *sunnah.* If these sources were silent on the issue in question, they used their reason to extrapolate or deduce, then consulted with the other companions, and acted on the consensus emerging from the consultation. Their judgments accumulated quickly into a viable tradition. Before their age passed away, 'Umar I instituted their corpus of legal opinions as a tertiary source after the Qur'ān and the *sunnah,* necessary for future legalists to consult before making new judgments. At the same time, there was the need for principles of lawmaking, or directives for judges as to how to proceed in new cases. When 'Umar appointed Shurayḥ as judge, he gave him a testimony which became the fountainhead of Islamic jurisprudence. It included the following principles:

1. Rendering justice to those who seek it is both an Islamic duty and inevitable.
2. In the court of law all men are equal.
3. The burden of proof falls on the complainant; that of swearing on the defendant.
4. Any party's request for time to produce the relevant evidence must be granted, within reason. Failure to produce the evidence is evidence to the contrary.
5. A judgment proven to be false by evidence ought to be revoked.
6. All adult Muslims are legal persons—*'adl*—except those convicted of perjury or of a *ḥadd* (crime).
7. No human may be charged for his intentions. Only his actions may be so charged and under legal evidence.
8. Where you find the Qur'ān and *sunnah* silent on any matter, find the comparable case or principle and deduce or extrapolate the law from it.
9. That which the Muslim collectivity has found good and desirable is so from the standpoint of God.

The need for law in this early period and the entry into Islam of large numbers of non-Arabic-speaking people posed another problem, that of the correct rendering and understanding of the tenets of the Qur'ān and *sunnah.* This called upon the jurists to establish rules for the understanding on the linguistic as well as on the juristic levels. Thus a discipline of linguistic hermeneutics as well as one of legal exegesis developed. The former built a formal logic into Arabic grammar and elaborated the relations of general terms *(al 'āmm)* and specific terms *(al khāṣṣ),* and their possible conversion to one another, in great detail. The latter distinguished between the Qur'ān's credal, liturgical, ethical, and prescriptive laws (including the criminal, civil, contractual, personal status, public, and procedural laws), and analyzed the nature of the legal force attaching to each. They distinguished between categorical and probable evidence, and between final and instrumental imperatives.

Also during this period the Prophet's actions, sayings, and attitudes became verbalized, that is, they were retrieved from the memories of the companions and rendered in discursive form as a statement made by the Prophet or a companion and transmitted by a chain of narrators who received it from one another. Obviously, the prestige of the narrators, their closeness to the Prophet, and the frequency of the narration by the companions constituted so many arguments for authenticity of what was being reported and were used as ground for new legislation.

The Flowering

A century after the death of the Prophet, none of his companions were alive to give an eyewitness report. While the text of the Qur'ān was established beyond doubt, its meanings and the relations they bore to the laws claimed to be founded upon them were subject to critical review. On the other hand, the *sunnah* was established neither in its text nor in its meanings. Its transmission was distant enough to be given detached examination. The earlier generations knew the situational contexts and causes of the revelation and were sufficiently imbibed with the spirit of the Prophet to perceive the Islamic meaning or purpose without difficulty. Presently a new age was dawning, characterized by distance from the two sources of revelation, by novel problems pressing for solution, and by a linguistic consciousness not so sure of itself. Often, too many different opinions, reports, and judgments were circulating concerning the same matter. The reassurance that religious conscience demanded was not always present. The question was no longer whether or not a certain action or measure was Islamic, but how its Islamicity could be demonstrated, and how critical conviction could be reached.

The verbalization, verification, and canonization of the *sunnah,* as described in Chapter 6, were launched. The yield was the establishment of the *Ṣiḥāḥ* (the six collections of verified traditions) and of *'ulūm al ḥadīth,* the sciences of the *hadīth.* At the same time, *'ulūm al Qur'ān,* or "sciences of the Qur'ān" were established (see Chapter 10). The ground was ready for a new science, *uṣūl al fiqh,* to lay down its principles for validating the derivation of law from the revelation.

Wāṣil ibn 'Aṭā' (130/748), founder of the Mu'tazilah movement (Chapter 14), had previously elaborated some principles relevant to *uṣūl al fiqh,* such as the sources of knowledge, the distinction between statement of fact and judgment or command, between particular and universal, between part and whole. Although these issues pertained to the philosophical matters raised by the interreligious dialogue of the time, by the conversion of Christians with a penchant for theology and metaphysical disputation, and by the translation of Greek philosophical texts, they did have some consequence for jurisprudence. Without a doubt, the intellectual atmosphere helped to raise and sharpen the theoretical issues concerning the law.

The man who rose to the challenge and founded the new discipline was Muḥammad Idrīs al Shāfi'ī (204/820). He learned from Mālik ibn Anas, the foremost leader of the jurists in Madīnah and a spokesman of the traditional school, and from Abū Ḥanīfah, leader of Kūfah and spokesman of the liberal school. He traveled widely and was familiar with the problems of the Muslim world and the thinking of the jurists everywhere. In his work, he defined the principles of deduction *(qiyās)* from the texts, and established criteria for the validation of their application. He examined the *ḥujjiyyah* or validating weight of the *sunnah,* equating its juristic power with that of the Qur'ān; of *istiḥsān* (juristic preference), which he declared void of validating power; of the traditions of the Prophet's companions, which he found weak unless supported by the *sunnah;* and of *ijmā'* which he declared nonexistent except in rituals and the transmission of the Qur'ān itself.

In the third century A.H., the Muslim world witnessed a great influx of ideas from classical antiquity, Persia, and India, and Muslim knowledge grew significantly. Differing schools of thought arose, some remaining close to the original faith, and others wandering away from it. It was in this period that the problem of the createdness vs. eternity of the Qur'ān arose, exposing the revelation to the relativization of history. Under the leadership of Aḥmad ibn Ḥanbal the view of createdness was defeated and the threat removed. These currents naturally affected juristic thinking. Publication of al Shāfi'ī's *Risālah* evoked numerous thinkers to write for or against its views. 'Īsā ibn Ibbān (221/836) rose to the defense of liberalism, as expounded in the School of Iraq, founded by Abū Ḥanīfah (150/768). Al Naẓẓām (221/836) added a dialectical argument against *ijmā'* and its possibility; and Aṣbagh ibn Faraj (225/840) wrote a defense of the Shāfi'ī view. The raging controversies did not fail to bring about a conservative reaction. Dawud ibn 'Alī al Ẓāhirī wrote against both parties, pleading for the sanctity of the letter of the revelation and hence the meanings that attach to it. His work, *Al Wuṣūl ilā Ma'rifat al Uṣūl* remains to this day the best defense of the literalist interpretation. The law itself was being developed furiously by the disciples and followers of Abū Ḥanīfah, such as Sufyān ibn 'Uyaynah (198/814), Muḥammad 'Abdul Raḥman ibn Abū Laylā, Supreme Judge of Kūfah (148/756), 'Abdul Malik ibn Jurayj (150/768), 'Abdul Raḥman al Awzā'ī (157/775), and al Layth ibn Sa'd al Fahmī (175/792), all of whom took advantage of the pragmatism and liberal rationalism of the Ḥanafī school and operated under the intellectual impetus its methodology provided.

In the fourth century A.H., the early beginnings of *uṣulī* thinking grew and matured into a full discipline. The law had been developing for three centuries, covering every conceivable action or problem-situation, under the guidance furnished by each of the notable thinkers, imāms, or jurists of the earlier centuries. Upon the thinkers of the fourth century now fell the task of exposing the methodological principles implicit in this lawmaking and to justify them against critique by the other schools, which had reached the same or different dispensations but by using different methodological assumptions. Abundant were the examples from which the theoreticians of the law could draw justification for their systematic constructions. Naturally, the writings on *uṣūl al fiqh* from that century on belonged to the same schools which they defended, and with which they sought to consolidate their formal principles.

The Shafi'ī school was the first to be established, armed as it were with the *Risālah* of its founder. Ibn Burhān al Fārisī (305/919) produced two books on *uṣūl,* elaborating and clarifying the *uṣūlī* principles of the *Risālah.* Only one of them is extant, *Al Dhakhīrah fi Uṣūl al Fiqh.* In the same vein, among others too numerous to mention, Muḥammad 'Abdullah al Ṣayrafī (330/642) produced three works, a commentary, a treatise on *ijmā',* and *Al Bayān fi Dalā'il al A'lām 'Alā Uṣūl al Aḥkām,* and Ibrahīm Aḥmad al Marwazī (340/952) wrote *Al Fuṣūl fī Ma'rifat al Uṣūl,* in which they clarified and defended the Shāfi'ī views. Another Shāfi'ī jurist, Aḥmad bin 'Umar bin Surayj (306/920) engaged Ibn Dāwūd al Ẓāhirī in debate in defense of the Shāfi'ī principle of *qiyās* which al Ẓāhirī condemned. Rising to the defense of *qiyās* as a source of new and certain knowledge was the great Mu'tazilah thinker turned anti-Mu'tazilah, Abū al Ḥasan al Ash'arī (324/936). He wrote a treatise in defense of deductive logic entitled *Ithbāt al Qiyās* and another on particulars and universals, *Al Khāṣṣ wal 'Āmm.* Abū Manṣūr al Māturīdī (333/945) joined the discussion on the highest philosophical level in his book, *Al Jadal fī Uṣūl al Fiqh,* meant to present and defend the Ḥanafī view.

In the Mālikī school, 'Amr Muḥammad al Laythī (331/943) wrote *Al Lumā',* Abū Bakr 'Alā' al Qushayrī (344/956) wrote *Kitāb al Qiyās* and *Uṣūl al Fiqh,* and Muḥammad 'Abdullah al Abharī (375/986) wrote his *Al Uṣūl fil Fiqh* and a treatise defending the *ḥujjiyyah* of the consensus of Madīnah, *Ijmā' Ahl al Madīnah,* in explanation of the views of Mālik ibn Anas, founder of the school.

Important as the foregoing works may be in the history of their respective schools of law, they did not make significant changes in, or contributions to, the discipline as such. Surpassing both the Mālikī and Shāfi'ī works in importance for the discipline were the works of the Ḥanafī jurists 'Ubaydullah Dalāl al Karkhī (340/952) and his pupil, Abū Bakr al Rāzī al Jaṣṣāṣ (370/981). The main contribution of the former is his introduction to the discipline of thirty-nine legal rules, thus ending its formal nature and making it a general philosophy of law in addition to being a formal methodology of law derivation. The latter established the historical and critical method in the discipline. Systematically, al Jaṣṣāṣ gave all matters the same treatment: definition; reporting and elaborating the predecessors' views; assessing, criticizing, amending, and complementing them with those of the author; presentation, evaluation, and criticism of the opponents' views; synthesizing and summing up the position; and marking its strength, weaknesses, and spots where further research was necessary.

The greatest contribution of al Jaṣṣāṣ, however, lay in his refutation of Shāfi'ī's arguments against *istiḥsān* and his establishment of it as the necessary condition of all creative legal thinking. Under Shāfi'ī, the ability of the jurist to attend to the welfare of the community was reduced, and that of responding to novel problems with novel solutions as inspired by the ultimate purposes of the *sharī'ah* was eliminated. Without *istiḥsān,* Islamic law stood condemned to fossilization. However, *istiḥsān* is not to be equated with juridical license, for the purposes of the *sharī'ah* guard it against any possible aberration.

In the fifth century the discipline of *uṣūl al fiqh* saw great flowering. The number of scholars specializing in it, and the books they wrote — systematic treatments and discussions of various aspects of the discipline and its problems — expanded significantly. After being a specialty of the jurists, the subject became an important component of any school's curriculum, as its relevance to Islamic learning as a whole came to be understood and appreciated by all. Moreover, *uṣūl al fiqh* joined the general battle of ideas raging at the time. *Uṣūlī* scholars rose to defend the Qur'ān against the Mu'tazilah claim of createdness, which demanded of them the establishment of a viable theory of hermeneutics and language, of prophecy and prophethood. They alone rose to counter the Ṣūfī claim for a *bāṭinī* (esoteric) meaning behind the Arabic words reached through allegorical interpretation or on authority of the initiated. The forces of sectarianism were no less the target of *uṣūlī* thinkers who had to refute their claims by Islamic universalism on sure epistemological and ethical foundations. The conservatives at one extreme and the radicals at the other had to be refuted and the *sharī'ah* had to be established as the law of the golden mean. Finally, the schlolastic rigor and preference for a priori reasoning of the *uṣūlī* scholars themselves had to be bent and tempered so as to keep the *sharī'ah* responsive to the empirical needs of the *ummah.* There had to be viable methods to gauge the welfare of the masses, which *uṣūl al fiqh* affirmed to be a definitive source of law.

Partly responsible for this flowering and expansion of *uṣūlī* scholarship was the fragmentation of the Muslim empire into small states governed by princely dynasties which vied with one another for prestige and competed to bring to their respective courts the greatest luminaries of the day. The Ḥamdānī dynasty

Illustration 14.3

King Fayṣal Mosque, Mindanao State University, Marawi City, Philippines, 1977. [Courtesy A. A. Tamano.]

Illustration 14.4

Ushak rug from Turkey, seventeenth century. [Courtesy Ministry of Culture and Tourism, Government of Turkey.]

in northern Syria and Iraq had two capitals, Ḥalab (Aleppo) and al Mawṣil. The Ṭūlūnī and Ikhshīdī dynasties, coming in the wake of the Fāṭimīs in Egypt, continued and developed the institutions of higher learning — especially al Azhar. The Saljūqs in Khurāsān held their court at Marw; and the Ghaznawīs, farther east in Ghazna (Afghanistan). Also at this time, Muslim Central Asia prospered under the Sāmānī dynasty, making Bukhārā and Samarqand glorious centers of Islamic learning, and Ṭabaristān prospered under Qābūs bin Washamgīr at Khiwā, near the Caspian Sea. South Persia and Iraq prospered under the Buwayhīs, who kept their court at Iṣfahān and al Rayy. Last but not least was the court of the Umawīs in Cordoba, which equaled the cities of the Muslim East in splendor and refinement, attracting to its universities and institutions the greatest minds of Europe.

Among the greatest works of *uṣūl al fiqh,* works that exercised a lasting influence on the discipline as well as on Islamic thinking, were the following:

Shāfi'ī scholars

1. Aḥmad Muḥammad al Isfarāyīnī (406/1016), *Kitāb Uṣūl al Fiqh.*
2. Ibrahīm 'Alī al Fīrūzabādī (476/1083), *Al Luma' fī Uṣūl al Fiqh, Al Tabṣirah fī Uṣūl al Fiqh.*
3. Imām al Ḥaramayn al Juwaynī (478/1085), teacher of al Ghazālī, *Al Burhān fī Uṣūl al Fiqh, Al Tuḥfah fī Uṣūl al Fiqh,* and *Al Waraqāt.*
4. Abū Ḥāmid al Ghazālī (505/1111), *Tahdhīb al Uṣul, Al Mankhūl min 'Ilm al Uṣūl,* and *Al Mustaṣfā min 'Ilm al Uṣūl.*

Mālikī scholars

1. Abū Bakr Muḥammad al Bāqillanī (403/1012), *Al Taqrīb min Uṣūl al Fiqh* and *Al Muqni' fī Uṣūl al Fiqh.*
2. 'Abdul Wahhāb 'Alī al Baghdādī (421/1030), *Al Ifāḍah fī Uṣūl al Fiqh.*
3. Aḥmad Muḥammad al Ma'āfirī (429/1037), *Al Wuṣul ilā Ma'rifat al Uṣūl.*
4. 'Alī Ibn Ḥazm (456/1063), the famous Biblical critic and comparativist of religion in Cordoba, *Al Iḥkām fī Uṣūl al Aḥkām.*

Ḥanbalī scholars

1. Al Ḥasan ibn Ḥāmid al Baghdadī (403/1012), *Kitāb Uṣūl al Fiqh.*
2. Abū Ya'lā al Farrā' (458/1065), leader of the Ḥanbali school in Baghdād, *Al 'Uddah fī Uṣūl al Fiqh, Al 'Umdah fī Uṣūl al Fiqh,* and *Al Kifāyah fi Uṣūl al Fiqh.*

Ḥanafī scholars

1. Aḥmad Ḥusayn al Bayhaqī (458/1065), *Al Yanābī' fī al Uṣūl.*
2. 'Abdullah 'Umar al Dabbūsī (430/1038), *Taqwīm al Adillah fī Uṣūl al Fiqh* and *Asrār al Uṣūl wal Furū'.*
3. 'Alī Muḥammad al Bazdawī (482/1089), *Kanz al Wuṣūl ilā Ma'rifat al Uṣūl.*
4. Abū Bakr al Sarakhsī (490/1096), *Uṣūl al Fiqh.*

Mu'tazilah scholars. Though not reputed for their position on law and jurisprudence but on *kalām* (theology and philosophy), some Mu'tazilah thinkers produced classics in *uṣūl.* Certainly the following constitute such classics whose influence reached far outside the Mu'tazilah ranks.

1. Muḥammad 'Alī al Baṣrī (436/1044) wrote a masterpiece, *Al Mu'tamad fī Uṣūl al Fiqh.*
2. Al Qāḍī 'Abdul Jabbār (415/1024) devoted a whole

volume of his encyclopaedic *Al Mughnī* to the science of *uṣūl,* and wrote as well five other treatises on the subject: *Al Ikhtilāf fī Uṣūl al Fiqh, Uṣūl al Fiqh, Al 'Amad, Majmū' al 'Ahd,* and *Al Nihāyah.*

Muslim scholars throughout the centuries have regarded eight of the foregoing thinkers as the foremost authorities and have referred to them constantly in their thinking and writing. These were 'Abdul Jabbār, al Baṣrī, Abū Ya'lā, al Juwaynī, al Ghazālī, al Dabbūsī, al Sarakhsī, and al Bazdawī. 'Abdul Jabbār and Baṣrī founded the disciplines of deontology and axiology, which they regarded as necessary conditions for knowledge of *uṣūl al fiqh* and law. They were led to undertake this task by two premises of Islamic law. First, it follows from God's nature that commands must issue from Him for man and creation to follow. Knowledge of the command as command, as something that ought to be done, is of the essence for all ethical and legal knowledge. Second, the commandments of God are rational and hence supported by *al ma'ānī* (purposes or values), as found in nature or pertaining to man's ethical and spiritual life, which correspond to the commandments as their ontological grounds. These values or grounds are knowable by reason and are the subjects of immediate intuition by humans with the requisite level of moral and spiritual sensitivity.

Abū Ya'lā al Farrā', al Juwaynī, and al Ghazālī were collectively responsible for exploring the nature of evidence and developing the theory that became the cornerstone of jurisprudence as well as of religious and philosophical knowledge. In their view, the *data revelata* were *ma'ānī* for which the Qur'ān and the *sunnah* as discursive revelation were the *bayān* or clarification. Further, *bayān* was the equivalent of evidence and hence the words of the Qur'ān and of the *sunnah* constituted the reportative part of the evidence. Agreement with the reportative evidence is the first condition of validity. There is yet another necessary part to evidence, the rational. Here the tests of internal coherence *(dalālah bil manẓūm),* of adequacy *(dalālah bil mafhūm),* and of correspondence with reality *(dalālah bil iqtiḍā')* are the components. But where all this is not adequate to prove the point, a higher level of rational evidence may be invoked to overarch the varying testimonies and overcome their differences. Al Ghazālī called this higher evidence "rational," defined it in intuitive terms, and identified it as the a priori eidetic content of thought *(dalālah bil ma'nā al ma'qūl).*

Finally, al Dabbūsī, al Sarakhsī, and al Bazdawī, the Ḥanafī jurists, reknitted with ever firmer threads the bond between the law and religion, making the former the instrument and form of man's vicegerency for God on earth. This linkage was the guarantee of success for the *sharī'ah.* For it provided the community with cohesion in the face of ethnic diversity, and the individual with moral uprightness in the face of temptation. It planted in the conscience of the average man, in the masses by the millions across the centuries and the world, the *wāzi'* (or inner restrainer) to bolster man's defenses against evil, the *ṭama'nīnah* (or reassurance) of right-walking with God, and the *'izzah* (or dignity) which rightly belongs to the human who can see the world and history as an object to be shaped, by him, for the greater glory of God.

Islamic law made Islamic civilization, not vice versa. It disciplined and united the Muslims across the generations, the centuries, and the continents, in every aspect of their lives, branding their minds, their hearts, and their deeds with the brand of Islam. By its agency, the convert was often lifted from the Stone Age to modernity in one swoop, from myth and superstition to empiricism and rational evidence, and from struggle for individual or tribal survival to that of divine vicegerency of human history.

CHAPTER 15

Kalām (Theology)

THE EARLY MANIFESTATIONS

The Rise of *Kalām*

The first manifestation of Islamic thought occurred outside of Arabia, and on three fronts. The first was that of jurisprudence. Confronted with new situations and new problems, and in the absence of the Prophet on whom they could call for fresh instruction in the divine imperatives, the Muslims were thrust upon themselves to translate the ideals of Islam into prescriptions to meet the new situations of daily life and devise solutions for the new problems. They had to invent the science of jurisprudence to govern and regulate the process of lawmaking, as we have seen in Chapter 14. To this end they had to raise and answer questions regarding the purposes of the *sharī'ah,* the nature of human acts, the meaning of obligation and of good and evil, and to establish rules for the understanding of the revelation. Thus, they involved themselves in elaborating and establishing logic, a system of rules concordant with Arabic grammar to govern their comprehension of linguistic meanings, deduction of secondary meanings, rules for extrapolation, and methods for ascertainment of empirical truth. Likewise, as previously noted, *ḥadīth* criticism led them to establish a whole set of critical disciplines, including historiography and biography. These challenges and the efforts the Muslims directed to meet them produced a positive, rational, and critical philosophy bent on meeting the needs of an exuberant and flourishing civilization.

There is no doubt that all these considerations were present in the Arabian Peninsula as well as outside of it in the provinces brought under the dominion of Islam. However, apart from the influx of wealth which the empire brought to Arabia, the nature and quality of life there did not change. The ideological and social change which Islam brought was radical and pervasive. It succeeded so well that after the Prophet and his generation had passed away, no thinker defended, or even presented, idolatry, associationism, tribalism, hedonism, *dahr,* or fatalism, as an issue. These problems, which dominated thinking and living in pre-Islamic Arabia, were no longer problems for the Muslims of the Peninsula. It was otherwise in the provinces where life presented different problems. Land tenure, irrigation and intensive agriculture, continuous trade between large urban centers which had hitherto dominated world empires, and the physical and social mobility which Islam and the Islamic state brought — all these created problems for which no ready-made answers were available precisely because life in the Peninsula presented no parallel. The new situations called for an intellectual effort to discover the relevance of Islam to them.

The second front, equally internal to the situation of Muslims, was the inclination, natural in humans, to think out and systematize the truths presented by the new Islamic vision. The earlier generations, which witnessed the revelation, and their children and grandchildren were too close to the extraordinary phenomenon of prophecy and could only be absorbed in the vision it imparted. In the presence of ultimate reality, human tendency is to acknowledge and acquiesce, to proclaim and enter into adoration and obedience. The Muslim's consciousness had been completely dominated by the vision of the divine pattern that commanded the adherent of the faith to transform space-time; and in his life, the Muslim had been too engaged in the business of making history to articulate his mission and ideology in a systematic manner. He certainly argued about it, but controversy had no appeal for him. The greatest and final argument he had was to point to himself and his fellow Muslims as exemplars of the faith; and both he and his opponents were convinced by this argument. The spectacle of the Muslim giving himself completely over to the new religious and moral values and realizing them with a completeness that hardly knew or tolerated exceptions while making history in the process, was as great as it was disarming. However, the human mind, in an epiphenomenon, wanted to propound and elaborate the new faith, and to systematize and deduce applications to all fields. Where this kind of work requires a minimal effort, as in the case of Islam—with its *kitāb mubīn* (clear book), *sunnah mubayyinah* (clarifying exemplification), and *sharī'ah muḥaqqiqah* (actualizing law)—sheer contemplation of the phenomenon of Islam and the revolution it brought about in all aspects of human life forced the mind to ponder and seek answers, if not to the questions of whence and whither, then surely to that of why.

Revelation, in the past as in Islam, is seldom systematic or comprehensive. It is always contextual in that its pronouncements speak to given situations. It does not purport to deal with all situations, nor to classify and order them so as to apply itself to them systematically. Rather, it pours itself out into one or another aspect of human living or concern, in bolts of intense light and heat, exposing the darkest recesses and the highest peaks. The tasks of ordering and categorizing, of applying the light of revelation to other situations, is not the work of revelation but of scholarship and thought acting under its guidance and light. Likewise, if revelation is ever comprehensive—as the Qur'ānic revelation certainly is—it is so on the level of first principles and values, never on that of specific materials for actualization. Since the aim of

Illustration 15.1

Mausoleum of Mughal ruler Jahangīr, near Lahore, Pakistan, seventeenth century. [Photo by L. al Fārūqī.]

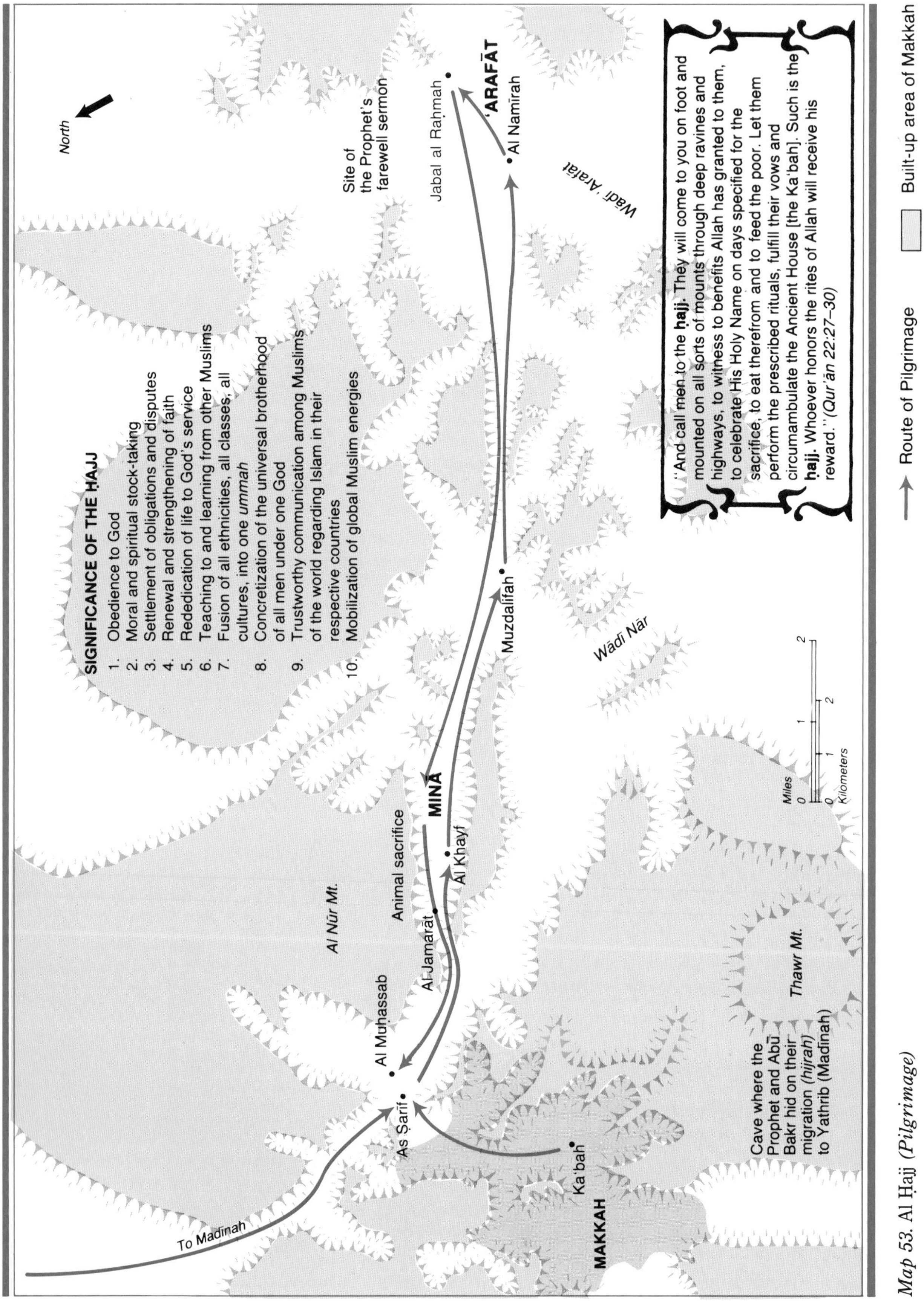
North
SIGNIFICANCE OF THE ḤAJJ
1. Obedience to God
2. Moral and spiritual stock-taking
3. Settlement of obligations and disputes
4. Renewal and strengthening of faith
5. Rededication of life to God's service
6. Teaching to and learning from other Muslims
7. Fusion of all ethnicities, all classes, all cultures, into one *ummah*
8. Concretization of the universal brotherhood of all men under one God
9. Trustworthy communication among Muslims of the world regarding Islam in their respective countries
10. Mobilization of global Muslim energies
Site of the Prophet's farewell sermon
Jabal al Raḥmah
'ARAFĀT
Al Namīrah
Wādī 'Arafāt
Muzdalifah
Wādī Nār
MINĀ
Al Khayf
Animal sacrifice
Al Jamarāt
Al Nūr Mt.
Al Muḥassab
As Sarif
Thawr Mt.
Cave where the Prophet and Abū Bakr hid on their migration (*hijrah*) to Yathrib (Madīnah)
Ka'bah
MAKKAH
To Madīnah
Miles 0 1 2
Kilometers 0 1 2
"And call men to the **ḥajj**. They will come to you on foot and mounted on all sorts of mounts through deep ravines and highways, to witness to benefits Allah has granted to them, to celebrate His Holy Name on days specified for the sacrifice, to eat therefrom and to feed the poor. Let them perform the prescribed rituals, fulfill their vows and circumambulate the Ancient House [the Ka'bah]. Such is the **ḥajj**. Whoever honors the rites of Allah will receive his reward." *(Qur'ān 22:27–30)*
Route of Pilgrimage
Built-up area of Makkah

Map 53. Al Ḥajj *(Pilgrimage)*

THE PROGRESS OF THE ḤAJJ

Before Starting the Ḥajj

1. Settle obligations.
2. Provide for dependents.
3. Settle disputes and begin a saintly life.
4. Resolve to perform the *ḥajj* for Allah's sake alone.
5. Budget adequately for trip from *ḥalāl*-earned money (honestly come by), on which *zakāt* has been paid.

En Route

1. Hold *ṣalāt* at each prescribed time.
2. Increase reading of the Qur'ān.
3. Take stock of your past.
4. Observe saintly behavior.

Five Mawaqit (sing. miqat); see Map 54

1. Dhūl Ḥulayfah, Northeast
2. Al Juḥfah (near Rābigh), Northwest
3. Qarn al Manāzil, East
4. Yalamlam, South
5. Dhāt 'Irq, Northeast

First Day

At *miqat:*

1. Take shower, or at least perform ablutions
2. Put on *ihram* clothing (two pieces of white unsewn cotton or linen cloth). Women are exempt.
3. Recite intention to perform *ḥajj.*

From *miqat* to Makkah:

Recite "Labbayka Allahuma . . ." (At your call, o God, here I come. There are no associates to You. Praise, gratitude, and the Kingdom are all Yours.)

At *Makkah,* within the Holy Sanctuary (*Al Ḥaram al Sharīf*):

1. Circumambulate the Ka'bah seven times, counterclockwise, beginning from the Black Stone corner.
2. Perform *ṣalāt* of two *rak'āt,* near the Ka'bah
3. Jog seven times between Ṣafā and Marwah hills, within the Holy Sanctuary.
4. Proceed to 'Arafāt.

At 'Arafāt:

1. Perform Ẓuhr and 'Asr *ṣalāt* jointly.
2. Listen to the sermon of the *imām.*
3. Stand up in prayer facing Makkah until sunset.
4. Proceed to Muzdalifah.

At Muzdalifah:

1. Perform Maghrib and 'Ishā' *ṣalāt* jointly.
2. Spend the night.
3. Perform Fajr *ṣalāt.*
4. Proceed to Minā.
5. Pick up pea-sized stones on the way.

Second Day

At *Minā:*

1. Sacrifice an animal and distribute its meat to the poor.
2. Throw seven pebbles at each of Satan's three *jamarāt* (shrines or pillars), saying with each throw: "Alah is Greatest."
3. Desacralize by shedding iḥrām, cutting hair, shaving, etc.
4. Spend the night at Minā, or proceed to Makkah.

Third Day

At *Makkah,* within the Holy Sanctuary:

1. Circumambulate the Ka'bah seven times, as on first day.
2. Perform a *ṣalāt* of two *rak'āt* near the Ka'bah.
3. Jog between Ṣafā and Marwah seven times.
4. Desacralize and return home.

revelation, and that of religion, is to reorder human life *in toto,* it is natural for it to speak on the highest levels of generality. Later, religious teachers and scholars fill in the detail.

On the third front, the early Muslims were met by Jews, Christians, Sabaeans, and Zoroastrians who questioned the claims of Islam and demanded satisfactory answers before they could convert to the new faith. Naturally, when they converted to Islam, they brought with them some religio-ideational baggage which predetermined their understanding of their new faith. As Muslims, they thought out their difficulties in understanding the faith, and gave them erroneous interpretations. The fundamental perceptions of their older faiths and cultures were too imbedded in their consciousness to be erased by Islam overnight; their own categories of understanding forced them to cast the Islamic truths in their own light. The Near East into which Islam had intruded was anything but a philosophical vacuum. The legacies of Ancient Mesopotamia and Egypt, of Greece and India, of Judaism and Christianity, of the region's religions and cultures were all alive and well. They may have allied themselves with the religions and cultures dominant at the

PILGRIMAGE STATISTICS

A. Number of People Who Made the Pilgrimage in 1977, 1979, and 1983

	1977	*1979*	*1983*
Pilgrims from Saudi Arabia	888,270	2,217,169	1,497,795
Pilgrims from other countries	739,319	862,510	1,002,911
Total	1,627,589	3,079,679	2,500,706

B. Number of People Who Made the Pilgrimage in 1977, by Country of Origin

Country	*Number*	*Country*	*Number*
Afghanistan	6,590	Mauritius	315
Algeria	53,230	Morocco	22,674
Bahrain	2,269	Niger	2,854
Bangladesh	5,815	Nigeria	104,577
Benin	205	Oman	2,429
Brunei	201	Pakistan	47,591
Cameroon	990	Palestine	1,434
Central African Republic	621	Philippines	784
Chad	1,720	Qatar	1,139
Djibouti	590	Senegal	4,825
Egypt	30,951	Sierra Leone	20
Ethiopia	1,121	Singapore	731
France	642	Somalia	4,786
Gambia	99	South Africa	765
Ghana	2,982	Spain	52
Greece	197	Sri Lanka	407
Guinea	1,244	Sudan	32,353
India	21,113	Syrian Arab Republic	24,829
Indonesia	35,703	Tanzania	1,086
Iran	36,942	Thailand	233
Iraq	34,909	Tunisia	7,914
Ivory Coast	1,129	Turkey	91,497
Jordan	14,211	Uganda	4,621
Kenya	590	United Arab Emirates	3,560
Kuwait	3,187	United Kingdom	1,309
Lebanon	3,815	Upper Volta	1,995
Liberia	80	Yemen Democratic Rep.	7,599
Libya	20,770	Yemen Arab Republic	79,347
Malaysia	4,278	Yugoslavia	1,115
Mali	2,740	American countries	473
Mauritania	1,084	Other countries	2,661

C. Number of People Who Made the Pilgrimage, 1927–1977, excluding Saudi Arabia

Year	*Number*	*Year*	*Number*
1927	90,764	1939	9,024
1928	81,666	1940	23,863
1929	39,045	1941	24,743
1930	29,065	1942	62,590
1931	20,181	1943	37,857
1932	25,291	1944	37,630
1933	33,898	1945	61,286
1934	33,830	1946	55,244
1935	49,517	1947	75,614
1936	76,224	1948	99,069
1937	59,577	1949	107,652
1938	32,152	1950	100,578

advent of Islam in the seventh century; but they were certainly capable of resisting and questioning the new religion.

Philosophical or theological thought in Islam began with three problems: the nature of *īmān* (faith) and the status of the grave sinner *(ṣāḥib al kabīrah);* determinism and freedom; and the nature of the divine attributes. The first two arose out of the Muslims' division regarding the claimants to caliphal rule and the violent conflicts that followed. When some Muslims called their opponents non-Muslim on account of their violent behavior, the issue of whether *īmān* is compatible with sin had to be met. And when those responsible for violence were brought to account for their deeds and they pleaded innocent because they acted under God's all-out determination, the issue of determinism and free will could not but be confronted and solved. The third problem stemmed from a source foreign to Islam. The Arabic-speaking Muslims had no trouble comprehending the Qur'ān in a direct and immediate way. Qur'ānic meanings bristled and shone in their words and expressions, too conspicuous to be missed. But when other Muslims sought to understand the texts, the road of immediate, intuitive apperception was not open to them. Barring it were the categories of understanding they inherited from their non-Arabic languages and their non-Islamic religions. Such a predicament threatened *tawḥīd,* the essence of Islam, when it affected the divine attributes.

Kalām (literally "words" or "speech," and referring to oration) was the name the Muslims applied to the discipline studying the afore-said issues, and *mutakallim* (pl. *mutakallimūm*) was used for the person committed to its pursuit. No word could have fitted better. *Khuṭbah,* oration or ex tempore speech, was the primary means of teaching, debating, proselytizing, or simply communicating information. Although writing was becoming more and more in use, it had not yet become central. Upon the able orator fell the task of defending the faith, of clarifying and elaborating it, of bringing it to the understanding of the people.

The First *Kalām* Schools

Al Qadariyyah. Founded by Ma'bad ibn Khālid al Juhanī (79/699), this school took its name from the view that man is capable of action *(qadar* or *qudrah)* and hence is responsible for his deeds. Ghaylān ibn Marwān al Dimashqī succeeded the founder in leading the school which taught the following principles. First, man is free and capable and therefore author of his deeds, whether good or evil. On the Day of Judgment, God will reckon with him, rewarding him for his good deeds and punishing him for his evil deeds. They quoted the Qur'ānic verses that obviously confirmed their view and interpreted those that seemed to do otherwise. Second, *īmān* is the consequence of knowledge and understanding, of acquiescence to the prophetic call of Muḥammad, and hence related to action but not necessarily requiring it. The grave sinner, they held, was indeed a Muslim despite his sin; but God will surely punish him on Judgment Day. Third, the attributes that pertain to the divine person, such as hand, sight, and hearing, were to be taken figuratively, so that the transcendence of God may be preserved. Predication of the attributes to God, they warned, is unlike that of an accident or quality of the substance to which it adheres. For the attribute, they claimed, is another index for the divine self.

PILGRIMAGE STATISTICS (Continued)

C. Number of People Who Made the Pilgrimage, 1927 – 1977, excluding Saudi Arabia

Year	*Number*	*Year*	*Number*
1951	148,515	1965	294,118
1952	149,841	1966	316,226
1953	164,072	1967	318,507
1954	232,971	1968	374,784
1955	220,722	1969	406,295
1956	215,575	1970	431,270
1957	209,197	1971	479,339
1958	207,171	1972	645,182
1959	253,369	1973	607,755
1960	285,948	1974	918,777
1961	216,455	1975	894,573
1962	199,038	1976	719,040
1963	266,555	1977	739,319
1964	283,319		

Al Jabriyyah. Founded by Jahm Ibn Ṣafwān (127/745) of Tirmidh in opposition to al Qadariyyah school, this school is sometimes known by the name of its founder as *al Jahmiyyah.* It adhered to the following principles. First, man is determined in all actions by divine power, including the acts of faith and virtue or faithlessness and vice. They quoted those Qur'ānic verses that obviously confirm their thesis, such as 76:29 – 30, and subjected the verses quoted by their adversaries such as 41:40 to allegorical interpretation. They thus reduced Qur'ānic freedom to a warning. Second, like al Qadariyyah, the school sought to preserve divine transcendence by interpreting the attributes pertaining to the self of God. They claimed that because only action and creation may be predicated of God, it is legitimate to attribute those qualities to the divine self. Third, the transcendence of God precluded that the world ever be visible to man. Hence, they interpreted verse 75:22, which says that the blessed shall behold God in Paradise, as meaning only that they will be in His presence. And they denied eternity of Paradise and Hell because they presumed God alone to be eternal.

Al Ṣifātiyyah. The foregoing schools became popular and began to divide the *ummah.* Arguments and counterarguments were heard everywhere. To some, their claims seemed exaggerated and their adherents removed from the immediate comprehension of the Arabic meanings of the Qur'ānic words. Naturally, this group rose to the defense of the silent Muslims who found their faith misinterpreted by both schools, and were known as *Ṣifātiyyah* or "attributists." A third school was thus founded by 'Abdullah ibn Sa'īd al Kullābī, which taught two principles. The first affirmation was that of the divine attributes in their known Arabic lexicographic meaning; and condemnation of all questioning regarding their nature or predication to God. They denied that the "hand" or "eye" of God is like anything human. They thus preserved transcendence and affirmed the attributes. Second, al Ṣifātiyyah denied the position of Qadariyyah on human freedom and the capacity for action. They held man to be determined by God in all that he does, and judgment (reward or punishment) is equally dictated by God, thus removing the apparent contradiction between them.

Al Khawārij. When 'Uthmān ibn 'Affān was elected to be the third caliph in 12/644, some leaders of the Muslim community were happy and others were not. The former were the clan of Umayyah, for 'Uthmān belonged to their house; the latter were the clan of Hāshim, for their candidate, 'Alī ibn Abū Ṭālib, lost his bid for the caliphate. The expectations of the Umayyah clan were met: the caliph appointed a number of the governors of the provinces from his clan, and thus invited the envy of others and the charge of nepotism from some. Soon, the anti-'Uthmān forces gathered strength and assassinated the caliph (35/656). The same body that elected 'Uthmān to the caliphate now elected 'Alī to replace him. The Umayyah clan was furious. Mu'āwiyyah ibn Abū Sufyān, governor of Syria, and 'Amr ibn al 'Āṣ, governor of Egypt, both of the Umayyah clan, united and asked 'Alī to identify and punish the assassins, or he would be disqualified from the caliphate by implication. Much as he personally might have wished to comply with the request, 'Alī was too weak to do so because insurrections were breaking out in many regions of the realm. Hence, Mu'āwiyyah and 'Amr joined forces

Illustration 15.2

Turfan Mosque, Xinjiang Province, People's Republic of China, seventeenth century. [Photo by Ingrid Larsen.]

and declared their independence of 'Alī's caliphate. Their contest for power became open defiance.

When their respective armies confronted each other at Ṣiffīn, south of al Raqqah on the Euphrates (36/657), and the forces of 'Alī were about to carry the day, the contesters resorted to a ruse and offered to accept arbitration. Anxious to spare blood and exhausted, 'Alī accepted the offer and withdrew. The offer of arbitration was a hoax and Mu'āwiyyah regrouped his forces for another round. The arbitration took place in 38/659, at Adhruḥ on the caravan route from Madīnah to Damascus, between Ma'ān and Petra. A group of 'Alī's followers strongly disagreed and insisted that arms should settle the issue. They were led by 'Abdullah ibn Wahb al Rāsibī and counted several thousand soldiers. 'Alī had to fight them to prevent an upset of the arrangement. He attacked and nearly annihilated Rāsibī's followers in the same year. But in the course of his encounter with them, he was assassinated at the hand of one of their men, 'Abdul Raḥman ibn Muljam, in 40/661. With 'Alī out of the way, Mu'āwiyyah declared himself legitimate caliph the same year.

The opponents of arbitration were expelled from the ranks of 'Alī's followers and declared heretics. They were charged with going against the consensus of the *ummah* and given the name of *Khawārij* or seceders. Subsequently, they were fought by everybody. Al Ḥajjāj, the Umawī governor of Iraq, fought many battles against them. They were fierce and dedicated, and they overran southern Iraq under the leadership of Nāfi' ibn al Azraq, and eastern Najd under that of Najdah ibn 'Āmir. Qaṭarī ibn al Fujā'ah was their greatest poet and hero. They recognized as legitimate only the first two caliphs, Abū Bakr and 'Umar; and they held that any capable man may hold that office if he is both competent and elected by the community. Theologically, they held the sinner as a *kāfir,* an outlaw or apostate, whom it is legitimate and religiously imperative to fight. Some remnants of this group survive to this day on the shores of the Arabian Gulf, in East Africa, and in Tunisia and Algeria; they are known as Ibāḍīs or Ibāḍiyyah, in reference to 'Abdullah ibn Ibāḍ who tempered their isolation by teaching that it is lawful for them to live among and mix with ordinary Muslims who disagreed with them. They are remembered today for their beautiful pietistic poetry.

Al Mu'tazilah. The three schools discussed above were also known by other names depending on the position they took regarding the issues involved. Regarding their position on the divine attributes, the schools were known as *Mu'aṭṭilah* (neutralizers) if they subjected the attributes to allegorical interpretation; *Mushabbihah* (anthropomorphists) if they affirmed them literally; and *Ṣifātiyyah* if they affirmed them and condemned any entertainment of how they were predicated of God. Concerning their position on human freedom, they were known as *Qadariyyah* and/or *Mu'tazilah* if they held man free, capable, and responsible; *Murji'ah* (deferrers) if they deferred judgment of the sinner to God and the Day of Judgment; and *Khawārij* (seceders) if they declared the Muslim sinner a non-Muslim and made of him an outlaw.

From Wāṣil ibn 'Aṭā', who died in Baṣrah in 131/749, to Abū al Ḥasan al Ash'arī, who died in Baghdād in 322/935, runs a line of brilliant thinkers who constitute the Mu'tazilah tradition.[1] This tradition was founded by Wāṣil ibn 'Aṭā' and was divided into two schools: that of Baṣrah comprising among its distinguished members 'Amr ibn 'Ubayd, Abū al Hudhayl al 'Allāf, Ibrahīm al Naẓẓām, 'Amr al Jāḥiz, Abū 'Alī, and Abū Hāshim al Jubbā'ī; and that of Baghdād, founded by Bishr ibn al Mu'tamar (210/826) and counting among its great members Abū Mūsā al Murdār, Aḥmad ibn Abū Du'ād (the favorite of the caliphs al Ma'mūn, al Mu'taṣim, and al Wāthiq, 204–232/820–848), Thumāmah ibn al Ashras, the two Ja'fars (Ja'far ibn Ḥarb and Ja'far ibn Mubashshir), Muḥammad al Iskāfī, and 'Abd al Raḥīm al Khayyāṭ. Abū al Ḥasan al Ash'arī was the last great *Mu'tazilī* who, having mastered their thought and method, overturned the tables against the *Mu'tazilah* and established the first crystallization of Sunnī theology. The *Mu'tazilah's* rise and flowering coincided with the formative period of Islamic thought. It was a time when the array of ideas presented to the observer was most bewildering. The job of controverting the opponents' opinions, of weighing alternatives and exposing their shortcomings, fell on the shoulders of the *Mu'tazilah;* and they certainly proved themselves in the many battles of ideas in which they engaged. Their history was as brilliant as that of their brethern — the military, the leaders of government and administration, of agriculture and industry, of trade and communications, of learning and the sciences — who had spent themselves in the realization of the divine pattern within as well as without, in themselves as in the world around them.

In the field of abstract thought, it was inevitable that questions of great importance would arise that demanded answers satisfying both reason and faith. *Al Mu'tazilah's* answers went a long way to achieve this but fell short of the goal. Their efforts opened the gates of controversy in matters that were basic to religion and ethics. The mood of the age was favorable and *Mu'tazilah* leaders were invited by caliph al Ma'mūn to assume power and lead the *ummah.* However, controversy permeated their ranks. Trusting their political power rather than their reason, they committed the tragic mistake of forcing acceptance of their doctrines upon the rank and file. Those who opposed the *Mu'tazilah* doctrine were forced out of office or thrown into jail. Aḥmad ibn Ḥanbal was imprisoned for his opposition of this *Mu'tazilah* view. Aḥmad ibn Abū Du'ād (160–240/777–855), the *Mu'tazilah* leader, was appointed chief justice by caliph al Mu'taṣim, on the testament his father, caliph al Ma'mūn, gave before his death in 218/833, but he had exercised great influence under the latter since 204/820. Caliph al Mutawakkil (232–247/847–862) discharged him from office in 229/851 and ordered his property confiscated. Since then, *al Mu'tazilah* as a movement fell from favor and was banned. It became the minority view and soon joined other Muslim dissenters — the Shī'ah — and alienated itself from the "orthodox" majority where some of its principles persisted.

Map 54. Al Ḥajj: Miqat al Ihram *(the points at which the pilgrims and visitors to Makkah don* ihram *clothing)*

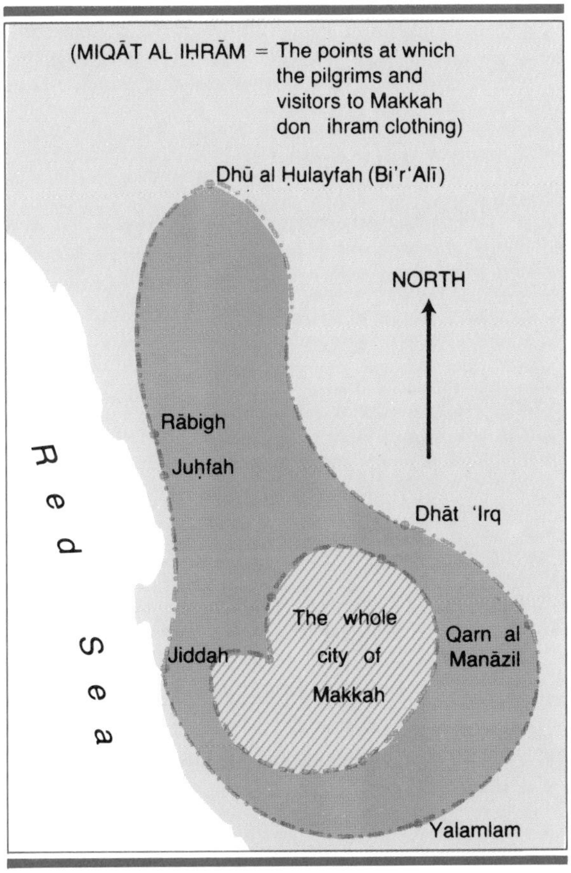

Outer Perimeter of sacred area
Inner Perimeter of sacred area (entire city of Makkah).

Mu'tazilah doctrine was founded on five axioms[2]: first, *al tawḥīd,* or uniqueness of God. This axiom was emphasized against the contentions of the Karaites (Jewish anthropomorphists), of the Manichaean dualists, of the Christian trinitarians, and of the Near Eastern philosophers who were for the most part gnostic emanationists. Under this principle the *Mu'tazilah* sought to establish the existence, uniqueness, and transcendence of God, which were threatened by those schools. Among Muslims, however, the *Mu'tazilah* claim of *tawḥīd* had an altogether different purport. It demanded that the divine attributes be "neutralized." If, as ordinary Muslims claim, the attributes were not God and eternal, then transcendence could no longer be maintained. Their argument was simple and straightforward. Divine knowledge is either eternal or it is created. If eternal, it is either in God, outside of God, or nowhere. If in God, then God is a theater where change takes place. If outside of God, then God is not omniscient and someone else is. And knowledge cannot be nowhere. It is somewhere and eternal. But it cannot be outside of God for that involves polytheism. It must therefore be in God and intrinsic to Him.

Similarly, all divine attributes must be declared either negative, denying that their opposites are

TABLE 15.1. AL MU'TAZILAH, BAṢRAH BRANCH

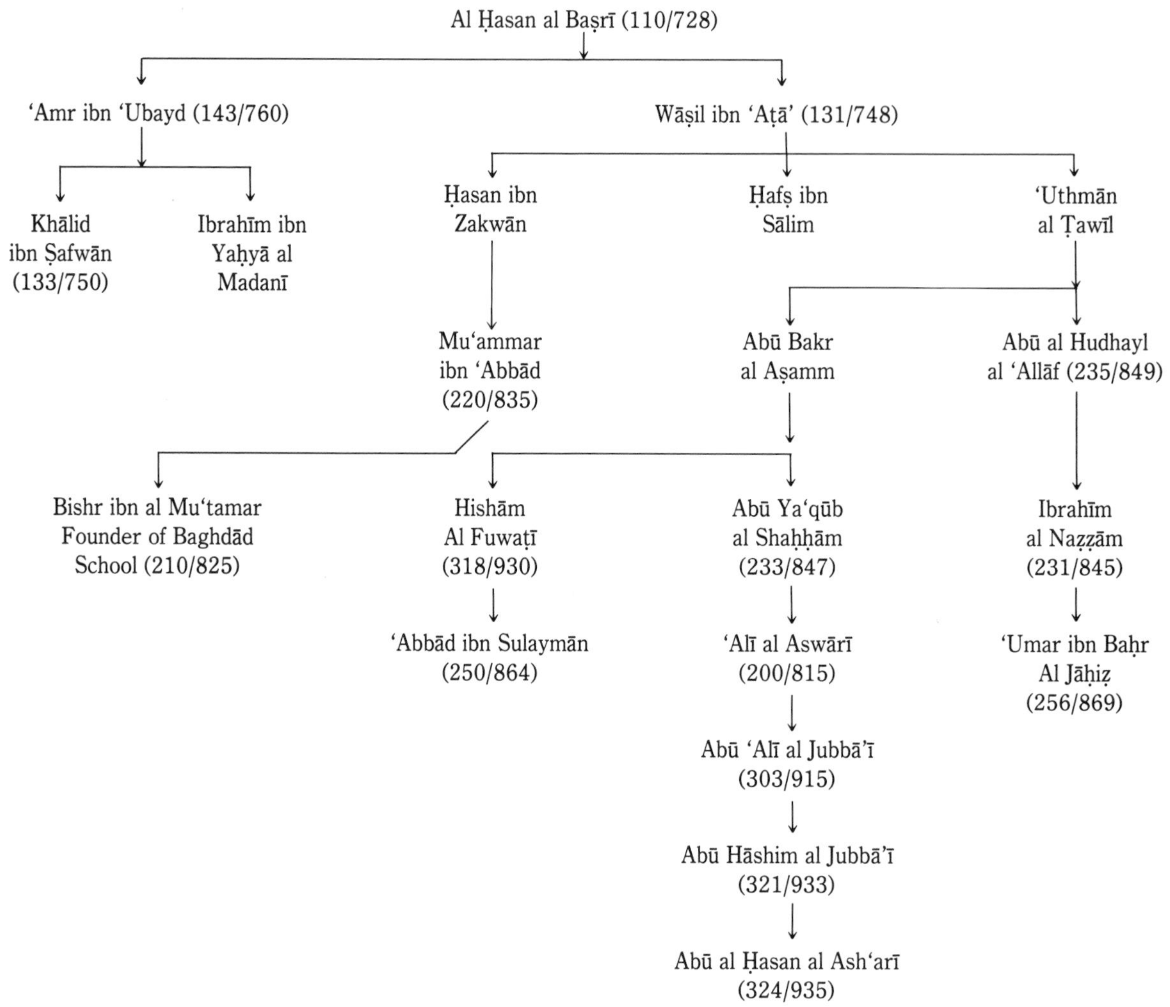

Later Mu'tazili Thinkers
1. Al Qāḍī 'Abd al Jabbār ibn Aḥmad al Ḥamdānī (415/1024)
2. Al Zamakhsharī (538/1143)

→ Teacher to student

predicable of God; or positive, affirming a facet of the divine self, not an accident or quality. The Islamic notion that the Qur'ān was the eternal word of God invited the same kind of argument. The *Mu'tazilah* maintained that the Qur'ān was created by God in time to fulfill a purpose He had for man and creation. The evidence they adduced was that the Qur'ān was composed of language, of sounds and meanings established by human custom, that it was kept in ink and paper and memorized completely by humans. It cannot be "in" or "of" God. On the other hand, to hold that the Qur'ān is "outside" of God and eternal is to affirm the existence of another eternal being besides God. Finally, the Mu'tazilah addressed the same argument against the beatific vision in paradise. God, they claimed, cannot be beheld by the human eye, even in Paradise, for only material bodies can be seen. Hence, the Qur'ānic verses affirming same (75:22) must be interpreted to mean something else, such as consciousness of the divine presence.

The second doctrine of the *Mu'tazilah* was that of *al 'adl* (justice). This axiom was emphasized against the contentions of the advocates of racialism, election, predestination, irrationalism, and justification by faith among all the above-mentioned groups, as well as against those Muslims who were determinists, intercessionists, and advocates of the primacy of revelation over reason. Here, the *Mu'tazilah* sought to establish the universalism, rationalism, humanism, and moral freedom of Islam. The Qur'ān contains verses that support both freedom and determinism (74:41, 41:46, 76:3 for the former; 9:51, 7:188, 11:36 for the latter; 13:13 for both). The *Mu'tazilah* regarded freedom as basic to the whole of religion and its enterprise. For this they presented five arguments: *taklīf*, or moral obligation, the phenomenon of prophethood and the sending of prophets, the affirmation of divine justice, the omnigoodness of God, and the rationality of good and evil — all of which, they claimed, were essential to religion and ethics and implied human freedom, capacity for action, and responsibility. Concerning the first, they divided human actions into necessary and free, absolving the former of, and charging the latter with, responsibility. They also denied intercession as interference with divine justice. Regarding the second, they argued that prophecy would be vain — indeed absurd — if humans were not free to be warned and instructed by the prophets. Such a view undermines all revelation, including the Qur'ān. As to the omnigoodness of God, it is absolute and may not be compromised by His willing injustice and evil, which He must do if He were the author of human deeds. That divine justice precludes any injustice equally implies that good and evil must be discoverable by reason as well as given by revelation. For it is injustice to consign to hell those who lived before the revelation and those whom it did not reach.

The third and fourth axioms, *al wa'd wa al wa'īd* (the promise of reward and threat of punishment) and *al manzilah bayna al manzilatayn* (the intermediate station between salvation and damnation) were subsidiary to the principle of justice. On the one hand, reward and punishment were held to be necessary if God's disposal of man's destiny was to be an absolutely just one. If all man's deeds ended in forgiveness and paradise, or in punishment and hellfire, or in neither, divine righteousness would be gravely compromised. On the other hand, an intermediate station between faith and unfaith, between salvation and damnation, was necessary on account of the faithful who slipped into grave sin. This axiom rehabilitated such a person in opposition to two kinds of extremisms: that which regarded adherence to the faith as all that is necessary for salvation, under which the sinner is complacently regarded as saved; and that which regarded all salvation as logically and materially

TABLE 15.2. AL MU'TAZILAH, BAGHDĀD BRANCH

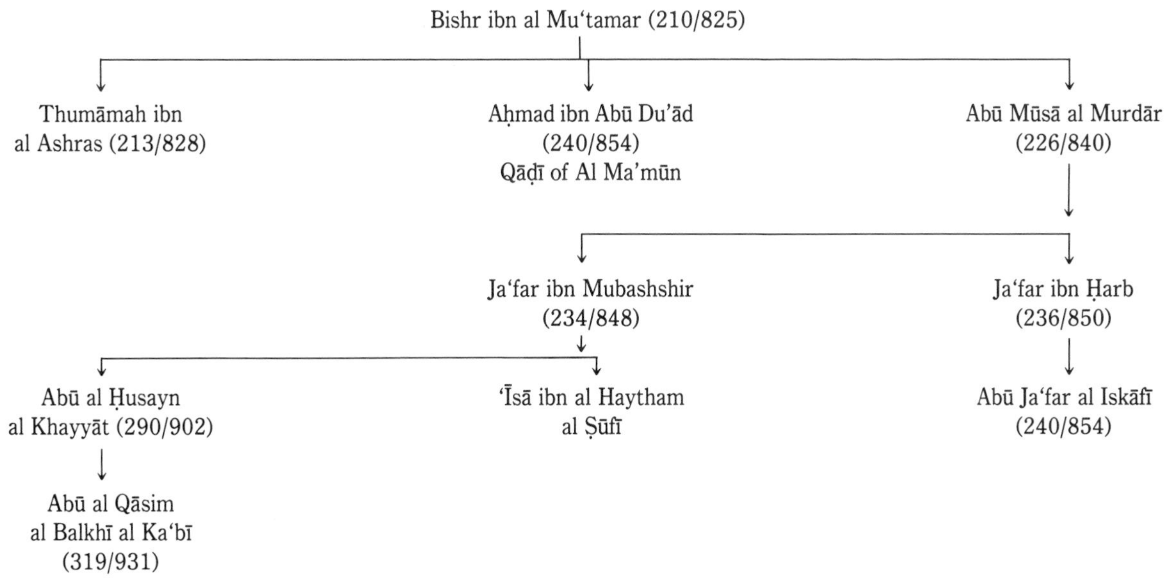

→ Teacher to student

Illustration 15.3

Prayer carpet from Ladik, Turkey, eighteenth century, Dennis R. Dodds Collection, Philadelphia. [Photo by L. al Fārūqī.]

equivalent to works, under which view the sinner is summarily condemned to punishment in this world and the next. Against both extremes, this principle kept the faithful, as faithful as well as sinner, under God's accusing finger for the sin of which he was guilty.

The fifth axiom was *al amr bi al ma'rūf wa al nahy 'an al munkar* (the enjoining of good and prohibition of evil), whose role was to establish the necessity of an imperfect yet perfectible creation for man's moral self-realization or fulfillment of the divine command; hence the need for man to engage himself in its warp and woof, to take history into his own hands, and to knead and remold the world into the likeness of the divine pattern God had revealed.

These five axioms were cardinal to the *Mu'tazilah*.[3] Contention or denial of any one of them removed the contender from *Mu'tazilah* rank. And yet, if we were to characterize *Mu'tazilah* doctrine by a single dominant idea, we are compelled to say that the whole thrust of their movement revolved around the problem of man's ethical nature, which they regarded as the central problem of the self. Their concern was a very Islamic one, since in Islam the end-all and be-all of human life — indeed, of all creation — is the realization in space-time of a divine trust. And their reasoning was clear. If God is transcendent — and the Muslim believes He is — He may not be said to invade, or be invaded by, creation. God is forever unique. Therefore, there is in Islam neither incarnation nor pantheism; neither emanation from God nor fusion into God. These are all constructs devoid of foundation. The only unquestionable, given reality is that man, the creature, stands under an imperative, namely, the command of value; that he is commanded as well as moved by value to seek its realization in the realm of the actual.

According to the *Mu'tazilah,* four different principles follow from this given reality, and their establishment is the task of all religious and philosophical thought. These are, first, that there is a command, a law, or *sharī'ah* — a divine pattern which is the divine will for man; and that this pattern is not man's creation but is *sui generis,* for though the law is relational to man, it is not relative to him. Otherwise, if value or the so-called divine command is man's creation or is relative to him, ethics is either the satisfaction of instincts and desires or the rule by convention. In either case the imperativeness and justification of the command are jeopardized.

The second principle is that man has an innate capacity to know that command or divine pattern, a capacity cultivable and susceptible of higher and lower degrees of perceptive strength, but nonetheless internal to man's realities and devolving upon him. Otherwise skepticism and cynicism become unavoidable. Furthermore, such capacity liberates man from traditions, which can never by themselves be critical.

The third principle is that man, whether as subject or as *matériel* of value realization, has the capacity to act or not to act in accordance with the command. The aspect of man as subject of value realization is precisely his moral freedom; his aspect as *matériel* is his malleability as well as that of creation, the openness of all space-time to in-formation by the divine pattern.

The fourth and last principle is that there must be an order in which the doing or non-doing of man, his realization or violation of the divine pattern, will not be in vain, but will be of consequence for him as well as for the cosmos; that while the consequence for the cosmos is objective, the consequence for the subject is

TABLE 15.3. THE SHĪ'AH IMĀMS

- 1. 'Aliyy ibn Abū Ṭālib (41/661)
  - 2. Al Ḥasan (49/669)
  - 3. Al Ḥusayn (61/680)
    - 4. 'Alī Zayn al 'Ābidīn (94/712)
      - Zayd (Imām of the Zaydīs of Yaman)
      - 5. Muḥammad al Bāqir (113/731)
        - 6. Ja'far al Ṣādiq (148/765)
          - Isma'īl (143/760) — Imām of the Isma'īlīs or Seveners
          - 7. Mūsā al Kāẓim (183/799)
            - 8. 'Alī al Riḍā (203/818)
            - 9. Muḥammad al Jawād (221/835)
            - 10. 'Alī al Hādī (254/868)
            - 11. Al Ḥasan al 'Askarī (261/874)
            - 12. Muḥammad al Muntaẓar (al Mahdī) (265/878) — Last Imām of the Imāmī or "Twelvers"

personal reward or punishment. Upon this principle depend the immortality of the soul, the resurrection of the body, the Day of Judgment, and Paradise and Hell. It was the *Mu'tazilah* thinkers' investigation of these problems that led to the establishment of these principles in the tradition of Islamic thought.

THE FLOWERING

Al Ash'arī

'Alī ibn Isma'īl al Ash'arī (258–322/873–935) started his career as a member of the *Mu'tazilah* and as student of Abū 'Alī al Jubbā'ī of the Baṣrah branch. At the age of forty, he abandoned the *Mu'tazilah* and countered its views, preaching against it in the mosque of Baṣrah. His views gained popularity when Niẓām al Mulk opened the *Niẓāmiyyah* school in Baghdād with branches in Naysābūr, Balkh, Herat, Iṣfahān, Marw, Baṣrah, and Mawṣil, and commissioned teachers to teach the views of al Ash'arī. Since then, *al Ash'ariyyah* has been the view of the majority of Muslims in most of the philosophical-theological matters affecting Islam.[4]

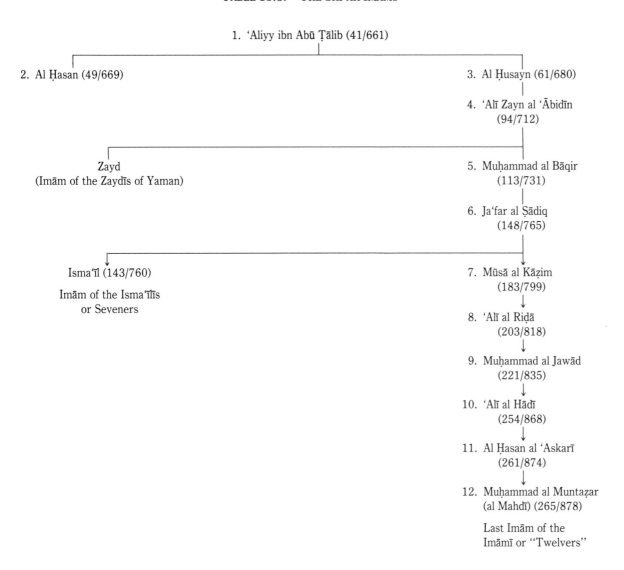

Tradition tells us that al Ash'arī one day confronted his teacher al Jubbā'ī with the following problem: Three brothers, one evil, one righteous, and one a minor, died. What was the fate of each of them? Al Jubbā'ī answered that the righteous was in Paradise; the evil in Hell; and the third belonged to the vague class of "People of Peace." Al Ash'arī asked: If the minor asked for permission to visit his brother in Paradise, would it be granted? Al Jubbā'ī's answer, based on the *Mu'tazilah* doctrine of justice, was, No, because Paradise can be earned only with good deeds. Al Ash'arī rejoined: But what if the minor claimed: Had I been allowed to live, I would have earned it. Basing his stance on the *Mu'tazilah* principle of divine omnigoodness, al Jubbā'ī answered that the boy would be told that it was better for him to have died early. Al Ash'arī then drove to his conclusion: But if the evil brother were then to ask God: You have known the good of the minor and decided to terminate his life in order to prevent him from doing evil and ruining himself. You knew my future as well. Why then did you do him the favor and not me? Al Jubbā'ī was confuted and al Ash'arī made his exit from the *Mu'tazilah* ranks.

Dissatisfaction with *Mu'tazilah* doctrine was certainly directed against the *Mu'tazilah*'s absolutization of the principles of justice and omnigoodness; but it extended to other areas as well. First, its neutralization of the divine attributes was repugnant to Islam. Subject and predicate cannot be one and the same; neither can God and His attributes. These are neither God, nor not-God; neither what the *Mu'tazilah* affirmed (that they are intrinsic to God and hence His self) nor what they denied (that an eternal attribute is another God besides God). Their question was fundamentally false. The attributes are indeed attributes of

TABLE 15.4. THE FĀṬIMĪ CALIPHS OF CAIRO, 297-567/909-1171

'Ubaydullah al Mahdī	297-322/909-934
al Qā'im	322-334/934-946
al Manṣūr	334-341/946-953
al Mu'izz	341-365/953-975
al 'Azīz	365-386/975-996
al Ḥākim	386-411/996-1021
al Ẓāhir	411-427/1021-1036
al Mustanṣir	427-487/1036-1094
al Musta'lī	487-495/1094-1101
al Āmir	495-524/1101-1130
Regency of al Ḥāfiẓ	524-525/1130-1131
al Ḥāfiẓ	525-544/1131-1149
al Ẓāfir	544-549/1149-1154
al Fā'iz	549-555/1154-1160
al 'Āḍid	555-567/1160-1171

God since He described Himself in their terms. To them belong the transcendent quality that belongs to Him, which makes any questioning superfluous, since the transcendent is by definition beyond human examination. To raise the question, therefore, is irrational; to answer it is denial of transcendence and hence blasphemy. Second, al Ash'arī agreed that the words, sounds, and their meaningful associations are created and established by convention. These, however, are not the Qur'ān, but merely its empirical substrate. The Qur'ān is the personal speech of God; as such, it constitutes a reality of a different order, a spiritual reality comprehensible to us through our minds. It is eternal because it is of God; and like God, it is uncreated. Third, the *Mu'tazilah* were wrong in denying the beatific vision in Paradise. Their claim assumed that in Paradise, vision takes place as it does on earth. But Paradise belongs to the transcendent realm where nothing is like nature. Since God promised the vision of Him to the righteous in Paradise, we have neither right nor evidence to deny it. On the contrary, Muslims ought to affirm it as it is described in the revelation (Qur'ān 75:23).

Illustration 15.4

National Mosque, Sembilan, Malaysia. [Photo by L. al Fārūqī.]

The existence of the unity of God. Al Ash'arī did not oppose only the *Mū'tazilah.* He elaborated a complete system of ideas with which to refute the other schools and present the Islamic claim rationally. Against the atheists al Ash'arī presented three arguments. First, the world is made of bodies, and bodies are divisible downward into atoms — the smallest of all existents. Since atoms are created, and the bodies composed of them, it follows that everything is created, requiring an uncreated cause which is God. Second, things are either necessary or contingent, the former constituting its own cause and the latter being caused by another. God cannot be contingent; for if He were, He would require another being by which He had to come to be, and so *ad infinitum*. The infinite regression is not a rational possibility. The nexus of cases must come to an uncaused cause in which to rest. That is God. Nor can the world be necessary; for that would make it another eternal being. Third, orderliness, design, and providence are evident throughout creation, which would be impossible without them. They imply the existence of an ordering, a provident being, a unique being that cannot be plural without upset to the order of creation. This being is God.

The doctrine of *kasb*. Al Ash'arī was also responsible for the doctrine of *kasb* (acquisition). He distinguished between the capacity to act, that is, to create or produce, or change beings, and that of willing the same. He denied to man the former on the ground that only God has such capacity. Man only wills things, and the power of God causes the willed object to be; man gains the merit or demerit of the event not because he did it but because he willed it. God's absolute mastery of the universe, His authorship of all events, His justice, and man's responsibility —which Islam affirms—are thus reconciled. Al Ash'arī's doctrine of *kasb* is consistent with the modern view of reality as a closed system free of causal gaps, and of man's action as no more than an intervention which deflects the causal flow from one effect to another chosen by him.

Divine pattern, not necessary causality. Islam's assertion that God is the Author of all events is the corollary of God's unique mastery of the universe, His total providence. No causal sequence is necessary in itself; its order and flow are contingent, determined by God to be what they are. Against the Greeks, al Ash'arī taught that matter does not generate matter, nor does it cause matter to change. It is God that does. This is tantamount to denying causality; and al Ash'arī did so in the conviction that God's almightiness precluded the existence of other primary or ultimate causal agents. Rather than laws of nature, al Ash'arī preferred to speak of God's patterns in nature. This position was meant to satisfy the religious as well as the philosophical requirement.[5]

Revelation and reason. We have already seen that the *Mu'tazilah* claimed for reason priority over revelation regarded good and evil as rational considerations confirmed by revelation, and that al Ash'arī asserted the opposite. Elaborating the priority of revelation over reason, al Ash'arī linked the questions of good and evil, of the nature of *īmān* and sin, and resurrection and judgment together. These, he held, were all given by revelation, not by reason. For they are not in themselves necessary; nor is their opposite necessarily true. If good and evil were purely affairs of reason, then they could exist in God's kingdom but outside God's will. Men's evil deeds would then take place against the will of God, exposing weakness in Him. As for the claim that God can do no evil, al Ash'arī argued that it is improper to lay down any conditions upon the Absolute. Should God seem to be doing evil, the truth is that such would be contrary to His nature though possible, and that what seems to us evil may not be so in reality at all. Likewise, al Ash'arī rejected the incompatibility of *īmān* and evil works, arguing that faith does not necessarily imply virtue, and that the evildoer may be either punished by God or forgiven. The same, he claimed, is true of prophecy. God did not have to send prophets; nor was sending them an impossibility. But now that He did send them, acquiescing to what they brought from God was obligatory to humans.

These ideas were elaborated by al Ash'arī's pupils and followers into a full system which they taught in turn and identified with the Islamic Sunnī view. Al Ash'ariyyah soon became the view of the majority of

Illustration 15.5

"Nurani," done in acrylic, dye, and yarn by Sulaymān 'Īsā, contemporary Malaysian artist. [Courtesy Sulayman 'Īsā.]

Muslims. The greatest followers were Abū al Ma'ālī al Juwaynī, al Bāqillānī, al Māturīdī, al Qushayrī, and Abū Ḥāmid al Ghazālī.

NOTES

1. For a biographical and bibliographical study of the Mu'tazilah, see Ibn al Murtaḍā, *Ṭabaqāt al Mu'tazilah,* ed. S. Diwald-Wilzer (Beirut: Catholic Press, 1961). For a systematic presentation of Mu'tazilah doctrine and extensive accounts of their history, see Zuhdī Ḥasan Jār-Allah, *Al Mu'tazilah* (Cairo: Al Nādī al 'Arabī fī Yāfā Publications, 1366/1947); A. N. Nādir, *Falsafah al Mu'tazilah: Falāsifat al Islām al Asbaqīn,* 2 vols. (Alexandria: Dār Nashr al Thaqāfah, 1950-1951); A. N. Nādir, *Le système philosophique des Mu'tazilah (Premiers penseurs de l'Islam)* (Beirut: Editions des Lettres Orientales, 1956). For works by members of the Mu'tazilah, see 'Abd al Raḥīm al Khayyāṭ's *Kitāb al Intiṣār wal Radd 'Alā Ibn al Rawandī,* ed. A. Nyberg (Cairo: Lajnah al Ta'līf wal Tarjamah wal Nashr, 1925); and A. N. Nādir's Arabic edition and French translation (Beirut: Catholic Press, 1957), English edition and commentary by I. R. al Fārūqī forthcoming; Al Qāḍī 'Abd al Jabbār, *Al Mughnī fī Abwāb al Tawḥīd wal 'Adl,* in serial volumes published by the Ministry of Culture and National Guidance (Cairo, 1959-); Al Qāḍī 'Abd al Jabbār, *Sharḥ al Uṣūl al Khamsah* (Cairo: Dār Iḥyā' al Kutub al 'Arabiyyah).

2. A brief statement of these five cardinal principles of Mu'tazilah doctrine may be read in D. B. MacDonald, *Muslim Theology, Jurisprudence and Constitutional Theory* (New York: Scribner's, 1903), pp. 119-164; A. S. Tritton, *Muslim Theology* (London: Luzac, 1947, pp. 79-106; W. Montgomery Watt, *Free Will and Predestination in Early Islam* (London: Luzac, 1948), pp. 61-92; T. J. De Boer, *History of Islamic Philosophy,* trans. E. R. Jones (London: Luzac, 1933), pp. 41-64; H. A. R. Gibb, *Mohammedanism* (London: Oxford University Press, 1949), pp. 110-117; Baron Carra de Vaux, *Les penseurs de l'Islam* (Paris: Geuthner, 1923), vol. IV, chap. IV, pp. 133-156.

3. Al Khayyāṭ, *Kitāb al Instisār wal Radd 'Alā Ibn al Rawandī,* p. 93.

4. Al Ash'arī wrote many books, one of which was a refutation of his own views which he held earlier when he was a Mu'tazilī. The most famous of his works are: *Al Ibānah fī Uṣūl al Diyānah, Istiḥsān al Khawḍ fī 'Ilm al Kalām, Maqālāt al Islāmiyyīn,* and *Al Luma'.*

5. It has often been claimed that al Ash'arī borrowed this doctrine of atomism from the Greeks (T. J. de Boer, *History of Muslim Philosophy,* pp. 57ff). The facts are otherwise. Greek atomism held the atoms to be dynamic beings carrying within them the potentiality for change, as it were, by definition. They were portions of matter which Democritus regarded as dynamic and capable of generation. Al Ash'arī's atoms were dead, inert, and immobile without God's action upon them.

CHAPTER 16

Taṣawwuf (Mysticism)

ORIGINS

Taṣawwuf, or the donning of wool, is the name given to a movement that dominated the minds and hearts of Muslims for a millennium, and is still strong in many circles of the Muslim world. It nourished their souls, purified their hearts, and fulfilled their yearning for piety, for virtue and righteousness, and for closeness to God. It grew and rapidly moved to every corner of the Muslim world. It was responsible for the conversion of millions to Islam, as well as for a number of militant states and sociopolitical movements. It was equally responsible for the eclipse of Muslim power, for the Muslims' exchange of rational for intuitive, and critical for superstitious knowledge; for their forsaking of this world and its concerns for the other. *Taṣawwuf* was a movement of both great good and great evil in the history of Islamic civilization.

Three independent streams of thought fed the river of *taṣawwuf* and determined its content and character. First, Islam brought with it some of the asceticism of the desert, an aversion to the life of urban and settled luxury. The Qur'ān and its constant recitation, Arabic poetry and the pietistic invocations and prayers composed in praise of God, and the adoring love of God and His divine presence which Islam emphasized created a tradition of saintliness as possession by the God-idea and absolute devotion to Him and His Prophet. This ascetic pietism militated against indulgent involvement in worldly affairs. It received exemplary expression in the life of the Prophet's contemporary, Abū Dharr al Ghifārī (31/652), the administration of the Umawī caliph 'Umar ibn 'Abdul 'Azīz, and the conduct of the learned scholar al Ḥasan al Baṣrī (109/728). The piety of *taṣawwuf* seems to have completely dominated the life of Abū Hāshim al Kūfī (158/776), who spent most of his time in prayer at the mosque of Kūfah. The vision of *taṣawwuf* inspired the exquisite poetry of Rābi'ah al 'Adawiyyah (184/801). She taught the love of God, pure and unadulterated by fear of punishment or desire for reward.

Second, Pythagorean Hellenism and Alexandrian gnosticism, which had penetrated Judaism and Christianity, had dominated the Near East for a thousand years before the advent of Islam. When the masses of the Near East and North Africa converted to Islam, it was natural that gnostic ideas and metaphors were brought in with their spiritual baggage. The dialectic of spirit and matter, of light and darkness, of high heaven and lowly earth had penetrated everywhere. Two Egyptian thinkers influenced by Hellenic gnosticism directed the current to join its waters to those of

TABLE 16.1. THE RIVER OF *Taṣawwuf* (MYSTICISM)

Origin

The river of *taṣawwuf* was formed by three brooks of thought. The first brook contributed to *taṣawwuf* the following ideals:

- Arab desert asceticism
- thorough-going devotion
- strong love of God
- poetic expression

The major figures of this first movement were:

- Abū Dharr al Ghifārī, Madīnah (32/652)
- 'Umar ibn 'Abdul 'Azīz, Dimashq (101/720)
- Al Ḥasan al Baṣrī, Baṣrah (110/728)
- Rābi'ah al 'Adawiyyah, Baṣrah (185/801)

The second brook of thought feeding *taṣawwuf* was characterized by:

- *gnosis* as certain knowledge
- imagery of light/darkness
- praise of spirit and condemnation of matter
- promotion of contemplative life over that of active commitment

The major thinkers of this school of thought were:

- Al Ḥārith ibn Asad al Muḥāsibī, Baghdad (243/837)
- Dhūl Nūn al Miṣrī, Alexandria (245/859)
- Abū Hāshim al Kūfī, Baṣrah (160/776)

A third brook, or movement, expounded the following ideals:

- body mortification
- spiritual elevation
- anti-worldism
- anti-societism

Major proponents of this movement were:

- Ibrahīm ibn al Adham (Amīr of Balkh, Khurāsān) (161/777)
- 'Abdullah ibn Mubārak, Marw (181/797)
- Shaqīq of Balkh, Balkh (194/810)
- Ḥitām al Aṣamm, Balkh (237/852)
- Abū Yazīd al Bisṭāmī, Bisṭām (261/875)

Flowering

The three brooks met to run in one stream. At their confluence stood Junayd al Baghdādī (298/910) who

- united and systematized all Ṣūfī ideas (the three brooks)
- established the categories of logic and knowledge, of metaphysics and ethics, pertinent to *taṣawwuf*
- Islamized the vocabulary of *taṣawwuf* by vesting it with Qur'ānic terms
- initiated allegorical interpretation of the Qur'ān to serve Ṣūfī purposes

Dominance

After Junayd al Baghdādī *taṣawwuf* ran like a mighty river and covered the entire Muslim world. The major thinkers of this period were:

- 'Umar ibn al Fāriḍ, Cairo (632/1234)
- Abū Ṭalib al Makkī, Kūfah (386/996)
- Abū Naṣr al Sarrāj. Dimashq (388/998)
- Abū Na'īm al Isbahānī, Iṣfahān (430/1038)
- Abū al Qasīm al Qushayrī, Naysābūr (465/1072)
- Abū Ḥāmid al Ghazālī, Baghdād (505/1111)
- Ibn 'Arabī, Andalus (638/1240)
- Jalāluddīn al Rūmī, Turkey (672/1273)
- Ibn 'Atā' Allah al Sakandarī, Alexandria (709/1309)

Decay

The seeds of decay were internal to the system of *taṣawwuf*, and they grew in time:

- compromise of transcendence with immanence
- compromise of intuitionism with esotericism
- compromise of societism with monkery and individualism
- compromise of reason with superstition
- compromise of *tawḥīd* with saint worship
- compromise of the authority of the *Sharī'ah* with that of the brotherhood-leader
- compromise of activism with contemplation

Reform

The following thinkers tried to counter the above-mentioned compromises:

- Taqiyyuddīn Aḥmad ibn Taymiyah, Dimashq (727/1326)
- Aḥmad Sirhindī, India (1024/1615)
- Waliyyullah al Dihlawī, India (1176/1762)
- Muḥammad ibn 'Abdul Wahhāb, Arabia (1206/1792)
- 'Uthmān dan Fodio, West Sudan (1233/1817)
- Muḥammad 'Alī al Sanūsī, Libya (1275/1859)
- Muḥammad Aḥmad (al Mahdī), Sudan (1303/1885)

the native Arabian stream of ascetic love of God: Al Ḥārith ibn Asad al Muḥāsibī (222/838) and Dhū al Nūn al Miṣrī (246/861). The first taught the doctrine of truth by illumination *(ishrāq)*, and the other the desirability and possibility of reunion with God in spirit following an ascent through virtue and contemplation.

Third, being the dominant religion of most of the provinces of Asia acquired by Islam, Buddhism was soon to exercise its influence. Buddhist condemnation of this world, its total abnegation in favor of the contemplative and monkish life, found its mouthpiece in Ibrahīm ibn al Adham (159/777). As told by his followers later, his life was not unlike that of the Buddha. Ibn al Adham was of noble birth, a ruling prince of Balkh, who suddenly decided to give up his post and property, his family and loved ones, and lead an ascetic, solitary life in the mosque, bent on his recitations and prayer, oblivious to food and all that belongs to the world. Abū Yazīd al Bisṭāmī (260/875) propounded the Hindu-Buddhist ideal of Nirvana as the goal *(baqā')* of a life of self-denial and mortification *(fanā')*. Hellenic and Buddhist ideas circulated in the Muslim world as alien imports until Junayd al Baghdādī (296/910) joined them to the Arab ascetic love-of-God stream and vested them with Islamic, indeed Qur'ānic, terms. Henceforth, the three streams were one and ran like a mighty river.

DEVELOPMENT

The Fraternal Order

The Ṣūfīs, or adherents of *taṣawwuf,* devised for themselves an order and institutionalized for it an ideology, an organization, a program, and initiation and adoration rites. At the time of al Kūfī and Ibn al Adham, the mosque was the place where the Ṣūfī exercise took place. Soon the Ṣūfīs extended the exercise beyond the *ṣalāt* times and rather than interrupt the *ṣalāt* of non-Sufis, they chose to found a separate quarter, away from any interference. Thus the *zāwiyah, takiyyah,* or *ribāṭ* was born as an institution separate from the mosque. There, the Ṣūfīs spent their days and most of their nights in prayer, invocation, and *dhikr,* or remembrance of God. They had little to eat, one woolen garment to wear, and the floor to sleep on away from the pleasures and comforts of home. Together, they constituted a fraternal order, an autonomous community, separate from the *ummah.* Although the fraternity was open to anyone, certain conditions for membership had to be met. Among them were: (1) the decision to join should be absolutely deliberate and personal; (2) all property must be given up; if not to the fraternity, then to one's relatives or the poor, so that the member would be free of all attachment to worldly goods; (3) absolute obedience to the elder or *shaykh,* the superior of the *ṭarīqah,* or mystical way, organization or brotherhood, and to those delegated by him to discipline the prospective members was required; (4) a probationary period was prescribed for each novice, after which the candidate was initiated into membership and given his garment of blue wool.

Once admitted, the member had to pass through a number of stages. First he became a *murīd,* or an applicant under training. Then he became a *sālik,* or fellow traveler. If he spent enough time at the *zāwiyah* with success, he would become a *majdhūb,* that is, attracted to the Ṣūfī way. Later, he would become a *mutadārak,* or one saved from the evils and temptations of the world. The members of the *ṭarīqah* classified themselves as follows: *Al Mubtadi'* (the beginner); *al Mutadarrij* (the successful practitioner); *al Shaykh* (the teacher, elder, or head of the *zāwiyah*); and *al Quṭb* (the pole, the highest authority of the *ṭarīqah* with all its branches and houses. The life of the Ṣūfī was regarded as a sort of journey or *safar,* punctuated by a number of stations *(maqāmāt)* in progressively higher order. The member's soul or consciousness was said to move through a series of states *(aḥwāl,* sing. *ḥāl)* as success in the Ṣūfī practice was proven. The *maqāmāt* or characteristics of the proper Ṣūfī were seven: repentance *(tawbah),* awe *(wara'),* asceticism *(zuhd),* poverty *(faqr),* patience *(ṣabr),* reliance *(tawakkul),* and satisfaction *(riḍā).* The *aḥwāl* or states were also seven in number: nearness *(qurb),* love *(maḥabbah),* fear *(khawf),* hope *(rajā'),* longing *(shawq),* witnessing *(mushāhadah),* and conviction *(yaqīn).*

For many centuries, the Ṣūfī fraternities existed without acquiring for themselves any reified presence in the community. Their ideology militated against it. When the *zāwiyah* (lit. corner) of the mosque was the meeting place, and later when the Ṣūfīs moved into a building of their own near the mosque, members walked in, worshipped and adored to their heart's content, gave in charity, and walked out. Later, the fraternities acquired enough property to be called rich, or they included all or most of the members of a certain profession and thus became the base of a guild, labor union, or partnership. The earliest to be founded as a legal personality with extensive endowments was begun by 'Abdul Qādir al Jīlānī (560/1166) in Baghdād. In the following two centuries, it branched out into most Muslim countries, where it was known as the *Qādiriyyah.* About the same time, another fraternity was founded by Aḥmad al Rifā'ī (570/1175). It too spread throughout the Muslim world and was known as the *Rifā'iyyah. Al Shādhiliyyah,* founded by 'Alī al Shādhilī (655/1258), spread mostly in Egypt and North Africa; the *Mawlawiyyah,* founded and developed by the followers of Jalāl al Dīn al Rūmī (670/1273) in Qoniah, Turkey, acquired fame, but few members, throughout the Near East. The same was true of *al Shishtiyyah,* the fraternity founded by Mu'īnuddīn Shishtī (633/1236) in India. Other fraternities were founded in nearly every region or province, but did not succeed in acquiring a worldwide constituency. Such were the *Bektāshiyyah* in Turkey, the *Tījāniyyah* in Morocco, and the *Aḥmadiyyah* founded by Aḥmad al Badawī (675/1278) in Ṭanṭā, Egypt.

Rituals

While all Ṣūfīs practiced the rituals of Ṣufism, each *ṭarīqah* institutionalized its own organization of them.

Illustration 16.1

Members of the Halveti-Jarrāḥī Order during a *dhikr* ceremony in the United States. [Courtesy The Jarraḥī Order of America, Spring Valley, N.Y.]

First and common to all was the ritual of *dhikr,* which consisted of repetitive invocations and litanies which were sometimes brief and simple, consisting of one name of God, and at other times were more detailed and involved. *Dhikr* was often practiced until the worshipper's consciousness lapsed or he fell from exhaustion. It had the merit of emptying consciousness of all the cares and concerns of human life and of concentrating it on God, His word and law, or the person of the Prophet Muḥammad. The exercise was for the Ṣūfī, as it was for mystics in many other religious traditions, the surest way to the ecstatic mystical experience. If the mystics of the world differ, their difference lies not in the induction of mystical experience, for every religion and culture has known a variety of ways of bringing it about. The difference that counts lies in the visible outcome of the experience for the subject and for society. Whereas in Taoism the outcome may be contemplation of nature, in Theravada Buddhism it is world- and self-denial. In Christianity, it is self-mortification and/or withdrawal from society; its marketplaces and battlefields. In Islam, it may well be self-dedication to a trade or craft, or to a holy war. It is possible to find examples of all these forms in the religious traditions of mankind; but the different mystical traditions can be differentiated according to the kind of visible outcome to which the mystics of that tradition were led by their experience of the holy.

Samā' (listening to Qur'ānic recitation or to the chanting of Ṣūfī prayers and special invocations), *ghinā'* (recitation of Ṣūfī poetry and other literature with moving appeal), *mūsīqā* and *raqṣ* (playing, listening or dancing to beautiful music) were other Ṣūfī activities calculated to bring about *ṭarab* (the special joy and intense pleasure through hearing), *nashwah* (emotional transport), and *ghaybah* (passage into the world beyond and communion with transcendent reality). In his mystical experience, the Ṣūfī felt he heard the call of heaven to rise above the world of sense and commune with the supernal plenum. If these rituals did not succeed in bringing about the mystical experience, they could be assisted by the drinking of wine or the consumption of drugs, to which the Ṣūfīs gave the fascinating name of *banj al asrār* (the anesthetic of [heavenly] secrets). Finally, the Ṣūfīs instituted self-mortification as another means to the same goal of mystical experience. Fasting, the exposure of the body to cold, heat, and coarse textiles, even the voluntary infliction of pain, were regarded as means of self-discipline in the exodus from this world, which they regarded as a prison in comparison to the freedom of the beyond.

Literature

Taṣawwuf has been responsible for a great legacy of literature in Arabic and all other Muslim languages. The Ṣūfīs sang their themes in exquisite poetry; they adored God and invoked His blessings and help with the most moving *saj'* or rhymed prose. Among the poets, the greatest honor belongs to Ibn al Fāriḍ (632/1235), Sa'dī, Ḥāfiẓ, and Jalāl al Dīn al Rūmī, whose *Mathnawī* is an encyclopaedia of religious and ethical knowledge as well. The foremost prose presentations of the Ṣūfī vision and practice were written by Abū Naṣr al Sarrāj (377/988) in his *Kitāb al Luma'* (The Book of Flashes); Abū Ṭālib al Makkī (385/996) in his *Qūt al Qulūb* (Nourishment for the Hearts); Abū Ḥāmid al Ghazālī (606/1111) in his world-famous *Iḥyā' 'Ulūm al Dīn* (Revivification of the Sciences of Religion); Abū al Qāsim al Qushayrī (466/1074) in his *Risālah;* and Muhyiddin ibn 'Arabi (636/1240) in his *Al Futūḥāt al Makkiyyah* (The Makkan Inspirations). Abū 'Abdul Raḥman al Sulamī (410/1021) wrote the most authoritative Who's Who in Ṣūfīsm up to his day.

Ṣūfī literature is so rich in metaphors, similes, and allegories that it can claim a lexicography of its own. Symbolism has never seen a brighter day in the whole history of Islam and in the range of its literature than with the Ṣūfīs. As long as Ṣūfī diction remained spiritual and refined, it attracted the people. At times, however, it degenerated to using such terms as embracing, hugging, and talking to God, or uniting with

Him, thereby causing revulsion in the minds of most Muslims.

Speculative Thought

From the time *taṣawwuf* invaded the ranks of the *ummah,* and scholars from every field of knowledge accepted it, its legacy of thought and literature was tremendous.

Al Ghazālī. Abū Ḥāmid al Ghazālī studied under al Juwaynī who recommended him to Niẓām al Mulk for appointment as a professor of philosophy at the Niẓāmiyyah School in Baghdād. At the apogee of al Ghazālī's fame as a scholar he was struck by doubt regarding most of what he taught. As a consequence, he left his post. He roamed for ten years, visiting Damascus, Jerusalem, Makkah and Madīnah, Naysābūr, and finally Ṭūs, where he was born. He wrote *Maqāṣid al Falāsifah* and *Tahāfut al Falāsifah,* criticizing the current philosophical views; *Iḥyā' 'Ulūm al Dīn,* his major opus; *Al Munqiẓ min al Ḍalāl,* his spiritual autobiography; and two small treatises of counsels and advice — *Ayyuhā al Walad* and *Mizān al 'Amal.* He also wrote many other works on the Qur'ān, on *taṣawwuf,* and on law and jurisprudence.

Illustration 16.3

Shaykh Muẓaffar of the Halveti-Jarrāḥī Order welcomes new Ṣūfī converts in New York City, 1984. [Photo by L. al Fārūqī.]

Illustration 16.2

Shaykh Muẓaffar and the Halveti-Jarrāḥī Dervishes of Isṭanbūl on a visit to the United States, 1979. [Courtesy The Jarrāḥī Order of America, Spring Valley, N.Y.]

Al Ghazālī anticipated Descartes in his methodical doubt, but he arrived not at any certain *cogito* but at the phenomenon of *yaqīn* (epistemological certainty) which critically reviews and rationally evaluates the data of reality but only after the consciousness has been illuminated by the light of *īmān* which God grants to the sincere seeker. Such a person continues to perceive rightly through an intuitive faculty called *dhawq,* which al Ghazālī borrowed from the Uṣūlī jurists. The latter spoke of "juristic *dhawq*" as a faculty by which one knows the purposes of the *sharī'ah* and relates them to the juristic problems at hand. Al Ghazālī took issue with the *mutakallimūn,* the Bāṭinīs, the Ṣūfīs, and the philosophers.

Al Ghazālī granted that the *mutakallimūn* defended the faith against its enemies and misinterpreters, and that they articulated its principles and categories to make it readily available for the use of the understanding. But in their enthusiasm, they adopted some of the methods of their enemies, especially the postulates of Greek logic and metaphysics which removed them farther from Islamic knowledge. The *mutakallimūn* relied on revelation rather than reason and conceded to their enemies that they had done so, thus rendering themselves unconvincing. Their *kalām* did not succeed in stopping the raging controversies, and it may have fueled them. Finally, the *mutakallimūn* did not succeed in reaching the rock of apodeictic knowledge which is the goal of all thinking.

As for the Bāṭinīs, al Ghazālī chastised them for appealing to the simple-minded and for taking advantage of the uneducated, by teaching them destructive esoteric doctrines on the authority of occult leaders whom they declared infallible. The Bāṭinīs' objection to the Sunnī recourse to text as well as to *ijtihād* (creative interpretation based upon the text of revelation) was misplaced, al Ghazālī argued, because "the finite texts cannot comprehend the infinite cases of reality," and because one ought to abide by the text wherever it is available and resort to creative interpretation in the absence of text. The Bāṭinīs' search for a living infallible leader was wasted effort since no one is infallible, and Islam had already had a teacher — Muḥammad — whose revelation and *sunnah* were extant. The Bāṭinīs' recourse to Pythagoreanism to justify their claims was in vain. That was the philosophy Aristotle rightly despised and all sensible people rejected as beneath them.

Reaffirming his view that *taṣawwuf* is both knowledge and action, al Ghazālī chastised those who sought to reach the mystical experience in a hurry. He also rejected the Ṣūfī claim that in the mystical experience one reaches God through fusion into or unity with the divine Being. Such a claim he regarded as blasphemous. The true perception of God is always perception of the presence of the transcendent as a commanding being; knowledge of Him is never a knowledge of His self but of His will. Al Ghazālī therefore could not countenance the preaching of Manṣūr al Ḥallāj (309/922) who went about Baghdād claiming that through the mystical experience he and God had become one. By reaffirming that Islam implies action, al Ghazālī meant to repudiate those Ṣūfīs who preached monkery and withdrawal from society, any form of asceticism or mortification, or nonobligation to observe the rituals and all other laws of the *sharī'ah*. Al Ghazālī thus made *taṣawwuf* respectable and conformant with the *sharī'ah* and spirit of Islam.

The critique of the philosophers and their craft was al Ghazālī's greatest contribution. He knew their doctrines well for he learned them as a student and taught them as a teacher. Among the philosophers, al Ghazālī distinguished the atheists whom he condemned because of their denial of God and their assertion that the world existed by itself; the naturalists who accepted God's existence but denied His relevance and His judgment, and permitted themselves to indulge in the pursuit of the pleasures of this world; and the philosophers proper such as al Fārābī and Ibn Sīna whose doctrines he subjected to critical analysis. He acknowledged their contributions to mathematics, astronomy, logic, the sciences of nature, politics, and ethics. According to al Ghazālī, it was in metaphysics that the philosophers committed their greatest errors; among them were the denial of bodily resur-

Illustration 16.4

Modular rug design in a nineteenth- or twentieth-century kilim from Turkey. [Courtesy Ministry of Culture and Tourism, Government of Turkey.]

rection on Judgment Day, restriction of God's knowledge to the universals rather than the particulars, and their assertion that the universe is eternal and uncreated.

Regarding the first error, al Ghazālī reviewed the philosophers' arguments that matter is corruptible but the soul is not, and that therefore it is a separate material entity; that it alone is immortal because it is of the essence of the *logos* which is spirit. Against these claims al Ghazālī argued that justice demands that the same person—both soul and body—meet whatever is due him on the Day of Judgment; that anything less would compromise divine justice, let alone contradict the divine word. Re-creation of the body and its reunion with its soul should be no more surprising than their combination on earth. Regarding the philosophers' second error, al Ghazālī repudiated the claim that knowledge of the particulars changes as they do; that a changeless foreknowledge of the changing particulars is indeed possible. Since God cannot suffer change, His knowledge must be of the universals alone which do not change. Al Ghazālī argued that neither the knowledge nor the subject of knowledge changes when, having been informed of change before its taking place, the object of knowledge goes through the preknown change. Likewise, al Ghazālī rejected the philosophers' claim that man is known to God only as a universal. Such knowledge, he held, is unnecessarily restrictive as well as inadequate. Knowing the particular, al Ghazālī held, is no threat to the absolute and transcendent nature of the knower; and besides, it is absolutely necessary for a sound judgment. Finally, al Ghazālī argued, it is as non-self-evident and as intellectually puzzling to distinguish between eternity of time and eternity of being as it is to distinguish between an eternal creator and a creation which took place *ex nihilo* and initiated the processes of time and change.

Regarding the third error, and despite Ibn Sīnā's distinction of eternity of time and eternity of being, al Ghazālī held that in neither case can that which is not eternal proceed from that which is eternal. Al Ghazālī rightly concluded that the distinction the philosophers had made had availed nothing. Further, the philosophers argued that the command to create the world must signify a change in God's mind and will. This would imply that God once did not know, and at a later time did know, thus imputing change and movement to God. Since that is impossible, the philosophers thought it was safe to deduce the eternity of the world. Al Ghazālī criticized the philosophers for assuming that any event in time implies a change in God's consciousness. The fact that, at a certain time and place in the future, a certain something is going to come to be, may itself be a piece of eternal knowledge in God. Therefore, when it does come true, it signifies no change in the subject of knowledge at all. Moreover, al Ghazālī argued, since God acts through secondary and tertiary causes, the chain leading to a certain event may have been launched in eternity with the full foreknowledge of its whole course well known to God. The philosophers he said, were wrong in claiming a time before the world had come to be. In fact, both space and time are impossible without creation. They came to be at the same time.

Thus al Ghazālī built his system on God as starting point and foundation, unlike the philosophers who started with the senses or reason. He anchored reason in *īmān,* whence it drew its ultimate postulates; and then gave it the freedom to be as critical as it wished. Without such anchoring, reason is fallible and untrustworthy. God is knowable through His works, His order and design of nature, His ubiquitous providence—all of which reason is capable of discerning in tentative but not definitive form. Between God and the world stands the realm of *malakūt* and *amr,* by which al Ghazālī meant the realm of values constituting the ought of all that is or will be, a realm that is absolute, a priori and transcendent *(malakūt),* as well as normative and imperative *(amr).* Knowledge of it is *yaqīn* (apodeictic certainty) and such knowledge is the ground of all other knowledge. Al Ghazālī, we may concede, taught the primacy of axiological knowledge, which relates man to God, over the knowledge of the world, which would be faulty and groundless without the first.

Illustration 16.5

Stylized floral arabesques in ceramic decoration, Mosque of Sulṭān Aḥmad, Isṭanbul, Turkey. [Photo by L. al Fārūqī.]

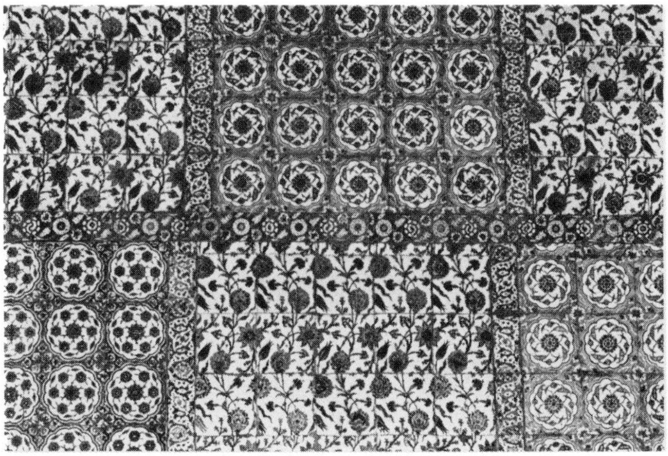

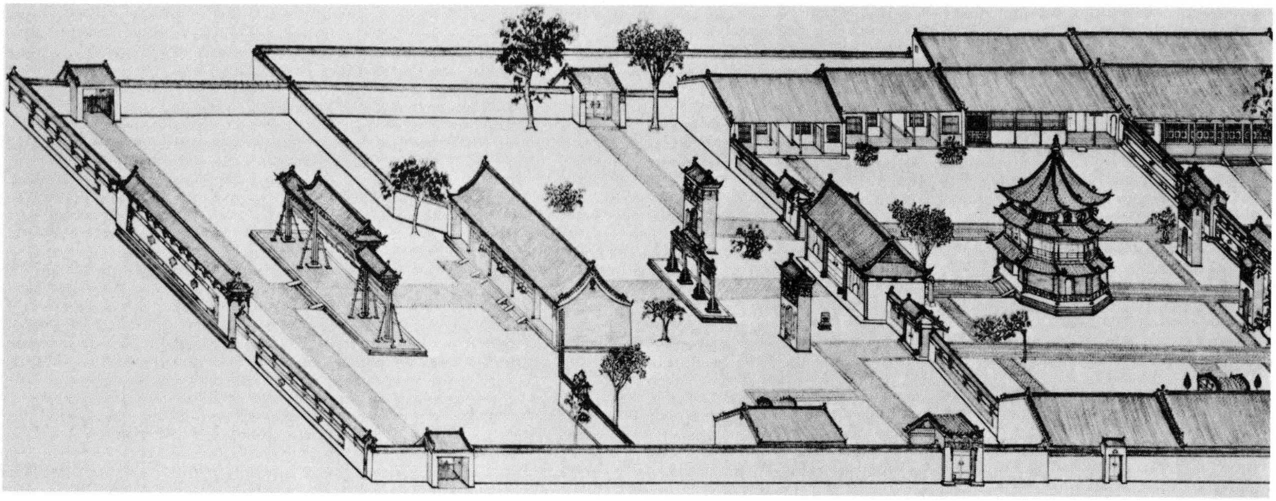

Illustration 16.6

Grand Mosque, Xian, People's Republic of China. The mosque was founded in the seventh century C.E. by Arab traders on the silk route.

Al Ghazālī's breakthrough lay in his critique of causality. The philosophers had mistaken simple customary perception for the truth. They acknowledged as necessary that which was not so. The relation of cause and effect falls into that category. The philosophers argued that, given the cause, the effect must follow without adducing proof except that the effect had in the past appeared following the cause which in no way proves the necessity they affirmed. "Following after" never implies "following from." It takes a different kind of proof to establish that the alleged cause was the real and only cause of the effect. It is mere custom and habit that lie at the root of our thinking, not rational evidence. What binds the effect to its cause, al Ghazālī affirmed, is God's action, which we can trust to repeat itself in patterns because God does not seek to cheat and mislead us. If causes operate and are establishable through science, it is because the action of God is patterned, not, as the philosophers claimed, because of any necessary power in the cause to bring about its effect.

Ibn 'Arabī. Muḥyiddīn ibn 'Arabī was born in Mursiah (Andalus) in 559/1165, and brought up in Seville, Cordoba, and Granada. He visited the lands of the East, settled in Cairo in 596/1201, and moved to Makkah two years later. He also visited Baghdād, Jerusalem, and Damascus, where he died and was buried in 636/1240. Tradition ascribes to him a huge number of works, but only three are extant: *Al Futuḥāt al Makkiyyah* (mentioned above), *Fuṣūṣ al Ḥikam* (Gems of Wisdom), and *Tarjumān al Ashwāq* (Expressions of Longing). His thought was the most speculative in Islam. God, in his view, is One, Absolute, the Source of all being, Whose essence is being. The world is both created and eternal; created in so far as it is in space and time, eternal in so far as it is in the knowledge of God. Indeed, the world is God and God is the world. They are indistinguishable from each other except in abstract human knowledge. Man never becomes God; nor God man. But it is possible through knowledge to achieve spiritual unity with God. Every prophet is *a* word of God and Muḥammad is *the* word of God, the focal point of all other prophethoods which Ibn 'Arabi declared partial. Behind the Prophet stands *Al Ḥaqīqah al Muḥammadiyyah* (the Muḥammadan truth or essence) which is the creative force of God. The purpose of creation is *al insān al kāmil* (the perfect man), who is also the microcosm reflecting the glory of God, the macrocosm. In so far as the prophets of history were reflections of the perfect man, they were the *awliyā'* (sing. *waliyy* or friend) of God. This quality is higher than prophecy. Ibn 'Arabī suggested that he too was a *waliyy* of God, indeed that he was the *khātim* (seal or last) of the friends of God just as Muḥammad was the *khātim* of the prophets. The relation binding God and the perfect man, Ibn 'Arabī claimed, is love; and this love is not exercised for its own sake, or for the sake of either party. Rather, it has a purpose it serves and to which it stands as effect to cause, namely, beauty.

This theory of *wilāyah,* coupled with that of the

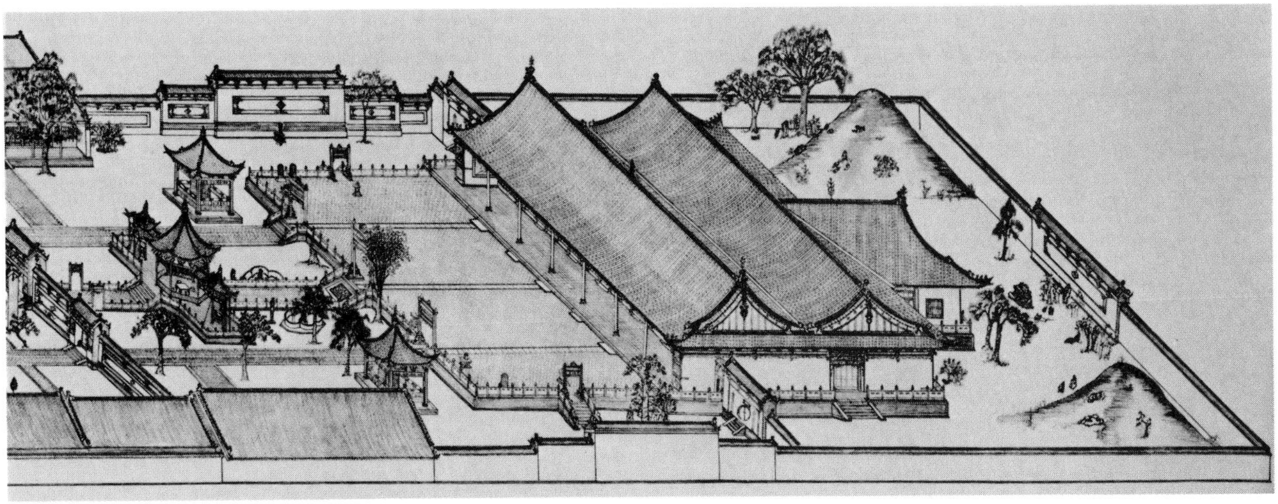

identification of God with the world, gave notoriety to Ibn 'Arabī. His theories gave the Ṣūfīs arguments with which to counter the sobering influence of al Ghazālī, and impetus to stray farther away from normative Islam. The *'ulamā',* guardians of the *sharī'ah,* the orthodox and orthoprax Muslims, were revulsed by Ibn 'Arabī's flights of speculative thinking. In pantheism, distinctions between good and evil dissolve since both are equally existent, and existence and divinity are one and the same reality. The same is true of our distinctions of ugliness and beauty, of sin and righteousness, which Ibn 'Arabī regarded as purely relative. The ultimate conclusion of this line of reasoning is the dissolution of differences between the religions, including Islam. Ibn 'Arabī did reach and express the conclusion that all religions are one, and that religious controversy, dispute, and competition is utterly senseless. Even argument and contention in religion Ibn 'Arabī regarded as meaningless.

DECAY

Unfortunately, and despite his tremendous influence, al Ghazālī's reform of *taṣawwuf,* his attempt to restrain the exaggeration to which the movement was by nature bent, did not succeed. The horses of mysticism lapsed into their wild nature and became indomitable. The *ummah* suffered an eclipse from which it has been trying painfully to recover in the last two centuries. Instead of continuing to discipline man to obey God and observe the *sharī'ah,* to deepen his commitment to Islam and purify and lift his soul on the path of righteous action, *taṣawwuf* became a disease causing or exacerbating the following symptoms:

1. *Kashf* or gnostic illumination was substituted for knowledge. Under *taṣawwuf,* the Muslim world abandoned its commitment to and pursuit of rational, scientific knowledge for the vision of mystical experience. It forsook the critical weighing and verification

Illustration 16.7

Grand Mosque, Xian, People's Republic of China. [Courtesy C. and A. Larsen.]

Illustration 16.8

Prayer Hall, Beijing Mosque, People's Republic of China, founded 349/960. Five *suwar* of the Qur'an are said to be embossed on its walls and ceiling. [Courtesy C. and A. Larsen.]

of alternatives for the esoteric, oracular, and authoritarian pronouncements of the Ṣūfī *shaykh* or leader. Once the attitude of the mind to reality changed and the subjective, esoteric inclination took over, all the sciences suffered. When men believed that truth could be reached in a shorter and less painful way, the will to critical, rational, and empirical knowledge suffered. In due course, mathematics was mixed up with numerology, astronomy with astrology, chemistry with alchemy, and, generally, the engineering of nature with theurgy.

2. *Karāmāt* or "little miracles," which *taṣawwuf* taught were possible in the state of union or communion with divinity and which it justified as favors granted by God to the most pious, destroyed the Muslim's respect for natural causation and taught him to seek results by the methods of spiritualistic conduction. In his mind, the natural relation of cause to effect, of means to objective, was destroyed and replaced by his connection to the Sūfī master capable of performing a *karāmah* for him.

3. *Ta'abbud,* the deliberate giving up of social, political, and economic activity for the sake of full-time ritualistic worship, and the commitment of all energies to *dhikr* or pious devotion became the highest goal. Surely, Islam imposed performance of the institutionalized five pillars of Islam, but it equally imposed fulfillment of man's *khilāfah* or "vice-gerency" and of *amānah,* "the divine trust."

4. *Tawakkul,* the total reliance upon the spiritual factor to produce the empirical results, replaced the Muslim's conviction of the certain efficacy of God's inexorable laws in nature and, hence, of the absolute necessity of human intervention into the causal nexus of nature, if the projected ends were to be realized.

5. *Qismat,* the passive acquiescence to what happens as being the action of arbitrary supernatural forces, replaced *taklīf,* or man's obligation to re-knead, recut, and remold space-time so as to realize therein the divine pattern. Rather than *amānah,* or man's assumption of this divine purpose for space-time as his own personal raison d'être, *taṣawwuf* taught a shortcut through *dhikr* or repeated prayers, and cultivated the hope for manipulation of the arbitrary supernatural forces, which opened the door to magic, talismanship, and charlatanism.

6. *Fanā'* and *'Adam,* the unreality, ephemerality, and nonimportance of the world, replaced the Muslim's seriousness regarding existence. It beclouded his consciousness of his cosmic status as the sole bridge through which God's will as moral value could be realized in space and time. Ṣūfīsm taught that life on earth is but a brief journey to the beyond. Against the Islamic principle that the final realization of the absolute in space-time is not only a distinct possibility but the supreme human duty, *taṣawwuf* taught that the world is no such theater after all, that such realization belongs to the beyond. Following al Ghazālī, it denigrated the world beyond reason or common sense.

7. *Ṭā'ah,* absolute, unquestionable, unreasoned, and totalistic obedience to the *shaykh* of one's Ṣūfī fraternity replacd *tawḥīd,* the recognition of no lord as Lord but He. Cultivation of the mystical trance came to replace the *sharī'ah* or fulfillment of the daily duties and lifelong obligations. This, together with *taṣawwuf's* pantheistic metaphysics, blurred all of Islam's ethical notions.

These symptoms ruined the health of Muslim society during half a millennium, from the fall of Baghdād to the Tatars in 655/1257 to the rise of the Wahhābiyyah, the first anti-Ṣūfī reform movement, in 1159/1747. Under the Ṣūfī spell, the Muslim had become apolitical, asocial, amilitary, anethical, and hence nonproductive, unconcerned for the *ummah* (the world brotherhood under the moral law), an individualist, and, in the last resort, an egotist whose prime objective was to be saved himself, to be absorbed into the consuming majesty of the divine being. He was shaken neither by the misery, poverty, disease, and subjection of his own society nor by the lot of mankind in history.

CHAPTER 17

Hellenistic Philosophy

It is proper to say that the translation of Greek scientific and philosophical texts into Arabic became a movement toward the end of the second/eighth century because of its massive programs and the speed with which its materials were digested and incorporated into Islamic culture. The process was aided by Christians who converted to Islam, as well as by those who sought fortune and prosperity in the new order Islam had established in the Near East. These were the instruments of that process. The movement was prompted by the new converts' questioning, as well as by that of those who remained Christians and countered the missionary efforts of Muslims with arguments drawn from Greek philosophy. To respond adequately to them, it was necessary that the Muslims learn these arguments, discover their underlying postulates and logic, and use them against their opponents. A third factor contributing to the rise of Hellenistic philosophy among Muslims was the fact that philosophy was not unrelated to the medical and natural sciences which the Muslims avidly sought. The texts of both science and philosophy were intertwined, and were often included in the same work or manuscript, following each other as chapters in the same systematic work. It was ideationally difficult, if not impossible, to separate them from each other. The Mu'tazilah were the first to seek, to study, and to use the philosophical legacy of the Greeks. The Muslim intelligentsia followed their example.

ABŪ YA'QŪB AL KINDĪ

Al Kindī (d. 251/866) was the first Muslim to elaborate a system of thought based on the logic of Greek philosophy. It was he who first established an Arabic lexicon of philosophical terms and laid down the definitions of the various categories. To this purpose he devoted a whole book, *Risālah fī Ḥudūd al Ashyā' wa Rusūmiha,* the first treatise in epistemology and logic. He was also the first to realize the gap between Islamic and Arabic thought, on the one hand, and the Greek ideas which he introduced on the other, and hence the first to seek to bridge that gap. Between religion and philosophy, between the *sharī'ah* and Greek logic, he claimed, there is a coincidence of purpose despite the difference in method. He defined philosophy as "the establishment of what is true and right," and argued that both religion and philosophy are equally necessary and legitimate, complementing each other. Contradiction or variance between them is never real, never final, but always apparent. It arises from application of the wrong method; for each kind of human pursuit there is a methodology proper to it which if violated or exchanged will result in contradiction. Al Kindī inclined toward the Mu'tazilah but he accepted the gnostic doctrine of illumination as the proper method to arrive at religious truth.

IKHWĀN AL ṢAFĀ

The Ikhwān al Ṣafā (c. 313-363/927-975), literally the Brethren of Purity, was an association of men founded in Baṣrah about 350/961 whose *Rasā'il* (Treatises) were known c. A.H. 375. There is wide disagreement about their identity and their projected role in society. The identity of the Ikhwān — authors of the treatises, the *Rasā'il Ikhwān al Ṣafā* — has been established by diaries of Abū Ḥayyān al Tawḥīdī (414/1023), a contemporary of the Ikhwān. These diaries were edited by Aḥmad Amīn and published under the title of *Al Imtā' wa al Mu'ānasah* in Cairo (1939-1944). Al Tawḥīdī mentions Zayd ibn Rifā'ah, Abū Sulaymān Muḥammad ibn Ma'shar al Bistī (alias al Maqdisī), Abū al Ḥasan 'Alī ibn Hārūn al Zanjānī, Abū Aḥmad al Mihrajānī, and al 'Awqī as members of the fraternity and authors of the *Rasā'il* which he read, took to his teacher, and discussed with them and others in A.H. 373. According to the *Rasā'il,* the Ikhwān were many and widespread; yet their organization was close-knit. "We have Ikhwān and friends among the notables and virtuous, scattered all over the country. Some are of royal blood, some are viziers, governors, men of letters; others are noblemen, merchants, 'ulamā', jurists, artisans and their children. To every class of these we have delegated a worthy and wise *Akh* (singular of Ikhwān) to serve and counsel them."[1] On this issue, al Qifṭī (646/1249) wrote: "As the authors have not disclosed their identity, people disagreed about them. Some said that the *Rasā'il* were the work of some descendants of 'Alī; others said they were the work of Mu'tazilī philosophers of the first period. None were able to establish their claim by any manner of means; for it is all guesswork."[2] Confirming al Qifṭī's insight, modern scholarship has ruled such claims out on the grounds that the persons in question all lived and died before a number of poets and thinkers (Ibn al Rūmī, al Mutanabbī, Abū al 'Alā' al Ma'arrī) whose authorship of many verses and quotations in the *Rasā'il* is beyond question, and on the evidence which the discovery of al Tawḥīdī's diaries has brought.

The Ikhwān sought to achieve two tasks: first, to recover in the main body of Islam, the *ummah,* its original Islamic ethical significance; and second, to enable the *sharī'ah,* by infusing it with liberal rationalism, to guide a recalcitrant, awakened human intellect that refuses to adopt imperatives without inner, personal, rational conviction. We have it on the authority of Abū Ḥayyān al Tawḥīdī that the Ikhwān came together to "elaborate a philosophy which, they claimed, brought them close to God's grace. The *sharī'ah,* they said, had been mixed up with falsehood and there was no way to purify it except through philosophy because only philosophy can give doctrinal truth and practical wisdom. For when Greek philosophy is harmonized with the Arab *sharī'ah,* there is perfection."[3]

The discovery of al Tawḥīdī's diaries shed further light on the nature of the Ikhwān's argument with the traditionalists. They speak of the Ikhwān as regarding the *sharī'ah* as medicine for the sick and a means to restore to them their lost health. They considered philosophy as medicine for the healthy, meant to preserve health and enable man to acquire virtue and prepare him for divine life and heavenly eternity. Thus, according to the Ikhwān, philosophy grants the *sharī'ah* a place in its scheme though the latter repu-

Illustration 17.1

Ṣabāḥ State Mosque, Kota Kinabalu, Malaysia. [Photo by L. al Fārūqī.]

diates the former. With *sharī'ah* man would come closer to God's grace by mere obedience; but with wisdom he wins that grace by grasping God's power and providence in the cosmos. It is a proof of God's goodness that there exist two mutually complementing ways for salvation, reason and revelation. Thus each would add to the excellence of the other: philosophy by giving the pious proof of the truth, conviction, and wisdom; and revelation by giving the wise piety, temperance, and love of God.

The Ikhwān accepted Greek dualism as far as the nature of man was concerned, but they assigned to body and soul functions in accordance with the imperatives of the *sharī'ah* and the *desiderata* of Islam. "Food for the body and knowledge for the soul" was for them a sort of war cry. To knowledge and its pursuit, the Ikhwān assigned first place among the virtues. Not one of all the duties imposed by the *sharī'ah* was more necessary, worthier, or closer to God, once He and His prophets were recognized, than knowledge and its pursuit and propagation. This enthusiasm for knowledge carried the Ikhwān to a perfect Socratism where knowledge, the good, and virtue are identified with one another. Knowledge is declared to bring in its train every good virtue and moral and material advantage. It makes the miser generous and gives the weak strength, the lowly, grandeur, the proud, humility.[4]

Following their allegorical interpretation of the Qur'ān, the Ikhwān moreover identified *Iblīs,* or Satan, with evil-doing, and defined evil-doing as blind belief in false opinions without knowledge or insight. They contrasted the good soul with the evil soul which does all its bad work without thought or deliberation. They concluded from such comparison that all ethical deeds and moral acts attributed to the rational soul are the results of that soul's true knowledge and beautiful belief; that all true knowledge and belief is the result of *ijtihād* (creative intellectual effort) and deliberation. To the man who seeks salvation, they counseled a self-purification through the washing off of false opinions and deliverance from the darkness of untruth. For education, that is, enlightenment, is the main — nay, the only — business of society and state. Knowledge should be taught to brother and neighbor, for it is the only medium of interpersonal moral relationships. The Ikhwān's neighborly love consisted not in charitable and altruistic sacrifices or in desiring ethical results in the persons of others, but first and foremost in educating one's neighbor, in bringing to him knowledge, man's most precious possession. To teach and educate and spread knowledge is the very essence of everything good. The Ikhwān were particularly interested in teaching the young, because these are the "pure in heart" and "anxious to win paradise" and "beginners in science." The older people, on the other hand, are "blindly attached to their sect, overconfident and prejudiced." They emphasized that teaching should proceed "in stages in proportion to the assimilative capacity of the candidate, with kindness and sympathy."[5]

The Ikhwān endeavored to cover all the sciences of their times and to organize in a *summa* all the departments of knowledge bound together by a single structure. The *Rasā'il,* fifty-three in number, covered all the fields from mineralogy, botany, and gynecology to ethics and religious laws.[6] That the unifying structure is ethical is obvious. Even numbers were studied not as pure quantity but as interpreting natural phenomena, and this significance of number was cosmos-pervading. The sciences were classified by order of their ethical significance, the highest being that which brings man knowledge of the divine kingdom, and the lowest, that which instructs him about objects in this world. The animal kingdom was ordered on an evolutionary basis, but not with regard to the physical characteristics of the species, in the manner of Darwin, but to the order of rank of the values each species had realized. Thus for their fidelity, memory, and nobility of disposition, the horse and the elephant rank far higher, and therefore closer to man, than the apes despite the closer physical resemblance of the latter. By order of the avenues of sense and thought leading to them, the sciences were thought to be empirical (having to do with the reports of sense), discursive (having to do with pure thought such as logic and mathematics), rational (dealing with ethical and valuational knowledge and the divine world-law), and illuminative (bestowed by God and directed to His nature and to the cosmic mysteries). Since the last science cannot be sought and is the prerogative of prophets, man's energies should be directed to the highest possible, to ethical knowledge.

AL FĀRĀBĪ, IBN SĪNĀ, AND IBN RUSHD

Abū al Nasr Muḥammad al Fārābī (d. 339/950) learned five languages and studied philosophy, medicine, mathematics, chemistry, and music; he was an excellent lutanist. He spent most of his life in Aleppo, enjoying the protection and patronage of its ruler, Sayf al Dawlah. His first concern was the reconciliation of the *sharī'ah* with philosophy which he saw represented by the polarity of Plato and Aristotle. He tackled the issue in a book he entitled *Union of the Two Wise Men — Plato and Aristotle,* and he derived his view of their union from the Plotinian treatise

Theology, which he, along with the whole Alexandrian and Christian traditions, mistook for a work of Aristotle's. Al Fārābī saw the two branches of learning dealing with materials (natural laws and moral laws) stemming from the same source—God. He held that they must be facets of one and the same reality, however different the approaches may be. The *sharī'ah* and philosophy, he concluded, unite in objective and purpose as well as in the material they study; for both focus their attention on the same reality—God's creation and order.

In logic and epistemology, al Fārābī followed Aristotle and added to his logic Porphyry's *Isagogia* and the illuminations of *The Theology of Aristotle.* Al Fārābī combined the rationalism of the *sharī'ah* with the *ishrāq* intuitionism of *taṣawwuf.* The cosmolgy of Plotinus further confirmed his view. The angel who brought down the revelation, he claimed, was also the active intelligence *(logos)* who gave the forms to the philosophers. Prophecy and philosophy are, he claimed, genuinely one and the same. The difference is not in the content given to the percipients, but in the percipients themselves being philosopher or prophet. In metaphysics, al Fārābī built his system on God as necessary ground of all being, and found in the gnostic legacy confirmation of this primary premise of Islam. Dividing reality into necessary and contingent, he distinguished the necessary-by-itself, the contingent-by-itself-necessary-by-another, and the contingent-not-yet-necessary. He identified God with the first, creation with the second, and the future of creation and the would-be actions of man with the third. Like al Kindī before him, al Fārābī defined God as the necessary being whose essence is to be, to live, to know, to create, to love. According to him, God does not know except Himself. As in the case of the Plotinian system, God contemplates Himself; He knows nothing of the affairs of the world. The charge al Ghazālī brought against the philosophers was thus justified; for the system they advocated had no room for the God of Islam, the active, provident Being by whose leave and will everything is or happens. The philosopher's God was indeed a *deus otiosus.* Nor did it help the philosophers to claim that the series of minds *(logoi)* that emanate from God, the absolute, terminate in the Active Mind which is the dynamic source of Forms and hence of creation. Such claim brought them to the blasphemy of polytheism.

Al Fārābī was more successful in his social theory, where he combined the sound insights of Plato with the requisites of Islam, and avoided what contradicted it. In his utopia, elaborated in *Ārā' Ahl al Madīnah al Fāḍilah,* the ruler is at once philosopher and prophet, combining the prerogatives and virtues of both. Al Fārābī perceived Islamic brotherhood as requiring that the citizens be like members of an organic body, that labor be according to competence and reward according to capacity. He avoided Plato's communion of husbands and wives, knowing how quickly such a view would arouse the Muslims to condemn him. Al Fārābī also wrote *Iḥṣā' al 'Ulūm* (Classification of the Sciences), crystallizing an effort begun by al Kindī to separate philosophy from *kalām,* and justifying adopted Greek philosophy as a discipline dependent entirely upon reason, unlike *kalām,* which he declared to be dependent upon revelation, the given data of faith. Philosophy was in the philosophers' view rational and critical; *kalām,* dogmatic. Little did al Fārābī and al Kindī appreciate the critical rationalism implicit in *tawḥīd;* and little did al Fārābī realize that his attempt to reconcile the *sharī'ah* and philosophy—such reconciliation being the epistemological basis of knowledge—was doomed to fail, even if the *Theology of Aristotle* had indeed been written by Aristotle.

Abū 'Alī al Ḥusayn ibn Sīnā (d. 428/1037), known in the Western world as Avicenna, was born in Afshānā, near Bukhārā. He studied mathematics under al Khawārizmī and medicine under 'Īsā ibn Yaḥyā and distinguished himself in both at the age of seventeen. He worked at the courts of a number of princes and produced the first systematic statements of philosophy and medicine in comprehensive compendia of all available knowledge in those fields. He wrote *Al Najāt, Al Shifā'* in philosophy, *Al Qānūn fī al Ṭib* in medicine, *Aḥwal al Nafs* in psychology. He also wrote two short stories, *Risālah al Ṭayr* and *Ḥayy ibn Yaqẓān,* in symbolic style to express social and religious truths in a way not readily comprehensible to the general reader. Apart from his excellence in medicine (his book was the world's undisputed authority for better than half a millennium, from its publication until the end of the seventeenth century), he deepened and added detail to the speculative theories of al Fārābī in logic, epistemology, and metaphysics. The general frameworks of their thought were identical: both accepted the intuitionism of gnostic illumination and the Ṣūfī ethic of contemplation as method of return to the absolute. Unlike al Fārābī, who envisaged the ideal society as one based on brotherhood and wisdom and led by a prophet-king, Ibn Sīnā denigrated society by declaring it hopelessly committed to mediocrity and opposition to the elite philosophers. His divergence from the cosmology and social ethics of Islam was all the greater. It was against him in particular that al Ghazālī launched his attack on philosophy. Ibn Sīnā's thought was the very embodiment of what was objectionable to Islam in the discipline as a whole.

Muḥammad Abūl Walīd Ibn Rushd (d. 593/1198),

Illustration 17.2

Top row, left: Front and back of a coin of Arab-Sasanian origin, bearing the name of Khusru II. Date: 36/656. Dimashq Museum.
Top row, right: Front and back of a coin minted during the reign of Umawī Caliph Hishām Ibn ʻAbd al Malik in 105/723. The inscription consists of the *shahādah* in angular Kūfī script. Dimashq Museum.
Middle row, left: Coin minted during the reign of Kākawayhī Sulṭān Muḥammad bin Dashmanzār, Iṣfahān, 406/1015. The inscription consists of the *shahādah* and the name of the sulṭān. National Museum of Qatar.
Middle row, right: Front and back of coin minted during the reign of the Fāṭimī, Al Āmir bi Aḥkām Allah, Alexandria, 514/1120. The inscription includes the *shahādah.* Dimashq Museum.
Bottom row, left: Front and back of coin minted during the reign of Saljūq Sulṭān Sulaymān Shāh in 597 A.H./1200 C.E. The inscription includes the *shahādah.* Damascus Museum.
Bottom row, right: Front and back of coin minted during the reign of Mamlūk Sulṭān Baḥrī al Ẓāhir Baybars in Cairo, 661/1262. The inscription consists of the *shahādah* and the name and title of the sulṭān. Dimashq Museum. [Courtesy Muḥammad Abū al Faraj al ʻUsh.]

known in the West as Averroës, was born in Cordoba. He studied medicine under the doctors of Āl Zuhr, especially Marwān; and he studied philosophy, religion, law, and jurisprudence for some time under the patronage of the Muwaḥḥidūn caliph in Marrākish who had a liking for philosophical investigations. But he found favor with the ruler of Seville who appointed him Chief Justice. He returned to his native city, Cordoba, to fill the post of Chief Justice, but left it soon to return to Marrākish to become vizier. He then fell out of favor, and was tried and banished to Alisanah, near Cordoba. He was subsequently forgiven and permit-

Illustration 17.3

Dayabumi Complex, Kuala Lumpur, Malaysia. Contemporary structure built by the government of Malaysia in Islamic style. [Courtesy Wan Muḥammad Yusuf.]

ted to spend the rest of his life in Marrākish, where he died. His remains were transported to Cordoba where they were buried in the graveyard of his ancestors.

Ibn Rushd wrote *Al Kulliyāt,* a compendium of medical knowledge, surpassing that of Ibn Sīnā in clarity, wealth, and organization of materials; *Bidāyat al Mujtahid wa Nihāyat al Muqtaṣid* in law and jurisprudence; *Faṣl al Maqāl fī mā bayna al Ḥikmah wal Sharī'ah Min al Ittiṣāl,* as a further attempt to reconcile religion and philosophy; and *Tahāfut al Tahāfut* in philosophy in which he sought to refute al Ghazālī's charges against the philosophers. He also wrote what became the standard commentary on Aristotle's works and standard style in subsequent literature in all fields of knowledge: *Al Sharḥ al Aṣghar* (The Lesser Explanation), a systematic and brief presentation of Aristotle's thought; *Al Sharḥ al Wasaṭ* (The Middle Explanation), in which Aristotle's writing was quoted according to subject matter and commented upon; and *Al Sharḥ al Kabīr* (The Great Explanation), in which Aristotle's writing was quoted verbatim, paragraph by paragraph, discussed, and commented upon.

Ibn Rushd was to Ibn Sīnā what the latter was to al Fārābī and al Kindī, namely, the producer of more detailed, clearer, and more systematic presentation of Greek philosophy. This was so well achieved by Ibn Rushd's three commentaries on Aristotle that they earned for him the title "the Second Master," after Aristotle, and established themselves as the only highway to Aristotle's thought. His attempt to reconcile philosophy to the ***sharī'ah*** was doomed even more than al Fārābī's because the contrast between the respective methodologies of the two disciplines was made sharper. For him, the theologians—*mutakallimūn*—were "preachers" needed by the populace to instill in them some moral restraint, beginning and ending with the *data revelata* which they must accept *ex hypothesi.* The philosophers, on the other hand, were real "teachers" moving from one logical step to another only after questioning and proving critical consideration of the evidence by the highest and noblest faculty—reason. Thus the gap between philosophy and religion was truly unbridgeable. Indeed, Ibn Rushd may be said to have anticipated the modern theory of religion in the West as determined by feeling and personal experience, the bases on which the truths of revelation are accepted. Ibn Rushd supported and elaborated the points on which Ibn Sīnā and al Fārābī were accused of heresy. His dismissal of al Ghazālī's charges was based on an allegorical interpretation of the dicta of religion, thus diluting the religious claim in order to accommodate philosophy.

IBN KHALDŪN

Ibn Khaldūn (d. 808/1406) lived at a time when the Islamic empire in the West was crumbling. First the Murābiṭūn and then the Muwaḥḥidūn movements had rallied the people around one flag; but the lack of leadership again dissolved the central authority and refragmented the realm into petty princedoms competing with and plotting against one another. Banū Ḥafṣ in Tunis, the Marīnīs in Morocco, the Mahdīs in Bijjāyah, Banū Naṣr in Granada, and other petty dynasties and states sometimes not larger than their capitals, had reached a nadir of division and mutual opposition. In the meantime, the Spaniards were uniting their kingdoms, consolidating their gains, extracting more concessions from the Muslims, and encroaching upon the territories the latter controlled. For two centuries, one province after another of Muslim Spain fell to the Christian invaders from the North—Toledo in 1085, Cordoba in 1236, and Seville in 1248. It was an age of political intrigue, of quick and violent succession of power among the Muslim states whose general condition was certainly one of decline and dissolution. Muslims plotted against one another, shifting their loyalty from one government and prince to another in pursuit of self-interest. Ibn Khaldūn fit perfectly into this milieu, as if he was not only born in it but for it.

Ibn Khaldūn was born in Tunis and studied law and

literature there. He worked at the Tunisian court for a while, waiting for an opportunity for self-advancement. It did not matter that the occasion that presented itself implied treason to his employer. The Moroccans were preparing the ground to invade Tunis; as for Ibn Khaldūn, his advancement was sufficient cause for providing them with the needed information. When the Moroccan campaign failed, Ibn Khaldūn ran for his life. He landed in Fās where his patron, Abū 'Inān al Marīnī, brought him into the court and assigned to him the post of secretary-general of the government. Ibn Khaldūn soon found out that the opportunities for advancement were greater elsewhere, so he plotted against his new employer to the advantage of the ruler of neighboring Bijjāyah, asking for the post of vizier there as reward for his treason. The Marīnī ruler of Fās uncovered the plot, and Ibn Khaldūn was thrown in jail for two years. From prison he corresponded with the Sulṭān of Qassantīnah, whose employ he joined when he gained his freedom. This leader was also betrayed by Ibn Khaldūn, this time for the benefit of the Sulṭān of Tilimsān; and the latter met a similar fate when Ibn Khaldūn tried to win the favor of the Sulṭān of Marrākish. The same scenario was repeated in Marrākish and Granada until his bad reputation made it impossible for Ibn Khaldūn to stay anywhere in the Maghrib, from Tunis to the Atlantic. He then decided to try his fortune in the East. He came to Egypt and offered his services to its ruler. The latter sent him on a precarious mission to Timurlank (Tamerlane), who at that time occupied Damascus. The mission succeeded and Ibn Khaldūn was amply rewarded. It was not the first time he succeeded in a diplomatic mission. He did succeed in every such mission entrusted to him by his numerous employers — a fact that proves his brilliance and correct assessment of the conflicts he was assigned to solve. However, he longed to return to the Maghrib, there to start all over again. In 774/1375 he found himself imprisoned in the fortress of Ibn Salāmah, and he thought it was time to write down what he had learned of the fate of nations throughout his life and the experience of their rise and fall.

As concerns method, Ibn Khaldūn followed in the footsteps of the Muslim Hellenistic philosophers — al Fārābī, Ibn Sīnā, and Ibn Rushd — in dividing knowledge between two domains: that of rational truth where reason is the criterion and judge, and that of spiritual truth where revelation and prophecy are supreme. In fact, he blamed the philosophers for trying to reconcile the *sharī'ah* and revelation with reason and philosophy. He argued that the two are forever disparate, with different faculties and methods applying to them. The philosophers tried to reconcile the irreconcilable. Reason will never reach the spiritual truths, because the latter are not its object, just as it is not possible for the eye to see sound or the ear to hear light. All transcendent truth falls outside the jurisdiction of reason, without becoming any less true. Transcendent truth must be sought in prophecy, not reason. It is possible that his classification of all religious knowledge outside the realm of reason prompted Ibn Khaldūn to fill the void with the sciences of man. None of the philosophers had restricted the jurisdiction of reason so radically; and they all wished, and hinted, that it was large enough to judge all matters including the spiritual. In Ibn Khaldūn's classification, the division is categorical. The two realms cannot and will not meet under reason and must remain separate. Reason, therefore, was judged as dealing only with the realm of nature. Ibn Khaldūn added to this realm that of human relations and history. This is what made him the first social scientist. Ibn Khaldūn did not doubt the necessity of causality in order to accommodate the providence and almightiness of God. In his view, causality is an iron-clad necessity which dominates the realm of social relations as well as that of nature. This novel perspective on human society was responsible for Ibn Khaldūn's effort to search for and find the laws governing society as he would those governing the phenomena of nature. Auguste Comte, the father of modern social science, brought social relations under the governance of empirical reason out of awe at the greatness and promise of science, following its achievements and victories over the magisterium of

Illustration 17.4

Mosque in Musqaṭ, the Sultanate of 'Umān. [Photo by L. al Fārūqī.]

the Church. Ibn Khaldūn anticipated Comte by half a millennium. He brought social relations under the governance of reason because of his clearer vision of the nature of the scientific enterprise and that of human reality. The latter seemed to defy science and lie beyond it, inciting Ibn Khaldūn to examine the problem more closely. Having located the turbulence in the religious sphere, Ibn Khaldūn separated that area from the realm of human affairs, denied reason's jurisdiction to judge in it, and secured a sure and permanent place for the remainder—the social relations—under the dominion of reason.

Social relations have their causes and effects like any natural phenomenon. The historian must seek them out and establish them with proof and evidence, like any scientist examining the events of nature. For such an investigation, history is the laboratory, and sociology—the science of human society—the product. He had no doubt that such a search was science, autonomous as well as new, with a subject matter, purpose, and method as clearly defined as any other. Before Ibn Khaldūn, many a book was written describing kings and rulers and distinguishing the successful from the failing among them. Many others dealt with how to establish and maintain social order, or depicted the ideal society for which humans should aim. The Greek works never went beyond these objectives. Ibn Khaldūn did. He searched for the laws under which all societies develop, flower, and decline; and he sought to establish them as guidelines for any prediction of the future of any society.

Illustration 17.5

Mosque in Musqaṭ, the Sultanate of 'Umān. [Photo by L. al Fārūqī.]

THE NEW SOCIAL SCIENCE OF IBN KHALDŪN

The most important perspective of society is that it is an organism that grows, matures, and ages not by chance or by divine fiat but because of real causes operating upon it. The relation between the social effects and the causes leading to them is universal and necessary. There are no accidents in social history but simply causes and their effects, some obvious and well known, others less so. The prime cause of formation of society is need. Human individuals are far less capable than the animals to preserve themselves. They need one another to complement their powers to survive. In food and agriculture, in housing and industry, as well as in defense, humans must cooperate and come together. In doing so, other causes besides need affect the outcome: geographic location and its consequences in biological formation and economic life. Ibn Khaldūn attributed most physical and psychic variations in society to these physical causes. Cold, mild, and hot temperatures were responsible for skin pigmentation (against the biblical myth of Noah and his descendants); for personalities being light, active, serious, or lethargic; and for food being abundant or scarce. In turn, these factors condition the life of society. Much food and luxury corrupt both the body and the mind, and little food and absence of luxury and comfort contribute to self-discipline and greater seriousness. Even religious piety does not escape being affected by these factors. The populations of the arid zones are thereby more given to religious demands and piety than those of the fertile zones.

Once launched into history in consequence of these formative factors, society runs a course of childhood, youth, maturity, and old age. Ibn Khaldūn equated the childhood stage with the life of the pastoral and agricultural peoples. He called it the stage of *badw* or nomadism, the period in which a society depends on pasture and the cattle it can support. It includes agriculture, whether irrigated or depending on rainfall; in either case the dominant feature is satisfaction of the barest necessities of survival. Population growth and food scarcity compel the *badw* society to enter the stage of *ghazw* (aggression) when it begins to fill its needs by raiding other societies in the same or weaker stage. Intertribal wars among the Arabs and the encroachment of the nomadic and pastoral peoples upon the irrigational lands belong to this category. The experience of a life of plenty, though for a brief while, will push the society in the *ghazw* stage to seek permanent settlement in those areas that guarantee abundance. When this happens, society enters the third stage, that of *ḥaḍar* (civilization). This stage begins when the society becomes a satellite of a more advanced state and receives regular subsidies, the justification for which may be defense against other raiding societies. But the advanced state continues to age and become weaker. Soon, the satellite state takes over and establishes itself in its stead. A life of civilization then begins, with the new society inheriting all the advances of the old, and imitating it in its living customs. Being the less civilized, the new ruler-society seeks to be like the old state. It copies and imitates the vanquished. This process takes three to four generations to be completed. At the same time, the vanquished society copies the new ruler-society because the latter is deemed to be superior, and its superiority is taken to be the explanation and justification for its victory. Inevitably, the ruling society is regarded as worthy of emulation. The result is the emergence of a more homogeneous society, fully civilized, but beginning to sink in the satisfaction of wants and exposing itself to the attacks of outsiders.

Ibn Khaldūn also analyzed the rise of society. Here he discovered that their animal nature impels humans to fight with one another over the material goods they need. In this situation of conflict, someone rises who is endowed with power and prestige, who imposes his authority upon society. Thus a state is born. It has nothing to do with religion. The ruler does not need religion to legitimize or sanction his sovereignty. The sovereignty of the ruler exists by virtue of his power and the confidence he inspires in his peers to acquiesce to that power and to entrust him with the task of protection. To name this cohesiveness between them Ibn Khaldūn chose the pre-Islamic notion of *'aṣabiyyah* (the bond between members of the same tribe), which the Qur'ān (48:26) and the Prophet condemned in no uncertain terms. Ibn Khaldūn made it the base of all political power, and declared sovereignty to belong to that group with the stronger *'aṣabiyyah*. Its essence is brute force and coercive power which no opponent can resist. Ibn Khaldūn estimated the average duration of *'aṣabiyyah* as that of four generations, naming the first as "experiencer," the second as "follower," the third as "tradition keeper," and the fourth as "tradition loser."

These views led Ibn Khaldūn to a cyclical view of history. Societies are born and grow and die, and other societies take their place, only to grow and die like their predecessors. Evidently, Ibn Khaldūn's view of human history runs counter to the Qur'ānic philosophy that the rise and fall of nations are conditional upon fulfillment or violation of the divine imperatives, either of which is always possible. Under Ibn Khaldūn's terms, the rise and fall of nations are ruled by a necessary law of nature; their actualization may be delayed for one or two or three generations, but it is inevitable. Ibn Khaldūn thought the moral law to be irrelevant to the unfolding of history. The only relevant factor was the cultivation of *'aṣibiyyah* or the will to use it to advantage. Since this philosophy was actualized in Ibn Khaldūn's own personal life, it will forever remain a question whether his life was ruined by his mind, or his mind was led astray by his life.

NOTES

1. *Rasā'il Ikhwān al Ṣafā* (Beirut: Dār Ṣādir-Dār Beirut, 1958); Vol. II, p. 165.

2. *Tārīkh al Ḥukāmā'*, ed. J. Lippert (Leipzig, 1903), p. 82.

3. Al Tawḥīdī, Abū Ḥayyān, in *Al Imtā' wa al Mu'ānasah*, ed. Aḥmad Amīn (Cairo, 1358-1364/1939-1944), p. 11.

4. *Rasā'il*, Vol. III, p. 346. Quoting the Prophet, the Ikhwān write, "Seek knowledge; for its acquisition is the fear of God, its pursuit is worship, its discussion is prayer, the search for it is holy war, its propagation is charity, its teaching is fraternity. For it is the index of right and wrong, the lighthouse of the road to paradise. It provides consolation in loneliness, friendship in estrangement, fidelity through thick and thin, protective arms against the enemy, rapprochement towards the foreigners, decor among friends. . . . For their friendship, the angels seek the men of knowledge, caress them with their wings, remember them in their prayers. . . . By knowledge is God obeyed, through it He is worshipped. . . . In knowledge the good is revealed, loved and implemented, for it is the prius of action, the first principle of every good deed."

5. *Rasā'il*, Vol. X, pp. 50-51.

6. The first complete edition of the *Rasā'il* was published in Bombay in 1306/1888. This was corrected by Nūr al Dīn Jiwā Khān, an Isma'īlī, and was mistakenly ascribed to Aḥmad 'Abdullah. It included fifty-two tracts, and failed to mention the manuscript from which it had been taken. Another edition was published in Cairo in 1347/1928, edited by Khayr al Dīn al Ziriklī from a manuscript in the National Library in Cairo. A third edition was published in Beirut by Dār Sādir-Dār Beirut in 1378/1958. *Al Risālah al Jāmi'ah* was published by the Arab Academy of Science in Damascus in 1347/1948, edited by Jamīl Ṣalībā.

CHAPTER 18

The Natural Order

To raise the question of the relation of Islam to the natural order is to seek Islam's answer to three different inquiries at once: What is nature? How is nature knowable? How is nature to be used? The first is a question of metaphysics; the second, of epistemology or science of nature; the third, of axiology and ethics. In the view of Islam, the three parts are interdependent. The answer given to one is not only relevant to but determines the other two. Together, the three inquiries constitute an integral theory of nature peculiar to Islam.

WHAT IS NATURE?

Islam takes nature very seriously. A large portion of the Qur'ān deals with nature, whether directly or indirectly. The nature of nature is determined by five principles: profanity, createdness, orderliness, purposiveness, and subservience.

Profanity

The living religions of the world can be divided between those that see nature as sacred—the naturalist—and those that see nature as profane—the transcendentalist. Taoism, Mahayana Buddhism, Hinduism, and archaic religions fall in the first category; Theravada Buddhism, Judaism, Christianity, and Islam fall in the second. Common to the first group is the view that God and nature are distinguishable only in the mind; that in reality they are one and the same. Nature, they all claim, is indeed God, or Ultimate Reality, or the Absolute; but the modality in which God and nature are presented and understood may be different.

This association is often expressed in myth, because the language of myth readily lends itself to such expression. Under its terms, naturalistic religions hold nature to be numinous, that is, mysterious, terrifying, and fascinating. Mystery (hiddenness, incomprehensibleness, impenetrability), almightiness (overwhelming power, absolute superiority, awesomeness), and sublimity (beauty, attractiveness, and moving power) are all qualities ascribed to nature. In some naturalistic religions the net balance is condemnation of nature as evil, demonic, a degradation of the Absolute; in others, the net balance is approbation, love, and respect. Both prescribe adoration: the one out of reverential fear, the other out of reverential love.

A wall of difference separates the naturalistic religions from those of transcendence. In the latter, na-

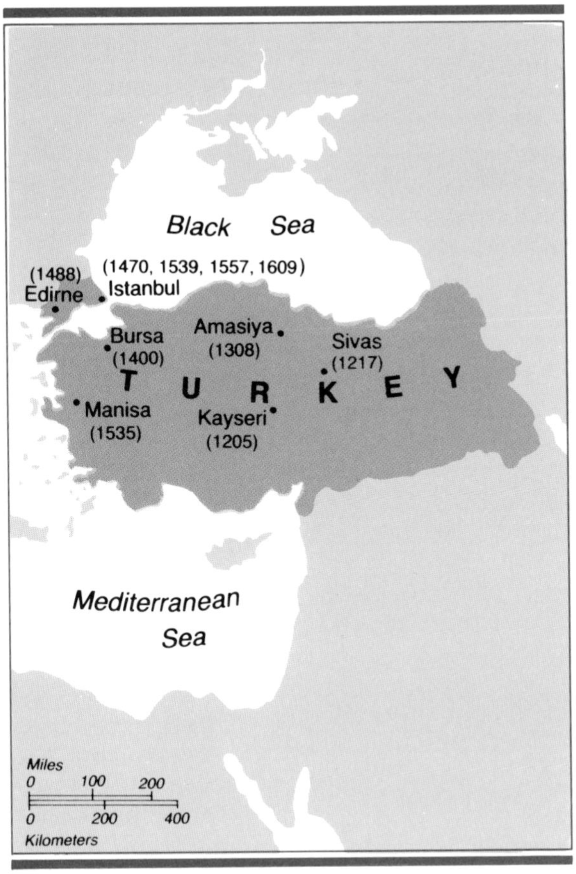

Map 55. Principal Medical Schools and Hospitals in Turkey, 1250–1609 C.E.

GREAT MEDICAL SCHOOLS AND HOSPITALS IN TURKEY

City	*Date Founded*	*Founder(s)*
Kayseri	1205	Sulṭāna Naṣībah Khātun and her brother, Sulṭān Ghiyāthuddīn Qaykhusro
Ṣivas	1217	Sulṭān 'Izzuddīn Qayqawūs
Amasiya	1308	'Anbar bin 'Abdullah
Bursa	1400	Bāyazīd Yilderim
Istanbul	1470	Fātiḥ Hospital
Edirne	1488	Bāyazīd II
Manisa	1535	Ḥafsah, wife of Salīm I
Istanbul	1539	Khunam, wife of Sulaymān
Istanbul	1557	Sulaymān
Istanbul	1609	Sulṭān Aḥmad, Aḥmad I

ture is profane, the opposite of the sacred. It is devoid of numinous qualities. It is neither terrifying nor mysterious nor fascinating. It is itself, an inexorable process of generation and decay, a clockwork whose power is inherent in itself. Whether in its totality, in its elements or species, or in its individual objects, nature is always itself, not-God, not-sacred, not-Ultimate Reality. As the religions of transcendence divide between theistic and nontheistic varieties, nature is regarded as either eternal or ephemeral, as either good or evil. For Theravada Buddhism, nature is eternal but evil. *Tanha,* the desire or tendency to change, and suffering constitute its essence. For Judaism, Christianity, and Islam, nature is ephemeral. In itself, it is good; but with reference to what man makes of it, or how he conducts himself toward it, it can become either good or evil. Generally, this is the substance of the agreement among the transcendentalist religions in the matter of nature. Certainly, differences among them qualify their transcendentalist position, diluting and compromising, or strengthening and emphasizing it. Islam stands at the extreme end of this spectrum where the profanity of nature is complete and absolute. Nothing is sacred but the sacred, namely, God; and everything else is profane, totally profane in all its aspects. That is the meaning of the Islamic profession of faith, *Lā ilaha illā Allah* (Qur'ān 3:18). To attribute sacredness to nature or to anything in it is to commit *shirk* or association of other beings with God. Islam condemned predication of sacredness to nature in no uncertain terms. To make of His creatures a part of Him (Qur'ān 43:15), to call upon anything other than God for help (39:43), to adore any part of nature beside God (40:66), to claim a genealogical connection between Him and humans or *jinn* (37:158), to take from the earth anything as divine (21:21)—is the capital crime, the unpardonable sin (4:48, 116). In Muslim eyes, *shirk* or the ascription of any sacredness to the profane, to anything in creation, is the vilest abomination. When in mystical transport, Manṣūr al Ḥallāj claimed that sacredness belonged to him, he was subjected instantly to the worst possible punishment—crucifixion. Previously, when 'Umar ibn al Khaṭṭāb, under the shock of the Prophet's death, claimed some nonprofane status for him, Abū Bakr pushed him aside from the pulpit and said, to the approval and delight of all Muslims: "Whoever worshipped Muḥammad, let him know that Muḥammad is dead. But whoever worshipped God alone, let him know that God is eternal and never dies" (Ibn Hishām, *Sīrat Rasul Allah,* vol. IV, p. 1070).

Createdness

Nature, in Islam, is a creature of God, created *ex nihilo,* by the sheer commandment of God for it to be. It is absolutely different and other than God Who is defined as "the totally other" or *laysa ka mithlihi shay'* (Qur'ān 42:11). The otherness of God, meaning that reality is dual, one realm being occupied exclusively by God, the transcendent Creator, and the other by all else, the creation, is the most emphatic lesson Islam had taught. To confuse the creature with the Creator, the Qur'ān teaches, is a terrible mistake because God alone is Creator (13:16). If there were more than one unique Creator, heaven and earth, Creator and creature, would have fallen to the ground and dissolved (21:22). God alone creates and re-creates; and no one else does (10:34). Heaven and earth and all that is in them are creatures, partaking of creatureliness, that is, of coming into being and passing away under all the relativities of space and time (11:7; 46:3). All creatures were created out of nothing, commanded to be and they were (2:118; 3:47, 59; 6:73: 16:40; etcetera). God is indeed capable of destroying creation and creating it all again in an instant (30:40, 10:34). His creation is not a generative act ["He has no counterpart, no female co-worker. . . . He never begets, and is never begotten. He has neither match nor parallel" (6:101–103; 112:1–4)] but a mere command (36:80–83).

Orderliness

Islam holds nature to be an orderly realm: an event occurs as a result of its cause; in turn, its occurrence is the cause of another event. The same events point to the same causes, and the same causes point to the same consequences (Qur'ān 65:3, 36:12). Nature is, furthermore, a complete order, because all events follow the same laws and nothing stands outside of them. Indeed, for a creature to be at all, it is to be in nature, to fall under its inexorable laws. To be other than nature or to stand outside of its laws is to be God and Creator of nature. This order was implanted in nature by God, the Creator Who created and fashioned it as it is. Nothing in it escapes His knowledge, and everything in it stands under the laws pertinent to it. That is what gives it its orderliness. The causal efficacy of each creature is measured; and so are its effect and time. Nature is thus a complete and integral system of causes and effects without flaw, without gap, perfectly patterned by its Creator. "Look into His creation for any discrepancy! And look again! Do you find any gap in its system? Look again! Your sight, having found none, will return to you humbled" (Qur'ān 67:3–4). This perfection will qualify nature as long as it exists; for God's creation will always be the same. The reason is that the patterns of God are immutable (48:23). He does not change His ways because He stands beyond change.

Purposiveness

Each of the objects that constitute nature has been assigned a purpose which it must, and will, fulfill. "God created everything and assigned to it its *qadar*," or measure, destiny, role, and purpose (Qur'ān 25:2, 87:3). Such purpose is built into the object as its nature, toward which it moves with inexorable necessity. It may be obvious and well-known or hidden and almost unknowable. But it is certainly there, a *"qadaran maqdūrā,"* specific and precise (Qur'ān 33:38). Purposiveness is the other side of orderliness. The very same relation of two objects in nature is causality when viewed theoretically and purposiveness when viewed axiologically. Better still, as our philosophers have said, notably Ibn Sīnā, the relation *in toto* is called causality, but within it, the formal, material, efficient, and final or purposive aspects are clearly discernible. Purpose pervades the whole of creation without exception. Such exception would fall outside God's knowledge and providence and would constitute a denial of divine unity and ultimacy. The Qur'ān affirms: "We have not created heaven and earth and all that stands between them in sport. . . . [Rather] We have created them in righteousness . . . for the purpose of confuting evil and error with truth and value" (44:38, 21:16). As object in nature, man is, in the Islamic view, equally purposive; for he is an integral part of the finalistic system that is creation. Indeed, Islam declares him to be the purpose of all the finalistic chains of nature. This constitutes his ecological interdependence with all that is in nature.

Subservience

Islam further affirms that purposiveness is not only an attribute of every object in nature but is also a predicate of the totality of nature. God did not create the world (in the Qur'ān, "heaven and earth") in vain but for a purpose, namely, that man may do the good works (Qur'ān 11:7, 18:7, 67:2). Islam therefore affirms an end, a purpose to creation, and conceives of that purpose as the moral works of man. To this end, God provided the necessary instruments. He equipped man with eyes and sight, with hearing and language, and with reason and understanding, so that he would be able to perform in the world (17:36, 46:26, 22:46). As to those who neglect to use this God-given equipment with which to understand nature, Islam declares them worthy of chastisement.

The subservience of nature to man means that the purpose that God assigned to each object is ultimately to lead to man's good, that man can use it to achieve felicity. It also means that God has made nature malleable, capable of receiving the causal efficacy of man, of keeping its causal threads open to further determination by him, and to make his input successful in bringing about the desired objective of human action. This is what the Qur'ān has expressed by the idea of *taskhīr*. Sun, stars and moon, heaven and earth, animals, plants and things, clouds, air and all the elements are all subservient to man (Qur'ān 13:2, 31:20, 22:65, etcetera). It is man's title to use nature as he pleases. For *taskhīr* of nature is not only for survival but for *zīnah* or pleasure as well (37:6). Indeed, the teleological system of nature itself is purposive in the higher sense of fulfilling the instrumental ends necessary for man's moral exercise. Such higher instrumentalism of nature is impossible without nature's orderliness. Nature, therefore, is essentially good; and its goodness is its perfect instrumentality to man's actualization of value which in turn is the purpose of creation. The Qur'ān affirmed that God created men only to serve Him (51:56), and defined that service as a divine trust which neither angels (2:30), nor heaven, earth, and mountains could carry because it requires moral freedom. According to Islam, this is the meaning of human life, of time and history: man is God's *khalīfah* or vicegerent on earth, to the end of realizing the moral values that are the higher part of God's will. This significance of man is indeed cosmic, since the cosmos itself was created for his sake.

HOW IS NATURE KNOWABLE?

Necessity of Natural Knowledge

Islam holds that the totality of the world was created out of nothing. Within the world, things are created or come to be through natural causes, by means of material, formal, efficient, and final causes built by the Creator into nature. The relations of these causes to their effects are always the same, thus constituting patterns in nature, or ways by which things are generated, by which they grow, change, die and decompose, and are regenerated. These patterns are the laws of nature. They govern all existents in nature, whether in their coming to be, their "life" or relations with other existents, or their passing out of existence. It is this aspect of creation that makes it a cosmos, an orderly realm, a theater where objects are, and events happen, in accordance with laws; where observation, study, and discovery of these laws are possible because of their permanence and constancy, and where prediction of events is possible. The orderliness of the universe requires that there be no causal gaps in it. Everything is the effect of causes, and the cause of other effects. Like causes produce like effects; and like effects necessarily imply like causes, thus making the world a web of interrelated, interdependent causal relations, repeating and thus making themselves discoverable. To discover and establish the validity of these patterns or laws, of their application or instantiation in the events of nature, is science. Science, therefore, requires—and its possibility implies—causality as first law of all that is or happens in nature. Without causality, that is, without the certainty that identical causes will lead to identical effects, the possibility of science suffers and may itself fall altogether. If some rocks could fall toward the center of the earth when not impeded in their fall by another cause, and other rocks could fall away from the center of the earth under identical conditions, then no law of gravity could ever be established, or even discovered. Natural order tolerates no causal gaps. It is universal as well as necessary.

The old comparison of nature to clockwork is indeed true. Within the cosmos, regularity is both regulative and constitutive. It distinguishes our world from chaos. Islam fully affirms cosmic regularity or causality within nature. Unequivocally, Islam declared nature to be a perfectly ordered realm and systematically removed from the Prophet Muḥammad every doubt that by, through, or for the sake of man, the natural order could be broken.

All the foregoing qualities of nature, therefore, are necessary for science. On the one hand, the necessity of profanity and regularity are obvious. Without them, there may be myth, but no science. On the other, purposiveness and subservience are necessitated by morality. Purposiveness is another perspective of causality and is inseparable from it. It does not matter whether or not the processes of nature are determined by man's welfare. Indeed, earthquakes, explosions, floods, droughts, fires, pestilences, and other natural catastrophes tell a different tale than the service of man. What is important is that the processes of nature be so interrelated as to provide for nature's continuity and regularity. Whether nature serves God or some other power, its continuity and regularity are sufficient to make it a viable arena for man's endeavor. Subservience is necessary if man is to be effective as a moral agent, if his actions are to make any difference at all in history. Actually, morality and ethics, revelation and religion, would all be in vain if creation were unchangeable, if man lived in an environment where nature is not malleable, where humans are unable to translate their decisions and desires into facts of nature. In such a world, the work of religion would all be done and finished. A human life whose total net effect in creation and history is nil is not the ideal contemplated by any religion, certainly not by Islam. The value of life as well as that of religion and morality are both based upon the possibility of contributing some change to creation. Otherwise, the notions themselves of good–evil, righteous–vicious, desirable–undesirable would become meaningless. No one would stand under any moral or religious obligation because that necessarily implies the capacity to change the course of nature.

Possibility of Natural Knowledge

Islam strongly affirms that a continuing and regular nature such as we find creation to be is indeed possible as object of human knowledge. First, it is observable and measurable since it functions according to laws or patterns. The Qur'ān repeatedly affirms that the patterns of God are immutable (30:30, 33:62). Human knowledge of these eternal patterns may be immediate through revelation; or painstakingly slow, tentative, and always incomplete, through rational examination. Islam maintains that the will of God is legible in either of two books: The Qur'ān,

Map 56. Qurṭūbah (Cordoba): Jewel of the West, 950 C.E.

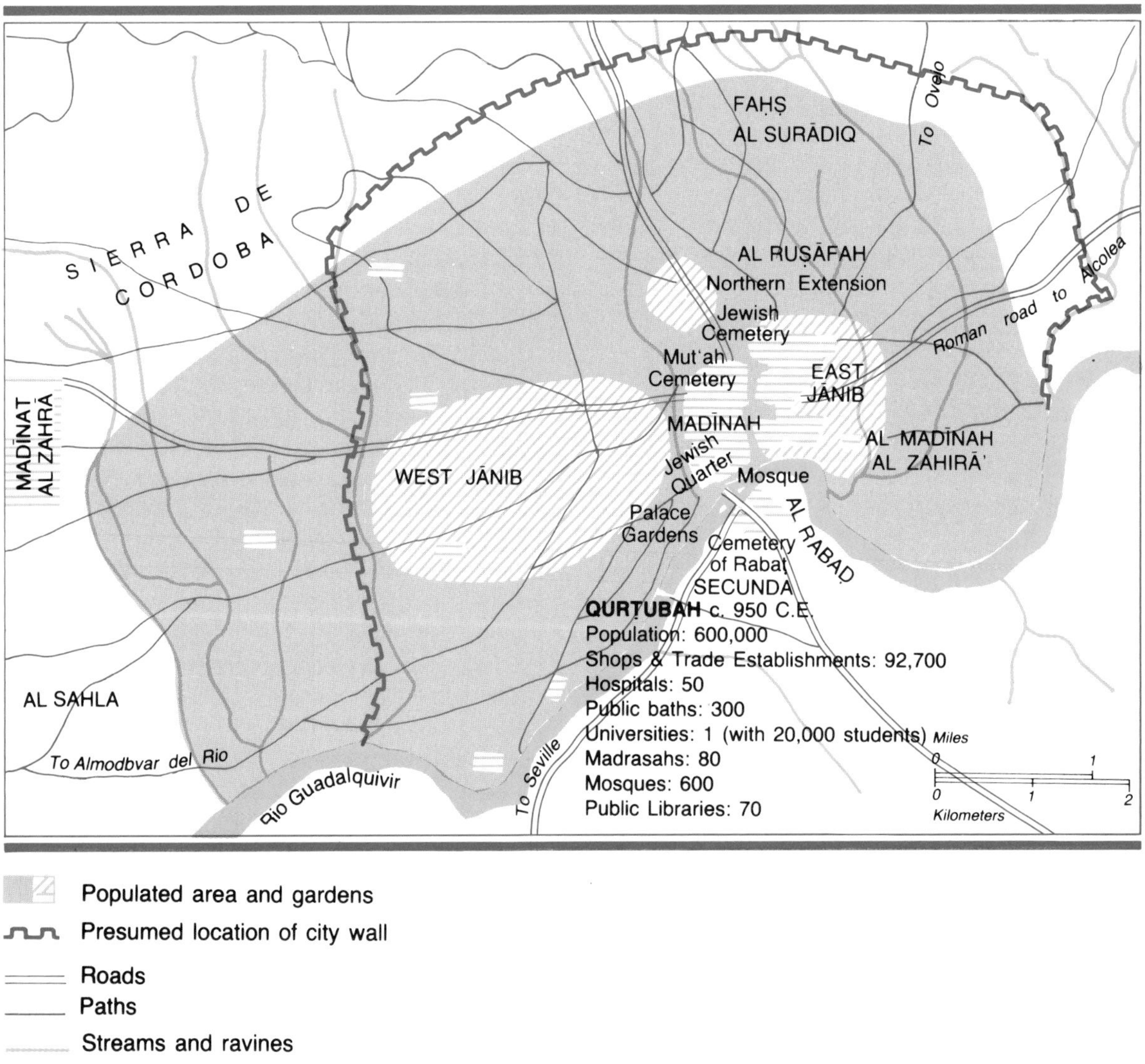

revealed by God to His Prophet in clear Arabic; and nature, the book for anyone to "read" through observation, measurement, *naẓar* or intellection and consideration, and testing in experience. Nature will not fail to yield its secrets—the eternal divine patterns—to anyone seriously applying himself to the task and allowing nature to speak for itself through experience. The laws of nature are hypotheses reached through observation and experimentation. This involves isolation of the factors or causes and effects operating in a phenomenon, their observation and measurement, and the amendment or confirmation of the hypotheses in experience.

Qurṭubah (c. 950 C.E.)	
Population	600,000
Shops and Trade Establishments	92,700
Hospitals	50
Public Baths	300
Universities	1 (with 20,000 students)
Madrasahs	80
Mosques	600
Public Libraries	70

The knowledge of nature is never complete. It is infinite at both extremities, the microcosmic and the macrocosmic. Creation is infinitely small, infinitely large, and infinitely complex. Investigation of any natural phenomenon reveals a baffling complexity of determinants affecting it, and an equally baffling complexity of effects arising from it. A whole "field" of causes and a whole "field" of effects is a truer description of any phenomenon of nature than a single line or nexus of cause and effect. A "field" is an infinite number of factors which converge on any point of space-time and diverge therefrom in another infinite "field" of effects. It is not surprising, therefore, that an examination of the works of nature is an infinite proposition; for such is in fact an examination of the work of God. Obviously, infinite knowledge is not the prerogative of humans but of God.

Two questions remain to be answered by Islam if we are to clarify its relation to natural science. First, may humans possess an adequate portion of it? Second, is such knowledge trustworthy? Islam's answer to the first question is a dynamic affirmation. Man's fulfillment of the tasks of vicegerency is directly proportional to the command one has of the laws of nature. "Those who know," The Qur'ān asks rhetorically, "are they the equals of those who don't?" Indeed, the more one knows, the more apt he is to recognize God as God.[1] Consequently, the works of the former must exceed and excel those of the latter, and so does their respective merit. In the same vein, the Prophet equated the ink of the scholar with the blood of the martyr. Since there is no limit to the individual's or group's effort to seek knowledge, adequacy is a function of their self-application and success in obtaining knowledge.

Islam's answer to the second question is no less affirmative. The knowledge of nature is indeed trustworthy, Islam affirms, on three counts. First, natural knowledge is a part of the general knowledge of the divine will which is trustworthy with a necessity flowing from the whole purpose of creation. The relevance of the divine will for anything and the validity of the divine purpose fall to the ground unless real knowledge of the divine will is possible for man. Second, the trustworthiness of human knowledge of nature is necessary because morality and religion demand it. As we have seen earlier, without reasonable assurance that a certain cause will and does in fact lead to a certain result, moral striving as well as living in general lose their mooring and become questionable. Third, Islam teaches that human knowledge of nature, if sought carefully and honestly, is trustworthy because God, the Author of the patterns as well as the drama of humanity, is not a mischievous trickster but a most beneficent and merciful God. Humans were not given their faculties of knowledge to be fooled by them, nor were they placed in an arena where they were required by God to do the good but were not equipped to bring about its actualization in creation. To say, however, that human knowledge of nature is trustworthy is not to say that it is apodeictically certain. The difference between trustworthiness and apodeictic certainty is great; and it occupied a fair portion of the thought of Muslim philosophers.

Al Fārābī, Ibn Sīnā, and Ibn Rushd maintained that knowledge of nature, because it takes nothing for granted and subjects everything to evidence, is rational, necessary, and true. Its conclusions are apodeictically certain on account of these grounds. When evidence confirms an observed regularity, the resultant knowledge is certain. The philosophers agreed that nature was patterned and regular, and so they were confident that rational knowledge of it was certain knowledge of reality. In nature, they thought, discrepancies were only apparent and could be corrected with further research. When the possibility of discrepancy is removed with critical application of the scientific method, the result is rational knowledge that is true and certain. The philosophers' view was an absolutization of the regularity of natural phenomena coupled with overconfidence in the human power of rational intellection.

It was Abū Ḥāmid al Ghazālī (d. 505/1111) who rose to the challenge the philosophers presented. Their position was unassailable as far as the regularity of nature in itself was concerned. That is also the position of the Qur'ān. But whereas Islamic theology assumes natural regularity to be a product of divine providence, philosophy assumes it to be a factum of nature as such, without recourse to divine providence or need for a divine being at all. Without divine providence, natural regularity is asserted as a fact of metaphysics, capable of standing by itself.

Like David Hume a millennium later, al Ghazālī questioned this claim for metaphysical regularity in his *Tahāfut al Falāsifah.* What the philosophers claimed to be proof, al Ghazālī charged, was merely a claim devoid of proof. The claim stated that a certain state or phenomenon B follows upon A when it contains all the factors necessary for B to emerge. "Following after," however, is not "following from"; and no matter how regular it is, "following after" cannot constitute evidence for "following from" nor explain or justify it. For that a different kind of evidence than mere repetition is needed. "Following after" is repetition; "following from" is causality. The latter, if known, gives apodeictic knowledge, capacity to predict, and necessary repetition. But repetition by itself can never constitute evidence of necessity; the suspicion that it may be accidental or contingent may never be removed.

How then does man classify phenomena as causes and effects when there is nothing but a repetition of them? And how does it happen that in most cases of prediction based upon repetition, the predicted effect does come to be? Al Ghazālī answered, as George Santayana was to do in our times, that repetition breeds habit of mind; and that humans, like Pavlov's dog, become accustomed to associate what follows with that which precedes and call them cause and effect. Necessary causality is therefore not a fact of nature but an invention of the mind ascribed to nature in the faith that, given a "cause," its so-called effect will follow. This faith of the scientist-observer of nature who does not postulate divine providence and the divine agency of all events in nature is naive, a mere tendency of animal nature. It is devoid of metaphysical foundation, supported by no epistemological evidence, a mere piece of wishful thinking. But where divine providence and active agency are recognized as a necessity of reason, the faith that, given cause A, its effect B will follow becomes a necessary conclusion of a rational system. God, the Creator of the universe, its unique and supreme Lord, Master, Sustainer, and Cause, has ordered nature so that it may be the arena in which humans live their lives and distinguish themselves in their moral deeds.

Causality, therefore, is neither necessary nor a metaphysical factum of an autonomous nature. Rather, it is the ordering of nature by the beneficent God. It is necessary by and through this divine beneficence. Contingency or indeterminacy will always characterize it; and this fact does not preclude the scientist convinced of the divine agency of all events to think and speak of causality in terms of necessity. For such a scientist is apodeictically certain that God will not alter His patterns arbitrarily, but will maintain them eternally and immutably, as He promised, to enable man to act morally and justify himself. This conception of nature to which al Ghazālī's reasoning led him nearly a thousand years ago is essentially the same as that which is dawning upon modern man today. For several centuries scientists struggled against the magisterium of the Church regarding cosmology and nature. They succeeded in establishing an autonomous science devoid of metaphysical foundations. They claimed, like the Muslim philosophers, that causality was the necessary law of nature; and they conceived of nature as an autonomous, closed mechanical system, devoid of gaps, but needing nothing outside of it to put it in order. This view reigned unquestioned in the nineteenth century. At present, hardly any scientist entertains this view of the universe. Relativity, indeterminacy, space and atomic research, and ecology have shaken that view. Today, the world of science is groping for a new view that will do justice to the new discoveries. Certainly, the Islamic view which crystallized in al Ghazālī's vision is a strong contender. For the Muslim, however, scientific knowledge of nature will remain inadequate as long as it does not take into consideration both the presence and the content of the divine will.

Desirability of the Knowledge of Nature

Islam taught these lessons to its adherents and prompted them to look into nature. The verses of the Qur'ān that command, warn, advise, and entice humans to observe the phenomena of nature — the succession of day and night; the movement of stars, sun and moon, and other heavenly bodies; generation and decay; life, growth, and death; of psychic events in individuals; and of social events in groups and in the broader movement of history, are too numerous to list. The variety and beauty of flowers, trees, and fruits; of tribes, nations, cultures, and ethnic entities; of mountains, valleys, rivers, and plains; of seas, climates, and storms — all are *āyāt* (signs or indices) pointing to the Creator and Source of order, according to the Qur'ān. Humans are enjoined to look into them, to investigate and understand them, to see them in the right perspective which applies to them as well as to the overall order or pattern of God. Islam called everyone to be a scientist investigating every field and aspect of nature; a historian examining every chapter of human and group behavior through the centuries. It called for this widest possible scholarship, confident that men will find Islam's claims for God and His providence, for nature, for man and history, confirmed. It made it a point of faith to discern the patterns of God in nature, an act of piety to articulate those patterns correctly and adequately; and an act of charity to teach them to others. It required its adherents to ascertain the movement of time and to locate precisely their geographical position on the earth, especially when they travel, and to find water and expurgate themselves of dirt, as prerequisites of worship and performance of ritual.

Under the impetus Islam provided, the science of nature became the hobby of the masses. Paupers and kings competed to obtain knowledge. In the search for knowledge that followed the ***Futūḥāt*** (the campaigns to spread Islam) and after coming into contact with the heirs of ancient knowledge — Greek, Mesopotamian, Persian, and Indian — everybody felt himself to be a conscript. No energy and no wealth was too precious to spend on this enterprise. Islam's religious encouragement of science broke the monopolies of the hermits, of churches and temples, and caused the treasuries and warehouses of knowledge to be invaded and their contents popularized among the masses. Islam was responsible for the fantastic tales of bags of jewels and gold paid for a few pages of a forsaken pharmacological or astronomical manuscript; of adventurous travel of thousands of miles in search of a person who might provide an insight into a mathematical problem. Science became the occupation of the masses; human history had never seen such a vast proliferation of scientific research and knowledge before. The scientific advances made by new converts to Islam were spectacular. In Central and Southeast Asia and in Africa particularly, men moved from Stone Age shamanism and animism directly into modernity upon conversion to Islam. The artifacts they left us from their first Islamic century (Stone Age tools, the highest available technology in the world at that time) testify to this tremendous jump of the human spirit under the aegis of Islam.

God, Islam held, created the world and implanted in it His immutable patterns that make it a cosmos. He designed it in a way calling for wonder: perfect, orderly, malleable, its parts causally and teleologically bound to one another, and its totality subservient to man. He invited man to study and investigate nature, to make the necessary deduction, and thus to recognize, worship, and serve Him. Indeed, He severely chastised those who were slow in looking into nature and did not reach the necessary conclusion regarding Him.

Islam and the Scientific Method

The fragmentation of knowledge into pursuits that use the scientific method and those that do not is a modern phenomenon. It came in the West with the rise of the sciences of nature in the sixteenth century. As scientists succeeded in liberating themselves from the magisterium of the Church and established a viable legacy, the "social sciences" followed and, in the hands of Auguste Comte, wrestled their freedom from the same magisterium, leaving the knowledge of man — philosophy, literature, the arts, language, and religion — to the "humanities." Underlying this outcome was the judgment that the sciences of nature follow a critical method and therefore lead to a sure knowledge of the truth. The social sciences dissociated themselves from the humanities and called themselves "sciences" because they adopted the scientific method and thereby guaranteed for themselves a portion of the truth alongside the sciences of nature. In an age dominated by romanticism, the humanities were left to cover what was left of human life — the realms of passion and feeling, of hope and beauty. But the division had already condemned them to the realm of opinion, where subjective truth may be expressed, but where no objective truth can be found. Philosophy remained uncategorized until in the twentieth century empiricism and analysis had swung it either on the side of the natural sciences or on that of conventional instrumentalism where it lost its relevance.

The cause of this development was the scientific method; and this was defined as the method of arriving at the truth of nature by observation, hypothesis, and experimentation. The method was further characterized by defining data and evidence in purely material terms, observable by sense and quantitatively measurable. Muslim thinkers have raised serious questions regarding the propriety of this "scientific method" when applied to the social sciences.[2] They have raised no less crucial questions regarding its adequacy when applied to the natural sciences in an age where valueless, amoral science seems to be leading the world to ruin.[3] Such criticisms, however, do not affect observation, hypothesis, and experimentation based on sensory, measurable data. In them-

Illustration 18.1

Miniature painting from an Islamic manuscript depicting a professor of applied science and his students. [Courtesy Kuwait Foundation for Scientific Progress.]

selves, these measures of seeking knowledge remain immune and valid. The question therefore is whether this method is the exclusive invention of modern Europe.

'Ilm or *fiqh* (science or knowledge) was first used by Muslims in connection with the knowledge of the revelation, its data, traditions, and meanings. As such it preserved its linguistic meaning. It began to acquire a technical meaning when it was applied to the knowledge of the law of God. There it meant knowledge through *istidlāl* (calling for evidence), seeking through evidence to make the unknown known. For all, *istidlāl* implied observation of the data and their examination through experimentation, measurement, and more observation. A further distinction was made between *istiqrā'* (allowing the data to speak for themselves) and *istinbāṭ* (drawing from the data what is internal to themselves). The former is identical to the empirical, inductive method, the latter is so to the analytical method. This is in evidence everywhere, especially in the medical achievements of Jābir ibn Ḥayyān (d. 198/813), Ibn al Haytham (d. 431/1039), and Abū al Rayḥān al Bīrūnī (d. 440/1048).

It is evident from their works that the Muslim scientists were quite critical of the ancients—Greeks, Near Easterners, Indians and Persians—whom they regarded with utmost respect, as well as of their own predecessors. Ibn al Nafīs declared that dissection had proven both Galen and Ibn Sīnā wrong; and al Bīrūnī refused to accept any statement of the masters without testing it in experience and confirming it by examination. The Muslims were aware both of the importance of sensory evidence and of the weakness and default of the human senses. Hence they developed instruments to correct and expand the sensory evidence, and would repeat experiments as a means to test results and avoid error. Jābir ibn Ḥayyān had a special name for scientific experiment, *al tadrīb;* and Ibn al Haytham called it *al i'tibār.*

HOW IS NATURE TO BE USED?

Islam's answer was direct and unequivocal. "It is God Who created heaven and earth . . . that you may distinguish yourselves by your better deeds" (Qur'ān 11:7). In another passage, the Qur'ān asserted: "God created life and death that you may prove your moral worth in your good deeds" (67:2). All Muslims therefore agree that nature was meant to be used for a moral end. It was not created in vain or sport (21:16) but as the theater and means for moral striving. In itself it is neither good nor beautiful; but it was made by God both good and beautiful to the end of serving man and enabling him to do the good deeds. Its goodness is derived from that of the divine purpose. For the Muslim, nature is a *ni'mah,* a blessed gift of God's bounty, granted to man to use and to enjoy, to transform in any way with the aim of achieving ethical value. Nature is not man's to possess or to destroy, or to use in any way detrimental to himself and to humanity, or to itself as God's creation. Since nature is God's work, His *āyah* or sign, and the instrument of His purpose which is the absolute good, nature enjoys in the Muslim's eye a tremendous dignity. The Muslim

Illustration 18.2

Anatomical drawing of a horse from a fifteenth-century manuscript in the Library of Istanbul University. [Courtesy Saudi Arabian Airlines.]

treats nature with respect and deep gratitude to its beneficial Creator and Bestower. Any transformation of it must have a purpose clearly beneficial to all before it can be declared legitimate.

Thus Muslims suffer from no hangups or complexes regarding their use of nature. God has ordained it for their use which they exercise innocently without any feeling of guilt. Nor do they see nature as an evil spirit, fallen god, or enemy worthy of defiance, capture, and subjugation. It is not a demonic force. Nor do Muslims see nature as an embodiment of a god or a good spirit, as anything numinous, which they should fear, love, or adore. The Qur'ān's statement that anything of nature is an *āyah* does not mean that there is any ontological relation between Creator and creature. The creature is in no sense the Creator; but, because it is a creature, it points to a Creator that caused it to be and sustained it in space-time. Between man and nature, there is in Islam neither enmity and war nor adoration; indeed, there is no personal relation whatever. As the work of God, nature commands respect and awe. Its complexity and regularity, its design and organic character, its malleability and subservience to man are cause for man to wonder, to appreciate God's creation, and to turn to Him in praise and obedience.

THE MUSLIMS' ACHIEVEMENTS IN HISTORY

The achievements we are to survey in this section may well be termed "Arab" despite the fact that a fair number of them were brought about by men who were not Arab. The reason is twofold. First, even non-Arabs wrote in the Arabic language, which they regarded as their own and of which they were extremely proud. Second, nobody — except Westerners and those Muslims who were indoctrinated by them — defined Arabness in terms of ethnicity. For all of them, as for the Arabs of the Peninsula through the ages, Arabness was always and invariably a matter of language.

The same achievements may well be termed Muslim or Islamic despite the fact that some were the achievements of Sabaeans, Jews, and Christians. There are again two reasons. First, the works of non-Muslims constitute a very small portion of the whole and belong either to the preparatory period or that of collection and systematization, but not to that of creative flowering. Second, the non-Muslim contributors were in the service of Muslims as their employees, directed to produce what Muslims desired to see produced. Their non-Islamic religions had nothing to do with their works, these being totally determined by the Islamic categories and values of their employers, colleagues, and the milieu in which they lived. Their works were part of an Islamic culture, determined by an Islamic worldview, ordered by Islamic categories. Hence the two appellations — Arab and Islamic — are justified; and the latter is preferable because it is more general and more inclusive and has the prior connotation of first principles and values, the culture as a whole, rather than merely its linguistic medium.

Medicine and Public Health

In Islam, the human body, its faculties and functions, and its consequent health and welfare, were object of wonder and appreciation. The Qur'ān referred to them on many occasions and declared them areas where the patterns of God obtain (23:14). The Prophet, in pursuit of that spirit, affirmed: "Do take medicines for your ills. God created no ailment but established for it an antidote except old age. When the antidote is applied, the patient will recover with God's permission." These directives provided the positive impetus necessary for the development of a science of medicine built upon empirical laws tested in everyday experience. The condemnation by the Qur'ān and the *ḥadīth* of magic and its practices alienated the Muslims against those pursuits, and oriented them toward

Illustration 18.3

Illustration of treatment for fractures and dislocations from Islamic Scientific Manuscripts. The excerpt deals with bone setting: 1. vertebrae column; 2. shoulder; 3. collarbone; 4. arm; 5. thigh; 6. lower leg; 7. foot; 8. jaw. [Courtesy Kuwait Foundation for Scientific Progress.]

genuine medicine and public health care. The faith that every disease has its antidote urged the Muslims to scan the world of minerals, plants, and animals in search of an antidote, to develop a sophisticated science of pharmacology. This was an occasion in which religion became allied to an exact and empirical science of the body, encouraged its development, and condemned all previous practices that were not scientific.

The general pursuit of scientific knowledge which Islam highly recommended found in medicine an extremely attractive field, partly because of the immediate benefits of which it was capable, and partly on account of the veneration with which the medical knowledge and profession had been held in the past. In a number of centers such as Ruhā, al Ḥīrah, Jundishāpūr, and Ḥarrān, Christian and Sabaean doctors, many of whom had run away from Church persecution and found refuge in the buffer states between Persia and Byzantium, had built a viable tradition of medical knowledge. The Muslims employed them, sat at their feet to learn from them, and commissioned them to translate their books and records into Arabic. Jurjī bin Bakhtīshu‘ (d. 215/830) was employed by al Manṣūr as court physician. Taught by their father, Bakhtīshū‘'s sons continued in the same employment. Yūḥannā ibn Māsawayh (d. 243/857) was asked to teach his profession to Muslims. Ḥunayn ibn Isḥaq (d. 260/873) was appointed by al Ma'mūn as head of Dār al Ḥikmah (The House of Wisdom), and was commissioned with his colleagues and pupils to procure and translate the whole legacy of medical and scientific knowledge into Arabic.

Thus Islamic medicine was born and began to grow rapidly. Its first achievement was the general assessment and review of the legacy of classical antiquity, and of Persian and Hindu scientific writings. This legacy was researched and proofed, systematized and translated, and given new categories agreeing with the general principles of Islamic religion and culture. Among its earliest Muslim masters were ‘Abdullah ibn Sahl Rabbān al Ṭabarī (d. 241/855), author of *Firdaws al Ḥikmah,* and Ya‘qūb al Kindī, the founder of Muslim Hellenized philosophy (d. 260/873). Medicine found its honorable place as the queen of the sciences of nature. Knowledge of nature and knowledge of religion were inseparable twins, complementing and supporting each other. That is why a fair number of the treatises on the sciences of nature were included under the general rubric of *tawḥīd.*[4] Enriched by scores of new words and concepts which the translators devised in order to give a precise rendering to the new sciences, the Arabic languages provided the medium for communicating as well as developing the new knowledge. So ample were its resources that soon medical treatises, like those of grammar a century earlier, began to be composed in poetry. The science of medicine prompted the development of pharmacology, and this, of botany and chemistry, of physiology and surgery. Baghdād counted 869 physicians who presented themselves to the licensing examination set up by the government of Caliph al Muqtadir in 319/931. From that date on, physicians, pharmacists, and hospitals were supervised by the *muḥtasib,* the officer in charge of the *ḥisbah* (see Chapter 7).

The art of diagnosis consisted of three parts: history of the case, which included the health situation of the household and all its members; investigation of the patient's urine *(al tafsīrah),* body temperature, smell, and other apparent conditions; examination of the pulse.

The city of Baghdād had already built its medical schools and attached to them hospitals and outpatient clinics in which the students practiced, and the teachers taught and did research. The first hospital was built by Walīd ibn 'Abdul Malik, the Umawī caliph, in 88/706, according to al Maqrīzī. Later, Muslim hospitals divided into those dealing with either mental or physical diseases, the latter being divided between contagious and noncontagious diseases. The Muslims also invented the ambulant hospital: a hospital carried on camelback in caravan style complete with beds, food, water, medicines, operating and isolation rooms, and a crew of doctors, nurses, attendants, officers, and servants. The ambulant hospital traveled from city to city or village to village, to attend to epidemics and the victims of natural catastrophes. Muslim hospitals were also equipped with recreational materials and some employed musicians. The ambulant hospital had the privilege to set up camp within the prisons as well, in order to attend to prisoners and guards. Whenever it came to a town that did not have a permanent hospital, the poor, the handicapped, the wayfarer, the miserable, and the outcast all enjoyed its benefits. There were hospitals for men and hospitals for women. Every hospital had its own pharmacy, kitchen, clothes-making factory, and library. As in modern times, Muslim physicians taught in their colleges and hospitals in the morning, and attended to their private practices in the afternoon.

Hospitals were built, maintained, and operated either at the expense of government or of perpetual endowments *(waqf,* pl. *awqāf)* by individual donors. Their services were always free. The resident physicians and their students were regarded, like all other college professors and students, as public servants dedicating their time and energy to the pursuit of knowledge in fulfillment of a major commandment of God.

One of the most famous hospitals was built by Aḥmad ibn Ṭūlūn in Cairo in 259/872. It opened its doors to all patients whatever the ailments afflicting them. The patient was divested of clothing, jewelry, and any personal possessions carried on the body; and these were kept for him in the hospital safe until departure from the hospital. Dār al Shifā' Hospital, built in Cairo in 683/1284 by Qalāwūn, remained in operation up to the Napoleonic invasion of Egypt in 1213/1798, when it was turned into a psychiatric hospital exclusively. It is still in existence today. Al Muqtadir built a new hospital in Baghdād in 303/915 which became famous because of the medical expertise of its director, Sinān ibn Thābit. Later in the same century, Baghdād saw the construction of another great hospital, Al 'Aḍudī, which had twenty-four resident physicians, a huge medical library, lecture halls, and hundreds of students from all corners of the Muslim world. It was Ibn Abū Uṣaybi'ah (668/1269) who preserved this and much more information about Islamic medicine, hospitals, and physicians in his *Ṭabaqāt al Aṭibbā',* a history of medicine and a Who's Who of its great men.

Islamic medicine was divided into two main parts: theory and practice. Under the former, knowledge was divided into five disciplines. Under physiology seven constituents of the human body were recognized, each of which became the subject of a specialized discipline. The practice part was divided into therapeutics or the science of curing disease, and hygiene or preventive medicine. The former was divided into surgery, drug therapy, and dietary therapy and regimental therapy, which included such measures as cauterization, diaphoresis, vomiting, leeching, massage, physical exercise, fomentation, purging, venesection, cupping, etcetera. To these, the Muslims added in the following century the specializations of dentistry, obstetrics and gynecology, opthalmology, pediatrics, and psychiatry. Their practice was governed by an expanded Hippocratic oath which combined medical service with devotion to God.

Prevention of ill health was regarded as requiring balance and harmony between six pairs of opposites: Excretion and retention, psychic movement and rest, bodily movement and rest, sleep and wakefulness, too much and too little food and drink, and too much or too little air. The Muslims devoted a great deal of their medical talent to preventive medicine, in the faith that it was more important than the science of therapeutics. The physician 'Alī ibn 'Abbās devoted thirty-one chapters of his book *Al Ṣinā'ah al Ṭibbiyyah* (The Medical Profession) to the prevention of disease and maintenance of good health.

In order to teach anatomy to their students, the Muslim colleges of medicine resorted to dissection of dead bodies, as a number of reports have affirmed. For example, in his book *Al Ifādah wal I'tibār,* 'Abdul Laṭīf al Baghdādī reports that he had access to a large pile of human skeletons and corpses from which he learned truths contrary to what he read in the works of Galen and others. The claim that the *sharī'ah* had prohibited dissection to Muslims is not true; for the *sharī'ah* permits the prohibited if it leads to the good of the people. Later Muslims in their decay stopped practicing dissection and justified their action by claiming *sharī'ah* prohibition. Thanks to the understanding of the earlier generations, dissection was practiced, anatomy learned, and surgery developed. Khalaf Abūl Qāsim al Zahrāwī (d. 414/1013) was the greatest surgeon of his century. He wrote *Al Taṣrīf Liman 'Ajiza 'an al Ta'līf* and devoted a great portion of it to surgery and its tools and practices. He was the inventor of methods to break up and extract stones in kidney or bladder.

The Muslims were the first to discover that epidemics arise from contagion through touch and air. Touching the clothing of the patient also led to contagion. They were the first to use anesthesia in surgery, which they called *al murqid* (that which puts to sleep), by placing a sponge soaked with the liquid on the patient's nose and mouth. They were also the first to cauterize wounds in surgery, and to stop bleeding by applying ice or cold water.

Some of the greatest physicians the Muslim world has produced were the following:

Abū Bakr Muḥammad al Rāzī (d. 311/932) was undoubtedly the greatest physician of the world in the Middle Ages. He began his career as a musician (a lutanist), then switched to the study of philosophy under Abū Zayd al Balkhī and finally to medicine at the Baghdād hospital. There, he wrote his book *Al Mujarrabāt.* In 290/902, at the call of Manṣūr ibn Isḥaq, he moved to Al Rayy to head its hospital. There, he wrote most of his medical books and dedicated them to his patron, entitling one of them *Al Ṭibb al Manṣūrī* in his honor. He also wrote a book on psychiatry, which he entitled *Al Ṭibb al Rūḥānī.* He was the first to insist that his students continue with postgraduate studies in medicine in order to enrich the discipline. His crowning work was *Al Ḥāwī fī al Ṭibb,* an encyclopedia of all the medical knowledge of his age. It was translated into Latin by Faraj ibn Salīm and printed in 1486 C.E., the first medical book ever printed in Europe. He was the first to make use of music to heal his patients. He arranged his students in concentric circles around patients so all could participate and to enable the newer students (outer circle) to learn from the older (inner circles). For the first time in human history, he distinguished between smallpox and measles. He established pediatrics as an autonomous discipline and wrote a textbook on the subject. He discovered the relation of sunstroke to the circulation of the blood, and produced several works on the chemical properties of elements—mineral, animal, and vegetal—and on their powers to cure certain diseases.

Abū 'Alī Ḥusayn Ibn Sīnā (d. 428/1037) was famed both as physician and as philosopher. His work *Al Qānūn fī al Ṭibb* was the largest ever written. It remained the ultimate reference in medicine for centuries and did not cede its place of superiority until the nineteenth century, being the standard textbook of medicine the world over for over 700 years. Wherever he traveled, Ibn Sīnā conducted experiments and examined medical records and live cases to confirm his older findings. He conducted surgical operations for the treatment of cancerous tissue, and established the effect of music on the patient's recovery. The princely court of Ḥamadān at Aleppo extended its patronage to him, but his metaphysical thoughts and personal arrogance did not contribute to any political success. Often, he had to flee and suffer his philosophical works to be destroyed. Ibn Sīnā discovered that stomach ulcers may be formed by either of two causes: a psychic cause such as worry or depression, and a material or organic cause acting on the stomach itself. He diagnosed cancer and urged an early treatment through surgical removal.

Khalaf ibn 'Abbās al Zahrāwī (d. 414/1013) was born, raised, and educated at Qurṭubah (Cordoba). He was called to al Zahrā', the new royal city built by Al Nāṣir, grandson of 'Abdul Raḥman, founder of the Umawī dynasty in Spain. There, al Zahrāwī lived and worked till he died. Only one of his works has survived. In his *Al Taṣrīf Liman 'Ajiza 'An al Ta'līf,* he included a treatise on surgery, the first independent treatment of the subject. He included in it more than 200 drawings of surgical instruments and of surgical operations he had conducted. He was extensively quoted by European surgeons down to the end of the sixteenth century.

Abūl Walīd Muḥammad Ibn Rushd (d. 595/1198) was a physician, philosopher, and judge. Ibn Rushd divided medical knowledge into seven branches: anatomy; health and its conditions; disease and its varieties; symptoms of illness and health; the instruments of health such as foodstuffs and medicines; methods of health preservation; and methods for illness removal. He was the first to discover and appreciate the role of physical exercise in the preservation of health.

Pharmacology and Chemistry

Under the patronage of Islam, pharmacology was separated from medicine and achieved independent status as a discipline and profession. This growth process started in the first century A.H., when the Umawī Khālid ibn Yazīd learned and adopted the medicinal preparations of the Greek School of Alexandria. Ja'far al Ṣādiq (d. 140/757) learned this Greek tradition from Khālid. Jābir ibn Ḥayyān, al Kindī, and al Rāzī all contributed significantly to the discipline, which was perfected and established as an autonomous science by al Bīrūnī (d. 443/1051), who defined the discipline, established its methods and principles, and wrote the most complete text for it. Until then, Muslim pharmacists depended upon two pharmacopoeiae by the same title, *Al Aqrabadhin,* written by Ṣābūr ibn Sahl (d. 255/868) and Ibn al Tilmīdh (d. 560/1164). The Muslims prepared nitric acid, sulfuric acid, nitro-hydrochloric acid; they discovered potassium and prepared its nitrate, as well as that of silver. They also prepared mercury chloride and oxide, as well as iron sulfate, boric acid, and a large number of new chemical products.

As far as vegetal pharmacology is concerned, Muslim pharmacists began with the *Materia Medica* of Dioscorides and soon absorbed the knowledge of India, Persia, and the Mediterranean world. They gave Arabic names to those plants or medicines which they came to know for the first time, and many are

Illustration 18.4

Cover from an Islamic manuscript of the eleventh century. The Arabic calligraphy says: "The Chief Master, the Best of the Latecomers, Abū 'Alī Ibn Sīnā of Bukhārā." [Courtesy Kuwait Foundation for Scientific Progress.]

Illustration 18.5

Illustration from a fifteenth-century Persian manuscript dealing with pharmaceutical information. [Courtesy Saudi Arabian Airlines.]

still known by their Arabic names. The work of Dioscorides, supplemented by the additions of Muslim researchers, remained unchallenged in its authority until Ibn al Bayṭar of Malaga, who lived in the middle of the seventh/thirteenth century. After completing his own researches, which included visits to Byzantium, Greece and Italy, and other European regions, Ibn al Bayṭar produced his *Al Mughnī fī al Adwiyah,* which he presented to King Ṣāliḥ al Ayyubī in Cairo. He followed this book with two other works — *Jāmi' Mufradāt al Adwiyah wal Aghdhiyah* and *Mīzān al Ṭabīb.*

Another great Muslim pharmacologist, who was a contemporary of Ibn al Bayṭar, was Rashīd al Dīn Ibn

Illustration 18.6

Pages from a fourteenth-century pharmaceutical text translated from the Greek.

al Ṣūrī (d. 639/1241), who lived in the eastern provinces. He was so meticulous in his research that he took with him an experienced painter and went to the fields and mountains recording every important species of medicinal plant by having the painter paint it for inclusion in his book.

Some other great pharmacologists and chemists of the Muslim world were the following:

Jābir Ibn Ḥayyān (d. 193/808) led the life of an ascetic Ṣūfī and spent most of it at his home in Damascus, where he also had his laboratory. He contributed so much to chemistry that the discipline was itself nicknamed "the craft of Jābir." He wrote more than 200 books of which eighty were in chemistry; of these only a few are extant. *Al Khawāṣṣ al Kabīr* (The Great Book of Chemical Properties), *Al Aḥjār* (The Minerals), *Al Sirr al Maknūn* (The Secrets of the Elements), *Al Mawzāzīn* (Weights and Measures), *Al Mīzāj* (Chemical Combination), *Al Khamā'ir* (Fermentation), *Al Aṣbāgh* (The Dyes), and numerous others he published by the score. He built a precise weighing scale which was capable of weighing items 6,480 times smaller than the *raṭl* (which is approximately one kilogram). He defined chemical combination as union of the elements together in small particles too small for the naked eye to see without loss of their character, as John Dalton was to discover ten centuries later. He thus refuted the older notion that combination destroys the combinants and creates a new element. He correctly defined combustion as the process in which the latent energy in the burning element is released, leaving behind the incombustible remainder. In response to Ja'far al Ṣādiq's wishes, he invented a kind of paper that resisted fire, and an ink that could be read at night. He invented an additive which, when applied to an iron surface, inhibited rust and when applied to a textile, would make it water repellent. He was concerned with the production of steel, and with protecting humans from toxic elements—vegetal, animal, and mineral—and wrote books about both, reporting about his experiments and describing their results in clear, precise terms for the benefit of the people. He counseled that chemical laboratories should be located far away from populated places.

'Izz al Dīn al Jaldakī (d. 762/1360) was responsible for several significant contributions: that dangerous gases arising out of chemical reactions should be protected against by application of masks; that clothing could be protected against caustic soda present in soap by mixing an additive to the soda before it was used for soap-making; and that silver was separable from gold by dissolving it in nitric acid which does not affect the gold. He insisted on purifying suspected water by means of evaporation and condensation, not mere filtration, because, he discovered, the latter process removed only the larger, more visible impurities. Among his numerous books were two volumes of over 1,000 pages each, entitled *Nihāyah al Ṭalab* (?) and *Al Taqrīb fī Asrār al Tarkīb.*

Physics

Muslim philosophers divided philosophical knowledge into two main groups: *Al Ilahiyyāt* (literally, divinity), which included *tawḥīd,* God's attributes and existence, and *al Ṭabī'iyyāt* (studies of nature), which included the material bodies and their movement or change and its causes. Heat, light, sound, magnetism and, mechanics fell into the latter division and were given as much importance as the divinity studies.

Muslim scientists invented instruments for the measurement of specific weights and gravities of elements. Some gold coins struck by Muslims a thousand years ago have been found to have a weight variance of three-thousandths of a gram—a fact that betrays a very high level of precision in weighing. Muslims also invented the clock pendulum and the magnetic compass and the astrolabe.

Ibn al Haytham (d. 431/1039) was invited by al Ḥākim to visit Egypt after a wish he once expressed to increase the benefit derivable from the Nile River. After examining the river in its long course, Ibn al Haytham suggested the construction of a mountain at

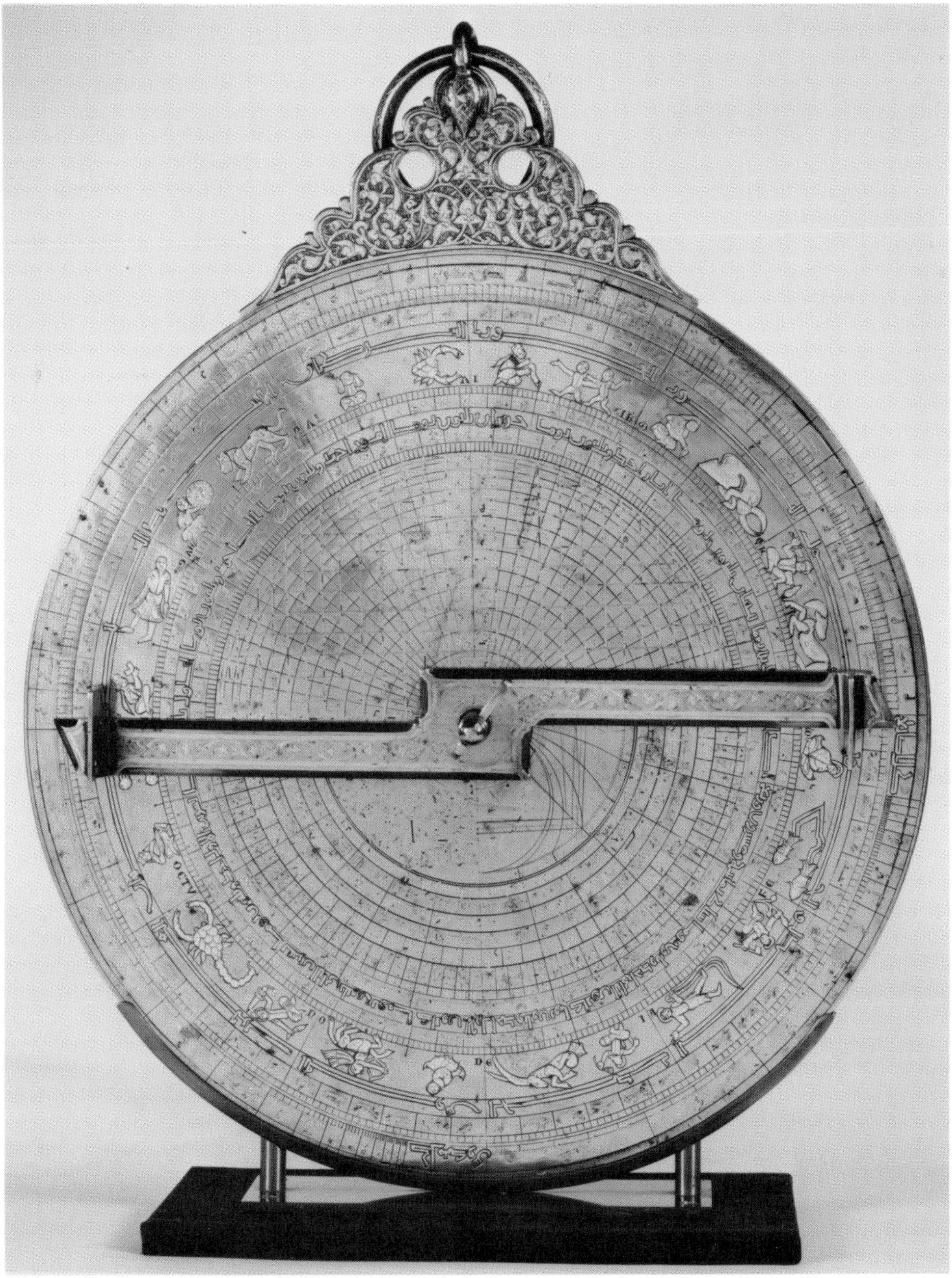

Illustration 18.7

Brass astrolabe inlaid with silver and copper, made in Cairo by ʿAbd al Karīm al Miṣrī al Asturlābī, dated 633/1236.

[Courtesy of the British Museum, London.]

Aswān which would dam the waters and raise their level to increase the area under irrigation. Al Ḥākim, however, could not rise to such level of imagination, and the project was not seriously considered. Ibn al Haytham was also responsible for determining the effects of atmospheric pressure and the earth's magnetic force on weight. He wrote some 200 books, 47 of which were in mathematics, 58 in engineering. His most famous achievements were in the realm of optics, where his studies began with the refutation of the view that vision is caused by a ray that issues from the eye, hits the object, and returns to the eye. He studied the phenomenon of light and was the first to explain refraction and reflection and lay down their laws. Certainly he was the founder of the science of optics, combining mathematical methods and physics principles. His book *Al Manāẓir* (The Visual World) laid down a new theory of visual perception, based on the eye's absorption of light rays issuing from the object, passing through the pupil, and reaching the brain through vision or eye nerves. Ibn al Haytham laid down the basis of explanation of the rainbow and of the camera obscura, elaborated later by Kamāluddīn al Fārisī, by observing the behavior of light passing through spheres of glass, of the light of an eclipsed sun and of a crescent, and light through a small aperture of a dark room. Explanation through observation and experimentation and the crystallization of results through mathematical formulae made his work the best prototype of the Islamic scientific method.

Illustration 18.8

Geomantic instrument from Syria or Mesopotamia of brass and copper inlaid with silver and gold. Signed by Muḥammad Ibn Khutlukh al Mawṣilī, dated 693/1241–2. [Courtesy of the British Museum, London.]

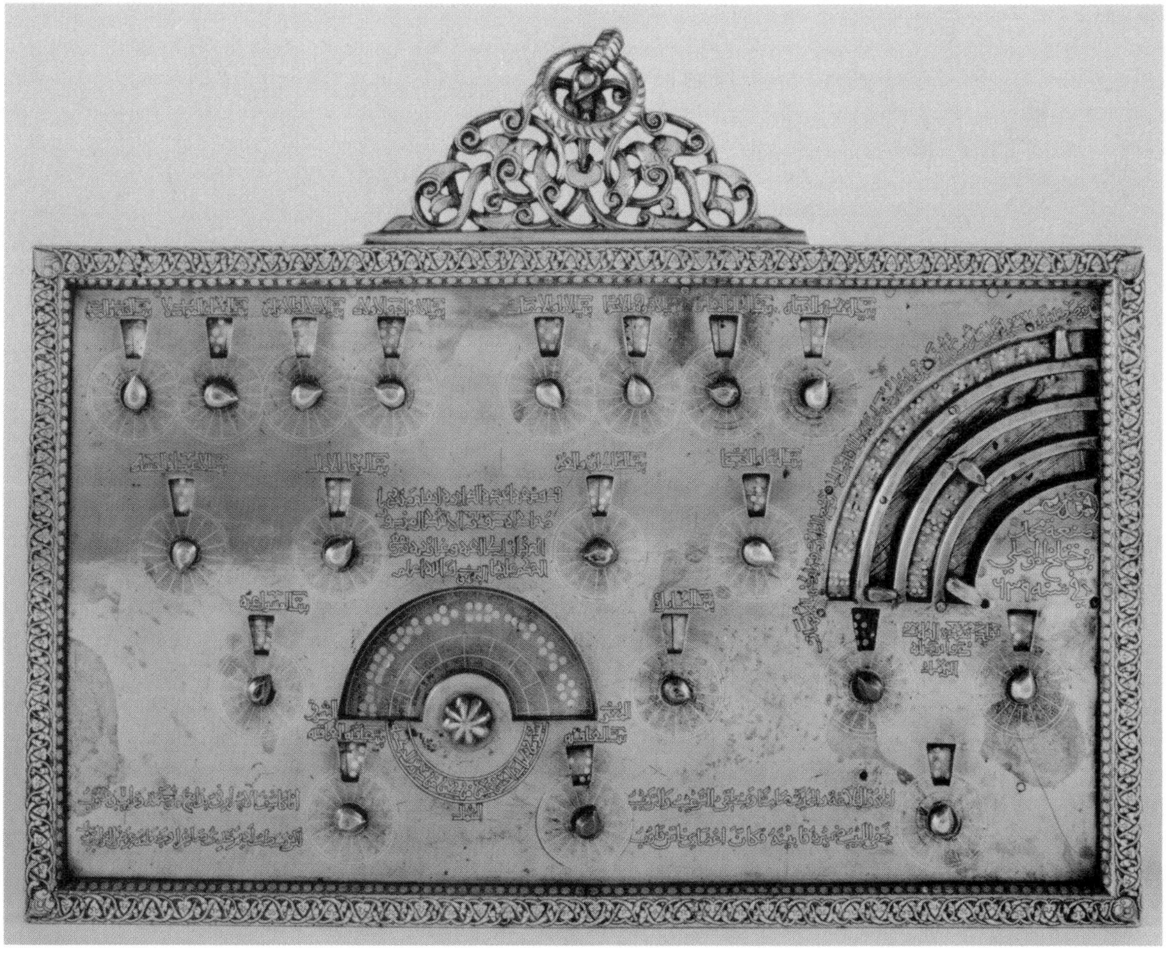

Mathematics and Astronomy

Perhaps the most distinguishing characteristic of the Muslims' contribution to the exact sciences was their vision of correspondence between mathematics, geometry, and astronomy. This vision was imparted to them by the Qur'ān, which affirmed, "We shall show mankind Our signs/patterns in the horizons/universe as well as in themselves until they become convinced that this revelation is the truth" (Qur'ān 41:53). The heavens and the earth were ordered rightly, and were made subservient to man, including the sun, the moon, the stars, and day and night. Every heavenly body moves in an orbit assigned to it by God and never digresses, making the universe an orderly cosmos whose life and existence, diminution and expansion, are totally determined by the Creator (Qur'ān 30:22). Upon this vision as base, Muslim astronomers built their view of the skies. It was the criterion by which they sifted the knowledge they had gathered from the pre-Islamic world, especially from Mesopotamia where astronomy was quite advanced. Pre-Islamic astronomy was a field in which mythology was pervasive, and the Muslims had to purge it clean of myth. Islam launched a fierce battle against astrology. Astrologers practice a profession built on falsehood. Hence, they are false even when their predictions come true, the Prophet said. The Qur'ānic faith of Muslim astronomers was their prime motivation and guide. Ascribing all causation and all movement to God, and perceiving His dominion as patterned and immutable, the conditions necessary for a scientific astronomy were realized and the skies could become the object of objective examination. The Muslims applied the knowledge they inherited from classical antiquity, Persia, and India; and they expanded and transformed that inheritance with their own creations.

Illustration 18.9

Astronomers at work, from a sixteenth-century Persian manuscript.

As far as theory of numbers is concerned, Thābit bin Qurrah departed from the Euclidean legacy by proposing a theory of infinite numbers being part of another infinite series of numbers. 'Umar Khayyām (d. 525/1130) and Nāṣir al Dīn al Ṭūsī (d. 645/1247) succeeded in constructing formulations in which magnitudes were expressed in numbers. In the field of arithmetic, Muslims made a unique contribution. India possessed a number of forms for expressing numbers which the Muslims acquired. They combined some, and reorganized them into two series, naming one series "Indian" and the other "Ghubārī." They used both. The latter was adopted by the West on account of its wide usage in Spain and North Africa and was called by Westerners "Arabic numerals." More important was the Muslims' invention of a symbol for zero (the Indians used to leave the place blank!), and gave it the name *ṣifr* (cipher, zero). They then organized the numbers into the decimal system where digital location acquired a numerical value beside the intrinsic value of its own. This development was of crucial importance to the progress of all sciences of nature. Before it, numbers were expressed in words with recourse to the fingers to complete an operation. Muḥammad ibn Mūsā al Khawārizmī (d. 236/850) was the mathematician who introduced the system of symbols representing the nine numbers and the inventor of *sifr* or zero to represent the absence of any. He was also the first to express numerical value by digital position. The two systems, the one expressing number by a symbol rather than a word and the other expressing value by digital position, were continued in the work of Ibrahīm al Uqlidīsī, and were popularized by Ghiyāth al Dīn Jamshīd al Kāshī. It then spread to Europe. It was al Khawārizmī who invented *al jabr* or algebra. He called the new discipline *al Jabr wal Muqābalah* ("linkage and juxtaposition") to describe what happens in an algebraic calculation. Muslims also invented the symbol to express any unknown quantity, namely *x* (or *s*, standing for the Arabic *shay'*), which was adopted by Europe from the Spanish who had simply transliterated it from the Arabic.

In astronomy, the Muslims not only cleansed the field of myths. They also denied that the observations and calculations of the Greeks were final. Declaring them all tentative and probable, they opened the gates for their revision. One of their most significant achievements was reached by Fakhr al Dīn al Rāzī (d. 606/1209) who questioned Aristotle's claim that stars were immobile and equidistant from the earth, as well as the claim that the movements of other heavenly bodies were all alike and similar. In his commentary on the Qur'ānic passage 2:258, al Rāzī affirmed that there is no evidence that the contrary may not be the case, that the real movement of the heavenly bodies may be different from what is observable by the unaided senses. The classical statement, however, belongs to al Bīrūnī: "In these and similar matters [of astronomy] one must resort to experimentation, and rely only on close examination of the data or results."[5]

A Greek book on astronomy attributed to Hermes Trismegistus was the first to be translated into Arabic in 125/742. Al Manṣūr, the second 'Abbāsī caliph, regarded astronomy with such approval as to ask the Persian astronomer Nawbakht to be his constant companion; and when the latter died, to appoint his son in his place, along with Ibrahīm al Fazārī, his son Muḥammad, 'Alī Ibn 'Īsā al Astrolābī, and others. In 156/772, the caliph commissioned Abū Yaḥyā al Baṭrīq to translate into Arabic the works of Ptolemy and other Greek sources which he had requested from the Byzantine emperor, and Muḥammad al Fazārī to translate the Sind-Hind book which contained the knowledge of India in the same field. These translations were used by al Khawārizmī to produce his famous *zīj* or Table of Calculations Indexing the Positions of the Heavenly Bodies. From then on began a wide scramble for the legacy of all previous learning, which the Muslims digested and corrected. These works placed the Muslims on the frontier of astronomy, as in the other sciences; and they began the creative task of transforming them into the modern sciences we know today. The Muslims took to observation, testing, and measurement. They were the first to draw and measure areas on the surface of a sphere which they took the earth to be, of measuring the length of a longitudinal and latitudinal degree, of representing the motion of the planets in relation to the sun. Abū al Wafā' al Buzajānī (d. 338/998) first discovered the shortcoming in the movement of the moon, and al Baṭṭānī calculated the length of the solar year and missed it by two minutes and twenty-two seconds. Some building of observatories took place under the Umawīs; al Ma'mūn completed one on Mount Qaysūn near Damascus, and another at al Shammāsiyyah in Baghdād. Later, Muslim observatories proliferated throughout the provinces and were responsible for a number of significant discoveries and measurements. The greatest observatory in the then known world was built at Maraghah in 657/1258, under the direction of Nāṣir al Dīn al Ṭūsī, who equipped it with a number of astronomical instruments built for him by a team of the best astronomers whom he had assembled from all corners of the Muslim world. Other observatories that distinguished themselves by their discoveries and/or the precision of their calculations were those of Ibn al Shāṭir and al Baṭṭānī in Damascus, al Dīnawarī in Iṣfahān, al Bīrūnī at Ghaznah, and Ulug Beg at Samarqand. In short, it can be said without hesitation that the world is obliged to the Muslims for their preservation of the knowledge of the ancients, for their significant corrections, for their new inventions and discoveries, for their

Illustration 18.10

Waterwheel in Ḥamāh, Syria. [Courtesy ARAMCO.]

Illustration 18.11

Astrolabic quadrant of brass, made by Muḥammad Ibn Aḥmad al Mizzī, Dimashq (734/1334–5). Sailors used the astrolabe to locate their north–south position. [Courtesy of the British Museum, London.]

establishment of astronomy as an empirical science, and for their cleansing of the discipline from magic and myth.

Geography

The Qur'ān commanded the Muslims to cross the earth in search of God's patterns in nature and in the affairs of men and women. Islamic law prescribed that each Muslim should find the *qiblah* (orientation toward Makkah) for the performance of rituals, which necessitates some knowledge of geography. It also prescribed travel to Makkah for the pilgrimage which, before the age of the train and plane, necessitated geographical knowledge of the areas to be crossed. This geographical knowledge was popularized because of the repetition of these rituals and their performance by the powerful and rich as well as by the lowly and poor. The Muslims were avid traders and travelers, undaunted by the usual perils and risks of long trips. They were encouraged by the worldwide spread of Islam, of the Arabic language as medium of communication, and of the Islamic ethic which placed great premium on hospitality and the welfare of the wayfarer. Indeed, Islam relieved the traveler of a number of religious duties, such as fasting or the performance of *ṣalāt* on time. Al Maqdisī wrote that geography is an absolute prerequisite for the merchant, the traveler, the sulṭān, the judge, and the *faqīh* (jurist). As in the case of astronomy, it was the Muslims who liberated geography from myth and gossip and raised it to the status of an empirical science. In the preface to his ***Murūj al Dhahab wa Ma'ādin al Jawhar,*** al Mas'ūdī (d. 346/957) wrote: "Every country has secrets which only its own people know. The reports of those who have not visited it and are satisfied to believe what has been said about it by others cannot be the equals of the empirical studies of those who did travel thereto, who witnessed and extracted every fact and ascertained every datum." He castigated Abū Yazīd al Balkhī for "reporting about countries he never visited, data he never beheld." The Qur'ānic commands prepared the Muslims for exploring the earth and for ascertaining geographical realities for the benefit of mankind. Their trade in pre-Islamic times had already prepared them for the task. They were experts in desert crossing; they plied the seas between Arabia, East Africa, India, and

Southeast Asia, and learned the arts of navigation by day and night.

It is no wonder, therefore, that the Muslims produced a rich legacy of geographical knowledge. Their descriptions of lands and people came in maps as well as texts. Their texts were the result of first-hand observation and on-the-scene confirmation. Their map-making developed as their knowledge of the earth grew. Al Khawārizmī (236/850) was the first to produce a global geography; and Abū al Qāsim 'Abdullah Ibn Khurdādhbih (d. 300/912) gave a full map and description of the main trade routes of the Muslim world in his *Al Masālik wal Mamālik.* Later, the Muslims began to produce atlases of their countries for popular and professional use. Such were the works of Isḥaq al Isṭarfī (d. 322/934), Aḥmad al Balkhī (d. 322/934), Muḥammad Ibn Ḥawqal, and Muḥammad al Maqdisī (d. 493/1101). Al Maqdisī was the first to produce maps in natural colors in order to bring geographical knowledge closer to human understanding. The crowning of Muslim achievements in geography came in the sixth/twelfth century following their discovery of ways to bring about exact measurements of the earth's surface. At this time they began to produce maps of the whole known world. This period found its apogee in the work of al Sharīf al Idrīsī (d. 562/1166) who was invited by Roger II, the Norman king of Sicily, to produce an up-to-date world map. Al Idrīsī asked for a ball of silver 400 rotols in weight (approximately 400 kilograms) and drew on it the seven continents, their lakes and rivers, cities, routes, mountains and plains, and trade routes, and noted on each the distance, height, or length as measured. Al Idrīsī wrote a book, *Nuzhat al Mushtāq fī Ikhtirāq al Āfāq,* to accompany the first globe ever built. The same period witnessed a surge of great travelers who left a rich legacy of geographical descriptions of the countries they visited and of anthropological descriptions of their peoples. Among them were Ibn Jubayr (d. 614/1217), Yāqūt al Ḥamawī (d. 626/1229), 'Abdul Laṭīf al Baghdādī (d. 629/1231), al Qazwīnī (d. 682/1283), Abū al Fidā' (d. 732/1331), and Ibn Bazṭūṭah (d. 779/1377).

NOTES

1. Qur'ān 39:9, 35:28.
2. I. R. al Fārūqī and 'Umar A. Nasseef, *The Social and Natural Sciences* (London: Hodder & Stoughton, 1981).
3. Ibid.
4. One of the most detailed experiments designed to establish the specific gravities of the elements was part of the work on *tawḥīd* entitled *Sharḥ al Maqāṣid* by Sa'd al Dīn al Taftazānī (d. 792/1389).
5. Quoted in Jalāl A. H. Mūsā, *Minhāj al Baḥth al 'Ilmī* (Beirut: Dār al Kitāb, 1392/1972), p. 259.

CHAPTER 19

The Art of Letters

THE MATRIX OF ARABIC

The discipline of the history of religions instructs us that all revelations must be contextual, fitting into the milieu in which they occur. Otherwise, the prophet's message would fall on deaf ears, and the divine purpose would be frustrated. On the eve of Muḥammad's prophecy, the Makkans and the Arabs generally had nothing to serve as the matrix for revelation except their language, and the taste for literary excellence which they had developed. Their language had generated a significant capacity to express wide ranges of experience; it coined words to suit every reality. It distinguished between the camels of different ages, different wools, different colors, and different numbers of offspring, as well as between the countless topographies of the desert, by giving to each a different name. It distinguished the hours of the day and the night, and their occurrences in the months, and gave each a different name. Arabic was so rich in nouns and adjectives that eloquence was defined as the accord between the expression and the reality as presented to the consciousness. The role of the literary artist was that of selection, from an infinity of possibilities, of the proper words for the proper ideas. Moreover, the Arabs had created Arabic poetry, a form of literary expression that marked the ultimate degree of discipline in the craft of letters.

THE QUR'ĀN AS THE LITERARY SUBLIME

This linguistic and literary preparation served as prerequisite for the advent of the Qur'ān. The Qur'ān claimed itself to be and was regarded by Muslims as a miracle of sublime form absolutely fitting sublime content and producing sublime effect. This aesthetic or literary miraculousness of the Qur'ān was accepted by all Muslims as evidence of its divine authorship. In order to be accepted and appreciated as a message from Heaven, the audiences the Qur'ān addressed had to be of such level of literary development as to perceive that it was not of human composition. The historical phenomenon of *i'jāz al Qur'ān,* the Qur'ān's challenge to match any portion of it in literary beauty, necessitated that the Arabs who contended as well as those who judged and arbitrated the contest, have the ability to recognize the literary excellence of what was being presented. Without it, it is doubtful that the Qur'ān could have exercised its shattering, terrifying, fascinating, stirring, and moving power. And without this power, the Arabs would not have acknowledged it as divine. The case of Muḥammad's prophethood is unique in that it rested its case on something literary, not physical, and made the truthfulness or validity of its claim, the very divinity of its source, hang on the thread of literary beauty. The sublime character of its message was absolutely without parallel! The audience, equipped with the highest possible level of literary awareness and sophistication, agreed.

Indeed, the Qur'ān shattered all the norms of literary excellence the Arabs had known. Every verse of it accorded with and fulfilled the known literary norms —and yet surpassed those beyond measure. The Arabs had notions of the literary ideals of which their language was capable, and they had witnessed in their poets, orators, and *kuhhān* (pl. of *kāhin* or oracular minister) numerous more or less perfect actualizations of these norms. The Qur'ān's actualization surpassed anything they ever knew. That is why they deemed it to be miraculous, or *mu'jiz,* a challenge to match it that could never be met. The Qur'ān completely disarmed its opponents upon sheer presentation. Its very recitation so overwhelmed their resistance, so stirred and moved them to the highest possible pitch of literary transport, that they acknowledged its divine origin and submitted themselves to its imperatives. The literary ideals were realized—and shattered!—to the Arabs' highest delight.

THE NATURE OF THE LITERARY SUBLIME

Sublimity of Form

Muslim minds applied themselves to the study of the Qur'ān as a literary work and sought to uncover the secrets of its beauty and miraculousness. These, they called *awjuh* or *dalā'il al i'jāz,* the aspects or causes that make the Qur'ān irrestible and unmatchable. Almost all thinkers touched on the subject in their writings, and some devoted to it treatises of considerable length and depth. Among these authors, al Jāḥiẓ (d. 255/868), Abū al Ḥasan al Jurjānī (d. 366/976), al Kummānī (d. 384/994), al Khaṭṭābī (d. 388/996), al Bāqillānī (d. 403/1013), 'Abd al Qāhir al Jurjānī (d. 470/1078), Fakhruddīn al Rāzī (d. 606/1209), al Zamlakānī (d. 651/1253), and, in modern times, Muṣṭafā Ṣadiq al Rāfi'ī (d. 1355/1937), Muḥammad Aḥmad Khalafallah, and 'Abdul Karīm al Khaṭīb have contributed the most important works. There is near-unanimity of the following characteristics or manifestations of the Qur'ānic sublime.

First, the Qur'ān is neither *shi'r* (poetry) nor *saj'* (rhymed prose). The first consists of verses identical in their meter (number, duration, and position of syllables) and rhyme (consonants and vocalization of the last syllable). The second is prose whose sentences and phrases are punctuated by a rhyme which is maintained throughout the composition. The Qur'ān is neither, though some of it contains some of the characteristics of both. Rather than be controlled by them and on occasion give up eloquence in favor of discipline, as often happens even in the best examples, the Qur'ān makes free use of them in order to enhance its objective. The Qur'ān's use of the elements of *shi'r* and *saj'* is always of the best and most eloquent, but it is never such as to make the remotest resemblance to or confusion with them possible. That is why a new category had to be invented for classifying the Qur'ān beyond poetry and prose, namely, *al nathr al muṭlaq* or absolutely free prose.

Second, the Qur'ānic verse is composed of words and phrases that fit the meanings perfectly. Its diction is always absolutely true and perfect. Any change, however small, is a change for the worse. No word may be omitted without destruction of the flow and meaning of the verse. None may be added without redundancy or imposition of the strange upon the familiar or organic.

Third, the Qur'ānic words and phrases of one verse, or of one part of a verse, compare or contrast perfectly with those of a preceding or following phrase or verse, whether in construction or meaning. The flow of its words thus produces the greatest tension and expectation, and the greatest quiescence and fulfillment possible. This quality of the Qur'ānic composition is called *tawāzun* or balance, and it operates in the form as well as in the content of the text.

Fourth, the Qur'ānic words and phrases express the richest and strongest meanings in the briefest of forms. It is never verbose and no word ever is superfluous. Any paraphrasing of a phrase, sentence, or verse requires far more words and always appears belabored, artificial, long-winded and, consequently, less powerful, less eloquent, and less moving than the Qur'ānic original. And yet brevity is not an absolute principle to be observed on each and every occasion. There are instances in the Qur'ān where repetition and extension are necessary. But there they must, and in fact do, have their special justification; brevity needs no justification and is the general rule of Qur'ānic prose.

Fifth, the Qur'ānic similes and metaphors, its conjunctions or disjunctions of concepts and precepts, carry the greatest possible appeal. They impinge upon the imagination with such mighty power that

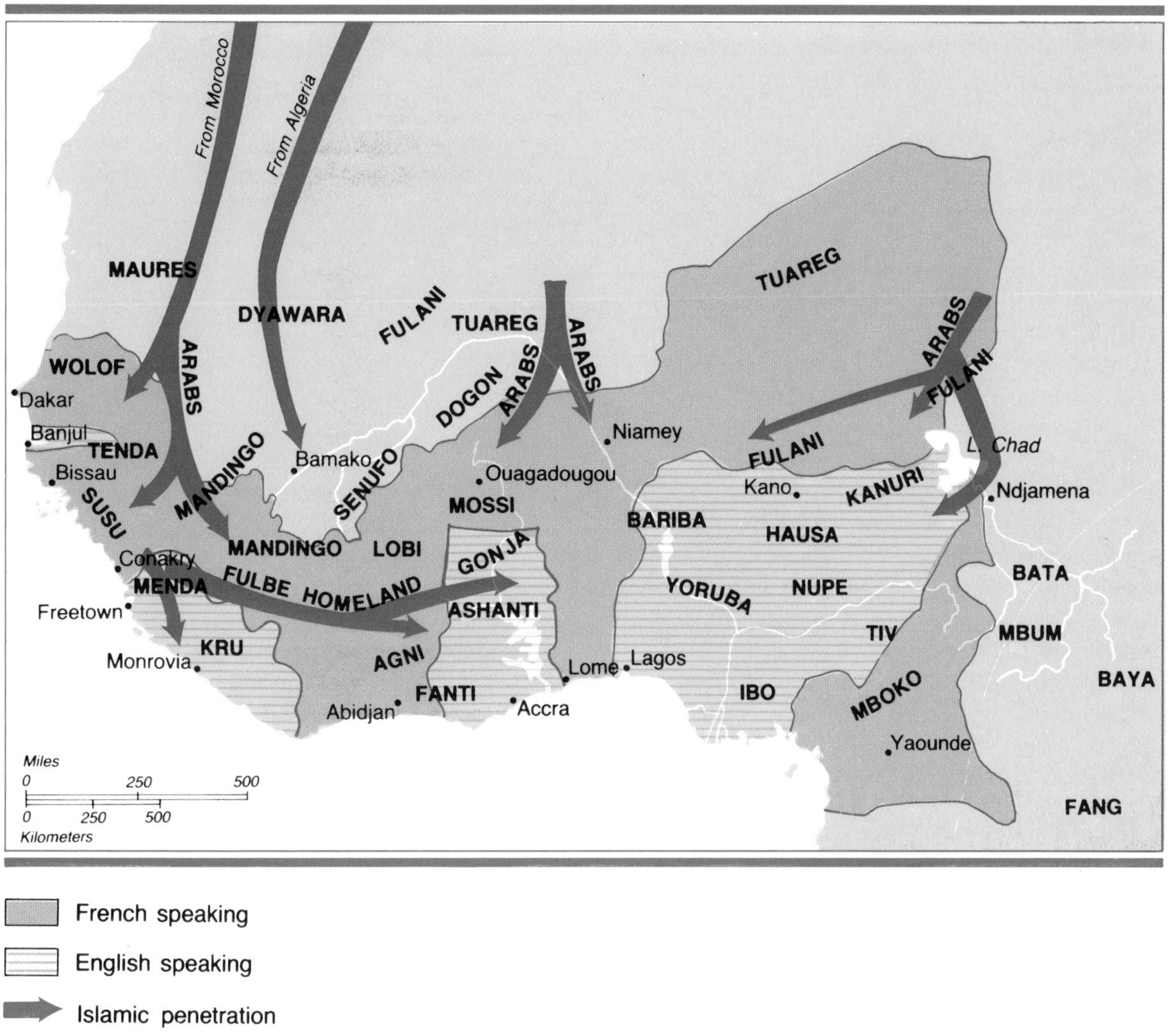

Map 57. Ethnic Groups in West Africa

they leave it "breathless" in its shock and fascination. For this unique quality of the Qur'ān, the Arab literary aestheticians invented the term *badī'* (the sublimely creative) and predicated it of the Qur'ānic phrases and expressions.

Sixth, the Qur'ānic composition is always precise, well-knit, truly rendered, like an artwork of absolute perfection. Its flow and construction is utterly free of gaps or weak spots. There are numerous instances where a word or a whole phrase is missing but the meaning is always clear though *sous-entendu.* The missing word or phrase has been omitted deliberately in order to make what is presented to the consciousness yet more taut.

Seventh, the Qur'ānic style is strong and emphatic and assertive, as well as smooth and delicate. The reader can feel it fall down upon him like rocks or with infinite finesse and tenderness. This is what is called *ḥusn al īqā'* (the beauty of falling upon the consciousness). Whether it murmurs like a serene brook, pounds like a torrent, or jumps and hurtles itself like a cavalry charge, its *īqā* is always perfect.

Eighth, Qur'ānic composition has no structure in the usual sense of the term. It combines the present, past, future, and imperative tenses in the same passage. It moves from the reportative third-person speech to the addressive second person; from the descriptive to the normative, from the interrogative to the exclamatory and hortatory. It is repetitive, though in each repetition a different message is conveyed. And finally, the Qur'ānic text is not arranged either topically or chronologically, for its purpose is neither systematic analysis nor reporting nor historiography. It is above all, first and last, a body of literature in which each phrase, verse, group of verses, or *sūrah* constitutes an autonomous unit, complete in itself, and the units are strung together *seriatim*. The sudden change of tense and mood exercises a most affective power upon the imagination and compels the understanding to move from reception to participation, and from perception to a judgment that is always affirmative, agreeing with the Qur'ān. The repetition is never redundant, since a novel lesson based on a novel aspect of the already known event is taught and emphasized. No narrative of the Qur'ān is given for information. Rather, assuming familiarity of the audience with the general outline of the story or event, the Qur'ān uses it as carrier for the fresh lesson it seeks to inculcate in the mind of the hearer. Finally, the continuous flow of reports, descriptions, account-renderings, and lessons of the Qur'ān seeks to convince and persuade by the beauty and force of its phrases, verses, or clusters of verses. A person with the requisite competence in Arabic may perhaps resist the call of a verse or cluster by itself; but none is able to resist the call emerging from the seemingly infinite flow. The Qur'ānic flow generates a momentum that sacks the hearer's recalcitrance, closed-mindedness, or obstinacy by its variegated pounding and ultimately carries that hearer to its destination.

Sublimity of Content

The sublimity of the message of the Qur'ān is expressed in many ways:

First, the Qur'ān affirms common sense and reasonableness as the ideal attitude of the human mind. It teaches freedom from contradiction, incoherence, and ambiguity; from paradox, myth, and any kind of obscurantism. It recognizes no papacy and no church magisterium with which to impose arbitrary opinions or dogmatic judgments. Barring a few prescriptions regarding rituals, its content claims to agree with reason, to carry its own grounds of reasonableness and truth. The Qur'ān assigns priority neither to revelation nor to reason, but declares their equivalence, explaining all discrepancies between them either as a failure to understand the revelation or as an error in the processes of reason. The Qur'ānic position is therefore optimistic as far as man's capacity for knowledge is concerned. The truth, it holds, is and is knowable; untruth is never final, and may always be overcome with better knowledge. Islam predicates this capacity for knowing the truth of all humans and affirms it as the base of Islamic universalism. It rejects any categorization of humans that discriminates between them at birth as to their capacity or as to their relationship with God, their Creator.

Second, the Qur'ān justifies man as he is, having been created in the best of forms, free from any predicament from which no extrication is possible. On the contrary, the Qur'ān regards man as eminently qualified to fulfill his function, and defines that function as vicegerency of God on earth. It does not deify man; nor does it regard him as the measure of all things. That, it judges, would be sheer exaggeration. Rather, the Qur'ān affirms man to be the purpose of creation, and his moral achievement the ultimate objective of all life and death. To this end, the Qur'ān regards all other creatures, including the earth, the sun, the moon and the stars, all that they contain as subservient to man. It grants man the right of usufruct of all there is. Hence, the Qur'ān knows of no conflict of man with God, or of man with nature. It holds man to earth though it declares him to be the goal and crown of creation. Man is free and enjoys unlimited power, but he must be responsible or lose his dignity and place as crown of creation, as vicegerent of God. This responsibility is thoroughly moral; and it is by his compliance with the moral law that man is ultimately judged. Man's person, life, and judgment are all endowed with inviolate integrity and sanctity. They are of intrinsic value. Indeed, they would be ultimately valuable were it not for the will of God, for His commandment which is the moral law and which stands above man and constitutes the criterion of his worth.

Third, the Qur'ān blesses and promotes the processes of life, and regards countering them as a sign of ill health rather than morality. In themselves, the desires for food and drink, for sex and procreation, for comfort and prestige, for wealth and power, for pleasure and beauty, for companionship and family and society, for wisdom, possession, and eternity are honorable propensities which God implanted in man to be fulfilled, not combated. God's bounty in nature is to be had and enjoyed, not denied. History is not to be abandoned, either to the Caesars or to fate. Rather it is to be turned around and directed by man toward moral excellence, worldly felicity, and human happiness. And in order to prevent any devaluation of the world on account of man's expectation of resurrection, or fear of judgment, the Qur'ān takes care to emphasize that this world is the only "world" there is; that the "other world," with its paradise and hell, is not an alternative to this world, something that counterweighs the miseries of this world. The Qur'ān affirms that this world is to be managed by man, the steward or vicegerent, as if it were eternal; that the other world is only a judgment and a consummation of judgment — a happy paradise if conduct in this world merits it, and a painful fire otherwise. Hence, to fill this world with goodness, to make the earth a garden and to fill it with healthy and strong people, to educate humanity so that everyone's life may embody as much genius, heroism, and saintliness as possible, and to do so in freedom and in accordance with the moral imperative — these are the ideals of human endeavor, the criteria of human felicity and merit.

Fourth, the Qur'ānic message is both intentional and actional. The criteria of its ethic go beyond intention, beyond the determinants of the subject. These are the domain of the conscience; and the conscience is the only capable judge of them. Islam does not deny the personalist values attaching to intentions and conscience. Rather, it emphasizes them, recognizing morality's need for purity and nobility of intent. Having called for their cultivation, the Qur'ān carries a deeper moral insight, namely, that moral worth is a function of both intention and action. It teaches that moral striving should lead to action, to the actual determination of space-time. There, conscience is inadequate. Public law and the judiciary are required to determine what is just and equitable. The public welfare, the equity of contracts, altruism and concern for others, citizenship and the exercise of human rights, the use of power for justice and for the good of the world — *ummah* — these are the hallmarks of the Qur'ānic society.

Fifth, the message of the Qur'ān is family-bound. Islam regards man as perfected only when married and only when the person has taken his place in society, enjoying its privileges and fulfilling its obligations. The Qur'ān declares marriage to be a civil contract between two equal partners whose agreement to and responsibility for its terms are constitutive. The Qur'ān's concern for the success of family life led it to undergird the family with a very detailed and comprehensive law which regulates every aspect of the life of each one of its members. In the Qur'ānic view, parents and children, brothers and sisters, grandparents and grandchildren, uncles and aunts, nephews and nieces, maternal and paternal cousins all constitute a single family with mutual rights and obligations.

Sixth, the message of the Qur'ān is universal. Addressed to all humans without distinction, it teaches them that they are all creatures of God, equal in their creatureliness, in their relationship to God, in their essential obligation to obey Him and fulfill His will, in their vicegerency for Him. It never tires of reminding them that on the Day of Judgment all humans will stand absolutely equal before the law; that each will receive absolutely his due, undiminished and without the slightest increase. According to the Qur'ān, there will be neither favoritism nor intercession, neither vicarious or group guilt nor merit. The mercy of God is not contrary to justice; it is His just judgment of all men. Islam has no countenance for a "chosen," "elect," or "remnant" status, neither for the Muslims nor for anyone else. It abhors every variety of particularism, tribalism, nationalism, racism, or ethnocentrism; and it teaches that no innate characteristic earns any priority for anyone. Every human must and will get exactly what he deserves.

Seventh, the Qur'ānic message is ecumenical. The Qur'ān invites mankind to accept its message rationally, critically, and in freedom. It calls their attention to the patterns of nature and history and asks men to judge for themselves the veracity of the Islamic claim. It commands the Muslims to be positive in their mission, to emphasize the areas of agreement and build upon them, "to call unto God with wisdom, goodly exhortation, and fair and gentle arguments" (Qur'ān 16:125), and never to coerce anyone in matters of faith (Qur'ān 2:256). Everybody's personal judgment must be respected, and his freedom to believe and order his life according to his faith must be honored. The Qur'ān declares the *ummah* a universal brotherhood within which a plurality of legal and cultural systems may operate at the same time. The Qur'ānic message reduces the difference between Islam and other religions to a domestic, internal development not intrinsic to either religion, and calls upon scholars of both sides to expose the historical roots of the divergence. It declares all humans to be born with the same religion, endowed by their Creator with a sense of the sacred, capable of recognizing the Holy and of acting upon the moral imperatives. Furthermore, the Qur'ān declares all humans to be recipients of one and the same identical message from God, thus acknowledging the better part of their religions as true and divine de jure. This principle made the Qur'ānic message and the religion built upon it the sibling of all the religions of humanity, a brotherhood evident in numerous and still extant elements of other religions which the Qur'ān affirms to belong to that original message. As to areas of disagreement, Islam identifies them as belonging to those parts of the original message that were lost, forgotten, misinterpreted, or abandoned, whether innocently and inevitably or deliberately. The Qur'ānic message calls on scholars and great men of faith in the religions to study the history of their faiths and restore to their religions the integrity of their holy writ and revelations. Thus, Islam regards its differences with other religious traditions as something manageable, capable of being explained, exposed, and removed, and ultimately causing all religions to unite under the divine banner. This attitude of the Qur'ānic message toward the religions of the world is both universal and dynamic; and it has made possible a critical world theology of the religions of humankind.

Eighth, the Qur'ānic message is comprehensive; and so is the *sharī'ah,* the law system built upon it. It does not divide worldly reality into sacred and profane, human life into religious and secular, nor social activity into moral and amoral regions. All reality and all events are subject to its criteria and determination. However, the relevance of the message of the Qur'ān, as well as that of the *sharī'ah,* is not a closed book. It is forever open to new realities. *Uṣūl al fiqh* (Islamic jurisprudence) has proved the necessary mechanisms by which the law is to be changed, suspended, increased, or reinforced. The *sharī'ah* is both law and philosophy of law, providing for both self-criticism and self-renewal.

Ninth, the Qur'ānic message commands beauty and aesthetic enjoyment in absolute terms. It declares beauty essential to, and hence an index of, revelation. The reason for this elevation of beauty is that it is a facet of the transcendence of God. No higher position could be conceived. Muslims are commanded to seek and establish beauty on every occasion, everywhere.

Sublimity of Effect

By itself, form is empty. It is endowed with a neutrality that makes it amenable to any use should an apt author wish to take advantage of it. This notwithstanding, form has a tendency to increase in beauty if wedded to ideas that are themselves beautiful. The nobler the content, the greater the form; the more banal the content, the weaker the form. In pre-Islamic Arabia, the values of *murū'ah* or chivalry — bravery, eloquence, hospitality, fidelity, and lineage — helped to produce beautiful forms of poetry. But these forms were also used to express the less respectable, romantic values of tribalism and ethnocentrism, the hedonistic values of wine and sex, or the cynical values of temporality, irresponsibility, and ultimate inconsequence. It was the latter use of poetical form which the Qur'ān condemned as prostitution of beautiful form (26:224–227).

On the other hand, content by itself is inert. Its value or nobility remains hidden until good form has exposed it for understanding, enjoyment, and appropriation. Without good form or as expressed in unattractive form, content loses its appeal. For ideational goodness is not goodness unless it is experienced. Although the value of good ideas is never nil, form can so reduce it as to make them "dead," "fallen on deaf ears," "out of tune with the situation in which they occur." When clothed with good and appropriate form, content exercises its power to move, to inspire, and to energize the percipient. Its value or goodness then shines with all its intrinsic glory. Indeed, good form acts mysteriously upon content by bringing it to life and enhancing its appeal.

The relation between form and content is not static, therefore, but dynamic. When form is given to content, neither remains the same. The result is always a greater, deeper, more moving, and lasting effect. The goals of communication — appropriation by the understanding, determination of judgment, and effective initiation of action — are the ultimate objectives of the literary art. The effect is the result of the combined action of form and content, not a function of

Map 58. West Africa Today

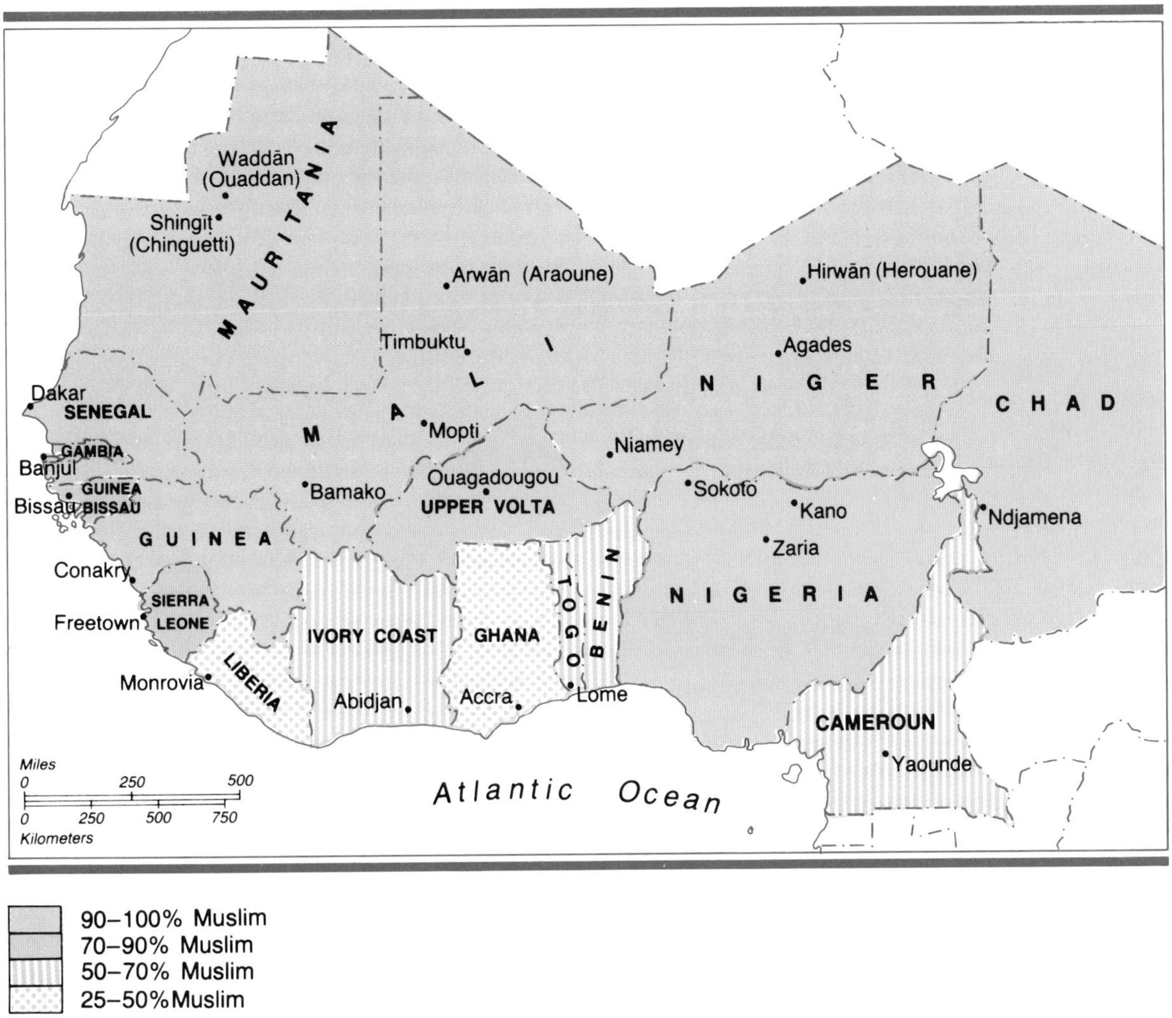

Map 59. West Africa: Percent Muslim Population, 1980

either factor alone; and the exact proportion of each may never be assessed. But the measure of effect as such is the degree of intensity of awareness, or depth of commitment, which the percipient experiences as a result of the presentation. Great ideas properly expressed in beautiful form are mighty forces. They can convincingly impart a new worldview, dictate a new judgment and will, and take possession of a person's consciousness and bring about radical transformation.

From this it follows that sublime effect is the result of sublime content wedded to sublime form. Sublime effect is the radical transformation of the percipient. The presentation impinges upon the consciousness with such force that the subject can only acquiesce and surrender to its moving and determining power. In response to the perceived sublime, one can only exclaim: That's just it! That is just as it ought to be! If the sublime is claimed to be the word of God, the

MUSLIM POPULATION OF WEST AFRICA

Country	*Population in Millions*	*Percent Muslim*
Benin	3.3	26
Cameroon	7.0	55
Chad	4.6	85
Gambia	.4	86
Ghana	12.0	26
Guinea	4.9	95
Guinea-Bissau	.9	70
Ivory Coast	5.0	56
Liberia	1.8	30
Mali	6.2	90
Mauritania	1.4	100
Niger	5.0	91
Nigeria	91.0	75
Senegal	4.6	95
Sierra Leone	3.1	85
Togo	2.4	55
Upper Volta	6.3	70

subject's response to it is the same as in the encounter of ultimate reality, namely, Your word is the truth! Thou alone art Holy! This is exactly the purport of the Muslim's exclamation, *"Ṣadaqa Allah al 'Aẓīm!"* (God Almighty does tell the truth!), interjected at the end of every Qur'ānic recitation.

Perception of the sublime in content and form and suffering of the sublime effect consequent upon it are shattering experiences which bring about a confutation of old norms and standards. But it is also a constructive experience insofar as it remolds the consciousness according to the new perceived norms and principles. The perceiving subject is hence never the same after the experience. New patterns come to determine the attitudes and faculty of judgment, issuing in conversion to the new vision which the experience has provided and a desire to convert others. Experience of the sublime may also impose the reorganization of nature—the habitat, environment, or countryside—to give form to the patterns implicit in the vision. The sublime effect constitutes its own evidence and justification. It ensues from the experience of the sublime in form and content, since it is their natural consequence. The effect is said to be necessary and universal in the sense that it must be and is realized in the person in whom the requisite preparation or capacity is present.

The sublime, we may therefore conclude, is never the sublime in form alone, nor that in content alone, nor that in effect alone. It is all three at once. Sublime form without sublime content, or sublime content without sublime form, produces little or no effect, certainly not effect that is sublime. On the other hand, a "sublime effect" which is not the product of sublime form and content is indistinguishable from madness or severe psychic derangement. *Ex hypothesi,* such effect has no cause to which it is anchored, and no principle or criterion by which it is disciplined. Hence, it leads to erratic behavior. *Per contra,* when the sublime effect is genuine, it is the product of sublime form and sublime content which give it direction and style, and constitute its cause and cultural essence.

EFFECT OF THE QUR'ĀN ON THE ART OF LETTERS

The advent of the Qur'ān in history produced far-reaching results. Where the audience was Arabic-speaking, conversion took place upon sheer presentation of the Qur'ān—a perfect exemplification of the sublime in form and content producing the sublime effect.

The consciousness of the Semitic world, especially the Arabic-speaking members of it, was overwhelmed; and large numbers of peoples converted to Islam *en masse.* Their literary awareness, prepared and disciplined by the centuries, perceived and absorbed the Qur'ānic sublime in form and content, and succumbed under the impact. The sublime effect of radical self-transformation and commitment to the cause of transforming the world and history into the likeness of the pattern they saw in the divine revelation took possession of their souls, their minds, their hearts, and their wills.

As for their literary faculties, they were stunned. Naturally, experience of the sublime had stupefied them. They had thought highly of themselves because of their literary excellence; and now something came to them that surpassed them in that realm and left them hopelessly fallen behind. Naturally, the Qur'ān knocked out their pride. The poetry of the most inspired literary genius paled before the mighty Qur'ān. Naturally, it humbled them and placed a temporary halt on their literary productivity. While some poets vowed never to compose poetry again, others chose to behold the Qur'ān perpetually, reciting its verses on all occasions, in response to or comment upon any matter. Everyone memorized most, and was familiar with all, of the Qur'ān; everyone recited its verses evening and morn; and everyone gave himself the greatest delight by contemplating its terms and phrases. No book ever commanded as wide or as deep a reverence as did the Qur'ān; none has been copied and recopied, passed from generation to generation, memorized in part or *in toto,* recited in solemn worship as well as in salons, marketplaces, and school rooms as much as the Qur'ān. Above all, no book has ever been the cause of such deep religious, intellectual, cultural, moral, social, economic, and political change in the lives of millions, or of peoples as ethnically diverse, as has the Qur'ān.

As we saw earlier, the advent of the Qur'ān froze the Arabic language as well as the categories of logic, understanding, and the beautiful embedded in the language. Overnight Qur'ānic Arabic became the standard and norm of the Arabic language as far as its vocabulary, syntax, grammar, and eloquence *(balāghah* or *faṣāḥah)* were concerned. Everybody looked to it as the ultimate criterion of literary composition and excellence. It was the guide of every writer and orator. Its expressions and figures of speech, its similes and metaphors, its idioms and artifacts became parts of everyday speech, and they were used as jewels and ornaments with which to embellish any literary composition. The result was the preservation of Arabic through fourteen centuries, free of adulteration and change. If Arabic is today the language of daily discourse for 150 million Arabs, and the language of culture, morals, religion, and law for a billion Muslims, it is so by virtue of the Qur'ān alone. It is indeed a unique phenomenon in the history of human culture that it is possible today for any person in the world of the Malays, or that of the Zulus, thousands of miles away from Arabia, fourteen centuries away from the Prophet, and an infinite distance away from the ethnic characteristics of the Arabs, to understand the Arabic Qur'ān just as the Prophet and his contemporaries did.

It is all too natural therefore that the Qur'ān has affected the culture—and *a fortiori* the literatures—of all Muslims. In the Arab world it even affected the literatures of Christians and Jews. On becoming Muslim, the non-Arabic-speaking peoples appropriated the language of the Qur'ān, and of the religious sciences that emerged later, into their own languages. It was thus that Pahlawi became the Fārisī of Firdawsī, Turkic became 'Uthmanlī Turkish, Sanskrit became Urdū, Bantu became Hausa in the West and Sawāḥilī in the East. The cultures of these languages were equally transformed into Muslim cultures, bearing the same values and patterns. Everyone of these Muslim languages adopted a large number of new terms and phrases, sometimes as many as half of their vocabularies. Everyone adopted the categories of thought and understanding embedded in the Arabic Qur'ān, the values and norms, the criteria and principles of piety and virtue, of goodness and beauty. Naturally, the literatures of these languages reflected all these changes and were transformed into Islamic literatures. In many cases (for example, Malay, Turkic, Hausa, Sawāḥilī), the languages were merely verbal and had no written literature. Islam brought to them the alphabet, made them heirs to the great legacy of Arabic literature, put them in contact with the intellectual currents of the world, created for them a new literature in their Islamized tongues, and launched their writers, thinkers, orators, and poets on illustrious careers of literary creativity and excellence.

Throughout the Muslim world as well as Muslim history, the Qur'ān has been the unchallenged, absolute literary ideal. Before the time of colonialism, when foreign powers forced replacement of the Arabic script with the Latin and began to influence the literary tastes of the Muslim peoples, first through the Western educational system and later through the Westernized mass media, nearly all the literatures produced by Muslims reflected the traditional characteristics of the Qur'ān. The literary genres of Islamic literature were universal. The *khuṭbah* (oration), the *risālah* (essay or epistle), the *maqāmah* (short story expressive of the linguistic/literary precocity of the hero), the *qiṣṣah* (a short story with a moral), the *qaṣīdah* (poem), the *maqālah* (an essay that revolves around one idea which is the center) of prose, and the more specific varieties of poetry, were produced and enjoyed by all Muslims. Muslim poetry followed the same rules of Arabic poetry, namely the *abḥur* or rhythmic modes, the division of the verse into two, three, four, and five hemistiches (if more than two, they were separated by a repeated choral hemistich), the *qāfiyah* or rhyme, and the total autonomy of the *bayt* (verse) or *maqṭa'* (section). Everywhere, the creative powers of the literati were concentrated on the selection of precise words and meanings, on the refinement of composition and style. In their productions, the verse of poetry shined by its own light and yielded its beauty through the refinement of its terms and phrases.

Muslim prose, on the other hand, followed the rules of Arabic prose. These included *ṣiyāghah,* or the delicate molding of the best words together to fit a certain meaning; *al muqābalah* or *tawāzun,* the balancing or juxtapositioning of symmetrical words, phrases, or meanings; repetition, or the expression of a form, modality, or theme a number of times, each different from the others yet focusing attention on the same subject matter; *al tarassul* or nondevelopmental continuation, that is, the succession of themes, parts, or chapters without organic interconnection but with standard phrases or themes to open and close each passage, and generating a momentum toward infinite continuation; *al ījāz,* brevity, precision, and simplicity, or use of the least number of words to pack the greatest meaning; *al īqā',* or the setting of each word in the place proper to it; *al intiqāl,* or the sudden change of tense, form of address, or meaning, to another contrasting with it as a means of reinforcing both; *tamthīl al ma'ānī,* or the conveyance of an abstract meaning through impressions given to senses, thus making the absent present, the illusory real, the abstract concrete; *al bayān,* clarity of expression, or absence of crypticisms, symbols, and hidden meanings; and finally, *muṭābaqah al 'ibārah li muqtaḍā al ḥāl,* propriety of expression, its fittingness to the occasion, or the selection of terms and styles befitting the reader/audience as well as the topic under discussion.

Observance of all these criteria, because they were derived from the Qur'ān, their ideal exemplification, was universally sought by all Muslims. Actualization of these criteria was the measure of success, of literary, aesthetic fulfillment of author as well as audience.

ACHIEVEMENTS IN PROSE

Ṣadr al Islām (The Early Period, 1–100/622–720) or The Age of Simplicity

This early period of Islam was a continuation of the pre-Islamic period. The Arabs had known writing, and their business transactions required them to keep some records. The greater part of the legacy of that period, nonetheless, was transmitted orally, having been committed to memory. It was the writers of the second century of the *Hijrah* who recorded what they had heard and received from the earlier generations. That their reportage was not always exact may be granted without damage to the thesis that the literature, in its totality, constituted a homogeneous body, reflecting the same literary characteristics as the fewer but absolutely genuine records. Moreover, the corpus contains much internal evidence, historical and formal, to establish its authenticity beyond question. At any rate, the materials of the *ḥadīth* especially, because of their religious importance as well as their relevance to the *sharī'ah,* were subjected to the rigors of *ḥadīth* criticism, which invented textual criticism and a number of sciences to complete its task.

Ṣadr al Islām includes the Prophetic period as well as the periods of the Rāshidūn and Umawī caliphates. The area in which the relevant materials were produced included Arabia proper, and the territories of West Asia and North Africa, which were added to the Islamic state. Though Islamized, the territories were still being Arabized, and hence their natives contributed nearly nothing. The materials were almost exclusively produced by peninsular Arabs whether within the Peninsula or, having migrated, taking root in the Islamized provinces. Contributions from provincial natives were premature at this stage, though they surpassed the productions of peninsular Arabs in the succeeding period. Besides the Prophet, the writers and orators who authored the materials were largely his companions and other contemporaries; and their style of speaking and writing is in evidence everywhere. Undoubtedly, that style had evolved from ancient times and served as a matrix for the new phenomenon of Islam. It was common to all, high and low, rich or poor.

The materials may be divided into three categories: (1) the *ḥadīth*—the treaties, sermons, and epistles of the Prophet; (2) the common sayings; and (3) the *khuṭab*—speeches, treaties, messages, and *waṣāyā* (sing. *waṣiyyah* or testament) of the early caliphs and leaders. The first two show little or nothing of Islam's literary influence, since they represent the matrix into which Islam was born. The third does so remarkably and constitutes the median between the literature in which Islam was born and that which it created to carry forth its ideas and ethos.

The *ḥadīth*. Sifted and collected in the six canonized anthologies, the *ḥadīth* represents, together with the treaties, messages, and sermons of the Prophet, the Prophet's style. Though personal, the style was perfectly at home in the wider environment of Arabia and that of the intellectual aristocracy of Makkah. This principle of stylistic harmony with all the literary legacy of *Ṣadr al Islām* was the canon of internal criticism used by the *ḥadīth* scholars to sift the true from the fabricated traditions. By this principle as well as by other canons of internal and external textual criticism, the *ḥadīth* materials were classified according to the degree of authenticity each report enjoyed under testing. Generally, *ḥadīth* scholars distinguished three levels of truthfulness or validity: the valid *(ṣaḥīḥ)*, the good *(ḥasan)*, and the weak *(ḍa'īf)*, as well as numerous subcategories under each of these levels. The tests used applied to both *isnād* (the chain of narrators who passed the *ḥadīth* from one reporter to another) and *matn* (the text transmitted), its content, and its form. Application of these criteria to the hundreds of thousands of *aḥādīth* circulating in the second and third centuries established *'ulūm al ḥadīth* (the disciplines of textual criticism, biography, and oral-tradition criticism). The operation was carried out with thorough-going honesty and criticality. The *aḥādīth* with a lesser degree of validity or authenticity were kept and assigned to the place proper to them in footnotes and exegetical commentaries, rather than be swept away into oblivion.

The term *ḥadīth* is often used to include the treaties the Prophet contracted and the texts he dictated, the epistles or messages he sent to distant correspondents, whether his own agents or the monarchs and chiefs of the neighboring regions, and the sermons he delivered on great occasions. Among those that belong to the first group are the texts of the treaties of Al 'Aqabah (621–622 C.E.) and Ḥudaybiyah (6/628), and the first constitution of the first Islamic state which the Prophet founded upon arrival in Madīnah on the first day of the *Hijrah.* Notable among the second group are the letters the Prophet sent in 8/630 to the emperors of Byzantium and Persia and the heads of the Churches of Egypt and Abyssinia; among the third is the last sermon he delivered on the occasion of his farewell pilgrimage to Makkah. To this category belong the treaties and messages of the Rāshidūn and very early Umawī caliphs (10–124/632–749).

The common sayings *(al Amthāl)*. Inherited from pre-Islamic times, the proverbs and common sayings of the peninsular Arabs were continuously used by the Muslims because of their literary eloquence and insights as well as the wealth of vocabulary, they presented, which, along with pre-Islamic poetry, aided the new Muslim converts to understand the vocabulary and syntax of the Qur'ān and the *ḥadīth.* This corpus of materials was later collected in anthologies by al Mufaḍḍal al Ḍabbī (168/775), Abū 'Ubaydah (211/827), and al Aṣma'ī (213/829).

The *khuṭab* (orations) and *waṣāyā* (testaments). Oratory is as old as humanity. Extraordinary events like war or moments of extreme emotional tension, whether joyful or sorrowful, usually call for unusual oratorical exercise. Through Islam, the Muslims were given a cause for which to strive; and they were so possessed by the new vision that they personally became its mouthpieces and missionaries. No church or organization was there to relieve them from the individual obligation to call for Islam. Thus, the call for Islam was everyday business for everyone, and everyone practiced it with greater or lesser eloquence. The extraordinary occasions and events helped to break into flames a fire that was constantly glowing in their hearts and imagination. The *khuṭbah* was the instrument of this new mass proselytization effort; it was the medium of communication between the masses and the leadership anxious to sway them to support its political role.

In the *khuṭbah* the Muslim found realization for this call from the depths of his being. In it, therefore, he pressed all his literary powers; upon its eloquence and moving appeal depended the exhortation, persuasion, and conversion of his audience to the ideals of Islam. And since those ideals were already couched in sublime form in the Qur'ān, the practice of weaving Qur'ānic materials into the *khuṭbah* fabric became the prime method of achieving literary strength and appeal. Thus, the art of improvisation with different words and constructs on the themes and verses of the Qur'ān or *ḥadīth* was born. This new venue for the art of letters produced a flood of new writings and became the national pastime of a whole people.

Add to the foregoing three more significant facts. First, the *futūḥāt* (campaigns for the spread of Islam) brought a great many peoples in southwest Asia to proselytization, who were speaking or capable of understanding Arabic. Second, the outbreak of political antagonism between the Arabs themselves, especially since the Caliphate of 'Uthmān (12–39/644–650), fired their need for oratory to sway the masses behind the various camp leaders. Third, the expanded territory and larger numbers of people brought new points of view—religious, social, legal, and cultural—and new problems which called for fresh interpretation of the practices of Islam known in Madīnah. All these provided the Muslims with more fuel, more occasion, and more cause to resort to oratory, the main mass medium of the times. Memorized instantly, the best *khuṭbah* were recited on frequent occasions, and were passed from generation to generation for literary enjoyment, just like the poetry of pre-Islamic times.

From the standpoint of literary aesthetics, the literature in *Ṣadr al Islām* continued the old tradition of Arabic prose, while it laid down the foundation for the new Islamic style. The following qualities were definitive:

1. Brevity, or the pressing of ideas and meanings in the fewest possible words. Fewer words would have made the expression obscure; more would have made it detailed or redundant. The composition was utterly free of repetition and of decorative, explanatory, or hortatory addenda.
2. Simplicity, or the smooth flow of composition, unhampered by complex structure, protracted exemplification, drawn out similes and metaphors, belabored rhyming, or conjunctions and disjunctions. *Ṣadr al Islām* prose is consistently free of embellishments; and it is beautiful without their aid.
3. *Talmīḥ,* or the pointing to the meanings intended without giving them express mention, thus baiting the mind and inciting the imagination to grasp the meanings, as it were, under cover. Provided that the intended meaning is not missed or rendered opaque, *talmīḥ* can add tremendous charm to a statement. It gives the mind the pleasure of seeking and finding.
4. *Jazālah,* or the solid weaving of ideas and words while preserving sweet enunciation and pleasing sound. Arab prose in this period was remarkably free of distension, of contrived elaboration, of dilation. It fell naturally and ran swiftly and thus conveyed its message effortlessly. The *khuṭab* fulfilled these literary canons or ideals—and more. They provided ample occasion for literary creativity, expansion, and direct quotations from the Qur'ān and *ḥadīth.* Gradually, incorporating the *data revelata* into a composition became the hallmark of literary craftsmanship.

Ḍuḥā al Islām (The Middle Period: Late Umawī to Early 'Abbāsī, c. 100–360/720–972): The Age of *Tawāzun*

The new age began with the Umawī caliph al Walīd ibn 'Abdul Malik who reigned between 85–96/705–715. We have it on the authority of al Qalqashandī that

Illustration 19.1

Cover of a book written for the private library of the 'Uthmānlī sulṭān Fātiḥ Muḥammad, fifteenth century, held in Topkapi Saray Museum, Isṭanbūl, Turkey. [Photo by L. al Fārūqī.]

writing under the Umawīs followed the style of the ancients until al Walīd, who brought great improvement to the government secretariat, to official writing and correspondence, and to calligraphy.[1] Al Walīd's new style remained in effect until 360/972 except for an interval of return to the ancient style under 'Umar ibn 'Abdul 'Azīz (98–101/717–720) and Yazīd ibn al Walīd, whose reign lasted less than a year in 125–126/744. It was in the literary spirit of al Walīd that Marwān ibn Muḥammad (126–132/744–750), the last Umawī caliph, commissioned 'Abdul Ḥamid ibn Yaḥya, the greatest essayist of the time, to develop the more flowery style of writing for which he is known. The messages of government became so long that it is said that 'Abdul Ḥamīd wrote for his employer an epistle that by itself took a camel to carry over to its addressee.

The new style was called *tawāzun* or literary symmetry, and was introduced in imitation of the Qur'ānic style. It consisted of writing in phrases with an equal number of syllables, of equal duration, and of equal construction. That was its highest form. Complete symmetry, however, was not necessary. A composition was said to belong to this style if some clusters of syllables in each phrase or sentence conformed to this requirement. It was essential, though, that the symmetrical clusters be sufficiently close to one another that one could associate any two or three without effort. Where they occurred in pairs, the rule was that the later phrase should never be longer than the earlier, so that the symmetrical clusters were not too far removed from each other. The weakest instance of *tawāzun* was that in which only the last cluster of syllables in each phrase or sentence conformed to the requirement. Without a doubt, *tawāzun* is characteristic of Qur'ānic prose. Indeed, the Qur'ān is the best —nay, sublime—example of *tawāzun*. *Tawāzun* was also known in pre-Islamic literature, especially in common sayings and the oracular pronouncements of the seers (*kuhhān*, sing. *kāhin*).

The greatest authors of the *tawāzun* style were 'Abdul Ḥamīd al Kātib (130/749), Abu 'Amr 'Uthmān al Jāḥiẓ (253/868), and Abū Ḥayyān al Tawḥīdī (375/987).

'Abdul Ḥamīd al Kātib served the last three Umawī caliphs as chief scribe. He learned the art of letters under Salīm, a student of Hishām ibn 'Abdul Malik, and served the latter when he was governor of Armenia. When Hishām became caliph and moved to Damascus, 'Abdul Ḥamīd moved with him and assumed leadership of the caliphal correspondence. Al Mas'ūdī described him as the first writer ever to open every composition with mention of God's name *(basmalah)*, the praise of Allah *(ḥamdalah)*, and the invocation of blessings upon His Prophet (ṣalāt).[2] 'Abdul Ḥamīd was also the first to lengthen the composition beyond the normal practice of the times, for no other reason than beautification. This was called *tarassul* (indulgence in extending the writing). Together with *tawāzun*, these characteristics quickly became the fashion, associated with 'Abdul Ḥamīd, their originator. He left a legacy of over 1,000 sheets of materials, according to Ibn al Nadīm.[3] The most famous and important of these are the essay addressed to the scribes of the kingdom on the art of writing, and an essay written on behalf of the caliph to his son, 'Abdullah ibn Marwān, who was sent to subdue a Khārijī rebellion.[4] Both works fully illustrate the new style. In both, extension is carried out by the addition of synonyms to the individual words, parallel phrases, and explanatory details.

Born in Baṣrah (150/767), Abū 'Amr al Jāḥiẓ studied under al Aṣma'ī and Abu 'Ubaydah, and was the undisputed leader of his day in oratory and writing, the greatest in quick wit, and the sharpest in criticism. He left 160 books of various lengths, the most famous of which carried the following titles: Dialogue between Winter and Summer; Squaring and Rounding Up; The Virtues of Turkomen; On Nobility, On Reconciliation and Pardon; Eloquence and Clarity; On the Animals; The Avaricious; *I'jāz* of the Qur'ān; Compositional Style of the Qur'ān; Proofs of Prophecy.

The style of al Jāḥiẓ was true to his age. His writing realized its norms to a preeminently high degree. He described these norms as follows:

Agreement of expression with meaning. "The speaker/writer should be aware of the proportions of meaning, of his audience, and of the situation, if his words are to accord with all of them. In this case, every situation would call for a different expression, as would every different meaning. . . . His composition would be free of jingoisms, of expressions which are strange to the audience. . . . Just as people are of different character, so are words and meanings. Mediocre words inevitably carry mediocre meanings; noble ones carry uncommon, beautiful meanings. Words and meanings are both hot or both cold; and nothing is more suffocating than words and meanings which are neither."[5]

Illustration 19.2

Leather cover for *Dīwān* of Ḥāfiẓ, held in the Library of the Sulaymāniyyah, Isṭanbūl, Turkey. [Courtesy Ministry of Culture and Tourism, Government of Turkey.]

***Al Bayān* or clear signification.** Meanings, al Jāḥiẓ held, are hidden in the consciousness. There, they lie in a state of deadened anonymity. When given proper expression, they come to life, they rise and exercise their moving power, making the distant near, the absent present, the complex simple, the strange familiar. Meanings are alive and influential in direct proportion to the propriety of their expression. Indeed, *al bayān* is everything that discloses and exposes meaning.

Brevity and nonartificiality. "The best composition," al Jāḥiẓ taught, "is that where the fewer words obviate the need for more; where the meanings are carried by the words in full view. And if both are appropriate to each other, they fall upon the heart like rain upon the good soil."[6] "Meanings and words run ahead, overtaking and overtaken by each other in their race toward the hearer's heart."[7]

***Al Iftinān* (artistry).** Al Jāḥiẓ's writing is always replete with examples, exceptions, and variations. His arguments for or against anything come in showers so penetrating and so abundant that the reader or audience is totally disarmed when the purpose is to disarm, and transported when the author wants his audience to be moved. "Throughout the composition, Qur'ānic words and phrases, ideas and percepts are set like shining jewels in a massive flow of precious metal." Al Jāḥiẓ was truly the creator of a style and its best example.[8] He was also the creator of the literary form called *al risālah,* an essay that has an ostensible topic which is also its title, but that treats its subject in detached paragraphs each of which focuses on an aspect of the subject matter. In *al risālah,* the treatment does not develop so as to make a structure with compartments organically related to one another. Each of the compartments, paragraphs, or sections is autonomous, self-propelled, and self-contained, and they follow one another *seriatim.* The root verb *tarassala* from which the name *risālah* is the participial object, means to orient oneself toward a topic and to compose as many paragraphs, analyses, discussions, elaborations, and commentaries around it as one can or pleases. *Al risālah* is nondevelopmental, nonsystematic, nondramatic. Its value resides in the individual insights of its words and expressions, of its sentences or clusters of sentences. With all the literary characteristics described above, *al risālah* as a literary form was fed by the literary norms of the Qur'ān and was created to express the message of an author standing in the midst of a civilization in full and resplendent bloom.

We have seen that 'Abdul Ḥamīd was the originator of the new style and that al Jāḥiẓ was its exemplar standing at the apogee of the period characterized by it. As the style changed and a new set of norms began to determine literary production, Abū Ḥayyān al Tawḥīdī rose to affirm that style which had by then become traditional and resistant to the innovations of the new. His model was al Jāḥiẓ, whom he eulogized as "the dearest to the heart, the noblest friend of the soul, the grand shaykh of letters, and the justification of the Arabs."[9]

Al Tawḥīdī grew up in Baghdād and earned a meager living in copying and bookselling. Aware that men of letters around him attached themselves to one princely court or another and derived all sorts of gifts and benefits from their patrons, he decided to approach the famous court-writer and vizier Ibn al 'Amīd in the hope of securing a job in the palace. When this initiative failed, he went to Ibn al 'Amīd's competitor and rival, al Ṣāḥib ibn 'Abbād, the court-writer and vizier in al Rayy. This expedition also failed. In bitter disappointment, he wrote his *Mathālib al Wazīrayn* (The Villainies of the Two Viziers), a strong satire against both ministers. He tried a third time, with Ibn Sa'dān, another vizier, but with little success. When Ibn Sa'dān was assassinated, al Tawḥīdī feared for his own life and escaped to Shīrāz where he joined a Ṣūfī brotherhood.

Al Tawḥīdī left a superb legacy of literature beside the *Villainies: Al Muqābasāt, Al Imtā' wal Mu'ānasah, Al Ḥawāmil wal Shamā'il, Al Baṣā'ir wal Dhakhā'ir,* and *Al Ishārāt al Ilahiyyah,* as well as a large number of *rasā'il* (plural of risālah).

Al Tawḥīdī was the first to put his literary production in the form of a diary of successive salon gatherings, each of which records the conversations of friends on a different topic, thus constructing a "super-*risālah*" out of several shorter ones. His writing fulfilled the literary norms of his tradition admirably. His innovation lay in the things about which he wrote, not in the form. He combined *adab* (literary writing) with philosophical thought and Ṣūfī ideas.

The Climax (Late 'Abbāsī Period, c. 360–600/972–1203): The Age of *Saj'* and *Badī'*

The middle style did not go out of fashion abruptly. A number of great writers continued to observe it as the new *saj'* style gained ground around them. Muḥammad ibn Yaḥyā al Ṣūlī (d. 335/947) wrote a superb *risālah* entitled "The Discipline of Letters" as a complement to 'Abdul Ḥamīd's famous *risālah* addressed to the scribes of the realm. 'Alī ibn 'Abdul 'Azīz al Jurjānī (d. 392/1001) wrote another on the role of the writer as medium between the ruler and ruled, entitled *Al Wasāṭah.* Abū Hilāl al 'Askarī (d. 395/1004) contributed a book entitled *Al Ṣinā'atayn* (The Two Crafts—that of letters and that of government). All these authors fulfilled the norms of *tawāzun* to the highest possible degree.

Although *saj'* was well known before Islam, and was present throughout Islamic history, it was never dominant before the advent of this climactic period in the fifth century of the *Hijrah.* It began to make inroads in the fourth century, and achieved masterly dominion over literature in the fifth. Since the Qur'ān was full of *saj',* or rhymed phrases that combined this quality with *tawāzun* and all other norms of literary beauty, the advocates of the new style pointed to it in justification of their own writing.

Saj' consists of prose whose phrases are rhymed in clusters of two or more parts. Its conditions include that the words be sweet and sonorous; that each of the rhymed phrases carry a different meaning; that the rhymed phrases fulfill the requirements of *tawāzun;* that the later phrase be always shorter than the earlier. *Badī',* on the other hand, which includes *saj'* and more, can be of many forms. Some men of letters counted fourteen varieties of *badī',* and others doubled that number or more. *Badī'* consists of creating phrases that are identical in syllabic structure, sometimes even in the shape of letters without their diacritical marks, but different in meaning. Such differences may be of the kind that exists between parallels and likes, opposites and contraries, or that expresses dualisms or quality, or of time and place,[10] and thus make the beginning of a sentence indicative of its end both in meaning and in form—a quality known as *tawshīḥ.*

The greatest exemplars of *saj'* and *badī'* were the following:

Caliphal correspondence. Caliphal correspondence was entrusted to the court *dīwān* or secretariat. The caliphal court employed the ablest writers and through them set the style and popularized it. The messages of the great matters of state depended for their outcome upon the moving power of the composition to bring about the desired solution, as was the case of Ibn Balkā's rebellion against the caliph Rukn al Dawlah (337/949). Ibn al 'Amīd wrote the epistle that, on Ibn Balkā's own confession, brought the rebel to his knees and transformed his heart. Other famous writers were Abū al Faḍl Muḥammad Ibn al 'Amīd (d. 360/970), Abū Isḥaq al Ṣābī (d. 384/994), al Qāḍī al Fāḍil (d. 596/1200), Lisān al Dīn Ibn al Khaṭīb (d. 776/1375), and al Ṣāḥib Ibn 'Abbād (d. 385/995). Less famous than these but equally eloquent in their writing for the caliphs were 'Abdul 'Azīz bin Yūsuf, Abū al 'Abbās al Ḍabbī, 'Alī al Iskāfī, and Abū al Fatḥ al Bustī of the fifth and sixth centuries A.H.

Literary essays. Literary essays were composed by their authors to describe conversations, report speeches, tell stories, or elaborate Islamic, moral, or human themes. Among the most famous were *Risālat al Ghufrān* (Forgiveness) written by Abū al 'Alā' al Ma'arrī (d. 449/1059), which described an imaginary conversation with the inhabitants of Paradise among whom al Ma'arrī included many evil-doers on the grounds that God had forgiven them their misdeeds, conversations with the inhabitants of Hell, as well as discussions of the various faiths of mankind. This *risālah* initiated a genre of writing that quickly spread to Europe where Dante produced his *Divina Comedia* in imitation of it. Al Ma'arrī wrote a number of other *rasā'il* of which *Al Risālah al Ighrīdiyyah* was deeply appreciated for its outstanding literary beauty. *Al Risālah* of Ibn Zaydūn (d. 463/1072) and *Risālah al Shukr* of Abū 'Abdullah al Ghāfiqī (d. 540/1146) were both written by Andalusian authors. Al Qalqashandī's *Mufākharah bayna al Sayf wal Qalam* (Contest for Honor by the Sword and the Pen) was written in 794/1383. Tāj al Dīn al Bazyarī wrote an essay in 740/1340 describing the hunt of Sulṭān Manṣūr ibn Qalāwūn, which immortalized him and his master in the annals of literature. Abū Bakr al Khawārizmī, a great *risālah* writer as well as a poet, met with fortune under the patronage of al Ṣāḥib ibn 'Abbād, and wrote a large number of exquisite literary essays. He entered into a competition with al Ḥarīrī and lost.

The *maqāmāt*. In the singular form, a *maqāmah* is a description of a session in which a number of people speak on a certain subject. Usually one of them tells the others a short story revolving around a man who distinguishes himself by his brilliance and eloquence in that subject, and the others comment upon it. Although this kind of literary session was known in the past, it was Badī' al Zamān al Hamadhānī (d. 398/1008) who gave it its form and established it as a literary genre. Of the near 400 *maqāmāt* he wrote, only fifty-one have survived. Abū Muḥammad al Qāsim al Ḥarīrī (d. 516/1119) brought the genre to perfection in his fifty *maqāmāt*, which became famous as soon as he completed them. In *Mu'jam al Udabā'*, Yāqūt related that al Ḥarīrī autographed 700 copies of his *Maqāmāt* at once, in the very year he completed the composition. Other famous users of the genre were Ibn al Ishtarākūnī (d. 538/1134); Muḥammad Ibrahīm al Dimashqī (d. 727/1327), who added to his *maqāmāt* a philosophical dimension; and Shahāb al Dīn al Khaffājī (d. 1069/1659). The *maqāmah* remained a classic form of literary expression until modern times when it was abandoned as a result of Muslim decay. Among the later writers, Aḥmad al Barbir (d. 1226/1811), Shahāb al Allūsī (d. 1270/1854), Naṣīf al Yāzijī (d. 1288/1871), Aḥmad Fāris al Shidyāq (d. 1303/1887), Ibrahīm al Aḥdab (d. 1308/1891), and 'Abdullah Fikrī (d. 1307/1890) wrote between fifty and eighty *maqāmāt* each.

In all three forms of Islamic writing, literary artistry achieved tremendous heights. The Qur'ānic style was the absolute model throughout, and its literary values were the unquestionable norms of all literary production. A point of superior excellence was reached by al Ma'arrī's *risālah* called *Al Fuṣūl wal Ghāyāt*, which was a marvelous work of pietism and thanksgiving to Allah, but whose excellence won for its author the charge of daring to parallel the Qur'ān in its *sūrah* and verses. Al Ma'arrī never intended any such thing; and his pupils, followers, and friends exonerated and defended him against the charge. It was a unique case in which a very high degree of excellence threatened the conscience which found its quiescence in the sublime.

ACHIEVEMENTS IN POETRY

Ṣadr al Islām (1–100/622–720)

The Prophetic and Rashidūn period. The Qur'ān did not condemn poetry, though it denied that it itself was poetry. The Qur'ān did condemn those poets who sold their talents and put their poetry behind any cause (26:224–227). Anxious to read in the Qur'ān a condemnation of all artistic creativity including the literary art, G. E. von Grunebaum deliberately omitted from consideration the verse that excepted from condemnation the poets who believe in God and do the works of righteousness, and thus misled his readers.[11] The Prophet, for his part, was extremely sensitive to the Arabs' predicament of being too prone to hostility and violence with partisan poetry. Hence, in some cases he discouraged poetry. But whenever poetry promoted wisdom and virtue, he praised it. Both Labīd and Umayyah ibn Abū al Ṣalt were highly regarded by him on account of the piety and morality evident in their poetry despite the fact that they were nonbelievers. As further proof, the Prophet called on three Muslim poets — Ḥassān ibn Thābit, Ka'b ibn Mālik, and 'Abdullah ibn Rawāḥah — to rise to the defense of Islam in poetry, which they did to the utter dismay of the Makkan enemies. When non-Arabs, whose command of the Arabic language and its meanings left something to be desired, began to enter Islam, the Caliph 'Umar ibn al Khaṭṭāb urged the new converts to learn poetry, and thus to develop their mastery of Arabic. As Muslims began to interpret the Qur'ān, Ibn 'Abbās, the first exegete, told them to seek what they failed to understand of the Qur'ān in the poetry of pre-Islamic Arabia. Indeed, the Rāshidūn caliphs often recited poetry, whether to exhort the Muslims to virtue or to arouse them to battle in defense of the faith.

The Umawī period. The Umawī period witnessed a significant rise in the composition and recitation of poetry. Three factors contributed to this development. First, the early *Futūḥāt* had brought large masses of non-Arabs under Islamic rule; and many of them had already converted to Islam. Their understanding of Arabic, and consequently of Islam, was far from perfect. To help them complete their Islamization, the Islamic state had to promote the Arabic language. Cultivation of poetry was an additional means to this objective. Second was the love the Umawī caliphs had for poetry, and the generosity with which they met those who sang their praises, or excelled in the art. Mu'āwiyah, 'Abdul Malik, and Hishām were exceptionally fond of poetry and did much to patronize the poets and their art. It was in this period that Jarīr and Farazdaq, the greatest Umawī poets, divided the whole of society into partisans of the one or the other who would recite their verses on every occasion to prove the superiority of their favorite.

Umawī poetry reveals three distinguishing characteristics. First, its diction was clean, pure, and precise. Being so near to the Prophet's period, nearly all Arabs spoke a language closely following the pre-Islamic and Qur'anic style. Umawī poetry was free of strange, complex, or difficult terms. Second, whereas the Rashidūn caliphs charged the poets with bad taste if they opened their compositions with praise of their beloved women, many of the Umawīs were lax and permitted the practice. Under them, describing the beloved *(al tashbīb)* became an established custom. Perhaps the intermixture of the desert Arabs with the settled populations of the conquered provinces was a contributing cause. Jamīl's praise of Buthaynah was so beautiful that she became the sweetheart of all poets, and these began their compositions with an innovative eulogy to her charms. Thus a myth of an "eternal feminine" called Buthaynah, Layla, Hind, or Da'd was born; and a new poetry *(ghazal)* was created around it. Third, criticism, satire, and sarcasm were practically unknown in pre-Islamic poetry, despite tribal hostility and competition. Under the Umawīs, the political tensions between the parties not only mobilized the poets in their service but also permitted them to attack the opponents. This involvement of the poets led to the creation of a new genre, hitherto unknown, of political and satirical poetry. In consequence, what was once condemned as selling of talent became normal, and the poets produced in direct proportion to the rewards received or expected. Later, political poetry led to literary satire as a genre pursued for its own sake, whether the enemy was real or imaginary, as was the case with *ghazal.* Fourth, the general laxity of the poets' morality and the spread of Christian poets opened the door for wine to become a popular subject of poetry.

The number of poets in each of the tribes during the pre-Islamic and Umawī periods are as follows:

Tribe	*Pre-Islam*	*Umawī*
Qays	27	26
Rabī'ah	20	11
Tamīm	12	13
Muḍar	16	9
Quraysh	10	23
Yaman	22	16
Quḍā'ah	4	8
Iyād	2	—
Arab Jews	4	—
Mawālī (Non-Arabs under Arab patronage)	1	21

Having won the political battle of the times, the Quraysh tribe showed the greatest increase, along with the rise of a new class of poets, the clients or *mawālī* from among the conquered peoples. Besides the ones already mentioned, the greatest poets of *Ṣadr al Islām* were Abū al Aswad al Du'alī (d. 69/689), the first systematizer of Arabic grammar, and al Akhṭal (a Christian poet from Ṣalt, Jordan, and of the tribe of Taghlib (d. 95/714). Jarīr (d. 111/730) and Farazdaq (d. 110/729) challenged the contemporary poets to support or oppose them in verse. This was often done by composing poems with the same meter and rhyme as the contending poems of Jarīr and al Farazdaq. The poetical battles that ensued forced everybody to listen and to take part in the dispute. 'Umar ibn Abū Rabī'ah (d. 93/712) and Qays ibn al Mulawwaḥ, better known as Majnūn Laylā (the one "possessed" by Laylā, the sweetheart) led the poets in *ghazal,* the poetry of love.

Ḍuḥā al Islām (100–656/720–1258)

With the passing of *Ṣadr al Islām,* the processes of urbanization and cosmopolitanization reached their peak under the 'Abbāsīs. Al Baṣrah, Al Kūfah, and Baghdād rose to full splendor and eclipsed the older cities of Syria and the Eastern Provinces of Persia and Central Asia. Affluence and luxury became the rule, replacing the ascetic discipline of the desert, and life took on a million colors and a highly complex structure, contrasting sharply with the straightforward simplicity of earlier times. Poetry was quick to be affected. As the mirror of consciousness, it entertained the ideals of its age.

The first change took place in the content of poetry. The city poets of the new age could not be satisfied with the repertory of ideas of earlier times used in the effort to Islamize and Arabize the population. Under the Umawīs, wine, women, and politics had become legitimate subjects of poetry; under the 'Abbāsīs, they became popular and common. Likewise, the imagination was enriched by new similes and metaphors, and discursive reason with new knowledge and ideas, all of which were at the disposal of the poets. In addition to these subjects, horticulture and its gardens, aquaculture and its fountains and streams, architecture and its palaces and mosques spread before the poetical imagination the richest table. Often, this exercised a mischievous influence on the poet's morality. We have already seen how, under the Umawīs, the poets learned to sell their talents to their princely patrons. Under the 'Abbāsīs, this tendency increased; and soon, poetry degenerated into permissiveness on the moral as well as the doctrinal level. Abū Nuwās (d. 198/811) was the king of the immoral poets; Ibn al Muqaffa' (d. 108/727), that of the heretical ones.

The successful poets quickly became very rich; many were among the richest persons in the land, so large were the donations and gifts made to them by their patrons. Often, they also wielded immense power, not excluding the caliph's power of life and death which they manipulated. The poetry of Sadīf caused the victorious 'Abbāsī leadership to exterminate the Umawī house; and that of Mālik ibn Ṭawq and of Rabī'ah brought revocation of capital punishment imposed upon them. The scribes who wrote for the caliph never enjoyed such power. Poetry was on every lip, in every place, on every occasion, either as an ex tempore composition by the poets or as memorized and recited by others. Pre-Islam had its *'ukāẓ* where poets competed every year. The 'Abbāsī realm had its *al Marbad* in Baṣrah where competition was in perpetual session. The Arabs, under the 'Abbāsīs, pushed their love for poetry to heights hitherto unknown. They knew so much of it that they pointed to the poet by a verse of his, or to a specific verse of poetry by the mere mention of the poet's name on an occasion befitting the verse in question. Poetry decorated the walls of houses inside and out, doors and window screens, curtains and cushions, glasses and utensils, jewelry and musical instruments, inner and outer clothes, even sandals and shoes. With henna, poetry was more or less permanently inscribed on faces and arms.

The 'Abbāsī period was blessed with a very large number of great poets. Seven outstanding poets filled the early part of that period (up to the caliphate of al Mutawakkil in 222/838) with their poetry and set a new style of life, of patronage, and of poetical composition.

Bashshār ibn Burd (d. 167/784) was a blind son of a slave, manumitted by his master for his eloquence. He composed poetry at the age of ten, and left a legacy of 12,000 poems. Al Sayyid al Ḥimyarī (d. 172/789) inclined toward the party of 'Alī and composed 2,300 poems. He refused any donation, including that of the caliph. Al Ḥasan ibn Hāni' Abū Nuwās (d. 198/811) was the first to liberate poetry from the rules and standards of pre-Islam and *Ṣadr al Islām,* both as to content, diction, and style of composition. His legacy of over 13,000 verses fall into every known poetical category. Muslim ibn al Walīd (d. 209/825) composed poetry while working as postmaster of Jurjān, and excelled in *ghazal.* Isma'īl Abū al 'Atāhiyah (d. 211/827) was an itinerant vase-seller, carrying his wares on his back. Passing by a group of youth who were reciting poetry, he challenged them to compose the other hemistiches of two or three verses he recited. He wagered the value of his wares on their inability to comply. He won the wager and became famous. He created new meters, inclined toward the ascetic life, and refused to compose *ghazal* even when ordered to do so by the caliph Al Mahdī. Ḥabīb Abū Tammām (d. 232/847) began his career as water-dispenser in a mosque in Fusṭāṭ (Old Cairo) and soon traveled to Baghdād and achieved fame. Immobilized by a heavy snowfall at the house of his host Ibn Salāmah in Khurāsān, he wrote down from memory a huge compendium of pre-Islamic poetry known as *Dīwān al Ḥamāsah,* as well as four volumes of his own poetry. Finally, Da'bal al Khuzā'ī (d. 246/861) was the most feared poet, by princes and commoners alike, for his caustic satires. His verses spread instantly, and the reputation of any target of their satire was ruined. He too rejected all gifts and lived off the bounty of relatives, pouring his copious praises on the family of the Prophet.

The middle part of the 'Abbāsī period (from al Mutawakkil's caliphate to the rise of the Buwayhī state in 334/946) witnessed a decline in caliphal patronage of the poets because the caliphs themselves fell captive to their servants and soldiers who had become sultans. It was a time of general insecurity and little or no freedom of expression. Moreover, the tremendous influx of ideas from the outside through the translations of the preceding century made themselves felt. Poetry withdrew from public causes and focused on the personal. It was also at this time that *al badī'* invaded poetry and absorbed its geniuses.

The most famous poets of this period were Ibn al Rūmī (d. 283/898), the first to give priority to meaning and content over diction and form, and Abū 'Ibādah al Buḥturī (d. 284/899), who resisted that trend and insisted on beauty of form. He wrote a larger compendium of pre-Islamic poetry than that of Abū Tammām (including works of some 600 poets), to which he gave the same title, *Dīwān al Ḥamāsah,* but for which he used a new classification of 174 categories rather than Abū Tammām's ten. Ibn al Mu'tazz (296/909), a son of the 'Abbāsī caliph of that name and a grandson of al Mutawakkil, besides composing poetry, wrote several books. Among these are a book of literary criticism, one on the history of poetry, one on the forms of *badī',* and two on royal poetry and the poetry of wine.

The late 'Abbāsī period began with the establishment of the Buwayhī state in 334/946 and ended with its supersession by the Saljūq Turkish state in 447/1056. This period was remarkable for its achievements in all fields of intellectual and spiritual endeavor because the 'Abbāsī empire broke up into a number of autonomous petty states which vied with each other in patronizing poetry, the arts, and the sciences. Poetry became more philosophical or theological, cultivating in specialized ways the values of urban society and civilization, of history and asceticism. Unlike earlier times, the poets counted numerous men of law, medicine, and philosophy among them. Exaggeration and extremism became popular in every field, including poetry. Even the meters *(al abḥur)* were increased by the addition of novel ones such as *al muwashshaḥāt* of al Andalus.

Some of the greatest poets of this period were the greatest of all times. Among them are Abū al Ṭayyib al Mutanabbī (d. 354/986), whose poetry exploded with a giant will to power and the making of history, and has remained the subject of a lively controversy to the present day. There is unanimous agreement among men of letters that al Mutanabbī's poetry was great in all the kinds of compositions he wrote, and he wrote in all the known kinds. Abū Firās al Ḥamdānī (d. 357/969) was a prince of the house of Ḥamdān which ruled the Ḥamdānī state in northern Iraq and Syria. Referring to him, al Ṣāḥib ibn 'Abbād commented that Arabic poetry began with royalty (the pre-Islamic king Imru' al Qays) and ended with royalty. Al Ḥamdānī was wounded by the Byzantines in battle and taken prisoner to Constantinople where he wrote exquisite poetry in captivity. Finally, Abū al 'Alā' al Ma'arrī (d. 449/1058) was the last of the great line of

Illustration 19.3

Marginal sectic.ı from Maragha Gulshan, late sixteenth century, showing the Mughal Emperor Jahangīr hunting. [Courtesy Islamic Information Service, Iran.]

Illustration 19.4

"Laylah and Majnūn at School," an illustration from a copy of the Khamsah of Niẓāmī dated 1574. [Courtesy The University Museum, University of Pennsylvania.]

poets. Blinded by smallpox at the age of three, he had a photographic memory which caused him to retain with precision everything he heard. Before he reached the age of eleven, he was a confirmed poet, acknowledged by all. He spent the last forty-nine years of his life in his home, feeding on a vegetarian diet, and living off an endowment left to him by his ancestors. He wrote profusely in many fields besides poetry. His *Al Luzūmiyyāt* and *Ṣaqt al Zand* include thousands of verses; and his *Al Rasā'il* contains over 800 poems which treat of almost every subject under the sun. His *Risālah al Ghufrān* has already been mentioned.

NOTES

1. *Subḥ al A'shā* (Cairo: Al Maṭba'ah al Amīriyyah, 1913-1918), Vol. 6, p. 391.
2. *Murūj al Dhahab* (Cairo: Al Maṭba'ah al Tijāriyyah, 1385/1965), Book 6, p. 81.
3. *Al Fihrist* (Leipzig, 1871), p. 117.
4. Full texts of both compositions may be read in al Qalqashandī, *Subḥ al A'shā*, Vol. 1, pp. 85-89, and Vol. 10, pp. 195-233, respectively.
5. *Al Bayān wal Tabyīn* (Cairo: Al Maṭba'ah al 'Ilmiyyah, 1311/1893), Vol. 1, pp. 77-78.
6. Ibid., p. 83.
7. Ibid., p. 49.
8. Al Bāqillānī, *I'jāz al Qur'ān* (Cairo: Dār al Ma'ārif, 1964), p. 58.
9. *Al Muqābasāt* (Cairo: Al Maṭba'ah al Raḥmaniyyah, 1929), p. 181.
10. See the listing of various kinds and forms of *badī'* in Ḍiyā' al Dīn Ibn al Athīr, *Al Mathal al Sā'ir* (Cairo: Būlāq Press, 1282/1865), pp. 114-118, 147-151; Qābūs ibn Washinkir, *Kamāl al Balāghah* (Cairo: Salafiyyah Press, 1341/1922), pp. 19-22; Ibn Shīt al Qurashī, *Ma'ālim al Kitābah* (Beirut, 1913), pp. 68-85.
11. See this author's refutation of Gustav von Grunebaum's claim in al Fārūqī, "Misconceptions of the Nature of Art in Islām," *Islam and the Modern Age* (1970), pp. 29-49.

CHAPTER 20

Calligraphy

In order to examine the unifying characteristics of the Islamic arts which the Qur'ānic message of *tawḥīd* produced, as well as the tremendous versatility and ingenuity in achieving ever new and creative forms of those characteristics, it is necessary to view products of wide geographic provenance and produced over many centuries of Islamic history. Only in this way can the unique qualities of overall unity within the Islamic arts be revealed and the special achievements of the various regions and periods be flavored.

The geographic scope of any exposition of Islamic art is tremendous. This makes difficult any attempt to be comprehensive, for the artistic examples are found in places as far removed as Spain and the southern Philippines, Central Asia and Tanzania (see Map 62). Equally wide is the time span of their creation. The study of Islamic art deals with materials from the seventh century all the way to the present day — over fourteen centuries of artistic expression with all the different materials, motifs, and techniques of production known during that long span of time.

To simplify our task, we will divide the Muslim world into seven subregions or artistic areas for our treatment of the visual arts in Islamic culture.[1] Although there are historical as well as aesthetic grounds for the demarkation of these areas, the reader is warned that the artistic areas represented in Map 62 are not easily limited by precise boundaries. Interaction between areas has resulted in frequent overlapping of regional characteristics, and the styles of one area may carry many similarities with those of another area because of reciprocal influences and common underlying characteristics. The reader should be aware that stylistic traits interpenetrate areas rather than originate or desist in a sharply definable manner. Structural characteristics are generally found to have the widest significance, while particular motifs, techniques of execution, or materials reveal a tendency for greater variability.

The styles which these subdivisions represent were not necessarily static over time. Though any one of the art regions reveals a good deal of unity in the art creations of its various periods, differences can also be found. We therefore speak of specialties or proclivities of certain periods — luster-ware ceramic production in ninth-century Iraq, ceramic mosaic in sixteenth-century Iran, *pietra dura* inlays in sixteenth- and seventeenth-century India, brocade and velvets of fifteenth-century Turkey, and so on. Yet even these specialties of period and place are both based on earlier artistic production and harbingers of later aesthetic creations.

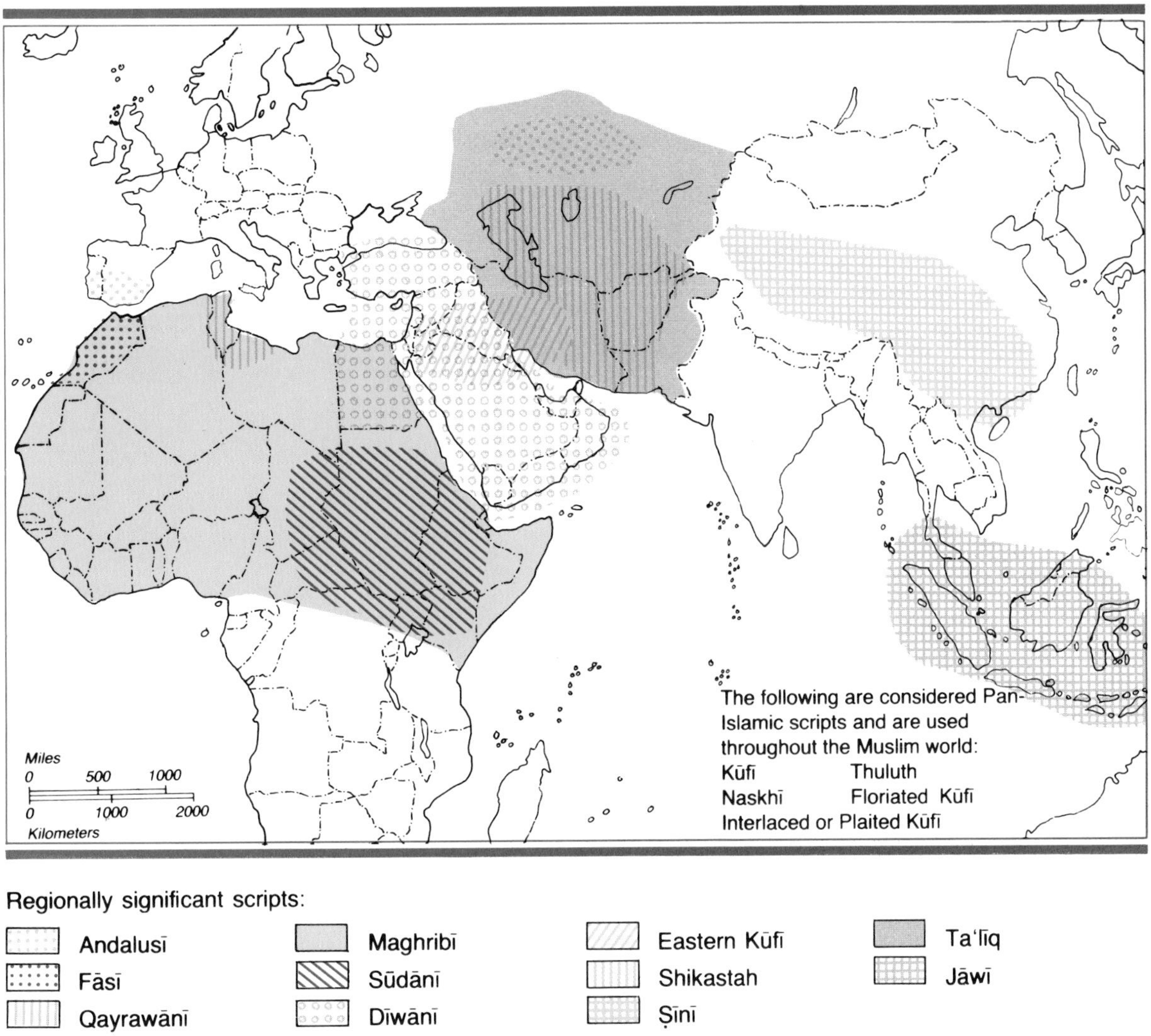

Map 60. Use of Arabic Calligraphy Styles in the Muslim World

The numbering of the areas proceeds from West to East. It implies no hierarchical status. Area I comprises the Maghrib or "Western" region, that is, the countries of Mauritania, the Western Sahara, Morocco, Algeria, Tunisia, and Libya, as well as Moorish Spain. Area II includes the regions of Middle Africa with a predominantly Muslim population and obvious aesthetic influences from Islamic culture. We prefer the expression "Middle Africa" to "Sub-Saharan Africa" for the area including those non-Arab parts of Africa that show strong Islamic influence. As indicated on Map 62, they include both Saharan and sub-Saharan regions, both non-Arab and Arab ethnic groups, and non-Arabic- as well as Arabic-speaking peoples. It includes major portions of at least twenty-five nations. Area III is that of the Mashriq, or "Eastern" region of the Arab world. It corresponds approximately to the countries of Egypt, Palestine/Israel, Jordan, Syria, Lebanon, Iraq, the Arabian Peninsula, and the Gulf region. Turkey will be treated as a separate Area IV because of the regional variations that distinguish it from its geographic neighbors. Area V, Iran-Central Asia, includes the countries of present-day Iran and Afghanistan, as well as major portions of the southern Soviet Union. Area VI corresponds to the predominantly Muslim regions of the Indian subcontinent—Pakistan, Bangladesh, and parts of India. The portions of East Asia with major Muslim populations—Malaysia, Indonesia, the southern Philippines, and parts of China—are included in Area VII. Although other regions within the medieval Mediterranean world (for example, Sicily, southern Italy, and certain regions of southern France and southeastern Europe) have also evidenced Islamic artistic influences, they will not be included in the present discussion nor accorded representation on the artistic areas map. This should be regarded not as a denial of the significance of those regions in the total picture of Islamic art but as an omission dictated by the generalized nature of this discussion.

All of the above-mentioned areas provide ample evidence of a determination of their artistic creations by the Islamic aesthetic core characteristics. Although it will be our main task to exemplify that unity in the aesthetic production, we will also endeavor to clarify how that unity has been embodied creatively in regionally significant variations.

Four chapters dealing with the visual and musical arts are included here: the present one on Calligraphy; Chapter 21 on Ornamentation in the Islamic Arts; Chapter 22 on The Spatial Arts; and Chapter 23 on *Handasah al Ṣawt,* or the Art of Sound. The literary arts have already been dealt with in Chapter 19. Of course, these chapters are not inclusive of all the art products created under the influence of the Islamic ideology; but they either deal with or lay down principles for the total realm of aesthetic creativity.

HISTORY AND DEVELOPMENT

As has been noted in Chapter 8, Qur'ānic influence made of calligraphy the most important art form of

Map 61. Diffusion of Islamic Art, 7th–20th centuries

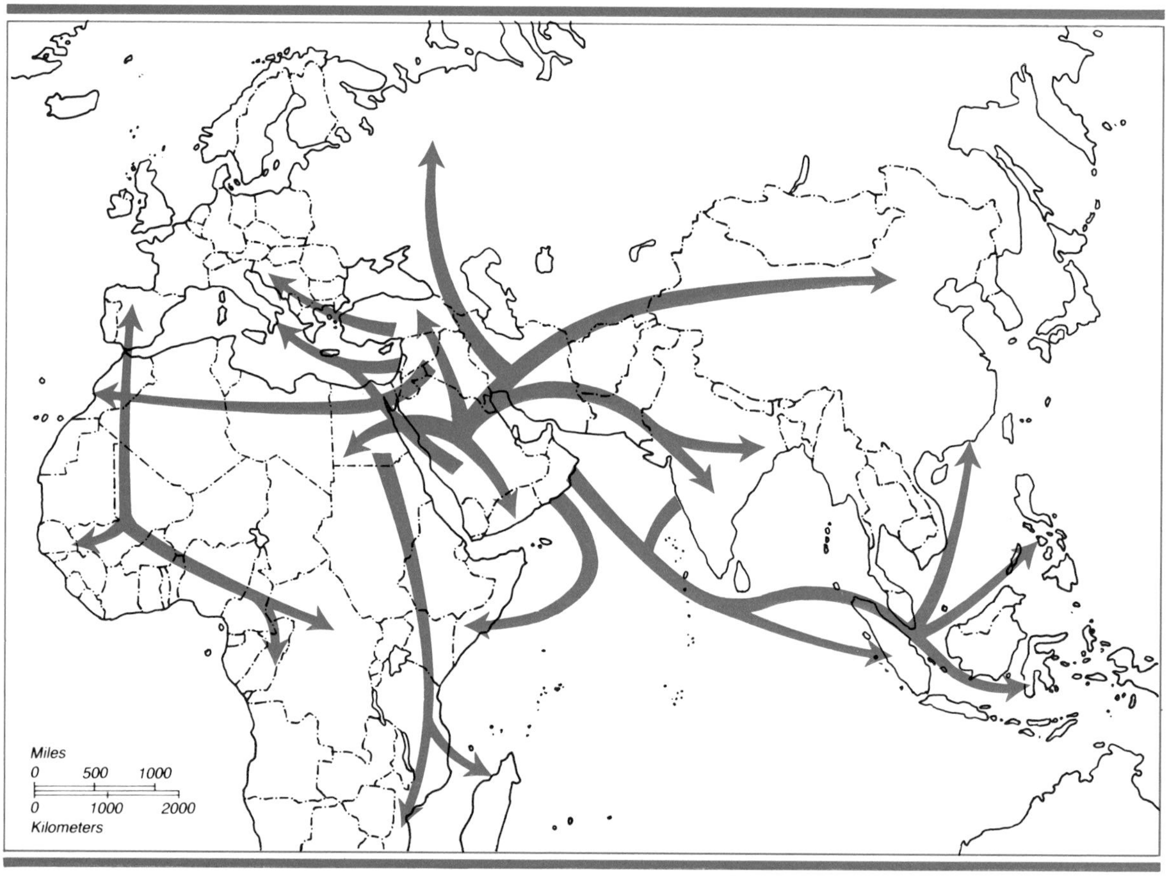

Avenues for the diffusion of Islamic artistic features (7th–20th c.)
Including: Language and literary forms
Visual motifs and structures
Architectural forms and decoration
Vocal styles and forms
Musical instruments

TABLE 20.1. IMPORTANT MUSLIM CALLIGRAPHERS

Zayd ibn Thābit, secretary of the Prophet Muḥammad.

'Alī ibn Abū Ṭālib (d. 661), fourth Rāshidūn Caliph, who was known for his beautiful calligraphy.

Abū al Aswad al Du'alī (d. 688), believed to have been the inventor of the system of large colored dots used in the early Islamic period as vowel markings.

Quṭbah al Muḥarrir, early Umawī calligrapher who is credited with inventing four major scripts, *ṭūmār, jalīl, niṣf,* and *thuluth.*

Khālid ibn al Hayyāj, official calligrapher of the Umawī Caliph al Walīd ibn 'Abd al Malik (705–715). He copied many large Qur'āns in *ṭūmār* and *jalīl* scripts.

Khalīl ibn Aḥmad (d. 786), developer of the diacritical markings.

Al Ḍaḥḥāk ibn 'Ajlān (8th c.), Syrian calligrapher of note in early 'Abbāsī period.

Isḥaq ibn Ḥammād (8th c.), Syrian, master of *thuluth* script.

Ibrahīm al Sijzī (d. 815), Syrian, brother of Yūsuf, and an accomplished calligrapher.

Yūsuf al Sijzī (d. 825), Syrian, pupil of Isḥaq ibn Ḥammād; a master of *thuluth* script and refiner of *jalīl* script.

Khwaja Tāj al Salmānī (9th c.), Iṣfahān, credited with developing the *ta'līq* script.

Al Aḥwal al Muḥarrir (9th c.), pupil of Ibrahīm al Sijzī, who derived a number of cursive scripts and invented the *ghubār* script.

'Alī Ibn 'Ubaydah al Rayḥānī (d. 834), inventor of the *rayḥānī* script.

Abū 'Alī Muḥammad Ibn Muqlah (d. 939–940), pupil of Al Aḥwal al Muḥarrir. He was a master of the cursive scripts popular at his time—the *Sittah*—and he developed a new method of perfecting and standardizing the writing of Arabic letters. The method was known as *al Khaṭṭ al Manṣūb.*

Abū al Ḥasan 'Alī ibn Hilāl, known as Ibn al Bawwāb (d. 1022), who further perfected the *Sittah.* He copied the complete Qur'ān 64 times.

Aḥmad ibn Muḥammad (Ibn al Khāzin) (d. 1124), second-generation pupil of Ibn al Bawwāb and master of the *tawqī'* and *riqā'* scripts.

Yāqūt al Musta'ṣimī (d. 1298), a native of Abyssinia who was a slave of the 'Abbāsī caliph al Musta'ṣim. He perfected earlier scripts and developed new ones, trained many subsequent calligraphers, and introduced a different cutting of the reed pen.

Mīr 'Alī Sulṭān al Tabrīzī (d. 1416), credited with inventing the *nasta'līq* script and trainer of many outstanding calligraphers.

Ibrahīm Munīf (15th c.), developer of the *dīwānī* script in Turkey.

Ḥamdullah al Amasī (d. 1520), considered to be the greatest calligrapher of the Ottoman period and refiner of the *dīwānī* script.

Isma'īl ibn-'Abdullah, known as Ibn al Zamakjalī (d. 1386), famous exponent of the *ghubār* script.

Qāsim Ghubārī (d. 1624), famous exponent of the *ghubār* script.

Ḥāfiẓ 'Uthmān (d. 1698), Turkey, who developed the *dīwānī jalī* script.

Shafī' of Herat, credited with inventing the derivative style *shikastah.*

Darwish 'Abd al Majīd Ṭāliqānī, the most important master of the *shikastah* script.

Islamic culture. Its effect and importance are found in every area of the Muslim world, in every century of Islamic history, in every branch of aesthetic production or media, and in every type of art object imaginable. Of all the categories of Islamic art, calligraphy is the most prevalent, the most significant, the most widely appreciated, and the most revered by Muslims.

By the early seventh century C.E., little development of writing had taken place among the peoples of the Arabian Peninsula. Rudimentary scripts existed, as is evidenced by archeological findings (inscriptions on stones, pillars, and so on) in the Peninsula. In addition, certain paleographic remains (writings on such perishable materials as parchment and papyrus) give proof that the Arabs of the time possessed a knowledge of the art of writing. It was not, however, a skill widely practiced by the contemporaries of Muḥammad. Though some of his companions and relatives were able to read and write, the Prophet himself never learned these skills. Poetry and prose, in large part, were committed to memory and recited in exact or improvised forms by their creators or other local bards. Long practice in the skill of memorizing had resulted in a highly developed capacity for verbal retention among the members of Arab society. Poetry was the Arabs' primary aesthetic interest, and seasonal fairs in Makkah and other centers provided occasion for competitions between the poets of the region. This vying for poetic-verbal supremacy generated in the citizenry an interest more passionate and more widespread than that aroused by the soccer or football matches of modern times in Western society. It is no wonder, therefore, that it was a literary masterpiece — the Qur'ān — that was to ignite the desert Arabs and their Semitic neighbors in the Mesopotamian region with religious zeal.

The revelations to Muḥammad which were to be compiled as the Holy Qur'ān were immediately committed to memory by the Prophet and his companions. In addition, those among the Prophet's associates who were able to write transcribed the *suwar* (chapters) on bits of clay, stone, bones, papyrus, or any other material that could be found.[2] Some of the Qur'ānic fragments were stored in the mosque of the Prophet, some in his home, and some in the homes of friends. With the death of the Prophet in 10/632, and the death in the subsequent battles of many of his followers who had memorized the entire Qur'ān, the community felt a strong need to record the revelation in more permanent form. At the urging of ʿUmar ibn al Khaṭṭāb, Abū Bakr, the first caliph, ordered the Prophet's secretary, Zayd ibn Thābit, to collect and write down all its passages in the order indicated by the Prophet.

Later, as the religion spread to ever wider horizons, a concern developed that the revelation would be lost or distorted unless a standard text could be sent to each politico-religious center of the Islamic state. As the message of the Qur'ān was appropriated by the new converts, many of whom were not Arabic-speaking, it was imperative that a single edition be made available for the teaching and propagation of the faith. The copy of Zayd ibn Thābit and all the Qur'ānic excerpts and fragments were again collected and checked in 31/651 on the orders of the caliph ʿUthmān, and a number of exact copies of the full text were produced (Chapter 5).

This process of preservation and instruction of new converts also brought new demands for improvement of the script and refinement of its rendering. The letters of the Arabic alphabet had until the early seventh century C.E. been executed separately, as is still common in Hebrew and certain other Semitic scripts. Gradually rules were established for linking many of the Arabic letters. Pointing was added to distinguish between those letters that were rendered by a single shape (for example, ب, ت, ث, ج, ح, خ, د, ذ, etcetera).[3] Short-vowel markings above and below the letters (the *fatḥah* for short "a" sound, *ḍammah* for short "u," *kasrah* for short "i") were developed to complement the consonants and long vowels.[4] Precise methods for indicating the diphthongs, the *hamzah* (glottal stop), the *maddah* (vowel prolongation), *shaddah* (double consonent), and *sukūn* (vowelless consonant) were also subsequently added.

The interest in writing grew commensurately with the newly awakened interest in the Qur'ānic text as guide to all thought and activity, and the desire to preserve it and render it accurately. As the orthographic improvements of written Arabic were being made, a number of scripts or styles of writing were also being developed. One of the early scripts, thought to have been developed in Iraq by the second half of the eighth century C.E., was angular in form. Its name, *Kūfī*, linked its origin to the new Islamic city of Kūfah and its popularity in the region around Baṣrah and Kūfah. It is thought to have developed from Aramaic and Syriac predecessors. Other styles of a more rounded and cursive quality were also in use for official and personal writings from the earliest decades.[5] These rounded scripts developed from the earlier neo-Sinaitic and Nabataean writing. Varieties of rounded scripts were especially popular in and around Makkah and Madīnah in the first centuries of the Islamic period. They were not, however, commonly used for Qur'ānic manuscripts in those times. For several centuries *Kūfī* was the preeminent script for copying the Qur'ān as well as for artistic inclusion on textiles, ceramics, coins, utensils, epitaphs, and architectural monuments.

In early copies of the Qur'ān, the horizontal lines of *Kūfī* script were often elongated to produce a squat and compact script (Illus. 20.1). This variety is most often designated as "Early Kūfī." In the late tenth century C.E., vertical lines were elongated in a new style developed by the peoples of Persia (Illus. 20.2). This form is commonly known as "Eastern Kūfī," because examples of it are most prevalent in copies of the Qur'ān made in the East. It was also called "Bent Kūfī" because of the inclination to the left of its short vertical strokes. Elaborate flourishes of its letters were often included below the lines of writing. On the whole, it was a much more delicate script than the other forms of *Kūfī* of the time.

After the initial problems of developing a complete and accurate writing system had been solved, the early Muslims set for themselves the task of beautifying their scripts. In addition to the variations of style produced by the horizontally or vertically elongated *Kūfī* scripts, Muslim calligraphers developed new variants of the basically angular form. The three most widely known variants of *Kūfī* script all resulted from an elongation of the letters themselves into various noncalligraphic motifs. One of these styles, in which the verticals of the script are extended into leaf and flower shapes, is known as "floriated Kūfī" (Illus. 20.3). A second, in which the verticals form decorative plaitings, is called "interlaced" or "plaited Kūfī"

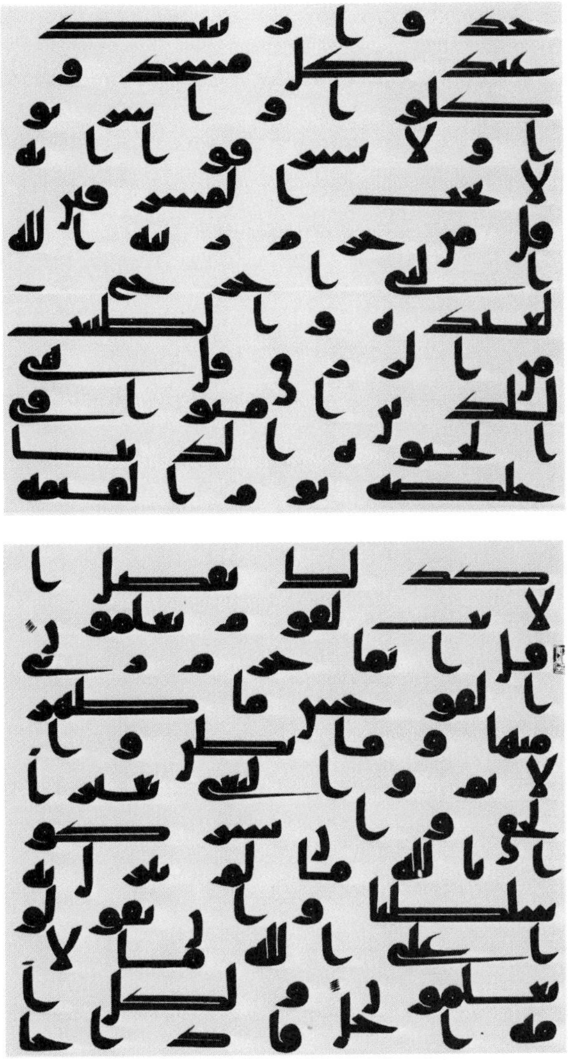

Illustration 20.1

Two folios (nos. 341 and 342) from the oldest Qur'ān manuscript known to exist and claimed to be one of the five copies canonized by Caliph 'Uthmān in the year 28/648. The manuscript is preserved in Bukhārā, U.S.S.R. A photographed edition of the entire manuscript was published in 1980 by Muḥammad Ḥamīdullah (Philadelphia: 'Ā'ishah Begum, Hyderabad House). The passage is from Qur'ān 7:31–34. [Courtesy 'Ā'ishah Begum, Hyderabad House, Philadelphia.]

(Illus. 20.4). A third style has been designated as "animated Kūfī," for the letters end in stylized animal or human figures. The last of these styles was used chiefly in Iran, where examples of stylized figural art (for example, the miniature paintings) were also more prominent than in other regions of the Muslim world.

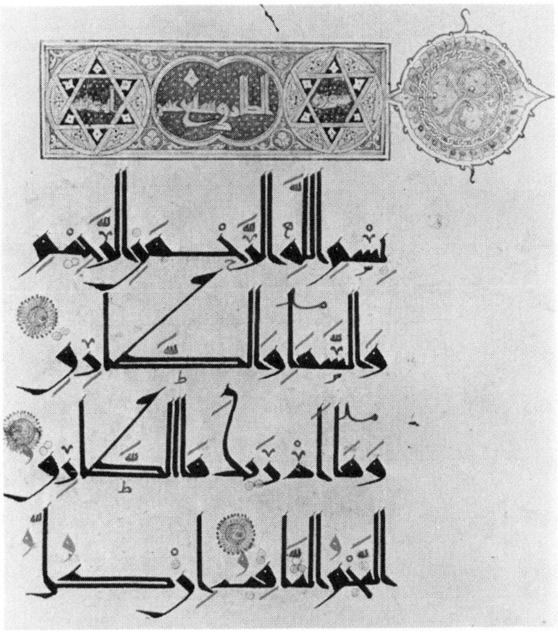

Illustration 20.2

Qur'ān 86:1–3, 4a, in Eastern Kūfī script, fifth/eleventh century. Collection of H. H. Prince Sadruddin Aga Kahn, Geneva, Switzerland.

Many other styles evolved from the basic angular and rounded scripts. Some derivatives included features from both categories. Each new script was given a special name and precise rules for its execution. In many cases, however, variant styles were little more than individual or regional variations of a general type. By the late ninth century C.E., more than twenty cursive styles were commonly used in addition to the angular scripts.

In the tenth century, the famous calligrapher and vizier Ibn Muqlah (d. 329/940) brought reform and systematization to the writing of the proliferating variants of cursive Arabic calligraphy. He devised rules of proportion for all the letters based on the rhombic dot (◆). According to his rules, the *alif* was to be a vertical equivalent in length to seven of these dots. Other letters were similarly given precise measurements for their vertical, horizontal, and curved strokes. In this manner Ibn Muqlah standardized each of the major cursive styles known at the time.

From the eleventh century, though *Kūfī* script continued in use for ornamental bands for manuscript, architectural, and small objects decoration, a more cursive and rounded script called *Naskhī* came into

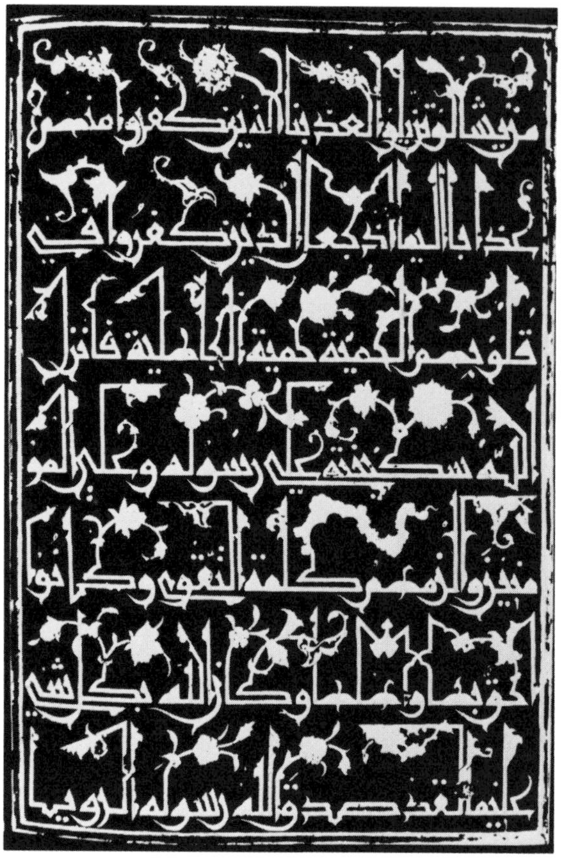

Illustration 20.3

Qur'ān 48:25b–27a in floridated Kūfī. [Courtesy Ministry of Culture and Tourism, Government of Turkey.]

Illustration 20.4

Floriated and plaited Kūfī script, carved stone at the Abdullah Anṣārī Shrine, Gazur Gah, Afghanistan, 1428–1429. [Photo by L. al Fārūqī.]

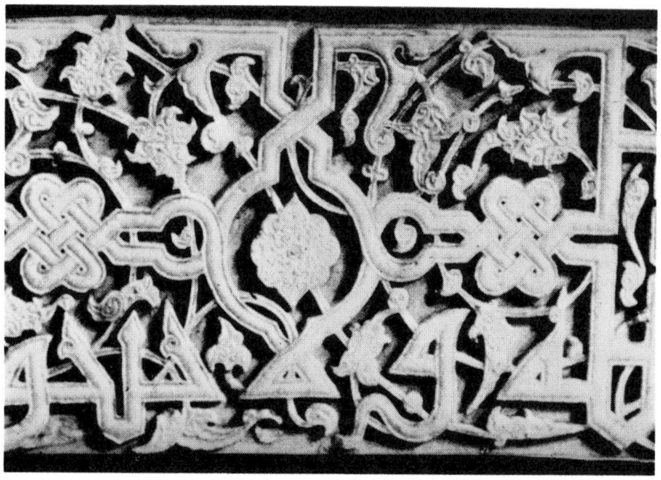

prominent use (Illus. 20.5).[6] Distinguished by its clarity, simplicity, and legibility, it is thought to have been developed by Ibn Muqlah, who introduced it at the court in Baghdād. Though it may have been used much earlier, Ibn Muqlah no doubt played a major role in developing and popularizing this variety of the rounded scripts. Another vizier, Ibn al Bawwāb (d. 423/1032), is the second of a trio of famous Muslim calligraphers. He followed the rules set down by his predecessor, Ibn Muqlah, but produced still more graceful versions of the six best known styles of cursive script of his time. Ibn al Bawwāb is thought to have initiated use of the rounded script for Qur'ānic copies. The oldest extant Qur'ān in *Naskhī* script is one done by Ibn al Bawwāb himself. It is held today in the Chester Beatty Library of the University of Dublin, Ireland. Because of its legibility, the *Naskhī* script gradually gained favor over *Kūfī* for copying the Qur'ān. Like the *Kūfī* script, *Naskhī* spread to all regions of the Muslim world.

Illustration 20.5

Qur'ān, Sūrah "Al Fātiḥah" in Naskhī script. Thuluth script in upper and lower identification panels. [Photo by L. al Fārūqī.]

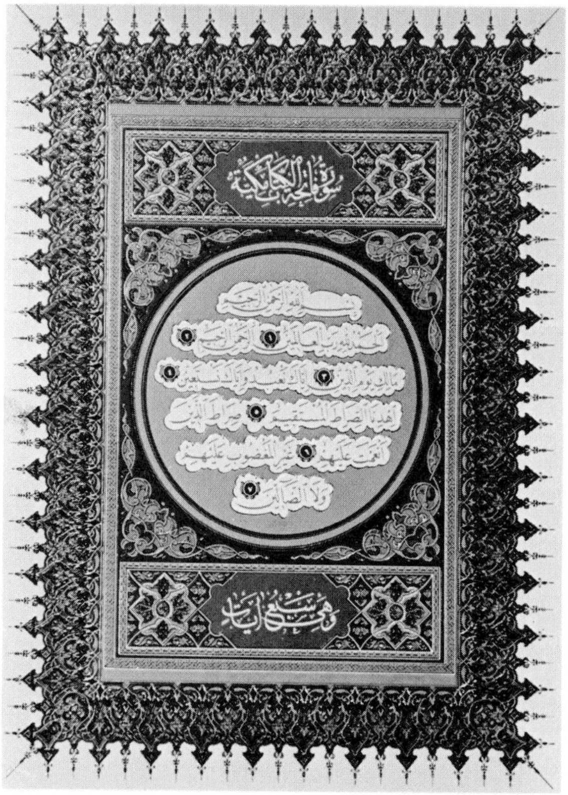

The rounded and cursive scripts were further elaborated and refined by a third celebrated calligrapher, Yāqūt ibn 'Abd Allah al Musta'ṣimī (d. 698/1298). Although he is sometimes said to have originated the *Sittah,* "the six" popular forms of cursive script of his time, they were probably known much earlier. He did, however, refine them further by inventing a new system for trimming the reed pen and preparing its nib for writing.

While the major traditions of the rounded Arabic scripts had been established, perfected, and refined by the time of Yāqūt al Musta'ṣimī, later generations were to make use of these materials in the production of larger, more decorative, and more extravagant copies of the Qur'ān, as well as of books of poetry and prose. The elegance in writing and its decoration found in copies of the Qur'ān executed in the following centuries is unexcelled. Each ruler, each dynasty, each wealthy patron competed in commissioning or writing the most beautiful Qur'ān of the day. Calligraphers were a prized addition to any court, and every learned person strove to attain the greatest possible mastery of the art. The interest in calligraphy spread from the execution of Qur'āns to its use in the decoration of objects made of metal, glass, ivory, textiles, wood, stone, stucco, and ceramics (Illus. 20.6). Every possible material and object was ornamented with

Illustration 20.6

Luster plate from Persia, thirteenth century, with inscriptions in Naskhī script. [Courtesy University Museum, University of Pennsylvania.]

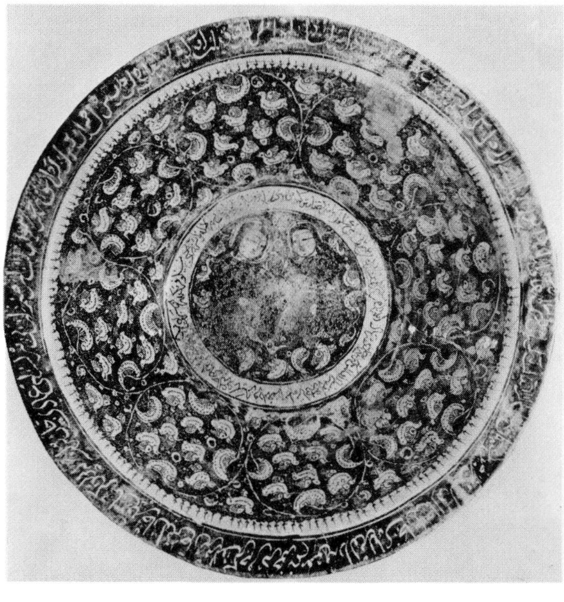

Illustration 20.7

Calligraphy panels, Madrasah al 'Aṭṭārīn, Fās, Morocco, 1323–1325. [Photo by L. al Fārūqī.]

bands (Illus. 20.7), medallions, motifs, or overall designs based on the art of writing.

Each of the various angular and rounded scripts evidenced a particular style and carried a distinguishing name (*Thuluth, Naskhī, Muḥaqqaq, Riqā'ī, Rayḥānī, Tawqī',* etcetera). Features of style that produced a different script included the way in which the hooked heads of verticals were made, the form of letter endings, the compactness of the letters, the degree of slant of the letters, the amount of horizontal or vertical elongation, the degree of rounding of corners, and so on. One of the most important rounded scripts to be developed, used in all regions of the Muslim world, is that known as *Thuluth* (Illus. 20.8). *Thuluth* is a decorative script used for architectural and small object decoration, as well as for decorative lines or titles and colophons for Qur'ānic and other manuscripts (Illus. 20.9–20.11). It is a very old script, having been popularized in the early decades of the 'Abbāsī period, that is, in the late eighth century C.E. It was regarded as one of the six major scripts (the *Sittah*). In use in various forms until the present day, *Thuluth* evidences a pronounced plasticity which allows letters to be extended or compressed to fit any given space or shape. Superimposed lines and elongated verticals are other common features of this script.

Though varieties of *Kūfī, Naskhī,* and *Thuluth* were used in all regions of the Muslim world (see Map 60), evidence of regionally significant scripts is also found. One of these is a script known as *Maghribī* (Illus. 20.12). Used in Moorish Spain and Western North Africa, this script was used for Qur'ān copies, other manuscripts, and small object decoration. Even in the Maghrib, it never gained prominence in the field

Illustration 20.8

Interior view, Ulu Jāmi', Bursa, Turkey. [Courtesy Embassy of Turkey, Washington, D.C.]

Illustration 20.9

Ince Minare Madrasah, Konya, Turkey, 1260–1265. [Courtesy Embassy of Turkey, Washington, D.C.]

of epigraphy, where the pan-Islamic scripts held sway. *Maghribī* script, which seems to have been flourishing around 400/1000, has been characterized as a cross between the angular qualities of *Kūfī* and the rounded forms of *Naskhī.* It has the distinguishing feature of exaggerated loop extensions below the lines of the final forms of certain letters. The system of diacritical marks used in the Maghrib did not differ greatly from that used in the Mashriq. The proportioned *(mansūb)* system of writing devised by Ibn Muqlah, however, was never widely adopted in the western regions of Islam.

Despite their conformity to certain general characteristics, four substyles of *Maghribī* script have been distinguished in history. The earliest of these is called *Qayrawānī,* after the center of its importance, the city of Qayrawān. This variant of *Maghribī* script is distinguished by very short verticals. The script called *Andulusī* or *Qurṭubī* ("of Andalusia" or "of Cordoba") has finer lines and is more compact than the other related scripts and evidences considerable elongation of horizontal and under-line strokes (Illus. 20.13). It became the most important style of Muslim Spain and from there spread to North Africa with the

Illustration 20.10

Interior of the Tomb of Sulṭān Muḥammad I, Bursa, Turkey, 1421. [Courtesy Embassy of Turkey, Washington, D.C.]

Illustration 20.11

Embroidery in black velvet used to cover the Ka'bah. [Photo by L. al Fārūqī.]

expulsion of the Muslims from the Iberian Peninsula. *Fāsī,* the third variety of *Maghribī* script, was larger, heavier, and more elaborate. In the early seventeenth century, it combined with the *Andalusī.* This amalgamation has been known simply as *Maghribī.* It became an important script in Morocco, Algeria, Tunisia, and, to a lesser extent, Libya. *Sūdānī* is a regional variety of *Maghribī* script developed and favored by the Muslim peoples of Middle Africa (Illus. 20.14). It has the common *Maghribī* script characteristics but the lines are heavier and the texture is denser. Today *Sūdānī* is the only one of the *Maghribī* styles to retain its separate name.

Three other regional scripts which achieved wide influence are attributed to Iranian innovators of the thirteenth and fourteenth centuries C.E. These are the *Ta'līq,* the *Nasta'līq,* and the *Shikastah* scripts. The latter two of these are considered variants of the parent *Ta'līq* script. Of these rounded and cursive scripts, *Ta'līq* can be recognized by a slanting form which gave rise to its name, "hanging" (Illus. 20.15). Rarely used for Qur'ānic copies, it has been primarily a script for the copying of other literary works and decorative additions to small objects. Probably originated sometime in the ninth century C.E., *Ta'līq* did not achieve widespread use until the time of the famous artist and calligrapher Mīr 'Alī of Tabrīz (late fourteenth and early fifteenth centuries C.E.).

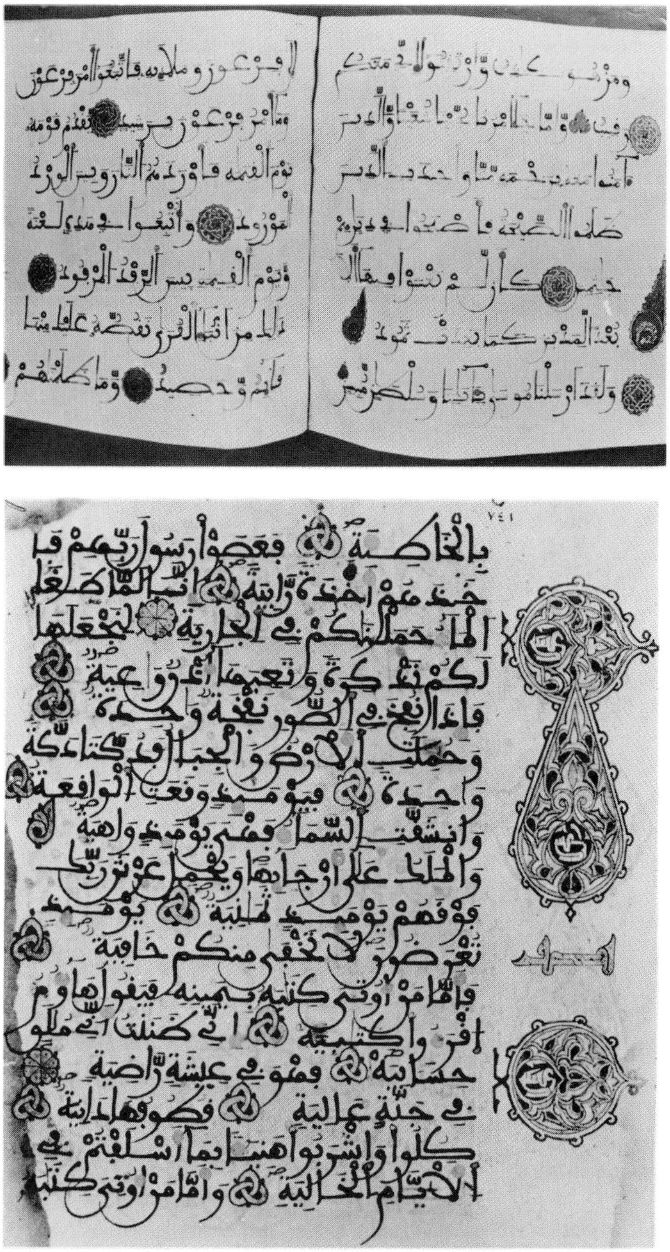

Illustration 20.12

Pages from two Qur'āns written on parchment in Maghribī script, eleventh-twelfth century.

A later elaboration of *Ta'līq* resulted in the *Nasta'līq* script. This was a lighter and more elegant system of writing. Among its distinguishing characteristics are the extravagantly elongated and flowing horizontal curves of many of its letters, the filling in of small circles, very thin and pointed letter endings, emphasis on horizontal rather than vertical move-

Area IV – Turkey
·Edirne ·Istanbūl ·Iznik ·Bursa ·Ankara ·Konya
·Amasya ·Sivas ·Divriği ·Kayseri ·Erzurum
·Bilecik ·Eyüb ·Safranbolu ·Birgi ·Üsküdar
·Nevşehir ·Manisa ·Payas ·Luleburgaz
·Adilevaz ·Karapinar ·Babaeski ·Bozüyük
·Diyārbakr ·Karaman ·Aksaray ·Niğde
·Beyşehir
Area V – Iran and Central Asia
·Shirāz ·Iṣfahān ·Natanz ·Kāshān ·Qūm ·Saveh ·Rayy ·Tehran
·Varamin ·Zawārī ·Ardistān ·Nayin ·Yazd ·Kirmān ·Damghān ·Tabrīz
·Marāghah ·Ardabīl ·Sulṭāniyyah ·Mashhad ·Turbat-i-Shaykh
·Hamadān ·Bisṭām ·Ṭūs ·Sangbast ·Qazwīn ·Bukhārā ·Khīwā ·Marw
·Samarqand ·Nakhjawān ·Ṭashqand ·Tirmidh ·Shahr-i-Sabz ·Balkh
·Ghaznah ·Herāt ·Kābul ·Bust ·Tayabad ·Gazur Gah ·Jam
Area I – The Maghrib
·Toledo ·Badajoz ·Qurṭubah ·Seville
·Granada ·Malaga ·Almeria ·Zaragoza
·Madīnah al Zahrā' ·Tinmal ·Marrākesh
·Maknās ·Fās ·Tlemcen ·Algiers ·Tūnis
·Qayrawān ·Ṣūsah ·Monastir ·Mahdiyyah
·Sfax ·Tripoli ·Ajdabiyyah ·Nedroma
·Qala'ah Bānī Hammād ·Taza
Area III – The Mashriq
·Cairo ·Al Quds ·Dimashq
·Raqqah ·Aleppo ·Baghdād ·Anjar
·Sāmarrā ·Mawṣil ·Baṣrah
·Quṣayr 'Amrah ·Ramlah
·Qaṣr al Hayr ·Mushattā
·Madīnah ·Makkah ·Sanā' ·Ibb
Area VII – East Asia
·Turfan ·Xian ·Canton ·Kuala Lumpur
·Kuala Kangsar ·Malacca ·Kota Baru
·Durian Burung ·Semarang ·Demak
·Banda Acheh ·Jakarta ·Samudra-Pasai ·Riau
·Yogjakarta ·Solo ·Marawi City ·Jolo
·Bandar Seri Bagawan ·Singapore ·Seoul
Area VI – Indian Subcontinent
·Lahore ·Thatta ·Uchch ·Multān ·Delhi ·Agra
·Fatehpur Sikri ·Ajmir ·Ahmadabād ·Bhopal ·Mandu
·Bijapur ·Banaras ·Juanpur ·Khandesh ·Champanir
·Ṭughluqabād ·Sasaram ·Jahanpana ·Shāhjahānabād
·Tribeni ·Chhota Pandua ·Hazrat Pandua ·Gaur
·Bagerhat ·Rampal ·Malda ·Dacca ·Sura ·Sherpur
·Rajmahal
Area II – Middle Africa
·Gao ·Timbuktu ·Goundam ·Larabanga ·Namou
·Chinguetti ·Bobo-Dioulasso ·Agadez ·Kano ·Sokoto
·Dakar ·Jenne ·Zaria ·Ilorin ·Kilwa ·Mogadishu
·Umm Durman ·Lamu ·Siyu ·Gedi ·Mwanza
·Mombasa ·Mnarani ·Kaole ·Ungwana ·Muhembo
·Songo Mnara ·Kizimkazi ·Pemba ·Suakin
Miles
0 500 1000
0 500 1000 1500
Kilometers

Map 62. Artistic Area of the Muslim World: Important Sites

TABLE 20.2. TIME CHART OF ISLAMIC CALLIGRAPHY

Pan-Islamic Scripts

	600 C.E. 700 800 900 1000 1100 1200 1300 1400 1500 1600 1700 1800 1900
Angular Scripts: Variants of *Kūfī*	Proto-*Kūfī*
	Early *Kūfī*
	Eastern or Bent *Kūfī*
	Floriated *Kūfī*
	Interlaced or Plaited *Kūfī*
	Animated *Kūfī*
Rounded Scripts	Proto-*Naskhī*
	Naskhī
	Ṭūmār
	Muḥaqqaq
	Thuluth
	Rayhānī
	Tawqī'
	Riqā'
	Ghubārī

Regionally Significant Scripts

Variants of *Maghribī:* Iberian Peninsula, North and Middle Africa	Qayrawānī
	Andalusī
	Fāsī
	Maghribī
	Sudānī
Variants of *Ta'līq:* Turkey, Iran and Central Asia, North India	*Ta'līq*
	Nasta'līq
	Dīwānī
	Shikastah
	Dīwānī Jālī
Iran and Central Asia	Ta'līq
	Nasta'līq
	Dīwānī
	Shikastah
	Dīwānī Jalī
The Far East	*Ṣīnī* (China)
	Jāwī (Malay Basin)

ments, and great contrast in width of lines (Illus. 20.16). In the sixteenth century, *Nasta'līq* practically replaced *Naskhī* as a script for copying Persian literary works. The name, *Nasta'līq,* is thought to be a contraction of ***naskh*** and *ta'līq*. Since the development of the script in the late fifteenth century C.E., it has been the national script of Persia (Illus. 20.17). *Nasta'līq* has been used primarily for secular literary

Illustration 20.13

Andalusī script from a twentieth-century work on art and artists. [Photo by L. al Fārūqī.]

works or calligraphy pages *(muraqqa')* created for album collections. It has almost never been used as a Qur'ānic script, though after about 900/1500 it became popular in Iran and Central Asia for epitaphs and inscriptions on architectural monuments. The style spread rapidly in those eastern regions where the Persian language and Iranian-Islamic influence was strong. Little or no influence of the Persian scripts can be discerned beyond these areas.

The *Shikastah* ("broken form") script was developed in Herat about the middle of the eleventh/seventeenth century. It is a complicated and difficult to read variation of *Ta'līq*.[7] This extremely dense script is written with tiny letters having very low and inclined verticals. It has no vowel markings. Lines are placed at various angles on the page. *Shikastah* has been used primarily for personal, business, or official correspondence in Persian and Urdu (Illus. 20.18).

One other script that had wide significance and usage in the Muslim world is the *Dīwānī* script, which was popularized by the scribes of the Ottoman sultanate in the late ninth/fifteenth century (Illus. 20.19). It is also considered to be a variant of *Ta'līq,* although the relation to the earlier Persian script is not as clear

Illustration 20.14

Pages from a manuscript on theology in Sūdānī script. [Courtesy 'Uthmān Ḥasan Aḥmad, Cultural Counselor, Embassy of the Sudan, Washington, D.C.]

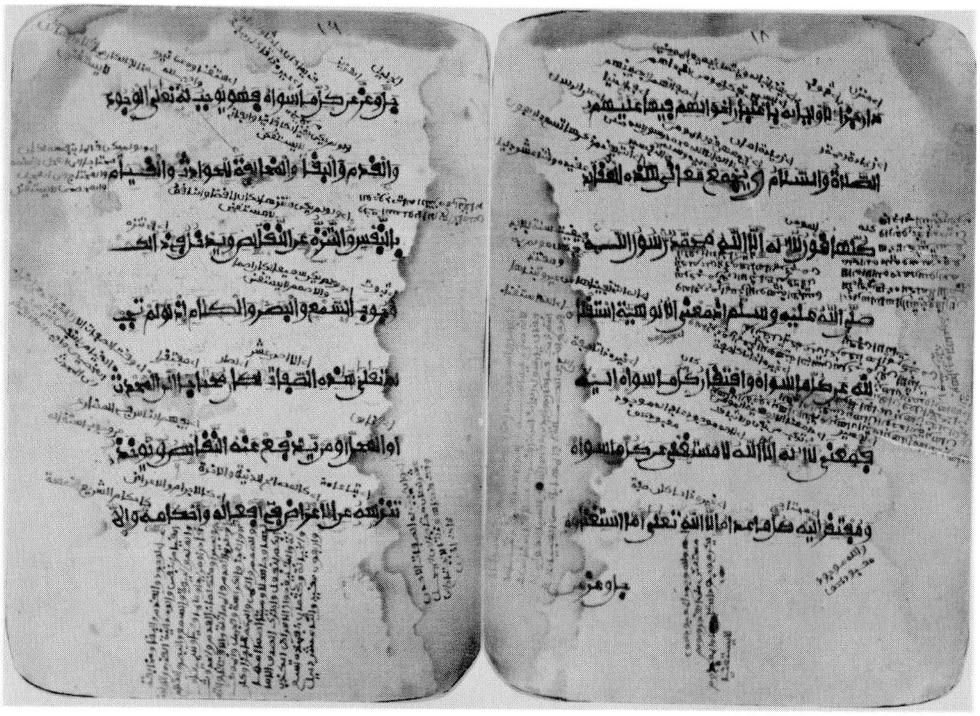

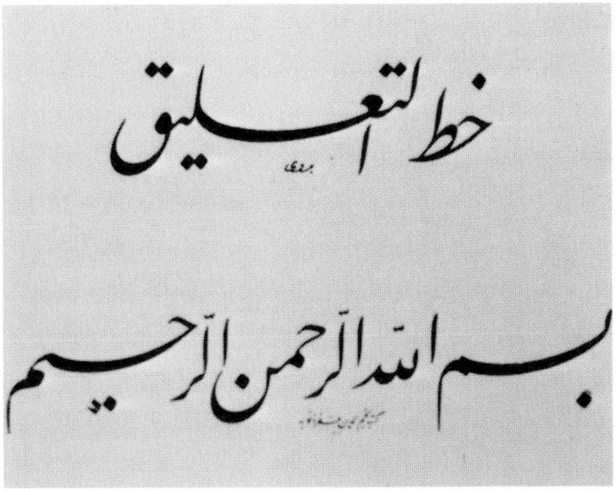

Illustration 20.15

Basmalah in Ta'līq script. [Photo by L. al Fārūqī.]

Illustration 20.16

Nasta'līq script, sixteenth century, Iran, with elaborate borders including human figures. [Courtesy Islamic Information Bureau, Tehran, Iran.]

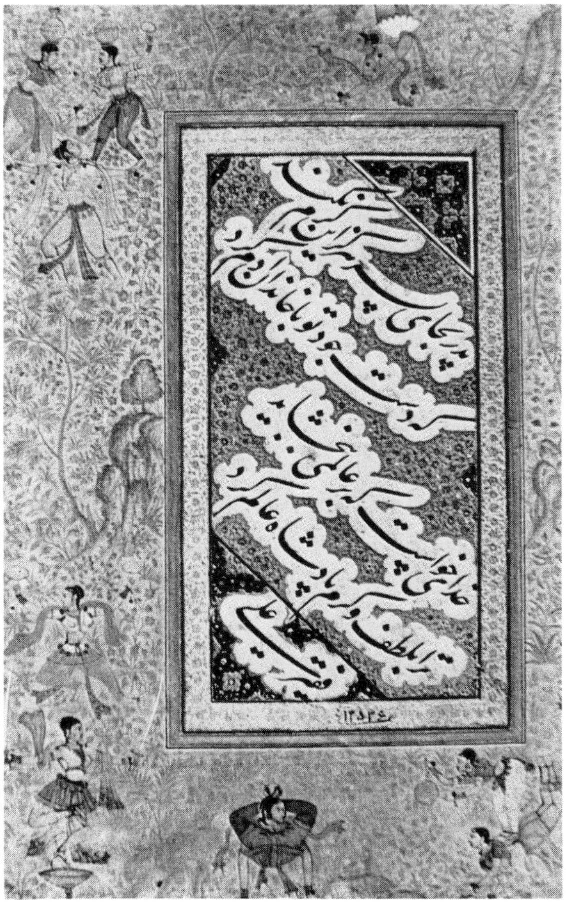

Illustration 20.17

Floriated Nasta'līq script, nineteenth century, Iran, Mīr 'Ali Shirāzī. [Courtesy Islamic Information Bureau, Tehran, Iran.]

Illustration 20.18

Shikastah script in cloud banks, eighteenth century, Iran. [Courtesy Islamic Information Bureau, Tehran, Iran.]

Illustration 20.19

(1) Dīwānī script; (2) an elaborated script known as Dīwānī Jalī. [Photo by L. al Fārūqī.]

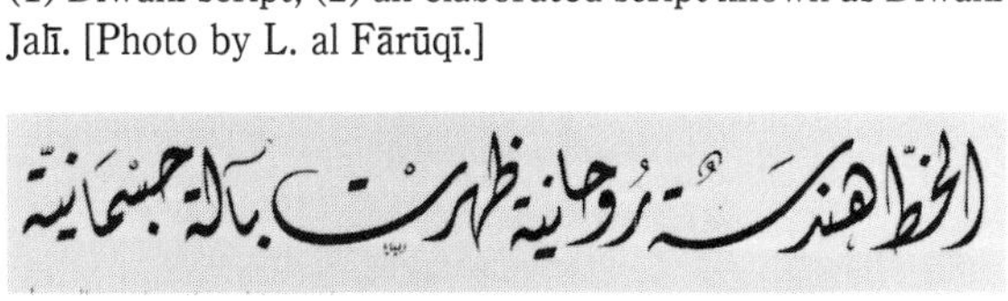

Illustration 20.20

Tughrā'. "Muḥammad Sayyid al Kawnayn wal Thaqalayn" (Muḥammad, Master of the Two Worlds [earth and paradise]). Museum of the Sulaymāniyyah, Isṭanbūl. [Courtesy Ministry of Culture and Tourism, Government of Turkey.]

Illustration 20.21

Calligraphy in Dīwānī Jalī. Calligrapher: Hāshim Muḥammad al Baghdādī, A.H. 1377. [Photo by L. al Fārūqī.]

as with *Nasta'līq* and *Shikastah.*[8] *Dīwānī* has been used particularly for official documents, proclamations, and the official signature seals (sing. *ṭughrā'*) which were created for each of the Ottoman sultans (Illus. 20.20). *Dīwānī* never enjoyed popularity for execution of Qur'ān copies or for epigraphic inscriptions. It is a rounded script which can be recognized by its extravagantly flowing movements and its gradual elevation and extension of letters at the ends of lines (Illus. 20.21). It features a marked tendency to superpositioning and unconventional joining of letters. Vowel marks are usually not included.

CONTEMPORARY CALLIGRAPHY IN THE MUSLIM WORLD

As the rise of Islamic awareness is felt among contemporary Muslim peoples and a new sense of ethnic, national, and religious identity moves the people of the Third World, Muslim calligraphers are again exploring and experimenting with their art. An increased interest in calligraphy is evident today among Muslim patrons as well as artists in all parts of the Muslim world. Although certain features of these new examples of calligraphy differ from region to region, it is not possible to discern distinct regional or national styles in the new efforts to practice an old Islamic art. This does not mean that contemporary efforts by calligraphers reveal no variety. Just the opposite is the case! But that variety is based more on variant adaptations of influences from the non-Islamic world than on national or regional particularisms. If one were to make an attempt to categorize the trends in the contemporary calligraphy of the Muslim world, most examples of that art would fit into one of the following categories: (1) "Traditional"; (2) "Figural"; (3) "Expressionist"; (4) "Symbolic"; and (5) "Pure Abstractionist."

Traditional Calligraphy

Examples of "Traditional" calligraphy are being produced by contemporary Muslim calligraphers in many of the styles and scripts known to earlier generations. We chose the term Traditional for the examples of this category because it signifies a conformance to long-established customs as well as to the more standard elements in the Islamic tradition. Traditional, therefore, implies not only correspondence with the past but also general conformance to the mainstream, or the dominant aspects, of the total calligraphic output of the Muslims. The other types of contemporary calligraphy show a relationship to less traditional aspects of the heritage, and to influences borrowed from alien traditions.

The contemporary Traditional calligraphers are usually trained in an apprentice system by one of the leading calligraphers of their locality. Some Muslim nations have had schools for the training of calligraphers, but these institutions have fallen on hard times in recent decades as the effects of colonialism, Westernization, and cultural/economic depression have made themselves felt. The *kuttāb* religious schools, which used to train Muslim children, contributed significantly to the survival of the interest in and capability for beautiful Arabic penmanship in all parts of the Muslim world. These strongholds of the calligraphic tradition have been severely weakened, however, by the presence of colonialist and missionary educational institutions. Even many of the schools of the Muslim nations which are operated by natives to the area have been so anxious to imitate their foreign competitors that the cultivation and refinement of Arabic calligraphy has fallen a hapless victim. Despite these adverse conditions, exponents of Traditional calligraphy still survive. Probably the most important reason for this persistence of the tradition is the unique compatability of this art with the aesthetic demands of the Muslim peoples. As an art form, it is particularly suitable for evidencing the basic characteristics described in Chapter 8 that make up the Islamic infinite pattern or arabesque.

The Traditional calligraphers of this century remain true to the demand for abstract quality through their choice of an abstract subject matter for their art. They emphasize the discursive message and the beautiful arrangement of the letters rather than the representation of figures from nature. Stylized leaf or flower motifs and geometric patterns are found in combination with the calligraphic figures, but the overall effect in the contemporary works of the Traditional calligraphers is abstract (Illus. 20.22).

Illustrations 20.23 and 20.24 provide examples of the second core characteristic of the Islamic arts as exemplified in the designs of the Traditional calligraphers: their modular quality. In Illustration 20.23 this is achieved by the two-segment *muthannā* ("doubled") treatment of the Arabic word *Allah.*[9] Such symmetrical organization of a word, phrase, or sentence in a right/left or up/down mirror arrangement has been practiced in Islamic calligraphy from at least the seventh/thirteenth century and perhaps even earlier.

Another example of modular quality (Illus. 20.24) uses a longer unit and combines it with not one but

Illustration 20.22

Calligraphy design in Tuluth script. Calligrapher: ʻAbd al Ghanī al Baghdādī, A.H. 1384. The passage, "We have granted you a manifest victory" (Qur'ān 48:1), is rendered in "mirrored" image and plaiting. [Photo by L. al Fārūqī.]

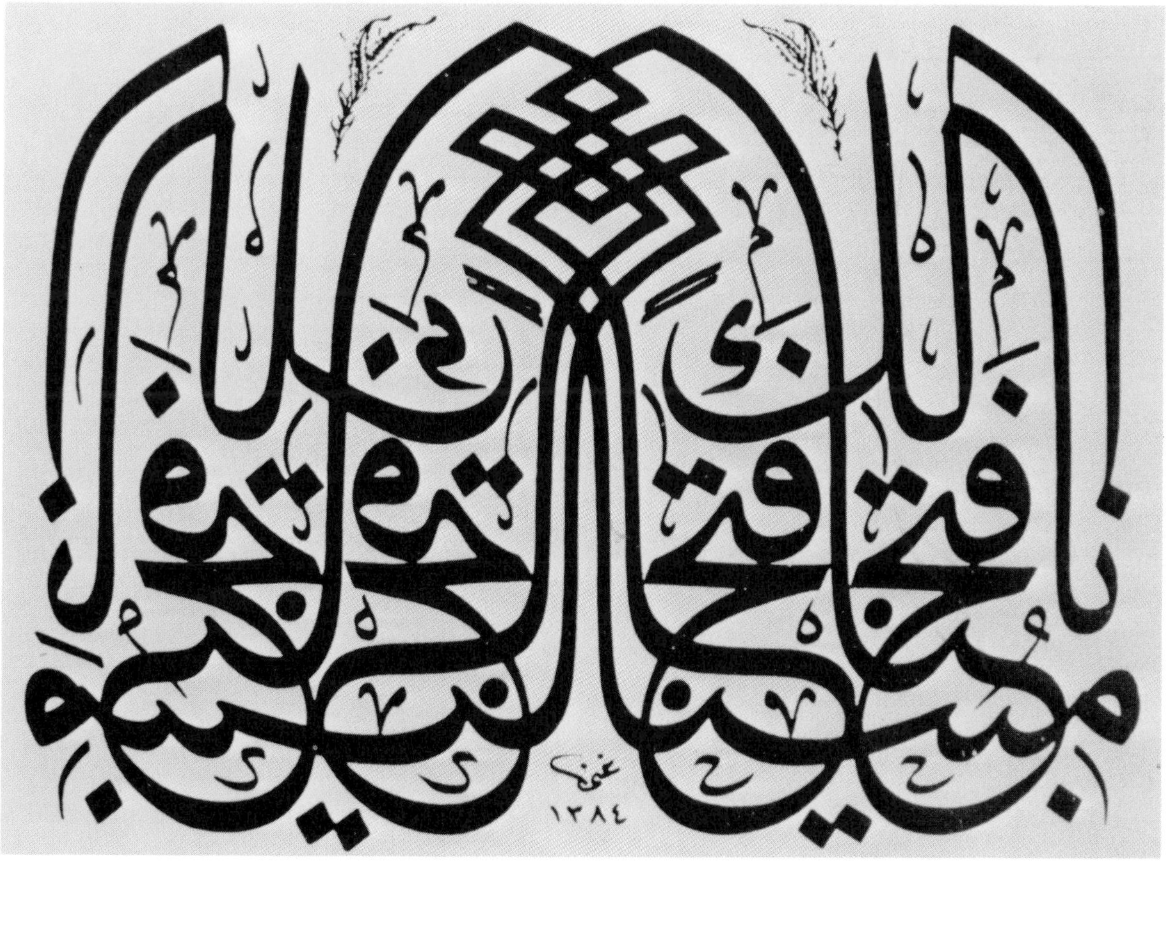

Illustration 20.23

"Traditional" contemporary calligraphy by Emin Berin, Iṣtanbūl, Turkey. "Allah" and its mirrored *(muthannā)* image. [Photo by L. al Fārūqī.]

three additional repetitions which complete a circular design. Here not only modular quality but also the third and fourth core characteristics — successive combination and repetition — are clearly represented.

Illustration 20.24

Contemporary calligraphy design by Emin Berin, Turkey. "We have granted you a manifest victory" (Qur'ān 48:1).

Any of these examples must be experienced with the successive investigation of the constituent modules. The movement and dynamism that this entails is the fifth of the core characteristics of any work of Islamic art. Each discursive-aesthetic segment is comprehended as an entity, after which the eye and the mind of the spectator move to the next unit within the pattern. The experience of the work of Traditional calligraphic art can thus be both discursively and aesthetically viewed as a dynamic continuum.

The sixth core characteristic, intricate detail, is also found in the Traditional calligraphy of contemporary Muslim artists. In Illustration 20.25 the artist, 'Ādil al Ṣaghīr, has produced a complicated calligraphy design in acrylic. Other contemporary artists who represent this Traditional category are Muḥammad Sa'īd al Saggar, Muḥammad 'Alī Shākir, and 'Iṣām al Sa'īd.

Figural Calligraphy

The second category of contemporary calligraphy could be designated as "Figural" since it combines figural motifs with the calligraphic elements in various ways. Some are combinations of addition, that is, the calligraphic and figural motifs are merely juxtaposed within the work of art. This is the essence of the Figural quality found in the calligraphy example of Illustration 20.26. This manner of combination has been used in the past (Illus. 20.27), but the figural elements were generally restricted to leaf or flower motifs that were stylized or denaturalized to better suit the abstract quality of Islamic art. Zoomorphic

Illustration 20.25

Calligraphy design by 'Adil al Saghīr. [Courtesy *Arts and the Islamic World.*]

Illustration 20.26

Calligraphy, "Allah," with "addition" of leaves in border. [Photo by L. al Fārūqī.]

Illustration 20.27

The Green Tomb, calligraphy of Miḥrāb niche, fifteenth century, Bursa, Turkey. [Photo by L. al Fārūqī.]

Illustration 20.28

Thuluth calligraphy molded in pear shape, reading: "Amān Marwat, O Master of the First and Last Ones." [Photo by L. al Fārūqī.]

and human figures were not included in Qur'ānic copies, in the decoration of mosques, *madrasahs,* or their furnishings, though they are found on vessels and utensils for domestic use.

A second form of combination of figural motifs with calligraphy in the art of the Muslims of both the past and the present in that which could be designated as molded (Illus. 20.28). In such designs the letters are elongated and shortened, spread out and squeezed, or elaborated with extensions, swirls, loops, or additional marks and fillers to make them conform to the shape of a noncalligraphic, geometric, vegetal, zoomorphic, or human figure. The *basmalah* ("in the name of Allah, the Merciful, the Compassionate"), which opens every written or recited Qur'ānic passage as well as any book or shorter work written by a Muslim, is a favorite motto for such calligraphy designs. Sayyid Naqīb al 'Aṭṭās is one of the many con-

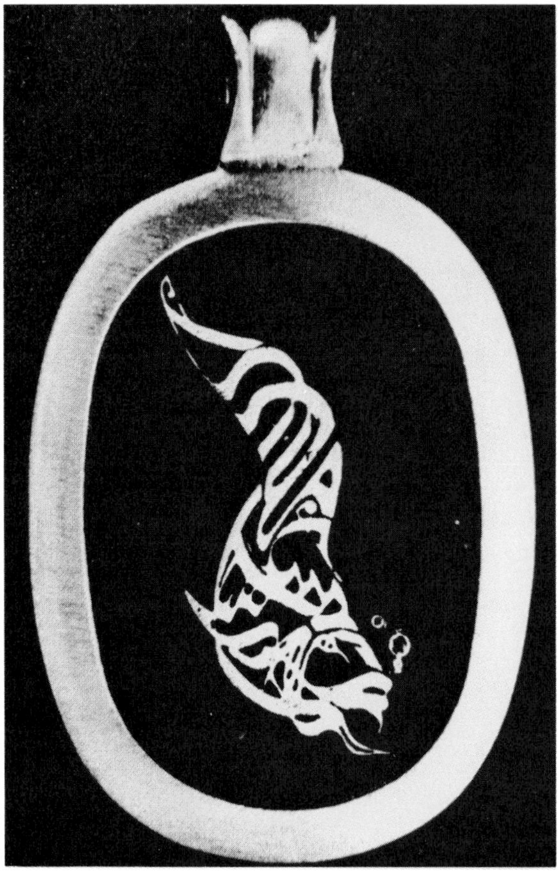

Illustration 20.29

Basmalah in shape of a fish, calligraphy design of Sayyid Naquib al ʿAṭṭas. [Photo by L. al Fārūqī.]

Illustration 20.30

Molded calligraphy by Pakistani artist Ṣādiqayn. The passage is from Qur'ān 55.

temporary Muslims who has created molded examples of Figural calligraphy (Illus. 20.29). In the works of Ṣādiqayn, a well-known Pakistani calligrapher, molding of the letters to achieve a Figural depiction is a prominent technique (Illus. 20.30).

Contemporary Islamic calligraphy features a third form of combination with figural motifs which could be designated as a design of integration (Illus. 20.31). In these, the letters themselves are extended into plant, animal, or human motifs. As the word implies, integration involves the impossibility of separating the constituent elements of design — the calligraphic and the figural. The letters of these examples have become constitutive of the figural element. The removal of either would destroy the design.

Expressionist Calligraphy

"Expressionist" calligraphy is a third type of contemporary calligraphic art of the Muslim world. This style, like other recent calligraphy creations, is related to comparable Western aesthetic movements. They are the result of the acculturation of Muslim art and artists with Western art in recent times. Although Expressionist calligraphers use the "vocabulary" of the Islamic artistic heritage, they are far removed from exemplifying its "grammar."[10]

The term Expressionist has been used to categorize that calligraphy in which emotion or emotive elements, usually expressed through violent distortion and exaggeration, are prominent (Illus. 20.32). As a modern movement in the Western world of the late nineteenth and twentieth centuries, it is exemplified by the works of artists who sought to convey to the viewer their own subjective emotions. They also wished to depict a personal, visual, and emotional response to objects, persons, or events represented. They certainly did not aim at realistic portrayal.[11] Such an art movement embodies the representational and the individualistic. It features a striking lack of rapport with — even a sharp antagonism to — the abstract and universal qualities of Islamic art. The Muslim artist has sought to draw the spectator away from the personal and the creaturely toward a concentration on transcendence. Expressionist art, in contrast, emphasizes human emotion, mood portrayal, subjective feelings, and individualistic concerns. It presents a "dive" into nature, and often into its least uplifting and ideal aspects, rather than an elevation to contemplation of a higher order of existence.

Despite the sharply alien premises of Expressionist art, a number of contemporary Muslim calligraphers have tried to adapt these aesthetic characteris-

Illustration 20.31

Calligraphy design by Ṣādiqayn, Qur'ān 55:66–67. [Photo by L. al Fārūqī.]

tics to Islamic calligraphy. They seem to be so imbibed with an alien tradition, rather than with the basic premises of the Islamic tradition and ideology, that they do not realize the incongruity of their efforts to produce calligraphy in this strange and un-Islamic way. The works of Qutaiba Shaikh Nouri represent such an orientation. Buland al Haidari has accurately described his works as an attempt to employ the letter "in the expression of his [the artist's] most intimate feelings and ideas, and its form is therefore affected by what is alive in his own consciousness."[12] Though they may utilize motifs from an Islamic heritage — the letters and words of the Arabic language — such works are part and parcel of a Western art tradition. They have little to offer a Muslim artistic revival or a Muslim audience. To judge them as Islamic art is little different from dressing a Western Christian in a turban and calling him a Muslim.

Symbolic Calligraphy

A fourth category of contemporary Muslim calligraphy includes examples of what we shall call "Symbolic" calligraphy. Despite the peculiar inapplicability of literal symbolism for the Islamic arts, some contemporary Muslim calligraphers have followed this direction. In such calligraphy, Westernization has again intruded on the artistic orientation and process. Evidence of such acculturation can be seen in the designs of contemporary calligraphers who use a particular letter or word to serve as a symbol of an idea or a complex of ideas. Also included are works in which a chosen Arabic letter is associated with objects, the names of which begin with its sound, for example, س with *sayf* ("sword") or *sikkīn* ("knife"). The symbolic letter or letters are juxtaposed in such compositions with representations of the objects of association in order to convey a specific message.[13] The ideas thus expressed pertain to the objects rather than to a discursive message carried by the writing. The meaning behind the objects is often accentuated by the very

Illustration 20.32

Contemporary calligraphy ("pure abstraction") by Ḍiyā' al 'Azzāwī (Iraq), textile wall decoration. [Courtesy *Funoon Arabiah.*]

shape or manner of execution of the letter or letters. Such combinations hold significance only as revelations of the artist's choice and feelings. By being forced into association with such an artificial combination of meanings, the letters are denied their role as conveyors of a discursive message. In this associative and symbolic guise, they are usually found in compositions expressing a message of protest or social reform. Such a motivation for artistic creation is not one that has played an important role in the history of Islamic art. One wonders if such close connections with the day-to-day life of mankind can possibly gain validity for the Islamic art of our time or of the future. This would be a sharp departure from the orientation toward transcendence of the Islamic aesthetic tradition.

Some art historians who have accomplished outstanding achievements in their study of the historical, linguistic, and archeological data pertaining to Islamic calligraphy have fallen into particularly un-Islamic symbolic interpretation of the Islamic calligraphic art products. One such claim is that, when written, the vertical letters of the *shahādah* (the confession of faith) are "calligraphic evidence for both the divine origins of the script and the truth of the faith." The same author continues: "Almost all the letters could be employed metaphorically."[14] In fact, the epigraph is claimed to function "as a manifestation of the intangible and eternal divine."[15] To the Muslim, there can be no such manifestation of Divinity. To ascribe divine representation to any figure or object would be regarded by most members of the community to be not just erroneous but even blasphemous.

Pursuing a similar symbolic and un-Islamic line, certain art historians have even dug up the "old bones" of those medieval conceits that attributed to the letters themselves a numerical value and magical significance.[16] The resemblance of the Arabic form of the Prophet's name to the worshipper bowed in prayer, which was mentioned in the writings of some early authors of the Islamic period, has been cited as evidence of this symbolic significance of the word in Islamic art and its widespread acceptance by Muslims. The argument, based on a limited acceptance of such an idea and in a limited period of time, is mistakenly suggested as a universal within Islamic history.

Pseudo-Calligraphy or Pure Abstraction

There is a fifth type of contemporary use of calligraphy by Muslim artists. It might be designated as "Pseudo-Calligraphy" or "Pure Abstraction." Pseudo-Calligraphy, of course, indicates that the motifs of this type of art resemble letters and/or words, but the forms do not carry any of the conventional meanings associated with them. Pure Abstraction is another label drawn from a twentieth-century Western art movement to label an aesthetic type within Muslim aesthetic production. Although the term abstraction has been used in Western art circles to categorize a number of quite different art movements, its combination with the adjective "pure" has generally specified a particular movement within abstractionism. Piet Mondrian, a Dutch painter who specialized in geometrically pure abstraction, was one of the most important contributors to this movement. He is described as producing art in which "shapes, lines and colours have their own absolute, autonomous values and relationships, divorced from any associative role whatsoever."[17] The fifth group of Muslim calligraphers take direction from such views. Letters, geometric shapes, or any other motif are used by the Muslim Pure Abstraction artists as pure form, divorced of any of their traditional meanings or significance. Stripped of their linguistic meaning, the letters are used as sheer elements of design. If the calligraphic motifs retain any meaning, it comes from the Expressionist qualities of their rendering or ascribed literary symbolic implications.

Some artists of the Muslim world who use calligraphy in this way have tried to establish a new school of art which they call the "One Dimension Group." Their goal is to make use of the Arabic script as if it were no different from a geometric or figural motif. Exploiting the plastic potentialities of the alphabet, these Pure Abstraction calligraphers deal with the letters as shapes to be manipulated rather than as elements of a discursive message.[18] With these artists, the letters are no longer the motifs of doubly-rich meaning that they were in the Islamic calligraphy of earlier times. In fact, for Muḥammad Ghanī, a sculptor, the form of the letters is so modified and mingled with the preceding or succeeding letters, as well as with the space surrounding it, that its very identity is jeopardized. Najā Mahdāwī, a contemporary Tunisian artist, produces compositions of inscriptions that are studies in pure form rather than something to be read (Illus. 20.33 and 20.34). These works sometimes lean toward Expressionism; others are completely free of any attempt to convey meaning. Thus they deny the very essence and function of Islamic calligraphy — to present a discursive message in the beautiful visual forms of the infinite pattern.

The works of the Pure Abstraction calligraphers can generally be regarded as outside the pale of Islamic art. They may be considered "Muslim" art only in the sense that their creators are statistical Muslims. But their denial of the integrity of the letters and

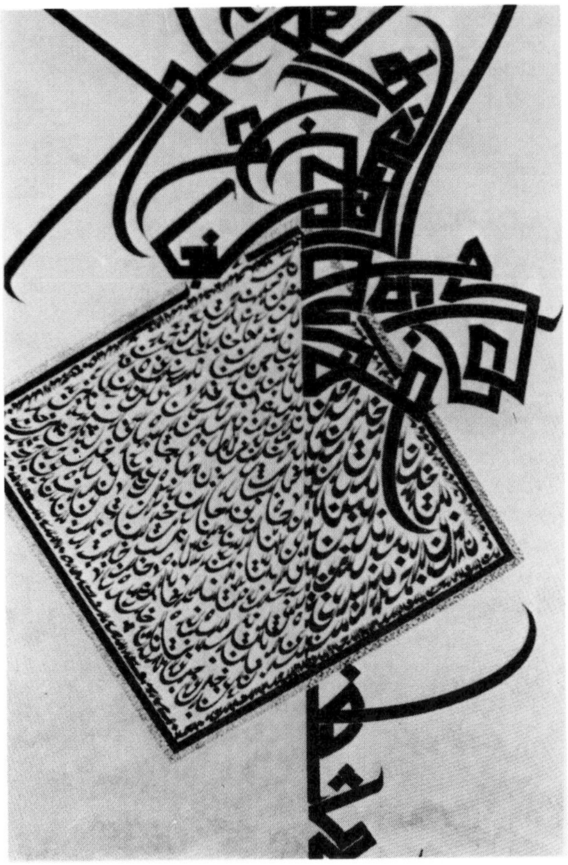

Illustration 20.33

Calligraphy design by Naja al Mahdawi, Tunisia. [Courtesy *Arts and the Islamic World.*]

Illustration 20.34

Calligraphy design by Naja al Mahdawi, Tunisia. [Courtesy *Funoon Arabiah.*]

words associated with the Arabic language, and therefore their denial of a relationship between their art and the Qur'ānic message, is antagonistic to that element of artistic creativity which has been held by Muslims throughout the centuries to be its most noble content. In addition, examples of Pseudo Calligraphy or Pure Abstraction that lean toward Expressionism, that is, try to visualize the artist's emotions and feelings, are inimical to Islamic abstract goals. The experiments in Pure Abstraction that are examples of "art for art's sake," that is, simply exercises in color and form, are equally un-Islamic. Islam and the doctrine of *tawḥīd,* which emphasize so strongly the telic nature of human existence and of every aspect of nature and human activity, cannot foster or support an art that exists selfishly and incongruously "for its own sake." In fact, such an art, Islam would maintain, is an impossibility. For if it is not expressive and reinforcing of one truth or set of truths, it must necessarily be expressive and reinforcing of another truth or set of truths. Even the expression and reinforcement of the denial of truth is a claim of truth for nihilism. In any case, that art which expresses other than Islamic principles could never warrant the regard or commendation of Islamic culture and the Muslim peoples.

Though some examples of contemporary calligraphy in the Muslim world seem more related to Western than to Islamic art, the very strong interest and concern with abstract motifs — the Arabic letters and words — is itself an indication of the importance and survival of the Islamic aesthetic core characteristics and their significance for future aesthetic activity. Rather than making use of the figural motifs emphasized so strongly in other cultures, and even practiced by recent sculptors and painters of noncalligraphic art in the Muslim world, many Muslim calligraphers have remained close to the tradition in choosing their abstract iconographic materials.

In addition to their use of abstract motifs, even the nontraditional contemporary calligraphers often give evidence of the relation of their work to the core characteristics of Islamic art.

In the acrylic by 'Ādil al Ṣaghīr (Illus. 19.25), the Islamic characteristics of both modular units and successive combinations are strikingly evident and excitingly achieved. Flowing lines of yellow, blue, green, and bronze varying in width carry the calligraphic lines and discursive content of the composition. Each segment or shape is a module within the whole. These

Illustration 20.35

Calligraphy, contemporary *Basmalah.* Calligrapher: Muḥammad Saʿīd al Ṣakkār. [Courtesy *Funoon Arabiah.*]

colored bands are combined to achieve a second level of organization; and on a third level, the composition reveals a highly stylized figural representation of a human figure. The work, therefore, like any successful Islamic work of art, must be viewed successively in parts and combinations of parts, as a series of "views" rather than as a single unity. Such additive structures demand the use of repetition, timed viewing, and intricacy, which are the other core characteristics of the Islamic arts.

Given the considerable production of the Traditional calligraphers, and despite certain incongruous borrowings by a limited number of non-Traditional calligraphers, it is clear that there is a strong tendency in the contemporary Muslim world to retain the features that have in-formed Islamic art and created a recognizable tradition throughout the centuries and in every region of the Muslim world. The lively renewal of interest, on the part of both artists and viewers, in calligraphy, as well as the refreshing experimentation to discover new ways of expressing the Islamic spirit through beautiful writing, are hopeful signs for the future of this most respected of the Islamic arts.[19]

NOTES

1. Chapter 23 on *Handasah al Ṣawt,* or the Art of Sound, makes use of an alternative subdivision of the Islamic world for elucidating the correspondence of musical genres to the aesthetic core characteristics. This, however, does not deny the suitability of the seven-part subdivision for dealing with other aspects of regional variety in the art of sound.

2. Bishr ibn ʿAbdul Malik and Ḥarb ibn Umayyah are believed to have introduced the Makkans to the art of writing the North Arabic script, a derivation from the earlier Nabataean. Ḥarb is credited with popularizing it among the aristocracy of the Quraysh, the tribe of Muḥammad. Among the contemporaries of the Prophet who became experts in writing were ʿUmar ibn al Khaṭṭāb, ʿUthmān ibn ʿAffān, and ʿAlī ibn Abū Ṭālib, three of the first four Rāshidūn caliphs.

3. This innovation was ordered by al Ḥajjāj, the powerful Muslim leader who controlled, for the caliphate in Damascus, the eastern regions of the Muslim empire at the turn of the eighth century C.E. Probably the system of "pointing" with one, two, or three black dots, which was devised under his direction, was not a new creation but an elaboration and perfection of earlier practices.

4. Abū al Aswad al Du'alī (d. 69/688) is thought to have invented the system of large colored dots used in that early period as vowel markings. These were to be supplanted in the eighth century by the diacritical markings developed by Khalīl ibn Aḥmad (d. 170/786). The latter are essentially those used today.

5. Nabia Abbott, *Studies in Arabic Literary Papyri I, Historical Texts* (Chicago: University of Chicago Press, 1957); see also Yasin Hamid Safadi, *Islamic Calligraphy* (Boulder, Colo.: Shambhala, 1979), p. 14.

6. According to one authority, it received this name because it canceled *(nasakha)* other forms of writing (Ibn Mīr-Munshī al Ḥusaynī Qāḍī Aḥmad, *Calligraphers and Painters,* trans. V. Minorsky [Washington, D.C.: Freer Gallery of Art, 1959], pub. 4339, p. 56, n. 135). Others relate the use of this term to the meaning of "transcribing," "transcription," or "copying" inherent in the root verb from which it is derived.

7. Safadi, *Islamic Calligraphy,* p. 30.

8. Ibid.

9. Other names for this type of design are *ʿaynālī* ("identical repetition"), *maʿkūs* ("reflected"), or *mutaʿākisah* ("the thing that has been reflected").

10. This analogy to the vocabulary and grammar of speech was used by the contributors to *Architecture as Symbol and Self-Identity,* Proceedings of the Aga Khan Seminar Four, "Architectural Transformations in the Islamic World," Fez, Morocco, 1979.

11. A few exemplars of this trend in Western art are Van Gogh, Gauguin, Seurat, Rouault, Klee, and Kandinsky. Their art has been described as "an artistic 'documentation' of emotional states and ideological conventions" (Umbro Apollonio, "Expressionism," *Encyclopedia of World Art* [New York, Toronto, London: McGraw-Hill, 1965], Vol. V, col. 317). Their art "was only the vehicle for emotionally intensified content; representation of external phenomena was completely subordinated to the visual statement of inner feelings" (ibid., col. 311).

12. Buland al Haidari, "Calligraphy in Modern Arab Art," *Arts and the Islamic World,* Vol. I, No. 1 (1983), p. 21.

13. Ibid.

14. Anthony Welch, *Calligraphy in the Arts of the Muslim Word* (Austin: University of Texas Press, 1979), pp. 25–26. See also Erica Cruikshank Dodd, "The Image of the Word," *Berytus* 18 (1969), pp. 35–58.

15. Welch, *Calligraphy,* p. 23.

16. Ibid., p. 25.

17. Article on Mondrian in *Encyclopaedia of the Arts,* ed. Geoffrey Hindley and Herbert Read (New York: Meredith Press, 1966) p. 636.

18. Shākir Ḥassan al Saʿīd regards the letter "as pure plastic value" (al Haidari, "Calligraphy," p. 20).

19. "It is quite natural for some artists in the developing countries to be captivated, at certain stages in their development, by artistic forms already perfected in more advanced countries, and by the products of those countries in the form of artistic schools, trends and plastic adventures. It is as equally natural that such superficial enchantment should not last long and that in a moment of awakening, the value of tradition for inspiration and confirmation of national identity will be recognized" (al Haidari, "Calligraphy," p. 17).

CHAPTER 21

Ornamentation in the Islamic Arts

The six general or core characteristics of the work of Islamic art having been laid down in Chapter 8, and calligraphy having been discussed in Chapter 20, the reader might expect that we would now proceed to investigate architecture, manuscript painting, metal work, ceramics, woodworking, leather-tooling, rugs, and textiles—in that or in any other order. We thought, however, that another organization of the materials of Islamic art was necessary to achieve a true appreciation of the beauty and significance of Islamic ornamentation. In fact, to deal with the various arts separately might lead one to think that they adhere to sharply varying characteristics of creative method and aesthetic perception. This is certainly not the case. The unity of the Islamic arts is such that, whether the artist makes use of paint, wood, bricks, stone, metal, clay, or textiles, the results are similar in effect. The function and significance of the decorative elaboration of these works, as well as their structures and forms, reveal an outstanding conformance of purpose and effect.

It will be the purpose of this chapter to discuss the unique functions of ornamentation in the Islamic arts, thereby revealing the significance of the application of infinite patterning to any work of art. In addition, this chapter describes some of the significant structural organizations which are revealed in all categories of Islamic art. Such purposes are not served by a purely historical or archeological study in which details of geographic and dynastic provenance, local influences, techniques of workmanship, and details of unique design motifs are enumerated. Such detailing, of course, would demand individual treatment for each medium. But that is not our purpose here. Studies fulfilling that need are already available in general books on the Islamic arts.[1] Other writings describe the arts produced in a particular region or country of the Muslim world.[2] Still other books and articles of historical and archeological importance that deal separately with a single medium or one type of Islamic art are to be found in contemporary libraries[3]; and individual articles on one object from that medium, or even one design on one object from one medium, are too numerous to list.[4]

Of course, additional research in all the categories of Islamic art is necessary. The materials still to be investigated will provide important research projects for art historians for decades, even centuries, to come. At the present stage of development, however, there is another need which seems more crucial to the understanding of Islamic art: an analysis that would put the information of the particularized studies mentioned into some understandable frame of reference. In other words, there is need to fit the many pieces of information now available into an analytical mosaic of the Islamic arts.

This chapter will discuss the special and unique relationship of the arts of Islam to ornamentation. This relationship is not peculiar to any particular category of art or medium. It overarches the visual arts as well as those of sound and movement. Islamic ornamentation includes the decoration of portable objects made of wool, metal, ceramics, fabrics, or any other material. It also encompasses what is generally labeled as architectural decoration, as well as the embellishment in the arts of sound and movement. Regardless of the materials or techniques used, Islamic ornamentation features striking aspects of unity — in its functions and significance as well as in the formal structures upon which it is based. The wide use of ornamentation makes a chapter on this subject essential to the understanding of the Islamic arts.

THE FUNCTIONS OF ORNAMENTATION IN THE ISLAMIC ARTS

A Western art historian has described ornamentation as "that component of the art product which is added, or worked into it, for purposes of embellishment. . . . [It] refers to motifs and themes used on art objects, buildings or any surface without being essential to stucture and serviceability. . . . This entire range of expression is used for ornamental purposes."[5]

This definition may be accurate for describing ornamentation in most other art traditions. Unfortunately, many Western or Westernized scholars who have dealt with the Islamic arts have regarded such a definition as a universal in the arts of all cultures and civilizations, and have been influenced by it in their analysis and description of Islamic art. This has resulted in their misunderstanding of some of the most crucial premises of that art. Since ornamentation is for them only a superficial addition to an aesthetic entity, they have judged the proliferation of ornament in Islamic art to be indicative either of the hedonism of the Muslim peoples, or of a cultural *horror vacui* (an abhorrence of empty space).[6] Not understanding the unique function and significance of ornamentation in Islamic aesthetic creation, many scholars cannot appreciate the positive contributions of this aspect of the art works of the Muslims. They can attribute to it only a negative and denigrating role.

In Islamic art, ornamentation or *zukhruf* ("decoration") is not something added superficially to the completed work of art in order to embellish it in an unessential way. It is also not a means of satisfying the appetites of a pleasure-seeking people. It should never be regarded as a mere filling of space to escape emptiness. Instead, the beautiful and intricate designs one finds on art objects of every region, and in every century of Islamic history, fulfill four specific and important functions which define their significance.

Reminder of *Tawḥīd*

First, the patterns of beauty found in the Islamic arts are concretizations of that ubiquitous aesthetic effort of the Muslim peoples to create art products that would lead the viewer to an intuition of divine transcendence. The ornamentation of the works of art are the outcome and the very substance of that effort. Since the need for such reminders of the Islamic ideology of *tawḥīd* is deemed an important addition to the environment, at work, at home, and in the mosque, the infinite patterns that comprise the ornamentation of the Islamic arts are to be found everywhere. It is not just the pages of the Holy Qur'ān that are made up of elaborate examples of calligraphy and illumination; the copy of a collection of stories or poems made for a caliph or prince is similarly decorated. It is not just the mosque that reveals transcendence-reminding ornamentation; a caravansary, a school *(madrasah),* or a private dwelling are similarly embellished. It is not just the lectern *(kursī)* on which the Qur'ān is supported in the mosque that is covered with infinite patterns; even the plate from which the Muslim eats his food, the armour or sword of the soldier, and the fabric of a head scarf are ornamented in similar fashion. It is quite proper, therefore, to regard Islamic art as uniquely inclusive of all types of beautiful and beautified objects, regardless of the use for which they have been designed.

Although in some sense the secular creations of any culture partake of a correspondence with the objects created for religious use during any particular period of time, it is a generally accepted notion that the expression "Christian art" pertains only to those art objects and buildings created for a specifically religious use in Christian culture. This is particularly true after the Renaissance, when the unity of life in Christianity was broken by the increasingly accentuated separation of the religious from the secular. In fact, some writers have maintained that, after the Renaissance, the production of "Christian art" ceased.[7] The art of subsequent periods may have been produced by artists who were nominally Christians, but their art no longer fulfilled the goals of Christian aesthetics and could no longer be related to the Christian theology.

Following the trend that progressively isolated religious from secular activities after the fourteenth century, the realms of religious and secular art tended to diverge more and more from each other and to develop in their separate ways. This reached such an extent that only the former is now regarded as "Christian art."

A comparable development could not occur in Islamic culture. There, from the very inception of the faith, the idea has been firmly entrenched that every activity, every idea, every occasion, and every object must not only be affected but also determined by the Islamic ideology. Art, like everything else, is considered to be part of the inclusive and comprehensive system that permeates the life of the *ummah.* For this reason, all types of objects used or made by Muslims are elaborately ornamented with those infinite patterns that tie them to the religion and the Islamic whole. Ornamentation thereby guards against the bifurcation of life into a religious realm, in which *tawḥīd* has power and influence, and a secular realm, for which the ideology has little or no relevance. Instead of being an unessential component added superficially to a work of art after its completion, ornamentation is at the core of the spiritualizing enhancement of the Islamic artistic creation and of the Muslim environment. By providing the ubiquitous infinite patterns, ornamentation raises any object from the realm of pure utility and makes of it an expression of the Islamic ideology.

Transfiguration of Materials

We have characterized the Islamic arts as emphasizing abstraction or denaturalization in their choice and use of subject matter. But subject matter was not the only thing determined by Muslim artists' desire to express *tawḥīd.* Their use of materials was also affected significantly by the wish for a mode of expression that accorded with their ideology. We would like to use the word "transfiguration" to designate the techniques that constitute a second function of ornamentation in the Islamic arts. That term is deemed suitable here, first of all, because it implies that the object transfigured by ornamentation has undergone a change in form or appearance but not in substance. This is certainly true of the ornamented work of Islamic art. The wood out of which it is made has not lost its natural properties; the granite is still as hard; the metal, as relentlessly opposed to being pierced as it was before the ornamentation process began. But the form and appearance of the materials have been drastically altered.

Second, the term "transfiguration" implies that the change is not mere change but an exalting, glorifying, or spiritualizing one. This is equally fitting of the contribution of ornamentation in the Islamic arts. The art work embellished with infinite patterns does indeed have an enhanced status in the mind of the Muslim, and especially so if the decorative designs includes Qur'ānic or other pious calligraphic elements.

Since the aesthetic goal of Islamic art is to lead the spectator away from concentration on self and this world, and toward contemplation of *tawḥīd* and a God Who is beyond and completely other than nature, the artist needs to deal with artistic materials in special and consistent ways. If the treatment of materials causes the viewer to concentrate on their naturalistic qualities, the aesthetic purpose of *tawḥīd* would not be served, and the adherence to abstract quality would be denied. Much has been written about the abstract and stylized nature of Islamic art, about its rejection of figural art as significant material for its creative expressions. Little attention, however, has been paid to the other ways Muslims have developed for denaturalizing and transfiguring nature in their arts. We have already discussed in Chapter 8 how the motifs and subject matter of Islamic art have been chosen and stylized to achieve those ends. We shall now consider the methods which Muslim artists have developed, in their use of ornamentation, to transfigure — that is, stylize, denaturalize, and beautify — the materials with which they work.

Overlay. One technique common to the various Islamic arts is to overlay the basic materials of any object or building with a decorative covering of infinite patterning (Illus. 21.1). The wooden box that holds a set of writing instruments is covered with intricate inlays of mother-of-pearl, ivory, or colored pieces of wood. One is not aware of, or concerned with, the material of the box itself. It matters little to the viewer if it is made of oak or teak, pine or mahogany, since all visible parts are covered with ornamental infinite patterning. In ceramic work, complicated meshlike or braided patterns have been affixed to those objects known as "Barbotine" ware. In this pottery, a semiliquid clay is applied from a tube, in a manner similar to that used by a cake decorator.

Architectural monuments can be equally revealing of the overlay method. Almost every important monument or simple structure includes evidence of such transfiguration (Illus. 21.2). The actual materials of construction for a building — be it palace or mosque, *madrasah* or caravansary, tomb or pavilion — are never emphasized. That would be too distracting to the goal Islamic art holds of reminding the viewer of a divine realm that is completely other than nature; it would orient the viewer toward the materials of na-

Illustration 21.1

Helmet ornamented with gold, rubies, and turquoise, sixteenth century. Topkapi Saray Museum, Isṭanbūl, Turkey. [Photo by L. al Fārūqī.]

ture rather than toward transcendence. A building could be made of bricks, rough stones, or even rubble; but no Muslim architect worthy of his profession would draw the attention of the viewer to those base materials with which he works. Instead, he emphasizes the transfiguring patterns with which they are overlaid. A covering of ornamental brickwork or ceramic tiles, a veneer of intricately sculpted stone or stucco, or an overlay of carved and painted wood hides the base materials. Overlay is one of the most important and prevalent devices for transfiguration of materials in the Islamic arts. It conforms to the pervasive cultural demand for abstraction from and denaturalization of the created world.

Disguise of inherent qualities of the materials. The transfiguration of materials through Islamic ornamentation makes use of a second means for enhancing denaturalization and transfiguration. This involves the treatment of materials in ways that would deny emphasis of their naturalistic qualities—in other words, render them more abstract or stylized. The elaborate carving of a stone façade often creates a light and supple, even a lacelike quality rather than an impression of weight and solidity which are the natural qualities of that material (Illus. 21.3). Ornamental bricks can become a meshlike covering for a building. Ceramics, for both small objects and architectural decoration, can be treated by glazing which

Illustration 21.2

Shrine of Fāṭimah, Qum, Iran (sixteenth–nineteenth centuries). [Photo by L. al Fārūqī.]

Illustration 21.3

A lacy "mesh" of carved stone in geometric and calligraphic ornament. Main gate of 'Alā al Dīn Mosque, Niğde, Turkey (1223). [Courtesy Embassy of Turkey, Washington, D.C.]

gives the finished luster ware product a metallic sheen and appearance. The grain and color of the wood, which would identity its type and emphasize its naturalistic qualities, are reduced to insignificance by inlaid or painted designs (Illus. 21.4). The viewer's attention is always drawn away from the material itself to concentrate instead on the ornamental patterns executed in that medium, patterns that lead to an intuition of the transcendence of Allah.

Lack of concern for preciousness of materials. As further evidence of the abstraction or transfiguration and deemphasis of materials in Islamic art, one finds little concern for the preciousness of materials themselves. Although gold, silver, mosaics, lead crystal, and other precious materials are sometimes used, the work of Islamic art derives its character and excellence from the "working" of those materials rather than from their intrinsic value.

The abundance of less precious metals in objects remaining from earlier centuries has sometimes been attributed to an ascetic tendency in Islamic religion and culture. This has little basis in fact. Certain passages from the ***ḥadīth*** literature, which discourage the extravagant use of gold and silver utensils,[8] have been regarded by non-Muslims as well as some Muslims as proof of a dominant asceticism in Islam. These texts must, however, be viewed in light of the passages in the Qur'ān itself that provide clearly anti-ascetic directives.[9] The more plausible explanation of the examples of ***ḥadīth*** in question is that these point to an authentic cultural tendency to downgrade the importance of wealth and material goods in order to stress more important things. The use of common and even prosaic materials for objects of elaborate intricacy and richness of detail is, therefore, another aspect of the transfiguration of materials in the Islamic arts. The extravagance of workmanship stands in sharp contrast to the frugality evidenced in the choice of basic materials. The peasant's clay pot, the iron skillet, the wooden door — all may be treated to elaborate ornamentation schemes, the labor for which might seem to go far beyond what the materials and their use warrant. The Muslim craftsman or artist thereby refuses to regard the material as an impor-

Illustration 21.4

Platter, its wooden materials disguised by elaborate inlays, twentieth century, Egypt. [Photo by L. al Fārūqī.]

tant ingredient in the aesthetic appreciation of the art work. Instead, priority is given to the infinite patterns that cover the object and meet the eye wherever it falls.

Transfiguration of Structures

Whereas many art traditions of the world may seek to emphasize the underlying structures of a particular work, Islamic art strives for a disguise of that basic framework. Contribution to this quality can be considered as a third function of ornamentation in the Islamic arts. It is another feature of the art product designed to draw the attention away from mundane ingredients and characteristics to a higher order of expression and meaning.

Ornamentation of any Islamic work of art plays the role of transfiguring it structurally, by hiding the basic forms or minimizing their impact on the viewer. For example, the outer surface of a beaker may be only a perforated cover for the waterproof container within (Illus. 21.5). The ceramic overlay of a façade or interior wall rarely delineates architectural members. Only when these architectural members provide outlines for design units of the infinite patterning are they exposed. In such cases, however, they are experienced as entities within the design structure, within the infinite pattern, rather than as units or members of architectural structure. To emphasize the design structure of an Islamic work of art is always desirable since it promotes a *tawḥīd*-based aesthetic perception of the art work. Emphasis on the actual building structure is rejected since that would emphasize the naturalistic, the rude earthly factors, the sticks-and-stones organic makeup of the object or architectural structure. It could not provide an aesthetic reminder of the other-than-nature qualities of Divinity. For this reason, Muslim artists have tended to mask construction details with overlays of transfiguration ornament.

Illustration 21.5

Vase with perforated exterior wall, Pakistan, twentieth century. [Photo by L. al Fārūqī.]

Beautification

The fourth function of ornamentation in the Islamic arts is one shared by the artistic traditions of all cultures, and is thus a universal in aesthetic creation. That is the use of ornament to beautify and embellish. Islamic ornamentation can be said to perform this function with great success, since the patterns it creates on the decorated object are themselves intrinsically pleasing to the eye. This fact, based on their symmetry, their pleasing colors, and their graceful and varied shapes, has been acknowledged by non-Muslims who are unable to appreciate those arts from within the cultural matrix, as well as by the Muslims themselves. The ornamentation found in these works of art imparts an additional dimension of beauty for the Muslim percipient; for any figure or object, any phrase or movement, any line or anecdote that expresses *tawḥīd* is for the adherent of Islam an expression of truth and goodness. It is therefore, a fortiori, an expression of beauty.

Many scholars have recognized the unity of Islamic art.[10] However, though recognized, the details of its embodiment are rarely enunciated. We have attempted in Chapter 8 and in this chapter to establish a number of dominant characteristics which pertain to the Islamic arts generally. These characteristics constitute its unity. They can be found in the arts of any medium or technique, in every region of the Muslim world, in every century of the Islamic period.

Scholars have been no less aware of variety in the Islamic arts. Variety has usually been attributed to the effect of ethnic, racial, or regional preferences. Despite acknowledgment of their existence, such elements of variety within the overall unity have rarely been enunciated or analyzed for a better understanding. There has been a "feeling" of regional emphasis or uniqueness with little attempt to understand its nature. Without losing sight of the numerous characteristics that give a comprehensive continuity to ornamentation in the Islamic arts, we shall make an attempt here to describe those elements of variety that typify the use of ornamentation in various parts of the Muslim world. For this purpose, we will use the same seven regions delineated on Map 62 (p. 364), which approximate recognizable artistic subdivisions within the whole. Though the borders indicated on Map 62 appear as precise boundaries of the seven regions, it should be understood that such framing of cultural aspects is susceptible to the "leakages" resulting from acculturation and diffusion. Any element described as characteristic of a region, therefore, may not be statistically unique to that region; but the prevalence of its use there and its limited and uncharacteristic use in other regions contribute to the region's characteristic style. Three factors will be considered here as possible elements providing regional specificity. These are techniques, materials, and motifs.

There is little in the field of ornamentation techniques that distinguishes one region from another. Carving, painting, weaving, veneering,[11] engraving or etching,[12] embossing,[13] leather-tooling, enameling,[14] filigree,[15] glass-blowing, and casting[16] are found in every region. It would be impossible to provide evidence for exclusivity for any region in any of these techniques. In fact, this conformance of techniques in the different regions is one aspect of the unity of Islamic art.

Materials are only slightly less homogeneous in the Islamic arts regardless of region and period of time. This element of possible regional particularity is governed, of course, by the availability of materials in the different regions. Stucco, paint, wood, metal, fibers for weaving, and clay for ceramic production are so widespread in their provenance that they can be regarded as typical of all seven regions. One difference can be seen in the production of carpets to embellish public and private spaces. In Turkey, Iran-Central Asia, and the Indian subcontinent production of carpets has been most important. Stone ornamentation, whether by carving or veneering, has of course been most prevalent in those regions where large quantities were locally available and easily quarried. Egypt, Turkey, and the Indian subcontinent are outstanding in this regard. Because stone was less commonly found in the Maghrib, Middle Africa, Iran-Central Asia, and East Asia, those regions have made greater use of bricks, wood, ceramic, and plaster ornamentation.

It is to the last of the three aspects — motifs — that the most striking differences between the arts of the different regions can be attributed. We shall discuss the seven regions separately in order to set forth the major elements of the motif vocabulary. (For a typology of motifs in the Islamic arts, see Figure 21.1.)

Although both figurative and nonfigurative motifs are used in Area I, the Maghrib, the arts of that region evidence a predominance of the latter category. All the subdivisions of nonfigurative motifs — calligraphy and the various types of geometric shapes, both rectilinear and curvilinear — are prominent in decoration of both architectural and smaller objects of the region. Polygons and star shapes are found with particular frequency. As for the figurative motifs used, most often they represent vegetal or lifeless objects rather than those suggestive of human beings, animals, or hybrid creatures. Figurative objects are heavily stylized and abstracted from their naturalistic forms.

In addition to these general characteristics of motif selection in the Maghrib, a few motifs are used with such consistency that they help distinguish a Maghribī style in ornamentation. These are found on small objects as well as on the larger structures of the "spatial arts." Probably the most distinctive of these is a special form of interlace. This patterning incorporates lozenge as well as arch shapes in intricate designs. It is particularly prominent as architectural decoration on the walls of buildings and towers (Illus. 21.6) where it is found in an infinite number of creative variants. Other motifs used frequently enough to constitute an element of particularity for a Maghribī regional style are the shell motif, the lobed and horseshoe arch, and arcade forms (Illus. 21.7, 21.8, 21.9).

Two characteristic features of motif representation in Area II, Islamic Middle Africa, are the prominence of rectilinear geometric shapes and the freehand aspect of their rendering (Illus. 21.10, 21.11). Human and animal motifs, always highly stylized, are more frequent here than in many other parts of the Muslim world (Illus. 21.12). This can be seen as a strong influence from the pre-Islamic artistic culture of the area. In West Africa, the influence of the Maghrib is often clearly discernible in the choice of motifs of decoration.

In Area III, the Mashriq, all the elements of the Islamic motif vocabulary can be found. It is difficult to assign predominance to any particular item, for all

TABLE 21.1. ARTISTIC MOTIFS OF THE MUSLIM WORLD

(For examples of each style of ornamentation, see Figure 21.1.)

Styles of ornamentation used throughout the Muslim world:
- Calligraphy
- Geometric patterns
- Stylized figures from nature (vegetal, animal, and lifeless objects)
- Architectural motifs

Ornamentation used in Area I (Maghrib, North Africa, and Spain)
- Lozenge interlace
- Shell motifs
- Lobed arches/arcades
- Horseshoe arches/arcades
- Interlaced arches

Ornamentation used in Area II (Middle Africa)
- Styles influenced by Area I motifs
- Rectilinear geometric shapes
- Freehand rendering of designs

Ornamentation used in Area III (Mashriq)
- Fluted domes
- Sculptured domes
- Alternating bands of color

Ornamentation used in Area IV (Turkey)
- Triangular arch
- Turkish triangles
- Triangular or conical domes

Ornamentation used in Area V (Iran and Central Asia)
- Stylized figures from nature (very important)
- Delicate rendering of motifs

Ornamentation used in Area VI (Indian Subcontinent)
- Lobed arches/arcades
- Inverted lotus figures at crest of domes
- Greater naturalism in rendering of figures from nature
- Bulbous domes

Ornamentation used in Area VII (East Asia)
- Wave motifs
- Boat prow motifs
- Voluptuous plant and animal forms
- Umbrella motifs
- Dragon motifs
- Lobed arches/arcades
- Bulbous domes

Illustration 21.6

Carved stucco ornamentation, Alhambra Palace, Granada, Spain. [Photo by L. al Fārūqī.]

FIGURE 21.1 MOTIF VOCABULARY OF THE ISLAMIC ARTS

I. Nonfigurative or Abstract Motifs

A. Calligraphy

B. Geometric Shapes

1. Rectilinear

a. Polygons

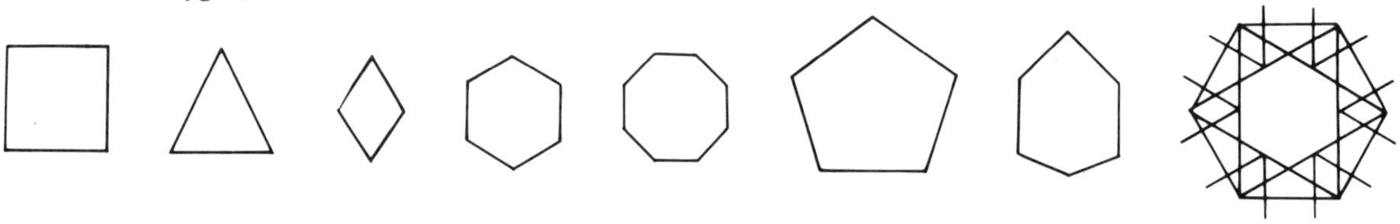

b. Stars and crosses

c. Swastikas and frets

d. Angular meanders

i. Key meander

ii. Chevron meander, zigzag

e. Chevron patterns

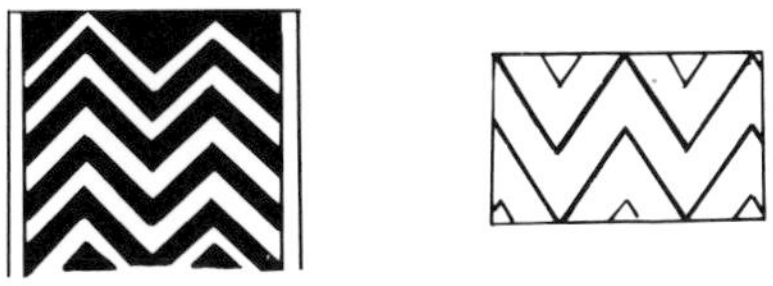

f. Lattice, checkerwork, hatching, and dotting

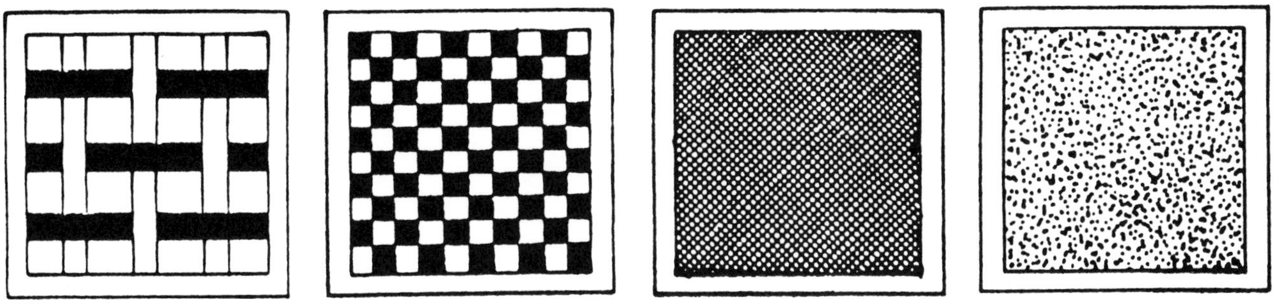

2. Curvilinear
   a. Circles (single, concentric, and interlocking)

   b. Scallops

   c. Curvilinear meanders and S curves
      i. Ribbon or undulating

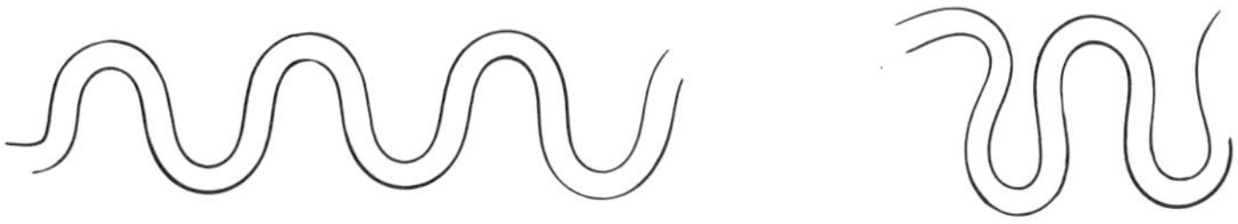

      ii. Wave

      iii. Guilloche

(Continued on next page)

FIGURE 21.1 *(Continued)*

iv. Spiral

Planar

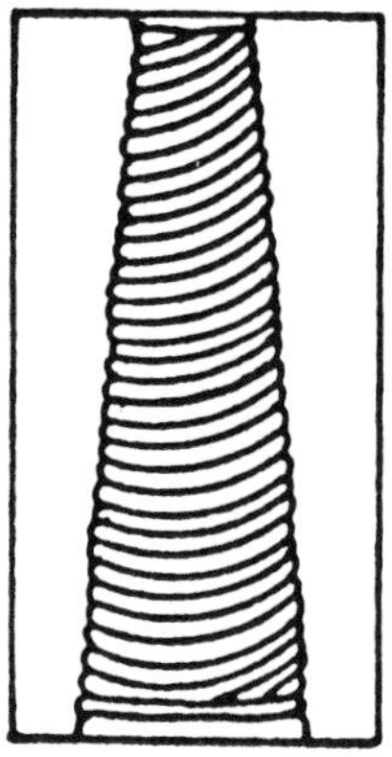

Three-dimensional

3. Mixed
   a. Counterchanged patterns

Angular

Curvilinear

B. Medallion, cartouches, and lozenges

II. Figurative Motifs

A. Living Figures

1. Vegetal

a. Rosettes

b. Flowers

c. Leaves

d. Trees

(Continued on next page)

FIGURE 21.1 *(Continued)*

e. Vines

f. Fruits

2. Human beings

3. Animals

4. Hybrid creatures
   a. Sphinx
   b. Centaur
   c. Griffin
   d. Harpies

B. Lifeless Objects from Nature
   1. Stylized objects
      a. Vases, pitchers

(Continued on next page)

FIGURE 21.1 *(Continued)*

b. Lamps

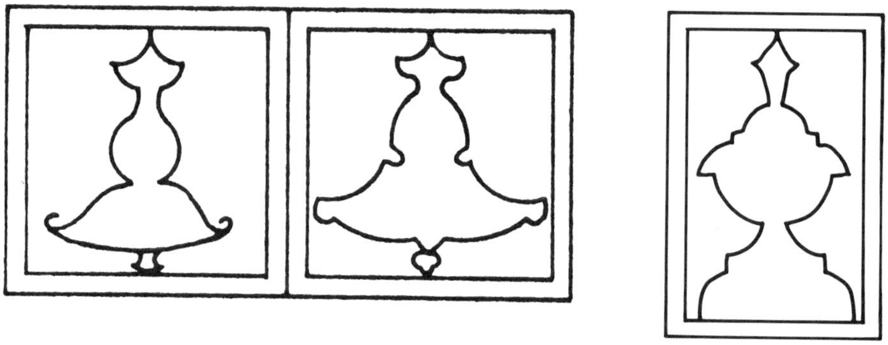

c. Shells

d. Interlace, ropes, and braid

e. Shields, emblems

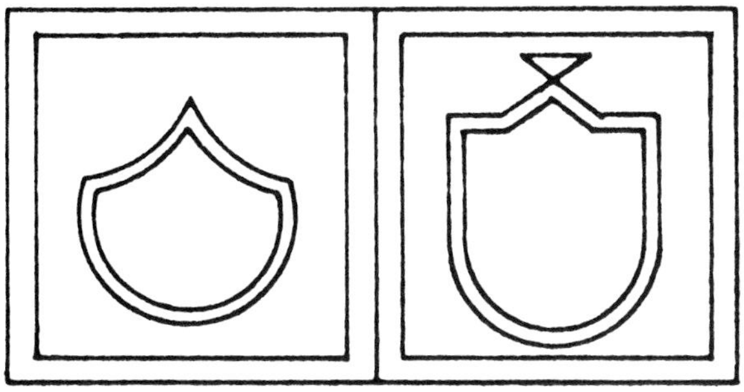

f. Cloud bands

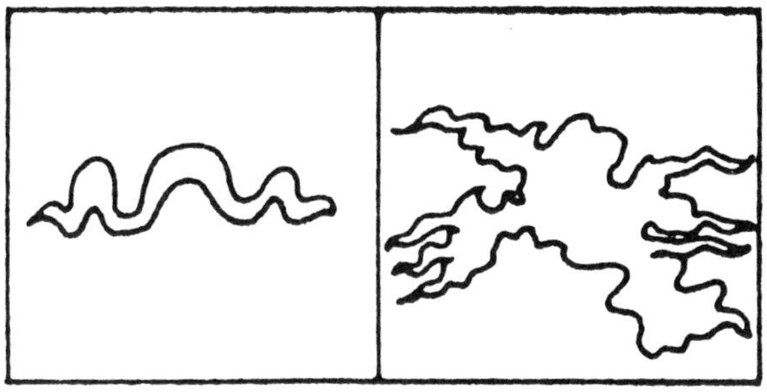

g. Water and wave motifs

2. Architectural motifs
a. Arches (blind and open)

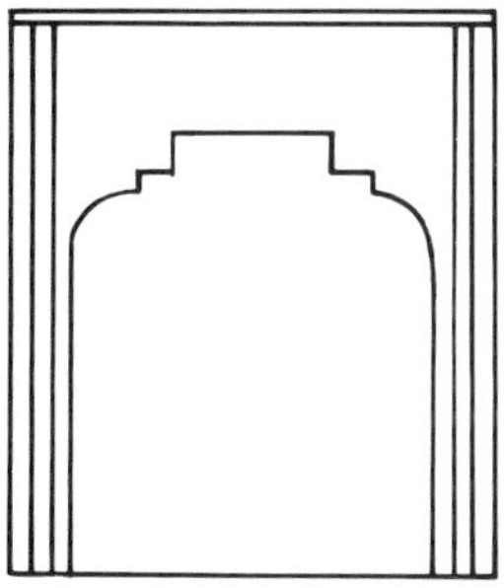

i. Square

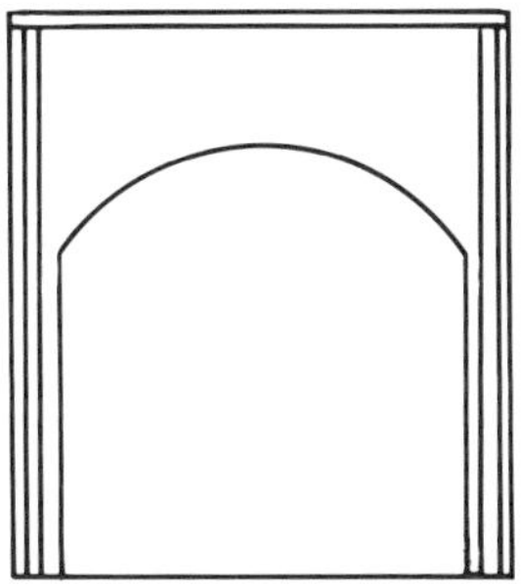

ii. Round

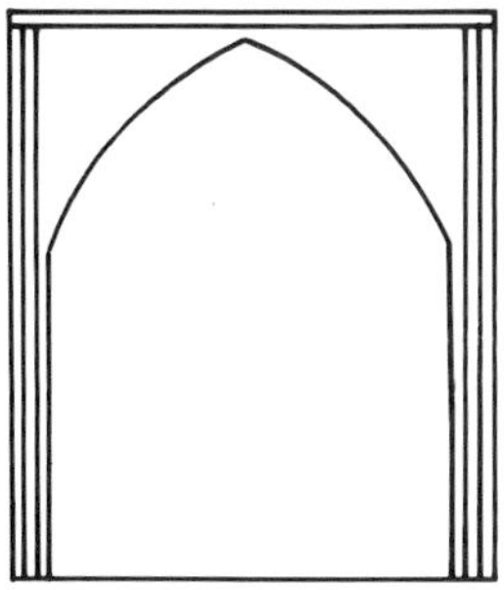

iii. Pointed

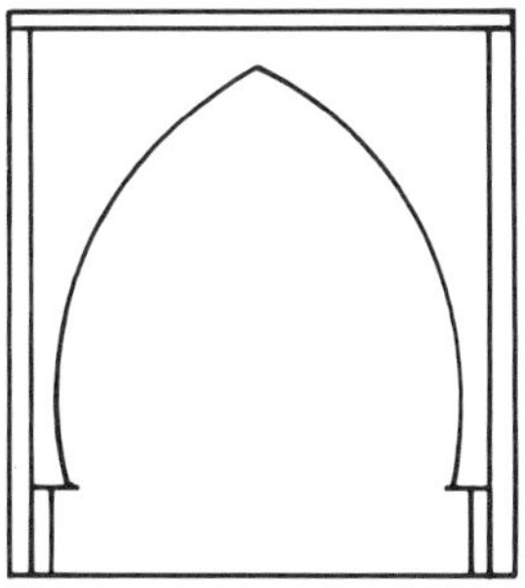

iv. Horseshoe

(Continued on next page)

FIGURE 21.1 *(Continued)*

v. Cusped, lobed

vi. Lambrequin

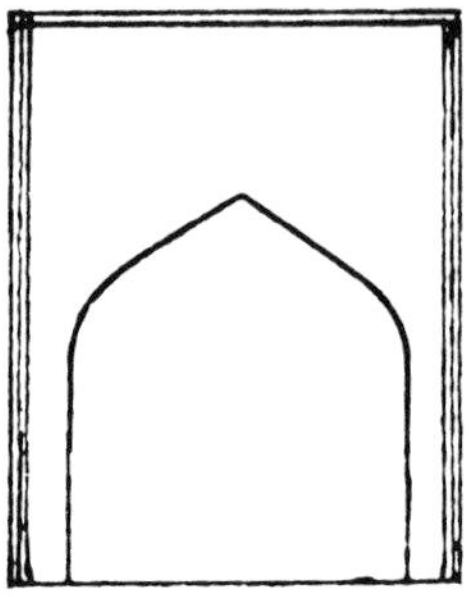

vii. Keel

viii. Interlaced

b. Arcades (blind and open)

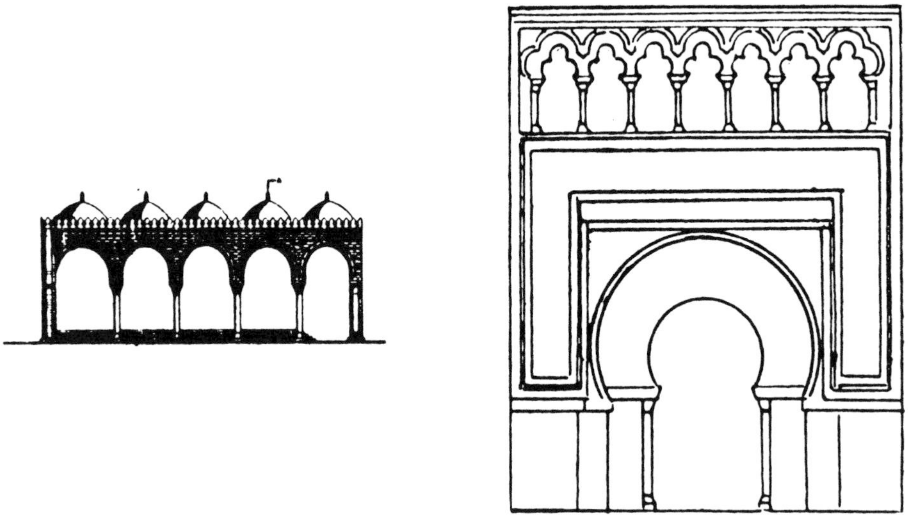

c. Columns and pillars (with or without structural role)

d. Domes and cupolas

e. Crenellations/merlons

f. Niches

i. Two-dimensional

ii. Three-dimensional *(muqarnas)*

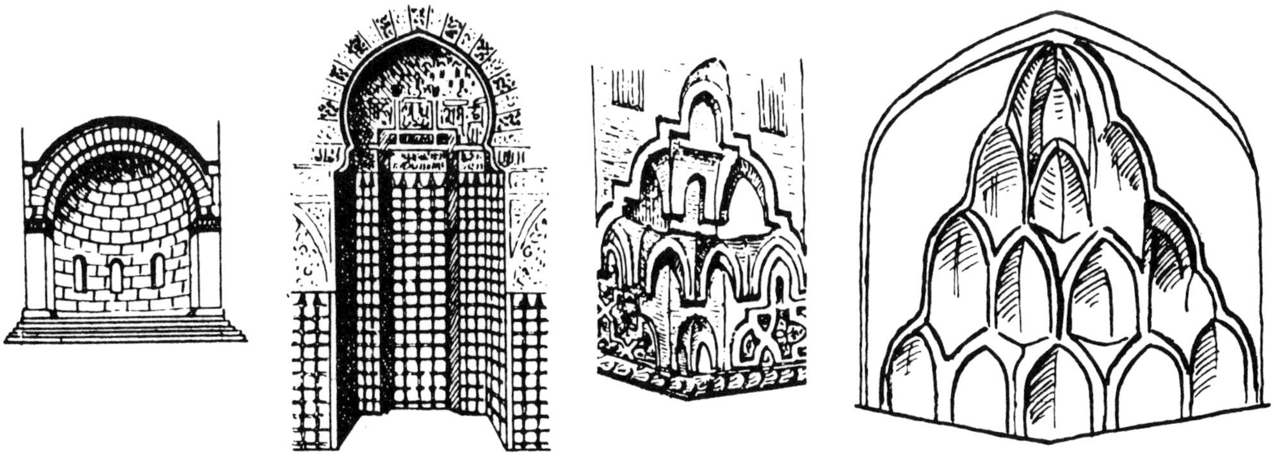

Illustration 21.8

Portal with horseshoe, lobed and interweaving arches, and crenellations, Mosque of Qurṭubah, Spain. [Photo by L. al Fārūqī.]

Illustration 21.7

Lobed arches and stucco interlaced patterns, Mausoleum of Muḥammad V, Rabāṭ, Morocco. [Photo by L. al Fārūqī.]

Illustration 21.9

Qaṣbah Gate, Rabāṭ, Morocco, twelfth century. [Photo by L. al Fārūqī.]

Illustration 21.10

Decorations on the mud architecture structure of the Amīr of Zaria's palace, Zaria, Nigeria. [Courtesy A. R. Doi.]

Illustration 21.11

Gate ornamentation of mud mosque in Zaria, Nigeria. [Courtesy A. R. Doi.]

Illustration 21.12

Stylized figures of Hausa carved designs, Nigeria. [Courtesy A. R. Doi.]

Illustration 21.13

Muqarnaṣ portal decorations, Green Mosque, Bursa, Turkey, 1414–1424. [Photo by L. al Fārūqī.]

have been artfully used in some or all periods. If any were to be singled out as regionally typical, they would probably include the fluting and sculpture decoration of domes and the alternating bands of color which are often found in both architectural and small object ornamentation.

Area IV, Turkey, like its neighbors in the Mashriq, has used a wide motif vocabulary. Artistic calligraphy has been particularly prominent and distinguished. Geometric and vegetal forms as well as lifeless objects from nature were all popular motifs in Turkish art during both the Saljuk (1078–1308) and Ottoman periods (1300–1922). Motifs particularly associated with Turkey are the pointed, triangular arch (Illus. 21.13) and the distinctive figures known as "Turkish triangles" (Illus. 21.14). The latter are triangular prismatic surfaces forming a kind of belt around the inner base of domes to facilitate the transition between round and square, smaller and larger entities. Although this is primarily an architectural element, both in origin and in function, it provided a motif for architectural decoration as well.

Iran-Central Asia, Area V, might be characterized as a region that has concentrated more than most other regions on stylized human and animal figures (Illus. 21.15). These depictions are often related to court life—for example, a ruler seated with his attendants or friends, hunting expeditions, or battle and tournament scenes.

Symmetrical confronted animals and two-headed birds are also popular motifs for decoration of all types of artistic products. Like the pre-Islamic art of Persia and the Fertile Crescent areas, many of the animal forms are hybrid creatures incorporating the head of one animal and the body of another. Though animals have sometimes been represented with considerable liveliness, they are always stylized to accord with the denaturalization tendency of Islamic art. It is difficult to assign prominence to any particular motif used in this area, but the aesthetic products of Iran-Central Asia reveal a refinement and delicacy in ornamentation which, regardless of motif used, contribute significantly to their aesthetic regional particularity.

In the Indian subcontinent, Area VI, Islamic art motifs from the figurative category have generally been treated more naturalistically than in other regions of the Muslim world. This applies to human and animal figures as well as to vegetal forms (Illus. 21.16). In addition, arch and arcade motifs of the lobed and bulbous varieties are particularly prominent (Illus. 21.17, 21.18). Fluting and inverted lotus figures topping domes and cupolas are also common ele-

Illustration 21.14

"Turkish triangles" of porch domes, Mosque and Madrasah of Murād I, Bursa, Turkey, 1365–1385. [Photo by L. al Fārūqī.]

Illustration 21.15

Lacquered pen box showing a doctor and his patient, by Muḥammad Ibrahīm Ḥusaynī, late eighteenth or early nineteenth century. [Courtesy Islamic Information Service, Iran.]

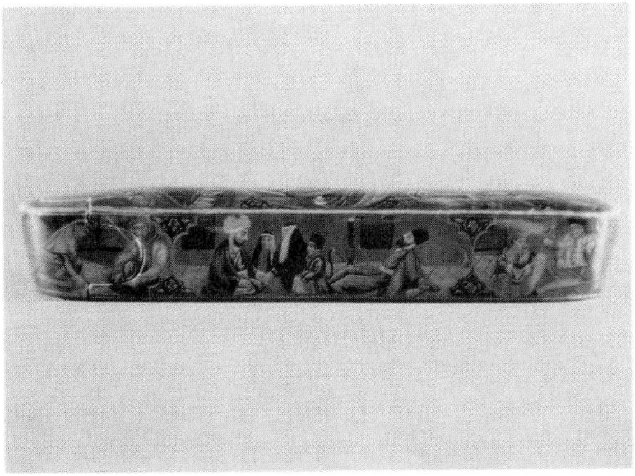

Illustration 21.16

Maḥabbat Khān Mosque, Peshawar, Pakistan. [Photo by L. al Fārūqī.]

ments in the Indian subcontinent; though many other motifs have also been frequently represented.

The proximity to the ocean of many of the Muslim-dominated areas of East Asia has resulted in a prominent use of boat prow decorations and wavelike motifs in Area VII. Even plant and animal forms are flowing and undulating. The rich vegetation of such places as Malaysia, Indonesia, and the southern Philippines has contributed to an almost voluptuous rendering of vegetal motifs which characterizes ornamentation of art products of those lands (Illus. 21.19). Added to this element of regional particularity is an influence from India and Indian Islam for lobed and bulbous arch and dome motifs (Illus. 21.20). The use of umbrellas as a physical protection from sun and rain and a symbolic sign of royalty in southeast Asia has made a parasol-like folding and pleating motif prominent in architectural decoration. In the art works of Chinese Muslims, decorative elements are drawn primarily from Central Asia (Illus. 21.21, 21.22) or from indigenous Chinese art (Illus. 21.23, 21.24).

In addition to these identifying characteristics of the various regions, we find the plant motifs varying somewhat from region to region, in conformance with the vegetation of each part of the Muslim world. For example, the tulip is typical of Turkish ornamentation but almost never found in that of other regions of the Muslim world; the mango (also called "paisley") de-

Illustration 21.17

Interior of Badshāhī Mosque, Lahore, Pakistan. [Courtesy Embassy of Pakistan, Washington, D.C.]

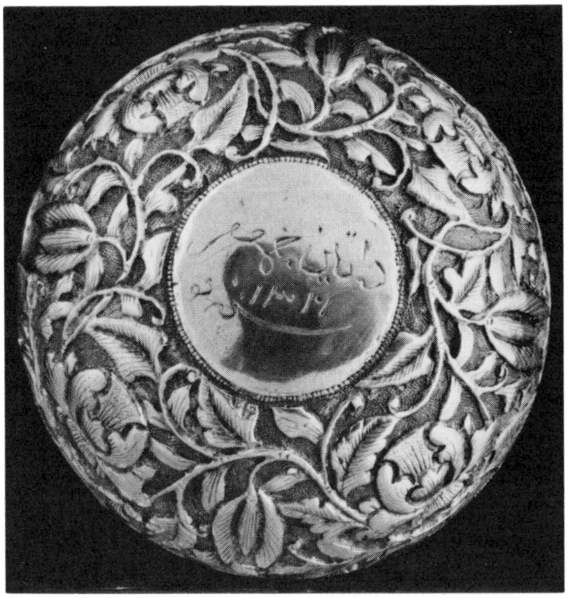

Illustration 21.18

Silver bowl with Jāwī script giving the Islamic date for its production (1319–1901), Johar, Malaysia. (Private collection of Puan Azah Aziz, Kuala Lumpur, Malaysia.) [Courtesy National Art Gallery, Kuala Lumpur.]

Illustration 21.19

Lobed arch arcading of Jāmi' Mosque, Kuala Lumpur, Malaysia. [Photo by L. al Fārūqī.]

Illustration 21.20

Minaret, Turfan Mosque, Xinjiang Province, People's Republic of China, seventeenth century. [Photo by Ingrid Larsen.]

Illustration 21.21

Entrance, Xian Mosque, People's Republic of China. [Courtesy Robert H. Garvin.]

Illustration 21.22

Gold tray made in Iran, early nineteenth century. [Courtesy Islamic Information Service, Iran.]

Illustration 21.23

Floral and geometric panels on carved wooden ***minbar,*** Grand Mosque of Qayrawān, Tunisia, ninth century. [Photo by L. al Fārūqī.]

sign is particularly important in Iran-Central Asia and the Indian subcontinent. Despite such minor variations in use or prominence of motifs, the degree of homogeneity even in this aspect of visual artistic materials is outstanding. In fact, the application of all the categories of the Islamic motif vocabulary in all regions is so consistent as to constitute still another element of unity in the Islamic art.

Illustration 21.24

Decorative façade of a villa, Kuwait. [Photo by L. al Fārūqī.]

ARABESQUE STRUCTURES

In addition to understanding the four important functions of Islamic ornamentation and thereby becoming aware of its significance, it is necessary to examine the structural organizations that underlie its infinite patterns. The Islamic infinite pattern or arabesque, whether used in the decoration of a Qur'ānic manuscript, the designs of a carpet, the improvisations of the lutanist, or the intricate ceramic ornamentation of a building, are found to conform to a number of structural types which recur in countless varieties. These formal categories can be discovered and distinguished in art works created throughout the Muslim world over the past fourteen centuries.

Four general categories of arabesque structure have been identified as representative. This does not imply a closed system to which no additional structures could be added. The exact opposite is the case. Any new structural "species" that fulfills the aesthetic demands of Islamic infinite patterning and conforms to its core characteristics would be a creative and welcome addition to the repertoire of Islamic art. The art inspired by *tawḥīd* involves a conceptual approach for which the possible manifestations are in fact infinite. Understanding the use in ornamentation of the four structures to be presented will help clarify the versatility and limitless possibilities of the Islamic aesthetic mode.

The visual arts—and for that matter, the Islamic arts of literature, sound, and movement—reveal some remarkable similarities to the Arabic language in which the revelation to Muḥammad was sent. Arabic, in addition to holding this key to Muslim interest and need, has been the medium for participation in the religious rituals as well as the *lingua franca* of the Muslim world for the past fourteen centuries. Even in the other so-called Islamic languages (Turkish, Persian, Urdu, Swahili, Malay, etcetera), the structures inherent in Arabic seem to have had wide significance.

Arabic is an intricate language based on a system of core meanings expressed through its trilateral roots. Since there is no limit to the number of such root words, the extensiveness of meanings in the language is potentially infinite. The three-consonant roots achieve specific nuances of the base meaning according to the highly regularized forms (*taf'īlāt,* sing. *taf'īlah*) of the Arabic language. Through the addition of prefixes, suffixes, or the internal addition of vowels, consonants, and doublings, these *taf'īlāt* provide all the varied parts of speech without losing their relationship to the trilateral root. For example, ḍ-r-b has a root meaning of "to strike"; *s-b-q* means "to race, to proceed." By adding a long "a" after the first consonant and a short "i" after the second, the root becomes *ḍārib,* "one who strikes"; and *sābiq,* "one who races or precedes." In another form, a "u" sound before the first consonant and following the second *(uḍrub)* produces the masculine singular imperative ("strike!"). Similarly, *ụsbuq* is the command to "go ahead!" Every verbal, nominal, adjectival, and adverbial meaning has its related and particularized form. The sixty or more commonly used *taf'īlāt* present another potentially limitless dimension of the Arabic language. Many more forms have been described and used by the masters of the language, and more could be added if the need should arise.

The structural types or forms of the Islamic arts are analogous to these *taf'īlāt* of the Arabic language. While the language *taf'īlāt* provide the beautifully regular and repeating framework for the combination of letters in words, the aesthetic *taf'īlāt* are the frame for artistic motifs and figures to create the patterns of Islamic art.

In similar fashion to the linguistic forms, the structures of the infinite pattern evidence a bi-leveled limitlessness. At least four basic arabesque structures have been found to be prevalent in the Islamic arts, but the discovery of new arabesque structures embodying the core characteristics of Islamic art would be desirable. At the same time, the variety in execution of these structures is limitless. The possible techniques, materials, and motifs are endless; and the different ways of manipulating the basic structures are equally without bounds. Given the rich variety of these structures in Islamic art history, it is obvious that the embodiment of the infinite pattern offers unlimited creative possibilities.

In some examples of infinite patterning the artist seems to have used more than one of the basic forms in a single arabesque design, each one in a different segment of the work, or by combining their features into an overall structure for the design. In such cases it is usually possible to determine a dominant influence of one or the other of the structures, or to define the design as exemplifying the combination of two or more identifiable structures.

Of the four basic structural categories of Islamic infinite patterns which have been recognized in numerous works, two are basically disjunct (*munfaṣilah)* or discontinuous in organization, while the other two are basically conjunct *(muttaṣilah)* or continuous. This characterization, like the identity of structural types, may be sharply delineated in some works, while in others its exemplification is veiled or verging on the other genus. Despite the resultant problems of classification, we will try to define archetypes and to relate specific examples of art to one or more of the theoretical models.

Multi-Unit Structure

The first of the disjunct *munfaṣilah* structures could be called the "multi-unit" arabesque or infinite pattern. It is composed of distinct parts or modules combined in an additive and repetitive fashion. Rarely does one module take precedence over another. Each unit maintains an emphatically separated identity, though it may be joined with other units to create a larger combination. As in any Islamic design, no single focalization of eye and mind is proper for its viewing or appreciation.

This structure, which lends itself readily to any medium and method, is widely used in Islamic art. The multi-unit organization has been found on the decorations of a ceramic or metal vessel (Illus. 21.25), on the weapons or armor of the soldier, on the decorative passages or illuminations of a Qur'ān or other book, on the designs of furniture (Illus. 21.26), carpets, and fabrics, as well as on the decorative overlays of architectural monuments (Illus. 21.27, 21.28). Even min-

Illustration 21.25

Carved stucco decoration, Madrasah al Sharrātīn, Salé, Morocco. [Photo by L. al Fārūqī.]

Illustration 21.26

Miniature painting depicting scene from "Chogan Bazi," by Ḥusayn Bihzād of Tehran, early twentieth century. [Courtesy Islamic Information Service, Iran.]

Illustration 21.27

Interior of cupola in a contemporary mosque in Kuwait. [Courtesy 'Iṣām Tājī.]

Illustration 21.28

Tile work in prayer hall of the ʻAbdallah Ansārī shrine, Gazur Gah, Afghanistan, 1428–1429 C.E. [Photo by L. al Fārūqī.]

Illustration 21.29

Detail of geometric design, wooden door, Green Mosque, Bursa, Turkey. [Photo by L. al Fārūqī.]

iature painting, which many would consider to be the art form least affected by the Islamic aesthetic premises, often exemplifies a multi-unit structural organization. The illustration may be a collection of separate "views" set off from each other by architectural elements (room dividers, arches, windows, doorways, and so on) or natural barriers (Illus. 21.29). Such partitions separate these figural embodiments of multi-unit structure into separate modules. Each mini-scene is perceived in turn, as the eye and mind are drawn from one unit to another.

The modules of a multi-unit arabesque can be appreciated singly, on one level of investigation, but they are often also organized in some form of second-level (and perhaps also third-level) combination. This might entail a symmetrical arrangement of units to right or left (Illus. 21.28) or up and down from a central point; or it might take the form of a combination of modules into a ring or chainlike structure (Illus. 21.30).

Interlocking or *Mutadākhilah* Structure

A second structure commonly found as the basic organizing principle behind an Islamic ornamentation pattern will be called "interlocking" or ***mutadākhilah***. Here, as in the multi-unit structure, a number of modules are combined; but an interpenetration of the elements of the design resulting from the combination of these units replaces the simple additive juxtaposition of the multi-unit designs. Repetitions and the multiplicity of focal points are equally important here, to give the impression of never-ending succession. The interpenetration of design elements may occur

Illustration 21.30

Frontispiece of a Qur'ān from the Sulaymāniyyah Library, Isṭanbūl. [Courtesy Ministry of Culture and Tourism, Government of Turkey.]

on any level, on that of the combination of individual motifs or that which involves more complex organizations of modules and complexes within the pattern. Each module or modular combination in this ornamentation can be experienced separately, but parts of each entity or the entity as a whole may also be viewed as fulfilling a different role in another part of the design. For example, each of the small six-sided units containing geometric motifs that make up the interlocking arabesque of Illus. 21.4 may be appreciated separately. On another level, each of these figures can be viewed as one part of a larger hexagon. On still another structural level, each border unit module of the larger hexagon has a double function in the structure; it interpenetrates (is ***mutadākhilah***) with another six-sided combination. Such interpenetrations become highly complex in many Islamic decorative patterns.

Both of the disjunct structures—the multi-unit and the interlocking structures—comprise organizations of a number of modules which retain their separate and distinct identity despite their combination into larger artistic entities. Both structures fulfill the infinite pattern requirements of a multiplicity of focal points in their repetitive patterning and give the impression of unending continuity. Both feature the six basic characteristics of the Islamic arts: abstraction, modules, successive combinations, repetition, dynamism, and intricacy.

The third and fourth structures used for the Islamic arts have been classified as "conjunct" rather than "disjunct." These structures are also examples of infinite patterning, but they present a visual, aesthetic expression of ***tawḥīd*** that is more representative of continuity rather than of disjunction.

Meander Structure

Of the conjunct or ***muttaṣilah*** structures, the first and least complicated is the "meander" arabesque, in which a seemingly never-ending succession of calligraphy, leaves, flowers, tendrils, and/or abstract shapes follow each other but are not readily divisible into the separate or distinct modules of the multi-unit arabesque. The motifs may be mounted on a trailing vine or may themselves provide the "track" for a continuing evolution. They defy assignment of beginning or middle, of climax or conclusion, to the pattern. Such continuous, additive organizations of motif components can be found in the arabesque panels for a small object as well as in panels or borders for architectural members or design units. In the former case, panels evidencing meander organization of the design elements are often combined with other modules of similar or dissimilar shape to create another level of design unit combination. The internal structure for such an arabesque is conjunct, while the overall structure for the work may be based on another artistic ***taf'īlah*** or form.

Expanding Structures

The second species of conjunct structure, and the fourth of the commonly used basic forms of Islamic ornamentation, shall be designated as the "expanding" arabesque; for it gives the impression of an ever-unfolding sunburst or explosive design. Its central modular core provides one "view" within the infinite pattern, but not by any means the only one. Border after border, and figure after figure are added successively to that central core, either by the artist in creation, or by the viewer in perception. Each addition furnishes a new composite and a new vision of the arabesque. Eventually the border of the page, the edges of the platter, the extremities of the wall panel, the façade of the building are reached, and the pattern must be cut, without completion or finality. That inconclusiveness is not to be disguised or avoided; in fact, it is of the essence of the Islamic pattern that, through this inconclusiveness, the design demands continuation beyond its empirical limits by the viewer's imagination. The mind is eventually unable to continue this process, and must submit to the realization of its incapacity in front of the demand. In this aesthetic exercise, in the experience of awe which it engenders, the percipient gains an understanding that there exists an inexplicable Reality, which is beyond space-time, but which is the Source and Determiner of all that comprises creation.

Given its significance in every branch of Islamic art, ornamentation can be seen as one of the most important elements, if not *the* most important element, in the aesthetic tradition of the Muslim peoples. It is not a superfluous addition to the art object which can be added or subtracted without aesthetic damage or consequence. Instead, it is of the very essence of the Islamic arts—an essence that determines the use of materials, molds the perception of forms, and generates a series of structures that can be recognized in every branch of artistic production. This essential element is not, therefore, simply a result of sociological, economic, or geographic factors and influences. It is not merely a component to be "worked into" the art product "for purposes of embellishment." Rather, it results from the underlying motivation, the raison d'être of the whole culture and civilization of the Muslim peoples. It has been necessitated and determined by the message of *tawḥid.*

NOTES

1. For example, Titus Burckhardt, *Art of Islam: Language and Meaning* (London: World of Islam Festival Publishing Co., 1976); Ernst Grube, *The World of Islam* (New York: McGraw-Hill, 1966); Ernst Kühnel, *Islamic Art and Architecture,* trans. Katherine Watson (London: G. Bell and Sons, Ltd., 1966); G. Marçais, *L'Art musulman* (Paris: 1962); David Talbot Rice, *Islamic Art* (New York: Praeger, 1965).

2. See, for example, Oktay Aslanapa, *Turkish Art and Architecture* (New York: Praeger, 1971); G. Marçais, *L'Architecture musulmane d'occident: Tunisie, Algérie, Maroc, Espagne, et Sicile* (Paris, 1954); Arthur Upham Pope, *Persian Architecture: The Triumph of Form and Color* (New York: George Braziller, 1965); A. Volwahsen, *Living Architecture: Islamic Indian* (New York, 1970).

3. Thomas W. Arnold, *Painting in Islam* (New York: Dover Publications, 1965); Arthur Urbane Dilley, *Oriental Rugs and Carpets: A Comprehensive Study,* revised by Maurice S. Dimand (Philadelphia: J. B. Lippincott Co., 1959); Martin Lings, *The Quranic Art of Calligraphy and Illumination* (London: World of Islam Festival Trust, 1976); Arthur Lane, *Later Islamic Pottery,* 2nd ed. (London, 1971).

4. Two examples: Arthur Upham Pope, "Foliate Patterns on the Alp Arslan Salver," *Bulletin of the American Institute for Persian Art and Archaeology,* 4 (1908), pp. 75–78; and R. Nath, "Depiction of Fabulous Animals (Gaj-Vyala) at the Delhi Gate of Agra Fort," *Medieval India,* 2 (1972), pp. 45–52.

5. Vinigi L. Grottanelli, "Ornamentation," *Encyclopedia of World Art* (New York: McGraw-Hill, 1965), Vol. 10, col. 831.

6. E. Herzfeld, "Arabesque," *Encyclopédie de l'Islam* (Paris: Picard, 1913), Vol. 1, pp. 367–372; M. S. Dimand, *A Handbook of Mohammedan Decorative Arts* (New York: Metropolitan Museum of Art, 1930), p. 12; Anthony Hutt, *Islamic Architecture, North Africa* (London: Scorpion Publications, 1977), p. 21; Derek Hill and Lucien Golvin, *Islamic Architecture in North Africa* (Hamden, Conn.: Archon Books, 1976), p. 64.

7. Titus Burckhardt, *Sacred Art in East and West: Its Principles and Methods,* trans. Lord Northbourne (London: Perennial Books, 1967), Introduction; and Ananda K. Coomaraswamy, *Christian and Oriental Philosophy of Art* (New York: Dover Publications, 1956), chap. 2.

8. See *Ṣaḥīḥ al-Bukhārī* (Arabic-English), trans. Muḥammad Muḥsin Khān (Al-Medina al-Munauwara: Islamic University, 1974), Vol. 7, pp. 365–367.

9. For example, Qur'ān 7:30–33, 57:27, 18:7, 16:8, 15:16, 37:6.

10. "Nous avons reconnu que ces oeuvres, créées à plusieurs milliers de kilomètres les unes des autres et à quelques siècles d'intervalle, présentaient entre elles un air de famille" (George Marçais, *L'Art musulman* (Paris: Presses Universitaires de France, 1962), p. 2.

11. This word designates a category that includes all those types of artistic ornamentation involving the fitting together of pieces of material to produce an overlay for an underlying base—marquetry, mosaic of stones and ceramic pieces, metal inlay, etcetera.

12. Engraving is the more inclusive term. It includes the process of cutting a design on a surface, or of using acid to produce the design. The latter is known as etching.

13. In this process, raised designs are created in metal objects through hammering from the reverse side.

14. The process of fusing a glassy, colored, opaque substance to the surface of metal, glass, or pottery.

15. Filigree ornamentation is composed of fine wires, most often of silver and less frequently of copper or gold. When these wire arabesque designs are affixed to solid pieces of metal—boxes, caskets, or vessels—the technique of decoration is known as *encrusting.*

16. To cast anything (metal, clay, plastic) is to form it into a particular shape by pouring or pressing the material into a mold.

CHAPTER 22

The Spatial Arts

Having dealt with the essence of Islamic art (Chapter 8), with calligraphy as the most important art form of Islamic culture (Chapter 20), and with the functions, significance, and structures of Islamic ornamentation (Chapter 21), we now turn to another field of the visual arts of Islamic civilization, the "spatial arts." This expression is inclusive of a number of creative efforts and products of the Muslim peoples, which have so many features in common as to make their conjoined treatment more suitable than an isolated presentation of each art form.

WHAT ARE THE "SPATIAL ARTS?"

Space has sometimes been described as the opposite of mass, as the negation of the solid in architecture.[1] According to that definition, the spatial arts would include only those architectural monuments with interior spaces which it is possible to enter. A significantly different view contends that all the visual arts could be regarded as "spatial arts" since they embody two and sometimes three of the spatial dimensions.[2]

Neither of these interpretations of the expression "spatial arts" is suitable for our purpose. The former is unduly limited since it excludes creations involving exterior space, the importance of wall treatments and ornamentation, and the aesthetic significance of the exteriors of buildings. All of these features have been crucially important in the experience and appreciation of an Islamic-built environment. The second theory is equally rejected here, since it prevents our organizing the Islamic visual arts into the appropriate and meaningful subdivisions needed.

What then are the perimeters of the "spatial arts" that best suit a discussion of Islamic art? Would this category include, for example, sculpture in the round, an art that reproduces zoomorphic, human, or other figures from nature in stone, metal, wood, or plaster? Such works certainly involve spatial dimensions, but they are almost nonexistent in Islamic art.[3] Their inclusion as examples of "spatial arts" would therefore be superfluous for this presentation. The use of naturalistic representations has not been favored for expression of the Islamic ideology, nor has it earned wide appreciation.

That does not mean that there is no sculpture in Islamic art, as some art historians have maintained. There is in fact a great deal of Islamic sculptured art; but, in keeping with the characteristic demand for abstraction, its examples have evidenced little concern for plastic modeling and naturalistic figures. Instead, the most frequent and appreciated examples of

Illustration 22.1

Islamic sculpture on arch and façade of the tomb of Jan Baba (d. 1608), Thatta, Pakistan. [Photo by L. al Fārūqī.]

sculpture done by Muslims have been those relief carvings that delineate infinite patterns. Such works can be found in abundance in all parts of the Islamic world; they use a great variety of materials as well as motifs (Illus. 22.1). Despite the importance of its examples, we will not treat Islamic sculpture in this chapter on the spatial arts, since in Islamic culture it is subsumed under the category of ornamentation (Chapter 21). It draws its characteristics, functions, and forms from that aspect of artistic production.

The first category, therefore, to be included in the Islamic "spatial arts" is one which, though it has sculptural and ornamental characteristics, plays an extra-ornamentation role in Islamic art. Its examples make use of the horizontal and vertical dimensions of space, as well as the plastic quality of volume. These "volume units," as we shall refer to them, include such free-standing or semi-attached items as fountains, columns, towers, triumphal arches, bridges, and aqueducts. As three-dimensional objects, they are designed to be seen from the exterior only. Like sculpture in the round, they can be contemplated and experienced from a number of viewpoints as the observer moves to different positions around the objects. They usually have no interior space that can be entered. They present the viewer with a succession of views and often incorporate a number of sides, planes, or superimposed bands, as well as the succession of units integral to the arabesque ornamentation covering their surfaces. These structures differ from the arts of ornamentation by including the pronounced spatial qualities of volume and mass. They are affective not only in themselves but in the alteration of the exterior and interior spaces of the surroundings.

A second category of the spatial arts includes those artistic creations that add interior space and enclosure to the horizontal and vertical dimensions and give the perception of depth, volume, and mass. These are the arts commonly designated as "architectural."

A third constituent of the spatial arts is landscaping, an art form developed extensively and with outstanding success by the Muslim peoples. It includes the creative and beautiful features of horticulture (the planting and care of plants) as well as that of aquaculture (the science of the artistic use of water in canals, ponds, fountains, and waterfalls).

The aesthetic treatment of space involves a fourth component, which can be described as the relationship of one building to proximate buildings, to the open spaces around them, and to the compound, complex, village, urban quarter, or city of which the building is a member. Such features of the built environment are no less important to Islamic art. Sometimes the expression "urban planning" is used to designate this subdivision of the spatial arts. That label is misleading, however, since it ignores the significance of such features in rural as well as in urban design. For the purposes of this discussion, we shall identify this fourth category of the spatial arts by the more precise though cumbersome expression "urban and rural design." The spatial arts of Islamic culture, therefore, will include four important subdivisions of artistic creation: (1) volume units, the free-standing or semi-detached edifices without interior space; (2) architecture, or structures with interior space; (3)

BASIC MOSQUE PLANS

Area I

Hypostyle Hall (usually with arcaded courtyard)

Marrakesh:	Mosque of the Qasbah (c. 1185–1190)
	Kutubiyyah (1125–1130)
Rabāṭ:	Hasan Mosque (1195–1196)
Tinmal:	Jāmi‘ Mosque (1153–1154)
Algiers:	Grand Mosque (end 11th cent.)
Tripoli:	Al Naqah Mosque (8th–10th cent.)
Qurṭubah:	Grand Mosque (785–987)
Fās:	Bū ‘Ināniyyah (1350–1355), with domical vaulting
	Qarawiyyīn (857)
Qayrawān:	Grand Mosque (836)
Tunis:	Jāmi‘ al Zaytūnah (864)
Ṣūṣah, Tunisia:	Grand Mosque (850–851)
Sfax:	Grand Mosque (998)
Mahdiyyah, Tunisia:	Grand Mosque (916)
Tlemcen:	Masjid al Manṣūr (14th cent.)
	Grand Mosque (1082, 1136)

Domed Unit(s)

Toledo:	Bāb Mardūn (999)

Centrally Domed Plan

Algiers:	Mosque of the Fishery (1660)

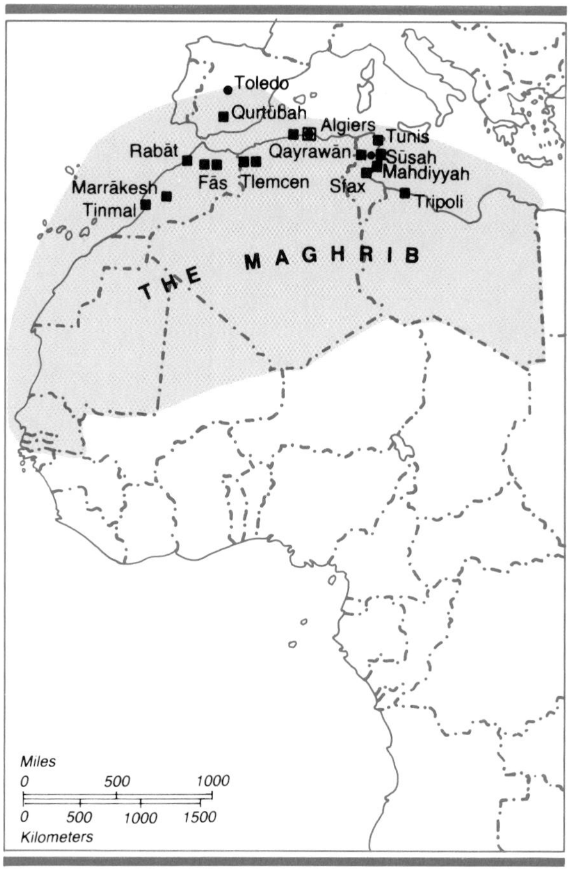

■ Hypostyle Hall
• Domed Unit
▣ Centrally Domed Plan

Map 63. Mosque Plans Used in the Maghrib

landscaping (both horticulture and aquaculture); and (4) urban and rural design.

Like the other arts of Islamic culture, all the spatial arts give evidence of a determination by the Islamic worldview and God view—in other words, by *tawḥīd.* Volume units, architecture, landscaping, and urban and rural design, as executed under the stimulus of Islamic culture, are as much expressions of Islam and its ideology as the calligraphic arts and those two- and three-dimensional ornamentations that transfigure Islamic art products. We shall see below that these four categories of artistic creation are based on the same core characteristics relevant to all the Islamic arts.

THE CORE CHARACTERISTICS

Abstraction

It may be fairly easy for the reader to imagine and comprehend the consequences of abstraction in the arts of ornamentation—a general rejection of figures as iconographic content, and the stylization or denaturalization of motifs used—but it may be less obvious how a tower, a building, a landscape design, or a city can give evidence of abstract quality. In the Islamic spatial arts, special methods and techniques have been developed and used to deemphasize nature and thus fulfill Islamic aesthetic goals. The transfigurations of nature as exemplified in the spatial arts belong to at least five major categories.

Overlay. One of these transfigurations runs parallel to a method discussed in Chapter 21, namely, the overlay of materials. This applies to volume units, individual buildings, rest houses and pavilions which form an important part of Islamic landscaping, as well as to complexes of buildings that make up major or

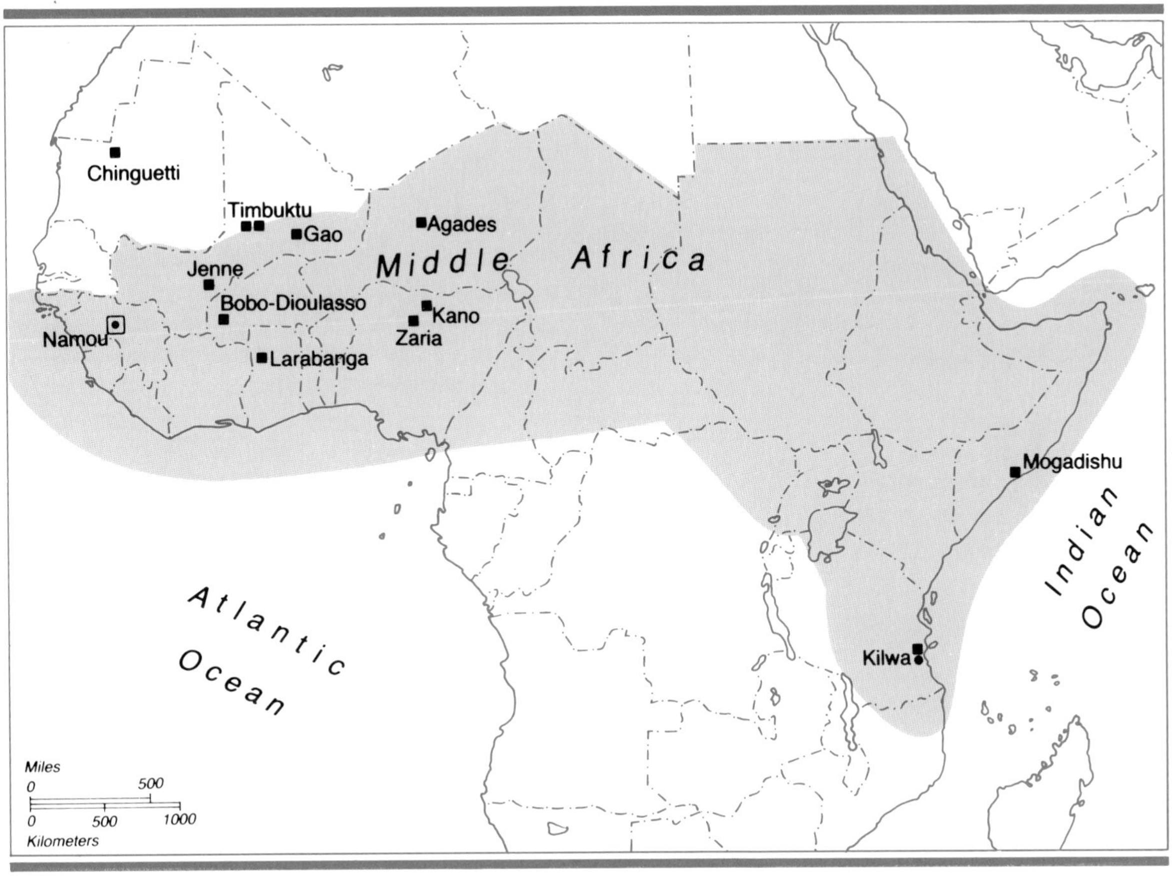

- ■ Hypostyle Hall
- ● Domed Unit
- ⊡ Centrally Domed Plan

Map 64. Mosque Plans Used in Middle Africa

minor portions of the rural and urban built environment. Since the ideas presented in the discussion on ornamentation are equally applicable here, there is little need for further elaboration of this feature. We would like to reemphasize, however, that abstraction in the spatial arts would not be complete without the techniques of overlay which have been so consistently used by Muslim builders.

Transfiguration of materials. The transfiguration of materials in the spatial arts again conforms to that described earlier in connection with the arts of ornamentation. The perception of the naturalistic qualities of the materials used is rendered aesthetically unimportant, and the attention of the viewer is directed instead toward the beauty and intricacy of

Area II

Hypostyle Hall

Kilwa, Tanzania:	Grand Mosque (15th cent.)
Agadez:	Grand Mosque (16th–19th cent.)
Bobo-Dioulasso:	Jāmiʿ Masjid (19th cent.)
Chinguetti:	Grand Mosque (13th–15th cent.)
Jenne:	Grand Mosque (14th–20th cent.)
Gao:	Askia al Ḥajj (1325)
Kano:	Jāmiʿ Masjid (15th–19th cent.)
Larabanga:	Jāmiʿ Masjid (17th–19th cent.)
Maska:	Jāmiʿ Masjid (19th cent.)
Mogadishu:	Fakhr al Dīn (13th cent.)
Timbuktu:	Grand Mosque (1325)
	Sankore Mosque (14th–15th cent.)
Zaria:	Jāmiʿ Masjid (19th cent.)

Domed Unit(s)

Kilwa:	Small Domed Mosque (15th cent.)

Centrally Domed Plan

Namou:	Jāmiʿ Masjid (18th–19th cent.)

Illustration 22.2

Terra cotta decoration, Bagha Mosque (built 1523), District Rajshani, Bangladesh. [Courtesy Department of Antiquities, Government of Bangladesh.]

the infinite patterns. Textures, grains, and other natural properties of construction materials are denied attention by the infinite patterns that cover their surfaces.

As a result of the abstraction achieved through transfiguration of materials, the Islamic spatial structure that one finds in village or city does not draw attention to the heaviness or lightness, the hardness or softness, the imperviousness or penetrability of the structural materials. The weight of a façade is visually dissipated by indentations, blind arches, windows, doorways, and decorative patterns (Illus. 22.2, 22.3, 22.4). The slender pillars supporting a wall disguise its actual mass and weight (Illlus. 22.5). Domes are constructed with apertures and ornamentations that deny the bulk and heaviness of the bricks, stone, or concrete out of which they are made (Illus. 22.6, 22.7). In addition to the two-dimensional painted, ceramic, brick, or stucco decorations, three-dimensional *muqarnas* overlays hide the underlying materials (Illus. 22.8).

The art of landscaping makes some use of building materials for the construction of pavilions and other structures that are incorporated into the Islamic garden. Features similar to the transfiguration of materials found in major buildings pertain here, despite the limited size of these structures. Landscaping features another manner of transfiguration of materials which

Illustration 22.3

Massive gateway to the area surrounding Jahangīr's Tomb, near Lahore, Pakistan, early seventeenth century. [Photo by L. al Fārūqī.]

Illustration 22.4

A village mosque of mud construction with "broken architecture," Ilorin, Nigeria. Such buildings are fast disappearing and are being replaced by buildings made of concrete blocks. [Courtesy A. R. Doi.]

Illustration 22.6

Interior of Mosque of Sulṭān Aḥmad, Isṭanbūl (1617). [Courtesy Embassy of Turkey, Washington, D.C.]

Illustration 22.5

Court of the Lions, Alhambra Palace, Granada, Spain. [Photo by Anmār al Zayn.]

Illustration 22.7

Cupola of the Hall of the Sisters, Alhambra Palace, Granada, Spain. [Photo by Anmār al Zayn.]

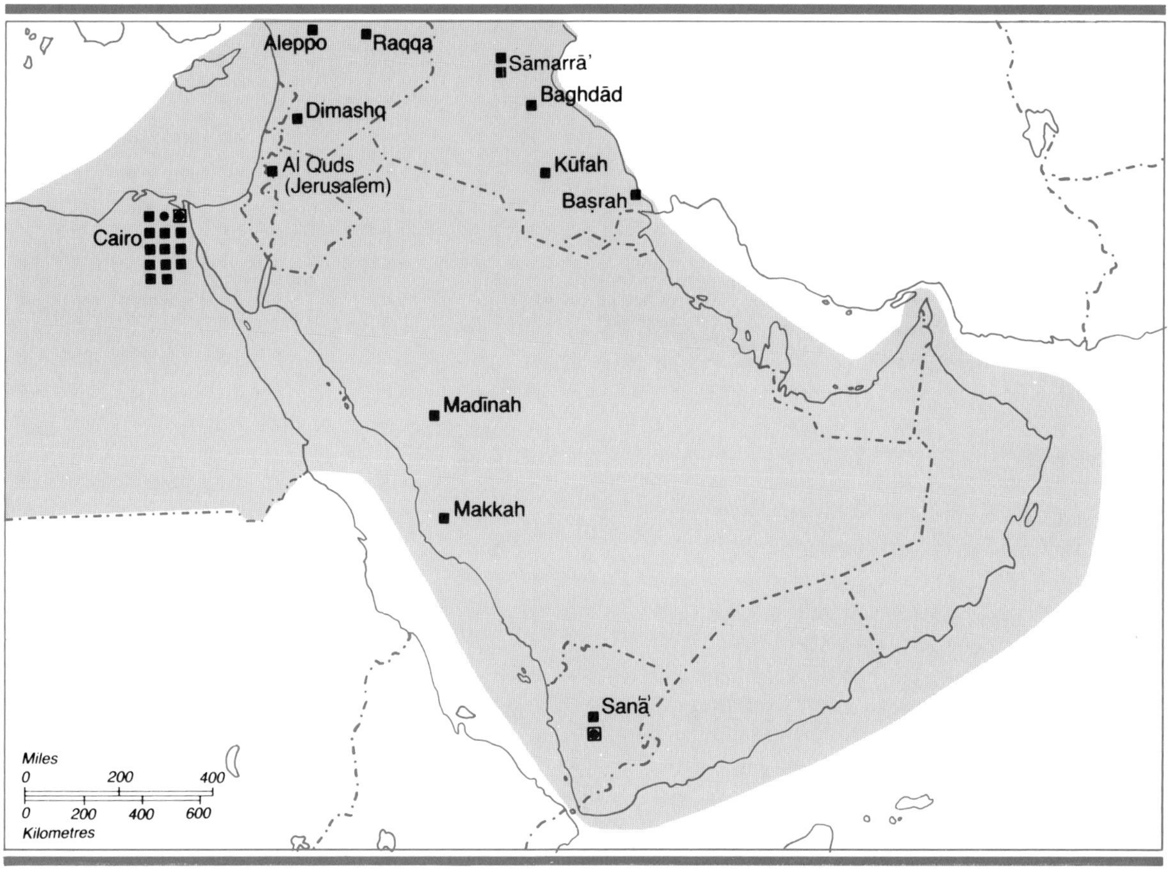

■ Hypostyle Hall
● Domed Unit
◙ Centrally Domed Plan

Map 65. Mosque Plans Used in the Mashriq

Area III

Hypostyle Hall

Raqqa, Syria:	Grand Mosque (772, rebuilt 1165-1166)
Baghdād:	Jāmi' al Kāẓimiyyah (19th c.)
Sāmarrā':	Grand Mosque of Abū Ḍulaf (859-861)
	Jāmi' Mosque of Al Mutawakkil (847-861)
Damascus:	Grand Mosque (705-715)
Aleppo:	Grand Mosque (1090)
Cairo:	Mosque of al Ṣāliḥ Talā'i' (1160)
	Mosque of Sulṭān Muḥammad Ibn Qalāwūn (1283-1285)
	Al Aqmār (1125)
	Al Azhar (970-972)
	Al Ḥākim (990-1012)
	Al Mu'ayyad Shaykh (1415-1420)
	Al Nāṣir Muḥammad (1318)
	Al Ẓāhir Baybars (1267-1269)
	Amīr Altunbughā (14th cent.)
	'Amr Ibn al 'Āṣ (641)
	Ibn Ṭūlūn (876-879)
	Barqūq (1392)
Ṣan'ā':	Grand Mosque (7th-17th cent.)
Baṣrah:	Mosque of 'Umar (8th cent.)

Domed Unit(s)

Cairo:	Al Juyūshī Mosque (1085-1092)

Centrally Domed Plan

Cairo:	Muḥammad 'Alī (1824-57)
Ṣan'ā':	Al Bāqiriyyah (16th cent.)

is peculiar to itself. The "materials" of the garden planner are trees and bushes, fruits and flowers, vines and grass, water and fountains. In the treatment of these materials, Muslim designers have displayed strikingly characteristic and innovative methods for achieving an abstract quality.

For example, there is a pronounced effort to present the fanciful and the denaturalized in the landscape artistry of Islamic culture. The Islamic garden is a formal one in which horticulture and aquaculture are applied to create stylized and infinite patterns. The Muslim landscaper does not preserve or imitate the uncultivated state of nature — however beautiful that may sometimes be. Instead, trees and bushes are planted, pruned, and trained in such a way as to create symmetrical and never-ending patterns. Rather than the earthly environment, it is the paradisiacal one that is cultivated. Water and plantings are never incorporated in their rough and natural state. A spring is not left to gush forth unrestrained from the mountainside, nor is the garden built to contain the natural bed of a brook or stream. Even waterfalls are rarely the result of natural phenomena in the Islamic garden. Their inclusion always entails a disciplining and transfiguration of the materials of nature. The controlled and patterned use of water disciplines and alleviates the natural characteristics of the surrounding environment rather than emphasizing them. Thus the treat-

Illustration 22.8

Entrance to Masjid-i-Shāh, Iṣfahān, Iran, 1612–1620. [Courtesy Muḥammad Thaqafī.]

ment of these materials is again reflective of the desire of Muslims to shape object and environment into an expression of Islamic identity and an example of infinite patterning.

Transfiguration of structures. The transfiguration of structures, like the overlay characteristics and the transfiguration of materials, is often a function of ornamentation in the Islamic arts. As such, it pertains to the embellishment of the spatial arts as well as to that of movable objects by providing another means of abstraction or denaturalization in the Islamic arts. The transfiguration of architectural structures has already been covered in Chapter 21, but there are some aspects of this particular method of transfiguration of nature that apply specifically to the spatial arts, contributing further to the fulfillment of Islamic aesthetic goals. Let us investigate these additional methods for abstraction which Muslims have incorporated in the tower or bridge, the mosque or palace, the garden or the plan of a city incorporating built up areas, passages for movement, and open spaces for commerce and recreation.

Whether seen or experienced from an internal or an external vantage point, the volume unit, the building, the garden, the complex, or the city give little hint of an overall plan. This is not to say that there is no plan. On the contrary, the spatial arts of Islamic culture have carefully organized and intricate structures which become apparent and clear on investigation of a detailed blueprint or by experiencing the spatial work of art in a temporal way, that is, by moving around and through it. For example, the much-used aisled hall or hypostyle plan as embodied in the Mosque of Qurṭubah (Illus. 22.9) cannot be experienced except by leisurely walking through its many aisles (Figure 22.1).[4] Upon entering the mosque from the courtyard, the casual visitor has no idea of the overall design of the building or of the intricate decorative treatment of the area near its *miḥrāb*. Despite the richness of the *miḥrāb* decoration and that of the areas nearby, the structure denies a single aesthetic focus for the building as a whole. Instead, this mosque is an additive composition of repetitive arches and aisles. This fact made successive enlargements to the original construction possible without damage to its aesthetic quality and perfection.[5]

The exterior impression given by any example of the Islamic spatial arts is no less revealing of its transfiguration of structure. An Islamic structure is rarely set off on a mountain top or isolated from its surroundings in ways that would provide visual perception of its overall plan. On the contrary, there is no understanding of the whole until each of its parts has been experienced by moving in and out and through and around its structures and the spaces between them. The *īwān* façade (Illus. 22.8) or the monumental gateway (Illus. 22.10) is so massive that it hides all notion of the rest of the building or buildings beyond. Structures are enmeshed with their surroundings in a way that disguises their outer limits. Even external borders merge with adjacent structures as mosque walls are backed to shops or dwellings, and the walls of one *ḥayy*, or quarter, blend with those of another (Figure 22.2).

Illustration 22.9

Mosque of Qurṭubah, Spain, interior view. [Photo by L. al Fārūqī.]

Transfiguration of enclosure. A fourth way in which the Islamic spatial arts enhance abstraction or denaturalization is through the transfiguration of enclosure. This consists not in the destruction or actual elimination of enclosing walls but in such treatment as would deemphasize their solidity and thus the impression they give of spatial limitation and confinement. We have already spoken briefly of the effect Islamic ornamentation has had on reducing the massiveness and opaqueness of walls, vaults, domes, and roofings. These features are, of course, equally important in the deemphasis of the solidity of enclosure.

Figure 22.1

The Mosque of Qurṭubah at four periods of its history

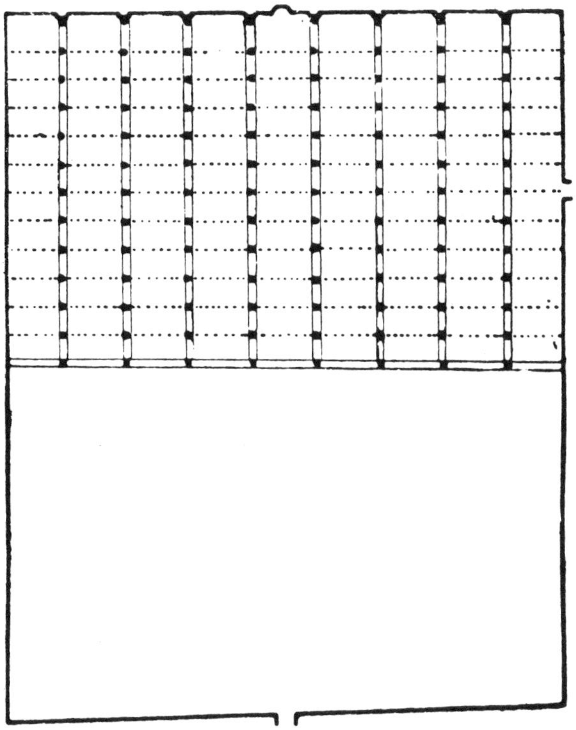

1. As built by Caliph 'Abd al Rahmān in 170/786.

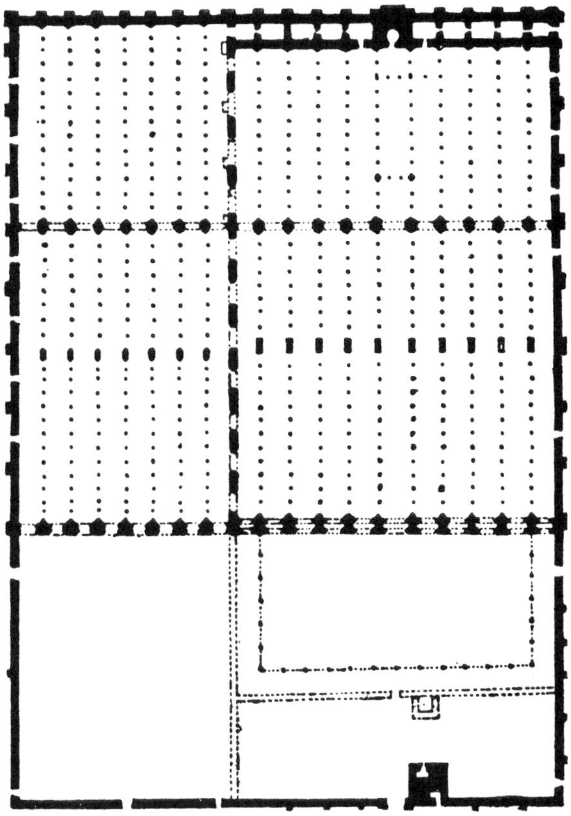

3. As enlarged in 377/987.

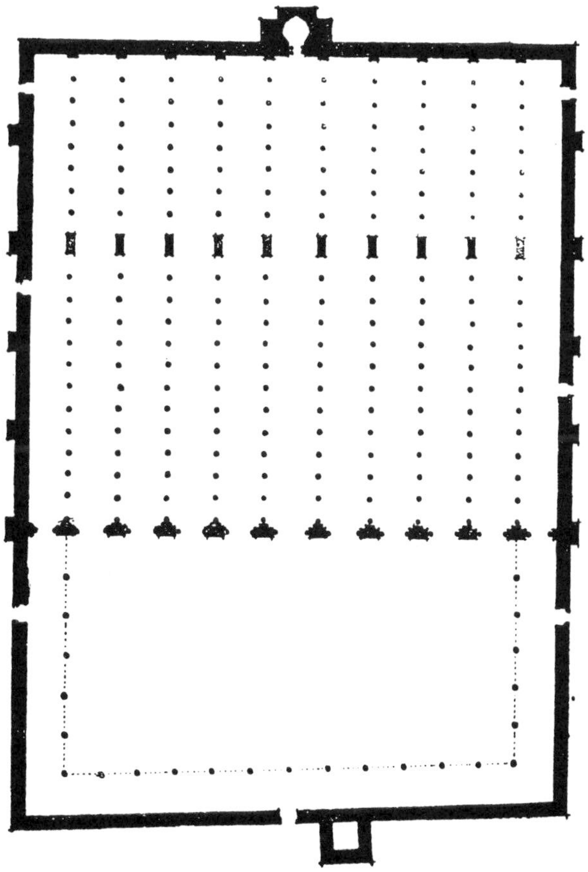

2. As enlarged in 234/848.

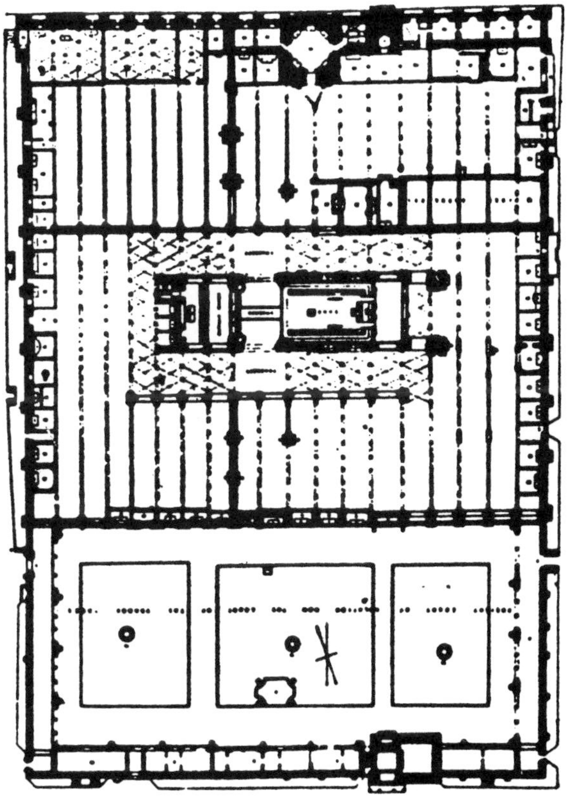

4. As a church after the expulsion of the Muslims from Spain.

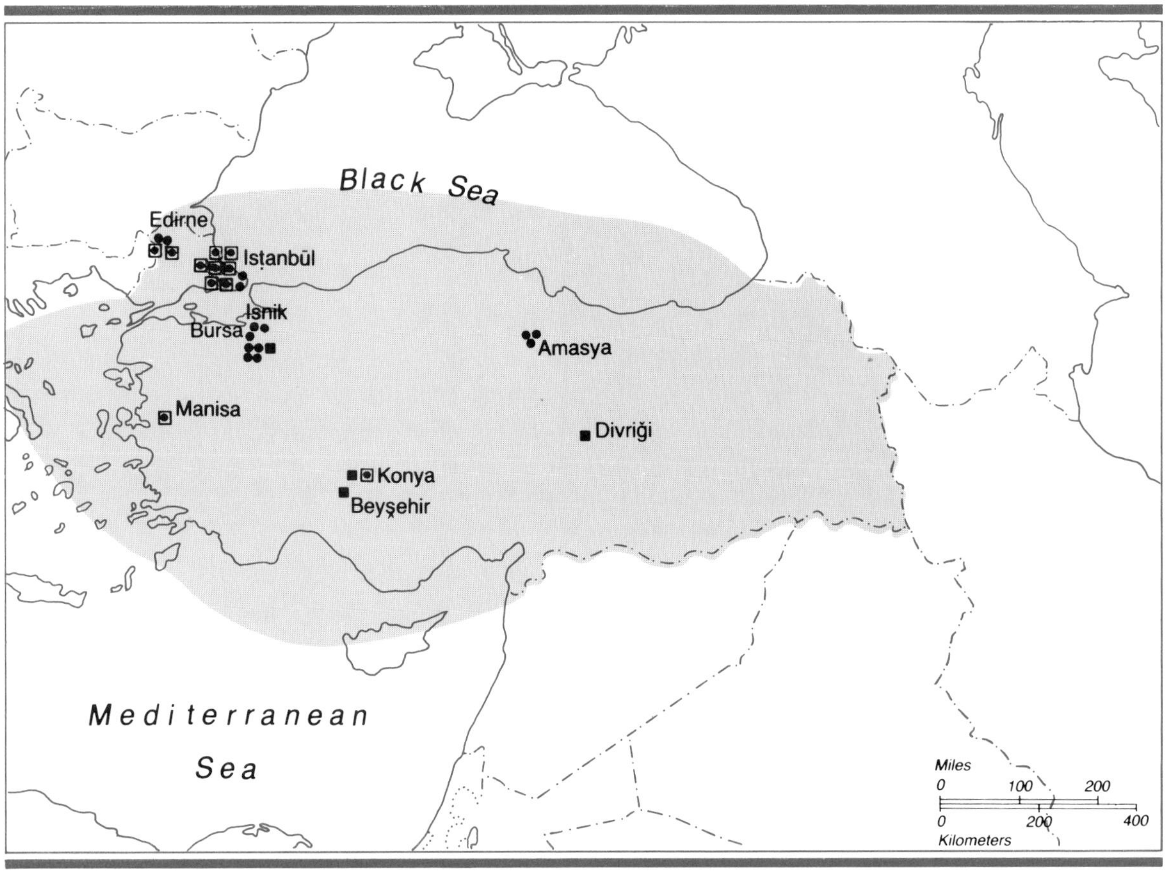

■ Hypostyle Hall
● Domed Unit
▣ Centrally Domed Plan

Map 66. Mosque Plans Used in Turkey

Area IV

Hypostyle Hall

Bursa:	Grand Mosque (1394–1413)
Beyşehir:	Eşrefoğlu Mosque (1297–1299)
Divriği:	Ulū Jāmi' (1228–1229)
Konya:	'Alā' al Dīn (1220)

Domed Unit(s)

Amasya:	Bāyazīd Pasha (1414–1419), multi-unit
	Yorguc Pasha (1428), multi-unit
	Mehmed Pasha (1486), multi-unit
Bursa:	Mosque of Orhan (1339–1340), multi-unit
	Yildirim (1390–1395), multi-unit
	Yeşil Cami (1412–1419), multi-unit
	Murād II (1424–1426), multi-unit
	Ḥamzah Bey (mid 15th c.), multi-unit with cross-axial īwāns
Edirne:	Murādiyyah (1435), multi-unit
	Eski Cami (1402), multi-unit
Iṣtanbūl:	Murād Pasha (1469), multi-unit
	Maḥmūd Pasha (1462), multi-unit
Iznik:	Yeşil Cami (1378–1392), single unit
	Haci Ozbek (1333), single unit

Centrally Domed Plan

Edirne:	Selimiyyah (1569–1575)
	Üç Şerefeli (1447)
Iṣtanbūl:	Nurosmaniyyah (1748–1755)
	Şehzade Mehmet (1548)
	Sokullo Mehmet (16th cent.)
	Sulaymāniyyah (1550–1556)
	Sulṭān Aḥmad (1609–1617)
	Rustam Pasha (1560)
	Yeni Cami (1597)
Manisa:	Murādiyyah (16th cent.)
Konya:	Şeref al Dīn Cami (1636)

Illustration 22.10

Gateway of Badshāhī Mosque, Lahore, Pakistan (1674). [Photo by L. al Fārūqī.]

Figure 22.2

Typical plan for urban-rural organization of
(a) clusters of residential-commercial units around an access street;
(b) successive combination of those modules in a larger complex made accessible by a larger street (after Stefano Bianca).

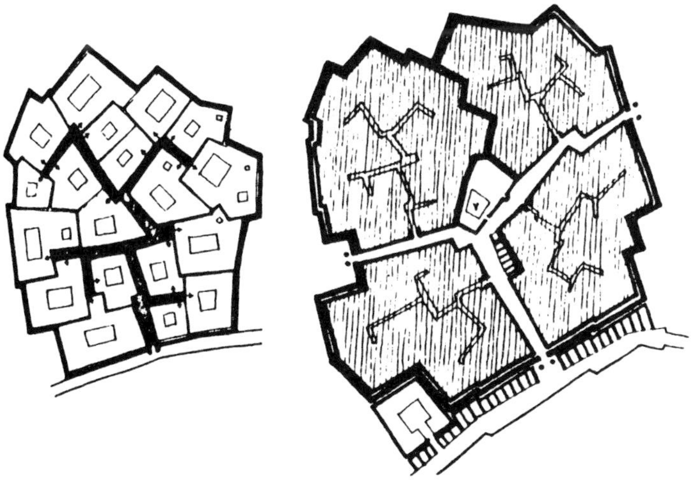

Another characteristic feature that exemplifies transfiguration of enclosure occurs in those structures that incorporate an internal courtyard. Where solid walls surround three sides of an enclosed space, a fourth side is often left open to the adjacent courtyard. This device for transfiguration of enclosure has the effect of visually denying any antagonism or opposition between man and the spatial enclosure or environment in which he lives and moves. Niche-like rooms abound in Islamic structures. While maintaining their identity as enclosures, they are, at the same time, part and parcel of the adjacent open or enclosed court into which they expand and for which they provide an element of protection and of enlargement of space. Windows sometimes proliferate (Illus. 22.11, 22.12) until walls could accurately be described as window screens rather than enclosing masonry barriers marking off human space from that of the larger world beyond. Archways and doorways are enlarged

Illustration 22.11

Mosque of Sulṭān Aḥmad, Isṭanbūl, Turkey, windows from interior (1617). [Photo by L. al Fārūqī.]

Illustration 22.12

Sulaymāniyyah Mosque, arches and side window wall, Isṭanbūl, Turkey (1557). [Photo by L. al Fārūqī.]

and multiplied to facilitate physical and aesthetic movement from one spatial module to another (Illus. 22.13) and to defy any impression of confinement (Figure 22.3). Arcades link the surrounding rooms to an open courtyard of a dwelling, mosque, or ***madrasah,*** thereby negating the feeling of sharply defined inner and outer spaces (Figure 22.4). Balconies and terraces, courtyards and squares provide exterior additions to the living and working areas of a building. Even domes lose their impression of enclosure and confinement as decorative overlays and the proliferation of windows cause the viewer to move aestheti-

Figure 22.3

Arcades surrounding the courtyard of the Grand Mosque of Qayrawān, Tunisia (836)

Illustration 22.13

Court of the Myrtles, Alhambra Palace, Granada, Spain. [Photo by L. al Fārūqī.]

Figure 22.4

Arcade archways lining *Ṣaḥn* of Al Ḥaram al Sharīf

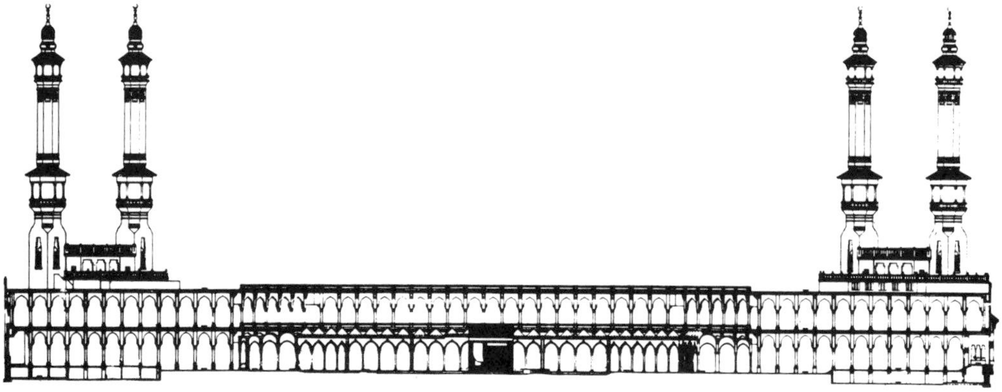

Illustration 22.14

Dome of Sulaymāniyyah Mosque, Isṭanbūl, Turkey (1557). [Photo by L. al Fārūqī.]

Illustration 22.15

King Khālid International Airport, Riyadh, Saudi Arabia. [Courtesy Aḥmad Totonji.]

cally and imaginatively into the space beyond. Sometimes a series of semidomes and exedrae bubble forth from the central dome to visually expand its limits (Illus. 22.14, 22.15; Figure 22.5), or a series of small domes replace the more confining barrier of a flat ceiling (Illus. 22.16; Figure 22.6). Space seems to be set free for human movement as well as aesthetic perception in these examples of the spatial arts.

Transfiguration or ambiguity of function. As a fifth feature of abstraction, the Islamic spatial arts exemplify the transfiguration or ambiguity of function. The individual room is not restricted to a single use.[6] Furniture is sparse and leaves much of the space free for a variety of activities. Both public and private needs may be filled by a single room at different times of the day. Utilization of rooms may also vary from season to season with the changes of weather — the warmer parts of the house serving for more general

Figure 22.5

Ṣehzade Mehmet Cami (centrally domed structure), Isṭanbūl (1548)

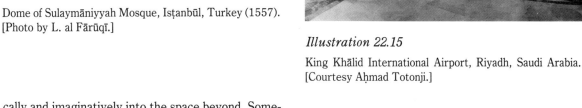

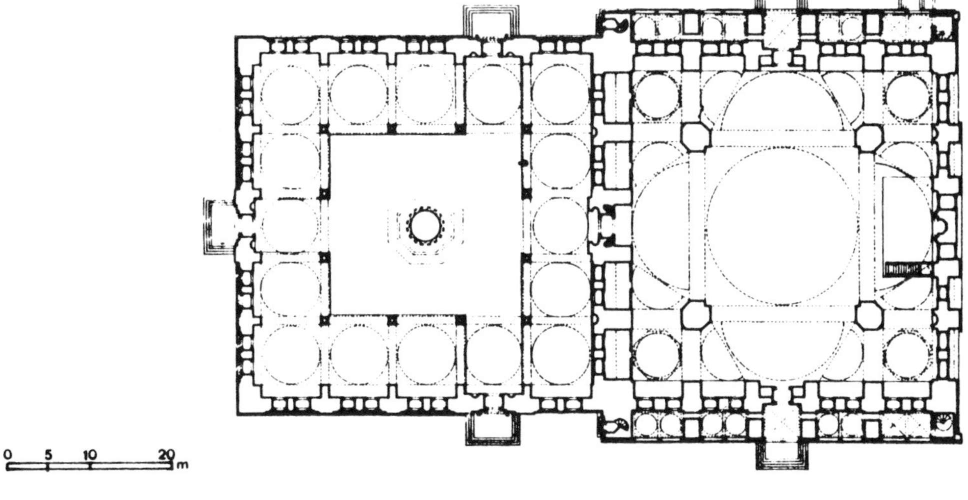

Illustration 22.16
Mosque of Ulu Jāmi', Bursa, Turkey (1396–1399). [Photo by L. al Fārūqī.]

Figure 22.6
Plan of Wazīr Khān Masjid (domed units structure), Lahore (1634–1636)

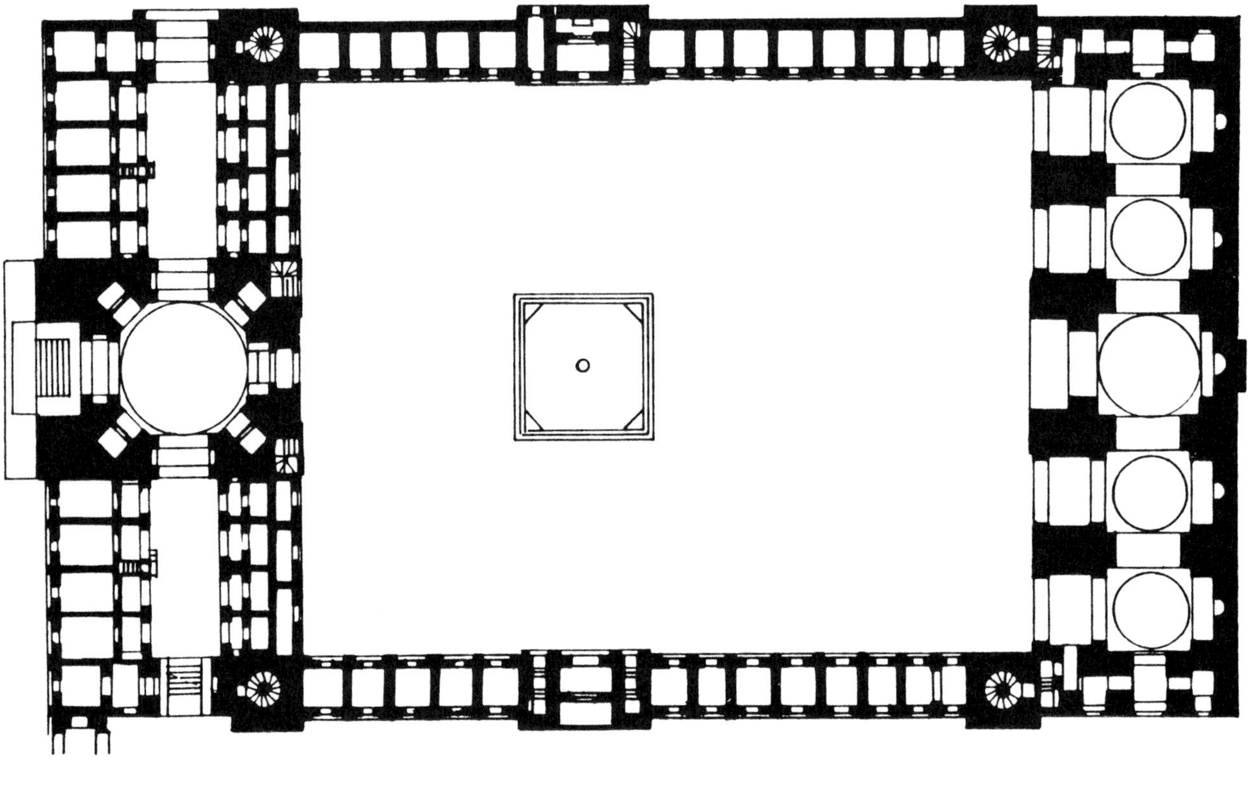

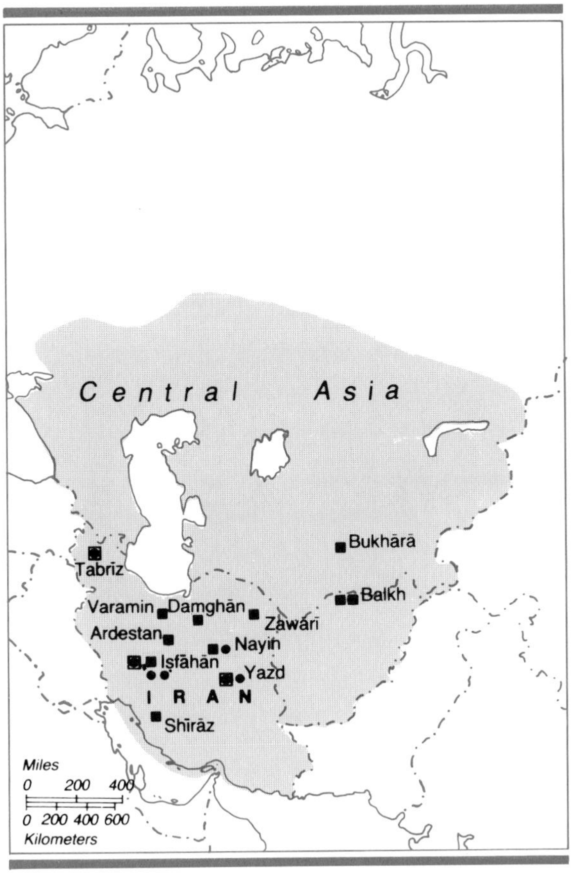

■ Hypostyle Hall
• Domed Unit
◧ Centrally Domed Plan

Map 67. Mosque Plans Used in Iran and Central Asia

Area V

Hypostyle Hall	
Bukhārā:	Masjid al Kalān (1514)
Ardestan:	Jāmi' Mosque (1072–1092), with court and four īwāns
Balkh:	Masjid al Tārīkh (c. 830–840)
Damghān:	Tarik Khānah (mid 8th cent.), with domical vaulting
Varamin:	Jāmi' Masjid (1322–1326), hypostyle with dome, four īwāns, and courtyard
Iṣfahān:	Masjid al Jāmi' (11th–18th cent.), combination of hypostyle hall with domical vaulting and four-īwān plan
Nayin:	Jāmi' Masjid (960), with domical vaulting
Shīrāz:	Wakīl Masjid (18th cent.), with two īwāns
Zawārī:	Jāmi' Masjid (1135–1136, 1156), domed hypostyle hall with court and four īwāns
Domed Unit(s)	
Iṣfahān:	Masjid-i-Shah (1612–1638)
	Shaykh Luṭfullah (1602–1628)
Nayin:	Masjid-i-Bāb 'Abdullah (1300?)
Yazd:	Jāmi' Masjid (1324–1364), two domed chambers and one īwān
Centrally Domed Plan	
Balkh:	Abū Naṣr Parsa Masjid (15th cent.)
Iṣfahān:	Masjid-i-'Alī (1522)
Tabrīz:	Blue Mosque (1462–1465), with eight smaller domes
Yazd:	Masjid-i-Waqt wa Sa'āt (1326)

use during the winter months, and the cooler ones during the summer. Whether built as a school, a dwelling, or a mosque, there is little evidence in an Islamic building that it must be used for one specific purpose only. The architectural members regarded as characteristic of the mosque have not only been used in that context. A wide variety of other structures built for public as well as private use have incorporated the same elements. The *ṣahn* or open courtyard, for example, has been a predominant feature in domestic structures of both palatial and modest dimensions throughout the centuries of Islamic history (Figure 22.7). It has also been a common feature of such public buildings as the mosque, the caravansary, the *madrasah,* the hotel, and the office building (Figures 22.8, 22.9). The *miḥrāb* niche, which indicates the direction of prayer in a mosque, is an aid to the worshipper wherever he lives or works. Therefore, this element is often included in buildings for which the major purport is not that of worship. The niche as an architectural element has in fact been used for a great variety of purposes—for entrance or portal, vending stall, or semi-secluded area for sleeping, eating, or conversation. Arcades are another element of mosque construction which are found as well in other private and public buildings. They are even outstanding elements of those spatial constructions that include no interior space, the aqueducts, bridges, fountains, triumphal arches, and so on, identified as volume units (Illus. 22.17). The dome is commonly identified as an outstanding feature of mosque architecture, but it plays an equally important role as roofing for other types of buildings.

Function is also transfigured or disguised in the spatial arts by the fact that practically the same tech-

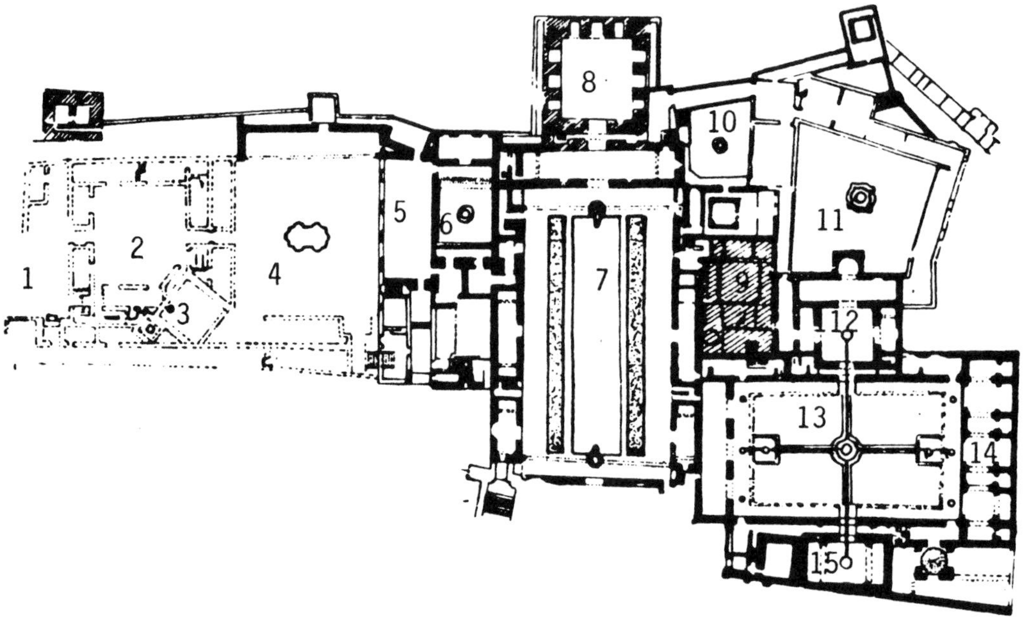

1. Entrance
2. First court
3. Mosque
4. Court of Machuca
5. Mexuar
6. Court of the Cuarto Dorado
7. Court of the Myrtles
8. Tower of Comares and Hall of the Ambassadors
9. Baths
10. Court of the Screen
11. Garden
12. Hall of the Two Sisters
13. Court of Lions
14. Hall of Justice
15. Hall of the Abencerajes

Figure 22.7

Alhambra Palace, Granada (13th–14th century.)

Figure 22.8

Plan of Masjid Ibn Ṭūlūn (hypostyle structure), Cairo (876–879)

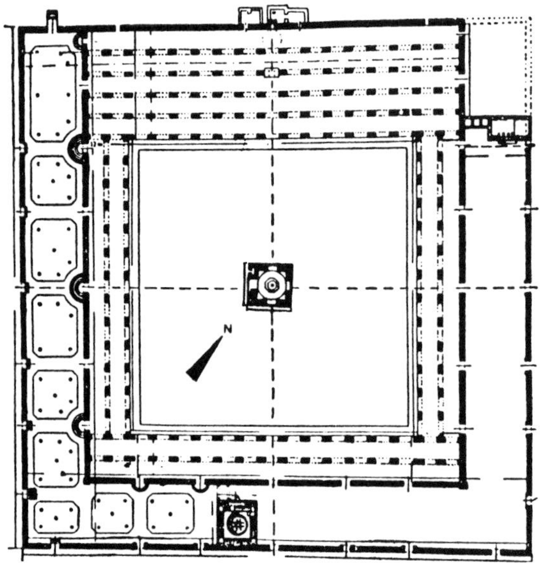

niques, materials, and motifs of ornamentation are applied to all structures, whether built for what would be considered a primarily religious purpose or a secular one. Although in specifically religious structures figural art is consistently avoided, most other examples of the Islamic spatial arts also make use of nonfigurative artistic motifs. Calligraphy, geometric figures, and vegetal motifs have been the ubiquitous vocabulary of decoration throughout Islamic history, in every region of the Muslim world, regardless of the function of the building or architectural complex. Building techniques and materials have differed according to locale and availability, but never because of the function of the finished construction.

Related to the transfiguration of function is the fact that, in an Islamic context, there is little desire to provide an isolated environment for any human activity. The life of the Muslim community is, in fact, a constant intermingling of religious activities with secular pursuits. Such integration of the secular and the religious is also evident in the spatial arts. A poly-

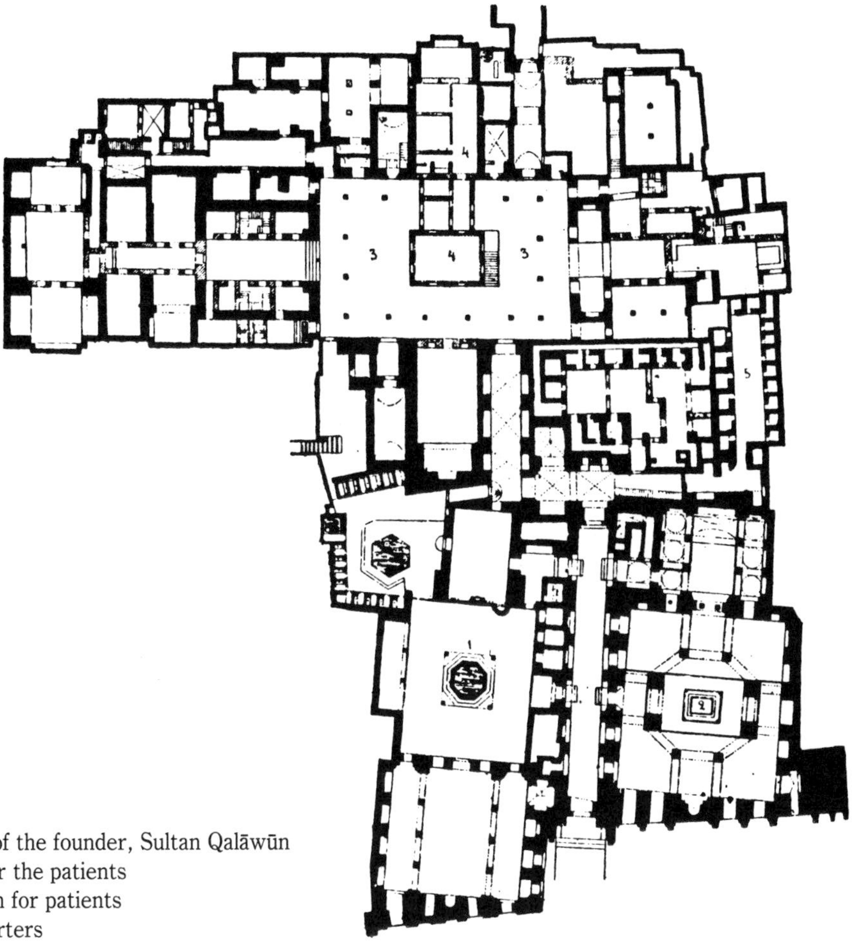

1. Mosque
2. Mausoleum of the founder, Sultan Qalāwūn
3. Courtyard for the patients
4. Waiting room for patients
5. Visitors' quarters

Figure 22.9

Hospital of Qalāwūn, Cairo (13th century.)

Illustration 22.17

Khwājū Bridge over the Zayandah River, Iṣfahān, Iran, a seventeenth-century engineering and artistic masterpiece.

Area VI

Hypostyle Hall

Agra:	Moti Masjid (1646–1653)
Aḥmadabād:	Jāmi' Masjid (1423)
Bagerhat:	Sath-Gumbad Masjid (c. 1440)
Champanir (in Gujarat):	Jāmi' Masjid (1523)
Delhi:	Jāmi' Masjid (1644–1658), with domical vaulting
	Khirki Masjid (c. 1375), with domical vaulting
	Moti Masjid (17th cent.), with domical vaulting
	Quwwah al Islām (1311–1316)
Fatehpur Sikri:	Jāmi' Masjid (c. 1570–1580), with domical vaulting
Gaur:	Tantipara, with domical vaulting
	Bara Sona Masjid (1526), with domical vaulting
Hazrat Pandua (Firozabad):	Quṭb Shāhī Masjid (1582)
	Adina Mosque (1375), hypostyle encircling a central court
Mandu:	Baba Adam's Mosque (1483), with domical vaulting
Tribeni:	Ẓafar Khān Ghāzī Mosque, with domical vaulting

Domed Unit(s)

Dacca:	Allakuri's Mosque (late 17th cent.), single unit
	Lalbagh Mosque (1678–1679), three domed units
	Bibi Maryam's Mosque, three domed units
Gaur:	Latton Masjid (1475), single dome
Lahore:	Badshāhī Mosque (1674)
	Masjid Wazīr Khān (1634–1636)
Sherpur:	Kherua Mosque (1582), three domed units
Sylhet:	Sankarpasa Mosque

Centrally Domed Plan

Gaur:	Chamkatti Mosque (1475)

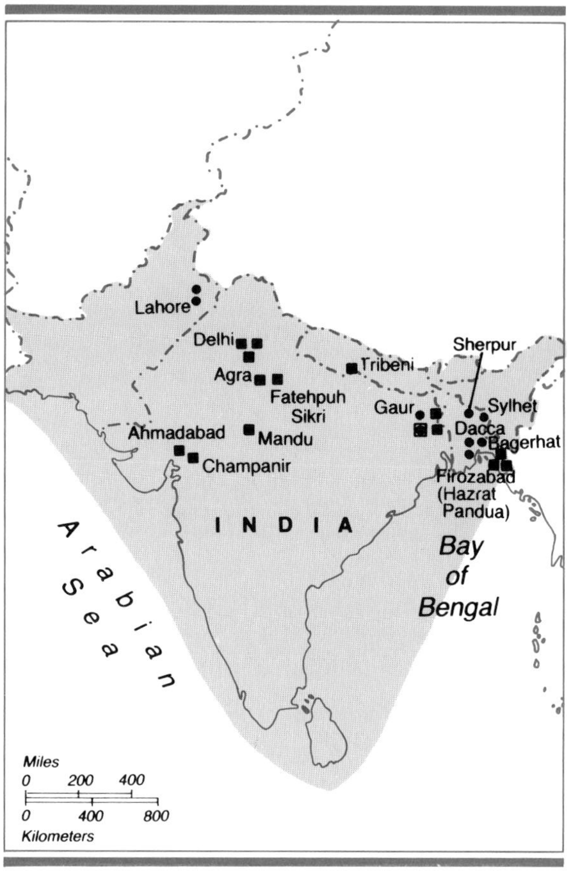

■ Hypostyle Hall
• Domed Unit
▣ Centrally Domed Plan

Map 68. Mosque Plans Used in the Indian Subcontinent

valent use of public and private space characterizes the Islamic-built environment.

Although the *sūq* (bazaar) is an urban quarter where much of the buying and selling of the Islamic city is negotiated, it is not isolated from the other activities of life. In addition to the shops, banks, and warehouses, which are necessary for the shopkeepers' trade, the mosque of the quarter is always close at hand for customers' and proprietors' use. The shopkeepers make their homes over their stores or in nearby low-income apartments. Residential facilities, as well as the caravansary, often interpenetrate the space of the *sūq,* and are themselves multifunctional buildings or complexes. The caravansaries or hostels of the Islamic world have traditionally included living space for both residents and travelers on the upper floors, while space for storerooms, shops, and even accommodations for animals was provided on the lower levels. Every ***madrasah*** has its mosque, and architectural complexes of all regions and periods give evidence of this multipurpose character which is implied in the transfiguration of function (Figure 22.10).[7]

The mosque itself exemplifies transfiguration of function in still another way by often being flanked with commercial spaces, the rent of which provides a permanent source of income for maintaining the structure. It is frequently combined with areas for educative, funerary, and residential purposes.

This lack of explicitness in function, which is an-

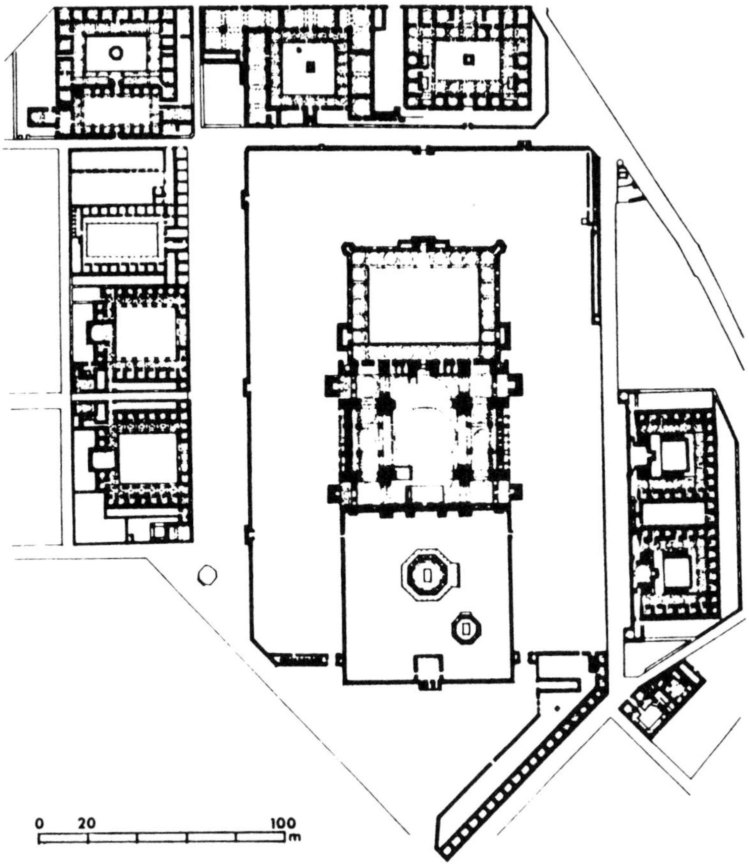

The complex includes four madrasahs, schools for the study of the hadīth, primary school, medical school, hospital, caravansary, public guesthouse for travelers, mosque, tombs, Turkish bath, soup kitchen, and marketplace.

Figure 22.10

Sulaymāniyyah Complex, Istanbul (1550–1557)

other aspect of abstraction, has not only been demanded by the desire to create artistic expressions of *tawḥīd;* it has also been required by the social and religious customs of the Muslim peoples. The Muslim believes that religion has an important role to play in every aspect of life, and, as a corollary, that all aspects of life are in some sense religious. There is no sharp differentiation between the sacred and the profane, no cleavage between the religious and the secular. The aesthetic transfiguration of function through the varied use of buildings and architectural elements has provided the individual architectural monument, as well as the built environment, with a generally multifunctional character. All monuments, even those of primarily secular function, are linked somehow to the religious dimension of Islamic life by inclusion of a place for prayer, a well or fountain donated by the pious for the benefit of the poor, or a religiously significant inscription added for decoration on a wall.

Units/Modules

In discussing the various aspects of abstraction in the Islamic spatial arts, we have touched on a number of the other five core characteristics of the Islamic arts in general. In the remainder of this section on the spatial arts, we will discuss specific examples of these other aesthetic aspects as they pertain to the spatial arts.

Just as the transfiguring ornamentation patterns on small objects or architectural monuments feature a number of internal modules or units which are combined in an additive way, the spatial arts are collectives of smaller modular entities. The Islamic palace is not a single block of rooms leading to one important

Area VII	
Hypostyle Hall	
Jakarta:	New Mosque
Turfan:	Masjid Turfan (17th cent.)
Domed Unit(s)	
Kuala Lumpur:	Jāmi' Masjid (early 20th cent.)
Centrally Domed Plan	
Kuala Lumpur:	Masjid Negara (mid-20th cent.)
Taipei:	Taipei Mosque

hall or throne room. Instead, it is often a combination of courtyard units, each open court acting as a nucleus surrounded by its ancillary rooms. The *madrasah* comprises a number of self-contained segments: one for prayer; four wings for each of the schools of law; a dormitory section; and perhaps an apartment complex or a mausoleum. The landscaped garden is made up of a series of carefully laid out and planted modules of ground interspersed with separate pools, pavilions, and arbors. The apartment complex has various internal segments, some for the reception of guests, and others for family use, storage, or commerce. The caravansary has one module for guest rooms, another designated as a mosque, others for shops, animal quarters, and so on. Even the urban quarter, or the city as a whole, is divided into a number of self-contained architectural-social-administrative-living units. Each of these is known as a *ḥārah* ("place for

Map 69. Mosque Plans Used in East Asia

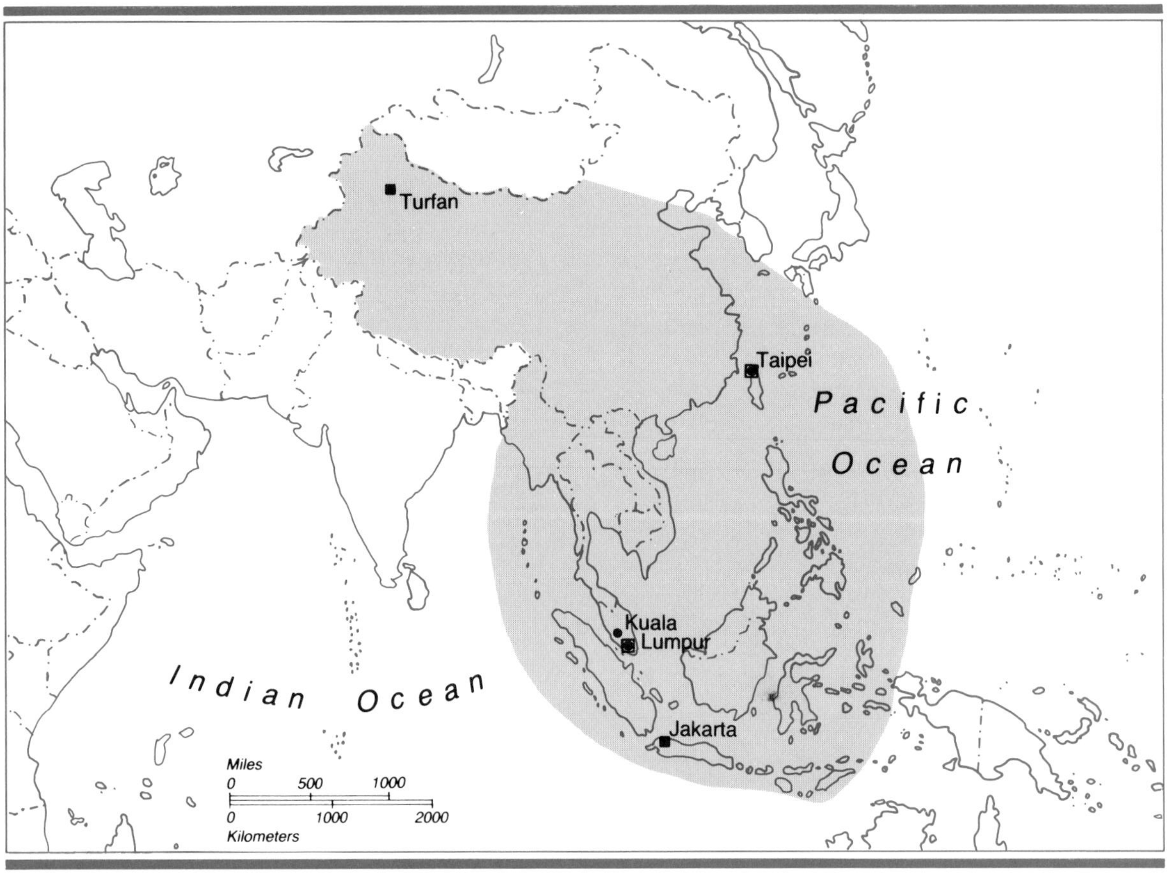

- ■ Hypostyle Hall
- ● Domed Unit
- ▣ Centrally Domed Plan

Illustration 22.18

Panoramic view of city of Lahore with Badshāhī Mosque in background. [Courtesy Embassy of Pakistan, Washington, D.C.]

turning") or *ḥayy* ("living space"). The former is generally equivalent to a small street open only at one end, which leads to a number of houses or places of business. The term *ḥayy* is used for a larger, autonomous segment of the town or city. In an Islamic environment, every neighborhood is a complete and integrated entity, an environmental module, with its mosque, shops, restaurants, residences, and areas for recreation.

Successive Combinations

The modules of the spatial arts are combined to form larger combinations on a number of levels. For example, separate rooms of a dwelling, which constitute the most basic and simple of spatial modular elements, are combined to form the bordering rooms of an open courtyard. On a successively more expansive level of combination, a number of courtyard and room units produce the domicile or palace. On a still wider level, they are added to an adjoining garden module or to one or more adjacent structures.[8] The mosque may comprise an additive series of domed units on one level of combination. These may be joined to an arcaded courtyard, a gateway, or a pavilion on a more inclusive level (Illus. 22.18). As we have seen, a religious complex may contain a prayer hall, a mausoleum, a *ṣahn* or courtyard, dormitories, a hospital, a museum, as well as separate sections or modules for teaching. Each section retains its identity as a self-contained unit while forming part of a larger identity as it combines with similar or different modules around it. City planning evidences a similar series of combinations which assures "a clear functional subdivision of the urban system, but also a total integration of single buildings into a comprehensive urban fabric."[9] Each dwelling is a tight enclosure ensuring privacy and security, its walls often built back-to-back with an adjacent structure (Illus. 22.19). A number of such buildings, and perhaps open spaces for movement and recreation, form a more comprehensive urban combination. These in turn combine as an urban quarter, and on still another level, a number of such neighborhood combinations are joined to produce the town or city. None of these additive segments takes aesthetic precedence over another. Instead, the integral parts of the built environment fit together like the tesserae of a giant mosaic.

Illustration 22.19

Village of Takrūnah, Tunisia. [Photo by L. al Fārūqī.]

Repetition

The characteristic of repetition, which was found to be so important for the creation of two- and three-dimensional ornamentation in Islamic art, is also a common factor in the spatial arts. The units that are the components of successive combinations of open or enclosed spaces are repeated in identical or varied form in these additive spatial structures. This also occurs in the internal units of individual buildings and gardens, as well as in the combinations of buildings that constitute a public or private religious, domestic, economic, or educational complex; an urban quarter; or a complete village or city. The repetition of rooms and open courts, of garden plots and foundations, of *aḥyā'* (sing. *ḥayy*) and neighborhoods contributes to the symmetrical organization of the Islamic design, the denial of particularism of its parts, and the additive quality of the spatial arabesque.

Dynamism

The comprehension and appreciation of any example of the Islamic spatial arts must be achieved by moving sequentially through its spatial units. A total impression or view is never possible from afar. There is no development or architectural evolution to a single point of aesthetic climax. The individual building is so enmeshed and intertwined with its surroundings that it is difficult to know where it ends and an adjacent structure begins. Even city walls are "virtually invisible and materialize only by gates. . . . Otherwise they are totally entrenched in the urban structure, being composed of the walls of individual houses located on the border of the corresponding spatial zone."[10] The example of Islamic spatial art must therefore be experienced in a dynamic way, not in a single, static moment of time. Like the other Islamic arts, it must be comprehended through a sequential appreciation of its multiple parts.

Intricacy

Comparable in intricacy to that of the two- or three-dimensional decorations of Islamic art are the combinations of spatial units that make up a volume unit, a building, a garden, or an Islamic built environment. No less than the inlaid, sculpted, or painted design, the examples of spatial art is a complex organization of artistic elements.

In part, the quality of intricacy is enhanced by the ubiquitous patterns of interior and exterior decoration (Illus. 22.20). This is true for all the spatial arts. But structural complexity is also present.

Contemplating or experiencing an aesthetic product with an overall unity may enable the percipient to gain a quicker and easier grasp of the whole than can

Illustration 22.20

Karatay Madrasah, Konya, Turkey (1251). [Courtesy Embassy of Turkey, Washington, D.C.]

be achieved by a similar perusal of a nondevelopmental work. Some measure of intricacy in the process of perception is thus inherent in the Islamic art work. Its many-layered organization, its repetitions, and the dynamism of experiencing it all contribute to its impression of intricacy.

Although the modules on each level of combination within the built environment provide autonomous divisions ensuring internal separateness and privacy, that seclusion is not achieved through an external isolation of the structures from each other. On the contrary, adjacent buildings in a traditional Islamic city form a contiguous and intricate mass, broken only by the openings for air and sun provided by the inner courtyards. Only the major passageways for movement are highly visible, for pedestrian thoroughfares are often semiprivate, or roofed passages providing access from public sectors into private space.

Still another factor in creating the impression of intricacy in the spatial arts is the fact that the structures of an Islamic village or city are not confined to the identical square blocks created by the intersection of perpendicular roadways. Instead, the arteries of movement are determined by the extremities and access needs of the internal modules and modular combinations. This can be seen as a sharp contrast to the earlier Roman plans with their parallel and perpendicular street grids. Figure 22.11 shows a reconstruction with dotted lines of the Roman city Hadrianopolis, and the plan of the center of the later Islamic city of Edirne, Turkey, built on the same site. The lack of regularity or obvious grid plan is an important factor contributing to intricacy in the Islamic-built environment.

The Islamic city has often been compared to a maze by visitors who did not understand its internal logic. Intricate it is, like any other Islamic infinite pattern; but chaotic, it is not. Recent studies of the traditional built environment in Muslim cities have proven the social, economic, political, and religious logic of these towns and cities and their compatibility to the human beings who inhabited them.[11] We would only wish that those in charge of contemporary building and renovation schemes were as knowledgeable and would see to it that the new environments be in accordance with, supportive of, and representative of the residents' life and traditions.

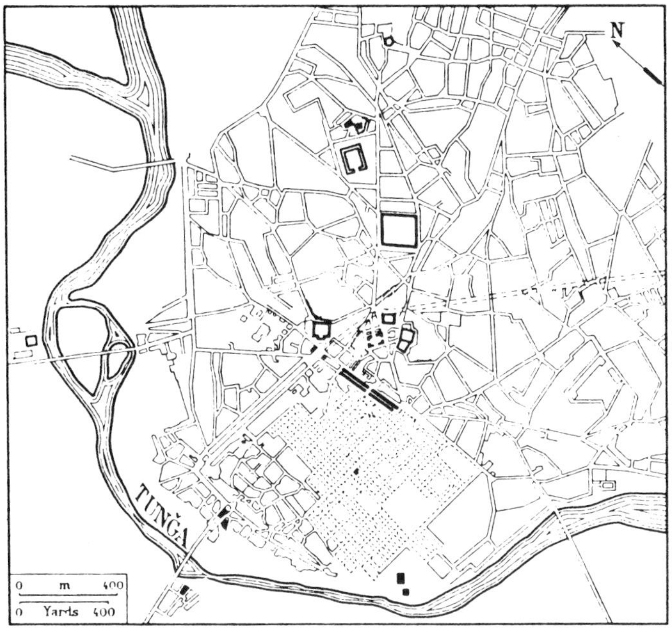

Figure 22.11

Plan of Edirne, Turkey, showing a reconstruction of the ancient Roman city of Hadrianopolis on the same site in dotted lines.

THE USE OF THE ARABESQUE STRUCTURES IN THE SPATIAL ARTS

The four structures that were found to be embodied in the designs of Islamic ornamentation (see Chapter 21) are also relevant for the spatial arts of the Muslim peoples. It would be impossible here to describe and discuss all the different kinds of structures that have been created by Muslim architects, landscapers, and rural/urban planners throughout more than fourteen centuries of Islamic history. The following examples must therefore be acknowledged as only a sample of the many representations of these structural types. We make no attempt to be exhaustive of the spatial art materials found in the Muslim world. Instead, the examples show the relevance of those organizational models and thereby help readers to discover and recognize other representations on their own.

Multi-Unit Structure

The disjunct "multi-unit" plan has been given a wide range of different realizations in the Islamic spatial arts. It has been used as the framework for individual buildings, for garden plans, as well as for rural or urban complexes. One of the most common architectural realizations of multi-unit structure is the mosque with multiple domes. Such buildings have constituted a particularly significant model for Turkey (Figure 22.12) and the Indian subcontinent (Illus. 22.21, 22.22, 22.23). Some of these buildings consist of a series of two or three rooms, each covered by a dome

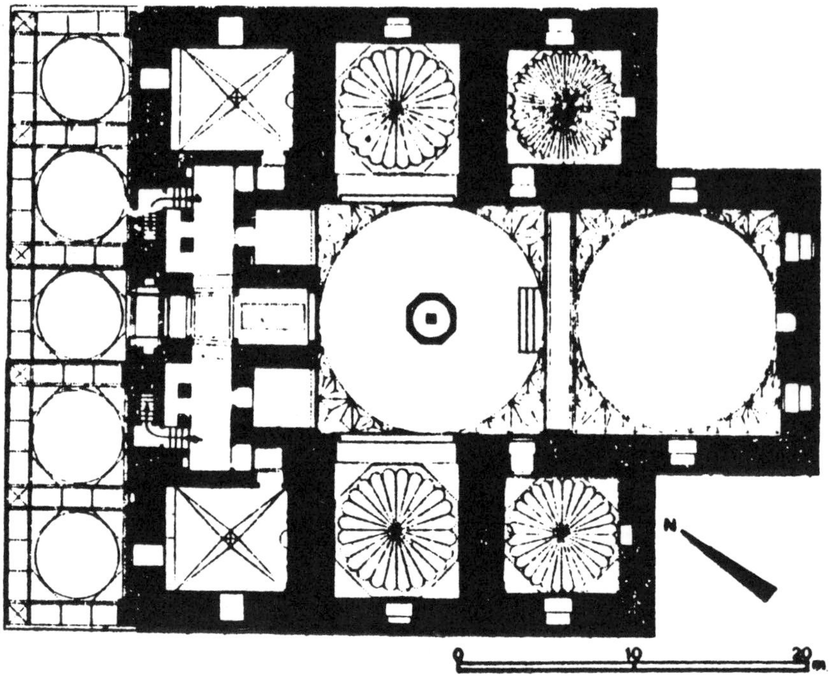

Figure 22.12

Plan of Yeşil Cami (domed units structure), Bursa, Turkey (1412–1419)

and serving as one module of the overall plan. Other plans typical of the multi-unit structure combine a large number of smaller domed units to roof an enclosed space (Illus. 22.16).[12] The domes of the latter type rest on heavy columns or piers, thus providing a segmentation of floor space, roofing, and spatial volume without division of the interior into separate rooms.

Not only religious structures have used the multi-unit plan. The *sūq* of Isfahan is an example of a similar

Illustration 22.21

Mosque of Murād II, "Murādiyyah," at Bursa, Turkey (1425). [Photo by L. al Fārūqī.]

Illustration 22.22

Quṭb Mosque, decorated with terra cotta panels, at Ashtagram, District Mymensingh, Bangladesh (sixteenth century). [Courtesy Department of Antiquities, Government of Bangladesh.]

Illustration 22.23

Mosque at Bhong near Ṣādiqabād, Pakistan. [Courtesy Embassy of Pakistan, Washington, D.C.]

structure for secular use. Garden plans are made up of a number of separate plots, with points of emphasis or punctuation provided by fountains, pools, and pavilions (Illus. 22.24). The descriptions and maps of traditional cities show them to be no less representative of this disjunct structure. In such cases the constitutive modules are neighborhoods rather than individual rooms.

Interlocking Structure

Like Islamic ornamentation, spatial art constructions often combine modules in ways that result in an ambiguous role for the individual segments of the structure. Rather than detracting from the effectiveness of the design, this feature enhances it by stimulating multiple interpretations and different ways of viewing the constituent parts. This method of combination, which has been referred to as an "interlocking" structure or arabesque, realizes all of the important core characteristics of an Islamic art work.

A stunning example of interlocking arabesque structure in the spatial arts is found in the Tāj Maḥal complex (Illus. 22.25). It contains the mausoleum built by the Mughal ruler Shāh Jahān in 1631 – 1648 for his wife Mumtāz Maḥal, as well as elaborate gardens and a number of subsidiary buildings. The main building, the mausoleum, is composed of a central domed chamber flanked by four subsidiary domed rooms (Figure 22.13). Each room represents one unit within the modular combination of this architectural masterpiece. The central domed chamber has a num-

Illustration 22.24

Shalimar Gardens, Lahore, Pakistan, built by Shāh Jahān (seventeenth century). [Courtesy Embassy of Pakistan, Washington, D.C.]

Illustration 22.25

Tāj Maḥal, Agra, India. [Photo by L. al Fārūqī.]

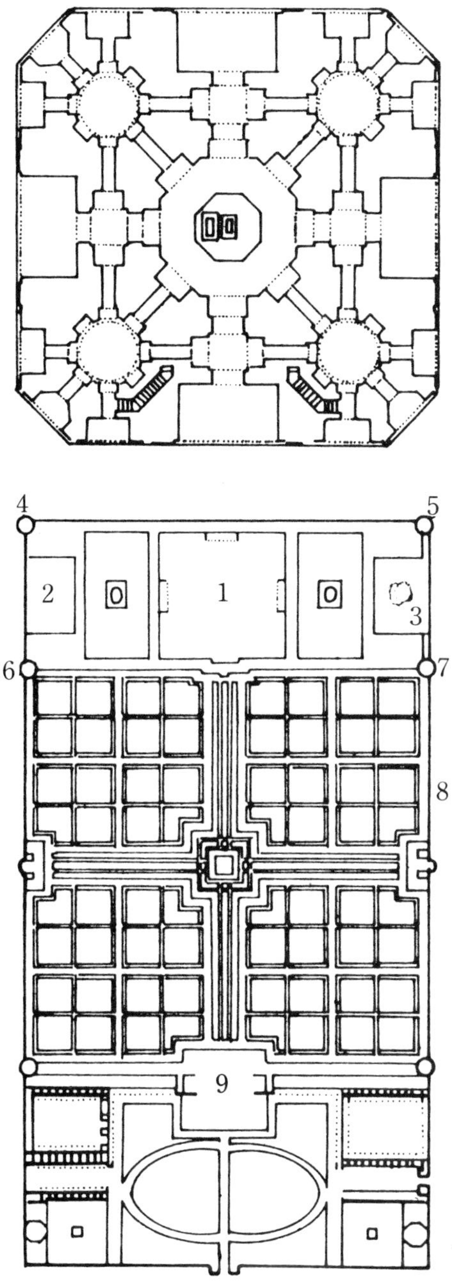

1. Mausoleum
2. Mosque
3. Guesthouse
4–7. Minarets
8. Gardens
9. Gatehouse

Figure 22.13

Tāj Maḥal, Agra (1631–1648)

ber of roles to play. It is a satisfying entity which includes many walls and panels of Islamic decoration. It also acts as a nucleus of the four repetitive chambers that surround it. The building provides only one level of combination in a much larger design. Four towers or minarets approximately 140 feet in height are placed at the corners of the plinth on which the mausoleum rests. These represent additional modules which, in combination with the domed mausoleum, contribute to a larger structural complex. Each minaret, like the individual rooms of the main building, can be appreciated as an individual module or as part of a larger combination.

In a still larger combination, two other buildings flank the funerary structure at opposite extremities of a rectangular environment. To the left is the mosque; to the right, a guest house of symmetrically balanced size and shape. Each of the three buildings—mausoleum, mosque, and guest house—is a self-contained design unit as well as part of a larger organization. Nearby, another area, nearly three times as large, provides still another segment of this "spatial" design. This is the garden of the complex. Within that landscaped area, a number of smaller combinations of modules are arranged in an intricate and symmetrical example of Islamic design. Instead of emphasizing the naturalistic qualities of the river which flows nearby, the landscaper has led its waters into small troughs and canals which divide the garden area into four large units of equal size. Each of these segments is further partitioned into four smaller modules; and those are subdivided into four still smaller segments. Each segment serves as a modular entity and as a constituent part of a successive series of larger combinations. Several garden pavilions, smaller tombs of relatives or ladies-in-waiting, and a gatehouse act as additional modular units within the overall plan.

Meander Structure

The "meander" arabesque structure evidenced in the spatial arts, like its counterpart in ornamentation designs, reveals a less regular and less symmetrical organization of internal parts than is generally found in the multi-unit or interlocking structures. It is exemplified, for example, in the plans of those buildings in which internal design modules exist without pronounced disjunction. An architectural plan that exemplifies the meander arabesque with great success is the aisled or hypostyle hall (Figure 22.14). This plan, which was used from the time of the Prophet Muḥammad (in his seventh-century mosque in Madīnah), has been a favored plan for mosque construction throughout the Muslim world (Figure 22.15). It has been especially prominent in the Maghrib, Middle Africa, and the Mashriq.[13]

One example of a spatial meander arabesque is the Mosque of Qurṭubah (Figure 22.9). The organization

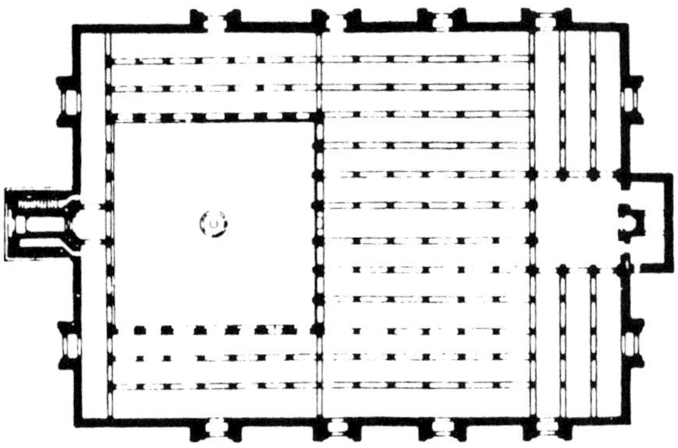

Figure 22.14

Plan of the Mosque of Manṣūrah (hypostyle structure), Tlemcen (1303, 1336)

of aisle or arch units in that building constructed in the eighth century and enlarged and enhanced in the ninth and tenth, cause the visitor to move visually in all directions: to the front and back, to left and right, as well as diagonally toward the unseen extremities of the building. There are no sharply separating boundaries between the constituent modules nor an organization into interpenetrating combinations. Instead, arch after arch and aisle after aisle provide contiguous units of the meander arabesque. There is no aesthetic impression of finality as the last arch or aisle on any side is encountered. The builder could have added another arch or another aisle without destroying the beauty of this infinite pattern. In fact, successive architects who enlarged the Mosque of Qurṭubah actually made such additions. The original structure was repeatedly increased in both length and breadth without destroying the aesthetic appeal and basic organization of the structure.

A landscaped garden or a complex of buildings can also feature the characteristics of a meander arabesque. One example of such organization utilizing both open and enclosed spaces is the complex of Fatehpur Sikri in India, a city built for Akbar, the Mughal ruler who reigned from 1556 to 1605 (Figure 22.16). The buildings of that royal city number more than two dozen entities. Placed in and around several open courtyards, they include palaces and domiciles, public and private reception halls, a mint and treasury house, a school and playground, mosques and tombs, a hospital and bathhouses, a gatehouse and caravansary, pavilions and gardens, a records house, and servants' quarters. Building succeeds building, garden follows garden, and open courts abound. Each structure or garden of the complex acts as one module of a meander design. None is placed in a position of unique importance or emphasis, and there is no impression of a single focus for aesthetic emphasis. Unfortunately, the royal city was abandoned by the emperor shortly after its construction, when the water supply of the area proved inadequate to fulfill the royal needs.

Expanding Structure

A fourth kind of arabesque structure that has been successful for ornamentation and transfiguration designs of the Muslim peoples has been designated as an "expanding" arabesque. It gives the impression of a core or nucleus that is progressively enlarged through its combination with additional motifs or modules. The additions to the nucleus produce a series of new and successively larger entities. Such structures can also be found in the spatial arts of Islamic culture. Here, the spatial expanding structure is composed of individual rooms, interior spatial volmes, segments or plots of a garden, or the districts or quarters of a town.

A particularly successful example of the expanding structure is a mosque built for Sulṭān Salīm II in Edirne, Turkey (1569–1674). The mosque was designed by Sinan, master architect of the Ottoman sultanate, when he was eighty years old. This version of the expanding arabesque has an octagonal central core beneath its massive dome. A primary-level combination of floor plan segments and spatial volumes adds four semidomes to the large, centrally domed area. These are placed at the corners of the building's outer rectangular walls (Figure 22.17). On a second level of combination, arcaded galleries on the east and west sides of the building are joined to the expanded central space. They are constructed in such a way that they seem to meld with the area under the dome as they fill in the space between the semidomes spanning the four corners of the building. So many windows pierce the side walls below the dome that the impression is that "no wall space remains."[14] Thus even the masonry boundaries of this architectural expanding arabesque draw the imagination of the viewer toward exterior space and to another level of combination.

One can find many examples of expanding structures in the spatial arts. Numerous are the garden plans, for example, that include repetitive and successive additions to a star-shaped center (Figure 22.18). These can be found in many regions of the Muslim world, in fact, wherever Muslims have lived and Islamic culture has flourished. The plan of Caliph Manṣūr for ninth-century Baghdād is a historical example in urban planning of the expanding structure (Figure 22.19). Whether done consciously or unconsciously, it was another attempt to produce an envi-

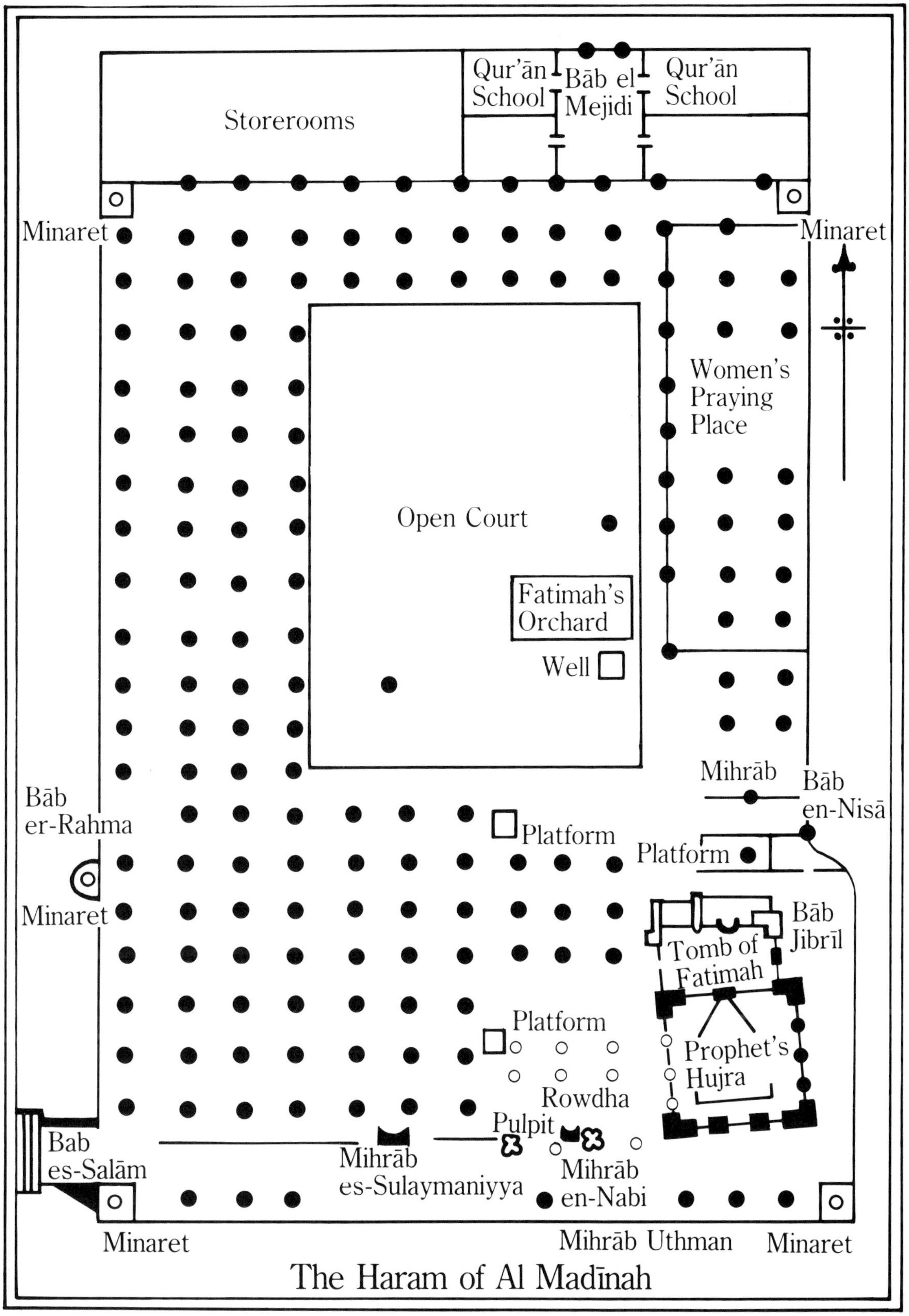

Figure 22.15

The Mosque of the Prophet (hypostyle structure), Madīnah

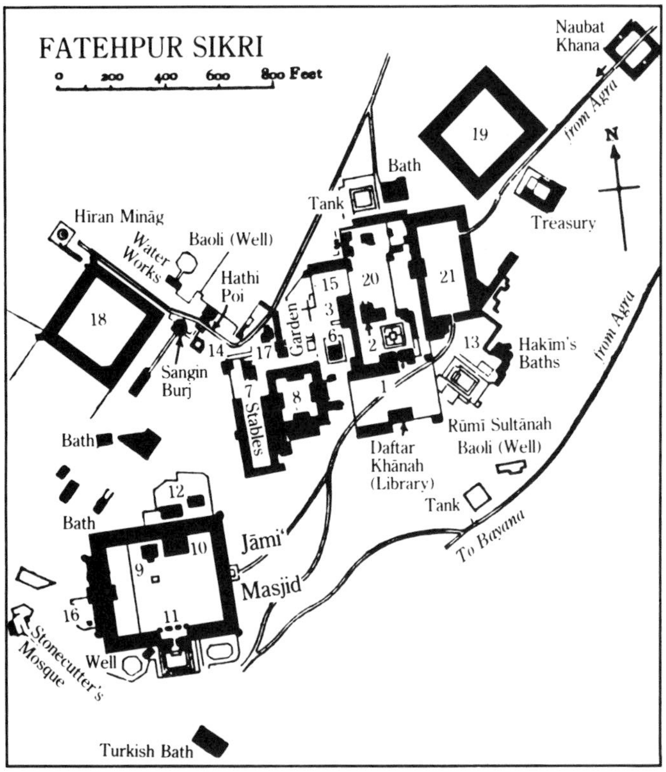

1. Khwabgah, or Sleeping Apartment, literally "House of Dreams."
2. Girls' School.
3. Panch Mahal, probably a pleasure palace for ladies of the court.
4. Diwan-i-Khas, hall for private audiences, sometimes known as Ibadat Khanah or "worship house."
5. Ankh Michauli, probably used for records.
6. House of Miriam, mother of Emperor Jahangir, with nearby garden and bath.
7. House of Raja Birbal, an important Hindu who embraced the new religion of Emperor Akbar.
8. Palace of Jodh Bai, wife of Emperor Jahangir.
9. Tomb of Shaykh Salim Chishti (d. 1571).
10. Tomb of Islam Khan, grandson of the saint and governor of Bengal.
11. Gate of Victory (Buland Darwazah), the "high gate" on south wall of the Jāmi 'Masjid.
12. House of Fazl and Fayzi, two brothers who were favorites of Akbar.
13. House of the Hakim ("doctor"), near Hakim's Baths.
14. Pigeon House.
15. Hospital.
16. Tomb of Salim Chishti's Son.
17. Nagina, or Ladies Mosque.
18. Caravansary.
19. Mint.
20. Chessboard Court.
21. Diwan-i-'Am, Public Audience Hall.

Figure 22.16

Plan of Fatehpur Sikri

ronment that would be consistent, aesthetically as well as politically, economically, and socially, with and supportive of the Islamic ideology.

NOTES

1. "Space, in contrast to plasticity, encounters its limitations where it strikes against the plastic masses; it is defined from the interior" (A. E. Brinckmann, ***Baukunst des 17. und 18. Jahrhunderts in der romanischen Ländern*** [Berlin, 1915]); "The enduring value of architecture is space. . . . Architecture must be seen and felt and understood from the inside out" (E. W. Rannels, "The Study of Architecture as Art," *College Art Journal,* 3 [1949]). Both quotations appear in Bruno Zevi's summarizing report on this view in "The Spatial Concept," a subdivision of his article, "Architecture," *Encyclopedia of World Art* (New York: McGraw-Hill, 1959), Vol. 1, cols. 633ff.

2. This theory follows an old-fashioned classification of all the arts as either spatial or temporal. It has been proven inconsistent and distorting of the true nature of both architecture and the other arts (Zevi, "Architecture," cols. 636ff).

3. Egypt's statues of Ibrahīm Bāshā, Muṣṭafā Kāmil, Sulaymān Bāshā, and Muḥammad 'Alī in the public places of Cairo cannot be considered as anything but an importation, in the land of the colonized, of the art of the colonizer.

4. Other prominent examples of the hypostyle or aisled hall are the mosques of Ibn Ṭulūn (Cairo), the Grand Mosque of Damascus, Al Azhar (Cairo), Qayrawiyyīn (Fās), the Grand Mosque of Qayrawān, and Al Ḥaram al Sharīf (Makkah).

5. Constructed in the eighth century, the building underwent major renovations and enlargements in the ninth and tenth centuries.

6. For example, see the description of the ambiguous quality of rooms in a Muslim palace, Oleg Grabar, *The Alhambra* (Cambridge, Mass.: Harvard University Press, 1978), pp. 48–90.

7. For example, the complex built for the University of Kuwait; Masjid Negara in Kuala Lumpur, Malaysia; the Sulṭān Ḥasan complex in Cairo, Egypt; the Qarawiyyīn Madrasah complex in Fās, Morocco; the Sulaymāniyyah complex in Istanbul, Turkey.

8. Bianca designates these successive combinations as "hierarchic levels" (Stefano Bianca, "Unity and Variety in the Domestic Architecture of Islam," unpublished paper presented at the Symposium, "The Common Principles, Forms and Themes of Islamic Art," Istanbul, April 1983, p. 7). See the plans of Dār al Imārah (Kūfah), Mushattā (Syria), Ukhaydir (near Baghdād), Bulkawara Palace (Sāmarrā'), Madrasah of Sulṭān Ḥasan (Cairo), the Topkapi Saray (Istanbul), and the Alhambra Palace (Granada, Spain), in John D. Hoag, ***Western Islamic Architecture*** (New York: George Braziller, 1963).

9. Bianca, "Unity and Variety," p. 7.

10. Stefano Bianca, "Traditional Muslim Cities and Western Planning Ideology—An Outline of Structural

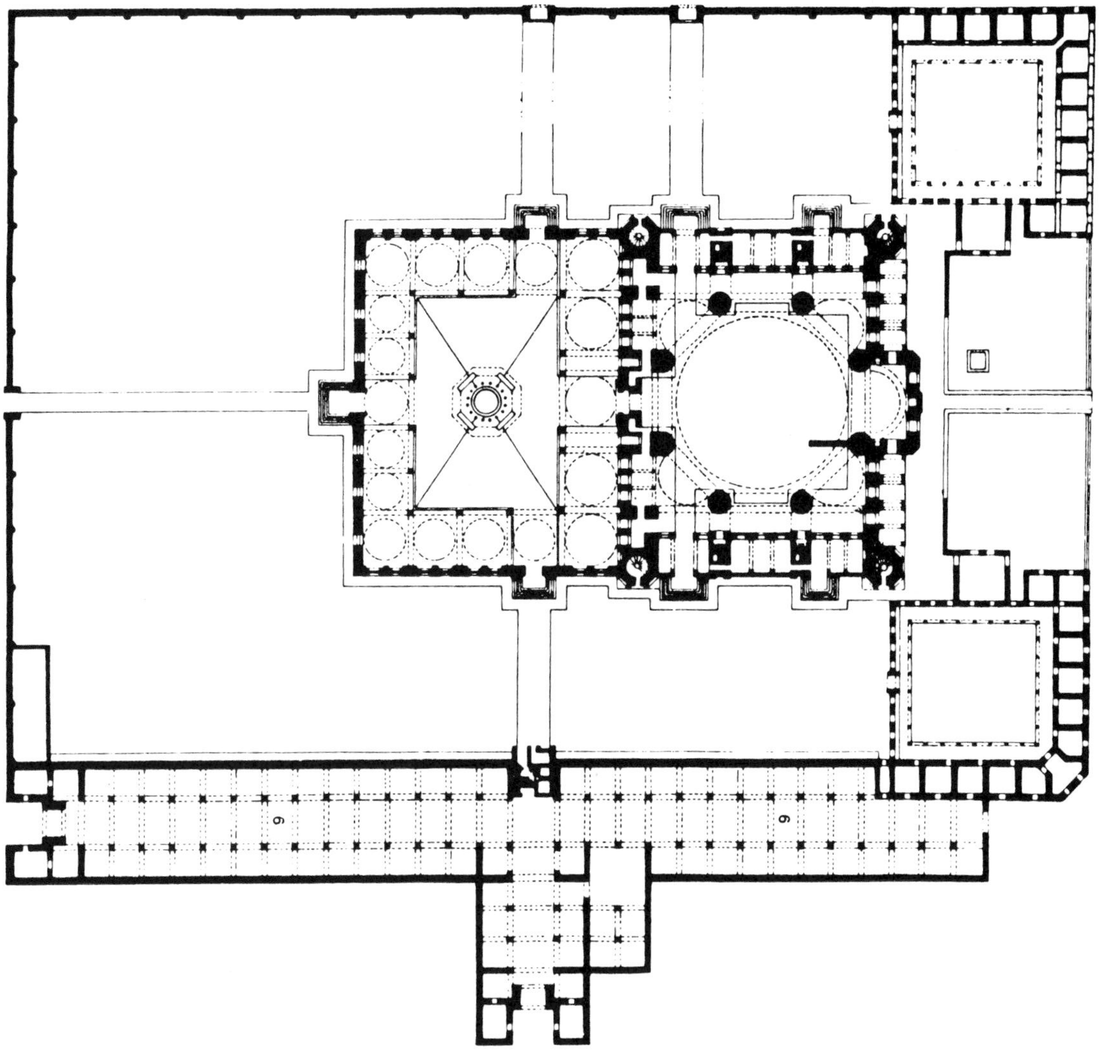

Figure 22.17

Salīmiyyah Masjid (centrally domed structure), Edirne, Turkey (1569–1575)

Figure 22.18

An Islamic garden exemplifying the expanding arabesque

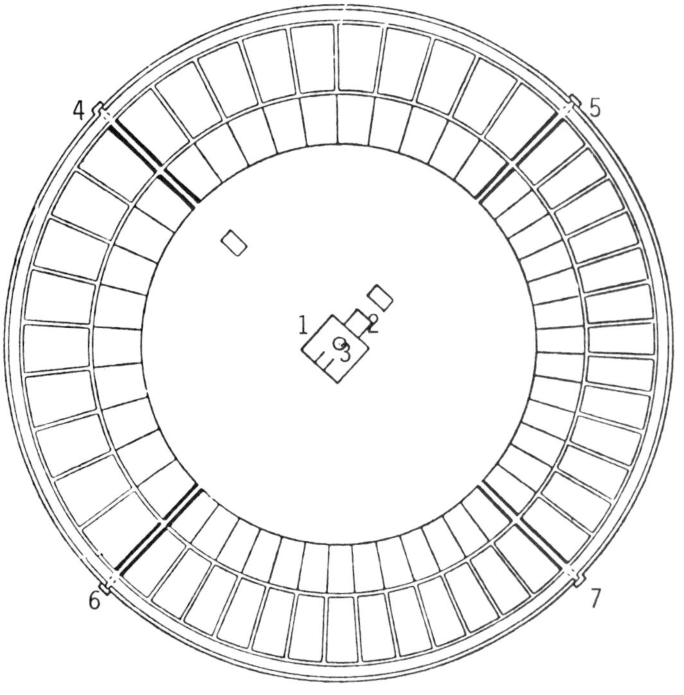

1. The Golden Palace
2. Masjid al Manṣūr
3. The Green Dome of the Palace
4. Dimashq Gate
5. Khurasan Gate
6. Kufah Gate
7. Basrah Gate

Figure 22.19

Baghdād, plan of the circular city of Caliph Al Manṣūr (762–767)

Illustration 22.26

Mosque of Turfan, Xinjiang Province, People's Republic of China, seventeenth century. [Courtesy Ingrid Larsen.]

Conflicts," unpublished paper presented at the "Symposium on the Arab City, Its Character and Islamic Cultural Heritage," Madīnah, Saudi Arabia, 1981, pp. 12–15.

11. See Stefano Bianca, *Architektur und Lebensform im islamischen Stadtwesen* (Zurich: Verlag für Architektur Artemis, 1979); A. Raymond, "La Géographie des ḥāra du Caire," B.I.F.A.O. (Cairo, 1980); Besim Hakim, ed., *Sidi Bou Said, Tunisia: A Study in Structure and Form* (Halifax, Nova Scotia: School of Architecture, 1978); and the work of the architects and planners affiliated with the Fās Master Plan (1975–1978) or with the Ḥajj Center, King 'Abdul 'Azīz University, Jiddah, Saudi Arabia.

12. For example, the Ūlū Jāmi' of Sivas and Bursa, Turkey; and the Sath-Gumbad Mosque at Bagerhat, Bangladesh.

13. See Nader Ardalan, "The Visual Language of Symbolic Form: A Preliminary Study of Mosque Architecture," *Architecture as Symbol and Self-Identity,* Proceedings of Seminar Four in the Series, "Architectural Transformations in the Islamic World" (Fez, Morocco, October 9–12, 1979), pp. 18–42, where that author provides a typology of mosque plans documenting the high incidence of mosques with hypostyle organization in the three regions mentioned. This does not imply that it is nonexistent in other regions; it can even be found in mosques built in the Far East by Chinese Muslims (Illus. 22.26).

14. Oktay Aslanapa, *Turkish Art and Architecture* (New York: Praeger, 1971), p. 224.

CHAPTER 23

Handasah Al Ṣawt *or The Art of Sound*

This chapter on the aesthetic materials usually designated as "music" has been given the title of *Handasah al Ṣawt,* or the Art of Sound. This calls attention to the fact that "music" or *mūsīqā,* the Arabic term, does not apply to all types of artistic vocal and instrumental arrangements of pitches and rhythms, as does the English term and its equivalents in other European languages. Instead, *mūsīqā* applies only to particular genres of sound art; and for the most part it has designated only those that have a somewhat questionable or even disreputable status in Islamic culture.[1] Therefore, to deal with "music," as it is understood in Islamic culture, would confine the discussion to a limited segment of the sound art genres of the Muslim peoples, and would exclude the more important and accepted types. On the other hand, to use that term as inclusive of Qur'ānic chant and other forms of sound art not judged to be music in that culture, would result, for the Muslims, not only in inaccuracy but even in blasphemy. In order to avoid any such misrepresentation, distortion, and irritation, the sound art materials described in this chapter will be regarded as examples of *handasah al ṣawt.* This recently coined Arabic expression will stand for all artistic combinations of tones and rhythms arising within Islamic culture.[2] It should not be understood as an equivalent for the much more limited *mūsīqā.* Because of an unavoidable association with the term *mūsīqā* and its limited relevance, the word "music" will be avoided as an equivalent for the totality of sound arts in the Islamic context. When used in reference to music generally, or to that of the non-Muslim world, it will carry its usual wide significance. When the adjectival form of that term is needed for the discussion of sound art in the Islamic context, *ṣawtī* will stand for "musical" in its wide, inclusive sense.

The religion of Islam prescribes, and Muslims seek to achieve, a unity of all thought and action under God's command. Just as the Qur'ān has served as a model for other aesthetic expressions, so it has provided the figurization of essence for aesthetic manifestation in the art of sound. It has affected *handasah al ṣawt* in two important ways: first, in a sociological way, by causing performers and listeners to regard and use *ṣawtī* art in uniquely Islamic ways; and second, in a theoretical way, by molding the characteristics of the actual sound art examples as performed and enjoyed by the Muslim peoples. We shall deal with the sociological materials, the first of the two categories of Qur'ānic influence, in the sections below on "The Art of Sound in Islamic Society," and "Model for Creativity: The Chanted Qur'an." The section on "The Core Characteristics as Manifested in *Handasah al Ṣawt*" presents materials pertaining to the second or theoretical type of effect the Qur'ān has had on the art of sound.

THE ARTS OF SOUND IN ISLAMIC SOCIETY

Despite the absence of a general term for musical expression, attitudes toward *handasah al ṣawt* as well as its use in Islamic societies around the world reveal many factors of homogeneity. These include (1) the categories of musical genres (religious, secular, folk, art, etcetera); (2) the contexts for performance; (3) performers of various genres; (4) audience participation; (5) historical extension; and (6) interregional relevance.

Categories of Musical Genres

The rejection in Islamic civilization of a separation of the religious from the secular realm has been carried into the area of the art of sound as well. Not only is *tawḥīd* relevant to the use of the religious genres of *handasah al ṣawt,* but it also infuses the Muslim's thinking about, and his participation in, other forms of sound art. In an Islamic context, therefore, categories generally used to distinguish one type of music from another—religious music from secular, art music from folk, and classical music from popular—fail to carry their usual distinctions. As we have endeavored to show elsewhere,[3] *handasah al ṣawt* reveals an "extensive unity" which bridges genre types and genre categorization. Karl Signell describes "mosque music" as a "sub-genre of classical music."[4] Amnon Shiloah writes of the "close links" and the "interaction" between religious and art music in the Muslim nations,[5] and of an "infiltration" of art music into the folk repertoire.[6]

Illustration 23.1

National Men's Champion, Qur'ān Reading Competition, Malaysia, 1981. [Courtesy Federal Department of Information, Government of Malaysia.]

Contexts for Performance

Homogeneity in Islamic societies' use of *handasah al ṣawt* is also evident in the lack of precise contexts for performance of many of the genres. There is little sense of isolation of the so-called religious genres to a strictly religious context in this culture. For example, Qur'ānic chant is a genre of religious *handasah al ṣawt* that has wide significance (Illus. 23.1). It is used each day in the performance of *ṣalāt,* the Islamic formal worship. In addition, it is heard at many other religiously significant occasions: at the special *ṣalāt* offered on each of the major holidays (*'Id al Fitr* and *'Id al Aḍḥā*), at the funeral and in the mourning rites for friends and relatives of the deceased, at the *tarāwīḥ* prayers offered each evening during the month of fasting (Ramaḍān), and so on. But Qur'ānic chant or *qirā'ah* ("recitation") is not only used in religious contexts. It is also heard in the public meeting, in the social gathering, on festive occasions, and in the daily programs of radio and television. Many other examples of *ṣawtī* art—chanted poetry, vocal and instrumental improvisations, and metered songs with serious words—are also performed in a wide range of contexts. It is only those genres of limited acceptability that are heard in restricted and specific performance contexts. It should be noted that even though Qur'ānic chant is used in a wide range of contexts, it is the only *handasah al ṣawt* genre accepted as part of the formal worship *(ṣalāt).*

Performers of Various Genres

The distinction between performers of different genres is much less pronounced in Islamic society than it is in others. An instrumentalist such as Benny Goodman, who can successfully cross the boundaries separating classical music from jazz, is an exception in Western musical culture. In Islamic culture, the same performers often play or sing quite different genres and for quite different functions.[7] Many of the successful singers of so-called secular music have actually received their early training as reciters of the Qur'ān. The late Umm Kulthūm was one of the most famous examples. Because of a cultural disdain for the professional musician, there are few specialists who devote themselves exclusively to musical performance. The participation in all types of sound art by nonprofessionals, therefore, is significant—whether it be Qur'ān and other religious chant, or vocal and instrumental performance for social entertainment. The amateurs are often as important to a *ṣawtī* performance as the professionals.[8]

Audience Participation

Audience participation also shows the homogeneity of the use of the art of sound in Muslim societies. Since there is little distinction sharply separating categories of *ṣawtī* performance, no genre of the traditional forms is beyond the aesthetic appreciation of any segment of the population. It is, in fact, only the contemporary Westernized popular and classical musics, coming from an alien tradition, that have a limited and particularized audience appeal that depends on special training of the potential listeners. As for the traditional sound arts, their correspondence to the Qur'ānic prototype has made them aesthetically accessible to all. There is no need for enforced listening or formal appreciation courses.

Historical Extension

The essential unity or homogeneity of *handasah al ṣawt* also has a historical dimension. Many of the characteristics which the careful observer finds in the musical examples of this century can be documented in the materials describing *handasah al ṣawt* performance of earlier centuries. Baron d'Erlanger writes that, both in melodic and in rhythmic features, the general characteristics of the music of the contemporary tribal Arabs can be considered a "faithful echo" of that of the pre-Islamic period[9]; and George Sawa has detailed the continuity between medieval and contemporary Arabic performance practice.[10] In his description of one anonymous work on Arabic music theory, Amnon Shiloah writes that that document is "a key . . . for understanding of the modal system which goes back to Ṣafī al-dīn [7th/13th century] and 'Abd al Ḳādir Ibn Ghaybī [d. 839/1435], and which lies at the base of the system still practiced today."[11]

Interregional Relevance

In addition to the above-mentioned elements of homogeneity, *ṣawtī* expressions in Islamic society reveal an interregional homogeneity. Although differences in music theory, in instruments, in genres, and in performance practice have existed from country to country and city to city, a remarkable number of characteristics unite the musical cultures of the Muslim peoples. These characteristics are evident in those countries that have a Muslim majority and even in many of those where Islam exists only as a significant minority religion.

Certain *ṣawtī* characteristics are achieved better or more easily with certain types of instruments than with others. This fact caused the spread of the most typical instruments of the early Muslims in the Arab cradleland to all regions of the Muslim world. The diffusion of instruments was aided and reinforced by the increased interaction between peoples which followed on the heels of the rise of Islam. This interaction was stimulated by increased trade, by political conquest, and by travel for education and pilgrimage. Gradually the most important instruments of the early Muslims were found in every region (Illus. 23.2). Sometimes they carried the same names and characteristics of construction as their ancestors; at other times, they were renamed and adapted to fit regional preferences and the availability of materials. The interregional homogeneity of instruments for *handasah al ṣawt* performance (Illus. 23.3–23.8) is visually expressed in Maps 71–77: one for chordophones (instruments in which the sound is produced by the vibration of strings); a second for aerophones (instruments with a sound-producing air column); and a third for membranophones (in which the sounding material is a tightly stretched skin). Idiophones, instruments made of a sonorous material that produce the sound themselves by shaking, percussion techniques, or concussion, are also represented among the instruments of the Muslim peoples. These instruments, however, have not played as important a role

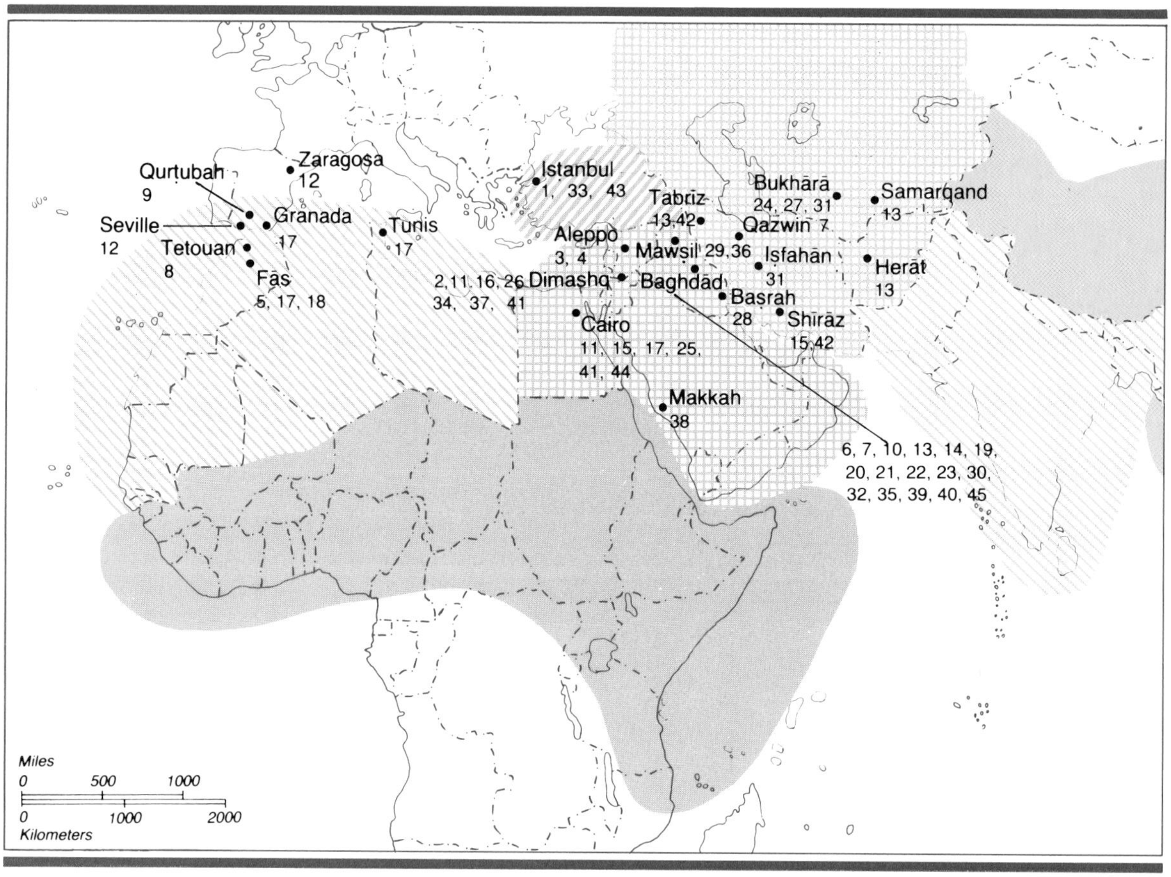

Map 70. Major Authors on Handasah al Ṣawt

MAJOR AUTHORS ON HANDASAH AL ṢAWT

1. al Anqarawī/al Anqirawī
   Galata (Isṭanbūl)
2. al ʻAṭṭār
   Dimashq
3. al Bisṭāmī
   Aleppo
4. al Fārābī
   Aleppo
5. al Fāsī
   Fās
6. al Ghazālī (Abū Ḥāmid)
   Baghdād
7. al Ghazālī (Majd al Dīn)
   Baghdād, Qazwīn
8. al Ḥā'ik
   Titwān
9. Ibn ʻAbd Rabbihi
   Qurṭubah
10. Ibn Abī al Dunyā
    Baghdād
11. Ibn Abī Uṣaybiʻah
    Dimashq, Cairo
12. Ibn Bājjah
    Zaragosa, Seville
13. Ibn Ghaybī
    Samarqand, Tabrīz, Baghdād, Herat
14. Ibn al Jawzī
    Baghdād
15. Ibn al Jazarī
    Cairo, Shīrāz
16. Ibn al Kayyāl
    Dimashq
17. Ibn Khaldūn
    Fās, Granada, Tūnis, Cairo
18. Ibn al Khaṭīb
    Fās
19. Ibn Khurdādhbih
    Baghdād
20. Ibn al Munajjim
    Baghdād

21. Ibn al Nadīm
Baghdād
22. Ibn Qaysarānī
Baghdād
23. Ibn Salamah
Baghdād
24. Ibn Sīnā
Bukhārā
25. Ibn Taghrī Birdī
Cairo
26. Ibn Taymiyyah
Dimashq
27. Ibn Zaylah
Bukhārā
28. Ikhwān al Safā'
Baṣrah
29. al Irbilī
Mawṣil
30. al Iṣfahānī
Baghdād
31. al Khwārizmī
Bukhārā, Isfahān
32. al Kindī
Baghdād
33. al Lādhiqī
Isṭanbūl
34. Mashāqah
Dimashq
35. al Mas'ūdī
Baghdād
36. al Muslim al Mawṣilī
Mawṣil
37. al Nābulusī
Dimashq
38. al Qāri'
Makkah
39. Ṣafī al Dīn al Ḥillī
Baghdād
40. Ṣafī al Dīn al Urmawī
Baghdād
41. Shihāb al Dīn
Dimashq, Cairo
42. al Shīrāzī
Shīrāz, Tabrīz
43. al Shirwānī
Isṭanbūl
44. al Suyūṭī
Cairo
45. al Ṭūsī
Baghdād

Illustration 23.2

Five of the most common instruments of the Muslim world: (clockwise from top) psaltery, short-necked lute, frame drum, end-blown flute, and long-necked lute. [Photo by L. al Fārūqī.]

Illustration 23.3

The short-necked lute ('ūd) as played by Munīr Bashīr, a virtuoso performer from Iraq. [Courtesy Ministry of Culture, Iraq.]

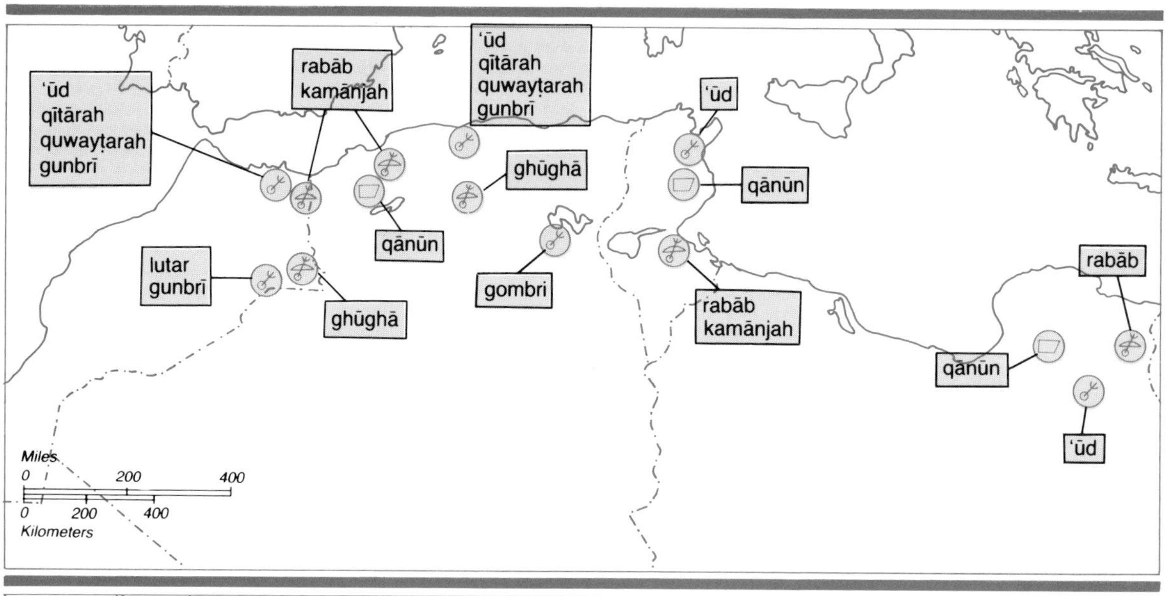

'ūd qītārah quwayṭarah gunbrī
rabāb kamānjah
'ūd qītārah quwayṭarah gunbrī
'ūd
ghūghā
qānūn
qānūn
lutar gunbrī
ghūghā
gombri
rabāb kamānjah
rabāb
qānūn
'ūd
Miles
0 200 400
0 200 400
Kilometers

A.

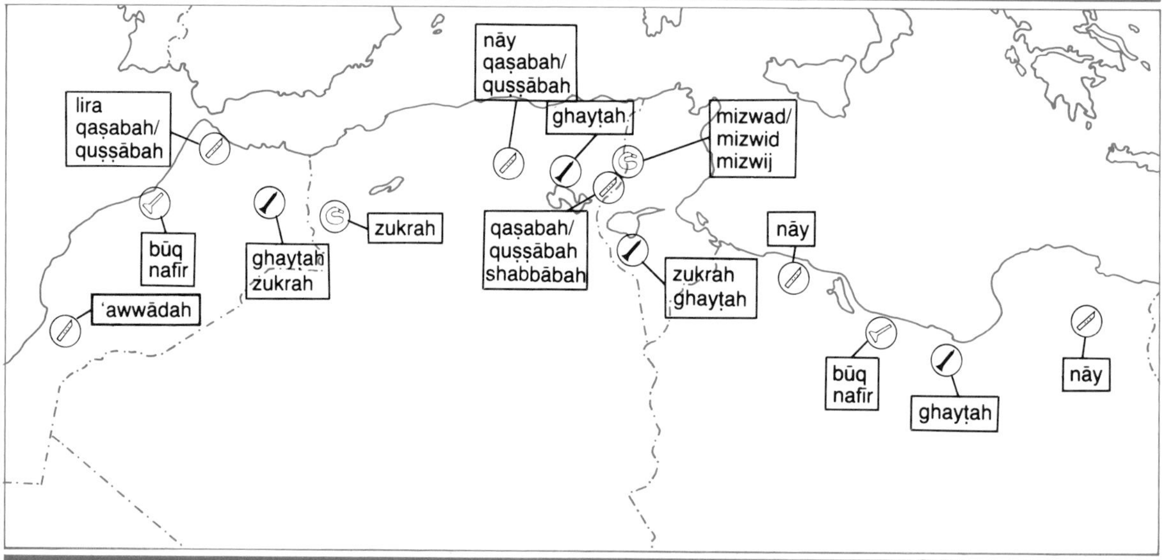

nāy qaṣabah/ quṣṣābah
lira qaṣabah/ quṣṣābah
ghayṭah
mizwad/ mizwid mizwij
zukrah
būq nafīr
ghayṭah zukrah
qaṣabah/ quṣṣābah shabbābah
nāy
zukrah ghayṭah
'awwādah
būq nafīr
ghayṭah
nāy

B.

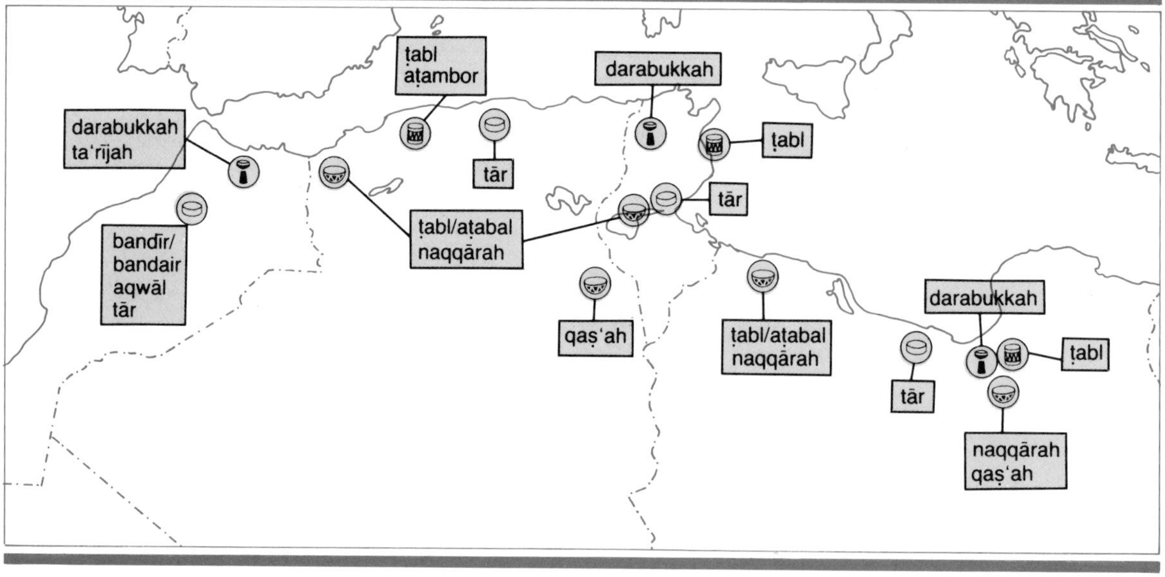

ṭabl aṭambor
darabukkah
darabukkah ta'rījah
ṭabl
ṭār
ṭār
bandīr/ bandair aqwāl ṭār
ṭabl/aṭabal naqqārah
qaṣ'ah
ṭabl/aṭabal naqqārah
darabukkah
ṭabl
ṭār
naqqārah qaṣ'ah

C.

Chordophones

- Plucked lute
- Bowed lute
- Psaltery
- Dulcimer
- Lyre

Aerophones

- End-blown flute
- Oboe-type instrument
- Bagpipe
- Trumpet

Membranophones

- Frame drum
- Goblet drum
- Kettle drum
- Double-headed drum

Map 71. Musical Instruments in the Maghrib
A. Chordophones
B. Aerophones
C. Membranophones

CHORDOPHONES

PL = Plucked lute (long- or short-necked)
BL = Bowed lute
P = Psaltery
D = Dulcimer
L = Lyre

AEROPHONES

E = End-blown flute
O = Oboe
B = Bagpipe
T = Trumpet

MEMBRANOPHONES

F = Frame drum (tambourine)
G = Goblet drum
K = Kettle drum (single or paired)
DC = Doubled-headed cylindrical drum

Aerophones found in Area I

E: Qaṣabah/quṣṣābah, nāy, shabbābah, lira, ‘awwādah
O: ghayṭah, zūkrah
B: zukrah/zūkrah, mizwad/mizwid, mizwij
T: nafīr, būq

Chordophones found in Area I

PL: quwayṭarah (kwītra), qītārah, ‘ūd, lutar, genibri/gunbrī
BL: rabāb, ghūghā, kamānjah
P: qānūn

Membranophones found in Area I

F: Bandīr/bandair, ṭār, ghirbāl, ṭār, quwwāl
G: darabukkah, aqwāl, ta‘rījah
K: ṭabl/aṭabal, naqqārah, qaṣ‘ah
DC: aṭambor, ṭabl

in the performance of *ṣawtī* genres as have the chordophones, aerophones, and membranophones. Therefore, we have not included a corresponding map for this category of musical instruments.

Interregional homogeneity may have been even stronger in earlier centuries than in contemporary times. In the early periods of Islamic history, there were no national boundaries to restrict movement of persons and ideas. Arabic, the language of the Qur'ān, was known by many of the people. It provided a common medium of cultural exchange for Muslims, and even for many non-Muslims, throughout those lands where Islamic culture was a dominant force. It was this common language and the similiarities of *ṣawtī*

Illustration 23.4

The psaltery (qānūn), a much used chordophone. [Courtesy Ministry of Culture, Iraq.]

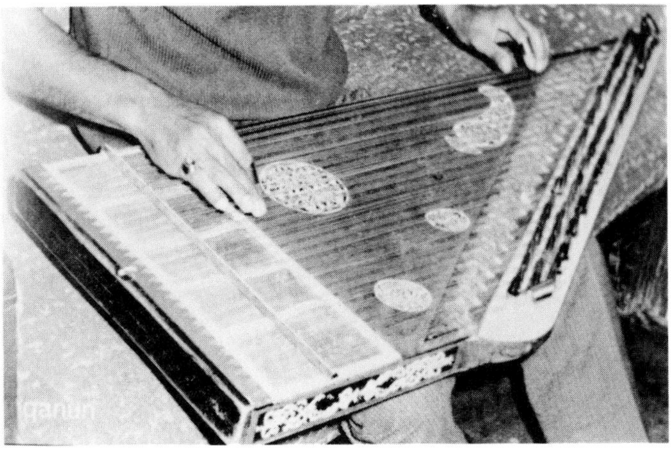

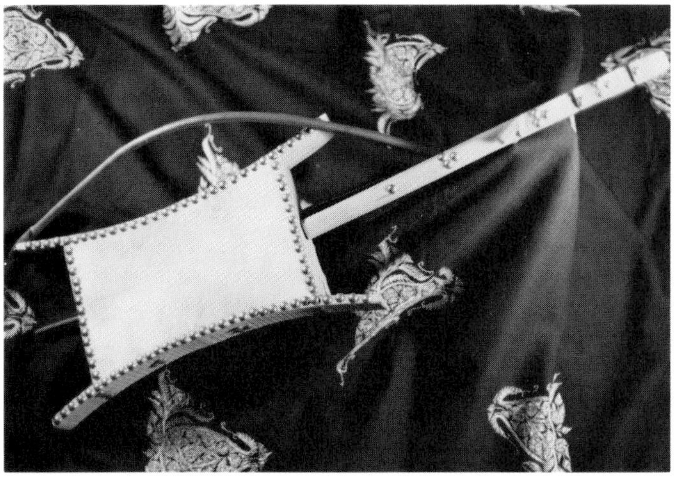

Illustration 23.5

Bowed folk instrument of the spiked fiddle variety (Lebanon). [Photo by L. al Fārūqī.]

practice, despite regional differences, that made it possible for many of the *sawtī* theorists of the Islamic world to be widely influential. Their treatises were not only read by members of their own century and their particular political enclave or geographic region. Writers on *handasah al ṣawt* such as al Fārābī (d. 339/950) and Ṣafī al Dīn al Urmawī (d. 693/1294) were copied and quoted for centuries after their deaths by interested theorists and laymen alike (Map 70). Figure 23.1 reveals the wide range of literary works pertinent to *handasah al ṣawt.*

Illustration 23.6

End-blown flute. [Photo by L. al Fārūqī.]

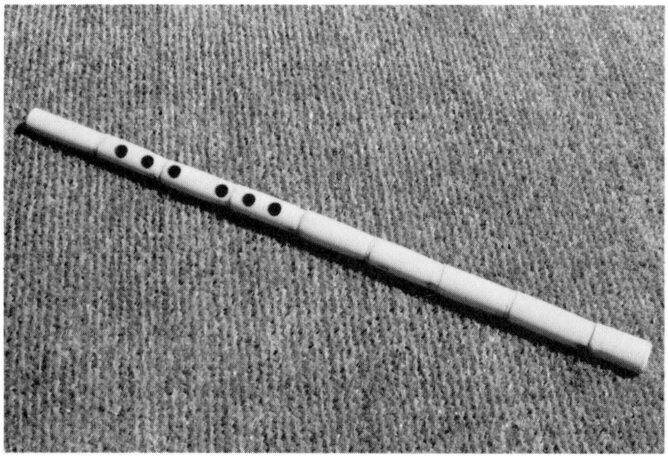

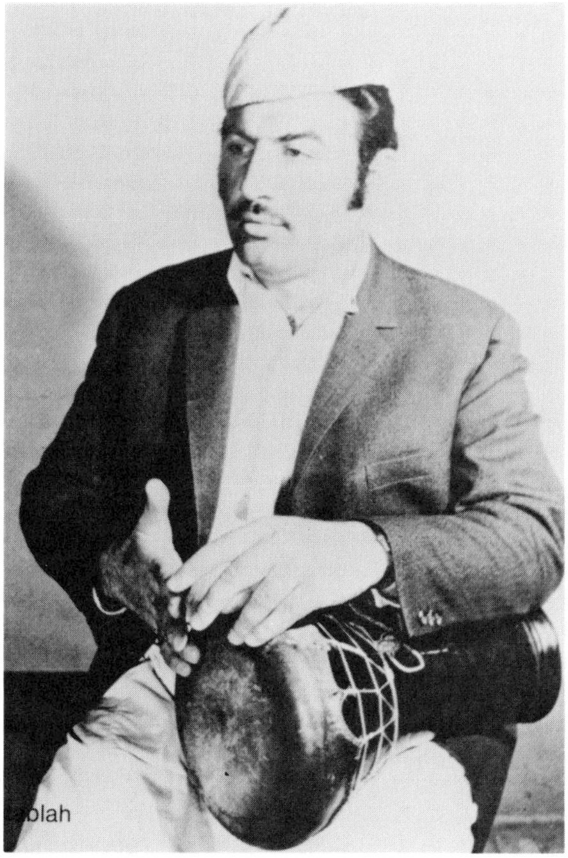

Illustration 23.7

Goblet drum *(ṭablah),* a popular membranophone in the Muslim world. [Courtesy Ministry of Culture, Iraq.]

Illustration 23.8

Another popular membranophone, the frame drum or tambourine. [Photo by L. al Fārūqī.]

TABLE 23.1. AUTHORS OF EXTANT ARABIC LITERATURE ON *Handasah al Ṣawt* (2–1300 A.H./800–1900 C.E.)

In the following listing, authors have been assigned to the century in which the major portion of their adult life was lived. Further information about the authors and their works can be gained from the following sources: Ibn Khallikān, Aḥmad Ibn Muḥammad. *Wafayāt al A'yān wa Anbā' Abnā' al Zamān* (Cairo: Būlāq, 1858), 2 vols.; idem, *Biographical Dictionary,* trans. Mac Guckin de Slane (Paris, 1843–1871), 4 vols.; Dodge, Bayard, ed. and tr. *The Fihrist of al-Nadīm* (New York: Columbia University Press, 1970), 2 vols.; Farmer, H. G. *The Sources of Arabian Music* (Bearsden, 1940; 2nd ed., Leiden: E. J. Brill, 1965); Shiloah, Amnon. *The Theory of Music in Arabic Writings (c. 900–1900), International Inventory of Musical Sources* (Munich: G. Genle Verlag, 1979). Relevant articles may be found in: *Encyclopedia of Islam* (Leiden: E. J. Brill, rev. ed., 1960–19); *The New Grove Dictionary of Music and Musicians,* ed. Stanley Sadie (London: Macmillan, 1980). A quick survey of the "Types of Literature That Include Materials on *Handasah al Ṣawt*" can be found in Figure 23.1.

Name	*Date of Death*	*Major Location of Life and Work*	*Main Field(s) of Relevant Work*
Ninth century			
Ibn Abū al Dunyā, Abū Bakr 'Abdullah Ibn Muḥammad	281/894	Baghdād	Lawfulness of *samā'*; musical instruments
Ibn Khurdādhbih (Khurradādhbih), 'Ubayd Allah Ibn 'Abdullah	300/911	Baghdād	Music; musical instruments
Ibn al Munajjim, Yaḥya Ibn 'Alī Ibn Yaḥya Ibn Abī Manṣūr	300/912	Baghdād	Music theory
Ibn Qutaybah, Abū Muḥammad 'Abdullah Ibn Muslim al Dīnawarī	274/887	Baghdād	*Tartīl al Qur'ān* and biographies of its reciters
Ibn Salamah, Abū Ṭalib Ibn 'Āṣim al Ḍabbī al Mufaḍḍal	c. 292/905	Baghdād	Musical instruments
al Jāḥiz, Abū 'Uthmān 'Amr Ibn Baḥr al Fuqaymī	255/869	Baṣrah	*Adab* (literature)
al Kindī, Abū Yūsuf Ya'qūb Ibn Isḥaq	after 256/870	Baṣrah, Baghdād	Music theory
Tenth century			
al Fārābī, Abū Naṣr Muḥammad Ibn Muḥammad Ibn Ṭarkhān	339/950	Aleppo	Music theory
Ibn 'Abd Rabbihi, Abū 'Umar Aḥmad Ibn Muḥammad	328/940	Qurṭubah	*Adab*
Ikhwān al Ṣafā' (a brotherhood that flourished during the second half of the tenth century)		Baṣrah	Encyclopedia of science and philosophy
al Iṣfahānī, Abū al Faraj 'Alī Ibn al Ḥusayn Ibn Muḥammad	356/967	Baghdād, Aleppo	*Adab,* biography, songs and song collections
al Khwārizmī, Abū 'Abdullah Muḥammad Ibn Aḥmad Ibn Yūsuf	387/997	Bukhārā	Encyclopedia of the arts and sciences
al Makkī, Abū Ṭalib Muḥammad Ibn 'Ali al Ḥārithī	386/996	Baṣrah, Baghdād	Sufism
al Mas'ūdī, Abū al Ḥasan 'Alī al Ḥusayn	345/956	al Fusṭāṭ (Cairo)	History
al Raffā' al Sarīyy, Ibn Aḥmad al Kindī al Mawṣilī	after 366/976	Aleppo, Baghdād	*Adab*
al Sarrāj, Abū Naṣr 'Abdullah Ibn 'Alī Ibn Muḥammad Ibn Yaḥyā Ṭa'ūs al Fuqarā'	378/988	Ṭūs	Sufism, *samā'*
al Sulamī, Abū 'Abd al Raḥman Muḥammad Ibn Ḥusayn al Azdī al Naysābūrī	412/1021	Naysābūr (Nishapur)	Sufism

(Continued)

TABLE 23.1 *(Continued)*

Name	*Date of Death*	*Major Location of Life and Work*	*Main Field(s) of Relevant Work*
Eleventh century			
al Ghazālī, Abū Ḥamīd Muḥammad Ibn Muḥammad al Ṭūsī	505/1111	Ṭūs, Baghdād	Religious sciences
al Ghazālī, Majd al Dīn Aḥmad Ibn Muḥammad al Ṭūsī	520/1121	Ṭūs, Baghdād	Lawfulness of *samā'*
al Ḥasan, Ibn Aḥmad Ibn 'Alī al Kātib	11th c.	Northern Syria	Music theory
al Ḥuṣri, Abū Isḥaq Ibrahīm Ibn 'Alī Ibn Tamīm al Qayrawānī	413/1022	Manṣūriyyah, near Qayrawān	*Adab*
Ibn al Qaysarānī, Abū al Faḍl Muḥammad Ibn Ṭāḥir Ibn 'Alī Ibn Aḥmad	507/1113	Baghdād	Lawfulness of *samā'*
Ibn Sīda, Abū al Ḥasan 'Alī Ibn Isma'īl	458/1066	Denia (Spain)	Dictionary
Ibn Sīnā, Abū 'Alī al Ḥusayn Ibn 'Abdullah	428/1037	Bukhārā	Encyclopedia
Ibn Zaylah, Abū Manṣūr al Ḥusayn Ibn Muḥammad Ibn 'Umar	440/1048	Isfahan, Bukhārā	Music theory
al Qushayrī, Abū al Qāṣim 'Abd al Karīm Ibn Hawāzin	465/1074	Baghdād, Naysābūr	Sufism
al Rāghib al Isfahāni, Abū al Qāṣim al Ḥusayn Ibn Muḥammad Ibn al Mufaḍḍal	502/1108	not known	*Adab*
al Ṭabarī, Abū al Ṭayyib Ṭāhir Ibn 'Abdullah Ibn Ṭāhir	450/1058	Baghdād, Naysābūr	Lawfulness of *samā'*
Twelfth century			
Ibn Abī al Ṣalt, Umayyah Ibn 'Abd al 'Azīz	529/1134	Denia (Spain), Cairo	Music theory
Ibn Bājjah, Abū Bakr Muḥammad Ibn Yaḥya Ibn al Ṣa'īgh al Andalusī	533/1139	Zaragosa, Seville	Acoustics
Ibn al Jawzī, 'Abd al Raḥman Ibn 'Alī Ibn Muḥammad Abū al Faraj	597/1200	Baghdād	Religion, *adab*
Ibn Qudāmah, Muwaffaq al Dīn Abū Muḥammad 'Abdullah Ibn Aḥmad Ibn Muḥammad	620/1223	Dimashq	Lawfulness of *samā'*
Ibn Sanā' al Mulk, Hibātullah Ibn Ja'far	608/1211	Egypt	Song collection
al Rāzī, Fakhr al Dīn Abū 'Abdullah Muḥammad Ibn 'Umar Ibn al Ḥusayn	606/1209	Rayy, Khwārizm, Herat	Encyclopedia
al Suhrawardī, Ḍiyā' al Dīn Abū Najīb 'Abd al Qāhir	563/1168	Baghdād	Sufism
al Turṭūshī, Ibn Abī Randaqah Abū Bakr Muḥammad Ibn al Walīd Ibn Muḥammad	520/1126 or 525/1131	Alexandria	Lawfulness of *samā'*
al Zamakhsharī, Abū al Qāṣim Maḥmūd Ibn 'Umar	538/1144	Khwārizm	Ethics
Thirteenth century			
al Firkāḥ, 'Abd al Raḥman Ibn Ibrahīm	691/1291	Syria	Lawfulness of *samā'*
Ibn Abī Uṣaybi 'ah, Muwaffaq al Dīn Abū al 'Abbās Aḥmad Ibn al Qāṣim Ibn Khalīfah Ibn Yūnus al Khazrajī	668/1270	Dimashq, Cairo, Ṣarkhad	Bibliographical dictionary
Ibn al 'Arabī, Muḥyī al Dīn 'Abdullah Muḥammad Ibn 'Alī Ibn Muḥammad	638/1240	Seville, Dimashq	Sufism

Name	*Date of Death*	*Major Location of Life and Work*	*Main Field(s) of Relevant Work*
Ibn Khallikān, Aḥmad Ibn Muḥammad Ibn Ibrahīm Abū al 'Abbās Shams al Dīn al Barmakī	681/1282	Dimashq, Cairo	Biographical dictionary
Ibn al Qifṭī, Jamāl al Dīn Abū al Ḥasan 'Alī Ibn Yūsuf Ibn Ibrahīm	646/1248	Aleppo	Biographical dictionary
Ibn al Ukhūwwah, Ḍiyā' al Dīn Muḥammad Ibn Muḥammad Ibn Aḥmad	729/1329	Egypt	Jurisprudence
al Maqdisī, Ibn Ghānim 'Izz al Dīn 'Abd al Salām Ibn Aḥmad Ibn Ghānim	678/1279	Cairo	Sufism
al Nawawī, Muḥyī al Dīn Abū Zakariyyā Yaḥyā Ibn Sharaf	676/1277	Nawa, south of Dimashq	Religious lessons
Ṣafī al Dīn 'Abd al Mu'min Ibn Yūsuf Ibn Fākhir al Urmawī	693/1294	Baghdād	Music theory
al Sāqizī, Muḥammad Ibn Yūsuf al Ḥalabī	fl. 693/1294	probably Syria	Sufism
al Ṣarkhadī, Tāj al Dīn Muḥammad Ibn 'Ābid Ibn al Ḥusayn al Tamīmī	674/1275	Dimashq	Lawfulness of *samā'*
al Shīrāzī, Quṭb al Dīn Maḥmūd Ibn Mas'ūd Ibn Musliḥ	710/1311	Shīrāz	Dictionary of the sciences
al Suhrawardī, Shihāb al Dīn Abū Ḥafṣ 'Umar	632/1234	Baghdād	Sufism
al Ṭūsī, Nasīr al Dīn Abū Ja'far Muḥammad Ibn Muḥammad Ibn al Ḥasan	672/1274	Marāghah, Baghdād	Music theory
Yāqūt al Rūmī Shihāb al Dīn Abū 'Abdullah Ya'qūb Ibn 'Abdullah al Ḥamawī	626/1229	Aleppo, Baghdād	Biographical dictionary
Fourteenth century			
al Adfuwī, Ja'far Ibn Tha'lab Ibn Ja'far	748/1347	Cairo	Lawfulness of *samā'*
al Bisṭāmī, Badr al Dīn Muḥammad Ibn Aḥmad Ibn al Shaykh Muḥammad al Ḥalabī	807/1404	Aleppo	Lawfulness of *samā'*
al Damīrī, Muḥammad Ibn Mūsā Ibn 'Īsā Kamāl al Dīn	808/1405	Cairo	*Adab*
al Dhahabī, Shams al Dīn Abū 'Abdullah Muḥammad 'Uthman Ibn Qaymāz Ibn 'Abdullah	748/1348 or 753/1352	Dimashq	Lawfulness of *samā'*
al Dhahabī, Shams al Dīn al Ṣaydāwī	14th c.	Syria	Music theory
al Ḥiṣnī, Taqī al Dīn Abū Bakr Ibn Muḥammad Ibn 'Abd al Mu'min	829/1426	Dimashq	Lawfulness of *samā'*
Ibn Abi Hajālā, Abū al 'Abbās Aḥmad Ibn Yaḥyā Shihāb al Dīn al Tilimsānī	776/1375	Cairo	Anthology of poetry
Ibn al Akfānī, Abū 'Abdullah Shams al Dīn Muḥammad Ibn Ibrāhīm Ibn Sā'id al Sinjārī	749/1348	Cairo	Encyclopedia of the sciences
Ibn al 'Aṭṭār, Abū al Ḥasan 'Alī Ibn Ibrāhīm Ibn Dāwūd	724/1324	Dimashq	Lawfulness of *samā'*

(Continued)

TABLE 23.1 *(Continued)*

Name	*Date of Death*	*Major Location of Life and Work*	*Main Field(s) of Relevant Work*
Ibn Baṭṭuṭā, Shams al Dīn ʻAbdullah Ibn Muḥammad Ibn Ibrāhīm Ibn Yūsuf al Lawātī al Ṭanjī	770/1368 or 779/1377	Fās	Travel
Ibn al Ḥājj, Abū ʻAbdullah Muḥammad al ʻAbdarī al Fāsī	737/1336	Fās	Jurisprudence
Ibn Jamāʻah, Burhān al Dīn Abū Isḥāq Ibrāhīm Ibn ʻAbd al Raḥīm	790/1388	Dimashq	Lawfulness of *samāʻ*
Ibn Khaldūn, Walī al Dīn ʻAbd al Raḥman Ibn Muḥammad Ibn Abī Bakr Muḥammad Ibn al Ḥasan	808/1406	Fās, Granada, Tūnis, Cairo	Philosophy of history
Ibn al Khaṭīb, Lisān al Dīn Abū ʻAbdullah Ibn Saʻīd Ibn ʻAlī Ibn Aḥmad	776/1374	Fās, Granada	Music theory
Ibn al Muqri', Sirāj al Dīn Ismaʻīl Ibn Abū Bakr	837/1433	Taʻizz, Zabīd (Yemen)	Poetry
Ibn Rajab, Zayn al Dīn Abū al Faraj ʻAbd al Raḥman Ibn Aḥmad	795/1392	Dimashq, Baghdād	Lawfulness of *samāʻ*
Ibn Taymiyyah, Taqī al Dīn Aḥmad	728/1328	Dimashq	Lawfulness of *samāʻ*
al Irbilī, Shams al Dīn Muḥammad Ibn ʻAlī Ibn Aḥmad al Khatīb	fl. c. 729/1329	Mawṣil	Music theory in poetic form
al Jawziyyah, Shams al Dīn Abū Bakr Muḥammad Ibn Abū Bakr al Zarʻī Ibn Qayyim	751/1350	Dimashq	Lawfulness of *samāʻ*
al Jīlī or al Kilānī, ʻAbd al Karīm Quṭb al Dīn Ibn Ibrahīm	832/1428	Aden, Zabid (Yemen)	Sufism
al Jurjānī, ʻAlī Ibn Muḥammad	816/1413	Shīrāz	Dictionary of scientific terms
al Mardīnī, ʻAbdullah Ibn Khalīl Ibn Yūsuf Jamāl al Dīn al Qāhirī	809/1406	Dimashq	Music theory in poetic and prose form
al Nuwayrī, Shihāb al Dīn Aḥmad Ibn ʻAbd al Wahhāb al Bakrī al Kindī al Shāfiʻī	732/1332	Tripoli, Cairo	Encyclopedia
al ʻUmarī, Ibn Faḍl Allah Shihāb al Dīn Aḥmad	749/1349	Dimashq	Geography, administrative manual
Fifteenth century			
al ʻAjamī, Shihāb al Dīn	after 900/1494	not known	Music theory
al Ḥamawī, Uways	fl. 901/1496	Tripoli	Anthology of poetry
al Ḥaṣkafī, Muẓaffar Ibn al Ḥusayn Ibn al Muẓaffar	fl. 15th c.	not known	Music theory
Ibn Ghaybī, ʻAbd al Qādir al Ḥāfiẓ al Marāghī	839/1435	Baghdād, Samarqand, Tabrīz, Herat	Music theory
Ibn Ḥijjah, Abū al Bakr Taqī al Dīn al Ḥamawī al Azrārī	836/1434	Cairo	*Adab*
Ibn al Jazarī, Shams al Dīn Abū al Khayr Muḥammad Ibn Muḥammad Ibn ʻAlī Ibn Yūsuf	833/1429	Dimashq, Shīrāz	*Tajwīd al Qur'ān*
Ibn al Khaṭīb, Muḥyī al Dīn Muḥammad Qāṣim Ibn Yaʻqūb	940/1533	Istanbul	*Adab*
Ibn Taghrī Birdī, Abū al Maḥāsin Jamāl al Dīn Yūsuf	874/1470	Cairo	History

Name	*Date of Death*	*Major Location of Life and Work*	*Main Field(s) of Relevant Work*
Ibn Zaghdūn, Jamāl al Dīn Abū al Mawāhib Ibn Aḥmad Ibn Muḥammad al Tūnisī al Wafā'ī al Shādhilī	882/1477	Tūnis, Cairo	Lawfulness of *samā'*
al Ibshīhī or Abshīhī, Bahā' al Dīn Abū al Fatḥ Muḥammad Ibn Aḥmad Ibn Manṣūr	after 850/1446	Maḥallah al Kubrā, Cairo	Anthology of *adab*
al Lādhiqī, Muḥammad Ibn al Ḥāmid	c. 900/1495	Istanbul	Music theory
al Maqdisī, Abū Ḥāmid Ibn Muḥammad	893/1488	not known	Anthology of *samā'*
al Shirwānī, Mawlānā Fatḥ Allah al Mu'min	15th c.	probably Isṭanbūl	Music theory
al Suyūṭī, Abū al Faḍl 'Abd al Raḥman Ibn Abū Bakr Ibn Muḥammad Jalāl al Dīn	99/1505	Cairo	Historical encyclopedia and Qur'ānic sciences
Sixteenth century			
al 'Ādilī, Badr al Dīn Abū 'Umar Muḥammad Ibn 'Umar Ibn Aḥmad	970/1562	Egypt	Religious subjects
al Anṭakī, Dawūd Ibn 'Umar al Ḍarīr	1008/1599	Antioch, Damascus Cairo, Makkah	Medical writings
al Burhānpūrī, Shaykh Muḥammad 'Īsā Sindhī	fl. 16th c.	India	Lawfulness of *samā'*
al Ḥamawī, 'Alwān 'Alī Ibn 'Aṭiyyah Ibn Ḥasan Ibn Muḥammad al Ḥaddād	936/1527	Ḥamāh (Syria)	Jurisprudence
al Haythamī, Abū al 'Abbās Aḥmad Ibn Muḥammad Ibn 'Alī Ibn Ḥajar	974/1567	Cairo, Makkah	Lawfulness of *samā'*
Ibn Kamāl or Kamāl-Pāshā-Zādah, Shams al Dīn Aḥmad Ibn Sulaymān	941/1535	Adrianpole, Isṭanbūl	Lawfulness of *samā'*
Ibn al Kayyāl, Shams al Dīn Abū al Barakāt Muḥammad Ibn Aḥmad Ibn Muḥammad al Shāfi'ī	938/1532	Dimashq	*Tartīl/Tajwīd al Qur'ān*
Ibn Ṭūlūn, Shams al Dīn Muḥammad Ibn 'Alī Ibn Aḥmad al Ṣāliḥī	953/1546	Dimashq	Encyclopedia of arts and sciences
Jamāl al Dīn, Ḥasan Ibn Aḥmad	16th c.	not known	Music theory
al Kīzawānī, 'Alī Ibn Aḥmad Ibn Muḥammad al Ḥamawī al Shādhilī	955/1548	Ḥamāh (Syria)	Sufism
al Muqṣirī, 'Afīf al Dīn 'Abd al Salām Ibn Shaykh al Islām Wajīh al Dīn 'Abd al Raḥman Ibn 'Abd al Karīm Ibn Ziyād	fl. 973/1565	Zabīd (Yaman)	Sufism
al Muttaqī al Hindī, 'Alī Ibn Hishām al Dīn 'Abd al Malik Ibn Qāḍī Khān	975/1567	Burhanpur (India), Multan, Makkah	Collection of maxims
al Qāri', 'Alī Ibn Sulṭān Muḥammad al Harawī	1014/1605	Makkah	Lawfulness of *samā'* and *ghinā*
al Shāmī, 'Umar Muḥammad Ibn 'Iwaḍ	fl. 993/1585	Bukhārā	Jurisprudence
Shams al Dīn Ibn Ḥāmid al Shāfi'ī	16th c.	Syria	Jurisprudence
al Sigetwārī, 'Alī Ibn Muṣṭafā 'Alā' al Dīn al Bosnāwī	1007/1598	Bosnia	Encyclopedia of scientists

(Continued)

TABLE 23.1 *(Continued)*

Name	*Date of Death*	*Major Location of Life and Work*	*Main Field(s) of Relevant Work*
Tashkopruzade, Aḥmad Ibn Muṣṭafā Ibn Khalīl	968/1561	Iṣṭanbūl	Encyclopedia of scientists, Qur'ānic sciences
Seventeenth century			
al Anqarawī or al Anqirawī, al Shaykh Isma'īl Ibn Muḥammad al Mawlawī	1042/1636	Galata (Turkey)	Lawfulness of *samā'*
al Dilusī, Mawlā Jihād al Dīn	17th c.	Samarqand	Music theory in poetic form
al Fāsī, 'Abd al Raḥman Ibn 'Abd al Qādir	1096/1685	Fās	Music theory in poetic form
Ḥajjī Khalīfah, Muṣṭafā Ibn 'Abdullah	1067/1657	Istanbul	Bibliography
al Ḥuṣrī al Ḥusaynī, Naṣrī Ibn Aḥmad	1085/1674	Dimashq	Lawfulness of *samā'*
Ibn Bisṭām, Muḥammad al Khashshābī Wānī Effendī Wānqūlī	probably 1096/1685	not known	Jurisprudence
al Makkī, 'Ali Ibn Muḥammad	17th–18th c.	not known	Anthology
al Maqarrī, Abū al 'Abbās Aḥmad Ibn Muḥammad Ibn Aḥmad Ibn Yaḥyā al Tilimsānī	1041/1632	Fās, Cairo	Literary history
al Nābulusī, 'Abd al Ghanī Ibn Isma'īl	1143/1731	Dimashq	Lawfulness of *samā'* and Sufism
al Rūmī, Aḥmad Ibn 'Abd al Qāhir	1041/1631	not known	Sufism
al Sahāranpūrī, 'Iṣmatullah Ibn A'zam Ibn 'Abd al Rasūl	fl. 1089/1678	India	Lawfulness of *samā'*
al Shirwānī Mullāzādah, Muḥammad Amīn Ibn Ṣadr Amīn	1036/1628	Turkey	Lawfulness of *samā'*
al Uskudārī, 'Azīz Maḥmūd Ibn Faḍlullah al Hudā'i	1038/1628	Turkey	Lawfulness of *samā'*
Eighteenth century			
al 'Attār, Muḥammad Ibn Ḥusayn	1243/1828	Dimashq	Music theory
al Dikdikjī, 'Abd al Wahhāb	1189/1775	Dimashq, Istanbul	Lawfulness of *samā'*
al Ḥā'ik, Ibn Aḥmad	fl. 18th c.	Tiṭwān (Tetouan)	Music theory
al Qābisī, Ḥusayn Ibn al Shaykh Aḥmad	end 18th c.	probably Tunisia	Music theory in poetic form
Kalīm Allah, Ibn Nūr Allah Ibn Aḥmad	1142/1729	Delhi	Sufism
al Muslim al Mawṣilī, Abū Ṣāliḥ Aḥmad al Rifā'ī Ibn 'Abd al Raḥman	1124/1712	probably Mawṣīl	Music theory
al Rampūrī, Salām Allah Ibn Shaykh al Islām	1229/1814 or 1203/1788	India	Lawfulness of *samā'*
al Tāfilātī, Muḥammad Ibn Muḥammad al Maghribī al Azharī	1191/1777	probably Jerusalem	Lawfulness of *samā'*
Nineteenth century			
al Bulāqī, Muṣṭafā Ibn Ramaḍan Ibn 'Abd al Karīm al Burullusī	1263/1847	Cairo	Lawfulness of instruments and singing
al Dāmūnī, Muḥammad Ibn Muḥammad	fl. 1215/1800	Egypt	Lawfulness of *samā'*
Mashāqah, Mīkhā'īl Ibn Jirjis Ibn Ibrahīm Ibn Jirjis Ibn Yūsuf Baṭraqī	1305/1888	Dimashq	Music theory
Shihāb al Dīn, Muḥammad Ibn Isma'īl al Ḥijāzī	1274/1857	Cairo	Music theory
Sulaymān Ibn Muḥammad Ibn 'Abdullah Ibn Isma'īl Abū al Rabi' al Sharīf al 'Alawī, Sulṭān of Morocco	1238/1822	Morocco	Lawfulness of *samā'*

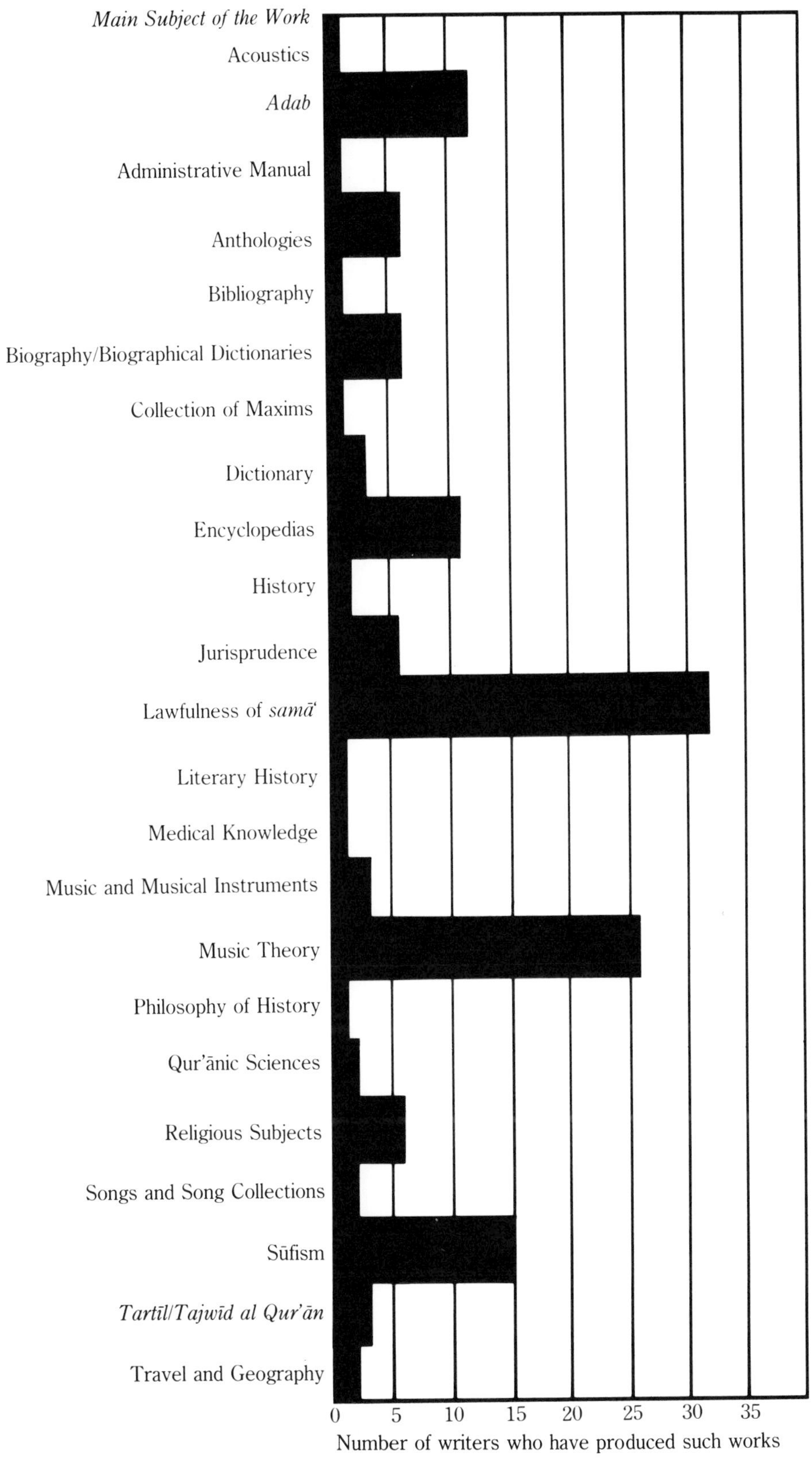

Figure 23.1

Types of literature that include materials on *Handasah al Ṣawt*

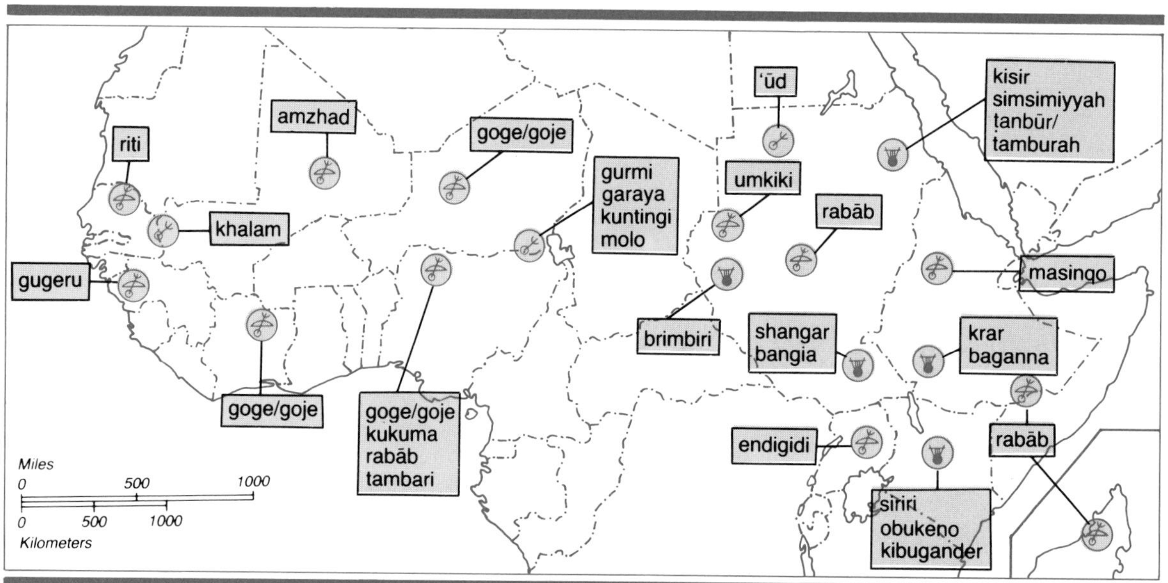

riti
amzhad
goge/goje
'ūd
kisir
simsimiyyah
tanbūr/
tamburah
gurmi
garaya
kuntingi
molo
umkiki
khalam
rabāb
gugeru
masinqo
brimbiri
shangar
bangia
krar
baganna
goge/goje
goge/goje
kukuma
rabāb
tambari
endigidi
rabāb
siriri
obukeno
kibugander
Miles
0
500
1000
0
500
1000
Kilometers

A.

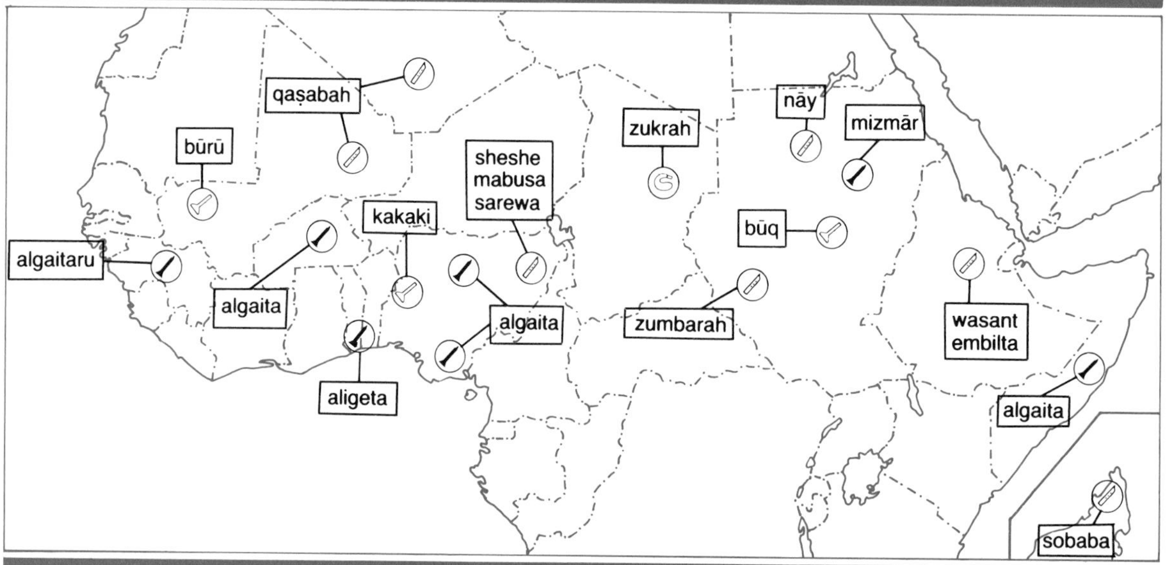

qaṣabah
nāy
zukrah
mizmār
būrū
sheshe
mabusa
sarewa
kakaki
būq
algaitaru
algaita
algaita
zumbarah
wasant
embilta
aligeta
algaita
sobaba

B.

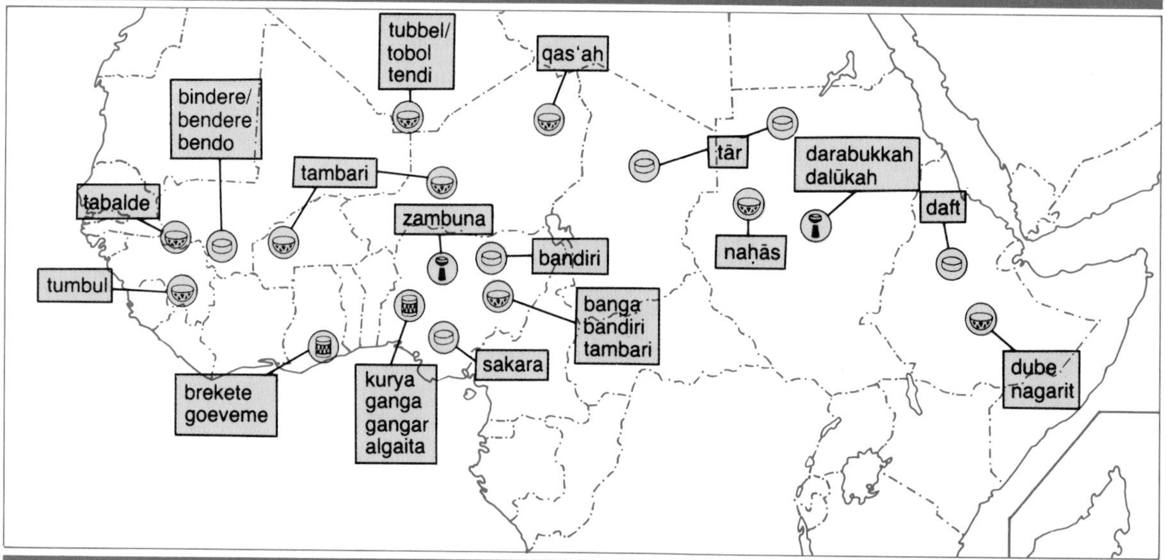

tubbel/
tobol
tendi
qas'ah
bindere/
bendere
bendo
tār
darabukkah
dalūkah
tambari
tabalde
zambuna
daft
naḥās
bandiri
tumbul
banga
bandiri
tambari
sakara
brekete
goeveme
kurya
ganga
gangar
algaita
dube
nagarit

C.

Map 72. Musical Instruments in Middle Africa
A. Chordophones
B. Aerophones
C. Membranophones

Chordophones found in Area II

PL: garaya, gurmi, kuntingi, molo (Hausa), 'ūd, khalam (Wolofs of Senegal and Gambia)
BL: amzhad (Tuareg), rebāb (West and East Africa), riti (Senegal), masinqo (Ethiopia), tambari (Hausa), goge/goje (Hausa), kukuma (Hausa), gugeru (Fulani), endigidi (Uganda), umkiki (West Sudan), mngoli and kaligo (Malawi)
L: ṭanbūr, simsimiyyah (East Africa), krar, baganna (Ethiopia), obukeno, siriri, kibugander (Kenya), brimbiri (West Sudan), shangar, bangia (South Sudan), kisir (Sudan)

Aerophones found in Area II

E: sarewa, mabusa, sheshe (Hausa), wasant (Ethiopia), sobaba (Madagascar), embilta (Ethiopia), qaṣabah (Tuareg), zumbarah (Sudan)
O: algaita (Hausa, Yoruba, East Africa), algaitaru (Fulani), aligeta (Togo), mizmār
B: zukrah (near Lake Chad)
T: būrū (Mandingo of West Africa), kakaki (Hausa)

Membranophones found in Area II

F: ṭār (Sudan), bandiri (Hausa), sakara (Yoruba), daft (Ethiopia), bindere and bendo (West Africa)
G: zambuna (Hausa), dalūkah (Sudan)
K: banga, bandiri, tambari (West Africa), tubbel/tobol and tendi (Tuareg), tabalde (Fulani), tambari (Nigeria), tumbul (Mandingo of West Africa), dube and nagarīt (Ethiopia), qaṣ'ah and nahās (Sudan)
DC: kurya, ganga, gangar algaita (Hausa), brekete, goeveme (Ghana), and many varieties

Interregional relevance is even evident in the attitudes of recent converts to Islam in Western Europe and America. These new Muslims are anxiously seeking, in every aspect of their lives, to acculturate and relate themselves to the Muslim *ummah* ("community"). Their religious "leap" into Islam has influenced their aesthetic interests and appreciations as well as their religious beliefs. As far as the *ṣawtī* arts are concerned, Qur'ānic chant is crucial for them. It is the most appreciated genre of artistically rendered sounds in the lives of the new Muslims, regardless of their backgrounds. The desire for cultural affinity by these converts has also made *handasah al ṣawt* genres from various regions of the Muslim world newly appreciated.

MODEL FOR CREATIVITY: THE CHANTED QUR'ĀN

Though it has never been regarded by Muslims as *mūsīqā,* Qur'ānic chant is the *handasah al ṣawt* genre to be heard in almost any context, with every type of audience, in every corner of the Muslim world. It is even an inescapable sound art experience for non-Muslims living in a region with a sizable Muslim population. Qur'ānic chant is therefore the most pervasive genre of *handasah al ṣawt* in Islamic culture. Although the Qur'ān's verses and chapters say little that can be interpreted as determining of *ṣawtī* experience,[12] the omnipresent chanted scripture plays a crucial, though subtle and usually subconscious, role in determining the characteristics of other genres of sound art in Islamic culture. The Qur'ān is a prototype for artistic expression in *handasah al ṣawt.*

Despite the factors of homogeneity mentioned above, the unifying *handasah al ṣawt* characteristics exemplified in the chanted Qur'ān follow a pattern of varying significance. By this we mean that certain genres of *handasah al ṣawt* reveal a higher level of conformance than others to those characteristics, This can best be understood by imagining a series of stepped concentric rings or cylinders representing the various categories of *handasah al ṣawt* genres (Figure 23.2). At the top and center is Qur'ānic chant, which faithfully embodies the core characteristics in every period and region. It is in Qur'ānic recitation that the greatest amount of effort has been exerted, and the greatest success achieved, in avoiding deviations from the chanting norms established in the time of the Prophet Muḥammad. This is the essence and heart of the *ṣawtī* tradition, the center of the concentric cylinders representing its variable and staged influence. It is the main carrier and purest form of the core characteristics of *handasah al ṣawt.*

Every century has had its "guardians" of the Qur'ānic *qirā'ah* tradition who wrote, preached, or acted to preserve the integrity of this vocal tradition.[13] Fortunately, their efforts did not result in a fossilized tradition; this was precluded by the improvisational nature of the art, a quality well guarded up to the present time.[14] It did, however, provide a continuity and homogeneity in the chant tradition which makes it possible for the Muslim to feel comfortable with the competent Qur'ānic recitation heard in any part of the Muslim world. This does not mean that individual reciters will be indistinguishable from each other or that they will all be equally satisfying to their

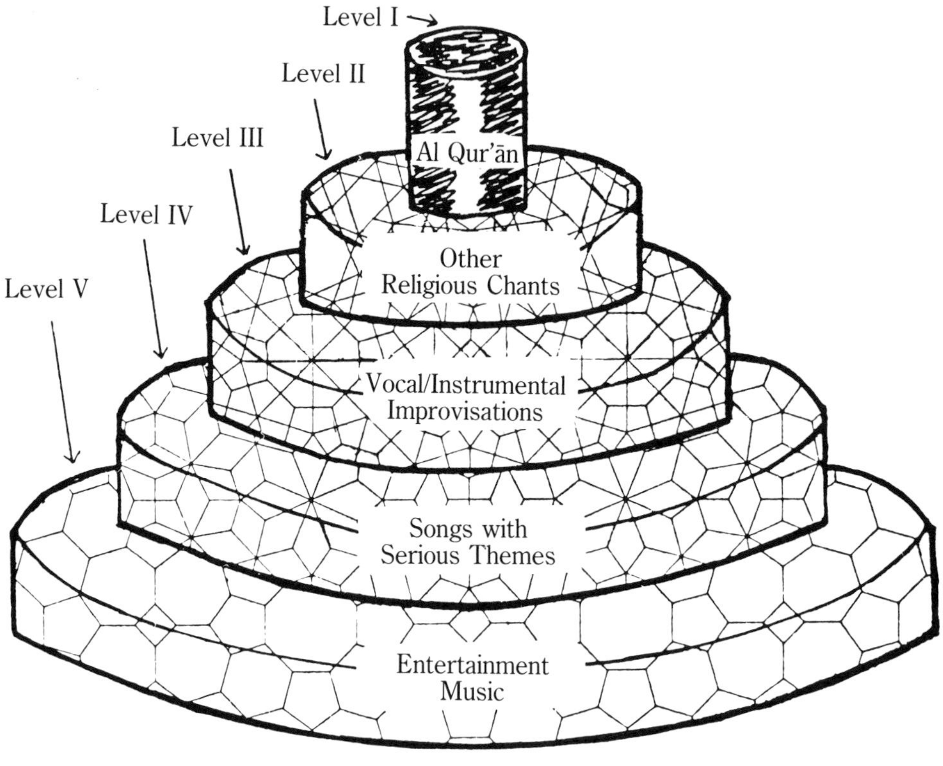

Figure 23.2

Genre relevance to the core characteristics of *Handasah al Ṣawt*

hearers since *qurrā'* (sing. *qāri';* "readers") vary significantly in linguistic, vocal, and aesthetic capabilities. It does imply that the recitation of the Qur'ān has strong boundaries which the culture's "aesthetic conscience" protects from being broken. The chant of Malaysia, therefore, does not differ appreciably from that of Egypt, Turkey, or Iran; and what we read of Qur'ānic cantillation of earlier periods indicates no allowable marked deviance from the norm.[15]

The second level or circle in our model is that of the chants associated with the call to prayer (the *adhān*) or pilgrimage, and the pitched recitation of religious poetry. Sometimes such poetry is in praise of the Prophet Muḥammad *(madīḥ)*. At other times it conveys thanks to Allah *(taḥmīd, ḥamd)* or mystical expressions. These *ṣawtī* renderings reveal a level of correspondence to the core characteristics of Islamic aesthetic creativity only slightly less consistent than that of *qirā'ah.* They are performed in all regions of the Muslim world, in private as well as at public gatherings, in the home or in the mosque, at religiously important occasions as well as at other times. Lyrics may be in Arabic, although indigenous languages are also used. Examples include the *na't* or *na'tiyah* of Afghanistan, the *marhaban, barzanji, rebanah* or *kompang, hadrah,* and *rodat* of Malaysia, the *marsiyā* and *sōz* of Pakistan, and the *nâat, miraciye,* and *mevlit* of Turkey, as they are commonly called in those lands.

The third cylinder or ring in the model includes instrumental and vocal improvisations (Illus. 23.9), for example, the *taqāsīm, layālī,* and *qaṣīdah* of Turkey and the Mashriq, the *āvāz* of Iran, the *shakl* of Afghanistan, the *dā'irah* and *istikhbār* of the Maghrib, *sayil* or *baqat* vocal music in southeast Asia, and the *rok'wan Allah* and *jinjin* of the Hausa of West Africa. Though some may depart from the strictly vocal rendering of the first two genre categories, such examples of improvised, free-rhythmed performance reveal a pronounced conformity to the core characteristics of the Islamic arts, of *handasah al ṣawt,* and of the Qur'ānic model. Here, however, the elements of regional diversity tend to be more frequent and pronounced in both vocal and instrumental examples.

A fourth category, which displays still less correspondence to the core characteristics revealed in Qur'ānic chant, is that of songs with religious themes:

Illustration 23.9

The late Umm Kulthūm, one of the most respected and admired vocalists of the Muslim world. Trained as a child to recite the Qur'ān, she later used that skill in singing a wide range of poetic-musical compositions. [Photo by Celebrity Foto Enterprises, Inc.]

the *qaṣīdah* of Malaysia, the *ghazal* of Iran-Central Asia and the Indian subcontinent, the *ilâhî, nefes,* and *ṣuğul* of Turkey, the *muwashshaḥ dīnī* of the Mashriq, *nashīd* of southeast Asia (Illus. 23.10), *wak'a addini* of the Hausa, and so on. These are metered compositions which are usually performed by groups of male and/or female performers singing in unison, that is, with a single melodic line simultaneously performed by all voices. Instrumental accompaniment may or not be included. The lyrics are often in Arabic, but regional languages of the Muslim world are also used. In some cases, the word content is a mixture of Arabic and the indigenous languages. Despite their metered base and the possible use of instruments (two features avoided in *qirā'ah*), they evidence many of the characteristics of Qur'ānic chant.

Generally revealing still less continuity with Qur'ānic content, form, and performance style are the solo or choral songs with secular themes and the instrumental compositions of the fifth level. Where genres among these show a high level of conformance, they have undoubtedly been influenced by the Qur'ān and by musical styles carried by Muslim travelers, settlers, and pilgrims. Other items included in this category show more obvious determination by alien or pre-Islamic cultures.[16] The degree of their conformance to the core characteristics has determined either their toleration or their rejection as entertainment and aesthetic expression. Association with disapproved activities such as the use of alcohol and drugs and the promiscious mixing of the sexes is another reason for the condemnation of certain genres belonging to this level, and for their being indulged in only with some sense of culpability and apology on the part of both performers and listeners.[17]

These concentric levels of decreasing conformity are applicable to all regions of the Muslim world. In all regions and areas, however, the highest degree of conformance exists in examples of Qur'ānic chant. Though there is a tendency toward increasing divergence as one proceeds outward from Level 1, even this factor is not uniform in all parts of the Muslim world. Divergence from the core characteristics in some regions is rarely experienced even in the music of the fifth level, while in other regions, it may be evident in features of an inner level or levels. In order to better understand this feature of Islamic *ṣawtī* cul-

Illustration 23.10

Women's chorus performing a *nashīd* (hymn) in connection with Qur'ān reading competition, 1981. [Courtesy Federal Department of Information, Government of Malaysia.]

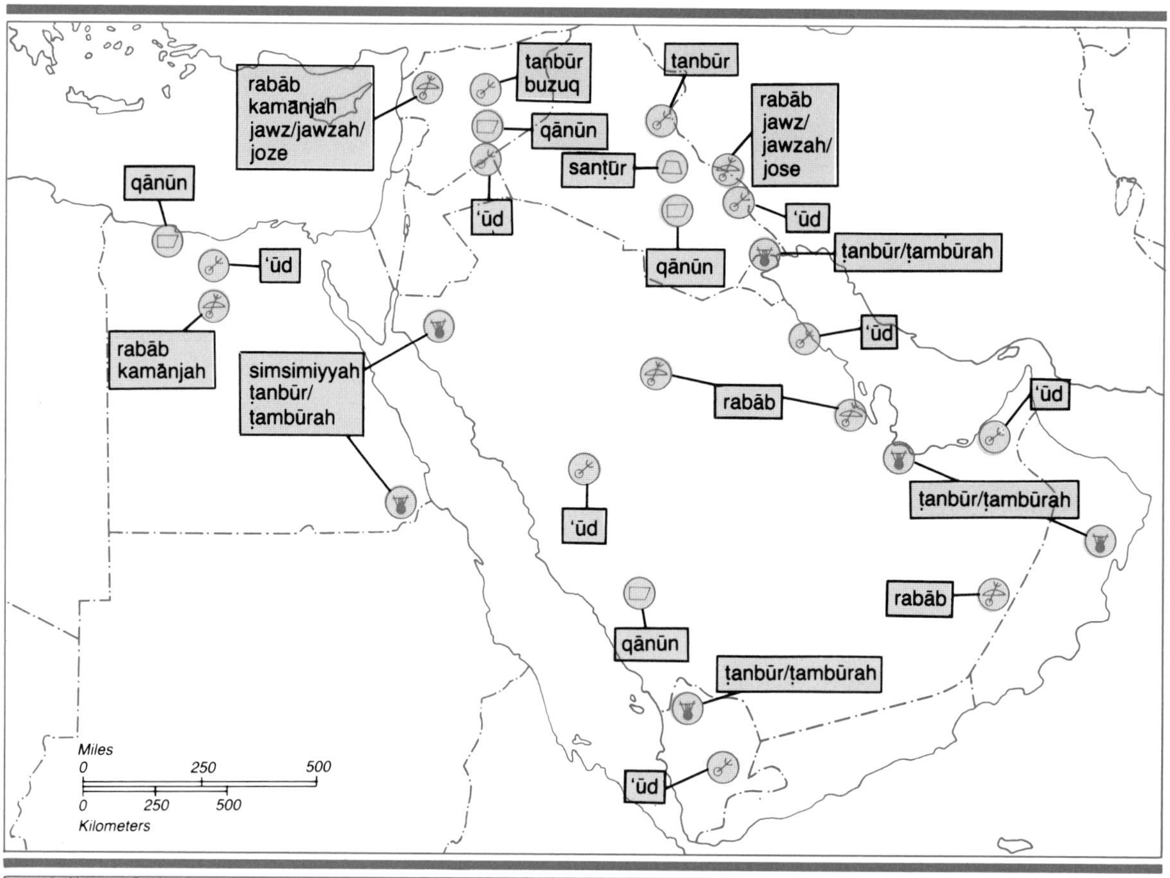
rabāb
kamānjah
jawz/jawzah/
joze
tanbūr
buzuq
qānūn
tanbūr
santūr
rabāb
jawz/
jawzah/
jose
'ūd
qānūn
'ūd
ṭanbūr/ṭambūrah
qānūn
'ūd
rabāb
kamānjah
simsimiyyah
ṭanbūr/
ṭambūrah
'ūd
rabāb
'ūd
ṭanbūr/ṭambūrah
'ūd
rabāb
qānūn
ṭanbūr/ṭambūrah
'ūd
Miles
0 250 500
0 250 500
Kilometers

A.

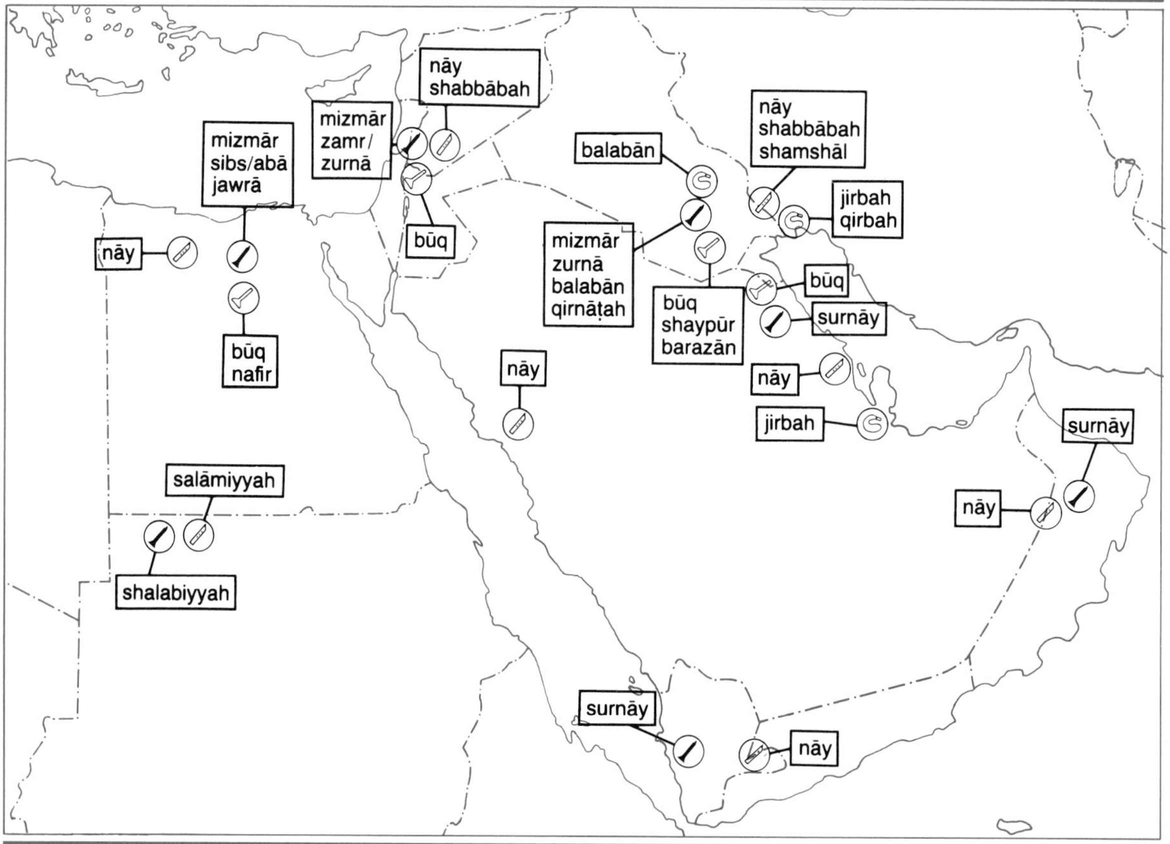
nāy
shabbābah
mizmār
zamr/
zurnā
mizmār
sibs/abā
jawrā
balabān
nāy
shabbābah
shamshāl
jirbah
qirbah
būq
nāy
mizmār
zurnā
balabān
qirnāṭah
būq
būq
shaypūr
barazān
surnāy
būq
nafir
nāy
nāy
jirbah
surnāy
nāy
salāmiyyah
shalabiyyah
surnāy
nāy

B.

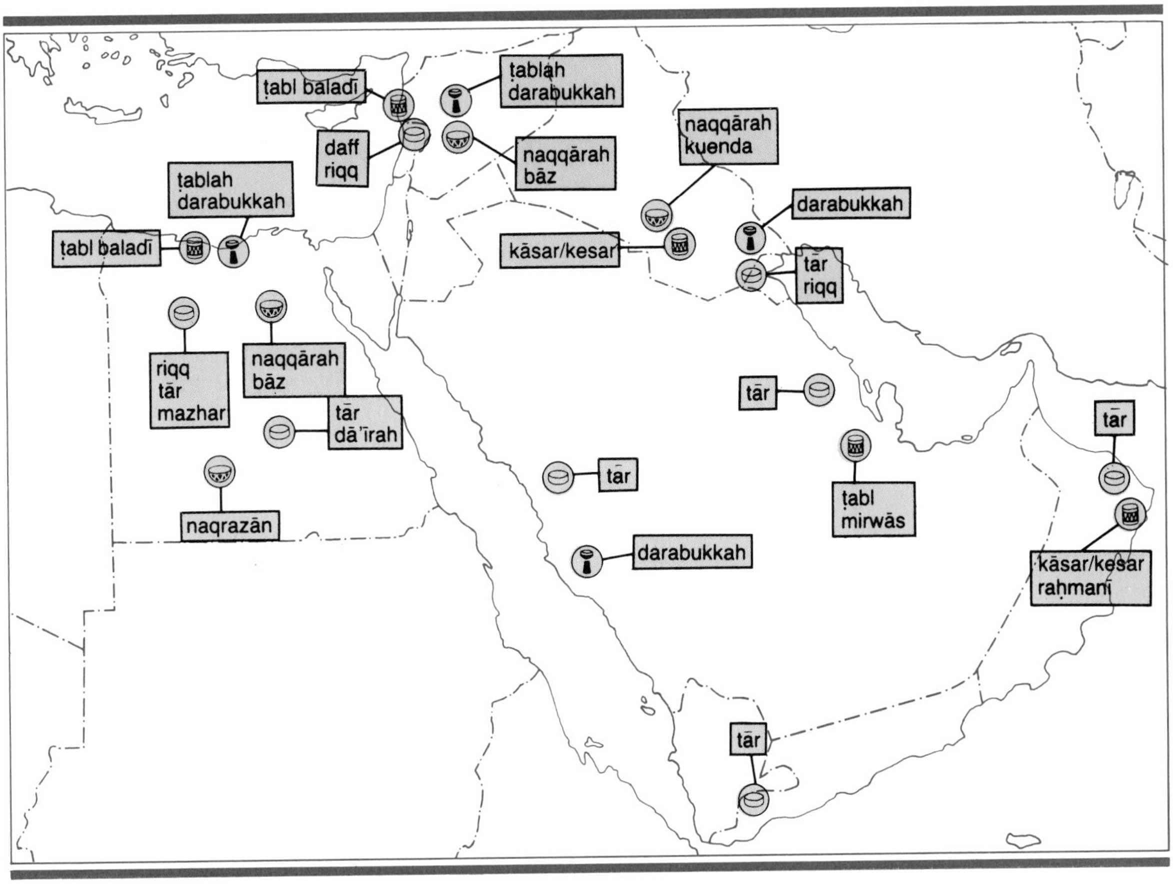

C.

Map 73. Musical Instruments in the Mashriq
A. Chordophones
B. Aerophones
C. Membranophones

ture, the Muslim world has been divided into three *handasah al ṣawt* areas representative of the varying degrees of conformity which the sound art genres show to the Qur'ānic prototype (Figure 23.3). Despite the apparent rigidity of boundary lines, such divisions should not be understood to mean that these areas exist with precise borders. Instead, one area melds into another without sharply definable perimeters. Neither does the division imply an identity of performance practice within the constituent subregions of any area. On the contrary, though each area may evidence striking conformity in the genres of the upper/inner levels of Figure 23.1, it may reveal significant variance in the types of performance of Level 5.

Such discrepancies in the applicability and influence of the Qur'ānic model depend primariliy on four factors. These are: (1) proximity to the Middle Eastern cradleland of the religion and culture; (2) the de-

Chordophones found in Area III

PL: 'ūd (short neck), ṭanbūr, buzuq (long neck)
BL: rabāb, kamānjah, jawz/jawzah/joze
P: qānūn
D: sanṭūr
L: simsimiyyah, ṭanbūr/ṭambūrah

Aerophones found in Area III

E: nāy, shabbābah, shamshāl, salamiyyah
O: mizmār, zurnā, surnāy (Gulf States), balabān or qirnāṭah (Iraq), jawrā, abā, sibs (Egypt), shalabiyyah (Upper Egypt)
B: jirbah, qirbah (Iraq), balabān (North Iraq)
T: būq, nafīr, shaypūr and barazān (Iraq)

Membranophones found in Area III

F: daff, mahzar, riqq, ṭār (Gulf States)
G: darabukkah, ṭablah
K: naqqārah, kuenda (South Iraq), naqrazān (Upper Egypt)
DC: ṭabl (Gulf States), ṭabl baladī (Egypt and Eastern Mediterranean), mirwās (Gulf States), kāsar/kesar (South Iraq, 'Umān), raḥmanī ('Umān), ḥoqa (Upper Egypt)

Illustration 23.11
Soloists and instrumental group of the Shadliki folklore ensemble, Uzbekistan, U.S.S.R. [Photo by L. al Fārūqī.]

gree of conformity of the pre-Islamic cultural base; (3) the duration of the Islamization process; and (4) the intensiveness of the Islamic encounter in the region.[18] The three ***handasah al ṣawt*** areas of the Muslim world represented in Figure 23.3 indicate varying degrees of conformance or nonconformance to the six core characteristics of aesthetic expression in Islamic culture. Constituent subregions within each of the areas are sometimes, though not always, geographically contiguous. Those parts of a subdivision that are widely separated, of course, vary more from each other than contiguous regions.

Subdivision I is roughly inclusive of the Mashriq, Maghrib, Turkey, and Iran. This is the area that shows the greatest identity with the Qur'ānic core characteristics. Its conformance is due to the following reasons. First, this subdivision includes those parts of the Muslim world that are in closest proximity to the cradleland of Islam. Second, the pre-Islamic cultural base of these regions was the most conformant to the subsequent Islamic overlay. With the exception of Turkey, these regions had participated for millennia in a larger Semitic complex of peoples and cultures before the coming of Islam. They had much in common, therefore, with the culture that developed under the banner of Islam. Their peoples were already aesthetically and musically prepared for the Islamization process. They were already capable of being moved by those aesthetic and musical characteristics that were to be fostered during the Islamic period. Since musical characteristics, like other cultural features, move with greatest ease where greater correspondences exist, the conformity to the core characteristics has been considerable in Area I. Third, this area includes those lands that have had the longest exposure to Islam, for it was here that large numbers of the population embraced the religion during the first century after the rise of Islam. Fourth, in this area the largest percentage of people have become adherents of the faith, thus widening the cultural impact in the society.

Subdivision II encompasses Central Asia and the Indian subcontinent. The somewhat decreased influence of the core characteristics on the ***handasah al ṣawt*** genres of these lands results from the following. First, these regions of the Muslim world are geographically farther removed than those of Subdivision I from the Middle Eastern cradleland. This has made interaction and aesthetic influence more difficult. Second, the pre-Islamic cultural bases on which the Islamic ideology was to build were more diverse in this area when compared with Subdivision I. Third, the Islamic influence has not been felt as long in this area because of the generally later conversion period for the Muslims of this region. Fourth, larger numbers of non-Muslims are represented in the population of the area. Since these peoples are less affected than Muslims by the Islamization process, the Islamic aesthetic encounter here is less intense than in Subdivision I. Given these differences of proximity, pre-Islamic cultural traditions, duration of Islamization, and intensity of the Islamic encounter, the level of penetration of the core characteristics exemplified in Qur'ānic chant into other genres of ***handasah al ṣawt*** has been somewhat less pervasive in Subdivision II than in Subdivision I. Central Asia and North India share many musical traditions with the Mashriq, Maghrib, Turkey, and Iran. The genres of ***handasah al ṣawt*** near the center of the concentric circles (Qur'ānic chant, nonscriptural religious chants, and vocal or instrumental improvisations) reveal no significant variance in core characteristics from the comparable genre levels of Subdivision I. In the genres at greater distance from the center, however, there is an increasing influence from the indigenous cultural background and a lessening determination by the core characteristics, not only on the number of genres affected but also in the density of influences evidenced in the various genres.

Subdivision III includes the regions of Middle Africa and the Far East where Islam is an important religio-cultural force. In these regions there is still powerful evidence of the core characteristics in certain genres of musical art, though variants from the norm in the genres themselves and their use in the culture are more prominent than in either of the other two areas. Whether in Middle Africa or the Far East, these regions are, first of all, farthest removed from the geographic origins of Islam. Second, they evidence many more factors of disparity between Islam and their pre-Islamic indigenous cultures. Third, the move of Islam into these lands was, in general, much

Figure 23.3

Handasah al Ṣawt: Subdivisions of the Muslim world

Regions where Qur'ānic influence on *handasah al sawt* genres is most pervasive

Regions where Qur'ānic influence is somewhat less pervasive

Regions where Qur'ānic influence is least pervasive

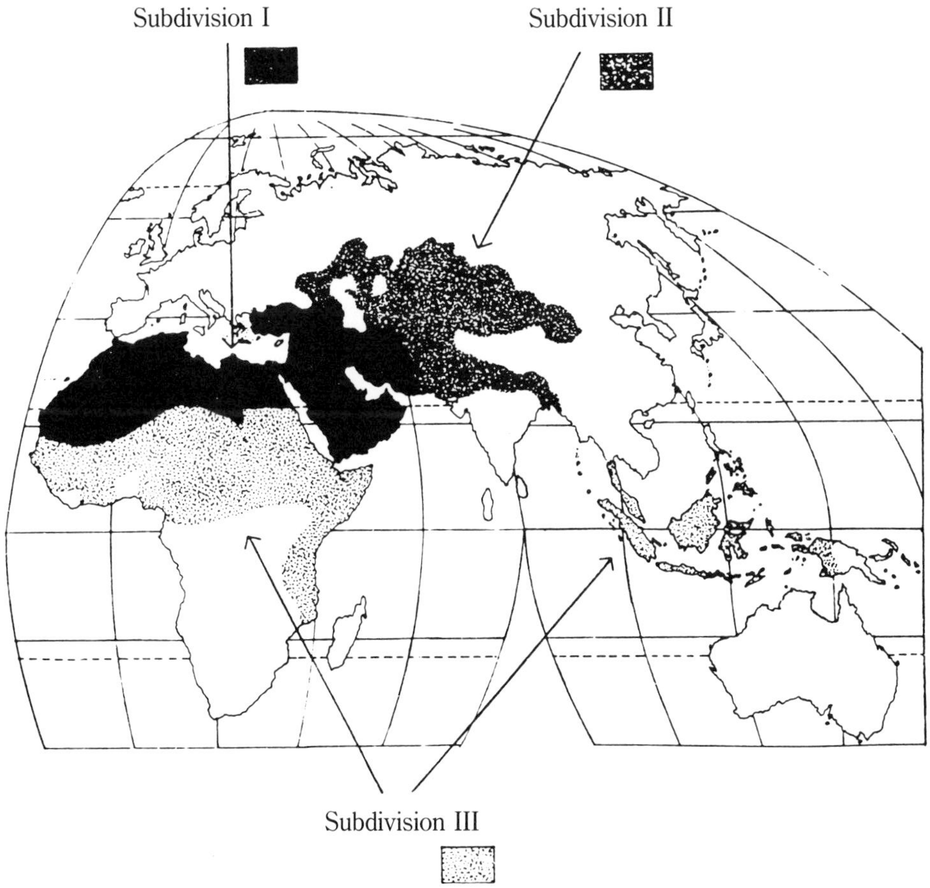

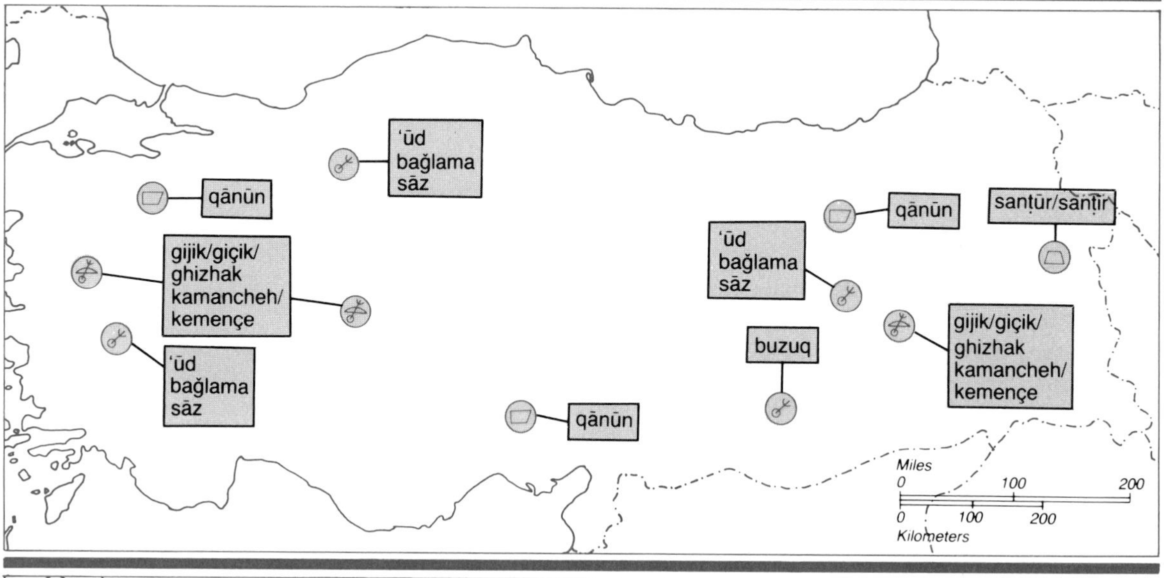
'ūd
bağlama
sāz
qānūn
gijik/giçik/
ghizhak
kamancheh/
kemençe
'ūd
bağlama
sāz
qānūn
qānūn
'ūd
bağlama
sāz
santūr/santīr
buzuq
gijik/giçik/
ghizhak
kamancheh/
kemençe
Miles
0 100 200
0 100 200
Kilometers

A.

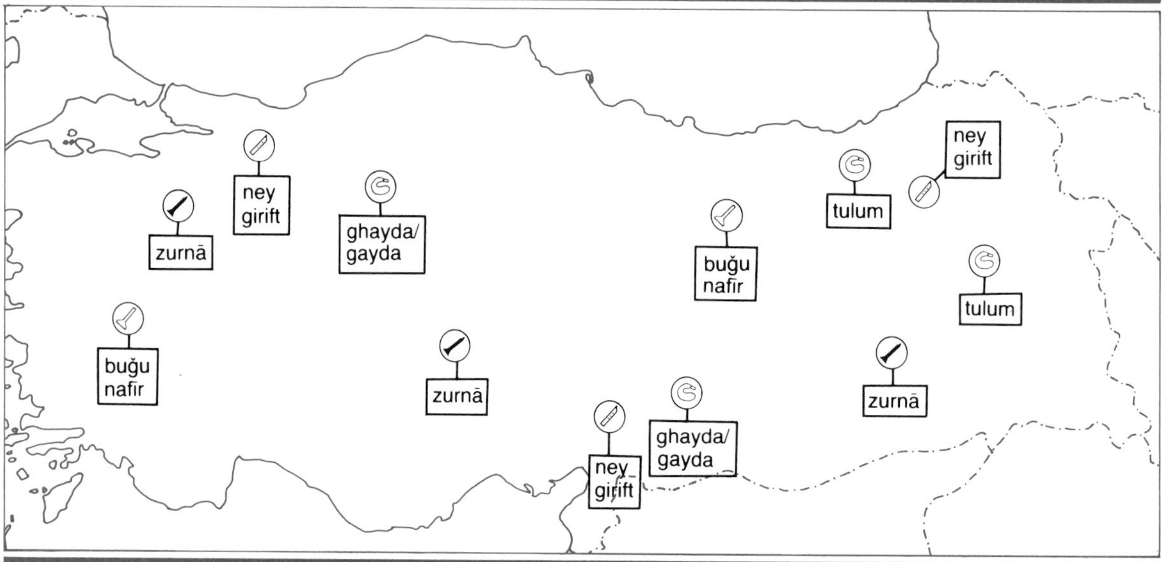
ney
girift
zurnā
ghayda/
gayda
buğu
nafir
zurnā
ney
girift
ghayda/
gayda
buğu
nafir
tulum
ney
girift
tulum
zurnā

B.

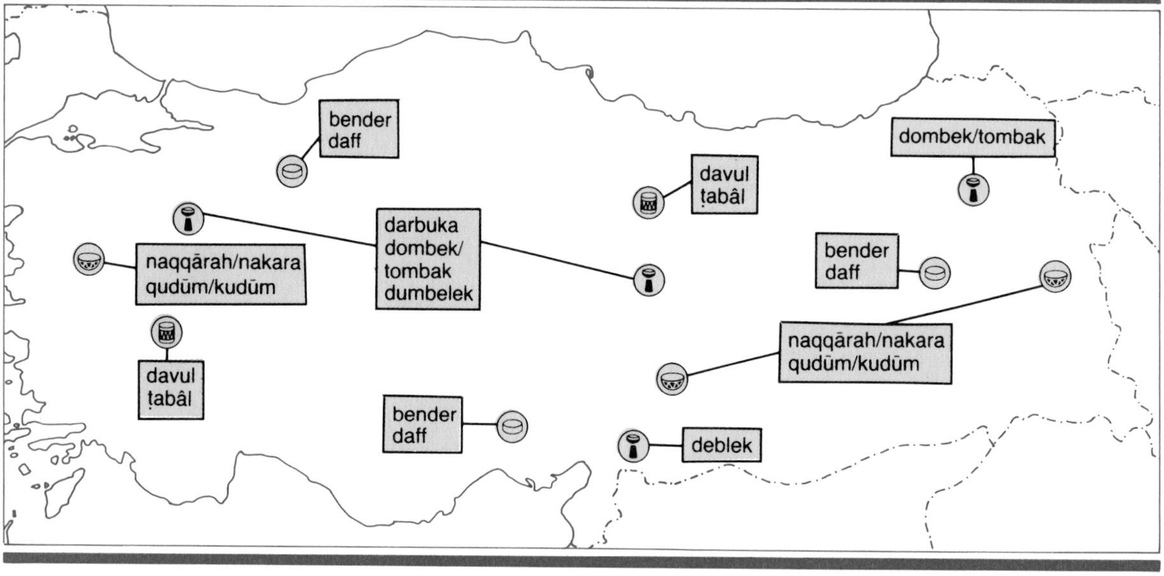
bender
daff
darbuka
dombek/
tombak
dumbelek
naqqārah/nakara
qudūm/kudūm
davul
tabâl
bender
daff
davul
tabâl
dombek/tombak
bender
daff
naqqārah/nakara
qudūm/kudūm
deblek

C.

Map 74. Musical Instruments in Turkey
A. Chordophones
B. Aerophones
C. Membranophones

Chordophones found in Area IV

PL: ʻūd, buzuq, sāz, bağlama
BL: kamancheh/kemence, ghizhak/giçik/gijik
P: qānūn
D: sanṭūr/sanṭīr

Aerophones found in Area IV

E: ney, girift
O: zurnā
B: ghayda/gayda, tulum (East Turkey)
T: nafīr, buğu

Membranophones found in Area IV

F: daff, bender
G: darabukkah, tombak/dombek, dumbelek, deblek (South Turkey)
K: naqqārah/nakara, qudūm/kudūm
DC: dauul/davul, ṭabal

later than in the other two areas. Fourth, although these are lands with a majority Muslim population, the percentages of non-Muslims are considerably greater than in either of the other two areas. Indonesia is an exception in this regard, for its population is 99 percent Muslim. The influence of the other three factors under consideration, however—geographic distance, greater contrast in cultural base, and later conversion—offset the population figures in that case.

Despite the factors militating against continuity of the core characteristics in Subdivision III, genres of the inner levels are closely related to the core characteristics of Subdivision I. Qur'ānic recitation expectations are identical. For example, many a southeast Asian *qāri'* and *qāri'ah* (fem.) figure prominently in competition with Qur'ānic reciters from all regions of the Muslim world (Illus. 23.12, 23.13).[19] Religious chants, solo improvisations on those instruments that are amenable to the core characteristics, songs with

Illustration 23.12

National Women's Champion of Qur'ān Reading Competition, Malaysia, 1981. [Courtesy Federal Department of Information, Government of Malaysia.]

Illustration 23.13

Champion in Children's Section of Qur'ān Reading Competition, Malaysia, 1981. [Courtesy Federal Department of Information, Government of Malaysia.]

serious themes, and even some instances of the purely entertainment repertoire often strongly exemplify the core characteristics. On the other hand, other items from the musical traditions of Subdivision III provide radical departures from the Qur'ānic norms. The music of the ***kulintang*** of the Philippines, of the *gamelan* of Indonesia, or of the polyphonic, polyrhythmic music of Middle Africa represent types of *handasah al ṣawt* that are strongly connected to pre-Islamic traditions. Consequently, the Islamic core characteristics have often been ignored or countered, and numerous alien influences have been retained or added to produce examples of sharply contrasting features. There must be some, perhaps subconscious realization of the lack of cultural rapport with their Muslim identity; for the Indonesians argue over the advisability of fostering the *gamelan* tradition,[20] their nobles make a kind of penance donation to the mosque for using the *gamelan* during the fasting month,[21] and the Muslims of the Philippines refrain from playing the ***kulintang*** during the fasting month, inside the mosque, or in connection with Islamic rites or holidays.[22]

We should also mention cases in which certain individuals, nominally Muslims, participate in rites and activities clearly carried over from pre-Islamic or non-Islamic religious beliefs and practices. Understandably, the music connected with such doctrines and activities often deviates from the core characteristics of Islamic culture. Both such religious practices and their musical accompaniments, therefore, are anachronistic to the Islamic environment and have been omitted from this presentation. If they were to be included, they would occupy still another genre level (a sixth, including genres related to non-Islamic religious rites) at the farthest remove from the Qur'ānic core of Level 1.*

THE CORE CHARACTERISTICS MANIFESTED IN *HANDASAH AL ṢAWT*

In this section, we shall describe the core characteristics of the Islamic arts as represented in ***handasah al ṣawt***. As will soon be evident, the *ṣawtī* elements that embody this correspondence are not necessarily exclusive to the sound art of Islamic culture. Many can be found as elements of other musical traditions. Nor have they necessarily originated in Islamic culture. Much has been borrowed from pre-Islamic or neighboring cultures whenever compatible elements have been encountered. But the particular emphasis and "mix" of characteristics is unique; it features a selective incorporation of old and new elements and an assimilation of the latter into a culturally determined framework. This framework has been stimulated by the doctrine of *tawḥīd* and its first and foremost figurization, the Holy Qur'ān.

Abstraction

One Qur'ānic characteristic that has determined artistic expression in Islamic culture is its abstract or nonprogrammatic quality. Since *tawḥīd* teaches that God cannot be identified with any object or being from nature, He cannot be musically associated with sounds that arouse psychological or kinesthetic correspondences to beings, events, objects, or ideas within nature. We have discussed many aspects of the visual arts that exemplify this characteristic. We shall now explain how abstract quality is achieved in the artful combination of pitches and musical durations.

Melodic and rhythmic elements in the sound arts of Islamic culture are not used or altered in order to match a dramatic unfolding of events and ideas. The genres of *handasah al ṣawt* make little or no attempt to be musically imitative of the creatures of nature. Neither are these elements manipulated to create specific and changing moods. Tempo, volume, style, pitch level, register, soloist, or performance group—all may change; but such changes result from the demands of aesthetic structure rather than in accordance with extramusical ideas of either implicit or explicit nature. A precise content or subject matter for a *handasah al ṣawt* performance is rare. Vocal as well as instrumental performances are named and identified by their melodic mode or by the opening line of the lyrics. Descriptive titles are rare even in those genre levels far removed from the central core. Vocables with little or no meaning, as well as stockwords and phrases that do not belong to the text, abound as external and even internal additions to the vocal line (see Figure 23.5, lines 4, 5 & 6). Since a tonal setting is not irrevocably bound to a single set of words, different melodies have often been conjoined with a single poem; and different poems, with a single tune.

Abstraction is particularly apparent in Qur'ānic chant, where no changes in mood are apparent from beginning to end of a single recitation, nor from one recitation to another. The other religious chants, the vocal and instrumental improvisations, and even

* The foregoing section on the varying applicability of genres in the three *handasah al ṣawt* subdivisions is a revision of an earlier publication by Lois L. al Fārūqī, entitled "Factors of Continuity in the Musical Cultures of the Muslim World," *Progress Reports in Ethnomusicology,* Vol. 1, No. 2 (1983–1984), pp. 1–18.

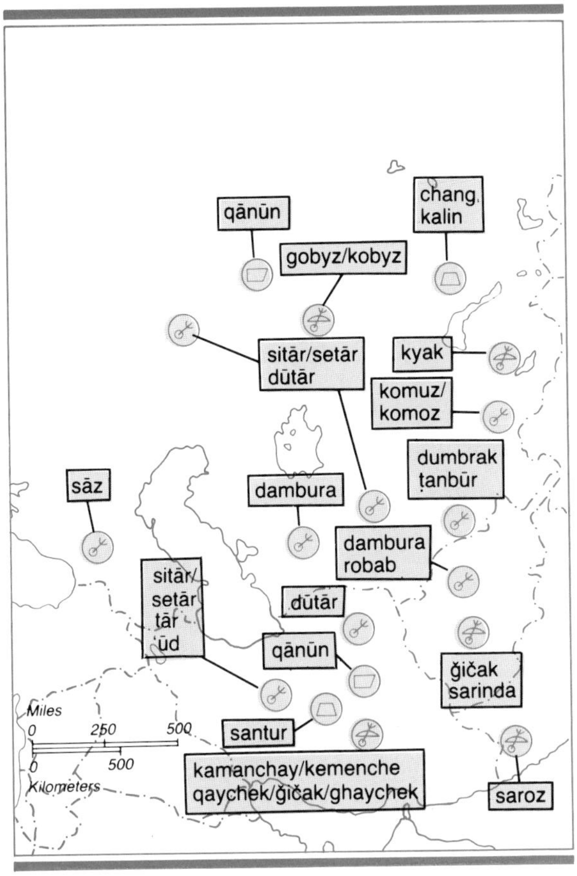

A.

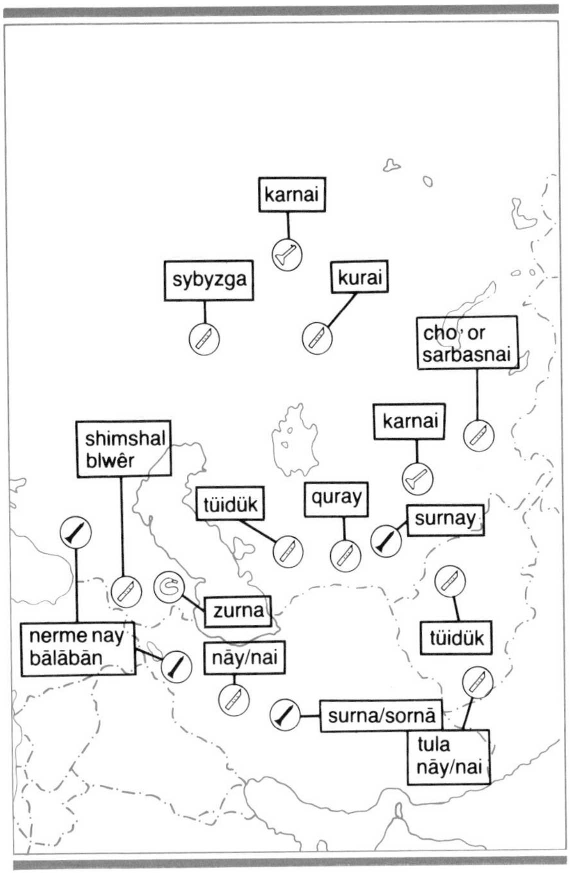

B.

Map 75. Musical Instruments in Iran and Central Asia

A. Chordophones
B. Aerophones
C. Membranophones

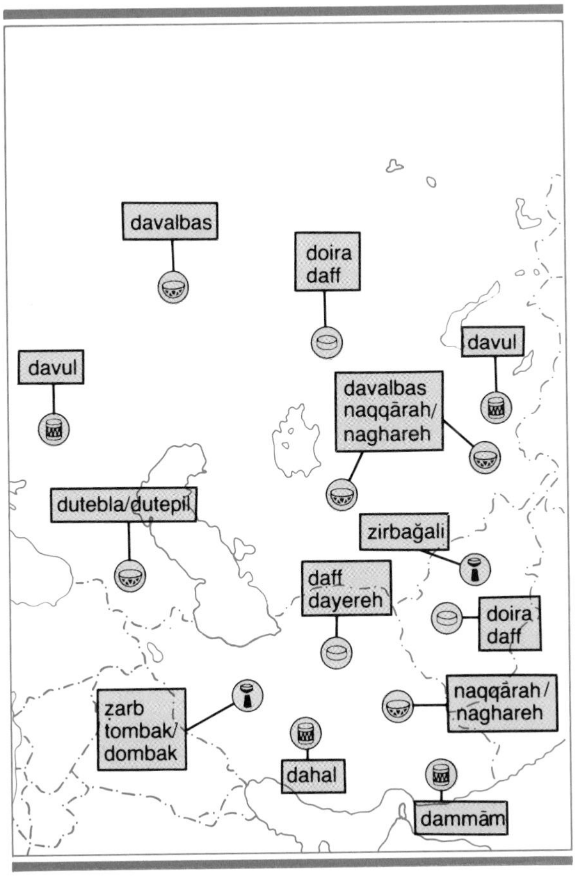

C.

Chordophones found in Area V

PL: sitār/setār, tār, dambura, dumbrak, dūtār, ṭanbūr, 'ūd, komuz/komoz, sāz, chogār, robab (Afghanistan)
BL: kamanchay, ğičak/ghaychek, saroz, sarinda (Afghanistan), kyak (Kirghiz), gobyz/kobyz
P: qānūn
D: sanṭūr, chang, kalin

Aerophones found in Area V

E: nāy/nai, tüidük, cho'or and sarbasnai (Kirghiz), sybyzga (Kazakh), tula (Pashtun and Baluch), shimshāl or blwêr (Kurdish), quray (Uzbek)
O: surnay, surna/sornā, nerme nay or balabān (Azerbaijan and Kurdistan)
B: zurna
T: karnai

Membranophones found in Area V

F: daff, doira, dayereh
G: tombak/dombak, ẓarb, zirbağali
K: naqqārah/naghareh, dutebla/dutepil (Kurdistan), davalbas
DC: dahal, dammam (South Persia), davul (Central Asia)

Important Ajnās of the Arabian Musical System

Ajnās with half (½) and whole (1) tone intervals:

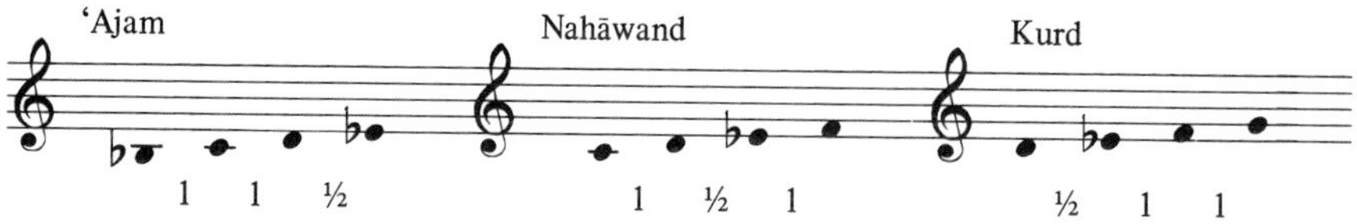

Ajnās with step-and-a-half (1½) interval:

Ajnās with three-quarter (¾) tone interval (𝄳 indicates a tone lowered by approximately ¼ tone):

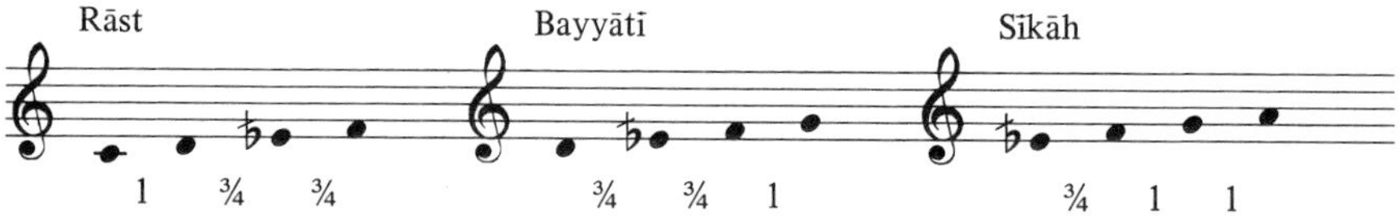

Such *ajnās* have a wide significance in the Muslim world, although their combination to form one- and two-octave scales and their names may vary from country to country and from region to region.

International Relevance

In Turkey we find such changes of name and pitch level as the following:

Turkish Kürdī (similar to Arab Kurd transposed)

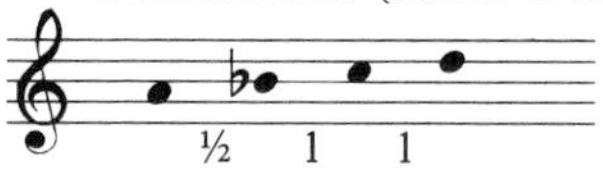

Turkish Çargâh (similar to Arab 'Ajam transposed)

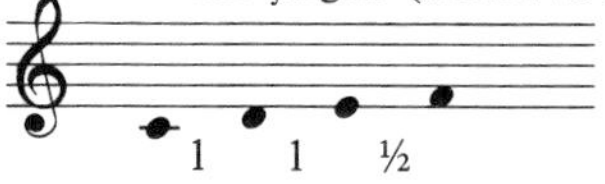

Turkish Puselik (similar to Arab Nahāwand transposed)

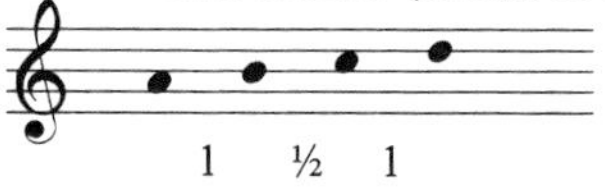

Turkish Rast (similar to Arab Rāst transposed)

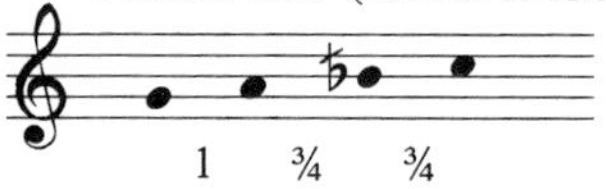

Many other examples from Turkey and other parts of the Muslim world could be cited.

Figure 23.4

The *Ajnās* (modes) of *Handasah al Ṣawt*

Combination of Ajnās

Ajnās are combined to achieve a modal scale as in the following *maqāmāt* scales of Arabian music of the Mashriq.

Maqām Rāst

Maqām Ṣabā

Maqām Ḥijāz

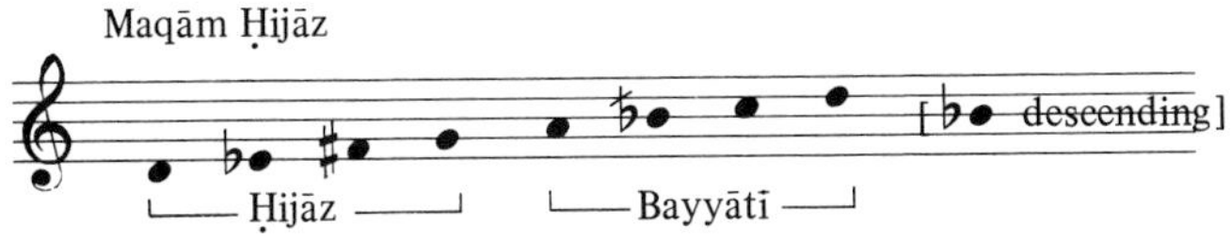

In addition to intervals and their manner of combination, many other features define Arabian music. These include starting tone, prescribed tonic or final resting tone, other important tones of stability, pitch and range, typical motifs, as well as prescribed succession and use of the tonal material.

music for light entertainment are generally free of the obvious musical "depiction" or symbolization of non-musical aspects. If any does occur, it is to be found only in the outermost level of genres, at the farthest remove from the Qur'ānic prototype and from cultural acceptability.

Regardless of the medium (vocal or instrumental) or the context (for religious or secular occasions, for artistically sophisticated or simple social events), *handasah al ṣawt* is always a composed or improvised creation of infinite patterning. Through manipulation of pitches and durations, the musical progression seeks to convey to the listener an impression of an unfolding pattern that never ends. This creation in tones and durations can also be designated as an arabesque. It is analogous to the similarly named creations in lines, colors, and forms of the visual arts of Islamic culture.

Modular Structure

The second of the aesthetic core characteristics, modular structure, casts further light on the nature of a *handasah al ṣawt* performance. The division into internal units, one of the most important structural features of the visual arabesque, is achieved in the art of sound in a great variety of ways. In Qur'ānic chant, for example, the phrases corresponding to a literary *āyah* (verse) or part thereof are clearly separated from each other by periods of silence. This aesthetically important separation is called a *waqfah* ("stop"). It can occur wherever the *qāri'* ("reader") wishes, so long as it does not interfere with logical comprehension of the chanted text. As each sound module nears completion, its closure is marked by a descent in pitch and a cadencing on an important tone of the scalar materials being used. As has been shown elsewhere,[23] these module endings are often accented by repetitive tonal and durational motifs which coincide with and reinforce the poetic rhyme and assonance. It is at the endings of particularly satisfying modules that the listeners respond with such exclamations of appreciation as *Allah* and *Allahu Akbar* ("God is the Greatest").

The religious chants of the second level as well as the vocal and intrumental improvisations of Level 3 are segmented in similar manner. Silences of varying lengths clearly separate one phrase from another, and complications of ornamentation and musical motifs proliferate near the closure to provide emphasis. The overall descending contour of the phrases and the closure on a tone of stability are similar to that of Qur'ānic chant despite possible differences in performance medium and function for these genres. Repeated closing phrases known as *qaflah, taslīm,*

Yā Man La'abat bihi Shumūl

Each melodic line corresponds to a nine-beat rhythmic cycle of three internal parts, each containing three beats.

Figure 23.5

Example of a *Muwashshaḥ*

forud, and so forth, emphasize the modular structure of these unmetered improvisations.

Another much-used device for accentuating the separation between phrases of vocal and instrumental improvisatory genres is the instrumental interjection known as a *lāzimah.*[24] This interlude or separating passage comprises a tonal motif or phrase, or may be a repetitive rhythmic figure performed on a percussion instrument at the end of each sound art module. The *lāzimah* varies in length from a few tones to a full refrain. In all cases, it emphasizes the closure of the musical module and readies performer as well as lis-

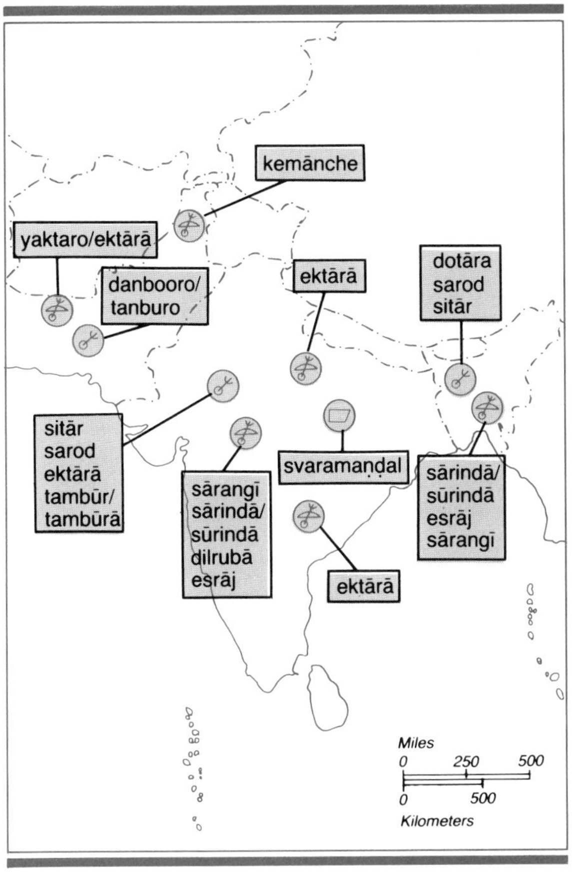

A.

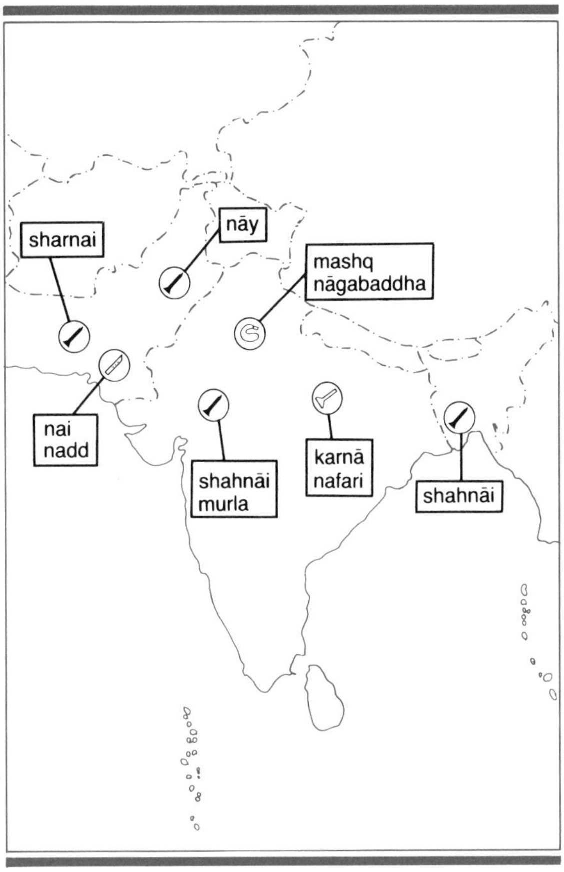

B.

Map 76. Musical Instruments in the Indian Subcontinent

A. Chordophones
B. Aerophones
C. Membranophones

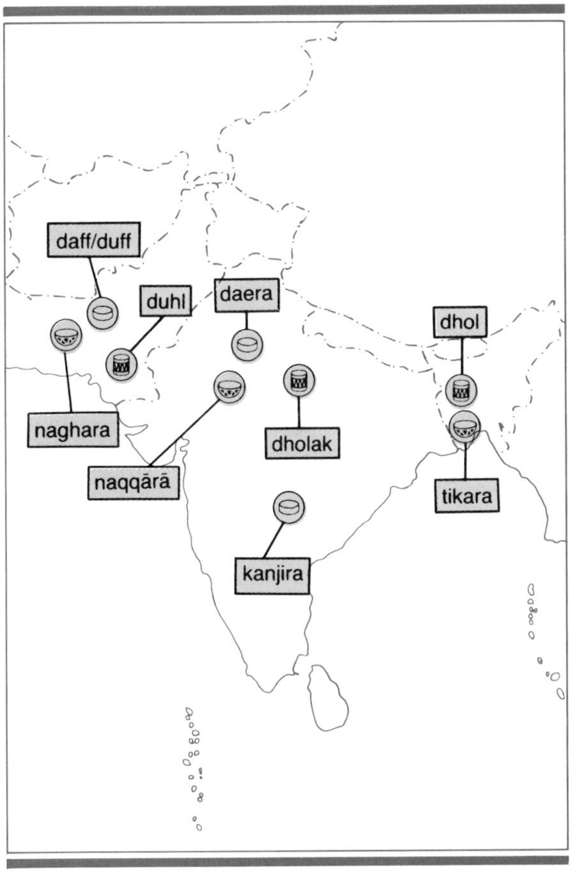

C.

Chordophones found in Area VI

PL: sitār, sarod, tambūr, bīn, nadd, danbooro/tanburo (Sind), rabāb, ektārā, dotārā (Bangladesh)

BL: Sāraṅgī, yaktaro (Sind), dilruba, sārindā/sūrindā, esrāj, kemānche

P: svaramaṇḍal

Aerophones found in Area VI

E: nai, nadd (Sind)

O: shahnai, sharnai (Sind), surnai, nāy (Punjab), murla

B: mashq, nāgabaddha (North India)

T: karnā, nafari

Membranophones found in Area VI

F: daff/duff, daera, kanjira (South India)

K: nāgārā/naqqārā/naghara, nahabat, mahānāgārā, tikara (Bengal)

DC: duhl (Sind), ḍholak (North India), dhol (Bangladesh)

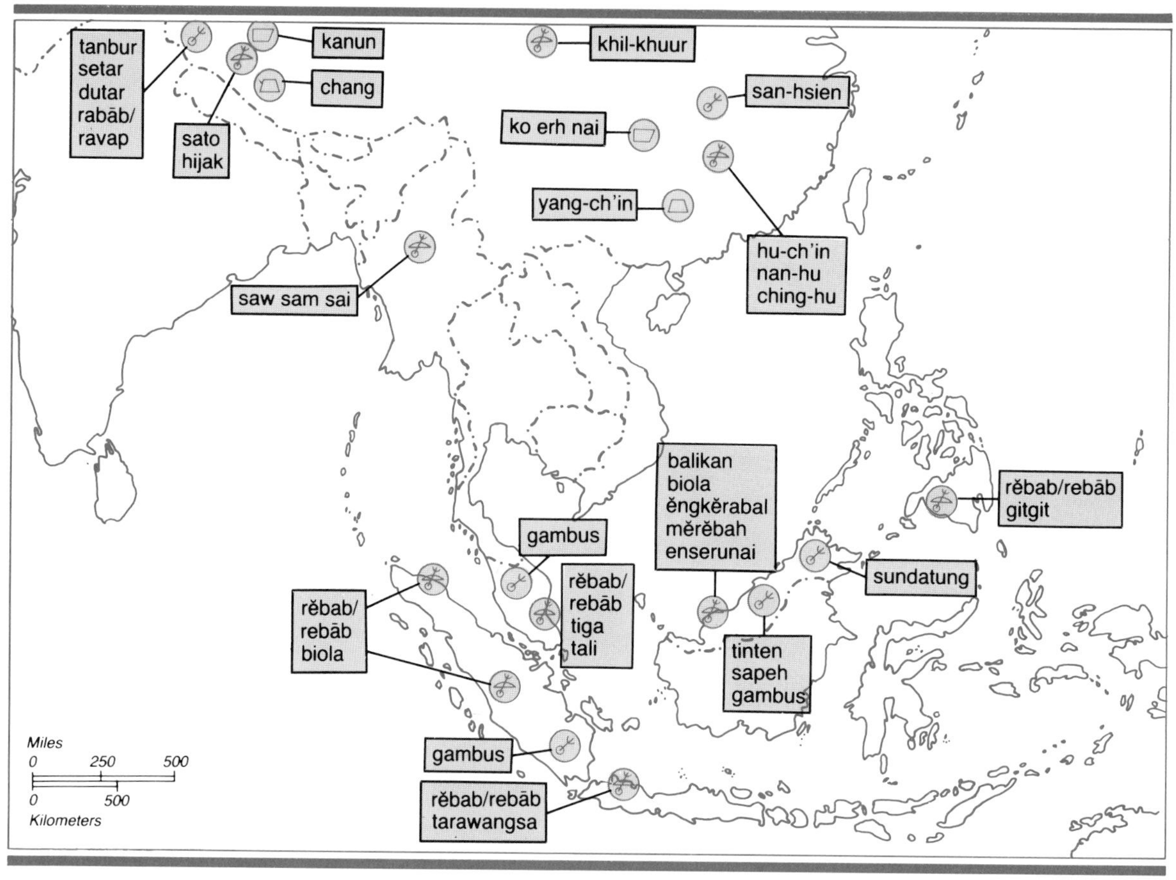
tanbur
setar
dutar
rabāb/
ravap
sato
hijak
kanun
chang
khil-khuur
san-hsien
ko erh nai
yang-ch'in
hu-ch'in
nan-hu
ching-hu
saw sam sai
balikan
biola
ĕngkĕrabal
mĕrĕbah
enserunai
rĕbab/rebāb
gitgit
gambus
rĕbab/
rebāb
tiga
tali
sundatung
rĕbab/
rebāb
biola
tinten
sapeh
gambus
gambus
rĕbab/rebāb
tarawangsa
Miles
0 250 500
0 500
Kilometers

A.

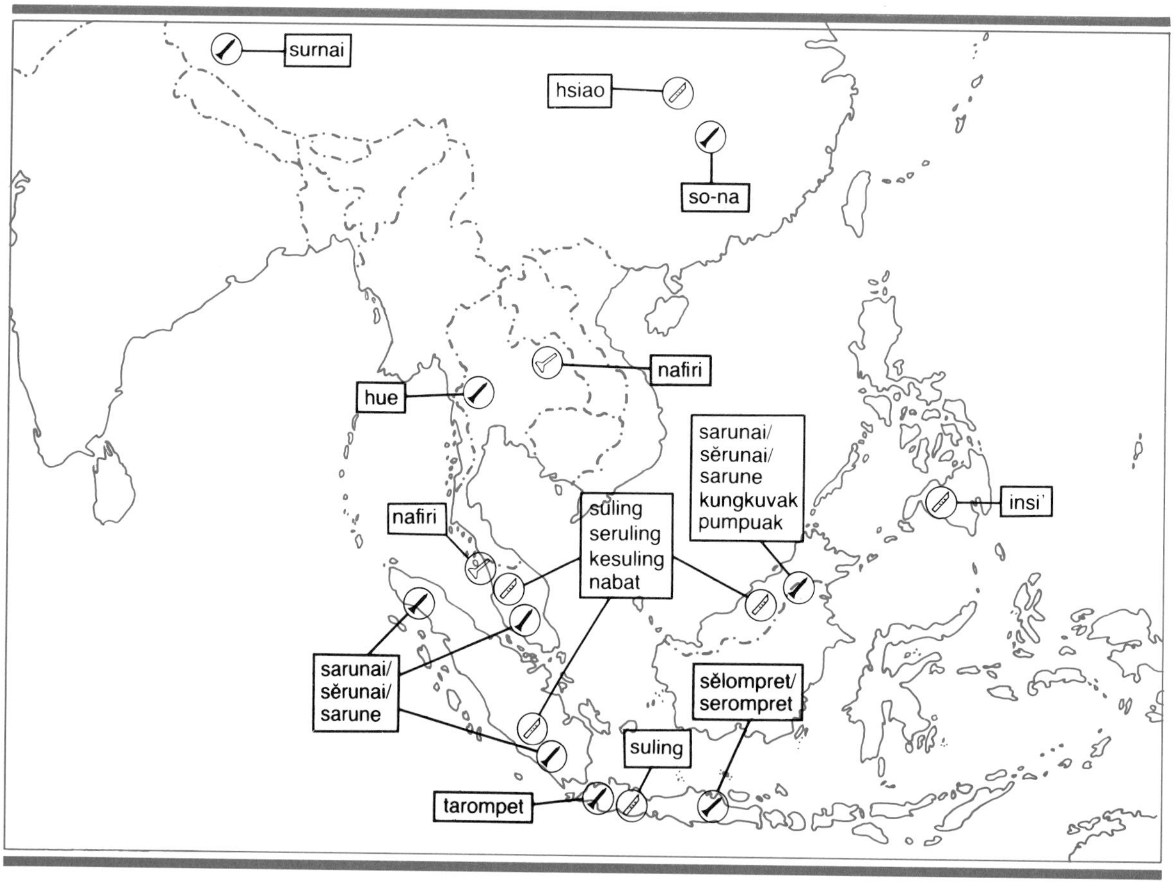
surnai
hsiao
so-na
nafiri
hue
sarunai/
sĕrunai/
sarune
kungkuvak
pumpuak
insi'
nafiri
suling
seruling
kesuling
nabat
sarunai/
sĕrunai/
sarune
sĕlompret/
serompret
suling
tarompet

B.

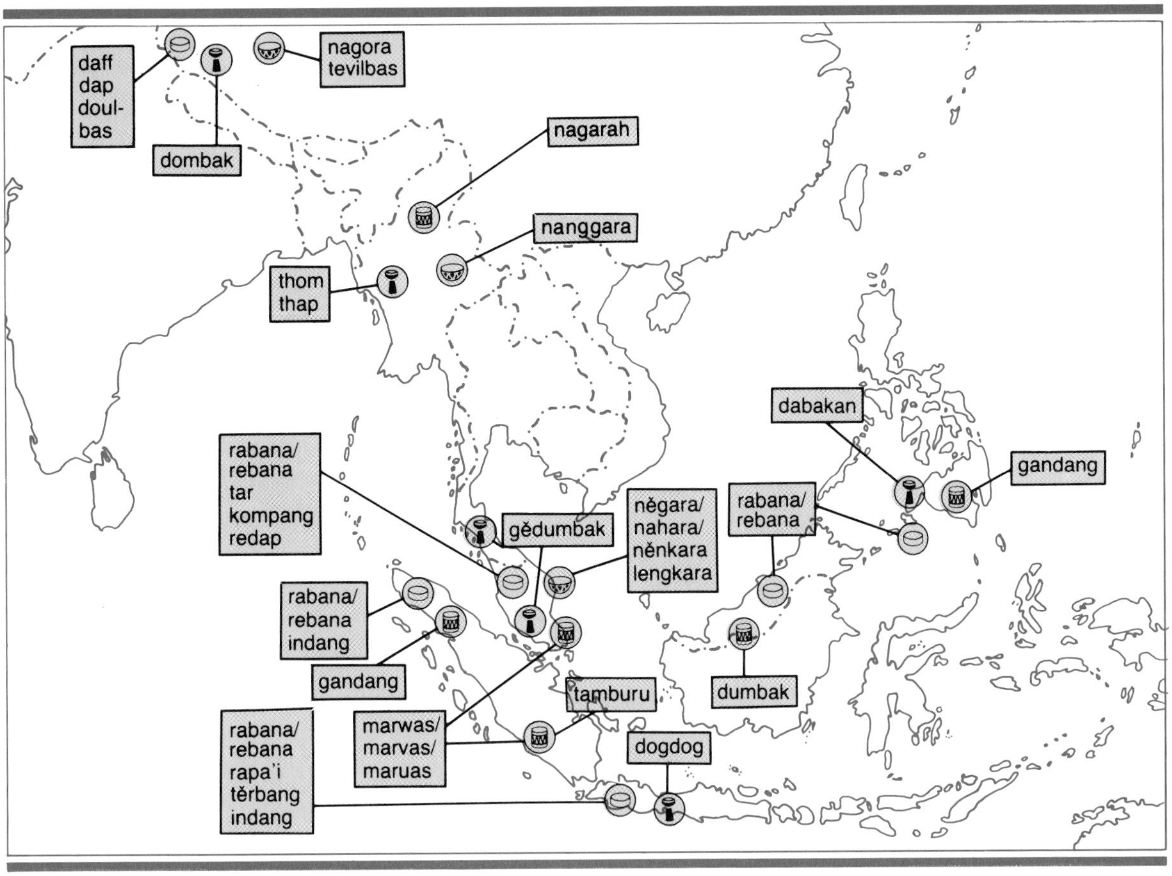

C.

Map 77. Musical Instruments in East Asia
A. Chordophones
B. Aerophones
C. Membranophones

tener for the next module. Though the name changes, this *ṣawtī* element can be heard in sound art performances in all parts of the Muslim world.

In genres dominated by a musical meter, that is, those of Levels 4 and 5 (Figure 23.1), rather than the free-rhythmed quality of the improvised forms, modular structure is no less a standard element, though it is evidenced by somewhat different means. Here the *waqfah* silence is not typical, but the descent to a tone of stability and the repetitive cadential motifs coincide with the closure of the metered segment just as in the free-rhythmed forms. If the piece is based on a rhythmic cycle of some length (ten beats or more), the musical segment will often coincide with one repetition of the rhythmic pattern, thus further reinforcing the melodic segmentation. A repetitive closing passage, either internal to the module or filling the break between modules, is a common feature of this music

Chordophones found in Area VII

PL: gambus, sundatung (Sabah), bĕlikan (Iban, Malaysia), tinten (Sarawak), san-hsien (China), setar, rabāb, dutār, tanbur (Uighur)

BL: biola, rebāb, gitgit (Southern Philippines), saw sam sai (Burma), balikan, enserunai, ĕngkĕrabal and mĕrĕbah (Iban, Malaysia), rebāb and tiga tali (Malaysia), hu-ch'in, nan-hu, ching-hu, and many other varieties (China), tarawangsa (West Java), sato, hijak (Uighur), khilkhuur (Mongolia)

P: ko erh nai (China), kanun (Uighur)

D: yang-ch'in (China), chang (Uighur)

Aerophones found in Area VII

E: suling (Malay Basin), insi' (Philippines), hsiao (China), seruling, kesuling, and nabat (Malaysia)

O: sarunai/sĕruna/sarune (Malay Basin), tarompet (West Java), sĕlompret/serompret (East Java), so-na (China), surnai (Uighur), kungkuvak and pumpuak (Sabah, Malaysia)

T: nafiri (Malaysia, Burma)

Membranophones found in Area VII

F: rabana/rebana (Malay Basin), rapa'i and tĕrbang (Indonesia), tar, redap, and kompang (Malaysia), indang (Indonesia), daff, dap, doul-bas (Uighur)

(Continued)

G: dabakan (Phillippines), thom or thap (Burma), gĕdumbak (Malaysia, South Thailand), dombak (Uighur), dogdog (West Java)
K: neğara/nahara/nĕnkara and lengkara (Malaysia), nanggara (Burma), nagora, tevilbas (Uighur)
DC: marwas/marvas/maruas (Malay Basin), tamburu (Indonesia), nagarah (Burma), dumbak (Sarawak, Malaysia)

(Figure 23.6; see *lāzimah* repetitions).[25] It may be performed by one or more instruments or by a chorus. It may comprise a single phrase repeated after each *ṣawtī* segment or a cadential formula within the module. It may also be extended into a contrasting refrain that separates one module from another (Figure 23.6).[26]

Contrasts of musical texture and style are other important means for setting one section off from another in *handasah al ṣawt* examples. Successive segments may alternate between vocal and instrumental performance, between a soloist and the accompanying ensemble or chorus, between male and female voices, between different soloists or ensembles of instruments, between contrasting melodic and rhythmic modes, between improvised and composed performance, between free-rhythmed and metered textures, between low tessitura and higher pitch levels.

Successive Combinations

The third aesthetic characteristic of the Islamic arts is the successive combination of its constituent modules. Performances of *handasah al ṣawt* com-

Yâ Hilālan, Ghāba 'Annī

The seven-beat rhythmic cycle is subdivided into two parts, one of three and one of four beats.

Figure 23.6

Example of a *Muwashshaḥ*

prise various kinds of additive combinations—of motifs to form phrases; of phrases to form periods of refrain or new materials; of periods or sections to form an improvisation or composition; of improvisations and compositions to form suitelike entities in a chosen melodic mode (the *faṣl, waṣlah, nawbah, ṣan'ah, shashmaqam,* and *chashni* of various parts of the Muslim world). This repetitive combination of parts on every level of performance is an important structural device for enhancing the impression of infinite pattern. Muslim musicians, as well as non-Muslims influenced by the same cultural environment, find their creativity to be fulfilled more in the artful combination and repetition of these internal modules than in the creation of totally new entities.

Repetition

Repetition is a fourth characteristic of the Islamic arts in general, and *handasah al ṣawt* in particular. Repetition is of course a feature of any musical tradition, but the frequency of its use in *handasah al ṣawt* examples is outstanding. Notes are successively repeated rather than sustained. Important tones of the modal scale are made prominent by repeated returns. Motifs, whether used as integral elements in the improvised or composed line or as vocal or instrumental interjections marking the completion of a musical unit, are another repetitive item. Refrain phrases are common within both composed and improvised *ṣawtī* modules, and refrain segments provide more extended material for repetition in many contexts and styles.

The extensive use of repetitions is not the result of a poverty of musical ideas among the adherents to Islam. Instead, it is one of the structural features which the Muslim peoples find necessary for the creation of infinite patterns. Repetition not only denies individualization of musical entities but also contributes to the never-ending quality that the aesthetic expression of *tawḥīd* should manifest. In addition, it emphasizes the successive combinations of musical modules on all levels of the improvised and composed performance.

Dynamism

Since all forms of *ṣawtī* art must be experienced through time, the element of dynamic character is built into every example of *handasah al ṣawt.* No specimen of musical art can fail to exemplify this element of dynamism. The dynamic quality specific to *handasah al ṣawt,* therefore, must be the result of additional causes. However, many of the causes that might be supposed to contribute to this quality actually have little influence in this direction.

For example, it is not a wide overall range or melodic extension that suggests dynamism in *handasah al ṣawt.* The genres generally confine melodic and rhythmic elaboration to a small scalar segment, often encompassing no more than four or five tones (Figure 23.4). Even when the range is extended to an octave or more, the improvisation or composition treats segments of that range successively in different modular segments, rather than in its entirety. The *qāri'* improvises on one *jins,* the Arabic term for a tetrachordal or pentachordal scalar segment, for an unspecified time, then moves to another *jins* or group of contiguous tones. Other religious chants and vocal/instrumental improvisations are equally representative of this feature. Even songs and instrumental compositions often use one *jins* of the melodic scale in one segment and move to a higher or lower one only as an element of contrast in a subsequent segment. Overall range cannot, therefore, be seen as a determinant of dynamism in this sound art.

Neither can wide leaps within the melodic line be regarded as factors for dynamism in *handasah al ṣawt.* Chordal melodies are almost nonexistent in the genres representative of the Islamic core characteristics, and intervals of more than a third rarely occur except at the opening of a phrase.

Multiplication of melodic lines is a third musical element that might be suggested as conducive to the impression of musical dynamism. This element is equally unrepresentative of *handasah al ṣawt,* for this sound art is predominantly monophonic. That is, it consists of a single melodic line without polyphony or harmonic accompaniment. Qur'ānic chant is always a solo vocalization, and many of the other religious poetic genres and vocal/instrumental improvisations are similarly executed by a single performer. Even when two or more people play or sing together, they generally follow a single melodic line, with only the slight departures from the unison performance which the improvisatory quality of their performance allows. When an instrument with melodic capacity accompanies a solo line, it performs in unison with the soloist or "shadows" that line with reduced or ornamented versions of the main melodic content. Such approximated, rather than precisely single-line performances, are known as heterophony. They can be heard in many performances by two or more vocalists or instrumentalists. The only other musical elements that provide a divergence from the generally monophonic texture of *handasah al ṣawt* are drones, ostinato figures, and certain types of ornamentation.[27]

Since all these suggested elements of dynamic

quality do not pertain, what are the features of this art that exemplify this fifth core characteristic of the Islamic arts? Three features, in addition to the inherent time-based quality of all musical expression, reinforce this characteristic: (1) density of activity; (2) emphasis on manipulation of motivic materials rather than presentation of themes; and (3) nondevelopmental form.

Density of activity. The infinite patterning which is the hallmark of all the Islamic arts focuses the listener's concentration on a single-line melody whether executed by vocalist, instrumentalist, chorus, or instrumental ensemble. But this melody, while eschewing the complications of an extended range, wide intervals, and multipart counterpoint or harmony, puts emphasis instead on the density of activity in that single line. The knowledgeable listener is attracted, at the opening of a sound art module, to "mount" the melodic line of the performer and follow it through a dense labyrinth of tonal and durational progressions. With few if any long notes or rests, the melody moves continuously until the conclusion of a phrase or segment is realized with a return to a tone of stability, a repetitive cadential motif, and/or some other indication of modular disjunction. Here both performer and listener "catch their breath" in preparation for a subsequent excursion of equally dense activity. The modular segments, as well as the improvisation or composition as a whole, reveal a progressive increase in density as the performance progresses.

Manipulation of short motifs, not extended themes. A second common attribute of *handasah al ṣawt* performances that reinforces dynamic quality is its emphasis on manipulation of short but melodically or rhythmically distinctive motifs, rather than the presentation of extended melodic themes.[28] This sound art allows for greater performer creativity in the "working out" of the melodic materials than in the presentation of the extended theme. The proliferation of small segments creates an impression of increasing activity and dynamism.

Nondevelopmental form. Dynamism is also enhanced by the manner of aesthetic experiencing which it stimulates. Instead of exhibiting a developmental form with steady evolution toward one overall climax and a conclusive ending, the sound art performance of Islamic culture defies its experience as a single unity. Since its parts are not inextricably joined, but succeed each other as autonomous entities, the aesthetic impression is one of the suppression of the impact of the overall *Gestalt* in order to emphasize the separate modules that make up the whole. Each self-sufficient part is experienced and considered on its own; each imparts some aspect of the whole while being structurally separable from it. This additive combination of entities generates an impression of activity and fluidity which is denied the developmental structure with its unified closed structure.

The unity of Islamic art in general, and of *handasah al ṣawt* genres in particular, is of a different kind. One cannot describe it by citing a single theme; by detailing the features of a single person, object, or scene; or by singing one well-remembered theme. Instead, the percipient must experience the art work as an open-ended and indefinitely expandable structure. The listener must move with it through some of its constituent segments, savoring each one is succession, thrilling at the release of gradually mounting tension near the end of each module, marveling at the ingeniousness and creativity of the organization of visual or aural motifs. Such a structure contributes significantly to the dynamic quality of *handasah al ṣawt* genres. This is not, however, a dynamism of excessive tension, of emotional anxiety or frustration. It is instead a dynamism that activates the human mind with the discovery of beautiful patterns, that stimulates the contemplation of a greater cause, that leads it from concern for mundane matters and personal problems to a higher reality.

Intricacy

Since the goal of the Muslim vocal or instrumental performance is to lead the listener to an intuition of the other-than-nature Ultimate Reality, since the best aesthetic means to achieve such an intuition is the creation of abstract patterns implying never-ending continuity, and since such patterns can more effectively attract the attention and concentration of the listener if they are sufficient involved and complex, the Muslim peoples have found tonal and durational intricacy preeminently suited to their needs. This intricacy, which parallels so closely the elaborate detail of Islamic creations in the visual arts, is musically embodied in ornamentation practices as well as in a number of theoretical elements.

Handasah al ṣawt performances abound with ornamental melodic and rhythmic figures. This applies to all forms of religious chant, to serious vocal or instrumental performance, as well as to the entertainment or social music of home or coffeehouse environment. The melismatic (highly decorative) quality of the melodic line has been so characteristic of the sound arts in Islamic culture that its presence has been judged to be an indication of Islamic influence.[29] It is incorrect, however, to treat the repetitive and motivic figures of the many free-rhythmed and improvisatory genres as optional or expendable decorations of a more basic melody. These figures, which anticipate, delay, and emphasize the arrival at a particular pitch position within the modal scale, comprise instead the actual substance of their melodic lines.

In the other type of performances—the metered compositions and traditional tunes—ornamentation is no less prominent, though basic tunes, with their ordered succession of pitches and durations, exist to be embellished. Trills, slides from one pitch to another, repetition of single tones to retain activity in a sustained pitch, short grace notes, either as a neighbor tone or those at a great distance—these are a few of the many tonal devices that provide embellishment and intricacy in *handasah al ṣawt* melodies. Durational ornaments have also been numerous and varied. They include shifts of accent, supplementary percussions added between the beats of the metric cycle, alteration of the note values while pitches are maintained, acceleration or slowing down, and so on.[30]

Another rich source of intricate detail results from the wide choice of different-sized intervals from which to draw in creating the melodic lines. Instead of using the European or Western theoretical scale composed of twelve tempered (that is, equalized) half-steps per octave from which certain tones are chosen to create a scale, the Muslims divide the octave into microtones from which they achieve many different sizes of intervals. Over the centuries, and in different parts of the Muslim world, these divisions and the choices of intervals favored to form scales and modes have varied. This principle has contributed to the characteristic of intricacy, while its varied realization has provided historical and regional diversity.

Added to the intricacy of the octave division and interval vocabulary, a proliferation of stepwise melodic progressions provides another element of intricate melodic movement in *hadasah al ṣawt* performance. The melodic progression is sinuous in its movement from one note to its upper or lower neighbor. Occasional intervals of a third seem only to serve as counters for the predominantly stepwise and chromatic progression (see Figures 23.5, 23.6). Instead of concentrating on melodic themes of extensive range, this music consists of numerous repetitions and variations of short motifs. Its conjunct, intricate patterning takes place within the boundaries of a scalar segment of only four or five tones. The profuse ornamentation which increases density also contributes to the intricacy of this sound art.

The rhythmic elements of *handasah al ṣawt* genres can also be characterized as detailed and intricate. In regularly rhythmed compositions complicated meters comprising not only cycles of 2, 3, and 4 beats but of 5, 7, 10, 12, 24, 32, and even more beats can be found. Cycles are divided internally into feet of varying length. The cycle also specifies the positioning of rests and the stronger and weaker beats (Figures 23.5, 23.6). The internal divisions of the rhythmic cycle may be binary or ternary, or may include both binary and ternary groupings within a single cycle. Performers, whether vocalists or instrumentalists, do not merely reproduce the rhythmic pattern. They fill in the pulses of the meter with such extra percussions or ornaments of which their improvisatory skills are capable.

Unmetered improvised performances convey an equal impression of rhythmic intricacy and detail. Because there is no prescribed pattern for rhythmic accentuation and duration, the performer is free to use any succession of beats and rests he or she chooses. The genres of this style consist of numerous short durations that match the equally intricate tonal possibilities from which the melodic line is made. Long notes are rare if not nonexistent in *handasah al ṣawt* genres.

The above description of the manifestation in *handasah al ṣawt* of the core characteristics of the Islamic arts confirms that the sound arts of Islamic culture have not been a mere collection of regional styles borrowed from various peoples and juxtaposed to constitute a "music of the Muslim peoples." It is, instead, a manifestation of an integral relation to the religion of Islam, to *tawḥīd,* to the Qur'ān, and to its chanted recitation.

Just as there was a religio-cultural "crucible" from which Islam burst forth in the seventh century, there was a musical crucible from which the genres of *handasah al ṣawt* evolved in the early centuries of the Islamic period. This crucible, when combined with the stimulus of the new ideology and the fervor of the commitment it engendered, produced a flowering of the sound arts, the effects of which are still evident in every part of the Muslim world today. This flowering was strongly determined by the religion of Islam. *Tawḥīd* and its figurization in the Qur'ān have not only affected many sociological aspects of attitude and usage pertaining to the *ṣawtī* arts but they have molded the very pitches, the durations, and their combinations in order to embody the six core characteristics of the Islamic arts.

NOTES

1. See entry "MŪSĪQĀ or MŪSĪQĪ" in Lois Ibsen al Fārūqī, *An Annotated Glossary of Arabic Musical Terms* (Westport, Conn.: Greenwood Press, 1981), p. 209; also section on "Terminology" in L. al Fārūqī, "The Sharī'ah on Music and Musicians," *Islāmic Thought and Culture,* ed. I. R. al Fārūqī (Washington, D.C.: International Institute of Islamic Thought, 1982), pp. 29ff. Mark Slobin finds a different term *(sāz)* used for "music" in another part of the Muslim world (northern Afghanistan), but it equally "excludes most of the 'innocent' manifestations . . . and tends to focus on the sphere in which music plays a potentially dangerous role . . ." (*Music in the Culture of Northern Afghanistan,* Viking Fund Publications in Anthropology, No. 54 [Tucson: University of Arizona Press, 1976], p. 26). Similar situations have been documented in studies of Muslims living in sub-Saharan Africa (David W. Ames and Anthony V. King, *Glossary of Hausa Music and Its Social Contexts* [Evanston, Ill.: Northwestern University Press, 1971], pp. ix–x); and the southern Philippines (Ricardo Diosdada Trimillos, "Some Social and Musical Aspects of the Music of the Taosug in Sulu, Philippines," University of Hawaii, unpublished master's thesis, 1965, p. 16; Thomas M. Kiefer, *Music from the Tausug of Sulu, Moslems of the Southern Philippines,* Introduction to a two-disc set of records [Ethnosound, Anthology EST 8000/1, 1970], p. 1).

2. First used in "Music, Musicians and Muslim Law," a paper prepared by this author for the conference on "The Musician in Muslim Society," Columbia University, spring semester, 1982.

3. See Lois Ibsen al Fārūqī, "The Status of Music in Muslim Nations: Evidence from the Arab World," *Asian Music,* 12 (1981), pp. 56–84, for a discussion of the inappropriateness of applying the usual categories of religious, art, folk, and popular music to the sound arts of the Arab peoples, as one ethnic-regional group within Islamic culture. For a similar view, based on research among Muslim peoples in Indonesia, see Margaret J. Kartomi, *Matjapat Songs in Central and West Java* (Canberra: Australian National University Press, 1973), pp. 12–13.

4. *Makam: Modal Practice in Turkish Art Music* (Seattle, Wash.: Asian Music Publications, 1977), p. 12.

5. Amnon Shiloah, "The Status of Traditional Art Music in Muslim Nations," *Asian Music,* 12 (1981), pp. 46–49.

6. Ibid., pp. 44–46.

7. See L. I. al Fārūqī, "The Status of Music in Muslim Nations," pp. 56–84; Kristina Nelson, "The Art of Reciting the Qur'ān," Ph.D. dissertation (University of California, Berkeley, 1980), pp. 102–104; Regula Burckhardt Qureshi, "Islamic Music in an Indian Environment: The Shi'a Majlis," *Ethnomusicology,* 25 (1981), pp. 45–47; Ja-Fran Jones, "The 'Īsāwīya of Tunisia and Their Music," University of Washington, Ph.D. dissertation, 1977, pp. 56–59, for evidence of this from many regions of the Muslim world.

8. Speaking about the music of the Berber Muslims of the High Atlas in Morocco, Bernard Lortat-Jacob writes: "Music belongs to everyone and everyone is a musician. In such a society, professionalism is virtually non-existent ("Community Music as an Obstacle to Professionalism: A Berber Example," *Ethnomusicology,* 25 (1981), p. 88). See also Bruno Nettl, "The Role of Music in Culture: Iran, a Recently Developed Nation," *Contemporary Music and Music Cultures,* ed. Charles Hamm et al. (Englewood Cliffs, N.J.: Prentice-Hall, 1975), p. 75.

9. *La Musique arabe,* Vol. 5 (Paris: Paul Geuthner, 1949), p. 64.

10. "The Survival of Some Aspects of Medieval Arabic Performance Practice," *Ethnomusicology,* 25 (1981), pp. 73–86.

11. Amnon Shiloah, *The Theory of Music in Arabic Writings (c. 900–1900)* (Munich: G. Henle Verlag, 1979), p. 367.

12. The only passages from the Qur'ān that have import for *ṣawtī* expression are the ones commanding its *tartīl* ("chanting") (for example, 73:4; 25:32); or involving its *tilāwah,* from the root verb *talā,* meaning "to give a deliberate, poised, pleasing recitation" (29:45; 18:27, etc.).

13. See Lamyā' al Fārūqī, "Tartīl al-Qur'ān al-Karīm," *Islamic Perspectives: Studies in Honour of Sayyid Abul A'lā Mawdūdī* (Leicester, England: The Islamic Foundation, 1979), pp. 108–113.

14. In order to preserve that improvisational creativity, religious leaders have always opposed both descriptive and prescriptive notation of the chanted Qur'ān. See Lamyā' al Fārūqī, "Tartīl al-Qur'ān al-Karīm," p. 119, n. 30.

15. M. Talbi, "La qirā'a bi-l-alḥān," *Arabica* (1958), Vol. 5, p. 185.

16. See a more comprehensive treatment of the reasons for differential acculturation of musical elements in different regions of the Muslim world, in Lois Ibsen al Fārūqī, "Factors of Continuity in the Musical Cultures of the Muslim World," *Progress Reports in Ethnomusicology,* 1 (1983–1984). The influence of a pre-Islamic tradition is evidenced in the gong tradition of southeast Asia; the polyphony and polymetric music of sub-Saharan Africa; and the Western-style classical music of Egypt which incorporates nationalistic themes, melodies, or instruments. William P. Malm's description of music in Kelantan, Malaysia, includes genres revealing varying levels of Islamic, Indian, and indigenous influences ("Music in Kelantan, Malaysia and Some of Its Cultural Implications," *Studies in Malaysian Oral and Musical Traditions* [Ann Arbor: University of Michigan, 1974], pp. 1–46). See also Margaret J. Kartomi's discussion of the "musical strata" of Indonesia ("Musical Strata in Sumatra, Java, and Bali," *Musics of Many Cultures: An Introduction,* ed. Elizabeth May [Berkeley: University of California Press, 1980], pp. 111–133); and the material on "Music Areas of Africa," which documents the results of interaction between Islam and the indigenous African cultures (Alan P. Merriam, "African Music," *Continuity and Change in African Cultures,* ed. William R. Bascom and Melville J. Herskovits [Chicago: University of Chicago Press, 1970], pp. 76–79).

17. The conflict among the Indonesians over the *gamelan* tradition is not merely an issue of national tradition vs.

modernism, as described by Becker (Judith Becker, *Traditional Music in Modern Java* [Honolulu: University Press of Hawaii, 1980], chap. 3). The surface turbulence gives evidence of a much deeper conscious and unconscious struggle for cultural homogeneity by a predominantly Muslim population which suffers from sharply divergent social, political, and cultural layers remaining from earlier times, as well as a strong contemporary challenge from Western culture. Analogous problems exist in many other regions of the Muslim world.

18. David W. Ames suggests that technology and ecology also play a role in different acculturation patterns among Muslims of Africa ("Contexts of Dance in Zazzau and the Impact of Islamic Reform," *African Religious Groups and Beliefs,* ed. S. Ottenberg, [1982], pp. 110–147).

19. In recent years, the champions in the international Qur'ān chanting competitions held annually in Kuala Lumpur have often been the national entires of East Asian nations. In 1978, a *qāri'* from Thailand and a *qāri'ah* from Malaysia were the winners; in 1979, a *qāri'* from Iran and a *qāri'ah* from Indonesia; in 1980, the two winners were from Malaysia and Indonesia; in 1981, from Libya and Malaysia; in 1982, both winners were from Malaysia.

20. See *supra,* n. 17.

21. Jaap Kunst, *Music in Java: Its History, Its Theory and Its Technique,* ed. E. L. Heins, 2 vols. (The Hague: Martinus Nijhoff, 1973), Vol. 1, p. 267, n. 1).

22. Usopay H. Cadar, "The Role of Kulintang Music in Maranao Society," *Ethnomusicology,* 17 (1973), pp. 234–249.

23. Lois Ibsen al Fārūqī, "Accentuation in Qur'ānic Chant: A Study in Musical *Tawāzun," Yearbook of the International Folk Music Council,* 10 (1978), pp. 53–68.

24. The term *lāzimah* means "necessity," an apt designation for a musical phenomenon of such aesthetic importance in Islamic culture.

25. See Habib Hassan Touma, *La Musique arabe,* trans. Christine Hetier (Paris: Editions Buchet/Chastel, 1977), pp. 87–88; and Signell, *Makam,* pp. 89–92, for representative descriptions of the *taslīm* (Turkish *teslim*) in various regions. In Persian music it is designated as *forud* (Ella Zonis, *Classical Persian Music: An Introduction* [Cambridge, Mass.: Harvard University Press, 1973], pp. 45–46).

26. Choral or instrumental responses have various names; see "Refrain" in Index of English Musical Terms, L. al Fārūqī, *An Annotated Glossary.* A Choral response with such separating effect is known as *amshi* in a Hausa context (Ames and King, *Glossary of Hausa Music,* p. 132).

27. A drone involves repeating an important tone of the mode by one instrument or voice while another vocal or instrumental melody progresses independently. An ostinato is a rhythmic or pitched motif which is sounded repeatedly as accompaniment for the monophonic line. It is most commonly used as underlay for an unmetered improvisation. Ornaments that combine one melody tone with another at a distance of an octave, a perfect fourth, or a perfect fifth have been used from early times till the present day. Ibn Sīnā (d. 428/1037) named such an embellishment *tarkīb* ("combination") when it involved an ornamental tone a perfect fourth or fifth from the main tone. When the auxiliary was an octave away, Ibn Sīnā called it *taḍ'īf* ("doubling"). Such embellishing tones have sometimes been sounded simultaneously with the melody tone; at other times they have preceded it like a disjunct grace note (Ibn Sīnā, *Al Najāt,* Arabic text and German introduction in *Ibn Sina's Musiklehre,* ed. Maḥmūd A. al Ḥafnī [Berlin: Otto Hellwig, 1930], p. 99).

28. A motif is "a short figure of characteristic design that recurs throughout a composition or a section as a unifying element. A motif is distinguished from a theme or subject by being much shorter and generally fragmentary. . . . As few as two notes may constitute a motif, if they are sufficiently characteristic melodically and/or rhythmically" (Willi Apel, "Motif, motive," *Harvard Dictionary of Music,* 2nd ed. [Cambridge, Mass. The Belknap Press of Harvard University Press, 1977], pp. 545–546).

29. Alan P. Merriam, "African Music," p. 83.

30. An outline of the different kinds of tonal and durational ornamentation described by Ibn Sīnā and still used today can be found in Lois Ibsen al Fārūqī, *An Annotated Glossary of Arabic Musical Terms,* under "TAḤSĪN AL LAḤN," pp. 335–336.

Al Taḥqīq fī Aḥādīth al Khilāf 259
taḥsīnāt 274
Al Ṭā'ī 133
Ṭā'if 17, 29, 119, 124, 209, 215, 242
Taipei, Mosque of 428
Taiwan 269
Ta'izz 452
Tāj al 'Arūs 239
Tāj Maḥal 433-35
Tajrīd Aṣmā' al Ṣaḥābah (by 'Izzud dīn ibn al Athīr) 255
Tajrīd Asmā' al Ṣaḥābah (by Muḥammad ibn Aḥmad al Dhahabī) 255
tajwīd al Qur'ān 452, 453, 455
takbīrāt 145
takiyyah 297
taklīf 74, 81, 288, 304
Takrūnah, Tunisia 430
talā 478n.12
Ṭalā Kārī Madrasah, Samarqand 167
Ṭalḥah 215, 274
Talifu 225
Ta'līq script 357, 363-7
Ṭāliqānī, Darwīsh 'Abd al Majīd 357
Tall al 'Amārnah 32
Tall Ḥalaf 7
Tall al 'Ubayd 10
al Tall, Ṣafwān 25
talmīḥ 345
Tamachek language 259
ṭama'nīnah 279
al tamassuk bil aṣl 267
tambari 457
tambūr 471
ṭambūrah 461
Tamerlane (Timurlank) 217, 311
Tamīm tribe 8, 350
tamthīl al m'ānī 343
ṭanbūr 457, 461, 467, 473
tanburo 471
T'ang Dynasty 224
Tanha 315
Ṭanṭā, Egypt 297
Tantipara (mosque) 426
Tanūkh tribe 7, 13, 14, 221
Tanzania 259, 268, 270, 284, 354
Taoist 90n.2, 298, 314
taqāsīm 458
Al Taqrīb fī Asrār al Tarkīb 328
Al Taqrīb min Uṣūl al Fiqh 251, 278
taqwā 110
Taqwīm al Adillah fī Uṣūl al Fiqh 251, 278
ṭār 447, 457, 461, 467, 473
ṭarab 298
Ṭarafah ibn al 'Abd 14, 69n.62
tarassala 347
al tarassul 343, 346
tarawangsa 473
tarāwīḥ 442
Al Ta'rīfāt 239
ta'rījah 447
Tarik Khānah 423
Tārīkh al 'Arab Qabla al Islām 69n.61
Tārīkh al Ḥukamā' 313n.2
Tārīkh al Umam wal Mulūk 228n.2
Ṭāriq ibn Ziyād 217, 226
ṭarīqah 297
Tarjumān al Ashwāq 302
tarkīb 479n.27
tarompet 473
Tarsus 18
tartīl 478n.12
Tartīl al Qur'ān 449, 453, 455
taṣawwuf 295-300, 303, 304, 308; *see also* mysticism, *Ṣūfī*
al tashbīb 350
Tashkand (Tashkent, Shāsh) 216, 225
Tashkopruzade, Aḥmad Ibn Muṣṭafā Ibn Khalīl 454
tashrī' 108
taskhīr 317
taslīm 469, 479n.25
taṣrīf 236
Al Taṣrīf Liman 'Ajiza 'an al Ta'līf 326
Tatars 15, 217, 304; language 259
Tatar Asian Soviet Socialist Republic 259
tat twam asi 46
Taṭawwur al Ḥurūf al 'Arabiyyah 25
tawakkul 297, 304
Tawāzun 336, 343, 345-46, 348
tawbah 297
tawḥīd 73-74, 76-77, 79-85, 88-89, 89n.2, 90n.3, 91n.47, 107, 109, 134, 142, 158, 163, 165, 169, 173, 176, 179, 193, 284, 287, 296, 304, 324, 328, 354, 375, 379-80, 383, 403, 406-407, 410, 427, 442, 466, 475, 477
Tawḥīd: Essays on Life and Thought 111n.27
al Tawḥīdī, Abū Ḥayyān 306, 313n.3, 346, 348
Ṭawqī' script 357, 361
tawshīḥ 348
Ṭāwūs 244
Ṭay tribe 7, 11, 213
Taym 9
Taymā' 14, 17, 207
Al Taysīr fī al Qirā'āt al Sab' 240
Teda language 259
tendi 457
tĕrbang 473
teslim 479n.25
Tetouan (Tiṭwān) 444, 454
tevilbas 470
al Tha'ālibī 233
Thābit bin Qurrah 331
Thābit ibn Qays 211
Thābit ibn Yazīd 28
Thailand 269, 284, 474
Tha'lab, Abūl 'Abbās 236
Tha'labah tribe 205
Thalabiyyah 215
Thamūd 65
Thamūd, tribe of 62
Thanesar 218
thap 474
Thaqīb 8
Thaqīf, tribe of 209
Thatta, Pakistan 409
Theodora, Empress 57
Theodora, daughter of Kartakuzinos 218
Theodoret 69n.48
Theodorus 214
Theodosius, Emperor 216
Theology (by Plotinus) 308
Theology of Aristotle, The 308
Theory of Music in Arabic Writings (c. 900-1900), The 449, 478n.11
theotokos theology 63
thom 474
Thousand and One Nights 26
Thrace 18
Thuluth script 175, 357, 361-62, 371
Thumāmah ibn al Ashras 286, 289
Thumulah tribe 7
Thut-mose IV 12
Al Ṭibb al Manṣūrī 326
Al Ṭibb al Rūḥānī 326
tiga tali 473
Tiglath-Pilezer I 35
Tiglath-Pilezer III 35, 37
Tigré 20
Tigris-Euphrates basin 26
Tigris River 3, 26-27, 198, 213, 215
Tihāmat (Tihāmah) 7, 47-48
Tījāniyyah 227, 297
tikara 471
tilāwah 478n.12
Timbuktu 226, 227, 411
Timurlank *see* Tamerlane
Tinmal 410
tinten 473
al Tirmidhī 114, 260
Titus 40
Tiṭwān *see* Tetouan
Tlemcen, Grand Mosque 410
Tobago 269
tobol 457
Togo 268, 270, 341
Toledo 217, 243, 310, 410
tolerance 79, 269
tombak 465, 467
Topkapi Palace (Saray), Istanbul, Turkey 260, 438n.8
Torah 38, 41n.1, 51, 54-55, 137, 191, 194-95
totalism, Islamic state as 159
Tours 217
Touma, Habib Hassan 479n.25
Tower of Ḥasan, Rabāṭ, Morocco 210
Toy, Crawford Howell 41n.6
Traditional Music in Modern Java 479n.17
transcendence 163, 165, 292, 296; *see also* God, transcendence of
transcendentalist faith 61, 63; see, Abrahamic faith; Mesopotamian tradition; God, transcendence of
transcendentalistic religions 314, 315
transfiguration in art 380-3, 411-6, 416-27
Trans-Jordan 53
Transoxania 224
Treaty of Ḥudaybiyah 125, 135-37, 202, 207
Trengganu 228
tribalism 67, 203, 211-2
Tribeni 426
triliterality 23
Trimillos, Ricardo Diosdada 478n.1
Trinidad 269
Tripoli 33, 216, 410, 452
Tsung, Su 225
Tsung, Emperor Hsuan 225
tubbel 457
Ṭubba' (kings of Yaman) 14
Ṭubba' Abū Karib As'ad 151
Ṭughluq, Fīrūz 233
Ṭughluq sulṭānate 218
ṭughrā' 368-9
Al Tuḥfah fī Uṣūl al Fiqh 278
tüidük 467
tula 467
Ṭulayḥah 211
tulum 465
Ṭūlūnī dynasty 278
Thuluth script 371
Ṭūmār script 357, 365
tumbul 457
Tunis 18, 216, 222, 226, 310-11, 406, 444, 452-53
Tunisia 16, 268, 270, 284, 286, 355, 363, 454; Tunisian court 406
Tunjar Arabs 226
Turfan, Xinjiang Province, People's Republic of China 286, 401, 428, 440
Turkestan 5, 216, 224
Turkey 217, 259, 268, 270, 284, 297, 315, 354-55, 360, 384, 398, 431, 454, 458-59, 462-63, 468
Turkic language 259, 343
Turkish art 398-9
Turkish Art and Architecture 407n.2, 440n.14
Turkish Cargah 468
Turkish Kurdi 468
Turkish language 21, 259, 403
Turkish Puselik 468
Turkish Rāst 468
Turkmenistan (Turkmenia) 259, 268
Turkomen 15, 16, 217
al Ṭurṭūshī, Ibn Abū Randaqah Abū Bakr Muḥammad Ibn al Walīd Ibn Muḥammad 450
Ṭūs 299, 449-50
Tushratta, King 33
al Ṭūsī, Naṣr al Dīn Abū Ja'far Muḥammad Ibn Muḥammad Ibn al Ḥasan 445, 451
Tyre 18, 33

al 'Ubayd period 27
'Ubayd al Qāsim ibn Salām, Abū 235

Yemen Arab Republic (North) 268, 284; *see also* Yaman
Yeni Cami 418
Yeşil Cami 418, 421, 432
Yibnah 17, 97
Yiddish 41n.1
Yildirim 418
Yorguc Pasha (mosque) 418
Yoruba 227
Yugoslavia 223, 259, 269, 284
Yūḥannā ibn Ru'bah, Bishop 208
Yunnan 225
yusr 79
Yūsuf ibn 'Abd al Barr 254

Zabīd, Yemen 452–3
Ẓafar Khān Ghāzī Mosque 426
Al Ẓāfir 292
Al Ẓāhir ('Abbāsī caliph) 133; (Fāṭimī caliph) 292
Al Ẓāhir Baybars Mosque 414
al Ẓāhirī, Ibn Dāwūd 276
Al Zahr al Maṭlūl fī al Khabar al Ma'lūl 258
al Zahrā' 326
Zahrah 9
al Zahrāwī, Abūl Qāsim Khalaf ibn 'Abbās 326
Zaire 270
al Zajjāj, Abū Isḥaq 237
zakāt 116, 145–47, 154, 211, 273, 283
Zakī, Aḥmad 69n.60
al Zamakhsharī, Abū al Qāsim Maḥmūd Ibn 'Umar 245, 288, 450
Zambia 270
zambuna 457
al Zamlakānī 336
Zamzam 149
ẓann 77
ẓannī 247
ẓanniyyah 114
Zaragosa (Saragosa) 217, 444, 450
Zaranka 37
Zarathustra 15
ẓarb 467
Zaria, Nigeria 118, 397, 411
Zawārī 423
zāwiyah 297
Zayandah River 425
Zayd ibn 'Alī 227
Zayd ibn Aslam 244
Zayd ibn Ḥārithah 123, 129, 208, 210, 291
Zayd ibn al Khaṭṭāb 211
Zayd ibn Rifā'ah 306
Zayd ibn Thābit 244, 274, 357–8
Zaydīs of Yaman 291
Zayla' tribe 227
Zaynab 122, 123
Zaynab bint Jaḥsh 123
Zeus 18
Zidonians 53
Ziggurat of Ur 22
zīj 332
Zimmi 199; *see also Dhimmah*
zīnah 317
Zion 54
zirbağali 467
Zoroastrian(s) 138, 198, 207, 221, 224, 283
Zoroastrianism 13, 14, 17, 39, 50; Zoroastrianized 55
Zubayd tribe 212
al Zubayr Ibn 'Abdul Muṭṭalib 9, 123, 275
Zubayr (fortress in N.W. Arabia) 207
Zuhayr ibn Abū Salmā 67, 69n.62
zuhd 297
Āl Zuhr 309
zukhruf 379
zukrah/zūkrah 447, 457
zumbarah 457
Zunbīl 216
zurnā/zurna 461, 465, 467

Map Index

This index contains not only place names but also other information contained in the maps. The names of battles, of battle commanders, of musical instruments, of different Arabic scripts — all are listed here with a reference to the map on which they appear. The numbers below are map numbers, not page numbers.